Introductory Foods

Thirteenth Edition

Marion Bennion

Barbara Scheule

Kent State University

Prentice Hall

Upper Saddle River, New Jersey
Columbus, Ohio

Library of Congress Cataloging-in-Publication Data

Bennion, Marion, 1925—
  Introductory foods / Marion Bennion, Barbara Scheule.—13th ed.
    p. cm.
  ISBN 0-13-233926-9
  1. Food. 2. Cookery. I. Scheule, Barbara. II. Title.
  TX354.B46 2009
  641.3—dc22

                                        2008054673

Editor in Chief: Vernon Anthony
Acquisitions Editor: William Lawrensen
Editorial Assistant: Lara Dimmick
Development Editor: Linda Cupp
Project Manager: Alicia Ritchey
Operations Specialist: Deidra Schwartz
Production Editor: Lisa S. Garboski, bookworks editorial services
Art Director: Candace Rowley
Interior Design: Ilze Lemesis
Cover Designer: Diane Lorenzo
Cover image: iStockphoto
Director of Marketing: David Gesell
Campaign Marketing Manager: Leigh Ann Sims
Curriculum Marketing Manager: Thomas Hayward
Marketing Assistant: Les Roberts

This book was set in JansonText-Roman by TexTech and was printed and bound by R.R. Donnelley & Sons Company. The cover was printed by Lehigh-Phoenix Color.

Pearson Education Ltd., London   Pearson Education Australia Pty. Limited
Pearson Education Singapore Pte. Ltd.   Pearson Education North Asia Ltd., Hong Kong
Pearson Education Canada, Inc.   Pearson Educación de Mexico, S.A. de C.V.
Pearson Education—Japan   Pearson Education Malaysia Pte. Ltd.

Prentice Hall
is an imprint of

PEARSON

10 9 8 7 6 5 4 3 2

ISBN-13: 978-0-13-233926-1
ISBN-10:   0-13-233926-9

CONTENTS

PRINCIPLES OF COOKERY

FATS, FRYING, AND EMULSIONS

SWEETENERS, CRYSTALLIZATION, STARCH, AND CEREAL GRAINS

FEATURE BOXES

Focus on Science

PREFACE

The thirteenth edition of *Introductory Foods* has been written and revised to introduce beginning college students to the basic fundamental principles of food preparation and to alert them to many innovations and emerging trends in food science and technology. The scientific basis for ingredients and techniques used in food preparation are provided throughout. This text is designed to be one of the first courses in food preparation for students studying nutrition and dietetics, hospitality management, family and consumer science education, and culinary arts.

NEW TO THIS EDITION

Over 60 new tables and charts have been added to present concepts in a concise and student-friendly format. Chapter content has been updated and reorganized to improve clarity and readability while maintaining the depth of the material. The listing of key chapter topics at the beginning of each chapter and the increased number of subtitles provide a stronger "roadmap" for students. The chapter references at the end of the book are extensive and have been updated with over 350 new sources. The feature boxes, introduced in the last edition, include such topics as "Multicultural Cuisine," "Healthy Eating," "Hot Topics," and "Focus on Science." Additional sidebars provide students with a discussion of specialized topics. Web resources are listed by chapter at the end of the book to guide students in their Internet exploration of food topics.

ORGANIZATION

The chapters in this book are independent, so that instructors may present them in any order that best fits the structure and objectives of the course. Cross-references to other chapters are indicated periodically in the text.

Chapters 1 through 4 contain introductory material about food choices, sensory analysis, economics, food safety, and regulations. Foundational principles of cooking are given in Chapters 5 through 8. The discussion of carbohydrates, fats, and proteins in Chapter 9 may be used as a review for students who have had chemistry courses or as an introduction for those who have not studied chemistry. The remaining chapters are divided into eight sections: "Fats, Frying, and Emulsions"; "Sweeteners, Crystallization, Starch, and Cereal Grains"; "Bakery Products"; "Fruits, Vegetables, and Salads"; "Dairy Products and Eggs"; "Meat, Poultry, and Seafood"; "Beverages"; and "Food Preservation."

FEATURES

- Tables and charts present concepts in a concise, student-friendly format
- Definitions of key words are provided in a glossary to assist students in learning new terms
- Chapter summaries and study questions aid in the review and understanding of the material
- Feature boxes highlight Multicultural Cuisine, Healthy Eating, Hot Topics, and Focus on Science
- In-depth coverage of specialized concepts in sidebars
- Web resources guide student exploration of topics
- Extensive reference lists with over 350 updated sources
- For instructors, Power Point slides and an instructor's manual are available

ACKNOWLEDGMENTS

To my husband Doug and sons Colin and Nathan, thank you for your understanding, patience, and encouragement throughout the revision of this text. My parents, Emaline and Lamoine Einspahr, are recognized for the value they always placed on the quest for knowledge and a quality education. Appreciation also is extended to my colleagues and students at Kent State University for their support and encouragement.

Frank Conforti, PhD, Associate Professor of Human Nutrition, Foods, and Exercise at Virginia Polytechnic Institute and State University, is appreciated for his contributions to the new Focus on Science features found in every chapter. Samantha Wait Knight, a graduate student at Kent State University, is recognized for her assistance in seeing that the figures and tables were properly numbered throughout. Breanna Harris, who helped to find over 150 new photographs and illustrations for the twelfth edition, is again acknowledged because many of these photographs can be found in this edition. We also are grateful to everyone who shared the photographs and illustrations found in this edition.

Our editors Bill Lawrensen and Linda Cupp are recognized for all of their efforts in successfully navigating this revision from a draft manuscript to a book in print. Christine Caperton of O'Donnell & Associates is thanked for her patient and helpful guidance throughout this revision. Appreciation is extended to all of the reviewers of this edition for their insightful and constructive comments: James Daniel, Purdue University; Zisca Dixon, Florida International University; Faye C. Johnson, California State University, Chico; Frank Conforti, Virginia Tech University; Kathy Knight, University of Mississippi; Janet Sass, Northern Virginia Community College; and

Kimberly S. Lukhard, East Carolina University. The recommendations of the reviewers were incorporated whenever possible.

INSTRUCTOR RESOURCES

To access supplementary materials online, instructors need to request an instructor access code. Go to *www.pearsonhighered.com/irc*, where you can register for an instructor access code. Within 48 hours after registering, you will receive a confirming e-mail, including an instructor access code. Once you have received your code, go to the site and log on for full instructions on downloading the materials you wish to use.

FOOD CHOICES AND SENSORY CHARACTERISTICS

1

The food choices that we make and the development of our behavior and habits concerning food are influenced by many interacting factors, including availability, income, culture, concerns about health, social values, religion, and even genetics [14, 55]. Yet, for most persons and in ordinary circumstances, foods must be palatable or have appetite appeal if they are to be eaten. A palatable food is one that is both acceptable to an individual and agreeable to his or her taste. Various sensory impressions or sensations, including odor, appearance, taste, and mouthfeel or touch, are involved in our judgment of palatability and food quality.

Learning to prepare foods with great appetite appeal includes learning to discriminate and evaluate the quality of food through the intensity of the sensations received when food is sampled. Individuals vary in their capacities to experience flavors and odors, but sensitivities to pleasurable encounters with food may be heightened as they learn more about food characteristics and quality.

A taste or liking for a variety of foods may be acquired. Learning to like new foods will provide ample rewards from increased enjoyment and enhanced aesthetic experiences. Eating a wide variety of foods also is an excellent practice from a nutritional perspective. You are encouraged to develop a discriminating taste as you begin to learn basic reasons why foods behave as they do during preparation and/or processing.

In this chapter, the following topics will be discussed:

- Factors affecting food selection and consumption
- Sensory characteristics of food
- Objective evaluation of food

FACTORS AFFECTING PATTERNS OF EATING

Humans, as biological beings, require food to sustain life. Humans eat to satisfy hunger and to meet a basic drive for food. The decision of what and when to eat is not solely driven by biological needs, however. Food consumption patterns are influenced by family and friends, cultural traditions, religious beliefs, health and nutrition factors, economic concerns, technological developments, psychological influences, and sensory quality.

Family and Social

The family structure and interactions among family members are important influences on the development of our food habits. Children learn that food provides comfort when they are hungry and is a pleasurable dimension of family activities, celebrations, and time with friends (Figure 1-1). Several studies have shown an association between children's food preferences and the food practices of their parents [1, 13, 51]. Peers, schools, daycare providers, and the media also influence eating patterns of children and adolescents [1, 13, 16, 51]. Adults share meals with friends, family, and coworkers as part of their social interactions.

The food patterns of families in the twenty-first century are being influenced by time restraints. Nearly 70 percent of women with children under 18 are working outside the home [6]. Food preparation time is further limited by a variety of extracurricular family activities. Families are coping with this time challenge by increasingly eating out [6], consuming food in the car [25, 46], purchasing home meal replacement and convenience foods [23], and simplifying menus to include fewer sidedishes [6]. Meals purchased outside the home accounted for 49 percent of total food expenditures in 2006 [61].

Regular, shared meals have been declining under the pressures of modern society. Nevertheless, the family meal plays an important role in human communication—communicating love, values, and information. It can be especially effective in increasing the well-being of children. Even in our changing society, older ideals about the importance of family meals have persisted [6]. Nearly 80 percent of the time, Americans eat dinner at home [33].

1

Cultural

Cultural forces shape our food behaviors. The culture in which we develop determines, to a large extent, our food patterns or habits. Foods are eaten in combination with other foods in ways that are determined and perpetuated by our culture. Food patterns differ markedly from one culture to another. Grasshoppers or roast dog may be delicacies in some parts of the world, whereas in other areas it would be unthinkable for humans to consume these products. Not everyone in a cultural group eats exactly alike because of the development of individual and family preferences.

The influence of ethnic groups is also seen in geographical areas in which individuals from these cultures represent a large percentage of the population. Food habits learned in other areas of the world tend to continue, when possible, as individuals or groups move to new locations. In the United States, some regional food preferences can be traced to the influx of immigrants into the region. Each culture passes on its food habits and patterns by training children from infancy in their unique patterns [10, 20]. In the United States, cultural food habits are modified as acculturation with the "American" diet occurs [68, 69].

The study of foods should help you understand and appreciate the food patterns of other cultures or ethnic groups as well as different taste preferences among various regions of the United States [32]. America is becoming increasingly more global in its tastes for food, resulting

FIGURE 1-1 Two children enjoy each others' company while enjoying a healthy snack. *(Photo by Keith Weller, Courtesy of U.S. Department of Agriculture)*

from a more diverse population, increased travel, and rapid communication [57]. Each ethnic group has developed a cuisine with its distinctive combination of flavorings for basic foodstuffs. When eating out, many people choose a culinary experience involving different and sometimes exotic foods. The food industry is accepting the challenges presented by demographic changes with new menu items featuring Japanese, Thai, Vietnamese,

MULTICULTURAL CUISINE

Ethnic Foods in America—So What Is the Typical Meal?

The U.S. Census Bureau estimates in 2050 the Hispanic population will be nearly one-fourth of the total U.S. population, or potentially 96.5 million. Asian and Pacific Islander populations are also anticipated to increase to 34 million. The non-Hispanic White population is still expected to be the largest ethnic group with 206 million, while non-Hispanic Blacks are estimated to be 54 million. Only time will tell if these predictions will materialize. Meanwhile, how will ethnic trends influence what we eat?

In the decade ahead, Mexican, Chinese, Caribbean, and Thai foods are expected to have the fastest develop-

ment. Latin cuisine is gaining in popularity as well. The flavors and ingredients from South American and Caribbean cuisines characterize Latin food. Latin food can be hot because of the use of chilies or refreshing with citrus fruits and assorted vinegars. Look for *empanadas* (a beef dish), Peruvian blue potatoes, *postones* (fried plantain), mango fruits, *dulce de leche* ice cream (based on a South American sweet caramel-like milk product), and many other Latin-inspired dishes. ■

Source: References 2, 47, 48

Korean, Middle Eastern, Caribbean, Jamaican, and Mediterranean foods [49]. With this, great variety of food choices are available. Fascinating experiences await the adventurer who learns to enjoy, and prepare, the foods of many different cultures.

Religious Beliefs

Food has significance in relation to many religious beliefs. Food laws within religious life may set strict guidelines dictating the types of food to be consumed, the procedures for processing and preparing foods, the complete omission of certain foods, and the frequency of eating other foods. To take advantage of the large markets available in religious communities, the food industry must serve the needs of these various groups.

Christian. The foods consumed, or not consumed, vary by the church denomination, although few dietary restrictions are common in most Christian denominations. Some churches, such as Catholic, may encourage members to avoid meat consumption during specific days in Lent.

Judaism. The kosher dietary laws, *kashruth*, are observed to varying degrees by members of the Jewish faith [32, 44]. These laws include a prohibition against eating blood and thus dictate rules concerning the slaughter of animals and their further processing [29]. Milk products and meat products must be kept separate. Only certain species of animals are considered to be suitable for consumption. Pork and shellfish, among others, are prohibited. Kosher laws also extend to ingredients that are used in food processing. Even many non-Jewish individuals choose kosher products because they are regarded as clean, high-quality foods.

Islam. Islam also prescribes a set of food laws [8, 32]. Foods that are lawful for Muslims to consume are called *halal* [29]. As a general principle, most foods are permitted; however, some prohibitions are specified. Prohibited foods include swine and all their byproducts, intoxicants of all types, birds of prey, land animals without ears such as snakes, flowing or congealed blood, and animals killed in a manner that prevents their blood from being fully drained from their bodies. Thus, there are strict requirements for the slaughtering of animals. Food products may be certified by the Islamic Food and Nutrition Council of America.

Hinduism. Hindu dietary practices emphasize the avoidance of foods that may interfere with the development of the body or mind [32]. Although not required, many Hindus are vegetarian. The consumption of cows is prohibited because cows are considered sacred. Pork is also frequently avoided by Hindus. Fish or meat must first be sanctified before it is consumed.

Vegetarianism and Religious Belief. Several religions advocate vegetarianism, although vegetarianism may be chosen for ecological, health, or other reasons as well. Chinese Buddhists advocate vegetarianism because they believe in compassion [26]. A vegetarian diet is recommended by the Seventh-Day Adventist Church but is not required for membership [5]. In the United States, approximately 2.5 percent of the population, or 4.8 million people, are vegetarians [24]. The majority of these are lacto-ovo vegetarians. Others are strict vegetarians or vegans.

Nutrition and Health

An interest in healthful lifestyles, including recognition of nutrition as an important part of the health improvement process, is flourishing among Americans. At the same time, obesity rates for adults and children have increased dramatically since 1991 (Figure 1-2) [58]. The National Health and Nutrition Examination Surveys (NHANES) found 65 percent of adults were overweight with 31 percent being considered obese in the 1999–2002 surveys [38]. National nutrition objectives are included in the U.S. Public Health Service's broad-based initiative *Healthy People 2010: National Health Promotion and Disease Prevention Objectives* [62] and are supported through the U.S. Dietary Guidelines, Food Guide Pyramid, and Nutrition Facts labeling on food products. How Americans respond to government health and dietary recommendations by adjusting their dietary habits will become more apparent in the years ahead, although an increased interest in healthy choices is evident in some segments of the food marketplace [50].

Dietary Guidelines. *Dietary Guidelines for Americans*, first published in 1980 by the U.S. Departments of Agriculture (USDA) and Health and Human Services, is now in the sixth edition [11, 63]. The *2005 Dietary Guidelines* differs from previous guidelines in scope and purpose. The *2005 Dietary Guidelines* includes more technical information and is geared toward health professionals and health policy makers. As in the past, the goal of the guidelines is to promote health and reduce the risk for major chronic diseases. Nine focus areas and key recommendations are provided within the *Dietary Guidelines* (Table 1-1) [65]. Two publications, based on the *Dietary Guidelines*, have been developed with consumers in mind. These consumer publications include a brochure entitled *Finding Your Way to a Healthier You* which includes topics such as "how to mix up your choices within each food group" (Figure 1-3) and a book entitled *A Healthier You* [66].

Food Guide Pyramid. The Food Guide Pyramid was introduced by the USDA in 1992 to illustrate the dietary guidelines graphically [11, 59]. The first major revision of the Food Guide Pyramid was published in 2005

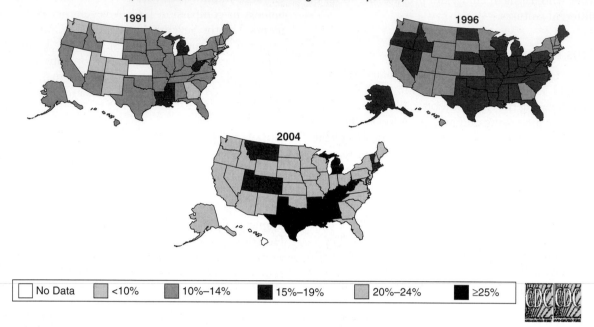

Obesity Trends* Among U.S. Adults
BRFSS, 1991, 1996, 2004
(*BMI ≥ 30, or about 30 lbs overweight for 5'4" person)

	No Data		<10%		10%–14%		15%–19%		20%–24%		≥25%

FIGURE 1-2 Obesity trends among U.S. adults. *(Courtesy of U.S. Centers for Disease Control)*

(Figure 1-4). The new *My Pyramid* focuses on an individualized approach to healthy eating and physical activity. Through the website www.mypyramid.gov, consumers may obtain guidance designed with their age, gender, activity level, and height and weight taken into consideration. A significant change in the new pyramid recommendations is the emphasis on cups as a method of measuring portion size. The 1992 pyramid guidelines used standardized serving sizes, which were often not consistent with portion sizes in the marketplace.

HEALTHY EATING

How Does America's Diet Measure Up?

To be consistent with the *2005 Dietary Guidelines,* Americans need to eat more fruits (about one more cup each day), vegetables (about one more cup each day), and milk (about two more cups per day if female, one more cup if male). Within the vegetable group, more legumes and more dark green and orange vegetables should be consumed. Iceberg lettuce, potatoes, and potato chips make up 52 percent of the vegetables in our diets, reflecting little variety. Overall, the consumptions of grains should decrease slightly (about one ounce per day), but the emphasis needs to be on more whole grains instead of refined. In general, fewer fats and added sugars should be eaten. Americans need to increase their activity levels and decrease their caloric intake. Americans are more sedentary but have increased food consumption by 16 percent (523 calories per day) since 1970. ■

Source: References 11, 15, 43, 64

TABLE 1-1 *2005 Dietary Guidelines for Americans:* Summary of Selected Key Recommendations

Chapter Topic in Dietary Guidelines	Key Recommendations Summarized (See http://www.healthierus.gov/ for recommendations for specific population groups)
Adequate Nutrients within Calorie Needs	Consume a variety of nutrient-dense foods and beverages while choosing foods that limit the intake of saturated and trans fats, cholesterol, added sugars, salt, and alcohol. Meet recommended intakes within energy needs by adopting a balanced eating pattern.
Weight Management	Balance calories from food and beverages with calories expended to maintain a healthy body weight. Prevent weight gain by decreasing caloric intake and increasing physical activity.
Physical Activity	Engage in regular physical activity and reduce sedentary activities. Achieve physical fitness by including cardiovascular conditioning, stretching exercises, and resistance exercises.
Food Groups to Encourage	Consume a sufficient amount of fruits and vegetables while staying within energy needs. Two cups of fruit and 2 1/2 cups of vegetables per day are recommended for a reference 2,000-calorie intake. Choose a variety of fruits and vegetables each day. Consume three or more ounce-equivalents of whole-grain products per day. In general, at least half the grains should come from whole grains. Consume three cups per day of fat-free or lowfat milk or equivalent milk products.
Fats	Consume less than 10 percent of calories from saturated fatty acids and less than 300 mg/day of cholesterol; keep trans fatty acid consumption as low as possible. Keep total fat intake between 20 and 35 percent of calories, with most fats coming from sources of polyunsaturated and monounsaturated fatty acids. When selecting and preparing meat, poultry, dry beans, and milk or milk products, make choices that are lean, low fat, or fat-free. Limit intake of fats and oils high in saturated and/or trans fatty acids, and choose products low in such fats and oils.
Carbohydrates	Choose fiber-rich fruits, vegetables, and whole grains often. Choose and prepare foods and beverages with little added sugars or caloric sweeteners. Reduce the incident of dental caries by practicing good oral hygiene and consuming sugar- and starch-containing foods and beverages less frequently.
Sodium and Potassium	Consume less than 2,300 mg (approximately one teaspoon) of sodium per day. Choose and prepare foods with little salt. Consume potassium-rich foods, such as fruits and vegetables.
Alcoholic Beverages	Those who drink alcoholic beverages should do so sensibly and in moderation—defined as the consumption of up to one drink per day for women and up to two drinks per day for men. Alcoholic beverages should not be consumed by some individuals, including those who cannot restrict their alcohol intake, women of childbearing age who may become pregnant, pregnant and lactating women, children and adolescents, individuals taking medications that can interact with alcohol, and those with specific medical conditions. Alcoholic beverages should be avoided by individuals engaging in activities that require attention, skill, or coordination, such as driving or operating machinery.
Food Safety	To avoid microbial foodborne illness: *Clean* hands, food contact surfaces, and fruits and vegetables. Meat and poultry should not be washed or rinsed. *Separate* raw, cooked, and ready-to-eat foods while shopping, preparing, or storing foods. *Cook* foods to a safe temperature to kill microorganisms. *Chill* (refrigerate) perishable foods promptly and defrost foods properly. *Avoid* raw (unpasteurized) milk or any products made from unpasteurized milk, raw or partially cooked eggs or foods containing raw eggs, raw or undercooked meat and poultry, unpasteurized juices, and raw sprouts.

Source: Reference 66

Food Labeling. In 1990, the Nutrition Labeling and Education Act resulted in the provision of standardized nutrition labels on nearly all processed foods. The Nutrition Facts labels do appear to be used by consumers seeking to make informed choices about the foods purchased [11]. Nutrition labeling is discussed further in Chapter 4.

Economic and Marketplace Factors

Food Availability. Geography of an area and variations in climate influence the types of food that can be, and usually are, grown. Historically, this fact has had a profound influence on the availability of particular foods and, in turn, on the eating patterns of people in the area. Examples are the widespread use of pinto beans and chili peppers in the southwestern United States and the extensive use of seafood in coastal areas. With the development of rapid transportation and modern food-handling facilities, however, the influence of geography and climate on our food habits has decreased greatly. For example, 40 percent of the fresh fruit consumed by Americans is imported. During the winter months especially, many imported vegetables may be found in American grocery stores [42]. U.S.

Mix up your choices within each food group.

Focus on fruits. Eat a variety of fruits—whether fresh, frozen, canned, or dried—rather than fruit juice for most of your fruit choices. For a 2,000-calorie diet, you will need 2 cups of fruit each day (for example, 1 small banana, 1 large orange, and ¼ cup of dried apricots or peaches).

Vary your veggies. Eat more dark green veggies, such as broccoli, kale, and other dark leafy greens; orange veggies, such as carrots, sweetpotatoes, pumpkin, and winter squash; and beans and peas, such as pinto beans, kidney beans, black beans, garbanzo beans, split peas, and lentils.

Get your calcium-rich foods. Get 3 cups of low-fat or fat-free milk—or an equivalent amount of low-fat yogurt and/or low-fat cheese (1½ ounces of cheese equals 1 cup of milk)—every day. For kids aged 2 to 8, it's 2 cups of milk. If you don't or can't consume milk, choose lactose-free milk products and/or calcium-fortified foods and beverages.

Make half your grains whole. Eat at least 3 ounces of whole-grain cereals, breads, crackers, rice, or pasta every day. One ounce is about 1 slice of bread, 1 cup of breakfast cereal, or ½ cup of cooked rice or pasta. Look to see that grains such as wheat, rice, oats, or corn are referred to as "whole" in the list of ingredients.

Go lean with protein. Choose lean meats and poultry. Bake it, broil it, or grill it. And vary your protein choices—with more fish, beans, peas, nuts, and seeds.

Know the limits on fats, salt, and sugars. Read the Nutrition Facts label on foods. Look for foods low in saturated fats and *trans* fats. Choose and prepare foods and beverages with little salt (sodium) and/or added sugars (caloric sweeteners).

FIGURE 1-3 Dietary recommendations from the consumer brochure entitled "Finding Your Way to a Healthier You." *(Courtesy of U.S. Department of Health and Human Services and U.S. Department of Agriculture)*

supermarkets have, on a regular basis, fresh fruits from tropical areas and live seafood, even though most are located far from the tropics or the ocean.

Economics. Whether we consume the variety of foods available in supermarkets and restaurants depends, to a considerable extent, on our purchasing power. Economics is a powerful factor in limiting or expanding our dietary patterns, although these changes may be transitory in some cases. When food budgets are restricted because of financial problems, less expensive foods must comprise a larger share of the menus offered. When budgets are liberal, more convenience items and snack foods are often purchased, and "eating out" occurs more frequently. These trends can be observed nationally when the country is in recession or in a period of economic prosperity [9].

Income and household size are the most important factors determining where and how Americans spend their food dollars [4]. Low income families spend 48 percent of their income on food, whereas middle income and high income households spend 13 percent and 8 percent, respectively. High income households spend a larger share of their food dollars on eating out.

Some households in America do not enjoy **food security** [45, 62]. In 2004, 12 percent of U.S. households were insecure at some point during the year [39]. There are a number of nutrition assistance programs available to help families, such as food stamps and the National School Lunch Program. The USDA calculates costs for four levels of food plans [60]. Understanding food preparation and food quality is an advantage whether working with limited or generous household food budgets.

Technological Development

The food-processing industry is sharing in the many ideas, innovations, and technological developments that are bringing about major changes in our society. The industry's growth and continued development keep an ever-increasing supply of new and convenient foods on the market and affect the purchasing habits of the consumer and the types of meals served both at home and in foodservice establishments.

Processing. The development of technological expertise in transportation, food preservation, and processing extends the seasons of food availability. **Irradiation** may be used to decrease bacterial contamination on poultry and meat and increase the shelf life of fresh fruits. **Aseptic packaging** decreases processing time and results in more flavorful food products. Flavor specialists are designing systems to improve the flavor of many foods. New-generation refrigerated foods offer fresh and flavorful entrees that may be stored under refrigeration for several weeks before reheating and service [30].

Anatomy of MyPyramid

One size doesn't fit all

USDA's new MyPyramid symbolizes a personalized approach to healthy eating and physical activity. The symbol has been designed to be simple. It has been developed to remind consumers to make healthy food choices and to be active every day. The different parts of the symbol are described below.

Activity

Activity is represented by the steps and the person climbing them, as a reminder of the importance of daily physical activity.

Moderation

Moderation is represented by the narrowing of each food group from bottom to top. The wider base stands for foods with little or no solid fats or added sugars. These should be selected more often. The narrower top area stands for foods containing more added sugars and solid fats. The more active you are, the more of these foods can fit into your diet.

Personalization

Personalization is shown by the person on the steps, the slogan, and the URL. Find the kinds and amounts of food to eat each day at MyPyramid.gov.

Proportionality

Proportionality is shown by the different widths of the food group bands. The widths suggest how much food a person should choose from each group. The widths are just a general guide, not exact proportions. Check the Web site for how much is right for you.

Variety

Variety is symbolized by the 6 color bands representing the 5 food groups of the Pyramid and oils. This illustrates that foods from all groups are needed each day for good health.

Gradual Improvement

Gradual improvement is encouraged by the slogan. It suggests that individuals can benefit from taking small steps to improve their diet and lifestyle each day.

(a)

(b)

FIGURE 1-4 (a) Anatomy of MyPyramid. *(Courtesy of U.S. Department of Agriculture, Center for Nutrition Policy and Promotion)* (b) My Pyramid: Steps to a Healthier You recommendations. *(Courtesy of U.S. Department of Agriculture, Center for Nutrition Policy and Promotion)*

Biotechnology.   Conventional breeding and selection of plants and animals over the centuries has been used to improve food supplies. Now, with a group of genetic tools that falls under the heading of biotechnology, the variety, productivity, and efficiency of food production can be targeted in less time and with greater predictability and control than was possible with traditional methods [21]. Genetic engineering may be used to increase crop yields and disease resistance and to produce faster-maturing, drought-resistant varieties. Biotechnology could be used to improve the nutritional quality of the food supply and reduce the use of chemicals [3]. However, in spite of the benefits, biotechnology has not been without controversy [27]. Public education about biotechnology is needed so people will acquire a base of knowledge with which to make judgments about these new tools as they make choices in food purchasing [54].

Technology in the Home.   Refrigeration and freeze processing within the modern home allow patterns of cooking and eating that cannot exist in developing countries where methods for keeping foods fresh are limited. Different types of cooking equipment, including the microwave oven, have markedly affected patterns of eating. Even the social aspects of food may be influenced by developments in food technology as we need to rely less on other family members to prepare the food we eat. Almost anyone in the household can retrieve an entree from the freezer and quickly heat it in the microwave oven.

Emotional and Psychological Effects

With all of today's technological influences, it is important that the meanings of food, other than the biological

and economic ones, be considered (Figure 1-5). Food means security, hospitality, and even status. Infants learn about security when mothers respond to their crying by giving them food. Familiar foods bring back memories of home and family and make one feel secure. Feeling full and physically satisfied and knowing that there is more food available for other meals bring security. Food is a symbol of hospitality and is used to show that one cares about others and is a friend. Gifts of food are given in times of both happiness and sorrow.

SENSORY CHARACTERISTICS OF FOOD

Sensory characteristics are important factors in determining whether we will first taste, then eat, and enjoy the food. Those involved in food preparation, both in the home and in commercial establishments, must take into careful account the appearance, flavor, and texture of the dishes prepared. Humans assess their food using the five senses: taste, smell, sight, touch, and hearing. For example, consider how the sounds of crisp foods such as raw carrots and the sizzle of fajitas when brought to the table influence the total experience with these foods. Understanding these sensory characteristics is essential in the study of food.

Appearance

Appearance often creates the first impression of food. Such qualities as color, form, consistency, size, and design or arrangement contribute to what may be called "eye appeal" of foods. Without an attractive and appealing appearance, foods may be rejected without being tasted.

(a)

(b)

(c)

FIGURE 1-5 (a) Mexican women chat while they roast chili peppers. *(Photograph by Kay Franz)*
(b) A brother and sister can get to know each other over ice cream cones. *(Photograph by Roger P. Smith)*
(c) Eating spaghetti requires real concentration. *(Photograph by Chris Meister)*

For the commercial vendor of prepared foods, the appearance of the food is extremely important, because this is the first opportunity to impress the potential buyer with the quality and desirability of the product.

Color is an especially important attribute. Try eating a jelly bean and guessing the flavor without prior knowledge of the color. Not only does color influence expectations of flavors, but it provides a perception of quality. Olive-green broccoli or a fruit tray with slices of apples and pears that have surfacing browning would not be favorably received.

Taste

Although *flavor* and *taste* are used synonymously, in a strict sense, taste is only one part of flavor. Taste involves the sensations produced through stimulation of the **taste buds** on the tongue. There are five primary taste sensations: sweet, sour, bitter, salty, and umami, also called savory. Sweet tastes are primarily associated with hydrocyl (-OH) groups, whereas salty tastes occur due to the ions of salts. Sour substances are generally the result of hydrogen ions (H^+) found in acids. A number of compounds taste bitter, including, in part, caffeine and theobromine. Umami is a taste associated with amino acid-based substances and is often described as "savory," "meaty," or "brothy." Monosodium glutamate is one example of a substance providing a umami taste. Other foods contributing umami include tomatoes, eggs, seafoods, cheese, and soy sauce.

Taste Buds. Taste buds are found in small elevations, called **papillae**, on the surface of the tongue (Figure 1-6). Taste sensations are produced when bitter, salty, sweet, or acid substances in a solution contact **taste receptors** in the **taste pore** leading to the taste bud. Sweet and sour are perceived most intensely on the tip of the tongue, although both may also be perceived at the back of the tongue or on the hard palate. Sensation of bitter tastes is generally delayed rather than immediate and is perceived at the back of the tongue and on the hard palate. Sour tastes are detected on the sides of the tongue. Figure 1-6 shows a diagram of a taste bud. A message is sent to the brain from the taste cells via nerve fibers with endings in the taste cells. The brain interprets and identifies the specific taste.

Influence of Temperature. Temperature may affect the blending of primary tastes and other factors contributing to flavor. The temperature range at which most foods are eaten, from ice cream to hot chocolate, affects the apparent intensity of some of the primary tastes. Sugar seems sweeter at higher temperatures than at lower temperatures. Just the reverse seems to be true of salt. Some substances, such as menthol, feel cool because of the sensitization of receptors in the mouth and throat,

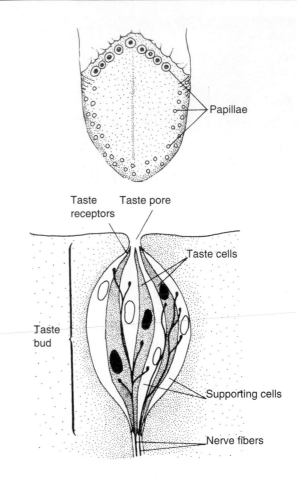

FIGURE 1-6 Drawing of the tongue, showing papillae on the surface. Taste buds are located on the sides and at the base of many of the papillae. Taste buds near the tip are more sensitive to sour, and those near the back are more sensitive to bitter. Diagram of an individual taste bud containing tiny taste receptors that come in contact with the substance being tasted, taste cells, and nerve fibers that carry the message from the taste bud to the brain for interpretation.

thereby exaggerating the feeling of coolness. Conversely, some foods such as chili peppers produce a hot or biting sensation by irritating the mucous membranes lining the mouth. The compound primarily responsible for the "hotness" of chili peppers is capsaicin.

Odor

An odor may be pleasing or offensive. The term *aroma* is usually applied to a pleasant odor. The smell of fresh baked bread, hot apple cider, freshly cut cantaloupe, and many other foods are considered appealing and, when experienced, encourage tasting of the food. In contrast, the odor resulting from burnt food is offensive. Some foods, especially those that are cold, have a limited odor. Ice cream is an example of this.

The olfactory center is found at the top of the nasal cavity, as shown in Figure 1-7. To stimulate the olfactory

Sensory Characteristics of Food

Flavor

Flavor is a complex mixture of taste, smell, texture, and temperature. The nose and mouth work together to deliver signals that the brain translates into the flavor of food. Some other facts about taste:

- Salt can hide bitter flavors.
- The heat of chili peppers is actually not a flavor but a response of pain receptors on the tongue.
- Aging tends to cause a loss of taste buds and sensitivity to food decreases—food tastes more bland to older people.

"The nose knows." How does the nose participate in tasting food?

Most of what is called "flavor" actually comes from odors that reach nerves via nasal passages at the back of the throat. A person could detect 10,000 odors, but how one could be detected from the other is still unknown. Scientists think that a person has many different receptors that "light-up" in various combinations in response to different scents.

Scientists also have found a strong link between smell and memory. Consider how a dinner experience could be enhanced if guests could enjoy the food with a smell associated with a pleasant experience.

Umami—What is it?

Umami is a Japanese word meaning "savory" or "meaty" and thus applies to the sensation of savoriness—specifically to the detection of glutamates which are especially common in meats, cheese (Parmesan, Roquefort), soy sauce, fish sauce, walnuts, grapes, broccoli, tomatoes, and mushrooms. The action of umami receptors explains why foods treated with monosodium glutamate (MSG) often taste fuller or better.

The glutamate taste sensation is most intense in combination with sodium. This is one reason why tomatoes exhibit a strong taste after adding salt. Sauces with savory and salty tastes are very popular for cooking, such as tomato sauces and ketchup for Western cuisines, and soy sauce and fish sauce for East Asian and Southern Asian cuisines.

---

center, substances must be in gaseous form. The gaseous molecules enter the nose as food is placed in the mouth and are drawn toward the olfactory center, where they stimulate nerve endings. Nerve impulses are thus sent to the brain to be interpreted. The sense of smell is estimated to be about 10,000 times as sensitive as the sense of taste in detecting minute concentrations, and it can differentiate hundreds, or possibly thousands, of distinct odors.

Flavor

Flavor is a blending of **taste** and **odor**. Millions of flavor sensations are experienced in a lifetime. For most, the perceived pleasantness of the flavor will determine if the food will be consumed. Flavor perceptions change over time, and foods not liked when one is young may become favorites later in life. Older adults may have less sensitivity to some flavors and therefore are inclined to add more sugar, salt, or other flavoring substances to enhance eating enjoyment [41].

Perceived flavor results from an integrated response to a complex mixture of stimuli or sensations from the **olfactory** center in the nasal cavity, the taste buds on the tongue, **tactile** receptors in the mouth, and the perception of **pungency**, heat, cooling, and so on when a food is placed in the mouth [28]. The process involved in this integration that produces flavor is not well understood because of its complexity. The flavor of food can be affected by every step in the production process, from selection of ingredients to processing to packaging and storage of the final product [34].

Brain

Olfactory
Center

FIGURE 1-7 Gaseous molecules enter the nose and stimulate the olfactory center, from which nerve fibers send messages to the brain concerning the odor of food.

Analysis of Flavor. Countless numbers of molecules contribute to our perception of odor or aroma and taste. One single flavor may be produced from the interaction of many different chemical molecules. Did you know, for example, that more than 200 different compounds are used to make artificial banana flavor? Many of the odorous substances in foods occur in such vanishingly small concentrations that it is difficult to show that they are even present. With the development of analytical tools such as the gas chromatograph, tracings from which are shown in Figure 1-8, the chemist has been able to separate, isolate, and identify many of the molecules that are responsible for aroma and taste in such foods as onions, strawberries, and beef.

Analytical tools used to great advantage by the flavor researcher are high-performance liquid chromatography (HPLC), the electronic nose, and the electronic tongue [31, 37, 56]. HPLC is especially useful for studying nonvolatile and/or labile flavor components (see Figure 1-9). Among other things, it can be used to test for adulteration of flavoring materials from natural sources. The electronic nose is a chemical sensing system that offers the advantage of the rapid detection of volatiles (Figure 1-10).

Impact of Heat on Flavor Development. The flavors of some foods are readily perceivable in the raw "natural" state, whereas cooking other foods produces flavors from nonflavor substances called flavor precursors. The method of cooking also has an impact on flavor development. For example, flavors produced when meat is cooked in water are different from those produced when it is roasted in an oven surrounded by dry heat. The tantalizing odors that develop during the baking of bread are additional examples of flavor substances produced by heating. Many of the volatile substances that waft from the oven where bread is baking are initially the products of yeast fermentation. The browning of the bread crust in a hot oven contributes to a pleasant flavor as well as an attractive appearance.

Natural Flavors. Flavors also may be produced during processing by enzymatic reactions, such as cheese flavors, or by microbial fermentation, such as butter flavors. Flavor substances that occur naturally or that are generated during heating, processing, or fermentation are considered to be "natural" flavors [28].

Artificial or Synthetic Flavors. Biotechnology can be used to generate natural flavor substances from enzymatic or microbial reactions. Natural flavors are simulated as closely as possible through the production of synthetic compounds. Synthetic compounds that are added to foods either individually or as part of a mixture are considered in the United States to be "artificial" or "synthetic" flavors. Both natural and artificial flavorings are combined in many foods.

Flavor Researchers. Knowledge of flavor chemistry and ways of simulating natural flavors is especially important as the world population increases and global markets expand. Foods must be flavored so that they are accepted by consumers in their unique cultural environment. To apply the science of flavor successfully to the development of new products and the improvement of old ones, the flavor researcher must first identify the substances that are responsible for the acceptable flavor and the mechanism by which people eating the food experience flavor. New food-flavor ingredients can then be developed, and foods can be processed in a manner that results in the most desirable flavors [22, 34].

Texture

The physical properties of foods, including texture, consistency, and shape, involve the sense of touch or feeling, also called the tactile sense. When food is contacted, pressure and movement receptors on the skin and muscles of the mouth and tongue are stimulated. Sensations of smoothness, stickiness, graininess, brittleness, fibrous qualities, or lumpy characteristics may be detected [52]. The tingling feeling that comes from drinking a carbonated beverage is an attribute of texture. Terms describing extremes of texture and consistency may include dry or moist, solid or fluid, thick or thin, rough or smooth, coarse or fine, tough or tender, hard or soft, and compact or porous.

Texture includes those qualities that can be felt with the fingers, the tongue, the palate, or the teeth. It is an important attribute that affects consumer attitudes toward and preferences for different foods. Textural characteristics of food have both positive and negative connotations for the consumer [53]. Those textures that are universally liked are crisp, crunchy, tender, juicy, and firm. Those generally disliked are tough, soggy, crumbly, lumpy, watery, and slimy. Texturizing agents are often used by the food processor to impart body, to improve consistency or texture of a food, or to stabilize an emulsion [40]. Such agents, of which there are many, optimize the quality of a food product so that consumers will find it acceptable.

Sound

The sound made when a food is eaten is also part of palatability and the enjoyment of eating. We often evaluate crispness by the sound it makes and by its tactile sensations in the mouth. Try to imagine how crisp carrot and celery sticks would "taste" without the accompanying sound of crunching. When microwave popcorn was introduced, one of the significant sensory concerns was the squeaky, rather than crunchy sound, audible when eating.

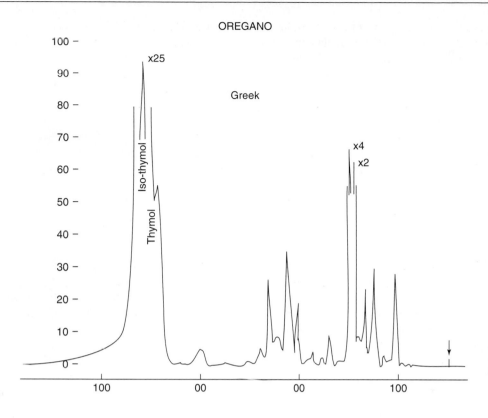

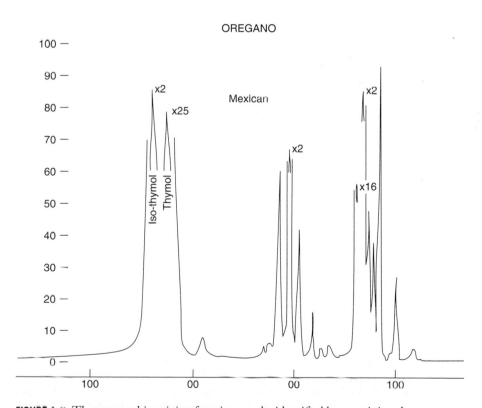

FIGURE 1-8 The geographic origin of a spice may be identified by examining the gas chromatographic tracing of its flavor components. Each peak on the tracing represents a different flavor substance. Oregano grown in Greece contains various flavor components in different amounts than oregano grown in Mexico. *(Courtesy of the R. T. French Company)*

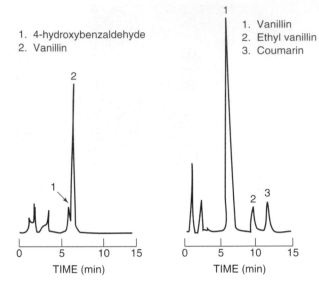

1. 4-hydroxybenzaldehyde
2. Vanillin

1. Vanillin
2. Ethyl vanillin
3. Coumarin

FIGURE 1-9 High-performance liquid chromatography (HPLC) may be used in testing vanilla for adulteration. The tracing on the left is from a true vanilla-bean extract, and the one on the right is from a sample that has been adulterated with coumarin, a substance banned as a flavor source in the United States. *(From Kenney, B. F. "Applications of high-performance liquid chromatography for the flavor research and quality control laboratories in the 1990s." Food Technology 44(9), 80, 1990. Copyright © Institute of Food Technologists)*

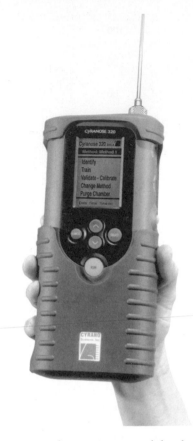

FIGURE 1-10 A piece of equipment named the electronic nose is used to pick up and record the aromas of various foods. *(Courtesy of Cyrano Sciences)*

Sensory Evaluation of Food

When the quality of a food is judged or evaluated by the senses (taste, smell, sight, touch, and hearing), it is said to be a sensory evaluation. Because food is prepared for the primary purpose of being eaten and enjoyed through the senses, sensory evaluation is most appropriate. No machine has yet been devised that can totally substitute for the human senses in evaluating the quality of human food. However, the human instrument used in sensory evaluation is very complex, and many problems need to be managed as data are collected and analyzed.

Flavor perceptions are difficult to characterize verbally. For example, think about how a strawberry tastes; then try to describe it to someone else. The character of a taste or aroma may be described using a wide variety of terms. Often the terms used to describe the flavor of a food indicate that the flavor is similar to that of some other familiar food product. For example, prepared cereal may be described as being nutty, starchy, haylike, floury, oily, or buttery. The primary tastes—sweet, sour, salty, and bitter—are relatively easy to describe. Other terms used to describe flavors in foods include caramel, stale, rancid, metallic, cardboardlike, musty, fragrant, flowery, fruity, sharp, pungent, tart, chalky, branny, burnt, spicy, astringent, sulfury, diacetyl (butterlike), malty, effervescent, earthy, chemical, putrid, yeasty, fishy, grassy, bland, toasted, and **aftertaste**. You may enjoy the

FOCUS ON SCIENCE

Gas Chromatography—How and Why Is It Used?

Gas chromatography is used as a means of identification and for quantification determination. The procedure is relatively simple. A small quantity of sample is introduced, typically by a micrometer syringe through a self-sealing diaphragm onto a column. The sample is vaporized on being injected onto the head of the column by striking a heated plate. Inert gas carries the sample along. The sample travels at various speeds depending on solubility, volatility, and gas pressure. Various components present in the sample will emerge at different times from the discharge end of the column. The time between injection of the test sample and the peak maxima shown on the chart printout is known as the retention time for the component.

challenge of finding new descriptive words for flavor evaluation.

Trained Sensory Panels. In food research, small groups of trained individuals, called judging panels or sensory panels, are commonly used to determine differences among food samples. These panels often consist of 5 to 15 individuals who have had training and experience in testing the particular food products being evaluated.

A variety of scoring, ranking, or difference tests are used by sensory panels. It may sometimes be desirable to do a complete analysis of all flavor components, such as sweet, buttery, burnt, fragrant, grainy, and metallic, in a particular food. Such a flavor profile of the food, giving a picture of its palatability, may be determined by a panel of trained judges working together (Figure 1-11). Aroma and taste are studied separately to complete the total flavor analysis.

Because any food product will likely contain many flavor components of differing degrees of volatility, these flavor components will impact the olfactory center at different times. Thus, aroma, taste, and texture may change as we eat and drink, especially for foods, such as chocolate, that melt in the mouth. These dynamic aspects of taste may be examined by using a time–intensity curve. The intensity of the flavor may be weak, moderate, strong, or someplace in between. Using a computer, the taster may record the changing intensity of a particular flavor attribute over a 30-second to 2 or 3-minute period [67]. Combining time–intensity curves for the various flavor components in a particular food may produce what has been called a dynamic flavor profile [12].

FIGURE 1-11 A sensory panel is used to evaluate the taste of foods. *(Courtesy of CCFRA)*

Consumer Panels. As new food products are developed, food manufacturers need to know if they can capture a large enough share of the market to warrant the cost of development and marketing. Many new products are introduced and fail each year. Sensory-evaluation professionals and marketing personnel may conduct consumer tests to obtain information on product quality and preference. Consumers and producers may not always agree on quality or preference. Trained sensory panels and consumer panels both involve people. However, trained panels are usually more objective than consumer panels. By correlating the two panels, the consumer can be better understood and the likelihood of product

FOCUS ON SCIENCE

Sensory Testing—Can You Identify the Food That Is Different?

Discrimination testing is a class of tests that represents one of the most useful tools available to the sensory professional. All of these methods are intended to answer a seemingly simple question: "Are these samples perceived as different?" It is on the basis of perceived differences between two products that can lead to a descriptive evaluation in order to identify the basis for the difference.

The identification of the samples is an important aspect of testing. Perhaps the researcher wants to know if a lowfat product can be identified as different from the standard product. If the product is labeled as lowfat, bias would be introduced.

Therefore, food and beverage samples used in sensory testing are usually identified with a numerical or alphabetic code.

Three types of discrimination tests are:

- *Paired Comparison.* Sensory panelists are asked to distinguish between two samples by identifying the sample that has more of a designated characteristic. For example, panelists may be asked to identify the spicier or sweeter sample.

- *Triangle Test.* Three samples are presented to the panelists for testing. The sensory panelists are asked to pick the two samples that are the same, thereby identifying one sample as different.

- *Duo-Trio Test.* Three samples are provided to the panelists for tasting. One of the samples is designated as the reference or control sample. From the remaining two samples, panelists are asked to identify the sample that matches the reference or control sample.

FIGURE 1-12 A hedonic scale for children has easy to interpret faces.

success enhanced. Consumer input is important from the very beginning of the development process.

In some cases, particularly in consumer preference testing that involves large groups of people, a hedonic scale is used without a description of the flavor components. A hedonic scale for children is shown in Figure 1-12. An example of a scale for adults follows.

____Like extremely well ____Dislike slightly

____Like very much ____Dislike moderately

Like moderately well Dislike very much

____Like slightly ____Dislike extremely

____Neither like nor dislike

OBJECTIVE EVALUATION OF FOOD

Objective evaluation of food involves the use of laboratory instruments to determine certain characteristics that may be related to eating quality. Devices and the objective measurements that may be made in the laboratory include a viscometer to measure viscosity (thickness or consistency) of a tomato paste or a starch-thickened pudding, a gelometer to measure the firmness or strength of a gelatin gel or a fruit jelly, a pH meter to measure the acidity of lemon juice, a colorimeter to measure the color of red apples, a compressimeter to measure the compressibility or softness of a slice of bread, and a shear or cutting apparatus to measure the tenderness of a sample of meat (Figure 1-13). These types of tests do not directly involve the human senses and thus are not part of a sensory evaluation.

The use of judging panels to evaluate food is often time consuming and expensive. Therefore, the use of laboratory instruments that give useful information with less time and expense is desirable when the information thus collected correlates well with sensory characteristics. Objective tests can usually be reproduced with reasonable precision. In the overall evaluation of the quality of a food product, sensory and objective methods complement each other [18].

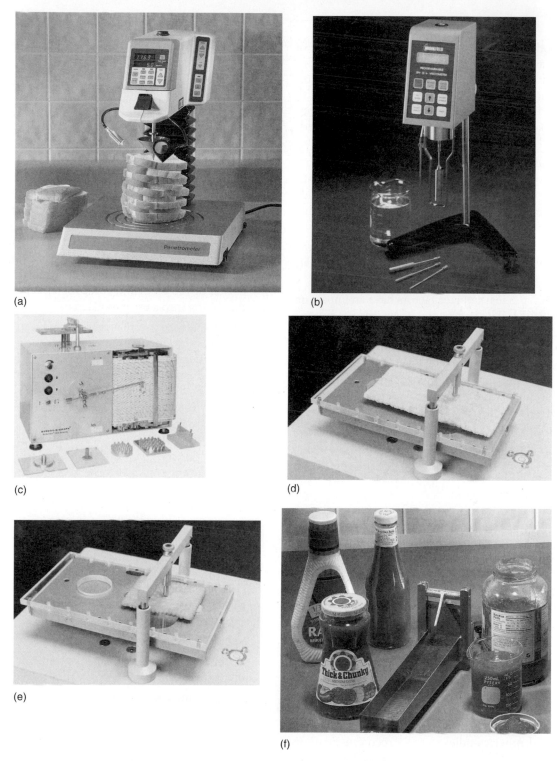

FIGURE 1-13 A variety of instruments are used in the objective measurement of food quality. (a) A micro processor–based digital penetrometer measures such characteristics of foods as the softness of bread. (Courtesy of Cole-Parmer Instrument Co., 800-323-4340)

(b) A Brookfield viscometer. (Courtesy of Brookfield Engineering Laboratories, Inc.)

(c, d, and e) The Brabender® Struct-O-Graph® may be used for testing mechanical parameters of foods that describe texture and structure. For example, textural characteristics of crackers and cookies may be measured. (Courtesy of C.W. Brabender Instruments, Inc.)

(f) The viscosity of food products such as sauces, salad dressings, and salsas may be measured by use of a consistometer. (Courtesy of Cole-Parmer Instrument Co., 800-323-4340)

CHAPTER SUMMARY

- The food choices we make and the development of our behavior and habits concerning food are influenced by many factors, including family, social, cultural, and religious traditions. Additionally, health and nutrition, food availability, economic resources, technological developments, and emotional considerations have an impact on what we eat.

- The food selections of families in the twenty-first century are increasingly influenced by time restraints. More convenience foods and foods prepared outside the home are being consumed. Nevertheless, family meals are still a priority for most families.

- Guidance has been provided to encourage healthy eating habits through the *2005 Dietary Guidelines*, *My Pyramid*, and nutrition labeling on food products.

- Economic and marketplace factors have an impact on food selection. The geography of an area has historically influenced the foods consumed in that region. Today, transportation and preservation methods have permitted a wide variety of foods to be served nearly anywhere. From an economic perspective, income and household size are important factors determining where and how Americans spend their food dollars.

- The food industry continues to develop innovative products, new packaging, and improved preservation methods to enhance the quality and availability of foods. Aseptic packaging, irradiation, and other biotechnology developments all influence the type and quality of food we consume.

- Sensory characteristics often determine whether we will first taste, then eat, and enjoy food. Appearance creates the first impression and includes such qualities as color, form, size, and design. Much of "flavor" is a blending of taste and odor. There are five primary taste sensations: sweet, sour, bitter, salty, and umami. The sense of smell is estimated to be about 10,000 times as sensitive as the sense of taste in detecting minute concentrations and differentiating hundreds of distinct odors. Texture includes the qualities that we feel with the fingers, the tongue, the palate, or the teeth and is accompanied by the sound that biting into a crisp food creates.

- The analysis or evaluation of food can be accomplished using human sensory test panels or through objective measurements with laboratory instruments. A combination of both of these types of tools provides the most complete understanding of the sensory qualities of a food.

STUDY QUESTIONS

1. Why is it important for the student of food science to be able to evaluate the palatability and quality of foods?

2. What is meant by *palatability*?

3. Discuss how family, society, culture, and religious practices may affect the eating patterns that an individual develops.

4. Identify several regional or ethnic food patterns, and then discuss how these foods are becoming integrated into home and restaurant menus.

5. Summarize the recommendations for health found in the USDA Food Guide Pyramid and the USDA Dietary Guidelines and identify suggested changes in the typical American diet to meet recommendations more closely.

6. Explain how economic, marketplace, and technological changes have an impact on food selection and availability.

7. Give an example of how the appearance of a food may influence your evaluation of its flavor or other quality characteristics.

8. Define and distinguish among the terms *flavor*, *taste*, *odor*, and *aroma*.

9. List the five primary tastes.

10. Briefly describe how the heating of food produces the sensations of taste and smell in humans.

11. Discuss what effect the temperature of a food has on your perception of its flavor.

12. Of what practical importance to humanity is research on flavor chemistry?

13. Which human sense(s) perceives the texture and consistency of a food?

14. Food quality may be evaluated by sensory or objective methods. (a) Provide examples of each type of evaluation, and (b) describe several situations or conditions under which quality evaluation of specific food products may be desirable or necessary.

FOOD ECONOMICS AND CONVENIENCE

2

Economics has been defined as the efficient use of resources to achieve a desired goal. Food economics, then, is our wise use of all available resources to obtain food that is acceptable, enjoyable, and healthful to an optimal extent. To achieve our goal, we use money as well as time, energy, knowledge, skills, and equipment, as well as our values or philosophy.

We are all consumers. Throughout our lives, we exchange money for goods and services. The responsibility for spending an individual's or a family's income is tremendous, and the cost of food is usually an appreciable expenditure for a household. In high income countries such as the United States, Japan, and Western Europe, the average share of the total budget for food is 13 percent. However, in low income countries such as Bangladesh, 47 percent of the total budget is used for food [38]. Likewise, among U.S. families, the highest income families spend more money for food than do low income families (Figure 2-1) [47, 48]. The responsibility for food purchasing is a major one, and the choices made with regard to convenience and the types of foods purchased can have significant impact on resources available for other expenses. For those involved in purchasing food for a foodservice establishment, financial responsibility is even greater.

To be most effective in the economic world, both the individual consumer and the professional in foods and nutrition need some knowledge of trends in food consumption. An understanding of factors affecting the cost and quality of food and amount of food waste is also important, especially as decisions are made about the use of convenience foods.

In this chapter, the following topics will be discussed:

- Trends in food use
- Food waste
- Factors influencing the cost of food
- Availability and use of convenience foods

TRENDS IN FOOD USE

What do people eat? And how much? Answers to these questions are important to those who work in the various fields of food and nutrition. Information on food consumption by populations and individuals may be collected in different ways using various sources.

Food Disappearance Data

One method of obtaining information on the food consumption or food use of populations is to measure directly (or to estimate through sampling and statistical procedures) the quantities of food that "disappear" into the nation's food distribution system. The total available food supply is measured using three components: total food production, total imports of food, and beginning-of-the-year inventories. From this total of available food is subtracted food that was exported, used by nonfood industries, used for seed by farmers, and year-end inventories. Food consumption calculated in this manner is called a *residual component*—what is left over when other uses are subtracted from the available total supply. The Economic Research Service of the USDA has periodically collected data since 1909 for up to 350 commodities, such as beef, eggs, wheat, and various fruits and vegetables [34, 35].

Food disappearance or food availability data, as a method of measuring food consumption, should be interpreted with an understanding of data collection strengths and limitations. The method of sampling, incomplete reporting, and estimation techniques all may contribute to errors. Strengths of this data are that they provide an independent measurement of food consumption without the errors inherent in consumer survey data [46].

Food Consumption Surveys

The USDA's Continuing Survey of Food Intakes by Individuals (CSFII) and the Health and Human Services' (HHS) National Health and Examination survey (HHANES)

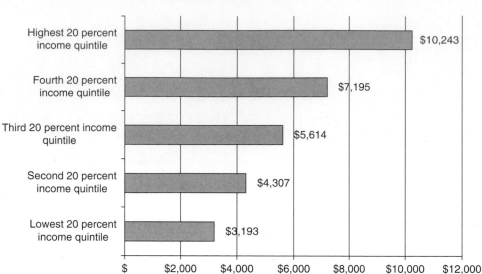

FIGURE 2-1 Per capita food spending by income quintile, 2006. Low income households spend less per person on food as compared to high income households. *(U.S. Department of Labor, Bureau of Labor Statistics, Consumer Expenditure Survey)*

provided information about food consumption and health prior to 2002. Beginning in 2002, these two surveys were conducted jointly under the NHANES/CSFII survey [10]. This new integrated survey is called "What We Eat in America" [27, 44].

Unlike the information about food consumption obtained from the food disappearance studies, the data for "What We Eat in America" are obtained from a nationally representative sample of Americans over a two-day period. In the 2001–2002 data set, 10,477 individuals participated in a physical examination at a mobile exam center, and 9,701 completed a dietary interview. This first integrated survey includes 2001 data from the NHANES and thus represents data collected in 2001 and 2002 [44].

As with the food disappearance data, these data should be interpreted with an understanding of their strengths and limitations. Survey data of Americans provide insight into Americans' food consumption patterns and allow a check on the accuracy of the USDA food disappearance data. Furthermore, these survey data allow an analysis of food patterns by age, region of the country, and other variables. However, individuals may not clearly recall exact consumption of foods or may be uncomfortable being entirely candid about the foods consumed. Researchers have developed the survey method to minimize these potential inaccuracies [45].

Changes in Food Consumption

Although food habits may be quite firmly established, people are receptive to change with sufficiently compelling reasons. Diet and health concerns, as well as changing prices and increasing or decreasing real disposable income, have probably contributed to changes seen in U.S. food

consumption. Other factors influencing these changes are the plethora of new products on the market (especially convenience items), the aging population, expanded advertising campaigns, smaller households, more two-earner households, and an increasing proportion of ethnic minorities in the U.S. population [49].

CONSUMER FOOD WASTE

Trends toward increasing food prices, coupled with growing concerns about conservation of resources, have focused attention on food loss or waste. It is important to know how much food is generally being wasted by consumers to attack this problem sensibly and try to change wasteful practices [22]. Discarded food does have associated expenses; thus practices to avoid food waste are suggested from an economic perspective. The impact of food and packaging waste on the environment is another factor to consider [1].

What is food waste? Different definitions may be used. In a broad sense, however, any food that was once usable but has since been discarded and not eaten by humans may be considered waste. Food eaten by household pets may be counted as waste if this food was originally prepared for human consumption.

Storage Loss

Food loss may occur at different stages of handling and preparation. As food is taken home from the market and transferred to cabinets, refrigerators, and freezers, it should be handled to minimize any potential losses. While food is in storage, even on a very temporary basis,

FOOD CONSUMPTION

What Is Known about Food Consumption in the United States Using Food Disappearance Data?

The Economic Research Service, under the U.S. Department of Agriculture, provides on-line access to food disappearance or food supply data. Go to http://www.ers.usda.gov/Data/FoodConsumption/FoodAvailIndex.htm or visit www.usda.gov and search using the key term Food Availability or Food Consumption to locate this information. Spreadsheets or tables and charts may be obtained for the foods and dates you specify.

Using this data source, the following food quantities per capita on an annual basis were obtained to highlight changes in food consumption since 1970. ■

	1970	2005	Percent Change
Meat (includes red meat, poultry, fish, and shellfish)	178 #	200 #	+12 %
Eggs	309 eggs	254 eggs	−18 %
Fruits	242 #	273 #	+12 %
Vegetables	336 #	415 #	+24 %
Flour and Cereal Products	136 #	192 #	+41 %
Cheese	11 #	31 #	+181 %
Beverage Milk	31 gallons	21 gallons	−32 %
Caloric Sweeteners	119 #	141 #	+19 %
Total Fat	56 #	87 #	+55 %

waste may result from microbial spoilage, contamination by insects and rodents, and spilling as a result of broken or open containers. If food is held or stored too long, particularly with improper packaging or temperature control, it may be discarded simply because it is not fresh.

Preparation Loss

Additional waste may occur during preparation as a result of discarding edible portions of the food before cooking, improper cooking procedures such as scorching or overcooking, preparing too much for the number of people to be served, and spoilage because of inappropriate holding of the food before service. Not serving leftovers also creates waste.

Plate Waste

Plate waste, food left on plates by individual diners (Figure 2-2), accounts for a significant portion of total food loss. Food may be left on plates at home or in the foodservice setting. In a study of a university dining hall serving 850 male and 490 female students who were on

board plans, an average of 17 percent of the food items selected was wasted [33]. Considering the number of students served, the total cost of food wasted was substantial.

FIGURE 2-2 Plate waste. *(Courtesy of the U.S. Department of Agriculture)*

There may be various reasons for food waste in foodservice settings. For example, overall plate waste was reduced from 40 percent to 27 percent when elementary students in grades 3, 4, and 5 had recess before rather than after lunch [4]. In another study, plate waste decreased from 43 to 27 percent when elementary students in grades 3, 4, and 5 had 30 minutes for lunch as opposed to 20 minutes [3]. Children who are hurried when eating lunch, either because of a short meal period or a desire to go out to recess, waste more food. In a continuing-care retirement community, there was less food waste when residents received family-style service or waitstaff service than when they were served trays [17].

SOME FACTORS INFLUENCING FOOD COSTS

At the least, modestly rising food prices are a reality in the United States (Figure 2-3), although U.S. food costs are among the lowest in the world. Low food costs allow Americans to spend a smaller percentage of their incomes on food and more on other goods and services or on savings. Overall, Americans spend only 9.5 percent of their disposable income on food [41]. Of course, the total family income affects the proportion of this income that is spent for food [5]. For example, in 2004, 7 percent of affluent Americans' income went for food, whereas low income households spent 32 percent of their income for food [47, 48]. In addition to the general effects of inflation, a number of other factors affect the cost of food.

Marketing

The USDA calculates marketing costs for food purchased by consumers in the United States, including food purchased both in retail markets and in foodservice establishments. In 2006, marketing expenses accounted for 81 percent of the cost of a food product (Figure 2-4). These marketing expenses include the cost of food processing, packaging, transportation, advertising, energy use, and other costs incurred in bringing food from the farmer to the consumer [14]. The farm-value share of food purchased in grocery stores was 19 percent. Thus, for every dollar consumers spent on food grown in the U.S., the farmer received 19 cents.

Crop Production

Food production is costly, yet farmers receive a relatively small percentage of the consumer food dollar. Substantial initial investments must be made by farmers in property and equipment. Farmers have become increasingly dependent on fuel to operate their equipment and on the fertilizers, herbicides, and insecticides that they must purchase to promote high crop yields. Additionally, some crops in particular are very labor intensive, and prices for these crops are therefore influenced by the cost of wages.

Poor weather conditions often reduce the size of crops of fruits, vegetables, and grains. Droughts, floods, and unexpected freezes all have a significant impact on crops. The weather is not controllable, and efficient management of commodity production thus becomes quite difficult. Crop shortages translate into higher prices in the marketplace when demand exceeds the supply.

Trade Policies

The United States presently enjoys a competitive advantage for a number of products in world agricultural trade. U.S. agricultural exports average $62.4 billion per year as compared to $57.7 billion in agricultural imports [42]. Top sources of agricultural exports and imports are found in Figure 2-5. Abundant natural resources and technological developments have contributed to the U.S. becoming a net exporter of agricultural products. However, changing international economies, world demand for certain commodities, and government policies concerning production or international sales can change trade advantages and affect prices. Ecology and food-safety regulations may also be controversial trade issues [16, 37, 43]. Sound policy decisions help control wide fluctuations in export sales.

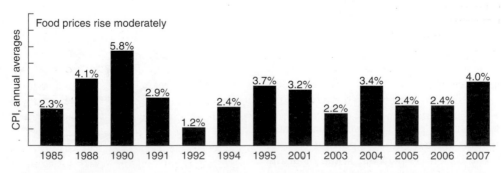

FIGURE 2-3 The percentage of increase in annual retail food prices is shown for several years. *(Courtesy of the U.S. Department of Agriculture)*

What a Dollar Spent for Food Paid for in 2006

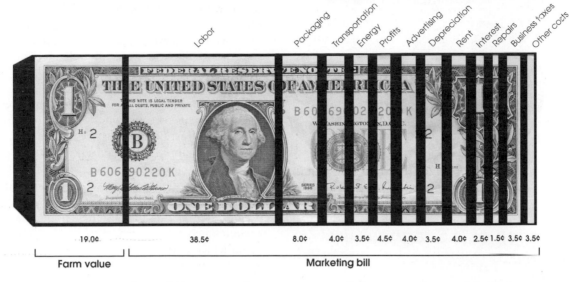

FIGURE 2-4 81 percent of every dollar spent on food goes to pay marketing costs. *(Courtesy of the U.S. Department of Agriculture, Economic Research Service)*

Food Processing and Packaging

Much of the food on supermarket shelves has been processed to some degree. Even the trimming of retail meat cuts and the packaging of fresh vegetables are types of processing, though minimal, that increase the cost of the food. Examples of highly processed foods include fabricated breakfast cereals, meat substitutes produced from textured vegetable proteins, frozen ready-to-eat entrees of various descriptions, and packaged salads.

Food processing and food production are both costly. Large investments in equipment, facilities, and human resources are essential. Additional processing costs include packaging materials and labeling to meet governmental regulations. New, expensive packaging materials continue to be developed to provide greater quality and options for consumers. As a result, packaging costs are sometimes substantial in proportion to the cost of the food itself.

Technological developments have made possible many new food products scarcely dreamed of a century ago that are marketed domestically and internationally. The research and development necessary to produce new food products are costly. Once new foods are developed, they require extensive promotional campaigns and test-marketing procedures. Typically, only about one-third of all new products are successful [18]. Losses to the manufacturer due to a new product's lack of success in the marketplace are reflected in increased prices at the consumer level.

An increasing number of today's foods have built-in "maid service," with partial or complete preparation having been accomplished before the food is purchased.

These so-called convenience foods must include the costs of preparation in their prices. In foodservice operations as well as at home, informed decisions must be made regarding the cost advantages of buying prepared and partially prepared food products versus paying labor costs to completely prepare the foods on the premises. However, in today's labor market, produce foods such as cleaned, ready-to-eat broccoli and peeled carrots may be more economical to purchase than to prepare on premises. There will be more discussion about convenience foods later in this chapter.

Food Purchasing Practices

Consumers have many options to consider when purchasing foods. Perhaps the first decision is where to buy food and in what form the food will be purchased. Price, quality, and convenience are all factors to be taken into account. Food preparation skills for some consumers may be a significant concern, whereas others enjoy new culinary challenges and experiences and therefore may seek out exotic ingredients without regard to cost.

Eating Out or Cooking at Home. In 2004, consumers spent 49.7 percent of their total food expenditures on food consumed at home [41]. These figures, however, should not imply that consumers eat half of their meals in restaurants and other foodservice establishments. Food purchased from a foodservice includes the cost of labor, entertainment, service, and ambiance, and therefore is more expensive. The menu price reflects a food cost markup to cover these additional expenses when providing

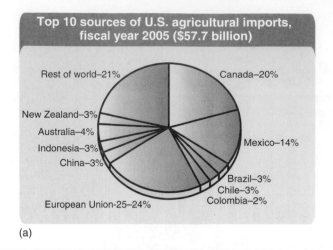

Top 10 sources of U.S. agricultural imports, fiscal year 2005 ($57.7 billion)

Rest of world–21%
Canada–20%
New Zealand–3%
Australia–4%
Indonesia–3%
China–3%
Mexico–14%
Brazil–3%
Chile–3%
Colombia–2%
European Union-25–24%

(a)

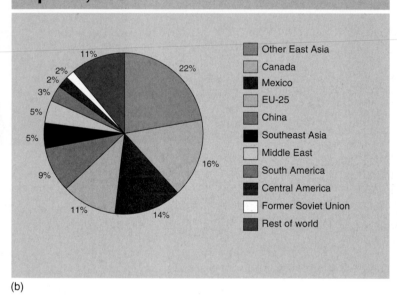

Major destination of U.S. agricultural exports, 2004

11%
2%
2%
3%
5%
5%
9%
11%
14%
22%
16%

Other East Asia
Canada
Mexico
EU-25
China
Southeast Asia
Middle East
South America
Central America
Former Soviet Union
Rest of world

(b)

FIGURE 2-5 (a) Top ten sources of U.S. agricultural imports in 2005. (b) Major destination of U.S. agricultural exports in 2004. *(Courtesy of U.S. Department of Agriculture, Economic Research Service)*

service. These costs may account for as much as 60 to 75 percent of the menu price, leaving 25 to 45 percent in actual food cost.

In a study examining where Americans eat, the researchers found 75 percent of adults purchase over half of their food from retail food stores as measured by weight [9]. In this study, nearly half of the adult population were classified as a "home cookers." The "home cookers" purchase 93 percent of their food from a store and were older than the other groups studied. In contrast, working families purchase 70 percent of their food from a store and 22 percent from carryouts. Young professionals purchase 40 percent of their food from carryouts, which

is a greater percent than that purchased from stores. Consumers valuing high service consumed 44 percent of their food at a restaurant. Students, faculty, and office employees purchased 25 to 52 percent of their food from cafeterias. Thus, income level, employment status, and lifestyle were all influencing factors on where consumers purchased food.

Types of Food Stores.   There are a number of different types of stores through which food is marketed on a retail basis. For foodservice institutions, a variety of vendors supply different types of food products, generally on a wholesale basis. In the retail sector, *specialty stores*, such as bakeries and fish markets, offer only one type of food. *Food cooperatives, or co-ops*, are organized by groups of consumers to purchase food on a wholesale basis. *Farmers' markets* are open seasonally as outlets for local farm produce. *Convenience stores*, almost miniature supermarkets, carry a limited stock of merchandise that has high turnover. They are often part of a large chain of stores and usually remain open 24 hours a day. This type of store has become very popular in the United States in recent years. It usually offers fast service but at somewhat higher prices. *Warehouse or discount markets* forego some consumer services such as bagging of groceries. They generally buy in very large quantities and pass some of their cost savings on to the customer. Grocery sales in *wholesale clubs* have increased markedly in recent years. *Supercenters* are giant stores that include a wide range of merchandise from clothing to groceries. Wal-Mart, Kmart, Target, and other major retailers are pursuing these stores as a way to corner the market on consumers seeking to purchase multiple products including food in one stop [11, 20]. Other means for consumers to obtain food include the Internet purchase of groceries and takeout foods.

Supermarkets handle the largest volume of retail food sales in the United States. These stores stock thousands of food items and, usually, other merchandise including beauty aids, pharmaceutical supplies, kitchen tools, flowers, and plants. The concept of supermarkets as full-service centers is growing. These may include florist shops, bakeries, ethnic food takeout services, catering, delicatessens, tortillerias, sushi bars, pharmacies, photofinishing shops, and even branch banks and post offices. In addition, some stores offer cooking classes, home delivery, and valet parking [20]. Nevertheless, supermarket sales have flattened since 1990 as consumers spend more on meals outside the home [32] and increasingly purchase from nontraditional retailers such as supercenters [24]. The term *home meal replacement* is being used to describe ready-made meals that can be taken home for eating. Supermarkets, in cooperation with food manufacturers, are expanding in this area of food merchandising. Currently, 80 percent of supermarkets sell ready-to-eat foods [20].

Prices are influenced by services offered and can vary between stores by as much as 5 to 15 percent [24]. Consumers should evaluate the various kinds of markets in terms of the services and benefits desired and the price they are willing to pay. The following items may be considered in this evaluation:

1. Quality and variety of merchandise carried
2. Layout and organization of the market
3. Pricing policies, such as specials, discounting, advertising, availability of in-store brands and generic or unbranded products, coupons, trading stamps, and games
4. Location of market
5. Sanitation and food safety
6. Customer services, such as bagging, carryout, and rapid service, and availability of printed information concerning nutrition and food.

Shopping Aids. Food manufacturers and retailers offer the consumer several conveniences to facilitate efficient shopping for food. These include unit pricing, open-date labeling, and nutrition labeling. Computerized checkout systems are the norm in supermarkets. Some of these aids involve additional labor and skill in producing and/or marketing food products and may thus increase the cost of food to the consumer.

Unit Pricing. The cost per pound or ounce for products sold by weight or the cost per quart, pint, or fluid ounce for products sold by volume is printed on a label, which is usually attached to the edge of the shelf where the products are displayed. This information allows the shopper to compare prices per unit for different-sized packages of the same product. The most economical size to buy can thus be readily determined. Generally, the smaller package sizes and individual-size convenience items are more expensive per unit because of the basic package cost. Unit pricing is mandatory in some states, but voluntary in others.

Open-Date Labeling. A date code is on each packaged food product for the customer to read and interpret. The date may appear in different forms on different packages. It may represent the last recommended day of retail sale, the end of the period of optimum quality, or the date of processing or final packaging. Open-date labeling provides some information for the shopper, but the conditions, such as temperature, under which the products are handled and stored greatly affect the quality.

Food Labeling. The basic requirements for all food labels include net weight of contents, manufacturer's or distributor's name and address, and ingredient declaration. Regulations governing the labeling of most food products are prepared by the U.S. Food and Drug Administration (FDA), but the labeling of meat and poultry products is under the jurisdiction of the USDA. In the early 1970s, the FDA completed a major revision of labeling requirements which included regulations governing nutrition labeling. Under these regulations, nutrition labeling was voluntary, except when the products contained added nutrients or when nutrition claims were made. Current mandatory food labeling is discussed in greater detail in Chapter 4.

The cost to manufacturers for nutrition labeling may be appreciable because they are required to have accurate nutrient information from laboratory analyses of samples of their food products. This expense ultimately affects the cost of food to the customer. Consumers, however, benefit by having access to accurate information about the nutrition content of the food being purchased. An evaluation of food expenditures by nutritional quality is another way to look at food cost.

Computerized Checkout Systems. Computer-assisted electronic cash register systems are commonly used in supermarkets. The cost of the items in the customer's shopping cart is tabulated by using a laser optical scanner to read Universal Product Code (UPC) symbols, which are affixed to each food package. The scanner is connected to a computer that then retrieves the necessary information from its storage and prints the name and price of each item on a screen for the customer to see. It also prints this information on the sales receipt. The computer must be properly programmed at all times with current price information. The UPC symbol contains a series of dark lines and spaces of varying widths, as shown in Figure 2-6. The left half of the symbol identifies the manufacturer, and the right half identifies the product. Most of the items on supermarket shelves carry a UPC symbol.

Use of a computerized system allows pricing of items to be done on the display shelves only and not on each individual product. It also speeds up checkout time and reduces errors at the cash register. Additional advantages are a meaningful record of purchases for the customer and improved inventory control for the retailer. However, a disadvantage is not having cost information readily available on the item itself for later reference.

FIGURE 2-6 *Universal Product Code.*

Price Conscious Buying A study was made of primary food preparers in the United States who agreed or disagreed with the following: *I run my household on a strict food budget.* Those participants who reported using a strict food budget were more likely than others to be concerned whether the meals they served were nutritious [12]. However, several of the most commonly recommended planning and budgeting tools for food shoppers were not widely used by those on a strict budget. These strategies include (1) making a complete list before shopping, (2) stocking up when preferred brands are on sale, (3) comparison shopping, and (4) redeeming coupons. Many useful suggestions may be made for the food shopper. Here are a few general guidelines to follow:

1. Compare prices for specified quality items; use unit pricing; consider cost of packaging; watch advertised specials.

2. Buy only quantities that can be utilized well; do not overbuy in terms of storage facilities available.

3. Buy staples in quantity but store them properly.

4. Buy in-store brands or generic items when the quality is acceptable for a particular use.

5. Purchase less expensive cuts of meat and use appropriate cooking techniques for high quality meals.

6. Buy fruits and vegetables in season when prices are lower.

7. Make reasonable substitutions when desired items are too expensive or unavailable.

8. Assess price per serving. Some foods may be less per pound or less as packaged but are actually more expensive per serving.

9. Factor in the cost of convenience products. Compare cost of frozen juice to refrigerated-prepared or the cost of a frozen entrée as compared to preparing the item "from scratch" using basic ingredients.

10. Plan ahead and purchase on a regular basis; use specifications or a written list; avoid impulse buying.

11. Choose vendors or markets that generally have reasonable pricing.

AVAILABILITY AND USE OF CONVENIENCE FOODS

Convenience foods may be defined as fully or partially prepared foods for which significant preparation time, culinary skills, or energy use have been transferred from the consumer's kitchen to the food processor and distributor. Most of the foods in a supermarket have had some preparation treatment. However, the term *convenience food* commonly applies to a food that has undergone a comparatively large amount of processing or market services and may be served with a minimum of effort and skill. Other names for these types of foods are *service ready*, *prefabricated*, *ready prepared*, or *efficiency* foods.

Ease of Preparation

Habits of cooking in an American kitchen are undergoing pronounced change. One survey indicated that 72 percent of consumers reported spending between 16 and 45 minutes preparing dinner during the work week. More than two-thirds of Americans say they struggle with cooking. Nearly 80 percent of households purchase pre-trimmed and washed produce, and 86 percent buy convenience entrees. Sales of take-out suppers have more than doubled in recent years [39].

Convenience foods help consumers to prepare dinner in a minimum amount of time. Convenience foods also help those who have limited preparation skills by providing high quality foods requiring minimal preparation. Although it could appear that a "homemade" item made from "scratch" is becoming an endangered species, many consumers are very sophisticated in their tastes and abilities. Home-cooked meals generally provide more nutritional value [25] and allow consumers to be creative in the development of their own special dishes.

Developments by Industry

The food industry is actively involved in the production of convenience foods. Many different processes are used in their preparation, including dehydrating the food to variable moisture levels by freeze-drying and other methods, precooking and freezing, and using various flexible packaging materials or pouches that withstand both high and low temperatures. Retort pouches were developed as a new food technology in the 1960s to be used even at the temperatures well above boiling needed for canning low-acid meats and vegetables. Retort pouches have been successfully used in the production of military rations for a number of years. With the introduction of retort pouch tuna in 2000, more commercial uses are anticipated in the years ahead (Figure 2-7) [7]. Another type of packaging called *modified atmosphere packaging* (MAP) aids in the retention of desirable qualities in products such as fresh-cut produce and salad ingredients (Figure 2-8).

The production of convenience foods actually began many years ago with the development of canning. Several canned products are now well-established convenience foods. In the twenty-first century, canned foods have a "new look" with contoured cans and fruit packaged in multilayer barrier plastic cups with peelable closures (Figure 2-7b). Other "canned" foods are sold in glass containers for a more upscale product or polyester bottles for the convenience of a see-through nonbreakable container [7].

Frozen foods were perfected by Clarence Birdseye in the 1920s [2]. Today, many frozen foods have entered

(a)

(b)

(c)

FIGURE 2-7 (a) Starkist provides consumers with convenient new retort packaging for tuna. *(Courtesy of Starkist Seafood)*
(b) Perfect for packed lunches or on-the-go snacks, Dole Fruit bowls are a shelf stable, travel-ready food. *(Courtesy of Dole Food Company, Inc.)*
(c) Yoplait has made yogurt readily accessible with its "no-spoon-necessary" packaging. *(Courtesy of Yoplait USA, Inc.)*

FOCUS ON SCIENCE

More About Retort Systems

Retort systems use steam or superheated water to cook food in its own package, extending shelf life and ensuring food safety. The processing time of retort packages is shorter than that required for traditional canned foods because retort packages have a thin profile and a high surface-area-to-volume ratio.

Consequently, heat penetrates the food much more quickly, thereby preventing overcooked, excessively soft food. The shorter processing time also results in a better flavor and a higher nutrient value.

Retort packaging has been slow to catch on in the United States because of the existing can-making and can-filling infrastructure. Companies need the necessary machinery—retort chamber—and the knowledge and experience to use retort systems. Soups and stews are starting to be available in stand-up pouches.

Source: Mykytiuk, A. (2002, October). Retort flexible packaging: The revolution has begun. *Flexible Packaging.* 19–25.

FIGURE 2-8 Dole ready-made salads in modified atmosphere packaging. *(Courtesy of U.S. Department of Agriculture)*

the market through widespread product availability, consumer desire for convenience, and the use of home freezers [13]. Also plentiful are dehydrated convenience items.

Special Needs Convenience Foods

Space travel and military training and operations have necessitated the ultimate in convenience foods. The development of convenience foods for these specialized environments and circumstances has resulted in new products and food processing technologies.

Space-Age Convenience. Travel into space brought special requirements with regard to food for the astronauts. The demanding specifications for weight, volume, and ease of preparation are met by convenience-type foods [6, 31]. Because the astronauts have much work and experimentation to do in space, the time required to

FOCUS ON SCIENCE

Modified Atmosphere Packaging (MAP)

The atmosphere within modified atmosphere packaging (MAP) is changed so that the composition is different than air. Air is composed of oxygen (O_2), carbon dioxide (CO_2), and nitrogen (N_2). The choice of the gas for MAP depends on the food product being packed and may be used alone or in combination with other gases. Storage of foods in a modified gaseous atmosphere can maintain quality and extend product shelf life by slowing chemical and biochemical deteriorative reactions. The growth of some spoilage organisms also can be slowed because of their inability to grow in low oxygen environments.

In addition to maintaining quality, MAP can improve product presentation. Foods packaged in MAP include:

- Dairy products such as whole milk powder and cheddar cheese—to improve shelf life.
- Red meat—to maintain bright red color (oxymyoglobin pigment).
- Raw poultry—to prevent growth of spoilage bacteria.
- Cooked, cured, and processed meat—to prevent microbial growth, color changes, and rancidity.
- Fish and fish products—to prevent microbial contamination, reduce oxidation reactions, or reduce deterioration by enzymes found in the fish.
- Fruit and vegetables—to reduce respiration (senescence), thereby slowing ripening and maturing. Also to prevent or reduce bacterial contamination and mold growth.

prepare and eat must be kept to a minimum. Foods must be stable to store at temperatures up to 100°F (38°C). Packaging must be flexible and able to withstand extremes of pressure, humidity, temperature, and vibration that could cause breakage or cracking. Food packages also must be convenient to handle (Figure 2-9 and Plate I).

Food developed for space travel is researched at the Food Systems Engineering Facility (FSEF) at the National Aeronautics and Space Administration (NASA) Johnson Space Center. Food scientists, dietitians, and engineers analyze the foods for nutritional, sensory, and packaging quality. Before foods are used on space flights, FSEF personnel test the foods on NASA's Zero-Gravity KC-135 airplane [31].

Military Convenience Foods. Military rations for battlefield foodservice have also undergone many changes over the years. During World War II, canned meats such as Spam were common. The basic combat ration used today is the Meal, Ready-to-Eat (MRE). MREs provide a full meal consisting of 9 or 10 components that provide about 1,300 kcal. The packaging consists of retort pouches, flexible packaging, in a meal bag (Figure 2-10).

The MRE must be able to be dropped out of aircraft, withstand environmental extremes from –60°F to +120°F, shelf stable for three years at 80°F, resistant to wildlife, and taste good. MREs may be eaten cold, or if heated, heated by a variety of ways including with a flameless heating device provided in the meal bag. MREs have improved considerably since they were used during Operation Desert Storm in the Persian Gulf War of 1991. Product developers go into the field with soldiers to assess performance of the MREs and interview the soldiers. This approach has increased soldiers' satisfaction [26].

Cost of Convenience

How much does convenience cost? In making cost comparisons between various convenience foods and similar home-prepared products, some difficulties may be encountered. Although food labels list ingredients from the greatest amount to the least, the exact proportions of ingredients contained in convenience foods are not identified and, therefore, home-prepared products may not contain the same amounts of component ingredients. The eating quality of the two products may also be very

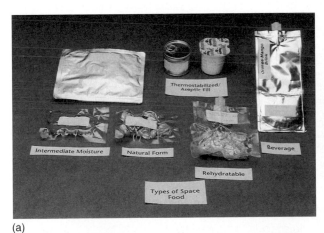

(a)

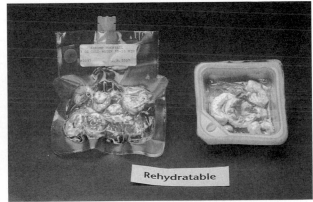

(b)

(c)

(d)

FIGURE 2-9 (a) Several types of foods and packaging are used in space. (b) Shrimp cocktail is ready to rehydrate as part of a space meal. (c) A typical meal tray in space. (d) This astronaut demonstrates one way to make sure the candy melts in your mouth and not in your hand. *(Courtesy of NASA)*

UP CLOSE

The Evolution of Food in Space

Mercury flights	It was learned a person could chew and swallow while weightless. Early space foods were either pureed to be forced into the mouth through tubes or compressed into compact, bite-sized pieces that were coated to avoid any loose crumbs that would float in zero gravity.
Apollo flights	A spoon, rather than a tube, was used to eat moist foods, and hot water was available for the first time to make the rehydration of foods easier.
Skylab program	Space was available for a dining room with tables, and a refrigerator and freezer. Astronauts had knives and forks available to them and ate from a food tray with cavities to hold containers of food.
Space Shuttle	A galley has been designed on the shuttle for astronauts' foodservice needs. The galley has hot and cold water, an oven, and a small refrigeration unit, but no freezer. The food includes (a) rehydratable foods such as macaroni and cheese; (b) thermostabilized foods in cans, plastic cups, or flexible retort packages such as puddings, fruits, and tuna; (c) intermediate moisture foods such as dried peaches; (d) natural form foods such as granola bars; and (e) irradiated meat. Condiments such as salt and pepper are packaged with liquid so that these seasonings can be used without floating into equipment on the shuttle. Many foods are dehydrated to reduce weight at takeoff, but water produced onboard as a byproduct of the spacecraft's fuel cells was readily available for use in space.
Space station	Foods are frozen, refrigerated, or thermostabilized, then heated to serving temperatures with an onboard microwave/forced air convection oven. Few dehydrated foods are used on the space station because the solar panels used to provide electricity do not produce water. In 2005, the space station crew enjoyed some gourmet creations of Chef Emeril Lagasse.
Future space travel	Future space travel is likely to involve manned flights of longer duration. NASA is cooperating with universities and the food industry in the research and development of controlled ecological life-support systems. Such a system includes biomass production, food processing, waste treatment, atmosphere regeneration, and water purification. Imagine the challenge to food scientists and engineers as they discover how to produce nutritious, safe, palatable foods from a limited amount of biomass materials, with serious constraints in space and facilities for food processing and preparation.

Source: References 8, 15, 28, 29, 30, 31

(a)

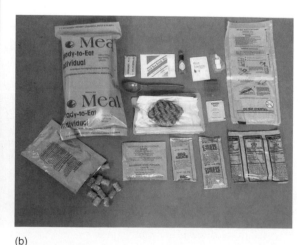

(b)

FIGURE 2-10 (a) Foods for the military must offer special conveniences as well as high quality.
(b) Components of a Meal, Ready-to-Eat. *(Courtesy of U.S. Army Soldier Systems Center)*

different. Nevertheless, cost comparisons may be made with these limitations in mind.

Eating Quality

Today's convenience foods offer the consumer variety, high quality, interesting culinary flavors, dietary modifications, and convenience [36]. Consumers now seek convenience with few compromises in quality, and the food industry has responded [19]. However, no convenience food can match individual tastes perfectly; thus, home cooking provides quality attributes that will continue to be difficult for the industry to match.

Nutritive Value

Nutritive value of convenience foods should be an important consideration in purchasing, but it should be considered on the basis of individual items. In commercial products, the more expensive components, particularly meat, fish, and poultry, may be present in somewhat lower quantities than in home-prepared dishes. The sodium content of processed foods may be a concern to some consumers.

The dehydration of potato products causes substantial loss of vitamin C, but instant potatoes are often fortified with this vitamin to make them more comparable to the fresh product. Many canned and dehydrated soups contain very small amounts of protein or other nutrients. Soups made at home vary greatly in the amount and type of ingredients used and thus in nutritional value, so comparisons with commercial soups are difficult to make. Extra ingredients may be added to purchased soups to make them more hearty and nutritious.

Saving Time and Effort

A major consideration for many when purchasing convenience foods is the promise of reduced preparation time and effort, including fewer cleanup chores such as dishwashing. From annual supermarket sales figures, it is obvious that households rely heavily on convenience foods. Some of them, such as frozen orange juice and gelatin or pudding mixes, have become so well established and widely used that they are probably not considered to be convenience foods in the same sense as frozen entrees. A relatively new trend is called "speed scratch." For example, in the preparation of lasagna, you might use frozen or fresh prepared noodles and canned sauce as ingredients to reduce the preparation time for this dish. Components of this dish are homemade, but convenience products are used for other ingredients to speed the preparation.

There are both advantages and disadvantages to the use of convenience foods. Personal preferences vary from one household to another. We need to consider several factors when deciding whether to purchase convenience foods: time, equipment, and storage space available; comparative costs; aesthetic appeal; our ability to cook and the joy and pride that we, and others around us, may feel when we cook "from scratch"; and concerns regarding nutrition and health.

HEALTHY EATING

Nutraceuticals or Functional Foods—A Lucrative and Challenging Market?

Although the word *nutraceuticals* is already an accepted dictionary term, meaning bioactive compounds (or chemicals) that have health benefits, only 10 percent of shoppers are familiar with this name. They know nutraceuticals or functional foods (a term previously used) only as health-promoting foods. The nutraceutical food market is large—and expanding rapidly as consumers seek to ensure overall good health and lessen their risk of disease development.

Nutraceuticals include nutrients, such as vitamins C and E and beta-carotene, and foods fortified with nutrients—a few examples are fortified cereals, orange juice with added calcium, and lowfat milk fortified with extra calcium. They also include nonnutrients, such as lycopene, which Heinz Ketchup stresses in its advertisements as "America's Favorite Source of Lycopene." Nutraceuticals are found in foods naturally e.g., garlic, soy, broccoli, tomatoes, tea, almonds, oats—for those who prefer naturally nutritious foods to supplements or fortified foods. These characteristics may be valuable advertising slogans in marketing. Functional beverages and snacks also are becoming popular, with nutrition bars being prominently displayed. In any case, a great market awaits, targeting both genders, all ages, and ethnic populations. ■

Source: References 21, 23, 40

CHAPTER SUMMARY

- Food economics is the wise use of all available resources to obtain food that is acceptable, enjoyable, and healthful to an optimal extent. The percent of the budget spent on food varies with the income level of the family. Food purchasing is a major responsibility because the choices made will have a significant impact on the resources available for other expenses.

- Food consumption in the United States is estimated by use of food disappearance data collected by the Economic Research Service of the USDA and a joint USDA and HHS survey of individuals called "What We Eat in America."

- Food is wasted in commercial foodservice operations and in households for a variety of reasons. Careful purchasing, planning, food preparation, and storing will reduce waste. Food waste can represent a considerable expense depending on the amount that is wasted. The environmental impact of waste should also be taken into consideration.

- Food costs generally increase over time. Crop production, trade policies, food processing, food packaging, and marketing all add to the cost of food.

- Food may be purchased on a retail basis through a variety of stores. Supermarkets, specialty stores, food cooperatives, farmers' markets, convenience stores, warehouse markets, supercenters, and wholesale clubs are some of the store formats available for food purchases.

- There are a number of shopping aids available to assist consumers in making good food selections. Unit pricing simplifies the price comparison of products. Open-dating provides consumers with information to assess the freshness of the product. Food labels, regulated by the government, provide information for consumers about the ingredient and nutrient content.

- Convenience foods help consumers prepare dinner in a minimum amount of time and enable the consumption of safe, palatable foods in space or during military exercises. The production of convenience foods began many years ago with the development of canning. Frozen foods were perfected in the 1920s and have led to a wide variety of foods for the consumer to choose from. Dehydrated foods also are plentiful in the marketplace. Retort pouches were developed in the 1960s.

- Consumers should evaluate the cost, quality, and nutritional content of convenience foods as compared to homemade foods. The quality of convenience foods has increased considerably over the years. However, no convenience food can match individual tastes perfectly; thus, home cooking provides quality attributes that will continue to be difficult for the food industry to match.

STUDY QUESTIONS

1. Explain the relationship among food choices, family income, and economics.

2. Describe two different methods that have been used by the USDA to obtain information on what and how much food is eaten in the United States. Evaluate the advantages and inaccuracies that may be associated with each method.

3. (a) Describe several findings from food disappearance data that give information concerning the types and amounts of food being consumed in the United States. (b) What types of information collected from these surveys may be useful to professionals working in the areas of food and nutrition?

4. (a) What is *food waste*, and how may food be wasted at the household level? (b) Identify multiple ways in which food waste in commercial food services and in households may be reduced.

5. List several factors that are likely to influence food cost to the consumer and briefly explain how they exert their influence.

6. Describe what is meant by *unit pricing* and *open-date labeling*. Explain their possible usefulness to the consumer.

7. Suggest several useful guidelines to follow when purchasing food.

8. Define the term *convenience foods* and give several examples.

9. Identify several challenges to developing foods for the military or the space program.

10. Explain how the widespread availability of convenience foods may affect food preparation techniques used in the home.

11. Convenience foods are sometimes compared with similar home-prepared products. Discuss how they generally compare in these factors: (a) cost (both food cost alone and cost that includes energy use and preparer's time), (b) eating quality, (c) nutritive value, (d) preparation time and effort.

FOOD SAFETY 3

ood safety is everyone's responsibility. From the farmer to the processor, packager, wholesaler, retailer, foodservice operator, and consumer, everyone should recognize potential health hazards related to food and know how to control them. Why is food safety so important? Foodborne microbes remain one of the most common causes of illness in the United States. Young children, pregnant women, elderly people, people with weakened immune systems, and people taking medications are at the highest risk for foodborne illness.

Exactly how many people become sick each year from foodborne illness is not clear. Estimates suggest that 5,000 deaths, 76 million illnesses, and 325,000 hospitalizations in the United States are caused by foodborne illness [51]. In 2005, the surveillance data provided documentation of 16,614 laboratory-diagnosed cases of foodborne diseases [76]. The Centers for Disease Control and Prevention (CDC) collects this surveillance data from 10 states including 44.5 million people (15 percent of the U.S. population). Thus, the number of foodborne illnesses reported by this system provides useful data about the prevalence of foodborne illness, but it reflects only a fraction of the cases nationwide.

In this chapter, the following topics will be discussed:

- The role of the government, industry, consumers, and others in the prevention of foodborne illness
- Four keys to safe food handling
- Hazard Analysis Critical Control Points (HACCP)
- Technologies such as pasteurization and irradiation to improve food safety
- Microorganisms and other causes of foodborne illness such as toxins and contaminants
- Food allergies and intolerances
- Biotechnology and bioterrorism

PREVENTING FOODBORNE ILLNESS

Who Has a Role in Preventing Foodborne Illness?

The concept of food safety from farm to table was emphasized in the 1997 report to the President prepared by the Food and Drug Administration (FDA), U.S. Department of Agriculture (USDA), Environmental Protection Agency (EPA), and Centers for Disease Control (CDC) [36]. Foodborne illness is prevented through the multifaceted efforts of all who have a role in producing, processing, regulating, and preparing food.

Government. The government promotes food safety through oversight and monitoring by the FDA, USDA, EPA, CDC, as well as other selected agencies. The USDA, for example, requires safe handling instructions on packages of all raw or partially cooked meat and poultry (Figure 3-1). Both the FDA and USDA regulate as well as inspect processors. Local health departments inspect foodservice establishments to enforce safe food-handling practices in the commercial sector. (Regulations are discussed further in Chapter 4.) All of these components help to ensure that the American food supply remains the safest, most wholesome in the world.

Producers, Processors, and Retailers. On the farm, good agricultural practices help to prevent or reduce contamination of produce foods [37] and promote healthy herds and flocks. The food-processing industry utilizes a variety of measures to limit potential food hazards. It pasteurizes, sterilizes, uses specialized packaging, freezes, refrigerates, dehydrates, and applies approved antimicrobial preservatives to various food products. Food retailers have a responsibility to store food at recommended temperatures and to turn over inventory so consumers have access to fresh foods. With the many

SAFE HANDLING INSTRUCTIONS

This product was prepared from inspected and passed meat and/or poultry. Some food products may contain bacteria that could cause illness if the product is mishandled or cooked improperly. For your protection, follow these safe handling instructions.

Keep refrigerated or frozen.
Thaw in refrigerator or microwave.

Keep raw meat and poultry separate from other foods. Wash working surfaces (including cutting boards), utensils, and hands after touching raw meat or poultry.

Cook thoroughly.

Keep hot foods hot.
Refrigerate leftovers immediately or discard.

FIGURE 3-1 The USDA requires safe handling instructions on packages of all raw or partially cooked meat and poultry products. *(Courtesy of the American Meat Institute and the U.S. Department of Agriculture)*

takeout food choices in today's grocery stores, these foods must be prepared and held to prevent food-safety hazards.

Foodservice Establishments. Well over 926,000 restaurants and many other foodservice establishments serve the American public [58]. Workers in the foodservice industry—including those employed in fast-food and carry-out restaurants, delicatessens, self-service food counters, mobile refreshment stands, family and gourmet restaurants, schools, hospitals, and other establishments—must be educated about potential food-safety hazards. The ServSafe program developed by the Educational Foundation of the National Restaurant Association has been widely used by the industry to provide education and food-safety certification [27]. Some states mandate that commercial foodservice operations have a food-safety certified employee or manager on premise during all hours of operation. Education is vitally important so the sanitary procedures that ensure microbial quality and safety in the food served to the public are fully understood. The primary responsibility of foodservice managers and dietetic practitioners is to supply consumers with safe products that are as free as possible from pathogenic microorganisms and other health hazards [2, 3, 27].

Consumers. Consumers have important responsibilities for food safety through the selection, preparation, and proper storage of foods. Consumers, however, may lack the necessary information to prepare food safely. Consumers in one study erroneously believed that contaminated food could be identified by taste or smell and did not refrigerate hot foods quickly as recommended, but instead left foods to cool slowly at room temperature before refrigeration [53]. A multistate survey of consumer food-handling practices found nearly 20 percent did not adequately wash hands or cutting boards after contact with raw meat or chicken [1]. A number of food-handling errors were observed by researchers at

Utah State University, who concluded that consumers report safer food-handling practices on surveys than observations of actual food preparation reveals [7, 8]. In general, many consumers do not appear to be acting on the messages concerning food safety that have been used for years by both government and industry groups by consuming undercooked eggs and other risky behaviors [68]. Consumer food-safety education campaigns are listed in Table 3-1 and include the USDA's cartoon thermometer called "Thermy" (Figure 3-2).

Four Keys to Safe Food Handling

The consumer education campaign of the Partnership for Food Safety Education (Figure 3-3) focuses on four critical messages:

1. Wash hands and surfaces often.
2. Don't cross-contaminate.
3. Cook to proper temperatures.
4. Refrigerate promptly.

Wash Hands and Surfaces. Following simple rules of sanitation such as washing hands before handling food, putting clean bandages on cuts and sores before working with food, and wearing plastic gloves can prevent numerous outbreaks of illness. Poor personal hygiene accounts for as much as 37 percent of the known causes of foodborne illness [61]. Although Americans may say they wash their hands, researchers observed handwashing practices of the general public in six public attractions in four metropolitan areas and found only 83 percent washed their hands after using the restroom [6].

When working with food, handwashing is necessary before food preparation and multiple times during food preparation. Additionally, hands must be washed properly. Hands should be washed in hot running water, with soap, and scrubbed for at least 20 seconds with care taken to clean under the fingernails. Hands should be rinsed under clean running water, and then dried with a single-use towel [27]. Saying the "ABCs" is one way to see that hands are washed for the appropriate length of time. In a study where the food preparation practices of consumers were videotaped, researchers found the average length of handwashing was only 4.4 seconds and 34 percent of the handwashing attempts were without soap [8].

Surfaces in kitchens need to be cleaned thoroughly as well. Fight BAC recommends the use of paper towels. If cloth towels are used, they must be clean and not left damp for extended periods of time, such as between meals. A damp dish towel contaminated with even small amounts of food soil is a perfect growing medium for bacteria which will cross-contaminate the surfaces later being "cleaned." In commercial foodservice operations, towels are either used clean from the laundry or, if to be used again a short while later, the towels are stored in a solution of a food-safe chemical sanitizer.

TABLE 3-1 Food-Safety Education Resources

There is a wide range of web pages, brochures, and flyers to use in educating consumers about safe food handling. A few of these food-safety education resources are provided below. Please note that Internet content changes rapidly, and the web addresses may change over time.

Worldwide Food-Safety Education Sources	Type of Information Available
Partnership for Food Safety Education http://www.fightbac.org/	A wide variety of consumer education resources focus on four key messages: Clean, Separate, Cook, Chill.
Home Food Safety: It's in Your Hands American Dietetic Association and ConAgra Foods Foundation http://www.homefoodsafety.org	Home food-safety statistics, information about foodborne illness, and safe food-handling information are provided.
FDA/National Science Teachers Association Partnership http://www.foodsafety.gov/~fsg/teach.html	Science and Our Food Supply Middle and High School Science Curriculum Teacher guides contain hands-on experiments and activities focusing on food and food safety.
Food Safety for Moms-to-Be Food and Drug Administration, Center for Food Safety and Applied Nutrition http://www.cfsan.fda.gov/~pregnant/tools.html	Materials, including PowerPoint slides, to use in providing food-safety education for pregnant women.
Food-Safety Education U.S. Department of Agriculture, Food Safety and Inspection Service http://www.fsis.usda.gov/Food_Safety_Education/index.asp	Information is provided for consumers on a variety of timely food-safety concerns. Some of the links include: • "Ask Karen" questions about food safety • Links to the USDA Meat and Poultry Hotline • "Thermy" and "Is It Done Yet" education programs about safe cooking temperatures • Links for kids and teens including games and quizzes
Food Safety for Seniors U.S. Food and Drug Administration, Center for Food Safety and Applied Nutrition http://www.cfsan.fda.gov/~dms/seniors.html	Food-safety information targeted for seniors is available through this site. Topics such as why some groups face special risks and how times have changed are included.
State Cooperative Extension	Food-safety materials are available through the State Cooperative Extension Service in many states across the U.S.

All dishes and equipment used in food preparation should be carefully cleaned. Machine-washed dishes, both in the home and in commercial foodservice establishments, may have a very low, if not almost nonexistent, bacteria count because hot water and strong sanitizing agents are used in machine washing. In homes where infectious diseases exist, it is important to keep all dishes used by patients separate from other dishes until they are sanitized. Hand-washed dishes and cutting boards may be sanitized in a solution of one tablespoon of chlorine beach per gallon of water. Porous surfaces, such as wood, should be sanitized in a solution of three tablespoons of chlorine bleach per gallon of water [20].

Don't Cross-Contaminate. Cross-contamination can occur because of a dirty cloth, unclean surfaces, contaminated cutting boards, dirty hands, or poor storage techniques. In the Utah State University study, dirty hands accounted for 51 percent of the cross-contamination cases observed. Another key problem was the storage of raw meat on the middle or top shelf of the refrigerator that could drip into other foods, such as lettuce or fruit, that would be consumed without cooking [8]. Foods should be stored in the refrigerator so that ready-to-eat foods are placed above raw foods that may be contaminated with pathogenic bacteria (Figure 3-4).

Cook to Proper Temperatures. Foods such as poultry, eggs, ground beef, pork, and seafood must be cooked to specified temperatures to enhance sensory qualities and also to kill pathogenic organisms such as *Salmonella*, *Escherichia coli*, *Listeria monocytogenes*, *Staphylococcus aureus*, *Trichinella spiralis*, *Anisakis simplex*, *Vibrio parahaemolyticus*, *Vibrio vulnificus*, and others that may be present. Food cooking temperature guidelines provided from the USDA as part of the "Is it done yet?" consumer education materials are shown in Figure 3-5. The temperatures, recommended for consumer use, include an additional

FIGURE 3-2 Thermy, the cartoon thermometer, promotes the use of thermometers in the home. *(Courtesy of U.S. Department of Agriculture)*

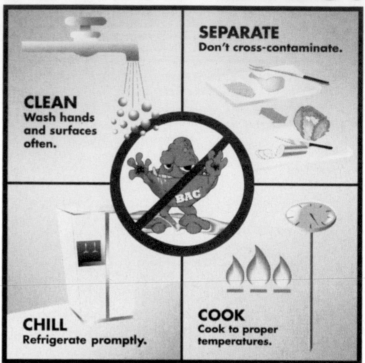

FIGURE 3-3 An eye-catching Fight BAC™ character is used to attract attention of the public in a campaign to teach consumers about food safety. *(Courtesy of the Partnership for Food Safety Education)*

margin of safety and thus are different from the temperature recommendations published in the FDA Food Code for use by foodservice operators (Table 3-2) [27, 79].

More consumer education about food temperatures and the use of thermometers is needed. For example, ground beef that is cooked to less than the recommended temperature of 155 to 160°F (68 to 71°C) has been found to be brown throughout [49, 65]. Consequently, color alone as a measure of doneness is ineffective. Many consumers in the Utah State University study undercooked chicken, meatloaf, or fish. Only 5 percent of the consumers in the Utah study used a thermometer, but many of the consumers who used a thermometer did not know the recommended temperatures [8].

Accurate temperature readings when using a thermometer depend on proper use and maintenance. A stem

FOCUS ON SCIENCE

How Does Bleach Inactivate Bacteria?

The American Red Cross recommends 1/4 cup of chlorine bleach per gallon water. Chlorox™, a sodium hypochlorite bleach, breaks down proteins in cell walls, rendering bacteria inactive. Sodium hypochlorite breaks down into little more than salt water once it completes killing microorganisms. It should be noted when a solution of bleach becomes "dirty," it will be inactivated. Thus, a bleach solution must be periodically remixed fresh, or it will be ineffective as a sanitizer.

Different concentrations of bleach are recommended depending on the task or purpose. For example, one concentration may be recommended for water to be sanitized for drinking and another level for the cleaning of surfaces and food contact equipment.

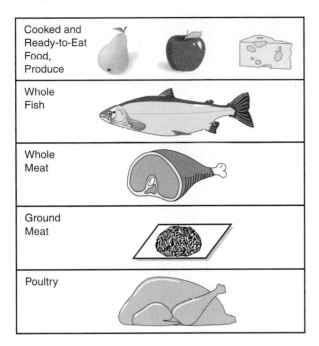

Cooked and Ready-to-Eat Food, Produce	
Whole Fish	
Whole Meat	
Ground Meat	
Poultry	

FIGURE 3-4 Proper placement of food in the refrigerator helps to reduce chances of contracting a foodborne illness by preventing cross-contamination of harmful bacteria into foods that may not be cooked before consumption.

thermometer (Figure 3-6a) must be inserted up to the dimple on the stem (typically about two inches) and sufficient time allowed for the temperature to register. When taking the temperature of a thin food such as a hamburger or chicken breast, the thermometer should be inserted from the side (Figure 3-6b). Thermocouples often are used in foodservice operations. Thermocouples record the temperature quickly and often require only one-fourth inch of food contact to provide an accurate reading; however, the cost is high so home use is not common. Most thermometers must be calibrated periodically to provide accurate measurements. Thermometers may be calibrated in ice water to 32°F (0°C) or in boiling water to 212°F (100°C) (Figure 3-6c).

Refrigerate Promptly. High risk, hazardous foods must be held hot or cold. Any temperature between 41° and 135°F (5° and 57°C), a temperature danger zone, permits growth of food-poisoning bacteria (Figure 3-7). Improper holding and inadequate cooling accounted for 76 percent of the reported foodborne illness outbreaks [61]. More than one researcher has documented that a significant number of consumers leave perishable foods at room temperature to cool before refrigeration [7, 8, 53]. Bacteria grow most rapidly between 70°F (21°C) and 125°F (52°C); therefore keeping food at room temperatures is very hazardous.

Even when foods are placed under refrigeration quickly following a meal, the food may still not cool quickly. Foods should not be in the temperature danger zone for more than four hours, including the preparation, service, and cooling times. To accomplish rapid cooling, the hot foods should be put in cool, shallow containers (preferably less than two inches deep) and promptly placed under refrigeration. Large roasts of meat should be cut into smaller portions before refrigerating. Additionally, the refrigerator must be at or below 41°F (5°C). Many consumers may have the refrigerator temperature regulator set too high [8] and may not be aware of the actual temperature being maintained. Using refrigerator

FIGURE 3-5 USDA-recommended temperatures for the safe cooking of meats, poultry, eggs, and fish are presented on this consumer-friendly flyer. *(Courtesy of U.S. Department of Agriculture, Food Safety and Inspection Service)*

TABLE 3-2 Cooking Temperatures Recommended in the 2005 FDA Food Code

Product	Temperature
Poultry	
Stuffing, stuffed meat, and dishes combining raw and cooked food (including soups and casseroles)	165°F (74°C) for 15 seconds
Ground meats (beef, pork, or other meat or fish)	155°F (68°C) for 15 seconds
Injected meats (including brined ham and flavor-injected roasts)	155°F (68°C) for 15 seconds
Pork, beef, veal, lamb	Steaks/chops:
	145°F (63°C) for 15 seconds
	Roasts:
	145°F (63°C) for 4 minutes
Fish	145°F (63°C) for 15 seconds
Fresh shell eggs for immediate service	145°F (63°C) for 15 seconds
Any potentially hazardous food cooked in a microwave oven	165°F (74°C); let food stand for 2 minutes after cooking

Source: Adapted from Reference 27.

6. Establish procedures for verifying the HACCP system.

7. Establish record-keeping procedures that document the hazard analysis so that the problems can be effectively traced.

The HACCP system is an important part of food processors' overall quality-assurance programs and helps to ensure the safety of their products. In 2001, the final rule requiring the adoption of HACCP systems by juice processors was announced by the FDA [80]. Five years earlier, in 1996, the USDA announced the final rule that requires the more than 6,200 slaughter and meat-processing plants that operate under federal inspection to adopt the HACCP system and to meet government standards for *Salmonella* microorganisms [25]. In addition, slaughter plants must test for generic *Escherichia coli* bacteria to verify that their control systems are preventing fecal contamination, the primary source of these organisms in the plant. The USDA is also requiring plants to adopt and follow written **standard operating procedures** (SOPs) for sanitation as part of good manufacturing practices. These requirements were phased in over a period of 6 to 42 months [24]. Likewise, HACCP regulations for seafood manufacturers were implemented in 1997. These rulings are designed to reduce contamination of juice, meat, poultry, and seafood in the processing plant. After the product leaves the plant, it is the responsibility of the wholesaler,

and freezer thermometers and checking them regularly will both enhance food quality and promote safe food storage. For the most accurate temperature, place the thermometers on a shelf within the refrigerator or freezer and not in the door.

Hazard Analysis and Critical Control Points—A Systematic Approach

One methodology designed to ensure food safety is the use of the Hazard Analysis and Critical Control Points (HACCP) system [27]. This preventative attempt in safety is built into the entire process of food manufacture. It is a quality control tool that focuses on critical factors directly affecting the **microbiology** of foods. HACCP operates on a set of basic procedures and involves the following steps (Table 3-3):

1. Analyze **hazards** and assess **risks**.

2. Identify **critical control points** in the process for each hazard where loss of control may result in an unacceptable health risk.

3. Establish preventative measures with critical limits for each control point.

4. Establish procedures to monitor the control points.

5. Establish corrective action to be taken if a deviation occurs at a critical control point.

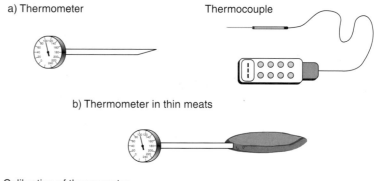

a) Thermometer Thermocouple

b) Thermometer in thin meats

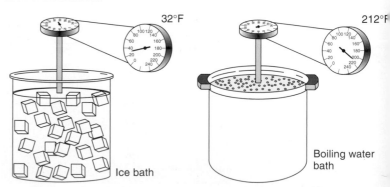

c) Calibration of thermometer

32°F   212°F

Ice bath   Boiling water bath

FIGURE 3-6 (a) Stem thermometer and thermocouple. (b) Proper use of thermometer in thin meats. (c) Method of thermometer calibration.

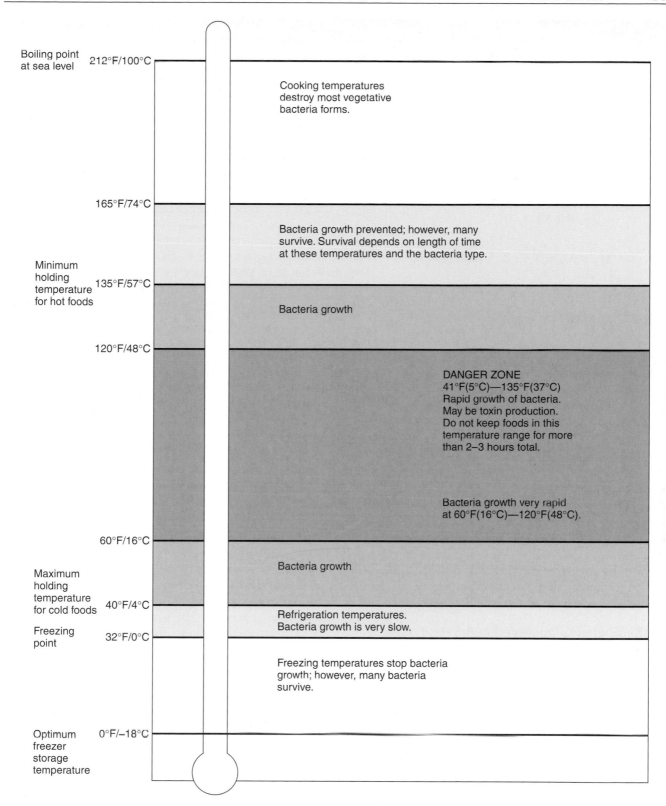

FIGURE 3-7 Effect of temperature on growth of bacteria.

retailer, and consumer to handle, store, and cook the product properly to ensure safety.

Many restaurants use the HACCP system as part of their quality-assurance program [27]. The following safeguards are essential for safe foodservice: control time and temperature through appropriate heating and cooling of high risk or potentially hazardous foods, good personal hygiene, and prevention of contamination and cross-contamination in preparation and storage [27]. At each of these critical control points in production, a schedule for

TABLE 3-3	What Do the Seven HACCP Steps Really Mean?
HACCP Steps	**What Should Be Considered?**
1. Analyze hazards.	What potential hazards exist with the food being prepared? For example, chicken and ground beef are high-protein foods that will readily support the growth of microorganisms, and both of these foods could be contaminated.
2. Identify critical control points.	How will the hazards be controlled? Storage at appropriate temperatures, cooking, sanitation, methods to avoid cross-contamination, or other measures?
3. Establish preventative measures.	Highly perishable foods such as meat, poultry, fish, and dairy must be refrigerated to safeguard against rapid microbial growth. Ground beef must be cooked to 160°F (71°C) and chicken must be cooked to 165°F (74°C) to kill any pathogenic organisms that may be present. Foods such as meat, potato, and pasta salads, generally served cold, must be kept out of the temperature danger zone. If taking a salad to a picnic, it must be kept cold.
4. Establish procedures to monitor critical control points.	How will you know if food is kept cold or cooked to proper temperatures? Thermometers in the refrigerator and thermometers used to check cooking temperatures are needed to allow accurate monitoring of the critical controls.
5. Establish corrective action.	If ground beef is only at 140°F (40°C), the corrective action would be to continue cooking. When monitoring cold foods, if a salad has been in the danger zone for longer than the recommended time period, the corrective action is to discard the salad.
6. Establish procedures to verify the system is working.	Especially in foodservice organizations, procedures must be in place to establish how the organization will know the system is working. In the home, methods of making sure your system is working may include checking your thermometers periodically to be sure the readings are correct. Is your refrigerator thermometer in a location where it is checked on a frequent basis?
7. Establish record keeping.	In the home, you may be unlikely to record the temperature of your refrigerator on a log; however, in foodservice organizations, this record keeping is an important way of keeping the HACCP system on track.

monitoring should be established and followed precisely. If monitoring reveals a potential hazard, a clearly defined corrective action must be taken and documented.

Technologies to Improve Food Safety

Pasteurization. A number of foods including milk, fruit juices, and eggs may be pasteurized to reduce the risk of foodborne illness. Pasteurized foods have been heated to kill pathogenic bacteria. The heat process may be very brief (161°F/72°C for 15 seconds) or a longer process (145°F/63°C for 30 minutes). Foods which have been ultrapasteurized have been heated to a higher temperature (280°F/138°C for 2 seconds) and as a result have a longer shelf life even though refrigeration is still necessary.

Milk and egg products such as liquid or dried eggs must be pasteurized because the risk of foodborne illness from these products is significant. Fruit juices must include a warning label if not pasteurized or otherwise treated to reduce foodborne pathogens sufficiently.

Irradiation. Irradiation has been found to be a safe and effective method of reducing foodborne pathogens through more than 50 years of research [70]. It is approved for use on several foods by the FDA and the USDA. Irradiation has also been referred to as cold pasteurization because it destroys harmful bacteria without heating the food. The sources of radiation energy allowed for food processing include gamma rays (produced from cobalt 60 and cesium 137), electron accelerators, and machine-generated X-rays [4]. The electron-beam (e-beam) system uses commercial electricity to accelerate electrons that kill harmful bacteria in frozen beef patties [55]. Food irradiated using gamma rays, electron-beams, or X-rays does not become radioactive [70].

The improved microbiological quality of the food is an important benefit from the use of ionization radiation. Consumers can prepare foods such as ground beef and chicken with greater confidence, if these are irradiated, because 99.9 percent of any *E. coli* 0157:H7 or *salmonella* is destroyed [4] while maintaining sensory qualities of the food. Irradiated foods are labeled "Radura," and the words "treated by irradiation" or "treated with radiation" (Figure 3-8). Consumers have been slow to purchase and use irradiated foods. Consumer education about this method of processing has been shown to increase consumer acceptance [41, 50, 59].

HOT TOPICS

Raw Milk? Is It Safe?

Milk has been pasteurized since the early 1990s and as a result illness and death caused by contaminated milk have been dramatically reduced. Today a renewed interest in raw milk (milk not pasteurized) is occurring. What are the issues?

Pasteurization is a heat process used to destroy harmful bacteria. It does not significantly change the nutritional value of the milk. Federal law, enforced by the Food and Drug Administration, prohibits the sale of raw milk across state lines. Sale of raw milk within a state is governed by the laws within the state and therefore may be different from state to state.

Why is the sale of raw milk prohibited in many jurisdictions? Consider that in 2001 and 2002 over 500 people became ill from raw milk or soft cheeses made from raw milk including Queso Panela, Asadero, Blanco, and Ranchero. Raw milk has been found to be contaminated with *Salmonella, Escherichia coli* 0157:H7, *Listeria, Campylobacter jejuni,* and other microorganisms. Proponents of raw milk suggest it is healthier. Research, however, does not support the arguments that significant amounts of nutrients and enzymes are destroyed thereby making pasteurized milk less healthy. ■

Source: References 14, 28, 29

FOCUS ON FOOD SCIENCE

Pasteurization and Sterilization: What Is the Difference?

Pasteurization is a heat process with temperatures between 140° and 180°F (60° and 82°C) that will lower the bacterial load. Sterilization includes boiling (212°F/100°C), steaming, or heating to completely destroy microorganisms.

Pasteurization is targeted to destroy pathogenic bacteria. Milk undergoes pasteurization to destroy pathogens, such as *Salmonella, Listeria monocytogenes, Escherichia coli,* and *Campylobacter jejuni.* However, some (~1 percent) of the non-pathogenic bacteria remain, and thus milk should be refrigerated. If at any time, milk remains at room temperature for two hours or more—for example, creamer used for coffee—it should be discarded and not poured back into its original container because the bacteria remaining after pasterization will multiply when held in the danger zone.

FIGURE 3-8 An irradiated food on the retail market should bear the international symbol along with either of the statements "treated with radiation" or "treated by irradiation."

MICROORGANISMS AND OTHER CAUSES OF FOODBORNE ILLNESS

Food provides nutrients needed to maintain health, yet may include harmful microorganisms or toxins which may cause foodborne illness. Bacteria, viruses, parasites, and fungi are examples of some microorganisms. Of these, bacteria are responsible for most foodborne illness outbreaks. Causes of foodborne illness should be understood so food can be prepared and served safely.

There are three general types of foodborne illness: infections, intoxications, and toxin-mediated infections. **Food infection** results when food containing live pathogenic microorganisms is consumed. Illness does not

FOCUS ON SCIENCE

of vegetative cells. Illness is caused by the ingestion of a large number of these vegetative cells. When these vegetative cells reach the intestine, they form spores and release an enterotoxin that causes symptoms.

Clostridium Perfringens—A Common Toxin-mediated Infection

The *Clostridium perfringens* microorganism forms spores that are highly heat resistant and may survive some of the cooking procedures. These spores may germinate to form a large number

---

appear immediately. Food intoxication can occur due to the consumption of a food contaminated with toxin-producing microorganisms or a food contaminated with a biological or chemical toxin. Symptoms of food intoxication usually occur within a few hours. Toxin-mediated infections occur when a food contaminated with microorganisms is consumed, and these microorganisms then produce toxins in the intestine [27].

Although this chapter will focus on microorganisms which may result in foodborne illness, not all microorganisms are pathogenic and may perform some extremely useful functions in food preparation and processing. For example, the delightful flavors and characteristic textures

of a variety of cheeses result from the activity of various bacteria or molds. Sauerkraut and pickles are made by using bacterial fermentation. Baker's yeast leavens bread and other baked products and contributes flavor. Those who enjoy Oriental foods with soy sauce are indebted to molds used in its manufacturing process. Various bacteria and molds are also used in industries that manufacture such things as citric acid and a great number of different enzymes.

Bacteria

Bacteria are tiny one-celled microbes smaller than either molds or yeasts and may be rod shaped (bacilli) or round

HOT TOPICS

Probiotics—Friendly Bacteria?

The Nobel prize-winning Russian scientist Elie Metchnikoff suggested in the early 1900s that the long, healthy lives of Bulgarian peasants resulted from their regular consumption of Bulgarian milk—now known as yogurt. He claimed that live friendly bacteria, such as lactic acid bacteria, needed to be ingested regularly through fermented dairy products to minimize putrefactive fermentations in the intestine and promote general health of the body [69]. This concept now goes by the name *probiotics* and has exciting market potential for food manufacturers in the United States. In Japan and Europe, these products are already common.

Probiotic foods are those containing live microorganisms which, when consumed in sufficient numbers, actively enhance health by improving intestinal microbial balance [67]. There are many health claims for probiotics—including

suppression of pathogenic bacteria, improvement in lactose metabolism, and anticarcinogenic activity—but definitive scientific studies are limited at present. An FDA advisory committee is considering the safety and potential health effects of probiotics in discussing GRAS status [22]. Safe use is founded on centuries of consumption of fermented foods.

There are challenges in formulating probiotic foods because bacteria often die during manufacturing, storage, and passage through the acid stomach. Organisms commonly used in regular yogurt manufacture do not survive in the gastrointestinal tract. Thus a trend is to add probiotic bacteria—*Lactobacillus acidolphilus, bifidobacteria,* and *Lactobacillus casei*—to the yogurt. A microencapsulation process has been suggested as a way to overcome the major hurdles of the gastrointestinal (GI) tract [69]. ■

(cocci). Generally, bacteria require more moisture than either molds or yeasts and grow best where concentrations of sugar or salt are low and where the pH is about neutral (neither acid nor alkaline). Some bacteria love the cold; these are called *psychrophilic* and thrive at refrigerator temperatures. Others are heat loving (*thermophilic*) and may create particular hazards in cooked foods. Many others, however, are *mesophilic*, meaning that they do best at moderate temperatures. Bacteria also vary in their need for oxygen or air. *Aerobic* bacteria must have oxygen, *anaerobic* bacteria can grow only in the absence of oxygen, and *facultative* bacteria can grow either with or without free oxygen.

Some bacteria are able to form spores or endospores that have special protective coatings, making them highly resistant to destruction by heating. These spores are especially resistant in low-acid environments, such as many vegetable and meat dishes. Table 3-4 identifies common foodborne infections, toxin-mediated infections, and intoxications.

Salmonella. *Salmonella* bacteria are one of the leading causes of foodborne illness. An estimated 1.4 million cases of salmonellosis, including 500 deaths, occur annually in the United States [35]. The approximately 2,000 different strains of salmonella are all capable of causing infection in humans, although two types are responsible for most illnesses. In most cases, recovery occurs within five or seven days; however, some individuals develop complications that persist for weeks or even months [16]. Death may sometimes occur with this disease, especially among the very young, the aged, and the infirm. The organisms, which appear under the microscope as short rods (Figure 3-9), usually enter the body orally in contaminated food or water and may produce a food-poisoning syndrome as they multiply in the intestinal tract. Even relatively small numbers of bacteria can result in infection.

Food Sources. A variety of foods have been associated with the outbreak of salmonellosis. Eggs and poultry, however, are frequently implicated. Eggs must be properly refrigerated from the time they are laid. New governmental regulations effective in 2001 require retail establishments to hold eggs at or below 45°F (7°C). Chicken has also commonly been associated with salmonella. It is not unusual to find that a significant percent of a particular lot of broiler chickens are carrying salmonella. Melons, especially cantaloupe, and other kinds of produce may be contaminated with salmonella as well.

Prevention of Foodborne Illness. Foodborne illness caused by salmonella can be significantly reduced by careful processing to avoid cross-contamination, careful time and temperature control of foods, proper cooking, and good personal hygiene. At present, processing methods cannot ensure that raw meat, poultry, and eggs

are free of salmonella unless the food has been irradiated; thus these foods should be handled with potential contamination in mind. The prevalence of salmonella contamination on foods has been reduced through HACCP implementation by processors and testing by the Food Safety and Inspection Service of the USDA [25]. Operating procedures in poultry and meat processing plants are closely monitored, and techniques involving steam or various washes may be employed to control the spread of microorganisms from one carcass to another.

Salmonella are sensitive to heat and are destroyed by normal conventional cooking of foods and pasteurization of milk. Poultry should be cooked to a minimum of 165°F (74°C). Higher temperatures generally are recommended for whole birds or microwaved poultry to ensure adequate cooking throughout. Cutting boards used for cutting up raw poultry or meat should be disinfected (one to three tablespoons of chlorine bleach per gallon of water) before use for other foods to prevent cross-contamination of microorganisms.

Most of the outbreaks of illness traced to this organism have been associated with eggs. Raw eggs should not be used in foods, such as ice cream, eggnog, and mayonnaise, that do not receive heat treatments sufficient to kill salmonella. Pasteurized eggs are a good option to permit the safe preparation of products such as eggnog. Pasteurized eggs also are used in the foodservice setting to avoid the pooling of several dozen eggs. Eggs are "pooled" when a large number of eggs are cracked into a bowl. This practice is no longer allowed because it has been associated with foodborne illness. One infected egg will contaminate the entire mixture, and the potential for these eggs to be at room temperature for too long will lead to a high risk of foodborne illness if the eggs are undercooked when served. Cantaloupe has also been implicated in outbreaks of salmonellosis. Cantaloupe must be washed carefully to remove any bacteria on the rind before cutting and then kept under refrigeration.

Good personal hygiene and thorough handwashing are essential to reduce the risk of salmonellosis. People who have had salmonellosis may carry the infecting organisms in their digestive tracts for some time after the symptoms of the disease have disappeared and thus may contaminate foods that they handle improperly. Household pets (especially reptiles) also can carry salmonella. Unwashed hands that have handled raw eggs, raw poultry, or pets are likely to infect other foods.

Campylobacter jejuni. *Campylobacter jejuni* is the leading cause of diarrhea in the United States [34, 35]. The infectious dose of *C. jejuni* can be quite low, with illness resulting from the ingestion of only a few hundred cells. The organisms are slender, curved, motile rods and have a requirement for reduced levels of oxygen. *Campylobacter* is a relatively fragile organism and is sensitive to drying, normal atmospheric concentrations of oxygen, storage at room temperature, acidic conditions, and high heat. It

TABLE 3-4 Food Infections and Intoxications

Organism	Type of Illness	Time until Onset of Symptoms	Nature of Illness	Foods Involved	Control Measures
Salmonella spp.	Infection. May be toxin-mediated.	6–48 hours; typically 12–36 hours.	Nausea, diarrhea, abdominal pain, fever, headache. May be life threatening in infants, the elderly, and the immuno-compromised. May cause arthritic symptoms 3–4 weeks later.	Eggs, poultry, meat, fish, milk products, cantaloupe, and other fresh produce.	Cook all animal foods to recommended temperatures. Cook poultry to 165°F (74°C). Do not consume raw or undercooked eggs. No cross-contamination. Thoroughly wash melons and other produce. Refrigerate promptly after cutting fruit.
Campylobacter jejuni	Infection. Even with low numbers of bacteria.	2–5 days is common. Symptoms can present 1–10 days.	Diarrhea (watery or bloody), fever, nausea and vomiting, headache, and muscle pain. Severe complications are rare but can occur.	Poultry, raw milk, eggs, contaminated water.	Handle raw poultry to prevent cross-contamination. Cook all animal foods properly. Cook poultry to 165°F (74°C). Consume pasteurized milk. Avoid raw milk.
Listeria monocytogenes	Infection.	3–70 days; usually about 3 weeks.	Nausea, vomiting, diarrhea, headache, fever, backache. Meningitis, septicemia, miscarriage. High fatality rate in immunocompromised.	Unpasteurized milk and soft-ripened cheese, deli meats and uncooked hot dogs, poultry, seafood, and vegetables.	Consume pasteurized milk and pasteurized milk products. Cook foods to recommended temperatures. Thoroughly wash vegetables. If pregnant or immunocompromised, heat deli meats and hot dogs thoroughly before consumption.
Yersinia enterocolitica and *Yersinia pseudotuber-culosis*	Infection.	24–48 hours.	Fever, diarrhea, vomiting. Severe abdominal pain; may mimic acute appendicitis.	Meats (pork, beef, lamb, etc.), oysters, fish, and raw milk.	Cook foods to recommended temperatures. Consume pasteurized milk. Avoid cross-contamination with careful sanitation.
Vibrio parahaemolyti-cus and *Vibrio vulnificus*	Infection.	*V. parahaemolyticus* 4–96 hours; usually 15 hours. *V. vulnificus* 12 hours to several days; usually 38 hours.	Diarrhea, abdominal cramps, nausea, vomiting, headache, fever, and chills. Severe cases of *V. vulnificus* can include decreased blood pressure and septicemia. Fatality from *V. vulnificus* infection is high (50 percent or higher) in individuals with underlying illnesses (diabetes, cirrhosis, or immunocompromised).	Raw, improperly cooked, or cooked cross-contaminated fish and shellfish. More common in warmer months. *V. vulnificus* commonly in raw oysters, clams, and crabs.	Consume properly cooked fish and seafood. Avoid cross-contamination with good sanitation practices. Individuals with underlying medical conditions should not consume raw oysters, clams, or crabs.

TABLE 3-4 (continued)

Organism	Type of Illness	Time until Onset of Symptoms	Nature of Illness	Foods Involved	Control Measures
Escherichia coli 0157:H7	Toxin-mediated infection.	2–4 days.	Hemorrhagic colitis. Severe cramping; watery or bloody diarrhea. Hemolytic uremic syndrome characterized by kidney failure.	Raw and undercooked ground beef. Raw milk, unpasteurized apple cider, and juice. Contaminated produce and water.	Thoroughly cook ground beef to a minimum of 155–160°F (68–71°C) throughout. Use pasteurized milk and pasteurized juices. Avoid cross-contamination and use good sanitary practices.
Clostridium perfringens	Toxin-mediated infection.	8–22 hours; usually 10–12 hours.	Intense abdominal cramps, diarrhea, and nausea.	Temperature-abused foods. Generally meat and meat containing foods such as gravy are cooled improperly, then heated insufficiently before consumption.	Cool foods rapidly after cooking. Hold hot foods above 135°F (57°C). Reheat leftovers to a minimum of 165°F (74°C).
Shigella spp.	Toxin-mediated infection.	12–50 hours	Abdominal pain; cramps; diarrhea; fever; vomiting; blood, pus, or mucus in stools.	Meat, poultry, and fish salads and products. Tofu and other protein foods. Sliced melons and other fresh produce.	Good personal hygiene practices. Avoid cross-contamination from hands and working surfaces. Properly cook foods to recommended temperatures.
Staphylococcus aureus	Toxin.	1–7 hours; usually 2–4 hours.	Severe vomiting, diarrhea, abdominal cramping. In severe cases, headache, muscle cramping, changes in blood pressure and pulse rate.	Reheated meat and other protein foods. Custard- or cream-filled baked goods. Salads such as egg, potato, meat, or pasta.	Good personal hygiene practices. Avoid cross-contamination from hands and working surfaces. Rapidly cool prepared foods under refrigeration.
Clostridium botulinum	Toxin.	4 hours to 8 days; usually 18–36 hours.	Fatigue, headache, dry mouth, double vision, muscle paralysis, respiratory failure. High mortality rate if not treated promptly.	Low-acid canned foods, meats, sausage, fish. Improperly processed or preserved garlic-in-oil.	If canning foods in the home, proper procedures must be followed. Rapidly cool leftover foods. Infant botulism: Infants should not consume honey until more than 12 months of age.
Bacillus cereus	Toxin (emetic) or toxin-mediated (diarrheal).	30 minutes–6 hours (vomiting); 6–15 hours (diarrhea).	Nausea and vomiting. Abdominal cramps or diarrhea.	Rice products; starchy foods; food mixtures such as sauces, puddings, soups, and casseroles. Meats, milk, vegetables, and fish.	Careful time and temperature control of foods. Cook foods to recommended temperatures. Cool food quickly.

Source: References 16, 27, 34

How Water Activity (a$_w$) Controls Bacteria Growth in Food

Bacteria need moisture for growth. So why do bacteria not grow particularly well in some foods that seem to be moist? And why are high sugar or high salt foods less likely to spoil?

The answer is water activity level. Foods with a low water activity level do not support bacterial growth. The water activity level of food can be reduced by the following:

- Drying—water is removed
- Freezing—formation of ice crystals makes the water unavailable
- Addition of solutes such as salt or sugar—the salt or sugar binds the water ■

cannot grow at temperatures below 86°F (30°C), grows slowly even under optimal conditions, and does not compete well with other bacteria. It grows at temperatures between 86° and 117°F (30° and 47°C) and is preserved by refrigeration, but it is readily destroyed by heat sufficient to cook foods. Therefore, *C. jejuni* is not likely to be a problem in properly cooked foods or in processed foods that have been pasteurized or dehydrated.

Food Sources. *C. jejuni* is often found in the intestinal tract of cattle, swine, sheep, chickens, and turkeys. Therefore, the most likely sources of human infection are raw or inadequately cooked foods of animal origin and foods that are contaminated after cooking through contact with *C. jejuni*-infected materials. Raw meats and poultry become infected during processing when intestinal contents come into contact with meat surfaces. Research has shown that up to 88 percent of retail chickens carry *C. jejuni* [45]. Undercooked poultry and ground beef have been suspected in several outbreaks of illness. Raw milk and nonchlorinated water have been implicated in some infections.

FIGURE 3-9 Salmonella is a rod-shaped bacterium with multiple flagellum. *(Courtesy of U.S. Department of Agriculture)*

Prevention of Foodborne Illness. Illness can be prevented by thorough cooking of poultry and meat, pasteurization of milk, and proper handling of foods both before and after preparation for service. Care must be taken when storing and handling potentially contaminated foods such as poultry to prevent cross-contamination. Raw poultry should be stored so liquids cannot drip into other foods, especially foods that will not be cooked before consumption.

Listeria monocytogenes. Although the occurrence of *Listeria*-related illnesses have declined since the late 1990s, there are still an estimated 2,493 cases of illness and 499 deaths annually [26, 51]. This organism can be responsible for a variety of health problems, including meningitis, septicemia, and miscarriage. Pregnant women are about 20 times more likely than the general population to get listeriosis [16]. In addition to pregnant women, illness occurs principally in individuals whose immune system is compromised in some way by such conditions as cancer, cirrhosis, AIDS, or transplantation of organs. In these cases, the mortality rate is high. Healthy individuals are usually able to overcome the infection with considerably fewer problems.

Food Sources. Soil is a common reservoir of *L. monocytogenes*, which may be carried in the intestinal tracts of a variety of animals, including humans. Home environments may be contaminated with *L. monocytogenes*. This organism is found most often in raw milk, soft-ripened cheeses, ice cream, raw vegetables, fermented raw sausages, raw and cooked poultry, raw meat, and seafood products [34]. It may also be present in some vegetables. Listeriosis was in the national spotlight in 1998, when 21 deaths and 80 illnesses were traced to a single plant producing deli meat and hot dogs [83].

Prevention of Foodborne Illness. Six of the 21 deaths in 1998 from contaminated hot dogs and deli meats were due to miscarriages or stillbirths. Therefore, pregnant women must thoroughly cook hot dogs; avoid soft cheeses such as feta, Brie, Camembert, blue-veined, and Mexican-style cheeses; and may be advised to avoid deli meats or heat deli meats before consumption [9].

Since the late 1990s, there have been a number of meat recalls, especially involving products such as sausages, hot dogs, and soft cheeses, because of *Listeria* contamination. Listeria grows well in the manufacturing environment that is usually cool and moist. Many methods to reduce the possibility of post-cooking contamination of products in manufacturing are being implemented and researched [26]. In 2000, the Food Safety and Inspection Service (FSIS) announced that the levels of sodium lactate and sodium diacetate could be increased in meat products to further control *Listeria* [56]. Refrigerator storage temperatures must be carefully controlled because fluctuations in temperature are likely to affect the growth of this and other organisms. *L. monocytogenes* can grow well at temperatures as low as 32°F (0°C) but is sensitive to heat and is destroyed by pasteurization.

Yersinia enterocolitica. An infection caused by *Yersinia enterocolitica*, known as yersiniosis, may cause gastroenteritis. Pigs are the primary animal source of this organism [16]. Foods involved in outbreaks of yersiniosis have included chocolate milk, pasteurized milk, and tofu that was packed in unchlorinated spring water [34]. The precise manner by which the organism contaminated these foods was not determined, but in each case it was thought to be a lack of good sanitary practice. *Y. enterocolitica* can grow at refrigeration temperatures but is sensitive to heat; therefore, to control illness from this cause, it is important to eliminate the organism from foods by pasteurization or cooking. Care should be taken to cook pork thoroughly; to avoid cross-contamination of processed, ready-to-eat foods with pork and porcine wastes; and to practice good hygiene and handwashing practices.

Vibrio parahaemolyticus and Vibrio vulnificus. These bacteria are associated with the consumption of raw or improperly cooked fish and shellfish [34]. The growth of *V. parahaemolyticus* is slowed or arrested at refrigeration temperatures. Most important with respect to human infections is prevention of bacteria growth in uncooked seafoods and avoidance of the contamination of cooked foods. Consumption of raw seafoods should be avoided, particularly during the warmer months of the year when the *Vibrio* organisms tend to increase in numbers [27]. It is important that the elderly and those whose immune systems are compromised because of cancer, HIV, renal disease, and so on, be informed of the dangers associated with eating raw shellfish [16]. The fatality rate from *V. vulnificus* can be 50 percent or higher in susceptible individuals.

Escherichia coli. *Escherichia coli* is the leading cause of kidney failure in children and the fourth most common cause of bacterial diarrhea in the United States [35]. It is a normal inhabitant of the human intestinal tract and occurs in high numbers in fecal material. In recent years, certain strains of *E. coli* have been identified as the causative factors in several food poisoning outbreaks in the United States and Canada (Figure 3-10). Each year in the United States, 73,000 cases of infection and 61 deaths are estimated to occur [16].

A subgroup of *E. coli* called enteropathogenic *E. coli* can produce foodborne illness. One particular strain of this subgroup, *E. coli* 0157:H7, causes hemorrhagic colitis, producing bloody diarrhea and severe abdominal pain. Children are most likely to develop a complication of this foodborne illness called *hemolytic uremic syndrome* (HUS). HUS is characterized by renal injury and can lead to permanent kidney damage or death [35]. Damage to the central nervous system can be another complication. As few as 10 organisms may result in illness; therefore, the careful handling of foods that may be contaminated with *E. coli* 0157:H7 is essential.

Food Sources. *E. coli* 0157:H7 is generally associated with cattle and their products—beef and milk. Ground beef is especially of concern because the bacteria, if present, are spread throughout the meat when it is ground. *E. coli* food poisoning has also been associated with water, unpasteurized apple cider and apple juice, and produce foods such as lettuce that have been cross-contaminated either in the field or in the kitchen. The FDA recommends that children, older adults, and people with weakened immune systems drink *only* pasteurized cider and juice.

Prevention of Foodborne Illness. To avoid illness caused by *E. coli*, foods should be adequately cooked and post-cooking contamination avoided through careful handwashing and cleaning of

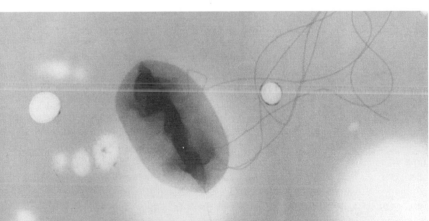

FIGURE 3-10 Transmission electron micrograph of *E. coli*. *(Courtesy of the Centers for Disease Control and Prevention, Public Health Image Library, Peggy S. Hayes)*

surfaces and equipment that have come in contact with raw meat. Consumers should cook ground meat to an internal temperature of 155 to 160°F (68 to 71°C). Although consumers were initially encouraged to check whether ground beef products were throughly cooked by the color of the meat in the center [54], research has shown that ground beef may be light gray or brown when below the safe temperature of 160°F [49, 65]. Consequently, consumer education efforts are now directed at encouraging the use of thermometers. Fresh fruits and vegetables should be washed thoroughly before eating. *E. coli* 0157:H7 can survive freezer storage as well as refrigeration [52].

The USDA requires that the HACCP system be used by livestock slaughter operations and meat-processing plants operating under federal inspection. The plants must also test for generic *E. coli* bacteria to verify that fecal contamination is not occurring. Processing methods such as steam pasteurization of the carcass, sprays, and organic washes are helping to reduce contamination during processing [56]. In 1999, irradiation of meat products was approved by the FSIS as another method to assure the safety of meat products [56]. Consumers, however, have been slow to embrace irradiated foods, unless education about the irradiation process is provided [66].

Clostridium perfringens.   The mechanism causing illness seems to involve the ingestion of large numbers of live vegetative cells of *C. perfringens*. These cells then form encapsulating spores in the intestinal tract and release an enterotoxin. The toxin produces the characteristic symptoms [34]. Thus, this microorganism exhibits characteristics of both a food infection and a food intoxication.

Foods responsible include beef, chicken, turkey, stews, meat pies, and gravy that have been mishandled. These foods may have been cooled too slowly after cooking or kept several hours without refrigeration, then improperly reheated. Because *C. perfringens* will grow at relatively warm temperatures, foods that have been held at a temperature below 130°F (55°C) for an extended period are another common cause of illness. *C. perfringens* organisms multiply rapidly under these conditions of poor temperature control during cooling, heating, or hot holding. Leftovers should be cooled rapidly and then reheated to a minimum of 165°F (74°C).

Shigella.   The major cause of shigellosis is infected food handlers who are carrying the organism in their intestinal tracts and who practice poor personal hygiene. Most outbreaks result from contamination of raw or previously cooked foods during preparation in the home or in food-service establishments. The best preventative measure is education of the food handler, with an emphasis on good personal hygiene. Relatively small numbers of the organisms can cause disease.

Staphylococcus aureus.   Certain strains of *Staphylococcus aureus* produce a potent toxin that is recognized as a common cause of food poisoning. It is called an *enterotoxin* because it produces gastroenteritis or inflammation of the lining of the stomach and intestines. The food-poisoning strains of *S. aureus* are present in the nasal passages and throats and on the hair and skin of 50 percent or more of healthy people [34]. Boils and some wounds may also be infected with them. Food may be contaminated with these potentially dangerous organisms when transfer occurs from the nasal passage or a sore on the hands of the food handler to the food being prepared. *Staphylococcus* organisms are shown in Figure 3-11.

Food Sources.   A wide variety of foods may provide excellent media for the growth of staphylococcal bacteria. Cooked poultry, baked ham, tuna, egg products, potato

The World Is Changing, and So Are Foodborne Pathogens

One key to understanding food safety is to appreciate that what we have done safely in the past may not continue to be safe in the future.

The consumption of rare ground beef at one time was common. What changed? *E. coli* 0157:H7 was identified as a relatively new pathogen. In 1993, more than 700 people in the northwestern United States became seriously ill after eating undercooked hamburger at a chain of fast-food restaurants. Four children subsequently died.

Likewise, recipes in many older cookbooks include raw eggs. The recommendation used to be that if an egg was "intact," meaning the shell was not cracked, then it was safe to consume raw. What changed? In the early 1980s, it was found that ovarian tissues of some hens were contaminated with *Salmonella enteritidis*, and these hens produced eggs with contaminated yolks in the intact egg. Current recommendations are that no eggs should be consumed raw or undercooked unless irradiated or pasteurized. ■

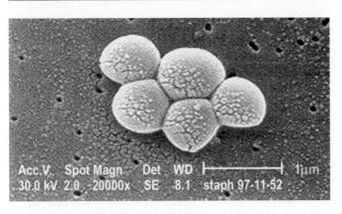

FIGURE 3-11 Scanning electron micrograph of *Staphylococcus aureus*. *(Courtesy of the Centers for Disease Control and Prevention, Public Health Image Library, Jim Biddle and Janice Carr)*

salad, and custard- or cream-filled baked goods are often involved. These foods, in particular, should be refrigerated at 35° to 40°F (2° to 4°C). Failure to refrigerate foods that have been contaminated with the microorganisms, thus allowing the toxin to form, is the usual reason for an outbreak of the disease. The toxin does not necessarily affect the taste of the product so individuals consuming such foods are not aware that they are eating "spoiled" food.

Prevention of Foodborne Illness. Prevention is accomplished by the sanitary handling of food during preparation and by proper refrigeration of prepared foods. Because staphylococci usually get into food by way of human handlers, contamination can be controlled by such simple rules as washing hands before preparing food and rewashing hands after using a handkerchief or tissue. Rubber or plastic gloves should be worn if cuts or sores are present on the hands, which not only keeps staphylococci from being transferred to the food from the cuts, but also prevents additional bacteria from getting into the sores.

Rapid cooling and refrigeration of foods at or below 41°F (5°C) are critical. Foods contaminated with staphylococcal organisms that are cooled very slowly or are held without refrigeration will provide favorable conditions for the growth of organisms and production of the toxin responsible for illness. Once the toxin has formed in the food, the staphylococcal toxin is not easily inactivated or destroyed; thus prevention is critical. The toxin is stable to heat and may withstand boiling for 20 to 60 minutes.

Clostridium botulinum. Botulism is a condition that results from the action of a potent toxin on the neurological system of the body, causing paralysis. The toxin is produced by the bacterium *C. botulinum*. Symptoms include nausea, vomiting, diarrhea, double vision, drooping eyelids, slurred speech, difficulty in swallowing, inability to talk, and, finally, respiratory paralysis and death. Infants with botu-

lism are lethargic, feed poorly, are constipated, and have a weak cry and poor muscle tone [16].

C. botulinum is able to form spores (Figure 3-12) that are very resistant to destruction by heat in a low-acid environment. It is also *anaerobic*, meaning that it can grow and produce toxin only in the absence of free oxygen. The organism itself and its spores are not pathogenic or disease producing in adult humans, but the toxin that it produces is one of the most potent known.

Food Sources. Inadequate processing of home-canned foods that are low in acid—particularly vegetables, low-acid varieties of tomatoes, and meats—creates the greatest problem with respect to botulism. The last reported outbreak of botulism from commercially canned food was more than 25 years ago [73]. Toxin production has also occurred in such foods as fresh mushrooms kept in tight plastic bags, baked potatoes wrapped in foil and left at room temperature for several days before being used to make potato salad, and seasoned cooked onions that were kept warm for extended periods of service. If fresh garlic cloves are placed in oil to season the oil, a danger of botulinum toxin production exists [27] because the oil creates an anaerobic environment favorable to *C. botulinum*.

C. botulinum spores may be found in honey, which has been implicated in some cases of infant botulism. Although adults can consume the *C. botulinum* cells that may be present in honey without ill effect, infants up to one year of age should not be fed honey. Out of about 110 cases of botulism reported in the United States each year, 72 percent are infant botulism [16]. *C. botulinum* is apparently able to colonize, grow, and produce toxin in the colons of certain infants, causing typical signs of neurological distress. Possibly because infants' intestinal bacteria are colonized after birth, *C. botulinum* organisms may grow before other bacteria that inhibit their growth have become well established.

Prevention of Foodborne Illness. When home-canning foods, procedures recommended by the USDA [11, 77] or by established companies that manufacture home-canning equipment should always be carefully followed for low-acid foods to guard against any possibility of toxins developing. Various strains of the organism vary in their temperature resistance, but low-acid foods are never safely processed unless they are heated at temperatures considerably above the boiling point of water, 212°F (100°C). It is recommended that temperatures no lower than 240°F (115°C) be used for low-acid foods. These temperatures can be achieved by processing in a pressure cooker at 10 to 15 pounds pressure. Canning procedures are discussed further in Chapter 30.

Spoiled foods containing the botulinum toxin may have off-odors and gas and appear to be soft and disintegrated. However, cases of botulism have been reported from eating foods that had little or no abnormal appearance or odor. Because of this problem and because the

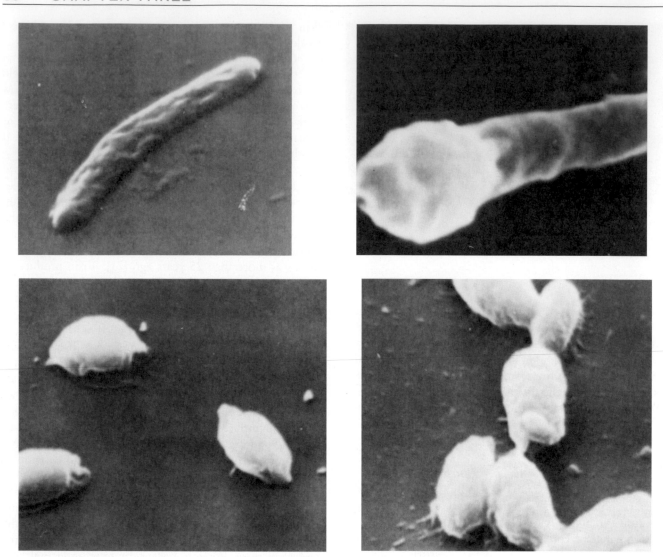

FIGURE 3-12 *Clostridium botulinum* spores are especially difficult to destroy and require temperatures above boiling when canning low-temperature foods. Scanning electron photomicrographs of (top left) a cell of *Clostridium botulinum*, type A, prior to formation of a spore and (top right) another type A cell during actual sporulation. At the bottom are spores of type B (left) and type E (right). *(Courtesy of the U.S. Department of Health and Human Services, Food and Drug Administration. D. A. Kautter and R. K. Lynt, Jr. (1971). Botulism, FDA Papers, 5(9), 16.)*

toxin can be inactivated by boiling temperatures, the USDA has recommended that home-canned low-acid foods (including low-acid tomatoes) that have not been processed using recommended procedures be boiled for 10 to 15 minutes before being tasted.

Commercially canned foods should be discarded if the can is damaged or the food appears suspect. Garlic-in-oil should be used immediately after preparation, or commercially prepared garlic-in-oil mixtures should be used. Honey should not be served to infants under 12 months of age.

Viruses

Viruses are an important cause of foodborne disease in the United States [47]. Essentially all foodborne viruses are transmitted to humans enterically, that is, by the fecal–oral route. They are shed in feces and infect by

being ingested. Infection may come directly by person-to-person contact or indirectly via the vehicles of food and water. Infection often results from mishandling of food by infected persons. Thus, sanitary personal hygiene habits and the avoidance of cross-contamination of ready-to-eat foods is critical. Viruses cannot multiply in foods and can usually be inactivated by cooking.

Hepatitis A. Foodborne illness due to the hepatitis A virus usually presents as a mild illness characterized by sudden onset of fever, malaise, nausea, anorexia, and abdominal discomfort, followed in several days by jaundice. The onset of symptoms occurs in 10 to 50 days. The infectious dose is presumed to be 10 to 100 virus particles [34]. Water, mollusks such as clams and oysters, and salads are frequently implicated in outbreaks. Other foods involved include sandwiches, fruits and fruit juices, milk and milk products, vegetables, salads, shellfish, and iced drinks.

Norovirus or Calicivirus. Gastroenteritis, characterized by vomiting and diarrhea, may be caused by Norwalk-like viruses that are shed in the feces. Norwalk viruses, also called *noroviruses*, have been implicated in a number of the outbreaks of gastroenteritis on cruise ships, often a result of cross-contamination of food or surfaces from an ill guest or employee. Food is not the only means by which these viruses can be spread; however, it is a very effective one. Shellfish and salad ingredients are foods most often implicated in Norwalk outbreaks. A high risk of infection is associated with the consumption of raw or insufficiently steamed clams and oysters [34]. The Norwalk virus is notable in that it has been spread through ice contaminated by unsanitary water or the poor personal hygiene of those who handled the ice.

Fungi

Fungi include molds, yeasts, and mushrooms. Fungi may be microscopic single-celled organisms to large multicellular organisms. Molds and yeasts have many beneficial functions in foods. Molds develop the characteristic flavors of some varieties of cheese, and yeast plays an important role in the leavening of yeast breads and the production of alcoholic beverages such as wine. Food spoilage or foodborne illness can also result from these organisms.

Molds. Molds are multicellular, filamentous microbes that appear fuzzy or cottonlike when they grow on the surface of foods. The growth may be white, dark, or various colors, such as green or orange. Mold **spores**, by which molds reproduce, are small, light, and resistant to drying. They easily spread through the air and can contaminate any food on which they settle. Molds may grow readily on relatively dry foods such as bread or stored cereal grains because they require less moisture than most other microorganisms. They thrive at ordinary room temperatures but, given sufficient time, can also grow under cool conditions in refrigerators. Some molds can grow even at relatively high temperatures.

Mycotoxins are toxins produced by molds that can contaminate foods such as grains, nuts, and fruits. *Asperillus, Fusarium,* and *Penicillium* species are three fungi naturally associated with foods that can produce mycotoxins. Several mycotoxins of concern include aflatoxins, patulin, ochractixin, zearalenone, trichothecenes, and fumonisins. When present in foods in sufficiently high levels, mycotoxins can cause liver or kidney deterioration, liver cancer, skin irritation, immunosuppression, birth defects, and death [57, 60].

Mycotoxins may be produced by *Fusarium* molds when adverse weather conditions, including both unusually wet spring and summer months and certain drought environments, occur during the growth of cereal crops (Figure 3-13). Contamination of the harvested grains by

FIGURE 3.13 A healthy wheat head (left) and one with *Fusarium* head blight disease (right). *Fusarium* can produce mycotoxins. *(Courtesy of U.S. Department of Agriculture)*

the toxin is a problem because the toxins survive most processing methods. Fortunately, accumulation of mycotoxins on cereal crops is not a significant problem during normal growing seasons [12]. The FDA has established regulatory limits for aflatoxins on both human and animal food. Monitoring programs are important in controlling the levels of mycotoxins in foods [39].

In the home, foods that develop mold growth should be discarded; however, solid cheeses may be trimmed of mold and the nonmoldy portion used if the cheese has been kept under refrigeration. Studies indicate that aflatoxins do not develop under refrigeration and that other toxins may be produced only in very small amounts or not at all. In the holding or storing of foods, precautions should always be taken to minimize mold growth by such practices as adequate refrigeration and use of foods within a reasonable time [78].

Yeast. Yeasts are one-celled organisms that are often spherical in shape. They usually reproduce asexually through budding, during which new daughter cells are pinched off from the parent cell (Figure 3-14). Unlike molds, most yeasts grow best with a generous supply of moisture. They also grow in the presence of greater concentrations of sugar than do most bacteria. The growth of many yeasts is favored by an acidic reaction (**pH** 4.0 to 4.5), and they grow best in the presence of oxygen. Thus, yeasts thrive particularly in acidic fruit juices, where they can ferment the sugar, producing alcohol. The range of temperature for the growth of most yeasts is, in general, similar to that for molds, with the optimum around 77° to 86°F (25° to 30°C).

Animal Parasites

The globalization of the world's food supply is causing exposure to parasites not previously common in a given geographical area. Consequently, the risk to American

FIGURE 3-14 Photomicrograph of baker's yeast, *Saccharomyces cerevisiae*. The yeast cell in the lower right corner is in the process of reproducing by budding; a new daughter cell is being created. *(Courtesy of Universal Foods Corporation)*

consumers of parasites has increased significantly. Only 13 species of parasitic animals were of concern in the United States in the 1990s. In 10 years that number has increased to over 100 species [62]. Current estimates suggest that up to 2.5 million cases of illness annually in the United States are due to food- and beverage-borne parasites [51].

In some parts of the world, infestation by such parasites as roundworms, flatworms, and certain species of protozoa may be common problems, and food or water may be carriers of these infecting agents. Protozoa include *Entamoeba histolytica*, the cause of amoebic dysentery, which is spread principally by fecal contamination of water, food, and diverse objects. Food handlers can spread this parasite. *Ascaris lumbricoides* is a roundworm or nematode that is spread fecally and is resistant to sewage treatment. It may survive for years in the soil and contaminate vegetables. *Trichinella spiralis*, another nematode, becomes encysted in meat and may be spread by this route. Certain tapeworms (flatworms) may also be encysted in meat, while other types may be acquired by eating raw or insufficiently cooked fish [62].

Trichinella spiralis. There is a continuing, though small, risk in the United States from the tiny roundworm, *Trichinella spiralis* (Figure 3-15). Legislation controlling hog feed, the increased freezing of pork, and public understanding of the need to cook pork products properly have all promoted a reduction in cases.

Trichinella now is most often associated with the consumption of meats other than pork, including undercooked game meats such as bear, boar, and rabbit. When meat from these animals is consumed before it has been sufficiently cooked to destroy the larvae in it, trichinosis results. The larvae are freed in the digestive tract after consumption of the meat and enter the small intestine, where they develop into mature worms. Their offspring (newborn larvae) migrate throughout the body via the circulatory system and invade striated muscles. Here they become encysted and may persist for years. In the first few weeks after ingestion of trichinae, symptoms include nausea, vomiting, diarrhea, sweating, and loss of appetite. Later, after the larvae reach muscles in the body, muscular pains, facial edema, and fever may occur. Several medications are available to treat trichinosis.

The USDA has recommended a procedure for processing cured pork products so that any trichinae present are destroyed. Therefore, these pork products should be free of trichinae. Poultry products that contain pork are subject to the same requirements concerning treatment for trichinae as are meat products containing pork. Thorough cooking of fresh pork to an internal temperature of at least 137°F (58°C) should ensure the destruction of any trichinae that may be present; however, a minimum of 145°F (63°C) is generally recommended for pork products. Cooking pork to an internal temperature of 160° (71°C), as recommended by the USDA "Is It Done Yet" temperature chart, allows a margin of safety. Pork cuts that are less than six inches thick can be frozen for 20 days at 5°F (–15°C) to destroy any trichinae present. However, the freezing of game does not consistently protect against trichinosis; thus, game meats must be thoroughly cooked regardless of freezing [18]. Precautions must be taken when cooking pork or game meats by microwaves to ensure that a final

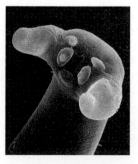

FIGURE 3-15 Scanning electron micrograph of a *Trichinella spiralis* tail. This parasite harbors itself in capsules inside flesh and in large quantities can cause severe muscular problems. *(Courtesy of J. Ralph Lichtenfels)*

temperature sufficient to destroy any trichinae is achieved throughout the meat.

Anisakis simplex. *Anisakis simplex* is a roundworm that can be found in cod, haddock, fluke, Pacific salmon, herring, flounder, monkfish, and fish used in sushi and sashimi. Fish must be cooked properly; if consumed raw, the fish must have been previously frozen. To protect against anisakiasis by freezing, the fish must be maintained at –4°F (–20°C) for seven days. Marinades are not protective, and marinated fish must still be properly cooked or previously frozen [27].

Toxoplasma gondii. This single-celled parasite causes a disease called *toxoplasmosis*. Toxoplasmosis infection is of concern for pregnant women because infants infected in the womb may develop serious eye or brain damage. Immunocompromised individuals also have a higher risk of complications. This parasite is frequently associated with cat feces and thus may be found in cat litter or contaminated soil. Raw and undercooked meat, however, can also be a source of toxoplasma gondii. Therefore, those at highest risk should be advised to cook all meat to a minimum of 160°F (71°C). Raw meats should be handled in storage and during preparation to avoid cross-contamination of other foods and surfaces [19].

Cyclospora cayetanensis. In the United States, the protozoa *Cyclospora cayetanensis* became a focus of public attention in the summer of 1996 [48]. This organism was recovered in multiple, clustered cases of prolonged diarrhea in the United States and Canada. More than 1,400 cases appeared from the Rocky Mountains eastward and were associated with the eating of fresh raspberries. The implicated raspberries were grown in Guatemala, but the *Cyclospora* was not actually found on the fruit. None of the available standardized tests for protozoan contamination of raw products was specifically intended for use on raspberries, creating difficulties in analysis.

Prions

Prions are normal proteins found in animal tissue that can become infectious. It is believed these misfolded, infectious proteins transform normally shaped proteins into abnormally shaped prions through contact. Prions are associated with bovine spongiform encephalopathy (BSE), often called "mad cow" disease. BSE and the human illness variant Creutzfeldt-Jakob disease (vCJD) appear to be caused by the same agent. These diseases result in irreversible damage of the central nervous system after an extended incubation period of several years [30].

The concern for consumers is the potential contamination of meat products. Worldwide, there have been 155 confirmed or probable cases of vCJD. In the United States, the one reported case of vCJD is believed to be related to consumption of potentially contaminated BSE meat while living in the United Kingdom where BSE was first reported in 1986. High-risk tissues include the cattle's skull, brain, eyes, tonsils, spinal cord, and part of the small intestine [30]. As of 2006, three BSE-infected cows have been confirmed in the United States by the USDA [75]. Since 1989, the FDA and the USDA have had regulations in place to prevent BSE among U.S. cattle and to protect consumers through active testing and surveillance [32].

Natural Toxins and Sources of Contamination

Although the term *natural* is generally associated with safety, certain plants and animals may contain natural constituents that are toxic, thereby producing gastrointestinal disturbances or even death when they are consumed in sufficient quantities.

Plant Toxins. Many toxic substances are found in tiny amounts in plant foods as normal components. Poisonous varieties of mushrooms, mistaken for edible kinds, are a well-known example of toxic plants. Oxalic acid is a constituent of plants such as spinach and beet greens. In large amounts, these may be responsible for oxalic acid poisoning in certain individuals. A very high content of oxalic acid is found in leaves of the rhubarb plant, which is why the leaves are not consumed.

Solanine is a water-soluble toxin that may be present in potatoes and increases during sprouting or exposure to light. This toxin is found principally in the skin and in the green portion directly underneath the skin, which may be removed by paring. However, the amounts of oxalic acid, solanine, and several other natural toxins in foods have not been shown to be toxic in the amounts usually eaten. These toxins, therefore, represent only minor hazards [23].

Vegetables of the cabbage family contain substances called goitrogens that can depress the activity of the thyroid gland. Legumes contain protease inhibitors that may interfere with the digestion of proteins. These inhibitors are destroyed by cooking. Substances called hemagglutinins, which cause agglutination of red blood cells, are found in soybeans, peanuts, kidney beans, and wax beans. Most of these substances are destroyed or inactivated in the human digestive tract. Seeds of the *Senecio* genus grow among, and may contaminate the harvest of, grains and contain substances that are toxic to the liver.

Marine Toxins. Toxins have been associated with seafood. Marine toxins are naturally occurring chemicals that generally do not affect the appearance, flavor, or smell of the seafood.

Ciguatoxin. Consuming predatory tropical reef fish, such as barracuda, contaminated by microscopic sea plants (dinoflagellates) causes ciguatera poisoning. Although barracuda is the fish most commonly associated with this toxin, grouper, sea bass, snapper, and mullet also have caused illness. Symptoms occur within a few minutes to 30 hours after consumption of the contaminated seafood. Nausea, vomiting, diarrhea, sweating, headache, and muscle aches are common. A sensation of burning or "pins-and-needles" may occur in some cases [17].

Scrombrotoxins. Scombrotoxic fish poisoning can occur when fish such as tuna, mackerel, bluefish, skipjack, swordfish, and bonito have begun to spoil, resulting in high histamine levels in the fish. Symptoms of scrombroid poisoning include flushing, rash, sweating, a burning or peppery taste in the mouth, dizziness, nausea, and headache. These symptoms occur within two minutes to two hours of consumption [17, 27]. Seafood must be kept cold; if temperature abused, it should not be purchased or consumed.

Paralytic Shellfish Poisoning. Often known as "red tide," paralytic shellfish poisoning is caused by a toxin produced by another dinoflagellate found in high concentrations in the ocean. The characteristic color of the tide is the result of the red-brown color of this organism. Shellfish such as mussels, cockles, clams, scallops, oysters, crabs, and lobsters typically from the colder coastal waters of the Pacific and New England states are most often affected. Symptoms of paralytic shellfish poisoning include numbness, tingling, and gastrointestinal upset that begin within one to three hours after eating the contaminated fish [17].

Chemical and Physical Contaminants

Toxic substances may contaminate the environment in which people, plants, and animals live. These substances include both inorganic elements—such as arsenic, cadmium, mercury, and lead—and organic substances—such as various chemicals used in pesticides. When contaminants persist in the environment, they may accumulate along the food chain in amounts that are toxic to humans when various animals and plants are consumed.

Mercury. Fish taken from water contaminated by the industrial use of mercury contain high levels of mercury, which may cause illness in humans if consumed in large amounts. Pregnant women, nursing women, and young children have been advised by the FDA to avoid shark, swordfish, king mackerel, or tilefish because these fish may contain high levels of mercury [81]. The EPA also provides water advisories to inform sport fishermen of the areas where fish may be contaminated [82].

Other Metals. Metals may enter foods from certain utensils. Galvanized containers are not suitable for foods because the zinc used for galvanizing is toxic. Cadmium and brass are also undesirable metals for use as food containers. Tin-coated cans are used in food processing, but only very small amounts of tin are generally found in most foods. Acid fruits and fruit juices packed in lacquered tin-coated cans and stored in the opened cans in the refrigerator contain increased amounts of both tin and iron [44]. Food stored in opened tin-coated

cans may also change in color or develop a metallic taste. Although these changes are undesirable, illness will not result from the canning materials currently used in the food-processing industry.

Small quantities of aluminum are dissolved from utensils in many cooking processes. This is apparently not harmful, but scientists are continuing to study the effects of aluminum in the diet. The element copper is nutritionally essential, yet certain salts of copper are toxic. Cooking green vegetables in copper containers to get a bright green color is no longer practiced because of the danger of toxicity. It has been reported that foods cooked in iron utensils, steel woks, and stainless steel cookware show increases in iron content [63]. Although the increase in iron is small, it is substantial enough to be considered in calculating dietary intake.

Packaging. Foods are packaged in various types of containers from which certain chemical molecules may migrate to the food contained inside. The FDA is responsible for approving food-grade packaging materials to ensure that the type and amount of material that may migrate into the food will not be harmful to the consumer.

Pesticide Residues. Consumer concern about pesticides residues has varied over the years. In a 1993 survey, 79 percent of the participants viewed pesticide residues on foods as a serious health hazard [10]. Today's consumers are less concerned about pesticide residues as compared to other potential food-safety issues [42]. Food scientists and an increasing number of consumers consider the predominant risk in the food supply to be microbiological, not chemical. At the same time, some consumers choose organic foods, in part because of a desire to avoid pesticides. Organic foods will be discussed in Chapter 4.

To protect the safety of our food supply, the FDA regularly monitors pesticide residues on foods, including in its program the completion of a yearly Total Diet Study [33]. Representative foods that might be consumed by various age and sex groups are purchased from grocery stores across the United States and analyzed in FDA laboratories for pesticide residues, as well as for other contaminants and some nutrients. In 2003, the FDA tested a total of 7,234 samples of domestic and imported foods for pesticide residues. Sixty-three percent of the domestically grown foods and 72 percent of the import samples (including foods from 99 countries) contained no pesticide residues [33]. Those samples with residues were within the limits set by the EPA. Research on pesticide residues will continue to ensure a safe food supply.

Food Allergies and Intolerances

Foods safe for the general population may be unsafe for selected individuals who are allergic to specified foods. True allergies are characterized by abnormal immune system response to naturally occurring proteins in foods [71]. Food allergy symptoms are varied and can include gastrointestinal, cutaneous, respiratory, or other symptoms. Some individuals experience anaphylactic shock that can result in death within minutes of consuming an offending food unless prompt medical attention is received [38]. Each year, approximately 150 Americans die from a severe allergic reaction, and 30,000 require emergency room treatment [31].

Prevalence of allergies in the U.S. population is estimated to be 2 to 2.5 percent of the population overall. Comparatively, children exhibit a higher rate of allergies, ranging from 5 to 8 percent [71]. Children will often grow out of their allergies, whereas adults tend to remain allergic throughout their lives. The "Big Eight" causes of food allergy are wheat, crustacea such as shrimp and crabs, eggs, fish, peanuts, milk, tree nuts, and soybeans [71]. Individuals who experience the most severe symptoms must carefully avoid even traces of the food responsible for the allergic reaction.

The Food Allergen Labeling and Consumer Protection Act of 2004 mandates that effective January 1, 2006, the "Big Eight" allergenic foods must be declared in plain language in the ingredient statement or a separate statement indicating "contains___" [31, 74]. Understandable and accurate food labels are essential if allergic individuals are to avoid offending foods. Good manufacturing practices to reduce cross-contamination of products during processing are another important strategy in the effort to provide safe food to those who are allergic [21, 72].

Food intolerances are different from allergies because food intolerances occur through nonimmunological means. Three categories of intolerances include anaphylactoid reactions, metabolic food disorders, and idiosyncratic illnesses. Sensitivity to strawberries is an example of an anaphylactoid reaction. Metabolic disorders include the intolerance of lactose or fava beans. Lactose-intolerant individuals have an impaired ability to digest lactose, the principal sugar in milk. Sulfite-induced asthma has been well documented and represents an idiosyncratic illness because the mechanism for this reaction is not understood [71].

ADDITIONAL FOOD-SAFETY ISSUES

Biotechnology

Biotechnology provides an important tool for growth and progress in the area of food and agriculture. The breeding of plants using cross-pollination has been a common, acceptable practice for many years in developing new plant varieties. With increased understanding of deoxyribonucleic acid (DNA) and genetics, beginning during the 1950s, a technology was developed by which DNA material (that is, genes) could be taken from an unrelated plant, bacterium, or animal and inserted into the genetic material of the plant being modified. Thus, this new biotechnology, called genetic engineering, offered the ability to introduce new and desirable traits more efficiently [40].

The main crops produced from biotechnology are corn, soybeans, cotton, potatoes, and rapeseed (grown for canola oil). These crops have been modified to resist insects or increase herbicide tolerance [5]. Biotechnology may also be used to improve the eating quality of a fruit or vegetable. In 1994, the "Flavr Savr" tomato was the first genetically altered food to be sold to U.S. consumers [40]. These tomatoes have increased resistance to softening so that they can be vine ripened, with consequent increased flavor.

The first food-processing aid produced by a genetically engineered microorganism was approved by the FDA in March 1990—the enzyme *rennin* or *chymosin*. Other enzymes, processing aids, and food ingredients are being developed. A growth hormone (rbST) given to cows to increase milk production is derived through the use of new techniques in biotechnology.

The safety of biotechnology products is regulated by the FDA, and potentially negative consequences to the environment are scrutinized by the USDA. Biotechnology, however, may cause safety concerns for some people. Most in the scientific community endorse the safety of genetic engineering stating that the risks are no different than the risks posed by traditional breeding methods [5, 46]. Biotechnology has the potential to ensure safe, abundant, affordable, and highly nutritious foods [43].

FOCUS ON SCIENCE

Sulfites—Why Are They Used?

Some individuals may become ill when exposed to sulfites. As a result of this risk, the use of sulfite in food has been limited, yet it is still used for some purposes. Sulfites are strong antioxidants that will prevent the darkening of light fruit such as apples, apricots, and bananas when dried. Because fruits cannot be blanched when dried, the enzyme polyphenoloxidase is still active. Sulfur dioxide will inhibit the activity of the enzyme and keep the fruit looking light.

Plants can be made resistant to insects and viruses, thus reducing crop losses and the use of chemical insecticides [13]. The public's concerns must therefore be addressed and satisfied by the scientific community. Consumers have been found to be more favorable toward biotechnology when educational information is provided about the risks and benefits [15].

Bioterrorism

Since 2001, FDA has conducted food supply vulnerability assessments, established with the CDC and the USDA. The Food Emergency Response Network hired more than 655 new field inspectors to monitor imports and updated labs to handle an increased number of food samples as efforts to protect the food supply from terrorism [52]. In 2002, the Public Health Security and Bioterrorism Preparedness and Response Act of 2002 was passed to "improve the ability of the United States to prevent, prepare for, and respond to bioterrorism and other public health emergencies" [64]. Under this new law, four major regulations with implications for food safety have been implemented. These include (1) registration of facilities that manufacture, process, pack, or hold food for animal or human consumption; (2) prior notification of imported food shipments to the FDA; (3) manufacturers, processors, packers, importers, and others are required to keep records identifying the source of food and where it is being shipped; and (4) the FDA has new authority to detain any food for 30 days if credible evidence exists that the food may be dangerous [52].

CHAPTER SUMMARY

- Food safety is everyone's responsibility. From the farmer to the processor, the packager, the wholesaler, the retailer, and the consumer, everyone should recognize potential hazards related to food and know how to control them.

- Foodborne illness is estimated to be the cause of 76 million illnesses per year. Young children, pregnant women, the elderly, people with weakened immune systems, and those taking medication are at the highest risk for foodborne illness.

- The government promotes food safety through oversight and monitoring by the USDA, FDA, EPA, and CDC.

- Consumers have important responsibilities for food safety. Studies have found many consumers do not follow safe food-handling practices.

- Four critical messages to reduce the incidence of foodborne illness include: Wash hands and surfaces often, don't cross-contaminate, cook to proper temperatures, and refrigerate promptly.

- HACCP is a coordinated system composed of seven steps for ensuring the safety of a food product. Through the assessment of risks and hazards, identification of critical control points, and establishment of preventative measures, corrective actions, system verification procedures, and record keeping, HACCP reduces the risk of foodborne illness.

- Pasteurization and ionizing radiation (irradiation) may be used for some foods to reduce the risk of foodborne illness. Pasteurization is the heating of foods to reduce foodborne pathogens and increase safety of the food. Foods are irradiated with gamma rays, electron beams, or x-rays to destroy bacteria in food. Irradiated foods are regulated by the FDA and USDA and must be labeled with the Radura symbol.

- There are a number of microorganisms (bacteria, viruses, fungi, and parasites) that are associated with foodborne illness. The characteristics of these organisms and methods to store, handle, and prepare food must be understood to prevent foodborne illness. Viruses are an important cause of foodborne illness in America and are commonly the result of poor personal hygiene on the part of food handlers or contaminated water. Molds may produce toxins called *mycotoxins*.

- Prions are proteins that have become infectious and are associated with bovine spongiform encephalopathy.

- Toxins may be another source of foodborne illness. Toxins natural in the environment include plant and marine toxins.

- Chemical and physical contaminants that may have a negative impact on food safety include mercury, other metals, packaging, and pesticide residues. The FDA has advised pregnant women, nursing women, and young children to avoid some fish due to the potential levels of mercury that may contaminate the fish. The FDA and EPA regulate and monitor pesticide residues in the food supply. Testing has shown pesticide residues to be low in the U.S. food supply.

- Foods safe for the general population may be unsafe for selected individuals who have food allergies or intolerances. The "Big Eight" causes of food allergy are wheat, crustacea such as shrimp and crabs, eggs, fish, peanuts, milk, tree nuts, and soybeans. Easy-to-understand, accurate food labels are essential so that allergic individuals can avoid offending foods.

- Biotechnology permits the development of new plants through more precise methods than cross-pollination. Genes may be inserted into a plant to provide resistance to pests, higher nutritional value, greater crop yields, or improved sensory qualities. Most in the scientific community endorse the safety of these biotechnology techniques.

- The Public Health Security and Bioterrorism Preparedness and Response Act of 2002 was passed to protect the safety of the food in the United States from terrorism.

STUDY QUESTIONS

1. Why is food safety so important and who is most at risk for foodborne illness?

2. Identify departments and agencies in the U.S. government who monitor and regulate the safety of food.

3. List and discuss several precautions that should always be taken in preparing, cooking, and storing food to ensure its safety for human consumption.

4. What is HACCP?

   (a) What general steps are involved in its implementation?

   (b) Discuss the role of HACCP in helping to prevent foodborne illness.

5. Identify the temperatures recommended for the safe endpoint cooking temperature for ground beef, chicken, and pork. What are some potential reasons why the temperature recommendations of the USDA (intended for consumers) and the FDA Food Code (intended for foodservice operations) are different?

6. Explain how to use a stem thermometer properly. Include a description of how to calibrate thermometers and how to take the temperature of thin foods such as hamburgers.

7. Discuss the proper refrigeration of foods. (a) How should food be stored in the refrigerator to prevent cross-contamination? (b) Describe storage methods for foods so that cooling is rapid.

8. Why is it extremely important that food handlers observe appropriate sanitary procedures when working with food? (a) Explain the process for washing hands thoroughly. (b) Identify multiple times before, during, and after food preparation that hands should be washed.

9. Compare the optimum conditions for growth of molds, yeasts, and bacteria in foods.

10. Explain the difference between *food infection, food intoxication*, and *toxin-mediated infection*. Give examples of each.

11. For each type of food poisoning listed below, (a) indicate if it is an infection, intoxication, or toxin-mediated infection; (b) list the usual symptoms; (c) list the types of food most likely to be involved; and (d) suggest measures that should prevent the occurrence of an outbreak of illness.

    (a) Salmonellosis
    (b) *Campylobacter jejuni* poisoning
    (c) *Escherichia coli* 0157:H7 poisoning
    (d) Yersiniosis
    (e) Listeriosis
    (f) Staphylococcal poisoning
    (g) *Clostridium perfringens* poisoning
    (h) Botulism

12. Describe some other types of bacterial food poisoning.

13. What is *trichinosis*? How is it caused? How might it be prevented?

14. Describe examples of potential food-related problems that may result from:

    (a) Mycotoxins
    (b) Animal parasites
    (c) Viruses
    (d) Environmental contaminants
    (e) Naturally occurring toxicants

15. What are food allergies and food intolerances? (a) Identify the "Big Eight" causes of food allergies. (b) Discuss the importance of food labels for those who are allergic to foods.

16. Describe the monitoring process for pesticides in the U.S. food supply.

17. What is meant by biotechnology? Give some examples of its use in improving the food supply.

FOOD REGULATIONS AND STANDARDS

4

Supermarket shelves hold thousands of different food items from which we may choose when shopping. As we make our selections, we all like to feel confident that we are getting our money's worth. But how can we be assured that we are receiving the quality and safety for which we are paying?

Most food processors and manufacturers work hard to establish and maintain reputations for good quality and safety in their products. They want to keep customers coming back again and again. The government also plays a role, through legislation and regulation, in ensuring quality and safety in the foods we purchase. Historically, as well as today, regulation of food safety has been regarded as an important function of government. Since passage of the first Pure Food and Drug Act of 1906, the role of the U.S. federal government has expanded in this area.

The Food and Drug Administration (FDA) and the U.S. Department of Agriculture (USDA) provide the primary oversight for our food supply. Various federal agencies also have responsibilities to regulate the food supply—including the setting of standards, control of adulteration and misbranding, promotion of good manufacturing practices (GMPs), approval of food additives, inspection, and grading. By promulgating regulations and setting standards, the government is attempting to implement the constitutional mandate to "promote the general welfare."

In this chapter, the following topics will be discussed:

- Role of U.S. government agencies in assuring the quality and safety of the food supply
- Key laws and regulations with impact on the food supply
- Some specific areas of government oversight including quality standards, food labels, food additives, biotechnology, pesticides, irradiation, inspection, quality grading, and organic foods.

FOOD AND DRUG ADMINISTRATION

The FDA is part of the U.S. Department of Health and Human Services (HHS) and includes the Center for Food Safety and Applied Nutrition (CFSAN). It is responsible for much of the policy and enforcement having to do with human food. The FDA regulates 80 percent of the food supply, including all foods except red meats, poultry, and certain egg products. Products regulated by the FDA account for 25 cents of each dollar consumers spend [48]. Food accounts for 75 percent of these regulated products.

In overseeing our food supply, the FDA performs several key roles to ensure food is safe, sanitary, wholesome, and accurately labeled. Regulations and laws, including the Federal Food, Drug, and Cosmetic Act of 1938 and its several amendments are administered by the FDA (Table 4-1). The safety of food additives, colorings, and foods developed through biotechnology is investigated and regulated. Scientific assessment of nutrition claims has led to nutrition labeling and health claims laws. Food industry surveillance and compliance is achieved in part through the efforts of FDA investigators and inspectors who oversee sanitation in food-processing plants, food-service sanitation, and interstate travel facilities. Both domestic and imported foods are inspected. Products identified as unsafe are prevented from coming to market. Products already in the marketplace may be detained or subject to voluntary or court ordered recalls. The FDA through the CFSAN also takes an active role in educating consumers about safe food handling [48].

History

Federal legislation of foods began in a serious way in 1906 with the passage of the Pure Food and Drug Act and the Meat Inspection Act [8, 13]. The USDA initially administered both of these. The chief chemist of the

fish are not included under USDA

important page

TABLE 4-1 Food and Drug Administration: Food Regulations to Protect the Health and Safety of the Public

Laws, Statues, and Regulations	Overview of Basic Provisions
1906 Pure Food and Drug Act	Prohibited misbranded and adulterated foods, drinks, and drugs in interstate commerce; addition of color additives to conceal poor quality; and use of "poisonous" colors in confections.
	• Authorized factory inspections.
	• 1913 Gould Amendment requires contents be plainly labeled on the outside of the food package with weight, measure, or count.
	"Loop hole" to this legislation which was repealed and replaced in 1938.
	Some manufacturers use "distinctive" names to market products that would have otherwise been illegal. For example, "Bred-Spread," a product that had no strawberries, yet was marketed as an alternative to jam and jelly.
1938 Federal Food, Drug, and Cosmetic Act	Food must be labeled by its common or usual name. Distinctive name provision in 1906 Act was removed.
	• Three kinds of food standards were authorized—identity, quality, and fill of container.
	• Colors had to be approved *before* use in foods, drugs, and cosmetics.
1954 Miller Pesticide Amendment	Defines procedures for setting safety limits for pesticide residues on agricultural commodities.
1958 Food Additives Amendment	Required manufacturers to establish safety before marketing. The generally recognized as safe (GRAS) list was published in 1958.
	Includes Delaney Clause prohibiting approval of any additive shown to induce cancer in humans or animals.
1960 Color Additives Amendment	Defined "color additive" and required manufacturers to establish safety before use in food.
1966 Fair Packaging and Labeling Act	All consumer products involved in interstate commerce must be honestly and informatively labeled. FDA enforces foods, drugs, cosmetics, and medical devices affected by this act.
1973 Low-Acid Processing Regulations Issued	Adequate heat treatment of low-acid foods is further regulated to prevent botulism resulting from commercially canned foods.
1980 Infant Formula Act	Required additional quality control procedures to assure nutritional content and safety.
1990 Nutrition Labeling and Education Act	Requires most foods to include nutrition labeling.
	• Starting in 1993, the "Nutrition Facts" label was required.
	• Health claims were regulated.
	• Use of terms "light," "low," "reduced," and others was legally defined.
	• Effective 2006, Nutrition Facts labels must include the trans fat content.
1996 Food Quality Protection Act	Amends the 1938 Food, Drug, and Cosmetic Act with regard to pesticides.
HACCP Regulations	In 1997, seafood processors required to use HACCP to ensure food safety.
	In 2001, HACCP regulations for fruit juice established.
2002 Public Health Security and Bioterrorism Preparedness and Response Act	Four regulations to address provision of Act were developed by FDA:
	• Food facility registration.
	• Prior notice of import foods.
	• Record-keeping of food received and shipped by all shippers, manufacturers, and others.
	• Procedures for FDA to detain suspect foods.
2004 Food Allergen Labeling and Consumer Protection Act	Starting In 2006, the major food allergens (peanuts, soybeans, cow's milk, eggs, fish, crustacean shellfish, tree nuts, and wheat) must be clearly labeled.

Source: References 13, 24, 39

USDA was Harvey Wiley. Dr. Wiley was an early pioneer involved in the struggle for adequate laws to protect the public's food supply (Figure 4-1). During the late 1800s and early 1900s, Dr. Wiley tried various tactics, including feeding measured amounts of chemical preservatives to 12 young volunteers in a so-called "poison squad" experiment, to increase understanding of food additive safety and highlight food-safety concerns. These volunteers were fed borax, salicylic, sulphurous and benzoic acids, and formaldehyde, over a five-year period to assess if these chemicals were injurious to health. The "poison squad" experiment gained the

(a)   (b)

FIGURE 4-1 (a) Members of the "Poison Squad" dine together consuming wholesome meals containing potentially harmful substances. This scientific investigation, conducted by Dr. Harvey W. Wiley, dramatized the need for pure food legislation. (b) William R. Carter was hired as the chef for the Poison Squad experiments. He later earned a degree in pharmaceutical chemistry and worked in FDA laboratories for 43 years. *(Courtesy of U.S. Food and Drug Administration)*

attention of citizens and helped to convince Congress and the president of the need for pure food legislation. Finally, in 1906, the first Pure Food and Drug Act was passed. It was a beginning.

Although the first legislation on foods was implemented by the USDA, it was later decided that, for products not of animal origin, the emphasis should be less on agriculture and more on health. Thus, in 1940, the FDA was transferred out of the USDA into the Federal Security Agency. In 1953, the FDA was moved again to the Department of Health, Education, and Welfare, which became the Department of Health and Human Services in 1979 [26].

The original 1906 Pure Foods Act was completely revised in 1938 and renamed the Federal Food, Drug, and Cosmetic Act. Among other things, the 1938 law required truthful labeling of additives. Several amendments to the Federal Food, Drug, and Cosmetic Act have been passed to strengthen the law and keep up with changes in food technology and medical science.

Federal Food, Drug, and Cosmetic Act of 1938

Under the Federal Food, Drug, and Cosmetic Act, the FDA sets three kinds of mandatory standards for products being shipped across state lines: identity, minimum quality, and fill of container. The public also is pro-

tected from food that may be unclean, decomposed, or contaminated.

Standards of Identity. The basic purpose for setting standards of identity for food products is to "promote honesty and fair dealing in the interest of consumers." Standards of identity define what a food product must be or must contain if it is to be legally labeled and sold by its common or usual name. The standard also lists optional ingredients that may be used but are not required. For example, the standard of identity for mayonnaise specifies the ingredients it must contain—oil, egg, and an acid component—and requires that at least 65 percent oil be included in the finished dressing. Prior to the establishment of standards of identity, consumers could not be assured that products, such as mayonnaise, ice cream, fruit jams or jellies, were composed of the generally expected ingredients. In fact prior to these standards, jam or jelly-like products were sold that did not contain fruit.

Standards of identity have been established for a large number of food products, including bakery and cereal products, cacao products, canned fruits and vegetables, fruit butters and preserves, fish and shellfish, eggs and egg products, margarine, nut products, dressings for foods, cheeses and cheese products, milk and cream, frozen desserts, macaroni and noodle products, and

FOCUS ON SCIENCE

prevalence of babies born with spinal bifada. Therefore, in 1998 the Food and Drug Administration mandated that folic acid be added to several enriched grain products including breakfast cereals, breads, pastas, flour, and rice.

Why Include Folic Acid in Enriched Grains?

Research studies found folic acid was important to the health of pregnant women and the unborn fetus. In particular, low levels of folic acid in the diet were associated with a higher

tomato products. Only after many public hearings and input from food industry representatives and consumers were the standards set.

Many of the standards of identity for food were established in the early years following passage of the Federal Food, Drug, and Cosmetic Act in 1938. The FDA has promulgated few new standards of identity since 1970. In 1998, the standards of identity for several enriched grain products were amended to require fortification with folic acid [35]. Although prior to 1993, foods with a standard of identity were not required to list ingredients, standardized foods now must list ingredients on the label [22]. Essentially, all foods, including those with a standard of identity, are subject to nutrition labeling under the 1990 Nutrition Labeling and Education Act. Modernization of the food standards of identity has been proposed, in part, to promote food technology innovations and to encourage development of food products with better nutritional profiles [38]. Thus, the standards of identity of foods, as currently established, may change significantly in the years ahead.

Standards of Minimum Quality.   Standards of minimum quality have been set for several canned fruits and vegetables, specifying minimum requirements for such characteristics as tenderness, color, and freedom from defects. If a food does not meet the minimum standard, it must be labeled "below standard in quality; good food— not high grade." Other words may be substituted for the second part of the statement to show in what respect the product is substandard, such as "below standard in quality; excessively broken." The consumer seldom sees a product with a substandard label at retail stores. Standards of minimum quality, as well as other grade standards, are indications of quality characteristics and are not concerned specifically with safety. Both lower- and higher-grade products are safe to eat.

Standards of Fill of Container.   Standards of fill of container state how full a food container must be for certain processed foods. These standards aim to avoid deception by preventing the sale of air or water in place of

Food Standards and the Nutrition Labeling and Education Act

When many of the food standards were developed, "recipes" for these products were based on the ingredients typically expected for a high quality food product. With an increasing emphasis on lower calorie and lower fat foods over the years, processors have developed foods to meet the public's desire for foods with a particular nutritional profile. Prior to the 1990 Nutrition Labeling and Education Act, reduced-fat foods that did not meet the standards of identity were labeled as *imitation* or with completely different names.

Today, reduced-fat versions of foods such as sour cream, mayonnaise, and ice cream may still be called by

their respective names even if the traditional standard of identity has not been met. For example, prior to 1990, "lowfat" or "reduced-fat" ice cream was called ice milk and by law could not be called ice cream because the standard of identity was not met. To maintain the standard name, reduced-fat versions of foods must (a) be labeled "lowfat" or "light" as appropriate, (b) not be nutritionally inferior (Vitamin A must be added to reduced-fat products to replace the Vitamin A lost when the fat was removed), (c) perform like the standard product, and (d) contain a significant amount of any mandatory ingredients [25, 37]. ■

food. They are needed especially for products that consist of a number of pieces packed in a liquid, such as various canned vegetables, or for products, such as nuts and ready-to-eat cereals, that shake down after filling.

Sanitation Requirements.   One basic purpose of the Federal Food, Drug, and Cosmetic Act is the protection of the public from articles that may be deleterious, that are unclean or decomposed, or that have been exposed to unsanitary conditions which may contaminate the article with filth or render it injurious to health. The law requires that foods be protected from contamination at all stages of production and that they be produced in sanitary facilities. Foods may not be distributed if they contain repulsive or offensive matter considered to be filth, whether or not it poses actual physical danger to an individual. Filth includes rodent hair and excreta, insects or insect parts and excreta, maggots, larvae, pollution from the excrement of humans and animals, or other materials that, because of their repulsiveness, would not be eaten knowingly.

The Federal Food, Drug, and Cosmetic Act declared any food prepared, packed, or held under unsanitary conditions to be adulterated. Therefore, the FDA has produced directives called *current good manufacturing practices* (GMPs). These directives establish regulations regarding many facets of the food-manufacturing process and include requirements for cleanliness; education, training, and supervision of workers; design and ease of cleaning and maintenance of buildings, facilities, and equipment; and adequate record-keeping to ensure quality control.

Food Additives and Colorings

What is a food additive? Under a broad definition, it is any substance that becomes part of a food product either when it is added intentionally or when it incidentally becomes part of the food. Examples of incidental additives are substances that may migrate from the packaging material into a food. The amount of additive involved in these cases is extremely small, but is nevertheless regulated [10].

The legal definition of *food additive* extends only to those substances that must receive special approval from the FDA after they have been thoroughly tested for safety and before they can be used in food. In addition to these specially tested and approved additives, the FDA maintains an official list of other substances added to foods that are "generally recognized as safe" (GRAS) for human consumption by experts in the field. Salt, sugar, and spices are examples of GRAS ingredients [10]. Although GRAS substances do not require the detailed clearance for safety that is specified for legally defined food additives, they are evaluated and reevaluated for safety by the FDA on a case-by-case basis. Ongoing industry assessment of GRAS substances also occurs. A Flavor and Extract Manufacturers' Association Expert Panel completed a comprehensive assessment of the GRAS flavoring substances in 1985, with the completion of a second

What Are Justifiable Uses for Food Additives?

Approved additives must serve a useful purpose. Additives may not be used to conceal damage or spoilage or to deceive the consumer. An additive may be intentionally used for one or more of the following general purposes:

1. To maintain or improve nutritional quality. Vitamins and minerals are used to fortify some foods when these nutrients may have been lost in processing or when they might be otherwise lacking in the usual diet.

2. To enhance the keeping quality with consequent reduction in food waste. Freshness may be maintained by the use of additives to retard spoilage, preserve natural color and flavor, and retard the development of rancid odors in fats.

3. To enhance the attractiveness of foods. Many additives will make food look and taste better. Natural and synthetic flavoring agents, colors, and flavor enhancers serve this purpose.

4. To provide essential aids in processing or preparation. A large variety of additives is used to give body and texture to foods as stabilizers or thickeners, to distribute water-soluble and fat-soluble particles evenly together as emulsifiers, to control the acidity or alkalinity, to retain moisture as humectants, to leaven or make rise many baked products, to prevent caking or lumping, and to perform other functions. ■

assessment in 2005 [18, 23]. Occasionally, substances may be removed from the GRAS list as more sophisticated analytical tools and methodologies for evaluation of safety are developed. It should be emphasized that there is an ongoing process of reassessment and evaluation by the FDA on all issues of food safety, including additives.

Food Additives Amendment. The Federal Food, Drug, and Cosmetic Act governs the use of additives in food entering interstate commerce. The 1958 Food Additives Amendment was designed to protect the public by requiring approval of new additives before they can be used in foods. The responsibility for proving the safety of additives rests with the manufacturer, who must file a petition with the FDA showing the results of extensive tests for safety. The FDA must approve the additive as safe before it can be marketed. The FDA also prescribes the types of foods in which the additive can be used and specifies labeling directions. Additives in meat and poultry products are under the jurisdiction of the USDA.

Color Additives Amendment. A color additive may be a dye, pigment, or other substance that imparts color to foods. Colors may be used to (a) offset color loss due to light, air, temperature, moisture and other conditions, (b) enhance natural colors, (c) correct natural variations in color, or (d) provide color. Colors may not be used to hide inferior or defective foods. Certified colors are synthetically produced and have historically been called "coal-tar" colors even though today most are made from raw materials obtained from petroleum [1, 42]. Certifica-

tion of colors applies to domestic and foreign manufacturers with a sample of each "lot" submitted to the FDA for analysis prior to use in food [6]. Colors that may be exempt from certification include pigments from natural sources, such as red or green from grape skin extract [10]. Colors exempt from certification must still comply with other FDA specifications for use [1].

All coloring substances added to foods are regulated under the Color Additives Amendment, passed in 1960. Rules regarding color additives were made stronger under this amendment, and previously approved certified colors were retested. An FDA batch certification of all synthetic colors is required. No color additives may be considered to be "generally recognized as safe" [1, 42].

Labeling of Additives and Colors. Food additives are required to be listed as ingredients on food labels. Spices and flavors may be simply mentioned as such, without each specific item being named. The presence of any artificial colors or flavors must be indicated. Certified colors, such as FD&C Yellow #5, commonly known as tartrazine, must be listed by name. Color additives, exempt from certification, may be listed as "artificial color."

Delaney Clause and Safety. Included in the Food Additives Amendment is a special clause carrying the name of Congressman James J. Delaney, who was chairman of the congressional committee that investigated, for two years, the use of chemicals in foods. Its report was issued in 1952. A similar clause is contained in the Color Additives Amendment. The Delaney clause provides

FOCUS ON SCIENCE

More Facts on Food Colors
Why use artificial instead of natural colorings in food?

The artificial water-solvent colorants used in a variety of foods are quite stable to heat, light, acid, and alkaline conditions. Natural colorants such as annatto extract (orange color), beet powder, and cochineal extract (red-blue color similar to beet powder) are unstable. Certain conditions such as heat, pH of the food, and storage will have a negative effect on the color brilliance of these natural colors.

What are "lake" colorants?

Water-soluble FD&C colorants can be transformed to an insoluble powder (lake) by precipitation with aluminum, calcium, or magnesium salts on a substrate of aluminum

hydroxide. These colorants are more stable to heat and light and do not "bleed" or migrate. Lake colorants are used extensively in confectionery products, bakery products, salad dressings, and chocolate substitutes in which the presence of water is undesirable. They are also used in the packaging industry in which films and inks are in contact with food and in pharmaceutical tablets.

Source: Francis, F. J. (1985). Pigments and other colorants. In *Food Chemistry* edited by Owen Fennema, p. 580. New York: Marcel-Dekker, Inc.

Can people be allergic to artificial colors?

Yes, tartrazine, also known as FD&C Yellow #5, is one such color. Tartrazine is a synthetic lemon azo dye that is derived from coal tar. Tartrazine appears to cause the most allergic and intolerance reactions of the azo dyes, particularly among those with aspirin intolerance and asthmatics. Because of tartrazine intolerance, the FDA requires the presence of tartrazine to be declared on food and drug products. In drug products, the colorant is declared as tartrazine, but in food products, it is declared on the label as FD&C Yellow #5.

"that no additive shall be deemed to be safe if it is found to induce cancer when ingested by man or animal, or if it is found, after tests which are appropriate for the evaluation of the safety of food additives, to induce cancer in man or animals" [50].

The Delaney clause has created much discussion and disagreement in the years since the legislation was passed. Science, in relation to the study of cancer and carcinogenesis (cancer development), has changed, and the causes and nature of cancer have become better understood. Many people believe that an absolute prohibition of carcinogens under the Delaney clause is unnecessarily restrictive. No distinction is made between cancer in humans or experimental animals, nor is there a specification on the amount of the substance to be consumed in testing. If the maximum tolerated dose of the substance to the test animals causes an increase in cancer incidence over that in the control group, the substance cannot be used as a food additive, regardless of its level of potency [52]. Some scientists have suggested that the debate about the Delaney clause should be viewed as a statutory issue, having to do only with the fine points of the law, rather than a true food-safety issue, because the health benefits provided by a strict interpretation of the clause would appear to be trivial [50].

Actually, there is no way in which the absolute safety of a food additive, either a legally defined or GRAS substance, can be guaranteed. Clearance through the FDA should ensure that the risk of adverse effects is minimal. However, benefits from the use of additives must also be considered—improved shelf life for many foods and reduced distribution costs, increased aesthetic qualities and convenience, and improved nutritional value. It has been suggested that there are three interacting components of risk issues—science, politics, and social communication (to the public) of the chemical food risks. Each component is complex and subject to limitations, subjectivity, and a reliance on value judgments [51]. Society must continue to work on the problem of developing appropriate policies concerning food chemical risks.

Irradiation

Through the legislation on food additives, the regulatory responsibility for irradiated foods was given to the FDA, although the USDA also has some involvement in the process [27]. The inclusion of irradiation under the food additive regulations has not been without controversy because irradiating food does not add ingredients to it.

Food irradiation is a recognized method for reducing postharvest food losses and ensuring hygienic quality. Irradiation is not a substitution for sanitary practices but does provides an added measure of safety because *E. coli* and other pathogenic organisms may be destroyed. Approval has been granted for the production and marketing of several irradiated food products, including herbs and spices, wheat flour, white potatoes, fruits and vegetables, poultry, and red meat [29, 31, 32]. Irradiated

food must be labeled with the Radura symbol and "treated by irradiation" or "treated with radiation." See Chapter 3 for more information on irradiation and its role in food safety.

Pesticide Regulation

The Miller Pesticide Amendment of 1954 was passed to establish a procedure for setting safe levels or tolerances for pesticide residues on fresh fruits, vegetables, and other raw agricultural commodities. Growers were using many new pesticides to produce more and better crops, but some of these chemicals left a residue on the food even at harvest. The safety of these incidental residues had to be determined and regulations set.

The Food Quality Protection Act was signed into law in 1996. This act amended the Federal Food, Drug, and Cosmetic Act and the Federal Insecticide, Fungicide, and Rodenticide Act to (a) include a new pesticide safety standard, (b) resolve inconsistencies in the regulation of pesticide residues on raw and processed commodities, (c) provide special protection for children and infants, and (d) require periodic reevaluation of pesticides [5]. The safety standard for pesticides is currently defined as "a reasonable certainty that no harm will result from aggregate exposure to the pesticide chemical residue, including all anticipated dietary exposures and all other exposures for which there is reliable information." Tolerance limits for all pesticide residues, whether carcinogens or not, are set by the EPA at "safe" levels. The maximum allowable levels for pesticide residues are established after careful consideration of the risks and benefits for all consumers, with special attention to children. These tolerances are monitored and enforced by the FDA and the USDA [5]. See Chapter 3 for more information about pesticides and safety monitoring.

Prior to the 1996 Food Quality Protection Act, when a pesticide residue was found to concentrate higher levels in a processed food than in the original agricultural product before processing, the EPA was required to treat the residue as a food additive. For example, when grapes are dried and become raisins, any pesticide residue present on the fresh grapes may be concentrated. As food additives, these pesticide residues were subject to the Delaney clause in the Food Additives Amendment that was passed in 1958. Thus, under the law, pesticide residues on raw and processed commodities had to be treated differently, causing confusion. The 1996 legislation provides for a single, health-based standard for all pesticides in foods. Pesticide residues on processed foods no longer come under the legal definition of food additive and are not subject to the Delaney clause.

What Must Be on a Food Label?

The FDA shares with the Federal Trade Commission (FTC) the responsibility for enforcing fair packaging and labeling laws. The USDA also is involved for some foods.

If a food is packaged, the following must appear on the label:

1. Name and address of the manufacturer, packer, or distributor
2. Accurate statement of the net amount of food in the package—weight, measure, or count
3. Common or usual name of the product (i.e., peaches) and the form (i.e., sliced, whole, or chopped)
4. Ingredients listed by their common names in order of their predominance by weight
5. Nutrition information, with few exceptions, as mandated by the 1990 Nutrition Labeling and Education Act

Nutrition Labeling

The Nutrition Labeling and Education Act was signed into law in 1990. Compliance with the law was required by 1994. The USDA Food Safety and Inspection Service established similar regulations for meat and poultry products. Nutrition labeling was designed to help consumers choose diets that are well balanced, health promoting, and at the lowest cost. This legislation established the Nutrition Facts label, nutrient content descriptors, and allowed health claims.

Nutrition Facts Label. The Nutrition Facts label (Figure 4-2) presents nutrition information as a percent of daily values. Daily Values are dietary standards used for labeling purposes, and include two types: Daily Reference Values (DRVs) and Reference Daily Intakes (RDIs). Daily Reference Values (DRVs) refer to fat, carbohydrates (including fiber), protein, cholesterol, sodium, and potassium. These are listed on the label for 2,000 and 2,500 calorie intakes. Reference Daily Intakes (RDIs) are for other nutrients including vitamin A, vitamin C, calcium, and iron. Additional vitamins and minerals, if provided on the label, are optional. RDIs replace the U.S. Recommended Daily Allowances (RDAs) that were previously used. Selected RDIs are listed in Table 4-2.

Starting in 2006, trans fats also must be included on the Nutrition Facts label [47]. Consumption of trans fats are associated with an increased risk of heart disease. A revision of FDA and USDA portion-size guidelines on the Nutrition Facts label is also under consideration, and changes may occur [36]. The proposed changes are related to the standardized portion size as compared to the packaged portion that the consumer may actually consume in one sitting. For example, 8 ounces is considered to be a standard beverage serving size. If a product is purchased in a 16-ounce container, the customer is likely to consume 16 ounces; therefore, the portion size for the purpose of Nutrition Facts may be better understood if calculated and labeled for a 16-ounce serving size.

Nutrient Content Claims. Prior to the 1990 Nutrition Labeling and Education Act, a consumer did not know how "light" or "lowfat" a product was, even if labeled with these terms. These nutrient content claims are now standardized and thus when used on a food label, have specific, legal definitions. Some of these nutrient content claim terms and their definitions are given in Table 4-3.

Health Claims. Health claims describe a relationship between the food and reduced risk of a health-related condition [41]. The FDA regulates health claims based on scientific evidence. Currently approved health claims are provided in Table 4-4. The following relationships between a nutrient or food and the risk of a disease have been approved for labeling purposes with some specific requirements governing their use.

Two additional nutritional health claims may be found on food labels. Qualified health claims may be used, following FDA authorization, when there is emerging evidence for a relationship between the food and reduction of a health risk [41]. For example, in 2003 FDA approved a qualified health claim for almonds stating "scientific evidence suggests, but does not prove that eating 1.5 ounces per day of most nuts, as part of a diet low in saturated fat and cholesterol may reduce the risk of heart disease" [19]. Structure and function claims may also be found on labels and include statements such as "calcium builds strong bones" [41].

Nutritional Labeling Requirements. Most foods are required to carry nutrition labels. Exemptions include food sold by small businesses; food sold in foodservice establishments; ready-to-eat foods prepared on site for later consumption; foods that contain insignificant amounts of nutrients, such as tea and spices; medical foods; and meat and poultry products produced or packaged at retail, such as sliced bologna. Fresh fruits and vegetables, raw single-ingredient meats, poultry, and raw fish also do not require nutrition labeling. If, however, a nutrition or health claim is made for any of these foods, nutrition labeling is required. The FDA has a voluntary program in which nutrition information about these products is displayed at the point of purchase in retail food markets.

Restaurants and other foodservice establishments may make certain health and nutrition claims for items on their menus. When they do so, they must explain how the food meets the FDA criteria for that claim and must have a reasonable basis for believing that the food meets the criteria. This information must be provided to the customer [15].

Food Allergen Labeling

As a result of the Food Allergen Labeling and Consumer Protection Act of 2004, the "Big Eight" allergenic foods must be clearly labeled on the package [43]. The "Big Eight" causes of food allergy are wheat, crustacean shellfish, eggs, fish, peanuts, milk, tree nuts, and soybeans.

Serving sizes are stated in both household and metric measures.

Nutrition Facts

Serving Size ½ cup (114g)
Servings Per Container 4

Amount Per Serving

Calories 90	Calories from Fat 30

% Daily Value*

Total Fat 3g	5%
Saturated Fat 0g	0%
Cholesterol 0mg	0%
Sodium 300mg	13%
Total Carbohydrate 13g	4%
Dietary Fiber 3g	12%
Sugars 3g	
Protein 3g	

Vitamin A	80%	•	Vitamin C	60%
Calcium	4%	•	Iron	4%

* Percent Daily Values are based on a 2,000 calorie diet. Your daily values may be higher or lower depending on your calorie needs:

		Calories	2,000	2,500
Total Fat	Less than		65g	80g
Sat Fat	Less than		20g	25g
Cholesterol	Less than		300mg	300mg
Sodium	Less than		2,400mg	2,400mg
Total Carbohydrate			300g	375g
Fiber			25g	30g

Calories per gram:
Fat 9 • Carbohydrates 4 • Protein 4

Calories from fat are shown on the label to help consumers meet dietary guidelines that recommend people get no more than 30 percent of their calories from fat.

% Daily Value shows how a food fits into the overall daily diet.

The list of nutrients covers those most important to the health of today's consumers, most of whom need to worry about getting too much of certain items (fat, for example), rather than too few vitamins or minerals, as in the past.

Daily values are something new. Some are maximums, as with fat (65 grams or less); others are minimums, as with carbohydrates (300 grams or more). The daily values on the label are based on a daily diet of 2,000 and 2,500 calories. Individuals should adjust the values to fit their own calorie intake.

FIGURE 4-2 An example of the Nutrition Facts label that appears on almost all packaged foods as a result of the 1990 Nutrition Labeling and Education Act. *(Courtesy of the U.S. Food and Drug Administration)*

Previously some of these ingredients could be labeled as "natural flavorings" or with terms such as "casein." Casein is a milk protein, and those allergic to milk must often avoid products containing casein. Using this example, labels now need to specifically list "casein (milk)" under the ingredients or state "contains milk." See Chapter 3 for additional information about food allergies in relation to food safety.

A proposed rule to strengthen labeling of gluten-free foods has been issued by the FDA. Individuals who have

celiac disease must avoid gluten and therefore will benefit by improved labeling.

Food Biotechnology

The FDA has developed a food biotechnology policy for foods derived from genetically modified plants. This policy is science based and reflects the FDA's understanding that changes in food composition can be accomplished by a process called *recombinant DNA technology* or *gene splicing* [13]. In many cases, the changes in plants involve

TABLE 4-2 Reference Daily Intakes (RDIs)

Nutrient	RDI Value
Vitamin A	5,000 IU
Vitamin C	60 mg
Thiamin (B$_1$)	1.5 mg
Riboflavin (B$_2$)	1.7 mg
Niacin	20 mg
Calcium	1,000 mg
Iron	18 mg
Vitamin D	400 IU
Vitamin E	30 IU
Vitamin B$_6$	2.0 mg
Folic acid	0.4 mg
Vitamin B$_{12}$	6 mcg
Phosphorus	1,000 mg
Iodine	150 mcg
Magnesium	400 mg
Zinc	15 mg
Copper	2 mg
Biotin	0.3 mg
Pantothenic acid	10 mg

familiar substances—proteins, carbohydrates, and fats—that raise no new safety questions. If, however, substances are produced with no history of safe use in foods, the same careful testing and approval used for other food additives is used to ensure the safety [11].

The first substance produced by genetic engineering to be approved by the FDA was an enzyme, *chymosin* or *rennin*, used in cheesemaking. This approval was given in 1990. The first genetically engineered vegetable approved was a tomato that ripens on the vine without undue softening, thus increasing its natural flavor while allowing normal shipping procedures. New rules for bioengineered foods are under discussion that include a premarket notification system [4] and appropriate labeling of both products that have or do not have genetically engineered components [9]. Biotechnology was discussed in Chapter 3.

FDA Food Code

In yet another food oversight role, the FDA publishes an updated Food Code every four years. The FDA Food Code provides food safety guidelines for all retail foodservice operations [44]. Because local restaurants and foodservice establishments are inspected and regulated by state and local government, local food codes may be

TABLE 4-3 Nutrient Content Descriptors Used on Food Labels*

Descriptor	Definition
Free	No amount or an amount that is of no physiological consequence based on serving size
Calorie-free	Less than 5 calories
Sodium-free	Less than 5 milligrams
Fat-free	Less than 0.5 gram of fat and no added fat
Cholesterol-free	Less than 2 milligrams
Sugar-free	Less than 0.5 gram
Low	Would allow frequent consumption of a food low in a nutrient without exceeding the dietary guidelines
Low-calorie	Less than 40 calories
Low-sodium	Less than 140 milligrams
Very low-sodium	Less than 35 milligrams
Lowfat	Less than 3 grams
Low in saturated fat	Less than 1 gram and less than 15 percent of calories from saturated fat
Low in cholesterol	20 milligrams or less, with less than 2 grams of saturated fat
Reduced	Nutritionally altered product containing 25 percent less of a nutrient or 25 percent fewer calories than a reference food
Less	Contains 25 percent less of a nutrient or 25 percent fewer calories than a reference food
Light	33 percent fewer calories or 50 percent of the fat in a reference food; if 50 percent or more of the calories comes from fat, reduction must be 50 percent of the fat; or sodium content of a low-calorie, lowfat food has been reduced by 50 percent: thus the term "light in sodium" may be used; or describes such properties as texture and color, as "light brown sugar" or "light and fluffy"
High	20 percent or more of the Daily Reference Value for a nutrient
Good source	Contains 10 to 19 percent of the Daily Reference Value for a particular nutrient

Source: Reference 14

* Per serving basis

TABLE 4-4 Health Claims Allowed for Conventional Foods

Barley and risk of coronary heart disease

Calcium and osteoporosis

Dietary fat and cancer

Dietary saturated fat and cholesterol and risk of coronary heart disease

Dietary noncarogenic carbohydrate sweeteners (sugar alcohols) and dental caries

Fiber containing grain products, fruits, and vegetables and cancer

Folic acid and neural tube defects

Fruits and vegetables and reduced risk of cancer

Fruits, vegetables, and grain products that contain fiber, particularly soluble fiber, and risk of coronary heart disease

Sodium and hypertension

Soluble fiber from certain foods (e.g., whole oats) and coronary heart disease

Soy protein and risk of coronary heart disease

Stanols/sterols and risk of coronary heart disease

Source: References 2, 45, 46

different from the FDA Food Code. Nevertheless, the FDA Food Code provides guidance to state and local governments when developing and updating their food safety regulations.

DEPARTMENT OF AGRICULTURE

The USDA is involved with food processing and marketing in several different ways. Under the auspices of the Food Safety and Inspection Service, the USDA inspects meat and poultry products for wholesomeness and truthful labeling, administering the Federal Meat Inspection Act and the Poultry Products Inspection Act (see Figure 4-3). The USDA Agricultural Marketing Service is responsible for administering the Egg Products Inspection Act, which requires inspection of all plants that process liquid, dried, or frozen egg products. It also offers grading services for meat, poultry, fruits, vegetables, eggs, and dairy products. Selected regulations and laws administered by the USDA are provided in Table 4-5.

How Can You Have Input into Government Regulations?

By law, anyone may participate in the rule-making process by commenting in writing on the FDA proposals [7] and sending these comments directly to the FDA. When the FDA, USDA, or other government agencies plan to issue a new regulation or revise an existing one, an announcement is placed in the *Federal Register*, which also provides background on the issue and gives the address for submitting written comments by a specified deadline. The *Federal Register* is available in many public libraries, colleges, and on the Internet.

Contacting your state representative or senator offers another opportunity for involvement in our government. In fact, public input was a significant factor in the passage of the 1906 Pure Food and Drug Act, 1906 Federal Meat Inspection Act, 1938 Federal Food, Drug, and Cosmetic Act, as well as the 2004 Food Allergen Labeling and Consumer Protection Act.

Here are some ways to keep in touch with our government. ■

Internet Web Address	Information Available
http://www.usa.gov/	Gateway to the U.S. government. Links are provided to help you get the information you need.
http://www.usa.gov/Contact/Elected.shtml	Contact your elected officials. This page provides links for the president, U.S. senators, U.S representatives, state governors, and state legislators.
http://www.gpoaccess.gov/fr/index.html	Main page for the *Federal Register,* the official daily publication for rules, proposed rules, notices of federal agencies, executive orders, and other presidential documents.
http://thomas.loc.gov	Legislative information from the Library of Congress is provided. You may search for a bill by text, bill number, or by the senator or representative sponsoring the bill.
http://www.regulations.gov	U.S. government regulations for all federal agencies may be found. Comments on regulations may be submitted on this website.

(a)

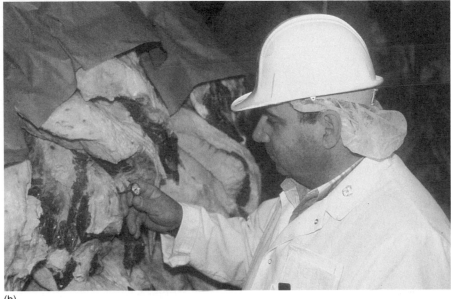

(b)

FIGURE 4-3 (a) U.S. Department of Agriculture meat inspectors, under regulation of the Federal Meat Inspection Act, examine cattle before slaughter and beef carcasses (b) for wholesomeness and freedom from disease. *(Courtesy of U.S. Department of Agriculture)*

TABLE 4-5 U.S. Department of Agriculture: Food Regulations to Protect the Health and Safety of the Public

Laws, Statues, and Regulations	Basic provisions
1906 Federal Meat Inspection Act	Mandates inspection of live animals, carcasses, and processed products. Also requires improved sanitary conditions for slaughter and processing.
1957 Poultry Products Inspection Act	Requires inspection of poultry products.
1967–1968 Wholesome Meat and Wholesome Poultry Products Acts	Meat Inspection and Poultry Product Inspection Acts were amended. The USDA gained authority to control unfit meat and meat products. Poultry products involved in interstate and foreign commerce must meet federal inspection standards.
1970 The Egg Products Inspection Act	Mandatory continuous inspection of liquid, frozen, and dried egg product processing.
1993 Nutrition Labeling of Meat and Poultry Products	Voluntary nutrition labeling guidelines established for single-ingredient raw meat and poultry products
	Mandatory nutrition labeling for all other meat and poultry products.
1994 Testing for *E. coli* O157:H7	*E. coli* O157:H7 declared to be an adulterant. Testing program for ground beef started.
1996–2000 Hazard Analysis and Critical Control Point (HACCP) Systems	Meat and poultry plants must develop and use HACCP plans to ensure safety of their products.
1999 Testing for *Listeria monocytogenes*	Testing for this pathogen implemented at plants processing high- and medium-risk ready-to-eat products (deli meats and other products).

History

Legislation creating the USDA was signed by President Abraham Lincoln in 1862 [34]. In the early years, the primary focus of the department was to promote food production by providing information for farmers. With the growth of the meatpacking industry after the Civil War, the Bureau of Animal Industry, a forerunner to the USDA Food Safety and Inspection Service, was created to prevent diseased animals from being used as food. Upton Sinclair's book *The Jungle*, which described filthy conditions in the Chicago meatpacking industry, led to the passage of the 1906 Federal Meat Inspection Act. Under this act, continuous government inspection of meatpacking plants was started and continues today. Over the years, new legislation has been passed to strengthen the role of the USDA.

Inspection

The USDA administers a mandatory continuous inspection program for meat and poultry that is sold in interstate commerce and in those states that do not have an inspection program of their own that is equal to the federal program. This inspection is for wholesomeness (safety) and proper labeling. The meat and poultry must be (a) from healthy animals or birds, (b) processed under strict sanitary conditions using good manufacturing practices and an HACCP system, (c) tested for the presence of some microorganisms, and (d) truthfully labeled. Meat and poultry slaughter and processing plants must test for generic *E. coli* to verify that the process is under control with respect to preventing and removing fecal contamination. The Food Safety and Inspection Service tests for salmonella on raw meat and poultry products to verify that pathogen reduction standards are being met for this organism. Prior to the USDA modernization of the inspection service with the implementation of HACCP, the USDA meat inspection was done by using sight, touch, and smell [3, 34].

USDA Grades

USDA inspectors may grade a food product using standardized quality criteria. Official USDA grading services are generally voluntarily requested but are sometimes required on a local level or for a particular industry program. They are performed by USDA inspectors but paid for by the manufacturer requesting the service. Grading may be done for meat, poultry, eggs, dairy products, some fish, nuts, rice, and fresh fruits and vegetables. Foods are inspected for grade determination, or "inspected for grade." However, the term *inspection* has different meanings when applied to various commodities. All meat and poultry must be inspected for wholesomeness before it can be graded for quality. The inspection determines wholesomeness; the grading determines quality.

Grade standards were originally established to aid in wholesale food trading, but many consumer grades have become useful. These consumer grades apply to small units of food that are usually sold in a retail market. The quality of the food at the time it was graded is indicated by the grade on the package, but no allowance is made for changes in quality that may occur during the handling and storage involved in the marketing process. Some products are more variable in quality than other products and therefore may require more grades. For example, there are eight grades for beef but only three for chicken. Most federal grades for consumers are preceded by the abbreviation *U.S.* and are enclosed in a shield-shaped mark (Figure 4-4). Even though a product may have been officially graded, the law still does not require that a designation of grade appear on the label. If the grade shield is used on a food product, however, the food must have been officially graded.

Because the grade standards for various products were developed at different times, the naming systems vary. For instance, the top-quality grade for cantaloupes is U.S. Fancy; for beets, it is U.S. No. 1; for carrots, it is U.S. Grade A; and for celery, it is U.S. Extra No. 1. U.S. Grades A, B, and C are used on poultry and on canned fruits and vegetables. To help achieve a more uniform grading system, the USDA has issued a policy statement that when future standards for fresh fruits, vegetables, and nuts are issued, revised, or amended, only the classifications U.S. Fancy and Grades 1, 2, and 3 may be used.

Food grading aids foodservice managers as they write specifications for the purchasing of various food products. The required quality of the product being ordered can be easily specified by grade, because the grade standards are known to both purchasers and vendors. Food grading is also an aid available to retail shoppers to help them meet their needs and desires more effectively. However, many consumers are not knowledgeable about specific details of the grading systems and may need more education to clarify differences between inspection and grading.

FIGURE 4-4 Shield-shaped marks used by the U.S. Department of Agriculture in grading food products. *(Courtesy of the U.S. Department of Agriculture)*

Organic Foods

The Organic Foods Production Act was passed by Congress in 1990 [33]. This act required that the USDA develop national standards for organically produced agricultural products to provide consumers with products

FIGURE 4-5 Government-certified organic symbol that can be placed on foods only after they meet government guidelines. *(Courtesy of U.S. Department of Agriculture)*

consistently and uniformly identified as "organic." Regulations developed through the Organic Foods Production Act and the National Organic Program established an organic certification program and labeling standards. These regulations prohibit the use of conventional pesticides, petroleum-based fertilizers, sewage sludge-based fertilizers, genetic engineering, and ionizing radiation. Animals to be marketed as organic must be fed organic feed, given access to the outdoors, and must not be given antibiotics or growth hormones [33].

Starting in 2002, the USDA labeling rules for organic foods were implemented. Certified foods labeled as "100 percent organic," or "95 percent organic" may include the USDA Organic seal (Figure 4-5). Foods containing 70 to 95 percent organic ingredients may be labeled "made with organic ingredients." Products with less than 70 percent organic ingredients may not include organic claims on the front of the package, but may list specific organically produced ingredients on the side panel (Figure 4-6). Products may still be labeled as free-range, hormone free, and natural. However, "natural" and "organic" are not interchangeable terms; only "organic" foods have been certified by USDA [17, 28, 30]. These labeling standards will help consumers to decide whether they want to pay a premium price for these products. With annual sales of over $5 million, the organic food industry has become an important component of the U.S. food system [17].

Other Areas of USDA Influence

Like the FDA, the USDA has an impact on the regulation of irradiation, biotechnology, additives, and labeling of foods. Specifically, the USDA oversees these

FIGURE 4-6 These sample cereal boxes show the four organic labeling categories. From left: 100 percent organic ingredients, 95–100 percent organic ingredients, at least 70 percent organic ingredients, less than 70 percent organic ingredients. *(Courtesy of U.S. Department of Agriculture)*

HOT TOPICS

A Single Food Safety Agency—Is This the Answer?

At the beginning of 2002, there were at least 12 different federal agencies and 35 different federal laws governing food safety [12, 16]. Although a number of these organizations—including the Bureau of Alcohol, Tobacco, and Firearms—are only peripherally involved in assuring food safety, several agencies play key roles that call for close coordination and collaboration with others. The FDA and the USDA are primary among these. The need for close working relationships among agencies became even more apparent when terrorism struck the United States on September 11, 2001. What is the answer to this problem?

A single agency that would consolidate all federal food safety responsibilities into a single, independent agency has been proposed. Others, however, believe such a reorganization of food safety responsibility would cause more problems than it solved [21]. Most agreed on two principles—first, that the United States now has the safest food supply in the world; second, that there are problems to be fixed in order to maintain that position.

Since early 2002 when the discussion about a single food agency was a key topic of discussion, the respective agencies have developed new areas of collaboration and have continued existing partnerships such as **FoodNet**, **PulseNet**, and **FORC-G**. Time will tell if there will be a major change in the regulation of food in the years ahead. ∎

---

related concerns with regard to foods regulated by the USDA, including meat, poultry, egg products, and foods containing meat or poultry. The USDA has approved the irradiation of meat and poultry to increase food safety. In the area of biotechnology, the USDA specifically oversees biotechnology applications with impact on foods regulated by the USDA and ensures plants developed through genetic engineering do not have an adverse impact on the agricultural environment. Specific labeling regulations of the USDA include the safe food handling labels found on eggs and meat packages as well as the organic labeling program previously discussed. These additional roles of the USDA will be addressed in greater depth in chapters focusing on USDA-regulated foods.

ENVIRONMENTAL PROTECTION AGENCY

The Environmental Protection Agency (EPA) protects the public health through the oversight of environmental risks from pesticides. It administers the 1947 Federal Insecticide, Fungicide, and Rodenticide Act that was amended by the 1996 Food Quality Protection Act. The EPA establishes maximum legally permissible levels for pesticide residues in food. Genetically engineered foods also may fall under EPA oversight if the alteration includes a component that functions as a natural pesticide.

CENTERS FOR DISEASE CONTROL AND PREVENTION

The Centers for Disease Control and Prevention (CDC) promote health by preventing and controlling disease. The CDC collaborates with the FDA and USDA in the Foodborne Disease Active Surveillance Network (FoodNet) system to measure the incidence and sources of bacterial foodborne diseases. The CDC manages the PulseNet system that is another collaborative effort with the FDA and USDA. PulseNet helps to control foodborne outbreaks through a national laboratory and computer database. Through this database, distinctive DNA "fingerprint" patterns for microorganisms may be identified, thereby permitting the tracing of foodborne illnesses that may be linked by one common food. Early identification of the source of foodborne illness helps the FDA and USDA to prevent further illnesses from the same food.

FEDERAL TRADE COMMISSION

The Federal Trade Commission (FTC) is an independent law enforcement agency charged with promoting free and fair competition in the marketplace. One major activity of the FTC is ensuring that fair and honest competition is allowed in the marketing of food products. The FTC attempts to protect the consumer from false or misleading advertising and misbranding, and shares with the FDA responsibility for enforcing labeling laws.

OTHER FEDERAL AGENCIES

The U.S. Department of Commerce National Oceanic and Atmospheric Administration (NOAA) oversees the management of fisheries in the United States. The Seafood Inspection Program of NOAA operates under the 1946 Agricultural Marketing Act. The voluntary inspection service provides product grading, establishment sanitation inspection, product lot inspection, process and product inspection, laboratory analysis, training, and consultation. The FDA, however, oversees the mandatory HACCP regulations and inspections for seafood processors through the FDA Seafood Regulatory Program [40]. The NOAA Seafood Inspection Program provides additional services for processors which include product grading.

The Bureau of Alcohol, Tobacco, and Firearms in the Department of the Treasury regulates most alcoholic beverages. The qualifications and operations of distilleries, wineries, and breweries are controlled. New products coming into the market are tested to ensure that alcoholic ingredients are within legal limits. Labels are examined to see that legal requirements have been met.

STATE AND LOCAL AGENCIES

The legislation and regulations previously discussed in this chapter are federal and apply only in interstate commerce. Within each state and within cities are many laws and regulations dealing with food processing, quality, and marketing. Each state has its own unique problems and attempts to solve them in individual ways, but federal laws and regulations are often used as models. States are usually organized with their own departments of agriculture and health and their own food and drug commissions. Assurance of sanitation, milk quality, inspection of meat and poultry, and protection of vegetable crops are some of the activities conducted by state organizations.

State and local governments provide for the inspection of foodservice establishments to protect the public who eat in restaurants, cafeterias, and other places where foodservice is offered. This service is usually the responsibility of state, county, and city health departments, which assess cleanliness and sanitary practices. In many cases, those working with food served to the public are required to obtain food-handling permits, sometimes involving both a physical examination and educational certification.

INTERNATIONAL STANDARDS

In our rapidly shrinking world, international trade in food is accelerating. The U.S. food industry plays a major role in international food marketing, and the world demand for processed foods continues to rise. In addition, an ever-growing number of food products made outside the United States are appearing on our supermarket shelves, probably because consumers' attitudes toward eating are changing. Most consumers today are more open and eager to try new foods and new **cuisines**. They are buying more specialty products and becoming familiar with imported items.

Increased international trade in foods has created an even greater need for international standards to safeguard the consumer's health and ensure fair food-trade practices. The Codex Alimentarius Commission was established in 1963 by a joint effort of the United Nations Food and Agriculture Organization (FAO) and the World Health Organization (WHO) to meet this need. Any nation that is a member of the FAO or the WHO may become a member of the commission. The international standards are quite comprehensive and include a description of the product; composition requirements; additives that may be allowed, if any; sanitary handling practices; fill of container, weight, and measure or count of units; labeling provisions; and methods of analysis and sampling necessary to determine that the standard is being met [49].

After the commission develops a recommended international standard, it is sent to the member nations for consideration of adoption. Individual members may adopt the standard for themselves. The World Trade Organization (WTO) accepts Codex food standards, guidelines, and recommendations as representing international consensus in this area [20].

CHAPTER SUMMARY

- The government, through legislation and regulation, plays a role in ensuring quality and safety in the foods we purchase. The FDA and USDA together are the primary agencies that oversee the food we consume.

- The FDA is part of the U.S. Department of Health and Human Services. All food except red meat, poultry, and eggs is regulated by the FDA.

- Under the Federal Food, Drug, and Cosmetic Act, the FDA sets three kinds of mandatory standards for products being shipped across state lines: identity, minimum quality, and fill of container.

- The FDA shares with the FTC the responsibility for enforcing fair packaging and labeling laws. The USDA is also involved for some foods. Several requirements are specified for food labels pertaining to the product name, ingredients, nutrition labeling, and amount in package.

- The 1990 Nutrition Labeling and Education Act provided regulations for the Nutrition Facts label, nutrient content claims, and health claims. The Food Allergen Labeling and Consumer Protection Act of 2004 mandates clear labeling of the eight foods most likely to cause food allergy.

- A food additive is any substance that becomes part of a food product either when it is added intentionally or incidentally. Food additives, as legally defined, must be thoroughly tested and receive approval for use in food. The "generally recognized as safe" (GRAS) list includes substances that do not require detailed clearance before use in foods; however, ongoing reassessment of these substances is done by the FDA and food industry.

- The 1958 Food Additives Amendment and 1960 Color Additives Amendment strengthened the regulation of additives. The Delaney Clause in the Food Additives Amendment specifies no additives found to cause cancer in humans or animals, when present in any amount, can be approved for use in foods. This clause has been debated over the years as the science, in relation to the study of carcinogenesis and cancer risk, has changed.

- The Miller Pesticide Amendment of 1954 and the Food Quality Protection Act of 1996 include standards for the use of pesticides in food and food products. The FDA monitors and enforces the EPA-established pesticide tolerance levels.

- The FDA has developed policies for foods derived from genetically modified plants. Both the FDA and USDA have regulatory responsibility for irradiated foods.

- The U.S. Department of Agriculture (USDA) is involved with food processing and marketing in several different ways. The USDA inspects meat, poultry products, and egg products for wholesomeness and truthful labeling.

- The USDA provides grading services for a variety of foods. The grade standards inform the consumer of the product quality.

- Regulations developed through the Organic Foods Production Act and the National Organic Program established an organic certification program and labeling standards.

- Additional agencies with involvement in the quality, wholesomeness, or marketing of our food supply include the Environmental Protection Agency; Centers for Disease Control and Prevention; Federal Trade Commission; Department of Commerce National Oceanic and Atmospheric Administration; Bureau of Alcohol, Tobacco, and Firearms; and state and local agencies. The Codex Alimentarius Commission works to develop international standards.

STUDY QUESTIONS

1. Which agencies of the federal government are particularly involved in setting standards and regulations for food? How is each involved?

2. What are the distinguishing characteristics of each of the following standards?
   (a) Standards of identity
   (b) Standards of fill of container
   (c) Standards of minimum quality
   (d) U.S. grade standards

3. What sanitary requirements for food processors are included in the Federal Food, Drug, and Cosmetic Act? Why does the FDA outline current good manufacturing practices (GMPs) for food processors?

4. Respond to the following:
   (a) Define *food additives* in a general sense.
   (b) What is the legal definition of *food additives?*
   (c) What are GRAS substances?
   (d) Give examples of intentional and incidental food additives.

5. Describe four justifiable uses for food additives.

6. Discuss implications for foods resulting from each of the following federal laws or amendments:
   (a) 1906 Pure Food and Drug Act
   (b) 1938 Federal Food, Drug, and Cosmetic Act
   (c) 1954 Miller Pesticide Amendment
   (d) 1958 Food Additives Amendment
   (e) 1960 Color Additives Amendment
   (f) 1996 Food Quality Protection Act

7. What is the Delaney clause, and why is it important to both the food processor and the consumer?

8. How can a consumer know that a food additive is safe? Discuss this.

9. List the four pieces of information that are required to be listed on food package labels.

10. What are daily values? Discuss how daily values help consumers to understand how a food may fit into their daily diet.

11. What are nutrient content claims, health claims, qualified health claims, and structure and function claims that may be found on food labels? How are each of these regulated?

12. What are organic foods? How can consumers know that they are truly getting organic food after they pay for it?

13. How is grading of food products useful to the wholesaler, the retailer, and the consumer? Discuss this.

14. Describe differences between inspection and grading of meat and poultry as applied to USDA regulations.

15. What is the Codex Alimentarius Commission, and what functions does it perform?

BACK TO BASICS 5

Correct proportions of ingredients are vital to success in the preparation of many food products. These proportions are best achieved when the measuring or weighing of each individual ingredient in a recipe is done accurately and consistently. Likewise, the use of standardized recipes and the proper use of selected tools and equipment will enable the preparation of many delicious and attractive foods. The development of good knife skills is important to protect your safety while at the same time allowing the efficient use of your time.

In this chapter, the following topics will be discussed:

- Small equipment and tools, including knives
- Weights, volume measures, and measurement techniques used in food preparation
- Metric as compared to U.S. customary measures and weights
- Recipes and recipe standardization

SMALL EQUIPMENT AND TOOLS

Knives are one of the most important tools used in the preparation of food. Understanding the best knife for each task and the development of good knife skills will enable you to prepare high quality foods, efficiently and safely. In addition to the measuring cups and scales to be discussed later in the chapter, whisks, spatulas, scoops, ladles, and multiple other tools each have an important purpose in food preparation.

Knives

A knife should be balanced and made from high quality materials for both the blade and the handle. The parts of the knife are shown in Figure 5-1. A full tang and bolster result in a well-balanced, durable knife. Handles may be made from wood or molded polypropylene. However, regardless of the material, the handle should be comfortable to hold and easily cleanable.

Knife Blades. Knife blades are generally made from carbon steel, stainless steel, or high carbon stainless steel. Carbon steel is an alloy of carbon and iron that sharpens easily. However, carbon steel blades also corrode and discolor easily. Stainless steel blades do not corrode or discolor, but these blades are difficult to sharpen. High carbon stainless steel blades share advantages of carbon steel and stainless steel by sharpening easily and not corroding [4].

Sharpening. A sharp knife is easier to use and reduces fatigue and, more importantly, the risk of injury. Sharp knives cut through food products more easily, thereby reducing the risk of dangerous slips. Knives should be sharpened regularly as the edge becomes dull. A sharpening stone or whetstone is used to place an edge on a dull blade (Figure 5-2). To use a stone, the blade is pressed evenly against the stone at a 20-degree angle as if slicing the stone. This step is repeated on both sides of the blade until sharp. Generally, the stone is lubricated with water or mineral oil. Vegetable oil is not recommended because it will become gummy. The final step in sharpening is to hone the blade with a steel. A steel is a long, thin, cylindrical metal tool that hones and straightens the blade immediately after sharpening and between occasions of sharpening (Figure 5-2). As with the sharpening process, a 20-degree angle is maintained.

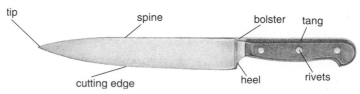

FIGURE 5-1 The parts of a chef's or French knife.

FOCUS ON SCIENCE

Carbon Steel, Stainless Steel, and High Carbon Stainless Steel—What Is the Difference?

Carbon Steel

Carbon steel is an alloy of iron that is approximately 1 percent carbon. It is easier to sharpen than stainless steel, holds its edge longer, but is vulnerable to rusts and stains.

Stainless Steel

Stainless steel is an alloy of iron, approximately 10 to 15 percent chromium, possibly nickel, and molybdenum with only a small amount of carbon. Lower grades of stainless steel are not able to take as sharp an edge as carbon steel, but they are resistant to corrosion, do not taint food, and are inexpensive. Expensive knives are the "exotic" stainless steel (mostly from Japan), are extremely sharp with excellent edge retention, and equal or outperform carbon steel blades.

High Carbon Stainless Steel

High carbon stainless steel contains a certain amount of carbon arbitrarily deemed "high." It is intended to combine the best attributes of carbon steel and ordinary stainless steel. High carbon stainless steel blades maintain a sharp edge and do not discolor.

(a) Three-Sided Sharpening or Whetstone

(b) Steel

FIGURE 5-2 (a) A whetstone is used to sharpen knives. (b) A steel is used to straighten the knife blade between sharpenings.

FIGURE 5-3 The most common grip: Hold the handle with three fingers while gripping the blade between the thumb and index finger.

There are other methods of sharpening knives including sharpeners available through local kitchen supply stores that may be used by simply drawing the knife blade through the sharpener. Other types of sharpeners are electric, but if not used with care, these may result in excessive wear to the blade. With practice the use of a stone and steel will provide the highest quality edge and maintain the life of the blade.

Using Knives. A variety of knives is available, each with a specific purpose. In foodservices, a number of different knives are used because using the proper knife for a given task is safer and more efficient. The same is true in the home. In addition to using the proper knife for the task, a cutting board is a must to protect you, the work surface, and the knife. Cutting on surfaces other than cutting boards will dull the knife and holding foods in the hands will increase the risk of cuts. When using a cutting board, secure it to the counter top by placing a damp dish towel between the counter and the board. The damp towel will prevent the cutting board from sliding on the counter surface.

A chef's or French knife is used for chopping, slicing, and mincing vegetables, such as onions, or meats, such as diced ham or turkey. This knife should be held with the thumb and index finger gripping the blade. The other three fingers hold the handle (Figure 5-3). This method of gripping the knife provides added stability and control. Although in foodservices, 10- to 14-inch blades are common, a 6- to 8-inch knife may be best in home use. Also, those with a small hand may find a smaller chef's knife easier to handle.

When cutting foods, the product should be held with all the fingers, including the thumb, curled back. The blade of the chef's knife is guided by the flat surface of the fingers between the first and second knuckles (Figure 5-4). With the fingertips tucked back, cuts are much less likely than when the food is held with the fingertips pointed outward. Initially, gripping the chef's knife and food as described may feel awkward. However, with

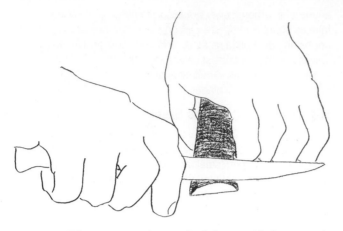

FIGURE 5-4 The proper cutting method shown with fingers and thumb curled back with blade of the chef's knife guided against the knuckles.

added practice these positions will become natural and will permit the rapid and safe dicing, mincing, and chopping of foods.

Several other kinds of knives are used for specific tasks (Figure 5-5). The utility knife is an all-purpose knife that may be used for cutting fruits and vegetables or carving poultry. A paring knife is usually two to four inches in length and is used for very detailed work. Although used by some for many tasks in the kitchen, it is not the best choice for most products that are to be sliced, chopped, or diced. The French knife is more efficient for these types of jobs. A slicer is used for carving cooked meat, whereas a serrated knife is typically used for slicing bread or pastry products. The butcher's knife is usually used to cut raw meats [4].

Hand Tools

Many hand tools are used in the kitchen to stir, whip, flip, peel, or grasp foods. Spoons may be solid, perforated, or slotted. Perforated spoons have round holes to drain away liquid from small foods such as peas, whereas slotted spoons have large slots to drain liquid from larger, more coarse foods. Whisks can be used to whip eggs, egg whites, or heavy cream by hand. Although whisks may be used to mix some bakery products, they may not be the best choice for delicate products that need to be mixed lightly. A number of common hand tools are shown in Figure 5-6.

Portioning and Measuring Tools

Scales and measuring cups will be discussed later; however, there are other tools that may be used to measure or portion foods. Ladles come in ounce sizes and may be used to measure liquids in the kitchen or for portioning food when served (Figure 5-7). Portion scoops or dishers are sized by a number that corresponds to the number of level scoops per quart [4]. For example, a number 12 scoop is equivalent to 1/3 cup because there are 12

portions of 1/3 cup per quart. Scoops not only measure the amount of food but also are the most efficient way to portion cookies onto a cookie tray or muffins into muffin tins for baking.

Thermometers are an essential item to have in the kitchen. Thermometers are used to measure the endpoint cooking temperatures and to monitor proper refrigeration and freezer temperatures, thereby promoting food safety (see Chapter 3). Food preparation can be better controlled by measuring the temperature of the oven, of oils when deep fat frying, and of the point at which a candy mixture should be removed from the heat (see Chapter 11).

Other Small Equipment

For draining liquid from large quantities of food, a colander, strainer, china cap, or chinois all have specific intended purposes (Figure 5-8). For example, both a colander and a china cap usually are constructed of metal bodies, whereas chinois and strainers are composed of fine mesh screens. The piece of equipment chosen will depend on the type of product being prepared.

Foods may be mixed using different hand tools depending on whether the product is to be stirred, folded, or whipped. Likewise, mixers have different attachments such as flat paddles, whips, or dough hooks. Each performs the mixing function in a specified way (Figure 5-9). The science behind food preparation provides an understanding of why a flat paddle is more appropriate for muffins than a whip, even though a whip is necessary for making angel food cake. Food processors, food choppers, and food blenders are additional pieces of small equipment that can make food preparation quicker and easier.

As you develop skill in food preparation and an understanding of food science, knowing the most appropriate knife, tool, or piece of equipment will come naturally. There are many more pieces of equipment available for use in the home and commercially that have not been discussed in this chapter. You are encouraged to learn how to use equipment to the best advantage to prepare high quality food. In some cases, you may find that some functions are best done by hand, even though using a mixer or processor would complete the task quicker. Safe and efficient work in a kitchen includes knowing how to use small tools and equipment.

WEIGHTS AND MEASURES

In the United States, recipes generally call for volume measurements, particularly in home cooking. Tablespoons, cups, pints, and gallons are the units commonly used. In some foodservice operations and in other countries, however, ingredients may be more commonly weighed than measured. Weighing is generally more accurate than measuring. Consequently, weights are often used in quantity cookery, especially in baking, because the need for accuracy is especially critical in

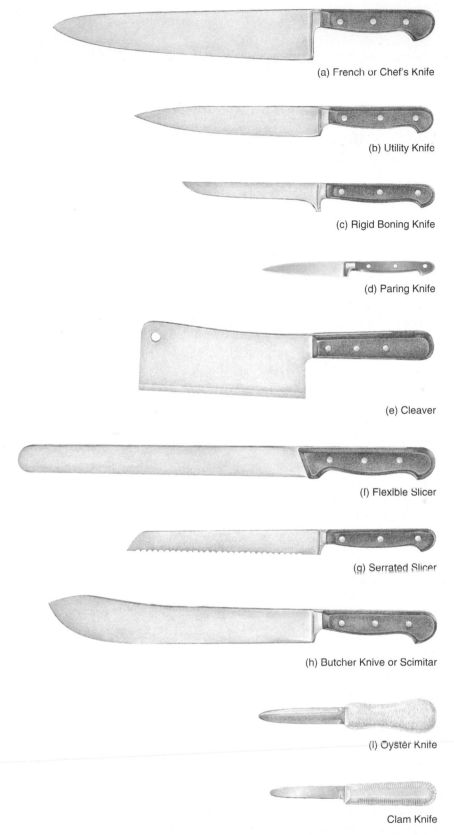

(a) French or Chef's Knife

(b) Utility Knife

(c) Rigid Boning Knife

(d) Paring Knife

(e) Cleaver

(f) Flexible Slicer

(g) Serrated Slicer

(h) Butcher Knive or Scimitar

(I) Oyster Knife

Clam Knife

FIGURE 5-5 Knife varieties: (a) French or chef's knife, an all-purpose knife for chopping, slicing, and mincing. (b) Utility knife used for cutting fruits, vegetables, and poultry. (c) Rigid boning knife is useful for separating meat from bone. (d) Paring knife is short for detailed work such as fruit or vegetable work. (e) Cleavers are used for chopping through bones. (f) Slicer is primarily used for cutting cooked meats. (g) Serrated slicer is used for cutting bread or pastry. (h) Butcher's knife is used to prepare raw meats. (i) Oyster and clam knives effectively open oyster and clam shells.

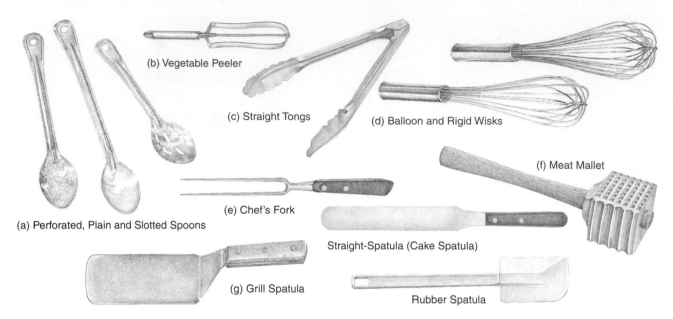

FIGURE 5-6 Variety of hand tools: (a) Perforated, plain, and slotted spoons. (b) Vegetable peeler. (c) Tongs. (d) Balloon and rigid whisks. (e) Chef's fork. (f) Meat mallet. (g) Grill, rubber, and straight or cake spatulas.

FIGURE 5-7 (a) Two ladle sizes used for portioning liquids. (b) Portion scoops are used for dishing cookie dough onto cookie sheets or ice cream into a dish.

baked goods. Some ingredients, such as flour, may pack down in the container [6], thereby resulting in inconsistent, and thus inaccurate, measurements. Weight and volume relationships also vary with certain chopped foods, such as onions, depending on the fineness and uniformity of chopping before measuring. Because of these differences in density, the use of standardized measuring techniques and equipment is particularly important.

When preparing food, a recipe may be increased or decreased in size, or ingredients may be provided in weights instead of measures. As a result, knowing measurement equivalents is beneficial. Some of the most frequently used U.S. customary measures are provided in Table 5-1. Additional measures, weights, and metric equivalencies may be found in Appendix A. It is important to realize that dry ingredients do not have the same **density** as liquids. For example, in U.S. standard weights, one cup of white flour equals only four ounces, whereas one cup of leaf tarragon is only one ounce [7]. Thus, if the recipe calls for weights, these units cannot be changed into measures, or vice versa, unless the appropriate conversion factor is known. Conversions are provided in books such as *Food for Fifty* [7].

Measuring Equipment

Liquid and Dry Measurements. Gallon measures (4-quart or 16-cup capacity), 1/2 gallon or 2 quart measures, and quart measures are commonly used in quantity food preparation. The liquid glass measuring cup of 1/2 pint or 8 fluid ounce capacity is usually used in home food preparation. For more accurate measurement of dry or solid ingredients, dry-measuring containers must be filled and leveled at the top. Fractional cups and one- and two-cup measures are available in addition to measuring spoons (Figure 5-10).

Accuracy of Measuring Equipment. The American Association of Family and Consumer Sciences (previously called American Home Economics Association) and the American National Standards Institute (previously called American Standards Association) published a set of standards and tolerances for household measuring

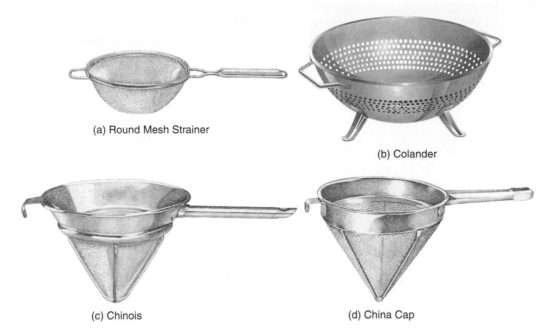

(a) Round Mesh Strainer

(b) Colander

(c) Chinois

(d) China Cap

FIGURE 5-8 (a) Round mesh strainer. (b) Colander. (c) Chinois. (d) China cap.

Flat Paddle

Whip

Dough Hook

20-Quart Mixer and Attachments

FIGURE 5-9 Mixer and three attachments: the flat paddle, the whip, and the dough hook.

utensils in 1963 [2]. These standards allow for a deviation of 5 percent from the precise measure indicated on the measuring utensil. Not all measuring utensils on the market meet the tolerance of 5 percent, however. The teaspoons and tablespoons that are part of flatware

or silverware sets should not be trusted as accurate measurements.

A scale or balance can be used to weigh foods (Figure 5-11). To be accurate, the scale must be of good quality and may need to be periodically oiled and calibrated. Weighing is often more practical than measuring, in terms of time and convenience, when large quantities are involved. Weighing also is generally more accurate than measuring volumes, particularly for foods that tend to pack down, such as flours and chopped ingredients. However, scales are not usually available in U.S. homes, and home-sized recipes are typically printed with measures.

Measurement of Staple Foods

Accurate measuring equipment and good measuring methods are needed to measure ingredients accurately. Most recipes allow small deviations in the amounts of ingredients used, and acceptable products are still produced. However, the quality of some products, such as shortened cakes, may be adversely affected by different methods of measuring the flour [3]. Accurate and consistent measurement of ingredients is important in producing uniform products of high quality time after time [1].

Flour.   To measure flour, sift, then spoon tablespoons of the flour lightly into a dry-measure cup until the cup is heaping full. Then level the top of the filled cup with the straight edge of a spatula (Figure 5-12). Do not pack the flour by shaking the cup while filling or hitting it with the spoon. Quantities of less than one cup should be measured in the smaller fractional cups such as 1/4, 1/3, or

TABLE 5-1	U.S. Customary Measurements and Fluid Weights

3 teaspoons (t. or tsp.) = ½ *fluid* ounces
                      = 1 tablespoon (T. or Tbsp.)
4 tablespoons = 2 *fluid* ounces = ¼ cup (c.)
16 tablespoons = 1 cup (c.)
1 cup = 8 *fluid* ounces = ½ pint
2 cups = 16 *fluid* ounces = 1 pint
4 cups = 32 *fluid* ounces = 1 quart
16 cups = 128 *fluid ounces* = 4 quart = 1 gallon

Note: A fluid, such as water, will weigh 8 ounces per cup. These conversions cannot be used for dry ingredients such as flour, spices, diced vegetables, and other similar ingredients.

1/2 cup. Likewise, when using measuring tablespoons or teaspoons, the spoon should be heaped full by dipping into the flour and then leveled with the straight edge of a spatula. Fractional spoons should be used to measure half and quarter spoonfuls. If fractional measuring spoons are unavailable, it is possible to use a teaspoon and remove the necessary fraction. Flatware or silverware teaspoons and tablespoons, however, will not provide accurate measurements.

Solid Fats.   Solid fats should be removed from the refrigerator long enough before they are measured so

that they will be plastic. Very hard fats are difficult to measure accurately except in the case of sticks of butter or margarine that have measurements marked on the wrapper. In this case, they may be cut, as marked, with a sharp knife. To measure plastic fats, press the fat into a dry-measuring cup with a spatula or knife so that air spaces are forced out. Then level the cup or fractional cup with a straight edge. For measurements up to 1/4 cup, level tablespoons may be used.

As an alternative, a water displacement method may be used if the water that clings to the fat does not affect the product. Pour cold water into a liquid-measure cup up to the measure that will equal one cup when added to the amount of fat to be measured. Then add enough fat to bring the water up to one cup when the fat is completely submerged in the water. Finally, drain off the water.

Sugar.   Granulated sugar is simply spooned into a dry-measure cup and then leveled with the straight edge of a spatula.

For brown sugar, any lumps should first be rolled out before the sugar is pressed into the cup firmly enough that it holds its shape when turned out of the cup. Measured in this way, one cup of brown sugar is approximately equal in mass to one cup of granulated sugar.

For the measurement of confectioners' or powdered sugar, sifting is followed by spooning the sugar into a cup, as for flour. Sifting the powdered sugar will remove any

FIGURE 5-10 Household measuring utensils can be labeled with metric or U.S. customary units. Dry measuring cups should be used for dry ingredients such as flour or sugar. Liquid measuring cups are best for liquids such as milk, water, or vegetable oil. *(Courtesy of World Kitchens, makers of Pyrex®, CorningWare®, and Baker's Secret®.)*

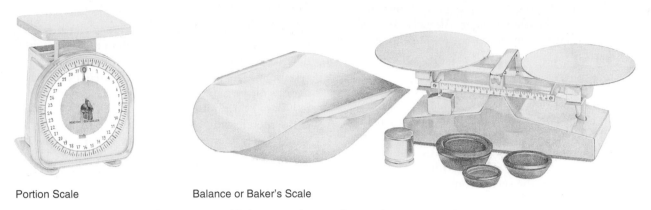

Portion Scale   Balance or Baker's Scale

FIGURE 5-11 Two types of scales, portion and balance, used to weigh ingredients accurately.

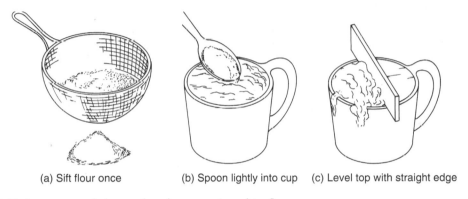

(a) Sift flour once   (b) Spoon lightly into cup   (c) Level top with straight edge

FIGURE 5-12 A recommended procedure for measuring white flour.

Why Sift Flour?

In a nutshell, flour is sifted to assure accurate measurement and sifted flour may blend into the other ingredients more easily.

Because most recipes are standardized for sifted flour, failure to sift flour will result in too much flour in the recipe. Unsifted flour is more tightly packed into the cup, and therefore more flour is in each cup. Flour is a difficult ingredient to measure consistently because it is composed of tiny particles of different sizes that tend to pack [3]. If unsifted white flour is substituted for sifted flour in a recipe standardized for sifted flour, the amount of flour may be adjusted by removing two level tablespoons from each cup of unsifted flour measured [6]. If weighing flour, one pound of flour will weigh one pound, regardless of whether it is sifted. When measuring other types of flour, issues to consider include:

- Graham or whole-wheat flours are usually not sifted before they are measured because the bran particles may be sifted out. Finely milled whole-wheat flour, however, may be sifted.
- Instantized flour, which contains agglomerated particles of quite uniform size, does not require sifting before being measured.
- The mass or weight of equal measures of white and whole-wheat flour also are not the same. One cup of whole-wheat flour weighs approximately 132 grams (4.4 ounces), whereas one cup of white flour weighs approximately 115 grams (3.8 ounces). ■

lumps. One cup of confectioners' sugar is slightly heavier than 1/2 cup of granulated sugar. About 1 3/4 cups of confectioners' sugar is equal in mass to one cup of granulated sugar.

Syrups. To measure syrups or molasses, place the cup or fractional cup on a flat surface and fill completely. Because it is thick, the liquid may tend to round up higher than level full. It should be cut off level with the straight edge of a spatula. Measure spoonfuls by pouring syrup into the spoon and cutting off level with the straight edge of a spatula. To keep the syrup from sticking to the measuring cup or spoon, the empty measuring utensil may be lightly sprayed with a nonstick vegetable spray, provided that minute amounts of fat will not compromise the recipe.

Liquids. For measuring liquids, a cup that extends above the largest measure mark should be used to increase ease and accuracy of measurement. Liquid-measuring cups have a lip for pouring. Only liquids are measured accurately in liquid-measuring cups; these cups should not be used for measuring dry ingredients. Place the cup on a flat surface and fill to the desired measure mark.

The eye should be at the level of the measure mark when reading the contents. In clear liquids, a meniscus can be seen at the upper surface as a curved concave line. The eye should read the lowest point of this meniscus (Figure 5-13). Some liquids, such as milk, honey, and corn syrup, do not form a meniscus and should therefore be measured at eye level where the liquid matches the desired measurement line.

The Metric System

During the French Revolution, France's lawmakers asked their scientists to develop a system of measurement based on science rather than custom. The result was the metric system, which has since been adopted by most of the nations of the world. The metric system is a decimal system based on multiples of 10. The basic unit of length is the meter, which is slightly longer than a yard. Each unit of measure may be divided by 10 for the next smaller unit of measurement. Thus, 1 meter equals 1,000 millimeters or 100 centimeters or 10 decimeters. The same prefixes are combined with the basic unit of **mass** or weight (gram) and the basic unit of volume or capacity (liter) to indicate designated amounts. Prefixes and symbols for mass, volume, and length are shown in Table 5-2. Other units and symbols associated with the metric system are given in Table 5-3.

Conversion to Metric

The United States is one of the very few nations in the world that has not fully converted to metric [8]. A change in the United States from the U.S. customary system of weights and measures to the metric system was recommended and became public policy with passage of the Metric Conversion Act of 1975. The change to metric was to be voluntary; however, the conversion process moved slowly. In 1988, an amendment to the 1967 Fair Packaging and Labeling Act required that manufacturers show both U.S. customary and metric designations on most consumer products. Some metric containers, such as one-liter soft drink bottles, are being used, but most food packages are labeled with the U.S. customary weight

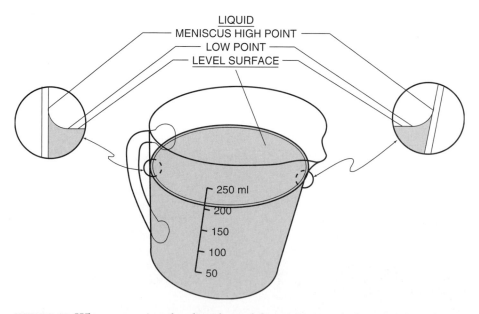

FIGURE 5-13 When measuring clear liquids, read the meniscus at the lowest point.

TABLE 5-2 The Metric System—Prefixes and Symbols

	Prefix	Mass	Symbol	Volume	Symbol	Length	Symbol
0.000001	micro-	microgram	μg	microliter	μL	micrometer	μm
0.001	milli-	milligram	mg	milliliter	mL	millimeter	mm
0.01	centi-	centigram	cg	centiliter	cL	centimeter	cm
0.1	deci-	decigram	dg	deciliter	dL	decimeter	dm
1.0		gram	g	liter	L	meter	m
10	deka-	dekagram	dag	dekaliter	daL	dekameter	dam
100	hecto-	hectogram	hg	hectoliter	hL	hectometer	hm
1000	kilo-	kilogram	kg	kiloliter	kL	kilometer	km

TABLE 5-3 Some Metric Units and Symbols

	Unit	Symbol
Energy	Joule	J
Temperature	Degree Celsius	°C
Pressure	Pascal	Pa
Frequency	Hertz	Hz
Power	Watt	W

first and then the metric weight. Legislation has been passed as recently as 1996 regarding the use of metric in the United States and progress, although gradual, is evident.

Metric and Recipes

The conversion of U.S. customary measures to metric measurements will require recipe testing and standardization to accommodate metric measuring cups and spoons. Metric measures are available in various equivalents of 1 liter and 500 and 250 milliliter capacities. Metric measuring spoons are available in 1 milliliter, 2 milliliters, 5 milliliters, and 15 milliliters. One cup converts to 237 milliliters; however, it would be more practical to use the 250 milliliter measure. Depending on the recipe, the small differences in amount from 237 milliliters (1 cup) to 250 milliliters could affect the final product. Therefore, standardization of each converted recipe is necessary.

Although the change to metric initially would offer some challenges, a strong benefit will be greater ease when adjusting recipes to smaller or larger sizes. Compared to the U.S. customary units, the conversions from ounces to pounds, tablespoons to cups, cups to gallons, and so forth will no longer be necessary because the metric system is based on multiples of ten. Selected equivalent weights or measurements between U.S. customary units and metrics are found in Table 5-4. A more comprehensive listing of conversions is found in Appendix A. Charts

Metric in the U.S. Marketplace

Metric measurements may be found on packages sold in the U.S. marketplace. The metric measurement labeling may be a *soft conversion* or a *hard conversion*.

Soft Conversion

When the container is sized and labeled in U.S. customary units followed by metric, this is a soft conversion. For example, the label on a 1.5 quart bottle of fruit juice may read "48 fl. oz. (11/2 qts.) 1.42 L." Home measuring cups also often provide both U.S. customary and metric units of measurement and are another example of a soft conversion.

The U.S. cups, quarter cups, and so forth are provided on one side of the measuring cup with the metric units provided on the other side.

Hard Conversion

When containers and packages are actually designed for the metric system with the U.S. customary units provided after the metric measurement as a conversion quantity, this is a hard conversion. For example, many soft drinks are now being marketed in one-, two-, or three-liter bottles. ■

TABLE 5-4 Selected U.S. Customary and Metric Equivalent Weights and Measures

U.S. Customary	Metric
Measures	
1 teaspoon	4.9 milliliters
1 tablespoon	14.8 milliliters
1 cup	237 milliliters
1 quart	946 milliliters or 0.946 liter
1.06 quarts	1 liter or 1,000 milliliters
Weights	
0.035 ounce	1 gram
1 ounce	28.35 grams
1 pound	0.454 kilogram
2.2 pounds	1 kilogram

for changing Fahrenheit and Celsius temperatures and formulas for these conversions are given in Appendix B.

RECIPES

A recipe lists the ingredients and the procedure for preparing a food product. Recipes may be found from a variety of sources such as cookbooks, friends and family, or the Internet. Comparing a recipe to other similar recipes will help to predict if the recipe is likely to provide good results. When using recipes from the Internet, you should assess the credibility of the source. You also may develop your own special dishes over time through experimentation in the kitchen. The study of food science will provide a foundation of knowledge on the ingredient functions that will enable you to adjust recipe ingredients successfully to suit your particular tastes or nutritional preferences.

Recipe Styles

To be effective, the recipe must be written simply and clearly so that it is easily understood. Four general styles of written recipes [1] are common. These styles include:

- *Standard Style.* Ingredients are listed in the order in which they will be used. Following the ingredient listing, the method of combining ingredients is provided in either step or paragraph form.
- *Action Style.* The narrative describing the action or method is interspersed with the listing of ingredients. The action or method and ingredients are provided in the order to be followed when preparing the recipe.
- *Descriptive Style.* These recipes are presented in a column format. Ingredients, ingredient quantity, and procedure are each in a column. The ingredient listing includes a description of any

modification necessary such as *sifted* flour, or *sliced* carrots.
- *Narrative Style.* The amounts of ingredients and the method are combined in narrative. This recipe style is best for very short recipes with few ingredients and brief instructions.

Regardless of the recipe style, a few key points in presenting recipes need to be followed.

1. Ingredients, as well as instructions, should be provided in the order of preparation. Do not list an ingredient first that is to be used at the very end of the recipe preparation.
2. Ingredients must be clearly described. For example, if an onion is needed, should it be white, yellow, or another variety of onion? Is it to be sliced, diced, or coarsely chopped? Are ingredients such as meats and vegetables to be prepared before or after measuring? For example, does it use 1 pound of cooked ground beef or 1 pound of raw ground beef? Likewise with vegetables, is it a purchased quantity (1 pound of potatoes) or prepared quantity (1 pound of peeled potatoes)? Foodservice recipes will often designate an ingredient as AP (as purchased) to indicate the meat is raw, the potatoes are unpeeled, and so forth. If the ingredient amount is a prepared or cooked quantity, the recipe may state EP (edible portion).
3. Instructions should be clearly understood by another person unfamiliar with the recipe. The audience for the recipe should be considered. Many will understand culinary terminology, whereas others may need an explanation for cooking terms such as fold, blanch, poach, and so forth.
4. Provide food safety recommendations, such as "Cook chicken to a minimum internal temperature of 165°F (74°C) throughout."
5. Provide the recipe yield. For example, four 1/2 cup servings.
6. Pan sizes, oven temperatures, and cooking times should be given.

Standardization and Recipe Adjustment

A recipe is considered standardized only after it has been tried and evaluated for quality, and any necessary adaptations or adjustments have been made. Equipment, types of ingredients available, and skill of the person preparing the recipe differ from one situation to another. Therefore, each recipe must be adapted and standardized for use in a particular situation. Once a recipe has been standardized for a particular setting, it is useful for making grocery and purchase orders and calculating food costs or nutritional content. Recipes that are standardized for inclusion in cookbooks generally use the methods for measuring

Four Basic Standardized Recipe Styles

Standard Recipe Style

1 cup sifted all-purpose flour
2 Tbsp granulated sugar
1 tsp baking powder
1/4 tsp salt
1/4 cup shortening (at room temperature)
(And so on.)

1. Preheat oven to 350°F (177°C).
2. Sift dry ingredients together into mixing bowl.
3. Add shortening. (And so on.)

Action Recipe Style

Measure and sift together in a mixing bowl:

1 cup sifted flour
2 Tbsp sugar
1 tsp baking powder
1/4 tsp salt

Add:

1/4 cup shortening
(And so on.)

Descriptive Recipe Style

Flour, all-purpose, sifted	1 cup	Sift dry ingredients together in mixing bowl.
Sugar, granulated	2 Tbsp	
Baking powder	1 tsp	
Salt	1/4 tsp	
Shortening	1/4 cup	Add to dry ingredients.
(And so on.)		

Narrative Style

Sift all-purpose flour once. Measure 1 cup sifted flour, 2 Tbsp granulated sugar, 1 tsp baking powder, and 1/4 tsp salt. Sift all dry ingredients together in a mixing bowl. Add 1/4 cup shortening. (And so on.)

Narrative style is best used with a recipe with few ingredients such as this recipe:

Thaw 2 pounds of frozen fish fillets. Cut into serving-size pieces. Place on broiler rack. Brush with melted butter or margarine. (And so on.) ∎

---

ingredients outlined earlier in this chapter. Recipes with eggs are generally standardized using large eggs.

Factor Method of Recipe Adjustment.   Recipe yields may need to be adjusted to meet individual situations. In enlarging home-size recipes for quantity use, it is best to first prepare the recipe and evaluate the result to be sure that it produces an acceptable product. Then the recipe may be adjusted for a larger or smaller yield by using the *factor method.* Many restaurant and home cooks increase or decrease recipe yields by the factor method. However, when the recipe yield is changed by a large factor, inaccuracies can occur because the relative proportionally of the ingredients change, and therefore product failure can occur [5].

The steps in adjusting a recipe using the factor method are as follows.

1. Divide the *desired* number of portions by the *current* recipe yield to obtain a factor to use for the increase or decrease of the recipe. When decreasing a recipe, the factor is less than one; when increasing, the factor is greater than one.

If desired portions = 32 and current portions = 8, then 32/8 = 4.

2. Multiply each ingredient measurement by the factor and convert to appropriate units of measure.

4 × 1 cup = 4 cups or 1 quart
4 × 1 tablespoon = 4 tablespoons or 1/4 cup

3. Check your calculations for accuracy.

Percentage Method of Recipe Adjustment.   Probably the most accurate method for yield adjustment, particularly when large volumes are involved, is called the *percentage method* [7]. When using the percentage method, if an ingredient, for example, is 25 percent of the recipe by weight, it will always be 25 percent by weight regardless of the amount of increase or decrease of the recipe. The steps in adjusting a recipe using the percentage method are as follows:

1. All ingredients must be in weights.
2. Add weight of each ingredient and total to obtain a total recipe weight.

Ingredient A	8 ounces (or 0.5 pound)
Ingredient B	+ 1 pound
Ingredient C	+ 4 ounces (or .25 pound)
Total recipe weight	= 1 pound and 12 ounces (or 1.75 pounds)

3. Calculate the percentage of each ingredient weight in relation to the total recipe weight by dividing the ingredient weight by the total recipe weight.

Ingredient A	0.5 pound / 1.75 pounds = 28.6 percent

4. Recipe increases and decreases can be made by multiplying the *desired* total recipe weight (yield) by the percentage of each ingredient.

If a total recipe weight of 5 pounds is desired, then

Ingredient A	5 pounds x 28.6 percent = 1.43 pounds

5. To check accuracy of calculations, total the new weight of each ingredient. This total should equal the new recipe weight, which in this example is 5 pounds.
6. The use of the percentage method is best used with digital scales so conversions of fractions of pounds do not need to be recalculated into pounds and ounces.

CHAPTER SUMMARY

- Knives and cutting boards are among the most important tools used in the preparation of foods. French or chef's, utility, paring, butcher's, and other knives are designed for specific tasks. The French knife is best for cutting or dicing a wide array of foods.

- Knives should be well balanced and made from high quality materials. High carbon stainless steel blades both sharpen easily and resist corrosion. A sharp knife is safer and easier to use than a dull one. Knives should be sharpened on a whetstone and honed on a steel.

- Many hand tools are used in the kitchen to stir, whip, peel, or grasp foods. Thermometers are an essential item to have in the kitchen to control food safety and quality.

- The correct proportion of ingredients is vital to success in the preparation of many food products. In the United States, recipes generally call for volume measurements, particularly in home cooking.

- Weighing is generally more accurate than measuring, particularly for ingredients such as flour that may pack. Weights are often used in quantity cookery.

- Dry ingredients do not have the same density as liquids. Therefore, one cup of most dry ingredients will not weigh the same amount per cup as compared to water. If a recipe provides weights for dry ingredients, appropriate conversion factors must be used to change into measures, or vice versa.

- The metric system is a decimal system based on multiples of 10. A change in the United States from the U.S. customary system of weights and measures to the metric system became public policy with passage of the Metric Conversion Act of 1975. A 1988 amendment to the 1967 Fair Packaging and Labeling Act required that manufacturers show both U.S. customary and metric designations on most consumer products.

- Recipe ingredients are measured with the use of dry-measuring cups, liquid-measuring cups, and measuring spoons or weighed with scales. Dry- and liquid-measuring cups should not be used interchangeably.

- Recipes list the ingredients and describe the procedure for preparing food products. To be effective, a recipe must be written simply and clearly so that it is easily understood. The four general styles of written recipes include standard, action, descriptive, and narrative.

- A recipe is standardized only after it has been tried and evaluated for quality, and any necessary adaptations or adjustments have been made.

- Recipe yields may be adjusted to meet individual needs. The factor method is commonly used in the home and smaller foodservice operations; however, this method may not provide consistently high quality products if large adjustments in yield are made. The percentage method of yield adjustment is most accurate, especially for large quantity food production.

STUDY QUESTIONS

1. What are the advantages and disadvantages of the three materials commonly used for knife blades?

2. Explain how to sharpen a knife and describe the tools that are used.

3. Explain how to grasp a knife and how to hold food when cutting or slicing.

4. Identify the purpose for which each of the following knives is best used: French/chef's, utility, paring, slicer, serrated, and butcher's.

5. Identify the purpose for each of the tools described in the text.

6. Discuss why accurate measurements are important in the preparation of quality food products.

7. What type of measuring cups should be used to measure liquids? What type should be used to measure dry ingredients? Explain.

8. How many tablespoons are there in one cup? How many teaspoons are there in one tablespoon? How many cups in a quart or in a gallon?

9. If a recipe calls for the weight for a dry ingredient and you want to measure the ingredient instead, can you convert the weight of any dry ingredient to a measure using the conversion of one cup is equal to 8 fluid ounces? Explain.

10. Describe appropriate procedures for measuring flour, liquid, solid fat, sugar, and syrups.

11. (a) What is the metric system of measurement? Where did it originate?

    (b) Identify advantages as well as challenges to a change from U.S. customary measurements to the metric system in the United States.

    (c) Name the basic metric units for length, volume or capacity, and weight or mass. What is indicated by the prefixes *deci-*, *centi-*, *milli-*, and *micro-?*

    (d) What is meant by *soft conversion* and *hard conversion* to the metric system?

12. What is a standardized recipe? Identify advantages to the use of standardized recipes.

13. Identify two methods of recipe yield adjustment and explain how they are used. Which method is most accurate when large changes in yield are to be calculated?

14. Describe several styles of written recipes and discuss the advantages of each.

HEAT TRANSFER IN COOKING 6

Heat is a form of energy that results from the rapid movement or vibration of **molecules** within a substance. This movement of molecules is called *kinetic energy*. With the use of a thermometer, we can measure the average intensity of the heat resulting from the molecular movement within a substance. We record it as *temperature*.

As the molecules move, they constantly collide with other molecules in the same substance or with molecules of another substance with which they come into contact. As molecules collide, their speed of movement may be changed. Rapidly moving molecules striking slower-moving molecules transfer some of their energy to the slower-moving ones. Thus, heat energy is transferred from a warmer substance to a cooler one.

Cooking results when heat is transferred to, or produced in, a food and is distributed from one part of the food throughout the whole. Heating or cooking produces many changes in foods that, when the cooking is properly done, increase their palatability and appetite appeal.

In this chapter, the following will be discussed:

- Effects of cooking food
- Changes in state (from solid to liquid to gas)
- Latent heat
- Types of heat transfer
- Media for heat transfer

WHY COOK FOOD?

There are several important reasons for cooking food. Ensuring that foods are edible and safe are essential outcomes of cooking. Additionally, cooking improves the digestibility and therefore nutritive value of some foods. Perhaps most important is the aesthetic appeal of foods that have been cooked.

Food Safety and Shelf Life

Proper cooking destroys most **pathogenic microorganisms** that may be present in these raw products (see Chapter 3). Meat, poultry, and seafood may be consumed raw in some instances and particularly within certain cultures. However, the potential for a foodborne illness can be significant when consuming these foods without cooking to recommended endpoint temperatures. **Pasteurization**, a relatively mild heat process with carefully controlled times and temperatures, is essentially a mild cooking process used to destroy pathogenic microorganisms in milk as well as some other food products such as eggs.

The keeping quality, or shelf life, of some foods is extended by cooking. For example, very perishable fresh peaches or other fruits keep somewhat longer if cooked. When cooked and canned, these foods keep for a considerably longer period.

Making Foods Edible

Some basic staple foods, such as dry legumes and whole grains, are not in an edible form when harvested. These products must be **rehydrated** and softened so that the raw starch is made more palatable and digestible. A remarkable transformation occurs when flour mixtures are baked or cooked, with many new flavor and color changes contributing to their increased palatability and appeal. Actually, these foods are generally more aesthetically pleasing, palatable, and acceptable when cooked.

Digestibility and Nutritive Value

Digestibility and nutritive value may, in some cases, be increased by cooking. Starch in cooked grain products and legumes becomes more readily available to digestive enzymes than that in compact raw **starch granules**. Some antidigestive factors in dry beans and peas are also destroyed by heating. Of course, cooking may bring about decreases in nutritive value as well. For instance, some loss of vitamins and minerals occurs when vegetables and meats are cooked. By avoiding overcooking and improper cooking methods, we can minimize these losses.

Aesthestic Appeal

Finally, let us not forget that food is to be enjoyed. Cooking foods makes possible the creation of many new delectable dishes, greatly increasing variety and interest in dining. Flavor, **texture**, and color of foods are affected in various ways by the cooking process. New flavors are formed by heating, as when meats are browned, breads are baked, and caramels are cooked. Flavor may also be lost or undesirable flavors may be produced by cooking, as when vegetables are overcooked or toast is burned.

Texture is often softened by cooking—the fiber of vegetables becomes limp, and the connective tissue of meat is tenderized. Some foods, however, become crisp on cooking (such as bacon, potato chips, and other fried foods). Eggs, both whites and yolks, become more firm on heating. The entire character of a texture may be changed by cooking. Note the great difference in texture between a cake batter and the finished cake or between bread dough and the baked loaf. A starch-thickened pudding or sauce also undergoes a remarkable change in texture after sufficient heating.

Color changes occur during cooking as well. Bright green vegetables turn dull and drab when they are overcooked or cooked with acid, whereas a short **blanching** period may actually enhance the color of fresh green peas. Rich brown gravy is made from drippings that have browned during the roasting of meat. Light brown crusts on baked goods enhance their eye appeal and improve flavor and texture characteristics. Thus, the effects of cooking on food are truly diverse and, in many cases, highly desirable.

MEASUREMENT OF TEMPERATURE

Thermometers are used to measure *sensible heat*—that which can be felt by the senses. Two thermometer scales commonly may be used to indicate the temperature of a substance. The Fahrenheit scale (F) is used in the United States in connection with the U.S. customary system of weights and measures. The Celsius (or Centigrade) scale (C) is used in most other nations and is used for scientific research in the United States.

Using the Fahrenheit scale, water at sea level freezes at 32° and boils at 212°. On the Celsius scale, water freezes at 0° and boils at 100°. The usual room temperature of 72°F is 22° on the Celsius scale (Figure 6-1). As long as the two scales are used in the United States, it may be necessary to convert from one to the other. The formula

$$1.8(°C) = (°F) - 32$$

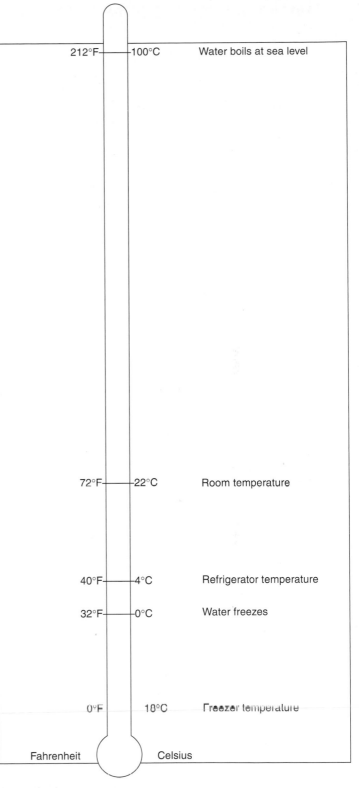

212°F — 100°C	Water boils at sea level
72°F — 22°C	Room temperature
40°F — 4°C	Refrigerator temperature
32°F — 0°C	Water freezes
0°F 18°C	Freezer temperature
Fahrenheit	Celsius

FIGURE 6-1 Two thermometer scales are used in measuring temperature: the Fahrenheit and the Celsius.

may be used for conversions from Celsius to Fahrenheit and vice versa [1]. Conversion charts also may be found in Appendix B.

HEAT INVOLVED IN CHANGE OF STATE

A substance may exist as a solid, a liquid, or a gas. When it changes from a solid to a liquid or from a liquid to a gas, we say that a *change of state* occurs. The physical state of the matter—solid, liquid, or gas—has changed. Energy is involved in this change of state and causes molecules to move more rapidly.

Change of State of Water

Water will be used as an example of change of state because water is commonly employed as a medium for applying heat in food preparation. Water changes from ice, to water, and then to steam with the addition of heat.

Solid.   The solid form of water is ice. In a chunk of ice, the water molecules have formed an ordered crystalline pattern and are held in a fixed arrangement in relation to each other. In a solid such as ice, the molecules may vibrate in place but do not move around freely.

Liquid.   Ice melts and becomes liquid water when heat is applied. The heat causes the water molecules to vibrate more rapidly and push against each other. In a liquid, the molecules have broken away from each other and are free to move about; however, they remain together and take the shape of the container in which they are placed.

Gas.   Water vapor and steam are both examples of the gaseous form of water. The molecules in a gas are widely separated and move freely in space. When liquid water stands in an open container, some of its molecules vaporize, or become gas, even at room temperature. This phenomenon can be observed when a glass of water, if left uncovered at room temperature, eventually becomes empty. The evaporation of water from a glass is an example of the conversion from liquid water to water vapor at room temperature. The random motion of the water molecules in this example was sufficient to allow escape into the atmosphere.

These gaseous molecules hovering over the surface of liquid water create a pressure called *vapor pressure*. As heat is gradually applied to liquid water, more gaseous molecules form, thus increasing the vapor pressure. When the vapor pressure is increased to a point just greater than the atmospheric pressure, bubbles that are formed in the liquid will begin to break at the surface, and boiling ensues. This process equalizes the vapor pressure and the atmospheric pressure. The water vapor coming from hot or boiling water is called *steam*.

At sea level, the temperature at which water boils is 212°F (100°C). At altitudes higher than sea level, the boiling point of water is decreased 1°C (1.8°F) for each 900 feet of elevation. Water boils at lower temperatures at higher elevations because the atmospheric pressure is lower at higher elevations. As a consequence, food must be cooked longer in mountainous regions because it is the temperature, not the boiling action, that influences cooking time. In contrast, vapor pressure builds up in a pressure cooker to levels greater than the atmospheric pressure, thereby increasing the boiling point of water to above 212°F (100°C). Thus, foods cook faster in a pressure cooker.

Heat Capacity of Water

Liquid water has a relatively large capacity to absorb heat. In fact, it is used as a standard for measuring the heat capacities of other substances. Water has been assigned a heat capacity of 1.00, called its *specific heat*, which indicates that one calorie is required to increase the temperature of one gram of water one degree Celsius. Thus, to take 100 grams of water (about 2/5 cup) from 0°C (32°F) to boiling at 100°C (212°F), 10,000 calories of heat or energy (1 calorie per gram per degree = 1 calorie × 100 grams × 100 degrees = 10,000 calories) are required. (These are *small* calories; 1,000 of these equal 1 kilocalorie, which is the unit used in nutrition.)

FOCUS ON SCIENCE

Why Does It Take Longer to Cook Certain Foods in the Rocky Mountains or Other High Elevation Locations?

Water boils at 212°F (100°C), right? Actually if you are cooking at a high altitude location such as Denver, Colorado, water will boil *before* 212°F (100°C). Bottom line—water boils at a lower temperature in high elevation areas.

Because Denver is at a high altitude, the external pressure on the water is decreased. At high altitudes, less energy is needed to break the water molecules free from the bonded energy. If it takes less energy, less heat is needed. If less heat is required, less temperature is required, and the water will boil at a lower temperature. Therefore, food cooked in water, like pasta or rice, will take longer to cook because it is cooking at a lower temperature than at sea level.

FOCUS ON SCIENCE

Boiling Water

To boil water requires energy, and this energy is in the form of heat which may be introduced by gas flame, electrical, solar, burning wood, etc. Energy has been introduced into the water to such a point that the bonding energy between the water molecules has exceeded the bond threshold and they have broken away and coalesced into steam.

Water boils at an extremely high temperature for its molecular size because of the extensive network of hydrogen bonds. The hydrogen (H) bonds are cohesive forces—these forces want to hold the water molecules together. Furthermore, there are a number of these bonds. The process of boiling requires that molecules come apart, and this process takes more energy than expected. Additionally, another result of the hydrogen bonding network is that water has a very high specific heat. Once heated, water takes a long time to cool off. Or in reverse, it takes a good deal of heat to make water hot.

Latent Heat

Latent Heat of Fusion and Solidification. Heat or energy that is required to change the physical state without changing temperature is called *latent heat.* This "hidden" heat or energy cannot be measured by a thermometer.

For each gram of ice that changes to liquid water, 80 calories of latent heat are needed even though the temperature remains at 32°F (0°C). These 80 calories of energy are absorbed by the melting ice and used to break up the ordered molecules of water in the ice structure. Heat absorbed during a change from solid to liquid state is called *latent heat of fusion.* Actually, the same amount of energy—80 calories per gram—was released from the liquid water as it froze and formed solid ice crystals. When energy is released during the change of a liquid to a solid, it is called the *latent heat of solidification.*

The latent heat of fusion is utilized when freezing ice cream using an ice-and-salt mixture. As the ice melts, the heat necessary for bringing about this change of state is taken from the ice cream mixture to be frozen, thus making it colder. Cold is really the absence of heat. Addition of salt to ice causes more rapid melting of the ice as equilibrium in vapor pressure is established for the mixture, thus lowering the temperature and enabling the freezing of ice cream in home-style ice cream makers (see Chapter 12). Although too low of a temperature for making ice cream, a mixture of one part salt to three parts ice, by weight, will result in a temperature of −6°F (−21°C).

Latent Heat of Vaporization and Condensation. When liquid water changes to a gas in the form of water vapor or steam, the energy absorbed is called *latent heat of vaporization.* For each gram of water vaporized at the boiling point (212°F/100°C), 540 calories are absorbed to produce steam at 212°F (100°C). The energy of latent heat does not change the temperature but is necessary to bring about the wide separation of water molecules from each other as they form a gas. In the reverse process—the condensation of steam to liquid water—the same amount of energy is released. This release of energy is called the *latent heat of condensation.*

We take advantage of this released heat when we steam foods. As steam touches the cooler surface of the food, it condenses to liquid and releases the 540 calories per gram of water condensed. This energy is absorbed by the food, thus actually aiding in the cooking process. It is this same energy absorption that accounts for the severity of steam burns when our skin comes in contact with steam.

TYPES OF HEAT TRANSFER

Conventional cooking methods transfer heat energy from its source to the food by means of conduction, convection currents, and radiation (Figure 6-2). In most cooking methods, more than one means of heat transfer is involved. Some cooktops may be specially designed to cook by magnetic induction (discussed later in the chapter).

Conduction

Conduction is the transmission of heat through direct contact from one molecule or particle to the next one. Heat moves from the heated coil of an electric unit, the touching flame of a gas unit, or other heat source to the saucepan placed on it and from the saucepan to the first layer of food, water, or fat in contact with the bottom and sides of the pan. Heat is then conducted throughout the mass of the food in the pan the same way, particle by particle (Figure 6-3). Using a pan with a flat bottom that comes in close contact with the heat source conserves heat and utilizes it most efficiently.

Although the process of conduction is similar for both fat and water, fat can be heated to a much higher temperatures than water; thus it is possible to bring more heat into the pan during the frying process. Water boils at 212°F (100°C), but it is common to fry foods at about 375°F (190°C).

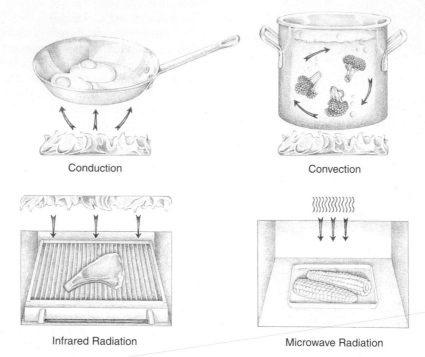

Conduction

Convection

Infrared Radiation

Microwave Radiation

FIGURE 6-2 Arrows indicate heat patterns during conduction, convection, and radiation.

Heat source

FIGURE 6-3 Conduction. Heat is transferred from an electric heating unit or from a gas flame that touches the bottom of the pan, through the pan, to the layer of the food that is next to the pan, and then throughout the food mass.

Quality of Materials for Conduction.   Materials used in the construction of cooking utensils vary in their ability to conduct heat efficiently. Metals that are good conductors include copper, aluminum, and iron. Pans are commonly made of either cast aluminum or aluminum formed from sheets (Figure 6-4). Cast-iron skillets and dutch ovens are heavy cooking utensils that likewise conduct and hold heat well.

Stainless steel is an alloy of iron with a small percentage of carbon and other metals, such as chromium and nickel. However, stainless steel does not conduct heat as well as copper, aluminum, and iron. Stainless steel is a very durable, easily cleaned metal and therefore is often used for cookware. To improve the conductivity of stainless steel cooking utensils, it is often combined in various ways with other metals to improve heating efficiency and eliminate "hot spots." For example, the heating base of a stainless steel pan may be clad with copper or aluminum, or a core of iron or other high-conductivity metal may be placed between the sheets of stainless steel used to form the pan. Heat-resistant glass and ceramic materials also offer some advantages as cookware but are not as effective in conducting heat as other materials.

Convection

Convection is the transfer of heat through air or liquid currents caused by the movement of different temperature areas of the gas or liquid. When gases and liquids are heated, they become lighter or less dense and tend to rise. The colder portions of these gases and liquids are more dense or heavier and move to the bottom. The lighter air rises and cooler, heavier air moves to the bottom, thus

FOCUS ON SCIENCE

How Does Conduction Work?

Basically, conduction is what happens when a piece of matter that is hot comes in direct contact with another piece of matter that is not. Because heat moves toward areas of lesser heat, the hot matter will make the less-hot matter hotter. The transferral matter in question can be anything from air to a piece of metal. However, different types of matter react differently when hot. Therefore, conduction will be different depending on the medium used.

Wok

Cast-Iron Skillet (Griswold)

Saucepan

Sautoir pan

FIGURE 6-4 Various styles of cookware allow for a variety of preparation methods.

setting up circular convection currents as illustrated in Figure 6-5.

Convection currents move the molecules around in their enclosed space and tend to distribute the heat uniformly throughout. Examples of the usefulness of these currents include cooking in a saucepan or other container with food particles dispersed in water (as is done with soups and stews), deep-fat frying, and baking in an oven. When foods are cooked in water or in fat as in deep-fat frying, convection currents move the heated molecules up and around the larger particles of food, transferring heat to the surfaces of the food. This heat can then be transferred into the particles by the process of conduction.

In conventional-oven baking, heated gas molecules of air rise from the energy source in the bottom and move around the surfaces of the baking containers. This movement particularly aids in the browning of the tops of baked products and other foods. Placement of containers in the oven is important to take full advantage of

What to Look for in High Quality Cookware

Ideally, pans should be made of materials that are good conductors and should be sturdy and warp resistant even with extended use. For efficient conduction, the pan should maintain contact on a flat heating surface. Warped pans therefore are less desirable.

The durability of a metal is determined to a great extent by its thickness, which is measured by its *gauge*. Gauge may be defined as the number of metal sheets of this particular thickness required to equal one inch. For example, 10 sheets of 10-gauge stainless steel or aluminum would equal a thickness of one inch; in other words, each sheet is 1/10 inch thick. Ten-gauge metal will produce a sturdy pan. To prevent warping, hot pans or skillets should never be placed immediately in cold water.

Nonstick finishes such as Teflon™ may be applied to the inner surfaces of pans and skillets. Nonstick surfaces allow the use of less oil in cooking. However, nonmetal spatulas and other utensils must be used to avoid scratching these finishes.

Iron skillets offer the advantage of holding heat well. Iron skillets and dutch ovens will also increase the iron content in the diet by absorbing into foods such as tomato sauce. However, due to the heat-holding capacity of iron skillets, use on glasstop ranges is not recommended because cracking of the range top may occur. Additionally, iron skillets must be well seasoned with a light coating of oil to prevent rust and the sticking of foods. ■

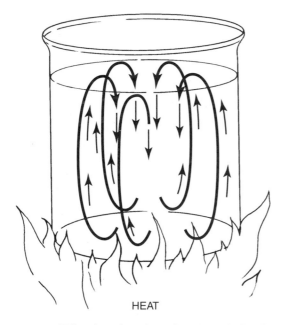

HEAT

FIGURE 6-5 When liquids and gases are heated, they become lighter (less dense) and rise, whereas cooler molecules of the liquid or gas move to the bottom of a container or closed compartment. These movements create convection currents that aid in distributing heat throughout the liquid or gas.

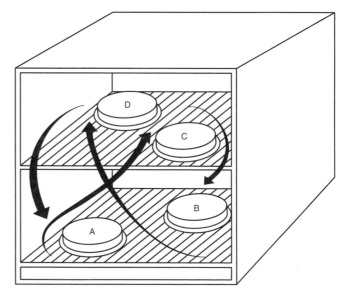

FIGURE 6-6 Convection currents move heated air around cake surfaces to aid in baking and browning.

convection currents in cooking and browning. When it is necessary to use two racks, the pans should be staggered so that one is not directly underneath the other (see Figure 6-6).

A convection oven employs a mechanical fan that increases air movement in the oven during baking, thus increasing the efficiency of heat transfer and decreasing cooking time. Convection ovens are common in foodservices and are becoming popular in the home. When using a convection oven, the baking time and temperature should be reduced to avoid overcooking. A temperature reduction of about 25°F (10°C) is suggested.

FOCUS ON SCIENCE

Convection Ovens—Why Reduce the Temperature?

In a convection oven, a fan blows the hot air around. Consequently, the convection currents move faster causing more hot matter (air) to come in contact with the item—in this case, food.

To help understand this phenomenon, consider wind chill. When cold air blows against you on a blustery winter day, you feel colder more quickly than you do on a windless day of the same temperature.

The rush of heat in the convection oven speeds up the chemical reactions that occur when food cooks. Overall, food cooked in a convection oven is usually done about 25 percent faster than it is in a conventional oven. Another benefit of convection ovens is even cooking. The circulating air reduces or eliminates hot and cold spots in the oven.

Radiation

Energy can be transmitted as waves or rays that vibrate at high frequency and travel very rapidly through space. An example of radiant energy is sunlight, which travels at the rate of 186,000 miles per second. Broiling, barbecuing, and toasting foods are examples of cooking methods that utilize radiant energy. The glowing coals of a fire, the red-hot coils of an electric heating unit, and the burning of a gas flame give off waves of radiant energy that travel from their source in a straight line to the surface of food that is placed in close proximity.

Radiant waves go directly from their source to the material they touch without any assistance in the transfer of energy from the air molecules in between. When radiant waves or rays reach the exterior parts of a food mass, energy is absorbed on the surface of the food and produces heat by increasing the vibration of the molecules in the food. Because the waves cannot penetrate below the surface, the interior is heated by conduction as the surface energy is transferred from one molecule to the next until it reaches the center of the food mass. Therefore, a combination of radiation and conduction is responsible for the heating of food in some cooking processes. In other applications of radiation such as baking, convection currents are also a factor in the transfer of heat.

Cookware Utensils.   The characteristics of the utensil being used affect the amount of energy absorbed from the radiant waves. When baking, the waves of radiant energy reach the exposed surface of the food and the outer surface of the utensil that holds the food. The utensil absorbs the energy and becomes hot, thereby transferring heat to the food by conduction. Dull, dark, rough surfaces absorb radiant energy readily, whereas bright, shiny, smooth surfaces tend to reflect the waves and absorb less energy, thus slowing the cooking and browning. Sometimes shiny aluminum bakeware is desirable, for example, to produce a light crust on layer cakes and cookies. Ovenproof glass dishes generally transmit radiant waves. Therefore, when glass bakeware is used, the oven temperature should be about 25°F (14°C) less than that used with aluminum bakeware.

Other Types of Radiation.   Infrared radiation is heat or energy from a slightly different wavelength. Infrared heat may be produced by high-energy lamps. These are sometimes used to keep food warm on a serving line. Infrared radiation has been used to dry fruits and vegetables and for heat blanching.

Although microwave cooking utilizes a form of radiant energy, microwaves are different from other radiant waves used in cooking food. In all cases, they are high-frequency electromagnetic waves, but microwaves have longer wavelengths and are somewhat lower in frequency than visible-light and infrared waves in the electromagnetic spectrum (see Figure 7-3). Microwaves cook food differently from how radiant waves cook. Microwave cooking is discussed in Chapter 7.

Induction Heating

Induction cooking utilizes a high-frequency **induction coil** that is placed just beneath the cooktop surface to produce friction and thereby generate heat. The induction coil generates a magnetic current that will heat a **ferrous** metal cooking utensil on the cooktop with magnetic friction. The cooktop is made of a smooth, ceramic material and remains cool (Figure 6-7). Only the cooking utensil gets hot. The hot utensil rapidly transmits heat to the food through conduction.

Flat cooking utensils made of cast iron, magnetic stainless steel, or enamel over steel are required for use on induction cooktops; utensils made of nonferrous materials

Induction Cooktop

FIGURE 6-7 Induction cooktops generate a magnetic current to heat cast-iron or magnetic stainless steel cookware.

cannot be heated. Heating by induction is rapid, and numerous power settings are available. Another advantage of the induction cooktop is the ease of cleaning. Because there is no exposed heating unit and the surface does not get hot, spills do not burn onto the unit.

MEDIA FOR HEAT TRANSFER

Media for transferring heat to food include air, water, steam, and fat. Combinations of these media are often used.

Air

Roasting, baking, broiling, and cooking on an outdoor grill are methods that use heated air as the cooking medium. These are generally considered to be *dry-heat* cookery methods, because the surface of the food comes into contact with dry air; however, in the interior of most foods, water participates in the transfer of heat. Also, where part of the product is in direct contact with a pan or cookie sheet, the heat from the air is conducted through the pan to the food. In convection ovens, a blower circulates the heated air, and the food heats more rapidly. When the surface of a food is dehydrated, temperatures higher than the boiling point of water may be attained, aiding in browning. The browning of food contributes to flavor development.

Water

Simmering, boiling, stewing, braising, and poaching are methods that use water as the primary cooking medium. For obvious reasons, these are called *moist-heat* cookery methods (Table 6-1). When water is the cooking medium,

---

TABLE 6-1 Dry, Moist, and Combination Cooking Methods

Type of Method	Media for Heat Transfer	Cooking Method	Description	Primary Method of Heat Transfer
Dry				
	Air	Broiling	Radiant heat from an overhead source is used to cook foods placed on a rack over a pan.	Radiation
	Air	Roasting	Roasting generally applies to meat and poultry. The food is cooked uncovered on a rack or roasting pan in a heated oven.	Radiation Convection Conduction
	Air	Baking	Baking generally applies to portion pieces of meat or poultry and other foods such as bakery products. Foods are baked, uncovered, in a heated oven.	Radiation Convection Conduction
	Air	Grilling	A heat source, such as coals in a barbeque, cooks food placed on hot grates.	Radiation Conduction
	Fat	Sautéing	A shallow pan is heated to a relatively high temperature with a small amount of oil to cook food. Stir-frying is a similar technique.	Conduction
	Fat	Pan Frying	A moderate amount of fat is used in a heated pan. The fat should come up to one-half or one-third the height of the food to be cooked. Pan-fried foods are generally breaded. Pan-frying uses less heat and more oil than sautéing.	Conduction
	Fat	Deep-fat Frying	Foods are submerged in oil heated to as high as 400°F (200°C). Deep-fat frying is a dry-heat cooking method because no water is used.	Conduction Convection
Moist				
	Water	Poaching	Food is placed in a liquid heated to 160°F to 180°F (71°C to 82°C). Water, broth, or other flavored liquids may be used. The food may be poached by submerging or placing in a shallow depth of liquid.	Convection
	Water	Simmering	Food is submerged in a liquid heated to 185°F to 205°F (85°C to 96°C). Often used to tenderize foods through long, slow cooking.	Convection
	Water	Boiling	Boiling liquid is used to cook foods. Water boils at 212°F (100°C) at sea level.	Convection
	Steam	Steaming	The food generally should not touch the liquid but is instead placed in a perforated or wire container above a boiling liquid.	Convection

TABLE 6-1	(Continued)			
Combination				
Fat Water	Braising	Food is browned in a small amount of fat, and then cooked covered in a small amount of sauce or other liquid. Because this method uses both dry and moist heat, it is considered to be a combination method of cooking.	Conduction Convection
Fat Water	Stewing	Stewing is generally associated with small pieces of food that have been browned in a small amount of fat. The food is immersed in a simmering sauce or liquid for final cooking.	Conduction Convection

Source: References 2, 3

the highest temperature attainable is that of boiling. At sea level, water boils at 212°F (100°C). Simmering and poaching use temperatures just below boiling.

Water is a better conductor of heat than air; therefore, foods cooked in water cook faster. Heat is transferred or conducted directly from the hot water to the food with which it comes into contact. Convection currents are also set up in hot water and help to distribute heat uniformly throughout the food mass.

Steam

Steaming is also a moist-heat method of cooking. Foods are steamed when they are placed on a rack above boiling water in a covered container that holds in the steam. Steaming also occurs when a food that contains water is closely wrapped and baked in the oven, such as a baked potato or a cut of meat wrapped in aluminum foil or placed in a cooking bag. Cooking a covered casserole in the oven involves cooking with steam, because the steam produced when the liquid boils is contained in the dish.

Heat is transferred from the steam to the surface of the food it touches. The food is often cooler than the steam, so the steam condenses on the surface, releasing the latent heat absorbed when the steam was formed from boiling water. This process aids in cooking and explains why a steam burn is likely to be more severe than one caused by boiling water.

In a pressure canner, steam is the cooking medium; however, because the close containment of the steam within the canner raises the vapor pressure, the boiling point of the water producing the steam is increased (Figure 6-8). Therefore, the temperature of cooking within the pressure canner is elevated above the boiling

FIGURE 6-8 A pressure canner is necessary to obtain temperatures higher than 212°F (100°C). *(Courtesy of National Presto Industries, Inc.)*

point of water at atmospheric pressure, and cooking is much more rapid. In a pressure saucepan, an adjustable gauge on the pan regulates the pressure and thus the temperature by releasing some steam during the cooking process. Canning is discussed further in Chapter 30.

Fat

Fat is the cooking medium in sautéing, pan-frying, and deep-fat frying. To *sauté* means to cook quickly in a very small amount of fat at a high temperature. Some sautéed foods may be lightly dusted with flour. Stir-frying is similar to sautéing, but it is commonly done in a wok (Figure 6-4). Pan-frying is cooking in a small amount of fat that comes about one-third to one-half of the way up the food to be cooked. Thus, more fat is used in pan-frying as compared to sautéing. Pan-frying is also at a more moderate temperature, and the foods are frequently coated in breading [2]. Cooking a food immersed in fat at a controlled temperature is deep-fat frying (Figure 6-9). In all of these cooking methods, heat is transferred by conduction from the energy source through the pan to the fat. Convection currents are set up in the heated fat and aid in distributing the heat. The heated fat then conducts heat to the food it touches.

Fat can be heated to a much higher temperature than the boiling point of water. Because some fat is also absorbed by the food, the flavor is changed to a considerable degree. Frying is discussed in more detail in Chapter 10.

Deep-Fat Fryer

FIGURE 6-9 Deep-fat fryers are equipped with wire baskets so fried foods can be raised from or lowered into the hot fat.

CHAPTER SUMMARY

- Heat is a form of energy that results from the rapid movement or vibration of molecules within a substance. A thermometer is used to measure the average intensity of sensible heat. Two thermometer scales are commonly employed: the Fahrenheit and the Celsius (or Centigrade) scales.

- Food is cooked to make it edible, increase palatability, increase digestibility, reduce or eliminate pathogenic microorganisms, improve keeping quality, and enhance enjoyment.

- Heat is involved in the change of a substance from a solid to a liquid, then to a gas. Ice is the solid form of water, whereas steam is the gas form.

- Latent heat is required to change the physical state of a substance. Latent heat does not result in a change of temperature; thus boiling water is at 212°F (100°C), as is steam. When liquid water changes to steam, 540 calories are needed. The amount of

energy needed to change ice to water without a change in temperature is 80 calories. These calories are small calories: 1000 calories equal 1 kilocalorie. The unit used in nutrition, although often called "calories," is kilocalories.

- In conventional cooking, heat is transferred from the energy source to the food by conduction, convection, or radiation. More than one type of heat transfer is typical when cooking.

- Materials used in the construction of cooking utensils vary in their ability to conduct heat efficiently. Copper, aluminum, and iron are excellent conductors. Although stainless steel is a high quality material that resists staining and corrosion, it is not one of the best conductors.

- Induction cooking utilizes a high-frequency induction coil that is placed just beneath the cooking surface to generate a magnetic current that heats ferrous metal cooking utensils placed on the cooking surface. Nonferrous cooking utensils will not heat up on induction cooktop surfaces.

- Air, water, steam, and fat are media for the transfer of heat. Roasting, baking, broiling, and cooking on an outdoor grill are methods that use heated air as the major cooking medium. Fat is the cooking medium

in sautéing, pan-frying, and deep-fat frying. These are called dry-heat cooking methods.

- Simmering, boiling, stewing, braising, and poaching are cooking methods that use water as the primary cooking medium. These are called moist-heat cooking methods. Steam is also a moist-heat cooking method.

STUDY QUESTIONS

1. List and explain five reasons for cooking food.

2. Give examples of changes in flavor, texture, and color of foods that may occur during cooking.

3. (a) Define and compare *latent heat* and *sensible heat*.

   (b) How much energy is involved in the latent heat of fusion for water? The latent heat of vaporization at boiling?

   (c) What is *vapor pressure*? How is it related to the boiling point of water?

   (d) What is meant by the *specific heat* of water?

4. Compare the Fahrenheit and Celsius thermometer scales.

5. Describe how heat is transferred in food preparation by (a) conduction, (b) radiation, (c) convection currents, and (d) induction heating.

6. (a) Name four different media commonly used for transferring heat to food and give examples of several cooking methods that use each medium.

   (b) What types of heat transfer are generally used in each method that you cited?

7. Describe each of the following cooking methods: broiling, roasting, baking, grilling, sautéing, pan-frying, deep-fat frying, poaching, simmering, broiling, steaming, braising, and stewing.

8. Identify moist, dry, and combination cooking methods.

MICROWAVE COOKING 7

Microwave heating stemmed from the development of radar during World War II. It was then recognized that radar antennas generated heat and that this principle might be useful in heating food. The first microwave oven (called the Radarange) became available for foodservice establishments in 1947, and the first one for consumer use was introduced in 1955. These early manufactured models were large, heavy, specially wired, and very expensive with pricetags around $1,300. Microwave ovens are now used in more than 90 percent of U.S. households [2]. The microwave oven of today is very different from the pioneer models; it is convenient, attractive, easy to use, and available in varying sizes, wattages, and prices (Figure 7-1).

Because of the widespread use of microwave ovens in food preparation and processing, it is important for students of food science to understand the principles of microwave cookery. Although the cooking of vegetables, meats, eggs, and some starch and flour mixtures by microwaves is discussed in the various chapters about these foods, general principles of microwave cookery are addressed here.

In this chapter, the following topics will be discussed:

■ Use of microwaves in the home, foodservice, and industry

■ How microwaves heat foods

■ Advantages and disadvantages of microwave cooking

■ Appropriate utensils and packaging materials for microwave use

■ Microwave cooking recommendations

FOOD-RELATED USES OF MICROWAVES

Microwave heating of food is useful in households, commercial and noncommercial foodservice, and also in the food industry for processing.

Home

Microwave ovens are used most frequently in the home to boil water, heat frozen foods, defrost frozen foods, or make popcorn [10]. Consumers have not been quick to embrace cooking entire meals in the microwave, even though there are a number of microwave cookbooks that provide recipes and guidance for those interested in cooking applications. Instead, consumers often use the microwave for speed and convenience (Figure 7-2). Younger members of the household also use microwave ovens. Some parents may be more comfortable allowing their older children to heat a snack in the microwave rather than in an oven. The interior of microwave ovens, as well as generally the food container, stay cool when heating a food item and thus may be perceived as safer even though the food itself can become very hot.

Microwave popcorn became very popular with consumers in the 1980s due to the development of susceptor technology in popcorn packaging [3]. Manufacturers are continuing to develop new microwavable foods that respond to consumers' desires for speed and convenience. Frozen juice can now be taken from the freezer and reconstituted in only one to two minutes when packaged in plastic microwavable cans [10]. A variety of other products including soups, rice and pasta entrees, pizzas, and sandwiches are being developed with packaging specifically designed for effective microwave heating [3,16]. These newly developed products provide a much higher level of quality for the consumer as compared to the microwavable foods of a decade earlier.

Foodservice

Heavy-duty commercial microwave units are often installed in foodservice establishments. These units have high-output capabilities and are designed to withstand frequent use. Microwave ovens in foodservice establishments are used primarily for reheating. For example, hospital foodservices may use microwaves as part of a system in which individual plates of chilled menu items are

FIGURE 7-1 Microwave ovens are a common appliance in today's kitchens. *(Courtesy of World Kitchens, makers of Pyrex®, CorningWare®, and Baker's Secret®.)*

reheated, one meal at a time, just prior to service to the patient [19].

The microwave cooking of foods is not frequently used in foodservice, unless for individual portions, because these are not time savings when large quantities are involved. A microwave tunnel oven allows continuous microwave heating of cooked portions foods. However, it is used primarily in specialized foodservice settings.

Food Industry

Meat tempering, bacon precooking, and sausage cooking represent the largest uses of microwave processing by the food industry [13]. Microwave processing equipment is used to temper 4 billion pounds of food each year. As the foods are tempered, they are brought to a temperature just below the freezing point of water, where they are not frozen but are still firm. Conventional thawing of these foods may take several days, whereas microwave tempering can be completed within minutes, with less drip loss and reduced microbial growth [8].

The precooking of bacon is another major use of microwave technology by food processors. In bacon processing, 80,000 slices may be precooked per hour in microwave processing equipment [13]. Currently, nearly all of the bacon processed for foodservice use is precooked in microwave ovens, and 10 percent of the bacon used in the home has been similarly precooked.

A combination of microwave and conventional heating can be used for drying pasta, saving both time and energy as compared with conventional drying. Microwave drying may also be used for fruit juice concentrates, herbs, bread crumbs, potato chips, and snack foods [8]. High-intensity microwaves may

be combined with external heat sources, such as hot-air or infrared energy, to cook products quickly while simultaneously producing a browned surface. Often high yields, superior quality, and more rapid processing result [13].

Fresh pasta, bread, granola, yogurt, meat products, and prepared meals can be pasteurized using microwave energy. Sterilization can be achieved with microwaves using overpressure conditions to produce temperatures of 230° to 266°F (110° to 130°C) when proper packaging materials are used. The proofing of yeast-leavened products can also be accomplished in a short time with the use of microwaves. Microwaves may be used for baking bread, pizza, cake, and pastry products, often in combination with conventional baking methods [8].

Specialized microwave equipment is used by the food industry. Conveyer belts are often used to move products through a microwave field, resulting in more uniformity in the distribution of energy throughout the food products. Mathematical modeling is an advance in microwave processing that uses software to model microwave heating patterns [13].

ACTION OF MICROWAVES IN HEATING

What Are Microwaves?

Microwaves are high-frequency electromagnetic waves of radiant energy. They can be described as radio waves of very short wavelength, falling between television and

FIGURE 7-2 A snack like nachos can be conveniently prepared in the microwave. *(Courtesy of World Kitchens, makers of Pyrex®, CorningWare®, and Baker's Secret®.)*

Some Microwavable Foods Have Special Packaging to Use When Cooking. Why?

Microwavable popcorn, pizza, sandwiches, and some other products depend on a concentration of heat in a microwave oven to produce a pleasing food. This concentrated heat is produced with a **heat susceptor.** Next time you pop microwave popcorn, look at the part of the package which is to be "this side down" or the pizza tray with the silver surface. These are heat susceptors.

Heat susceptors may consist of metallized paperboard, which strongly absorbs energy and becomes very hot. The metal itself does not absorb the microwave energy, but it readily absorbs the heat produced by the other materials in the packaging. Thus, the use of susceptors allows popcorn to become hot enough to pop. Likewise, susceptors are used for microwavable pizza, sandwiches, and other products where the concentration of heat is useful to promote browning or crispness. ■

infrared frequencies on the electromagnetic spectrum (see Figure 7-3). In comparing wavelengths, radio waves are measured in kilometers, television frequencies in meters, microwaves in centimeters, and infrared waves in microns [7]. Microwaves are generated in a vacuum tube called a *magnetron*, which converts alternating electric current from a household circuit into electromagnetic energy radiation. Microwaves radiate outward from their original source and can be absorbed, transmitted, or reflected. In most microwave ovens, a stirrer blade in the top of the oven helps to distribute the waves (Figure 7-4). In other ovens, foods are rotated by turntables as a means of uniformly distributing energy.

The Federal Communications Commission has assigned certain frequencies for microwave cooking to avoid interference with communication systems that operate in closely associated frequencies. These assigned frequencies are 915 and 2,450 megahertz (million cycles per second). Although microwave cooking can be satisfactorily accomplished at either frequency, only the 2,450 megahertz

frequency is used in the microwave ovens being manufactured today for commercial foodservice and home use [7]. The shorter wavelengths (approximately 4.8 inches) produced by a frequency of 2,450 megahertz result in more uniform heating and better results for small items being cooked.

How Do Microwaves Heat Food?

As the microwaves enter the product, they interact with electrically **polarized molecules,** sometimes called *dipolar molecules*, in the food. These dipolar molecules include water, proteins, and some carbohydrates. Dipolar molecules act like tiny magnets and align themselves in the microwave electromagnetic field. The field alternates millions of times each second, causing the polarized molecules in the food to rotate rapidly due to forces of attraction and repulsion between the oppositely charged regions of the field. Heat is produced by the friction that is created between the rapidly moving molecules, thereby cooking the food. Positive and negative ions of dissolved

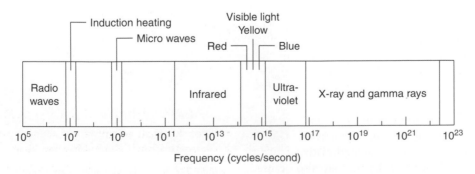

FIGURE 7-3 The electromagnetic spectrum, showing the frequency of microwaves located between the frequencies of radio waves and infrared-visible light.

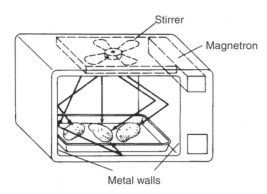

Stirrer

Magnetron

Metal walls

FIGURE 7-4 Microwaves are produced by a magnetron, from which they enter the oven. A stirrer deflects the microwaves and distributes them to various parts of the oven. They are reflected back from the metal walls of the oven. The food in the oven absorbs the microwave energy, and heat is created in the food as a result of the friction produced between the rapidly moving molecules.

salts in the food, including table salt or sodium chloride (NaCl), also migrate toward oppositely charged regions of the electric field and generate additional heat by their movement [8]. Microwaves are not hot and do not heat directly, heating instead by causing the movement of dipolar molecules.

Within a microwave oven, the microwaves reach the food that is to be cooked both directly from the magnetron unit and indirectly by reflection from the metal walls. The short, straight microwaves are reflected by metals. The metal walls of a microwave oven reflect and thus contain the microwaves within the oven cavity. Microwaves generally penetrate about one to two inches into the food, the depth varying with the frequency of the microwaves and the composition of the food. Further distribution of the heat, particularly toward the center of a relatively large mass of food, occurs by conduction, as it does in conventional heating. Microwaves do not, as is sometimes supposed, cook from "the inside out" [23]. Microwave cooking is faster, however, because microwaves penetrate farther into food than the infrared radiant waves used in conventional cooking and, therefore, deposit more energy at greater depths in the food.

Safety and Regulation

Since 1971, the FDA has regulated the manufacture of microwave ovens in terms of performance standards and design safety. A radiation safety standard enforced by the FDA limits the amount of microwaves that can leak from an oven throughout its lifetime [23]. The limit is 5 milliwatts of microwave radiation per square centimeter at a distance of 5 centimeters (2 inches) from the oven surfaces. This amount is far below the level known to harm people, and the exposure decreases as one moves away from the oven. For example, the exposure to microwave radiation at 20 inches from the oven is only one-hundredth of the level

at 2 inches. Microwave ovens also are required to have two interlocking systems to prevent the production of microwaves if the latch is opened. The FDA tests microwave ovens in commercial establishments, dealer premises, manufacturing plants, FDA labs, and in a limited number of homes to see that the standard for allowable leakage is met. The standard is believed to protect the public from radiation hazards. Nevertheless, research is conducted on an ongoing basis to assess the impact of microwaves on the human body [23].

Microwave Ovens

Microwave ovens are available with a variety of features to aid in food preparation. Variable power outputs, calculation of cooking times, and automatic features are some of the options available. Some manufacturers have combined a conventional electric oven with a microwave oven in the same compartment or a microwave–convection oven combination. Microwave ovens also have been designed to function as both a microwave oven and a ventilation cooking hood above a range, thus conserving space.

Microwave ovens may be purchased with varying power outputs. Microwave ovens for consumer use usually have an output capability of 600 to 700 watts, whereas commercial units often have a higher wattage. The design assumption for the heavy-duty units is that they will be used hundreds of times per day. Microwave ovens with lower power—400 to 500 watts—are also available for home use. These units heat more slowly than units with higher wattages but are more economical to purchase.

High-speed cooking can be slowed in most microwave ovens presently being manufactured, allowing cooking on various medium and low speeds. The reduced-power settings actually give full power intermittently, with on-off cycling, which reduces localized overheating and helps to protect sensitive foods. Variable settings have increased the adaptability of the oven for many different products and needs, including defrosting frozen foods.

Automatic features add convenience. For example, some ovens automatically determine the cooking time and power level when the weight of meat or poultry is entered into the program. Some sensor programs can automatically determine doneness of foods such as vegetables and then turn off the oven, or, alternatively, the product can be cooked and then held warm for a period.

ADVANTAGES OF MICROWAVE COOKING

Speed of Cooking and Reheating of Foods

One of the great advantages of using a microwave oven is the speed with which cooking can be accomplished—two to 10 times faster than conventional methods. The actual time required for cooking depends on the volume and type of food being cooked. Microwave ovens are not

Why Some Foods Cook More Quickly than Others in a Microwave Oven

The composition of a food affects the rapidity of heating. Fats and sugars have low **specific heats** compared with water; therefore, foods high in fat or sugar heat more rapidly than foods high in water. Foods with less **density** also heat more rapidly than high-density foods when similar weights of these products are heated. Dense foods limit the depth of penetration of the microwaves. For example, a dense brownie batter heats more slowly than a light, porous cake. ∎

generally designed for quantity cookery, and the time of cooking must be lengthened as the quantity of food to be cooked is increased. One potato, for example, cooks in 4 to 6 minutes in a microwave oven, whereas four potatoes require 16 to 19 minutes to cook.

Microwave cooking has special advantages in reheating precooked foods, both individually packaged and packaged in meals, and in thawing frozen foods. The microwave oven not only reheats precooked foods more rapidly than conventional methods, but it also avoids a reheated or warmed-over flavor [5]. Microwave oven owners often use these ovens for heating convenience meat items and casseroles, instead of using conventional heating appliances.

Reduction in Nutrient Loss

Microwaves are popular for cooking vegetables. A minimum amount of water is needed to cook vegetables in the microwave oven, thus conserving soluble nutrients. Additionally, researchers have found that microwave blanching of vegetables as compared to blanching in water resulted in less nutrient loss [17].

Energy Conservation

The microwave oven has a real advantage in saving energy when compared with conventional ovens, particularly for cooking up to about six servings at one time. In cooking pork sausage links, the microwave oven had the lowest energy requirement, followed by the convection oven, with the still-air oven requiring the most energy [12]. Additional energy savings from microwave use come from the lesser amount of dishwashing that is generally required. Containers used for microwave cooking are usually suitable for serving as well.

During warm seasons of the year, cooking methods that do not contribute to the warmth in the home are advantageous. In microwave cooking, the oven walls and surrounding air do not become hot. Only the food is heated. Furthermore, the container holding the food will only become hot if the cooking period is sufficiently long.

FOCUS ON SCIENCE

Warmed-Over Flavor and Microwaved Foods

What is warmed-over flavor?

Warmed-over flavor (WOF) occurs when food is reheated. The culprit is fat. Meats, especially those high in polyunsaturated fatty acids, are prone to oxidation, leading to rancidity development. Fish is also at risk, followed by poultry, pork, beef, and lamb. The oxidized fats produce volatiles; when the food is reheated, off flavors such as "cardboard," "rancid," "ice box," and even "freezer burn" are characterized.

How can microwavable foods avoid WOF?

In order to make some foods more acceptable, the manufacturer might include flavors that mask "warmed-over" tastes. Several flavor manufacturers encapsulate flavor systems so that they release flavor only upon microwave heating. Use of various spices that contain natural antioxidants is another method to avoid the problem of WOF. Also, the manufacturer may use technology that releases aromas in the heated food to enhance product appeal.

LIMITATIONS OF MICROWAVE COOKING

Surface Browning of Foods

Lack of surface browning is a disadvantage of microwave cooking for some foods, particularly baked products. A loaf of bread, for example, without a crisp, golden-brown crust does not have the same appeal as one that possesses this characteristic. Foods that require cooking for a relatively long time, such as a meat roast, may develop some browning, but most food items would be greatly overcooked before browning would occur.

The lack of browning of microwave-cooked products is due to the cool air temperature inside the microwave oven and to the cooling effects of moisture evaporation at the surface of foods cooked with microwaves. The temperature inside the microwave-cooked food is actually higher than it is at the surface [6]. To overcome to some degree the problems created by the lack of browning in microwave cooking, a special browning dish can be used to sear chops, meat patties, steaks, and similar products. A special coating on the bottom of the dish absorbs the microwave energy and becomes very hot (450° to 550°F/232° to 289°C).

Other Quality Considerations

Foods that need long cooking periods at simmering temperatures to tenderize or to rehydrate are not as satisfactorily prepared in a microwave oven as in a conventional oven. Dried pasta and rice are examples of foods that do not cook much more quickly in the microwave because rehydration must occur. In other foods, such as sauces and meats, flavors do not have an opportunity to develop in the short cooking periods of microwave ovens.

Stale bread is freshened with heating by conventional methods, but bread reheated in a microwave oven becomes tougher. The addition of certain emulsifiers, and increased water content (by use of fiber), has decreased the toughness of microwave-reheated bread [14]. Food processors are able to improve the quality of microwavable food products in part by the use of hydrocolloids, such as xanthan gum, carrageenan, and microcrystalline cellulose, which have high water-binding capabilities. These ingredients help to stabilize many microwavable products and prevent dry spots due to uneven heating and loss of moisture [4].

Overcooking and Erupted Hot Water Phenomena

It is relatively easy to overcook foods in the microwave oven, because heating is rapid. Caution must be exercised to avoid the dehydrating effects that may result from as little as a few seconds of overheating. Safety is also a concern when some products such as liquids are overheated. Superheated water has been reported to the FDA [23]. Superheated water is water that has been heated past its boiling temperature without appearing to boil. This is most likely to occur in a very clean cup when a liquid has been heated too long. When superheating has occurred, a slight movement such as picking up the cup or adding instant coffee may result in a sudden, violent eruption of boiling water that may cause a severe burn.

Unevenness of Heating and Food Safety

Unevenness of heating is a major disadvantage in the use of the microwave oven. This lack of uniformity in heat distribution raises some questions about the microbiological safety of certain foods heated with microwaves; sensory characteristics may also be affected. In the heating of meals made of ground meat patties, sauce, mashed potatoes, and carrots, it was reported that cold and hot spots were present near each other. The high–low temperature difference could be greater than 54°F (30°C) at spots within a few centimeters of each other [18]. When individual portions of meat loaf (beef), mashed potatoes, and green beans were heated in a microwave oven during one study that simulated procedures used in cook–chill

FOCUS ON SCIENCE

Starches and Hydrocolloids in Microwavable Foods

Starch and hydrocolloids are used to build viscosity in food, but they are a challenge to the food scientist to use in microwavable applications because the desired consistency needs to be obtained with shorter heating times. An instant starch or a cold-soluble colloid will aid in obtaining the desired viscosity with shorter cooking times.

What role do starches and hydrocolloids play in the quality of microwavable foods?

Even though a food may taste good, if the texture is dry, crumbly, mushy, or soggy, it may be unacceptable to the consumer. These texture variations can be associated with rapid heat and vaporization that occurs during microwaving. Texture is also affected by uneven heating that is common when using a microwave oven. Starches or hydrocolloids can benefit microwavable foods by (a) inhibiting the rapid loss of moisture during heating, (b) keeping water bound (as in meats), and (c) preventing syneresis (weeping or loss of moisture).

foodservice systems, a wide range (up to 83°F/46°C) of endpoint temperatures was observed [6].

It has also been reported that the usual procedures followed in cooking chicken by microwaves may not destroy all of the *Salmonella* organisms that may be present [11]. Concern has been expressed in regard to the destruction of *Trichinella spiralis* in pork prepared in the microwave oven (discussed in more detail in Chapter 25). It is important to ensure the safety of these foods by checking the final temperature in several locations within the product with a meat thermometer or the oven's temperature probe. Historically it has been recommended that meats cooked by microwaves be heated 25°F (14°C) higher than those attained with conventional heating. Current recommendations however, suggest cooking meats in a microwave oven to 165°F (74°C) throughout [15].

The voltage being fed to the microwave oven must be consistent at all times that the oven is operating to ensure quality control in the cooking process. The voltage may vary, however, particularly in metropolitan areas during peak periods of electricity use. Software programs are being designed to indicate to the oven when it is operating on less current and allow it to adjust appropriately [20].

PACKAGING MATERIALS AND COOKING UTENSILS

When cooking with a microwave in the home, plastic, ceramic, and glass containers that are labeled as microwave safe must be used [22]. Generally, materials that are transparent to microwaves should be utilized; the waves pass through these materials, as light passes through a window, and heat the food inside the container. Metal containers or glass containers with a metal glaze, rim, or trim are not acceptable for microwave use. Some utensils that are acceptable for use are shown in Figure 7-5. Recommendations for microwave cooking utensils by the type of material are given in Table 7-1.

If it is uncertain that a ceramic container is microwave-oven safe, it should be tested by placing it in the oven with a heat-resistant glass cup containing one cup of water and running the oven on high power for one minute. If the dish remains cool, it is suitable for microwaving. If it becomes hot, it has absorbed some microwave energy and should not be used.

A number of foods cooked in home microwave ovens use packaging provided when purchased. The commercial packaging of microwavable foods serves several functions. It protects the product in storage and distribution, controls the heating of the product, may function as a serving dish, and helps to sell the product [7]. Manufacturers are continuing to develop new packaging that allows the effective heating of foods and thereby enhances quality [3]. Special disposable packaging that uses heat susceptors is often beneficial for cooking such products as microwave pizza, french-fried potatoes, and some filled pastry products in which crispness and browned surfaces are desirable characteristics.

(a)

(b)

(c)

FIGURE 7-5 Several kinds of dishes may be used in the microwave. (a) This casserole dish may be used with a microwave-safe cover. (b) A variety of glass dishes are appropriate for microwave cooking. (c) This casserole dish comes with a microwave plastic pop-top lid that will vent steam. *(Courtesy of World Kitchens, makers of Pyrex®, CorningWare®, and Baker's Secret®.)*

TABLE 7-1 Microwave Cooking Utensils

Type of Material	Microwave Safe	Not Recommended
Glass, ceramic, and CorningWare®	Recommended if heat resistant	Some glazed ceramics are not recommended because these dishes become hot before the contents are heated. Dinnerware with silver or gold trim is not recommended.
Utensils with metal trim or screws in lids or handles		Not recommended because arcing is likely to occur, causing sparks.
Ceramic mugs or cups with glued on handles		Not recommended because handles may fail.
Paper products	White, microwave-safe papers towels may be used to absorb moisture and splatters during cooking. Paper plates labeled microwave safe are recommended.	Dyed paper products are not recommended to avoid migration of dye into the food product. Newspaper and brown paper bags should not be used because of inks and other chemicals that may have been used in manufacture.
Plastics	Microwave plastics designed for use in the microwave oven are recommended. When using microwave-safe plastic, slitting the top is recommended to prevent pressure buildup. Minimal contact between the food and the plastic is recommended to avoid migration of plasticizers into the food. Levels of migration have been found to be highest when direct contact occurs between the film and foods with a high fat content	Thin storage bags, plastic wrap on meats from the store, foam meat trays, take-out containers, and one-time-use plastic containers such as margarine tubs should not be used in the microwave oven. These plastics have not been produced for microwave use and may melt or distort.
Metal containers		Not acceptable for use in microwave ovens.
Aluminum foil	Some microwave manufacturers may indicate that very small strips of aluminum may be used to reduce excessive cooking of certain areas.	Do not use large pieces of aluminum. Do not use aluminum unless safe use is specifically described in the owner's manual provided by the manufacturer.

Source: References 7, 9, 21, 22

GENERAL COOKING SUGGESTIONS

Browning

Large pieces of food, such as meat roasts, brown during cooking in a microwave oven because cooking time is relatively long, but smaller quantities of food cooked for short periods need to be browned by some means other than the use of microwave energy. Small cuts of meat may be broiled conventionally after microwave cooking to develop browned color and flavor. Bacon is easily cooked in a microwave oven, however, and does brown. The fat on the surface of the bacon aids in browning. The optimum time for cooking should not be extended to increase the likelihood of browning. Foods dry out very rapidly with only slight overcooking when using microwaves.

Creative use of dark-colored toppings, sauces, crumbs, and spices can compensate for lack of browning in many dishes. Melted cheese and gravies also may be used to improve the appearance of casseroles and meat dishes. In addition, some formulated products are available for use in coating the surfaces of meats to encourage browning. Their major ingredient may be salt, which, when applied to a wetted surface, increases the electrical conductivity of the surface. Electrical conductors absorb microwave energy avidly and produce higher temperatures on the surface [7].

Stirring and Turning

Power is unevenly distributed in the microwave oven; therefore, foods need to be turned around, turned over, stirred, or relocated in the oven at various times during cooking. Multiple items such as individual potatoes, pieces of fish, and custard cups should be placed in a circle. Many microwave ovens are equipped with a turntable whose rotation automatically distributes power more evenly; turntables also can be purchased separately. Although metal is generally not acceptable for use in a microwave oven, small strips of aluminum foil may be used in many brands of microwave ovens to shield thin or sensitive parts of the food. The foil should not be allowed to touch the inside of the oven [1].

Standing Time

A food continues to cook for several minutes after it is removed from the microwave oven. This fact should be taken into account when cooking time is determined to avoid overcooking. During this standing time, heat continues to be conducted from hotter parts of the food mass to cooler ones, and the internal temperature of the food may increase. Allowance should be made for longer standing time for foods of large volume and density, such as meat roasts. Wrapping individual potatoes in foil after they have been cooked in the microwave oven and allowing them to stand for several minutes will complete the cooking process with limited danger of overcooking.

Defrosting

One benefit of a microwave oven is the ease of defrosting. Most ovens have a defrost setting with a low- to medium-power input. The oven cycles on and off, and during the off periods, the heat produced in the food is distributed or equalized throughout.

As defrosting proceeds, some attention to the product improves the outcome. Ground meat, stew meat, whole poultry, or whole fish should be turned. As soon as possible during the defrosting process, small pieces of meat, poultry, or fish should be broken apart and separated in the oven while defrosting is completed. Meat and poultry should be cooked immediately after defrosting.

Combining Microwave and Conventional Cooking

Many foods can be prepared most efficiently if they are cooked partly by microwaves and partly by conventional methods. Bread can be toasted conventionally and then combined with sandwich fillings prepared by microwaves. Cheese placed on top of a sandwich is easily melted in the microwave oven. A casserole can be cooked in the microwave oven, then a crumb topping placed on it, and the topping finished by broiling in a conventional oven. Chicken can be browned on a grill after it is cooked in a microwave oven. Sauces for pasta can be cooked in the microwave while the pasta is prepared conventionally. Because microwave energy does not increase the water-absorption rate of the starch granules in most cereal products, microwave cooking does not generally save time for such foods.

The microwave oven can increase efficiency in food preparation in other ways. For example, syrup for pancakes can be warmed by microwaving while it is in the serving pitcher. Sprinkling a few teaspoons of water over raisins, covering tightly, and microwaving 30 to 60 seconds will plump the raisins. Baking chocolate can be melted in its paper wrapper in the microwave oven, and butter or margarine is also easily melted. Brown sugar can be softened by placing an apple slice in the bag, closing tightly, and microwaving 15 seconds or until lumps soften.

Heating Meals

Factors affecting the heating in microwave ovens include, in addition to the oven itself, the packaging and the food. Because different foods have different **dielectric** (and thermal) **properties**, uneven heating may occur in meals with several different components. Temperatures near the edges of a plate or tray of food tend to be higher than in the center; the edge of the food seems to act as an antenna in the microwave field, absorbing energy. In the heating of a meal consisting of ground meat patties, sauce, mashed potato, and carrots, it was reported that the arrangement of the foods on the tray had the most pronounced effect on heating rates and final temperatures. The best heating effect was achieved when mashed potatoes were piled up along the sides of the tray. The saltiness of the food did not notably affect the heating uniformity [18].

Microwave ovens are widely used, in both homes and institutions, to reheat fully cooked, plated meals. Individual meal items should be chosen and grouped so that they are as compatible as possible in terms of heating rate and uniformity of heating. Dense meal items, including baked potatoes, mounded mashed potatoes, lasagna more than 1/2 inch thick, cabbage rolls, stuffed peppers, and thickly sliced meat or fish, heat relatively slowly. Therefore, such foods should be thinly portioned. Examples of meal items that heat more rapidly and easily are mashed potatoes with the center pressed down; thinly sliced meats, centered on the plate with gravy over them; and thinly portioned fish without sauce. Denser items should be placed toward the outside of the plate. Subdivided vegetables or loose rice and pasta may be placed in the center.

CHAPTER SUMMARY

- Microwave ovens are used most frequently in the home to boil water, heat frozen foods, defrost frozen foods, or make popcorn. Manufacturers are continuing to develop new microwavable foods that respond to consumers' desires for speed and convenience.

- Foodservices may use microwave ovens to reheat chilled or frozen foods generally for individual meals.

- The food industry uses specialized microwave equipment to temper meat, precook bacon, cook sausage, dry pasta, proof yeast breads, and more.

- Microwaves are high-frequency electromagnetic waves of radiant energy. They may be described as radio waves of very short wavelength, falling between television and infrared frequencies on the electromagnetic spectrum. Microwaves are reflected by metals and thus are contained within the oven cavity.

- Microwaves work by interacting with electrically polarized molecules in food such as water, proteins, and some carbohydrates. The polarized molecules in the food rapidly rotate, resulting in the production of heat due to friction. Microwaves penetrate one to two inches into the food, but do not cook from "the inside out," as has been suggested by some.

- The FDA has regulated the manufacture of microwave ovens since 1971. A radiation safety standard enforced by the FDA limits the amount of microwaves that can leak from an oven throughout its lifetime.

- Cooking in microwave ovens offers several advantages. Microwave cooking of foods is very fast, although varies with the quantity, density, and composition of the food. Energy usage is generally less than that required for cooking similar products conventionally. Some foods, such as vegetables, retain more nutrients when cooked in little or no liquid in a microwave oven.

- Limitations of cooking in a microwave oven include foods generally do not brown; foods that need long cooking periods at simmering temperatures to tenderize or rehydrate are not as satisfactorily prepared by microwave; heating is uneven and can pose food-safety concerns unless temperatures are carefully and appropriately monitored; burns can occur due to superheated liquids; and microwave-safe cooking utensils must be used.

- When cooking with a microwave oven, plastics, ceramic, and glass containers that are labeled as microwave safe must be used. Paper products such as white, microwave-safe paper towels are acceptable, but newspaper or brown paper bags should not be used.

- One-time-use plastic containers and foam containers or trays should not be used because they may melt or release undesirable chemicals. Some plasticizers, used in flexible packaging films, may migrate into the food during microwaving; thus, these plastics should not be in contact with foods being heated in a microwave oven.

- The use of specific cooking suggestions for browning, stirring, standing, and defrosting foods will enhance success when cooking in a microwave oven.

STUDY QUESTIONS

1. What are microwaves and how do they produce heat when they are absorbed by food?

2. Discuss several advantages and several limitations to the use of microwave equipment in home cooking, institutional foodservice, and industrial food processing.

3. What types of containers should be used to hold food during cooking in the microwave oven. Why?

4. Why should foods be stirred or turned at intervals during cooking in a microwave oven? Of what value is standing time after cooking? Explain.

5. What precautions should be taken when reheating fully cooked, plated meals in a microwave oven. Why?

6. Why are on and off cycles used for defrosting in a microwave oven?

7. Give several suggestions for using the microwave oven in combination with conventional methods of cooking.

8. What is superheated water? How can it be avoided?

SEASONINGS, FLAVORINGS, AND FOOD ADDITIVES

8

Our senses determine the pleasure of our experiences with food. We may eat to maintain life, but this becomes a difficult task without the enjoyment that comes from the blending of various sensations into what one might call a marvelous flavor bouquet. A steaming bowl of clam chowder, for example, may entice us to taste it because of its attractive appearance or perhaps because of its delicious aroma. Once we taste it, we relish its *flavor*—that complex combination of taste, aroma, and mouthfeel that is characteristic of that particular dish. We, therefore, enjoy this experience of eating and want to repeat it.

The natural flavors of many foods—fresh, ripe strawberries, for example—are enticing in themselves, but the judicious use of seasonings and flavoring materials can greatly enhance the natural flavors of many foods, either alone or combined in a recipe. Flavorful food is always the ultimate goal of the cook. Attainment of this goal requires the proper use of seasonings and flavorings.

Flavorings, including herbs and spices, represent the largest category of food additives. In addition to flavoring, food additives perform a number of desirable functions, which include improvement of nutritional value, reduction in spoilage, and enhancement of consistency.

In this chapter, the following topics will be discussed:

- Seasonings such as salt and pepper
- Flavor enhancers
- Spices and herbs
- Flavor extracts
- Vegetables, fruits, and fresh flowers as flavorings
- Alcohol
- Food additives

BASIC SEASONINGS

Seasonings, in general, are substances that enhance the flavor of a food or combination of foods. Basic seasonings—salt and pepper—are added to improve the flavor of foods without being specifically perceived or detected as themselves. They may bring out hidden flavors.

Salt

Salt is one of the oldest commodities known to man. It has played a major role in history. For example, Roman soldiers were sometimes paid in salt and our word *salary* comes from the Latin word *sal*, meaning "salt" [22]. Salt is one of the most widely used seasonings and is also found naturally in some foods. It is a crystalline substance with the chemical name sodium chloride ($NaCl$); it may be obtained from salt beds or from solar evaporation of saline waters from the oceans, and it is purified before being marketed for food use. Sometimes an anticaking agent is added to it, and it may be iodized for nutritional purposes. Several types of salt are available in the marketplace and are described in Table 8-1.

The optimal amount of salt in a dish depends on the food product being prepared and the preferences of the persons who will consume the food. For most cooked dishes, salt and other seasonings should be added in small increments, with a tasting after each addition, until the most desirable taste is achieved. Many recipes specify the amount of salt as "to taste" or "tt," which means salt is added just until the taste of salt is perceptible. In products such as soups and sauces which are likely to evaporate during cooking, salt should be added at the end of the cooking period to avoid the dish from becoming too salty as it cooks and concentrates.

Salt interacts with other flavors. Salt will enhance the sweet and sour flavors while suppressing bitter flavors. These interactions explain the preference by some of salting watermelon or cantaloupe to enhance sweetness and the salting of eggplant to reduce bitterness. In soup, the influence of salt on sweetness and bitterness has also been demonstrated [10]. Salt also affects the mouthfeel of the soup, giving the impression of increased thickness and fullness, as if the product were less watery and thin. The addition of salt produces an overall flavor balance that is

TABLE 8-1 Varieties of Salt for Use in Cooking	
Type of Salt	**Description**
Table salt	Usually produced by pumping water through underground salt deposits. The water is evaporated leaving crystals.
	Table salt may have a magnesium carbonate or another anticaking agent added to promote a free-flowing product.
	Iodized table salt has had iodine added for nutritional purposes.
Kosher salt	Purified rock salt with no iodine or magnesium carbonate.
Also called coarse or pickling salt	Has large irregular crystals and is used in the "koshering" or curing of meats.
	Some cooks may prefer Kosher salt because it dissolves more easily and will not cloud certain dishes.
Sea salt	Salt produced by evaporating sea water. Flavor is more complex due to additional minerals such as magnesium, calcium, and potassium that may be present. Color can vary depending upon region where it was produced.
Rock salt (edible and inedible)	Rock salt has been mined from underground deposits. The unpurified rock salt is used for making homemade ice cream or for de-icing a driveway or walk area. Edible rock salt, which has been purified, may be used in a salt mill.

Source: References 13, 20

more "rounded out" and "fuller." Figure 8-1 compares the flavor profile for tomato soup to which salt was added with those for soup to which dill seed or onion powder was added.

Pepper

Pepper was the first Oriental spice to arrive in Europe and today remains one of the most widely used spices in the world. The "hot spices," which include black and white pepper, red pepper, and mustard seed, represent 41 percent of U.S. spice usage [2]. Pepper is cultivated in the tropics, with 86 percent of the pepper imported into the United States coming from India, Indonesia, and Brazil [23].

Not all pepper is the same. Black and white pepper is produced from the berry of the vine *Piper nigrum*. Black pepper is made from berries picked while still green which are then fermented and sun-dried. For white pepper, the berry is picked when ripe, then the outer layer of skin is removed to reveal the white interior [13, 16, 20]. Red pepper, sometimes called cayenne red pepper, comes from plants of the genus *Capsicum*, and although hot, it is not botanically related to *Piper nigrum*, which produces the berries for black and white pepper.

Black table-ground pepper is used as a seasoning only in dark-colored foods; it spoils the appearance of light-colored foods. Light peppers, white and red, are used in both light and dark menu items. Red pepper in particular is known for its heat and pungency. Ground white pepper is good for all-around seasoning. It blends well, both in appearance and in flavor, in white dishes, and it has the necessary strength to season dark dishes. White pepper is generally perceived as milder than black pepper.

FLAVOR ENHANCERS

Flavor enhancers act somewhat differently from seasonings. A flavor enhancer does not itself bring flavor to a dish. Instead it acts to heighten the diner's perception of flavor. Examples of flavor enhancers include monosodium glutamate (MSG) and some other substances called 5'-ribonucleotides. The distinctive taste that MSG and the 5'-ribonucleotides produce, particularly in meat, fish, and poultry products, has been called *umami*. This word is derived from the Japanese word meaning "delicious" or "savory."

The umami taste appears to be distinct from the four classical tastes: sweet, sour, salty, and bitter (see Chapter 1 for more information about taste). The umami taste is associated with the amino acid glutamic acid and nucleotides found naturally in foods such as mushrooms, aged cheese, tomatoes, meats, soy sauce, and seaweed [15].

Monosodium Glutamate flavor enhancer

MSG is a crystalline material that looks something like salt. Chemically, it is the sodium salt of an amino acid called *glutamic acid*. In past years, MSG was often manufactured from wheat gluten or corn protein, but today it is usually made in a fermentation process that starts with molasses or some other carbohydrate food material.

The history of MSG as a flavor enhancer is long and interesting. Many hundreds of years ago, Oriental cooks used dried seaweed called *sea tangle* to make a stock. Dishes prepared from foods cooked in this stock had a remarkably full and rich flavor. With the 1908 discovery by a Japanese professor in Tokyo that glutamate in the seaweed was responsible for flavor enhancement, MSG

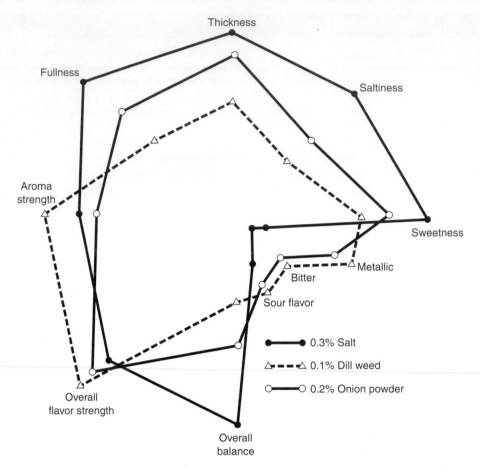

FIGURE 8-1 Aroma and flavor profiles for tomato soup with (1) 0.3 percent salt, (2) 0.1 percent dill weed, or (3) 0.2 percent onion powder. The farther away a point is placed from the center point, the more pronounced is the attribute. *(Reprinted from Gillette, M. (1985). Flavor effects of sodium chloride. Food Technology, 39(6), 47. Copyright © by Institute of Food Technologists)*

HEALTHY EATING

A Pinch of Salt?

The U.S. Department of Health and Human Services and the U.S. Department of Agriculture provide dietary guidance on salt intake in the Dietary Guidelines. Consumption of less than 2,300 milligrams of sodium (one teaspoon) per day may reduce the risk of high blood pressure [33]. However, because more than half of the salt consumed by Americans comes from commercially processed foods, advice on choosing these convenience foods in addition to low-salt preparation of foods is needed [14].

The use of other seasonings including herbs and spices has been suggested as one strategy to reduce salt consumption. Umami-rich ingredients have also been found to increase the perception of saltiness and are therefore another means to reduce the amount of salt used [15]. ■

FOCUS ON SCIENCE

Salt and Pickling

Adding salt to pickling brine is one important way to help lactic acid bacteria win the microbial race. At a certain salt concentration (as low as 5 percent NaCl) and a pH = 4, lactic acid bacteria have a competitive advantage and grow more quickly than other microbes. Below this "right" concentration, bad bacteria may survive and spread more easily, possibly out-competing lactic acid bacteria and spoiling the pickles. If too much salt is added, lactic acid bacteria will not thrive, the vegetables will not be pickled, and salt-tolerant yeasts will be able to thrive. These salt-tolerant yeasts consume the lactic acid, thereby making the pickles less acidic—and more hospitable to spoilage.

Pickles also may be brined in bulk with a controlled fermentation of cucumbers, producing a uniform product in a shorter time period. The controlled fermentation method employs a chlorinated brine of 25° salinometer, acidification with acetic acid, the addition of sodium acetate and inoculation with *P. cerevisiae* and *L. plantarum* or the latter alone with a 10 to 12 day fermentation required.

Source: Jay, J. M. (1986). Chapter 16. Fermented foods and related products of fermentation. In *Modern Food Microbiology*, 3rd ed., p. 382. New York: Van Nostrand Reinhold Co.

---

was formulated in Japan the following year [11]. In 1917, MSG was introduced into the United States [15].

MSG is generally considered to be a flavor enhancer or intensifier, bringing out the flavors of other foods. At the levels ordinarily used in cooking, MSG does not have a taste of its own; however, when used in sufficiently large amounts, it may add its own flavor. It has the greatest flavor effect in low-acid foods such as vegetables, meats, poultry, and fish. It does not improve the taste of high-acid foods, including fruits and fruit juices; neither does it enhance the flavor of milk products or sweet doughs. Approximately 1/2 teaspoon for each pound of meat or four to six servings of vegetables is generally recommended for use.

5'-Ribonucleotides

A group of compounds called 5'-ribonucleotides are present naturally in some foods, such as beef, chicken, fish, and mushrooms. They may act as flavor enhancers and, in combination with MSG, create the umami taste. Their action with MSG has been called synergistic. Synergism refers to cooperative action among two or more substances so that the total effect of the mixture is greater than the sum of the individual effects. Even a very small amount of the ribonucleotides increases the flavor-enhancing properties of MSG [11].

In crystalline form, the ribonucleotides are available to the food processor for use in flavoring various snack foods and other dishes. Commercially they are usually prepared from yeast extracts or yeast autolysates. These flavor enhancers are widely used in Japan, and various combinations of the ribonucleotides, such as a 50:50 ratio of disodium 5'-inosinate to disodium 5'-guanylate, have been marketed by Japanese companies for several years. The inosinate and guanylate compounds appear to have the strongest flavor effects of all the ribonucleotides. It is claimed that they unlock natural taste characteristics and suppress harsh flavor [22].

What Makes Pepper Hot?

Although we commonly think of heat in reference to our sensory reaction to peppers, the effect is really not thermal but rather a chemically induced irritation that stimulates the endings of the trigeminal nerve—quite different from the sense of taste or the sense of touch. The chemical responsible for this stimulation in black pepper is called *piperine*, and the active agent in red pepper is *capsaicin*. The chemical composition of capsaicin ($C_{18}H_{27}O_3N$) is similar to piperine ($C_{17}H_{19}O_3N$) [5]. However, capsaicin is about 100 times more potent than piperine. ■

Monosodium Glutamate (MSG)

Controversy exists over the safety of the widespread use of MSG in foods. Extensive study of its effects on a variety of animal species, however, has led to the conclusion that, in the amounts commonly used, it presents no public health hazard [9, 11, 19]. A comprehensive report was prepared for the FDA by the Life Sciences Research Office of the Federation of American Societies for Experimental Biology (FASEB) in 1995. It concluded that MSG is safe for the general population at levels normally consumed [19]. Some persons, however, may respond to large doses (3 grams or more) of MSG with temporary adverse reactions; some persons with asthma are sensitive to amounts of 1.5 to 2.5 grams of gluta-

mate consumed without food. These sensitivities are called *MSG symptom complex.*

The FDA requires that MSG be listed as an ingredient when it is added to foods. Consideration is also being given to requiring label declaration of the free glutamate content of foods that contain significant amounts of this substance. This requirement would allow consumers to make informed decisions in choosing to eat certain foods. Although MSG is commonly used in many manufactured foods, processed foods marketed primarily for babies and small children do not include this flavor substance as an ingredient. ■

SPICES AND HERBS

History

Used since antiquity, spices have always been treasured for their ability to flavor foods, but they were valued also for many nonfood purposes—as ingredients of incense, perfumes, cosmetics, embalming preservatives, and medicines. In early history, spices were used not only to improve the bland qualities of many foods, but also to help preserve food [25]. Spices became valuable commodities imported from India, China, and Southeast Asia, with the Arabians controlling the spice trade for many years.

The desire for and quest for tropical spices was instrumental in provoking trade wars and in encouraging exploration. Marco Polo went to the Far East in search of spices and precious stones, and Columbus was searching for a new trade route when he discovered America. Spices were so important, costly, and scarce—even being accepted as currency in the late thirteenth century—that wars were fought over them. The United States is now the world's largest importer of spices and herbs, which come mainly from the Orient, the Mediterranean area, India, and Central and South America. The spice market in the United States is growing as consumers demand more seasoning in their foods [8, 23].

Classification

The term *spice* is used to describe a wide variety of dried, aromatic vegetable products that are used in building the flavors of prepared foods. The American Spice Trade Association describes spice as "any dried plant used primarily for seasoning purposes" [3]. This definition includes tropical

aromatics (pepper, cinnamon, and cloves), leafy herbs (basil and oregano), spice seeds (sesame, poppy, and mustard), dehydrated vegetables (onions and garlic), and spice blends. The FDA does not include dehydrated vegetables and also requires spices such as paprika or turmeric to be labeled as spice coloring.

Spice. In common usage, many define spice more narrowly by only referring to those parts of aromatic plants, such as bark, roots, buds, flowers, fruits, and seeds, that are grown in the tropics [13, 20]. Using this definition, allspice, anise, cardamom, cayenne pepper, cinnamon, cloves, cumin, ginger, mace, nutmeg, paprika, and turmeric are all spices. Some spices are sweet, some are spicy sweet, and some are "hot."

Spices are available as whole or ground. Ground spices allow for more uniform distribution and more rapid release of flavor than whole spices and thus are often added near the end of cooking, as opposed to whole spices that are introduced earlier. Spice extractives also are available to food processors. Spice extractives are produced by grinding or crushing the spices, then extracting the spice with steam distillation, solvent extraction, or other processing methods [25].

Herb. The term *herb* usually refers to leaves and stems of soft-stemmed plants that grow in temperate climates; however, some woody-stemmed plants also produce culinary herbs, such as sage. Bay leaves come from an evergreen tree—the laurel [13]. Other herbs include basil, marjoram, mint, oregano, rosemary, savory, tarragon, and thyme.

Quality

Spices come from every part of the world. They are grown and harvested on many small farms; some are even found growing wild. Quality is therefore difficult to control. Cleanliness, insect and rodent infestation, and microbiological quality are important concerns.

Spices imported into the United States must meet American Spice Trade Association (ASTA) specifications and standards established by FDA and the USDA [25]. The ASTA quality specifications control for cleanliness, impurities, adulteration, moisture content, microbial growth, pesticide levels, micotoxin/aflatoxin levels, and particle size. Treatment with ethylene oxide, methyl bromide, irradiation, and heat have been used to reduce microbial contamination. Ethylene oxide has been banned in some European countries but is still approved by the U.S. EPA. Methyl bromide was phased out by the EPA in 2005 [25].

FLAVOR EXTRACTS

Extracts and essential oils from aromatic plants, dissolved in alcohol, are often used to flavor baked products, puddings, sauces, and confections. These include extracts of vanilla [20, 26], lemon, orange, and almond, and oils such as peppermint and wintergreen. Only small amounts of these flavorful materials are required, but they add their own distinctive flavors to the final products. The extraction solvent is often alcohol and, thus, very volatile. Consequently, the flavorings should be stored in tightly closed containers and kept in a cool place. In puddings and other products cooked on surface units, the flavorings should be added at the end of the cooking period. In baked products, they should be added to the fat during preparation to reduce volatilization.

Some flavoring materials are added to processed foods in encapsulated forms [21]. Flavors are encapsulated for a number of reasons: The process helps to retain flavor in food products during storage, protects the flavor from undesirable interactions with the food, minimizes oxidation, and allows the controlled release of flavors.

VEGETABLES, FRUITS, AND FLOWERS AS FLAVORINGS

We season and flavor foods not only with basic seasonings, herbs, and spices, but also by the ingredients we choose to include. Onions, garlic, tomatoes, mushrooms, peppers, and many other vegetables have pronounced flavors that influence the final taste of the product [20]. Many soup and sauce recipes use a *mirepoix* to flavor the dish. A standard mirepoix is a mixture of diced vegetables including 50 percent onions, 25 percent carrots, and 25 percent celery [13].

Hot Peppers

"Hot" peppers originated in the New World and were taken back to Europe by Christopher Columbus. Hot peppers, commonly called chilies (or chiles), are basic to many cuisines of the world and are increasing in popularity in the United States (Plate II). The worldwide capsicum crop exceeds 7.7 billion pounds annually and represents a greater tonnage than pepper [22]. In the United States, ethnic trends, including an interest in Caribbean, Mexican, and South American dishes, is promoting the consumption of "hotter" dishes. Worldwide,

FOCUS ON SCIENCE

Essential Oils and Vanilla Extract

Essential Oils

Essential oils found in the skin of citrus fruit (orange and lemon) contribute flavor and aroma thought to hold the essence of the plant. The flavor and aroma of spices are made by oil deposits in seeds (cumin), pods or fruits (nutmeg), bark (cinnamon), and even stems (sassafras). Essential plant oils, whether from orange zest or coriander seeds, are highly volatile—that is, they evaporate quickly when exposed to air.

Vanilla Extract

Vanilla is a plant (an orchid), and the beans are its pods. There are two varieties of vanilla used commerically: Bourbon that is from Madagascar and popular in the U.S. and Tahitian that is popular in Europe. The growing, location, and processing method greatly determine the final flavor. Much like coffee and chocolate, the beans are picked and dried or "cured" in order to develop flavor and aroma. In the United States, real vanilla extract must contain 35 percent ethyl alcohol and 13.35 ounces vanilla beans per gallon. Double-strength extracts (twofold vanilla) contain the same amount of alcohol, but twice the beans. Artificial vanilla is a combination of chemicals, vanillin, and other ingredients to replace the flavor and aroma of vanilla. Vanilla flavoring is a combination of imitation and pure extracts.

Source: Brown, A. (2004). Chapter 1. The parts department. In *I'm Just Here for More Food*, p. 78. New York: Stewart, Tabori, and Chang.

the cuisines of India, Asia, Africa, and many other countries utilize the hot flavors of capsicums in their dishes to convey distinctive flavors.

Chilies are from the capsicum genus that encompasses over 300 varieties of plants varying in hotness, color, and flavor [5, 23]. Some of the commonly used peppers include the *sweet green pepper, habañero* or *scotch bonnet, jalapeño, chipotle, poblano, ancho, anaheim,* and *paprika.* Sweet green peppers unlike many other chilies are not hot, but are nevertheless flavorful. The habañero or scotch bonnet is generally considered to be the hottest chili in the world at 100,000 to 300,000 Scoville Heat Units. Jalapeños are hot to medium-hot and are used in many Mexican dishes. The chipotle is a smoke-dried jalapeño with a deep smoky flavor. The ancho chili is a dried poblano chili; both types are mild to medium-hot. Paprika is the powder of a mild sweet chili and is frequently valued in cooking for the rich, red color it adds to a dish [18].

Even when handling chili peppers, "burning" of the hands can occur if latex gloves are not used. Likewise, care should be taken to avoid touching the face or eyes when working with chili peppers.

Fruits

Fruits also are used in some dishes for the distinctive flavor they can provide. Citrus fruits in particular are aromatic and flavorful. Lemons, limes, and oranges contribute to the flavor of many dishes including baked products, entrees, vegetables, or sweet desserts.

Edible Flowers

Edible flowers add flavor as well as beauty to foods. Nasturtium blossoms have a peppery taste and thus are very good in dishes such as salads where the flavor will be complementary (Figure 8-4). Roses, in particular, are sweet and therefore very pleasing with desserts.

Some suggestions for using flowers include nasturtium blossoms stuffed with crab meat, with each blossom affixed to a small cracker with a tiny amount of cream cheese mixture. The top of an iced white cake can be sprinkled with coconut and calendula petals before the icing has set. Edible flowers, such as roses, violets, and others, can be sugared by dipping them in gum Arabic (edible gum), then dusting them in granulated sugar, and placing them on waxed paper to dry [20]. Slightly beaten eggs whites may be used in place of the edible gum; however, if egg whites are used, it is best to use reconstituted powdered egg whites because they have been pasteurized. Sugared flowers can be used to garnish rose petal sorbet or other desserts.

In selecting flowers, be sure that they have been grown to be eaten and have not been subjected to various insecticide sprays. Also, you should be aware that all flowers are not edible. Some, like lily of the valley and daffodils, are poisonous. Rose petals, nasturtiums, Johnny-jump-ups, and pinks are good for eating.

ALCOHOL

Wines, liqueurs, and distilled spirits can be used in preparing main dishes, sauces, and desserts, creating new and interesting flavors. It has generally been assumed that, because of its low boiling point, the alcohol is evaporated from the foods during cooking; however, a study of six alcohol-containing recipes found that from 4 to 85 percent of the alcohol was retained in the food [4]. For a pot roast that was heated over two hours, the retention was 4 to 6 percent. For a sauce to which Grand Marnier was added when the sauce was boiling, the alcohol retention was 83 to 85 percent. Flamed cherries jubilee retained 77 to 78 percent of the alcohol. The presence of alcohol in significant amounts affects the energy value of a food because alcohol contributes approximately 7 kilocalories per gram.

Calendulas

Pansies

Nasturtiums

FIGURE 8-4 Calendulas, pansies, and nasturtiums are just a few of the edible flower varieties that can be used to liven up any salad or dish.

FOOD ADDITIVES

A number of additives are used in foods, each with a specific purpose. Many of the additives in foods are very familiar and include salt, vanilla, pepper, baking soda, and spices [12]. Food additives may be used in foods to do the following:

- Maintain or improve safety and freshness
- Improve or maintain nutritional value
- Improve taste, texture, and appearance

Additives cannot be placed in food to conceal damage or spoilage or to deceive the consumer. The FDA regulates the use of additives in foods and maintains a list of additives called "Everything Added to Food in the United States" [32]. Some additives, such as salt, are on the "generally recognized as safe" (GRAS) list and are not subject to the same regulatory process as other ingredients. More information about the regulation of food additives may be found in Chapter 4.

There are many different, specific functions of food additives, but most may be grouped into classes based on similar function. Some of the more important classes or types of additives follow. Examples of each class are given in Table 8-4.

TABLE 8-4 Some Additives and Food Ingredients in Use for Various Types of Foods

Type or Class	Purpose	Examples	Food in Which Used
Nutrients	Replace vitamins and minerals lost in processing (enrichment) or add nutrients lacking in diet (fortification)	Thiamine, riboflavin, niacin, folate or folic acid, beta carotene, iron or ferrous sulfate, ascorbic acid, Vitamin D, alpha tocopherols	Flour, breads, and cereals in enrichment process. Fruit juices, fruit drinks, dehydrated potatoes, and margarine.
Preservatives (includes antimicrobials and antioxidants)	Prevent food spoilage from bacteria, molds, fungi, or yeast; slow or prevent changes in color, flavor, or texture; delay rancidity; maintain freshness	Ascorbic acid (Vitamin C), citric acid, sodium benzoate, calcium propionate, sodium erythorbate, sodium nitrate, calcium sorbate, potassium sorbate, butylated hydroxyanisole (BHA), butylated hydroxytoluene (BHT), tocopherols (Vitamin E)	May be used in a variety of foods. Antioxidants often found in foods containing fats to prevent rancidity. Browning of fruits is prevented by ascorbic and citric acid. Propionates retard molding and development of "rope" in bread. Benzoates provide antimicrobial function in carbonated beverages and fruit drinks.
Coloring agents	Offset color loss, correct natural variations in color, provide color to colorless foods	FD&C Blue #1 and #2, FD&C Green #3, FD&C Red #3 and #40, FD&C #5 (tartrazine), and #6, Orange B, Citrus Red #2, beta-carotene, grape skin extract, and paprika oleoresin	Found in many processed foods.
Flavors and spices	Add a specific flavor, which may be natural or synthetic	Natural flavoring, artificial flavor, spices	Found in a wide variety of foods.
Flavor enhancers	Enhance flavors already in foods without providing a separate flavor	Monosodium glutamate (MSG), hydrolyzed soy protein, autolyzed yeast extract, disodium guanylate, or inosinate	Many processed foods.
Emulsifiers	Prevent separation, keep emulsified products stable, allow smooth mixing of ingredients, and control crystallization	Soy lecithin, mono- and diglycerides, egg yolks polysorbates, sobitan monostearate	Margarines and shortenings, salad dressings, peanut butter, frozen desserts, chocolate.
Stabilizers and thickeners	Produce uniform texture, improve "mouthfeel"	Gelatin, pectin, guar gum, carrageenan, xanthan gum, whey	Frozen desserts, dairy products, cakes, pudding, jams, jellies, sauces.
Sequestrants	Bind small amounts of metals which may be undesirable	Ethylenediamine tetraacetic acid (EDTA)	Wine and cider.
Humectants	Retain moisture	Glycerine, sorbitol	Marshmallows, flaked coconut, and cake icings.
Anticaking agents	Prevent moisture absorption; keep powdered foods free-flowing	Calcium silicate, iron ammonium citrate, silicon dioxide	Table salt, powdered sugar, and baking powder.
Bleaching and maturing agents	Improves baking properties of wheat flours	Chlorine, chlorine dioxide, benzoyl peroxide	Cake flour and all-purpose flour.

TABLE 8-4   (Continued)

Type or Class	Purpose	Examples	Food in Which Used
Leavening agents	Promote rising of baked goods	Baking soda, monocalcium phosphate, calcium carbonate	Breads and other baked goods.
Acids, alkalies, and buffers	Adjust and control pH	Citric acid and its salts, acetic acid, sodium bicarbonate, sodium hydroxide	Soft drinks, processed cheese, baking powders, Dutch processed cocoa.
Sweeteners	Add sweetness with or without added calories	Sucrose (sugar), glucose, fructose, sorbitol, mannitol, corn syrup, high fructose corn syrup, saccharin, aspartame, sucralose, acesulfame potassium (acesulfame-K), neotame	Beverages, baked goods, sweetener substitutes, many processed foods.
Fat replacers	Provide texture and creamy "mouth feel" in reduced-fat foods	Olestra (sucrose polyester), cellulose gel, carrageenan, polydextrose, modified food starch, microparticulated protein (as Simplesse®), guar guam, xanthan gum, whey protein concentrate	Baked goods, dressings, frozen desserts, confections, cake and dessert mixes, dairy products.
Bulking agents	Adds texture and body	Polydextrose	Baked goods, confections, puddings, and other foods.
Gases	Serve as propellant or create carbonation	Carbon dioxide, nitrous oxide	Oil cooking spray, whipped cream, carbonated beverages.

Source: Reference 12

Nutrient Supplements

Vitamins and minerals are often added to processed foods either to restore or to improve their nutritive value. Examples include the enrichment of bread and cereals, the addition of iodine to salt, and the fortification of milk with vitamin D. Some vitamins—for example, vitamins C and E—also play functional roles, such as acting as antioxidants.

Preservatives

Antioxidants are a group of preservatives. Fatty foods are particularly susceptible to spoilage as rancidity develops with unpleasant off-odors. Some antioxidants retard the development of rancidity. Another type of antioxidant may prevent enzymatic oxidative browning in fresh fruits and vegetables. Vitamin C is an effective antioxidant in this regard.

Antimicrobial agents are another group of preservatives. These additives prevent or inhibit spoilage caused by such microorganisms as molds and bacteria. The effectiveness of such preservation methods as refrigeration may be enhanced by the judicious use of certain antimicrobial agents.

Coloring Agents

Proper use of color makes foods more visually appealing and corrects natural variations and irregularities. Artificial colors must be certified to meet specifications set by the FDA on a batch-by-batch basis. Some natural pigments, such as carotenoids, are available for use in foods, although they are generally less stable than artificial colors.

Flavoring Materials

A wide variety of substances are used to improve the flavor of processed foods. These include natural extractives and essential oils as well as synthetic or artificial flavorings. Flavor enhancers are also used. Flavorings, which include herbs and spices, comprise the largest group of intentional additives.

Emulsifiers

Emulsifiers are widely used to mix two immiscible liquids, such as fat and water, uniformly together in the making and stabilizing of emulsions. They are also used to stabilize foams and suspensions. Emulsions are discussed further in Chapter 10.

Stabilizers and Thickeners

Texture and body are important characteristics of many foods. A variety of stabilizers and thickeners are used to achieve desired smoothness and consistency, including many vegetable gums, such as carrageenan, and a number of starch products.

Sequestrants

Sequestrants are used to bind (chelate) small amounts of metals, such as iron and copper, that may have undesirable effects on flavor or appearance.

Humectants and Anticaking Agents

Humectants are used to retain moisture and keep certain foods soft. Some humectants are added to finely powdered or crystalline foods to prevent caking as moisture is absorbed.

Bleaching and Maturing Agents

The baking properties of wheat flours are improved by the addition of certain oxidizing agents (maturing agents). Many of these also have a bleaching effect.

Acids, Alkalis, and Buffers

Acidity or alkalinity is very important in many processed foods. Acids, alkalis, and buffers are used to adjust and control the pH. Buffers will resist changes in acidity and alkalinity and thus help to stabilize the pH. The alkaline salt—sodium bicarbonate or baking soda—is also used to produce carbon dioxide gas to leaven baked products.

Alternative Sweeteners

A sweet tooth has apparently always been part of the human anatomy. The harvesting of honey and sugar cane has a long history. Substitutes for the taste of caloric sweeteners, including sucrose (table sugar), honey, and corn syrups, have been developed, however, only in the past century. A number of alternative sweeteners have been approved by the FDA for use in food and are discussed in Chapter 11.

Fat Replacers

Professional groups and public health agencies currently stress the important relationship between high fat intake and the risks of developing coronary heart disease and some cancers. This has generated much interest in lowfat substitutes for many traditional high-fat food products. The food industry is thus motivated to develop substances that can replace fat but leave flavor and texture unchanged or minimally changed. Some of the approved fat replacers are GRAS (generally regarded as safe), whereas others require special approval by the FDA as food additives.

Carbohydrate-based fat replacers include cellulose, various gums such as xanthan gum and carrageenan, dextrins, and modified starches. Microparticulated protein, whose trade name is Simplesse®, is a protein-based fat replacer produced from whey protein or milk and egg protein. Some emulsifiers can also replace part of the fat in a food product [7].

Sucrose polyesters (olestra) are nonabsorbable and thus noncaloric fat replacers. They may be used in cooking oils and shortenings, commercial frying, and snack foods [7]. Olestra was approved by the FDA in 1996 for use in snacks and originally was required to include a statement on the label indicating it may affect gastrointestinal function in some people. In 2003, the FDA concluded the label statement was no longer warranted [31].

Bulking Agents

Polydextrose contains only one calorie per gram and helps to add texture and body when fat and sugar are reduced in some food products. Some of the modified starches also add body and texture to lowfat products. When used to provide texture and body in reduced-fat or reduced-sugar food products, these substances are called *bulking agents*.

CHAPTER SUMMARY

- The natural flavors of many foods are enticing in themselves, but the judicious use of seasonings and flavoring materials can greatly enhance the natural flavors of foods.

- Seasonings, in general, are substances that enhance the flavor of the food or combination of foods without being specifically perceived or detected.

- Salt is a crystalline substance with the chemical name sodium chloride (NaCl). There are many varieties of salt that may be used in cooking. Salt is also found naturally in some foods.

- Black pepper and white pepper are produced from the berry of a climbing vine. White pepper is most appropriate for dishes in which black pepper would be unattractive.

- Flavor enhancers act differently by heightening the perception of flavors. Examples of flavor enhancers include monosodium glutamate (MSG) and some other substances called 5′-ribonucleotides.

- Spice may be defined broadly to include herbs or may be defined more specifically as parts of aromatic plants, such as bark, roots, buds, flowers, fruits, and seeds. Herbs may be described as the leaves and stems of soft-stemmed plants. When substituting fresh herbs for dried herbs in a recipe, approximately twice the amount of fresh herbs should be used. Spices, herbs, and seasoning blends should be stored in a cool, dry, and dark place in airtight containers to extend storage life.

- Flavorings are substances added for their own distinctive flavors, such as extracts of lemon. Flavor extracts and essential oils from aromatic plants, dissolved in alcohol, are often used to flavor baked products, puddings, sauces, and confections.

- Ingredients such as onions, garlic, tomatoes, mushrooms, and fruits also flavor foods. Wines, liqueurs, and distilled spirits can be used in preparing main dishes, sauces, and desserts, creating new and interesting flavors.

- "Hot" peppers are botanically different from black and white pepper. "Hot" peppers, commonly called chilies, are from plants of the genus *Capsicum*. There are many varieties of "hot" peppers that differ in hotness, color, and flavor.

- Edible flowers may be used for flavor and color in many dishes. Not all flowers are edible; therefore when using flowers, be sure that the flower is an edible variety and that it has not been contaminated with insecticide sprays.

- Additives may be used in foods for a variety of useful purposes. Additives may be used as nutrient supplements; preservatives; antimicrobial agents; coloring agents; flavoring materials; emulsifiers; stabilizers and thickeners; humectants and anticaking agents; bleaching and maturing agents; acids, alkalis, and buffers; alternative sweeteners; fat replacers; and bulking agents.

STUDY QUESTIONS

1. Distinguish among seasonings, flavorings, and flavor builders.

2. Describe the basic effects or roles of salt and pepper when properly used in cooking.

3. What is a flavor enhancer? Give examples.

4. What is MSG? How was it discovered? With which types of food is it most effectively used?

5. What is meant by the *umami* taste? Discuss.

6. In a strict classification, what are *spices*, and what are *herbs?*

    (a) Give examples of each.

    (b) Describe their basic roles in cooking.

    (c) Give suggestions for proper storage.

    (d) Suggest uses for fresh herbs.

7. Identify and discuss ingredients other than spices, herbs, and basic seasonings that add flavor in recipes.

8. List at least 10 different types or groups of food additives and give examples of specific additives for each group.

FOOD COMPOSITION 9

Foods contain different chemical molecules that are put together in a variety of ways. It is obvious, simply by looking, that some food products are not homogeneous. From casual observation of a sliced tomato, for example, you may note skin, seeds, and soft tissues, each with a different structural appearance. Even foods that appear to be homogeneous, such as cheddar cheese, are composed of an ultrastructure that may be seen by examining a sample of the food under a microscope. Even with the aid of the finest microscope, however, some molecules and structures still cannot be seen. Foods are very complex materials.

Determination of the amount of each chemical component in a food, called its *chemical composition*, may be made in the laboratory. Water, carbohydrates, fats, and proteins are the chemical substances found in largest amounts in foods. Enzymes are special types of proteins found in small amounts in unprocessed plant and animal tissues. Minerals, vitamins, acids, and many flavor substances, and pigments that give color, are also present in foods in minute amounts.

Comprehensive tables of food composition have been produced by compiling the results of numerous analyses of food samples done in laboratories. The Agricultural Research Service (ARS) in the U.S. Department of Agriculture (USDA) provides a database that reports nutrients in over 6,000 foods. This database, called the *USDA National Nutrient Database for Standard Reference, Release 20 (SR20)*, is available on CD-ROM or from the USDA website [17].

In addition to knowing the quantity of each chemical component present in foods, we need some knowledge of the characteristics and properties of the major constituents. Changes may occur in these components as a food is processed and prepared. For example, water is removed in large quantities from fruits, vegetables, and meats when they are dehydrated. Fat melts and is found in the drippings when meat is roasted. Oil and water or vinegar separate from each other when the emulsion in mayonnaise is broken. Addition of fresh pineapple to a gelatin mixture prevents setting of the gelatin, because the gelatin, which is a protein, is broken down into peptides or amino acids by an enzyme in the pineapple.

For those who have not previously studied chemistry, the information presented will be helpful in understanding the nature of foods as discussed in other chapters of this text. In this chapter, the following chemical characteristics of the major components of foods will be discussed:

- Water
- Carbohydrates
- Lipids
- Proteins
- Solutions and dispersions

WATER

Water in Foods

All foods, even those that appear to be quite dry, contain at least some water. Amounts present range from as low as 1 or 2 percent to as high as 98 percent, although most foods contain intermediate amounts. Table 9-1 gives the water content of selected foods. Examples of foods that are high in water are raw vegetables and juicy fruits. Fresh greens contain about 96 percent water, and watermelon has about 93 percent. Crackers, an example of a low-moisture food, usually contain only 2 to 4 percent water.

Free Water.   Much of the water in plant and animal tissues is held inside the cells (intracellular). In many cases, it is held within the cells as a hydrate, which means that it does not flow from the cells when the tissues are cut or torn. For example, by visual observation, lean broiled beefsteak does not appear to contain about 60 percent water, and a sliced stalk of celery does not appear to be

TABLE 9-1 Water Content of Selected Foods	
Food	**Water Content %**
Lettuce, iceberg, raw	96
Celery, raw	95
Broccoli, cooked	90
Carrots, raw	88
Milk, whole	88
Orange juice	88
Oatmeal, cooked	85
Apples, raw	84
Creamed cottage cheese	79
Eggs, raw, whole	75
Bananas	74
Chicken breast, cooked	65
Ice cream	61
Beef roast, lean, cooked	57
Pork, ham, cooked	53
Pizza, cheese, baked	46
Potatoes, french-fried	38
Cheddar cheese	37
Bread, whole wheat	38
Bread, white	37
Cake, white layer	24
Butter	16
Raisins	15
Brownies	10
Cookies, chocolate chip	4
Popcorn, popped, plain	4
Cornflakes	3
Peanuts, roasted in oil	2

Source: Reference 11

94 percent water. The ability of a food to hold water in this way is called its *water-holding capacity*. Although much of the water in plant and animal tissues is held as a hydrate, it is still available. That is, it may be removed by pressure, and it retains the properties of pure water—it can be frozen or act as a **solvent** to dissolve other molecules. It may be called *free water.*

Bound Water.   Some of the water in foods, however, is held in an extremely tightly bound form called **bound water.** Bound water actually becomes part of the structure of large molecules such as proteins and **complex carbohydrates,** has reduced mobility, and does not have the same properties as free water—it does not readily freeze or boil and cannot easily be pressed from the tissue. Some water is bound by the interaction with **ions** and small molecules.

Water Activity.   The more water that is bound in a food, the less the activity of the water. Water activity (a_w) is defined as the ratio of the **vapor pressure** of water in a food (p) at a specified temperature to the vapor pressure of pure water (p_o) at the same temperature, that is, p/p_o. The presence of **nonvolatile** substances in a food, such as sugars and salts, lowers the vapor pressure of the water present. Therefore, the water activity value of a food will be less than 1.0.

The perishability of a food is related to its water content, the food being generally more perishable with higher water content. This relationship occurs because microorganisms require water for their growth. However, an even closer relationship exists between the water activity and perishability. Water activity can be reduced by drying a food. In this case, some water is removed by vaporization, thus causing the substances that are dissolved in the water remaining in the food to become more concentrated and the vapor pressure, therefore, to be lowered. Water activity can also be reduced by freezing, because water is removed from the system when it forms ice. The addition of sugar or salt lowers the water activity of a food because some water is bound by these substances; that water is then unavailable for use by microorganisms. Intermediate-moisture foods normally have water activity between 0.7 and 0.9 and are not susceptible to microbial growth, although they are soft enough to eat without rehydration. Fresh meats, fruits, and vegetables have usual water activity values of 0.95 to 0.99 and are very susceptible to spoilage.

Uses of Water in Food Preparation

Water plays several important roles in food preparation, affecting both the sensory characteristics of food [10] and the processes by which heat is transferred and foods are cooked.

Universal Solvent.   Water has been called a *universal solvent,* indicating that it can dissolve many different substances. It acts as a solvent or a dispersing medium for most of the chemical substances in foods. For example, many of the flavor molecules in beverages such as coffee and tea are dissolved in water; sugars are dissolved in fruit juices and in syrups; and starch granules may first be dispersed in cold water and then, as they are heated, absorb large amounts of water to produce a thickened mixture, as a pudding or sauce. A negative aspect of water when it is used in cooking is that it may leach out and dissolve some important nutrients, particularly vitamins and minerals, found in vegetables. If the cooking water is not consumed, some major nutrient losses occur.

Heat Transfer.   In cooking, water is an important medium for applying heat. It may be used for this purpose both in its liquid form as hot or boiling water and in its vapor form as steam. When water boils, the forces of attraction between water molecules are overcome, and the water molecules become gaseous. They leave the container in bubbles of steam. At sea level, the temperature of boiling water is 212°F (100°C). Making water boil rapidly does not increase this temperature. Steam that is not under pressure has the same temperature as boiling water. However, a certain amount of energy, called **latent heat** or *heat of vaporization*, is necessary to change the state of water from its liquid form to its vapor form as steam. This heat is absorbed by the steam but does not register on a thermometer. When steam condenses on a cooler surface and returns to its liquid form, the latent heat is released and helps to cook the food. For example, steamed vegetables are cooked both by the heat of the steam itself and also by the release of latent energy from the steam as it condenses on the surface of the vegetables and changes back to its liquid water form. Heat transfer was discussed further in Chapter 6.

Freezing. Water is involved in the preparation of freezing mixtures that may be used to freeze ice creams and other frozen desserts, particularly those made at home. When crushed ice (water in its solid form) is mixed with salt, the salt dissolving on the surface of the ice increases the melting rate. As ice changes from its solid form to liquid (water), heat is absorbed. This energy is called *latent heat of fusion*. The same amount of heat is given off when water freezes to ice. Water freezes at 32°F (0°C).

Cleansing Agent. Water also performs an important function as a cleansing agent both for food itself and for utensils and equipment used in the preparation and serving of food. It removes soil particles and many microorganisms as well. Cleaning agents, such as soaps and detergents, increase the cleaning capacity of water.

Chemical Changes. Water promotes chemical changes in certain cases. Some mineral salts become ionized in solution—they break apart, and each part develops either a positive (+) or a negative (–) charge. For example, common table salt is known chemically as sodium chloride or NaCl. When this salt is placed in water, it dissolves and ionizes as follows:

$$NaCl \rightarrow Na^+ \, Cl^-$$

Ionization of salt in water increases the temperature at which water boils; however, the effect is minimal with the amount of salt typically used.

Ionization causes other chemical reactions to occur. As long as baking powder remains dry, for example, no chemical reactions take place; however, when it dissolves in water, some of the chemicals that it contains ionize and then react with each other to produce new chemical substances. Among these products is carbon dioxide (CO_2) gas, which rises in tiny bubbles and makes a baked product light or leavened.

Water also affects the reactions of acids and bases (or alkalies). The chemical phenomenon that characterizes an acid substance is the ionization of a hydrogen atom, producing a positively charged hydrogen ion (H^+). This hydrogen ion, among other things, stimulates our taste buds to give us the impression of sourness. The ion that is characteristic of bases or alkalies is a negatively charged hydroxyl ion (OH^-).

Water and pH. The degree of acidity or alkalinity affects the characteristics of many foods and food mixtures during preparation. The color of fruit juices and of vegetables during cooking, and the color of chocolate in baked products, is affected by the acidity. To simplify the quantification of degrees of acidity, the pH scale was developed. This scale runs from 1 as the most acidic to 14 as the most alkaline. A pH of 7, in the middle, indicates an essentially neutral solution (neither acidic nor basic).

Pure water that has an equal number of hydrogen (H^+) and hydroxyl (OH^-) ions has a pH of 7. Tap water, however, usually has small amounts of other ions that affect its acidity or alkalinity, thus changing the pH from 7. For example, the harder the tap water, the more calcium and magnesium ions it contains. The presence of these ions increases the alkalinity of hard water, so its pH is above 7. This alkaline or basic pH will affect the color of some vegetables cooked in the water. The pH values of selected foods are given in Table 9-2.

TABLE 9-2 pH of Selected Foods	
Food	**pH**
Limes	2.0
Lemons	2.2
Vinegar	2.9
Strawberries	3.4
Pears	3.9
Tomatoes	4.2
Buttermilk	4.5
Bananas	4.6
Carrots	5.0
Bread	5.4
Meat, ripened	5.8
Tuna	6.0
Potatoes	6.1
Corn	6.3
Egg yolk	6.4
Milk	6.6
Egg white	7.0–9.0

Source: Reference 2

Hydrolysis. Water has an active part in a special type of chemical reaction called *hydrolysis*, which refers to the breaking of a linkage between units of a larger or more complex molecule to yield smaller molecules. If a complex molecule is completely hydrolyzed, all of the linkages between the small building blocks that comprise the larger molecule are broken. In this process, a water molecule actually becomes part of the end product. For example, starch is a complex carbohydrate molecule made up of hundreds of small glucose (a simple sugar) molecules. When starch is hydrolyzed, the chemical linkages between the glucose units are broken. For each linkage that is broken, one molecule of water enters into the reaction and becomes part of the glucose molecules, as shown:

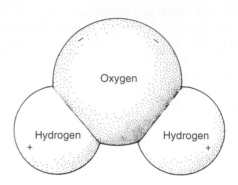

FIGURE 9-1 The water molecule is called a *dipolar molecule* because part of it is positively charged and another part is negatively charged

Part of a starch molecule   (Two linkages broken)   glucose   glucose

Hydrolysis + 2H₂O

The Nature of Water

Water is a small molecule containing two hydrogen atoms and one oxygen atom (H_2O) bonded strongly together by what are called **covalent bonds**. It is interesting to note, however, that water does not behave in the same manner as most other molecules of similar size with regard to such characteristics as boiling point, freezing point, and vapor pressure. Water is a unique molecule, fortunately for all of us living on Planet Earth, who depend so much on water for our very existence.

Water is unique chiefly because of its **polar** nature [4]. Although the hydrogen and oxygen atoms of water are joined by strong covalent bonds, the positive and negative charges are not evenly distributed over the whole molecule. Figure 9-1 is a representation of a water molecule with a negative (–) charge on the oxygen side and positive (+) charges on the hydrogen sides. The water molecule has positive and negative poles and thus is *dipolar*. Because opposite charges attract each other, the negative part of one water molecule is attracted to the positive part of another water molecule, causing these molecules to cluster together, as demonstrated in Figure 9-2. The attraction between the negatively charged oxygen and the positively charged hydrogen is a type of bonding in itself, although much weaker than covalent bonding. This special bond is called a *hydrogen bond* (see Figure 9-3).

Because water molecules have such a special attraction for their fellow molecules, considerable energy is necessary to separate them from each other. This fact is apparent when water is boiled and its state is changed from the liquid to the gaseous molecules of steam or water vapor. The boiling point of water (212°F /100°C at sea level) is quite high, considering the small size of this molecule.

The *vapor pressure*, which is the pressure produced by those water molecules that have already become vapor and are close to the surface of the liquid water even at room temperature (see Figure 9-4), is comparatively low. Therefore, because water does not readily change to a gaseous state, a considerable amount of heat must be applied to the water to overcome the special attraction of the molecules for each other and raise the vapor pressure before the water will boil. The amount of heat or energy required to change water from the liquid state to a gaseous state (called latent heat of vaporization) at its boiling point is 540 calories (0.54 **kilocalorie**) for each gram of water that is changed to steam. The temperature of the steam itself is the same as the temperature of the boiling water. The boiling point of water is discussed in more detail in connection with boiling sugar solutions in Chapter 11.

Water Hardness

Water is generally classified as being soft or hard to various degrees. What is it that makes water hard? Basically, it is the presence of various mineral salts.

Types of Hard Water. The two general types of hard water are temporary and permanent. *Temporarily hard water* contains calcium, magnesium, and iron bicarbonates that precipitate as insoluble carbonates when the water is boiled. These mineral deposits may accumulate as *scale* in hot water heaters and kettles used over a long

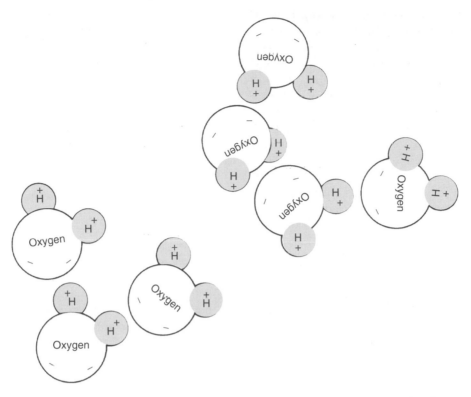

FIGURE 9-2 Water molecules cluster together because the positive charge on one molecule is attracted to the negative charge on another molecule, forming a weak bond.

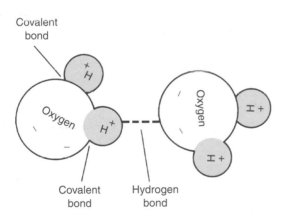

FIGURE 9-3 A hydrogen bond forms as water molecules are attracted to each other.

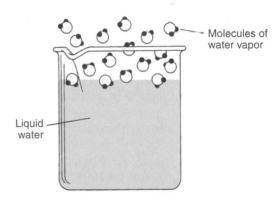

FIGURE 9-4 Vapor pressure is the pressure produced over the surface of a liquid, such as water, as a result of the escape of some of the liquid molecules into the vapor or gaseous state. This process causes water to gradually disappear or evaporate from an open container even at room temperature.

period primarily for boiling water. *Permanently hard water* contains calcium, magnesium, and iron sulfates that do not precipitate on boiling. They form insoluble salts with soap and decrease its cleaning capacity.

Hard Water and Food Preparation.   The mineral salts of hard water may affect food preparation in various ways.

Calcium retards the rehydration and softening of dried beans and peas during soaking and cooking. Hard water is often fairly alkaline and may thus affect the color of some of the pigments in cooked vegetables. Iced tea may be cloudy because some compounds in the tea (polyphenols) precipitate with the calcium and magnesium salts in hard water. Water that is naturally soft contains very few mineral salts.

Softening Water.   Hard water may be softened by several different processes. In one method, water-softening agents, such as washing soda and polyphosphates, may be added to water to precipitate the calcium and magnesium salts. Another method uses an ion-exchange process in which calcium and magnesium ions are exchanged for sodium ions. A resinous material may be contained in a water-softening tank through which the hard water flows. Sodium ions held by the resin are exchanged for calcium and magnesium in the hard water until the resin has exhausted its sodium supply. At this point, the resin may be recharged with sodium by flushing it with a strong salt solution. Water softened in this manner is, of course, higher in sodium than it was originally.

CARBOHYDRATES

What comes to mind when you hear the word *carbohydrate?* You may think of sugars and starch, and perhaps fiber. Sugars are *simple carbohydrates,* consisting of either one basic sugar unit or a few of these small units linked together. Starch and fiber belong to the class of *complex carbohydrates,* because they may have thousands of basic sugar units linked together to form very large molecules. Thus, carbohydrates are either sugars or more complex substances, such as starch, which are formed by the combination of many sugars.

Carbon (C), hydrogen (H), and oxygen (O) are the elements that comprise carbohydrates. The ratios of these elements to each other form a pattern: One molecule of water (H_2O), containing the hydrogen and oxygen, is present for each atom of carbon. *Hydrated carbon* is suggested by the ratio $[C_x(H_2O)_y]$ and from this the name *carbohydrate* has been derived.

Carbohydrates are formed in green plants through *photosynthesis,* by which process energy from the sun is harnessed to convert carbon dioxide (CO_2) from the atmosphere and water (H_2O) from the soil into the simple sugar, glucose ($C_6H_{12}O_6$). Oxygen (O_2) is given off by the plant during this photosynthetic process. Thus begins the cycle of nature on which animal life depends.

High carbohydrate foods, including various cereal grains, legumes, and starchy roots or tubers, are staples in the diets of millions of people throughout the world. Foods classified as largely carbohydrate include the following:

Sugars	Jellies and jams
Syrups	Flours
Molasses	Dried fruits
Honey	Legumes
Candies	Cereal products

Chemical Classification

Carbohydrates are classified according to the number of basic sugar units that are linked together. They may thus be grouped in the following way.

Monosaccharides:	simple sugars with one basic unit
Disaccharides:	simple sugars with two basic units
Oligosaccharides:	intermediate-size molecules containing approximately 10 or fewer basic units
Polysaccharides:	complex carbohydrates with many basic units (up to thousands)

Monosaccharides.   The simplest sugar carbohydrates are monosaccharides. *Saccharide* refers to their sweetness and *mono* to the fact that they are a single unit. Those with which we are most concerned in food preparation contain six carbon atoms and are thus called **hexoses**, although some five-carbon sugars, called **pentoses**, are important components of certain fibers and **vegetable gums**.

Three important hexose monosaccharides are glucose, fructose, and galactose. Another name for glucose is *dextrose;* fructose is sometimes called *levulose.* Each sugar has the same number of elements, $C_6H_{12}O_6$, but slight differences in position of the chemical groups produce differences in properties, including sweetness and solubility. Chemical structures for these sugars are shown in Figure 9-5, and some sources are given in Table 9-3. Sugars are discussed in more detail in Chapter 11.

Glucose.   The most widely distributed monosaccharide in foods is glucose, which is present in at least small amounts in all fruits and vegetables. The sugar that circulates in the bloodstream is glucose. A number of complex carbohydrates, including starch, have glucose as their basic sugar unit. Glucose is a major component of corn syrup, which is produced by the breakdown or hydrolysis of the complex starch molecule. Crystalline glucose and corn syrup are widely used in bakery products and other manufactured foods. Glucose is present in honey with relatively large amounts of fructose.

Fructose.   Probably the sweetest of all the common sugars is fructose. It contributes much of the sweetness to honey and is found in many fruits, sometimes being called fruit sugar. Because it is very soluble, fructose is not easily crystallized.

Technology has made possible the production of a high-fructose corn syrup by employing a special enzyme, called *glucose isomerase,* to change glucose to fructose. This syrup is widely used in processed foods, particularly soft drinks.

Galactose.   Although galactose is generally not found free in natural foods, it is one of the two building blocks of milk sugar (lactose). Some galactose is formed from the

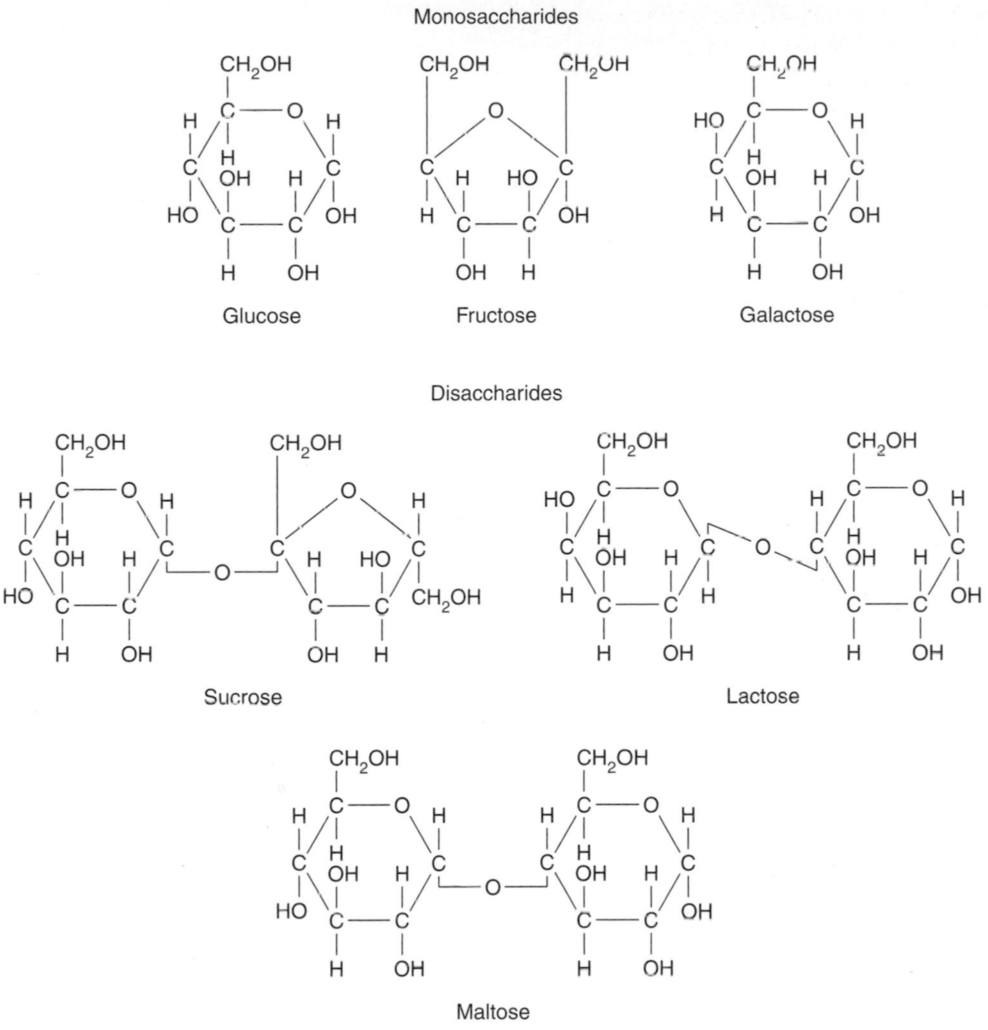

Monosaccharides

Glucose   Fructose   Galactose

Disaccharides

Sucrose   Lactose

Maltose

FIGURE 9-5 Chemical structures for monosaccharides and disaccharides of importance in food preparation.

breakdown or **hydrolysis** of lactose when fermented milk products, such as yogurt, are made. Galactose is also present in some oligosaccharides, such as raffinose; a derivative of galactose (galacturonic acid) is the basic unit of pectic substances. Galactose is a basic building block of many vegetable gums, which are complex carbohydrates.

Disaccharides. Monosaccharides are the building blocks of disaccharides, which consist of two monosaccharides linked together. Disaccharides of particular interest in the study of foods are sucrose, lactose, and maltose. Their chemical structures are shown in Figure 9-5, and some sources are listed in Table 9-3.

Sucrose. Sucrose is table sugar and is widely used in crystalline form for food preparation. It is usually extracted from sugar cane or the sugar beet. Sucrose is composed of one molecule of glucose and one of fructose. These two monosaccharides are linked through their most reactive chemical groups, the aldehyde group

(HC=O) of glucose and the ketone group (C=O) of fructose.

When sucrose is hydrolyzed, the linkage between glucose and fructose is broken, and a molecule of water is added in the reaction. The resulting mixture, containing equal molecular amounts of glucose and fructose, is sometimes called *invert sugar* and is important in controlling sugar crystallization during the process of making crystalline candies (see Chapter 11). Sucrose may be hydrolyzed by an enzyme called *sucrase* or *invertase*.

Lactose. Lactose, commonly called milk sugar, is found naturally only in milk and milk products. The two monosaccharides that comprise lactose are glucose and galactose. Whey, produced during cheese making, is a rich source of lactose and is sometimes used in processed or manufactured foods.

TABLE 9-3 Sugars, Their Sources, and Products of Hydrolysis

Sugar	Common Sources	Products of Hydrolysis
Monosaccharides, $C_6H_{12}O_6$		
Glucose or dextrose	Fruit and plant juices. Often present with other sugars. Honey. Formed by hydrolysis of sucrose, lactose, and maltose.	
Fructose or levulose	Fruit and plant juices. Often present with other sugars. Honey. Formed by hydrolysis of sucrose.	
Galactose	Does not occur free in nature. Formed by hydrolysis of lactose or galactans.	
Disaccharides, $C_{12}H_{22}O_{11}$		
Sucrose	Present with other sugars in many fruits and vegetables. Sugar cane and sugar beets are rich sources. Maple sugar and syrup. Used in many processed foods.	One molecule each of glucose and fructose. A mixture of equal amounts of glucose and fructose is called *invert sugar*.
Lactose	Milk and whey.	One molecule each of glucose and galactose.
Maltose	Malted or germinated grains. Corn syrup. Formed by hydrolysis of starch.	One molecule yields two molecules of glucose.
Oligosaccharides		
Raffinose (a trisaccharide)	The seed coats of legumes, nuts, and dried beans.	One molecule each of galactose, glucose, and fructose.
Stachyose (a tetrasaccharide)	Legumes, nuts, seeds, and dried beans.	One molecule of raffinose plus galactose.

Maltose. Two molecules of glucose link to form maltose. Maltose is one of the products of hydrolysis when the complex carbohydrate starch is broken down. Therefore, it is present in germinating or sprouting grains, where starch hydrolysis provides energy for the grain growth. It is also an important component of corn syrups, which are made by breaking down corn starch.

Oligosaccharides. The term *oligosaccharide* may be used to refer to carbohydrate molecules containing 10 or fewer monosaccharide units. (*Oligo* is a Greek word meaning "few.") This category includes the trisaccharide (three sugar units) raffinose and the tetrasaccharide (four sugar units) stachyose. These carbohydrates are not digested by humans and may be broken down by bacteria in the intestinal tract, resulting in some gas formation. They are present in dried beans.

In Japan, oligosaccharides are added to several foods, including soft drinks and cereals, to act as **prebiotics** by stimulating the metabolism of indigenous bifidobacteria in the colon [16]. Growth of bifidobacteria apparently suppresses the activity of putrefactive bacteria.

FOCUS ON SCIENCE

Prebiotics and Probiotics

Prebiotics and probiotics can restore the balance of bacteria in the digestive tract. So what is the difference between prebiotics and probiotics?

- *Probiotics* are beneficial bacteria that can be found in various foods. When you eat probiotics, you will add these healthy bacteria to your intestinal tract. Common strains are *Lactobacillus* and *Bifidobacterium* families of bacteria.

- Prebiotics are nondigestible foods that make their way through the digestive system and encourage good bacteria to grow and flourish. Prebiotics keep beneficial bacteria healthy. Prebiotics come from oligosaccharides: fruits, legumes, and whole grains. Fructo-oligosaccharides may be added to many foods. Yogurt made with bifidobacteria contains oligosaccharides.

Polysaccharides. Polysaccharides are complex carbohydrates containing monosaccharide units numbering from about 40 to thousands. These basic units are linked in various ways. Linkages may produce long, straight chains in some cases and branched-type molecules in other instances.

Starch and Dextrins. Starch is the basic storage carbohydrate of plants and is therefore found in abundance in seeds, roots, and tubers. Hundreds or even thousands of glucose molecules join to make a starch molecule. Basically, there are two kinds of starch molecules, sometimes called *fractions of starch*. One is a long chain or linear type of molecule called *amylose*. The other is a highly branched, bushy type of molecule referred to as *amylopectin*. Most natural starches are mixtures of these two fractions, each contributing its own properties in relation to thickening and gelling. Illustrations for the chemical structures of amylose and amylopectin are shown in Figure 9-6.

As starch molecules are produced in a growing plant, they are placed in a tightly organized formation called a *granule*. **Starch granules** are large enough to be seen under an ordinary microscope. When starch granules are heated in water, they swell tremendously in a process called *gelatinization*. The swollen starch granules are responsible for the thickening that occurs when starchy puddings and sauces are cooked. Starch and gelatinization are discussed in more detail in Chapter 13.

Dextrins are produced when starch molecules are partially broken down by enzymes, acid, or dry heat. We might think of dextrins as large chunks of broken starch molecules. They are formed from starch when corn syrup is made, when bread is toasted, and when flour is browned. They have less thickening power than starch.

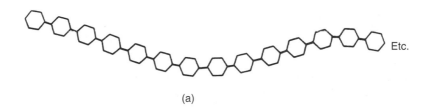

(a)

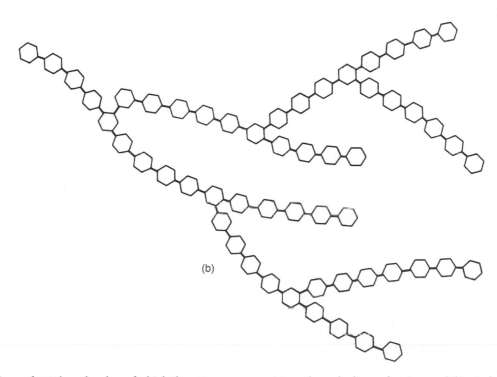

(b)

FIGURE 9-6 Portions of starch molecules, of which there are two types: (a) amylose, the linear fraction, and (b) amylopectin, the branched fraction. Each small unit represents one molecule of glucose.

Glycogen. Glycogen, a polysaccharide, is sometimes called *animal starch* because it is found in animal tissues. It is similar in structure to the amylopectin or branched fraction of starch. When completely hydrolyzed, it yields only glucose. The liver stores glycogen on a short-term basis until it is hydrolyzed to help maintain a normal blood sugar level. The muscles also temporarily store glycogen.

Plant Fiber Components. The term *dietary fiber* refers to the "edible parts of plants or analogous carbohydrates that are resistant to digestion and absorption in the human small intestine with complete or partial fermentation in the large intestine" [1]. Fiber is sometimes called *roughage* or *bulk* and is a complex mixture composed primarily of *cellulose, hemicelluloses, beta-glucans, pectins,* and *gums,* which are all polysaccharides. The fact that oligosaccharides are indigestible by human digestive juices may qualify them to be called low-molecular weight, water-soluble dietary fibers. A noncarbohydrate molecule called **lignin** also is part of the fiber complex, particularly in woody portions of vegetables. The Food and Nutrition Board at the National Academy of Sciences has proposed new definitions "Dietary Fiber" and "Added Fiber" that distinguish between intact fiber in plants and fiber that has been isolated and added to foods [3, 7].

The fiber components are found primarily in or around the cell walls of plants. Many of them play important structural roles, whereas some, including various gums, are nonstructural. The importance of fiber in our diets for the prevention or control of several chronic disorders, including colon cancer, cardiovascular disease, and diabetes, has been recognized by the health and scientific communities [3, 13]. The outer bran layers of cereal grains, legumes, nuts, and seeds, as well as fruits and vegetables, contain relatively large amounts of dietary fiber, many of whose components have the capacity to absorb water and swell.

Cellulose. Cellulose has thousands of glucose units linked together, as does the linear fraction of starch; however, the glucose molecules in cellulose are linked in a different way than the glucose units in starch and form long, strong fibers. The linkage of glucose molecules in cellulose is not subject to hydrolysis or breakdown by human digestive enzymes. Therefore, unlike starch, which is digestible, cellulose is indigestible. The cell walls of plant tissues contain cellulose in tiny fibrils, helping to give structure to these tissues.

Cellulose may be chemically modified to make it more soluble and able to form gels. Examples of modified cellulose include methylcellulose and carboxymethyl cellulose, which are used to thicken, stabilize, gel, and provide bulk in various processed foods [6].

Hemicelluloses. Also found in plant cell walls are hemicelluloses. These are a heterogeneous group of polysaccharides that contain a variety of different monosaccharide building blocks. In many cases, these molecules have branching side chains. Hemicelluloses, along with cellulose, play important structural roles in plants. Xylose and arabinose, which are pentoses (monosaccharides with five carbon atoms), are common components of hemicelluloses.

Beta-glucans. Beta-glucans are polysaccharides made up of glucose building blocks that are linked together differently from the glucose components of cellulose. Beta-glucan molecules are less linear than cellulose molecules and more soluble in water. Oats and barley are rich sources of beta-glucans [3, 12]. Foods high in beta-glucans are authorized by the FDA to be labeled with a health claim stating the food may reduce the risk of heart disease.

Pectic Substances. Pectic substances are polysaccharides found in the spaces between plant cells and in the cell walls, and aid in cementing plant cells together. **Galacturonic acid**, a derivative of the sugar galactose, is the basic building block of pectic substances. The largest of the pectic molecules, sometimes called the parent, is *protopectin*. It is present in largest amounts in unripe fruit and is hydrolyzed by enzymes in the tissues to the less complex *pectinic acid*, also called *pectin*, as the fruit ripens. *Pectic acid* is produced from pectin by additional hydrolysis of special chemical groups on the molecule called **methyl esters**. Pectin is the substance responsible for forming gels in various jams, jellies, and preserves; it also occurs naturally in many fruits.

Vegetable Gums. The term *vegetable gum* or *gum* describes a wide variety of water-soluble polysaccharides that have the ability to act as thickeners or gelling agents in food products [5]. They are a major part of a group of food-processing aids called **hydrocolloids**. Gums are long-chain **polymers** of monosaccharides; various hexose and pentose sugars and their derivatives are the basic building blocks. When they are dissolved or dispersed in water, they have a thickening or texture-building effect, creating *body* and improving mouthfeel in a variety of food products [14, 15]. They also make it more difficult for dispersed materials to separate. In other words, they *stabilize* suspensions (solids dispersed in water). Thus, gums may help to retain water, reduce evaporation rates, modify ice crystal formation, and produce other desired changes in the consistency and flow characteristics of various foods. The preparation of low-calorie and reduced-fat foods often requires the ingenious use of hydrocolloids; for example, gums can thicken and stabilize low-calorie salad dressings made with reduced amounts of oil or with none at all. The FDA regulates gums, classifying them as either food additives or GRAS (generally regarded as safe) substances [6]. Vegetable gums include the following:

Source	Examples
Extracts from seaweed	Agar
	Alginates
	Carrageenan
Seed gums	Guar gum
	Locust bean gum
Plant exudates	Gum arabic
	Gum tragacanth
	Gum karaya
Chemically modified materials	Methyl cellulose
	Sodium carboxymethyl cellulose
Fermentation products	Xanthan gum
	Gellan gum

Browning

Chemical reactions that cause browning of foods often occur during preparation and storage. In some cases this color is desirable, but in other cases it is not. It is important to be able to control browning so that it can be inhibited or encouraged as needed. Some browning reactions are **catalyzed** by enzymes. Those involved in the browning of fresh fruits and vegetables are discussed in Chapter 20. Other browning results from nonenzymatic reactions, some of which involve carbohydrates.

Carmelization. When sugars are heated to temperatures above their melting points, they undergo a series of chemical reactions that begin with dehydration and end with polymerization, which produces brown compounds. This process is called **caramelization**. If this operation is not too extensive, a desirable caramel flavor and a light brown color result. As heating is continued, however, many bitter compounds are produced, and the color becomes very dark.

Maillard Reaction. Another type of browning is produced by the *Maillard reaction*. This reaction also involves a carbohydrate—a sugar—in its initial step. The **carbonyl group** of a sugar combines with the **amino group** of an amino acid or protein with the removal of a molecule of water. After this, a series of chemical reactions occurs, including fragmentation and then polymerization, with the eventual formation of brown pigments. The specific compounds involved and the conditions of temperature, pH, moisture, and so on, under which the reaction occurs, all affect the final flavor and color, which may be desirable or not desirable. The browning of a loaf of bread during baking is due mainly to the Maillard reaction. The flavor and color, in this case, are desirable; however, the browning and off-flavor that may develop when nonfat dry milk solids are stored for a long time are not.

LIPIDS OR FATS

The term *lipids* is used to describe a broad group of substances with similar properties or characteristics of insolubility in water and a greasy feel. The lipid classification includes at least three major groups with which we are particularly concerned in the study of food and nutrition: neutral fats known as triacylglycerols or triglycerides, phospholipids, and sterols.

Triglycerides (Triacylglycerols)

Approximately 90 to 95 percent of the fatty substances in foods fall into the triglyceride group. Thus, when we talk of fats in food, we are actually talking about triglycerides or triacylglycerols. For our discussions in this text, we use

FOCUS ON SCIENCE

More on Caramelization

The caramelization reaction can be summarized as follows:

- First the sugar melts at temperatures above 300°F (149°C) which is followed by foaming.
- Sucrose decomposes into glucose and fructose.
- A condensation reaction occurs in which the individual sugars lose water and react with each other.

- Hundreds of new aromatic compounds are formed having a range of complex flavors.

Some flavors formed during caramelization are as follows:

- *Diacetyl (2, 3 butanedione)* is an important flavor compound produced during the first stage of caramelization. Diacetyl is responsible for a buttery or butterscotch flavor.
- *Esters* and *lactones* have a sweet, rum-like flavor.
- *Furans* have a nutty flavor.
- *Maltol* has a toasty flavor.
- Bitter flavors can be formed if caramelization is allowed to proceed too far because the original sugar will be destroyed.

How Is the Maillard Browning Different from Caramelization?

Maillard browning and caramelization are both nonenzymatic browning reactions, but Maillard browning is a chemical reaction between a free amino group or an amino acid (usually lysine) and a reducing sugar (glucose).

In Maillard browning, different types of sugars react more readily than others. In order of reactivity, are the following:

- Pentose sugars such as ribose. Pentose sugars are five-carbon sugars.

- Hexose sugars such as glucose, fructose, and galatose. Hexose sugars have six carbon atoms.

- Disaccharides such as sucrose, lactose, and maltose.

Likewise, different amino acids produce varying degrees of browning with lysine being the most reactive. Because, the Maillard reaction produces water, having a high water activity environment inhibits the reaction: therefore, intermediate water activity (a_w) values of 0.5 to 0.8 allow the reaction to proceed rapidly. The effect of pH is not clearcut, and reactions take place by different pathways with the pH of the system influencing the ratio of products formed. Therefore, pH<6 will favor the formation of furfurals, whereas a pH>6 will produce reductones and fission products.

---

the older term *triglyceride*, rather than *triacylglycerol;* both refer to the same kind of chemical molecule.

Triglycerides are made up of three fatty acids combined with one molecule of an alcohol called *glycerol.* Glycerol has three carbon atoms and three hydroxyl groups (−OH). Fatty acids are commonly composed of linked chains of carbon atoms, with an organic acid group

$$-\overset{O}{\underset{}{\overset{\|}{C}}}-OH$$

on the end of the chain. The fatty acids are joined to the glycerol molecule by what is called an *ester linkage,* as shown in the following, where R represents the chain of carbon atoms.

glycerol   3 fatty acids   triglyceride

Fatty Acids.   Most fatty acids in foods are not free fatty acids but rather are combined in triglycerides. Different fatty acids may be joined with the glycerol in the same triglyceride molecule. Fatty acids vary in two important ways—they differ in the length of the chain of carbon atoms and in the number of hydrogen atoms that are attached to the carbons.

The carbon chain in fatty acids may be as short as four carbons or as long as 24 or more carbons. Generally, however, the fatty acids in foods have an even number of carbons. Names of some common fatty acids and the lengths of their carbon chains are listed in Table 9-4.

A carbon atom has four bonds with which it joins to other atoms. Within a carbon chain, two of the bonds join with adjacent carbon atoms. Each of the remaining two bonds on a carbon atom may bond with a hydrogen

TABLE 9-4 Fatty Acids Found in Foods

Fatty Acid Common Name	Systematic Name	Number of Carbon Atoms
Saturated		
Butyric	Butanoic	4
Caproic	Hexanoic	6
Caprylic	Octanoic	8
Capric	Decanoic	10
Lauric	Dodecanoic	12
Myristic	Tetradecanoic	14
Palmitic	Hexadecanoic	16
Stearic	Octadecanoic	18
Arachidic	Eicosanoic	20
Monounsaturated		
Palmitoleic	Hexadecenoic	16
Oleic	*Cis*-Octadecenoic	18
Polyunsaturated		
Linoleic	Octadecadienoic	18
Linolenic	Octadecatrienoic	18
Arachidonic	Eicosatetraenoic	20

atom. Some fatty acids have all of the hydrogen atoms with which the carbon atoms can bond. There are no *double bonds* between carbon atoms, which might be broken to allow bonding with more hydrogens. These types of fatty acids are called *saturated*. Other fatty acids contain double bonds between some carbon atoms and are *unsaturated* in terms of the amount of hydrogen they contain. Examples of saturated fatty acids are butyric acid, which is present in butter, and stearic acid, which is a major component of beef fat. Palmitic acid, a saturated fatty acid with 16 carbon atoms, is widely distributed in meat fats, vegetable oils, and cocoa butter.

$$\begin{array}{c}
\quad\ \ H\quad\ H\quad\ H \\
\quad\ \ | \quad\ \ | \quad\ \ | \\
H-C-C-C-COOH \\
\quad\ \ | \quad\ \ | \quad\ \ | \\
\quad\ \ H\quad\ H\quad\ H
\end{array}$$

(butyric acid; 4 carbon atoms)

$$\begin{array}{c}
\ H\ H\ H\ H\ H\ H\ H\ H\ H\ H\ H\ H\ H\ H\ H\ H\ H \\
\ |\ \ |\ \ |\ \ |\ \ |\ \ |\ \ |\ \ |\ \ |\ \ |\ \ |\ \ |\ \ |\ \ |\ \ |\ \ |\ \ | \\
H-C-C-C-C-C-C-C-C-C-C-C-C-C-C-C-C-C-COOH \\
\ |\ \ |\ \ |\ \ |\ \ |\ \ |\ \ |\ \ |\ \ |\ \ |\ \ |\ \ |\ \ |\ \ |\ \ |\ \ |\ \ | \\
\ H\ H\ H\ H\ H\ H\ H\ H\ H\ H\ H\ H\ H\ H\ H\ H\ H
\end{array}$$

(stearic acid; 18 carbon atoms)

$$\begin{array}{c}
\ H\ H\ H\ H\ H\ H\ H\ H\ H\ H\ H\ H\ H\ H\ H \\
\ |\ \ |\ \ |\ \ |\ \ |\ \ |\ \ |\ \ |\ \ |\ \ |\ \ |\ \ |\ \ |\ \ |\ \ | \\
H-C-C-C-C-C-C-C-C-C-C-C-C-C-C-C-COOH \\
\ |\ \ |\ \ |\ \ |\ \ |\ \ |\ \ |\ \ |\ \ |\ \ |\ \ |\ \ |\ \ |\ \ | \\
\ H\ H\ H\ H\ H\ H\ H\ H\ H\ H\ H\ H\ H\ H
\end{array}$$

(palmitic acid; 16 carbon atoms)
Saturated Fatty Acids

Oleic acid contains one double bond (see diagram on page 140). It is thus a *monounsaturated* fatty acid. Linoleic, linolenic, and arachidonic acids contain two, three, and four double bonds, respectively. Fatty acids with more than one double bond are often called *polyunsaturated*. Polyunsaturated fatty acids that have a double bond between the third and fourth carbon atoms from the left are called omega-3 (ω-3) polyunsaturated fatty acids. Some ω-3 fatty acids appear to be of importance in body metabolism related to the prevention of coronary heart disease. Fish, particularly fatty fish, contains ω-3 fatty acids.

The body is not able to make linoleic acid (see page 140) with its two double bonds. Linoleic acid is therefore considered to be an essential fatty acid for both infants and adults, because it must be obtained in the diet. Skin lesions and poor growth have been reported in infants receiving a diet limited in fat, and these symptoms disappeared after a source of linoleic acid was added to the diet. It has been suggested by the Food and Nutrition Board of the National Research Council–National Academy of Sciences that a linoleic acid intake equivalent to 2 percent of the total dietary kilocalories for adults and 3 percent for infants is probably satisfactory to avoid any deficiency. The average American diet apparently meets this recommendation.

Good food sources of linoleic acid include seed oils from corn, cottonseeds, and soybeans (50 to 53 percent linoleic acid) and special margarines and peanut oil (20 to 30 percent). Corn oil contains more than six times as much linoleic acid as olive oil, and chicken fat contains up to 10 times as much as the fat of **ruminant animals** such as cattle. The fat from an avocado is about 10 percent linoleate.

Cis-trans Configuration. The shape of a fatty acid is changed by the presence of a double bond, because the double bond limits the rotation of the carbon atom at this point. The particular molecular shape produced by a double bond is dependent on the configuration of the bond. It may be either cis or trans. A cis configuration has the hydrogen atoms on the same side of the double bond, as illustrated at the top of the next page.

$$H-C-C-C-C-C-C-C-C-C=C-C-C-C-C-C-C-C-COOH$$

(oleic acid; 18 carbon atoms)

$$H-C-C-C-C-C-C=C-C-C=C-C-C-C-C-C-C-C-COOH$$

(linoleic acid; 18 carbon atoms)
Unsaturated Fatty Acids

In a trans configuration, the hydrogen atoms are on opposite sides of the double bond, as shown here.

cis — C — C — C

trans — C — C — C

Because it is part of a triglyceride molecule, the fatty acid's shape affects the melting point of the triglyceride. An unsaturated fatty acid with a trans configuration has a higher melting point than the same size molecule with a cis configuration, because the bending of the chain in the cis fatty acid does not allow the triglyceride molecules to pack as closely together when they crystallize in a solid state. Thus, less energy is required to separate them when they melt; therefore they melt at a lower temperature.

Types of Triglyceride Molecules.   A triglyceride molecule may be formed with three of the same kind of fatty acids, for example, three palmitic acid molecules. In this case, the triglyceride would be called a *simple* triglyceride and could be named tripalmitin. More commonly, however, triglycerides in foods are *mixed,* that is, they contain different fatty acids, either all three different or two alike and one different.

Phospholipids

Phospholipids are present in foods in relatively small amounts but play some important roles, chiefly as **emulsifying agents**. Lecithin is a phospholipid that is used as a food additive in various processed foods, including margarines. Phospholipids are present in buttermilk, resulting from the churning of cream. Certain baked products made with dried buttermilk may benefit from the emulsifying action of the phospholipids present. Egg yolk is a good source of phospholipids.

Structurally, phospholipids are much like triglycerides. They contain glycerol attached through an ester linkage to two fatty acids; however, they differ from triglycerides in that, instead of a third fatty acid, there is a phosphoric acid group joined to the glycerol. A **nitrogen base**, such as choline, is also linked with the phosphoric acid.

$$H-C-O-C-R_1 \quad \text{(fatty acid No. 1)}$$
$$H-C-O-C-R_2 \quad \text{(fatty acid No. 2)}$$
$$H-C-O- \text{phosphoric acid + nitrogen base}$$

FOCUS ON SCIENCE

Trans Fatty Acids and Foods

Trans fats can be found in vegetable shortenings, some margarines, baked goods, crackers, cookies, snack foods, and other foods made with, or fried in, partially hydrogenated oils.

Unlike other fats, the majority of trans fat is formed when the food manufacturers turn liquid oils into solid fats such as shortening and margarine. Also, oils may be lightly hydrogenated to preserve their quality and prevent rancidity because of their amount of unsaturated fatty acids which are prone to becoming rancid.

Because of the association between the consumption of trans fatty acids and heart disease, manufacturers are using different methods of hydrogenation to produce shortenings and other solid fats that may be labeled as trans fat free.

In a mixture, the fatty acid portions of the phospholipid molecules are attracted to other fat substances, whereas the phosphoric acid–nitrogen base portion is attracted to polar molecules such as water or vinegar. Thus, the phospholipid may act as a bridge between fat and water and allow them to be mixed in an emulsion. The phospholipid functions as an emulsifying agent.

Sterols

Cholesterol is probably the most widely known sterol and is found only in animal foods—meat, fish, poultry, egg yolks, and milk fat. Cholesterol is an essential component in the cells of the body, but too high a level of cholesterol in the bloodstream is one factor associated with an increased incidence of coronary heart disease. Vitamin D is also a sterol.

Plants do not manufacture cholesterol, but plant oils do contain some other sterols, generally called *phytosterols*. These sterols, however, are not well absorbed from the human digestive tract and actually interfere with the absorption of cholesterol. In 2000, the FDA authorized a health claim identifying the role of plant sterols or plant sterol esters in lowering the risk of heart disease [8, 9, 12]. Vegetable oil spreads high in plant sterols are available in grocery stores, but are not yet popular with consumers. The chemical structures of sterols are complex and quite different from those of the triglycerides.

Fats in Food Preparation

Several important roles are filled by fats in food preparation. They act as primary tenderizing agents in baked products, contribute to leavening when air is incorporated into a batter during the creaming of fat and sugar, and promote moistness. For example, contrast the marked tenderness of a croissant, which contains a high proportion of fat, with the chewiness of a bagel, which is made with very little fat.

Oils are major components of salad dressings and mayonnaise. Fats may be heated to high temperatures and act as a medium of heat transfer in the frying of foods. High-fat products such as butter and margarine are used as table spreads. Several flavor compounds are fat soluble and are carried in the fat component of many food products. The properties and processing of fats are discussed in Chapter 10.

Foods high in fat include the following (see also Table 10-1 in Chapter 10):

Butter	Deep-fat fried foods
Cream	Chocolate
Lard	Cheese
Oils	Nuts
Margarine	Fat meats
Hydrogenated shortening	

PROTEINS

Proteins are large, complex molecules found in every living cell. The name *protein* is derived from the Greek word *proteos*, meaning "of prime importance" or "to take the first place." Thus, all foods that were once living animal or plant tissues, including meats, vegetables, and cereal grains, contain some protein. Protein is an essential nutrient for human life and growth. In food preparation, proteins play important functional roles, for example, binding water, forming **gels**, thickening, producing **foams**, and aiding browning. In addition, enzymes, which are special kinds of protein molecules, catalyze many reactions that affect the characteristics of prepared foods.

Structure of Proteins

Proteins are unique because, in addition to the elements carbon, hydrogen, and oxygen, they also contain nitrogen. Often, sulfur is present as well, and some proteins contain phosphorus or iron. Proteins are large molecules made up of hundreds or thousands of small building blocks called *amino acids*, which are joined in a special chemical linkage called a **peptide linkage**. These linkages produce long chains that are said to constitute the *primary structure* of proteins.

The *secondary structure* of proteins results from the springlike coiling of the long peptide chains (see Figure 9-7). The characteristic coil is called an *alpha helix*, and special bonds, called **hydrogen bonds**, help to hold the coils in place.

The secondary coils of peptide chains may fold back on themselves, usually in an irregular pattern, to form more compact structures. This folding, which is characteristic for each particular protein, produces what is called the *tertiary structure* of a protein molecule. The long chains of amino acids, when coiled and folded, often produce a globular shape for the protein. A still higher level of organization, called the *quaternary structure*, may result when some globular proteins combine with others, and each forms subunits in a more complex whole. The structure of many protein molecules is indeed intricate, but the final shape of the protein is often of critical importance to its function in a living cell or in food preparation.

Amino Acids. About 22 different amino acids are used as building blocks for proteins. Each of these amino acids has two chemical groups that are the same for all of the

FIGURE 9-7 Representation of an alpha helix.

amino acids—an amino group ($H_2N–$) and a carboxyl or acid group.

$$-\overset{\overset{\displaystyle O}{\|}}{C} - OH$$

The remainder of the molecule differs specifically for each amino acid. A general formula for amino acids is written as follows, with the R representing a side chain of variable structure.

$$
\begin{array}{c}
\overset{\displaystyle O}{\|} \\
C - OH \\
| \\
H_2N - C - H \\
| \\
R
\end{array}
$$

The side chains or R groups give a protein its particular characteristics. Some R groups have short carbon chains, some contain sulfur, some have additional amino acid groups, and some have a cyclic structure. The side chain structures are shown in Table 9-5.

The peptide linkage is between the amino group of one amino acid and the acid or carboxyl group of another. Protein molecules are formed as hundreds of these linkages are made. The following hypothetical protein molecule shows several amino acids joined together by peptide linkages.

$$
\begin{array}{llll}
H_2N - CH - CO - NH - CH - CO - NH - CH - CO - (NH - CH - CO)_n - NH - CH - COOH \\
\quad\quad | \quad\quad\quad\quad\quad\quad\quad | \quad\quad\quad\quad\quad\quad\quad | \quad\quad\quad\quad\quad\quad\quad\quad\quad | \quad\quad\quad\quad\quad\quad | \\
\quad\quad CH_2 \quad\quad\quad\quad\quad\quad CH_3 \quad\quad\quad\quad\quad\quad (CH_2)_4 \quad\quad\quad\quad\quad\quad R \quad\quad\quad\quad\quad CH_2 \\
\quad\quad | \quad\quad\quad\quad\quad\quad\quad\quad\quad\quad\quad\quad\quad\quad\quad\quad\quad\quad\quad\quad | \quad\quad\quad\quad\quad\quad\quad\quad\quad\quad\quad\quad | \\
\quad\quad C_6H_5 \quad\quad\quad\quad\quad\quad\quad\quad\quad\quad\quad\quad\quad NH_2 \quad\quad\quad\quad\quad\quad\quad\quad\quad\quad\quad OH
\end{array}
$$

phenylalanine   alanine   lysine   serine

TABLE 9-5 Side Chain (R) Groups for Selected Amino Acids

Amino Acid	Structure for Side Chain (R) Group
Glycine	$-H$
Alanine	$-CH_3$
Valine	$-CH\begin{smallmatrix}\nearrow CH_3 \\ \searrow CH_3\end{smallmatrix}$
Leucine	$-CH_2-CH\begin{smallmatrix}\nearrow CH_3 \\ \searrow CH_3\end{smallmatrix}$
Isoleucine	$-CH\overset{\nearrow CH_3}{\underset{}{}}-CH_2-CH_3$
Serine	$-CH_2-OH$
Threonine	$-CH\overset{OH}{\underset{\searrow CH_3}{}}$

Sulfur-Containing

Cystine	$-CH_2-S-S-CH_2-\overset{\overset{\displaystyle O}{\|}}{\underset{NH_2}{\overset{\displaystyle C-OH}{CH}}}$
Cysteine	$-CH_2-SH$
Methionine	$-CH_2-CH_2-S-CH_3$

TABLE 9-5	Continued

Acidic

Aspartic acid	$-CH_2-\overset{\displaystyle O}{\overset{\|}{C}}-OH$
Glutamic acid	$-CH_2-CH_2-\overset{\displaystyle O}{\overset{\|}{C}}-OH$

Basic

Lysine	$-CH_2-CH_2-CH_2-CH_2-NH_2$
Arginine	$-CH_2-CH_2-CH_2-NH-\overset{\displaystyle \|}{\underset{NH}{C}}-NH_2$
Histidine	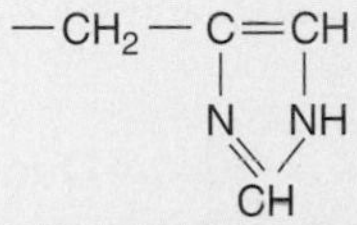 $-CH_2-C=CH$

Aromatic

Phenylalanine	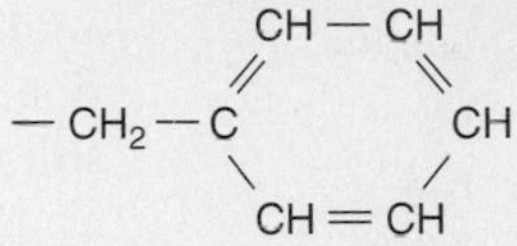
Tyrosine	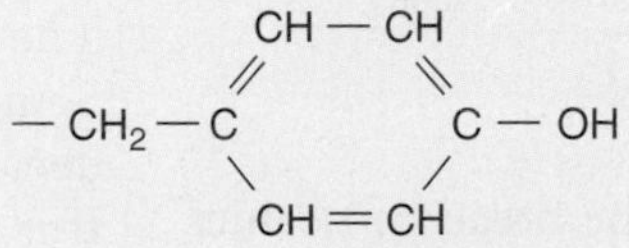
Tryptophan	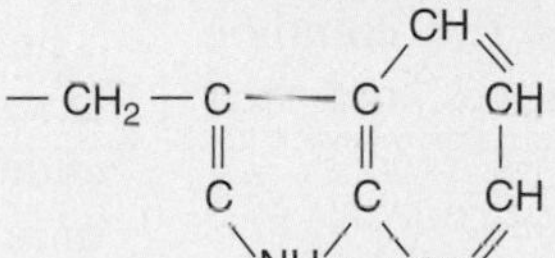

Protein Quality

Nine amino acids are considered nutritionally essential for tissue maintenance in the adult human, in the sense that the diet must furnish them in suitable amounts. These essential amino acids are isoleucine, leucine, lysine, methionine, phenylalanine, threonine, tryptophan, valine, and histidine. Histidine has been shown to be essential in the diet of adults and infants. The other amino acids, considered nonessential, may be synthesized in the body if nitrogen sources are available.

The balance of essential amino acids in a protein determines the biological value of that protein. Proteins of high biological value contain adequate amounts of the essential amino acids to promote the normal growth of animals and are sometimes called *complete proteins*, whereas proteins of low biological value do not. Because the amino acid requirement for growth is more rigid than that for the maintenance of tissues, some proteins that are inadequate for growth may function satisfactorily for maintenance or repair of body tissues. Specific examples

of proteins of high biological value are those found in milk, cheese, eggs, meat, poultry, and seafood.

Vegetable sources of protein are often lacking to some degree in one or more of the essential amino acids and have a lower score for biological value. In addition, the total amount of protein in relation to the total calories found in certain vegetable products, such as cereal grains, is low. An exception among plant protein foods is the soybean, which contains a relatively large amount of high-quality protein. Some protein foods of relatively low biological value may be combined with other protein sources that complement them, one supplying more of an essential amino acid(s) than the other is able.

Cereals or legumes are more valuable in the diet if they are combined with even a small amount of protein from an animal source, such as milk, cheese, egg, meat, fish, poultry, or with soy protein, which furnishes amino acids that cereals and most legumes lack. Cereals and legumes also complement each other to improve protein quality. For example, a peanut butter sandwich contains a

TABLE 9-6 Sources and Qualitative Values of Some Common Proteins

Protein	Source	Biological Value
Casein	Milk or cheese	High
Lactalbumin	Milk or cheese	High
Ovovitellin	Egg yolk	High
Ovalbumin	Egg white	High
Myosin	Lean meat	High
Gelatin	Formed by hydrolysis from certain animal tissues	Low
Gliadin	Wheat	Low
Glutenin	Wheat	High
Hordein	Barley	Low
Prolamin	Rye	Low
Glutelin	Corn	High
Zein	Corn	Low
Glycinin	Soybean	High
Legumelin	Soybean	Low
Legumin	Peas and beans	Low
Phaseolin	Navy beans	Low
Excelsin	Brazil nut	High

better quality protein mixture than the bread or peanut butter eaten separately. Table 9-6 lists the common names of several food proteins, their sources, and their general biological value.

Food Sources

Protein is present in many foods, but in varying amounts. Because it is an essential substance for living cells, one would expect to find it in both plant and animal tissues. Foods that are relatively high in protein (20 to 30 percent) include meats, fish, poultry, eggs, cheese, nuts, and dry legumes. Even after dry legumes are rehydrated and cooked, they make an excellent contribution to dietary protein requirements. Although milk contains only about 4 percent protein, it is an excellent source of good-quality protein because of the amounts usually consumed on a regular basis. Cereal grains contain lesser amounts of protein; however, in the quantities of cereal grains that are often eaten, they make an important contribution to protein needs.

Properties and Reactions

Buffering. Amino groups act as bases or alkalies, whereas carboxyl groups act as acids. As both of these groups are present on the same amino acid or protein structure, amino acids and proteins may act as either acids or bases and are said to be *amphoteric*. This characteristic is important for many aspects of food preparation when the degree of acidity or alkalinity affects the quality of a food product. Proteins may combine with either the acid or the base within a limited range and resist any change in acidity. Because of this characteristic, they are called **buffers**.

Denaturation and Coagulation. The large complex protein molecules may undergo changes in their structures when they are subjected to the various conditions commonly encountered in food processing and preparation. If the protein molecule unfolds to some degree yet still retains all of the peptide linkages between the amino acids that comprise the molecule, it is said to be *denatured*. The process of *denaturation* is illustrated in Figure 9-8. Some of the properties of the protein change when it is denatured. For example, it usually becomes less soluble. If it is an enzyme, it loses its ability to function as such. The extent of denaturation may be either limited or extensive. If the conditions causing denaturation persist, additional changes may occur in the protein. The unfolded parts of the molecule recombine in different ways to produce a new molecular shape, and protein molecules may bond together to form a continuous network. The term *coagulation* has been used to describe some of the later stages of protein denaturation in which denatured protein molecules bind together and produce a gel or a solid mass. The coagulation of egg white upon being heated is an example of this process.

Applying heat in the cooking of food produces denaturation and/or coagulation of proteins. An example is the roasting of meat, which denatures the meat proteins. Proteins may also be denatured by mechanical beating. For example, when egg whites are whipped to produce a

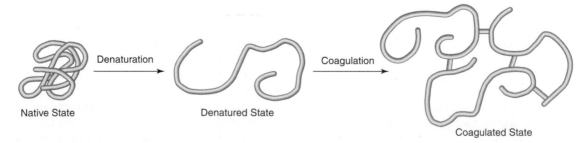

Native State → Denaturation → Denatured State → Coagulation → Coagulated State

FIGURE 9-8 Denaturation of a protein involves unfolding of the molecule. The denatured molecules may bond together again to form a coagulated mass.

foam, denaturation and coagulation of the egg white proteins occur. Changing the degree of acidity, changing the concentration of mineral salts, and freezing may also cause denaturation.

Enzymes.   Enzymes are protein molecules with a special function. Produced by living cells, they act as *catalysts* to change the rate of a chemical reaction without actually being used up in the reaction itself. Enzymes catalyze a wide range of reactions in living matter, from the digestion of foods in the digestive tract of animals to most of the complex processes occurring in plant and animal metabolism. Enzymes in plant and animal tissues do not stop functioning when the animal is slaughtered or the plant tissue is harvested. Thus, we must deal with enzymatic activity when we handle foods from these sources. Enzymes and enzymatic action in foods are mentioned frequently throughout the text.

Nomenclature.   Names of enzymes often include the substrate or substance on which they act, joined with an *-ase* ending. For example, *lactase* is an enzyme that works on lactose to bring about its hydrolysis, and *maltase* catalyzes the hydrolysis of maltose to yield glucose. Sometimes an enzyme is named for the product that results from its action. Sucrase, for example, is sometimes called *invertase* instead, because its action to hydrolyze sucrose produces an equimolecular mixture of glucose and fructose, which is commonly called *invert sugar*. In other cases, the name describes the reaction catalyzed; oxidase, for example, is the name of an enzyme involved in an oxidation reaction. Still other names, such as *papain* and *bromelin*, do not provide any information about the substrate, end products, or reaction.

A systematic nomenclature program that attempts to describe both the substrate and the type of reaction has been established; however, the names are often cumbersome and difficult to use on a practical basis. Numerical codes are sometimes used, but they, too, are difficult to use.

Mechanism of Action.   It has been suggested that enzymes function somewhat like a lock and key. They first combine with the substrate on which they will act, forming an intermediate compound sometimes referred to as the *enzyme-substrate (E-S)* complex. This complex formation undoubtedly involves a specific catalytic site on the enzyme. When the reaction is complete, the enzyme separates from the product and is free to react with another molecule of substrate. This process may be depicted as

enzyme (E) + substrate (S) → E-S → E + product (P)

Some Types of Enzymes.   Enzymes may be classified into groups according to the type of reaction they catalyze. For example, some enzymes catalyze hydrolysis reactions (*hydrolytic enzymes*), and some catalyze oxidation and reduction reactions. Hydrolysis is a chemical reaction that involves the breaking or cleaving of a chemical bond within a molecule. Water plays an essential role in this reaction, and the hydrogen and oxygen atoms of water are added to the two new molecules formed. Within the classification of hydrolytic enzymes, some are designated *proteases*, or *proteinases*, because they hydrolyze or digest proteins; *lipases* hydrolyze fats; and *amylases* act on starch. *Sucrase* breaks down sucrose into two simpler sugars. Some enzymes that catalyze oxidation-reduction reactions are commonly called oxidases or dehydrogenases.

Some hydrolytic enzymes occur in plant tissues and have importance in food preparation. For example, the enzyme bromelin, which occurs in pineapple, is a protease and causes gelatin (a protein) to liquefy when fresh or frozen uncooked pineapple is added to gelatin. It is necessary to inactivate (denature) bromelin by heating the pineapple before adding it to a gelatin mixture if the gelatin is to set. Bromelin has been used as a meat tenderizer because of its proteolytic action. Papain, which is obtained from the papaya plant, also acts on proteins to hydrolyze them. It forms the basis of some tenderizing compounds applied to less tender meats. Enzymes used as meat tenderizers do not penetrate very far into the meat and may tenderize only on the surface. Certain oxidases in plant tissues are involved in the darkening of cut or bruised surfaces of many fresh fruits and vegetables. *Chymosin*, or *rennin*, is an enzyme that brings about the clotting of milk and is used in the manufacture of cheese.

Enzyme Activity.   Each enzyme acts most effectively under optimal conditions. Temperature, degree of acidity or pH, amount of substrate, and amount of enzyme are all important. In general, the rate or speed of an enzymatic reaction increases as the temperature increases until a critical level is reached, at which point denaturation or coagulation of the enzyme by heat stops the activity. At its optimum temperature, enzymatic activity is greatest, and denaturation does not occur. For example, the optimum temperature for the activity of papain is 140° to 160°F (60° to 70°C). When it is used as a meat tenderizer, it does not begin to hydrolyze meat proteins to any significant extent until this temperature range is reached during the cooking process. The enzyme is then inactivated as the temperature rises above 160°F (70°C).

Each enzyme also has an optimal pH. Often, this pH range is quite narrow, outside of which activity does not occur. For example, chymosin (rennin) clots milk most effectively when the pH is about 5.8. Clotting does not occur if the pH is strongly alkaline.

The rate of an enzymatic reaction increases with increasing substrate up to a certain point and then remains constant. The rate of an enzymatic reaction also increases with increasing amounts of enzyme. Enzyme activity in foods may thus be at least partially determined by controlling the conditions under which the food is held or handled.

SOLUTIONS AND DISPERSIONS

Foods are usually mixtures of the various chemical substances that we have discussed—sugars, starch, fiber, fats, proteins, minerals, vitamins, water—and also air. To complicate things still further, some of these substances may be in different states—solid, liquid, or gas. Substances combined with other substances are often called *dispersion systems*. One (or possibly more) substance called the *dispersed phase* is scattered or subdivided throughout another continuous substance called the *dispersion medium* (Figure 9-9). For example, table sugar or sucrose may be dispersed in water; the individual molecules of sucrose are the dispersed phase, and the water surrounding each of the sucrose molecules is the dispersion medium or continuous phase.

Dispersion systems may be classified on the basis of the state of matter in each phase. According to this classification, a food system may have the following:

- gas dispersed in a liquid (air in whipped egg white [a foam]),
- a liquid dispersed in a liquid (oil dispersed in vinegar to make mayonnaise [an emulsion]),
- or a solid dispersed in a liquid (proteins such as casein dispersed in milk or ovalbumin dispersed in egg white).

Another classification of dispersion systems is according to the size of the dispersed particles (see Table 9-7). In this classification, the tiniest molecules or particles dispersed in a liquid are said to form true solutions. Particles of intermediate size, although still very small, form colloidal dispersions. Comparatively large particles, such as corn starch granules dispersed in cold water, form suspensions. In line with this classification, small molecules or ions such as sugars, salts, and vitamins are usually found in true solutions; larger molecules such as proteins, pectic substances, cellulose, hemicelluloses, and cooked starch are usually colloidally dispersed; and clumps of molecules such as fat globules and uncooked starch granules are usually suspended and readily separate from the dispersion medium on standing. In true solutions, the dispersed phase is called the solute, and the dispersion medium is referred to as the solvent. In food systems, water is the most common solvent or

TABLE 9-7	Particle Size in Various Types of Dispersion Systems
System	**Particle Size**
True solutions	Less than 1 nm[a] in diameter
Colloidal dispersions	1 nm to 0.1 or 0.2 μm[b] in diameter
Suspensions	Greater than 0.2 μm in diameter

[a] A nanometer (nm) is one thousandth of a micrometer.
[b] A micrometer (μm) is one millionth of a meter.

dispersion medium; however, in a few cases, such as those of butter and margarine, fat is the dispersion medium, and small droplets of water form the dispersed phase.

Characteristics of Solutions

Solutions are common phenomena with respect to food systems. Sugars are in water solutions in fruits, fruit juices, and vegetables. In fact, in all foods containing sugars or salts and water, a solution is formed.

The solutes in solutions are always tiny molecules or ions. These minute particles are in constant kinetic motion but are evenly distributed throughout the solvent; therefore, the mixture is homogeneous. Because solutions are very stable, they remain unchanged indefinitely unless water evaporates and the solute becomes so concentrated that it crystallizes out of solution. The solute is so finely dispersed that it passes through most membranes and filters and cannot be seen under a microscope. True solutions do not usually have the capacity to form gels.

Characteristics of Colloidal Dispersions

The colloidal state is intermediate between a true solution and a coarse suspension, with dispersed particles that are either large molecules, such as proteins or pectin, or clumps of smaller molecules, such as minute globules of fat containing small bunches of triglyceride molecules. Because colloidal particles are larger than those in a true solution, they do not have as much kinetic energy and do not move as rapidly in the dispersion medium. Therefore, they are not as homogeneous and not as stable. They do, however, remain dispersed under usual conditions of food preparation and storage.

Three major factors are responsible for the stabilization of colloidal dispersions. (1) The colloidal particles are moved back and forth by the smaller, faster moving water molecules of the dispersion medium in what is called *Brownian movement.* (2) There are similar net electric charges on the dispersed particles—either all positive or all negative—and like charges repel each other, keeping the colloidal particles separated. (3) The colloidal particles often bind water closely around them (called *water of hydration*), forming a somewhat protective shell.

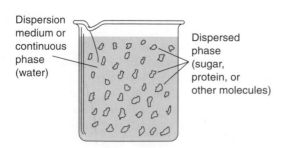

Dispersion medium or continuous phase (water)

Dispersed phase (sugar, protein, or other molecules)

FIGURE 9-9 A dispersion system.

A unique characteristic of many colloidal systems is the ability to form gels. Gels essentially are liquids trapped in a polymer network resulting in a more or less rigid system. A colloidal dispersion in a liquid, pourable condition is called a *sol*, thus distinguishing it from a true solution in which the dispersed particles are smaller. The sol, under proper conditions of temperature, pH, and concentration, may be transformed from a pourable mixture into a gel. It has been suggested that during gel formation, the relatively large colloidal particles loosely join to form a continuous network, sometimes called a *brush-heap structure*, trapping the liquid dispersion medium in its meshes. Figure 9-10 suggests how this might happen. Gel formation in foods may involve proteins, such as egg and gelatin gels, or carbohydrates, such as pectin jams or jellies and starch-thickened pies or puddings. See Chapter 22 for a discussion of gels in gelatins.

Foams, characterized as a gas dispersed in a liquid substance, are considered to be colloidal systems. Emulsions are also colloidal dispersions, where one liquid is finely dispersed throughout a second liquid with which the first liquid is generally considered to be immiscible or insoluble. The formation of a stable emulsion requires a third agent, called an *emulsifying agent*. Certain proteins and phospholipids often act as emulsifying agents in food products.

Characteristics of Suspensions

Suspensions are generally very unstable. The dispersed particles are composed of large groups of molecules, and the force of gravity tends to cause separation of the particles from the dispersion medium. The particles are large enough to be seen under an ordinary microscope. Examples of suspensions in food preparation include French dressings without added emulsifying agents. When the mixture is shaken, the oil becomes dispersed in the vinegar; however, the two phases separate immediately on standing. When corn starch and cold water are mixed together in the preparation of a starch-thickened pudding, the starch granules are suspended in the water; however, on standing only a short time, they settle to the bottom of the container. Tiny crystals of sugar in a crystalline candy such as chocolate fudge also represent an example of a suspension. In this case, the system is more stable; however, larger crystals may form, and the candy may become "sugary" if it stands too long in a dry atmosphere where moisture is evaporated from the product.

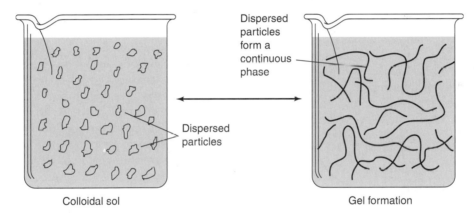

FIGURE 9-10 A representation of gel formation. This is sometimes called *sol-gel transformation* and is typical of colloidal dispersions.

CHAPTER SUMMARY

- Water, carbohydrates, fats, and proteins are the chemical substances found in the largest amounts in foods.

- All foods contain at least some water. Much of the water in plant and animal tissues is held inside the cells. Water in foods may be free water or bound water. Water activity is the ratio of the vapor pressure of water in a food at a specified temperature to the vapor pressure of pure water at the same temperature. Foods with a high water activity level are more perishable than foods with a low water activity level.

- Water plays several important roles in food preparation. It serves as a solvent, a medium for applying heat, and a cleansing agent, and it may promote chemical changes.

- Water is a small molecule containing two hydrogen atoms and one oxygen atom bonded by covalent bonds. Water is unique chiefly because of its polar nature.

- Water may be soft or hard. Water that is hard has various mineral salts that may affect food preparation.

- Carbohydrates are either sugars or more complex substances such as starch. Carbon, hydrogen, and oxygen are the elements that comprise carbohydrates.

- Carbohydrates are classified as monosaccharides, disaccharides, oligosaccharides, or polysaccharides according to the number of basic sugar units that are linked together. The simplest sugar carbohydrates are monosaccharides which include glucose, fructose, and galactose. Sucrose, lactose, and maltose are disaccharides consisting of two monosacccharides linked together. Polysaccharides are complex carbohydrates containing 40 to thousands of monosaccharide units. Starch, dextrins, glycogen, plant fiber, cellulose, hemicelluloses, beta-glucans, pectic substances, and vegetable gums are polysaccharides.

- Starch molecules are in a tightly organized formation called a *granule*. When starch granules are heated in water, they swell in a process called *gelatinization*.

- Dietary fiber refers to the remnants of plant cells that are resistant to hydrolysis or breakdown by human digestive enzymes. Fiber has been recognized as important in our diets.

- Some nonenzymatic browning reactions in foods involve carbohydrates. Sugar caramelizes when heated to temperatures above its melting point. The Maillard reaction is another type of browning reaction.

- Lipids are a broad group of substances with similar properties or characteristics of insolubility in water and a greasy feel. The lipid classification includes three major groups of importance in food preparation: triglycerides, phospholipids, and sterols. Approximately 90 to 95 percent of the fatty substances in foods are triglycerides. Triglycerides are made up of three fatty acids combined with one molecule of an alcohol called *glycerol*.

- Saturated fatty acids have all of the hydrogen atoms with which the carbon atoms can bond. There are no double bonds between carbon atoms that can be broken to allow bonding of more hydrogens. Unsaturated fatty acids contain double bonds between some carbon atoms and thus are unsaturated in terms of the amount of hydrogen they contain. Monounsaturated fatty acids contain one double bond. Fatty acids with more than one double bond are called polyunsaturated.

- The shape of a fatty acid is changed by the presence of a double bond. A cis configuration has the hydrogen atoms on the same side of the double bond. In a trans configuration, the hydrogen atoms are on the opposite sides of the double bond.

- Phospholipids, although present in relatively small amounts in foods, are important in food preparation, chiefly as emulsifying agents. Lecithin is an example of a phospholipid.

- Cholesterol is probably the most widely known sterol and is found only in animal foods. Plants do not manufacture cholesterol, but plant oils do contain some other sterols, generally called *phytosterols*.

- Fats have several important roles in food preparation. Fats are tenderizing agents and serve as a medium of heat transfer in the frying of foods.

- Proteins are large, complex molecules found in every living cell. In food preparation, proteins play important functional roles, for example, binding water, forming gels, thickening, producing foams, and aiding in browning.

- Proteins are unique because, in addition to the elements carbon, hydrogen, and oxygen, they also contain nitrogen. Proteins are large molecules made up of hundreds or thousands of small building blocks called *amino acids*.

- About 22 different amino acids are used as building blocks for proteins. Nine amino acids are considered nutritionally essential for adult humans. Nonessential amino acids may be synthesized in the body.

- Proteins function as buffers to resist a change in acidity. This characteristic is important in the preparation of some foods.

- Applying heat in the cooking of food produces denaturation and/or coagulation of proteins. Proteins also may be denatured by mechanical beating, as is done when egg whites are whipped. A protein molecule is said to be denatured when the molecule unfolds to a degree yet retains the peptide linkages. *Coagulation* is a term used to describe the later stages of protein denaturation in which the denatured protein molecules bind together and produce a gel or solid mass.

- Enzymes, a special kind of protein molecule, catalyze many reactions that affect the characteristics of prepared foods. Bromelin and chymosin (rennin) are examples of enzymes.

- Foods are usually mixtures of various chemical substances. These substances may be in different states—solid, liquid, or gas. Substances combined with other substances are often called *dispersion systems*. Dispersion systems may be classified on the basis of the state of the matter in each phase. Dispersion systems may also be classified according to the size of the dispersed molecules as true solutions, colloidal dispersions, or suspensions.

STUDY QUESTIONS

1. The chemical composition of food can be determined in the laboratory. List the major components and the minor components that are present in foods.

2. Give examples of foods that are high, intermediate, and limited in water content. Explain what is meant by *water activity*.

3. Describe four or five important functions of water in food preparation.

4. What is the pH scale? What does it indicate? Place several common foods on the scale.

5. Describe some unique characteristics of the water molecule.

6. (a) Name two types of hard water and the types of mineral salts contained in each.

   (b) Describe two methods of softening permanently hard water.

7. (a) What are carbohydrates? Simple carbohydrates? Complex carbohydrates?

   (b) In the following list of carbohydrates, indicate which are monosaccharides, which are disaccharides, and which are polysaccharides.

Starch	Fructose (levulose)
Glucose (dextrose)	Galactose
Lactose	Dextrins
Cellulose	Glycogen
Maltose	Sucrose

   (c) Identify the monosaccharide building blocks for each disaccharide and polysaccharide listed in Question 7b.

   (d) What are oligosaccharides? Give examples.

   (e) Give several examples of vegetable gums and describe some of their uses in food processing.

   (f) Name two fractions of starch and describe the major differences in their chemical structures.

   (g) List at least four chemical components of dietary fiber. Indicate which are carbohydrates.

8. (a) Describe in words the chemical structure of a triglyceride.

   (b) Distinguish among saturated, unsaturated, and polyunsaturated fatty acids.

   (c) For each of the following fatty acids, indicate if it is saturated, monounsaturated, or polyunsaturated:

   Palmitic acid
   Linoleic acid
   Butyric acid
   Stearic acid
   Oleic acid

   (d) Distinguish between cis and trans fatty acids.

   (e) What is a simple triglyceride? A mixed triglyceride?

   (f) In the following list of foods, check those that are rich sources of fat:

Whipped cream	Lard	Pork spareribs
Spinach	Walnuts	Potato chips
Pinto beans	Cheddar cheese	Shortening
Corn tortillas	Chocolate	White bread
Margarine	Corn oil	Apples

   (g) How do phospholipids differ from triglycerides in chemical structure? What useful role do phospholipids play in food preparation?

   (h) List several food sources of cholesterol.

9. (a) What chemical groups characterize amino acids?

   (b) How are amino acids joined to make proteins?

   (c) What is meant by the side chains or R groups of a protein? Explain why proteins may act as buffers in foods.

   (d) What is an essential amino acid and how many amino acids are so designated for adult humans?

   (e) From the following list of amino acids, identify those that are nutritionally essential:

Methionine	Threonine	Glutamic acid
Phenylalanine	Isoleucine	Cystine
Tryptophan	Glycine	Leucine
Serine	Alanine	Valine
Lysine	Tyrosine	Histidine

   (f) Explain the meaning of *biological value* in relation to proteins. Why do some protein foods, such as eggs and milk, have high biological value while others, such as kidney beans and wheat flour, have lower biological value?

   (g) Explain how proteins can supplement each other to improve the net nutritional value.

   (h) Name several food sources that are relatively high in protein.

   (i) Describe, in general, the primary, secondary, tertiary, and quaternary structure of proteins.

10. (a) Describe what probably happens when a protein is denatured. List at least four treatments, likely to be applied to foods, that can cause protein denaturation.

    (b) Explain what probably happens when proteins are coagulated and describe some examples of coagulation in foods.

11. **(a)** What is a catalyst? What are enzymes, and how do they act as catalysts?

(b) Suggest a general mechanism of action for enzymes.

(c) Give examples of hydrolytic enzymes.

(d) Explain why enzymes are important in food processing and preparation.

12. **(a)** Describe what is meant by the terms *dispersion system*, *dispersed phase*, *dispersion medium*, *solution*, *solute*, and *solvent*.

(b) Give examples of foods in which types of dispersion systems are classified according to the state of matter in each phase.

(c) Describe three types of dispersion systems classified on the basis of size of dispersed particles.

(d) Describe what probably happens during a sol–gel transformation in a food product. What types of dispersion systems are likely to show this phenomenon?

FATS, FRYING, AND EMULSIONS 10

Fat is present naturally in many foods; it may comprise an important part of their gross chemical composition. The fat present naturally is often referred to as invisible fat. Examples of foods containing appreciable quantities of invisible fat include meat, poultry, fish, dairy products, eggs, nuts, and seeds. Visible fats are shortening, lard, salad and cooking oils, margarine, and butter. Many of these products contain essentially 100 percent fat. The so-called visible fats are often incorporated by the food-processing or foodservice industries into baked products, such as cakes and cookies; into fried foods, such as french-fried potatoes and doughnuts; and into other manufactured foods and may seem invisible to consumers unfamiliar with food composition and food preparation.

In food preparation, we are concerned mostly with triglycerides, as these comprise the major part of the fat naturally found in foods as well as the more purified fats. The classification of lipids, including triglycerides (triacylglycerols), fatty acids, phospholipids, and sterols, was presented in Chapter 9.

In this chapter, the following topics will be discussed:

- Fat consumption and nutrition implications of fat in the diet
- Functions of fat in food
- Properties of fat
- Processing and types of fat
- Deterioration of fat including rancidity and flavor reversion
- Frying
- Fat replacers
- Emulsions, including salad dressings

FAT CONSUMPTION AND NUTRITIVE VALUE

Concern about fat has become one of the nation's primary nutrition issues. During the past decade, the American Heart Association, the surgeon general, and other health organizations have called for a reduction in total dietary fat to 30 percent of kilocalories with no more than 10 percent of total kilocalories from saturated fats [13, 51]. Relationships among the high intake of saturated fat and trans fats with high blood cholesterol levels and coronary heart disease have been reported. Total dietary fat also has been associated with some types of cancer.

Fats, however, also are a valuable part of the diet. Fats provide essential fatty acids, carry fat-soluble vitamins, and are a concentrated energy source. Linoleic acid, an omega-6 polyunsaturated fatty acid (PUFA), is an essential nutrient and thus is a necessary component of the diet. Vitamins A, D, E, and K are fat-soluble vitamins. Butter contains approximately 15,000 international units (IUs) or 3,000 retinol equivalents (REs) of Vitamin A per pound, and margarines are fortified with a similar amount of this vitamin. Refined vegetable oils and hydrogenated shortenings contain little or no vitamin A, but vegetable oils are good sources of vitamin E.

Fat provides nine kilocalories per gram compared to four kilocalories per gram of carbohydrates or proteins. Thus, on a weight basis, pure fat supplies more than two times the kilocalories of pure carbohydrate or protein. For those seeking to reduce caloric intake, high-fat foods can contribute excessive calories. Table 10-1 gives the approximate weight and measure of various fats and fat-rich foods required to furnish 100 kilocalories and the percent of fat found in each food.

The amount and type of fat in the diet of Americans is measured with food disappearance data and food consumption surveys called "What We Eat in America." Both of these data sources were discussed in Chapter 2. Although Americans have reduced the percentage of calories from fat in their diets, the annual per capita intake of calories, as well as fat, has increased [11]. From 1970 to 2003, the food consumption of Americans has increased by 16 percent resulting in an average of 523 additional calories per day per person [21]. In 2005, 87 pounds of fats and oils were consumed per year per person

HEALTHY EATING

Are Some Fats Healthier than Others?

In short—yes, some fats are healthier to consume. Saturated fats and trans fats have been associated with increased blood cholesterol levels and heart disease. Monounsaturated and polyunsaturated fatty acids have been found to have a favorable impact on blood lipids [3, 8]. Research into diet and health is ongoing, and some of the relationships among fat intake, type of fat intake, and health will be more fully understood in the years ahead.

Omega-3 fatty acids are polyunsaturated fats that in particular have been associated with a decreased risk of developing coronary heart disease and hypertension [16, 39, 47]. Plant sources of omega-3 polyunsaturated fatty acids (α-linolenic acid) include soybean oil, canola oil, walnuts, and flaxseed [51]. *Eicosapentaenoic acid* (EPA) and docosa-hexaenoic acid (DHA) are long chain omega-3 fatty acids found in fish which may be particularly beneficial. The body can make the hormonelike compound *prostaglandin* from EPA [27]. This particular prostaglandin reduces the blood clotting rate and thus the likelihood of a clot blocking the coronary arteries. In addition to the health benefits of omega-3 fatty acids, the value of these fatty acids as one of the methods to reduce trans fatty acids in foods is being explored [17].

So how does the consumption of fat in the United States measure up with regard to kinds of fat? The following table reveals that although our consumption of monounsaturated and polyunsaturated fats has increased since 1970, our saturated fat intake has not declined because our overall fat intake has increased. ■

U.S. Food Supply Grams of Fat Per Capita Per Day				
	Total Fat	**Saturated Fat**	**Monounsaturated Fat**	**Polyunsaturated Fat**
1970	145	51	58	25
2004	179	56	79	37

Source: U.S. Department of Agriculture, Economic Research Service Data Sets: Nutrient Availability. Available from http://www.ers.usda.gov/Data/FoodConsumption/NutrientAvailIndex.htm

TABLE 10-1 Approximate Amounts of Various Fat and Fat-Rich Foods Required to Furnish 100 Kilocalories

Food	Fat Content (%)	Weight (g)	Approximate Measure (Tbsp)
Butter	80	13	1
Margarine	80	13	1
Hydrogenated fat	100	11	1
Lard	100	11	1
Salad oil	100	11	1
Bacon fat	100	11	1
Peanut butter	46	16	1
Cream, light	20	50	3
Cream, whipping	35	33	2, or about double the volume if whipped
Cream, sour	25	48	4
Cheese, cheddar	32	24	1" cube
Egg, scrambled	11	61	1 egg
Ground beef, regular, broiled	21	35	1 ounce
Doughnut, yeast	21	26	1/2 doughnut

which is an annual increase of 31 pounds per person from 1970 intake levels [52]. Over the years, the types of fat chosen by consumers have changed as well. In 1970, 14 pounds of animal fat and 39 pounds of vegetable fats were used per capita annually. By 2005, the amount of animal fat per capita annually had decreased modestly (down to 11 pounds); however, vegetable fat increased considerably to 74 pounds.

FUNCTION OF FATS IN FOOD PREPARATION

Fats play a variety of roles in food preparation. They give flavor and a mouthfeel that is associated with moistness, thus contributing greatly to palatability and eating pleasure [15]. Some fats, such as butter and bacon fat, are used specifically to add flavor. As an ingredient in baked products, fats "shorten" strands of the protein gluten and thereby tenderize it. Some fats also contribute to the aeration of batters and doughs. Their capacity to be heated to high temperatures makes them an excellent medium for the transfer of heat to foods in the process of frying. Fats are major components of salad dressings, in which they usually constitute one phase of an emulsion. Lecithin, a phospholipid, is an example of a fat that may act as the emulsifying agent, or emulsifier. In addition, fats are a concentrated source of energy for the body. Functions of fats in food preparation are summarized in Table 10-2.

PROPERTIES OF FATS

Fats exhibit several unique properties that influence their use in food preparation. Solubility, melting point, smoke point, plasticity, and flavor will be discussed. The chemical structure of triglycerides and their component fatty acids was discussed in Chapter 9.

Solubility

Fats are insoluble in water and therefore do not mix readily with water-based food systems. They also have a greasy feel. In the laboratory, they are soluble in a group of organic solvents that include chloroform, ether, and petroleum ether.

Melting Point

In common usage, fats that have a relatively high melting point and are solid at room temperature are called *fats*, whereas those that have lower melting points and are liquid at room temperature are called *oils*. The melting point of a fat is influenced by the type, form, and length of fatty acids. These characteristics have significance for food preparation and nutrition.

Type of Fatty Acids. Saturated fats hold all of the hydrogen that may be attached to carbon atoms (see Chapter 9). In contrast, unsaturated fats are capable of

TABLE 10-2 Functions of Fat in Food	
Functions of Fat	**Examples**
Flavor	Fats such as butter and olive oil add distinctive flavors and may carry and enhance flavors in some foods.
Color	Butter adds a yellow, creamy color to some dishes.
	Foods fried in fat are browned.
Texture	In a properly prepared pastry, shortening or lard provides for a flaky texture (see Chapter 19).
	Shortening creamed with sugar when making a cake will contribute to a fine cell structure and moist crumb.
	Fried foods become crisp.
	Fat, such as dairy cream, contributes viscosity or creaminess.
Tenderness	In baked goods, fats and oils interfere with the development of gluten (see Chapter 15).
Emulsification	Vegetable oils are one phase of the emulsion in salad dressings.
Heat transfer	Fats can be heated to a high temperature which is well above the boiling temperature of water resulting in desirable texture, flavor, and color changes.
Control of crystallization	Crystal formation in ice cream is controlled in part by fat from dairy cream.
Moistness in meat	Fat contributes to the sensation of moistness.

binding more hydrogen. When fats contain a relatively high proportion of saturated fatty acids, such as palmitic and stearic acids, they have relatively high melting points and are usually solid at room temperature. However, when fats contain a relatively high proportion of unsaturated fatty acids, such as the monounsaturated oleic acid and the polyunsaturated linoleic acid, they have relatively low melting points and are oils at room temperature. Fatty substances that have a relatively high content of polyunsaturated fatty acids, or a high ratio of polyunsaturated fatty acids to saturated fatty acids (P/S ratio), are commonly called *polyunsaturated oils* or *fats*. Examples of such products are corn, soybean, cottonseed, and safflower oils, and many soft margarines. Figure 10-1 provides the percentage of polyunsaturated, monounsaturated, and polyunsaturated fats found in several kinds of dietary fat.

Trans Fatty Acids. The trans form of a fatty acid has a higher melting point than its cis form, likely due to the shapes of the molecules. The cis form is more bent and thus less able to pack tightly together with other molecules. Tightly packed triglyceride molecules require more heat or energy to move them apart, thus increasing the melting temperature. See Figure 10-2.

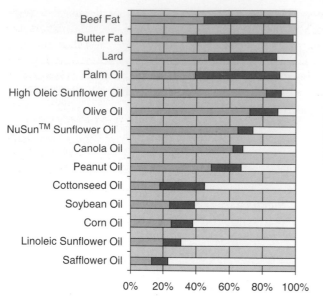

FIGURE 10-1 Dietary fats vary in the percentage of polyunsaturated, monounsaturated, and saturated fats. Saturated fats are associated with an increased risk of heart disease. Polyunsaturated and monounsaturated fats therefore are preferable from a health perspective.

cis hydrogen atoms are on the same side of the double bond

$$H \quad H$$
$$| \quad |$$
$$(-C=C-)$$

trans hydrogen atoms are on opposite sides of the double bond

$$H$$
$$|$$
$$(-C=C-)$$
$$|$$
$$H$$

FIGURE 10-2 The shape of the fatty acid is influenced by the presence of the double bond between the carbon atoms. This double bond limits the rotation of the carbon atom and therefore the placement of the hydrogen atoms. Some trans fatty acids occur naturally in certain fats; however, trans fatty acids most frequently are found in food as the result of hydrogenation.

Length of Carbon Atoms. Fatty acids usually contain an even number of carbon atoms ranging from 4 to 24 carbon atoms in length (see Chapter 9). As the number of carbon atoms in the fatty acids increases, thus making longer-chain fatty acids, the melting point increases. For example, butyric acid with four carbon atoms melts at a lower temperature than stearic acid with 18 carbon atoms. Both of these fatty acids are saturated. Butter contains a relatively large proportion of short-chain fatty acids, many of them saturated, and melts at a lower temperature than beef fat or hydrogenated shortenings, which contain more long-chain fatty acids.

Melting Point of Chocolate. All food fats are mixtures of triglycerides, although each contains different kinds of triglyceride molecules. Thus, fats usually do not have a sharp melting point, but rather melt over a range of temperatures. An exception is the fat in chocolate. Because many of its triglyceride molecules are alike in chemical structure, having similar component fatty acids, chocolate melts over a fairly narrow temperature range that is close to body temperature, thus releasing in the mouth, as it is eaten, its delightful flavor bouquet and smooth mouthfeel.

Smoke Point

The smoke point of a fat is the temperature at which smoke comes from the surface of the fat when heated. Fats have different smoke points; for example, whole butter has a smoke point of approximately 260°F (127°C) compared to the smoke point of soybean oil which is 495°F (232°C). Soybean, corn, canola, and peanut oils are types of fats better suited for high heat applications such as deep-fat frying or sautéing because of their high smoke points. Butter that has been clarified by melting and then skimming off the surface layer, composed of water and milk solids, to leave only the fat component also has a relatively high smoke point.

Plasticity

Most fats that appear to be solid at room temperature actually contain both solid fat crystals and liquid oil. The

FOCUS ON SCIENCE

Plasticity of Fats

The plasticity of a fat is related to the fatty acid profile and the arrangement of the fatty acids after they are heated and manipulated. After manipulation, fatty acid chains can form into

three different arrangements known as: α (alpha), β (beta), and β' (beta prime). β' crystals are smooth and creamy. Manufacturers of plastic shortenings and margarines use the β' stability of mixed glycerides to produce products with this desired creaminess. The fatty acids, which vary in saturation, isomerism, and length, require time to rearrange into the dense three-dimensional packing crystal. In the β' arrangement, alternate rows of triglycerides are at right angles. Cottonseed oil contains a fatty acid profile that promotes β' crystals, and for this reason it is used in the manufacture of some plastic fats.

liquid part is held in a network of small crystals. Because of this unique combination of liquid and solid, the fat can be molded or pressed into various shapes without breaking, as would a brittle substance. The fat is said to exhibit plasticity. The type and size of the crystals in a plastic fat influence the performance of the fat in baked products and pastry. Plastic fats can be creamed, that is, mixed with the incorporation of air.

Flavor

Some fats that are used for seasoning at the table and in salad dressings possess distinctive and pleasing flavors. These include butter, bacon fat, olive oil, sesame seed oil, and margarines. Margarines have a certain amount of butterlike flavor because, in their manufacture, the fat is churned with cultured milk or whey and additional flavoring substances are often added. In choosing fats for flavor purposes, the cost may also have to be considered. For example, olive oil and butter are more expensive selections compared to other oils or margarine.

The ability of fats to take up or dissolve certain aromatic flavor substances is frequently used in food preparation. Onions, celery, peppers, and similar flavorful foods are cooked in fat to produce a savory fat that can be incorporated into food mixtures. Aromatic fruit and other flavors are also dissolved by fat.

PROCESSING, REFINING, AND TYPES OF FATS

Fats and oils commonly used in food preparation are separated from various materials and refined. Many oils come from seeds or fruits, lard comes from pork tissue, and butter comes from cream. Further processing produces fats such as margarines and hydrogenated shortenings.

Hydrogenation

The process of hydrogenation changes liquid oils into more solid plastic shortenings. The fats produced by hydrogenation are neutral in flavor, have a high enough smoke point to make them useful for frying, and have good shortening power. Hydrogenated fats also resist oxidation which results in undesirable rancid flavors and odors. The plastic quality of hydrogenated shortenings is important in the preparation of certain baked goods when the fat is to be creamed into the sugar, as in cookies, or cut into the flour in products, such as pie crust and biscuits. Hydrogenation also changes a vegetable oil into margarine which may be spread on bread.

Hydrogenation, however, produces trans fatty acids (see Figure 10-2) which have been associated with an increased risk of heart disease. Shortenings, if not trans fat reduced, contain 25 to 29 percent trans fatty acids and 25 to 29 percent saturated fats [44].

How Oils Are Hydrogenated. Hydrogenation occurs in a reactor, where hydrogen gas is bubbled through the liquid oil in the presence of a nickel catalyst, which speeds the reaction. In the process of hydrogenation, some of the double bonds between the carbon atoms of the fatty acid portion of the triglyceride molecule are broken, and hydrogen is added. This chemical change makes the fatty acids more saturated and increases the melting point of the fat. With sufficient hydrogenation, it becomes a solid at room temperature. Often, products that have received different degrees of hydrogenation are combined to produce the desired effect [34]. Some oils, such as frying fats used in foodservice operations, are partially hydrogenated.

Various approaches are being used by manufacturers to reduce trans fatty acid content of shortenings and margarines [36, 50]. A modification of the hydrogenation process can reduce the development of trans fatty acids. Interesterification by a chemical or enzymatic process is one way to produce hydrogenated fats such as margarine with fewer trans fatty acids [10, 50]. The use of low temperatures, high pressures, and high catalyst concentrations has been found to reduce the trans fatty acids by 50 percent [17]. Fractionalization is another approach used to reduce trans fats and involves the batch cooling of the refined oil followed by batch filtration [12].

Health Implications of Hydrogenation. Although some trans fatty acids occur naturally in foods such as

FOCUS ON SCIENCE

What Is Interesterification?

Interesterification is basically a process in which the ester bonds linking fatty acids to the glycerol backbone are split, then the newly liberated fatty acids are randomly shuffled within a fatty acid pool and re-esterified onto a new position, either on the same glycerol (*intra*esterification) or onto another glycerol (*inter*esterification).

Interesterification has been industrially viable in the food industry since the 1940s to improve the spreadability and baking properties of lard. In the 1970s, there was a renewed interest in this process, particularly as a hydrogenation replacement in the manufacture of zero trans fat margarines. Today it plays a key role in the production of low-calorie fat replacers such as Procter and Gamble's olestra, or Olean®, and Nabisco's salatrim, or Benefat®.

Source: Rousseau, D. and Marangoni, A. G. (2002). Chapter 10: Chemical interesterification of food lipids. In *Food Lipids*, edited by C. C. Akoh and D. B. Min), p. 303. New York: Marcel Dekker, Inc.

butter, approximately 90 percent of trans fatty acids in the American diet are found in partially hydrogenated vegetable oil (margarines and shortenings) [54]. Research has shown a positive, linear link between trans fatty acid intake and the elevation of plasma cholesterol [23, 30]. Thus, trans fatty acids, like saturated fats, have been found to increase the risk of coronary heart disease [53].

The food label has been shown to influence consumers' fat intake [40]. Effective January 2006, the FDA requires manufacturers to include trans fat content on the Nutrition Facts label (see Chapter 4). Consumers are encouraged to compare fats or products containing fats by selecting the product with the lowest combined trans and saturated fatty acid levels and the lower amount of cholesterol [53].

Hydrogenated Shortening

Hydrogenated shortenings are used in many baked goods including cakes, pie crusts, biscuits, and cookies. Shortenings are also found in many commercially prepared crackers, cookies, and other snack foods. Hydrogenated shortenings often have emulsifiers, such as monoglycerides and diglycerides, added to them. The addition of emulsifiers to fats used in cakes makes possible the addition of higher proportions of sugar and liquid to fat, as is desired for some cake formulas. The presence of mono- and diglycerides in hydrogenated shortening, however, decreases the smoke point of the fat, thus making it somewhat less valuable for frying purposes. In the home, often only one type of general-purpose shortening is used. Commercial food-processing and foodservice establishments may use several different shortenings which have been formulated for specific purposes such as deep-fat frying, cake making, or icings.

Margarine

Oleomargarine was first developed in 1869 by a French chemist, Mège-Mouries, in response to the offer of a prize by Napoleon III for a palatable, nutritious, and economical alternate for butter. Beef fat was the chief constituent of the original margarine. Since that time, many changes have occurred in the composition and processing of margarine.

Ingredients. Margarine is made from hydrogenated vegetable oils; liquid vegetable oils; milk, buttermilk, or whey; and additives which provide desirable characteristics. Margarine is a *water-in-fat emulsion* and must contain not less than 80 percent fat according to the standard of identity for margarine established by the FDA (see Chapter 4 for more about food regulations). Most regular margarines contain about 80 percent fat.

Soybean and cottonseed oils, refined and partially hydrogenated to the desired consistency, are extensively used to produce margarines. Liquid oils may be blended with partially hydrogenated oils in such a way that the total polyunsaturated fatty acid content is higher than in ordinary margarines. If the first ingredient listed on the label is oil, rather than partially hydrogenated oil, the polyunsaturated fatty acid content of the margarine is likely to be relatively high.

Other ingredients permitted in margarine by the federal standard of identity are vitamins A and D for nutritive purposes; diacetyl as a flavor constituent; lecithin, monoglycerides, and/or diglycerides of fat-forming fatty acids as emulsifying agents; artificial color; salt; citric acid or certain citrates; and sodium benzoate, benzoic acid, or sorbic acid as a preservative to the extent of 0.1 percent.

Types of Margarine.   A variety of margarine products are available and are described on Table 10-3. The reduced-fat and whipped margarines, while desirable for use as table spreads, are generally not recommended for baking. Recipes for cookies and other baked items have been formulated for a specified amount of fat and thus the use of a lower-fat margarine will have an impact on quality. The functions of fat in baking are discussed in Chapter 15.

Plant stanol and sterol ester (also called *phytostanols* and *phytosterols*) based margarines were introduced in the United States in 1999 [29]. Stanol and sterol esters have been found to lower cholesterol levels up to 14 percent in adults [28]. The plant stanol and sterol esters function by blocking the absorption of dietary cholesterol [41]. In 2000, the FDA issued a rule allowing a health claim on stanol and sterol ester containing products for reducing the risk of coronary heart disease providing the foods are low in saturated fat and cholesterol. However, some concern has been expressed about the impact of these products on the absorption of beta-carotene, lycopene, and vitamin E.

Processing of Oils

Vegetable oils are obtained from fruits, seeds, and nuts. Soy and palm is the source of nearly two-thirds of the world's vegetable oil [12]. Oil most often is removed from oil-containing seed fruits or nuts by pressing in batches or a continuous expeller press. The meal leaving the expeller may contain some residual oil which is removed by solvent extraction. Hexane is the most common solvent used and is evaporated from the oil. The meal remaining after the oil has been obtained is used for animal feed, some select human food applications, fuel, or fertilizer [12].

The crude oils are further refined to remove free fatty acids, color, and suspended meal particles [12]. An alkaline material is added to remove the free fatty acids not attached to a glycerol molecule. Free fatty acids in excess can detract from the oil's flavor and decrease its effectiveness when used for frying. The unwanted products of this reaction are then removed by centrifuging and washing, with a final drying process, followed by bleaching and deodorizing to remove color pigments and further purify the oil [34]. *RBD* refers to an oil that has been refined, bleached, and deodorized.

TABLE 10-3 Varieties of Margarine

Type of Margarine	Description and Characteristics
Regular or standard	Will contain 80 percent fat. This is the type of margarine to use in recipes for baked goods such as cookies.
Light or reduced fat	Contain a lesser amount of fat, a greater amount of water, and a stronger emulsifying system than regular margarines. Amount of oil or hydrogenated oil varies between 45 and 75 percent.
	Generally not appropriate for use in a recipe for cookies and other baked goods. Also not desirable for sautéing because the added water will result in excessive spattering.
Whipped	May contain an inert gas to increase the volume and decrease the density, thus has six sticks to the pound instead of four.
Margarines made with canola oil, olive oil, or other.	May be made with specialized oils to add unique flavor, meet consumer preferences for type of oil, or to provide other desirable characteristics.
Trans fat free	Vegetable oils hydrogenated using a process to avoid trans fatty acids
Margarine and butter blends	Contain both margarine and butter to offer more butter flavor while having less cholesterol than 100 percent butter.
Unsalted	Does not contain salt.
Plant stanol or sterol ester	Margarine containing plant stanol or sterol esters which have been shown to reduce cholesterol levels.

Winterization. Some cooking oils become cloudy when stored in the refrigerator and thus are undesirable for salads and salad dressings that will be refrigerated. The cloudiness of these oils occurs because some of the triglyceride molecules in the oil have higher melting points than other molecules in the mixture and crystallize or become solid at the low refrigerator temperature. In the manufacture of oils intended to be used primarily for making salad dressings, a winterizing process is applied. In this process, the temperature of the oil is lowered to a

HOT TOPICS

Plant Sterol Esters—Natural Phytonutrients

It has been known for several decades that plant sterols can reduce blood cholesterol levels. They have been used to some extent as supplements and as drugs to lower cholesterol levels in hypercholesterolemic patients and appear to inhibit the uptake of dietary cholesterol from the intestine. In 1999, two margarines containing plant sterol esters were put on the market with brand names of Benecol® and Take Control® [29].

What are plant sterols, or phytosterols as they are commonly called? They are chemical cousins of cholesterol but are produced in plants, rather than in animals, where they stabilize cell membranes. Phytostanols are a related group of compounds that are chemically saturated, having two more hydrogen atoms in their ring structures. Because of their insolubility, it was not possible to add these compounds to foods until it was discovered that, when they were combined with fatty acids as esters, they could be readily incorporated into fatty foods [28].

Phytosterols and phytostanols are safe enough to be classified as GRAS and are highly effective in relatively small amounts. Two servings a day of the special margarines can reduce LDL cholesterol by about 10 percent. These products may be labeled with the FDA-approved health claim that "plant sterols esters and plant stanols esters may reduce the risk of coronary heart disease by lowering blood cholesterol levels" [29].

Phytosterols may be derived from the vegetable oil refining process. Phytostanols are often produced from "tall oil," a phytosterol-rich byproduct from the pulping of pine and other trees [28]. These substances are then purified and esterified with food-grade fatty acids. With the availability of these products, an entirely new line of heart-healthy foods may be marketed. ■

point at which the higher-melting triglycerides crystallize. Then the oil is filtered to remove these crystals. The remaining oil, referred to as *salad oil*, has a lower melting point and does not crystallize at refrigerator temperatures [34]. Thus, even under refrigeration, a winterized oil will remain a clear, liquid oil.

Kinds of Oils

Vegetables oils may be used in cooking as oils or hydrogenated to produce shortenings and margarines. A number of different oils may be found in the marketplace. The flavor, cooking characteristics, nutrition profile (Figure 10-1), and price influence the choice of oil.

Soybean. Soybean oil is one of the dominant edible oils in the United States. Until the early 1940s, it was not used in this country chiefly because of its susceptibility to oxidation and development of off-flavors described as being "grassy" and "painty." These off-flavors, or flavor reversion (discussed later in this chapter), appear to be related to the content of linolenic acid. Partially hydrogenated soybean oil has improved stability and is a major component of vegetable shortenings and margarines [19]. Also, low-linolenic acid soybean oil, with higher stability toward oxidation, has been developed using conventional plant-breeding methods [20].

Cottonseed. Cottonseed oil was America's first vegetable oil, developed over a century ago as a byproduct of the cotton industry. With lower cotton production, the supply of cottonseed oil has decreased. Much of the cottonseed oil used in the United States is consumed as a salad or cooking oil or is formulated into shortenings that are used in baking and frying. It has a neutral flavor that does not mask the flavor of other products [19].

Olive. The most expensive of the edible oils is olive oil, also one of the most ancient oils. It has always been prized for its flavor, particularly by those who have lived in the Mediterranean area, where olive oil is the major cooking and salad oil. The popularity of olive oil in the United States has grown as consumers embrace world cuisines and seek to use oils with perceived health benefits. Olive oil contains a high percentage (approximately 92 percent) of the monounsaturated fatty acid oleic. It is also more stable to oxidation than most oils because of its low content of linoleic acid, a polyunsaturated fatty acid.

Good grades of olive oil are those that have not been refined, deodorized, or otherwise processed. The terms *extra virgin*, *virgin*, and *pure* indicate the acidity level and amount of processing. *Virgin olive oil* applies only to oil obtained from the first pressing of the olives without further processing. *Extra virgin olive oil* is a top grade of virgin olive oil because of its low acidity level. The term *pure* can be used for blends of virgin and refined oils that have been processed from the pulp remaining after the first pressing of the olives. Pure olive oil is less expensive and less flavorful as compared to extra virgin and virgin olive oils [33]. Pure olive oil however, has a higher smoke point (468°F/242°C) compared to other types of olive oils and is therefore a better choice for higher temperature cooking techniques such as sautéing [7].

HOT TOPICS

Urban Legends—Canola Oil

Think of the information you have "heard through the grapevine" or perhaps through the Internet? Some of these tidbits may later be found to be true, partially true, somewhat misleading, or outright wrong. Urban legends can be easily circulated in today's high tech world. Dangers associated with food are a popular subject area for urban legends, and knowing where to sort out the facts is critical for any food or nutrition professional.

Canola oil has been the subject of urban legends which incorrectly state it is a highly dangerous, even potentially poisonous substance. Canola is not rapeseed. This is an important distinction because rapeseed contains erucic acid and glucosinolates which are undesirable. Canola was produced from traditional plant breeding to remove these undesirable components. Canola has been studied for over 20 years and has been found to reduce the risk of heart disease because of its desirable fatty acid profile. The FDA has approved Canola oil for use in the United States and has granted it GRAS status. Likewise, Canola oil is used widely in Europe. In Europe, however, this product is called oilseed rape or rape oil as they choose not to use the name developed in Canada.

There are more myths and questions you may find about Canola, as well as other foods; just take time to check out the scientific facts. ■

Canola. Canola is the name given to cultivars of rapeseed that are very low in erucic acid. Canola oil is a highly stable oil that is high in unsaturated fat (94 percent), 58 percent of which is the monounsaturated fatty acid, oleic [19]. This oil has increased in popularity during the 1990s because of its health advantages over other oils. Canola oil is relatively new on the market, compared to other oils. It is being used in salad dressings, margarines, shortenings, and fats produced for commercial frying operations.

Sunflower, Safflower, Peanut, and Corn. Sunflower oil has good flavor stability and is growing in popularity. Safflower oil, with 78 percent linoleic acid, has the highest polyunsaturated fatty acid content. However, it is more expensive than many other oils and lacks flavor stability [34]. Peanut oil, on the other hand, has excellent oxidative stability. It is preferred by some snack food manufacturers because of its flavor [19]. Corn oil has a naturally sweet taste and is used primarily in margarines. It is a relatively stable source of polyunsaturated fatty acids because of its low linolenic acid content [26].

Tropical Oils. Coconut, palm, and palm kernel oil are known as tropical oils. Coconut oil is solid at room temperature because it contains a high proportion of saturated fatty acids, about 92 percent. Many of these are short-chain fatty acids, particularly lauric acid. Coconut oil has a sharp melting point, similar to the fat found in chocolate, and is therefore useful in confections and cookie fillings.

Palm-kernel oil is much like coconut oil and composed of a high proportion of saturated fatty acids. Palm oil is different from palm kernel oil; it is extracted from the fruit rather than the kernel of the palm tree [5, 6]. Although half of the fatty acids in palm oil are saturated, it contains few short-chain fatty acids. It is semisolid at room temperature and has a long shelf life. Palm oil may be used in margarine and shortening and thus is on the labels of a number of processed foods. Recently, palm oil is being used in conjunction with soybean oils to produce trans fatty acid free margarines [36].

New Oils. Traditional plant breeding and genetic engineering are being used to enhance vegetable oil quality. High-oleic acid oils, including modified soybean, safflower, sunflower, and canola, are being developed through plant breeding. Advantages of these oils include increased stability to oxidation (without hydrogenation and the consequent increase in trans fatty acids) and nutritional effects of a low saturated fat in the diet [31, 38, 44]

Butter

Butter is the fat of cream that is separated more or less completely from the other milk constituents by agitation or churning. The mechanical rupture of the protein film that surrounds each of the fat globules in cream allows the globules to coalesce. Butter formation is an example of the breaking of an *oil-in-water emulsion* by agitation. The resulting emulsion that forms in butter itself is a *water-in-oil emulsion*, with about 18 percent water being dispersed in about 80 percent fat and a small amount of protein acting as the emulsifier. Buttermilk, a lowfat milk product, remains after butter is churned from cream. The key steps in butter production are provided in Table 10-4.

Sweet, Cultured, and Clarified Butter. Butter is made from either sweet or sour cream. Cultured butter is made from cream cultured with bacteria. It has a more pronounced flavor. Either sweet or cultured butter may be clarified by melting the butter and skimming off the top layer composed of water and milk solids. Recall that butter contains approximately 80 percent butter fat, 18 percent water, and milk solids. Clarified butter contains only the butter fat.

Salted or Unsalted. Some sweet-cream butter is marketed unsalted as sweet butter. Salted butter is preferred by most Americans; unsalted butter is used extensively in Europe and by European-trained chefs. Unsalted butter in cooking offers the advantage of allowing the cook to control more fully the seasoning of the dish. Unsalted butter may be especially desirable when baking.

TABLE 10-4 Key Steps in Butter Production

Step	Description
Cream	Cream is separated from milk and standardized to a fat percent level for quality control.
Pasteurization	By law, cream is heated to reduce pathogenic bacteria and enzymes.
Aging	Cream is held under refrigeration to ensure proper churning and butter texture.
Ripening (optional)	If cultured butter is desired, a culture of lactic acid bacteria is added to develop flavor and aroma characteristic of cultured butter.
Churning	Cream is agitated by a continuous or batch method.
Draining buttermilk	The liquid remaining after the fat globules coalesce is buttermilk. This lowfat byproduct of butter churning is drained from the butter.
Washing (optional)	The butter may be washed.
Working	The butter is worked (mixed) to remove any remaining water or buttermilk and to mix in salt and coloring if desired.
Packing and storage	Butter is packaged and cooled to storage temperature.

Source: Adapted from Reference 55

Coloring.   Butter produced when cows are on green feed is naturally more pigmented than butter produced when green feed is not consumed. Thus, the season of the year and consumer preferences for butter of different degrees of color determine the use of coloring so that a uniform color may be sold throughout the year. Carotene is the coloring agent commonly used.

Grade Standards.   The USDA has set grade standards for butter [1]. Grades for butter include U.S. Grade AA and U.S. Grade A. U.S. Grade AA butter must have a smooth, creamy texture, delicate sweet flavor, and be made from high-quality, fresh, sweet cream. U.S. Grade A butter rates close to the top grade, however, may not be as smooth and spreadable as Grade AA. Butter must have at least 80 percent milkfat by federal law.

Flavor.   Butter flavor is complex, resulting as it does from the combination of many flavor compounds. A substance called *diacetyl*, formed from bacterial action, is an important flavor component of butter. Butter is highly valued by many for its flavor.

Lard

Lard is one of the oldest culinary fats; however, the nutritional profile, lack of uniformity in the production of lard, as well as its flavor and some of its physical properties, such as a grainy texture, resulted in a reduction in the use of lard by many Americans as other shortenings became available. In 1970, the per capita annual availability of lard in the food supply was 4.5 pounds as compared to 0.7 pound in 2004 [52]. Lard is still the preferred fat in Mexican cuisine for such dishes as refried beans. It also has excellent shortening power resulting in tender pie crusts.

Lard is the fat rendered from the fatty tissues of the hog. Rendering involves subdividing the fatty tissue into small particles and heating. The melted fat then separates from the connective tissue and other cell residues. The quality of lard depends on such factors as the part of the body from which the fat is obtained, the feed used for fattening the animal, and the rendering process. Leaf fat, which lines the abdominal cavity, is used to make the better qualities of lard.

A chemical modification, called *interesterification*, can be applied to lard to improve its plasticity and creaming qualities. Interesterification involves treating the fat with a catalyst at a controlled temperature, which produces a movement of some of the fatty acids to other triglyceride molecules in the mixture. This creates a more random distribution of fatty acids on the triglyceride molecules. The degree of unsaturation is not changed, but the way the fat crystallizes does affect its creaming properties and improves its performance in such baked products as shortened cakes.

Lard is susceptible to spoilage by the development of rancidity. Antioxidants are added to lard in processing to increase its shelf life. Some lard samples have relatively low smoking temperatures and have not been commonly used for frying; however, lards with high smoke points can be produced.

Making Butter at Home

Butter may be made at home relatively easily with today's appliances. Here's how to do it:

Take one to two cups of heavy, pasteurized cream (preferably without added stabilizers) and blend in a food processor using the plastic blade, whisk, or normal chopping blade. You will see (a) soft whipped cream, (b) firm whipped cream, (c) coarse whipped cream, (d) seizing of the cream followed by fine bits of butter in buttermilk, and (e) yellowish butter separated from milky buttermilk. Drain the buttermilk, leaving the butter.

The butter produced at this stage may be eaten or additional steps may be followed for better storage. To further process the butter, add one-half cup of ice-cold water and blend. Discard the wash water and repeat until the water is clear. Finally knead the butter with a potato masher and pour out water as it separates. When most of the water is removed, you are ready to enjoy! ■

Source: http://webexhibits.org/butter/doityourself.html

DETERIORATION OF FAT AND ITS CONTROL

A special type of chemical spoilage that commonly occurs in fats and fatty foods is rancidity. It may develop on storage, particularly if the fats are highly unsaturated and the environmental conditions are appropriate for initiating the reaction. The chemical changes that result in rancidity are chiefly of two types: hydrolytic and oxidative.

Hydrolytic Rancidity

Hydrolysis involves breaking chemical bonds and, in the process, adding the elements of water—hydrogen and oxygen. When triglycerides are hydrolyzed, they yield free fatty acids and glycerol. This reaction may be catalyzed by the enzyme *lipase*. Release of free fatty acids does not produce undesirable odors and flavors in fats unless they are short-chain fatty acids, such as butyric acid and caproic acid. These fatty acids predominate in butter. They are volatile and largely responsible for the unpleasant odor and flavor of rancid butter. They may render butter inedible even when present in low concentrations. Long-chain free fatty acids, such as stearic, palmitic, and oleic acids, do not usually produce a disagreeable flavor unless other changes, such as oxidation, also occur.

Oxidative Rancidity

The characteristic unpleasant odor of fats in which oxidative rancidity has developed is difficult to describe but widely recognized. Oxidative rancidity requires oxygen but is more likely to occur when the fat also is exposed to heat, light, or metals such as iron and copper. Oxidative rancidity also may be caused by the action of an enzyme called *lipoxygenase*, which is present in some foods. Rancidity most often results from a strictly chemical reaction that is self-perpetuating, called a *chain reaction* (Figure 10-3).

Most susceptible to oxidative changes are the unsaturated fatty acid portions of triglycerides. Therefore, more highly unsaturated fats, such as linoleic acid, are most susceptible to oxidative rancidity. Highly hydrogenated fats and natural fats composed largely of saturated fatty acids are relatively resistant to this type of chemical change, but all natural fats contain some unsaturated fatty acids and therefore may become rancid.

Oxidative rancidity is responsible for most of the spoilage of fats and fatty foods. It may also be a problem in dry foods containing only small quantities of fat, such as prepared cereals. When rancidity develops in fatty foods, the fat-soluble vitamins A and E that are present also may be oxidized.

Flavor Reversion.   A special type of oxidative deterioration, *flavor reversion*, involves a change in edible fats characterized by the development of an objectionable flavor prior to the onset of true rancidity. The kinds of off-flavors that develop during reversion vary with the particular fat and with the conditions that cause the change. No fat is entirely free from the tendency to develop flavor reversion, but some oils, such as corn and cottonseed oils, are quite resistant to this type of deterioration. Soybean oil, which contains high levels of linoleic acid, is highly susceptible to flavor reversion. Reverted soybean oil has been described as "painty," "beany," "hay-like," "grassy," and, in the final stages, "fishy."

Reversion may develop during exposure of the fat to ultraviolet or visible light or heat. A small amount of oxygen seems to be necessary for the reaction, which is

FOCUS ON SCIENCE

Rancidity

Why do some fats become rancid more quickly than others?

The keeping quality of fat or oil is determined by its degree of saturated or unsaturated fatty acids. Fatty acids have a greater tendency to become rancid when more unsaturated. Therefore, a monounsaturated fatty acid (one double bond) has a better keeping quality than a polyunsaturated fatty acid (two or more double bonds). Linolenic acid (three double bonds) has a greater chance to become rancid than linoleic acid (with two double bonds). Additionally, for a food fat to become rancid, there must be a free fatty acid. This "clipping action" of the fatty acid from the glycerol is caused by light (ultraviolet rays), moisture, heat, metal (copper or iron), or enzymes.

Fat	H
This diagram depicts a fatty acid chain.	$[-C-C-C=C-C-]$ with H above and H below

Fat-Free Radical (-H)	H
The chemical oxidation of fat is initiated when a hydrogen atom (H) is lost from the fatty acid chain as shown here.	$[-C-C-C=C-C-]$ with H above and • below
The carbon atom is therefore left as a free radical which is a highly reactive chemical group.	

Peroxide-Free Radical (+O$_2$)	H
The free radical reacts with oxygen (O$_2$) in the environment to produce a peroxide-free radical as shown here.	$[-C-C-C=C-C-]$ with H above, then O, O, • below
Peroxide-free radicals also are quite reactive.	

Another fatty acid chain to continue reaction.	H
	$[-C-C-C=C-C-]$ with H above and H below

Hydroperoxide (+H)	H
The *chain reaction* is continued when the peroxide-free radical pulls a hydrogen atom from an adjacent fatty acid chain.	$[-C-C-C=C-C-]$ with H above, then O, O, H below
Hydroperoxide, as depicted here, and a fat-free radical, as shown in the next diagram, result from the reaction of the peroxide-free radical with the fatty acid chain (previous diagrams).	
Hydroperoxides do not appear to have unpleasant rancid odors and flavors, but these molecules readily break into pieces, producing smaller volatile substances that give the characteristic odors of rancid fat	

Fat-Free Radical	
With the formation of another fat-free radical, the chain reaction continues. Refer to the fat-free radical above and follow down the steps again and again!	H
	$[-C-C-C=C-C-]$ with H above and • below
Because the reaction shown in this series of diagrams is a chain reaction, once a fat develops a slight rancid odor, the production of more pronounced rancidity occurs rapidly.	

FIGURE 10-3 The chain reaction resulting in the chemical oxidation of fat is depicted and explained in the diagrams and narrative.

catalyzed by the presence of small amounts of metals such as iron and copper. Soybean oil is known to contain traces of iron and copper, which may act as **pro-oxidants**. Thus, the flavor of soybean oil is stabilized by the use of metal inactivators or sequestrants, which tie up the trace amounts of iron and copper that are present.

The chief precursors of the reversion flavor in oils are thought to be the triglycerides containing **linolenic** acid, although linoleic acid is probably also involved to some degree [46]. The fats that are most susceptible to reversion contain linolenic acid in larger amounts than the relatively stable fats. Selective hydrogenation of soybean oil to decrease the amount of linolenic acid aids in preventing flavor reversion. Plant breeding and genetic engineering are developing oils that are lower in linolenic acid content [31].

Antioxidants and the Prevention of Rancidity

Fats can be protected to some degree against the rapid development of rancidity by controlling the conditions of storage. Storage at refrigerator temperature with the exclusion of light, moisture, and air aids in rancidity prevention. Because only certain rays of light catalyze the oxidation of fats, the use of colored glass containers that absorb the active rays protects fats against spoilage. Certain shades of green in bottles and wrappers and yellow transparent cellulose have been found to be effective in retarding rancidity in fats and fatty foods such as bacon. Vacuum packaging also helps to retard the development of rancidity by excluding oxygen.

Antioxidants have been used in the United States since 1947 to stabilize fats and control the development of rancidity [18]. Several compounds with antioxidant activity, including the nutrients vitamin C and beta carotene, are naturally present in certain foods. Vitamin E (tocopherols), present in seeds and in the oil extracted from seeds, is an effective antioxidant that protects edible vegetable oils [42]. Four synthetic antioxidants approved as food additives by the FDA are butylated hydroxyanisole (BHA), butylated hydroxytoluene (BHT), tertiary butyl hydroquinone (TBHQ), and propyl gallate. These four substances have found widespread use in food processing [14, 42].

Some substances, such as citric acid, may be used with antioxidants in foods as *synergists*. A synergist increases the effectiveness of an antioxidant but is not as effective an agent when used alone. Metals such as iron and copper may be present in trace amounts in foods and will encourage the development of oxidative rancidity. Some synergists may be effective because of their ability to bind or chelate the metals and prevent them from catalyzing the oxidation process. Chelating agents are sometimes called *sequestering agents*.

Antioxidants generally appear to act as oxygen interceptors in the oxidative process that produces rancidity, providing a hydrogen atom to satisfy the peroxide-free radical (Figure 10-3). Thus, the chain reaction that perpetuates the process is broken or terminated, until another hydrogen atom is lost from a fatty acid chain, and the chain reaction begins again. Antioxidants, therefore, greatly increase the shelf life of fats, and foods containing fat such as processed meats, whole-grain and dry-prepared cereal products, nuts, fat-rich biscuits and crackers, potato chips, and flour mixes.

FRYING

The two methods of frying are pan-frying, in which a shallow layer of fat is used (Figure 10-4), and deep-fat frying, in which the food is submerged in heated fat (Figure 10-5).

Pan-frying

Pan-frying is used to cook such foods as hamburgers, chicken, fish fillets, bacon, potatoes, eggplant, and eggs. It is difficult when pan-frying to know the exact temperature of heating because of the shallow depth of the fat, which is usually less than 1/2 inch; however, smoking of the fat is a definite indication that decomposition is occurring and should never be permitted. Moderate temperatures are generally used. The frypan should be seasoned before its first use by pouring a small amount of shortening into the warm frypan and rubbing the pan surface with a cloth to produce a mirrorlike finish.

Pan-frying is often done using a vegetable oil, shortening, butter, or margarine. However, butter has a lower smoke point, and both butter and margarine contain water which can cause spattering. Diet butters or margarines are especially prone to splattering because of their even higher water content. In foodservice operations, a specialty griddle shortening is generally used. For frying, the skillet should be merely coated with fat, not filled with an excessive amount.

Deep-Fat Frying

Deep-fat frying is commonly used to prepare French fries, onion rings, breaded chicken tenders and nuggets, donuts, and a variety of other foods. Most deep-fat fried foods should be lightly brown, crisp on the exterior, moist and tender inside, and without the sensation of excessive fat. In the home, foods may be deep-fat fried in a heavy pan with a deep-fat frying thermometer to monitor temperatures, or more easily by the use of a small electric deep-fat fryer. Deep-fat fryers come in a variety of sizes for foodservice operations (Figure 10-5).

Frying Temperature. The temperature of the fat when deep-fat frying will influence the quality of the food and the degradation of the fat. Food fried at temperature that is too high will become too dark on the exterior prior to being cooked fully in the interior. When foods are

FIGURE 10-4 Pan-frying breaded veal cutlets produces a tender, juicy cutlet with a golden brown and crisp coating. Stir-frying asparagus and mushrooms in a wok or sauté pan uses only a small amount of oil and results in a flavorful dish.

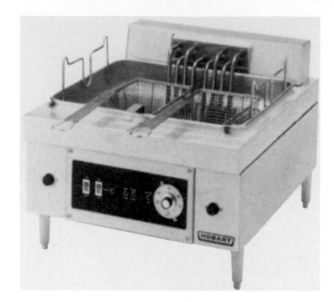

FIGURE 10-5 Deep-fat frying is common practice at many foodservice establishments. A small counter fryer holds 28 pounds of shortening. This large fryer can hold 50 pounds of shortening and produce 110 pounds, or about 440 servings of French fries per hour. *(Courtesy of Hobart Corporation)*

cooked at temperature that is too low, the food will absorb excessive fat.

In most deep-fat frying applications, the temperature of the fat is controlled by a thermostat which will automatically control the heat to the fryer based on the oil temperature. Some simple home deep-fat fryers have only one factory preset temperature which is satisfactory for most foods. Foodservice and more sophisticated home fryers allow for a choice of temperature. Smaller foods are generally cooked at higher temperatures, whereas larger foods such as a breaded chicken breast should be cooked at a lower temperature. Alternatively, these larger food items may be partially cooked in the fryer until the desired level of browning has been achieved and then immediately finished in the oven. Holding partially cooked foods before final cooking is not recommended for food safety reasons. Table 10-5 provides a range of temperatures that can be used for deep-fat frying.

Fat Absorption. A minimum level of fat absorption is desirable when frying foods. A reduction of fat in the diet is desirable from a nutritional perspective, and excessively greasy foods are of poor sensory quality. Fat absorption is influenced by (a) frying temperature, (b) length of cooking time, (c) food characteristics, and (d) condition of the frying fat.

Foods fried at low temperatures will absorb more fat because the food will be cooked for a longer period. As noted previously, it is necessary to fry certain foods at lower temperatures to allow complete cooking of the interior while avoiding a dark brown exterior. Some foods, however, are inadvertently cooked at a low temperature due to overloading the fryer. Overloading a fryer with an excessive amount of food will cause a significant temperature drop, and the food will be sitting in the fat but not frying. An overloaded fryer will require an extended period of time to recover to an appropriate frying temperature. While the fat temperature is too low, the food will absorb fat, and a greasy product will be the result.

The proportions and types of ingredients in doughnuts and various manipulative procedures affect fat absorption. Doughnuts or fritters will absorb more fat when the recipe or formula contains a higher level of lecithin (a phospholipid), eggs (which contain lecithin), or sugar and fat [37]. Doughnuts made from soft wheat flours and from soft doughs absorb more fat than doughnuts made from strong flours and from stiff doughs. The development of gluten by the extensive manipulation of the dough decreases fat absorption. Lastly, if the surface of the dough is uneven, surface area will increase, and therefore fat absorption will increase.

A pectin coating for French-fried potatoes and some breaded items such as fish and chicken reduces the amount of fat absorbed by these products. Barley flour that is β-glucan rich used in batters also appears to reduce the amount of oil uptake [35]. A protein substance extracted from muscle tissue is another approach that has been found to reduce food moisture loss and the amount of oil absorbed during frying [45]. The total calorie content of the fried items is therefore reduced when less fat is absorbed.

The type of fat used for frying does not appear to affect significantly the amount of fat absorbed. Under

TABLE 10-5 Temperature Ranges for Deep-Fat Frying

Type of Product	Temperature of Fat	Approximate Time to Brown a 1-inch Cube of Bread in Hot Fat in Seconds*
Doughnuts	350°–375°F (175°–190°C)	60
Fish	350°–375°F (175°–190°C)	60
Fritters	350°–375°F (175°–190°C)	60
Oysters, scallops, and soft-shelled crabs	375°F (190°C)	40
Croquettes	375°F (190°C)	40
Eggplant	375°F (190°C)	40
Onions	375°F (190°C)	40
Cauliflower	375°F (190°C)	40
French-fried potatoes	385°–395°F (195°–200°C)	20

*__Note:__ A thermometer or thermostat controlled fryer is the preferred method of controlling temperature. A bread cube, however, can provide another method of assessing temperature.

identical conditions of time, temperature, and type of food being fried, various fats commonly used for frying appear to be absorbed in similar amounts.

Fat Selection. Several factors may be considered in choosing a frying medium. Fats used for frying must produce foods with a desirable flavor and color. Frying fats must also be stable, resistant to foaming and gum formation, tolerant of high cooking temperatures, and have a relatively high smoking point. Lastly, although consumers enjoy fried foods, the preference for the use of fats with a more favorable nutritional profile is desired. Many restaurants, in the past, used a mixture of animal tallow and vegetable fat for frying. While this blend of frying fat had many desirable characteristics, consumers who are vegetarians and those concerned about saturated fat and cholesterol prefer all-vegetable frying fats which also are low in trans fatty acids.

Frying fats are processed to improve their functionality in frying applications. A certain amount of hydrogenation of the frying oil historically has been needed to provide good flavor stability and to increase the frying life of the fat before too much degradation occurs. New soy-based, low-linolenic oils are being developed that are resistant to oxidation, exhibit strong flavor stability, do not require hydrogenation, and yet function well as frying oils [45].

Functionality of frying fats may also be enhanced by adding antioxidants or methyl silicone. Antioxidants may be added to frying fats to lengthen the shelf life not only of the fat, but also of the fried product. Minute amounts of methyl silicone are often added to fats during processing to help retard foaming and deterioration during frying.

Care of Fat. To maintain high quality in fried foods, it is important to monitor the frying fat regularly. A frying fat may be used for a considerable period if the turnover with fresh fat is fairly high and if the fat is cared for properly. Fat is damaged by salt, water, high temperatures, food particles, and oxygen contact. Thus, food should not be salted above the frying fat, and ice crystals on foods should be removed as much as possible before frying. Not only will water damage the oil, but water in hot oil will cause spattering and can result in burns to anyone nearby. A smoking oil is an indication that the temperature is too high and, if the temperature is not reduced, the oil could reach a *flash point* and ignite. Thermostats on fryers should be checked with a fryer thermometer to assure the proper functioning.

Frying fats need to be filtered regularly. Filtering the fat removes charred batter, breading, and other materials that have accumulated in the frying fat, as these can ruin the appearance of the fried product, contribute bitter flavor, lower the smoke point, and darken the fat. The tiny crumbs that flake off products during frying are sometimes called *fines* and must be removed regularly to preserve the integrity of the frying fat.

Frying fat used in the home should be filtered after each use through cheesecloth or a fine metal mesh strainer and stored in a cool place out of contact with light and air. In the foodservice operations, the frying fat should be filtered at least daily. Various filtration systems are available for foodservice, including screens, cartridges, and paper filters with and without filter aids. Some filters are built into the frying equipment; portable filters are also available.

Frying fats that have darkened considerably, show evidence of a lowered smoke point, or are foaming should be discarded. Foaming of frying fats is distinctive and can be distinguished from the normal bubbling that occurs when frying by the very small bubbles which are present and the tendency of these small bubbles to proliferate much like sudsy water. Foods prepared with degraded fats will be of poor quality.

$$CH_2OH \qquad\qquad CH_2$$
$$| \qquad\quad heat \qquad \parallel$$
$$CHOH \longrightarrow \quad CH \qquad + 2H_2O$$
$$| \qquad\qquad\qquad |$$
$$CH_2OH \qquad\qquad C = O$$
$$\qquad\qquad\qquad\qquad |$$
$$\qquad\qquad\qquad\qquad H$$

glycerol   acrolein   water

FIGURE 10-6 Acrolein is produced when fats are heated to the smoking point. As shown, glycerol, when heated, produces acrolein and water.

Fat Turnover.   *Turnover* indicates the amount of fat in the fryer that is replaced by fresh fat in a given period. Because fat is absorbed by the foods that are fried, the amount of fat continuously decreases, and fresh fat will need to be added to maintain the correct depth of the fat. The rate of turnover varies depending on how much food is fried. When turnover is slow, it is necessary to discard periodically all of the fat in the deep-fat fryer and start again with fresh fat.

Changes to Fat Used for Deep-Fat Frying.   Frying fats change when used for deep fat frying. *Acrolein* and surfactants are chemicals that may be produced in frying fat. Food can interact with the fat and cause changes, including darkening of the fat.

Acrolein.   Acrolein is a substance produced when fats are heated to excessive temperatures and smoke. It may result in eye and throat irritation when you are near smoking cooking fat. Acrolein results from the dehydration of glycerol. The source of the glycerol is from the hydrolysis of triglyceride molecules in the fat to their component parts of free fatty acids and glycerol. The chemical change of glycerol to acrolein and water is shown in Figure 10-6.

Polymerization.   Polymerization occurs in fats that are held at frying temperatures (374°F/190°C) for extended periods. Polymerization is a reaction where free fatty acids are coupled into new compounds or *polymers*. These polymers contribute to increased viscosity and darkening of the fat.

Change in Smoke Point.   A high smoke point is desirable in a fat used for deep-fat frying. The smoke point of a fat will lower over time when used. It is one of the reasons frying fats must be replaced. The smoke point of fats will lower as the result of the following:

- free fatty acid formation resulting from high heat or the frying of high-moisture foods
- suspended matter such as flour or batter particles in the fat
- greater surface area of the fat exposed to air

Surfactants.   Oxygen from the air may react with the fat in the fryer at the oil–air interface, thus creating many different chemical compounds in the frying fat in addition to the basic triglyceride molecules that originally made up the fat. Some of the chemicals produced are surfactants—molecules that interact at the air–oil or oil–food interfaces and lower the surface or interfacial tension. A surfactant theory of frying suggests that the lowered surface tension allows oxygen to be drawn in, producing some oxidized compounds that aid in heat transfer. Also, the contact time between the hot oil and the aqueous food surfaces is increased, and more heat is transferred to cook the food. If surfactant levels become too high, however, degradation of the fat is enhanced, polymers are formed, increased viscosity results from the gum formation, and foaming is excessive [9].

Darkening of Fats.   As frying fat is used, darkening occurs. As the fat darkens, the foods fried in it darken more rapidly and may be uneven in color. Color is one of the indicators used commercially to determine when the oil should be replaced. The ingredients in the product being fried influence the color changes of the frying fat. Potatoes form little color in the frying fat, whereas chicken causes considerably more darkening. The composition

FOCUS ON SCIENCE

Why Does My Deep-Fat Fryer Basket Develop a Sticky Build-up?

The hydrolysis of triglycerides occurs during frying because of the heat and moisture from the food. As a result of triglyceride hydrolysis, free fatty acids are formed in the frying fat.

These free fatty acids join together (polymerize) and form long chains. These long compounds cause an increase in viscosity of the frying fat. This thickening is the reason the side walls of a fryer and the fryer basket will develop a sticky build-up.

More about Smoke Point

The smoke point of a fat or oil is influenced by its fatty acid profile. The higher the amount of long-chain fatty acids, the higher the smoke point. Because most foods are fried between 350° and 400°F (176° to 204°C), it is desirable to have a fat that has a smoke point that exceeds this temperature range. If not, the fat will reach flash point. The flash point is the temperature at which volatile substances are formed at a rate permitting ignition, but not combustion. If the flash point is ignored and the fat is maintained at this high temperature, a fire will occur.

During the Thanksgiving holiday period, food programs on the television may recommend peanut oil for turkey frying. Peanut oil contains C-22 (Behenic acid) fatty acid in its makeup which makes it a good choice for a frying fat because of its high smoke point. Other fats with high smoke points include soybean, canola, and cottonseed oils.

---

of the breading mixture also affects darkening. The presence of egg yolk in a batter or dough causes greatly increased darkening of the fat with continued use.

Changes to Food During Frying. In deep-fat frying, there is a direct transfer of heat from the hot fat to the cold food that continues until the food is cooked. Water present in the food to be fried plays some important roles in heat transfer and the frying process. Water is lost from the exterior surfaces of the food as it is converted to steam. The steam carries off energy from the surface of the food and prevents charring or burning. While water is being evaporated, the temperature of the food is only about 212°F (100°C). Water then migrates from the central portion of the food outward to the edges to replace that lost by evaporation. Finally, the interior of the food is cooked. Sufficient heat must be transferred to gelatinize starch and coagulate proteins that may be present in the food.

BUYING FATS

It is important when purchasing fats to consider their specific uses in food preparation and to select fats in accordance with needs and budget. Fats are often tailored for specific uses in foodservice operations, such as deep-fat frying, pan-frying or griddling, and cake making. Separate fats are generally purchased for each of the specific needs.

Most consumers probably do not need to keep more than three or four different household fats on hand. Butter, because of its flavor, is sometimes preferred for table use, as well as for use in some baked products and for seasoning certain foods. Margarine serves a similar purpose, usually at a somewhat lower cost, although the different brands of margarine vary widely in price. A blend of butter and margarine is also available. Margarines, particularly those types that are high in polyunsaturated fatty acids, may be chosen over butter for health reasons.

Most households require some shortening, but one general-purpose shortening can be used satisfactorily for both shortening and frying purposes. In foodservice, several different shortenings may be purchased which have been formulated for specific purposes. For health reasons, monounsaturated or polyunsaturated oils may be preferable when frying to reduce the level of trans fatty acids consumed. Lard is preferred by some for use in pastry, biscuits, refried beans, or tortillas. The use of fats for shortening is considered in Chapter 15.

COOKING LOWFAT

Consumers have been bombarded with messages concerning the detrimental health effects of high-fat diets and are encouraged to lower their fat intakes. Why do we like fat? It tastes good. Diets rich in fat tend to be more flavorful and heighten the pleasures of eating.

We can, however, lower the fat to some degree and still have delicious food. Acceptable muffins, yellow cake, and drop cookies can be prepared using less fat than typically is used [24]. Pureed cannelloni beans have been found to be a satisfactory substitute for shortening in brownies [48]. Plum puree and applesauce have been used as substitutes for fat in baked foods with success as well. Using questionnaires of restaurant patrons to evaluate acceptability of lower-fat menu items, it was found that customer satisfaction was actually higher for the lower-fat items than for the regular menu items [22]. This finding indicates that many consumers are interested in the availability of nutritious menu items and will choose them. If they do not taste good, however, consumers will not choose them repeatedly.

Many ideas for cooking low in fat have been suggested. These include choosing lean cuts of meat that are trimmed well of fat, using nonstick pots and pans that require less fat for cooking, using roasting or broiling methods instead of sautéing and frying, stir-frying with a small amount of vegetable oil cooking spray, and seasoning with a variety of herbs [32]. Favorite recipes can be modified to be lower in fat, for example, making lasagna with less meat or with vegetables and using less or lowfat cheese. Egg whites can be substituted for whole egg in some baked recipes and cocoa for chocolate, thus reducing the fat. Several cookbooks are available with emphasis on lowfat cooking. By adjusting ingredients and cooking methods, we can eat for health while maintaining taste and enjoyment.

FAT REPLACERS

Food processors are using a wide variety of ingredients to replace or partially replace fat in food products. As fat replacement technology has changed over the years, fat replacers increasingly are being used in customized applications [45]. Replacers are regulated by the FDA. Unless the fat replacer is generally regarded as safe (GRAS), it must be approved by the FDA as a food additive. The American Dietetic Association (ADA) has issued a position paper on fat replacers [4]. The position of ADA is that the "majority of fat replacers, when used in moderation by adults, can be safe and useful adjuncts to lowering the fat content of foods and may play a role in decreasing total dietary energy and fat intake."

Fat plays several roles in various food products. Although many of its functions are related to texture, it is very difficult, if not impossible, to find a fat substitute that will perform well in all food products [49]. Several different fat replacers are presently in use and are sometimes employed in combinations. Generally, fat replacers can be classified into two groups—fat substitutes and fat mimetics or imitators. Fat substitutes are macromolecules that chemically and physically resemble triglycerides and can replace fat in foods. They are often referred to as *fat-based fat replacers*. Fat substitutes are usually stable at cooking and frying temperatures [2].

Fat mimetics are substances that imitate sensory properties of triglycerides but cannot replace fat on a weight-to-weight basis. These products are often called *protein-based* or *carbohydrate-based fat replacers*. Many are modified common ingredients, such as starch and cellulose, and act to bind a substantial amount of water [2].

Fat-Based Replacements

Chemically, olestra consists of six to eight long-chain fatty acids combined as esters with sucrose to produce compounds called *sucrose fatty acid polyesters*. Olestra, or Olean®, is neither digested nor absorbed from the human digestive tract and is therefore noncaloric; yet olestra has characteristics similar to triglycerides when used in food preparation. It is heat stable and can be used in frying.

Several structured triglycerides have been developed as fat substitutes that have fewer kilocalories per gram than the usual triglycerides. One of these is salatrim (Benefat®). Salatrim consists of a family of structured triglycerides containing at least one short-chain fatty acid (two, three, or four carbon atoms long) and at least one long-chain fatty acid (predominantly stearic acid with 18 carbon atoms) esterified with the glycerol molecule, and yields 5 kilocalories per gram when metabolized in the body. Salatrim is used in confectionery products, baked goods, and some dairy foods [2].

The use of emulsifier systems that will "stretch" the function of the fat makes possible some fat reduction in many fat-containing products. For example, the addition of mono- and diglycerides as emulsifiers to cake shortenings allows a reduction in the fat content without sacrifice to quality. Emulsifier systems can be designed to function well in many lowfat products, but other ingredients must also be used in conjunction with the emulsifier system to help replace the fat that is lost. Included in the emulsifier group are fatty acid esters of sucrose that are similar to olestra but contain only one, two, or three fatty acid esters instead of the six to eight esterified in olestra. Lecithin is another emulsifier that can help in fat replacement in many food products.

Carbohydrate-Based Replacements

Many of the reduced-fat products introduced into the market have contained carbohydrate-based fat replacers [4]. These include derivatives of cellulose, maltodextrins, gums, modified starches, pectin, and polydextrose. Ingredient developers have produced several products marketed under specific brand names, using, in many cases, a combination of ingredients [19].

Carbohydrates such as starches, cellulose, and gums have a long history of use in the food industry. They often function as thickeners and stabilizers. When used to replace fat, they add form and structure, hold water as hydrophilic agents, and act as emulsifiers when a small amount of fat is used. They may produce a mouthfeel that is similar to that created by fat, but they do not taste exactly like fat. Stickiness and other textural problems may result if large amounts are used. A combination of gums, cellulose, and/or modified starches can be used to produce a fat replacement system.

Maltodextrins are nonsweet carbohydrates made from partially hydrolyzed starch. They can partly or totally replace fat in a variety of products, including margarine, frozen desserts, and salad dressings. They are classified as GRAS by the FDA and have the same caloric value as starch [19].

Polydextrose is a "designed" ingredient, prepared from a mixture of dextrose (glucose), sorbitol, and citric acid. It has multiple functions, which include acting as a bulking agent, a texturizer, and a humectant, and it may be used to replace sugar or fat. Polydextrose contains only one kilocalorie per gram, in comparison with four kilocalories provided by sugars and starch. It is approved by the FDA for use in such products as frozen dairy desserts, baked goods, confections, puddings, and salad dressings [25].

A variety of high-fiber ingredients have been developed to trim fat in products. Oatrim is produced by partial enzymatic hydrolysis of the starch-containing portion of the bran obtained from whole oat and/or corn flour. It contains 5 percent beta-glucan, a soluble plant fiber [2]. A research group of the USDA developed Oatrim,

Z-Trim, Nu-Trim, Soy-Trim, and Rice-Trim. Z-Trim is a zero-calorie fat substitute made from corn and wheat [45]. C-Trim is one of the most recent new products, and it functions as a fat replacer with the added benefit of beta-glucan which has been shown to regulate blood glucose and lower cholesterol [45].

Protein-Based Replacements

Several fat replacers come from protein sources, including egg, milk, whey, soy, gelatin, and wheat gluten. Some are microparticulated to form microscopic, coagulated round, deformable particles that give a mouthfeel and texture similar to fat. Others are treated in ways to modify their functional properties, such as water-holding capacity and emulsifying characteristics. These substances are generally not heat stable but are used in dairy products, salad dressings, frozen desserts, and margarines [2].

One microparticulated-protein fat replacer is Simplesse®, which has received approval by the FDA as a GRAS substance. It is produced by reshaping proteins from milk and egg into tiny round particles. These particles are so small that they are perceived as fluid. Microparticulated protein has a caloric value of four kilocalories per gram on a dry basis, compared with nine kilocalories per gram for the fat it replaces. A hydrated gel form provides one kilocalorie per gram. It cannot be used for frying but can be used in frozen desserts, yogurt, cheese spreads, cream cheese, and sour cream. It should also be suitable for use in baked products [2].

EMULSIONS

The term *emulsion* is applied to a system consisting of one liquid dispersed in another liquid with which it is immiscible. A third substance, an emulsifying agent or emulsifier, is necessary to stabilize the system and keep one liquid dispersed in the other on a permanent basis (see Figure 10-7).

Emulsions in Foods

Emulsions are found naturally in many foods, such as milk, cream, and egg yolk. In all such foods, the fat is divided into small particles or globules and dispersed

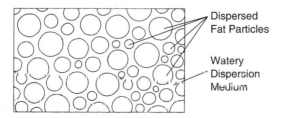

FIGURE 10-7 An emulsion consists of one substance dispersed in another substance with which it is immiscible. An emulsifying agent surrounds each dispersed particle. This diagram represents an oil-in-water emulsion; the oil droplets, surrounded by an emulsifying agent, are dispersed in water.

throughout the watery portion of the food. The homogenization of whole milk further divides the naturally emulsified fat into particles that are so fine they tend to remain in suspension and do not rise to the surface on standing, as does the fat in nonhomogenized milk.

Many food products are emulsions that have been formed during processing or preparation. The manufacture of emulsions is a highly energetic and dynamic process. Work is necessary to divide the fat into tiny globules or droplets. These newly formed globules must be rapidly protected against coalescence by the adsorption of an emulsifier at their surface. Shaking, beating, stirring, whipping, and high-pressure homogenization are some methods used to form an emulsion of one immiscible liquid dispersed in another.

From food preparation, examples of emulsions are mayonnaise and other salad dressings, sauces, gravies, puddings, cream soups, shortened cake batters, and other flour mixtures in which the fat is dispersed. Other emulsions are produced in the commercial processing of foods such as peanut butter, margarine, sausages, and frankfurters. The dispersing medium may be water, milk, dilute vinegar, lemon or other fruit juice, or some similar liquid. The dispersed substance may be any of the commonly used food fats and oils. Some emulsions, such as margarine, have fat as the dispersing medium and water as the dispersed substance. Even though the fat is not always a liquid at ordinary temperatures of holding, the food system is still called an emulsion.

A variety of substances act as emulsifying agents and stabilizers in manufactured food systems, including the isolated milk protein casein, whey proteins and concentrated whey products, isolated soy proteins, oilseed protein concentrates, gelatin, lecithin, cellulose derivatives, fine dry powders such as ground spices, various vegetable gums, and starch pastes. Several emulsifiers are present in some batters. For example, shortened cake batter may contain egg lipoproteins, casein from milk, gluten and starch from flour, and mono- and diglycerides that have been added to the shortening.

Temporary Emulsions

If oil and water alone are shaken together, an emulsion is formed, but on standing, the oil particles reunite and separate from the water. Emulsions of this kind are called *temporary emulsions*. They must be used immediately or, if made in quantity and stored, they must be reshaken or beaten before each use. Simple French and Italian dressings are examples of this type of emulsion.

Permanent Emulsions

Permanent emulsions, which can be held or stored without separation of the two immiscible liquids, require an emulsifying agent or emulsifier to form a protecting or stabilizing film around the dispersed droplets and prevent them from reuniting. The term *stabilizer* is also used to describe the emulsifier or the substance that assists the emulsifier in some food products. An example of a permanent emulsion is mayonnaise. Actually, any food containing fat that is distributed throughout and does not appear on the surface as a separate layer is a permanent emulsion.

The two general types of emulsions are an *oil-in-water* emulsion and a *water-in-oil* emulsion. Oil-in-water emulsions are more common in foods, but butter and margarine are examples of water-in-oil emulsions. The type of emulsion formed depends to a considerable extent on the nature of the emulsifier.

How does an emulsifier act to form an emulsion? Emulsifiers have a special type of chemical nature: They are amphiphilic molecules. Part of the emulsifier molecule is attracted to or soluble in water (hydrophilic), whereas another part of the same molecule is soluble in fat (lipophilic). Thus, the emulsifier molecule may be oriented at the interface of the two immiscible liquids with its hydrophilic group in the watery phase and its lipophilic group in the fat or oil phase. One of these amphiphilic groups is a little stronger than the other and causes one phase to form droplets that are dispersed in the other continuous phase, with the emulsifier between them as it surrounds droplets of the dispersed phase. Figure 10-8 suggests how an emulsifier might orient itself at an oil–water interface to form an emulsion.

If the emulsifier is more attracted to the water, or more water soluble, it promotes the dispersion of oil in water. If the emulsifier is more attracted to the oil, or more oil soluble, it tends to produce a water-in-oil emulsion. A photomicrograph of the fat-in-water emulsion of milk, both before and after homogenization, is shown in

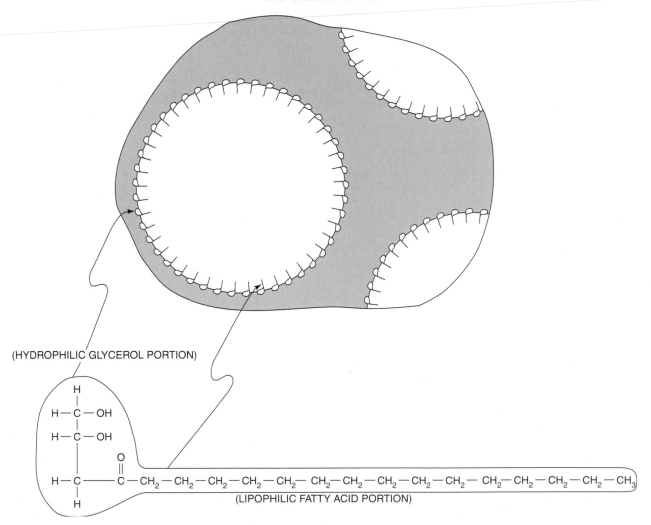

SECTION THROUGH OIL DROPLETS
DISPERSED IN WATER

(HYDROPHILIC GLYCEROL PORTION)

(LIPOPHILIC FATTY ACID PORTION)

FIGURE 10-8 An emulsifier stabilizes an emulsion by virtue of its chemical structure. In a simplified presentation, this structure includes one part that is attracted to water and another part that is attracted to fat. The attraction of one of the groups is somewhat stronger than the other. For example, a monoglyceride molecule is shown with the fatty acid portion being attracted to the oil and the glycerol portion attracted to the water, forming a filmlike layer around the oil droplets and keeping them dispersed in the continuous watery phase.

Figure 23-5 (Chapter 23). Breaking of emulsions or separation of the two phases may occur under certain conditions. In some cases, the emulsion can re-form.

SALAD DRESSINGS

Classification

Definitions and standards of identity for mayonnaise, French dressing, and salad dressing have been published by the FDA. If products are labeled and sold under these names, they must meet the standards of identity unless the product is labeled with a nutrient claim such as "reduced fat." These modified products must not be nutritionally inferior and must function like the standard product (see Chapter 4 for more about labeling and food regulations).

All three dressings contain an acidifying ingredient. Many variations of these three basic dressings are created by using different, optional ingredients. Thus, a wide variety of dressings are available commercially, for example, Thousand Island, blue cheese, bacon and tomato, creamy cucumber, Italian, ranch, and taco dressings. Citrus flavors in dressings have gained popularity in recent years [43]. Exciting new flavors in salad dressings may encourage healthful eating, bringing into the daily diet more vegetables, salads, and nutritious sandwich fillings (Figure 10-9).

Dressings for salads made in home kitchens are not, of course, governed by standards of identity. Many of these dressings are simple combinations of ingredients and are difficult to classify. In fruit dressings, fruit juices replace vinegar and other liquids. Sour cream, sometimes with added ingredients such as crumbled cheese, can be added to vegetable or fruit salads. Mixtures of vinegar or lemon juice and seasonings, with or without small amounts of fat-containing ingredients, are sometimes used as low- or reduced-calorie dressings.

Dry salad seasoning mixes can also be prepared. A mixture of seasonings and emulsifiers or stabilizers are included in dry salad dressing mixes. These are usually added to sour cream or to milk and mayonnaise to make a creamy dressing or to vinegar and oil to make a French-type dressing.

Salad Dressing

Salad dressing is the emulsified semisolid food prepared from edible vegetable oil, an acidifying ingredient, egg yolk or whole egg, and a cooked or partly cooked starchy paste prepared with a food starch or flour. Water may be added in the preparation of the starchy paste. Optional seasonings and emulsifying agents may also be used. Salad dressing must contain not less than 30 percent by weight of edible vegetable oil and not less than 4 percent by weight of liquid egg yolks or their equivalent unless a legally defined nutrient claim has been made. All of this is specified in the standard of identity for salad dressing.

Many different dressings for salads can be made in both home and foodservice operations. Some of these are cooked dressings and may be of the custard type, in which all thickening is accomplished with egg yolk or whole egg. More frequently, a starchy agent is used to aid in thickening because there is less tendency for curdling to occur when cream or milk is used as the liquid. Some cooked dressings made with milk or cream are of a consistency suitable for immediate use, but the dressing may be made thicker than desirable and highly seasoned to permit dilution without impairment of flavor.

French Dressing.   According to its standard of identity, French dressing is the separable liquid food or the emulsified viscous fluid food prepared from edible vegetable oil (oil content not less than 35 percent by weight), specified acidifying agents, and optional seasonings. Reduced-fat or calorie dressings may still be called French dressing with the appropriate nutrient claim. If it is emulsified, certain gums, pectin, or other emulsifiers, including egg or egg yolk, may be used to the extent of 0.75 percent by weight of the finished dressing. Large amounts of paprika and other powdered seasonings also help to keep the oil and acid emulsified. In unemulsified French dressing, a temporary emulsion is formed as the dressing is shaken or beaten. Oil and acid ingredients separate soon after mixing but can be shaken or mixed each time the dressing is used.

The usual proportions for French dressing are 3/4 cup salad oil for each 1/3 cup vinegar or lemon juice. Various seasonings can be used.

Reduced-Fat Dressings.   Reduced-fat salad dressings and mayonnaise are sold on the retail market and are prominently labeled as such. The caloric content of reduced-calorie dressings depends on how much oil is used. Those that contain essentially no fat in the finished dressing contain 6 to 14 kilocalories per tablespoon. Others, with up to 3 grams of fat per tablespoon of

FIGURE 10-9 A basic vinaigrette dressing adds flavor to this tomato, greens, and asparagus salad with fresh mozzarella cheese.

finished dressing, provide 30 to 40 kilocalories per table-spoon. A comparable full-fat salad dressing contains 60 to 80 kilocalories per tablespoon.

A mixture of emulsifying agents and stabilizers, including xanthan gum, alginate, cellulose gum, locust bean gum, and modified starch, is used to produce an emulsion and to substitute for the fat that is being elimi-nated. These stabilizers are hydrophilic and hold rela-tively large amounts of water, giving body or thickness to the product.

The 1990 Nutrition Labeling and Education Act requires that a product labeled as fat-free have less than 0.5 gram of fat per serving and no added fat. A product labeled as lowfat must contain less than 3 grams of fat per serving. A product labeled as light must contain 33 percent fewer calories or 50 percent of the fat in a reference food. If 50 percent or more of the calories in the product comes from fat, the reduction must be 50 percent of the fat.

No-oil low-calorie dry dressing mixes are also avail-able. The dry mix is added to water and vinegar, pro-ducing a product with about 6 kilocalories per tablespoon. Some reduced-calorie dry mixes require the addition of milk and mayonnaise. These produce creamy dressings with about 35 kilocalories per tablespoon. The dry mixes contain stabilizers and emulsifiers, plus various herbs and other flavoring materials.

Mayonnaise

According to its standard of identity, mayonnaise or may-onnaise dressing is the emulsified semisolid food pre-pared from edible vegetable oil, vinegar and/or lemon juice or citric acid, egg yolk or whole egg, and one or more optional ingredients, such as salt, mustard, paprika, a sweetening agent, and monosodium glutamate. If there is no qualified health claim, the edible oil content of may-onnaise must be not less than 65 percent by weight and is emulsified or finely divided in the vinegar or lemon juice. In mayonnaise, oil is dispersed in vinegar or lemon juice. Lecithin, found in the egg yolk, acts as the emulsifying agent, coating the dispersed particles of oil to keep them dispersed on a permanent basis.

Mayonnaise can be made in the home kitchen (Figure 10-10). The factors that affect the formation of mayonnaise, its stability, and the ease of preparation are similar wherever the product is made. However, recipes with raw egg yolks should be modified through the use of a pasteurized egg yolk to reduce the use of foodborne ill-ness. For food-safety reasons, in addition to the time involved in the preparation of mayonnaise, few make this product from scratch.

Factors Affecting Mayonnaise Preparation.　Cold oil is more difficult to break up into small globules than warm, less viscous oil. Thus, the start of emulsification is delayed by chilling, but after the emulsion is formed, chilling thickens and stabilizes the product.

Egg yolk is the chief emulsifying ingredient in may-onnaise. Salt, mustard, paprika, and pepper are used mainly for flavor, but both the salt and the powdery sea-soning ingredients help to stabilize the emulsion as well. Mayonnaise usually contains about 3/4 to 1 cup of oil per egg yolk and 2 tablespoons of acid ingredient.

Stable mayonnaise can be mixed by various methods. The acid may be added (a) to the yolk with the seasonings before any additions of oil, (b) at various intervals during the mixing, (c) alternately with the oil, or (d) after a large percentage of the oil is added to the egg yolk. The first additions of oil must be small to allow a stable emulsion to form. After the first two or three additions of oil, the volume that is added at one time may be increased to a variable extent, depending on the temperature of the ingredients, the rate of beating, and other factors, but in any case it should be less than the volume of emulsion that is already formed.

Breaking and Re-forming an Emulsion.　If oil particles coalesce, the emulsion breaks, and the oil sepa-rates from the watery portion of the dressing. When this occurs while the emulsion is forming, the cause is incom-plete preliminary emulsification, too rapid an addition of oil, too high a ratio of oil to emulsifier (or another wrong proportion), or an inefficient method of agitation.

FIGURE 10-10 Mayonnaise may be made in the home. The use of pasteurized eggs is recommended. (a) Whip egg yolks until frothy, (b) drizzle the oil slowly into the yolks while mixing to allow the emulsion to form, (c) the finished mayonnaise.

Prepared emulsified mayonnaise may separate during storage. Freezing may damage or rupture the film of emulsifying agents and allow the dispersed oil to coalesce, resulting in a broken emulsion. Mayonnaise stored at too high a temperature may separate because of differences in the rate of expansion of warm water and oil. Mayonnaise stored in an open container may lose sufficient moisture from the surface by evaporation to damage the emulsion. Excessive jarring or agitation, particularly during shipping and handling, can cause separation, but this occurrence is uncommon.

A broken mayonnaise emulsion may be re-formed by starting with a new egg yolk, or with a tablespoon of water or vinegar, and adding the separated mayonnaise to it gradually. Thorough beating after each addition of separated mayonnaise is important. If separation occurs in the preparation of mayonnaise before all the oil is added, the remainder of the original oil may be added only after reemulsification has been achieved as described.

Variations. Additions can be made to mayonnaise to vary the flavor and consistency. Chopped foods, such as vegetables, olives, pickles, hard-cooked eggs, and nuts, may be added with discretion. Chili sauce, sour cream, and whipped cream can also enhance flavor and consistency for certain uses.

CHAPTER SUMMARY

- Fat is present in many foods and plays a variety of roles in food preparation and nutrition. Fat present naturally is often referred to as *invisible fat*, whereas fats that are added to foods are called *visible fats*.

- To reduce the risk of heart disease, total dietary fat intake of 30 percent or less of kilocalories and saturated fat intake of 10 percent or less of kilocalories is recommended. Fats provide essential fatty acids and carry the fat-soluble vitamins and therefore, in moderation, are an important part of the diet.

- Fats contribute flavor, color, texture, tenderness, and moistness to foods. Fats are an effective method of heat transfer and are one phase of emulsions.

- Fats are insoluble in water. Fats that are solid at room temperature are called *fats*, and those liquid at room temperature are called *oils*. The melting point of fat is influenced by the type of fatty acids, form of fatty acids (cis or trans), and length of carbon atoms. Fats demonstrate plasticity because of a unique combination of liquid and solid crystals that allows the fat to be molded or pressed into various shapes.

- Hydrogenation changes liquid oils into solid fats such as shortening or margarine by adding hydrogen. Other methods of processing oils to produce the desirable characteristics of hydrogenation fats are being used to reduce trans fatty acids produced during hydrogenation. Interesterification and fractionalization are two such methods.

- Oils are obtained from fruits, seeds, and nuts generally by pressing. Winterized oils (salad oils) have been processed to remove the triglyceride molecules that crystallize or become cloudy under refrigeration.

- Butter is the fat of cream that is separated from the other milk constituents by agitation or churning. Butter is a water-in-oil emulsion.

- Lard is the fat rendered from the fatty tissues of the hog. Although lard is used less widely than in the past, it is still preferred by some for pie crusts and biscuits due to its shortening ability and for the flavor it provides in Mexican cuisine.

- Fat may deteriorate in flavor due to rancidity resulting from hydrolysis or oxidation. A special type of oxidative deterioration, flavor reversion, involves a change in edible fats characterized by the development of an undesirable flavor. Fats can be protected against rancidity to some degree by controlling the storage conditions and by using antioxidants.

- Pan-frying and deep-fat frying are two methods of cooking that utilize fat as the cooking medium. Fats selected for deep-fat frying must be highly stable, have a high smoke point, and have a neutral or desirable flavor. Fats that become excessively dark, foam, or smoke at normal temperatures for deep-fat frying should be discarded. Fats that are well maintained by routine straining and filtering will last longer. Several factors influence the amount of fat absorbed by foods when cooked by deep-fat frying.

- The amount of fat can be reduced when cooking through the careful selection of lowfat foods, cooking methods, and recipes. Favorite recipes can be modified to reduce the amount of fat.

- Food processors are using a variety of ingredients to replace or partially replace fat in food products. Fat replacers must be generally recognized as safe (GRAS) or must be approved by the FDA as food additives. Fat replacements may be fat-based, carbohydrate-based, or protein-based.

- Emulsions are found naturally in many foods or may be formed during processing or preparation. The term *emulsion* is applied to a system consisting of one liquid dispersed in another liquid with which it is immiscible. Temporary emulsions separate on standing. Permanent emulsions, such as mayonnaise, can be held or stored without separation.

- There are many types of salad dressings that can be purchased commercially or made in the home.

Mayonnaise, French dressing, and salad dressing all must meet standards of identity to be labeled with these names in the marketplace.

STUDY QUESTIONS

1. For what general purposes are fats used in food preparation? Name at least four uses.

2. Explain two chemical reasons why fats vary in their melting points so that some are liquid at room temperature, whereas others are solid.

3. Most fats used in food preparation are separated from other tissues and refined or processed. Briefly describe how each of the following fats is produced. Also indicate for which of the general uses listed in Question 1 each fat may be appropriate.
   - (a) Butter
   - (b) Margarine
   - (c) Lard
   - (d) Hydrogenated shortening
   - (e) Oil
   - (f) High oleic, low linolenic acid oil

4. (a) Explain what happens when oils are hydrogenated and when they are winterized.
   - (b) What purposes do these processes serve in the production of food fats?
   - (c) What is a *plastic* fat? Give examples.

5. (a) What is *rancidity?*
   - (b) Distinguish between hydrolytic rancidity and oxidative rancidity.
   - (c) Explain what probably happens when a fat is oxidized and becomes rancid.
   - (d) List several factors that may contribute to the development of rancidity. How can these be controlled?
   - (e) How does an antioxidant retard the development of rancidity?
   - (f) Name several antioxidants that may be added to, or are present in, fatty foods.

6. (a) What is *pan-frying?* What is *deep-fat frying?*
   - (b) Explain the importance of using a proper temperature in frying foods. What do smoke point and acrolein have to do with the proper temperature for frying?
   - (c) Discuss factors to consider when choosing a frying fat.

- (d) Give suggestions for the appropriate care of used frying fat.
- (e) What is meant by fat *turnover*? Why is it important in frying?
- (f) Discuss several factors that may influence the amount of fat absorbed during frying.

7. Discuss several factors to consider in deciding which fats to purchase.

8. Give several suggestions for cooking lower-fat, yet delicious, foods.

9. (a) What types of substances are being used or tested for use as fat replacers in food products? Discuss.
   - (b) Give examples of carbohydrate-based, protein-based, and fat-based fat replacers.

10. (a) What is an *emulsion?* What is necessary to produce a permanent emulsion?
    - (b) Give several examples of emulsions in natural foods and of emulsions in prepared or processed foods.
    - (c) Describe the difference between an oil-in-water emulsion and a water-in-oil emulsion.
    - (d) How does an emulsifier act to stabilize an emulsion?

11. (a) Standards of identity have been published for which three types of dressings for salads?
    - (b) What percentage of oil is specified for each type?
    - (c) Which governmental agency is responsible for these standards?

12. (a) Describe mayonnaise and list its major ingredients.
    - (b) Discuss several factors that may affect the formation of a stable emulsion in the making of mayonnaise.
    - (c) Describe what happens when an emulsion breaks. How can a broken mayonnaise emulsion be re-formed?

13. Describe French dressing and list its major ingredients.

14. Explain how salad dressing generally differs from mayonnaise.

SWEETENERS AND SUGAR COOKERY

11

Sweeteners have been used for food since prehistoric times, probably beginning with the discovery of honey. From drawings in Egyptian tombs we learn that, as early as 2600 B.C., beekeeping was practiced for honey production. It is doubtful, however, that the honey was available to anyone but the rich and powerful. Today, some type of sweetener is found in most people's diets.

Commonly used sweeteners are generally extracted from plant sources and refined. The term *sugar* usually refers to crystallized sucrose (table sugar). In addition, sweeteners include other concentrated sources of sugar such as corn syrups, maple syrup, molasses, and honey. Artificial or alternate sweeteners produce sweetness but are usually noncaloric substances.

In this chapter, the following topics will be discussed:

- Sweetener consumption and nutritive value
- Sugar properties
- Sugar types including crystalline sugars and syrups
- Alternative sweeteners
- Sugar cookery
- Candy

SWEETENER CONSUMPTION AND NUTRITIVE VALUE

From **disappearance data**, published by the U.S. Department of Agriculture (USDA), it is apparent that the consumption of sugar and sweeteners in the United States has increased since 1909 (Figure 11-1). In 2005, the U.S. per capita annual consumption of cane and beet sugar, edible syrups, honey, high fructose corn syrup, glucose, and dextrose was 142 pounds compared to 119 pounds in 1970 [32]. Disappearance rates of sugar, however, are only indicators of availability and may overestimate consumption. Food consumption surveys may underestimate consumption. See Chapter 2 for a discussion about food disappearance and consumption surveys.

Sugar provides only energy for the body; the dry product is essentially 100 percent carbohydrate. Therefore, foods that contain relatively large amounts of sugar generally have low nutrient density. Increasing the consumption of sugar-rich foods may contribute to an unbalanced diet by proportionately decreasing the consumption of protein, minerals, and vitamins. The Dietary Guidelines for Americans recommend that only moderate amounts of sugars be consumed. Molasses, which contains

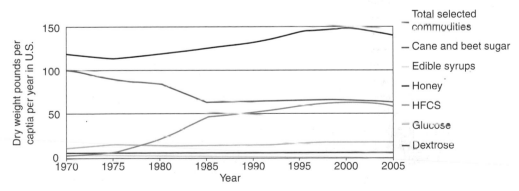

FIGURE 11-1 The amount of added sugars has increased over the years. (*Courtesy of U.S. Department of Agriculture, Economic Research Service*)

Food Consumption—Disappearance Data for Selected Sugars and Sweeteners

Food disappearance data collected by the USDA Economic Research Service suggest Americans have increased their consumption of sugar and sweeteners. In 1970, 119 pounds per capita of sugar and sweeteners were used in the food supply system as compared to 141 pounds in 2004. Cane and beet sugar use has declined since 1970, whereas the use of high fructose corn syrup has increased considerably (0.55 pound per capita in 1970 to 59 pounds in 2004) [32]. High fructose corn syrup use has increased in large part to beverage manufacters shifting from sugar to high fructose corn syrup in many soft drinks. The use of honey, edible syrups, glucose, and dextrose has changed very little in the past 30 years. ■

the natural ash of the plant juices from which it is made, furnishes some nutrients other than carbohydrates, such as a small amount of calcium and iron; however, the less-refined sugars and syrups, including honey, are still essentially energy foods and, on the whole, cannot be relied on to furnish other nutrients in significant amounts.

A position paper of the American Dietetic Association (ADA) points out that, on the basis of present research evidence, dietary sugars are not an independent risk factor for any particular disease, nor do they appear to be responsible for behavioral changes. Sugars can contribute, along with other fermentable carbohydrates, to acid production in the mouth, which promotes dental cavities [1]. Sugars have their proper place in food preparation, providing variety and satisfying the apparently inborn desire for sweet taste. However, the total caloric need, as well as the requirements for protein, vitamins, and minerals, must be carefully considered when adding sugar-rich foods to the diet.

PROPERTIES OF SUGARS

Properties of sugar including solubility, melting point, moisture absorption, fermentation, acid and enzyme hydrolysis, decomposition, and sweetness are discussed in the following section. The chemical classification of sugars as monosaccharides and disaccharides, and a description of some of the common sugars, was provided in Chapter 9.

Solubility

In the natural state of foods, sugars are in a solution. Crystallization of sugar occurs from a sufficiently concentrated sugar solution, a fact that is used in the commercial production of sugar from sugar cane and beets.

The common sugars vary in solubility. Fructose, a monosaccharide, is the most soluble; lactose, a disaccharide, is the least soluble. The relative solubility of sugars is provided in Table 11-1. The solubility of all sugars in water is increased by heating. As shown on Table 11-2, the amount of sucrose which may be dissolved in 100 grams of water more than doubles when the temperature increases from 68°F (20°C) to 212°F (100°C).

Saturated and Unsaturated Sugar Solutions. When small amounts of sugar are added to water and the mixture is stirred, the sugar dissolves, and the solution appears to be transparent. We call this solution *unsaturated* because it will dissolve more sugar if it is added. The solution becomes *saturated* when it has dissolved all of the sugar

TABLE 11-1	Relative Solubility of Sugar at Room Temperature Listed from Most to Least Soluble
Most Soluble	Fructose
	Sucrose
	Glucose
	Maltose
Least Soluble	Lactose

TABLE 11-2	The Solubility of Sucrose in Water Increases When the Temperature of the Water Increases
Grams of Sugar Dissolved in 100 Grams of Water	**Temperature**
203.9	68°F/20°C
320.5	158°F/70°C
487.2	212°F/100°C

that it can at that particular temperature. A solution is truly saturated when sufficient solute (sugar, in this case) has been added so that some remains undissolved in the bottom of the container.

Supersaturated Solutions. A solution is *supersaturated* when it holds more solute than is usually soluble at a particular temperature. To produce a supersaturated sugar solution, more sugar than can be dissolved at room temperature is added to water, and the mixture is heated to the boiling temperature, at which point all of the sugar dissolves. As this solution is carefully cooled to room temperature without being disturbed, the solution gradually becomes saturated and then supersaturated.

Only by careful cooling and avoiding factors that promote crystallization can a solution be held in the supersaturated state. Because supersaturation is such an unstable state, crystallization eventually occurs, and all excess solute beyond saturation is precipitated or crystallized. Some substances require more time to crystallize from a supersaturated solution than others, unless agitation or seeding (adding a few already formed crystals) starts the process of crystallization. The sugars that are the most soluble, such as fructose, are the most difficult to crystallize; those that are the least soluble, such as lactose, crystallize readily. In making candies, close attention is given to the solubility and ease of crystallization of sugars.

Melting Point and Decomposition by Heat

With the application of sufficient dry heat, sugars melt or change to a liquid state. Heating beyond the melting point brings about several decomposition changes. As sucrose melts at about 320°F (160°C), a clear liquid forms that gradually changes to a brown color with continued heating. At about 338°F (170°C), caramelization occurs with the development of a characteristic caramel flavor along with the brown color. Caramelization is one type of browning, called *nonenzymatic browning* because it does not involve enzymes. It is a complex chemical reaction, involving the removal of water, polymerization, and the formation of organic acids.

Caramel has a pungent taste, is often bitter, is much less sweet than the original sugar from which it is produced, is noncrystalline, and is soluble in water. Both the extent and rate of the caramelization reaction are influenced by the type of sugar being heated. Galactose and glucose caramelize at about the same temperature as sucrose (338°F/170°C), but fructose caramelizes at 230°F (110°C) and maltose caramelizes at about 356°F (180°C).

Granulated sugar, when heated dry in a heavy pan, caramelizes. When hot liquid is added, the caramelized sugar dissolves and can be used to flavor puddings, ice creams, frostings, and sauces. Caramel is also produced during the cooking of such foods as peanut brittle and caramel candy.

Absorption of Moisture

Sugars absorb moisture. For example, crystalline sugars become caked and lumpy unless they are stored in dry places. Baked flour mixtures that are rich in sugar take up moisture when surrounded by a moist atmosphere in tightly closed containers. Because of this tendency to absorb moisture from the atmosphere, sugars are said to be *hygroscopic*.

Rock Candy

Have you ever enjoyed a sweet treat called rock candy? Rock candy is crystallized sugar made from a supersaturated sugar solution. Here's how it is made:

- Collect a clean cotton string, popsicle stick, and clean pint-sized canning jar.
- Tie the string to the stick and place the stick across the top of the jar with the string hanging into the jar without touching the bottom.
- Using a heavy pan on a range, heat 2 cups of sugar in 1 cup of water until the sugar dissolves or the temperature on a candy thermometer reads 240°F (116°C).
- Remove the sugar mixture from the heat and add flavoring or coloring if desired.
- Carefully pour the hot sugar mixture into the pint-sized jar, being careful not to spill.
- Let the sugar mixture sit undisturbed for 3 to 10 days with the string hanging into the jar.
- Watch the sugar crystals grow.
- When ready to eat, remove from the jar and break the rock candy into pieces and enjoy!

The science behind rock candy is that a *supersaturated* sugar solution was made by heating more sugar in water than would dissolve without heat. Supersaturated sugar solutions are unstable, and the sugar will begin to crystallize. The string serves as a place for sugar crystals to collect, thereby making rock candy. ■

Fructose is more hygroscopic than the other sugars commonly found in food. Therefore, higher moisture absorption occurs in products containing fructose, such as cakes or cookies made with honey, molasses, or crystalline fructose. These baked products remain moist noticeably longer than similar products made with sucrose.

Fermentation

Most sugars, except lactose, may be fermented by yeasts to produce carbon dioxide gas and alcohol. Fermentation is an important reaction in the making of bread and other baked products; the carbon dioxide leavens the product, and the alcohol is volatilized during baking. Fermentation is also important to beer and wine making. The spoilage of canned or cooked products containing sugar may occur by fermentation.

Acid Hydrolysis

The disaccharides are hydrolyzed by weak acids to produce their component monosaccharides. Sucrose is easily hydrolyzed by acid, but maltose and lactose are slowly acted on. The end products of sucrose hydrolysis are a mixture of glucose and fructose. This mixture is commonly called invert sugar. The monosaccharides are not appreciably affected by acids.

The extent of acid hydrolysis in a sugar solution is variable, depending on whether the solution is heated, the kind and concentration of acid used, and the rate and length of heating. Application of heat accelerates the reaction, and long, slow heating tends to bring about more hydrolysis than rapid heating for a shorter period. The higher the acidity, the greater the rate and extent of decomposition. Hydrolysis may occur incidentally, as in the cooking of acid fruits and sugar, or it may be brought about purposely as a means of improving the textures or consistencies of certain sugar products, such as fondant, for which hydrolysis is often produced by the addition of cream of tartar, an acid salt.

Enzyme Hydrolysis

Enzymes also hydrolyze disaccharides. The enzyme *sucrase*, also called *invertase*, is used in the candy industry to hydrolyze some of the sucrose in cream fondant to produce invert sugar composed of fructose and glucose. This process produces soft, semifluid centers in chocolates. The enzyme is commonly added to the fondant layer around the fruit in chocolate-coated cherries. It must be added after the sugar solution is boiled and cooled so that the enzyme is not destroyed. The addition is usually made during beating or when the fondant is molded for dipping. The fondant must be dipped in chocolate shortly after the enzyme is added, and chocolate coatings must completely cover the fondant to prevent leakage as the enzyme acts on the sucrose. Because the enzyme acts best in an acid medium, the fondant is acidified.

Decomposition by Alkalies

The decomposition of sugars by alkalies also has significance in sugar cookery. Alkaline waters used in boiling sugar solutions may bring about some decomposition of sugars. The monosaccharides, which are only slightly affected by weak acids, are markedly affected by alkalies. Both glucose and fructose are changed into many decomposition products both by standing and by being heated in alkaline solutions. The stronger the alkali solution, the more pronounced are the effects on sugars. The decomposition products of glucose and fructose are brownish, and, when the process is extensive, the flavor may be strong and bitter. Examples of the decomposition of sugars by alkalies in food products is provided in Table 11-3. In complex food products, such as baked goods, browning may occur not only as a result of sugar decomposition by alkali but also because of the Maillard browning reaction. This reaction begins with the interaction of sugars and amino groups from proteins.

Sweetness

The flavor of purified sugars is described as being sweet. We humans love sweetness, as do virtually all mammals since history began, with honey, dates, and figs providing early sources of sweetness [3]. The degree of sweetness that we perceive is affected by several factors, including genetic variation among individuals as well as concentration of the sweetener, temperature, viscosity, pH, and the presence of other substances with the sweetener. It is therefore sometimes difficult to make consistent and

TABLE 11-3	Food Examples of the Decomposition of Sugars by Alkalies
Food Product	**Characteristics as a Result of Decomposition of Sugars by Alkalies**
Fondant	Cream of tartar is often added to a fondant mixture to make it more acidic to prevent the alkali decomposition.
	Fondant is less white when made with glucose or corn syrup *without* the addition of cream of tartar.
	Hard water is alkaline and when used for making fondant, an off-white color may be pronounced.
Baked beans	Baked beans are browner in color and have a greater caramelized flavor when made with glucose- or fructose-containing sweeteners, such as corn syrup, rather than table sugar.
Cakes and cookies	Cakes and cookies are browner in color and have a stronger flavor when made with honey and baking soda. Baking soda is alkaline and contributes to the decomposition of sugars.

reproducible comparisons of sweetness among the various sweeteners, including the common sugars.

Lactose is the least sweet of the sugars, followed by maltose, galactose, glucose, and sucrose, with fructose being the sweetest. However, these orders of sweetness do not hold at all temperatures or in all products. For example, fructose was reported to give sweeter lemonade than sucrose when added in equal weights, but sugar cookies, white cake, and vanilla pudding were sweeter when made with sucrose compared with fructose [11]. A maximum sweetness from fructose is most likely to be achieved when it is used with slightly acid, cold foods and beverages.

CRYSTALLINE FORMS OF SUGAR

Crystals will form in a supersaturated sugar solution. In the process of crystallization, molecules that are dispersed in a liquid solution pack closely together in a precise, organized, set pattern to form a solid substance. The tiny crystals, which have a characteristic shape for each substance crystallized, may sometimes be gathered into clusters of crystals.

The size of the crystals formed depends on a number of factors, including concentration, temperature, agitation, and the presence of other substances that interfere with crystal formation. These factors are carefully controlled both in the crystallization of commercial sugars and in the making of candies.

Granulated Sugar

Granulated sugar or crystalline sucrose, called *table sugar*, plays a variety of roles in food systems. To the food scientist, sucrose is much more than a sweetener. For example,

it affects the texture of many baked products, it improves the body and texture of ice creams, it is fermented by yeast to produce carbon dioxide gas which leavens breads, and it preserves jams and jellies by retarding the growth of microorganisms.

Table sugar is produced commercially from both sugar beets and sugar cane. The product, refined sucrose, is chemically the same from both sources. In the production of table sugar, the plant materials are crushed or sliced, and the high sugar content is extracted. The juice is filtered, clarified, and evaporated under a vacuum to form a concentrated sugar syrup, from which the sugar is crystallized. In the processing of cane sugar, an intermediate product with 2 to 3 percent impurities is *raw sugar*. Raw sugar is sent to refineries for further treatment through a series of steps involving dissolving, purifying, and recrystallizing to produce granulated sugar. The crude raw sugar is not suitable for human consumption. Beet sugar production is done in one continuous stage, without a raw sugar intermediate.

Many grades and granulations of refined sugar are available. Fine granulated sugar with uniform grain size is the principal granulated sugar for consumer use. Forms of sugar which may be found in the marketplace are described in Table 11-4.

Other Crystalline Sugars

A white crystalline form of glucose, 75 to 80 percent as sweet as sucrose, is produced by the complete hydrolysis of cornstarch. It can be obtained in various particle sizes, including powdered and pulverized, but is used chiefly in the food industry. The crystals sometimes found in honey are mostly glucose; the fructose remains in the syrup.

TABLE 11-4 Forms of Granulated Sugar

Forms of Granulated Sugar	Description
"Regular" white sugar	Sugar usually used in cooking or in sugar bowls. May be "fine" or "extra fine" crystal size.
Fruit sugar	Slightly finer than "regular" sugar. Often used in dry mixes and powdered drinks.
Baker's special sugar	Finer than fruit sugar. Developed for baking industry for cakes and sugaring cookies or donuts.
Superfine, ultra fine, or bar sugar	Finest crystal size of all of the crystalline sugars. Dissolves very easily and thus is ideal for meringues, delicate cakes, or iced-drinks. In England, is known as caster sugar.
Confectioner's or powdered sugar	Granulated sugar ground to a smooth powder and sifted. Contains about 3 percent cornstarch to prevent caking. May be ground to different degrees of fineness; powdered sugar sold in grocery stores is 10X.
Coarse sugar	Crystal size is larger than regular sugar. Is resistant to color changes and inversion to glucose and fructose (invert sugar). Used for making fondants, confections, and other products where this stability is desirable.
Sanding sugar	A large crystal size sugar used in the baking industry to sprinkle on baked goods. The large crystals appear to "sparkle" in light.
Liquid sugar	White granulated sugar which has been dissolved in water for use in recipes requiring dissolved sugar.

Source: Reference 31

Crystalline fructose that is more than 99 percent pure is available but, like crystalline glucose, is used mainly by food processors. When used in combination with sucrose, the sweetness is greater than when an equal amount of either sugar is used alone, thus allowing less sugar to be used. Compared with sucrose, fructose produces more rapid development of viscosity and increased gel strength in starch-thickened pies and puddings [28]. Crystalline lactose, which is about one-sixth as sweet as sucrose, and maltose also are available for special uses.

Maltodextrins, which are derived from cornstarch, are available as dry products and as concentrated solutions. The starch in maltodextrins is less completely hydrolyzed to glucose than corn syrup solids; therefore, they are less sweet and have a very bland flavor. They also contribute chewiness, binding properties, and viscosity to candy [10].

Brown Sugars

Brown sugar is obtained from cane sugar during the late stages of refining. It is composed of clumps of sucrose crystals coated with a film of molasses. Molasses is a byproduct of the sugar production process; it is the liquid remaining after most of the sugar crystals have been separated from it. Some invert sugar, which is an equal molecular mixture of fructose and glucose, is present in molasses and thus in brown sugar. A small amount of ash, an organic acid, and flavoring substances are also present in brown sugar, contributing to the characteristic pleasant caramel flavor and light yellow to dark brown color. The lighter the color, the higher the stage of purification and the less pronounced the flavor. Types of brown sugar are described on Table 11-5.

Cocrystallized Sucrose

An interesting process known as *cocrystallization* can be applied to the crystallization of sucrose, resulting in several novel functions for this product in the food industry. In the cocrystallization process, spontaneous crystallization of a purified supersaturated sugar solution is accomplished by rapid agitation, resulting in the production of aggregates of microsized crystals as cooling proceeds. The aggregates have a spongelike appearance, with void spaces and an increased surface area (Figure 11-2). In the presence of a second ingredient, an infinite dispersion of this ingredient occurs over the entire surface area of the sucrose aggregate. This cocrystallization process may be defined as one whereby a second ingredient is incorporated in, or plated onto, a microsized sucrose crystal by spontaneous crystallization [2]; there is no settling out of the second ingredient. The resulting sugar product is homogeneous and readily dispersed in food ingredients. The second ingredient may be flavorings such as honey, fruit juice, maple, peanut butter, chocolate, and alternate sweetener–sugar combinations. The incorporation of mixtures of ingredients into a crystallized sugar matrix is also used to make instant-type products with improved functions in gelling, aeration, and emulsification, such as pudding mixes, gelatin dessert mixes, flavored drink mixes, and icing mixes.

SYRUPS, MOLASSES, AND HONEY

Corn Syrups

Regular corn syrups contain about 75 percent carbohydrate and 25 percent water; however, the proportions of the various sugars present in the carbohydrate portion may vary from 20 to 98 percent glucose, depending on the manufacturing process and the proposed use of the product [10, 31]. Corn syrup also may be called glucose syrup on food labels.

Corn syrup has traditionally been produced in the United States by using acid and high temperatures to hydrolyze corn starch. The carbohydrate of the resulting product is composed of 10 to 36 percent glucose and 9 to 20 percent maltose, the remainder consisting of higher sugars and **dextrins** [16]. With the additional use of selected enzymes, a corn syrup that contains a much higher proportion of glucose and/or maltose may be prepared. The use of **glucoamylase** yields more glucose,

TABLE 11-5 Forms of Brown Sugar	
Forms of Brown Sugar	**Description**
Turbinado sugar	Partially processed raw sugar. Only surface molasses has been removed; thus it is blond in color and has a mild brown sugar flavor.
Light and dark brown sugar	Dark brown sugar is deeper in color and has more molasses flavor compared to light brown sugar.
Muscovado or Barbados sugar	British specialty brown sugar which is very dark brown with a strong molasses flavor. Sugar crystals are coarser and stickier in texture compared to "regular" brown sugar.
Free-flowing brown sugar	Produced by cocrystallization, free-flowing brown sugars are fine, powderlike and pour like white sugar.
Demerara sugar	A light brown sugar with large golden crystals which is popular in England.

Source: Reference 31

(a)

(b)

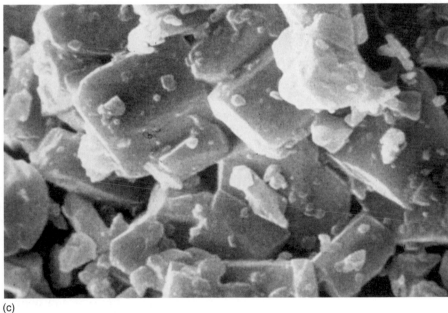

(c)

FIGURE 11-2 A new generation of sucrose products can be made by cocrystallization.
(a) Ordinary sugar crystals at 35× magnification.
(b) Cocrystallized sugar aggregates of microsized sucrose crystals at 175× magnification.
(c) Surface structure of cocrystallized sugar aggregates at 1,750× magnification.
(Reprinted from Food Technology, 47(1), 147. (1993). Copyright © by Institute of Food Technologists. Photographs courtesy of Ahmed Awad, PhD, Domino Sugar Corporation)

whereas the use of β-amylase yields more maltose. High-glucose syrups have lower viscosity and higher sweetening power.

The extent of conversion of starch to glucose is described by the term *dextrose equivalent* (DE), which is defined as the percent of reducing sugar calculated as dextrose (glucose) on a dry-weight basis. Dextrose or glucose thus has a DE of 100. Corn syrups are available with different sugar compositions having DEs of 20 to 95 [10].

Corn Syrup Solids. Dried corn syrups or corn syrup solids are produced by the spray or vacuum drying of refined corn syrup. The dried product is useful in such foods as dry beverage mixes, instant breakfast mixes, cereal bars, and sauce mixes.

High-Fructose Corn Syrup. A high-glucose corn syrup is used as the basis for production of a high-fructose corn syrup (HFCS) by use of the enzyme glucose isomerase.

FOCUS ON SCIENCE

More on Dextrose Equivalents and Reducing Sugar

What is meant by dextrose equivalents?

Dextrose equivalents (DE) is a term that is used to indicate the degree of hydrolysis of starch into glucose syrup (or corn syrup). DE is the percent of reducing sugars in the syrup, calculated as the dextrose (glucose) on a dry-weight basis. A simple way to remember this is that DE indicates what percentage of syrup is glucose. If the DE is low, then large numbers of linear chains or long-chain fragments have been retained, and strong gels may be formed.

What is a reducing sugar?

Aldoses (such as glucose) are called *reducing sugars* because of their ability to reduce an agent such as silver or copper (II) ions. In this reaction, the sugar's aldehyde group is oxidized to a carboxylate group. Fehling's solution, which is an alkaline solution of copper (II) salt, oxidizes an aldose (such as glucose) to an aldonate. In this process, the copper (II) is reduced to copper (I) which precipitates as a brick-red oxide Cu_2O as in the following reaction:

$$2CU(OH)_2 + R-\overset{\overset{\displaystyle H}{|}}{C}=O \rightarrow R-\overset{\overset{\displaystyle O}{\|}}{C}-OH + Cu_2O + H_2O$$

This enzyme catalyzes the chemical reaction that changes about half of the glucose in the mixture to fructose. HFCS containing about 42 percent of the carbohydrate as fructose was produced in the early 1970s. Syrups containing up to 90 percent fructose have since been prepared by a fractionation process that removes much of the glucose from a 42 percent HFCS. To produce a syrup of 55 percent fructose content, a stream of 90 percent fructose syrup is blended into a stream of 42 percent fructose syrup [22]. The primary feature of HFCS is sweetness.

HFCSs are widely used in the manufacture of soft drinks. They are also used in a variety of other products, including prepared cereals, chocolate products, icings, canned and frozen fruits, frozen desserts, confections, and sauces [8].

Molasses and Sorghum

Molasses is the residue that remains after sucrose crystals have been removed from the concentrated juices of sugar cane. It contains not more than 25 percent water and not more than 5 percent mineral ash. The sugar, which may be present in amounts up to 70 percent, is a mixture of sucrose, glucose, and fructose, but is chiefly sucrose.

Molasses differs in sugar and mineral content depending on the stage of the crystallization process from which it is derived. After the first crystallization of sucrose, the molasses is high in sugar and light in color. After the final process, a dark and bitter product with a relatively high mineral content, called *blackstrap molasses*, remains. Most molasses sold on the market is a blend of different types. Sorghum is made from cane sorghum and is similar to molasses in appearance. Its total sugar content is about 65 to 70 percent.

Maple Syrup

Maple sugaring has been an early-spring tradition in some parts of the United States ever since Native Americans first discovered that sap from the maple tree cooked over an open fire produced sweet syrup. Vermont is particularly well known for its delicious pure maple syrup.

Maple syrup is probably the most highly prized of all syrups used for culinary and table purposes. It is made by evaporation of the sap of the sugar maple to a concentration containing no more than 35 percent water. The special flavor that gives maple syrup its economic importance is not in the sap as it comes from the tree. It is developed in the processing or cooking down of the sap into syrup. Organic acids present in the sap enter into this flavor-developing process. It has been found that evaporating the sap at low temperatures through distillation or freeze-drying results in syrup that is practically flavorless and colorless. Approximately 40 gallons of sap are necessary to yield a single gallon of maple syrup.

Honey

Honey is flower nectar that is collected, modified, and concentrated by the domesticated European honeybee. Honey is a supersaturated solution and, with storage, glucose tends to crystallize out of the solution, producing granulation. Granulation is reversed by heating.

Honey contains about 17 percent water and 82.5 percent carbohydrate, with small amounts of minerals, vitamins, and enzymes. The carbohydrate portion of honey includes fructose (38 percent), glucose (31 percent), maltose (7 percent), and sucrose (2 percent). As specified by the FDA, honey may not contain more than 8 percent sucrose; a higher percentage is taken as an indication of adulteration. The addition of any other sugar substances—such as HFCS— to honey is also considered to be adulteration.

The USDA has set standards for grades of honey, including comb honey and extracted honey (filtered and strained; liquid and crystallized). The grades are based on moisture content, minimum total solids, flavor, aroma, clarity, and absence of defects. The flavor of honeys differs according to the characteristic flavoring compounds present in the nectar of different flowers. Over half of the honey produced in this country is mild-flavored sweet clover, clover, or alfalfa honey (Figure 11-3). Honeys also come from orange and other citrus blossoms, wild sage, cultivated buckwheat, and the tulip tree. Much of the honey on the market is a blend of different floral types. The color of honey may vary from white to dark amber. The color of fresh honey is related to its mineral content and is characteristic of its floral source. Grades of honey are independent of color, but darker-colored honey generally has a stronger flavor than the white or light-colored product.

Honey is stored in the comb by bees and in that form is marketed as comb honey. If the comb is uncapped and centrifuged, the honey is extracted. Extracted honey may optionally be pasteurized by a mild heat treatment to destroy yeasts and to delay crystallization. Honey may then be strained to remove wax particles and foreign matter. It also may be filtered to remove pollen, air bubbles, and other fine particles.

Controlled crystallization produces a product called *crystallized honey*. A process has also been developed for producing dried honey. This product has a color and flavor that are quite close to those of the original honey. It is granular in form, is free flowing, and has a long shelf life. Whipped honey may have part of the fructose removed,

leaving a higher proportion of glucose, which crystallizes to some degree resulting in a thickened mixture.

Table 11-6 lists some sugar and syrup substitutions that can be made in food preparation. Adjustment must be made for the liquid present in syrups.

LOW-CALORIE SWEETENERS AND OTHER SUGAR SUBSTITUTES

Although sugar has been used to sweeten foods for many decades, concerns about caloric excess in the diet, tooth decay, or specific dietary concerns such as diabetes have sparked a desire for alternatives. The food industry has responded with a variety of reduced-sugar products. The American Dietetic Association has taken the position that there is an appropriate use for nonnutritive, as well as nutritive, sweeteners when they are consumed in moderation and within the context of a diet consistent with the Dietary Guidelines for Americans and the Dietary Reference Intakes [1]. Terminology often used in relation to low-calorie sweeteners and substitutes is provided in Table 11-7.

Alternative sweeteners currently approved for use in the United States include saccharin, aspartame, acesulfame-K, sucralose, and neotame. Neotame and sucralose are the two most recently approved alternative sweeteners. The FDA approved neotame in 2002 and sucralose in April 1998. No one alternative sweetener is best for every food product [20, 26]. Therefore, sweeteners are chosen for the applications for which they will be best suited. Combinations of different alternative sweeteners, called *sweetener blends*, offer promise for improved taste and stability and can overcome the limitations of the individual sweeteners [20, 25].

Saccharin

Saccharin was first synthesized in 1879, when it was accidentally discovered that it has a sweet taste. It has been used in the United States since 1901 for both food and nonfood purposes. Intensely sweet, 300 to 500 times as sweet as sucrose, it is stable in a wide variety of products under extreme processing conditions [14]. It can be synthesized with relatively few impurities and is inexpensive. One major disadvantage of saccharin is its perceived bitter aftertaste, particularly at higher concentrations; however, when used in combination with other nonnutritive

FIGURE 11-3 Honey can be added to many foods for flavor. Here it is used to sweeten a biscuit. *(Courtesy of U.S. Department of Agriculture)*

TABLE 11-6 Substitution among Sugar and Syrup Products
1 cup brown sugar = 1/2 cup liquid brown sugar
1 cup honey = 1 1/4 cup sugar + 1/4 cup liquid
1 cup corn syrup = 1 cup sugar + 1/4 cup liquid

TABLE 11-7 Terminology Used for "Low-Calorie Sweeteners," "Alternative" Sweeteners, and Bulk Sweeteners

Definition	Terms Used	Examples in United States

Sweeteners with very intense sweet taste used in small amounts.
 	
Contributes very few or no calories to the food in which the sweetener is used.
	Low-calorie sweetener
	  Indicates the purpose for the sweetener and is term preferred by some authors.
	Alternative sweetener or sugar substitute
	  These terms are used but also may be used for other types of sweeteners thus resulting in confusion.
	High-potency sweetener
	  May confuse some consumers who may perceive the foods using these ingredients are extremely sweet.
	Nonnutritive sweetener
	  This term is used by some authors, but other authors suggest this description is not entirely accurate especially with regard to aspartame.
	Artificial sweetener
	  Another term used by some authors.
		acesulfame-K
		aspartame
		neotame
		saccharine
		sucralose

Sweeteners used in place of sugar to reduce calories while still providing the same "bulk" as sugar. Unlike the low-calorie or nonnutritive sweeteners which provide essentially no calories, polyols provide 0.2 to 3.0 kilocalories per gram. May be used in combination with a low-calorie sweetener.	Polyols Sugar alcohols Bulk sweeteners	sorbitol mannitol xylitol erythritol isomalt lactitol maltitol hydrogenated starch hydrolysates

Source: References 1, 17, 30

sweeteners such as aspartame or cyclamate, sweetness is enhanced and bitterness decreased somewhat.

Saccharin (sold under the trade name Sweet'N Low®) has been the only approved nonnutritive sweetener used in the United States during certain periods. Some concern about its safety, however, has been expressed over the years. In 1977, the FDA proposed banning this GRAS substance because an increase in bladder tumors in laboratory rats was found to be associated with the ingestion of high levels of dietary saccharin. Strong public protest influenced the U.S. Congress to impose a moratorium against any action to ban saccharin, in part due to the highly controversial methodology of the laboratory rat study. The moratorium was extended periodically to allow continued use of saccharin as further research clarified saccharin's role in the carcinogenic process [7]. The Congress ruled, as a compromise measure, that a warning statement had to be placed on labels of foods containing saccharin. Saccharin has since been found to be a carcinogen only in rats and only if administered over two generations. Epidemiological studies in humans have not shown the risk of developing bladder cancer to be increased with exposure to saccharin.

In December 1991, the FDA officially withdrew the proposed federal ban on saccharin, indicating that "the safety of saccharin is no longer of concern and that these 1977 proposals have become outdated" [4]. A National Toxicology Program panel, which reports to the National Institute of Environmental Health Sciences, removed saccharin from the list of substances known or anticipated to be human carcinogens in 2000 [17]. The warning label requirement was rescinded in 2001 [17, 30].

Aspartame

Aspartame was discovered in 1965 and initially was approved for use in several foods by the FDA in 1981 [17]. In 1996, the FDA approved the use of aspartame as a general-purpose sweetener which means it may be used in all categories of foods and beverages.

Aspartame is made by joining two amino acids—aspartic acid and phenylalanine—and adding methyl alcohol to form a methyl ester (see Figure 11-4). Aspartame is a white, odorless, crystalline powder that has a clean, sugarlike taste and a sweetness potency 180 to 200 times that of sucrose [15]. No bitter aftertaste is associated with aspartame. The registered trade name for aspartame as a food ingredient is NutraSweet®. Equal® is a tabletop low-calorie sweetener containing NutraSweet®. Another tabletop sweetener is Spoonful®, which consists of aspartame and maltodextrin. It is designed to measure like

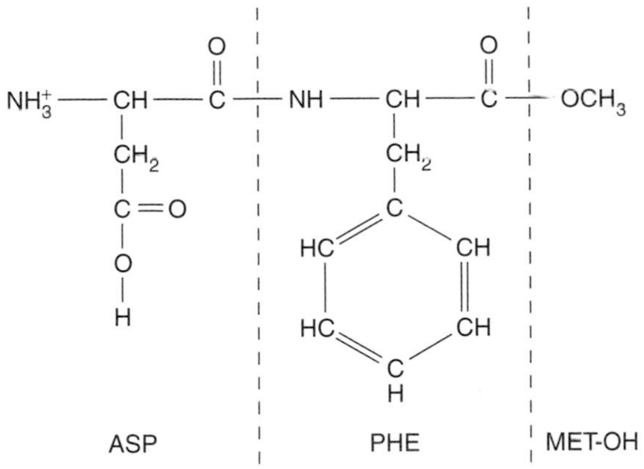

FIGURE 11-4 Chemical structure of aspartame. ASP, aspartic acid; PHE, phenylalanine; MET-OH, methyl alcohol.

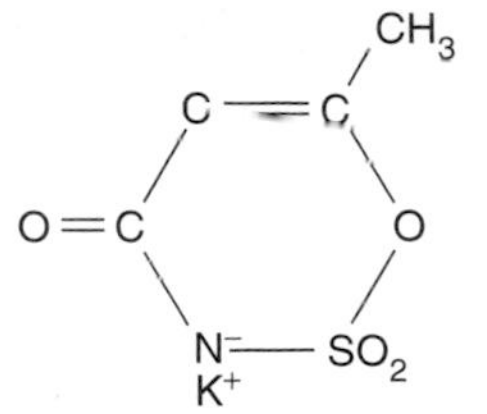

FIGURE 11-5 Chemical structure of acesulfame-K.

sugar. Aspartame can be utilized as an energy source in the body; however, it is used in such small amounts that its caloric value is insignificant.

Because aspartame is not stable to heat but changes chemically and loses sweetness, it has not been useful in such foods as baked layer cakes [12]. Its instability to heating can be corrected, however, by encapsulating a core of granulated aspartame with a water-resistant coating of polymer and/or a layer of fat. After the outer layer melts, the core layer slowly hydrates, releasing the aspartame in the final stages of baking. The use of low-calorie bulking agents with aspartame is also necessary to produce the effects on volume and texture that sugar provides in many baked products.

Rigorous testing has been done to ensure the safety of aspartame [14, 17, 20]. Although some have questioned the wisdom of its use, particularly in soft drinks kept at high temperatures, research from several sources has documented the safety of aspartame use by healthy adults and children, and by individuals with diabetes. Aspartame-containing foods should not, however, be used by individuals with phenylketonuria (PKU), because phenylalanine is released during its metabolism.

Acesulfame-K

Acesulfame is a synthetic derivative of acetoacetic acid. It is apparently not metabolized in the body and is excreted unchanged. This sweetener is characterized by a rapid onset of sweetness. It has little undesirable aftertaste, although at high concentrations it does exhibit lingering bitter and metallic flavor attributes [14]. Acesulfame-K, the potassium salt of acesulfame (see Figure 11-5), is up to 200 times sweeter than sucrose [1, 17].

Acesulfame-K was inadvertently discovered by a German chemist in 1967. The FDA approved this compound as a food additive in 1988 and for general use in foods except for meat and poultry in 2003 [30]. It is used in a variety of products and is marketed under the brand name Sunette® [14, 17].

Acesulfame-K is heat stable. It does not decompose under simulated pasteurization or baking conditions [20]. It thus has potential for use in cooked and baked products. In mixtures of acesulfame-K and aspartame (1 : 1 by weight) there is a strong synergistic enhancement of sweetness.

Sucralose

Sucralose is a white, crystalline solid produced by the selective addition of chlorine atoms to sucrose (Figure 11-6). It is 600 times sweeter than sugar, tastes very much like sucrose, and has no bitter aftertaste [20]. It is highly soluble in water and is stable under extreme pH conditions and at high temperatures; therefore, it can be used in retort applications, hot-filled and carbonated beverages, and baked goods. Sucralose does not interact with any other food components. Because absorption of sucralose is limited and the small amount that is absorbed is not metabolized, it imparts no caloric value to foods [1, 17, 24, 30].

Sucralose was approved by the FDA for use in several food and beverage categories in 1998 and then as a general-purpose sweetener in all foods the following year [30]. This sweetener was developed by a British firm and licensed for U.S. distribution. As a tabletop sweetener, it is marketed in packets, tablets, and granular form under the Splenda® brand.

Neotame

In July 2002, the FDA approved neotame for use as a general sweetener in foods (Figure 11-7). Neotame is 7,000 to 13,000 times sweeter than sucrose [20]. Thus, it is more potent than any of the other alternative sweeteners currently approved in the United States [21]. It functions

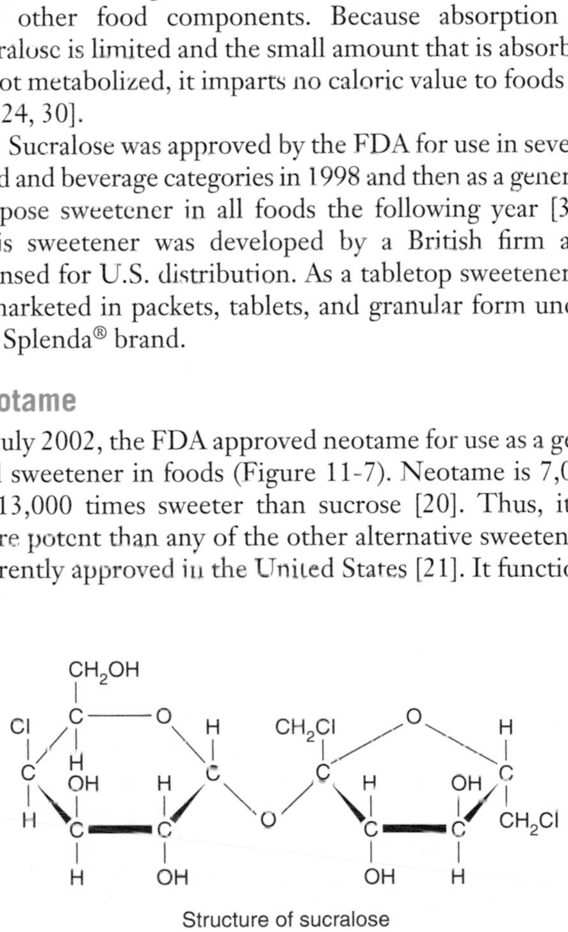

Structure of sucralose

FIGURE 11-6 Chemical structure of sucralose.

FIGURE 11-7 Structure of neotame. *(Source: Adapted from Reference 21)*

as a low-calorie sweetener and a flavor enhancer. Neotame has a clean sweet taste that is "sugarlike" without undesirable taste characteristics. It has been shown to enhance some flavors like mint and to suppress other flavors such as bitterness and the "beany" flavors in some soy products.

The stability of neotame has some similarities to aspartame, although neotame is more stable in neutral pH conditions and can be used successfully in dairy foods and baked products. Neotame is heat stable and can be used in cooking and baking [17].

French scientists Claude Nofre and Jean-Marie Tinti, in work with the NutraSweet Company, developed this alternative sweetener [21]. Neotame can be made by the reaction of aspartame with 3,3-dimethylbutyralde-hyde. However, unlike aspartame, neotame does not metabolize to phenylalanine, and thus no special labeling is needed for those with phenylketonuria (PKU). Neotame has been found safe for the general population, including children, pregnant women, and people with diabetes [1, 17, 21].

Other Alternative Sweeteners Not Yet Approved in the United States

Cyclamates. Cyclamates are 30 times sweeter than sucrose, taste much like sugar, and are heat stable. The sweetness has a slow onset and then persists for a period of time. Although cyclamates were considered GRAS by the FDA at one time and are currently approved for use in 50 countries, they are now banned from use in the United States [20]. A chronic toxicity study implicated sodium cyclamate as a possible bladder carcinogen in rats and resulted in the removal of cyclamates from the GRAS list in 1970. Since 1970, several additional safety studies have been done which have not been able to confirm the original findings of bladder cancer. A petition for approval of cyclamates as a food additive was again filed with the FDA; however, as of 2005 this petition is being held until further data are submitted to the FDA [17].

Alitame. Alitame is a peptide that is 2,000 times sweeter than a 10 percent solution of sucrose. It may be metabolized in the body, but would give minimal caloric value, because only a small amount of sweetener would be required to match the sweetness of sucrose. Alitame is highly soluble and has good stability under a variety of manufacturing conditions, although an off-taste may occur in warm acidic solutions. It may be used in combination with other low-calorie sweeteners. Alitame is already in use in several other countries, including Mexico [13]. A petition for the approval of alitame is being held in abeyance until additional data documenting safety are provided to the FDA [17].

Thaumatin. Thaumatin is a small protein extracted by physical methods from the berry of a West African plant—sometimes called the miraculous fruit. It is listed in the *Guinness Book of World Records* as the sweetest substance known—2,000 to 2,500 times sweeter than an 8 to 10 percent solution of sucrose. Although it is metabolized in the body and yields 4 kilocalories per gram, its low usage levels make it basically noncaloric. It is listed as GRAS in the United States as a flavor modifier but not as a sweetener [17]. This protein interacts with taste receptors on the tongue to mask unpleasant tastes, such

Acceptable Daily Intake of Low-Calorie Sweeteners

Acceptable daily intake (ADI) is the estimated amount of a substance, such as a low-calorie sweetener, that may be consumed over a lifetime without risk. The ADI is usually set at 1/100th of the maximum level found to cause no adverse effects in animal experiments [1, 17].

The U.S. Food and Drug Administration establishes the ADI of low-calorie sweeteners in the United States.

International and other government authorities establish ADI standards for food ingredients in other countries which may vary slightly from U.S. established levels. The ADI is one of the considerations influencing the approval of sweeteners for use in the food supply. ■

as metallic and bitter flavors. As a flavor enhancer, it acts in a similar fashion to monosodium glutamate and the 5'-nucleotides. It functions synergistically with other high-intensity sweeteners, allowing reduced levels of these substances [29]. A United Kingdom company produces and markets thaumatin under the trade name Talin®.

Neohesperidin dihydrochalcone. Neohesperidin dihydrochalcone is 1,500 times sweeter than sucrose, but it has a flavor profile which is different from sucrose [1, 17]. It is derived from grapefruit rinds and is approved in the United States as a flavor modifier but not for use as a sweetener.

Stevia. Stevia, steviol glycosides, or stevioside are all terms used to describe the sweetening substance extracted from a South American shrub of the chrysanthemum family. Stevia glycosides are 250 to 300 times sweeter than sugar. Stevia is not an approved food ingredient in the United States, but it may be sold as a "dietary supplement" because the regulations overseeing dietary supplements do not require approval before marketing. Products containing stevia, however, may not be advertised as sweeteners. Animal studies have raised concerns about the safety of stevia and so until additional scientific data are obtained, this substance is unlikely to be approved for use as a food additive in the United States [17].

Glycyrrhizin. Glycyrrhizin is 30 times sweeter than sugar but has a different flavor profile. It is derived from licorice extract and is considered GRAS in the United States as a flavoring agent, flavor enhancer, or surfactant. Glycyrrhizin, however, is not approved as a sweetener [17].

SUGAR ALCOHOLS (POLYOLS) AND NOVEL SWEETENERS

Low-calorie sweeteners lack the bulk needed for many food products. Sugar alcohols are therefore used with low-calorie sweeteners to improve bulk, mouthfeel, and texture [20]. Eight polyols (erythritol, mannitol, isomalt, lactitol, maltitol, xylitol, sorbitol, and hydrogenated starch hydrolysates) are approved for use in the United States. Foods sweetened with polyols may be labeled with "sugar free" or "does not promote tooth decay" claims; however, these foods may not meet the requirements of a "reduced-calorie food." Reduced-calorie foods must contain 25 percent less calories than the full-calorie product. Those who are following a diabetic or weight reduction diet should be aware of the caloric value of sugar alcohols [18]. The caloric values permitted by the FDA in the labeling of polyols are provided in Table 11-8.

TABLE 11-8 Caloric Values for Polyols

Sugar Alcohol (Polyol)	Kilocalories per Gram
Hydrogenated starch hydrolysates	3.0
Sorbitol	2.6
Xylitol	2.4
Maltitol	2.1
Lactitol	2.0
Isomalt	2.0
Mannitol	1.6
Erythritol	0.2

Source: References 17, 20

Erythritol

Erythritol is a monosaccharide polyol that is naturally present in a number of fruits and vegetables including pears, melons, and mushrooms [1, 17]. It is produced by the hydrolysis and fermentation of starch and purified by crystallization. Like other sugar alcohols, erythritol does not promote tooth decay or sudden increases in blood glucose. Unlike other sugar alcohols, however, it does not cause undesirable laxative side effects. It is about 70 percent as sweet as sucrose, has only 0.2 kilocalorie per gram, and, when used with other high-intensity sweeteners, may round off the flavor. The FDA, in 1997, accepted for filing a GRAS affirmation petition [13, 24]. Acceptance of this petition by the FDA allows manufacturers to produce and sell erythritol-containing foods in the United States. Erythritol is suitable for a variety of food products including chewing gum, candies, bakery products, beverages, and others.

Mannitol

Mannitol is used in food and pharmaceutical products. Mannitol is about 65 percent as sweet as sucrose [10]. It is often used as a dusting powder for chewing gum to prevent the gum from sticking with the wrapper. In medications, it effectively masks the bitter tastes of vitamins, minerals, and other ingredients. If the daily consumption of a particular food may exceed 20 grams of mannitol, the FDA requires the statement "excess consumption may have a laxative effect" on the label [17, 20].

Isomalt, Lactitol, and Maltitol

Isomalt is 0.45 to 0.6 times as sweet as sugar and can replace sugar in many products, often with minimal modifications in the formula [20, 25]. Unlike most polyols, it does not produce a cooling effect.

Lactitol is 0.3 to 0.4 times as sweet as sucrose [25]. It is produced by hydrogenation of the milk sugar lactose [5]. A low-calorie sweetener may need to be used in combination with lactitol to achieve the desired level of sweetness in some products [20].

Maltitol is made by hydrogenation of maltose [27]. It has a sweetness level that is 0.8 times that of sucrose. Like isomalt, maltitol does not produce a cooling effect. Maltitol can be used as a fat replacer in some products in addition to its use as a sweetener.

Xylitol

Xylitol is used primarily in confections such as chewing gums, candies, chocolates, and gum drops. Xylitol is as sweet as sugar and has a significant cooling effect that enhances mint flavors. It has the advantage of being associated with the significantly reduced formation of new caries [20]. Sugar alcohols, such as xylitol, are noncariogenic because they are not fermented by bacteria [10]. Xylitol appears to be the best nutritive sweetener with respect to caries prevention.

Sorbitol

Sorbitol has been used for half a century in processed foods [20]. It is 0.6 times as sweet as sucrose and exhibits a cool, pleasant taste. Sorbitol is used in many food products for its sweetening ability, moisture stabilizing, and texture properties. Similar to the requirement for mannitol, the FDA requires that if the consumption of a food might exceed 50 grams of sorbitol, the product must be labeled to inform consumers of the potential laxative effect [17].

Hydrogenated Starch Hydrolysates

Hydrogenated starch hydrolysates describes the broad group of polyols that contain hydrogenated oligo- and polysaccharides in addition to polyols such as sorbitol, mannitol, or maltitol. However, if the polyol mixture contains more than 50 percent sorbitol, for example, it would be called sorbitol syrup [20]. Hydrogenated starch hydrolysates are 40 to 50 percent as sweet as sugar, and like the other polyols discussed, they are used as bulk sweeteners, bulking agents, and humectants, along with other functional roles.

Novel Sugar Sweeteners

Two novel sugar sweeteners, trehalose and tagatose, are relatively new to the marketplace [17]. Trehalose is a naturally occurring disaccharide which provides 4 kilocalories per gram like sugar, but is less sweet and results in a lower glycemic response [17, 25]. This sweetener is valued for the ability to stabilize foods during freezing or hydration [17]. It was approved for GRAS status in the United States in 2000 and occurs naturally in mushrooms, yeast, seaweed, and lobster [25].

Tagatose occurs naturally in some dairy products. It is an isomer of fructose which is manufactured using lactose as the raw material. It is almost as sweet as sugar and is similar in bulk. Tagatose, however, provides fewer calories (1.5 kilocalories per gram) and a lower glycemic response due to differences in how it is metabolized [17, 26]. Tagatose has been approved for GRAS status and may be labeled with the claims "does not promote tooth decay" or "may reduce the risk of tooth decay" [25].

BULKING AGENTS

Although many consumers today are looking for foods that are low in calories or "light," they still want them to be good tasting. Often, good-tasting food is synonymous with sweet food. Although it is relatively easy, with the approved nonnutritive sweeteners, to make a low-calorie product sweet, it is more challenging to match the other functions provided by sugar in the formulation [9]. One method is to use a bulking and bodying agent—something that is low in calories but provides volume, texture, and a thickened consistency. Bulking agents are also called *macronutrient substitutes*.

Polydextrose is a bulking agent that has been shown to be safe through extensive testing. It is an approved food additive used—often with an artificial sweetener—in such products as frozen desserts, puddings, baked goods, frostings, and candies. Polydextrose contributes 1 kilocalorie per gram, only one-fourth of the calories that sucrose or other sugars provide. Therefore, when used

FOCUS ON SCIENCE

More about Sorbitol
Why does sorbitol prevent dental caries?

Sorbitol is derived from the hydrogenation of D-glucose. Sorbitol is used in sugarless gum and is about 70 percent as sweet as sucrose. When sorbitol is used in place of sucrose,

there is a reduction in dental caries because it is not metabolized by the microflora of the mouth to produce plaque.

What foods contain sorbitol?

Sorbitol is used in sugarless gums, mints, candies, and cough drops. In toothpaste, it functions as a humectant and plasticizer and imparts a cool sweet taste. Sorbitol also is used in nondietetic foods including shredded coconut, glazed and dried fruits, baked goods, and gelatin products for its humectancy and bodying effect.

HEALTHY EATING

Formulated Foods for People with Diabetes

Sedentary life styles and an abundance of food are contributing to the growing plague of obesity in the United States along with one of its side effects—the increased risk for developing diabetes. About 5.9 percent of the U.S. population has been diagnosed with some form of diabetes—Type 2 being the most common—and diabetes is the seventh leading cause of death in the U.S. [15].

Foods designed for diabetics are different from the usual low-sugar, lowfat foods found on the market and are not to be used for weight reduction. They attempt to provide a balance of nutrients for diabetics that work with drugs to control blood glucose levels more effectively. For example, Mead Johnson

Nutritionals has developed a *Choice DM®* line of ready-to-use beverages and nutrition bars and Ross Products Division of Abbott Laboratories markets the *Glucerna®* line of similar products. Both the beverages and the bars provide a balance of carbohydrate, fat, and protein with added vitamins and minerals and use alternative sweeteners such as aspartame and sucralose. The bars contain a special starch that is resistant to digestion, giving a lower glycemic response—that is, the blood glucose level does not rise as rapidly or as high after the bar is eaten. These products give diabetics greater choice in managing their daily diets. Research continues in an effort to improve these "designer" foods [19]. ■

with aspartame or saccharin, it can reduce the caloric content of an item by 50 percent or more [9]. The materials used in the production of polydextrose are an 89 : 10 : 1 mixture of dextrose, sorbitol, and citric acid. One polydextrose product is marketed under the brand name Litesse™.

Other bulking agents include cellulose and maltodextrins. Maltodextrins consist of glucose units with a dextrose equivalent (DE) of less than 20 and contribute 4 kilocalories per gram. Some fat-free products in which bulking agents may be used, such as fat-free cookies and granola bars, contain concentrated fruit juices and dried fruits as substitutes for added sugar.

SUGAR COOKERY

Sucrose, or table sugar, is the mainstay of the enormous worldwide chocolate and sugar confectionery industry. In the preparation of concentrated sugar products, such as candies and frostings, many of the chemical and physical properties of sugar are of particular importance. The foundation for cooked frosting and candies is a boiled sugar solution. Some properties of solutions, therefore, are discussed here.

Boiling Points and Solutions

Boiling Pure Liquids. The boiling point of a liquid may be defined as the temperature at which the **vapor pressure** of the liquid is equal to the atmospheric pressure resting on its surface. At the boiling point, the vapor

pressure of the liquid pushes against the atmospheric pressure to the extent that bubbles of vapor break and are released. Once boiling occurs, the temperature of the boiling liquid does not increase; an equilibrium is established.

The boiling point of a liquid varies with altitude, because atmospheric pressure is lower at high altitudes and higher at low altitudes. The boiling point of water at sea level, where atmospheric pressure is about 15 pounds per square inch or barometric pressure is 760 millimeters of mercury, is taken as a standard. At sea level, water boils at 212°F (100°C). At higher altitudes, water boils below this temperature. For each 960 feet above sea level, the boiling point of water drops 1°C (1.8°F). In mountainous areas, the low boiling point of water seriously interferes with many cooking operations, and thus methods and formulas usually require modification for use at high altitudes.

The boiling point of water may be lowered artificially by creating a partial vacuum, which is accomplished by withdrawing part of the air and steam above a boiling liquid, and thus lowering the air and steam pressure. Similarly, the boiling point may be elevated by an increase in air or steam pressure. The pressure cooker, which is a tightly closed utensil, increases pressure by preventing the vapor above the liquid from escaping. The pressure of the accumulated steam is thus added to that of the atmosphere above the liquid.

Boiling Solutions. Anything that decreases the vapor pressure of a liquid increases its boiling point. Substances in a true solution, such as sugar or salt, that do not become volatile or gaseous at the boiling point of water will decrease the vapor pressure of the water, because these molecules displace water molecules on the surface of the liquid. The boiling point is increased because it takes more heat to raise the lowered vapor pressure to the point where it is equal to atmospheric pressure (Figure 11-8). When dissolved substances ionize in solution, as does salt, the vapor pressure is decreased, and the boiling point of the water is raised to an even greater degree. The larger the number of particles of solute in the solution, the more the vapor pressure is lowered and the higher the temperature of boiling.

Boiling sugar solutions do not reach a constant boiling point as does water alone. As water evaporates and the remaining solution thus becomes more concentrated, the boiling temperature increases. This process continues until all of the water is evaporated or the solubility of the sugar is exceeded. The boiling points of some pure sucrose solutions of various concentrations are given in Table 11-9. These figures are for sucrose solutions alone and do not apply to mixed sugar solutions such as sucrose solutions containing corn syrup, glucose, or molasses, which are more commonly used in making candy than pure sucrose solutions. Candy mixtures are, however, predominantly sucrose.

Calibrating and Reading the Thermometer. The first step in candy making is to calibrate the thermometer by taking the temperature of boiling water. If the thermometer does not show the proper temperature for the altitude, an adjustment is made by adding or subtracting, as appropriate, the difference in degrees between the expected and observed temperatures.

In taking the temperature of boiling sugar solutions, the bulb of the thermometer should be completely immersed in the solution but should not touch the bottom of the pan. In reading the scale, the eye should be on a level with the top of the mercury column.

Inversion of Sucrose

The hydrolysis of some sucrose to produce equal amounts of glucose and fructose, a mixture called *invert sugar,* helps control sugar crystallization in candy making. Thus, it deserves some special consideration in our discussion.

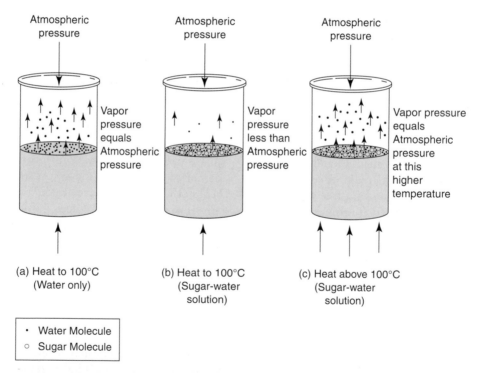

FIGURE 11-8 Pure water boils at 212°F (100°C) at sea level because its vapor pressure is equal to atmospheric pressure at this point: An equilibrium is established. When sugar or other nonvolatile solute is dissolved in water, some of the nonvolatile sugar molecules displace water molecules on the surface. The vapor pressure of the solution is therefore decreased. Heating to 212°F (100°C) does not increase the water vapor pressure enough to be equal to the atmospheric pressure at this point. More heat must be put into the solution to vaporize more water and increase the vapor pressure enough to equal the atmospheric pressure. Therefore, a sugar solution boils at a higher temperature than pure water. The higher the concentration of sugar or other nonvolatile solute, the higher the boiling point of the solution.

TABLE 11-9 Boiling Points of Sucrose Solutions of Various Concentrations at Sea Level									
Percent Sucrose	10	20	30	40	50	60	70	80	90.8
Boiling Point									
°F	212.7	213.1	213.8	214.7	215.6	217.4	223.7	233.6	266.0
°C	100.4	110.6	101.0	101.5	102.0	103.0	106.5	112.0	130.0

Source: Browne's *Handbook of Sugar Analysis*. Reprinted by permission of John Wiley & Sons, Inc.

Because a mixture of invert sugar and sucrose is more soluble than a sucrose solution alone, and thus less easily crystallized, the mixture allows the process of crystallization to be more easily controlled than when invert sugar is not present. Desirably small sugar crystals can therefore be produced in crystalline candies such as fondant and fudge. Although a small amount of invert sugar is formed by the long, slow heating of a plain sucrose solution, the reaction is accelerated by the presence of a weak acid. Cream of tartar, an acid salt, is probably the preferable acid to use in most candy making, because its composition is fairly uniform and measurements are usually quite accurate. In addition, fondant made with cream of tartar is snowy white.

The amount of inversion that occurs when sucrose is heated with water and acid varies greatly and is difficult to control. The rate of heating, the length of heating, and the quantity of cream of tartar used all affect the amount of invert sugar formed. If too much acid is used or if the period of heating is too long, too much inversion occurs, with the result that the fondant is extremely soft or fails to crystallize at all. It has been found that the presence of 43 percent invert sugar prevents crystallization completely.

Usually, about 1/4 teaspoon of cream of tartar is used with 2 cups of sugar in making fondant. In a fondant cooked to 239°F (115°C) in 20 minutes, 11 percent invert sugar was produced with 1/8 teaspoon cream of tartar and 1 cup (200 grams) sugar [33].

Glucose, fructose, or invert sugar may be added directly to sucrose solutions in candy making rather than producing invert sugar during cooking by the addition of cream of tartar. Direct addition of these substances makes control of their quantity easier than trying to regulate the amount of invert sugar produced by sucrose hydrolysis. Corn syrup, which contains a high proportion of glucose, is sometimes used instead of cream of tartar in fondant mixtures. The glucose in the sucrose solution has an effect similar to that of invert sugar in increasing the solubility of the sucrose and allowing better control of the crystallization process so that small sugar crystals are produced in the final product.

CLASSIFICATION OF CANDIES

Either *crystalline* or *noncrystalline* candies may be produced from boiled sugar solutions. Crystalline candies are generally soft. If properly made, they are so smooth and creamy that the tiny sugar crystals that comprise their microscopic structure cannot be felt on the tongue. The principal crystalline candies are fondant, fudge, and panocha. Divinity, with added egg white, also is a crystalline candy.

Noncrystalline candies are sometimes called *amorphous*, which means "without form." In their preparation, by use of various ingredients and techniques, crystallization of sugar is prevented. Noncrystalline candies may be chewy, such as caramels, or hard, such as butterscotch, toffees, and brittles.

FOCUS ON SCIENCE

The Chemical Reaction for Inversion of Sucrose

The chemical reaction for the inversion of sucrose is provided below. The acid or enzyme enables the reaction but is not consumed in the reaction.

$C_{12}H_{22}O_{11} + H_2O = C_6H_{12}O_6$ (glucose) $+ C_6H_{12}O_6$ (fructose)

Crystalline Candies

Fondant.   Fondant is a soft, smooth candy. It is made by cooking a sucrose solution to approximately 234°F (112°C), after which the solution is cooled and beaten until crystallization occurs. A simple sucrose and water solution sometimes makes good fondant; however, more satisfactory results are generally obtained by the addition of acid to accelerate inversion or by the direct addition of invert sugar, glucose, or corn syrup to aid in keeping crystals small. Use of milk or cream (as the liquid) increases the creamy character of fondant.

Essential steps in the making of fondant include (1) complete solution of the crystalline sugar, (2) concentration of the solution to the desirable stage, and (3) prevention of crystallization until conditions are favorable for the formation of fine crystals.

Solution.   Undissolved sugar crystals may cause seeding while the solution is cooling and start crystallization before it is desirable. Therefore, a complete solution of sugar is accomplished by (1) adding sufficient liquid to dissolve the sugar and (2) stirring then covering the pan at the beginning of cooking to allow steam to dissolve crystals on the sides of the pan. To allow for adequate evaporation which concentrates the solution, the pan must be uncovered after this initial cooking period. Alternatively, crystals may be washed from the pan with a small piece of moistened paper towel or cheesecloth wrapped around a fork instead of covering the pan during the initial cooking period (see Figure 11-9).

Stirring the solution during cooking does not start crystallization, but stirring and vigorous boiling may splash syrup on the sides of the pan above the liquid where it may dry, crystallize, drop into the cooling syrup, and start premature crystallization. The spoon used for stirring also may introduce dried crystals unless it is well rinsed between stirrings.

Concentration.   Table 11-10 gives the temperatures and tests of doneness for candies of various types. The temperature range for the final cooking of fondant mixtures at sea level is 234° to 240°F (112° to 115°C). Higher temperatures reduce the water content, thereby increasing the concentration of sugar. A drier, more moldable fondant is produced with a higher temperature. A lower temperature (less concentrated mixture) gives a very soft fondant. When the humidity is high, higher temperatures are desirable to evaporate the additional liquid absorbed by fondant in damp weather. When corn syrup is used in candy, slightly lower temperature are necessary to reach the desired stages of firmness. At altitudes above sea level, the final boiling temperatures should be lowered to the extent that the boiling point of water is decreased below 212°F (100°C).

The desired rate of cooking fondant mixtures depends partly on the proportions of ingredients used. Faster boiling is necessary if a high proportion of water is

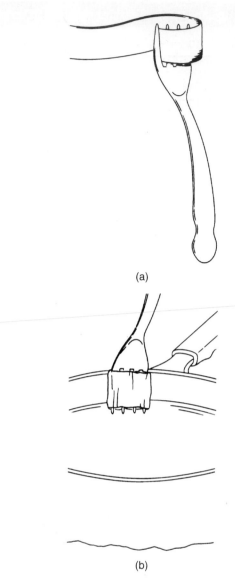

(a)

(b)

FIGURE 11-9 Complete solution of sugar. Wipe all sugar crystals from the sides of the pan as the candy mixture begins to boil. (a) Roll a small strip of moistened paper towel or cheesecloth around the tines of the fork. (b) Dip the covered fork in and out of a cup of clean water as the sides of the pan are wiped free of sugar crystals. The extra water on the wrapped fork goes into the boiling sugar solution.

used to avoid too long a cooking period and consequently the production of too much invert sugar. Violent boiling is usually to be avoided because of the larger amount of syrup that is splashed on the sides of the pan.

Testing the doneness of candy mixtures may be accomplished by the use of a thermometer or by evaluating consistency after dropping the hot candy mixture into very cold water. The results of the cold water tests of doneness are compared with the temperatures of cooking in Table 11-10 and are shown in Figure 11-10.

Once cooking of the syrup is complete, it may be cooled on a smooth flat surface, such as a marble-topped counter, or left to cool in the pan. Cooling will be more

TABLE 11-10   Temperatures and Tests for Syrup and Candies

Product	Final Temperature of Syrup at Sea Level*		Test of Doneness	Description of Test
	°F	°C		
Syrup	230–234	110–112	Thread	Syrup spins a 2-inch thread when dropped from fork or spoon.
Fondant	234–240	112–115	Soft ball	Syrup, when dropped into very cold water, forms a soft ball that flattens on removal from water.
Fudge				
Panocha				
Caramels	244–248	118–120	Firm ball	Syrup, when dropped into very cold water, forms a firm ball that does not flatten on removal from water.
Divinity	250–256	121–130	Hard ball	Syrup, when dropped into very cold water, forms a ball that is hard enough to hold its shape, yet plastic.
Marshmallows				
Popcorn balls				
Butterscotch	270–290	132–143	Soft crack	Syrup, when dropped into very cold water, separates into threads that are hard but not brittle.
Taffies				
Brittle	300–310	149–154	Hard crack	Syrup, when dropped into very cold water, separates into threads that are hard and brittle.
Glacé				
Barley sugar	320	160	Clear liquid	The sugar liquifies.
Caramel	338	170	Brown liquid	The liquid becomes brown.

*For each increase of 500 feet in elevation, cook the syrup to a temperature 1°F lower than the temperature called for at sea level. If readings are taken in Celsius, for each 960 feet of elevation, cook the syrup to a temperature 1°C lower than that called for at sea level.

rapid on a cool marbletop surface. As the hot syrup cools, it becomes saturated and then supersaturated because it is holding in solution more solute (sugar) than is normally soluble at the lower temperatures. As discussed earlier, supersaturated solutions are unstable. Thus, the candy must be handled to avoid premature crystallization. The syrup should be poured quickly from the pan. Scraping,

prolonged dripping from the pan, or jostling of the poured syrup will usually start crystallization and should therefore be avoided. Uneven cooling may start crystallization in those portions of the syrup that first become supersaturated. If a thermometer is placed in the syrup to determine when the syrup is ready for beating, it should be read without moving it in the syrup.

(a)

(b)

(c)

FIGURE 11-10 The concentration of sugar syrups is best measured with a candy thermometer. Spooning a few drops of the syrup into very cold water will provide another measure of concentration as shown by the soft, hard, and hard crack stages in these pictures. (a) Soft ball stage; (b) Hard ball stage; (c) Hard crack stage.

Crystallization. An important aim in making crystalline candies is to produce a very smooth texture. For this to be achieved, many fine crystals, rather than few large crystals, must be formed. For a small-crystal structure, conditions must be conducive to the formation, within the supersaturated solution, of many nuclei or small clumps of molecules. These act as centers around which crystal formation may begin. Some substances readily crystallize from a water solution with only a slight degree of supersaturation. With other substances, such as sugar, there must usually be a high degree of supersaturation before formation of nuclei and crystallization start.

The presence of glucose, corn syrup, invert sugar, fats, and proteins interfere with crystallization of sucrose in fondant and other candies. Glucose, corn syrup, or invert sugar affect crystallization because they make the sugar solution more soluble and, therefore, decrease the ease of crystal formation. Other substances, including fats from milk, cream, butter, margarine, and chocolate, and proteins from milk and egg white, do not themselves crystallize. They physically interfere with the process of sugar crystallization, retarding the growth of crystals. All of these interfering substances aid in fine crystal formation and smooth texture in crystalline candies.

The temperature at which crystallization occurs affects the size of crystals, primarily because it affects the rate of crystallization. In general, the higher the temperature at which crystallization occurs, the faster the rate of crystallization and the more difficult it is to keep the crystals separated, resulting in larger crystals. Cooling the candy mixture to about 104°F (40°C) before starting to beat, favors the formation of more nuclei and finer crystals. The viscosity of the solution is also greater at lower temperatures. High viscosity is a further aid in the production of fine crystals because it retards crystallization. Figure 11-11 shows the sizes of crystals formed in fondant beaten at different temperatures. The syrup could be cooled to so low a temperature that beating is impossible. Too low a temperature also may hinder the formation of many nuclei.

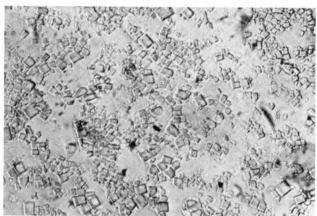

Crystals from fondant made with sugar, water, and cream of tartar, boiled to 239°F (115°C) and cooled to 104°C (40°C) before beating.

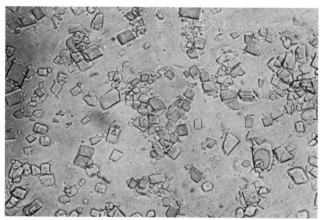

Crystals from fondant made with sugar and water with 7 percent glucose added, boiled to 239°F (115°C) and cooled to 104°F (40°C) before beating.

Crystals from fondant made with sugar and water only, boiled to 239°F (115°C) and cooled to 104°F (40°C) before beating.

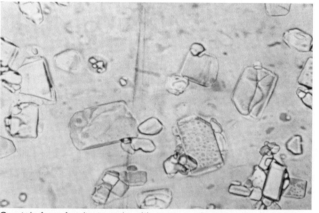

Crystals from fondant made with sugar and water only, boiled to 239°F (115°C) and beaten immediately.

FIGURE 11-11 Comparison of sugar crystal size with various methods of making fondant.   *(Courtesy of Dr. Sybil Woodruff and the Journal of Physical Chemistry)*

Agitation or stirring favors the formation of finer crystals than are produced spontaneously. Therefore, it is important to stir a crystalline candy, not only until crystallization starts, but until it is complete. As crystallization proceeds, the candy stiffens and becomes moldable. It can be kneaded in your hands (see Figure 11-12). It is important to work rapidly to prevent hardening and crumbling of the fondant before kneading is started. It is usually possible to see when the fondant is about to set in a more stiff mass. Its shiny appearance becomes dulled, and it seems to soften temporarily. The softening is the result of the heat of crystallization being given off as the crystals form.

Ripening. As crystalline candy stands after crystallization is complete, it becomes somewhat more moist and smooth and kneads more easily, because some of the very small crystals dissolve in the syrup. Changes that occur during the initial period of storage are called *ripening*. Adsorbed substances that interfere with crystallization aid in retarding the growth of crystals during storage.

Proportions for Fondant	
With Cream of Tartar	**With Corn Syrup**
2 cups (400 g) granulated sugar	2 cups (400 g) granulated sugar
1/4 tsp cream of tartar	1 to 1 1/2 Tbsp (21 to 39 g) syrup
1 cup (237 mL) water	1 cup (237 mL) water

Fudge. The principles of making fudge do not differ from those of making fondant. Usually the butter or margarine, the fat of chocolate, and the milk proteins and fat furnish the substances that interfere with crystallization. Acid is sometimes used, and corn syrup may be used. If brown sugar replaces part or all of the white sugar, some invert sugar is introduced into the mixture. Also, a small amount of acid in the brown sugar helps invert sucrose. Therefore, brown sugar fudge (panocha) crystallizes less rapidly than white sugar fudge. When crystallization is almost complete, the initially glossy fudge becomes dull, and the whole mass softens slightly, as it does for fondant (Figures 11-13 and 11-14). The fudge should be poured from the pan before it hardens.

Noncrystalline Candies

Sugar does not crystallize in noncrystalline candies. The crystallization is prevented by (1) cooking to very high temperatures so that the finished product hardens quickly or solidifies before the crystals have a chance to form, (2) adding such large amounts of interfering substances that the crystals cannot form, or (3) combining these methods.

Brittles. Brittles are cooked to temperatures that are high enough to produce a hard, brittle candy that solidifies before it has a chance to crystallize. The brown color and characteristic flavor of brittles result from nonenzymatic browning reactions, probably both the Maillard type and the caramelization of sugar. The development of caramel also helps to prevent crystallization of sugar in the brittles because it is noncrystalline.

Some brittles are made merely by melting and caramelizing sucrose. Soda is sometimes a constituent of brittles and is added after cooking is completed. It neutralizes acid decomposition products and forms carbon dioxide gas, which gives the candy a porous texture. The flavor is also made milder and less bitter by the use of soda. The degree of bitterness in a brittle depends on the extent of decomposition of the sugar. Brittles include butterscotch, nut brittles, and toffee.

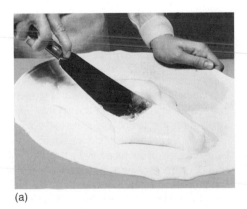 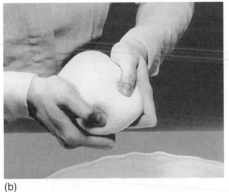

(a) (b)

FIGURE 11-12 Fondant is manipulated with a spatula after it has cooled to 104°F (40°C). Some form of agitation is needed until crystallization is complete. The fondant is then quickly formed into a ball and kneaded until smooth. *(Courtesy of General Foods, Inc.)*

(a) Fudge that has been beaten too long and has hardened in the pan.

(b) Fudge beaten to the correct stage for pouring into a dish to harden.

FIGURE 11-13 Fudge should be beaten to the correct consistency before it is poured out to harden. *(Courtesy of Best Foods)*

Chocolate fudge is made by adding unsweetened chocolate to the basic ingredients before starting to cook.

FIGURE 11-14 Blonde and chocolate fudge. *(Courtesy of Best Foods)*

FOCUS ON SCIENCE

What Is Happening when Fudge Is Cooling?

After boiling the solution and reaching the endpoint temperature, the syrup reaches saturation very soon after it starts to cool. If everything was done precisely, the sugar does not come back out of the solution. Instead, the syrup continues to cool as a supersaturated solution. The solid phase—in this case, sugar—cannot start to crystallize without something to serve as a nucleus. If a single sugar crystal is present, however, the syrup will start to crystallize, and the crystals will grow steadily as the syrup continues to cool resulting in grainy fudge.

That is why the inversion of sugar is important in the syrup. Large crystals of sucrose have a harder time forming when molecules of fructose and glucose are present. Crystals interlock together and form large molecules. If some of the molecules are a different size and shape, they will not fit together, and a crystal does not form.

Caramels. Caramels are firm, noncrystalline candies containing large amounts of interfering substances. They are cooked to temperatures between those for crystalline candies and hard brittle candies. The added substances that interfere with crystallization are usually butter or margarine and viscous corn syrup or molasses, which contain glucose, fructose, or invert sugar. Corn syrup also contains dextrins, which do not crystallize. Acid hydrolysis may be used to produce invert sugar, but more inversion is necessary for caramels than for fondant. Fats and proteins in milk or cream also aid in preventing crystallization. The final cooking temperature varies with the kind and proportion of ingredients. The brown color of caramels results chiefly from the Maillard reaction. The color and flavor of caramels develop better with long, slow heating than with rapid cooking. The characteristic flavor of plain caramels may be modified somewhat by the addition of chocolate or molasses.

Taffy. Taffy can be made from a simple sucrose syrup with the addition of cream of tartar, vinegar, or lemon juice to invert part of the sucrose and prevent crystallization. Flavoring extracts may be added when the solution has cooled sufficiently for pulling. Glucose, corn syrup, or molasses can be used instead of acid. Taffies are harder than caramels and therefore require higher cooking temperatures.

Fondant Confections

Fondant has many possible uses. It may be made into bonbons, which are fondant centers dipped in melted fondant, or into fondant loaves, which have fruit and nut mixtures added. Centers for chocolates are commonly made from fondant. Fondant patties are made from melted fondant that is flavored and colored as desired. Candy cookbooks suggest many specific combinations of fondant with other ingredients.

Fondant Dipping. Fondant centers are prepared ahead of time from fondant of a suitable texture for molding. The molded centers are allowed to stand on waxed paper until firm and slightly hardened on the outside. The fondant for melting may be of softer consistency than that used for molding.

Only a small quantity—about one cup—of fondant should be melted at one time. In a container of appropriate size, this quantity provides sufficient depth to coat the centers easily yet not enough to become too coarse and granular before it can be used.

The fondant is best melted over hot water. While melting, the solid fondant is broken up or turned frequently but with a minimum amount of stirring. Formation of coarse crystals by the stirring of a hot solution is as important here as in the making of the original fondant. While the fondant is melting, food colors in liquid or paste form may be applied on the point of a toothpick.

TABLE 11-11	Color and Flavor Combinations Used for Candy
Color	**Flavor**
Red	Oil of cinnamon or cloves
Green	Oil of lime
White	Oil of peppermint
Pink	Oil of wintergreen
Yellow	Oil of lemon
Orange	Oil of orange

Care should be taken to avoid adding too much color. Food flavors, if they are in the form of oils, must be added with equal care to avoid too strong a flavor. Extracts are more dilute.

After the fondant is melted, colored, and flavored, it must be cooled slightly to such a consistency that it clings to the molded fondant during dipping. The molded pieces of fondant are quickly dipped into the melted fondant and are then placed on waxed paper in a cool environment to set. Colors and flavors often used together are provided in Table 11-11.

Fondant Patties. Fondant patties are also made from melted fondant. After the melted fondant is colored and flavored, it is dropped on waxed paper from a teaspoon—1/2 to 1 teaspoon may be used, according to the size of patty desired. Speed is necessary to dip and pour the fondant before it begins to harden. If the melted fondant becomes too stiff to flow into a smooth patty, it should be remelted, or a very small amount of hot water should be added to it.

CHOCOLATE DIPPING

The chocolate used for ordinary culinary purposes is not generally suitable for dipping candies. Dipping chocolate should be of fine quality and contain sufficient cocoa butter to promote hardening with a smooth, glossy finish.

Centers to be coated with chocolate should be prepared several hours before dipping so that they are firm enough to handle easily. An exception is fondant centers to which invertase enzyme has been added; this type of fondant becomes softer the longer it stands.

Successful chocolate dipping depends largely on the use of a suitable chocolate; the control of temperatures and avoidance of a humid atmosphere; and thorough stirring or hand manipulation of the chocolate while it is melting and cooling, and, as much as possible, while dipping. Manipulation of the chocolate ensures uniform blending of the cocoa butter with the other chocolate constituents and produces a more even coating.

Temperatures and Techniques. Room temperature and humidity are well controlled in commercial chocolate dipping rooms. The temperature should be 60° to 70°F (15° to 20°C). A clear, cool day of low relative humidity is desirable. Drafts should be avoided, as uneven cooling affects the gloss and color of chocolates.

Even melting of the chocolate is facilitated by grating, shaving, or fine chopping. The chocolate should be melted over hot (not boiling) water; higher temperatures may allow the cocoa butter to separate out. While the chocolate is melting, it should be stirred continuously. Stirring prevents uneven heating and overheating and maintains a uniform blend. Water should not be allowed to get into the melting chocolate, as it can cause the chocolate to become lumpy.

After the chocolate has melted, it should be taken to a temperature of about 120°F (49°C) for tempering. It should then be continuously stirred while being cooled to about 85°F (29°C). At this point the chocolate is ready for dipping. The range of temperatures at which chocolates can be satisfactorily dipped is narrow; hence, rapid dipping is necessary. Fondant centers may be dropped into the chocolate, coated, and lifted out with a wire chocolate dipper or a two-tined fork. The coated chocolate is inverted on waxed paper. Another method of dipping chocolates is to pour the melted chocolate onto a marble-topped surface and stir it by hand. Fondant centers may be rolled in the melted chocolate; the surplus chocolate is removed by tapping the fingers lightly on the marble surface, and then the coated chocolate is dropped quickly onto waxed paper (see Figure 11-15).

Defects of Dipped Chocolates. The chief defects of dipped chocolates are gray or streaked surfaces, a broad base on the dipped chocolate, or sticky spots on the surface. Gray surfaces are caused by unfavorable room temperatures, incorrect temperatures during melting and handling the chocolate, direct drafts, excessive humidity, insufficient stirring of the chocolate, and not rapid enough cooling of the chocolate. The surface of a defective chocolate appears dull and gray because the fat of the chocolate has not crystallized in a stable form.

A broad base on the dipped chocolate results from dipping at too high temperatures or from failure to remove excess chocolate after dipping. Sticky spots result

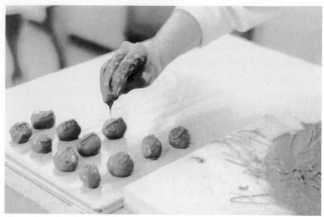

Chocolate is mixed until it reaches the correct temperature for dipping. A fondant center is rolled in the chocolate and then placed on waxed paper in a cool room. The chocolate should set up or harden immediately.

FIGURE 11-15 Chocolate dipping. *(Photograph by Roger P. Smith and Ava Winterton)*

from leakage of the centers because of incomplete coating with chocolate. These spots are particularly likely to occur in chocolates made from fondants that liquefy on standing.

THE CONFECTIONERY INDUSTRY

A variety of ingredients are available to the commercial confectioner to help improve texture, prevent defects, add gloss, enhance flavor release, and aid processing in the manufacture of candies. These include quick-setting starch to reduce drying time for jelly gum candies, encapsulated flavors and colors for customized products, blends of acidulants to improve taste properties of hard candies, lecithin products to act as emulsifiers in caramels and toffees, and polishing and sealing systems for chocolate-based products. Sugar-free and lowfat confections are being developed in increasing quantities. Various hydrocolloids, such as pectins, starches, gelatin, and gums, are playing important roles as textural or stabilizing agents in the manufacture of many confectionery products, including lower-fat and calorie-reduced items [6, 23].

CHAPTER SUMMARY

- Sugar provides only energy for the body. Therefore, foods that contain relatively large amounts of sugar generally have low nutrient density.

- In the natural state of foods, sugars are in solution. The crystallization of sugar occurs from a sufficiently concentrated sugar solution. Common sugars vary in their solubilities. Solutions may be unsaturated, saturated, or supersaturated depending on the amount of sugar that is dissolved in the solution.

- With the application of sufficient dry heat, sugars melt; with continued heat, sugar will caramelize. Caramelization is one type of browning called *nonenzymatic browning*.

- Sugars are said to be hygroscopic because of the tendency to absorb moisture from the atmosphere. Fructose is more hygroscopic than the other sugars commonly found in food.

- Most sugars, except lactose, may be fermented by yeasts to produce carbon dioxide gas and alcohol. Fermentation is an important reaction in the making of bread and other baked products.

- The disaccharides are hydrolyzed by weak acids to produce their component monosaccharides. The end products of sucrose hydrolysis are a mixture of glucose and fructose, commonly called invert sugar. Invert sugar is desirable in some sugar products, such as fondant, to improve the texture or consistency of the product.

- Enzymes also hydrolyze disaccharides. The enzyme sucrase, also called invertase, is used in the candy industry to hydrolyze some of the sucrose in cream fondant to fructose and glucose.

- The decomposition products of glucose and fructose by alkalies are brownish and may be strong and bitter if the process of decomposition was extensive. Baked beans, fondant, cakes, and cookies may be browner and stronger in flavor as a result of alkaline decomposition of the sugars in these foods.

- The degree of sweetness that we perceive is affected by several factors, including genetic variation among individuals as well as the concentration of the sweetener, temperature, viscosity, pH, and the presence of other substances with the sweetener. In general, lactose is the least sweet, with fructose being the sweetest.

- Table sugar is crystalline sucrose produced commercially from sugar beets and sugar cane. Sugar plays a variety of roles in food systems by affecting the texture of many baked goods, improving the body and

texture of ice cream, being fermented by yeast to leaven breads, and preserving jams and jellies by retarding the growth of microorganisms.

- Powdered sugar is machine ground or pulverized from granulated sucrose. Brown sugar is obtained from cane sugar during the late stages of refining and is composed of clumps of sucrose crystals coated with a film of molasses.

- Corn syrups, high-fructose corn syrup, molasses, maple syrup, and honey each offer unique properties and flavors that are useful in food preparation.

- Low-calorie or alternative sweeteners currently approved for use in the United State include saccharin, aspartame, acesulfame-K, sucralose, and neotame.

- Sugar alcohols (polyols) may be used with low-calorie sweeteners to improve bulk, mouthfeel, and texture. Eight polyols (erythritol, mannitol, isomalt, lactitol, maltitol, xylitol, sorbitol, and hydrogenated starch hydrolysates) are approved for use in the United States.

- Polydextrose, cellulose, and maltodextrins are bulking agents that may be used in low-calorie foods. Bulking agents provide volume, texture, and a thickened consistency in products using low-calorie sweeteners.

- Sugar solutions are boiled in the preparation of many candies. Boiling sugar solutions do not reach a constant boiling point as does water alone because as the water evaporates, the solution becomes more concentrated, resulting in an increase in the boiling temperature.

- Invert sugar is important in candy making because a mixture of invert sugar and sucrose allows the process of crystallization to be more easily controlled. Thus, desirably small sugar crystals can be produced in crystalline candies such as fudge and fondant.

- Crystalline candies include fondant, fudge, panocha, and divinity. An important aim in the preparation of crystalline candies is to produce a very fine texture. Agitation or stirring once the candy is at the desired temperature favors the formation of finer crystals.

- Noncrystalline candies include brittles, caramels, and taffy. Sugar does not crystallize in noncrystalline candies. The crystallization is prevented by (1) cooking to a very high temperature, (2) adding large amounts of interfering substances that prevent crystal formation, and (3) a combination of these methods.

STUDY QUESTIONS

1. Sugars have many properties that are important in the preparation of candies and other sugar-containing foods.

   (a) List the common sugars in order of their solubilities in water at room temperature. Describe how the solubility of sugars is affected by temperature.

   (b) Describe a saturated and a supersaturated solution. Explain the significance of a supersaturated solution in making crystalline candies.

   (c) What happens when sugar is heated in a dry state above its melting point? Why is this reaction important in food preparation?

   (d) What is meant by *hygroscopic?* Which is the most hygroscopic sugar?

   (e) Name the two monosaccharides that result from the hydrolysis of sucrose. What catalysts may cause sucrose hydrolysis? Describe examples of the importance of this reaction in food preparation, particularly in candy making.

   (f) Describe examples from food preparation of the effect of sugar decomposition by alkali.

   (g) Compare the common sugars for relative sweetness. Discuss several factors that affect these comparisons. Under what conditions is fructose likely to taste most sweet?

2. Various types of sugars and syrups are available on the market. Describe the major characteristics of each of the following:

   (a) Granulated sugar (sucrose)
   (b) Powdered sugar
   (c) Brown sugar
   (d) Corn syrup
   (e) High-fructose corn syrup
   (f) Molasses
   (g) Honey
   (h) Maple syrup

3. Discuss trends in sweetener consumption in the United States in recent years.

4. List some sugar alcohols and describe their possible uses in foods.

5. (a) Give several examples of nonnutritive, high-intensity, or alternative sweeteners.

   (b) What is the present legal status of saccharin in the United States? Discuss.

   (c) What is the chemical nature of aspartame? Of acesulfame-K? Of sucralose? Of neotame?

   (d) Discuss some advantages and limitations to the use of alternative sweeteners in manufactured foods.

   (e) Give examples of bulking agents and describe their role in the production of reduced-sugar foods.

6. (a) What is the effect of sugar on the boiling point of water? Explain.

   (b) Describe what happens as you continue to boil a sugar solution.

7. (a) Name two major classifications for candies. Describe the general characteristics of each type.

   (b) Classify caramels, toffee, fondant, taffy, butterscotch, fudge, brittles, and panocha into the appropriate groups described in Question 7a.

8. Describe the basic steps involved in the preparation of crystalline candies such as fondant and fudge. Explain what is happening in each step and how crystallization is controlled.

9. Describe the basic steps involved in the preparation of brittles and caramels. Explain how crystallization is prevented in each case.

10. Suggest several uses for basic fondant.

11. Describe and explain several precautions that must be observed for successful dipping of chocolates.

FROZEN DESSERTS 12

Frozen desserts have been enjoyed in one form or another since as early as the 2nd century B.C. Frozen ices and flavored snow evolved into ice cream and the wide variety of other frozen desserts we enjoy today. Until 1800, ice cream was rare and enjoyed primarily by the affluent. By the mid-1800s, however, ice cream became more widely available in soda fountain shops [10, 14]. Today, many consumers enjoy ice cream and other frozen desserts purchased from their local grocery stores, although ice cream parlors and custard stands remain a treat.

The ingredients, method of freezing, and storage all have an impact on the quality of frozen desserts. In this chapter, the following topics will be discussed:

- Consumption trends and nutrition
- Types of frozen desserts
- Characteristics of frozen desserts
- Ingredients in frozen desserts and light frozen desserts
- Commercial ice cream processing
- Preparation of ice cream in the home
- Storage

CONSUMPTION TRENDS AND NUTRITION

Consumption Trends

Total per capita sales of frozen desserts was 26 quarts in 2004 [8]. Ice cream represents 87 percent of the total sales with frozen yogurt, water ices, sherbets, and other products representing the remainder of the market. Vanilla is the most popular flavor with chocolate being next. Reduced-fat frozen desserts sales increased nearly 14 percent from January to June 2005 [8].

The U.S. Department of Agriculture food disappearance data figures are reported in pounds. In 2005, this data set reports the following annual per capita figures:

15.4 pounds ice cream, 5.9 pounds lowfat ice cream, 0.89 pound sherbet, 1.3 pounds frozen yogurt, and 0.57 pound of other frozen desserts [17].

Nutrition

Ice cream, frozen yogurt, and other frozen desserts contribute protein, calcium, vitamin A, riboflavin, as well as other nutrients to the diet. Those desserts containing higher percentages of milk will result in a greater contribution of nutrients. Fat and sugar are also found in frozen desserts, thereby resulting in a generally high caloric value. Frozen desserts must have a higher sugar content to taste desirably sweet compared to most other types of desserts because of the dulling effect of cold temperatures on taste sensations. Fruit ices, sherbets, and sorbets, although generally lower in fat than ice cream, have a higher sugar content (Figure 12–1).

Reduced-fat and reduced-sugar frozen desserts are available in the marketplace. Prior to the passage of the 1990 Nutrition Labeling and Education Act, reduced-fat ice creams were labeled "ice milk." Starting in 1994, reduced-fat, lowfat, light, and fat-free ice creams were sold in place of ice milk [13]. The regulatory limitations for these various types of desserts may be found in Table 12-1. (See Chapter 4 for more information about the Nutrition Labeling and Education Act.)

FIGURE 12-1 This lemon sorbet makes for a wonderfully refreshing dessert.

TABLE 12-1 Classification of Commercially Frozen Desserts

Frozen Dessert	Description
Ice cream	Ice cream is produced by freezing (while stirring) a pasteurized mix containing at least 10 percent milkfat, 20 percent total milk solids, sweeteners, and other optional ingredients that stabilize or flavor the mix. The finished ice cream must weigh at least 4.5 pounds per gallon and contain at least 1.6 pounds of food solids per gallon.
Frozen custard, French ice cream, French custard ice cream	Eggs are added to the ingredients found in ice cream. The total weight of egg yolk solids is not less than 1.4 percent of the finished weight. If it is a bulky ice cream, the egg solids must be not less than 1.12 percent of the finished weight.
Reduced-fat ice cream	Ice cream made with 25 percent less fat than in the standard reference ice cream.
"Light" ice cream	Contains at least 50 percent or less total fat or 33 percent less calories compared to the standard reference ice cream.
Lowfat ice cream	Not more than 3 grams of milkfat in a 4 fluid ounce serving.
Nonfat ice cream	Less than 0.5 gram of milkfat per serving.
Gelato	An Italian-style ice cream that is rich in egg yolk solids and total solids. Contains little air and no stabilizers or emulsifiers.
Bulky flavored ice cream	Contains a significant amount of ingredients such as nuts, fruit, confections, cookies, and cocoa. The minimum level of fat may be reduced in these ice creams.
Soft serve	Ice cream which is served after being drawn from the freezer without hardening.
Mellorine	Milkfat is replaced in whole or part by vegetable or animal fat. Must contain not less than 6 percent fat and 2.7 percent protein.
Paravine	A frozen dessert similar to ice cream; however, it contains no dairy ingredients.
Tofutti	Brand name of a frozen dessert that resembles ice cream but contains no dairy ingredients. Contains tofu or soybean curd with sweeteners, stabilizers, and a nondairy fat.
Frozen yogurt	Frozen yogurt is similar to ice cream; however, it is generally lower in fat, and it must contain bacteria cultures, which are typical for yogurt.
Fruit sherbet	A pasteurized frozen product containing fruit juices, sweeteners, stabilizers, 2 to 5 percent total milk solids, 1 to 2 percent milkfat, and a minimal acidity of 0.35 percent. Sherbet must be a minimum of 6 pounds per gallon which is equivalent to a 50 percent overrun. Sherbet is generally higher in sugar than ice cream.
Sorbet	Contains frozen fruit and/or fruit juice, sugar, and stabilizers. The volume of air whipped into the product may be up to 20 percent. Sorbet is generally high in sugar.
Italian ice	Composed of sugar, water, and flavoring. Large ice crystals are generally present. Frozen lemonade is an example of an Italian ice.
Frappé	An ice frozen to a slushy consistency and served as a drink. Contains fruit juices.
Novelties	Examples of novelties include ice cream sandwiches, ice cream bars, cones, cake rolls, and molded items.

Source: Reference 14

TYPES OF FROZEN DESSERTS

The three main types of frozen desserts are ice creams, sherbets, and water ices [3]. Some ice creams contain enough egg yolk solids to be considered a custard-type ice cream. Several ice creams also contain bulky flavoring ingredients such as fruits, nuts, chocolate syrup, cookie pieces, and peanut butter mixtures. Table 12-1 summarizes the distinguishing characteristics of commercial frozen desserts.

Ice cream may be further classified as *superpremium*, *premium*, *standard*, or *economy*. Superpremium ice cream contains a high fat content (12 percent or higher milk-fat), a very low overrun which indicates little air has been mixed into the product during freezing, and very high quality ingredients. Likewise, premium is high in fat and has little overrun. Both of these classifications of ice creams are rich and creamy but will have a high calorie and high fat content compared to standard ice cream. Standard ice cream is defined as containing the minimum requirements of the Food and Drug Administration (FDA) standard of identity which is 10 percent milkfat, 20 percent total milk solids, and 4.5 pounds per gallon. Economy ice cream meets the standard identity for ice cream, however, generally sells for a lower price. Refer to Chapter 4 for a discussion of FDA standards of identity.

Dippin' Dots®

In 1992, a patent was issued for the manufacture of a "free-flowing alimentary dairy product." Today this product is known as Dippin' Dots. It is produced by releasing droplets of the flavored ice cream mix into liquid nitrogen. Upon removal from the nitrogen, the product is stored at –22°F (–30°C). For consumption, it is warmed above this temperature. ■

Source: Reference 14

CHARACTERISTICS OF FROZEN DESSERTS

Frozen desserts are complex food systems. These frozen systems are foams with air cells dispersed in a continuous liquid phase that contains ice crystals, emulsified fat globules, proteins, sugars, salts, and stabilizers. Ice cream in particular, has a colloidal structure. (Refer to Chapter 9 for more about colloidal dispersions.) Small air bubbles and ice crystals are dispersed among liquid water and destabilized, clustered fat globules, thus contributing to the characteristic taste and mouthfeel of ice cream (Figure 12-2) [6, 14].

High-quality ice cream products are characterized by a smooth, creamy, somewhat dry and stiff texture with tiny ice crystals, enough body so that the product melts slowly and uniformly, and a sweet, fresh characteristic flavor. In addition, the flavor and the color should be pleasing. Table 12-2 provides an overview of some of the quality attributes and potential defects that may be present in ice cream.

Crystal Formation

All types of frozen desserts are crystalline products in which water is crystallized as ice. The aim in preparation is generally to obtain fine crystals and produce a smooth mouthfeel. Differences in crystal size and creamy texture are apparent among products, depending on the fat content and the use of stabilizers. For example, fruit ices containing no fat usually have a more crystalline texture than high-fat, creamy ice creams. Many of the same general factors that tend to produce fine crystals in crystalline candies, in which the crystals are sugar, also produce fine ice crystals in frozen desserts. Both fat and nonfat solids such as proteins interfere mechanically with crystal formation and growth. Many stabilizers, including vegetable gums, are hydrocolloids that bind large amounts of water, increase viscosity, and interfere with crystallization. Agitation of the mix during freezing also promotes the development of small ice crystals.

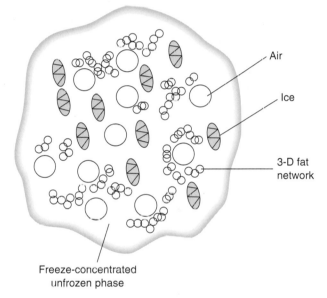

FIGURE 12-2 Ice cream has a three-dimensional structure of fat, air, and ice. The structure of ice cream can be described as a partially frozen foam with the majority of the space taken by ice crystals and air bubbles. Tiny fat globules surround the air bubbles with proteins and emulsifiers surrounding the fat globules. Finally, a very concentrated, unfrozen solution of sugars forms a continuous phase. *(Source: Adapted from Reference 14)*

Overrun

Overrun is the amount of ice cream obtained above the amount of mix frozen and results from whipping air into the mix during freezing. Ice cream, being a partly frozen foam, typically contains 40 to 50 percent air by volume [1]. Thus, during freezing, the volume of the ice cream mix increases by 70 to 100 percent. Homemade ice creams usually have no more than 30 to 40 percent overrun. The higher percentage of overrun in commercial ice creams in comparison with homemade products results from a better control of freezing conditions, such as the rate of freezing and the stage of hardness at which the

TABLE 12-2 Selected Quality Attributes and Potential Defects in Ice Cream	
Quality Attribute	**Potential Defects and Causes**
Flavor	Sweetness and flavorings—too much or too little
	• Amount or type of sweeteners and flavors may result in poor flavor.
	Off-flavors—cooked flavor or "lacks freshness"
	• Milk products were cooked to too high of a temperature, or ice cream was stored where the storage atmosphere allowed the absorption of undesirable volatile flavors.
Body	Crumbly—flaky or snowy
	• Overrun too high, low stabilizer or emulsifier, low total solids, or coarse air cells.
	Gummy—pasty or putty-like body
	• Overrun too low, too much stabilizer, or poor stabilizer
	Weak body—melts quickly into watery liquid
	• Overrun too high, low total solids, insufficient stabilizer
Texture	Coarse or icy—ice crystals are large
	• Most likely cause of large ice crystals is fluctuating temperatures during storage or distribution.
	• Other causes include insufficient total solids, protein, stabilizers in the mix; insufficient aging of the mix following pasteurization; slow freezing; slow hardening; incorporation of large air cells due to type of freezer; or rehardening of soft ice cream.
	Sandy—a rough, gritty mouthfeel that does not melt and disappear
	• Caused due to formation of lactose crystals.
	• Prevented by hardening ice cream quickly, maintaining low hardening temperatures, and preventing temperature fluctuations.
Volume	Shrinkage—ice cream pulls away from side of container, thus it "shrinks."
	• Is the result of a loss of air bubbles
	• Potential causes include too low of temperatures during hardening, too high or too low storage temperatures, excessive overrun, pressure changes as might occur when transporting ice cream from high to a low altitude
Melting	Ice cream should melt not too slow or too fast. Once melted, the product should form a homogeneous fluid base.
	Curdy—irregularly shaped curd particles are visible in melted product
	• caused by protein destabilization or over-stabilization by gums
	Does not melt—ice cream retains shape after 15 to 20 minutes at room temperature
	• excess fat destabilization
	• too much stabilizer
	Foamy—large air bubbles retain shape in melted product
	• too high a level of emulsifiers and egg yolks
	Wheying off— watery fluid appears that may have curd particles in the fluid
	• caused by protein destabilization or separation between proteins and polysaccharides
	Low viscosity—melted product is thin like milk
	• caused by low solids in mix

Source: References 4, 14

freezing is discontinued. **Homogenization** increases the viscosity of the mix and also favors retention of air.

Too little overrun produces a heavy, compact, coarse-textured frozen dessert, which is more expensive per serving, whereas too great an overrun results in a frothy, foamy product. Better ice creams are often sold by weight, and federal standards require weight of 4.5 pounds per gallon, thereby controlling the amount of overrun. Sherbet must weigh not less than 6 pounds per gallon [18].

Overrun may be calculated by volume or by weight using one of the following formulas:

$$\text{Percent overrun} = \text{(volume of ice cream made} - \text{volume ice cream mix)/} \text{(volume of mix used)} \times 100$$

$$\text{Percent overrun} = \text{(weight of gallon of mix} - \text{weight of gallon of ice cream)/} \text{(weight of gallon of ice cream)} \times 100$$

Locust bean gum, through its interaction with the carrageenan, converts the mix to a weak gel.

Guar gum is added to soften and make less chewy the gel structure formed with locust bean gum and κ-carrageenan. It helps to provide a smooth texture and creamy body.

Source: Whistler, R. L., and BeMiller, J. N. (1997). Chapter 11: Carrageenans: In *Carbohydrate Chemistry in Food Scientists,* pp. 193–194, St. Paul, MN: American Association of Cereal Chemists.

What Specific Stabilizers Enhance Body and Texture in Ice Cream?

Carboxymethylcellulose is used as the primary stabilizer.

Kappa (κ)-type carrageenan is added as a secondary stabilizer to prevent whey separation.

Body

The term *body* as used in connection with frozen desserts implies firmness or resistance to rapid melting. Homemade ice creams usually have less body than commercial ice creams because stabilizers used in the commercial products often add body. Homemade ice creams generally melt faster in the mouth and give the impression of being lighter desserts, although they may actually be richer mixtures than many commercial ice creams.

Texture

Texture refers to the fineness of particles, smoothness, and lightness or porosity. The size and distribution of ice crystals is a major factor influencing the texture of frozen desserts. Substances that interfere with large-crystal formation, such as fat and certain stabilizers, help to produce a fine, smooth texture in frozen desserts. Preference tests show that consumers generally like smooth, fine-grained ice cream.

INGREDIENTS IN FROZEN DESSERTS

Ice cream ingredients include milk, milkfat, sweeteners, and flavorings. Additionally ice cream may include eggs, emulsifiers, and stabilizers. Cream is typically the ingredient that supplies milkfat. Nonfat dried milk or whey may comprise part of the nonfat milk solids in ice cream. Table 12-3 provides a listing of several different types of ingredients that may be used in making ice cream.

Milkfat

An optimum amount of cream, supplying milkfat, gives desirable flavor to ice cream and also improves body and texture, resulting in a firm, smooth product. The amount of milkfat influences the viscosity of the mix, thereby affecting the incorporation of air. A moderate viscosity is desirable, as both a highly viscous mixture and a thin, nonviscous one resist the incorporation of air. The air

---

TABLE 12-3 Ice Cream Ingredients

Ingredient Category	Potential Ingredients Used
Dairy	Cream, milk, evaporated milk, condensed milk, dried milk, nonfat milk, whey, hydrolyzed milk protein, and others
Sweeteners	Sugar, dextrose, invert sugar, corn syrup, maple syrup, honey, brown sugar, malt syrup, lactose, fructose, aspartame, acesulfame-K, sucralose, high-fructose corn syrup, and others
Egg products	Whole eggs or egg yolks, which may be liquid, dried or frozen
Stabilizers and thickeners	Guar gum, locust bean gum, sodium carboxymethyl cellulose, sodium alginate, propylene glycol alginate, xanthan, gelatin, calcium sulfate, carrageenan, gum acacia, gum karaya, oat gum, gum tragacanth, furcellaran, and others
Emulsifiers	Mono- and diglycerides, polyoxyethlene sorbitan monostearate (60) or monoloeate (80), microcrystalline cellulose, dioctyl sodium sulfosuccinate, and others
Caseinates	Ammonium caseinate, calcium caseinate, potassium caseinate, sodium caseinate
Coloring	Natural or artificial colors
Mineral salts	Sodium salts of citric acid

Source: Reference 14

cells are desirably small, and the texture is smooth in a mixture with optimum viscosity.

Homemade ice creams with a high milkfat content may have a tendency to churn, producing agglomerated particles of butter. The homogenization of commercial ice cream mixes helps to avoid this problem. Commercial ice creams usually contain 10 to 14 percent milkfat.

Nonfat Milk Solids

Nonfat milk solids often are added to improve the flavor and texture of the ice cream. A relatively high percentage of milk solids reduces the free water content of ice cream and thus improves its texture by encouraging finer ice crystal formation. The added lactose found in the nonfat milk solids enhances sweetness [14]. Nonfat milk solids also promote the development of overrun.

Commercial ice creams can be reinforced with milk solids by the use of evaporated skim milk, nonfat dry milk, or dry whey solids. Whey solids, however, may substitute no more than 25 percent of the nonfat milk solids according to U.S. regulatory standards. Homemade ice creams usually are not reinforced with milk solids, although nonfat dry milk may be found in some recipes. Unless reinforced with nonfat dry milk, homemade ice creams probably contain not more than 6 percent milk serum solids compared with an average of about 9 or 10 percent in commercial ice creams.

Too high a percentage of nonfat milk solids gives a sandy ice cream as a result of the crystallization of lactose at the low temperature of holding. About 11 percent nonfat milk solids is close to the upper limit for prevention of a sandy product, unless the enzyme *lactase* is added to hydrolyze the lactose. In this case, a higher level of nonfat milk solids can be used without the development of sandiness. Too low a percentage of nonfat milk solids encourages high overrun, which creates fluffiness and poor body.

Sweeteners

Sweeteners, of course, affect flavor. Consumers generally seem to prefer a fairly sweet ice cream (one containing about 14 or 15 percent sugar). Sugar also lowers the freezing point and affects the amount of water frozen at the usual holding and serving temperatures for ice cream, thus improving texture. If too much sugar is added, the freezing point is lowered excessively, and freezing is retarded. If too little sugar is used, the freezing point is high enough that much of the water is frozen, adversely affecting the texture of the ice cream [15].

Although table sugar is the usual sweetener in homemade frozen desserts, various sweeteners are used in commercial products. These include corn syrups and high-fructose corn syrups (HFCSs), as well as sugar. The use of corn sweeteners is increasing. A comparatively large amount of HFCS, which produces a lower freezing point, has been reported to contribute to the development of iciness on storage of ice cream [19].

Eggs

Custards thickened with egg yolk or whole eggs are sometimes used in ice creams. Eggs or egg yolks have been a traditional emulsifier in ice cream mixes and are one of the reasons for the traditional smoothness found in French vanilla or custard ice creams [14]. Eggs also improve the whipping ability of the mix.

Commercially, eggs are added to the mix prior to pasteurization. In home preparation, the eggs should be cooked with the sugar, milk, and cream until a minimum temperature of 165°F (74°C) has been reached. Raw eggs should not be used in frozen desserts because of the possible presence of salmonella even in unbroken eggs. This cooked custard should then be cooled under refrigeration for several hours prior to freezing.

Stabilizers and Emulsifiers

Emulsifiers affect the fat-globule structure and the agglomeration of these globules during freezing, which contributes to improved whipping quality and texture. Stabilizers interfere somewhat with ice crystal formation, helping to keep the crystals small; they also give body to the mixture [16]. Some of the water in frozen desserts is bound by the stabilizers, thus inhibiting ice crystal growth, particularly during distribution and storage [19].

Several different stabilizers and emulsifiers are used in commercial frozen desserts in amounts up to 0.5 percent. Gelatin is one example of a stabilizer that may be used in home recipes. Although once commonly used in commercial ice cream, gelatin has been largely replaced by other polysaccharides of plant origin [14].

Acids

Citric acid is an acid commonly used in sherbets and ices. The addition of citric acid provides a tart flavor and reduces the perception of sweetness. Sherbets and ices generally have about twice the sugar content of ice cream to produce the desirable flavor, body, and texture [14]; thus, the reduction in sweetness perception is desirable in these frozen desserts.

Fruit and Flavorings

A variety of fruits and flavorings may be used in ice cream and other frozen desserts. Vanilla is a traditional flavoring for ice cream and may be added as pure vanilla extract or as imitation or artificial vanilla flavoring. Vanilla extract provides a more desirable flavor profile. Chocolate and cocoa also are popular flavorings for frozen desserts.

Fruit ice creams follow vanilla and chocolate in popularity. Strawberries, raspberries, and peaches are examples of fruits which may be used in ice cream, frozen yogurt, and other frozen desserts. Additional sugar is often used with fruit to form a fruit and sugar syrup and to counteract the tartness of the fruit.

Many different candies, cookies, and nuts may be used in frozen desserts. Co-branding is becoming increasingly

PLATE I

Food in space. (Courtesy of National Aeronautics and Space Administration (NASA))

NASA astronauts gather around to decide what's for dinner.

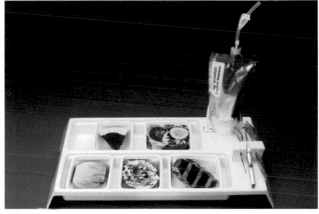

A typical space station meal tray with utensils anchored to the tray.

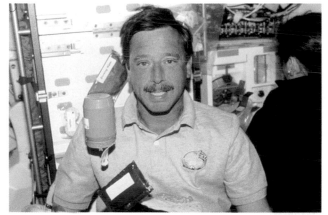

An ordinary PB&J sandwich made on a flour tortilla in a not-so-ordinary way.

Astronauts catching their food adds a whole new meaning to meals on the go.

PLATE II

Seasonings and flavorings.

Yellow onions are used in many dishes to add flavor. (Courtesy of U.S. Department of Agriculture)

Peppers not only add flavor but color as well. This group of peppers represents many colors as well as "degrees of heat." (Courtesy of U.S. Department of Agriculture)

PLATE III

Soup.

Rice and vegetables combined with chicken, cheese, and crispy tortillas makes a different and delicious soup. (Courtesy of Riceland U.S.A)

Black beans are mixed with peppers and topped with rice to create a hearty soup. (Courtesy of Riceland U.S.A)

Grains and Pasta.

This dish is made with couscous and accented with various vegetables. (Courtesy of Land O'Lakes)

Breaded and baked ravioli is a non-traditional way to serve pasta and makes a great appetizer. (Courtesy of Land O'Lakes)

PLATE IV

Grains and pasta.

These tomatoes are filled with rice and seasonings then baked producing an interesting way to eat your grains and veggies. (Courtesy of the USA Rice Federation)

Bulgur, a grain, can be combined with fruit to make a tasty breakfast dish. (Courtesy of Dole Food Company Inc.)

Herbs and bowtie pasta are tossed to create this Mediterranean style pasta salad. (Courtesy of McCormick & Company, Inc.)

Pasta can be combined with almost any type of food. Here a primavera is created using vegetables and surimi. (Courtesy of Alaska Seafood Marketing Inst.)

PLATE V

Quick breads.

These waffles are topped with berries and whipped cream for a dessert-like breakfast treat. (Courtesy of Land O'Lakes)

Muffins and scones such as these make great tea time snacks. (Courtesy of Land O'Lakes)

Sandwiches.

A cheeseburger can be garnished with cheese. (Courtesy of Cattlemen's Beef Board through the National Cattlemen's Beef Association.)

This sandwich made with cucumbers, cheese, tomatoes, lettuce, and dill cream cheese spread puts a new twist on lunch ideas. (Courtesy of Land O'Lakes)

This Hawaiian inspired sandwich features grilled chicken topped with pineapple rings. (Courtesy of Dole Food Company Inc.)

PLATE VI

Baking yeast breads can be a rewarding and creative experience. (Courtesy of Fleischmann's Yeast)

Breadsticks, white loaf bread, and seeded braid loaf

French bread, Italian bread, and Russian black bread displayed with fruit

Pecan caramel rolls

PLATE VII

Yeast breads.

These hearth breads are blended with various spices prior to baking. (Courtesy of Wheat Foods Council.)

Wheat before milling into flour. (Courtesy of Wheat Foods Council.)

A collection of bread types ranging from pretzels to bread sticks and loaves to pitas. (Courtesy of Wheat Foods Council.)

PLATE VIII

Cookies and desserts.

Cookies fresh out of the oven are always a family favorite. (Courtesy of Land O'Lakes)

Cookie bars, chocolate chip pie, and fudge can fulfill any chocolate lovers craving. (Courtesy of Nestlé.)

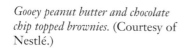

Gooey peanut butter and chocolate chip topped brownies. (Courtesy of Nestlé.)

PLATE IX

Quiche, pie, and tarts.

A New England chicken and corn quiche. (Courtesy of Land O'Lakes)

A dessert tart composed of fresh fruit, cream cheese, and a tart shell. (Courtesy of American Dairy Association)

An all-American classic—the apple pie. (Courtesy of the U.S. Department of Agriculture)

PLATE X

Varieties of apples. (Courtesy of Washington Apple Commission)

Red Delicious

Golden Delicious

Rome

Granny Smith

Winesap

Gala

Fuji

Criterion

Other fruits. (Courtesy of Washington State Fruit Commission; cherries courtesy of Northwest Cherry Growers)

Early Red Haven peaches

Red Gold nectarines

Empire plums

Lambert cherries

PLATE XI

Fresh fruits—pears. (1-5: Courtesy of Pear Bureau Northwest; 6: Courtesy of U.S. Department of Agriculture)

Bartlett

Red Bartlett

Anjou

Comice

Bosc

Pears growing on the tree

PLATE XII

Fresh fruits.

Freshly picked blackberries, strawberries, and blueberries. (Courtesy of U.S. Department of Agriculture)

Strawberry shortcake, one of the many delicious desserts that can be made using fresh fruit. (Courtesy of U.S. Department of Agriculture)

Cherries, grapefruit sections, and melon slices make an attractive fruit salad. (Courtesy of Northwest Cherry Growers)

Nectarine slices may be served with cheese for dessert. (Courtesy of Washington State Fruit Commission)

PLATE XIII

Specialty fruits.

Hawaiian papayas. (Courtesy of Agriculture Research Service, U.S. Department of Agriculture, photo by Scott Bauer.)

Carambolas, also called star fruit. (Courtesy of Agriculture Research Service, U.S. Department of Agriculture, photo by Scott Bauer.)

(Lower left) Asian pear, prickly pears, feijoas, fig (in front); (Right) passion fruit, tamarinds, tamarillos, carambola (star fruit); (Upper left) atemoya (black seeds), cherimoya. (Courtesy of the United Fresh Fruit and Vegetable Association).

PLATE XIV

Potatoes and vegetables.

Cucumber, garlic, carrots, and green onions. (Courtesy of the U.S. Department of Agriculture)

(Lower left) tomatillos, chayote (cut); (Upper right to lower right) cilantro, radicchio, arugula; (Upper left to lower right) enoki mushrooms, shiitake mushrooms, oyster mushrooms. (Courtesy of the United Fresh Fruit and Vegetable Association)

(Left to right outside colander) russet, round white, round red, long white, russet, yellow; (Inside colander) two round red and round white. (Courtesy of The National Potato Promotion Board)

PLATE XV

Salads can add variety to menus.

Greens can be combined with non-traditional items, such as mango, to create an exotic salad. (Courtesy of Land O'Lakes)

A salad can be a simple, yet attractive vegetable and dip tray. (Courtesy of American Egg Board)

Spinach adds green color to orange and grapefruit sections, red onion wedges, and sliced avocado, the mixture tossed with lemon sesame dressing. (Courtesy of Sunkist Growers)

Broccoli florets, red sweet bell pepper, and orange slices are served with a mustard-dill salad dressing. (Courtesy of Sunkist Growers)

PLATE XVI

Several varieties of cheese.

(Clockwise from lower left) butter, cheese powder in scoop, flavored butter in dark crock, cheese powder in two tan crocks, milk, Cottage Cheese in Wisconsin crock, Cheddar wheel, cold pack in tan crock, Gouda, Brie with strawberry garnish, Manteche, Italian-style Gorgonzola, large Cheddar wheel, and shredded mild Cheddar. (©1998, Courtesy of Wisconsin Milk Marketing Board)

Camembert cheese, bread, peaches, and wine make a delicious combination. (Courtesy of American Dairy Association)

Swiss, Colby and Jack marble, cheddar, pepper jack, and a parmesan cheese wedge pictured with bread and sesame sticks. (Courtesy of American Dairy Association)

popular in the marketplace as well-known candies, cookies, and other ingredients are used and advertised prominently with the ice cream. Oreo® Cookie ice cream and Snickers® candy ice cream are examples of this trend.

INGREDIENT MODIFICATIONS FOR "LIGHT" FROZEN DESSERTS

Major changes in the composition of frozen desserts are necessary to achieve reduced calories and/or fat and to attain "light" status. It is a complex process to produce acceptable frozen desserts with useful reductions in sugar and fat. Understanding the role of ingredients available for the production of acceptable light frozen desserts is essential if high quality products satisfying customers' appetite for low fat and low calorie desserts is to be achieved.

Fat Modifications

Fat contributes greatly to the flavor and richness that consumers have come to expect in frozen desserts that are similar to ice cream. The smooth mouthfeel of fat may be only partially replaced by the addition of low-calorie texturizers such as vegetable gums and cellulose derivatives. However, a variety of fat substitutes and fat-replacement technologies are available to produce a product of desirable texture. Maintaining flavor quality may be even more difficult. Fat serves as a reservoir of flavor as it interacts with many flavor components. Thus, flavor is slowly released in the mouth, resulting in a pleasant aftertaste. Flavor challenges are increased as fat is decreased in a creamy frozen dessert [7].

Fat replacers used in ice cream are usually carbohydrate, protein, or lipid based [14]. Microparticulated proteins, one marketed as Simplesse®, appear to be relatively successful fat replacers in frozen desserts. Fantesk™, another fat replacer that is composed of a starch-lipid composite, was tested in soft-serve ice cream and found to produce a product similar to standard commercial products [2]. More information about fat replacers may be found in Chapter 10.

Sugar Modifications

In frozen desserts, sugar has important functions beyond its sweetening power. For example, the freezing point of the mixture is markedly increased when sugar is replaced by a high-intensity sweetener such as aspartame. This exchange increases the amount of water frozen at any given temperature below the freezing point of the mixture and thus affects the texture and body of the frozen dessert [14]. It also affects the overrun of the finished product, which modifies its usual characteristics.

So-called **bulking agents** have been used to replace some of the nonsweetening functions of sugar in frozen desserts, including **polydextrose**, **maltodextrins**, and **sorbitol**. However, some disadvantages of one or more of these ingredients include the development of off-flavors and the possible development of gastrointestinal distress. In addition, some bulking agents have the same caloric value as sucrose [11]. Bulking agents and polyols were discussed further in Chapter 11.

Nonfat Milk Solids

Another adjustment sometimes made in light frozen desserts is an increase in the nonfat milk solids. A defect of frozen desserts with high levels of nonfat milk solids is sandiness. As nonfat milk solid levels increase, the amount of lactose in the mix also increases. Crystals of lactose may form at these higher levels and will create a sandy mouthfeel. If the enzyme lactase is added to the mix before processing, lactose is hydrolyzed to glucose and galactose. These sugars are more soluble and sweeter than lactose and allow an acceptable light product to be made with increased milk solids [12].

PREPARATION OF FROZEN DESSERTS

Most ice cream used in this country is commercially manufactured, although some ice cream is still prepared at home. The preparation of frozen desserts, whether made commercially or in the home, starts with the preparation of the mix. Ingredients are mixed together, heated, allowed to cool, frozen, and then hardened in a container in frozen storage. Even though commercial and homemade ice creams differ, the basic principles involved in their preparation are similar.

Commercial Ice Cream Processing

Pasteurization, Homogenization, and Aging. The steps in the manufacture of ice cream include blending of ingredients, pasteurization, homogenization, aging the mix, freezing, packaging, and hardening [5]. The mix is **pasteurized** to destroy pathogenic organisms. Pasteurization also aids in the blending of ingredients, makes a more uniform product, and improves flavor and keeping quality. Next, the hot mix is homogenized by forcing the liquid through a small orifice under conditions of temperature and pressure suitable to divide the fat globules finely, which are reduced to about one-tenth of their usual size. The texture and palatability of ice cream are improved by homogenization. The homogenized mix is cooled and aged for a minimum of four hours, but overnight is usually preferred. During this time, the fat globules solidify, and the viscosity increases, thereby improving the body and texture of the ice cream [14].

Freezing and Hardening of the Mix. The ice cream mix is frozen in continuous or batch freezers. The continuous method allows the continuous freezing and withdrawal of ice cream. Both methods utilize a liquid refrigerant, usually ammonia, which enters a chamber surrounding a cylinder containing the mix. The liquid refrigerant absorbs heat and results in the freezing of the mix. Some self-contained models operate with another type of refrigerant such as Freon® [14]. Within the cylinder, holding the ice cream mix, dashers scrape freezing ice cream from the walls of the chamber while whipping air into the mix. This agitation of the ice cream mix causes some of the fat globules to **agglomerate** into a form similar to a bunch of grapes. Although this agglomeration process is desirable, if too extensive, actual churning may take place resulting in clumps of butter. Emulsifiers and stabilizers in commercial ice cream mixes help to control the degree of agglomeration and thus decrease freezing time, improve whipping quality, and produce an ice cream with a fine, stiff texture that melts slowly and uniformly [1].

Ice cream produced in the continuous or batch freezers is essentially "soft-serve" ice cream at the end of this freezing process. To produce the ice cream purchased in grocery stores and in ice cream stores featuring "hand-dipped" ice cream, the soft ice cream is drawn from the freezer into packages and quickly transferred to cold storage rooms. Here the freezing and hardening process is completed without agitation [14].

Soft-Serve. Soft-serve ice cream and frozen yogurt are popular items in many fast-food and buffet-type foodservice establishments. These products are similar in composition to their harder frozen counterparts, but they are served directly from the ice cream maker and therefore do not undergo the hardening process. Additional stabilizers or emulsifiers may be used in soft-serve ice cream,

yogurt, and reduced-fat ice cream products. State regulations vary regarding the sale of soft-serve products.

Ice Cream Preparation in the Home

When homemade ice cream is prepared from pasteurized milk, cream, and eggs, the ice cream mixture does not require heating before the freezing process. Heating in a double boiler for 15 to 20 minutes at 145°F (63°C) can be advantageous, however, because it will blend the ingredients thoroughly. If raw eggs are added to the mix, the ice cream must be heated to a minimum of 165°F (74°C) to destroy pathogenic bacteria which may be present in the raw eggs. After it is heated, the mixture should be cooled quickly. A smoother ice cream and improved flavor will result from aging or holding the mix for 3 or 4 hours at refrigerator temperature before freezing.

Home Ice Cream Freezers. Figure 12-3 illustrates the structure of an ice cream freezer. Ice cream freezers may be electric or hand cranked. The outer container or bucket of the freezer is usually made of a material that conducts heat poorly, such as wood or plastic foam, which minimizes the absorption of heat from the air. The container that holds the ice cream mix inside the outer container is metal, which conducts heat readily and permits the rapid absorption of heat from the ice cream mix. A paddle or dasher inside the metal can agitates the ice cream mixture and scrapes mixture from the side walls as it is turned.

The ice cream mix should occupy two-thirds or less of the capacity of the inner metal can to allow for overrun or swell during freezing (Figure 12-4). If the container is

IN DEPTH

The Science Behind the Freezing of Liquids

Pure liquids have characteristic freezing points at constant pressure. For pure water, freezing occurs when the liquid water is in equilibrium with the solid state, which is ice. Thus, water freezes at 32°F (0°C) at a pressure of 760 millimeters of mercury. Unlike many substances, water expands during freezing to occupy more space than it did in the liquid form due to an expanded lattice-like structure when frozen. Although water freezes at 32°F (0°C), after freezing, the temperature of ice may be lowered below 32°F (0°C) if in colder surroundings.

Substances dissolved in a liquid to form a true **solution** cause the freezing point of the solution to be lower than the freezing point of the pure liquid. A sugar solution, which is the basis for frozen desserts, has a lower freezing point than pure water. Ices and sherbets that contain acid fruit juices have a higher percentage of sugar than ice creams, and therefore freeze at a lower temperature. ∎

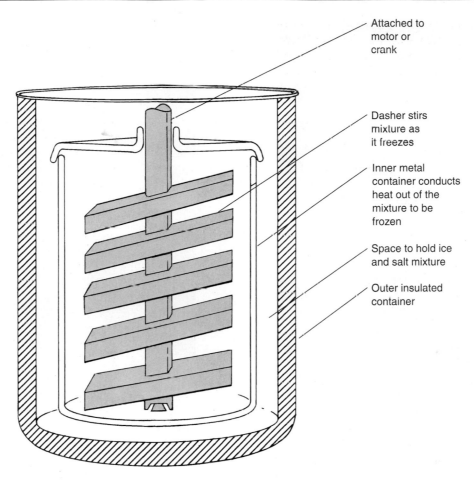

Attached to
motor or
crank

Dasher stirs
mixture as
it freezes

Inner metal
container conducts
heat out of the
mixture to be
frozen

Space to hold ice
and salt mixture

Outer insulated
container

FIGURE 12-3 Structure of an ice cream freezer.

filled to the top before freezing, the ice cream will overflow as air is incorporated, and the mix freezes.

Packing the Freezer with Ice and Salt. Although refrigerants are used to remove heat from the mix commercially, in the home setting, a mixture of ice and salt packed in the space between the metal can holding the mix and the outer container performs the same function. The container should be filled about half full with ice before beginning to alternate the addition of ice with salt. The type of salt used is usually coarse sodium chloride (NaCl), called *rock salt*. Regular table salt is undesirable because of expense, and it tends to lump and collect in the bottom of the freezer.

One part rock salt to six parts crushed ice by weight is an efficient proportion of salt to ice for home freezing. This amount is equivalent to about 1 to 12 by measure. For faster freezing, a proportion of about one part salt to eight parts ice, by measure, also is satisfactory. The higher the percentage of salt, the shorter the time required for freezing. If freezing is too rapid, however, not enough time is available to keep the ice crystals separated and small while stirring, and the crystals of ice formed may be large enough to produce a granular texture.

As the ice is melted by the salt, a water brine will be produced. This brine should not be drained off except through the small overflow drain hole found near the top of the outer ice cream container. This brine effectively draws heat from the mix and thus promotes rapid freezing.

Rate of Cranking the Mix. When cranking ice cream by hand, slow agitation of the ice cream mixture is desirable at the beginning of the freezing period until the temperature of the freezing mixture is lowered below the critical churning temperature. At 40°F (4°C) or above, agitation tends to cause the formation of clumps of butterfat, resulting in a buttery ice cream or in actual butter. Rapid agitation after the mixture is chilled incorporates much air and also favors the formation of many nuclei and fine ice crystals. Electric freezers will crank the ice cream at a rate preset at the factory.

Freezing of the Mix. As the salt melts the ice, heat is absorbed from the mix as well as the surrounding area. The rapid melting of ice that that occurs when salt is added to it increases the rate of heat absorption. When the mixture to be frozen reaches its freezing point, ice crystals begin to form and precipitate out. The dasher

(a) The ice cream mixture is placed in the freezing canister and the dasher is in place.

(b) The freezer is closed; crushed ice and rock salt are added .

(c) Brothers can help each other in turning the freezer as they eagerly await the final result.

(d) The freezing is completed, and the cover carefully lifted.

(e) The dasher is removed from the freezing caniser.

(f) Anticipation is finally at an end, and the boys can spoon out the delicious frozen ice cream.

FIGURE 12-4 Freezing ice cream at home can be a family activity.

IN DEPTH

How Do Salt and Ice Cause the Freezing of a Frozen Dessert?

When ice and salt are mixed, the surface of the ice is usually moist and dissolves some of the salt. The vapor pressure of the concentrated salt solution that is formed on the surface of the ice is lower than that of the ice itself. In an attempt by the system to establish equilibrium, more ice melts. More salt then dissolves, and the process is repeated.

As ice melts, it absorbs heat. The rapid melting of ice that occurs when salt is added to it increases the rate of heat absorption. Some heat is also absorbed as the salt dissolves in the film of water on the ice surface. The heat that is absorbed in both of these processes is taken from the brine, from the air, or from the mixture to be frozen. Because cold is actually the absence of heat, as heat is removed, the temperatures of the brine and mixture to be frozen are lowered.

The greater the proportion of salt to ice in the mixture, the lower the temperature of the mixture will be. This proportion holds true until no more salt will dissolve in the water coming from the melting ice, that is, until a **saturated solution** of salt is produced. The lowest temperature possible in a brine from a salt and ice mixture is about –6° to –8°F (–21° to –22°C). Few dessert mixes require a temperature lower than 14° to 18°F (–8° to –10°C) to freeze. ■

---

turned by hand or with an electrical motor scrapes the mixture from the side walls, permitting a new layer of mixture to come in contact with the can. This agitation also tends to form many nuclei on which ice crystals may form, which favors small crystal formation. As this mixture freezes, water is removed from the mix by becoming ice, thereby causing the mix to become more concentrated. This sweeter, more concentrated unfrozen mix will have a lower freezing temperature than the original mix. Thus as freezing proceeds, the freezing temperature is gradually lowered, just as the evaporation of water that occurs in the boiling of a sugar solution produces a gradual increase in the boiling temperature of the mixture.

The initial freezing of the mix is complete when the crank is too difficult to turn by hand or the electric motor is laboring, as will become apparent by the sound of the motor. The ice cream, if served at this point, will be similar in consistency to soft-serve. To harden the ice cream, drain off excess brine and repack with a freezing mixture of ice and salt containing a higher percentage of salt than used for the original freezing. The hardening of the dessert to a consistency desirable for serving is thus accomplished more rapidly.

Still-Frozen Desserts

Still-frozen desserts are prepared without the agitation of a dasher as is used in commerical or home ice cream freezers. It is difficult to produce fine crystals in ice creams that are frozen without stirring, because relatively few nuclei for ice crystal formation are present, and thus large crystal growth can occur. Mixtures that can be frozen most successfully without stirring are those rich in fat, such as whipped cream products, or mixtures containing gelatin, cooked egg custard, evaporated milk, or a cooked starch base. These substances interfere with the formation of large ice crystals. Because these mixtures are not stirred to incorporate air, air must be beaten into cream or evaporated milk prior to freezing. Partially frozen mixtures may be removed from the freezing trays and beaten once or twice during the freezing period. Air cells tend to interfere with coarse-crystal formation.

Still-frozen desserts may be frozen in a home freezer compartment or by packing in a freezing mixture. The time required for freezing refrigerator desserts depends on the quantity being frozen, the composition of the mixture, and the temperature. About four to six hours may be needed, and the cold control is best set on the lowest temperature. When the mixture is frozen without stirring, freezing quickly promotes the production of many small ice crystals. Faster freezing occurs if the mixture is stirred occasionally in the tray to permit unfrozen portions to come in contact with the tray.

If a still-frozen dessert is frozen in a freezing mixture, the proportion of salt to ice is about one to two by measure. Mixtures frozen without stirring require a longer time and a colder temperature to freeze than stirred mixtures. Removing heat from the center of the mass may be difficult in unstirred frozen desserts, because these desserts are high in fat and have air beaten into the heavy cream that is normally used as the basis of the mixture. Both cold fat and air are poor conductors of heat. The fineness of the division of salt and ice is also a factor influencing the rate of freezing in the preparation of frozen desserts. Finely crushed ice has more surfaces exposed to the action of salt than coarsely chopped ice; hence, the finer ice melts faster.

STORAGE OF FROZEN DESSERTS

Frozen desserts must be kept cold! Ice cream exposed to temperatures above 10°F (–12°C) will develop adverse changes in body, texture, and flavor. Temperature fluctuations are especially of concern and will cause the small ice crystals to turn into large crystals, resulting in an icy, crystalline texture. When purchasing ice cream, it should be –20°F (–28°C) and quickly returned to freezer storage in the home or foodservice. When storing ice cream, keep it between –5°F and 0°F (–21°C and –18°C) in an area of the freezer where temperature fluctuations will be minimized. Thus, storage in the door compartment is not recommended. Although many home freezers are self-defrosting, storage in a nondefrosting freezer, such as a deep-freeze, is preferable so the temperature fluctuations necessary for the defrosting feature can be avoided. Finally, because ice cream will absorb odors, store with the container lid tightly closed away from foods with strong odors [9].

CHAPTER SUMMARY

- According to the FDA standards of identity, ice cream must contain 10 percent milkfat, 20 percent total milk solids, and 4.5 pounds per gallon. Manufacturers must meet specific fat or calorie guidelines to label their ice cream product as reduced, light, or lowfat.

- Frozen desserts are complex food systems. These systems are foams with air cells dispersed in a continuous liquid phase that contains ice crystals, emulsified fat globules, proteins, sugars, salts, and stabilizers.

- Overrun is the amount of ice cream obtained above the amount of mix frozen. During freezing, the volume of the ice cream mix increases by 70 to 100 percent. Both too little and too much overrun have a negative impact on the quality of the product.

- The term *body*, as used in connection with frozen desserts, implies firmness or resistance to rapid melting. *Texture* refers to the fineness of particles, smoothness, and lightness or porosity. The size and distribution of ice crystals is a major factor influencing the texture of frozen desserts.

- Milkfat, nonfat milk solids, sweeteners, stabilizers, and emulsifiers have an impact on the quality characteristics of frozen desserts. An optimum amount of milkfat gives desirable flavor to ice cream and also improves body and texture. A relatively high percentage of milk solids reduces the free water content of ice cream and encourages finer ice crystal formation.

- Sweeteners affect flavor and lower the freezing point of the mix. If too little sugar is used, the freezing point is high enough that much of the water is frozen, adversely affecting the texture of the ice cream. Emulsifiers contribute to improved whipping quality and texture. Stabilizers interfere somewhat with ice crystal formation, helping to keep the crystals small.

- Major changes in the composition of frozen desserts are necessary to reduce calories or fat and still have a high quality product. A variety of fat and sugar replacers may be used. Nonfat milk solids may be added to reduced-fat or reduced-calorie ice creams; however, because lactose is less soluble than other sugars, high levels of nonfat milk solids can result in an undesirable "sandy" product.

- The steps in the manufacture of ice cream include blending of ingredients, pasteurization, homogenization, aging of the mix, freezing, packaging, and hardening.

- Ice cream prepared in the home begins with mixing the ingredients. If raw eggs are used, the mixture must be heated to a minimum of 165°F (74°C). An electric or hand-crank freezer includes an outer container and an inner metal container with dashers. One part salt to 12 parts ice by measure is an efficient proportion of salt to ice for freezing. As the ice is melted by the salt, heat is absorbed from the mix. The cranking of the freezer scrapes frozen mix from the sides of the container, whips in air, and promotes the development of small ice crystals.

- The freezing point is the temperature at which the vapor pressures of the pure liquid and its pure solid substance are equal, and the liquid and solid forms remain in equilibrium. Substances dissolved in a liquid to form a true solution cause the freezing point of the solution to be lower than the freezing point of a pure liquid.

- Still-frozen desserts are frozen without stirring. These mixtures are rich in fat, such as whipped cream products, or mixtures containing gelatin, cooked egg custard, evaporated milk, or a cooked starch base. These substances interfere with the formation of large ice crystals.

- Fluctuating temperatures during storage will increase the size of the ice crystals resulting in an icy, crystalline frozen dessert.

STUDY QUESTIONS

1. Describe the major characteristics of a well-prepared frozen dessert such as ice cream or sherbet.

2. Describe identifying characteristics of each of the following:

   (a) Sherbet

   (b) Water ice

   (c) Ice cream

   (d) Mousse

   (e) Sorbet

   (f) Frozen yogurt

   (g) Mellorine

   (h) Parevine

   (i) Reduced fat ice cream

3. What is the effect of each of the following on the flavor, texture, and/or body of a frozen ice cream?

   (a) Milkfat

   (b) Nonfat milk solids

   (c) Sweeteners

   (d) Stabilizers

   (e) Overrun

4. Discuss some of the problems often involved in the formulation of acceptable "light" frozen desserts. What are some possible solutions to these problems?

5. Explain how a mixture of ice and salt is able to act as a freezing mixture to freeze frozen desserts.

6. Describe an appropriate procedure for preparing homemade ice cream in an ice cream freezer. Explain what happens at each step.

7. What procedures should be used when freezing a frozen dessert without stirring. Why?

Starch is one of the most abundant substances found in nature. A storage form of carbohydrate in plants, starch is located in roots, seeds, fruits, and stems. In plants, as in humans, starch provides energy. For example, during germination of a seed, this stored polysaccharide molecule undergoes enzymatic hydrolysis to yield glucose, which then supplies energy for the germination and early stages of plant growth.

Starch is available to the food industry, and also to the consumer, as a purified material. In this form, it belongs to a group of substances called hydrocolloids, a group that also includes pectin and a number of gums, sometimes called vegetable gums. Hydrocolloids are colloidal substances. Hydrocolloids are water loving and absorb relatively large amounts of water. In manufactured foods, starches are often used as stabilizers, texturizers, thickeners, and binders. In the home, starch is used to thicken sauces, soups, puddings, and other foods.

In this chapter, the following topics will be discussed:

- Nutrition
- Sources of starch
- Starch structure
- Kinds of starch
- Gelatinization, gel formation, and retrogradation
- Factors affecting starch pastes
- Starch cookery

NUTRITION

Starch, as a component of breads, cereals, grains, potatoes, and other foods, provides 70 to 80 percent of the world's calories. Although starch in its purified form, such as found in cornstarch, for example, will be the focus of this chapter, the importance of "starchy" foods in the diet should be noted. Breads and grains provide not only calories, but also vitamins and other nutrients depending on the particular type of food.

Starch is a polysaccharide which is digested by humans to convert it into glucose. The human digestive system produces enzymes, called amylases, that break down or hydrolyze starch yielding the disaccharide maltose. Maltose is then hydrolyzed to glucose, which is absorbed and metabolized by body cells, providing energy.

SOURCES OF STARCH

Seeds, roots, and tubers are parts of plants that serve most prominently for the storage of starch. Thus, the most common sources of food starch are cereal grains, including corn, wheat, rice, grain sorghum, and oats; legumes; and roots or tubers, including potato, sweet potato, arrowroot, and the tropical cassava plant (marketed as tapioca). Sago comes from the pith or core of the tropical sago palm.

Corn is grown in temperate to warm climates with half of the world's production in the United States. Wheat is grown primarily in North America, Europe, and Russia. Approximately 90 percent of the world's rice supply is produced in southern and southeastern Asia, whereas about 70 percent of the world's potato supply is grown in the cool, moist climate of Europe and Russia. Tapioca, extracted from cassava, is grown near the equator.

Purified starch may be separated from grains and tubers by a process called *wet milling*. The wet milling of corn results in starch, germ, fiber, and protein. Approximately, 32 pounds of starch can be produced from one bushel of corn [5]. The steps involved in the wet milling of corn are explained on Table 13-1.

COMPOSITION AND STRUCTURE

The Starch Molecule

Starch is a polysaccharide made up of hundreds or even thousands of glucose molecules joined together. The molecules of starch are of two general types, called

TABLE 13-1	Steps in the Wet Milling of Corn to Produce Starch

Steps in the Wet Milling Process	Description
Inspection and cleaning	Dust, chaff, and other foreign materials are removed from shipments of corn.
Steeping	Corn is soaked in mildly acidic 50°F (10°C) water for 30 to 40 hours. Gluten bonds are loosened and begin to release starch. Coarse grinding, following the steeping period, breaks the germ loose from other components.
Germ separation	The low-density corn germs are spun out of the water slurry containing the coarsely ground corn. Corn oil is produced from the germ.
Fine grinding and screening	The corn and water slurry is ground more thoroughly to release the starch and gluten from the fiber. The starch–gluten suspension resulting from this step is called *mill starch*.
Starch separation	The mill starch is passed through a centrifuge to separate out gluten still present. The remaining starch is washed several times to remove any remaining protein. The starch, once dried, is 99.5 percent pure.

Source: Reference 6

fractions: amylose and amylopectin. Most starches found in nature are mixtures of the two fractions. Corn, wheat, rice, potato, and tapioca starches contain 16 to 24 percent amylose, with the remainder being amylopectin. The root starches of tapioca and potato are lower in amylose content than the cereal starches of corn, wheat, and rice.

Amylose. Amylose is a long chainlike molecule, sometimes called the *linear fraction,* and is produced by linking together 500 to 2,000 glucose molecules. A representation of the amylose molecule is shown in Figure 13-1. The amylose fraction of starch contributes gelling characteristics to cooked and cooled starch mixtures. A gel is rigid to a certain degree and holds a shape when molded.

Through genetic manipulation, high-amylose starches have been produced. For example, a high-amylose corn, called *amylomaize,* has starch that contains approximately 70 percent amylose. High-amylose starches have a unique ability to form films and to bind other ingredients.

Amylopectin. Amylopectin has a highly branched, bushy type of structure, very different from the long, stringlike molecule of amylose. In both amylose and amylopectin, however, the basic building unit is glucose. Figure 13-2 represents the chemical nature of amylopectin, with many short chains of glucose units branching from each other, much like the trunk and branches of a tree. Cohesion or thickening properties are contributed by amylopectin when a starch mixture is cooked in the presence of water, but this fraction does not produce a gel.

Certain strains of corn, rice, grain sorghum, and barley have been developed that contain only the amylopectin fraction of the starch. These are called *waxy* varieties because of the waxy appearance of the kernel when it is cut. Waxy starches are nongelling because of the lack of amylose and may be used successfully in products that will be frozen and thawed.

The Starch Granule

In the storage areas of plants, notably the seeds and roots, molecules of starch are deposited in tiny, organized units called *granules.* Amylose and amylopectin molecules are placed together in tightly packed stratified layers formed around a central spot in the granule called the *hilum.* The starch molecules are systematically structured in the

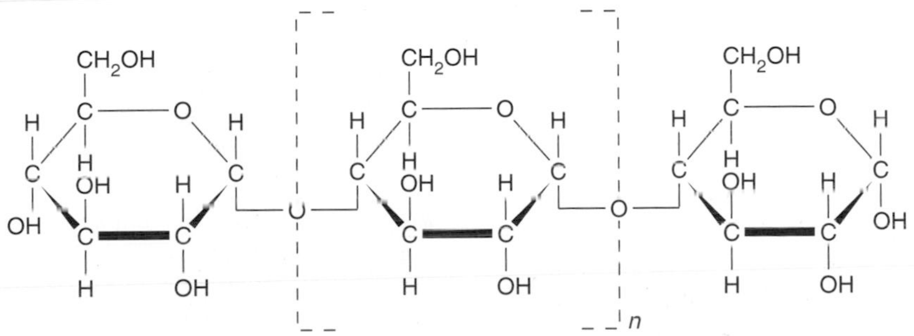

FIGURE 13-1 Amylose is a linear molecule with hundreds of glucose units linked together. A portion of the molecule is represented here. The glucose units are joined between the No. 1 carbon atom of one glucose molecule and the No. 4 carbon atom of the next one. The *n* may represent hundreds of similarly linked glucose molecules. See also Chapter 9.

FIGURE 13-2 Amylopectin is a bushy, treelike molecule with many short branches of glucose units linked together. A portion of the molecule is represented here. The glucose units in the chains are joined between the No. 1 and the No. 4 carbon atoms. However, at the points of branching, the linkage is between the No. 1 carbon atom of one glucose unit and the No. 6 carbon atom of the other. See also Chapter 9.

granule to form crystallinelike patterns. If the starch granules, in a water suspension, are observed microscopically under polarized light, the highly oriented structure causes the light to be rotated so that a Maltese cross pattern on each granule is observed (Figure 13-3). This phenomenon is called birefringence. The pattern disappears when the starch mixture is heated and the structure disrupted. The sizes and shapes of granules differ among

FOCUS ON SCIENCE

The Chemical Structures of Amylose and Amylopectin

Amylose

Amylose is a linear polymer of glucopyranose units with carbon atom No. 1 of one glucose connected to the hydroxyl of carbon atom No. 4 of the adjacent glucose unit forming an α (alpha)-(1 → 4) linkage. Amylose is a very flexible and mobile molecule and can easily assume random shapes. It has many hydroxyl groups that allow hydrogen bonding with other starch molecules. It is responsible for the three-dimensional gel structure in starch-containing food products.

Amylopectin

Amylopectin is composed of amylose subunits, that are joined by α-(1 → 4) and α-(1 → 6) linkages. The α-(1 → 6) linkages create branched points within the molecule which give it profoundly different characteristics from the amylose molecule. Amylopectin shows the primary structure within one growth ring. It shows clusters of short chains of different lengths. Each cluster has branch points in a narrowly defined region which allows close spacing (packing) of the linear short chains. The terminal end group of each chain is nonreducing, encouraging some double helix and crystal formation of parallel chains.

FIGURE 13-3 Potato starch seen under polarized light shows birefringent crosses resulting from the highly organized nature of the granules (magnified 700×). *(Courtesy of Eileen Maywald, Corn Products Company)*

starches from various sources, but all starch granules are microscopic in size. Figure 13-4 shows photomicrographs of starch granules from various sources.

KINDS OF STARCH

The kind of starch may be classified from more than one perspective. Starch may be described by the kind of plant from which it was derived, for example, corn, potato, and so forth. Another way to understand kinds of starch is whether the starch has been produced from a plant found in nature or from a plant developed through the use of biotechnology and genetic crossbreeding. Some starches, called *modified starches*, may be modified through chemical or physical means to produce starches with specific useful characteristics. Lastly, starches may be called *resistant* because this kind of starch may not be digested by the human digestive tract. All of these kinds of starch will be discussed in the following section.

Native Starches

Native starch is starch which was derived from plants without chemical or physical modification. Cornstarch is commonly used in cooking and is an example of a native starch. Tapioca, potato, arrowroot, and other kinds of native starches are described in Table 13-2. Each type of native starch has unique characteristics which should be considered when cooking.

Improved Native Starches

Improved native starches provide some of the functional benefits found in modified starches without chemical or physical modification of the starch. These improved native starches may be developed through traditional plant breeding methods or through the use of genetic

engineering. Genetic engineering was discussed further in Chapter 3.

Interest in improved native starches is due in part to strict government constraints on the amount and type of chemicals used to modify starches, thus encouraging starch producers to seek hybrid plants offering desired functional properties [9, 23]. A line of functional native starches providing better texture with enhanced taste qualities when compared with traditional modified starches is now on the market, produced by a patented technology [17, 18]. Soft white wheat with 100 percent amylopectin is being field tested, and it may be available in the future as another improved native starch [3].

Modified Starches

Starches may be modified using chemical or physical methods to tailor the functional characteristics of the starch to desired applications. Native starches from different sources (wheat, corn, potato, and tapioca) behave differently in food preparation because of varying compositions and ratios of amylose to amylopectin fractions. These differences should be considered when choosing a starch for a particular use. Natural or native starches may have limitations when used in food processing and manufacturing or in the home when freezing and thawing are desired. Consequently, chemical modification of natural starches is used in the food-processing industry to achieve a desired texture and flavor in a finished product that must undergo high temperatures, high shear, low pH, or freeze-thaw cycles during its production [16]. Clear gel is an example of a modified cornstarch that is used in foods to be frozen and thawed or in canned pie fillings because of its stability in these applications.

The U.S. Food and Drug Administration (FDA) has published regulations governing the modification of natural food starches, providing guidelines concerning the types and amounts of modifiers allowed, the residuals permitted, if any, and the combinations that are acceptable. Within these guidelines, starch manufacturers work to develop new and innovative starch derivatives. The most common chemical modifications of starch utilized by the food industry involve *hydrolysis, cross-linking,* and *substitution.* Chemically modified starches are listed as modified starch on food labels.

Hydrolysis or Acid-Converted Starch. Hydrolysis of starch may be accomplished by mixing starch with water and an acid to produce a random breaking of linkage points along the molecular chain. Most of the starch still remains in the form of granules and is dried after the acid treatment. This modified starch is known as *thin-boiling* or *acid-thinned starch.* It produces a paste with low viscosity when it is boiled, and it hydrates at a lower temperature than the unmodified starch, but then produces a stiff gel. Acid-thinned starch often is used in the confectionery industry [12].

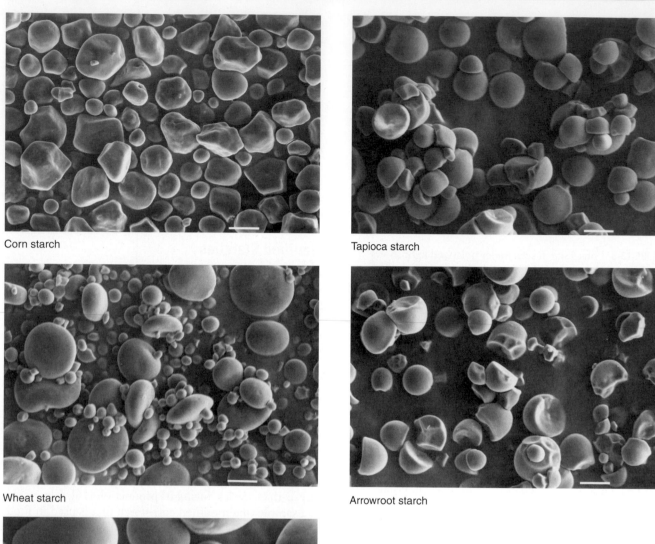

Corn starch

Tapioca starch

Wheat starch

Arrowroot starch

Potato starch

FIGURE 13-4 Starch granules from different plant sources have characteristic shapes. Granule size ranges from small to large within each plant source. The bar at the bottom of each photograph represents 10 μm (micrometers). *(Photographs courtesy of Dr. James BeMiller, Whistler Center for Carbohydrate Research, Purdue University)*

Cross-Linked or Cross-Bonded. Cross-linked starches are modified to lower viscosity and increase temperature for hydration. Additionally, stability in acid conditions, resistance to **shear** or stirring, and tolerance to heat are improved [12]. Food processors, therefore, have greater flexibility and control when they use cross-linked modified starches in manufactured foods. Starches modified by cross-linking are valuable for foods that are heated for

TABLE 13-2 **Kinds of Native Starches**

Native Starch	Description	Characteristics in Food Preparation
Cornstarch	Derived from the wet milling of dent corn. May be called maize. Common cornstarch contains about 25 percent amylase. Waxy maize starch is almost entirely amylopectin. High-amylose cornstarch contains 55 to 75 percent amylose.	Used to thicken sauces, gravies, and puddings. Compared to wheat starch (flour), results in a clearer, glossy sauce. Thickening is reduced when mixed with an acid. Common cornstarch should not be used in foods to be frozen and thawed.
Tapioca	Produced from the root of the cassava plant. Contains 15 to 18 percent amylose.	May be used to thicken pudding or pie fillings. Thickens quickly at a lower temperature than other starches. Is more tolerant of freezing and thawing than some other starches. Pearl tapioca (small or large) is characterized by the "pearls" of starch in the cooked product.
Wheat	Produced from the milling of wheat. Wheat starch has an amylose content of 25 percent.	Products thickened with wheat flour are not glossy like those thickened with other starches such as cornstarch or arrowroot.
Potato	Derived from potatoes. Contains 20 percent amylose.	Is gluten-free. May be used to thicken soups and gravies. Avoid boiling liquids thickened with potato starch.
Rice	Sweet rice flour or starch is produced from sweet rice. Sweet rice has a higher starch content as compared to other kinds of rice. Contains 20 percent amylose and 80 percent amylopectin.	Used in Asian desserts. Tolerates freezing.
Arrowroot	Extracted from the roots of plant growing in tropical countries. Bermuda arrowroot is grown in Central America. Arrowroot is similar to tapioca starch. Some commercial "arrowroot" starch is produced from the cassava plant and therefore would not be considered true arrowroot although it is often called Brazilian arrowroot.	Imparts a shiny gloss to foods. Is neutral in flavor. Thickens at a relatively low temperature and will tolerate acidic ingredients and prolonged heating better than some starches. May be frozen and thawed more successfully than other kinds of native starches. Is not recommended for dairy-based sauces because a slimy texture may result.
Sago	Prepared from the pith of palms native to the East Indies.	Used to thicken pudding or a variety of other dishes.

Source: References 1, 8, 12, 13

IN DEPTH

Hydrolysis of Starch

Hydrolysis is the breaking of a chemical linkage between basic units in a more complex molecule to produce smaller molecules. Water is involved in this reaction. Starch hydrolysis may be brought about or catalyzed by the action of enzymes called *amylases*. Acid may also act as a **catalyst** in the breakdown.

The complete hydrolysis of starch produces glucose because glucose is the basic building block for starch molecules. Intermediate steps in the hydrolysis of starch include:

- **Dextrins**—large chunks of starch molecules which are still large enough to be classified as polysaccharides

- **Oligosaccharides**—sugars which contain several glucose units

- Maltose—a **disaccharide** with two **monosaccharide** units, which yields only glucose ■

extended periods of time or are subjected to exceptionally high shear (for example, canned soup, spaghetti sauces, and certain pie fillings).

Cross-linking is produced by the use of reagents that have two or more reactive groups. These groups react with starch molecules at selected points and create a cross bond between two chains of the starch molecule. Reagents include phosphorus oxychloride and adipic acid. Cross-linking may be thought of as welding molecular starch chains together at various spots or locations, thus limiting the swelling of the granules.

An example of the improved properties that result from modification of starches is found in cross-linked waxy maize starch. The natural starch is nongelling because it contains no amylose fraction, only amylopectin. In this regard, it should make a good thickening agent for fruit pies, providing a soft, thickened but not rigid mixture; however, it is quite stringy in texture, which is an undesirable characteristic for fruit pies. When it is chemically treated to produce cross-linking, the resulting starch retains its nongelling properties but loses the stringy characteristic. It also is much more stable to heating and freezing and makes an ideal thickening agent for many of the frozen fruit pies that are marketed.

Substitution or Stabilization. Substitution is used to prevent retrogradation of cooked starch which may be likely to occur in frozen and refrigerated products [12]. Starches with a high percentage of amylose are most likely to experience retrogradation due to the linear amylose molecules which may re-associate. Substitution improves clarity and reduces *syneresis*, which is a weeping of liquid from the cooked starch mixture upon standing.

Starches are modified by substituting certain monofunctional chemicals (those having only one reactive group, such as acetate) on the hydroxyl groups (−OH) of the starch molecule at random points, which decreases the tendency of bonding between molecular chains of the starch and increases the stability of the starch-thickened product as it is frozen and then thawed.

Physically Modified Starch. Physically modified starches may be modified by drum-drying, extrusion,

spray drying, heat, or moisture treatment. Through one or more of these physical modifications, starches that hydrate or absorb water in cold liquid systems may be produced.

Instant or Pregelatinized Starches. Instant starches are made by cooking a starch in water, then cooking it on a drum dryer or extruder. This cooked starch is then ground and may be used in products that do not include further heat treatment. The integrity of the starch granules is lost; however, the finished product has a smoother texture providing the starch is adequately dispersed to prevent lumps [12]. Instant starches are utilized in instant dry-mix puddings, gravies, and sauces.

Cold-Water Swelling Starches. Cold-water swelling starches also are pregelatinized, but retain their granular integrity [12]. These starches swell in room temperature water and have a smooth texture. Cold-water swelling starches are produced by heating the starch in an ethanol–water solution or by a spray-drying cooking process.

Heat-Treated Starches. Starches may be treated by specialized heat processes to produce starches with desirable characteristics which may be labeled as "starch" and not "modified starch" because no chemicals are involved. Heat-treated starches have greater viscosity and stability [12]. The starch may be heated beyond its gelatinization point in insufficient water or heated with water below its gelatinization point for an extended period to result in the increased functionality.

Resistant Starches

Resistant starch is not digestible by the human body. There are four main types of resistant starch called RS1, RS2, RS3, and RS4. Of these, only RS4 is a chemically modified starch; the other types are found in nature. Although each of these kinds of resistant starch has different characteristics, all are useful in foods to increase total dietary fiber in food products without significantly impacting product quality as can occur with other sources of fiber [14].

FOCUS ON SCIENCE

Resistant Starches

Today's resistant starches are typically categorized into four classes and their sources are as follows:

RS1: Physically inaccessible or digestible resistant starch that is found in seeds, legumes, and unprocessed whole grains

RS2: Occurs in the natural granular form, such as uncooked potato, green banana flour, and high amylose corn

RS3: Formed when starch-containing foods are cooked and cooled. May be found in bread, corn flakes, and cooked-and-chilled potatoes or retrograded high amylose corn

RS4: Selected chemically modified; not found in nature

FOCUS ON SCIENCE

Starch-Based Fat Replacers

Many consumers want foods that are lower in fat content but, at the same time, are rich, creamy, flavorful, and satisfying. To meet this demand, the food industry has developed a variety of low-calorie, starch-based materials to replace fat in processed foods. These types of products are sometimes called *fat mimetics*. Carbohydrate fat replacers are usually modified starch hydrolysates (formed from hydrolysis), although several products are modified by substitution [19, 24].

It has been suggested that the fat-replacing properties of starch-based materials result from an association of water with the structure of the carbohydrate particle. The carbohydrate strongly binds and orients water in such a way as to provide a sensation in the mouth that is similar to that produced by fat.

Of course, formulating lowfat foods requires complete reformulation of traditional products. All attributes of the traditional food, such as flavor, sweetness, saltiness, acidity, texture, viscosity, mouthfeel, and appearance, must be considered and ingredient adjustments made to ensure that the desired characteristics continue to be present in the reformulated result [24].

Examples of Fat Mimetics

Maltodextrin is a fat mimetic made by partial enzyme-catalyzed hydrolysis of potato starch. It can replace up to 50 percent fat in food products. Another is tapioca maltodextrin derivatized to a low degree of substitution levels with an alkenylsuccinate. When 0.5 percent of a 25 percent suspension of the latter is added to ice cream containing the minimum of 10 percent butterfat, the ice cream has the eating quality of one containing 14 percent butterfat. Another fat mimetic is made by treating granular cornstarch with dilute acid or with α-amylase to a dextrose equivalence of less than 5, preferably about 2. In both cases, the amorphous regions of the granule are preferentially removed by hydrolytic erosion, leading to a more crystalline product.

EFFECT OF HEAT AND COOLING ON STARCH

When starch is used in food preparation, several steps occur. First, when starch is placed in water, but not cooked, it will absorb water. Without heat, this water absorption is reversible. When starch granules are heated in water, however, an irreversible change called *gelatinization* occurs. Gelatinization is the swelling of the starch granules giving a *starch paste* which is a viscous colloidal mass. Depending on the type of starch fraction, amylose or amylopectin, most prevalent in the starch used, gel formation may occur as the mixture cools. Cooling also may result in the reassociation of some of the starch molecules, thereby forming a tight gel matrix. This state is known as *retrogradation* and can cause *syneresis* or weeping. In the following section, the impact of dry heat, moist heat, and the influence of ingredients when cooking starch in a liquid will be explored as related to gelatinization, gel formation, and retrogradation.

Dry Heat

When dry heat is applied to starch or starchy foods, the starch becomes more soluble in comparison with unheated starch and has reduced thickening power when it is made into a cooked paste. Some of the starch molecules are broken down to dextrins in a process called *dextrinization*. Color and flavor changes also take place when starch-containing foods are subjected to high temperatures with dry heat. A nonenzymatic browning occurs, and a toasted flavor, which may turn to a burned flavor if the process is continued, develops.

Brown gravy or an espagnole sauce is usually relatively thin in consistency if the dry flour is browned or a brown roux is produced in the process of making the gravy without making adjustments to compensate for the decreased thickening ability of the roux. A larger proportion of flour to liquid, or more brown roux than is normally used, is necessary to obtain a thick gravy. Alternatively, some white flour may be used with the browned flour. Brown roux has a "peanut" flavor component as a result of browning. Another example is the dry-heat dextrins, known as *pyrodextrins*, which are formed in the crust of baked flour mixtures, on toast, on fried starchy or starch-coated foods, and on various ready-to-eat cereals.

Moist Heat

The starch granule is generally insoluble in cold water. A nonviscous suspension of starch is formed when raw starch is mixed with cold water and, on standing, the granules gradually settle to the bottom of the container. After this starch and water suspension is heated, a colloidal dispersion of starch in water is produced. The resulting thickened mixture is called a *starch paste*.

Gelatinization. As starch is heated in water, the set molecular order within each starch granule is disrupted as water is absorbed and the starch granules swell. This gradual process is called gelatinization. Gelatinization results in an increase in viscosity or thickness until a peak viscosity is reached. The dispersion also increases in translucency to a maximum as heating continues [11]. The degree of translucency varies with the type of starch.

Starches made with root starches, such as potato and tapioca, generally are clearer. The changes that occur during gelatinization are irreversible and include the swelling of granules, the melting of small crystallite areas within the granule, the loss of birefringence (the crosses seen when granules are viewed under polarized light—see Figure 13-3), and the solubilization of some of the starch molecules [2].

Gelatinization occurs over a temperature range that is characteristic for a particular starch and in part is related to the size of the starch granules. Figure 13-5 shows various stages in the heating of starch in water. Large granules swell first. Potato starch granules, generally larger than those of other starches, begin to swell at a lower temperature than cornstarch or tapioca. In any case, swelling is usually complete at a temperature of 190° to 194°F (88° to 92°C). Starch gelatinization temperatures for various starches are provided in Table 13-3.

Pasting. When the heating of the starch–water mixture continues after gelatinization, some further granular swelling occurs, as well as movement of more molecular components from the granule into the surrounding medium, and eventually total disruption of the granules. This process is called *pasting.* Gelatinization and pasting are generally described as sequential processes [2].

Gel Formation. Gel formation or *gelation* is different from gelatinization. Gelation takes place on cooling of the starch paste after the starch granules have been gelatinized. Gel formation in cooked starch pastes is a gradual process that continues over several hours as the paste cools. Starches containing relatively large amounts of amylose, such as cornstarch, form firmer gels than starches with a somewhat lower concentration of amylose, such as tapioca. Waxy varieties of starch without amylose do not form gels. Thus, nongelling modified

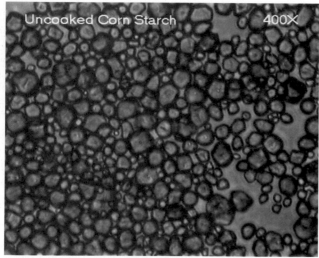

Unheated corn starch granules

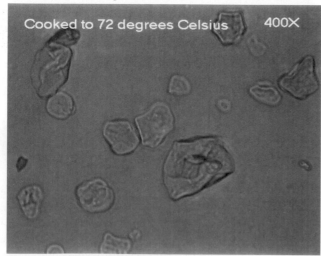

Corn starch granules heated in water to 162°F (72°C)

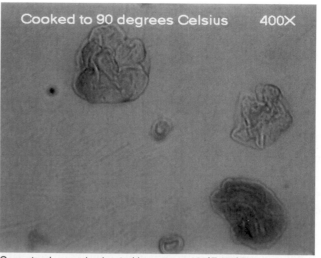

Corn starch granules heated in water to 195°F (90°C)

FIGURE 13-5 Photographs showing the change in corn starch granules (magnified 400×) as heating in water (causing gelatinization) proceeds. The slides were stained with iodine. *(Courtesy of Angela Macias, National Starch and Chemical Company)*

TABLE 13-3 Starch Gelatinization Temperatures for Selected Types of Starch

Type of Starch	Approximate Gelatinization Temperature
Corn (common)	149°–163°F (65°–73°C)
Corn (waxy)	149°–156°F (65°–69°C)
Corn (55 percent high amylose)	183°F (84°C)
Corn (70 percent high amylose)	199°F (93°C)
Wheat	136°–147°F (58°–64°C)
Tapioca	138°–149°F (59°–65°C)
Potato	135°–149°F (57°–65°C)

waxy starches are effectively used for products that are frozen or items such as a stir-fry sauce or gravy that is to be cooled and reheated for later use. A wheat flour or cornstarch sauce or gravy is difficult to reheat into a smooth sauce after cooling due to gel formation.

Retrogradation.   As starch-thickened mixtures continue to stand after gel formation is complete, the process of retrogradation may continue to produce changes as additional bonds are formed between the straight-chain amylose molecules. The amylose molecules associate more closely together. Some of these molecules aggregate in a particular area in an organized, crystalline manner. As the amylose molecules pull together more tightly, the gel network shrinks, and water is pushed out of the gel. This process of weeping, called *syneresis*, results from the increased molecular association as the starch mixture ages. Ultimately an ordered crystalline structure develops [2]. Gel formation and retrogradation are illustrated in Figure 13-6.

FACTORS AFFECTING STARCH PASTES

Certain conditions must be standardized and controlled to obtain uniformity in the cooking of starch pastes. These include temperature of heating, time of heating, intensity of agitation or stirring (shear), acidity (pH) of the mixture, and addition of other ingredients.

Temperature and Time of Heating

Starch pastes may be prepared most quickly by bringing to a boiling temperature over direct heat, constantly stirring during thickening, and simmering for approximately one minute. Longer cooking to improve the flavor is not necessary; however, if a starch mixture is not fully cooked, then a raw starch flavor and a less smooth or silky mouthfeel will be evident. Continued heating after gelatinization is complete can result in decreased thickness. Boiling or cooking starchy sauces and pudding in the home for longer periods usually does not produce thinner mixtures, however, because the loss of moisture by evaporation is not controlled. The loss of moisture results in an increase in starch concentration and therefore an increased thickness which then offsets the thinning from excessive heat.

Under carefully controlled conditions, starch pastes that are heated rapidly are somewhat thicker than similar pastes heated slowly [10]. More concentrated dispersions of starch show higher viscosity at lower temperatures than less concentrated mixtures because of the larger number of granules that can swell in the early stages of gelatinization.

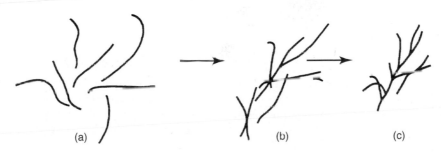

(a)   (b)   (c)

FIGURE 13-6 A diagram representing gel formation and further retrogradation of a starch dispersion: (a) solution, (b) gel, (c) retrograded. *(From Elizabeth Osman, Starch and other polysaccharides. In Food Theory and Applications edited by Pauline C. Paul and Helen H. Palmer. Copyright © 1972, John Wiley & Sons, Inc. Reprinted by permission of John Wiley & Sons, Inc.)*

IN DEPTH

Gel Formation

Many starch molecules are disrupted during the process of gelatinization as the starch granules swell. Some of the molecules of amylose, the linear starch fraction, leach out from the granule. Two or more of these chains may form a juncture point, creating a new bond, which gradually leads to more bonds and more extensively ordered regions. Bonding with the amylose molecules begins immediately after cooking.

Amylopectin, the branched fraction, usually remains inside the swollen granule where it more slowly forms new bonds between branches in a process of recrystallization [22]. Bonds formed between the branches of the bushy amylopectin molecules are weak and have little practical effect on the rigidity of the starch paste; however, bonds between the long-chain amylose molecules are relatively strong and form readily. This bonding produces a three-dimensional structure that results in the development of a gel, with the amylose molecules forming a network that holds water in its meshes. The rigidity of the starch mixture is increased. ■

Agitation or Stirring

Stirring while cooking starch mixtures is desirable in the early stages to obtain a smooth product of uniform consistency. If agitation is too intense or is continued too long, however, it accelerates the rupturing of the starch granules, decreases viscosity, and may give a slick, pasty mouthfeel. Stirring should therefore be minimized.

Acidity (pH)

A high degree of acidity appears to cause some fragmentation of starch granules and hydrolysis of some of the starch molecules, thus decreasing the thickening power of the starch granules [7]. In cooked starch mixtures containing fruit juices or vinegar, such as fruit pie fillings and salad dressings, the acidity may be high enough (pH below 4) to cause some thinning. Specially prepared modified starches resistant to acid breakdown are used in commercial food processing when this may be a problem. When a high concentration of sugar is also present in a starch paste, the sugar may help to decrease the effect of acid, because sugar limits the swelling of starch granules, and the starch molecules are therefore not as available for hydrolysis by acid. Proportions of ingredients in recipes for acid–starch products, such as lemon pie filling, have been adjusted to compensate for the usual effects of acid and sugar so that a desirable consistency results. Acid juices, such as lemon juice, should also be added after the starchy paste has been cooked, thus limiting the acid's contact with starch molecules.

Addition of Other Ingredients

Various ingredients are used with starch in the preparation of food. Some of these ingredients have a pronounced effect on gelatinization and on the gel strength of the cooled starch mixture. Sugar raises the temperature at which a starch mixture gelatinizes [4, 21]. The use of a relatively large amount of sugar delays the swelling of the starch granules and thus decreases the thickness of the paste, at least partially, by competing with the starch for water. If not enough water is available for the starch granules, they cannot swell sufficiently. In a recipe calling for a large amount of sugar, only part of the sugar need be added before cooking. After the starch mixture has been cooked, the remainder of the sugar can be added with much less effect on viscosity.

High concentrations of sucrose (table sugar) are more effective in delaying swelling or gelatinization than are equal concentrations of monosaccharides such as glucose and fructose. At a concentration of 20 percent or more, all sugars and syrups cause a decided decrease in the gel strength of starch pastes. The presence of fats and proteins, which tend to coat starch granules and thereby delay hydration, also lowers the rate of viscosity development.

STARCH COOKERY

Combining Starch with Hot Liquids

A potential problem in starch cookery results from the tendency of dry starch particles to clump or form lumps. Before hot liquids are combined with starch, the particles of starch must be separated to bring about a uniform dispersion of well-hydrated starch granules. This process can be accomplished by (a) dispersing the dry starch with melted fat to make a **roux,** (b) mixing the starch with cold water to form a **slurry,** or (c) blending the starch with sugar.

Roux. A roux is prepared by blending melted fat with flour to form a paste the consistency of wet sand. A roux may be may be white, blond, or brown. A white roux is cooked only briefly, whereas a blond roux is cooked until a light brown color. Brown roux is cooked until a darker color has been achieved. A brown roux will have less thickening power due to dextrinization as described earlier in this chapter. The roux is then incorporated into a liquid to thicken it. To avoid lumps, a cold liquid should be added to a hot roux, or alternatively, a cold roux should be added to a hot liquid with vigorous stirring until blended. Further cooking will result in the gelatinization of the starch.

Slurry. A slurry is prepared by mixing flour or starch with some of the cold liquid to form a "slurry" with the consistency of thick cream. The slurry is added to a hot liquid while stirring and then cooked over direct heat until the mixture boils. Although the slurry method is useful for many products, it may not provide as rich a flavor and generally will be less stable in a soup or sauce than when these products are prepared with a roux. A sauce or gravy, however, will be more clear and glossy when cornstarch is used instead of flour; therefore, some dishes such as stir-fry vegetables are best prepared with a cornstarch slurry.

Sauces

A variety of sauces may be made with starch used as a thickening agent. A white sauce is a starch-thickened sauce made from fat, flour, liquid, and seasonings. When the liquid is milk, the basic sauce is called *béchamel* (bay´-sha-mel *or* besh´-a-mel). When the liquid is a light stock of veal, chicken, or fish, the sauce is called a *velouté* (vayl´-oo-tay´). The five basic mother sauces are described in Table 13-4.

White sauces are used in the preparation of a variety of dishes, including creamed eggs, fish, and vegetables; cheese sauce; cream soups; soufflés; croquettes; and certain casserole mixtures. The finished sauce should be smooth, satiny, and free of lumps. The consistency depends on the amount of starchy agent used. Table 13-5 gives proportions for standard white sauces of various consistencies along with suggested uses. If cornstarch is substituted for flour in making a white sauce, only half as much cornstarch should be used compared to the original amount of flour.

TABLE 13-4 The Five Basic Mother Sauces. These basic sauces can be used as a base to make additional sauces.

Sauce Name	Description
Béchamel	Milk thickened with roux and flavored with onion, nutmeg, salt, and pepper. Cheese sauce, mornay, and other sauces may be made using béchamel
Velouté	Fish stock, chicken stock, or veal stock is thickened with roux and seasoned with salt and pepper. A suprême sauce is made by adding cream to a chicken velouté sauce.
Espagnole	Brown stock, such as a beef stock, is thickened with a brown roux and seasoned with tomato purée, diced carrots, onions, and celery and additional herbs and spices. This sauce is used to make demi-glace by adding equal parts espagnole to a brown stock and simmering until the mixture is reduced by half due to evaporation.
Tomato Sauce	Tomatoes, diced carrots, onions, and celery with additional herbs and spices are cooked together and may or may not be thickened with a roux depending on the desired use of this sauce. A vegetable or white stock also may be included.
Hollandaise	Composed of egg yolks, white wine vinegar, water, lemon juice, clarified butter, and seasonings, this sauce is thickened as a result of the egg yolks and the emulsion formed when making this sauce. A béarnaise sauce is made using hollandaise as a base.

Source: Reference 15

TABLE 13-5 Proportions of Ingredients and Uses for White Sauce

Sauce	Fat*	Flour	Liquid	Salt	Pepper	Uses
Thin	1 1/2 tsp (7 g)	1 Tbsp (7 g)	1 c (237 mL)	1/4 tsp (1.5 g)	fg**	Cream soups
Medium	1 Tbsp (14 g)	2 Tbsp (14 g)	1 c	1/4 tsp	fg	Creamed vegetables and meats; casseroles
Thick	1 1/2 Tbsp (21 g)	3 Tbsp (21 g)	1 c	1/4 tsp	fg	Soufflés
Very thick	2 Tbsp (28 g)	4 Tbsp (28 g)	1 c	1/4 tsp	fg	Croquettes

*Amounts may be adjusted, if desired. A roux should be the consistency of wet sand.

**fg is abbreviation for "few grains"

Cream Soups

Cream soups may vary in consistency, but their usual thickness corresponds to that of thin white sauce. One tablespoon of flour is used for each cup of liquid, which may be part milk and part vegetable cooking water or meat broth and finely diced vegetables. Combined vegetable waters sometimes produce a soup of better flavor than the water from a single vegetable. A **mirepoix**, composed of diced onions, carrots, and celery, is used in a number of soups because of the flavor provided. If starchy vegetables are used for pulp, such as is done in some purée or cream soups, the flour must be reduced to about one-half the usual amount. The fat must also be reduced, or, lacking enough flour to hold it in suspension, the fat will float on top of the soup. Some flour is desirable for starchy soups, such as potato or dried bean soup, to hold the pulp in suspension. In preparing a cream soup, a medium white sauce can be made from milk, fat, flour, and seasonings. An amount of vegetable juice and pulp equal to the milk used is then heated and added to the sauce, thus diluting the mixture to the consistency of a thin white sauce.

If acid juices, such as tomato, are used, the acid is added gradually to the white sauce at serving time to minimize the tendency to curdle. Fresh, recently opened milk will be more stable in resisting curdling, and whole or

FIGURE 13-7 This New England clam chowder has an attractive appearance and has been properly prepared so that the sauce is smooth and creamy.

reduced-fat milk generally is less likely to curdle than nonfat (skim) milk. Although a curdled cream soup is edible, it is aesthetically undesirable (Figure 13-7). Making a tomato sauce from the tomato juice, fat, and flour (roux) instead of making a white sauce is preferred by some cooks and is a common practice in the production of canned tomato soup.

Baking soda may be used by some in cream of tomato soup because the soda will offset the acid in the tomato and therefore reduce the tendency toward curdling. Baking soda, however, is not recommended because it may increase the alkalinity of the soup so much that vitamin C

MULTICULTURAL CUISINE

Soups—Less Traditional and More Diverse?

The image of soup is expanding! We may relate chicken soup to the comforting of a loved one who is ill—and this may still be an important role. But many different varieties of soup, some with exotic flavors and textures, can take us on culinary journeys across the globe.

Food technologists are assisting in the expansion by developing ingredients that capture Asian, French, Caribbean, and Italian cooking and can serve as key components in formulating soups. For example, coconut is used as both a flavor and a fat base in many Eastern and tropical cuisines, much the same as Western cuisines use butter, cream, or cheese. Interest in Indian and Thai cuisines is growing in the United States, and Kraft Foods has produced a dehydrated coconut, refined to a very fine particle size, that can be used in soups that are typical of these cuisines [20]. Soups also adapt well to the growing demand for vegetarian products

and are excellent vehicles for "hot" ingredients such as chilies, which are valued in many cultures.

Modified starches can aid in developing many food products, including soups and sauces such as instant cream-style soups, creamy jalapeño sauces, and microwavable spaghetti sauces, where high viscosity, smooth texture, and stability are desired. The bland or nonmasking flavor profiles of these starches allow more exotic flavors to come through in the finished recipe.

Soup is not just a first course or a side dish these days, either. It can also be the featured entrée, standing by itself. A variety of vegetables and savory flavor combinations may also add to both nutritional quality and esthetic enjoyment. Many traditional soups can be upscaled for greater diversity in exploring other cuisines (Plate III). Soup can truly be both a comfort and an indulgence [20]. ■

and some of the B vitamins are essentially destroyed by oxidation. The use of soda may also seriously mar flavor if an excess is used.

Starch-Thickened Desserts

Cornstarch pudding is probably the most common starch-thickened dessert. Although similar desserts are made from other cereal sources, including wheat flour alone or combined with tapioca or sago, puddings made with cornstarch are often considered to have a smoother mouthfeel and less "pasty" texture than those made with flour. The consistency of starchy puddings varies according to personal preference. If a pudding stiff enough to form a mold is desired, it will have better flavor and texture if it is made as soft as possible while still holding its form when unmolded. Many prefer pudding to have a relatively soft consistency, in which case it must be spooned into individual dishes. Tapioca and sago puddings, particularly, are usually more acceptable when they are relatively soft.

The preparation of puddings and pie fillings often combines starch and egg cookery to produce a creamy mixture (Figure 13-8). The product is thickened with starch before the egg is added, because starch tolerates higher temperatures than egg. The pudding is first prepared in the same manner as a cornstarch pudding containing no egg. After starch gelatinization is complete, a small amount of the hot starchy mixture may be added to the egg. This dilutes or tempers the egg so that it does not coagulate in lumps when it is added to the bulk of the hot mixture (Figure 13-9). Alternatively, a small amount of cold milk may be withheld in the beginning of the preparation and mixed with the egg to dilute it. This milk–egg mixture is then added all at once, with stirring, to the hot starchy pudding mixture, producing a smooth, creamy product.

Starchy puddings containing egg should be cooked sufficiently after the addition of the egg to coagulate the egg proteins. If this is not done, the pudding may become thin on standing. If a fairly large amount of egg is used,

FIGURE 13-8 Meringue is placed on this chocolate cream pie.

the temperature of the pudding after the egg is added should not reach boiling, because this may result in curdling of the egg with a consequent grainy texture of the pudding.

Numerous additions or substitutions may be made to the basic formula for cornstarch pudding to vary the flavor. These additions include chocolate or cocoa, caramelized sugar, shredded coconut, nuts, maple syrup, or diced fruits. Recipe books should be consulted for specific directions in preparing the variations.

Basic Formula for Cornstarch Pudding	
2 to 3 Tbsp (16 to 24 g) cornstarch	2 cup (474 mL) milk
1/4 cup (50 g) sugar	1 tsp vanilla
1/8 tsp salt	1 egg or 2 egg yolks (optional)

Mix sugar, salt, and starch. Add 1/2 cup of cold milk gradually to form a smooth mixture. Heat remaining milk in a saucepan and add the starch–sugar mixture (in which the starch particles have been separated by the sugar and then the cold milk) to the hot milk with constant stirring. Cook the mixture over direct heat, stirring constantly, until the mixture boils; continue simmering for 1 minute. Remove from heat and add vanilla. Chill. If egg is used in the pudding, add a small amount of the hot boiled mixture to the slightly beaten egg; then add this to the hot mixture

(a)

(b)

FIGURE 13-9 (a) Hot liquid is slowly poured into eggs while beating to warm the eggs gradually. (b) The egg and hot liquid are returned to the range to finish cooking.

in the saucepan. Cook over moderate heat for 3 or 4 minutes to a minimum of 165°F (74°C). After cooking is completed, add vanilla. Chill.

Microwave Cooking of Starch Mixtures

The microwave oven is a quick and convenient tool in the preparation of relatively small quantities of starch-thickened sauces and puddings. If preparing larger quantities, the use of the microwave oven will not necessarily be a timesaver.

A smooth, creamy chocolate pudding to serve only one or two persons may be prepared in just a few minutes. First, semisweet baking chocolate is heated in milk in a 2-cup measure with the microwave oven on high for 1 to 2 minutes until the mixture is hot. A blend of dry corn-starch and sugar is then added to the hot chocolate milk, and the mixture is heated on high for 1/2 to 1 minute,

stirring after each 30 seconds. Vanilla, butterscotch, and other types of starch-thickened puddings are prepared in a similar manner. Microwaved sauces and puddings need less stirring than conventionally cooked sauces and puddings, because there is no tendency for the material on the bottom of the container to scorch as in range-top cooking.

It is just as easy to prepare small amounts of a basic white sauce in the microwave oven. First, butter or margarine is melted by heating on high for 1/2 to 1 minute to make approximately 1 cup of sauce. The flour and seasonings are then added, and milk is blended into the fat-flour mixture. Microwaving 6 to 8 minutes then produces a smooth, creamy white sauce. The mixture is stirred at approximately 1-minute intervals during the cooking. Using a similar technique, gravies may be prepared in the microwave oven using meat stock and meat drippings.

FOCUS ON SCIENCE

Challenges Associated with Microwave Cooking of Starch

When cooking starch products in a microwave oven, it can be very difficult to produce an acceptable product. First,

because heating is uneven in the microwave, hot and cold spots will occur. Second, when cold, the starch is insoluble in the liquid and needs to be stirred constantly to keep the starch dispersed. Third, because the mixture cannot be stirred while heating in the microwave and the heat is uneven, the product will lump, undercook, and some of the starch granules will not open. A microwave-cooked product such as pudding may have a rough texture against the tongue. Thus, manufacturers of starch-based products, intended for microwave cooking, may use modified starches to overcome some of the challenges associated with the microwave cooking of starch.

CHAPTER SUMMARY

- The parts of plants that serve most prominently for the storage of starch are seeds, roots, and tubers. Thus, the most common sources of food starch are cereal grains, including corn, wheat, rice, grain, sorghum, and oats; legumes; and roots or tubers, including potato, sweet potato, arrowroot, and the tropical cassava plant. Purified starch may be separated from grains and tubers by a process called *wet milling*.

- Starch is a polysaccharide made up of hundreds or even thousands of glucose molecules joined together. The molecules of starch are of two general types, called *fractions*: amylose and amylopectin. The amylose fraction of starch contributes gelling characteristics to cooked and cooled starch mixtures. Amylopectin contributes to cohesion or thickening properties of a starch mixture.

- Molecules of starch are deposited in tiny, organized units called *granules*. Starch molecules are structured in the granule to form crystallinelike patterns.

- Starches include natural or native starch, modified starch, or resistant starch. Natural starches may

be improved through selective breeding or genetic engineering.

- Modified starches are modified using chemical or physical methods to improve the functional characteristics of the starch. Chemical modifications include hydrolysis, cross-linking, and substitution. Physical modifications of starch may be used to produce instant or pregelatinized starches, cold-water swelling starches, or heat-treated starches with greater viscosity and stability.

- Resistant starches are not digestible by the human body. There are four types of resistant starch that can be useful in foods to increase total dietary fiber.

- When dry heat is applied to starch or starchy foods, the starch becomes more soluble in comparison with unheated starch and has reduced thickening power when it is made into a cooked paste. Some of the starch molecules are broken down to dextrins. High temperatures also cause color and flavor changes.

- The starch granule is insoluble in cold water. After a starch-and-water suspension is heated, gelatinization, or swelling of the starch granules, is observed. The swelling of the starch granules results in colloidal dispersion of starch in water which is then called a *starch paste*. Gel formation or gelation may occur as the mixture cools, depending on the type of starch fraction. Waxy varieties of starch, without amylose, do not form gels. As a starch paste continues to stand after gel formation is complete, additional bonds are formed between amylose molecules in a process called *retrogradation*. Syneresis may occur as the result of retrogradation.

- Temperature, time of heating, degree of agitation, acidity, and addition of other ingredients such as sugar can have an impact on the cooking of starch pastes. Excessive cooking, stirring, agitation, acid, or sugar can result in the thinning of a starch paste. Undercooked starch pastes will have a raw starch flavor and a less smooth or silky mouthfeel. Excessive agitation may give a slick, pasty mouthfeel.

- Dry starch particles may clump or form lumps unless the dry starch is dispersed with melted fat, blended with sugar, or mixed with cold water. A roux is the name used in cooking to describe melted fat and a starch, such as flour, that are cooked together. A slurry is a mixture of starch and a cold liquid which is added to a hot liquid and cooked further.

- A variety of sauces and cream soups may be made with starch used as a thickening agent.

- In the preparation of starch-thickened desserts, the starch is first mixed with sugar. Generally the starch and liquid mixture is cooked together before the addition of the eggs. To prevent curdling, eggs should be tempered before adding to the hot starch mixture to complete cooking.

- Starch mixtures may be prepared in the microwave, providing relatively small quantities of starch-thickened sauces and puddings are to be made.

STUDY QUESTIONS

1. Starch is a storage form of carbohydrate deposited as granules in plant cells.

   (a) Describe the appearance of starch granules when viewed under a microscope. How do their size and shape differ from one plant source to another?

   (b) Name the two fractions of starch. Explain how they differ in structure.

   (c) Explain why some natural starches are chemically modified. Give examples of the types of chemical modification most commonly used.

   (d) How can native starches be improved for desirable uses in food processing, lessening the need for chemically modified starches?

   (e) What products are produced as starch is hydrolyzed? What may catalyze this process?

2. (a) Describe what happens when dry starches are heated. What is this process called?

   (b) Why is gravy made from browned flour usually thinner than gravy made from the same amount of unbrowned flour? Explain.

   (c) Describe what happens when starch granules are heated in water. What is this process called?

   (d) Distinguish between the process described in Question 2c and *pasting* of starch.

   (e) Describe the general effect of each of the following on the thickness of a cooked starch mixture: (1) rate of heating, (2) excessive stirring, and (3) addition of sugar.

3. Many starch-thickened mixtures become stiff or rigid on cooling.

   (a) What is this process called? What happens in the starch mixture to bring it about?

   (b) How does the amount of amylose in the starch affect the rigidity? Why?

   (c) What is meant by *retrogradation* of a starch paste?

   (d) What is *syneresis*? Why may it occur in cooked starch mixtures?

   (e) Which of the common starches forms the stiffest and which the softest pudding when used in equal amounts? Explain.

4. Distinguish between *gelatinization* and *gelation* of starch mixtures.

5. Describe three ways to keep powdery starches from lumping when they are added to hot liquid. Explain what is happening in each case.

6. Describe appropriate methods for preparing each of the following items. Explain why these methods should be successful.

   (a) White sauce

   (b) Cream of vegetable soup

   (c) Cream of tomato soup

   (d) Cornstarch pudding

   (e) Cornstarch pudding with egg

7. What two types of instant starch are available to the food processor? How do these differ from each other? Give examples of products in which the consumer may expect to find instant starches used.

8. Suggest appropriate procedures for preparing puddings and white sauces in the microwave oven.

PASTA AND CEREAL GRAINS 14

Cereal grains are seeds of the grass family. The word *cereal* is derived from *Ceres*, the Roman goddess of grain. Wheat, corn (maize), rice, oats, rye, barley, and millet are the most important cereals used for human food. Grain sorghum is used chiefly for animal feed, but starch is extracted from it for commercial food use. Triticale is a grain produced by crossbreeding wheat and rye. Although it is not a seed of the grass family, buckwheat is often classified with the cereal grains because buckwheat flour has properties and uses similar to those of cereal flours. A rediscovered cereal-like plant is amaranth, which produces an abundance of tiny seeds (Figure 14-1). About 1,000 of these seeds weigh approximately 1 gram. Amaranth is one of those rare plants whose leaves are eaten as a vegetable and the seeds are used as cereals [38].

Cereal is not limited to breakfast foods—it applies to a large group of foods made from grains, including flours, meals, breads, and alimentary pastes or pasta. The ease with which grains can be produced and stored, together with the relatively low cost and nutritional contribution of many cereal foods, particularly whole-grain products, has resulted in the widespread use of grain commodities throughout the world. Actually, cereal grains are the principal crops that have made the continuation of humankind possible. They are the staple in the diets of most population groups.

In this chapter, the following topics will be discussed:

- Consumption trends
- Structure and composition
- Nutritive value
- Common cereal grains
- Breakfast cereals
- Cooking of rice
- Pasta

CONSUMPTION

On the basis of disappearance data, per capita use of flour and cereal products in the United States, after falling dramatically from the levels of the first half of the century, has increased over the past 25 years, rising to 192 pounds annually in 2004 [43] (see Table 14-1). Wheat is the major grain eaten in the United States, with wheat products representing 71 percent of total grain consumption in 2003 [5]. However, rice, corn, and oat products are gaining favor and have increased their share of total grain consumption since 1970 (see Figure 14-2).

In spite of the information gained from the use of disappearance data for the available food supply, surveys of actual food intake by representative samples in the United States suggest that Americans are falling far short of consuming the amounts of grain products recommended by the Dietary Guidelines. Only 35 percent of Americans included in the 1999–2002 National Health and Nutrition Examination Survey (NHANES) met the total grain consumption recommendation. Even fewer Americans age 12 and over are meeting the whole-grain recommendation with only 4 percent consuming three

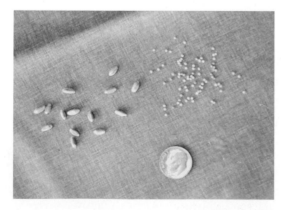

FIGURE 14-1 Amaranth seeds are very tiny, which is emphasized by showing them alongside small wheat kernels (on the left). The dime in the picture helps you to judge sizes by comparison. *(Photograph by Chris Meister)*

TABLE 14-1	Annual Per Capita Grain Consumption in the United States
Years	Flour and Cereal Products (lbs)
1910	295
1920	242
1930	228
1940	199
1950	167
1960	147
1970	136
1980	145
1990	181
2000	199
2005	192

Source: Reference 43

servings of whole-grain foods—such as brown rice, rolled oats, and whole-wheat products—per day [6]. Of the whole grains consumed by Americans, 36 percent are consumed at breakfast. One-third of the whole-grain servings consumed are snacks such as whole-wheat crackers and popcorn [6].

STRUCTURE AND COMPOSITION

All whole grains have a similar structure: outer bran coats, a germ, and a starchy endosperm portion, as shown in Figures 14-3 and 14-4. Cereal products vary in composition depending on which part or parts of the grain are used.

Bran

The chaffy coat that covers the kernel during growth is eliminated when grains are harvested. The outer layers of the kernel proper, which are called the *bran*, constitute

about 5 percent of the kernel. The bran has a high content of fiber and mineral ash. Milled bran also may contain some germ. The *aleurone* layer comprises the square cells located just under the bran layers of the kernel (see Chapter 15, Figure 15-1). These cells are rich in protein, phosphorus, and thiamin, and also contain some fat. The aleurone layer comprises approximately 8 percent of the whole kernel. In the milling of white flour, the aleurone layer is removed with the bran.

Endosperm

The *endosperm* is the large central portion of the kernel and constitutes about 83 percent of the grain. It contains most of the starch (Figure 14-4) and most of the protein of the kernel. The vitamin, mineral, and fat content of the endosperm is generally low. Milled white flour comes entirely from the endosperm.

Germ or Embryo

The *germ* is a small structure at the lower end of the kernel from which sprouting begins and the new plant grows. It usually comprises only 2 to 3 percent of the whole kernel. It is rich in fat, protein, ash, and vitamins. When the kernel is broken, as it is in certain processing procedures, the fat is exposed to oxygen in the air. This greatly reduces the storage life of the grain because the fat may become rancid. The broken or milled grain also is more susceptible to infestation by insects.

NUTRITIVE VALUE AND ENRICHMENT

Cereal grains are important dietary components for several nutritional reasons. Grains provide the world population with a majority of its food calories and about half of its protein. For the emphasis on dietary fat reduction and increased complex carbohydrate intake (starch and fiber), cereal grains are "made to order." Grains are excellent sources of starch, the nutritive polysaccharide, and indigestible fiber. Cereal grains are low in fat and supply

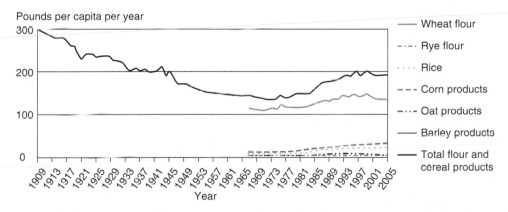

FIGURE 14-2 Since 1910, total grain consumption has declined; however, consumption has increased since the 1970s. (*Source: U.S. Department of Agriculture, Economic Research Service.*)

GRAINS FOR BREAKFAST CEREALS

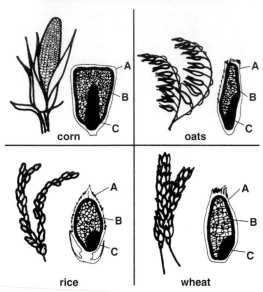

corn   oats

rice   wheat

A BRAN consists of several thin outer layers of the grain kernel and is its protective coat.

B ENDOSPERM is the stored food supply for the new plant which develops as the kernel germinates. It comprises about 85% of the kernel.

C EMBRYO or GERM is the miniature plant which enlarges and develops after the kernel germinates.

FIGURE 14-3 Several common grains have similar structures including bran, endosperm, and germ. Corn, oats, rice, and wheat may be consumed in a variety of ways as breakfast cereals or side dishes with a meal. *(Courtesy of Cereal Institute, Inc.)*

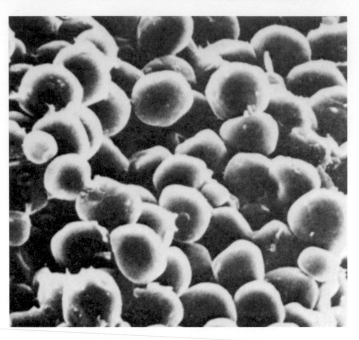

FIGURE 14-4 A scanning electron micrograph of the fractured surface of the endosperm of corn showing the cornstarch granules. *(Courtesy of the Northern Regional Research Center, U.S. Department of Agriculture)*

a number of valuable vitamins and minerals. A comparison of composition and nutritive value for various cereals is given in Appendix C.

Protein

The proteins of cereal grains are generally of relatively low biological value. Various cereals and legumes, however, supplement each other with respect to essential amino acid content so that the quality of the protein actually eaten is considerably increased. In a vegetarian diet, the lack of the essential amino acid lysine in cereal grains is complemented by lysine in legumes, including soybeans. Likewise, the amino acid methionine is lacking in legumes but found in cereal grains.

Refined and Enriched Grains

The nutritive value of cereal products varies with the part of the grain that is used and the method of processing. Refined flours and cereals are made from the endosperm which contains chiefly starch and protein. Therefore, refined cereals and flours furnish little more than starch or protein unless they are enriched with some of the vitamins and minerals lost in milling.

Enriched and fortified flour, according to a legal definition, is white flour to which specified B vitamins

(thiamin, riboflavin, and niacin) and iron have been added. In 1996, the U.S. Food and Drug Administration (FDA) mandated the addition of folic acid to help prevent birth defects due to a deficiency of this vitamin [16]. Optional enrichment ingredients include calcium and vitamin D. The standards for enriched white flour published by the FDA are listed in Table 14-2. Enrichment is required for refined cereal products that enter interstate commerce. Many states also have passed laws requiring enrichment of refined cereal products and flours sold within their boundaries.

Enrichment of white flour increases nutritional quality, but it does not make it nutritionally equivalent to whole-grain flour because only a few of the nutrients lost in milling are replaced by the enrichment process. Many breakfast cereals are highly fortified with vitamins and minerals, well beyond the usual enrichment standards. One study found that ready-to-eat cereals consumed by 10-year-old children made an important contribution to their diets in terms of vitamins and minerals [21].

Whole Grains

Whole grains are cereal grains with the endosperm, germ, and bran present in the same relative proportions as in the intact grain [44]. Whole grains may be intact, ground, cracked, or flaked. The Dietary Guidelines for Americans 2005 provide a specific recommendation for the consumption of whole grains. Per day, three or more ounce-equivalents of whole-grain products or at least half of the grains consumed should be from whole grains [39]. An ounce serving of whole grains is equivalent to one

HEALTHY EATING

Can You Identify Your Whole Grains?

Whole grains include cereal grains consisting of the intact, ground, cracked, or flaked grains which contain all of the bran, germ, and endosperm in the same relative proportions as found in nature [44].

To identify whole grains, look for the following:

Brown rice

Bulgur (cracked wheat)

Popcorn

Trilicale

Whole-grain corn

Whole rye

Wild rice

Buckwheat

Millet

Sorghum

Whole-grain barley

Whole oats or oatmeal

Whole wheat

Quinoa

Keep in mind that color is not a good indicator of whole grains because a brown color can be obtained through the addition of molasses or other ingredients. Furthermore, products made with whole, white wheat will not be brown but are whole grain. Lastly, label terms *wheat bread*, *stone-ground*, and *seven-grain bread* should not be assumed to imply the product is whole grain. Instead look for *whole* wheat as well as the other whole grains listed above on the ingredient label to identify whole grains [5]. ■

TABLE 14-2 Enrichment Standards Compared with Whole-Wheat Flour (milligrams per pound)*					
	Thiamin	Riboflavin	Niacin	Iron	Folic Acid
Whole-wheat flour	2.49	0.54	19.7	15.0	
Enriched white flour	2.0–2.5	1.2–1.5	16–20	13.0–16.5	0.43–1.4
Enriched bread, rolls, or buns	1.1–1.8	0.7–1.6	10–15	8.0–12.5	0.43–1.4

*One pound of flour is usually equivalent to 1 1/2 pounds of bread.

slice of whole-grain bread, one-half cup of brown rice or whole grain pasta, or one cup of most dried breakfast cereals [5].

Whole-grain products are higher in a number of micronutrients [9]. Diets high in whole grains are associated with a reduced risk of cancer, cardiovascular heart disease, diabetes, and obesity [4, 33, 35]. Whole grains provide fiber for the diet. The position of the American Dietetic Association states adequate amounts of dietary fiber should be consumed from a variety of plant foods [3].

COMMON CEREAL GRAINS

Wheat

Wheat has been cultivated since early times and is one of the most widely cultivated plants on earth. Wheat is commonly milled into flour, is used for the production of wheat starch and, in large quantity, for the making of various types of breakfast cereals. Wheat flour is uniquely suitable for bread making because it contains proteins that develop strong, elastic properties in dough. No other common cereal grain equals wheat in bread-making qualities.

Classes of Wheat.   Thousands of varieties of wheat may be grouped into six classes which include hard red wheat, hard red spring, soft red winter, durum, hard white, and soft white. These classifications are based on three factors: (1) winter or spring, (2) hard or soft, and (3) color. Winter wheats are planted in the fall, lie dormant over the winter, then grow in the spring for harvesting later in the summer. Spring wheats are planted in the spring and harvested during the same growing season. Hard wheats are higher in protein content than soft wheats and usually have greater baking strength in that

HEALTHY EATING

Whole-Grain Foods—How Many Servings Today?

How many servings of whole-grain foods have you eaten today? If you are an average consumer in the United States, the answer to this question is "less than one." According to the 2005 Dietary Guidelines for Americans, three or more ounce-equivalents of whole grains are recommended on a daily basis [39].

Joanne Slavin and David Kritchevsky, of the University of Minnesota and Wistar Institute of Anatomy and Biology, respectively, outlined some basic reasons why whole grains are so important to our health [34]. We know that whole grains provide dietary fiber, vitamins, and minerals. We can get these from other foods, but whole grains also provide **phytochemicals** that function as nutrients, antioxidants, and **phytoestrogens**. Whole-grain consumption also reduces the risk of certain cancers, stroke, diabetes, and cardiovascular disease.

The researchers point out that the whole is greater than the sum of the parts. The total protectiveness of whole-grain intake against heart disease appears to be greater than the sum of the protection seen with the parts—vitamins, minerals, soluble fiber, etc. that are found in whole grains. Consumers need to get this message and act on it by making significant changes in their diets.

The food industry can also help by overcoming barriers to whole-grain consumption—including flavor characteristics, price, informative labeling, and convenience. In 1999, the FDA approved a health claim for whole grains: "Diets rich in whole grains and other plant foods that are low in total fat, saturated fat, and cholesterol may reduce the risk of heart disease and some cancer." To qualify for this claim, the food must contain at least 51 percent whole-grain ingredients. Food manufacturers need to find ways to produce healthful whole-grain products that meet the taste test of consumers. Science supports the importance of this effort. So, how many servings of whole grains will you eat tomorrow? ■

they result in a loaf of bread of large volume and fine texture. Soft wheats are therefore commonly used to make pastries, cookies, crackers, and other products where a high protein content is undesirable [10].

White wheat is gaining favor for bread making because flour made from whole white wheat is whole grain, yet unlike whole red wheats, offers a white color. Whole white wheat flour has a fine, uniform particle size similar to that of refined flour due to a specialized milling process [17, 27]. Whole-wheat flours made from red wheats will have a characteristic light brown color.

Durum wheat is a very hard, non–bread-making wheat of high protein content. It is grown chiefly for use in making macaroni and other pasta. Nearly 73 percent of the durum wheat produced in the United States is grown in North Dakota [20]. Classes of wheat, milling, and flour are discussed in more detail in Chapter 15.

Processing.   Wheat is often ground into flour; however, a variety of forms of wheat may be found in the marketplace including wheat berries, bulgur, cracked wheat, and wheat germ. Wheat is also used to make a variety of breakfast cereals, which may be shredded, puffed, flaked, or rolled. Various types of wheat products are described in Table 14-3.

Corn

Corn is a plant that is native to America. Early settlers in the New World were introduced to the uses of corn by Native Americans. The United States produced 42 percent of the world's corn in 2005 and is the leading exporter of corn [45]. Corn used as a grain is called *dent* or *field* corn and is different from sweet corn that is consumed as a vegetable. Field corn is harvested in the fall when it is dry and the kernel has formed a dent. The corn kernel is versatile and can take a great variety of forms.

Processing.   Corn is processed for use in a wide variety of foods and other products. Corn millers process corn by one of the following ways: (1) tempering and degerming, (2) stone-ground or nondegerming, or (3) alkaline-cooked [22]. In the degerming process the majority of the outer bran and germ are removed. When the corn kernel endosperm is freed of the bran and germ, hominy is produced (see Figure 14-5). Hominy grits, fine grits, corn meals, and corn flours then may be produced using rollers, sifters, and grinders. Hominy grits are coarse compared to fine grits, meals, and flours. Hominy grits are used for the production of corn flakes.

TABLE 14-3	Types of Wheat Products
Types	**Description**
Wheat berry	Another name for the wheat kernel with only the inedible outer hull removed. When used for cooking will need to be cooked for an extended period of time to soften.
Bulgur	Made from white or red, hard or soft, whole-wheat kernels that are parboiled and then dried. A small amount of the outer bran layers is removed, and the wheat is then usually cracked. Also called *tabouli wheat*.
	Armenian restaurants serve cooked bulgur pilaf. Bulgur may also be found in vegetarian dishes. Additionally, bulgur may be present in recipes originating in Turkey, Greece, Cyprus, the Middle East, North Africa, and East Europe.
Cracked wheat	Made from the whole kernel which is broken into small pieces. Similar to bulgur, but unlike bulgur is not cooked and dried. Provides a nutty flavor and crunchy texture to baked goods. Presoaking or cooking before use is recommended.
Wheat germ	Germ of the wheat kernel. May be added to foods to provide a nutty, crunchy texture. Is high in protein, fat, B vitamins, and vitamin E. Due to fat content, can become rancid.
Wheat bran	Bran is the outer layer of the wheat kernel. Is a good source of fiber, B vitamins, protein, and iron. May be added to baked goods.
Farina	Coarsely ground endosperm of wheat. May be used as a breakfast cereal. Commonly known as Cream of Wheat.

Source: Reference 2

FIGURE 14-5 Hominy is the endosperm of the corn kernel, freed from bran and germ. *(Photograph by Chris Meister)*

of the corn in a boiling lime solution followed by steeping. Excess alkali and the loose pericarp tissue are washed away, and the remaining corn product is ground to form masa flour [22]. Masa flour is used for tortillas, corn chips, taco shells, and other similar products.

Uses for Corn.   Corn is used in a wide variety of products including breakfast cereals such as corn flakes, corn breads, grits, and corn tortillas. The most popular items in Mexican restaurants—tacos, quesadillas, and fajitas—contain corn. Corn oil, which contains a high proportion of polyunsaturated fatty acids, is extracted from the germ of the corn kernel. Corn syrups and glucose are produced by the hydrolysis of cornstarch, which is the principal starch used in the United States for culinary purposes (see Chapter 13).

Not only is corn used for food, but it is also used in all kinds of consumer and industrial products. For example, corn is the source of the ethanol that is blended with gasoline for cleaner-burning fuel, and cornstarch is used as a clay binder in ceramics, an adhesive in glues, and a bodying agent in dyes.

Mills using the stone-ground process most often use white corn to produce whole-grain hominy grits and corn meal. The alkaline-cooked process involves the cooking

FOCUS ON SCIENCE

acid composition. Studies have shown that oil content and composition of some corn lines are affected by the geographic locations in which corn is grown.

Corn Oil

Corn oil is a byproduct of corn wet milling industries and is recovered from the germ of dent corn. Dent corn has a very thick outer skin and has been shown to have a constant fatty

MULTICULTURAL CUISINE

Corn—A Key Ingredient in Mexican Cuisine

Corn is a major food for the peoples of Mexico and Central America and is a staple ingredient in America's fastest growing ethnic cuisine—Mexican. The corn tortilla plays a central role in Mexican cuisine, and the tortilla is becoming one of the fastest growing segments of the baking industry in the United States [36]. Either corn or flour tortillas make excellent "wraps" for a variety of food mixtures. Tortillas are traditionally made from corn that is **steeped** and cooked in alkali solution, washed to remove excess alkali, and ground on a stone mill into a dough called *masa*. Masa is pressed into flat, circular shapes, which are then cooked on a hot griddle [15]. This traditional procedure for making tortillas, however, is being replaced by large-scale commercial operations in which corn is cooked and ground immediately with little or no steeping, and the tortillas are cooked in large, automated cookers. ■

Pop, Pop, Popcorn!

Popcorn is a particular variety of corn that is uniquely designed to pop. Moisture inside the kernel surrounded by a hard outer surface will pop open and provide a tasty treat when heated due to a build-up of pressure from the expanding moisture.

Popcorn that fails to pop may be the result of popcorn that has dehydrated over time during extended storage. Recently however, scientists have found the chemical structure of the pericarp (outer hull) may play a major role in which popcorns pop the best [28]. The pericarp not only needs to function like a pressure cooker, holding in the moisture until a high level of pressure is produced during heating, but it also needs to hold the moisture in during storage. Those kernels that fail to pop had essentially leaky outer hulls which allowed the moisture to escape before cooking. ■

Rice

Considered as a world crop, rice is one of the most used of all cereal grains. It is the major food in the diets of many people living in Asia. In America, rice consumption has increased considerably in the last 20 years. U.S. Department of Agriculture (USDA) disappearance data report 20 pounds of rice per capita consumed annually in 2004 as compared to only 8.7 pounds per capita in 1984 [43]. Six states (Arkansas, California, Louisiana, Mississippi, Missouri, and Texas) produce more than 99 percent of the rice grown in America [31].

Varieties of Rice.   More than 40,000 different varieties of rice are grown worldwide [26], although only about 100 are grown commercially in the United States [40]. Rice is classified as long-, medium-, and short-grain varieties (Figures 14-6 and 14-7). The food industry also recognizes a fourth category called *specialty rices*. These are distinguished by characteristics other than shape and size and include varieties such as jasmine, basmati, arborio, and sweet glutinous or waxy rice. Some of these have fragrant aromas.

Long-, Medium-, and Short-Grain Rice.   Long-grain varieties of rice have comparatively high amylose content and are light and fluffy when cooked. The cooked kernels tend to separate. The medium- and short-grain varieties contain less amylose, absorb less water in cooking,

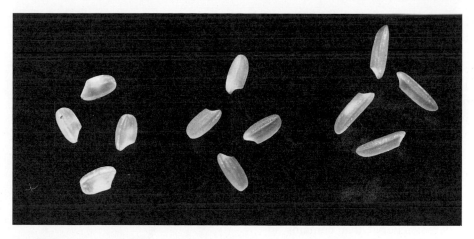

FIGURE 14-6 Short-, medium-, and long-grain varieties of rice. *(Courtesy of The Rice Council)*

FIGURE 14-7 This long-grain rice is grown in the United States. *(Courtesy of U.S. Department of Agriculture, Photo by Keith Weller)*

and the kernels are more clingy or sticky when cooked. The preference for fluffy versus sticky rice depends on the culture of the consumer and the desired characteristics of the dish being prepared.

Specialty Rices. Specialty rices have become more popular in the United States as the interest in ethnic cuisines and new flavors has increased (Figure 14-8).

Aromatic rices such as della, jasmine, and basmati have a flavor and aroma similar to roasted nuts or popcorn. Della and basmati are dry, separate, and fluffy when cooked, whereas jasmine tends to cling together [26]. Arborio is a medium-grain rice with a characteristic white dot in the center of the grain. Arborio is typically used in risotto, a classic Italian dish, because it will absorb flavors and produce a creamy texture.

Processing of Rice. Rice may be processed in several ways to produce brown rice, polished white rice, enriched rice, parboiled or converted rice, precooked or instant rice, and rice flour. These rice products are described in Table 14-4.

Oats

Many prepared breakfast cereals contain oats. In addition, oats are used in the making of cookies, granola bars, baby foods, variety breads, candy, and snack items. Oats are utilized in a rolled form as both old-fashioned and quick-cooking products.

Processing. When oats are processed, the outer hull is removed, but most of the germ and bran remain with the endosperm. Oat kernels with the outer hulls removed are called *groats*. Rolled oats are made by passing groats through rollers to form flakes. For quick-cooking rolled oats, the groats are cut into tiny particles that are then rolled into thin, small flakes. Regular or old-fashioned rolled oats are rolled without cutting. Rolled oats sold commercially, therefore, contain nearly the whole oat kernel. Because of the retention of most of the germ, rolled oats are higher in fat than most other cereals. They are also a good source of thiamin and other B vitamins and iron.

Beta-glucan. Oatmeal has been a common breakfast cereal for many years, but it has become even more popular with the publication of research indicating that oat bran is particularly effective in diets designed to lower elevated blood cholesterol levels. The use of oat fiber by the food industry thereafter increased greatly, as evidenced by a dramatic rise in the sale of oat bran by the Quaker Oats Company from 1 million pounds per year in 1986 to 2 million pounds per month by 1989 [29]. The benefit appears to come from oat bran's content of beta-glucan, a glucose polymer. Still, there are other cereal sources of beta-glucan, including barley, which is the subject of continuing nutrition research.

At the USDA Northern Regional Research Center, a process was developed for producing a granular or powdered material that contains an appreciable amount of beta-glucan from enzyme-treated oat bran or oat flour. This product is called *oatrim* and is being marketed commercially as a fat replacer.

Rye

Rye is grown and used in the United States chiefly as a flour, but it is also available as rye flakes and as a **pearled** grain. Although rye is a dark cereal grain, it actually has a mellow taste that may enhance the flavor of breads and cereals without overpowering them. Rye is used in the United States much less than wheat, but its use more

FIGURE 14-8 An array of rice varieties are pictured (from top left, going clockwise): black japonica, aromatic red rice, basmati, brown, precooked, sweet, arborio, short, medium, long, parboiled, and jasmine. *(Courtesy of USA Rice Federation)*

nearly approaches wheat in baking quality than other grains. In parts of Europe, rye is established as an important bread flour. Rye flour is available in three grades: light, medium, and dark.

TABLE 14-4 Kinds of Rice Products

Kinds	Description
Brown rice	Least processed form of rice. Only the outer husk or chaffy coat is removed from the kernel. Germ and most of the bran is retained. Rich in vitamins, minerals, and fiber. Takes longer to cook than more highly processed forms of rice.
White polished rice	Bran coats and germ are rubbed from the rice grain by an abrasive process, thus leaving the starchy endosperm. The polishing procedure also removes more than half of the minerals and most of the vitamins from the kernel.
Enriched rice	White polished rice may be enriched with vitamins and minerals lost in processing. Often, a powdery material is applied to the surface of the grain. Enriched rice should not be washed before cooking or rinsed after cooking to avoid loss of the enrichment nutrients.
Converted or parboiled rice	Is soaked in water, drained, and then heated, typically by steaming, before it is dried and milled. This heat process retains nutrients normally lost during milling in the rice kernel by causing nutrients in the outer coats to migrate to the interior.
	Benefits of parboiled rice include improved nutritive value, improved keeping quality, less disintegration during cooking, and better retention of shape and texture during cooking and hot holding.
	Parboiled rice takes somewhat longer to cook than regular milled white rice.
Instant or precooked rice	A long-grain rice that has been cooked, rinsed, and dried by a special process. It may be cooked quickly and therefore is convenient to prepare.
Rice flour	Made from grinding the grains that are broken during milling. Rice flour is relatively resistant to syneresis in frozen/thawed foods and may replace modified starch in some applications.
	Shown to reduce the absorption of oil by as much as 70 percent in donuts and 60 percent when used in a batter for fried chicken [26].
	Is a nonallergenic alternative to wheat flour products [23].
Rice bran	Is the outer brown layer removed during the milling of white rice. It deteriorates rapidly once it is separated from the rice kernel, because a lipase enzyme is exposed to the oil in the bran. The fat breaks down, and an unacceptable musty taste rapidly develops.
	May be heat treated so the enzyme is deactivated and the bran is stabilized [7].

FOCUS ON SCIENCE

What Is Lipase and How Does It Affect Quality of Rice Products?

Rice bran contains unsaturated fatty acids: linoleic acid and linolenic acid. Lipase, a hydrolytic enzyme specific to fatty acids, also is present in the bran. Lipase will cause the removal of the fatty acid from the glycerol. Once the fatty acid is free, and if it is an unsaturated fatty acid, rancidity will occur. Unsaturated fatty acids break down to volatile compounds that will produce off-aromas and flavors.

Genetically Engineered Grains

Genetic engineering is a precise way of introducing new traits into plants by moving genes from one plant to another, eliminating, or rearranging genes using recombinant DNA techniques [40, 41]. More precise and selective than traditional crossbreeding, genetic engineering allows plant developers to control carefully changes in plant characteristics. Biotechnology, which includes genetic engineering techniques, is regulated in the United States collaboratively by the USDA, FDA, and EPA [41, 42].

The prevalence of genetically engineered crops has increased considerably since the mid 1990s when only 5 percent of U.S. soybeans was genetically engineered. In 2006, the USDA estimated 61 percent of corn and 89 percent of soybeans were biotechnology varieties [40]. These genetically engineered crops are herbicide tolerant or pest resistant.

A second generation of genetically engineered crops is under development. Golden rice with enhanced levels of vitamin A is one such crop. In areas of the world where vitamin A deficiency is common and rice is a staple in the diet, this rice could have a positive impact on health [32]. More research is anticipated before golden rice can be approved for use [1]. Other researchers are working on rice with lower levels of phytic acid (Figure 14-9). Phytic acid binds several minerals including iron, calcium, magnesium, and zinc.

FIGURE 14-9 A geneticist compares two kinds of low-phytate rice. *(Courtesy U.S. Department of Agriculture, Photo by Scott Bauer)*

Because phytic acid is poorly digested, these minerals also become less available for use by our bodies when bound by phytic acid [11]. ■

Barley

Pearled barley is the chief form in which this grain is used at the present time in the United States. Pearling is a process that removes the outer hull of barley, leaving a small, round, white pearl of grain, the kind seen in some soups.

Barley may become a valuable source of beta-glucan for the food industry. Some barley flour is available and may be used in breakfast cereals and baby foods. Sprouted barley is a source of malt, which is rich in the enzyme amylase. A commercially available source of barley for

FOCUS ON SCIENCE

Beta (β)-glucans

β-glucans are nondigestible dietary polysaccharides that have gained prominence for lowering blood cholesterol. They are found in the bran of cereal and occur in especially high concentrations in oat and barley brans.

Chemically, β-glucan is a linear chain of β-D-glucopyranosyl units; about 70 percent are linked $(1 \rightarrow 4)$ and about 30 percent $(1 \rightarrow 3)$. The $(1 \rightarrow 3)$ linkages occur singly and are separated by sequences of generally two or three $(1 \rightarrow 4)$ linkages. Thus the molecule is composed of $(1 \rightarrow 3)$-linked β-cellotriosyl and cellotetraosyl units. A representative structure of a segment of oat and barley β-glucans is shown below where n usually is 1 or 2 but could be larger.

$$— \rightarrow 3)—\beta Glcp—(1-[- \rightarrow 4)—\beta Glcp—(1— \rightarrow]_n$$

Source: Whistler, R. L., and BeMiller, J. N. (1997). Chapter 7: Cellulosics. In *Carbohydrate Chemistry for Food Scientists*, pp. 166–167. St. Paul, MN: American Association of Cereal Chemists.

---

baking and cooking is malted barley, which is a byproduct of the beer-brewing industry. Although most of the beta-glucan is removed in the malting process, a concentrated oily substance called *tocotrienol* remains, and it appears to have blood cholesterol–lowering capabilities [29].

Other Grains

Wild Rice.   Wild rice is not true rice but rather the hulled and unmilled grain of a reedlike water plant. It is available only in limited quantity and is therefore usually relatively expensive. During the 1980s, methods were developed for cultivating wild rice. It is now grown in California, as well as in the Great Lakes region, where it was first discovered growing wild [12]. It is prized for its unusual nutlike flavor and uniquely long brown grains. Like many whole-grain cereals, it has relatively poor keeping quality, especially at warm temperatures.

Buckwheat.   Buckwheat is not a seed of the grass family; it is the seed of an herbaceous plant. Because it contains a glutenous substance and is made into flour, it is commonly considered a grain product. Fine buckwheat flour has little of its thick fiber coating included. In that respect, it is similar to refined white flour. It is prized for its distinctive flavor and is commonly used in the making of griddle cakes. The volume of buckwheat flour sold in the United States is relatively small.

Triticale.   Triticale is a hybrid plant produced by crossing wheat and rye. It combines desirable characteristics of each of the parent species. Generally, triticale has a higher protein content and better amino acid balance than wheat. It could be a valuable source of nutrients for many peoples of the world. Certain varieties of triticale have been shown to produce acceptable breads, snack crackers, and noodles [14, 30]. Although triticale is now used primarily for animal feed, it may find increasing use in the human diet as research on this grain continues [24].

Kamut and Spelt.   Kamut is a high-protein variety of wheat with large kernels. Kamut may be substituted for wheat berries, or the flour may be used similarly to wheat flour. Spelt is a grain which is a predecessor of wheat. It is used primarily as flour.

Quinoa.   Quinoa (pronounced *keenwah*) is a small seed which may be cooked like rice or ground into flour. Relatively high in protein, it was a staple of the ancient Incas.

BREAKFAST CEREALS

Breakfast foods made from cereal grains vary widely in composition, depending on the kind of grain, the part of the grain used, the method of milling, and the method of processing. They may be uncooked, partially cooked, or completely cooked. Considerable amounts of sugars, syrups, molasses, or honey are added to some cereals. In certain products, heating dextrinizes part of the starch and produces toasted flavors.

Ready-to-Cook and Instant Cereals

Raw cereals that are cooked in both home and institutional kitchens include whole grains, cracked or crushed grains, granular products made from either the whole grain or the endosperm section of the kernel, and rolled or flaked whole grains. Finely cut flaked grains cook in a shorter time and hence are described as being *quick cooking*. Disodium phosphate is sometimes added to farina to make it quick cooking. It changes the pH of the cereal, becoming more alkaline, and thus causes more rapid absorption of water with faster cooking.

The starch in instant cereals, such as instant oatmeal, has been pregelatinized by prior cooking. Therefore, when boiling water is added and the mixture is simply stirred, the cereal is ready for consumption.

Ready-to-Eat Cereals

Basic processes used in the production of prepared cereals include shredding, puffing, granulating, flaking, and extruding (see Figure 14-10). Mixtures of cereals or cereal flours are often used. Ingredients commonly added

GRAINS INTO BREAKFAST CEREALS

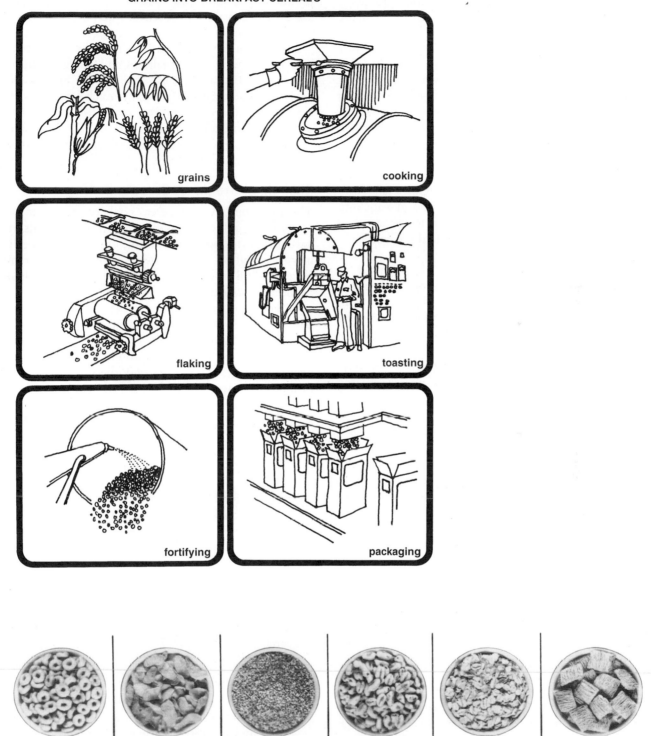

extruded | flaked | granulated | puffed | rolled | shredded

FIGURE 14-10 Major steps in the processing of grains into flaked cereals and types of prepared cereals. *(Courtesy of Cereal Institute, Inc.)*

to ready-to-eat cereals include sweetening agents, salt, flavorings, coloring agents, and antioxidants as preservatives. In most cases, the cereals are fortified to a comparatively high degree with minerals and vitamins added during processing to avoid heat destruction.

Puffed Cereals. In the production of puffed cereals, the whole grain is cleaned and conditioned and put into a pressure chamber. The pressure in the chamber is raised to a high level and then suddenly released. The expansion of water vapor on release of the pressure puffs up the grains to several times the original size. The puffed product is dried by toasting, then cooled and packaged.

Flaked Cereals.   Flaked cereals are made by lightly rolling the grain between smooth rolls to fracture the outer layers of the cleaned and conditioned whole grain. This grain is then cooked, and various flavoring or sweetening substances are added so that they penetrate the rolled grain. The cooked product is dried, conditioned, flaked on heavy flaking rolls, toasted, cooled, and packaged.

Granular Cereals.   In the preparation of granular breakfast cereals, a yeast-containing dough is made from a blend of flours. The dough is fermented and made into large loaves that are baked. The baked loaves are then broken up, dried, and ground to a standard fineness.

Shredded Cereals.   A white, starchy wheat is used for shredded cereals. The whole grain is cleaned and cooked with water so that it is soft and rubbery. The cooked grain is cooled, conditioned, and fed to shredders, which consist of a pair of metal rolls, one smooth and the other having circular grooves. The cereal emerges between the grooves as long parallel shreds. These shreds can be layered to form a thick mat. The mat is cut into the desired size, baked, dried, cooled, and packaged.

Extruded Cereals.   A number of fabricated products—snack foods and breakfast cereals—are extruded. In this process, the cereal-based material is made into a dough, which is fed into the extruder. Moisture content, time, temperature, and pressure are carefully controlled to achieve the desired result. A high-temperature, short-duration cooking period is used in many cases to produce expanded ready-to-eat cereals. Starch is gelatinized in the material as it moves through the extruder, and a colloidal gel is formed. When the product emerges from the nozzle of the extruder, the sudden drop in pressure permits the superheated water to form water vapor or steam. The mass then inflates with numerous tiny cells and is fixed in its expanded state [8].

Economics in Purchasing Cereals

Despite the large numbers of cereals on the market in the United States today, no federal standard of identity has been developed for breakfast cereals other than farina. The great variety available may cause some confusion in the purchase and use of cereals, particularly because a great deal of advertising of these cereal products is done in the mass media, much of it aimed at young children.

Information on nutritive value and cost are essential aids to making wise purchases. Too much food money is sometimes spent for products that are no better nutritionally than many others that are available at a fraction of the cost. A large amount of sugar, up to 35 percent of the product by weight, is used in the production of some prepared cereals. Nutrition labeling provides useful information when making comparisons between products.

In general, the more processing done to a breakfast cereal and the more ingredients added, the higher the retail price. Packaging costs also may be high. Cereals cooked in the kitchen are usually much less costly than ready-to-eat cereals; however, ready-to-eat cereals are popular and are convenient. Whole-grain cereals should be given preference because of the fiber content and generally higher nutrient density.

Cooking of Breakfast Cereals

The main purposes of cereal cookery are to improve palatability and digestibility. Historically, cereals may have first been consumed as whole grains with no preliminary preparation. Later, heat was applied in the parching of grains. Still later came the addition of water before the application of heat.

Cereal cookery is fundamentally starch cookery because starch is the predominant nutrient of cereals. Other factors involved are fiber, which is found chiefly in the exterior bran layers, and protein, which is a prominent constituent of the cereal endosperm. Until softened, or unless disintegrated mechanically, bran may interfere with the passage of water into the interior of the kernel and presumably may retard the swelling of starch. If cellulose is finely divided, its affinity for water is greatly increased. The temperatures necessary to cook starch are more than adequate for cooking the protein in the cereal.

Techniques for Combining Cereal and Water.   If the cereal is in a finely divided form, such as with farina and cornmeal, it should be added to water in a way that avoids lumping so that a uniform gelatinous mass is formed on heating. All cereal particles should be equally exposed to water and heat. If lumps form, dry material remains inside a gelatinous external coating. The following two methods are commonly used to combine cereal with water. (Salt is usually added to the boiling water before the cereal is added.)

1. Gradually pour the dry cereal into boiling water. Slight stirring may be required, but if the water does not cease boiling, stirring may be unnecessary.
2. Mix the cereal with cold water before adding it to the boiling water. The cold water tends to hold the particles apart.

Excessive stirring breaks up cereal particles so that they lose their identity. Even granulated cereals may be broken up to form a more gummy mass than would result from heating with the minimum amount of stirring.

Temperature and Time Periods.   Cereals may be cooked entirely over direct heat using low to moderate temperatures, or they may be placed in a double boiler after the cereal has been added to the boiling water. Cooking times are somewhat less over direct heat than in a double boiler.

The principal factors that affect the time required for the cooking of cereals are the size of the particle, the amount of water used, the presence or absence of the bran, the temperature, and the method used. Finely granulated endosperm cereals, such as farina, cook in less time than whole or cracked cereals. Quick-cooking and precooked cereals, of course, can be prepared much faster than completely raw and untreated cereals. For example, whole-wheat cereal may require 1 to 2 hours of cooking to soften the bran and completely gelatinize the starch granules.

Proportions of Water to Cereal. Proportions of water to cereal vary according to the type of cereal, the quantity cooked, the method of cooking, the length of cooking, and the consistency desired in the finished cereal. The majority of people appear to prefer a consistency that is fairly thick but not too thick to pour. The amount of water must be adequate to permit swelling of the starch granules. If the consistency is too thin, further cooking may be necessary to evaporate the excess water.

Table 14-5 provides the common proportions used for various types of cereals. The amount of salt will vary according to taste.

COOKING OF RICE

White Rice

The challenge of rice cookery is to retain the form of the kernel while at the same time cooking the kernel until it is completely tender. Rice is generally cooked with amounts of water that will be fully absorbed during cooking. Rice

can be cooked in about twice its volume of water, although the exact amount will vary with the variety of rice and the cooking method. Regular rice increases to about three times its volume in cooking. One-half teaspoon of salt per cup of uncooked rice may be used for seasoning. Enriched rice should not be rinsed before cooking because the enrichment mixture will be washed off. Guidelines for several rice cooking methods are provided in Table 14-6.

A number of different ingredients may be used when preparing rice dishes. Rice can be cooked in milk with the use of the double-boiler method. Cooking rice in chicken or beef broth can also give it a desirable flavor. Many ingredients such as herbs, spices, garlic, sautéed onions, or lemon zest can result in a delicious rice dish. A variety of hot and cold dishes may be made with rice as a basic ingredient (see Figure 14-11 and Plate IV).

In some parts of the country where the water is hard, the minerals in the water can produce a grayish green or yellowish tint to the cooked rice. The addition of 1/4 teaspoon of cream of tartar or 1 teaspoon of lemon juice to 2 quarts of water will maintain the white color.

TABLE 14-5 Approximate Proportions of Water to Cereal for Cooked Breakfast Foods

Type of Cereal	Water (cups)	Cereal (cups)
Rolled or flaked	2 or 2 1/2	1
Granular	4 or 5	1
Cracked grain	About 4	1
Whole grain	About 4 unless grain was soaked for several hours	1

TABLE 14-6 Rice Cooking Methods

Cooking Method	Description
Simmering range top	Cook in a kettle with water equal to approximately 2.25 the volume of the rice. Bring to a boil, add rice, and lower temperature to maintain a simmer. Cover with a lid. Rice should be cooked in 15 to 20 minutes depending on the type of rice.
	Due to evaporation, this cooking method requires more water in proportion to rice.
Double boiler	Place rice and water equaling 1 3/4 the volume of the rice in the top of a double boiler over boiling water and cover. Due to reduced evaporation, less water is necessary as compared to other methods. Rice should be done in about 45 minutes.
Oven	Place rice in a covered baking dish with an equivalent amount of water as used when cooking by simmering range top. Place in a 350°F oven for about 25 to 35 minutes for white or parboiled rice.
Microwave	Place rice and water in a microwave-safe dish and cook on high until boiling. Cooking should be completed on 50 percent power for 15 to 20 minutes, depending on the type of rice. Only a minimal amount of time is saved when preparing rice in the microwave because the rice kernel still must absorb water and soften during the cooking process.
Rice cookers	Follow instructions for the rice cooker. In general, less water is needed when using a rice cooker compared to other methods.

FIGURE 14-11 Rice tabbouleh is a cold salad that combines rice, cucumber, tomato, mint, olive oil, and spices, thereby creating an unconventional way to serve rice. *(Courtesy of USA Rice Federation)*

Brown Rice

Brown rice can be cooked by the same methods used to cook white rice, but it must be cooked about twice as long. Because of the longer cooking time, somewhat more water is needed to allow for evaporation—up to 2.5 times the volume of the rice. Brown rice can be soaked for an hour in water to soften the bran and to shorten the cooking period. It does not tend to become sticky with cooking.

Researchers are developing methods of processing brown rice to reduce the cooking time from 45 minutes to 15 minutes to encourage consumers to use brown rice. Brown rice is highly nutritious and higher in fiber than white rice; however, the longer cooking time discourages some from preparing it. Researchers have found that by "sandblasting" the rice grains with rice flour under 60 to 70 pounds of air pressure per inch the rice bran develops water-absorbing holes that result in a faster preparation time [37]. Also available is precooked brown rice, which has a slightly different flavor profile than regular brown rice, but cooks quickly.

Precooked or Instant Rice

Precooked rice can be prepared very quickly. Boiling water is added to the rice. The mixture is then brought back to a boil, removed from the source of heat, and allowed to stand closely covered until the rice swells.

Rice Pilaf

Browning rice in a small amount of hot fat before cooking it in water converts part of the starch to dextrins. Swelling will also be somewhat decreased. The rice develops an interesting color and flavor that make the method desirable to use as a basis for Spanish rice, as rice pilaf, or as a side dish. Chicken or beef broth rather than water is used as the cooking liquid for pilaf.

PASTA

The terms *pasta* and *alimentary paste* are applied to macaroni products, which include spaghetti, vermicelli, noodles, shells, linguine, rotini, ziti, couscous, and many other shapes. There are more than 600 pasta shapes available worldwide, with more being developed [25]. Several different shapes of pasta are shown in Figure 14-12. In general, delicate pasta shapes should be paired with a delicate sauce, and sturdy pastas should be complemented with a robust, hearty sauce.

The principal ingredient in the making of pasta is a flour coarsely ground from durum wheat called *semolina*. Durum wheat is a high-protein grain containing carotenoid pigments in higher concentration than is found in bread wheats, giving pasta its characteristic yellow or amber color. Nearly three-fourths of the durum wheat grown in the United States is grown in North Dakota (Figure 14-13).

Although pasta may be prepared from little more than semolina and water, pasta products may include additional ingredients. Egg noodles, for example, must contain 5.5 percent egg solids to be called a noodle according to U.S. government regulation. Gaining in popularity are whole-grain pastas, and pasta made with green pea, chickpea, and lentil flours combined with semolina. These products provide more fiber and, if made with lentils, a higher protein content as well. These additional ingredients do have an impact on flavor, texture, and color of pasta compared to traditional formulations [46]. Spinach and tomato powders may also be used in some pasta products to produce distinctive colors and flavors.

Manufacture of Pasta

In the commercial manufacture of pasta, the flour is mixed with water in large mixers under vacuum. If additional ingredients are used to produce a specialty pasta, it is added during the mixing phase. The tough dough produced during mixing is then shaped into the characteristic shapes by being (1) forced or "extruded" through dies, or (2) cut out of flat sheets of dough. Macaroni, for example, is forced through a die with a steel pin in the center to produce a hollow rod. A notch on one side of the rod causes the dough to curve as it passes through. Dough forced through dies are cut into the desired length by a revolving knife [20].

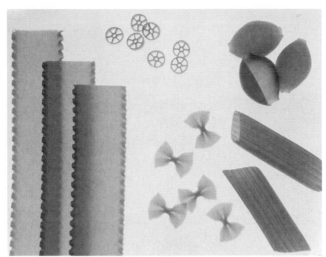

Lasagne, wagon wheels, bow ties, manicotti, and jumbo shells.

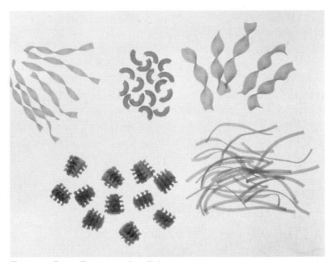

Egg noodles, elbows, and radiatore.

Fettuccine, linguine, spaghetti, thin spaghetti, and angel hair.

Penne, rotini, rigatoni, medium shells, and ziti.

FIGURE 14-12 Pasta comes in many shapes and sizes. *(Courtesy of National Pasta Association)*

FIGURE 14-13 Several types of pasta are shown with their main ingredient—durum wheat.
(Courtesy of Wheat Foods Council)

Next, the pasta is dried in dryers that may be as long as 320 feet. The temperature and humidity is carefully controlled during drying to produce high-quality pasta. Drying that is too rapid may result in pasta that breaks easily. The conventional drying process takes place at approximate temperatures of 140°F (60°C), but the high-temperature process uses temperatures above 212°F (100°C) [13]. Prior to the development of machines that can carefully control the drying of pasta, it was hung on racks to dry in the sun [19].

Preparation of Pasta

Macaroni, spaghetti, and other pastas are cooked by adding the pasta to boiling water, which is usually salted. Approximately 2 to 3 quarts of boiling water are used for 8 ounces of pasta product. The more water used, the less likely it is that the pasta will stick together, thus it is important to use an adequate amount of water. Addition of a small amount of oil to the cooking water may also help to keep the pasta pieces separate. The pasta should be added gradually so that the water continues to boil rapidly. Cooking continues in an uncovered pan with occasional stirring until the pasta is tender yet firm to the bite. The standard for final cooking is called *al dente* (to the tooth). If the pasta is to be further baked or simmered with other ingredients, it should be cooked until almost tender. Cooking then is completed after the pasta is combined with the other ingredients.

Pasta generally increases 2 to 2.5 times its original volume on cooking, although the amount varies with the type of shape of the pasta being prepared. Because of the very high protein content of the flour used in the manufacture of pastas of good quality, form is almost always retained on cooking. If cooking time is excessive, however, the pasta will become soft, sticky, and may break up.

When the boiling process is complete, the pasta should be drained thoroughly in a colander or strainer. Enriched pasta should not be rinsed in water after cooking to avoid the loss of vitamins and minerals. If cooked pasta must be held a while before serving, it may be placed over hot water in a strainer. Steam will keep the product hot and moist without further cooking. Stickiness is reduced by this procedure, compared with overcooking.

Pasta can be designed especially for use in microwave ovens. Most conventional pastas are too thick to be cooked properly and uniformly by microwaves and will not achieve the desired firm texture. Microwaveable pasta has thinner walls and has additional ingredients such as egg albumen [18]. The additional protein helps to form an insoluble network that traps starch granules and controls gelatinization more effectively [13].

Fresh or high-moisture pasta packaged in barrier trays under a modified atmosphere is being marketed successfully as a convenience food, along with companion sauces [13]. Because microbial safety is not ensured by the modified atmosphere packaging alone, care must be taken to keep the product refrigerated after it has been processed and packaged under carefully controlled conditions.

The variety of dishes that can be prepared with macaroni products is almost endless: soups, salads, main dishes, meat accompaniments, and even desserts can be prepared with pasta (Plates III, IV). For example, pasta may be combined with flavorful roasted vegetables or with fruits in dishes such as pasta salad with pineapple-mint salsa [25]. Pasta may also be used in dishes with hot and spicy ingredients including peppers and cayenne. Fish and seafood pair nicely with pasta. Traditional Italian sauces are not the only way to serve pasta as a main course.

FOCUS ON SCIENCE

Why Does Pasta Maintain Its Shape When Cooked?

Protein and starch in semolina play an important part in allowing pasta to maintain its shape when cooked. During cooking, the starch granules swell rapidly and tend to disperse and in part become soluble. The proteins, on the contrary, become completely insoluble and coagulate, creating a netlike structure around the starch. Because these mechanisms occur approximately at the same temperatures, the more rapidly the proteins form the netlike structure, the more limited will be the swelling of the starch. The starch components will remain trapped inside the protein network ensuring a firm consistency and absence of stickiness. If the protein is of poor quality, the starch granules will not be confined, and the soluble material will pass into the cooking liquid, producing a product that will be sticky and of poor consistency.

Source: Pagani, M. A., Lucisano, M., & Mariotti, M. (2007). Chapter 17: Traditional Italian Products from Wheat and Other Starchy Products. In *Handbook of Food Products Manufacturing*, (edited by Y. H. Hui), p. 327. Hoboken, NJ: John Wiley and Sons.

MULTICULTURAL CUISINE

Pasta—Reflecting Global Tastes?

Italians recognized a good thing when they adopted pasta as their national dish, but pasta is a favorite dish for many other nationalities also. Consumers in the United States eat pasta dishes more than once a week, and children eat more pasta than any other age group in this country [25].

Pasta—which simply means "dough" or "paste"—adapts itself to the unique flavoring spices and sauces of a wide variety of cuisines. Recipes utilizing pasta have been formulated by the thousands. To examine some of these, visit the National Pasta Association website at http://www.ilovepasta. org. As you browse through the many delectable recipes and photographs offered, your mouth may water in anticipation. Here are some of the tastes of many different cultures:

- *Sicilian* stuffed shells feature jumbo shells stuffed with yellow raisins, green olives, onion, and three kinds of cheese—ricotta, mozzarella, and parmesan—baked in tomato sauce.

- Bow ties with *Asian* chicken uses a marinade of soy sauce, honey, lime juice, and mustard for cubes of skinless chicken breast, before blending this mixture with the bow tie–shaped pasta.

- A *Japanese* pasta uses spaghetti with thin strips of flank steak, soy sauce, peppers, carrots, and scallions.

- *Thai* cuisine is represented in a recipe for linguine with spicy shrimp sauce. Ingredients in this dish include shrimp, red bell peppers, and scallions cooked in a mixture of sesame oil, chicken broth, red pepper flakes, jalapeño pepper, ground ginger, soy sauce, peanut butter, and white vinegar.

- A curried pasta salad, to be served cold, may remind you of *India*.

- Regional differences are represented in such recipes as *Tex-Mex* lasagna, which includes kidney beans and corn alongside chili seasoning and Monterey Jack cheese. A spicy Texas breakfast casserole, with egg noodles, sausage, eggs, cream of mushroom soup, diced tomatoes, and picante sauce should give even a Texan a good start for the day.

- There also is a pasta recipe with a Thanksgiving flavor that features radiatore with pumpkin sauce, turkey, and cranberries.

How about that? And all these recipes—and more—are available for trying. Enjoy your browsing! ■

CHAPTER SUMMARY

- Cereal grains are seeds of the grass family. *Cereal* refers to a large group of foods made from grains including flours, meals, breads, and alimentary pastes or pasta.

- All whole grains have a similar structure: outer bran coats, a germ, and a starchy endosperm portion. In the milling of white flour, the bran and aleurone layer is removed leaving the endosperm.

- The nutritive value of cereal products varies with the part of the grain that is used and the method of processing. Enriched flour, according to legal definition, is white flour to which specified B vitamins and iron have been added.

- Whole grains are cereal grains with the endosperm, germ, and bran present in the same relative proportions as in the intact grain. At least half of the grains consumed daily should be from whole grains.

- A variety of forms of wheat, in addition to flour, are available to consumers and include bulgur, wheat berries, and cracked wheat. Six different classes of wheat exist with durum wheat the preferred type for making macaroni and other pasta.

- The corn kernel is versatile and can take a great variety of forms. Hominy is produced when the corn kernel endosperm is freed of the bran. Hominy grits are made from breaking the hominy into fairly small pieces. Corn is also milled into cornmeal and cornstarch.

- Rice is one of the most used of all cereal grains. Rice may be long-, medium-, or short-grain. Aromatic rice varieties have a flavor and aroma similar to roasted nuts or popcorn.

- Rice may be processed to produce brown, polished white rice, enriched rice, parboiled or converted rice, instant or precooked rice, or rice flour. White rice may be enriched, and if so, it should not be rinsed before cooking or after cooking.

- Oats are utilized in a rolled form as both old-fashioned and quick-cooking products. In the processing of oats, most of the germ and the bran remain with the endosperm. Oat kernels with the outer hulls removed are called *groats*.

- Rye is used in the United States chiefly as flour, but it is also available as rye flakes and as pearled grain. Rye flour is available in three grades: light, medium, and dark.

- Barley is used as pearled barley and as malted barley. Pearling is the process that removes the outer husk of barley. Malted barley is used for making beer and other beverages.

- Wild rice is not true rice, but the hulled and unmilled grain of a reedlike water plant. Triticale is a hybrid plant produced by crossing wheat and rye. Buckwheat is the seed of a herbaceous plant but is commonly considered a grain product because it can be made into flour. Quinoa is a small seed which may be cooked like rice or ground into flour.

- A wide variety of breakfast cereals are made from grains. Raw cereals that are cooked in home and foodservice kitchens include whole grains, cracked or crushed grains, granular products made from either the whole grain or the endosperm, and rolled or flaked whole grains.

- Ready-to-eat cereals are produced using processes that include shredding, puffing, granulating, flaking, and extruding. Sweetening agents, salt, flavoring, coloring agents, antioxidants, vitamins, and minerals are ingredients commonly added to ready-to-eat cereals.

- The main purposes of cereal cookery are to improve palatability and digestibility. The time required for the cooking of cereals are influenced by the size of the particle, the amount of water used, the presence or absence of bran, the temperature, and the method used.

- Rice is cooked in about two times the volume of water compared to the volume of rice. Regular rice increases to about three times its volume in cooking. Brown rice takes about twice as long to cook as white rice.

- The principal ingredient in the making of pasta is semolina flour that is ground from durum wheat. Pasta also may include eggs and other optional ingredients.

- Macaroni, spaghetti, and other pastas are cooked by adding the pasta to boiling water. Approximately 2 to 3 quarts of boiling water are used for 8 ounces of pasta. Pasta generally increases 2 to 2.5 times its original volume on cooking. The standard for the final cooking is called al dente.

STUDY QUESTIONS

1. Name the most important cereal grains used for food.

2. The structures of all grains are somewhat similar.

   (a) Name three major parts of a grain. Describe the general chemical composition of each part.

   (b) What is the *aleurone* of a cereal grain? Describe its general composition and indicate where it usually goes during the milling of grain.

3. (a) What is meant by *enrichment* of cereals and flours? What nutrients must be added to meet the standards of the federal government?

   (b) Compare the general nutritional value of refined unenriched, enriched, and whole-grain cereal products.

4. Cereal grains are often processed in preparation for use. Indicate which grains are commonly used to make the following products. Briefly describe the processes involved in preparing the grain.

   (a) Uncooked breakfast cereals

   (b) Prepared breakfast cereals

   (c) Flour

   (d) Meal

   (e) Hominy

   (f) Grits

   (g) Pasta

5. What are the main purposes for cooking cereals?

6. Suggest appropriate methods for cooking each of the following cereal products. Explain why these methods are appropriate.

   (a) Granular cereals such as farina and cornmeal

   (b) Rolled oats

   (c) Rice

   (d) Macaroni or spaghetti

7. Describe the general processes involved in the production of each of the following types of ready-to-eat cereal.

   (a) Puffed

   (b) Flaked

   (c) Granulated

   (d) Shredded

   (e) Extruded

8. Discuss several factors to consider when purchasing cereals.

BATTERS AND DOUGHS 15

Batters and doughs, sometimes called *flour mixtures*, include a large variety of baked products such as muffins, biscuits and other quick breads, pastry, shortened and unshortened cakes, cookies, and breads. Producing the final result desired in a flour mixture depends on such factors as accuracy in measurements or weights (Chapter 5), skill in manipulation, control of oven or other temperatures, and knowledge about the kinds and proportions of ingredients used. The principal ingredients used in foundation formulas for doughs and batters are flour, liquid, fat, egg, sugar, leavening agent, and salt. Flavoring substances are added to some types of mixtures. Fat replacers and alternative sweeteners are important ingredients in reduced-fat or reduced-calorie items.

A so-called standard product may vary somewhat, depending on individual preferences; however, it is important to learn what characteristics are generally preferred in various baked products and what proportions of ingredients and techniques of mixing might be used to achieve these characteristics. Understanding ingredients and mixing methods will allow the production of the "standard" you desire.

In this chapter, the following topics will be discussed:

- Basic ingredients including flour, leavening agents, fat, liquids, eggs, sugar, and other sweeteners
- Classification, mixing methods, and structure of batters and doughs
- Dry flour mixes
- Baking at high altitudes

FLOUR

Wheat is the principal grain used in the United States for flour. White wheat flour is defined by the U.S. Food and Drug Administration (FDA) as a food made by grinding and sifting cleaned wheat (Figure 15-1). The flour is freed from the bran and germ of the wheat kernel so that specifications for moisture, ash or minerals, and protein content are met. Because of its protein and starch content, flour provides structure and body in baked flour products.

Classes of Wheat

Wheat may be classified on the (a) color of the kernel, (b) hardness or softness of the kernel, and (c) basis of the time of planting or the growing season. Some wheat kernels have a reddish appearance and are called *red wheat*. Wheat with comparatively white kernels is called *white wheat*. A hard wheat has a hard, vitreous kernel, whereas a *soft wheat* appears to be more powdery. Hard wheats are usually higher in protein than soft wheats, and the protein has more baking strength when flour from this wheat is made into dough. Therefore, flour from hard wheat is especially good for bread making.

Wheat varieties planted in the spring and harvested in the fall are called *spring wheat*, whereas those that are planted in the fall and harvested the following summer are called *winter wheat*. Winter wheat varieties are grown in areas with relatively mild weather because these wheats remain in the ground all winter. Winter wheats may be hard, semihard, or soft. Hard winter wheats have a fairly strong quality of protein and are suitable for bread-making purposes. Spring wheats include hard red varieties, hard white and soft white varieties, and durum wheats, which are used for the production of macaroni products.

The geographical areas in which most of the hard spring wheats are produced are the north central part of the United States and western Canada. Hard winter wheats are grown mainly in the middle central states. Soft winter wheat is grown east of the Mississippi River and in the Pacific Northwest. Because climatic and soil conditions affect the composition of wheat, wide variations can be expected within these classes. Wheat was also discussed in Chapter 14.

a Kernel of Wheat

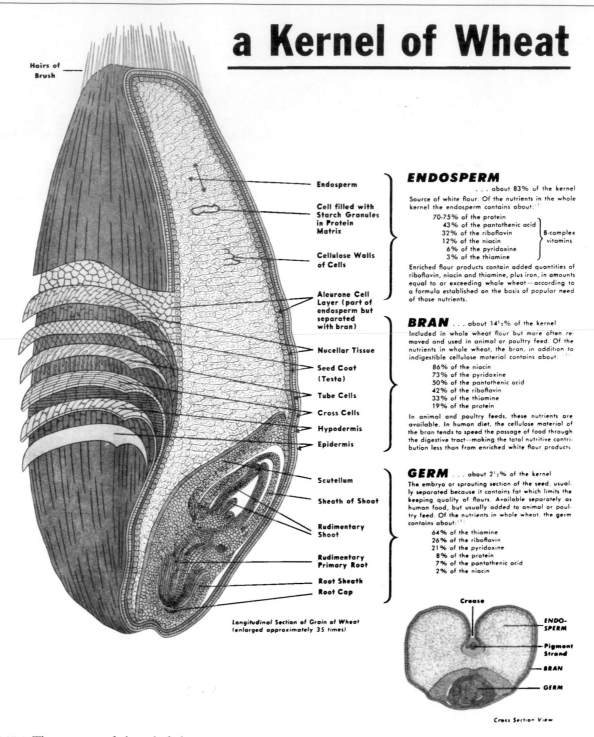

Hairs of Brush

Endosperm

Cell filled with Starch Granules in Protein Matrix

Cellulose Walls of Cells

Aleurone Cell Layer (part of endosperm but separated with bran)

Nucellar Tissue

Seed Coat (Testa)

Tube Cells

Cross Cells

Hypodermis

Epidermis

Scutellum

Sheath of Shoot

Rudimentary Shoot

Rudimentary Primary Root

Root Sheath
Root Cap

Longitudinal Section of Grain of Wheat
(enlarged approximately 35 times)

ENDOSPERM
... about 83% of the kernel

Source of white flour. Of the nutrients in the whole kernel the endosperm contains about:[1]

70-75% of the protein
43% of the pantothenic acid
32% of the riboflavin   B-complex
12% of the niacin   vitamins
6% of the pyridoxine
3% of the thiamine

Enriched flour products contain added quantities of riboflavin, niacin and thiamine, plus iron, in amounts equal to or exceeding whole wheat—according to a formula established on the basis of popular need of those nutrients.

BRAN ... about 14½% of the kernel

Included in whole wheat flour but more often removed and used in animal or poultry feed. Of the nutrients in whole wheat, the bran, in addition to indigestible cellulose material contains about:[1]

86% of the niacin
73% of the pyridoxine
50% of the pantothenic acid
42% of the riboflavin
33% of the thiamine
19% of the protein

In animal and poultry feeds, these nutrients are available. In human diet, the cellulose material of the bran tends to speed the passage of food through the digestive tract—making the total nutritive contribution less than from enriched white flour products.

GERM ... about 2½% of the kernel

The embryo or sprouting section of the seed, usually separated because it contains fat which limits the keeping quality of flours. Available separately as human food, but usually added to animal or poultry feed. Of the nutrients in whole wheat, the germ contains about:[1]

64% of the thiamine
26% of the riboflavin
21% of the pyridoxine
8% of the protein
7% of the pantothenic acid
2% of the niacin

Crease

ENDO-SPERM

Pigment Strand

BRAN

GERM

Cross Section View

FIGURE 15-1 The structure of a kernel of wheat. *(Courtesy of the Wheat Flour Institute)*

Milling

The milling of white flour is a process that involves separating the endosperm from the bran and germ and subdividing it into a fine flour. Many years ago, white flours were made by sifting wheat that had been ground in a stone mill. This method of separation yielded flour that was generally less white and of poorer baking quality than the flour produced in today's mills, where the wheat

passes through a series of rollers. The basic steps of milling include the following:

- Cleaning—dirt, stones, weed seeds, and other debris are removed
- Tempering—moisture levels are adjusted to facilitate the separation of the bran, endosperm, and germ

- Break—kernels are crushed between rollers to loosen the endosperm
- Separation and sifting—sieves and air currents are used to separate the finely ground endosperm from coarse particles as well as the bran and germ
- Grinding—the coarse endosperm (also called **middlings**) is ground into flour by reduction rollers [4]

The break, separation, and grinding steps are repeated to produce various streams of flour. Flour produced later in the process will contain less endosperm and more bran and germ than previous streams. Flour grades are determined by which streams are included in the final flour. The major steps in milling are shown in Figure 15-2.

The wheat kernel is divided into three main parts approximately as follows: 83 percent endosperm, 14.5 percent bran layers (including the aleurone layer), and 2.5 percent germ [15]. The endosperm contains many starch granules embedded in a cell matrix that includes protein (Figure 15-3). When the parts of the wheat kernel are not separated and the whole kernel is ground, the flour resulting from this process is called *whole wheat, entire wheat,* or *graham* flour.

Because the endosperm represents approximately 83 percent of the total kernel, about that same amount of white flour should theoretically be obtained by milling. In actual practice, however, only 72 to 75 percent is separated as white flour. The separation of endosperm from bran and germ is neither a simple nor an extremely efficient process. The inner bran layers and the germ are tightly bound to the endosperm, and it is impossible to make a complete separation. The usual 72 to 75 percent extraction produces white flour containing essentially no bran and germ and exhibiting good baking properties. In times of national emergency, the usual percentage of extraction has been increased as a conservation measure. It has been suggested that the regular extraction rate of white flour could be increased up to 80 percent without sacrificing baking quality [21].

Grades of Flour

The miller grades white flour on the basis of which streams of flour are combined. The grade may be confirmed by measuring ash content because bran is high in minerals [4]. *Patent* flours are the highest quality of commercial flours, coming from the more refined portion of the endosperm from the first streams of flour produced during milling [7]. Patent flours are essentially free of bran and germ and thus are whitest in color. Different grades of patent flour are available with the highest quality called *extra short* or *fancy patent*. Patent flour can be made from any class of wheat.

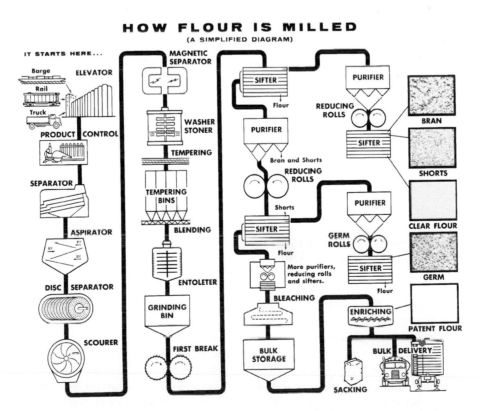

FIGURE 15-2 Steps involved in the milling of flour. Flour is sifted at various times during milling, and after each sifting, some of the flour stream may be removed. *(Courtesy of the Wheat Flour Institute)*

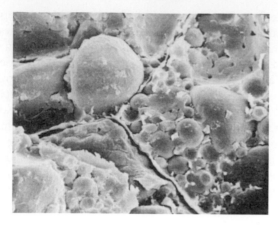

FIGURE 15-3 A scanning electron micrograph (2,100 ×) of fractured wheat endosperm cells showing small and large starch granules embedded in the cell matrix. *(Reprinted from Freeman, T. P., and Shelton, D. R. Microstructure of wheat starch: From kernel to bread.* Food Technology, *45: 165(3), 1991. Copyright © by Institute of Food Technologists. Photograph supplied by Thomas P. Freeman)*

Straight grade theoretically should contain all of the flour streams resulting from the milling process, but actually 2 to 3 percent of the poorest streams are withheld. Very little flour on the market is straight grade. *Clear grade* is made from streams withheld in the making of patent flours and is high in ash compared to patent flours. Clear-grade flours may be first clear or second clear with the second clear-grade having the highest ash content.

Maturing and Bleaching of Flour

White flours may be bleached or treated with additives to mature the flour. These processes favorably affect the baking properties of flours.

Maturing.   When freshly milled flour is used to bake bread, the result is a loaf of relatively low volume and coarse texture. A loaf with higher volume and finer texture can be made from the same flour after it has had an opportunity to mature or age. *Aging* involves simply holding or storing the flour for several weeks or months. During this time, not only does the flour lighten in color because the carotenoid pigments are being oxidized, but the baking quality also improves. The oxidation of portions of the glutenin and gliadin protein molecules, which occurs during aging, allows more bonds to form when gluten forms and thus results in higher quality breads [4]. Although the aging of white flour brings about both bleaching and maturing, these two processes are separate and distinct.

Bleaching.   Freshly milled, unbleached flour is yellowish in color, primarily because of the presence of carotenoid pigments. If this flour is held for a time, the yellow color becomes lighter. It is bleached because the yellow pigments gradually become oxidized. Instead of storing flour to permit natural oxidation, bleaching agents may be used. Benzoyl peroxide and chlorine are commonly used. Chlorine is used predominately in cake flours because it will weaken gluten and allow the starch to absorb water more easily which is desirable in cakes [4].

Maturing and Bleaching Agents.   The addition of certain chemical substances to freshly milled flour produces effects similar to aging but in a much shorter period. This process saves the cost of storing the flour. The FDA permits the use of specified chemical substances, one being benzoyl peroxide, which is primarily a bleaching agent. Chlorine dioxide, chlorine, and acetone peroxides have both a bleaching and a maturing effect. Azodicarbonamide may be added to flour as a maturing agent but does not react until the flour is made into a dough. Flour that has been treated with any of these chemicals must be labeled "bleached." Both bleached and unbleached flours are available to the consumer on the retail market.

Potassium bromide at one time was commonly used as a maturing agent. It strengthens the flour resulting in higher quality breads. Ascorbic acid, however, has gained favorability as an alternative due to safety concerns associated with potassium bromide.

Enrichment of Flour

Enriched flour is white flour to which has been added specified B vitamins (thiamin, riboflavin, niacin, and folic acid) and iron. Vitamin D and calcium are optional additions. Many states have laws requiring enrichment of flour and cereals, which is mandatory for those flour and cereal products that enter interstate commerce. Enrichment was discussed in Chapter 14.

Protein in Flour and Gluten Formation

Wheat flour is commonly used for bread baking in part because of proteins in wheat that form gluten when flour is mixed with water. The type of flour, other ingredients, and the mixing procedure for various baked goods are chosen in large part either to develop gluten, as in yeast breads, or to limit gluten development as in delicate cakes and pastries.

Proteins in Flour.   Various proteins have been extracted from wheat. Using the Osborne classification, wheat proteins include the more soluble albumins and globulins, and the insoluble gliadin, and glutenin. Albumins and globulins do not appear to play major roles in baking. Gliadin and glutenin, however, when moistened with water and thoroughly mixed or kneaded, form gluten, which is primarily responsible for the viscous and elastic characteristics as well as high loaf volume of wheat flour doughs [2, 7, 11]. The amino acids proline and glutamine, found in gluten, also appear to have an impact on dough development [3].

When the gliadin and glutenin fractions are separated from each other, the gliadin fraction is found to be a syrupy substance that can bind the mass together. It has little or no resistance to extension and may be responsible for the viscous properties of the dough. The glutenin fraction exhibits toughness and rubberiness (Figure 15-4). It resists the extension of the dough and contributes to elasticity [7].

Gluten Formation. Gluten is formed when the proteins found in flour—gliadin and glutenin—are hydrated with water and mixed. During the mixing of a dough, the long strands of glutenin are aligned in the direction of mixing and interact with gliadin molecules to form a strong, elastic, uniform film that envelops the starch granules in the mixture (Figure 15-5). As gluten develops, it becomes more difficult to stretch yet is more elastic and strong with the ability to "spring back" [4]. If a bread dough is overmixed, the gluten strands may tear and the gluten network will break down resulting in a soft and sticky dough unable to retain leavening gases [4]. Overmixing is most likely to occur when mixing mechanically with a mixer rather than when kneading by hand.

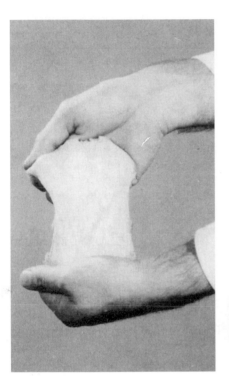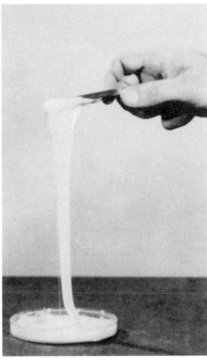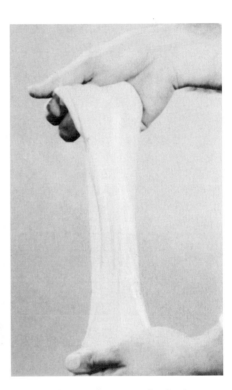

FIGURE 15-4 The glutenin fraction gives elasticity to dough (left); the gliadin fraction provides fluidity, stickiness, and cohesiveness (center); and gluten is a blend of both proteins (right). *(Courtesy of Baker's Digest and R. J. Dimler)*

FOCUS ON SCIENCE

Gluten Proteins

Gliadin and glutenin are the two proteins that make up gluten. Gliadin has a molecular weight of 30,000 to 80,000, whereas glutenin has a molecular weight ranging from approximately 80,000 up to the millions.

The glutenin protein is a "heavy-duty worker" in the dough. A variety of glutenin subunits are crosslinked by disulfide bonds which enhances the strength exhibited during mixing and the formation of the gluten structure [8]. Because of their large size, the glutenin protein forms a network that is mainly responsible for the elasticity and cohesive strength of the dough. The gliadin protein acts as a plasticizer and contributes mainly to viscosity, plasticity, and extensibility of the dough. The quality of these proteins in the wheat flour determine the bread-making performance because gluten quality depends on the gliadin : glutenin ratio of the proteins.

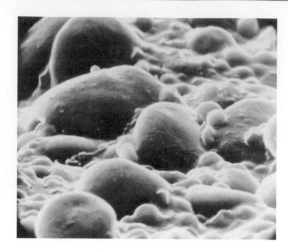

FIGURE 15-5 Scanning electron photomicrograph of a dough sample showing a developed gluten film covering starch granules of variable sizes. *(Reprinted from Varriano-Marston, E. A comparison of dough preparation procedures for scanning electron microscopy.* Food Technology, *31: 34(10), 1977. Copyright © by Institute of Food Technologists)*

The development of gluten requires an appropriate amount of water to form a dough. Adequate water is necessary to hydrate gliadin and glutenin. Large amounts of water will dilute these proteins, however, and prevent or reduce gluten development. As air and carbon dioxide gas bubbles are incorporated in the dough, a foam is produced. Interactions probably also occur in the dough between gluten proteins and lipids and other dough components as well [12]. Wheat-flour dough is a complex but interesting phenomenon.

Gluten Extraction. Gluten can be extracted from a flour-and-water dough that has been vigorously kneaded by thorough washing of the dough with cool water to remove the starch (Figure 15-6). When most of the starch has been removed from the dough, the water will be clear. The moist gluten thus extracted has elastic and cohesive properties similar to those of chewing gum.

Types of Wheat Flour

It is important to understand the differences in composition and characteristics of wheat flours in order to use them most effectively. Within certain limits, various types of flour may be interchanged in different recipes by altering the proportions of the nonflour constituents of the mixture. One of the factors that varies with different types of flours is the protein level. The percentage of protein for several types of wheat flour are provided in Table 15-1. The composition and nutritive value of some wheat flours are given in Appendix C.

Whole-Wheat Flour. Whole-wheat flour also may be called *graham* flour or *entire wheat* flour. It contains essentially the entire wheat kernel and may be ground to different degrees of fineness. The keeping quality of whole-wheat flour is lower than that of white flour, because it contains fat from the germ that may be oxidized on storage. Flour ground from freshly harvested wheat in home grinders may be stored at room temperature up to a month before rancidity develops and sensory quality decreases [6].

Whole-wheat flour is higher in fiber than white flour because it contains the bran. Although whole-wheat flour has a relatively high protein level, less gluten is formed; thus, whole-wheat doughs typically are denser and coarser than breads made with refined white flour. Gluten formation is negatively affected by the sharp bran particles that cut gluten strands and components in the germ that interfere with gluten development [4].

FIGURE 15-6 Gluten can be extracted from a flour-and-water dough by washing it carefully with cold water to remove the starch. The amounts and characteristics of gluten from various flours can thus be compared. Pictured are samples of unbaked and baked gluten. (Left) Cake flour; (center) all-purpose flour; (right) bread flour. The size of the gluten balls corresponds with the level of protein in the designated flour. *(Courtesy of the Wheat Flour Institute)*

Gluten-Free Diets

People who have *Celiac disease* (sometimes called gluten-sensitive enteropathy) must avoid foods containing gluten. For these individuals, an autoimmune response results in the production of antibodies that attack and damage the intestinal tract. Celiac disease tends to "run in families" although research into the causes and treatment are ongoing.

Given the important role of gluten in baking, what are the implications of a gluten-free diet? First of all, foods containing gluten must be avoided. Thus, wheat, rye, barley, spelt, kamut, and triticale grains, which form gluten, should not be used. In place of these grains, rice flour, potato starch, and tapioca flour may be used. Although baked foods made with these alternative flours may have some different characteristics than those made with wheat flour, a variety of resources and recipes is available to help those following a gluten-free diet to enjoy a wide variety of foods—including baked goods.

Check out these recipes from the Celiac Sprue Association and Land O' Lakes websites:

http://www.csaceliacs.org/recipes.php
http://www.landolakes.com/mealideas/
gluten-free-baking-recipes.cfm ■

TABLE 15-1 Percent of Protein Found in Various Types of Wheat Flour

Flour Type	Percent of Protein
Gluten flour	40–45
Durum flour	12.0–15.0
Bread flour	11.5–13.5
Whole wheat	11.0–14.0
All-purpose flour	9.5–11.5
Pastry flour	7.0–9.5
Cake flour	6.0–8.0
Vital wheat gluten	"Vital wheat gluten" is not considered flour, but instead an ingredient that may be added to "strengthen" doughs. It contains about 75 percent protein which can form gluten. It should not be confused with gluten flour.

Source: References 4, 22

Whole white wheat flour, produced from hard white winter wheat, is gaining in popularity. Due to a special milling technology, whole white wheat flour has a softer, smoother texture as compared to traditional whole-wheat flours produced from red wheat [17].

Bread Flour. Bread flour is a white flour made chiefly from hard wheat. It contains a relatively high percentage of protein that develops into gluten. Gluten contributes very strong, elastic properties when the flour is made into a dough. Bread flour has a slightly granular feel when touched and does not form a firm mass when pressed in the hand. It may be bleached or unbleached. Bread flour is used by commercial and foodservice bakers for yeast breads and also is available for use in the home kitchen. It produces breads of relatively high volume and fine texture with an elastic crumb.

All-Purpose Flour. A white flour, all-purpose flour is usually made from a blend of wheats to yield a protein

FOCUS ON SCIENCE

Why May Whole-Wheat Flour Become Rancid?

Whole flour contains the bran, germ, and endosperm. Lipoygenase and unsaturated fatty acids are present in the germ. Lipoygenase causes free fatty acids to occur and, at the same time, supplies oxygen to the unsaturated fatty acid. Consequently, rancidity, off-flavors, and aromas may develop in whole-wheat flour.

content lower than that of bread flour. It contains enough protein that it can be used for making yeast bread and rolls under household conditions. Foodservice operations, however, generally use a bread flour. All-purpose flour is used for making quick breads. The gluten that develops in doughs made from all-purpose flour is less strong and elastic than that produced in bread-flour doughs. All-purpose flour may be used for making pastry, cookies, and certain cakes. It usually has too high a protein content to make a delicate, fine-textured cake.

Pastry Flour. Primarily used in commercial baking, white pastry flour is usually made from soft wheat and contains a lower percentage of protein than is found in all-purpose flour. Its chief use is for baking pastries and cookies.

Cake Flour. Prepared from soft wheat, cake flour usually contains only the most highly refined streams of flour from the milling process and is a short patent grade of flour. The protein content of cake flour is very low in comparison with other types of flour. Cake flour is bleached with chlorine not only to whiten the flour but also to reduce gluten development [4, 14]. So finely milled that it feels soft and satiny, rather than a granular texture, cake flour forms a firm mass when pressed in the hand. The high starch content and weak quality of gluten produced from cake flour make it desirable chiefly for the preparation of delicate and fine-textured cakes.

Instantized Flour. Also called *instant, instant-blending,* or *quick-mixing* flour, instantized flour is a granular all-purpose flour that has been processed by moistening and then redrying to aggregate small particles into larger particles or agglomerates. The agglomerated particles are of relatively uniform size and do not pack; therefore, this flour does not require sifting before measuring. It flows freely without dust, is easily measured, and blends more readily with liquid than regular flour. Instantized flour is most useful when blended dry with a liquid, such as in the thickening of gravies and certain sauces. Some changes should be made in formulas and preparation procedures if this flour is substituted for regular flour in baked products.

Self-Rising Flour. Leavening agents and salt are added to self-rising flour in proportions desirable for baking. Typically, one cup of self-rising flour will contain 1 1/2 teaspoons of baking powder and 1/2 teaspoon of salt [22]. Monocalcium phosphate is the acid salt most commonly added in combination with sodium bicarbonate (baking soda) as leavening ingredients. Self-rising flours are popular for preparing quick breads, such as baking powder biscuits.

Gluten Flour. Wheat flour is mixed with dried extracted gluten to form gluten flour. This flour has a protein content of about 41 percent compared with the 10 to 14 percent protein content of most wheat flour. The gluten is extracted by the gentle washing of a flour-and-water dough and is dried under mild conditions to minimize any effects on its viscoelastic properties. Gluten that retains its desirable baking qualities is sometimes called *vital wheat gluten.* Gluten flour is used by the baking industry to adjust the protein level in various doughs. Gluten may also be used in breakfast foods.

Other Wheat Products

Cracked wheat, although not a flour, is used extensively in baking breads and quick breads. It should be soaked in double its volume of water for 24 hours before use. Cracked wheat may be combined in varying proportions with whole-wheat or white flour. Rolled wheat is also used to make cookies and quick breads.

Wheat germ, which contains essentially all the fat from the wheat kernel, is available as yellowish tan flakes that may have been toasted. Raw wheat germ, containing up to 10 percent oil, begins to develop rancidity as soon as it is milled. It may be vacuum packed to control the oxidative changes that produce rancidity. A process that involves careful, controlled heating to inactivate the enzymes *lipase* and *peroxidase* which catalyze the oxidation of fat can produce a stabilized wheat germ with a six-month shelf life. Stabilized wheat germ retains its vitamin and mineral content, including the antioxidant vitamin, vitamin E. Wheat germ is a good source of B vitamins and iron. It may be added to both yeast and quick breads. Defatted wheat germ also is available. It is

FOCUS ON SCIENCE

More on All-Purpose Flour

All-purpose flour is made up of a blend of hard and soft wheat that can be used for all purposes—cakes, cookies, biscuits, pie crusts, and breads. The protein content of all-purpose flour averages about 11 percent. The actual protein content of all-purpose flour may differ from region to region and from brand to brand. Regional differences have influenced manufacturers to place more protein in flour sold in the northern United States, where yeast breads are more popular, than in flour sold in the South, where biscuits requiring softer flour are more routinely consumed.

stable and is a good source of protein, fiber, and certain vitamins and minerals.

Commercial applications for the use of wheat germ include crackers, breakfast cereals, variety breads, and snacks. The vitamin potency of wheat germ is not appreciably decreased by baking in the yeast breads that contain it; however, the germ has been found to exert a deleterious effect on the baking quality of flour. For this reason, a relatively strong flour is best used with the wheat germ. The germ may be substituted to the extent of one-fifth to one-third of the flour.

Flours and Meals Other Than Wheat Flour

Flours other than wheat are used in quick breads and yeast breads.

Rye Flour. The sifting of rye meal results in rye flour. It has some gluten-forming properties, but it contains chiefly gliadin with only small amounts of glutenin. Therefore, bread made from rye flour, although not necessarily soggy or heavy, is more compact and less elastic than bread made with wheat flour. Some white flour is often combined with rye flour in making bread to yield a lighter, more porous product than is possible with rye flour alone.

Cornmeal and Corn Flour. Cornmeal, a granular product made from either white or yellow corn, is commonly used in several types of quick breads. Its chief protein, *zein*, has none of the properties of the gluten of wheat. If a crumbly product is to be avoided, cornmeal must be combined with some white flour, preferably all-purpose flour, to bind it. Corn flour has the same properties as cornmeal except that it is finer. It is used chiefly in commercial pancake mixes and prepared cereals.

Soy Flour. Made from soybeans, which are legumes, soy flour is high in protein, although the protein has none of the characteristics of gluten. Soy flour must be used with a strong or moderately strong wheat flour for good results in the baking of breads. An important advantage of using soy flour in baked products is the contribution it makes to the amount and quality of the protein. In baked items, soy flour also promotes moisture retention,

HEALTHY EATING

Designer Fibers—Into the Mainstream?

Health-conscious Americans are becoming even more aware of the health benefits of dietary fiber. They emphasize its positive role in preventing constipation, improving desirable weight loss, helping to prevent heart disease by lowering blood cholesterol levels, and helping to prevent cancer. Many say that they are trying to increase their fiber intake but still are not meeting the Daily Value of 25 grams per day recommended on the Nutrition Facts food labels [19]. At any rate, fiber is "in"; it is "trendy" in food and nutrition circles.

The old dietary fiber was defined as "the remnants of edible plant cells, polysaccharides, lignin, and associated substances resistant to digestion by the alimentary enzymes of humans" [5]. This definition is now being expanded to include, somewhere in the definition, new compounds, not necessarily derived from plant cell walls, that are important in creating positive physiological changes in the body. For instance, the carbohydrates **inulin** and fructooligosaccharides may act as **prebiotics** in stimulating growth of desirable bacteria, such as bifidobacteria, in the intestine. These prebiotics, which might be called "designer" fibers, are now being added to a wide range of food products in Europe and Japan, including cookies, pasta, brioche, nutrition bars, puddings, and breakfast drinks.

There is a flurry across the globe of new product activity that includes trends toward oat drinks, rye-based heart-friendly products, and heart disease–preventative cereals or nutrition bars as part of a new world of exciting product options [19]. One company has patented the technology for producing a stabilized rice bran extract. This process captures the nutrient-rich, water-soluble portion of rice bran (which includes soluble **pentosans**) in a spray-dried powder that is stable to oxidative changes. This designer product is being marketed as a dough conditioner and emulsifier combined to give bakery products with high moisture, longer shelf life, and improved consumer acceptance [16].

With a new image for dietary fiber and a worldwide market, food technologists are eager to produce new designer ingredients. Watch for them! ■

improves crust color, and extends shelf life. Federal standards for commercial white breads permit the use of 3 percent soy flour as an optional ingredient.

Miscellaneous Flours. *Buckwheat flour* does not have the same baking properties as wheat flour and therefore is often used with wheat flour in recipes. The principal use of buckwheat is in pancakes and waffles. Some of the pancake batters are fermented to increase the flavor.

Triticale flour, made from the cereal that is a cross between wheat and rye, may be used to make yeast bread of satisfactory quality. Its flavor has been reported to be like that of a very mild rye bread [10].

Rice flour is fundamentally rice starch. It is a low-protein flour which does not produce gluten. *Potato flour* is used in some countries and, like rice flour, is chiefly starch.

Amaranth flour, made by grinding the tiny amaranth seed, is used in some areas of Latin America, Africa, and Asia. Amaranth is now being cultivated in limited amounts in the United States. Amaranth flour has a high content of the amino acid lysine, which is limited in wheat flour. It may make a valuable nutritional contribution when combined in wheat breads, cookies, and other baked products [18].

MAJOR LEAVENING GASES

To *leaven* means to "make light and porous." Most baked flour products today are leavened. This process is accomplished by incorporating or forming in the product a gas that expands during preparation and subsequent heating. Three major leavening gases are air, steam or water vapor, and carbon dioxide. In some flour mixtures, one of these leavening gases predominates, whereas in other products, two or three of the gases play important roles.

Air

Air is incorporated into flour mixtures by folding and rolling dough, by creaming fat and sugar together, or by beating batters. Beating whole eggs will add some air, but the beating of egg whites can add a significant amount of air. In common practice, some air is incorporated into all flour mixtures.

Steam

Because all flour mixtures contain some water and are usually heated so that the water vaporizes, steam leavens all flour mixtures to a certain degree. Some products leavened almost entirely by steam are popovers, cream puffs, and éclairs (Figure 15-7). These mixtures have a high percentage of liquid, and baking is started at a high oven temperature, which rapidly causes steam to form. Because one volume of water increases more than 1,600 times when converted into steam, it has tremendous leavening power. The water available for conversion to steam may be added

FIGURE 15-7 The rapid expansion of the dough leaves a large air hole in éclairs that may be filled with pastry cream.

as liquid or as a component of other ingredients, such as eggs. Egg whites contain enough water to furnish two to three times more expansion in baking angel food cakes than the air that was added by beating. Even stiff doughs, such as pie crust, are partially leavened by steam.

Carbon Dioxide

Carbon dioxide may be produced in a flour mixture either by a biological process or by a purely chemical reaction. The biological production of carbon dioxide is usually because of the action of yeast. Bacteria, in some recipes, may be another source of biological carbon dioxide production. Baking powder and baking soda are chemical leavening agents which are commonly used to produce carbon dioxide in baked goods.

LEAVENING AGENTS

Yeast and Bacteria

Carbon dioxide is produced by the action of yeast and certain bacteria on sugar in a process called **fermentation**. Yeast ferments sugar to form ethyl alcohol and carbon dioxide. The alcohol is volatilized by the heat of baking. The fermentation is catalyzed by a mixture of many enzymes produced by the yeast cells. Sugar is usually added to yeast-flour mixtures to speed fermentation and the production of carbon dioxide gas. If no sugar is used, yeast can form gas slowly from the small amount of sugar that is present in flour. **Maltose** also is produced in flour from the action of **amylase** as it hydrolyzes starch. **Maltase**, an enzyme produced by yeast, then hydrolyzes the maltose to yield glucose, which is available for fermentation by the yeast. The use of yeast in leavening is discussed further in Chapter 17.

Certain bacteria also may produce leavening gas in flour mixtures. One type produces hydrogen and carbon dioxide gases in salt-rising bread. Although the organisms occur normally in the cornmeal used to make the sponge for salt-rising bread, they have, in addition, been isolated and put on the market as a starter for this type of bread. Sourdough bread also uses bacteria in producing leavening gas.

FOCUS ON SCIENCE

to stand overnight to ferment in a warm place, preferably between 90° and 100°F (32° and 38°C). This is the leavening agent that will be required for the bread; therefore, yeast in the conventional way is not used in salt-rising bread.

What Is Salt-Rising Bread?

Salt-rising bread is leavened by the fermentation of a salt-tolerant bacterium in cornmeal. The cornmeal must be stone ground. A mixture of cornmeal, milk, and sugar is allowed

Baking Soda

Sodium bicarbonate (baking soda) in a flour mixture gives off carbon dioxide (CO_2) gas when heated in accordance with the reaction

$$2NaHCO_3 + heat \rightarrow Na_2CO_3 + CO_2 + H_2O$$

sodium   sodium   carbon   water
bicarbonate   carbonate   dioxide

However, the sodium carbonate (Na_2CO_3) residue from this reaction has a disagreeable flavor and produces a yellow color in light-colored baked products. Brown spots also may occur in the cooked product if the soda is not finely powdered or is not uniformly distributed throughout the flour.

To avoid the problem of a bitter, soapy-flavored residue in the baked product, sodium bicarbonate is combined with various acids to release carbon dioxide gas. The flavor of the residue remaining after the gas is released depends on the particular acid involved in the reaction. The salts formed with many acids are not objectionable in flavor.

The following food ingredients contain acids and may be combined with soda in flour mixtures to release carbon dioxide gas:

> Buttermilk or sour milk (containing lactic acid)
>
> Molasses (containing a mixture of organic acids)
>
> Brown sugar (which has a small amount of molasses coating the sugar crystals)
>
> Honey
>
> Citrus fruit juices (containing citric and other organic acids)
>
> Applesauce and other fruits
>
> Vinegar (containing acetic acid)
>
> Cream of tartar (potassium acid tartrate)

The optimum amount of soda to combine with an acid food in a recipe depends on the degree of acidity of that food. The acid-containing foods listed vary in acidity and yield variable results when combined with soda; however, the usual amount of soda to combine with 1 cup of

buttermilk or fully soured milk is 1/2 teaspoon. Less soda is required for milk that is less sour. Because the pronounced flavor of molasses may mask any undesirable flavor resulting from an excess of soda, up to 1 teaspoon of soda is often recommended for use with 1 cup of molasses, but less may be used. The acidity of honey and of brown sugar is too low to allow their use in flour mixtures as the only source of acid to combine with soda.

Cream of tartar is an acid salt (potassium acid tartrate) and may be combined with soda to produce carbon dioxide gas when the mixture is moistened. The salt that is left as a residue in this reaction (sodium potassium tartrate) is not objectionable in flavor. The chemical reaction between cream of tartar and soda is

$$HKC_4H_4O_6 + NaHCO_3 \rightarrow NaKC_4H_4O_6$$

cream of   sodium   sodium potassium
tartar   bicarbonate   tartrate
$$+ CO_2 + H_2O$$
carbon   water
dioxide

Baking Powder

Baking powders, like baking soda, produce carbon dioxide to leaven baked goods. Baking powders were developed as one of the first convenience foods containing mixtures of dry acid or acid salts and baking soda. Importantly, *all baking powders are composed of soda plus an acid ingredient.* The carbon dioxide gas (CO_2) comes from the soda. Starch is added to standardize the mixture and help stabilize the components so premature reactions are avoided. Baking powders have been classified into different groups or types depending on the acid constituent used; however, not all types are available to the consumer.

According to federal law, all types of baking powders must contain at least 12 percent available CO_2 gas. Those powders manufactured for home use generally contain 14 percent, and some powders for commercial use have 17 percent available gas. Baking powder containers should always be kept tightly covered to avoid the absorption of moisture that causes the acid and alkali constituents to react prematurely with the loss of some carbon dioxide.

Double-Acting Baking Powder

The type of baking powder that is generally available for home use is called *SAS-phosphate* baking powder. It is a double-acting baking powder, which means that it reacts to release carbon dioxide gas at room temperature when the dry ingredients are moistened and reacts again when heat is applied in the process of baking.

SAS-phosphate baking powder contains two acid substances. Each reacts with soda to release carbon dioxide gas at different times in the baking process. One acid is a phosphate, usually *calcium acid phosphate*. This acid salt reacts with soda at room temperature as soon as liquid is added to the dry ingredients. Thus, the batter or dough becomes somewhat light and porous during the mixing process. The other acid substance is *sodium aluminum sulfate* (SAS). It requires heat and moisture to complete its reaction with soda. Therefore, additional carbon dioxide gas is produced during baking.

The reactions of calcium acid phosphate and baking soda are complex and difficult to write. Many different salts are probably produced in this reaction, and they may interact with each other.

$$CaH_4(PO_4)_2 + NaHCO_3 \rightarrow \text{insoluble} + \text{soluble}$$

calcium acid   sodium   calcium   sodium
phosphate   bicarbonate   phosphate   phosphate
             salts   salts
$$+ \; CO_2 + H_2O$$
       carbon   water
       dioxide

Sodium aluminum sulfate apparently reacts in two stages. The first reaction is with water and results in the production of sulfuric acid as heat is applied, after which the sulfuric acid reacts with soda to produce carbon dioxide gas, according to the following equations:

$$Na_2SO_4Al_2(SO_4)_3 + 6H_2O \xrightarrow{heat} Na_2SO_4$$

sodium aluminum   water   sodium
     sulfate   sulfate
$$+ \; 2Al(OH)_3 + H_2SO_4$$
      aluminum   sulfuric
      hydroxide   acid

$$3H_2SO_4 + 6NaHCO_3 \rightarrow 6CO_2 + 6H_2O + 3Na_2SO_4$$

sulfuric   sodium   carbon   water   sodium
   acid   bicarbonate   dioxide   sulfate

All baking powders leave residues in the mixture in which they are used. The sodium sulfate (Na_2SO_4) residue from the SAS-phosphate baking powder has a somewhat bitter taste which may be objectionable to certain individuals. Some people are more sensitive than others to this bitter taste.

Amount of Baking Powder to Use. An optimum amount of baking powder is desirable for any baked product. If too much baking powder is used, the cell walls of the flour mixture are stretched beyond their limit, and they may break and collapse. If too little baking powder is present, insufficient expansion occurs, and a compact product results. Use of the minimum amount of SAS-phosphate baking powder that leavens satisfactorily is particularly desirable because of the bitter residue formed with this baking powder. Between 1 and 1 1/2 teaspoons of SAS-phosphate baking powder per cup of flour should be adequate for the leavening of most flour mixtures.

Methods of Adding Baking Powder and Soda

Dry chemical leavening agents, including baking powders, are usually sifted or mixed with the flour. They are not allowed to become wet and thus begin to release their carbon dioxide gas until the later stages of the mixing process, when the liquid ingredients are combined with the dry ingredients.

Some recipe directions suggest that the soda be mixed with the sour milk or molasses called for in a recipe. When soda and molasses are mixed, gas tends to be lost slowly due to the high viscosity of the molasses. Carbon dioxide gas, however, is likely to be more rapidly lost from a mixture of buttermilk and soda compared to a batter made by mixing the soda with dry ingredients and then adding the buttermilk. Students in laboratory classes have compared the volumes of chocolate cakes containing soda and buttermilk when the soda was either sifted with the dry ingredients or added directly to the buttermilk. They found that when the soda–buttermilk mixture is added immediately to the batter, the volumes of the finished cakes are quite similar. Allowing the soda–buttermilk mixture to stand before adding it to the batter results in a lower cake volume.

Substitutions of Chemical Leavening Agents

Buttermilk and soda may be substituted for sweet milk and baking powder and vice versa in many recipes for baked products. One-half teaspoon of soda and 1 cup of buttermilk or fully soured milk produce an amount of leavening gas almost equivalent to that produced by 2 teaspoons of SAS-phosphate baking powder. Other approximately equivalent substitutes include 1/2 teaspoon of baking soda plus 1 1/4 teaspoons cream of tartar or 1/2 teaspoon baking soda plus 1 cup molasses. Sweet milk can be made sour by taking 1 tablespoon of vinegar or lemon juice and adding enough sweet milk to make 1 cup, or by adding 1 3/4 teaspoons of cream of tartar to 1 cup of sweet milk. An example of making a substitution in a recipe follows:

Original Recipe	
2 cups (230 g) flour	3 tsp (9.6 g) SAS-phosphate powder
1 cup (237 mL) sweet milk	

Recipe with Substitution of Soda and Sour Milk	
2 cups (230 g) flour	1/2 tsp (2 g) soda
1 cup (237 mL) buttermilk	1 tsp (3.2 g) SAS-phosphate powder

FAT

The major role of fat in flour mixtures is to tenderize or "shorten" the strands of gluten. This tenderizing effect is produced through formation of layers or masses that physically separate different strands of gluten and prevent them from coming together. To shorten effectively, a fat must have the capacity to coat or spread widely and to adhere well to flour particles.

Comparative Shortening Power of Fats

It is difficult to make definite statements concerning the comparative shortening power of various fats because many factors have been shown to modify their effects. For example, the manner in which a fat is distributed in a mixture, the extent of distribution, the temperature of the fat and of the mixture, the presence or absence of emulsifiers in the mixture, the type of mixture, and the method and extent of mixing, as well as the method by which the fat itself has been processed, may have an effect on the shortening power of the fat.

Smoothness of the batter and desirable texture in some finished baked products, such as shortened cakes, are related to the emulsification of the fat in the batter. The presence of some monoglycerides and diglycerides in the fat increases the degree of emulsification of the fat, allowing it to be dispersed in small particles throughout the batter. The addition of emulsifiers to shortened cake batters has been shown to yield cakes of increased volume and finer texture than usually result without the use of emulsifiers.

The *plasticity* of a fat is related to its shortening power. In a plastic fat, some of the triglyceride molecules are present in a liquid form and some are crystallized in a solid form. The presence of both solid and liquid phases in the fat means that the fat can be molded or shaped rather than being fractured or broken when force is applied to it. Fats that are more plastic are more spreadable and, presumably, can spread over a greater surface area of flour particles than less plastic fats. The temperature of fat affects plasticity. At 64°F (18°C), butter is less plastic than at 72° to 83°F (22° to 28°C). At higher temperatures, butter tends to become very soft or to melt completely.

A shortometer measures the weight required to break a baked wafer. This instrument can test the shortening value of fats on pastry. The results of these tests have been somewhat variable, but, in many cases, lards have been shown to have more shortening power than most hydrogenated fats, butter, and margarine. Oils that are high in polyunsaturated fats usually produce more tender pastries than lards. One explanation that has been offered is that these oils cover a larger surface area of flour particles per molecule of fat than fats containing a relatively high proportion of saturated fatty acids. The relationship between the degree of unsaturation and shortening power of fats, however, needs further clarification.

With other proportions and other conditions standardized, the higher the concentration of fat in a mixture, the greater the shortening power. This point deserves consideration in the substitution of one fat for another. Butter and margarines contain approximately 82 percent fat and about 16 percent water. Reduced-calorie spreads that are marketed as substitutes for margarine or butter contain even less fat. Lard, hydrogenated fats, and oils contain essentially 100 percent fat. Disregarding other factors that appear to affect the shortening power of fats, the mere substitution of an equal weight of a fat with a higher fat concentration for one with a lower concentration affects the tenderness of baked flour mixtures. Fats were discussed further in Chapters 9 and 10.

Fat in Leavening

Plastic fats appear to play important roles in some flour mixtures in the trapping of air bubbles that later contribute to the texture of the finished product. This role of

FOCUS ON SCIENCE

The single upper bar is brought down by means of a motor until it breaks the wafer, and the force is recorded. Therefore, in the case of a pie crust, a low value will indicate a tender crust, whereas a high value is indicative of a tough pie crust.

The Shortometer—A Measurement Method for the Comparative Shortening Power of Fat

The breaking strength of pastry, cookies, and crackers can be determined in a shortometer. This breaking strength is measured by placing the pastry or wafer across two horizontal bars.

FOCUS ON SCIENCE

cells, and these cells are dispersed in the batter. When the batter is baked, the air cells produce gas, and the product rises.

Plastic Fats and Leavening

A plastic fat is soft and moldable at room temperature. There is a certain ratio of liquid to solid fat present in the particular fat that makes it plastic. When the fat is beaten, it traps air

---

fat may be particularly important in the preparation of shortened cakes. It has been suggested that creaming fat and sugar crystals together and also vigorously beating fat-containing batters cause air cells to be entrapped in the mixture. Fats that incorporate air readily and allow it to be dispersed in small cells are said to have good creaming properties.

Fat Replacers

Substances used to replace fat in a flour mixture must mimic the effects of fat on the eating quality of the finished product [1]. This challenges the ingenuity of the food industry as new products are formulated. Cellulose, gums, maltodextrins, modified starches, and polydextrose are carbohydrate-based substances that are used as fat replacers. Dehydrated fruit products, such as banana flakes and prune paste, may be used in low- or no-fat bakery products to maintain a desirable texture. A microparticulated whey protein concentrate, Simplesse®, can be combined with selected emulsifiers for easy, effective use in lowfat baked products [20]. Specially designed emulsifier systems also are important components in fat-reduced products because they extend the effects of the fat. However, without jeopardizing the quality of the finished item, the fat in many baked product formulas can be reduced, at least slightly. Fat replacers were discussed in Chapter 10.

LIQUIDS

Liquids have various uses in flour mixtures. They hydrate the starch and gluten and dissolve certain constituents, such as sugar, salts, and baking powder. It is only when baking powders are wet that the evolution of carbon dioxide gas begins. The typical structure or framework of doughs and batters is not formed until the protein particles become hydrated. **Starch gelatinization** during baking requires moisture. Various liquids may be used in flour mixtures, including water, potato water, milk, fruit juices, and coffee. The water content of eggs is also a part of the total liquid.

EGGS

Eggs may be used as a means of incorporating air into a batter, because egg proteins coagulate on beating and give some structure or rigidity to the cell walls surrounding the air bubbles. Egg whites can form a particularly stable foam. As they are beaten, the cell walls become increasingly thinner and more tender to an optimum point. Beaten egg whites can be carefully folded into a batter, retaining much of the air in the foam.

Egg yolks add flavor and color to flour mixtures. They also aid in forming emulsions of fat and water because of their content of **lipoproteins**, which are effective emulsifying agents. Because egg proteins coagulate

---

FOCUS ON SCIENCE

fruit, and a function of pectin is to trap water or, in this instance, moistness. Therefore, these fruit-based products are able to function relatively well as fat replacers by promoting moistness in baked goods.

Moisture Retention in Lowfat Baked Goods

One of the main functions of fat in a baked good is that it contributes moistness. Banana flakes and prune paste are able to trap water or moisture in the baked good. Pectin is present in

on heating, the addition of eggs to flour mixtures increases the rigidity of the baked product.

SUGAR AND OTHER SWEETENERS

Sugar is an important ingredient in baked goods to sweeten, tenderize, retain moisture, contribute a brown color, aid in leavening, stabilize egg white foams, and provide foods for yeast. Granulated sugar is used in many flour mixtures for sweetening purposes. Brown sugar, honey, molasses, and syrups also may be used for the unique flavors and characteristics of these sweeteners. Brown sugar will produce baked goods that retain moisture longer than those made with granulated sugar. Brown sugar must be firmly packed into a cup when measured unless substituted by weight. Refer to Chapter 5 for more on weights and measurements.

Sugar has a tenderizing effect because it interferes with gluten formation, protein coagulation, and starch gelatinization [4]. Gluten development is affected because sugar ties up water, making less water available for the gluten. Therefore, more manipulation is necessary to develop the gluten structure when sugar is not present. Similarly, the holding of water by sugar interferes with starch and protein and thus delays the formation of structure in baked goods. The coagulation temperature of egg proteins is elevated by sugar. For example, sponge-type cakes contain relatively large amounts of egg as well as sugar. Sugar also increases the temperature at which starch gelatinizes, which is of particular importance in high-sugar products such as cakes of several types. The tenderizing affect of sugar also may result in baked flour mixtures with a greater volume because the tenderized gluten mass expands more easily under the pressure of leavening gases. Additionally, sugar helps to achieve a fine, even texture in many baked products [13].

The *hygroscopic* nature or water absorption tendency of sugar helps to retain moisture and improve shelf life of baked goods [4]. Sugar increases softness, moistness, and helps to reduce drying and staling. Sugar also contributes to the browning of outer surfaces of baked products and produces desirable flavors. Caramelization occurs at high oven temperatures as the surface of the product becomes dry.

Sugar contributes to leavening. Creaming of shortening and crystalline sugar adds air to the mixture. In yeast mixtures, sugar is a readily available food for the yeast plant. Sugar also stabilizes egg white foams, whipped whole eggs, and whipped yolks. As a result, whipped eggs are better able to hold air and are less likely to collapse or weep. Angel food, genoise, and chiffon cakes are examples of products with whipped eggs.

High-intensity or alternate sweeteners, including saccharin, encapsulated aspartame, acesulfame-K, and sucralose, are stable under high temperatures and retain sweetness in baked products. A bulking or bodying agent such as polydextrose must be added with high-intensity sweeteners to substitute for some of sugar's effects on texture. Compensation also must be made for the effect of sugar on the tenderness of the finished product. Again, the food industry faces challenges in formulating no-sugar baked products. Alternate sweeteners were discussed in Chapter 11.

CLASSIFICATION OF BATTERS AND DOUGHS

Flour mixtures vary in thickness depending largely on the proportion of flour to liquid. Based on thickness, flour mixtures are classified as batters or doughs.

Batters

Batters are classified as pour batters or drop batters, but considerable variation exists within each group; some pour batters are very thin, whereas others pour with difficulty. A pour batter contains 2/3 to 1 cup of liquid per cup of flour. A drop batter usually has 1/2 to 3/4 cup of liquid per cup of flour. In batters containing approximately 1 part liquid to 2 parts flour, gluten development readily occurs on mixing. Popovers and thin griddle-cake and shortened-cake batters are examples of pour batters. Some drop batters are stiff enough to require scraping from the spoon. Drop batters include muffins, many quick breads, and various kinds of cookies. A batter containing yeast is called a *sponge*.

Doughs

Doughs are thick enough to be handled or kneaded on a flat surface (Figure 15-8). Most doughs are rolled in the final stages of preparation, although yeast dough is not usually rolled except for the shaping of certain types of rolls. Doughs may be soft (just stiff enough to handle) or stiff. Soft doughs contain about 1/3 cup of liquid per cup

FIGURE 15-8 Yeast bread dough is thick enough to be kneaded by hand.

of flour. A stiff dough may contain only 1/8 cup of liquid per cup of flour. Examples of soft-dough products include baking powder biscuits, rolled cookies, yeast bread, and rolls. Pie crust is an example of a stiff dough.

GENERAL METHODS FOR MIXING BATTERS AND DOUGHS

General objectives in the mixing of doughs and batters are uniform distribution of ingredients, minimum loss of the leavening agent, optimum blending to produce characteristic textures in various products, and optimum development of gluten for the desired individual properties. Although many different methods are employed for the mixing of batters and doughs, three basic methods may be adapted for use with a variety of products.

Muffin Method

In the muffin method, dry ingredients are sifted together into the bowl used for mixing. The eggs are lightly beaten, and the liquid and melted fat (or oil) are added to the eggs. The liquid ingredients are then blended with the dry ingredients. The amount of stirring which is desirable will vary with the product.

For thin mixtures, such as popovers, thin griddle cakes, and thin waffle mixtures, lumping can be prevented by adding the liquid ingredients gradually to the dry ingredients. Conversely, the overstirring of thicker batters, such as thick waffle mixtures and muffins, can be prevented by adding liquid ingredients all at once to the dry ingredients. Thicker batters are stirred only until the dry ingredients are dampened to avoid an undesirable development of gluten and a resulting decrease in tenderness (Figure 15-9).

FIGURE 15-9 The muffin method of mixing is used to prepare waffles such as this one.

Pastry or Biscuit Method

In the pastry or biscuit method, the dry ingredients are sifted together. Fat is cut in or blended with the dry ingredients, and liquid is then added to the fat–flour mixture. The "cutting in" of the fat, instead of thorough blending, results in a more flaky product which is desirable in both biscuits and pie crusts. Although this method is used mainly for pastry and biscuits, it is also appropriate for other flour mixtures. The techniques of handling the dough after the addition of liquid differ for pastry and biscuits. Biscuits are generally mixed more thoroughly than pie crusts and are lightly kneaded before they are rolled out and cut into the desired shapes.

Conventional Method

Although cakes are mixed by more than one method, the conventional cake method, or simply the conventional method, is usually understood to mean the conventional way in which fat and sugar are creamed together, beaten eggs are added, and dry and liquid ingredients are alternately blended with the fat–sugar–egg mixture. This method may also be used for making cookies, various quick breads, and other flour products. Yeast bread, cream puffs, and sponge-type cake are mixed by special methods applicable only to these products. Whatever the method, the optimum amount of manipulation varies with the type of product, with the character and proportion of the ingredients used, and with the temperature of the ingredients.

STRUCTURE OF BATTERS AND DOUGHS

The structure that develops in batters and doughs varies according to the kind and proportion of ingredients used. In all mixtures, except those of high liquid content, hydrated gluten particles adhere and form a continuous mass that spreads out into a network. Some components of the mixture, such as salts and sugar, are partially or completely dissolved in the liquid. The starch granules from the flour tend to be embedded in the gluten network (see Figure 15-5). Other components act as emulsifying agents by separating or dividing the fat in the mixture into particles of varying fineness. The temperature and the physical and chemical state of the ingredients partially determine the degree of dispersion of the emulsion. Melted fats or oils may behave differently from solid fats in certain doughs and batters.

The texture of the finished product depends largely on the structure obtained in the mixing of the dough or batter. Texture is a combination of such characteristics as the distribution of cells, the thickness of cell walls, the character of the crumb (elastic, crumbly, velvety, or harsh), and the grain (the size of the cells). Optimum texture cannot be expected to be the same for all products, because of the variation in the kinds and amounts of constituents used. Typical textures for different baked products are discussed with those products in later chapters. Variations from typical textures and possible causes for variation are also discussed.

When all of the factors that affect texture are considered, it is not surprising that products made from the same formula may differ with several bakings. Although a certain degree of control of materials, manipulation, and temperatures is possible, it is difficult in practical baking in the kitchen to always control all factors that play a part in determining the quality of the end products obtained. In industrial operations and in many foodservice establishments, controls are sufficiently precise and reproducible that the same quality product is guaranteed each time. Quality assurance programs are geared to achieve just that.

DRY FLOUR MIXES

A wide variety of flour-based mixes for products such as cake, muffins, biscuits, pie dough, cookies, and so forth is marketed. Excellent directions to the consumer in the use of these prepared mixes tend to ensure uniform, good-quality finished products. In addition to flour, mixes may contain leavening, salt, fat (sometimes powdered shortening), nonfat dry milk, dried eggs, sugar, and flavoring ingredients, such as dried extracts, cocoa, ginger, and dried molasses, depending on the type of mixture.

Numerous additives are used and have contributed to the success of commercial flour mixes. These include various emulsifiers, modified starches, caseinate, gums, cellulose, and whipping aids. A combination of added substances is often necessary in the production of reduced-fat or reduced-calorie mixes.

Mixes are convenient timesavers and may cost no more (and sometimes even less) than a similar product prepared in the kitchen. Costs must be determined on an individual basis and are sometimes difficult to compare because of differences in ingredients and yields. (The cost of convenience foods was discussed in Chapter 2.)

Various flour mixes can also be made in the home kitchen, saving time by measuring and mixing at least some of the ingredients at one time. However, because the techniques used in the production of commercial mixes are not available for home use, homemade mixes do not have as long a shelf life. They should be adequately packaged and stored at cool temperatures. Commercial mixes usually contain a leavening acid that dissolves slowly, such as anhydrous monocalcium phosphate or sodium acid pyrophosphate, to prevent the premature reaction of the baking powder during storage. Also, off-flavors do not readily develop in the mixes with these acids.

BAKING AT HIGH ALTITUDES

Some balancing of ingredients and variation of baking temperature may be necessary at high altitudes. At high altitudes, as compared to sea level, the atmospheric pressure is less (Table 15-2). The decreased pressure at higher altitudes results in three key changes that affect cooking: (a) leavening gases meet less resistance and expand more quickly, (b) moisture evaporates more quickly, and (c) water and liquids boil at lower temperatures. From a quality perspective, the overexpansion of a baked product may stretch the cells to the extent that they break and collapse, producing a coarse texture and decreased volume.

Cookbooks with recipes designed for high altitudes may be used [9] or recipes may be adjusted using general guidelines. Leavening agents are usually decreased to reduce overexpansion. The strengthening of the cell walls of the product by decreasing the sugar or adding more flour will also counteract excessive leavening. Additional eggs may be added as another way to strengthen cakes and prevent falling. Oven temperatures may be increased 15° to 25°F (8° to 14°C) to "set" the structure before the leavening gases expand too much. Increased liquid may also be added because of greater loss by evaporation. Suggestions for several types of baked products are provided in Table 15-3 and specific ingredient adjustments for shortened cakes are given in Table 15-4.

TABLE 15-2 Atmospheric Pressure at Various Altitudes	
Altitude	**Atmospheric Pressure (Pounds of Pressure per Square Inch of Surface)**
Sea level	14.7
5,000	12.3
10,000	10.2
Source: Reference 9	

TABLE 15-3 High Altitude Suggestions for Baked Products

Baked Product	General Suggestions for High Altitude Preparation
Yeast breads	Dough will double in size in much less time at high altitudes. Do not allow to rise more than double in size. To develop good flavor, punch down dough twice to lengthen rising period without overexpansion of structure.
	Will likely need less flour at high elevations due to drier conditions.
Cakes	Decrease amount of leavening and/or increase the baking temperature.
	Reduce sugar and increase liquid to compensate for excessive evaporation of water at high altitudes.
	Rich cakes may need less shortening, oil, butter, or margarine.
	Addition of eggs will strengthen cell structure of rich cakes.
Angel food and sponge cakes	Avoid beating too much air into the eggs. At high altitudes, beat egg whites to the "soft" peak stage.
	Use less sugar, more flour, and increase baking temperature to strengthen cell structure.
Cookies	Many cookie recipes may produce good results at high altitude without modification. Improvement may be observed by a slight increase in oven temperature, liquid ingredients, or flour. Slight decreases in baking powder, baking soda, fat, or sugar may improve quality. Make small changes and test the product to avoid overcompensation for the altitude.
Biscuits	Biscuits often do not need adjustments to compensate for structural issues. A bitter or alkaline flavor can occur at high altitudes due to inadequate neutralization of the baking soda or powder. If flavor is a concern, reduce the amount of leavening agent.
Pie crusts	Some recipes may be improved by the addition of slightly more liquid.

Source: Reference 9

TABLE 15-4 Adjustments for Shortened Cakes

Adjustment	3,500–6,500 Feet	6,500–8,500 Feet	8,500–10,000 Feet
Reduce baking powder			
For each teaspoon, decrease:	1/8 tsp	1/8–1/4 tsp	1/4 tsp
Reduce sugar			
For each cup, decrease:	0–1 Tbsp	0–2 Tbsp	2 1/2 Tbsp
Increase liquid			
For each cup, add:	1–2 Tbsp	2–4 Tbsp	3–4 Tbsp

Source: Reference 9

CHAPTER SUMMARY

- Batters and doughs, sometimes called flour mixtures, include a large variety of baked products. The primary ingredients used for doughs and batters are flour, liquid, fat, egg, sugar, leavening agent, and salt.

- Wheat is the principal grain used in the United States for flour. Because of its protein and starch content, flour provides structure and body in baked flour products.

- The milling of white flour is a process that involves separating the endosperm from the bran and germ and subdividing it into a fine flour. Milled white flour

usually contains 65 to 70 percent starch and 8 to 13 percent protein.

- Various grades and types of flours are formulated from the many streams of flours resulting from the milling process. The miller grades of flour include straight grade, patent flours, and clear grade. These grades are determined on the basis of which streams of flour are combined.

- Aged flour produces breads with higher volumes and finer textures. Flours may be "bleached" by the addition of approved chemicals or may lighten in color due to the oxidation of the carotenoic pigments after extended holding.

- Several types of wheat flour are available and include whole-wheat, bread, all-purpose, pastry, cake, instantized, self-rising, and gluten flour.

- Rye, cornmeal, corn, soy, buckwheat, triticale, rice, potato, and amaranth flour may be used to make a variety of products. Because these flours contain little or no gluten, wheat flour is often used with flours from other grains so that high-quality baked goods may be produced.

- To leaven means to "make light and porous." Three major leavening gases are air, steam or water vapor, and carbon dioxide.

- Carbon dioxide may be produced in flour mixtures either by biological processes (yeast or bacteria during fermentation) or by a purely chemical reaction (baking soda or baking powder).

- Baking powders are mixtures of dry acid or acid salts and baking soda. SAS-phosphate baking powder, typically used in the home, is a double-acting baking powder. It releases carbon dioxide gas when the dry ingredients are moistened and when heat is applied in the process of baking.

- Baking soda may be substituted for baking powder in a recipe if the correct proportion of an acid ingredient, such as cream of tartar or buttermilk, is added to the recipe.

- The major role of fat in flour mixtures is to tenderize or "shorten" the strands of gluten. When substituting fats in recipes, the amount of fat in butter versus oils or hydrogenated fats should be considered. A product containing a higher percentage of fat will have a greater shortening power.

- Plastic fats, such as used in shortened cakes, trap air bubbles during creaming that later contributes to the texture of the finished product.

- Liquids hydrate the starch and gluten and dissolve certain constituents, such as sugar, salts, and baking powder. Starch gelatinization during baking requires moisture.

- Eggs may be used to incorporate air into the batter, add flavor, enhance color, aid in forming emulsions, and increase rigidity of flour mixtures due to coagulation of the egg proteins.

- Granulated sugar sweetens, contributes to browning, provides food for yeast, tenderizes, and increases the volume of baked goods. Sugar also may help to achieve a fine, even texture in many baked products.

- Flour mixtures are classified as batters or doughs. Batters may be thin and pour readily or may be stiffer and are called *drop batters*. Doughs are thick enough to be handled or kneaded on a flat surface.

- The general objectives in the mixing of doughs and batters are uniform distribution of ingredients, minimum loss of the leavening agent, optimum blending to produce characteristic textures in various products, and optimum development of gluten. Three basic methods of mixing are used for a variety of products: muffin method, pastry or biscuit method, and conventional method.

- For high-quality baked products at high altitudes, some balancing of ingredients and variation in baking temperature may be necessary to counteract the more rapid expansion of leavening gases, greater evaporation, and lower temperature of boiling which occur at high altitudes.

STUDY QUESTIONS

1. (a) What is meant by the *milling* of flour?

   (b) How is white flour produced?

   (c) How is whole-wheat or graham flour produced?

   (d) How do hard and soft wheat flours generally differ in characteristics and composition?

   (e) Name three grades of white flour and indicate which is usually found on the retail market.

2. For each of the following types of flour, describe the general characteristics and uses in food preparation:

   (a) Bread flour

   (b) All-purpose flour

   (c) Pastry flour

   (d) Cake flour

   (e) Instantized flour

   (f) Self-rising flour

3. About 85 percent of the proteins in white wheat flour are relatively insoluble and play an important role in developing the structure of baked products.

   (a) Name the two wheat-flour protein fractions that develop into gluten with moistening and mixing or kneading.

   (b) Describe the characteristics of wheat gluten. Discuss its role in the preparation of baked flour mixtures.

4. (a) What is meant by the term *leaven?*

   (b) Name three leavening gases that are commonly present in baked products.

(c) Describe several ways in which air may be incorporated into a batter or dough during preparation.

(d) Explain why steam is such an effective leavening gas. Name two products that are leavened primarily by steam.

5. Carbon dioxide (CO_2) gas may be produced by biological and by chemical means.

(a) Describe how CO_2 may be produced biologically in baked products.

(b) Describe examples of the chemical production of CO_2 in flour mixtures.

6. Although CO_2 will be released when soda is heated in a moist environment, explain why it cannot satisfactorily be used for leavening in baked products without an accompanying acid.

7. Baking powders always contain at least two active ingredients. Name them. Which one is responsible for the production of CO_2?

8. Name several acid foods that are commonly used with soda in baked products.

9. Generally, the only type of baking powder available to the consumer is SAS-phosphate baking powder.

(a) Explain why this baking powder is called "double-acting."

(b) Name the active ingredients in this baking powder.

(c) Explain how the active ingredients participate in the production of CO_2 gas.

10. (a) How much soda is normally used with one cup of buttermilk in a baked product?

(b) How much SAS-phosphate baking powder is normally used per one cup of flour to leaven a baked product?

11. Briefly describe the general role of each of the following ingredients in baked flour mixtures:

(a) Fat

(b) Flour

(c) Liquids

(d) Eggs

(e) Sugar

12. Why is it a challenge to produce acceptable baked products that are reduced in fat, sugar, and/or calories? Explain.

13. What are batters? Doughs? Give examples of each.

14. Describe each of the following general methods of mixing batters and doughs. Give examples of baked products commonly prepared by each method.

(a) Muffin method

(b) Pastry or biscuit method

(c) Conventional method

15. (a) Why do some adjustments need to be made in baked products when they are prepared at high altitudes? Briefly discuss this.

(b) Suggest appropriate adjustments for shortened cakes that are baked at high altitudes when using recipes standardized at sea level.

QUICK BREADS 16

Traditionally, quick breads have included a variety of products that can be prepared without the rising or proofing time required by yeast breads. Quick breads are often served warm. Examples of quick breads are popovers, pancakes or griddle cakes, waffles, muffins, biscuits, scones, coffeecakes, and loaf breads made with baking powder as a leavening ingredient. Cream puffs and éclairs may also be classified with quick breads.

Quick bread ideas and recipes are borrowed from many different ethnic groups. There are Swedish pancakes and pancake balls, Finnish oven pancakes, and German potato pancakes. In many parts of Mexico, flour tortillas are made in the home from a basic flour dough that usually contains baking powder; the dough is rolled into flat circles before being baked on a hot griddle. Sesame turnovers come from Greece; they are made of a pastry-like dough containing a small amount of baking powder and are filled with ground nuts and seeds. The variety of quick breads with ethnic origins is almost limitless.

Table 16-1 provides proportions of ingredients for some basic quick breads. Ingredients are balanced to produce the type of product desired. Structural ingredients, such as flour and egg, are balanced against tenderizing ingredients, primarily sugar and fat, so that the product will have form or structure yet be appropriately tender. The consistency of the batter or dough is generally determined by the ratio of flour to liquid ingredients.

In this chapter, the preparation and quality characteristics of the following quick breads will be discussed:

- Popovers
- Cream puffs and éclairs
- Pancakes and waffles
- Muffins, nut breads, coffeecakes, and fried quick breads
- Biscuits and scones

TABLE 16-1 Proportions of Ingredients for Quick Breads

Product	Flour	Liquid	Eggs	Fat	Sugar	Salt	Baking Powder	Soda
Popovers	1 c	1 c	2–3	0–1 Tbsp		1/4–1/2 tsp		
Cream puffs	1 c	1 c	4	1/2 c		1/4 tsp		
Muffins	1 c	1/2 c	1/2–1	1–2 Tbsp	1–2 Tbsp	1/2 tsp	1 1/2–2 tsp	
Waffles	1 c	2/3 c	1–2	3 Tbsp	1 tsp	1/2 tsp	1–2 tsp	
Pancakes								
Sweet milk	1 c	2/3 c	1	1 Tbsp	1 tsp	1/4–1/2 tsp	1–2 tsp	
Thick buttermilk	1 c	1 c	1	1–2 Tbsp		1/4–1/2 tsp	1/4–1/2 tsp (optional)	1/2 tsp
Thick sour cream	1 c	1 c	1			1/4–1/2 tsp	1/4–1/2 tsp (optional)	1/2 tsp
Biscuits	1 c	Rolled, 1/3 c Dropped, 1/3–3/8 c		2–3 Tbsp		1/2 tsp	1 1/2–2 tsp	
Scones	1 c	1/3 c cream	1	2–3 Tbsp	1 Tbsp	1/8 tsp	2 tsp	

POPOVERS

Ingredients

Popovers contain a relatively high proportion of liquid, usually milk, and are leavened chiefly by the steam produced in a hot oven in the early stages of baking. Popovers are usually mixed by the muffin method, as described in Chapter 15. Although either pastry or all-purpose flour may be used for making popovers, the crusts are usually more rigid when all-purpose flour is used. Because of the high percentage of moisture in the batter, the gluten particles, on becoming hydrated, tend to float in the liquid. The batter should be stirred until smooth and free of lumps. Excess gluten formation with mixing is unlikely to occur because the high liquid content in popovers prevents the gluten proteins (gliadin and glutenin) from adhering and forming gluten. With so small an amount of flour in relationship to liquid, the liquid is best added gradually at first until the lumps are stirred out.

Most of the structure of popovers is the result of the gelatinization of starch and the coagulation of eggs. As noted previously, little gluten development will occur because of the high liquid content. Thus, an inadequate amount of eggs in popover batter will result in a heavy product with a very small volume. Two eggs per cup of flour will result in enough extensible and coagulable material to form rigid walls. If the eggs are small or if pastry flour is used, three eggs per cup of flour will provide more desirable results than two eggs. Fat serves little purpose in popovers. It tends to float on top of the thin batter and thus chiefly affects the top crust. If as much as one tablespoon of fat is used, the top crust may have a flaky appearance.

Characteristics

Popovers are high rising and usually have irregular shapes. They are hollow, with thick crusty walls (Figure 16-1). Because of the high percentage of liquid in the mixture, the interior is moist but not similar to raw dough. Crusts should not be so brown that their flavor is impaired.

Baking

Muffin pans (preferably deep ones) or heat-resistant glass cups can be used for baking popovers. They are greased to keep the popovers from sticking. When iron pans are used, baking may be speeded up if the pans are pre-warmed, because iron requires more time to become hot than tin or aluminum. Because steam is the chief leavening agent in popovers, a hot oven temperature (450°F/232°C) is required to form steam quickly. After 15 minutes at 450°F (232°C), the oven is reduced to 375°F (191°C) for the remainder of the baking time, about 45 minutes. If popovers are baked for the whole time at a hot temperature, the crusts may become too brown in the time required to form rigid walls that do not collapse on removal from the oven. Popovers should be pricked with a fork to allow steam to escape upon removal from the oven to avoid a soggy interior. If a crisper popover is desired, turn off the oven and return the pricked popovers to the oven for several minutes.

Browning in popovers is apparently produced primarily by the Maillard reaction. The amount of milk sugar or lactose in the mixture is probably sufficient for this reaction to occur. Dextrinization of starch in the flour may also contribute to browning.

Causes of Failure

Probably the chief cause of failure in making popovers is insufficient baking. Popovers are not necessarily done when they are brown and may collapse on removal from the oven if the egg proteins are not adequately coagulated. Popovers will not rise to a sufficient volume unless they are baked in a hot oven for the first part of baking so that steam can quickly be generated. An inadequate amount of egg in the formula also may result in decreased volume.

FIGURE 16-1 Well-made popovers have a large volume and a moist, hollow interior. *(Photograph by Roger P. Smith)*

FOCUS ON SCIENCE

Popover Tips

How do eggs contribute to the structure of popovers?

The eggs form the framework of the popovers when the egg protein stretches with the expansion of steam and then coagulates on heating.

How can Maillard browning be reduced in popovers?

Browning can be reduced by baking the popovers on the lowest rack position in the oven. If baked on the middle or higher position, excess browning will occur because hot air rises, thereby contributing to a darker popover.

CREAM PUFFS AND ÉCLAIRS

Ingredients and Mixing

Cream puffs and éclairs contain the same proportion of liquid to flour as popovers and also are leavened primarily by steam, but they are made with eight times as much fat. Cream puffs and éclairs are therefore considerably more tender than popovers. A large proportion of egg is used in cream puffs to emulsify the high percentage of fat.

The method of mixing the cream puff batter, also called pâte à choux, is unique to this product. The fat is melted in hot water, and the flour is added all at once with vigorous stirring. Heating is continued until the batter is smooth and forms a stiff ball. **Gelatinization** of the starch occurs during this cooking process. The mixture is then cooled slightly, and the eggs are added (either one unbeaten egg at a time, or one-third of the beaten eggs at one time). Thorough beating is necessary after each addition of egg. The eggs contain lipoproteins that act as emulsifying agents to divide the fat into small particles throughout the mixture. At this stage, the batter is smooth, stiff, and glossy. The egg also plays a role in obtaining a large volume. Egg proteins aid in the stretching process during the first stages of baking and are later coagulated by heat to contribute to the rigid structure of the final product. Even though the cream puff batter is stiff, it can be beaten without danger of toughening the puffs. The high percentage of fat and water in relation to flour interferes with the development of gluten and prevents it from forming a tenacious mass.

Characteristics

Puffs are usually irregular on the top surface, although the surface may vary depending on the consistency of the batter before baking. The walls are rigid but tender because of the high fat content. The center of the puff is hollow and moist. Some of the moist interior strands may be removed, if desired, and the puff dried out in the oven. The crust should have a light golden-brown color

(Figure 16-2). The hollow center of cream puffs is usually filled. A wide variety of mixtures can be used as fillings, including chicken, tuna, and other types of salads; custards and starch-thickened puddings; flavored and sweetened whipped cream mixtures; and ice cream and other frozen desserts. Smaller puffs are generally used for hors d'oeuvres and larger ones for desserts.

Baking

The cream puff batter is dropped in mounds onto an ungreased baking sheet, allowing some room between mounds for expansion during baking. Éclairs are piped with a pastry bag into an oblong shape (Figure 16-3). A high oven temperature of 450°F (232°C) is necessary to form steam quickly and bring about the puffing or expansion of the batter. The high temperature may be maintained throughout the baking period, providing that overbrowning does not occur. The baking time is decreased to about 30 to 35 minutes if a high temperature is used continuously. If 450°F (232°C) is used for 15 minutes, followed by about 375°F (191°C) for the remainder of the baking time, about 45 minutes of total baking time will be required. The puffs should feel rigid and should not collapse on removal from the oven. Cream puffs are not necessarily done when brown.

FIGURE 16-2 Cream puffs.

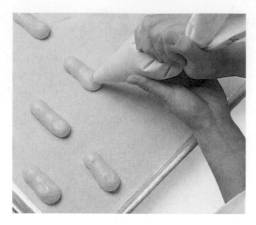

FIGURE 16-3 A pastry bag is being used to pipe the éclair batter into oblong shapes on a cookie tray prior to baking.

Causes of Failure

Causes of failure include insufficient baking, excessive evaporation of moisture during cooking of the paste, inaccurate ingredient measurements, and inadequate beating of the mixture. As in the making of popovers, cream puffs will collapse when removed from the oven if baked an inadequate length of time. The walls of the puffs should be rigid before removal from the oven.

The excessive evaporation of moisture during the cooking of the paste will alter the proportions of the ingredients and makes formation of a stable emulsion unlikely, thus leading to poor quality. Excessive evaporation may be caused by boiling the water and fat too long before adding the flour and by overcooking the flour–fat–water mixture. When the emulsion is destabilized, the fat tends to separate from the mixture. The batter appears oily and separated instead of shiny and viscous, and the fat oozes from the puffs during baking. A small amount of water should be beaten into the batter to reestablish the emulsion before proceeding to bake the puffs. Inaccurate measurements also may increase the percentage of fat in the mixture and result in similar problems as noted previously from too much evapora-

tion. Failure also may result from insufficient beating so that the mixture is not smooth, stiff, and glossy.

PANCAKES

Ingredients and Mixing

Pancakes, sometimes called *griddle cakes*, are more variable both in the proportion of flour to liquid and in the characteristics of the finished product than most flour mixtures. The cooked cakes may be thin and moist or thick and porous according to the proportions of ingredients used (Figure 16-4). Crepes are thin, tender pancakes that contain a high proportion of egg. Crepes are discussed in Chapter 24.

Pancake mixtures contain flour, liquid, a leavening agent, and salt. Egg is normally used but may be omitted. Cakes are more tender if they contain fat, but it is possible to omit fat. Sugar may be used as an aid in browning, because of its **caramelization**, and may slightly modify the flavor.

If thick buttermilk or sour cream is used in the cakes, the proportion of flour to liquid may be about one to one. In sweetmilk cakes, 1 1/3, 1 1/2, or 1 3/4 cups of flour may be used per cup of liquid, depending on the type of flour and on the desired thickness of the cake. Because the cream contains fat, shortening can be omitted in cakes made with cream.

Pancakes are leavened by carbon dioxide gas produced either from baking powder or from a sour milk and soda combination. Overstirred pancakes may be soggy because of a loss of carbon dioxide during stirring and may show some tunnel formation. Thin batters tend to lose more carbon dioxide gas on standing than thicker batters. More baking powder may be required if batters are to stand for some time than if they are baked immediately.

Pancakes are usually mixed by the muffin method described in Chapter 15. The stiffer the batter, the less the batter should be stirred, to avoid toughening the cakes by developing the gluten. Pancake batters, like muffin batters, are slightly lumpy, rather than completely smooth when mixed properly.

FOCUS ON SCIENCE

Lipoproteins and Cream Puff Quality

Emulsifiers allow immiscible substances such as water and oil to mix. Lipoproteins, found in eggs, are emulsifiers that hold cream puff dough together. In cream puffs, an emulsifier is needed because there are high amounts of fat and water, but not enough flour to hold everything together. When the dough is beaten vigorously, the lipoproteins in the eggs stabilize the fat by dispersing it throughout the dough. At the end of beating, the dough should feel "sticky." If it has a "greasy" feel, this is an indication that the fat is not completely emulsified. The stabilization of "greasy" dough can be accomplished by beating in a small amount of another egg into the dough to form an emulsion properly and enable the dough to puff when baked.

FIGURE 16-4 Pancakes or griddle cakes can be made thin and moist (left) or thick and porous (right). *(Photograph by Chris Meister)*

FOCUS ON SCIENCE

Leavening in Pancakes and Crepes

A true crepe does not contain a source of carbon dioxide (CO_2) in the form of baking powder and or baking soda. Crepes traditionally have a high ratio of eggs and water to flour,

and thus the coagulation of the egg is essential to their structure. Pancakes are leavened by CO_2 and are thicker in structure than the crepe.

Cooking

Seasoned griddles can be used without being greased, particularly if the batter contains two or more tablespoons of fat per cup of liquid used. Specially coated, nonstick cooking surfaces are normally used without being greased.

Much of the success in making pancakes depends on the temperature of the griddle. If the griddle is appreciably below the appropriate temperature, the pancakes cook so slowly that leavening gas is lost and expansion is insufficient producing pale and heavy cakes. Browning in pancakes is primarily the result of the Maillard reaction. Too hot a griddle may burn the cakes before they are sufficiently done. Even if the griddle is not hot enough to cause burning, it may produce uneven browning and a compact texture from too rapid cooking. The temperature of the griddle can be tested by cooking a few drops of batter.

A uniformly heated griddle is essential for the griddle cakes to brown evenly. Large griddles over small flames may be practically cold in the outer areas. As cakes cook on a griddle of a desirable temperature, bubbles of gas expand and some break at the surface. When the edges of the pancakes appear slightly dry, they should be turned. If the entire surface becomes dry, the cakes will not brown

evenly on the second side after turning. After being turned, the cakes rise noticeably and become slightly higher in the center. Peaks will not form, however, unless the pancake mixture is very stiff or was greatly overstirred. Pancakes are done when brown on the second side. Although pancakes may sometimes be turned a second time provided that they are almost done when turned, more desirable cakes usually result from one turning.

WAFFLES

Ingredients and Mixing

Waffle mixtures are similar to pancakes except that waffles contain more egg and more fat (Plate V). Waffles are leavened by carbon dioxide gas, usually from baking powder, although yeast may sometimes be used. Because tenderness and crispness are desirable characteristics in waffles, a flour of relatively low gluten content and weak gluten quality is a good choice (see Chapter 15 for a discussion on types of flours). By using a sufficient amount of fat and by avoiding overstirring, however, a stronger flour can be successfully used. In general, a stronger flour tends to yield a less tender, more breadlike waffle.

The proportion of flour in waffles may vary from 1 1/3 to 1 3/4 cups per cup of liquid. With appropriate mixing and cooking techniques, good waffles will be produced. Thinner batters lose their leavening gas more quickly, and it is more difficult, without loss of air, to blend beaten egg whites with batters of thin consistency. Ease of pouring is a point in favor of somewhat thinner batters.

Some waffle mixtures that are to be used as dessert or as shortcake are richer in fat than the proportions suggested in Table 16-1. These specialty waffles often contain sugar and may contain cocoa or molasses. Such mixtures require longer, slower baking than batters with no sugar, for the waffles to be crisp and done without scorching. Caramelization of the sugar contributes to browning.

Waffles of excellent quality usually result when the batter is mixed by a modified muffin method that involves separating the eggs and adding the beaten egg whites last. However, the whole beaten egg may be used successfully in the muffin method for mixing waffles. Refer to Chapter 15 for further discussion on the muffin method of mixing.

Baking

A waffle baker (iron) is preheated before the batter is poured on the grids. An automatic heat control with an indicator usually shows when the appliance is ready. The batter may stick to the grids if the waffle iron is too hot, insufficiently heated, or there is not enough fat in the batter. Waffle grids should be greased, at least for the first waffle, even if they have a nonstick finish. Manufacturer's directions should be followed in preconditioning and using new waffle bakers.

Very thin batters made with one cup of flour per cup of liquid are too thin to fill the waffle iron sufficiently to bake the waffle crisp and brown on both sides. Crispness depends partly on the depth of batter that the waffle baker holds. A thicker waffle has a tendency to be less crisp than a thin waffle.

What Happens During Baking?

Several key changes occur during baking and cooking which allow a batter or dough to come out of the oven or off the griddle with very different characteristics. These changes are described below.

Solid Fats Melt

Flaky biscuits and pie crusts occur when pockets of fat melt. Leavening in other products is enhanced when air and water trapped in solid fat escapes. Melting fat also coats gluten strands and thereby contributes to tenderness.

Gases Form and Expand

As gases expand—air, steam, and carbon dioxide—cell walls stretch, become thinner, and therefore become tender. Product size and volume also increase.

Microorganisms Die

Yeast, mold, bacteria, and viruses die. Salmonella, which may be present in raw eggs, is an example of an organism destroyed during baking. Yeast, used for leavening in some products, stops producing carbon dioxide once it dies.

Egg and Gluten Proteins Stretch and Coagulate

Initially the proteins will stretch as the mixture rises in the oven. Then as the protein molecules are heated, unfolding and bonding of the molecules occurs. The protein becomes rigid and is no longer able to stretch, thus "setting" the structure of the baked product.

Starches Gelatinize

Wheat flour contains about 70 percent starch. When starch is heated in the presence of moisture, gelatinization occurs. The starch granules absorb moisture and swell, thereby providing structure. Starch gelatinization is of minimal significance as a structure builder in low moisture products such as pie crust.

Gases Evaporate

As gases escape, a dry or crisp crust develops. The product also will lose weight as moisture is lost.

Caramelization and Maillard Browning Occur

Baked products develop a brown crust and a desirable "baked flavor" due to caramelization and Maillard browning. The absence of this browning can be observed if a product is prepared in a microwave oven where the interior temperature remains cool and browning does not occur. ■

Source: Reference 1

MUFFINS

Ingredients

Muffins usually contain flour, leavening, salt, sugar, fat, egg, and liquid. Sugar and eggs may be omitted from muffins, but better flavor and texture result from including both ingredients. Fat may be reduced to one tablespoon per cup of flour and still make reasonably acceptable muffins if sugar is present at a moderate level [2]. In commercial baking, modified waxy starches, substituted for flour at a 2 percent level, have been reported to enhance the eating quality of lowfat fresh-baked muffins. These starches also could be used in muffin mixes [3]. Composite flour blends may be used to extend wheat flour supplies or to enhance nutritional qualities. For example, wheat-flour formulations containing peanut, sorghum, cassava, or cowpea flours at levels of 12 to 33 percent have been reported to produce acceptable muffins [4]. There were no significant differences observed between the formulations tested and the control muffins made with 100 percent wheat flour for 22 of 31 sensory, physical, and compositional characteristics.

Muffins are leavened by carbon dioxide gas, usually produced from baking powder. Muffins that contain an acidic ingredient, such as buttermilk or mashed bananas, typically use baking soda or a combination of baking soda and baking powder. Structure is provided by the flour components, starch and some gluten, and by egg proteins upon coagulation during baking.

Characteristics

A well-made muffin is uniform in texture, but the grain is usually not very fine and the cell walls are of medium thickness. The surface is lightly browned, has a somewhat pebbly appearance, and is rounded but not peaked. The crumb of the muffin is slightly moist, light, and tender. The muffin breaks easily without crumbling. The flavor is, of course, characteristic of the particular ingredients

FIGURE 16-5 These berry muffins have a rounded, pebbly crust and tender crumb.

used, but is usually slightly sweet and pleasant tasting. Figure 16-5 shows well-made muffins.

Mixing

Muffins are generally mixed by the muffin method. The fat, if it is solid, is melted and combined with the liquid ingredients, including egg, which are then added, all at once, to the dry ingredients. The ratio of flour to liquid in a muffin mixture is approximately two to one.

The amount of stirring is more important for muffins than for most mixtures blended by the muffin method. The gluten forms most readily when a 2 : 1 ratio of flour to liquid is used and is easily overdeveloped with too much stirring.

In an overstirred muffin, peaks and tunnels tend to form. When a muffin batter is stirred only enough to blend the liquid and dry ingredients, dampening dry flour lumps carefully, the batter appears lumpy and drops sharply from the spoon. With continued stirring, an elastic gluten mass begins to form, and the batter becomes smooth and tends to string from the spoon (Figure 16-6).

FIGURE 16-6 Characteristics of muffin batter. (a) A properly mixed muffin batter results when dry ingredients are just moistened. The batter appears pebbly, not smooth; (b) In an overmixed muffin batter, the gluten has partially developed and the batter appears to be smooth and cohesive.

Moderately overstirred muffins tend to increase slightly in volume, but further stirring results in a decrease in volume. Carbon dioxide gas is probably lost with excessive stirring. A crust then forms on the overmixed muffin during baking, before additional carbon dioxide gas is produced by the heat of the oven. As the gas is produced, it is forced through the softer center of the muffin and contributes to tunnel formation.

The effects of overmixing a muffin batter can be clearly seen in Figure 16-7. A more compact texture, rather than an open grain, is associated with peaks or knobs and tunnels in the overmanipulated muffin. With extreme overmixing, sogginess may occur and, owing to the loss of much carbon dioxide gas, few tunnels may form.

Muffins containing relatively large amounts of fat may be mixed by the conventional method. Such muffins are more cakelike in texture. They are sweeter and more tender than plain muffins. Because sugar and fat interfere with the development of gluten in the batter, the effects of increased mixing are less pronounced than in a plain muffin, and tunnel formation is less likely [6].

Dry ingredients were just dampened.

Additional stirring was done. Some tunnels are beginning to form.

Muffins were overstirred. Tunnels and peaks are apparent.

FIGURE 16-7 External and internal characteristics of muffins made from batters mixed for varying lengths of time.

Variations

A wide variety of muffins can be made by modifying the ingredients. For example, cornmeal, bran, or whole-wheat flour can be substituted for part of the white flour. Nuts, dates, blueberries, apples, other fruits, or bits of crisp bacon may be added to the batter while it is being mixed. Maple syrup muffins are made by substituting maple syrup for half of the milk in the recipe. Preparation of orange-honey muffins calls for placing one teaspoon of honey and a thin slice of fresh orange in the bottom of each baking cup before adding the muffin batter. Another version is to place one teaspoon of jelly in a half-filled muffin cup and then add the remainder of the batter, resulting in a "surprise" muffin.

Bran and cornmeal muffins can tolerate more manipulation without undesirable results than muffins made entirely of all-purpose wheat flour. Bran interferes with the development of gluten, and cornmeal does not contain gluten proteins. In the making of bran muffins, flavor may be improved by first soaking or hydrating the bran in the liquid before combining it with the other ingredients. The substitution of wheat or corn bran for up to 25 percent of the weight of the flour still allows for an acceptable muffin while increasing the fiber content to a considerable degree [7].

Baking

Pans should be prepared before the muffins are mixed. The batter becomes full of gas bubbles and rises perceptibly if allowed to stand in the mixing bowl while the pans are being prepared. Cutting into the batter later to fill muffin pans permits gas to escape and decreases the volume of the finished muffins. The bottoms of the pans should be greased, but the greasing of the side walls is optional. The muffin structure may receive some support from clinging to ungreased sides of the muffin pan as the batter rises in baking; however, muffins may be removed from the pans more easily when the sides are greased.

An oven temperature of 400°F (204°C) is satisfactory for baking muffins in about 20 to 25 minutes. A product leavened by carbon dioxide gas must be allowed to rise before crust formation occurs. For that reason, a very hot oven must be avoided. A temperature slightly under 400°F (204°C) is satisfactory if sufficient time is allowed for baking. Browning appears to be chiefly the result of the Maillard reaction, but the caramelization of sugar also may contribute to browning. Muffins baked at too low of a temperature may not develop a pleasing brown crust without being overbaked.

NUT BREADS, COFFEECAKES, AND FRIED QUICK BREADS

Nut breads and coffeecakes, like muffins, contain flour, leavening, salt, sugar, fat, egg, and liquid. Nut breads are often characterized by the inclusion of ingredients such as bananas, pumpkin, apples, carrots, zucchini, and nuts that provide flavor and moistness. Nut breads may be baked in small or standard-sized loaf pans. A small crack down the center of the loaf is common and is not considered to be defect. Because of their larger size, nut breads are typically baked at a lower temperature (350°F/177°C) compared to muffins to prevent too dark of a crust when fully baked.

Coffeecakes are similar to muffins but are made in cake or pie pans. Many coffeecakes are distinguished by fruit, nut, or crumb toppings, which provide flavor, texture, and a decorative appearance. Although many coffeecakes are classified as quick breads because baking powder is the leavening agent, some coffeecakes are made from yeast bread dough.

Cake doughnuts, hush puppies, and fritters are similar to other quick breads. However, these quick breads are deep-fat fried rather than baked. Cake doughnut dough may be refrigerated and then rolled out before cutting into a doughnut shape that is fried in hot fat. Both hush puppies and fritters are batters that can be dropped by spoonfuls or with small dishers or scoops into the hot fat. Hush puppies typically contain cornmeal, whereas fritters may contain small pieces of fruit such as apple or a spicy ingredient such as jalapeños.

BISCUITS

Ingredients

Biscuits usually contain flour, fat, milk, baking powder, and salt. Soda and buttermilk, either the fresh cultured product or dried churned buttermilk, may be used instead of sweet milk and baking powder for the leavening of biscuits. Dried churned buttermilk contains phospholipids that act as emulsifiers and aid in the fine distribution of fat in baked products. Cultured buttermilk is usually made from fluid skim or lowfat milk, so it does not have the same composition as churned buttermilk.

Characteristics

Rolled baking powder biscuits may be compact and flaky or light and fluffy, depending on how much they are kneaded and how thin the dough is rolled before baking. A well-made biscuit usually has a fairly uniform shape, an evenly browned and tender crust, a tender crumb of creamy color, and good flavor (Figure 16-8). Flakiness is a desirable characteristic of biscuits that have been rolled. Easily separated sheets of dough can be seen when a flaky biscuit is broken open. The flakiness of a biscuit results from the distribution of fat particles coated with dough. The fat melts on baking and leaves spaces between the sheets of dough.

Dropped biscuits have slightly more liquid in the recipe and are not kneaded as a soft dough. They are dropped by spoonfuls onto a cookie sheet for baking. The resulting biscuit is usually irregular in shape and slightly coarse in texture, but tender with a crisp crust.

FIGURE 16-8 The proper amount of kneading improves the volume and quality of baking powder biscuits. The biscuit on the left was prepared from unkneaded dough; the one on the right was made from dough kneaded 15 times before rolling and cutting.

Mixing

Biscuits are mixed by the biscuit or pastry method, which involves cutting a solid fat into the flour, baking powder, and salt mixture before adding milk and stirring. The dough for rolled biscuits should be a soft, rather than a stiff, dry dough (Figure 16-9). Biscuit dough that is patted or rolled with no preliminary kneading yields biscuits that are very tender and have crisp crusts; however, they are coarse in texture, are small in volume, and have

slightly rough surfaces. Kneading lightly, using 10 to 30 strokes (depending on the amount of stirring used to mix the dough), produces a biscuit of fine texture that displays evidence of layering when broken open. It also rises to a larger volume than an unkneaded biscuit (Figure 16-8). The top crust is smoother, and the general external appearance is better in slightly kneaded biscuits than in unkneaded ones. Kneading past the optimum amount produces a compact, toughened biscuit.

For variation in the preparation of biscuits, cooked bacon chips, grated cheese, chopped chives, or other herbs may be added to the flour mixture before the liquid (Figure 16-10). Grated orange rind may also be added to the flour mixture, and a sugar cube soaked in orange juice can be placed on top of the biscuit before baking.

Baking

The baking sheet requires greasing for dropped biscuits but not for rolled ones. Rolled biscuits can be placed on the baking sheet about 1 or 1 1/2 inches apart if crusty biscuits are desired. Otherwise, no space is needed between biscuits. A hot oven of 425° to 450°F (218° to 232°C) for 8 to 10 minutes is satisfactory for baking biscuits. The hot oven produces steam that aids in separating sheets of dough as the fat melts. Biscuits may stand for at least an hour before baking without loss of quality.

(a)   (b)

(c)   (d)

FIGURE 16-9 (a) Sifting the dry ingredients together; (b) cutting in the fat can be done by hand as shown here or with the use of a pastry cutter; (c) kneading the dough; (d) cutting the biscuits.

FOCUS ON SCIENCE

Why Do the Proper Mixing Procedures for Biscuits Influence Quality?

Biscuits should have more structure (gluten development) compared to muffins. For a high, flaky, and tender biscuit, the following key steps should be followed.

1. Cutting fat into the flour—develops tenderness and flakiness
2. Stirring in milk—begins gluten development
3. Kneading of dough to a limited extent—causes more gluten development
4. Rolling dough out to 1/2 to 3/4 inch thickness—is essential to a high flaky biscuit
5. Cutting out biscuits with a straight down motion with no twisting—prevents toughness and uneven biscuits

FIGURE 16-10 These rosemary biscuits can be served alone or with a simple spread. *(Courtesy of Land O'Lakes)*

SCONES

Scones, although similar to biscuits, are much richer (Plate V). Scones usually contain eggs, butter, and half-and-half or cream [5]. The biscuit method of mixing is used when making many scones; like biscuits, scones are rolled out and baked on an ungreased cookie sheet.

CHAPTER SUMMARY

- Quick breads include a variety of products that can be prepared without the rising or proofing time required by yeast breads. Common leavening agents in quick breads are baking powder, baking soda with an acidic ingredient in the recipe, or steam.

- Popovers contain a high percentage of moisture. Steam produced in a hot oven is the chief leavening agent in popovers. Popovers are usually mixed by the muffin method and are characterized by a hollow center and thick, crusty walls.

- Cream puffs and éclairs contain the same proportions of liquid to flour as popovers and are also leavened primarily by steam, but they are made with eight times as much fat. The method of mixing cream puff batter is unique and should result in a smooth, stiff, and glossy batter. Like popovers, cream puffs and éclairs have a brown exterior with a large hollow center.

- Pancakes may be thin and moist or thick and porous depending upon the proportions of ingredients used. Pancakes are leavened by carbon dioxide gas produced either from baking powder or from a sour milk and soda combination. Overstirred pancakes may be soggy and show tunnel formation due to the overdevelopment of gluten.

- Waffle mixtures are similar to pancakes except they contain more egg and more fat. Waffles of excellent quality usually result when the batter is mixed by a modified muffin method that involves separating the eggs and folding in the beaten egg whites last.

- A well-made muffin is uniform in texture, lightly browned, has a somewhat pebbly appearance, and is rounded but not peaked. The crumb of the muffin is slightly moist, light, and tender. If overstirred, peaks and tunnels tend to form. Properly mixed muffin batter will appear lumpy and will drop sharply from the spoon.

- Nut breads and coffeecakes are similar to muffins. Nut breads are baked at a lower temperature for a longer time in loaf pans, and coffeecakes are baked in cake or pie pans. Cake doughnuts, hush puppies, and fritters are similar to other quick breads but are cooked by deep-fat frying.

- A well-made biscuit usually has a fairly uniform shape, an evenly browned and tender crust, a tender crumb of creamy color, and a good flavor. Flakiness is a desirable characteristic of biscuits that have been rolled.

- Scones are similar to biscuits but are richer. Scones usually contain eggs, butter, and half-and-half or cream.

STUDY QUESTIONS

1. For each of the following products, describe (1) the usual ingredients, (2) the usual method of mixing, and (3) any special precautions to be observed in their preparation or potential problems to be avoided.
   (a) Popovers
   (b) Cream puffs
   (c) Pancakes
   (d) Waffles
   (e) Muffins
   (f) Biscuits

2. What characterizes a quick bread?
3. Compare and contrast the following:
   (a) Cream puffs, éclairs, and popovers
   (b) Pancakes and waffles
   (c) Muffins, coffeecake, and nut breads
   (d) Cake doughnuts, hush puppies, and fritters
   (e) Biscuits and scones

Yeast breads include a wide variety of products including sandwich breads, rolls, bagels, pita bread, focaccia, and many more. The type of flour, grains, and other ingredients are chosen when making breads to produce honey wheat, crushed wheat, branola, oatnut, 12-grain, 7-grain, sour dough, dark rye, light rye, pumpernickel rye, light oatmeal, light stone-ground wheat, and Roman meal, as well as the usual white, whole-wheat, and French breads. What all of these breads have in common is that all are leavened with yeast. Flour, liquid, yeast, and salt are essential ingredients in yeast breads; however, other optional ingredients such as sugar, eggs, and fat may be included depending on the particular type of bread desired.

The making of bread has become a huge industry. Most Americans buy bread rather than make it at home. The making of bread at home, however, can be a particularly rewarding experience if you take the time to develop a certain amount of skill. Warm homemade bread can make any ordinary meal a special one, and automatic bread machines make this easy. Bread is not only a delicious menu component but also provides an economical and healthful source of calories. Breads and rolls account for 15 percent of the whole grains consumed by Americans [36].

In this chapter, the following topics will be discussed:

- Characteristics of yeast breads
- Ingredients and their functions
- Mixing and handling
- Fermentation and proofing
- Baking bread
- Rolls
- Whole-grain and variety breads
- Bread staling

CHARACTERISTICS OF YEAST BREADS

The texture of good-quality bread is fine, the cell walls are thin, and the grain is uniform (Figure 17-1). Cells tend to be slightly elongated rather than round, although the shape of the cell varies. The crumb is elastic and thoroughly baked so that when cooled it does not form a gummy ball when pressed between the fingers. The fresh crumb should spring back quickly when touched with the finger.

A well-shaped loaf of bread has a rounded top and is free from rough, ragged cracks on the sides. The shred on the sides of the loaf where the dough rises is smooth and even. Careful and uniform shaping of the loaf and placing the shaped dough in the center of the baking pan contribute to the production of a well-shaped baked loaf of bread. However, abnormalities in shape have numerous

FIGURE 17-1 Bread of relatively high volume and fine texture can be made using all-purpose flour.

causes in addition to problems created by the way the dough is shaped. Such factors as the stiffness of the dough, the strength of the gluten, the extent of **fermentation** and **proofing**, the baking temperature, and the position in the oven may all affect the shape of the loaf as well as its volume and texture. Bread of good quality is light, having a large volume in relation to the weight of the loaf.

If a loaf has been allowed to proof too long before being placed in the oven, the cells overexpand and collapse somewhat. The result is a loaf of bread that is flat or sunken on top and has overhanging eaves on the sides, somewhat like a mushroom shape. The texture of such a loaf is coarse, with an open grain and crumbly character (Figure 17-2). If a loaf has not proofed long enough before being placed in the oven, it may have wide cracks on the sides after baking, because the crust structure will have set before sufficient expansion of the loaf has occurred. The texture may be somewhat compact and coarse (Figure 17-3).

FIGURE 17-2 A loaf of bread that has proofed too long in the pan before being baked. The texture is open and coarse, and "eaves" are seen on the sides of the loaf.

FIGURE 17-3 A loaf of bread that did not rise sufficiently in the pan before being baked. A ragged crack appears on the end and side where the dough rose unevenly during the process of baking. The volume is relatively low and the texture rather coarse.

INGREDIENTS

The essential ingredients for yeast-leavened dough are flour, liquid, yeast, and salt. Other constituents, mainly sugar and fat, affect texture and flavor. Additives also are used commercially in the baking of bread and rolls. These include oxidants and vital wheat gluten, which strengthen the dough and assist in the retention of leavening gas.

Yeast

For thousands of years, yeast has been the leavening agent for baking bread, although it has been produced industrially for only about 150 years [34]. It is a microscopic one-celled plant (Figure 17-4) that undergoes **metabolic** activity in dough, affecting the dough's functional properties and bread quality. Among the metabolites are amino acids, which are necessary for the activity of the yeast and also serve as important sources of bread flavor **precursors** [5]. The yeast produces carbon dioxide gas, which makes the dough light, or leavened. Carbon dioxide, ethyl alcohol, and flavoring substances result from the breaking down of simple sugars in a series of chemical reactions collectively called *fermentation*.

Since yeast is a living one-celled plant, providing temperatures favorable to yeast is important for fermentation and leavening to occur. Water that is too hot will kill yeast whereas temperatures that are too cold will result in very slow rising bread. When yeast is dissolved directly in water, a temperature of 100° to 115°F (38° to 46°C) is suggested. A slightly warmer water temperature is acceptable (120° to 130°F/48° to 54°C) when the water is added to yeast mixed with dry ingredients. Most yeast cells die at temperatures around 140°F (60°C).

Baker's yeast is marketed as *instant quick-rising active dry yeast, active dry yeast, bread machine instant dry yeast, and compressed yeast*. The species of yeast used in making bread is *Saccharomyces cerevisiae*. Strains of this microorganism are carefully selected, grown, and sometimes crossbred to produce a final product with desirable characteristics for baking. (Changes during fermentation of yeast dough are discussed later in this chapter.)

Instant Quick-Rising Active Dry Yeast. Instant quick-rising active yeast often is used by home bakers. It hydrates rapidly and therefore may be mixed directly with the dry ingredients. Additionally it rises quickly compared to active dry yeast (Figure 17-5). Instant quick-rising yeast can reduce the time for the dough to rise by as much as fifty percent [9, 28]. Dry yeast also offers the advantage of being relatively shelf stable. It may be stored for as long as one year at room temperature if left unopened. The same properties of instant quick-rising yeast that allow rapid hydration, however, also contribute to its high instability in air. Therefore, it is packaged in a vacuum or in the presence of nitrogen gas with oxygen excluded to preserve its activity. After four-ounce jars are opened, the unused portion of the yeast

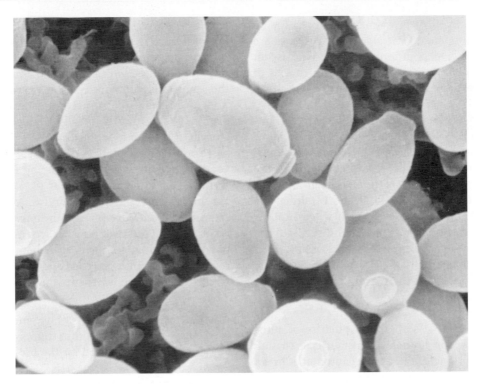

FIGURE 17-4 Photomicrograph of baker's yeast, *Saccharomyces cerevisiae*. The yeast cell in the lower right corner is in the process of reproducing by budding; a new daughter cell is being created. *(Courtesy of Universal Foods Corporation)*

FIGURE 17-5 Bread dough containing quick-rising yeast (left) rises substantially faster than dough containing the same amount of regular active dry yeast (right). Both doughs proofed for 15 minutes at 100°F (38°C). *(Reprinted from N. B. Trivedi, E. J. Cooper, and B. L. Bruinsma. Development and applications of quick-rising yeast. Food Technology, 38 (6), 51, 1984. Copyright © by Institute of Food Technologists)*

should be protected by resealing the jar and storing it in the refrigerator [34]. Use within three to four months is recommended after opening.

Instant quick-rising active yeast came into the marketplace in the early 1980s. The development of this quick-rising yeast was made possible because of advances in genetics and drying technology [34]. A specially selected strain of *Saccharomyces cerevisiae* is used, and drying is done in equipment that allows very rapid dehydra-

tion. No loss of optimal activity occurs in the drying process. The instant yeast consists of cylindrical and porous rod-shaped particles that are very fine and light, with a large surface area.

Active Dry Yeast.   Active dry yeast may be purchased for either home or commercial use. It became available in the mid 1940s and offered bakers a form of yeast that was not highly perishable. Like instant quick-rising active dry yeast, active dry yeast may be stored for up to a year when unopened. Packages of dry yeast are usually dated, after which time optimal activity is not guaranteed. The conditions that contribute to loss of viability in the yeast are mainly air, moisture, and warm temperatures.

Active dry yeast must be rehydrated for 5 to 10 minutes in water at 110° to 115°F (43° to 46°C), to allow proper reconstitution of the yeast without a loss of cell contents. Water above 130°F (54°C) begins to kill the yeast plants; cool water can shock the yeast, causing some of the cell contents to be leached out and resulting in a "slackened" dough that flows in the pan when proofed [6]. Active dry yeast should not be added directly to the dry ingredients as is done with instant quick-rising yeast. Compared to instant quick-rising yeast, active dry yeast has larger granules, which is the reason it does not rehydrate rapidly.

Bread Machine Yeast. With the popularity of automatic bread machines in homes, an instant quick-rising yeast specially developed for use in automatic bread machines is available. Although quick-rising active dry yeast also works well in automatic bread-making machines, bread machine yeast has added ascorbic acid (vitamin C) which functions as a dough conditioner. The ascorbic acid promotes stretching of the dough during rising. Whether bread machine yeast or instant quick-rising active dry yeast, the yeast should be placed in or near the flour and should not come into contact with liquid or salt, especially when the timer is being used to delay the mixing and baking of the bread.

Compressed or Fresh Cake Yeast. Compressed yeast is produced from a blend of wet yeast cells and emulsifiers that is extruded and then cut into a block form in a variety of sizes. It contains about 70 percent moisture and is therefore perishable and must be kept refrigerated. Fresh yeast should be used within 10 days of purchase. When held at room temperature for more than several hours, this yeast loses leavening activity. A fresh sample of compressed yeast is creamy white in color, is moist but not slimy, crumbles easily, and has a distinctive odor. When stale, the yeast becomes brownish and may develop a strong unpleasant odor. Because compressed yeast undergoes minimal processing, it is the most consistent in quality of all the baker's yeasts [6].

Compressed yeast must be softened in lukewarm liquid at approximately 85°F (29°C) so that it will blend with other dough ingredients. It may be softened either in a small amount of water or in the total amount of liquid used in the dough. Because compressed yeast contains added moisture and conditioners not found in active dry yeast, the dry yeast cannot be substituted interchangeably on a weight basis. The weight of active dry yeast used should be approximately 60 percent of the weight of compressed yeast.

Starters. Yeast may be introduced to bread dough by use of a starter. A *starter* is some of the sponge from a previous baking saved for future use. Sourdough starters were highly valued in early history, as the starter provided the only available source of yeast for making breads. Today, artisanal bakers prize their starters, because of the distinctive flavor of the breads produced by the bakery as a result of their unique starter.

Sourdough starters get their gaseous action and flavor components from wild yeast and lactobacilli bacteria from the air to ferment the mix [8, 39]. Similar bacteria are present in yogurt. Flour and water are the only two required ingredients for a sourdough starter; however, additional ingredients such as yogurt, milk, sugar, or potato water may be included depending on the starter recipe. Starters must be used and replenished frequently with fresh flour and water to avoid spoilage.

Amount of Yeast to Use. The amount of yeast to be used may be altered within limits according to the amount of time to be used for the bread-making process. Small amounts of yeast, such as 1/4 to 1/3 cake or package per 1 cup liquid, are satisfactory when the yeast is given enough time to activate. With small amounts of yeast, a sponge method of mixing permits more rapid growth of yeast. Excess yeast causes an undesirable odor and flavor in bread. Coarse texture, gray color of crust and crumb, and loaves of distorted shapes also may result from a great excess of yeast and too rapid fermentation. Bread can be made in about 2 1/2 hours using 1 cake or package of yeast per 1 to 1 1/4 cups of liquid. The use of quick-rise active dry yeast can shorten the rising time even further. For ordinary use, however, the smallest amount of yeast that will serve the purpose is desirable.

Flour

Wheat flour is unique in that it will produce a viscoelastic dough that retains gas [13]. The result is breads of high volume and fine texture with a cohesive, elastic crumb. Gluten, which is developed when the glutenin and gliadin proteins in wheat flour are hydrated and mixed, is responsible for extensibility and elasticity in the dough. After the gluten structure has been expanded by gas cells, heat coagulates the gluten proteins and sets the structure. Because of the weakening effect of fermentation on gluten, the flour best adapted to the making of bread is one of strong gluten quality, such as bread flour. A weak gluten becomes so highly dispersed that a bread of poor volume and quality is likely to result. Although bread flour is the most desirable for bread making, acceptable bread can also be prepared using all-purpose flour. See Chapter 15 for more information about gluten and types of flours.

The baking performance of flour is measured in the laboratory by food scientists. The relationship between laboratory tests and flour performance in production is complex. Among the factors that can contribute to a change in flour performance are genetics of the developed wheat varieties and changes in milling practices. The level of protein, however, appears to be the most important factor influencing loaf volume [13]. (See Chapter 15 for more on wheat and milling). Dough conditioners may be added to strengthen the desirable characteristics of the dough. Potassium bromide was used frequently in the past, but ascorbic acid is now the most commonly used oxidative flour improver [32].

A pound loaf of bread can be made with approximately 3/4 pound or 3 cups of flour and 1 cup of liquid. For good bread flours, about 60 to 65 percent of the weight of the flour as liquid gives a dough of the best consistency. Strong flours with a high protein content have a higher hydration capacity than flours of lower protein content. Thus, the amount of liquid used in making bread varies with the hydration capacity of the gluten-forming proteins in the flour. Weak flours have a low imbibition capacity and therefore require a lower percentage of moisture. If milk is used instead of water, a slightly higher proportion is needed because of the 12 to 14 percent of milk solids present. The amount of flour required in bread making also may vary with the level of humidity in the environment. Thus it is common to make small adjustments in the amount of flour in a bread recipe to achieve a soft, but not sticky dough.

Liquid

Liquid is essential in bread dough to hydrate flour proteins and contribute to the development of gluten. In addition, it is essential for the partial gelatinization of starch, which makes an important contribution to bread structure [14]. Other components, such as sugar or salt, are dissolved or dispersed in the liquid. The liquid used in making bread may be milk, water, potato water, or whey. Eggs also may serve as part of the liquid in bread dough. If the liquid is milk, it should be scalded. Heating destroys certain enzymes and changes some proteins so that an undesirable softening of the dough does not occur during fermentation. Dry milk used by commercial bakers has been heat treated.

The type of liquid used will affect the characteristics of the dough. Water is used in lean doughs when a crisp crust is desirable. The addition of milk and egg results in a rich, tender bread. Eggs also add color. A small quantity of mashed potato may be added to bread dough. Potato water and cooked potato introduce gelatinized starch into the mixture, which favors fermentation and also enhances the keeping quality and flavor of the baked bread. Milk and whey increase the nutritive value of bread to some extent.

Beyond the amount of liquid required to achieve maximum loaf volume, additional absorption of water dilutes gluten and results in decreased loaf volume. Too small a proportion of moisture may not provide enough water for optimal gluten development and may result in decreased loaf volume of the finished bread.

Sugar

Although it is not an indispensable ingredient in a bread formula, sugar plays several roles in bread making. It increases the rate of fermentation by providing readily available food for yeast so that the bread rises in a shorter period. If larger amounts of sugar are used, however, as in sweet rolls, the action of the yeast is somewhat repressed, and the fermentation and proofing periods must be longer. Flavor (primarily sweetness), texture, and browning are also affected by the use of sugar, although the browning of bread is primarily the result of the Maillard reaction. Sugar in bread dough comes from three sources: that present in the flour, that produced by the action of enzymes hydrolyzing starch, and that added as an ingredient [23].

For loaf breads, 2 teaspoons to 1 1/2 tablespoons of sugar per 1 pound loaf are common amounts used. Doughs for rolls usually contain slightly more sugar—about 2 to 4 tablespoons per cup of liquid used. Some recipes use honey, corn syrup, brown sugar, or molasses instead of granulated sugar because of the flavor and colors that these forms of sugar may supply.

FOCUS ON SCIENCE

Vital Wheat Gluten

Vital wheat gluten is concentrated dried gluten protein that has been derived from wheat flour by removing starch and the bran. Vital wheat gluten contains 75 to 80 percent protein. Although sometimes called *gluten flour,* vital wheat gluten and gluten flour are not the same. Gluten flour typically has a protein level 40 to 45 percent. Contrast either of these, however, to the protein levels found in all-purpose (9.5 to 11.5 percent) or bread flour (11.5 to 13.5 percent).

Because gluten retains the gas and steam formed during baking, vital wheat gluten is an essential ingredient when baking with soy flour or soya powder. Soy does not contain the proteins needed to form gluten; therefore, the soy-based doughs will not rise or hold shape like doughs made from wheat flour. Either vital wheat gluten or gluten flour may be used in variety of yeast bread recipes as a means to raise the protein content and therefore result in greater gluten development.

Fat

Fat is used in commercial bread making to facilitate the handling of the dough, to increase the keeping quality of the bread, and to improve loaf volume and texture [13, 22, 32]. The tenderness of the bread also is increased. Liquid oils do not perform the same functions that allow an increase in volume as solid shortenings; however, commercial bakers can combine various conditioners and softeners with liquid oil and produce a bread of acceptable quality [12].

For loaf breads, 1 to 1 1/2 tablespoons of fat per 1 pound loaf are sufficient to improve tenderness, flavor, and keeping quality. Two to 4 tablespoons or more per cup of liquid may be used in roll dough for increased tenderness.

Salt

Salt is added to bread dough for flavor, but it also has other effects. Salt retards yeast fermentation and therefore increases the time required for bread dough to rise. Salt has a firming effect on gluten structure [32]. Bread made without salt is often crumbly in texture and may easily become overlight.

The amount of salt usually considered to produce good flavor in bread is approximately 1 teaspoon per 1 pound loaf. An excess of salt should be avoided from the standpoint of both texture and flavor. It would appear, however, that the usual level of salt might be reduced in bread without sacrificing quality or acceptability. In one study, a panel of 40 untrained judges found both white and wheat breads acceptable when salt was reduced by 50 percent of the normal level [41].

Dough Conditioners and Other Ingredients

Dough conditioning formulations are commonly added to commercially prepared yeast doughs. These include oxidizing agents that act on the gluten structure to produce a better-handling dough and a bread with finer texture, better volume, and a softer crumb. The U.S. Food and Drug Administration (FDA) has approved several oxidizing substances for use as dough conditioners, including ascorbic acid, calcium iodate, azodicarbonamide, and calcium peroxide.

Emulsifiers enhance dough stability, produce a more flexible dough, and result in a finer and softer crumb [32]. A number of emulsifiers such as lecithin, mono- and diglycerides, diacetyl tartaric esters of mono- and diglycerides, and sodium stearoyl lactylates may be added to bread dough. In addition, yeast nutrients such as monocalcium phosphate and calcium sulfate may be used in commercial bread making.

Addition of certain enzymes, including **amylases** and **proteases**, to flours or doughs can initiate improvements such as retardation of staling, enhancement of bread crust color, and softer crumb. Most of the enzymes that are commercially available for use in bakery processing come from fungi and bacteria [7].

New bakery ingredients continue to be developed. Whey protein ingredients have been found to improve the mixing of bread dough, while producing high-quality breads with desirable characteristics [25]. Rice bran extracts offer functionality as both a dough conditioner and an emulsifier. Encapsulated flavorings offer advantages in flavor and bread quality. Savory Betrflakes™ is a lipid-based flavor delivery system that offers tomato-basil and cheddar-garlic flavors for breads such as focaccia [25]. The addition of garlic to wheat flour doughs has been shown to weaken the dough and result in an undesirable crumb and low volume; however, these negative effects are not present when the garlic has been encapsulated [18]. Encapsulated cinnamon, sold as Flavor-Shure™ Cinnamon, offers advantages in bread quality as well, because raw cinnamon added to bread dough will inhibit rise [25].

MIXING AND HANDLING

The mixing and kneading of bread greatly influences the final quality of the bread. During mixing, ingredients are blended into a mostly homogeneous mass, air is incorporated into the dough creating many small gas nuclei, and gluten is developed. Flour particles rapidly absorb water in the early stages of mixing. With continued mixing, moisture is distributed throughout the dough. The creation of many small gas nuclei during mixing is significant

FOCUS ON SCIENCE

How Do Dough Conditioners Strengthen the Yeast Dough?

Oxidizing substances are used as dough conditioners to produce a bread with finer texture, a softer crumb, and better volume. So how does this dough strengthening and conditioning

effect occur? Disulfide bonding strengthens gluten. Sulfer atoms on the protein molecules, however, can bind with hydrogen atoms. Sulfur bound to hydrogen cannot form a disulfide linkage. Oxidizers work to improve doughs by "stripping" hydrogen atoms from the sulfur–hydrogen (sulfhydryl) linkages, and therefore more sulfur is available for the formation of the gluten-strengthening disulfide bond.

because during fermentation yeast increases the size of existing gas cells but does not create new gas cells. Thus, for a fine crumb, air must be incorporated into the dough during mixing [32].

The characteristics of dough change during mixing and kneading (Figure 17-6). Initially upon homogenization of the ingredients, the dough tears easily and sticks to the hands. With increased mixing, the dough becomes smoother, is less sticky, and has more coherence. At this stage, the dough will pull away from the sides of a mixer. In the last stage, the dough is well developed. The dough displays strong coherence, and a small ball of dough may be stretched into a thin film without tearing or breaking. The dough cannot be similarly stretched in the earlier stages. If the dough is overmixed, the dough will become sticky, extensible, and excessively soft [32]. Overmixing is most likely to occur when using a mechanical mixer.

Two basic methods of mixing yeast bread are the straight-dough method and the sponge method. The batter method also may be used for some breads. Kneading is an important part of the bread-making process.

Straight-Dough Method

In the mixing of yeast bread by the straight-dough method, the liquid is generally warmed with the sugar, salt, and softened fat. If milk is used, it must be scalded then cooled to the proper temperature before adding the yeast to avoid killing the yeast. Depending on the type of yeast being used, the yeast will be mixed with the dry ingredients or rehydrated in warm water. Instant quick-rising active dry yeast hydrates quickly and therefore is mixed directly with the dry ingredients.

About one-third of the flour is then blended with the liquid ingredients and vigorously mixed. Beating the batter blends ingredients uniformly, starts the development of gluten, and incorporates air cells. The remainder of the flour is added gradually to form a dough that is "kneaded" in the mixer or transferred to a floured board for kneading by hand. The dough is kneaded (see

"Kneading" later in the chapter) until it has a smooth, satiny, outside surface.

Sponge Method

In the sponge method, a loose dough (sponge) consisting of liquid, sugar, yeast, and part of the flour is mixed as in the straight-dough method. When the mixture has stood until it is light and full of gas bubbles, it is then made into dough by the addition of the remaining flour, salt, and other recipe ingredients. The dough is kneaded and allowed to rise until it is at least double its original volume, after which it is shaped and placed in baking pans. Much of the bread made commercially in the United States is made using this method [13].

Batter Method

Breads may be made from batters that contain less flour than doughs. The straight-dough method is modified to eliminate the kneading and shaping steps. The batters are allowed to rise at least once in the bowl and/or in the baking pan. These unkneaded breads usually have a more open grain and uneven surface than kneaded breads and lack the elasticity of the crumb; however, less preparation time is required.

Automatic Bread Machines

Automatic bread machines have gained popularity in the home. With the convenience of these machines, you may, if you desire, plan to return home and find fragrant odors of baking bread permeating your kitchen. In using bread machines, the ingredients are placed in the pan, and the timing cycle is set according to the manufacturer's instructions. At the scheduled time, the loaf of bread will be mixed, proofed, and baked. To make specialty breads, the dough cycle may be used which will signal when the dough may be removed for shaping, final proofing, and baking in a conventional oven. Bread machine or instant quick-rising active dry yeast is well suited for use in bread machines.

FIGURE 17-6 Dough development. (left) Dough barely mixed; (center) dough partially developed; (right) dough developed. *(Courtesy of the Wheat Flour Institute)*

Kneading

Kneading of bread dough is essential for the development of strong elastic gluten strands from flour of relatively high protein content. During the kneading process, the swollen particles of the protein fractions, gliadin and glutenin, adhere to each other and become aligned in the long elastic strands of gluten. The development of gluten during kneading is important to provide structure and strength for the dough and the finished loaf of bread. Starch granules from the flour, entrapped in the developing gluten, also play an important role in bread structure.

Kneading by Hand. Skillful handling of the dough ball is necessary at the beginning of kneading. The mass may be collected into a ball of dough that, with proper handling, tends to remain smooth on the outer surface in contact with the board. All wrinkles and cracks are best kept on the side in contact with the hands to minimize the tendency for the dough to stick to the board. Wet spots on the outside surface may require frequent coating with flour until the dough becomes elastic enough to knead easily.

The kneading movement is a rhythmical one in which the fingers are used to pull the mass over into position for kneading and the lower part of the hand is used for applying pressure to the dough. Forcing the fingers into the dough or using too heavy a pressure tends to keep the mass of dough sticky and difficult to handle (see Figure 17-7.

Kneading by Machine. Various mixers are available with motors powerful enough to mix bread dough completely, thus eliminating the necessity of kneading by hand. The manufacturers' directions should be followed in the use of these mixers. Special attachments called *dough hooks* are commonly used in both commercial and commercial-style home mixers. The dough should cling to the dough hook in one ball as mixing progresses. If the dough is too soft to form a ball, additional flour should be added.

When kneading bread by machine, the dough can overheat due to friction during the mixing and kneading process. This effect can be observed when making large quantities of bread in foodservice or when using a food processor in the home setting. This undesirable rise in dough temperature can be controlled by a formula that calculates the desired temperature of liquid by taking into account the friction heat generated by the equipment, flour temperature, and room temperature [19]. Recipes provided by home food processors generally recommend a specific water temperature, which is cooler than used in traditional hand-mixed recipes, to control the dough temperature.

Quality Considerations. Whether kneading by hand or by machine, care must be used during kneading to avoid the incorporation of excess flour into the mixture, which results in too stiff a dough. With the development of a good hand-kneading technique, it is surprising how little flour need be used on a board for the handling of any kind of dough. Later handling can be done with practically no flour because of the increased extensibility of the dough after fermentation.

Although overmixing by hand is unlikely, dough may be kneaded too much by machine. As discussed earlier, overmixed dough will become sticky and excessively soft. Properly kneaded dough should be smooth, elastic, and have evidence of small air pockets or blisters under the surface of the dough.

FERMENTATION AND PROOFING

Fermentation may be described as the time between the start of mixing and the molding or shaping of the dough. Functionally, the fermentation period continues dough development while the dough rises or increases in volume. Proofing increases the volume of the shaped dough to result in desirable properties during baking. Decorative finishes may be added to the dough following shaping but prior to proofing and baking.

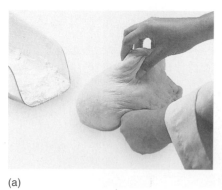

(a)   (b)   (c)

FIGURE 17-7 To knead bread: (a) bring the edge of the dough toward you; (b) push the dough away from you with your fist or the heel of your hand; (c) turn the dough one-quarter of a turn and repeat the process until the dough is elastic and smooth.

Fermentation

Fermentation initially is an aerobic reaction. The respiration of the yeast consumes the oxygen trapped in the dough during the first few minutes and thus the fermentation reaction in bread is predominately an anaerobic reaction [13, 32]. The fermentation reaction may be shown by the following formula [13].

$$C_6H_{12}O_6 + \text{Yeast} \rightarrow 2C_2H_5OH + 2CO_2$$
Glucose   Ethanol   Carbon Dioxide

The carbon dioxide gas produced during yeast fermentation causes the bread dough to expand or rise. Ethyl alcohol is volatilized during baking. Byproducts of the fermentation reaction also include many flavor substances. Organic acids, amino acids, and other substances produced during fermentation participate in complex reactions that result in characteristic bread flavor.

Favorable Conditions for Fermentation. During fermentation, the dough should be in a warm, moist environment. Fermentation can take place over a wide range of temperatures, but the best flavor is probably developed at 79° to 90°F (26° to 32°C). Cold inhibits yeast activity, and a temperature of about 130°F (55°C) destroys yeast plants. Excessively warm temperatures may favor the growth of organisms that produce undesirable flavors in bread.

Dough that is exposed to air develops a crust or film that must later be discarded to avoid the formation of heavy streaks throughout the dough. To avoid crust formation, a proofing cabinet should be used. Proofing cabinets control the temperature and the humidity to provide ideal conditions for the fermentation and proofing of the dough. If one is not available, the bowl containing the dough may be placed in a pan of warm water and then covered with another pan of the same size. The vaporization of moisture from the surface of the water maintains a humidity that keeps the bread surface from drying out. Alternatively, the surface of the dough may be lightly greased and the bowl covered with a plastic wrap.

Punching Down. Once the dough has doubled in size, the dough is punched down or is lightly mixed in the mixer (Figure 17-9). The key purpose of punching down the dough is to subdivide the gas cells to produce more smaller cells [13, 32]. A dough that has been punched down during fermentation and allowed to rise a second time before shaping will have a better crumb texture and larger oven spring [32]. A satisfactory bread, however, can be made at home with only one rising period prior to shaping of the loaf or rolls.

Optimal Fermentation. The number of times the dough should be allowed to rise in the fermentation period varies with the strength of the flour. Doughs made from strong gluten flours may be allowed to rise more times than doughs made from flours with lower protein content before the dough is placed in the pans. Weak glutens tend to become too highly dispersed with too long a fermentation period. Bread must be baked before gluten strands become so thin and weak that they break, thus allowing carbon dioxide gas to escape.

Overfermentation results in poor oven spring and is likely to produce a loaf that is flat or sunken on top. The

UP CLOSE

Gluten Development

Protein particles in the flour are moistened and start to swell as the dough is mixed. With mixing, interactions occur and include hydrogen bonding. The hydrogen atoms of −OH or −SH group in the protein molecules interchange and establish weak bonds [13]. Increased interaction leads to the development of the gluten complex. The gluten complex is composed of glutenin and gliadin.

Gluten may be envisioned as a coiled protein that contains a number of disulfide bonds (−S−S−) linking parts of the molecule together to provide more strength and rigidity (see Figure 17-8) [33]. During mixing, many of these bonds are broken, and the gluten becomes more expanded and relaxed so that it may be stretched by the leavening gases. The gluten is "developed" and becomes more extensible and elastic.

At one time, gluten development theory suggested glutenin and gliadin molecules merged to form a network of giant gluten molecules. Recent research, however, suggests the breakdown of glutenins occurs into smaller subunits which then aggregate into larger proteins after mixing [32]. ■

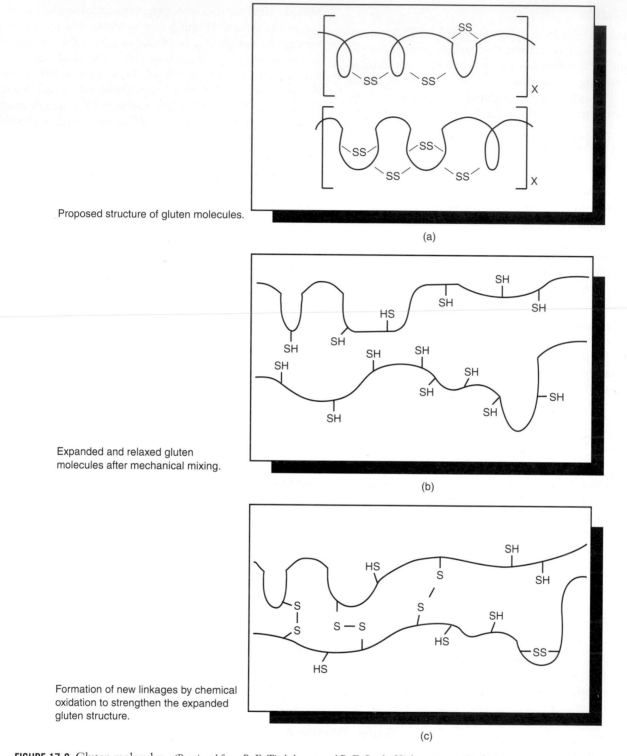

Proposed structure of gluten molecules.

(a)

Expanded and relaxed gluten molecules after mechanical mixing.

(b)

Formation of new linkages by chemical oxidation to strengthen the expanded gluten structure.

(c)

FIGURE 17-8 Gluten molecules. *(Reprinted from R. E. Tieckelmann and R. E. Steele. Higher-assay grade of calcium peroxide improves properties of dough.* Food Technology, *45(1), 108, 1991. Copyright © by Institute of Food Technologists)*

bread will have a coarse grain and thick cell walls. It also may have an unpleasant sour odor and flavor and a crust that does not brown well. The volume is small, and the loaf is heavy and compact. In contrast, underfermenta-tion produces bread that has thick cell walls and is heavy, small in volume, and less tender than bread that has fer-mented sufficiently to bring about a desirable dispersion of the gluten.

(a)   (b)

FIGURE 17-9 (a) The dough before rising; (b) Punching down the risen dough.

UP CLOSE

What Happens during Fermentation?

Growth of Gas Nuclei

The gas nuclei in the dough initially contain about 20 percent oxygen and 80 percent nitrogen. As the yeast consumes the oxygen, only nitrogen remains, and the fermentation process becomes an anaerobic reaction. Carbon dioxide, produced by the yeast, is diffused and retained in the dough as (a) gas within the gas cells and (b) dissolved in the aqueous phase of the dough [13]. Cell membranes stretch and the dough rises.

Action of Enzymes

Fermentation is catalyzed by a variety of enzymes produced in the yeast cells. A starch-splitting enzyme called *amylase* is present in flour. In commercial bread baking, additional amylase may be added. This enzyme catalyzes the hydrolysis of starch to dextrins and maltose. Dextrins help to maintain freshness of breads, and maltose may be fermented by the yeast or can contribute to the color of the crust [32].

Proteases soften gluten and thus at low levels can improve the handling of the dough during mixing [32]. These enzymes hydrolyze proteins to peptides and amino acids. If the proteases are too active, they may hydrolyze too much of the protein and produce harmful effects, such as poor texture and decreased volume.

Increase in Acidity

Acidity increases in bread dough from a pH of about 6.0 when first mixed to a pH of 5.0 during fermentation [13]. The increase in acidity is attributed largely to the carbon dioxide, but organic acids, chiefly acetic and lactic, are also formed. Increased acidity promotes fermentation and amylase activity and holds in check some unwanted organisms. Greater dispersion of the gluten with loss of elasticity and tenacity also occurs as acidity increases. ■

Proofing

After the dough has undergone fermentation and is molded into a loaf and placed in a baking pan, it is allowed to rise again (Figure 17-10). This final rising in the pan is called *proofing*. Proofing should be terminated when the loaf has approximately doubled in size and the dough does not spring back when it is lightly touched.

The inside bottom of the pan in which the dough is placed is greased to aid in removing the baked bread from the pan. The greasing of side walls is optional, but a

FOCUS ON SCIENCE

How Does Proofing Affect the Volume of the Baked Bread Loaf?

Proofing is the second rising of the yeast dough before it is baked. There are proofing ovens that are temperature- and moisture-controlled for dough rising. Proofing is an important step in bread making because it will affect the final volume of the baked bread. An indentation by the finger into the dough is a simple procedure to determine adequate proofing or rising. If the dough is under proofed, the baked bread will be small and dense. If the dough is over proofed, the bread will rise during baking, but because the dough is already overstretched, it will collapse in the oven and be sunken in the middle.

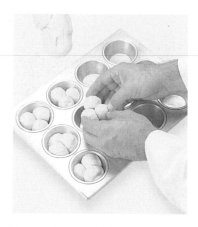

FIGURE 17-10 Placing three small dough balls into a muffin tin to make cloverleaf rolls. This is a simple yet attractive way to shape rolls before proofing.

somewhat larger volume of loaf may result from allowing the dough to cling to the side walls while rising.

Decorative Finishes

Before proofing, breads may be shaped into rolls or braided to create beautiful rolls and breads (Figures 17-10, 17-11, 17-12) Additional decorative touches may be added immediately before baking that change the appearance of the bread. A glaze or a wash may be brushed onto the dough to attach seeds, oats, and other toppings to the crust. A wash also may be used to create a shiny, crisp, or soft crust. A whole egg and water wash will promote a shiny crust, whereas a whole egg and milk wash will create a shiny, soft crust. Egg white and water is used when a shiny, firm crust is desired. Milk or cream will make the crust soft, and a water wash will create a crisp crust [15].

FIGURE 17-11 This panettone bread is braided to create a beautiful appearance.
(Courtesy of Wheat Foods Council)

FIGURE 17-12 Rolls can be formed into many different shapes. *(Courtesy of Fleischmann's Yeast®)*

Many breads are slashed to create an attractive design on the crust. Doughs are slashed by cutting lightly into the surface of the dough with a sharp knife just before baking. In addition to the decorative effect, hard crusted breads may be slashed to permit the escape of gases and allow additional rising during baking [15].

BAKING BREAD

Conventional Baking

As heat is applied to the bread during baking, gas production and expansion are greatly accelerated, which results in a sharp rising of the dough, called *oven spring*, for the first few minutes of the baking period. The temperature of the interior of the loaf gradually rises until a temperature is reached that destroys yeast plants, inactivates enzymes, and stops fermentation. Alcohol is volatile and is almost completely driven off during the baking of bread.

The maximum temperature of the interior of the loaf is approximately the boiling point of water, but as moisture evaporates from the exterior surface and crust formation occurs, the temperature of the crust becomes higher than that of the crumb. Gluten undergoes a gradual change in properties over a rather wide range of temperatures (122° to 175°F/50° to 80°C) and finally becomes firm as it coagulates. Partial gelatinization of starch occurs during baking. Starch absorbs only about one-third of its weight of water at room temperature, but because it constitutes about four-fifths of flour, it is responsible for about half the total water absorption of flours made into dough. As the gluten loses water during baking and the starch swells with the imbibition of additional water during heating, at least partial gelatinization of the starch is made possible [16]. In fresh bread, the gluten holds less water, and the starch holds more water than in the uncooked dough. The partially gelatinized starch contributes to bread structure as it is embedded within strands of coagulated gluten proteins.

The Maillard reaction appears to be chiefly responsible for the brown crust color in baked bread. The browning reaction probably also contributes to bread flavor. Browning of bread, as with other baked products, is influenced by the type of pan used. Pans with dark or dull finishes absorb heat more readily than bright shiny ones that reflect heat. Therefore, the surfaces of bread in contact with dull or dark pans brown more readily and uniformly.

Baking temperatures and times vary according to the type of dough and size of mass to be baked. Whether a hot or moderate oven is used at the beginning depends on the extent of rising before the bread is placed in the oven. Too hot an oven, however, sets the bread before optimum oven spring occurs, thus reducing the final volume and affecting the texture. Most recipes recommend temperatures of 375°F to 425°F (191°C to 218°C) for bread baking.

Microwave Baking

White bread is generally not acceptably cooked by microwaves because of the lack of crust formation; however, relatively dark breads, such as rye and whole-wheat or oatmeal wheat, have been satisfactorily prepared in the microwave oven with little additional heating in a hot conventional oven. Medium (50 percent) power is generally used. Brown-and-serve rolls are successfully prepared in the microwave. They are browned in a hot conventional oven before being served.

Frozen Yeast Doughs

Frozen bread dough that is already shaped into a loaf is marketed at the retail level. The dough is thawed at room temperature and allowed to rise before baking. This convenience food allows one to have the aroma of freshly baked bread in the kitchen without the mixing and kneading processes. The most significant problem associated with the freezing of dough is how to maintain the viability and gassing power of frozen yeasts. The longer the active fermentation time undergone by yeast before freezing, the less stable the yeast is to freezing. Thus, the addition of yeast at the end of mixing, a reduction in proofing time, and an increase in yeast amount are possible aids in producing acceptable frozen doughs. The addition of extra wheat gluten and oxidants, as well as other additives, may also help to ensure yeast viability and baking strength. The possibility of using yeast strains other than *Saccharomyces cerevisiae* in frozen doughs has been suggested [3].

ROLLS

Rolls usually contain somewhat larger amounts of fat and sugar than are generally found in bread. Eggs may also be added, although satisfactory roll dough can be made without eggs. The eggs may be beaten lightly and added in the early stages of dough making. An egg adds about 3 tablespoons of liquid.

Rolls require 15 to 25 minutes of baking at 425°F (218°C). Pan rolls require a longer baking time than single rolls separated on a baking sheet or in muffin pans. A pan of rolls may require almost as much baking time as a pound loaf of bread.

Although any roll dough can be held in the refrigerator for one or two days before baking, refrigerator rolls are probably best made from a dough of slightly different proportions from plain rolls. For refrigerator rolls, only a moderate amount of yeast is used to avoid overfermentation, and slightly more than the usual amount of sugar is added to serve as food for the yeast during the approximately one-week period that the dough may be held before baking. When the rolls are first mixed, they are kneaded and allowed to undergo one fermentation, after which they are punched to release gas and stored closely covered at refrigerator temperature to be used as needed. If the dough rises appreciably during holding, it is punched from time to time to release gas. When it is needed, part of the dough is removed from the refrigerator, shaped into rolls, and allowed to rise in a warm room until the rolls double in bulk. This process may require two to three hours, depending on the temperature of the

Commercial Bread Baking

Numerous technological advances have been applied in the baking industry. Many processes used in commercial bread making are, of course, very different from procedures used in the home kitchen.

Pure yeast cultures and standardized ingredients, including many chemical additives, are available to commercial bakers. Powerful mixers, fermentation rooms, dough dividers, and automatic proofing, baking, and wrapping systems are used. Through the 1940s, the predominant bread-making system in the United States was a sponge-and-dough system. Since then, several alternative methods have been developed, including a conventional straight-dough method,

a continuous-dough process, and a short-time bread-making system. Short-time doughs involve a single mixing step and little or no bulk fermentation of the dough before panning. Short-time breads are generally made with warmer doughs, more yeast, and higher levels of oxidants than are used in the preparation of conventional doughs [40]. High-speed mixing of doughs substitutes to some degree for the fermentation period. Addition of oxidizing and/or reducing agents also helps to develop the dough with less fermentation required. Shortening the fermentation period in commercial bread production saves time and labor expense. ■

dough and the room. Rolls can be formed into a variety of shapes and sizes (Figure 17-12 and Plates VI, VII).

WHOLE-GRAIN AND VARIETY BREADS

Artisan breads, flat breads, hearth breads and other specialty breads have gained in popularity among American consumers [30, 35]. Restaurants and bakeries are featuring more of these products to satisfy the changing tastes of customers. Contrast in the flavor and texture of breads is made possible by the use of a variety of grains in various forms (Figure 17-13). Flours, meals, and flakes can all be used.

Whole-grain flours contain essentially all the vitamins and minerals, as well as fiber, present in unmilled grain and thus offer nutritional advantages over highly milled flours. The importance of incorporating whole-grain products into the diet on a regular basis has been emphasized [4, 31, 37]. Four slices of most variety breads furnish appreciable amounts of minerals and vitamins to help meet daily nutritional needs [26, 27].

Other nutritive ingredients may be added to breads to meet the needs of particular groups. For example, some researchers developed a bread formulation designed to supply the elderly with essential nutrients that are often deficient in their diets. Soy-based ingredients have been developed for use in bread products marketed for women [25]. With the use of whey, a nutritive yeast product, and lowfat cheese, an acceptable bread was formulated that increased the calcium, thiamin, and riboflavin content 1.2, 2.0, and 1.2 times, respectively, over that of the best-liked commercial bread [21].

Whole-Wheat Bread

Whole-wheat bread is prepared with whole-wheat flour. If some white flour is used with the whole-wheat flour in commercial bread making, the bread is labeled simply wheat bread. Wheat bread generally contains about 75 percent white flour and 25 percent whole-wheat flour [38]. The procedure for mixing, fermenting, and baking whole-wheat dough is similar to that described for white bread dough, although the kneading does not have to be as extensive. The small particles of bran in whole-wheat flour interfere with the development of gluten. Even extensive kneading does not overcome this effect. The volume of the finished loaf of whole-wheat bread is therefore usually somewhat less than that of white bread. If the whole-wheat flour is very finely ground, however, the volume of the bread made from this flour may approach that of white bread.

Whole white wheat bread is relatively new in the marketplace. It is made from hard white wheat instead of hard red wheat, and thus is it fairly white in color. Because of a specialized milling process, the whole wheat is finely milled and thus produces a soft bread without the usual hearty texture associated with whole-wheat bread made from hard red wheat. See Chapter 15 for more discussion about types of wheat and whole grains.

High-Fiber Breads

With an emphasis on the need for increased fiber in the diets of most Americans, the baking industry has developed ways of adding extra bran to breads without sacrificing quality [29]. Vital wheat gluten and certain conditioners can be used to counteract the deleterious effects of up to 15 parts of bran per 85 parts of flour. Bran flakes or prepared bran cereals may be used at home as added ingredients in wheat bread or rolls to provide additional fiber.

A survey of breads marketed in one local area suggests that there are considerable differences in the amounts of dietary fiber found in specialty breads and breads labeled *wheat bread*. The fiber content ranged from 0.5 gram to about 2.0 grams per slice. Whole-wheat bread contains about 1.5 grams of dietary fiber per slice [20].

Use of Flours Other Than Wheat

Some wheat flour is needed in all yeast breads to provide gluten for bread structure and lightness. Flours milled from grains other than wheat may be combined with wheat flour to give varied and flavorful baked products. Of all the grains, rye flour comes closest to wheat in terms of gluten-forming properties, but rye flour alone does not make a light loaf of bread. Rye yeast bread generally contains some wheat flour. Approximately equal portions of

FIGURE 17-13 Variety breads and rolls truly do come in many different shapes and sizes. *(Courtesy of Kansas Wheat Commission and U.S. Wheat Associates)*

MULTICULTURAL CUISINE

Evolution of the Sandwich

It was an Englishman, John Montague, the fourth Earl of Sandwich, who in 1762 satisfied his hunger in a hurry by ordering two slices of meat between two pieces of bread. Thus was born the sandwich, of which about 45 billion are now being consumed each year in America. Lord Sandwich truly started something—and a very good thing at that.

The basis of a sandwich is bread. And bread is an important component of almost every cuisine around the world. Everybody loves bread—flat breads such as focaccia from Italy and tortillas (Plates XVIII, XIX) from Mexico or cha-patti from India, French baguettes and croissants, Jewish bagels, peasant breads of Eastern Europe, and many more. Bread—a great foundation for a vast variety of fillings—meats, fish, eggs, cheeses, tofu, vegetables, savory herbs, sauces, and condiments. The sandwich has been rejuvenated recently with a rise in the production of fresh-baked artisan and ethnic breads, promising a continuation of this food as an American favorite. And sandwiches are a great way to deliver nutritional benefits—healthy vegetables and protein foods, along with whole grains [30].

While the peanut butter and jelly sandwich remains a favorite of many, the possible variety for sandwiches is limitless.

We will mention just a few examples. Greek salad heroes—mushrooms, cucumbers, olives, oregano, garlic, tomato, vinegar, feta cheese on a big bun. Crescent roll dough wrapped around wieners and cheddar cheese, or chicken tenders and Swiss cheese, and baked. Rye bread with honey mustard, sliced turkey, Gouda cheese, and thin tart apple slices—buttered on the outside of the sandwich bread and grilled on both sides. Onion and Gorgonzola cheese stuffed in focaccia dough before baking. Pita bread stuffed with a mixture of crumbled tofu, shredded carrots, diced onions, sunflower seeds, turmeric, curry powder, mayonnaise, and mustard. Barbequed crab, olives, cheese, and tomato sauce spread on English muffins and broiled. Mashed avocados, chopped red onions, cilantro, garlic, and jalapeño wrapped in a warmed tortilla and fastened with a toothpick. The possible variety is limited only by your imagination.

Has the sandwich evolved since 1762? Certainly it has, and promises to continue to do so in the foreseeable future. Viva the sandwich! ■

---

rye and wheat flour yield good results. Pumpernickel bread is composed of dark rye flour and molasses.

The germ of wheat or other grains is a good source of protein, vitamins, and minerals, but it also contains a **reducing substance** that has a detrimental effect on bread volume. Heat treatment inactivates this substance. A gentle heat treatment may also be used to inactivate enzymes (lipase and peroxidase) that cause rancidity in raw wheat germ, thus producing stabilized wheat germ. Heat-treated wheat germ may be added to bread in amounts of up to 15 percent of the weight of the flour with no deleterious effect on bread volume.

Soy flour increases the protein content of breads and has been used commercially to make high-protein breads. Additives are commonly used by commercial bakers to overcome the adverse effects of soy flour on the absorption, mixing, and fermentation of dough. However, bread containing about 1/3 cup of soy flour to 5 cups of all-purpose flour can be satisfactorily made at home. This bread can

be made higher in protein by the use of extra nonfat dry milk solids.

Other grains that may be used in bread making, in combination with wheat flour, include oatmeal, corn-meal, barley flakes, and buckwheat flour. Molasses and honey are often used as the source of sugar in whole-grain breads to contribute flavors that blend well with whole-grain products. The relatively coarse textures and dark colors of some specialty breads lend variety to meals.

Other Specialty Breads

Artisan breads are old world–style breads that are sturdy and chewy. These breads are generally prepared with a starter. French baguettes are prepared from a lean dough, which is a dough that contains only water, yeast, bread flour, and salt. A crisp, chewy crust with a tender interior is produced when steam is produced in the oven from a pan of hot water or a specially designed oven capable of injecting steam (Figure 17-14). In contrast, brioche is a

FIGURE 17-14 These French baguettes have a golden, crisp crust.

tender bread made from a very rich dough containing butter and eggs. Challah, a traditional Jewish bread, is another rich bread that contains eggs as well as honey.

Flat breads are traditional in many parts of the world. Pita bread, from the Middle East, is a flat bread with a large pocket produced by steam. Stuffing the pocket with sandwich fillings can make delicious sandwiches. Other flat breads that do not contain a pocket but may be called pita bread are used for Greek gyros. Like pocket pita bread, the variety of sandwiches that can be made with this flat bread is only limited by your imagination. Ingredients of your choosing may be placed on this flat bread, gently folded, and enjoyed. Focaccia is an Italian flat bread that has gained popularity in America in recent years. It is distinguished by the use of olive oil and savory toppings such as fresh rosemary, Parmesan cheese, and cracked black pepper. Focaccia may be eaten alone or as a

sandwich bread (Figure 17-15). A muffuletta sandwich, a New Orleans–style hero sandwich, is often made using focaccia bread.

Bagels are a doughnut-shaped yeast bread that have been prepared from a yeast dough that is proofed, then molded, and boiled. After boiling, the bagel is dried and baked until brown in an oven. Traditional bagels, which are dense and chewy, are made from lean formulas with a low proportion of yeast. A higher proportion of sugar and yeast will result in a lighter bagel [1].

Pizza dough is generally made from a lean yeast dough which is allowed to rise for about 30 minutes before rolling into rounds. Cornmeal may be used on the bottom of the pizza pan for a distinctive texture and appearance. Pizza dough also may be used for calzones. Calzones are an Italian-American dish composed of pizza dough folded like a turnover with fillings such as an Italian tomato sauce, ricotta cheese, pepperoni, or spinach and then baked.

STALING OF BREAD

Staling refers to all the changes that occur in bread after baking. These include increasing firmness of the crumb, decreasing capacity of the crumb to absorb moisture, loss of flavor, crumbly texture, and development of a leathery crust. Bread staling is a complex phenomenon and involves multiple mechanisms [10]. Changes in crystallinity that can be detected in the laboratory in the starchy portion of bread have led to the conclusion that starch is mainly responsible for staling. It is apparently the **amylopectin** fraction of starch that is most involved in staling, as it undergoes a type of retrogradation. Retrogradation of **amylose** also occurs, but primarily during

FIGURE 17-15 Focaccia, a bread made with seasonings, adds flavor to any sandwich.
(Courtesy of Wheat Foods Council)

baking and initial cooling. However, the firming of bread, associated with staling, can be slowed if moisture loss is controlled, such as is done through the formulation and packaging of meal, ready-to-eat (MRE) breads [11]. Thus, bread has been shown to firm due to factors in addition to amylopectin recrystallization.

Monoglycerides seem to form a complex with amylose molecules, decreasing retrogradation, and to exert a softening effect on the crumb. Some interaction between starch and gluten has also been suggested in explaining staling [17]. Fat in the bread formula helps to retard staling, while emulsifiers added by commercial bakers have a similar effect, as do certain amylase enzymes.

If stale bread is reheated to 122° to 140°F (50° to 60°C) or above, the staling is reversed, and the bread regains many of the characteristics of fresh bread. The soluble fraction of the starch that decreased during staling is increased. The process can be reversed several times until the bread has lost too much moisture. In the practical application of this freshening process, moisture may even be supplied if rolls are covered with a slightly dampened cloth during heating. Freezing also seems to reverse the staling process. Freezing combined with heating to thaw the frozen product brings about considerable freshening of stale bread products. This process can be quickly accomplished in a microwave oven; however, microwave energy produces some toughening in bread, and caution must be exercised to avoid the dehydrating effect of microwaving too long. Bread stales more rapidly when it is held at refrigerator temperatures than when it is stored at room temperature.

Spoilage of Bread

Bread spoils most commonly by molding. Any mold spores in the dough are destroyed in baking, so mold growth on baked bread comes from contamination of the loaf after baking. Conditions favorable to mold growth are moisture and warm temperatures. Commercially, sodium or calcium propionate is added to the bread dough as an antimolding additive and is quite effective. In warm, humid weather, however, even bread containing this additive is likely to mold if it is held for more than a few days at room temperature. Refrigeration retards mold growth but also speeds the staling process. Bread should be frozen if it is not to be used within a few days.

Rope is a bacterial contamination that can originate in the flour bin or in the various constituents used to make the bread. The spores of this bacterium are not destroyed in baking, and within a few days the interior of the loaf becomes sticky and may be pulled into "ropes" of a syrupy material. The odor of the loaf becomes foul and somewhat like the aroma of overripe melons. Bread is inedible when rope has developed extensively. The cure consists mainly of eliminating the source of the bacteria, although acidifying dough to a pH of 4.5 or lower will prevent rope development. Sour milk or buttermilk may be substituted for one-fourth to one-half of the total liquid, or approximately one tablespoon of distilled vinegar per quart of liquid may be added. This addition does not change the flavor of the bread. Calcium or sodium propionate that is added to bread to retard molding is also effective in preventing rope.

Bread may be packaged in a plastic film under a modified atmosphere, which in most cases is carbon dioxide alone or in combination with nitrogen gas. This method limits the loss of moisture and microbial growth to extend the shelf life of the bread. The carbon dioxide also has an anti-staling effect, possibly due to a change in the ability of amylopectin to bind water in the bread [2]. Shelf-stable meal, ready-to-eat (MRE) bread is preserved by controlling water activity, pH, oxygen content, and initial microbial load [24].

CHAPTER SUMMARY

- The texture of good-quality bread is fine, the cell walls thin, and the grain uniform. The crumb is elastic and should spring back quickly when touched with the finger.

- A well-shaped loaf of bread has a rounded top and is free from rough, ragged cracks on the sides. A loaf of bread that is flat or sunken on top and has overhanging eaves on the sides has been proofed too long. A loaf that has not proofed long enough may have wide cracks on the sides after baking.

- The essential ingredients for yeast-leavened dough are flour, liquid, yeast, and salt.

- Yeast is a microscopic one-celled plant. Instant quick-rising active dry yeast, active dry yeast, bread machine yeast, and fresh compressed yeast may be used. Active dry yeast must be rehydrated in warm water (110° to 115°F/43° to 46°C); however, instant quick-rising yeast rehydrates rapidly and is therefore mixed directly with the flour.

- Yeast breads may be leavened with a starter which is some of the sponge from a previous baking saved for future use. Sourdough starters may be made from flour and water or from milk, yogurt, and flour.

- Wheat flour produces bread of high volume and fine texture with a cohesive, elastic crumb. The amount of flour needed to make bread dough will vary with the type of flour used, type of liquid, and level of humidity present in the surrounding environment.

- Liquid is essential in bread dough to hydrate flour proteins and for the partial gelatinization of starch. Milk, if used in yeast bread, should be scalded, and then adequately cooled before mixing with yeast.

- Sugar in bread dough comes from the flour, starch hydrolyzed by enzymes, and sugar added as an ingredient. Sugar provides food for the yeast; however, high levels of sugar repress yeast activity. Flavor, texture, and browning also are affected by the use of sugar.

- Fat is used in bread making to facilitate the handling of the dough, to increase the keeping quality of the bread, and to improve loaf volume and texture.

- Salt is added to the bread dough for flavor. It also retards yeast fermentation and has a firming effect on gluten structure.

- Two basic methods of mixing yeast bread are the straight-dough method and the sponge method. The batter method may also be used for some breads. Kneading of dough is essential for the development of strong elastic gluten strands.

- Fermentation occurs primarily when bread rises. During fermentation, enzyme action occurs, acidity increases, gluten quality changes, and carbon dioxide is produced. Both overfermented and underfermentated breads have quality defects.

- After the dough has undergone fermentation and is molded into the desired shape and placed in a baking pan, it is allowed to rise again. This final rising is called *proofing*.

- Decorative finishes may include slashing, braiding, or the use of a wash or glaze. The type of wash selected will have an influence on the color, texture, and shine of the crust.

- During baking, gas production and expansion greatly increase, resulting in oven spring. The temperature of the bread increases, destroying yeast plants, deactivating enzymes, driving off alcohol, and evaporating moisture. Gluten coagulates and partial gelatinization of starch occurs. Bread browns chiefly due to the Maillard reaction.

- Whole-grain breads are prepared with whole-wheat flour. The small particles of bran in whole wheat interfere with the development of gluten.

- Flour from other grains may be combined with wheat flour to give varied and flavorful products. Rye flour comes closest to wheat in terms of gluten-forming properties; however, rye yeast breads generally contain some wheat flour to produce a light loaf. Soy, oatmeal, cornmeal, barley flakes, and buckwheat are additional grains that may be used in bread making.

- Artisan breads are old world–style breads that are sturdy and chewy. Flat breads, bagels, and pizza dough are additional ways in which yeast dough is used to make products other than breads and rolls.

- Staling refers to all the changes that occur in bread after baking. Increasing firmness, decreasing capacity of the crumb to absorb moisture, loss of flavor, crumbly texture, and the development of a leathery crust are common signs of staling. Stale bread may be reheated to reverse staling. Bread stales more rapidly when stored under refrigeration; room temperature or frozen storage are preferred.

- Bread spoils most commonly by molding. Moisture and warm temperatures are favorable conditions for mold growth. Rope is a bacterial contamination that can originate in the flour bin or the various constituents used to make bread. Bread is inedible when rope has developed.

STUDY QUESTIONS

1. Describe desirable characteristics of yeast bread.

2. Explain the role played by each of the following ingredients in the making of yeast bread:

   (a) Yeast

   (b) Flour

   (c) Liquid

   (d) Sugar

   (e) Fat

   (f) Salt

   (g) Dough conditioners

3. Compare the similarities and differences among compressed yeast, active dry yeast, and instant quick-rising dry active yeast as they are used for the preparation of yeast breads.

4. Compare bread flour and all-purpose flour in terms of mixing, handling, and expected outcome in the making of yeast bread.

5. What steps are involved in mixing yeast bread by the straight-dough method? The sponge method? The batter method?

6. Explain why kneading is such an important step in the preparation of yeast bread at home.

7. What is meant by *fermentation* of yeast dough and by *proofing?* What occurs during these processes?

8. What are the purposes for *slashing* bread prior to baking?

9. Why may a *wash* be used prior to baking?

10. (a) Describe changes that occur during the baking of yeast bread.

(b) What is meant by *oven spring*?

(c) Why is it important to bake bread at precisely the right time after proofing in the pan?

11. How do ingredients and their proportions generally differ between rolls and bread?

12. What is the difference between wheat and whole-wheat bread?

13. Identify characteristics of some of the specialty breads available.

14. (a) What changes occur as bread stales?

(b) Which component of bread appears to be responsible for staling?

(c) How can somewhat stale bread be refreshened?

15. (a) Give suggestions on how to store bread appropriately.

(b) What is *rope* in bread, and how can it be controlled?

CAKES AND COOKIES 18

Although a wide variety of formulations are included in the class of baked products called *cakes*, these recipes can usually be classified into two major groups: shortened cakes or cakes containing fat, and unshortened cakes or cakes with no fat. A third category might be added—the chiffon cake, which has characteristics of both shortened and unshortened cakes. A chiffon cake usually contains a larger proportion of egg than a shortened cake, a proportion similar to that found in unshortened cakes. It does contain fat in the form of oil.

Cookies differ in several ways from cakes. Fine texture and velvety crumb are less prominent characteristics of cookies than of cakes, and often, less skill is required to prepare them. Special skills are required to make certain types of cookies, such as rolled cookies or meringue-type cookies; the inexperienced person may find the preparation of these products quite challenging.

Among the fat-reduced bakery items that are appearing on the market are a variety of reduced-fat, lowfat, or no-fat cakes, cake mixes, and cookies. These items are similar to shortened cakes and cookies in general characteristics but have been formulated using various fat-replacing systems.

In this chapter, the characteristics, preparation, and ingredient functions for the following will be discussed:

- Shortened cakes
- Unshortened cakes
- Cookies

SHORTENED CAKES

Types and Characteristics

Shortened or butter cakes are of two types: *pound cake* and *standard shortened cake*. Pound cakes have a close grain and are somewhat compact in character, yet they are very tender (Figure 18-1). Pound cakes should not be heavy or soggy, but lack the soft, light, velvety crumb of a well-made

shortened cake. Historically, pound cakes were prepared from one pound each of butter, sugar, flour, and eggs with no added leavening agent except for the air incorporated in the creaming of the fat and sugar and in the beaten eggs. Steam has been found to be responsible for about half the expansion during baking, provided that the air cells are retained. Theoretically, the moisture evaporates into the air cells, and the vapor expands during baking. In commercial pound cakes, improved textures have resulted from the addition of a small amount of baking powder.

FIGURE 18-1 A cherry pecan pound cake. Originally, pound cakes contained approximately one pound each of the main ingredients: eggs, butter, flour, and sugar. *(Courtesy of the American Egg Board)*

A good standard shortened cake has a fine grain, cells of uniform size, thin cell walls, and a crumb that is elastic rather than crumbly. Crusts should be thin and tender. Top crusts should be smooth or slightly pebbly and have top surfaces that are only slightly rounded. The standard shortened cake is leavened chiefly by carbon dioxide gas from baking powder or from soda and buttermilk. Air incorporated into the plastic fat or into the beaten eggs or egg whites also aids in leavening the mixture.

Ingredients

Usual ingredients in a standard shortened cake include sugar, fat, egg, liquid, a leavening agent, salt, and flour. A proper balance between the tenderizing effects of sugar and fat and the firming or structural effects of flour and egg is particularly important in shortened cakes. Proportions of ingredients, however, may vary widely for ordinary shortened cakes. Mixtures may be classified as lean or rich depending largely on the relationship of fat and sugar (the tenderizing ingredients) to the ingredients that give structure (flour and egg). Specific ingredients can be increased or decreased within certain limits without producing undesirable results. Changes in ingredient proportions may require an adjustment to the amount of mixing, however.

Sugar. Sugar adds sweetness and has an important effect on the texture and volume of shortened cakes. Sugar weakens the structure of cakes by interfering with gluten development in the flour. Sugar affects gluten development by attracting and holding water, thereby preventing sufficient hydration of the flour proteins. Consequently, less gluten can be produced, and the cake is tender. As sugar is increased in a formula, stirring must be increased to develop the gluten sufficiently to overcome the weakening effects of excess sugar. Without increased stirring, an increase in the percentage of sugar in a cake causes the cake to fall and to have a coarse texture and thick cell walls. Both crust and crumb are gummy. The crust may appear rough, sugary, and too brown (Figure 18-2).

The volume of cakes is influenced by sugar. Granulated sugar, when creamed with shortening, traps small air bubbles contributing to leavening of the batter. The temperature at which starch gelatinizes also affects volume. Sugar raises the temperature at which the starch gelatinizes and causes a decrease in the viscosity of the batter in the early stages of baking [16]. Thus, the cake has more time to increase in volume before the batter "sets."

Another way in which sugar influences volume is by decreasing cohesive forces. It has been suggested that the resistance to movement of a cake batter during baking, referred to as *cohesive forces*, influences the development of the structure of the finished cake. Various ingredients affect these cohesive forces in different ways. An optimum

FIGURE 18-2 A cake containing too much sugar may fall in the center and have a coarse, gummy texture.

quantity of sugar decreases the cohesive forces and allows the batter to move more freely. The volume of the cake therefore increases [24].

Most cake recipes or formulas use sucrose or table sugar. When other types of sugar are used, quality attributes of the cake can be affected. If glucose or fructose is substituted for sucrose, more fructose is required to attain the same starch gelatinization temperature [3]. Cakes made with fructose also tend to be darker because the browning (Maillard) reaction is more pronounced. Acceptable cakes have been made with 50 and 75 percent of the sucrose replaced with high-fructose corn syrup [20]. Researchers have found cakes prepared with high-fructose corn syrup are more brown and of somewhat lower volume [18, 20]. Kinds of sweeteners were discussed further in Chapter 11.

Egg. Eggs add air to cake batter when beaten and contribute to the structure of cakes by the coagulation of the proteins during baking. The optimum amount of egg in a given cake mixture produces finer cells, thinner cell walls, and usually larger volume than are obtained with a lower or higher percentage of egg. Although the way the eggs are added may modify the effects, an excess of egg gives a rubbery, tough crumb. When beaten egg whites are added last, the effects of increased egg are less noticeable. The cohesive forces in a baking cake batter are increased as egg white is added in increasing amounts [24].

Fat. Shortening, butter, and margarine are common fats used in shortened cakes. An important role of fat in cakes is increased tenderness. Fat weakens structure and tends to decrease volume when added beyond the optimum amount. Cohesive forces decrease with increasing amounts of fat [24], thus having a favorable influence on cake volume.

In addition to tenderizing, plastic fats aid in incorporating air into the batter. Most hydrogenated fats contain some inert gas as they are marketed. Creaming fat and sugar together adds additional air bubbles to the cake batter. It has been suggested that the air bubbles incorporated into fat during creaming act as a base for the distribution of leavening gas (carbon dioxide, particularly) during mixing and baking.

When substituting one type of fat for another in a shortened cake recipe, the characteristics of the fat should be considered. Shortening contains 100 percent fat compared to butter or margarine which contains approximately 80 percent fat. "Diet" butter or margarine will have even a lower percentage of fat and consequently is not recommended for baking. Different types of fat also will provide different results when creaming. Oils cannot be creamed with sugar. Butter and margarine have a narrow temperature range at which the fat is plastic; if too liquid or too hard, it will not cream as well with the sugar. Fats of good creaming quality, such as shortening, will yield a cake of better texture than soft or liquid fats unless the methods of mixing are altered. In comparing various fats, butter has been reported to make cakes that scored highest for tenderness and velvetlike texture, whereas hydrogenated shortening produced cakes with the highest rating for evenness of grain [19].

A reduction in the amount of fat in a cake recipe can be desirable to reduce calories or the fat content of the diet while still offering a pleasing cake (Figure 18-3). A variety of fat replacers are used by food technologists. All of the fat or oil in a cake can be replaced by one of the systems containing modified starches, gums, emulsifiers, and stabilizers. In the home, replacing a portion of the fat in

cakes with applesauce or fruit purée has produced acceptable, yet lowfat cakes. Researchers have found decreasing by half the amount of oil added to a commercial yellow cake mix batter did not appreciably change the appearance, moistness, flavor, or overall acceptability of the baked cake [4]. It has been reported that the shortening in yellow cakes made in the home kitchen may be reduced by half without substantially changing the acceptability, as evaluated by a trained sensory panel [12]. Thus, typical recipes may be adjusted in order to decrease fat consumption to some degree. Fats and fat substitutes were discussed in greater detail in Chapter 10.

Emulsifiers. Emulsifying agents in cake batter cause the fat to be distributed more finely throughout the mixture and allow the cake formula to carry more sugar than flour. Shortenings that contain small amounts of emulsifiers are sometimes called *high-ratio* shortenings because of the higher ratio of sugar to flour that is possible with their addition. When optimum amounts of an emulsifier are used, the cohesive forces in the cake batter are decreased, the batter moves or flows more readily because the viscosity is decreased during the early part of the baking period before the structure sets, and the volume of the finished cake is increased [16]. The emulsifier may interact with the starch as it gelatinizes. A fine and even texture in the finished cake is the result (Figure 18-4).

Emulsifiers are commonly added to shortenings that are to be used for making cakes. Hydrogenated shortenings on the retail market often contain small amounts (about 3 percent) of mono- and diglycerides. Polysorbate

FIGURE 18-3 Vanilla and butter extract add delicious, rich flavors to this cake prepared with a lowfat formula. *(Courtesy of McCormick & Company Inc.)*

FIGURE 18-4 The volume and quality of a shortened cake improve when an emulsifier is used. *(Courtesy of* Food Engineering *and C.D. Pratt, Atlas Powder Company. Photograph by R. T. Vanderbilt Company)*

60 (about 1 percent) is also frequently used in commercial emulsified shortenings. A larger variety of emulsifiers are available to commercial bakers [9].

Leavening Agents. Cakes may be leavened by baking powder, baking soda, air entrapped in creamed shortening or beaten egg whites, and steam. Too little baking powder in a cake produces a compact, heavy product. Increasing the baking powder increases cake volume until the optimum quantity is reached. Beyond that, volume decreases, and the cake falls. A coarse texture and a harsh, gummy crumb may also result from an excess of baking powder. Cakes made using SAS-phosphate powder may be disagreeably bitter if large amounts are used. Less baking powder is needed to produce the best volume and texture when more air is incorporated into the cake by means of a creamed fat–sugar mixture or beaten egg whites.

Baking soda is used in cakes that have an acidic ingredient such as sour milk, buttermilk, or fruit juice. Although cocoa generally does not provide enough acid to allow the use of only baking soda, some chocolate cake recipes will use both baking soda and baking powder as leavening agents. See Chapter 15 for a more extensive discussion of leavening agents.

Flour. Flour contributes structure to shortened cakes. Too little flour has the same effect on a cake as an excess of fat or sugar. The structure is weak, the texture is coarse, and the cake may fall. Excess flour, on the other hand, produces a compact, dry cake in which tunnels form readily. Tunnels, however, may form in a cake of good proportions if the mixture is overmanipulated or is baked at too high a temperature.

Cakes may be formulated to use all-purpose or cake flour. Cakes made with all-purpose flour, however, are generally lower in volume and have a coarser texture than similar cakes made with cake flour, in part because all-purpose flour has a higher protein content than cake flour. High-ratio cakes in particular benefit from the use of cake flour. High-ratio cakes have a high proportion of

sugar and water in relationship to flour and can collapse in the oven when cake flour is not used. Cake flour is lower in protein compared to all-purpose flour and has been treated with chlorine gas to improve favorably baking quality for delicate cakes.

All-purpose flour can be substituted for cake flour in a cake formula that specifies cake flour. One cup of all-purpose flour minus two tablespoons can be used in place of one cup of cake flour [1]. Others suggest replacing the two tablespoons of flour removed from the cup of all-purpose flour with two tablespoons of cornstarch and then substituting this flour–starch blend for cake flour. See Chapter 15 for more information about kinds of flour.

Liquid. The liquid ingredient in cakes dissolves the sugar and salt and makes possible the reaction of baking powder or baking soda. Liquid disperses the fat and flour particles and hydrates the starch and protein in the flour, allowing both starch gelatinization and gluten development. Some steam is produced from the liquid, which helps to leaven the cake. Various liquids may be used, including milk, water, and fruit juices. A moist cake of low volume results with excess liquid because the batter will be too thin to adequately trap air.

Chocolate. Because of the starch content of cocoa and chocolate, a smaller percentage of flour than that used in a yellow cake produces a more desirable chocolate cake. With the same proportions of flour, fat, and sugar that are used in plain shortened cakes, chocolate cake batters tend to be undesirably stiff, resulting in cakes that are dry, with a tendency to crack on top. Chocolate cake recipes usually contain relatively high percentages of sugar or fat or both, and therefore the proportion of flour may approach that usually used in other shortened cakes. Cocoa has a greater thickening effect than chocolate because the percentage of starch in cocoa is about 11 percent compared to 8 percent in chocolate. From the standpoint of flavor, color, and thickening effect, best results are usually obtained by using about two-thirds, by weight, as much

IN DEPTH

Why Use Cake Flour?

Cake flour produces tender and delicate cakes. High-ratio cakes, in particular, will fall or collapse in the oven when cake flour is not used.

Cake flours are finely milled from soft wheat which is low in protein and are treated with chlorine gas to improve baking quality for delicate cakes. Chlorine bleaches pigments in the flour, oxidizes flour proteins to reduce normal gluten-developing properties, and interacts with the starch to increase swelling capacity [13, 15]. Apparently some of the lipids in the flour are also affected [13]. Because cake batter is a complex system, the chlorine-treated flour undoubtedly reacts with other formula components to produce the texture and volume of the final product [22]. In making cakes with cake flour, the gelatinized starch is probably more important to structure than the small amount of gluten developed. The gelatinization of the starch helps to convert a fluid phase into a solid, porous structure.

Researchers have investigated methods and ingredients for cake making which will result in high-quality cakes without the use of chlorine treated flour. Cakes prepared with heat-treated flour and the addition of xanthan gum to the formula were found to have slightly greater volumes and a crumb grain that was essentially equivalent to the control cake prepared with chlorinated flour [29]. Other researchers found that nonchlorine-treated flour could be used to produce white layer cakes with better quality characteristics compared to the control cakes prepared with chlorine-treated flour. The formula of the nonchlorine-treated flour cakes was modified to include starch, soya lecithin, and xanthan gum, in addition to an increase in the concentration of dried egg albumen [8]. ∎

cocoa as chocolate in a recipe. This amounts to about 3 to 3 1/2 tablespoons of cocoa as a substitute for 1 ounce of chocolate.

The acidity of chocolate is not sufficiently high to necessitate the use of soda unless buttermilk is used in the cake mixture. The color of chocolate cakes gradually changes from cinnamon brown to mahogany red as the acidity decreases and the alkalinity increases. *Devil's food cakes*, which are characteristically mahogany red, contain enough soda to produce an alkaline pH in the batter. The

characteristic chocolate flavor, as well as the color, is changed with increasing amounts of soda.

Proportions of Ingredients. A satisfactory plain standard cake has, by measure, one-third as much fat as sugar, two-thirds as much milk as sugar, and about three times as much flour as liquid, as in the following example of a cake formula. Salt is used in cakes for flavor, and only small amounts are needed. Formula adjustments for high altitude baking were discussed in Chapter 15.

FOCUS ON SCIENCE

More about Chocolate Cakes and Leavening Agents

Early research conducted on chocolate cake found that a combination of baking soda and baking powder had a positive effect on the crumb structure of the chocolate cake. Baking soda alone produces a coarse crumb, whereas baking powder

produces a very fine crumb. This all has to do with how the carbon dioxide (CO_2) is evolved in the batter from the different leavening sources.

When a recipe contains a combination of baking powder and baking soda, the baking powder does most of the leavening. The baking soda is added to neutralize the acids in the recipe plus to add tenderness and some leavening. Baking soda alone will produce a batter with a pH = 7 resulting in a a red color or Red Devil's food. Increasing the amount of baking soda will darken the color but will also compromise the chocolate flavor with a soapy overtone. If baking powder is used alone, the pH will decrease below 7, producing a lighter brown color and a decrease in the chocolate flavor.

Sugar 1 1/2 cups	Eggs 2
Fat 1/2 cup	Salt 1/2 tsp
Milk 1 cup	Baking powder 3 tsp
Cake flour 3 cups	Flavoring 1 tsp

Recipe Calculations. In foodservice, recipes designed for household use are often adjusted for quantity production. Various methods may be used for making this adjustment, including multiplying the weight of each ingredient by a certain factor or calculating recipe percentages [21]. In the factor method, a factor is determined by dividing the desired yield by the yield of the current recipe. These calculations can be done quickly on a computer, and such software programs are available.

The way in which a particular computer program calculates the recipes is important. Five German chocolate cakes, in quantities serving 60 people, were prepared with formulations that were generated from a household recipe. Several different computer programs were utilized to perform the calculations for the same home-size recipe, and the prepared cakes were then evaluated for quality characteristics [17]. The five computer programs used for this study gave somewhat different ingredient quantities, and these differences affected quality. The percentage method of recipe calculation will provide the most consistent and accurate measurements when adjusting recipes [21]. More about recipe standardization may be found in Chapter 5.

Mixing

A variety of methods can be used to combine the ingredients in shortened cakes. Four commonly used methods are described here.

Conventional Method. The conventional method consists of creaming a plastic fat (Figure 18-5), adding the sugar gradually to the fat with continued creaming, adding the egg or egg yolks to the fat–sugar mixture, and beating until the mixture is well blended and very light.

FIGURE 18-5 Creamed butter and sugar are shown in this mixer bowl.

The dry ingredients are sifted together and added alternately with the milk in about four portions. The egg whites may be beaten separately until stiff but not dry and quickly folded into the batter at the end of mixing to avoid excessive loss of gas.

Flavoring extract may be added to the creamed mixture, to the milk, or when the dry and liquid ingredients are being added. The conventional method of mixing is more time consuming than the other methods described here. It should produce a fine-textured cake and may be conveniently used for mixing cakes by hand.

Conventional Sponge Method. The conventional sponge method is used with lean cake mixtures, in which the amount of fat is not sufficient to produce a light creamed mass when all the sugar is added to the fat. To avoid the dry, crumbly character of the fat–sugar mixture, about half of the sugar is reserved to be beaten with the eggs until this mixture is very stiff. The rest of the sugar is creamed with the shortening. The liquid and dry ingredients are added alternately to the fat–sugar mixture. The beaten egg–sugar mixture is then folded into the batter at the end of mixing. Note, however, that a surprisingly large amount of sugar can be creamed with a small or moderate amount of fat if the fat is at the most favorable temperature for creaming, 75° to 85°F (24° to 29°C), and if the addition of sugar is gradual. A good cake can be made from oil by using the conventional sponge method.

Muffin Method. In the muffin method, the eggs, milk, and melted fat are mixed together and added all at once to the sifted dry ingredients. This method is simple and rapid and is particularly useful for lean formulas when the cake is to be eaten while still warm.

Quick-Mix Method. The quick-mix method is known by several other names, including the *single-stage, one-bowl,* or *one-mix* method. It requires a change in the proportions of ingredients from those that are satisfactory for the conventional method of mixing. Higher proportions of sugar and liquid are used with the quick-mix method, and the shortening should contain an emulsifying agent. All of the ingredients, particularly the fat, should be at room temperature so that the ingredients can be readily dispersed. Use of this method is difficult when mixing by hand. An electric mixer is desirable; however, commercial cake mixes, which are designed for the one-bowl method of mixing, may be mixed by hand if the number of mixing strokes, rather than time, is used as the measure. The quick-mix method used with an appropriate formula yields a fine-grained, tender, moist cake of good volume that remains fresh for a relatively long period.

The mixing of the batter can be completed in two stages. In Stage 1, sift all dry ingredients into the bowl used for mixing. Add all fat, *part* of the liquid, and flavoring or add all fat, liquid, and flavoring. Beat for a specified time. In Stage 2, add unbeaten eggs or egg whites and the remaining liquid if part of the liquid was withheld in the first stage, then beat for a specified time.

In some recipes, the baking powder may be omitted from the first stage and stirred in quickly (all by itself) between the two stages. For uniformity of blending, both the sides and the bottom of the bowl should be scraped frequently during mixing.

Effects of Under- and Overmanipulation. The amount of mixing needed to produce the best cake texture varies with the proportions of ingredients and the quantity of batter. The temperature of the ingredients is also a factor, as is the quantity of baking powder and the time at which the baking powder is added.

The thoroughness of creaming the fat–sugar mixture affects the extent of subsequent mixing. Thorough creaming makes possible a wider range in the amount of mixing that will produce a good texture. A good creamed mixture is light and spongy but has enough body to prevent an oily, pasty, or frothy mass. When eggs are added to the creamed fat and sugar, the mass becomes softer but should retain enough air to remain light. When the fat–sugar mixture separates into large flecks or curds on the addition of eggs, the resulting cake usually has a coarser texture than a cake produced from an uncurdled batter. A more stable emulsion may result from adding eggs gradually to the fat–sugar mixture. The use of a shortening containing an emulsifier, such as mono- and diglycerides, also aids in forming a stable emulsion.

Mixing a cake batter barely enough to dampen the dry ingredients may yield a cake of good volume, but the texture is coarse and the cell walls are thick. The optimum amount of stirring produces a cake of good volume, uniform texture, small cells, thin cell walls, and a slightly rounded top. Overstirring tends to produce a compact cake of smaller volume. When cakes are greatly overstirred, they become heavy or soggy. As stirring is increased, peaks tend to form, and the side walls of the cake are not as high as those in cakes stirred the optimum amount. If cakes are cut or broken where the peaks occur, long tunnels will be found. Certain rich mixtures may show a concave surface if they are understirred.

The fact that cake mixtures contain more sugar and fat than most other flour mixtures decreases the tendency for toughness to result from stirring. Gluten development is retarded by sugar and fat. Stirring more than the optimum amount may appreciably toughen cakes, especially those made from lean mixtures and from flours of stronger gluten quality.

Preparation of Pans

Baking pans should be prepared before the cake batter is mixed so the batter can be transferred into the pans immediately after mixing. Allowing the batter to stand in the mixing bowl more than 15 to 20 minutes before placing it in the baking pans is undesirable because leavening is likely to be lost, resulting in an adverse effect on the volume and texture of the baked product.

Pans may be greased on the sides and bottoms, or the sides may be left dry (Figure 18-6). If the sides of the pan

FIGURE 18-6 Grease the bottom and sides of the pan and dust with flour before beginning to mix the cake.

Why Do Some Cake Mixes Create "Fluffy" Cakes Compared to Cakes Prepared from Scratch?

Box cakes are usually light, soft, and moist. These characteristics are in part because of box mix ingredients including mono- and diglycerides, cellulose gum, and other additives (leavening agents) that work in tandem. Emulsifiers such as mono- and diglycerides are more effective at incorporating air into the batter compared to eggs which are the sole emulsifiers in the homemade cakes.

Emulsifiers help to hold the ingredients together by enabling the fat to mix well with the milk and other ingredients. Furthermore, the effectiveness of the leavening agents, such as baking powder or baking soda along with monocalcium and dicalcium phosphates, are improved with emulsifying ingredients that help the batter to hold more of the gas produced by the leaveners. In box mixes, a greater retention of leavening gas is possible because of the added emulsifiers. Consequently, a cake with greater volume and lightness is produced.

Source: Ruperti, Y. (2008, March/April). Fluffy yellow layer cake. *Cook's Illustrated. 91,* 21–22.

are not greased, the cake volume may be somewhat greater because the cake structure is supported by clinging to the sides. Flouring the greased bottom of the pan aids in removing the cake from the pan, but the flour coating should be light. An alternative procedure is to cut a piece of paper, waxed or unwaxed, to fit the bottom of the pan. After the paper is placed in the greased pan, it is greased on the top surface, which will come in contact with the cake.

Baking

Baking Temperatures. The oven temperatures commonly used for baking shortened cakes range from 350° to 375°F (177° to 191°C). The optimal temperature may vary with the cake formula. Some data indicate that plain cakes increase in volume and in total cake scores (including such characteristics as texture, tenderness, velvetiness, and eating quality) when baked at temperatures up to 365°F (185°C) but decrease at 385°F (196°C). Chocolate cakes, which have often been baked at lower temperatures than other shortened cakes on the theory that chocolate scorches easily, also show increased volume and total cake scores when baked at higher temperatures—loaf cakes at 385° to 400°F (196° to 204°C) and layer cakes at 400°F (204°C). High temperatures are sometimes not recommended because of excessive browning and humping of the top. The browning of cakes is apparently the result of both the Maillard reaction and the caramelization of sugar.

The better results obtained with higher temperatures would seem to indicate that a more rapid coagulation of cake batter in relation to the rate of gas formation and gas expansion prevents the collapse of cells. Such collapse results in coarse grain and thick cell walls in the baked cake.

If dark, dull pans are used, the cake will brown more readily and uniformly than when bright, shiny pans are used. The shiny pans tend to reflect heat, whereas the dull pans absorb it more easily.

Cooling the Cake before Removal from the Pan. It is recommended that cakes not be removed from the pan until the interior reaches a temperature of about 140°F (60°C). At this point, they have usually become firm enough to handle without damage to the structure of the cake. Allowing the baked cake to stand about 10 minutes before removal from the pan is usually sufficient for this temperature to be reached (Figure 18-7).

Microwave Baking. Flour mixtures do not form a brown crust when cooked by microwaves. Because cakes are usually frosted, the lack of crust formation is of less importance from the standpoint of appearance for cakes than for some other baked products. However, the flavor associated with browning is not developed. A browning unit in the microwave oven may aid in browning the top surface of the cake.

Some cake mixes are specifically formulated to be cooked in a microwave oven and are packaged with special pans for use in the microwave oven (Figure 18-8). Because microwaved cakes rise higher than conventionally baked cakes, the pans should be filled no more than one-third to one-half full. The method of starting the cake at 50 percent power and finishing it at high power results in a more even top than cooking on high for the entire period. The top of a microwaved cake may be slightly moist when done, but the moisture will evaporate during standing time out of the oven.

UNSHORTENED CAKES

Unshortened cakes are of two types: white *angel food*, which is made from egg whites, and *yellow sponge*, which is made from the whole egg.

Angel Food Cake

Some may consider angel food cake the ultimate fat-free cake. Angel food cakes are often made using commercial mixes in which the egg white foam is stabilized by the addition of a whipping aid; however, excellent-quality cakes may be made at home using fresh egg whites. The proper incorporation and retention of air is critical in unshortened cakes to allow expansion and a typical texture. Air accounts for approximately half of the leavening in angel food cakes, but steam also plays an important role in leavening this product. Steam, formed from the vaporization of the water of egg white, brings about two or three times the expansion in baking angel food cake as is accounted for by the expansion of air.

Characteristics. A desirable angel food cake is porous or spongy, is of large volume, and has thin cell walls (Figure 18-9). Tenderness and moistness also are important characteristics. The size of the cells varies, but the grain is generally more open and less fine than that of good-quality shortened cakes.

Ingredients. The ratio of sugar to flour in the following cake formula is appropriate for tenderness yet not high enough to cause the collapse of the cake.

Egg whites 1 cup	Cream of tartar 1 tsp
Sugar 1 1/4 cup	Salt 1/4 tsp
Cake flour 1 cup	Flavoring 1 tsp

Egg Whites. Egg whites incorporate air as they are beaten to form a foam. Important in stabilizing the foam is the coagulation of egg proteins by the mechanical forces of beating (see Chapter 24 for a discussion of beating eggs). Fresh eggs are preferable to older eggs for making angel food cakes because the fresh whites are thicker and produce a more stable foam. Good-quality angel food cakes may be prepared using frozen or dried

Pour the batter into prepared pans. The batter should be divided evenly between the layer pans.

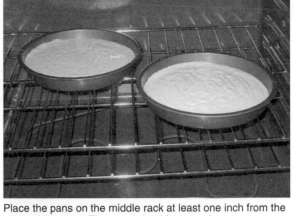

Place the pans on the middle rack at least one inch from the sides of the oven. The pans should not touch.

After minimum baking time, touch the center lightly. If no imprint remains, the cake is done. Or insert a wooden pick in the center.If it comes out clean, the cake is done.

Allow cakes to cool 10 minutes on wire racks before removing them from the pans. If cakes are left in the pans too long, they willsteam and become soggy.

The finished cake has a moist, velvety crumb and good volume.

FIGURE 18-7 Steps for baking a perfect cake.

FIGURE 18-8 Many kinds of pans are available for baking. Glass bowls, custard cups, and measuring cups are microwave safe. Glass bread and brownie pans can also be used for conventional oven cooking. *(Courtesy of World Kitchens Inc., makers of Pyrex®, Corning Ware®, and Baker's Secret®)*

FIGURE 18-9 A good-quality angel food cake has large volume and thin cell walls.

egg whites [11]. In addition to the important role of egg white proteins in foam formation and stabilization, some proteins in egg whites are coagulated by heat and give structure to the baked cake.

Flour. Cake flour, because of its low percentage of protein, its weak quality of gluten, and its fine granulation, produces a more tender, delicate angel food cake than flour of stronger gluten quality. Flour increases the strength of the cake crumb and contributes to the structure. As the amount of sugar is increased, the flour, within certain limits, must also be increased to provide a satisfactory ratio of sugar to flour so that sufficient structure is maintained in the cake.

Sugar. Sugar has a stabilizing effect on the egg white foam and allows more beating without overcoagulation of

the egg white proteins. Sugar also sweetens the cake and aids in browning. The higher the percentage of sugar in the formulation, the greater the tendency toward development of a sugary crust. Sugar interferes with gluten development and therefore tends to produce a more tender and fragile cake when used in increasing amounts. Sugar elevates the coagulation temperature of egg proteins and, if used in excess, may retard coagulation to such an extent that the cake collapses. In addition, the temperature for starch gelatinization is increased by sugar, and that structure of the cake for which gelatinized starch is responsible is affected by increasing amounts of sugar.

A fine granulated sugar is normally used in making angel food cakes; however, 25 percent of the sugar may be replaced by high-fructose corn syrup with little effect on the physical or sensory characteristics of the cake [7].

Cream of Tartar. Cream of tartar is an important constituent of angel food cake because of its beneficial effect on color, volume, and tenderness. The anthoxanthin pigments of flour are yellowish in an alkaline medium but are white in an acid or neutral medium. The Maillard or browning reaction between sugars and proteins is also less likely to occur in an acid than an alkaline medium. Therefore, the addition of cream of tartar (an acid salt) produces a cake that is more white than yellow or tan. Cream of tartar, as an acid substance, also stabilizes the egg white foam to allow heat to penetrate and bring about coagulation without collapse of the foam. Large air cells and thick cell walls (coarse grain) are the effects of an unstable foam that has partially collapsed. Cream of tartar prevents extreme shrinkage of the cake during the last part of the baking period and during the cooling period. Cream of tartar also produces a more tender cake. The optimal proportion is about one teaspoon per one cup of egg whites.

FOCUS ON SCIENCE

Cream of Tartar

Cream of tartar changes the pH of the egg white to an acidic range (pH of 5.6 to 5.7) by increasing the number of free-floating hydrogen ions (H$^+$) in the egg white. This pH range is near the isoelectric point of globulin G$_2$ and considerably below pH 8.0 at which the dissociation of ovomucin occurs. Globulin G$_2$ and ovomucin are both proteins found in egg whites.

At the more acidic pH range, the egg white foam becomes stable and is able to hold onto air whipped into the whites. During baking, this more stable foam reaches the temperature of coagulation before the foam collapses. Thus, the shrinkage of the cake during the last phase of baking and the cooling period is less likely to occur.

Mixing. The egg whites can be beaten with an electric mixer, a rotary beater, or a wire whisk. The whisk usually produces a somewhat larger volume of cake, but the cells also are larger. Egg whites should not be overbeaten, as this contributes to dryness and a lack of extensibility in the film surrounding the air bubbles. The air cells break and collapse, which results in a cake of low volume, thick cell walls, and coarse texture. The egg whites should be stiff, but the peaks and tails that form should bend over slightly, instead of standing rigid and upright.

Egg whites beat more easily to a foam of large volume when they are at room temperature than when they are beaten at a lower temperature. Therefore, eggs to be used in angel food cake should be removed from the refrigerator some time before they are to be beaten. Cream of tartar is added to the egg whites, and they are beaten until a foam begins to form. Sugar may be beaten into the egg whites as they are being whipped, or it may be folded in after the egg whites are completely beaten. In the first case, the sugar is added gradually as for meringue, starting after the cream of tartar is added. Beating the sugar into the egg whites is known as the *meringue method* and is preferable if an electric mixer is used. Beating some sugar into the egg white foam seems to have a greater stabilizing effect on the cake than folding all of the sugar in with the flour. Regardless of the method used for adding sugar, about two tablespoons of sugar at a time are sifted over the surface of the egg whites. Adding either sugar or flour in too-large portions results in the loss of air and often in the uneven blending of the sugar or flour.

After the sugar is added, the flour is gently folded into the mixture. If an electric mixer is being used, it should be turned down to the lowest speed setting. Part of the sugar may be reserved to be mixed with the flour. The flour mixed with some sugar unquestionably folds into the mixture more easily, but usually a better cake is obtained when as much of the sugar as possible is added to the egg white foam before the addition of any flour. Thorough mixing of the sugar with the egg white produces a mixture into which the flour blends easily.

The number of strokes needed by different individuals for folding the flour varies. Thorough blending is necessary, but overmanipulation results in a loss of air and in decreased tenderness.

The flavoring extract may be added after the whites are partially beaten. Adding the extract at this stage allows it to become thoroughly distributed without the necessity for overmanipulation later. Extract should never be added at the end of mixing because the extract is either incompletely blended with the batter or extra manipulation is needed to blend it uniformly. Alternatively, extract may be added while sugar or flour is being folded into the mixture. The salt may be added toward the end of the beating of the foam and before the addition of flour, because salt may have a slight destabilizing effect on the egg white foam if it is added earlier.

Preparation of Pans. Pans are not greased for either type of sponge cake. It is desirable to have the mixture cling to the sides of the pan until it is coagulated by the heat of the oven. After baking, the pan is inverted and allowed to stand until the cake is thoroughly cooled. This gives the delicate cake structure a chance to set with the least amount of strain placed on it.

Baking Temperatures. Baking at 350°F (177°C) has been found to result in a more tender and moist angel food cake of larger volume and thinner cell walls than baking at lower temperatures [2]. A wide range of oven temperatures would appear to be satisfactory, however, if the minimum time required to bake the cake is used. Longer baking tends to toughen the cake whatever the temperature, but greater toughening occurs with longer baking at higher temperatures.

Angel food cakes made from commercial mixes and baked at 350° to 375°F (177° to 191°C) scored higher in all quality characteristics than those baked at 400° to 425°F (204° to 218°C) [10]. Compact layers formed as a result of partial collapse of the structure after the cakes baked at 400° to 425°F (204° to 218°C) were removed from the oven. Angel food cakes made from commercial mixes, baking initially at 375°F (191°C) and then lowering the temperature to 350°F (177°C), 325°F (163°C), and finally 300°F (149°C) at 10-minute intervals, yields tender baked cakes of very high volume. When the

FOCUS ON SCIENCE

Why Is the Crust of an Angel Food Cake a Light "Macaroon" Color?

The angel food cake has a lighter crust color than other cakes because the pH of the batter is lower due to the amount of cream of tartar used in the cake. The Maillard browning reaction, which is responsible for browning, proceeds at a lower rate because of the acidic pH, resulting in a "macaroon" color.

---

baking cake begins to shrink, it may be tested with a toothpick or cake tester. If moist or sticky crumbs cling to the tester, the cake must be baked longer.

Sponge Cake

Ingredients. The usual ingredients and proportions for yellow sponge cake are as follows.

Eggs 6	Water 2 Tbsp
Sugar 1 cup	Lemon juice 1 Tbsp
Cake flour 1 cup	Grated lemon rind 1 Tbsp
Salt 1/4 tsp (lightly measured)	

Mixing. Yellow sponge cakes can be made by either separated or whole-egg methods. In the whole-egg method, the eggs are beaten until they are foamy. The water, lemon juice, and lemon rind are then added, and the mixture is beaten until it is as stiff as possible. (This mixture can be made very stiff.) The sugar is added gradually and beaten into the mixture. The flour and salt are mixed together and then sifted over the surface, about two tablespoons at a time, and folded into the egg mixture until all is well blended.

This method is desirable when preparing a very small recipe. It produces a cake no better than that produced by a method in which egg whites and yolks are separated, but it is difficult to beat one or two separated egg yolks as thoroughly as they should be beaten for best results.

In one separated-egg method, the egg yolks are partially beaten. The sugar, salt, water, lemon juice, and lemon rind are added, and the whole mass is beaten until very stiff. The flour is folded lightly into the mixture, after which the stiffly beaten egg whites are folded in [5]. Alternatively, the stiffly beaten mixture of yolks, sugar, water, lemon juice and rind, and salt is combined with the beaten egg whites before the flour is folded into the mixture.

In a meringue method, the sugar is boiled with about three-fourths the volume of water to 244°F (118°C). It is then poured gradually over the beaten egg whites with constant stirring until a stiff meringue is formed. The egg yolks, lemon juice, lemon rind, and salt are beaten together until very stiff. The yolk mixture is folded into the whites, and the flour is then gradually folded in.

Certain types of emulsifiers may be used by commercial bakers of sponge cakes. These allow the use of a simplified one-stage mixing procedure and result in a lighter cake of uniform grain, greater tenderness, and longer shelf life.

Baking. Baking temperatures for sponge cakes are similar to those used for angel food cakes. Sponge cakes are toughened by overbaking.

COOKIES

Classification

Cookies are of six basic types. *Rolled cookies*, when baked, may form either a crisp or a soft cookie depending on the proportions of the ingredients and the degree of doneness. *Dropped cookies* are made from a stiff batter that may be dropped or scraped from the spoon. *Bar cookies*, a cake-type mixture, are baked in a thin sheet and later cut into bars or squares. *Pressed cookies* are made from an extra-rich stiff dough that is pressed through a cookie press into various shapes. *Molded cookies* are made from a stiff dough that is shaped into balls, bars, or crescents and sometimes flattened before baking. So-called *icebox* or *refrigerator cookies* are made from a mixture so rich in fat that the dough is difficult if not impossible to roll; it is chilled in the refrigerator to harden the fat and is then sliced from the roll or molded and baked (Figure 18-10 and Plate VIII).

Ingredients

Formulas for cookies are at least as varied as those for cakes. In general, the same ingredients that produce good cakes also produce good cookies. Cake flour is not generally used for cookies because few cookies have a soft, velvety crumb or the texture of good sponge or shortened cakes. All-purpose flour is satisfactory for most cookies; however, pastry flour may be used in some foodservice operations.

HEALTHY EATING

Sugar or Sucralose? Tips for Baking

Although people with diabetes may include small amounts of sugar in their diets, they still have to include this sugar in a total allowance of carbohydrate for the day. Thus a diabetic's diet may be extremely *unbalanced* if a high-sugar—and usually also high-fat—dessert is consumed frequently. Sugar substitutes or alternative sweeteners come to the rescue to provide sweetness without carbohydrates or calories, making it easier to enjoy more frequently some of the foods they used to love.

Sugar substitutes have been used for many years, beginning with saccharin. (Alternative sweeteners were discussed in Chapter 11.) One of these products, approved by the FDA in 1998, is sucralose. Sucralose is a chlorinated derivative of sugar (sucrose) but is 600 times sweeter and is not absorbed and metabolized in the body. Also importantly, it does not have an aftertaste, as do some of the other sugar substitutes. In addition, it withstands prolonged heat treatment and can therefore be used in baking. Sucralose is now being marketed in granular form for easy measuring under the brand name of Splenda®. In this product, sucralose is blended with maltodextrin so that, for sweetness, one teaspoon or one cup of Splenda® is equivalent to one teaspoon or one cup of sugar. Splenda® is considerably more expensive than sugar, however.

As you know, sugar in baking does much more than sweeten. Sugar tenderizes, contributes to browning, aids in moisture retention, gives structure, and adds volume to a baked product. However, some adjustments for sucralose substitution must be made. Several tips may be useful as you begin to experiment in baking with Splenda®.

Proportions of other ingredients can be adjusted to make up for differences in the total volume of a recipe. The addition of small amounts of honey, molasses, cocoa, or other dark ingredients can help achieve browning and increase moistness. Addition of nonfat dry milk powder and baking soda may help in adapting a cake recipe. Check your baked goods sweetened with Splenda® for doneness a little earlier than for the sugar-sweetened product because they bake more quickly. The Splenda® sweetened products will last longer if stored in a refrigerator. Splenda® granular may be successfully incorporated into a recipe by (1) combining it thoroughly with other dry ingredients, (2) dissolving it in the liquid, or (3) creaming it with fat in the recipe [27].

Many recipes for cakes, cookies, and pies using Splenda® are available on the Internet [27]. You may enjoy experimenting with this product. ■

Crisp cookies are usually made from a mixture that is rich in fat or sugar or both. Many rolled cookie recipes call for little or no liquid. Because high volume is not desired in rolled cookies, the mixtures contain little or no leavening agent other than air incorporated into the creamed fat–sugar mixture.

Cookies are a major snack item in many countries of the world. Particularly in countries where wheat flour is imported but other flours are abundant, a composite flour may be used in the making of cookies. Cookies prepared from formulas containing 50 : 45 : 5 or 50 : 40 : 10 parts of wheat flour, rice flour, and defatted soy flour were found to be acceptable by both trained and consumer panels in Brazil [14]. These cookies were baked in a microwave oven as an alternative method for preventing nutrient degradation from extensive browning.

Cookie aroma is unique. Some of the volatile flavor compounds of cookies are formed during processing. For example, nonenzymatic (Maillard) browning reactions produce flavor compounds in the baking of cookies. Some of these sweet aroma compounds have been characterized [23], but a wide range of aromatic compounds is added to cookies during preparation, making the study of the final flavor profile more difficult. Extraction methods have been developed for the analysis of cookie aroma [25].

Texture is an important attribute in determining the acceptability of a cookie—some cookies are crisp, whereas others are soft and chewy (Figure 18-11). Shortening has an important impact on the final texture. Various ingredients may be used to produce fat-reduced and/or calorie-reduced cookies with desirable texture characteristics. One suitable replacement for at least one-fourth of the shortening and for a portion of the sugar in crisp oatmeal cookies has been reported to be Litesse®, which is a form of **polydextrose** [6]. Cellulose gums and mixtures of emulsifiers also are used in low- or reduced-fat cookies.

(a)

(b)

FIGURE 18-10 Several types of cookies are illustrated in this photograph. (a) Beginning at the bottom center of the tray with the rolled bear cookies and proceeding clockwise, there are two kinds of bar cookies, drop cookies, pressed spritz cookies, Bavarian refrigerator cookies, and molded crescent cookies. *(Photograph by Chris Meister)*

(b) Drop cookies are dropped onto the cookie sheet. Rolled-out cookies are cut into decorative shapes and placed carefully on the pan. *(Courtesy of World Kitchens Inc., makers of Pyrex®, Corning Ware®, and Baker's Secret®)*

(a)

(b)

FIGURE 18-11 (a) Many types of bar cookies can be prepared. Frosted cakelike bars, tender blonde brownies, and rich, fudge brownies are all tasty desserts. (b) Drop cookie dough may be baked on a cookie sheet for individually sized crisp cookies, in a pan and cut into squares, or into a round pie pan and decorated for a special treat. *(Courtesy of Nestlé USA)*

The acceptability of cookies prepared with fat substitutes has been reported in the literature. In one study, oatmeal, peanut butter, and chocolate chip cookies were prepared with applesauce or prune puree to reduce the fat content [28]. The reduced-fat peanut butter cookies were the most difficult to prepare with acceptable quality attributes. Flavor acceptability in all of the cookies was impaired somewhat when fruit purées were used. However, the sensory panel did find the reduced-fat oatmeal and chocolate chip cookies to be acceptable. The use of puréed white beans as a fat substitute in oatmeal chocolate chip cookies was also found to prepare an acceptable cookie [26]. The cookies became less acceptable when the amount of beans was increased.

Mixing and Handling

The conventional method is used for mixing most cookies, but beaten egg whites are seldom added last. Cookies of the sponge type are made by sponge cake methods.

Doughs for rolled cookies are usually soft but allow handling and rolling. Stiffer doughs and those rehandled and rerolled give dry, compact cookies. Many cookie mixtures must be chilled to facilitate rolling. Rolling only a portion of the dough at one time prevents continued rerolling. All trimmings can then be collected at the end for rerolling. Rolling between sheets of heavy waxed paper is sometimes done, but the usual method is to roll the dough on a floured board. Care must be used to avoid incorporating too much extra flour into the dough while rolling it and to avoid having the cookie covered with excess flour when it is ready for baking. If excess flour is on the surface of the cut cookie dough, it will remain on the cookie after baking and mar the external appearance and flavor. A pastry cloth and stockinet-covered rolling pin may also be used for rolling cookies.

The thickness of rolled dough ready for cutting is usually 1/8 or 3/16 inch. If the dough is to be used for cutouts, especially large ones, it is good to roll it to a 1/4 inch thickness (Figure 18-12). In removing cut cookies from the board to the baking sheet, the use of the side, rather than the end, of a spatula usually avoids marring the shape of the cookie. Sticky cookie dough and dough that is rolled tightly to the board are difficult to remove by any method.

Dropped cookie mixtures vary in consistency depending on the finished product desired. Some mixtures are meant to be spread into a round, flat cookie of about 3/8 to 1/2 inch thickness after baking. Such mixtures produce softer cookies than the average rolled dough. Other dropped cookies are meant to hold their form. Judgment and experience with the recipe are necessary to avoid too stiff or too soft a mixture. A mixture that is stiff enough to hold its form almost completely while baking usually produces a dry, breadlike cookie that may crack on top while baking. A cookie that only partially holds its shape during baking is usually of a more desirable texture and eating quality and has a better appearance. The type of mixture partially determines how stiff it can be without producing undesirable results. A mixture very rich in fat can be stiffer than a leaner mixture. Practically all mixtures will be stiff enough to require scraping rather than dropping from the spoon if they are expected to hold their form fairly well. Flour of strong gluten quality tends to produce a dry, breadlike drop cookie, particularly if the mixture is very stiff before baking.

Baking

Baking sheets rather than cake pans are more efficient for baking most cookies, because there are no high side walls to interfere with the circulation of heat. Cookies baked in pans with high sides may cook until they are done, but their tops may be only slightly browned, or not at all. Bar cookies are usually baked in pans with sides, however. Baking sheets require no greasing for rolled or refrigerator cookies, which are rich in fat, but do require greasing for dropped cookies or cookie bars. Cookie dough should be put on cool cookie sheets, because the dough will melt and spread if it is placed on a hot pan. You may want to bake a test cookie first to be sure that the consistency of the dough is just right. If the cookie is too flat, additional flour may be added to the dough. Rolled cookies spread little in baking, so little space is needed between them. Icebox cookies spread somewhat more, and dropped cookies must have space to spread.

The methods used to test for doneness of cakes are generally not effective for most cookies. Cookies should be lightly brown and may still appear to be slightly moist

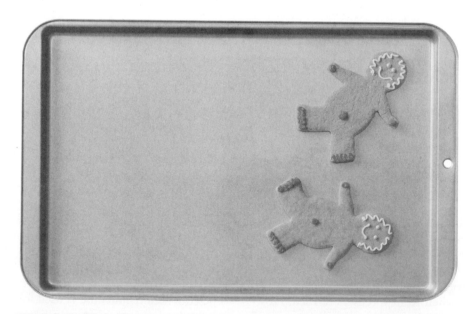

FIGURE 18-12 These decorated gingerbread cookies are an example of a rolled and cutout cookie. Decorations add the final touch. *(Courtesy of World Kitchens Inc., makers of Baker's Secret®)*

when ready to be removed from the oven. Cookies will be affected by carryover baking and therefore will continue to "bake" after removal from the oven. Failure to take into account this carryover cooking will result in cookies that are very crisp or hard after cooling. Fudge brownies and some other bar cookies can be especially difficult to assess. These bar cookies, unlike cakes, should be slightly moist when removed from the oven.

Several cookie doughs ready for baking are marketed in the refrigerated state. The dough is spooned or molded into balls and baked. One company markets cookie dough in the form of little balls or pieces that are frozen and packaged, which allows the option of baking part of the package, if desired. Ready-to-bake brownies are also available, as either frozen or refrigerated doughs, for both microwaving and conventional baking.

Some restaurants with buffet-type service bake cookies on a continuous basis for customer consumption. The dough is previously prepared but baked where customers can see the process and smell the aroma.

CHAPTER SUMMARY

- Cakes are generally classified into two major groups: shortened cakes and unshortened cakes. Chiffon cakes could be considered a third category.

- Shortened cakes are of two types: pound cake and standard shortened cake. The pound cake generally has no leavening agent except for air incorporated when creaming the fat and sugar and beating the eggs. Standard shortened cakes are leavened chiefly by carbon dioxide gas from baking powder or soda. A good standard shortened cake has a fine grain, cells of uniform size, thin cell walls, and a crumb that is elastic rather than crumbly.

- Sugar adds sweetness to a shortened cake. Sugar interferes with gluten development from the flour, delays the gelatinization of starch, and decreases the cohesive forces in the cake batter, thereby affecting tenderness and volume. Excess sugar in a cake formula may result in a fallen cake with a coarse texture and a gummy crust and crumb.

- The optimum amount of egg in a given mixture produces finer cells, thinner cell walls, and usually a larger volume than are obtained with a lower or higher percentage of egg. Excess eggs in a recipe give a rubbery, tough crumb.

- Fat weakens structure and tends to decrease volume when added beyond the optimum amount. In addition to tenderizing, plastic fats aid in incorporating air into the batter as a result of creaming the fat and sugar together.

- Emulsifying agents in cake batter cause the fat to be distributed more finely throughout the mixture and allow the cake formula to carry more sugar than flour. Shortenings that contain small amounts of emulsifiers are sometimes called *high-ratio shortenings*.

- Flour contributes structure to shortened cakes. Too little flour has the same effect as too much fat or sugar. Excess flour produces a compact, dry cake in which tunnels form readily. Cakes made with all-purpose flour are generally lower in volume and have a coarser texture than cakes made with cake flour.

- Liquid dissolves dry ingredients, allows the reaction of baking powder or soda, disperses ingredients, hydrates starch and protein, and produces steam when heated. Excess liquid in a cake formula results in a moist, low-volume cake.

- A smaller percentage of flour is used in chocolate cakes because of the starch content of the cocoa and chocolate. The color of chocolate cakes will vary as the level of acidity or alkalinity changes.

- Four common methods of mixing cakes are the conventional method, conventional sponge method, muffin method, and quick-mix method. The amount of mixing needed for a high-quality cake varies with the ingredient proportions and the batter quantity. Undermixed cakes may yield a cake of good volume, but the texture is coarse and the cell walls thick. Overmixing tends to produce a compact cake of smaller volume which may have tunnels or become heavy or soggy.

- Pans should be prepared either by greasing or by greasing and flouring before the batter is mixed. Cake batters that are allowed to stand in the bowl may result in cakes with less than an optimum volume and texture.

- The oven temperatures commonly used for baking shortened cakes range from 350° to 375°F (177° to 191°C). If dark, dull pans are used, the cake will brown more readily than if bright, shiny pans are used. Cakes cooled to about 140°F (60°C) will be firm enough to remove from the pan.

- Unshortened cakes are of two types: white angel food, which is made from egg whites, and yellow sponge, which is made from whole egg.

- A desirable angel food cake is porous, springy, tender, moist, of large volume, and has thin cell walls. Air accounts for approximately half of the leavening in angel food cakes, but steam also plays a role. Beaten egg whites incorporate air. Flour increases the strength of the cake crumb and contributes to structure. Sugar has a stabilizing effect on the egg white foam, sweetens the cake, and aids in browning. Cream of tartar has a beneficial effect on color, volume, and tenderness.

- Yellow sponge cakes may be made by either separated or whole-egg methods.

- Pans are not greased for angel food or yellow sponge cakes. After baking, the pan is inverted and allowed to stand until the cake is thoroughly cooled. Both angel food and sponge cakes will toughen if overbaked.

- Cookies are of six basic types: rolled, dropped, bar cookies, pressed cookies, molded cookies, and icebox or refrigerator cookies. Formulas for cookies, like cake formulas, are varied.

- Crisp cookies are usually made from a mixture that is rich in fat or sugar, or both. Shortening also has an important impact on the final texture. Acceptable cookies may be prepared using fat substitutes.

- The conventional method is used for mixing most cookies. The consistency of the cookie dough will vary with the type of cookie being prepared.

- Cookies should be lightly browned and may still appear to be slightly moist when ready to be removed from the oven. Cookies will be affected by carryover baking and therefore will continue to "bake" after removal from the oven

STUDY QUESTIONS

1. Shortened cakes are of two types. Name them and describe distinguishing characteristics of each.

2. Describe the usual role and the effect of an excessive amount of each of the following ingredients in the production of a shortened cake:
   - (a) Sugar
   - (b) Egg
   - (c) Fat
   - (d) Baking powder
   - (e) Liquid
   - (f) Flour

3. What role is played by an emulsifier in a shortened cake batter. What effect does it have on the finished product?

4. Briefly describe each of the following methods for mixing a shortened cake. Explain the advantages or disadvantages of each method.
   - (a) Conventional
   - (b) Conventional sponge
   - (c) Muffin
   - (d) Quick-mix

5. Describe the effects of under- and overmixing a shortened cake batter. What factors affect the desirable amount of mixing to be done?

6. Why is it important to prepare the pans for a shortened cake batter before the batter is mixed? Explain.

7. Suggest an appropriate temperature for baking a shortened cake. Explain why this temperature is recommended.

8. Why should a shortened cake be allowed to stand for about 10 minutes after baking before removal from the pan?

9. (a) Name and describe characteristics of two types of unshortened cakes.

   (b) What is a *chiffon cake*?

10. Describe the usual role of each of the following ingredients in angel food cake:
    - (a) Egg whites
    - (b) Sugar
    - (c) Cream of tartar
    - (d) Flour

11. (a) Describe appropriate methods for mixing angel food and sponge cakes.

    (b) Point out precautions that should be taken in mixing unshortened cakes to ensure finished cakes of good quality.

12. Suggest appropriate baking temperatures for angel food and sponge cakes.

13. How should angel food and sponge cakes be cooled after baking? Why?

14. (a) Describe six basic types of cookies.

    (b) Suggest some precautions that are necessary in the preparation of rolled cookies of good quality.

    (c) What types of baking pans are generally recommended for cookies? Why?

Pastries are products made from doughs containing moderate to large amounts of fat and mixed in a manner to produce flakiness. Note the following three examples:

- Plain pastry or pie crust is used to make all types of tarts, turnovers, and dessert pies, including single- and double-crust fruit pies (Figure 19-1); custard-type pies baked in the shell; and soft starch-thickened cream pies and gelatin-based chiffon pies in which the fillings are added after the pie shells are baked (Plate IX).

- Plain pastry is also used as a carrier of high-protein foods to be served as a main dish including various types of meat, poultry, and fish pies with single or double crusts; patty shells to hold chicken à la king and similar types of creamed mixtures; and quiches, which are pies that can be made with a variety of ingredients, such as bacon, ham, Swiss cheese, mushrooms, onions, and other vegetables, baked in a custard-type filling (Figure 19-2).

- Puff pastry—flaky layers of light, buttery dough—is used to make crisp, sugar-glazed, and cream-filled French pastry or flaky sweet rolls called *Danish pastry* (Figure 19-3). Puff pastry is made by rolling chilled butter in a well-kneaded flour-and-water dough, then folding and rerolling several times to make many thin layers of dough separated by thin layers of butter. During baking, the butter melts and permeates the dough.

FIGURE 19-1 A lattice-top fruit pie. *(Courtesy of Sun-Maid Growers of California)*

FIGURE 19-2 A quiche that contains fresh sliced mushrooms, sliced green onions, and shredded Swiss cheese. The custard base is made with eggs and light cream or milk. *(Courtesy of the American Egg Board)*

FIGURE 19-3 Puff pastry can be used to produce a variety of tantalizing products. In the center front is an apple turnover, behind this, the thin flakes of the pastry can be seen in elephant ears; three creme-filled French pastries are on the right; and at the top of the picture is a small Danish pastry. *(Photograph by Chris Meister)*

In this chapter, the following topics on the making of plain pastry will be discussed:

- Characteristics of pastry
- Ingredients
- Mixing, rolling, and baking plain pastry
- Other types of pastry and crusts

CHARACTERISTICS OF PLAIN PASTRY

Good-quality pastry is tender but does not easily break when served. It is flaky, with a blistered surface, is slightly crisp, evenly and lightly browned, and pleasantly flavored.

Flakiness

Flakiness is described as thin layers of baked dough separated by open spaces (Figure 19-4). Some factors that have been found to affect flakiness are (1) the character of the fat used (solid versus melted or liquid fat), (2) the consistency of solid fat, (3) the type of flour used, (4) the proportion of water, (5) the degree of mixing, (6) the method of mixing, and (7) the number of times the dough is rolled.

Flakiness is thought to result from a process in which small particles of fat are coated with moistened flour or dough and then flattened into thin layers when the dough mixture is rolled out. On baking, the fat melts, is absorbed by the surrounding dough, and leaves empty spaces between thin layers of the baked dough.

Solid fats yield a flaky crust more easily than melted or liquid fats; however, flaky pastry can be produced with melted fats or oils. Liquid fats generally tend to blend more completely with flour. They may yield a very tender and crumbly crust when used in the same proportion as solid fats.

Firm fats that remain in layers when they are rolled yield a flakier crust than soft fats. The method used in making puff pastry, in which the fat is reserved to be

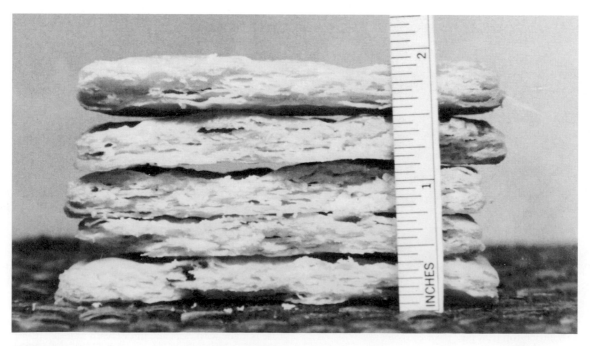

FIGURE 19-4 A very flaky pastry can be made with lard as the fat.

rolled between the layers of dough, increases flakiness. Merely rerolling increases flakiness, but unless the percentage of fat in the mixture is high, rerolling may also develop the gluten sufficiently to increase toughness. Rerolling as a means of increasing flakiness is valuable chiefly for puff pastry.

A regular pastry flour may yield a very flaky crust, but flakiness increases with the strength of gluten. Toughness may also increase with the use of a stronger flour unless additional fat is used and greater care is taken in manipulation.

Tenderness

Because tenderness is one of the most desirable characteristics of good pastry, it requires at least as much consideration as flakiness; yet some of the factors that produce flakiness tend to decrease tenderness, and vice versa. Tenderness is at a maximum when the fat spreads over the flour particles, interferes with the hydration of gluten proteins in the flour, and thus decreases the formation of gluten strands. If the fat blends too thoroughly with the dough, the crust is too tender to handle and tends to be crumbly. Adjustments in both ingredients and techniques of mixing and handling must be made so that both flakiness and tenderness are achieved in the baked pastry.

INGREDIENTS IN PLAIN PASTRY

Plain pastry contains only a few ingredients—flour, fat, salt, and water. Plain pastry is leavened primarily by steam, which is produced by baking in a hot oven. Leavening in plain pastry is not extensive, however.

Flour

Either pastry or all-purpose flour can be used; pastry flour requires less fat for optimum tenderness and is used primarily by commercial bakers. Because of the larger amount of gluten formed with all-purpose flour, about 1/3 cup of fat per cup of flour may be needed to produce a tender crust. This proportion also depends on the kind of fat used and the skill of the handler.

Water

The amount of water required for plain pastry varies with the hydration capacity of the flour, the amount and type of fat, the temperature of the ingredients, and the individual technique of handling. An excessive amount of water added in the making of pastry dough allows the hydration and development of more gluten than is desirable for optimum tenderness [3]. Toughness of pastry is therefore increased by too much water in the dough. Too little water produces a dry dough that is crumbly and difficult to handle. The amount of liquid should be sufficient to barely form a dough; the dough should not be wet and sticky [6].

Fat

Fat is responsible for the tenderness of pastry because it spreads over the particles of flour and retards their hydration. Fats vary in their tenderizing properties [5]. Liquid oils spread more than plastic fats and usually have greater tenderizing power. Reduction of the level of soybean or safflower oil in pie crust results in a product that compares favorably in quality characteristics with pie crust made with a standard level of shortening [1]. Softer plastic fats spread more readily than harder fats. Butter and margarine contain only about 80 percent fat and therefore have less tenderizing power than 100 percent fats such as lard and hydrogenated shortening when substituted on a weight basis. A cup of lard weighs more than a cup of hydrogenated shortening because the shortening has been precreamed and contains an inert gas to make it lighter. In addition to the role of fat in tenderizing, plastic fats, in particular, play an important part in the development of flakiness in pastry.

The fat should be cold enough to be firm rather than pasty or oily, but plastic enough to be measured accurately and to cut into the flour. In warm weather, some chilling of fat may be necessary. Likewise, some chilling of water may be desirable.

FOCUS ON SCIENCE

Why Does a Plastic Fat Perform Better Than Other Kinds of Fat in Pastry Dough?

A fat that is plastic covers the largest surface area and has the greatest "shortening power." A plastic fat contains both liquid and solid phases of fat. Depending on the fatty acid composition and distribution, at room temperature as much as 70 to 85% of the glycerides may be liquid with only 15 to 30% crystallized in solid form. Both chemical composition and physical structure affect the liquid/solid ratio and thus the plasticity of the fat.

TECHNIQUES OF MIXING

A standard plain pie crust may be prepared by cutting in the fat, then adding water with a minimum amount of mixing. Cutting of the fat into the flour coats the flour particles and therefore is one of the contributors to a tender pastry. The dough is then gathered into a ball and refrigerated for 15 to 30 minutes before rolling into the crust. During this period of holding, the water migrates throughout the dough, and the fat is chilled.

The fat can be cut into the flour with a pastry blender or with a knife or spatula. It can even be lightly blended with the fingers (Figure 19-5). A reasonably uniform blending of fat with flour produces a more uniformly tender crust sometimes called a *mealy crust*. Fat particles may vary in size. Cutting of the fat into particles the size of peas is generally suggested for a flaky crust. Those who favor a relatively coarse division of fat in the flour–salt mixture do so on the theory that flakiness is increased by rolling larger fat masses into thin layers.

Electric mixers or food processers can also be used both to mix the fat with the flour and to mix the liquid with the flour–fat mixture in the final stages of dough

FIGURE 19-5 Fat may be cut into the flour with a pastry cutter, knife, or by hand as shown here.

preparation. However, care must be taken to avoid overmixing. Excessive mixing when adding the water will toughen the crust. When mixing a pie crust by hand, the water may be lightly mixed into the fat and flour mixture by using a fork to toss the flour–fat mixture with the water (Figure 19-6).

1. After the flour and salt are measured and mixed together in the bowl, the shortening is cut in with a pastry blender.

2. Sprinkle the water, a tablespoon at a time, over the flour-fat mixture.

6. Divide dough approximately in half; round up larger part on a lightly floured cloth-covered board.

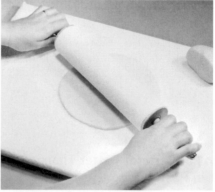

7. Roll out not quite 1/8 inch thick.

FIGURE 19-6 Preparation of pastry. *(Courtesy of Kitchens of Betty Crocker, General Mills, Inc.)*

Modified Mixing Method

Several methods of mixing pastry, other than the traditional pastry method, have been suggested. A satisfactory pastry product can be obtained by using any one of these methods. A modified method of mixing pastry has been developed in which 1/4 cup of a 2 cup portion of flour is reserved to be mixed with liquid to form a paste. After the fat and the remainder of the flour have been combined as described, the paste is added all at once and blended with the flour–fat mixture.

Hot-Water and Oil Methods

In the hot-water method of mixing pastry, solid fats can be melted by stirring them into boiling water; this mixture is then stirred into the flour and salt. If oil is used as the fat, it can be shaken with water and added in a similar manner. Alternatively, the oil can be sprinkled over the flour–salt mixture followed by stirring to disperse the oil. The water can then be added as in the traditional method. Pastry made by the hot-water and oil methods may be somewhat less flaky than pastry made by the traditional method.

Puff Pastry Method

Pastry can also be made by a modified puff pastry method: About two tablespoons of the flour–fat mixture are removed before the liquid is added. After the pastry has been rolled out, this flour–fat mixture is sprinkled over the dough. The dough is rolled up like a jelly roll and cut into two pieces. One piece is placed on top of the other, and they are then rerolled for the pie pan. This method tends to increase flakiness in pastry.

ROLLING PASTRY

Pastry can be rolled as soon as it has been mixed, but allowing the dough to stand for a few minutes increases the extensibility or elasticity of the dough, making it easier to handle and to roll. When the work area is warm,

3. Mix lightly with a fork until all the flour is moistened.

4. Gather the dough together with your fingers and press into a ball.

5. A canvas-covered board and a stockinet-covered rolling pin prevent the pastry from sticking while being rolled out.

8. Keep the pastry circular and roll it about 1 to 2 inches larger than the pie pan.

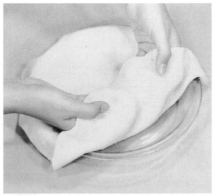

9. Fold the pastry in half. Quickly transfer to a pie pan and unfold.

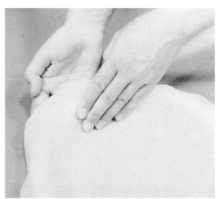

10. Fit the pastry carefully down into the pan. Avoid trapping air underneath the dough. Trim off the overhanging edges. Place the filling in the pastry-lined pan. Roll out the other part of the dough for the top crust.

FIGURE 19-6 Continued

FOCUS ON SCIENCE

How Does Flakiness Form in a Baked Pie Crust?

Some of the plastic fat forms discrete particles with flour adhering to them. These particles are flattened when rolled, thus creating layers of fat and dough. When the pie crusts are baked, steam is formed, the dough gelatinizes, and the fat melts into the dough, thereby leaving an empty space and flakiness. It is important that the fat has a high melting point, such that it remains solid until the dough gelatinizes.

refrigeration of the dough before rolling can help maintain flakiness. For ordinary pie crust, the dough is rolled to about 1/8 inch thickness. Enough flour is required for the board to keep the crust from sticking, but the minimum amount should be used to avoid toughening the pastry. Occasional lifting of the crust while rolling also tends to prevent sticking. The dough can be rolled on a canvas-covered board, onto which a small amount of flour has been rubbed, or between two layers of waxed paper. Crusts that are rolled very thin become too brown when baked as pie shells and break when handling or serving. If they are used for fruit pies, they may break during baking and allow juices to flow out.

Crusts are rolled into a circular shape. The dough for a lower crust or a pie shell should be about one to two inches greater in diameter than the top of the pan, which allows for variable pan depth (Figure 19-6). To avoid excessive rolling of dough, which toughens the pastry, each crust is rolled separately. For future use, the rolled pastry can be frozen before baking [2], or the baked shells can be frozen.

Although pie shells tend to shrink somewhat in baking, excessive shrinkage can be prevented if the dough is not stretched when it is fitted into the pan. Preparing enough dough to make a rim or a frilled edge is also an advantage if shrinking occurs. Overdevelopment of the gluten by rerolling may result in greater shrinkage during baking than occurs when gluten is not developed to an appreciable extent.

The formation of large blisters in pastry shells during baking can be prevented by forcing air from under the dough while fitting the dough into the pan and by pricking the dough adequately with a fork before baking. Crusts in which fillings are to be cooked are never pricked.

Top crusts for fruit pies are less likely to break under the pressure of steam if small openings are made near the center for the escape of steam. Large gashes should be avoided because they are unattractive and permit the loss of juices. Making the air vents into a decoration results in an attractive pie (Figure 19-7). Top crusts adhere more closely to lower crusts if the latter are moistened with water before the crusts are pressed together.

BAKING

Plain pastry that is baked prior to the addition of the filling is baked at a hot oven temperature (425°F to 450°F/218° to 232°C). This heat allows rapid production of steam, which separates the layers of dough formed as the fat particles melt. Baking is continued until the surface is delicately browned, which probably occurs chiefly as a result of the Maillard reaction.

Baking temperatures are adjusted according to the type of filling in pastry shells. The filling must be adequately cooked before the crust becomes too brown. Soaking of bottom crusts by fruit and custard fillings sometimes creates problems in baking.

Preventing Soaked Crusts

Many methods have been suggested and tried for preventing a soaked crust in fruit, custard, and pumpkin pies. Some methods—partially baking the crust, coating the

FIGURE 19-7 Air vents in the top crust can be attractive and functional. *(Courtesy of World Kitchens Inc., makers of Pyrex®, Corning Ware®, and Baker's Secret®)*

crust with raw egg white, or heating the crust until the egg white is coagulated—have no value. A partially baked crust becomes more soaked than one that is not baked. It also tends to be heavy or soggy. Raw egg white, being soluble in water, blends with the filling, thus offering no protection against the soaking of the crust.

So how can the crusts be protected? For fruit pies, you can coat the upper surface of the lower crust with melted butter, use a hot oven temperature for the first 15 minutes of baking, and thicken the filling before placing it in the pastry-lined pan. Thickening the filling gives you the added advantage of knowing the precise consistency of the juice before the pie is baked.

For custard and pumpkin pies, the problem of soaked crusts is even more difficult to solve. The lower baking temperatures required for egg mixtures prolong the baking time and permit increased soaking before the pie is done. A method that has been suggested to improve the crusts of custard pies is chilling the pastry for one hour before adding the filling, and using a high oven temperature (450°F/232°C) for the first 10 minutes of baking. Increasing the percentage of egg in the mixture (three eggs per pint of milk) lowers the coagulation temperature of the egg proteins and increases the ease of coagulation for the mixture. Scalding the milk used for the filling also shortens coagulation time. A coagulated custard does not penetrate the crust as readily as an uncooked mixture. An overcooked custard may exude sufficient water to produce a wet crust.

Using a Microwave Oven

Microwaved pastry is tender, flaky, and puffy, but it does not brown. A few drops of yellow food coloring can be added to the dough, or the pastry can be brushed with egg yolk before microwaving. A one-crust pastry shell is cooked on high power for about 6 or 7 minutes, the dish being rotated one-half turn after 3 minutes. Alternatively, the pastry shell can be baked in a conventional oven and the filling cooked in a microwave oven. Commercial pie filling mixes are easily prepared by mixing the packet contents with milk and cooking on a high-power setting for 2 to 3 minutes with periodic stirring.

The bottom crust of a two-crust pie can be cooked by microwave on a medium setting for 5 to 6 minutes, the uncooked filling added, the top crust put in place, and the pie cooked again. The pie should be turned midway in the cooking period. If a broiling unit is not available for browning, the pie can be finished by baking for 10 to 15 minutes in a hot conventional oven. Meringues can be cooked by microwaves but must be browned in a conventional heating unit.

Prepared Pie Crust

Homemade pie crusts can be frozen baked or unbaked for later use. Alternatively, partially prepared pie crust is available on the market in several forms. Ready-to-bake pie crust in aluminum pie pans is sold as a frozen product. Instructions generally suggest that the dough be thawed before baking. If the product is to be used in the preparation of a fruit pie, however, it should be filled with the fruit and baked without being thawed. Rolled sheets of pie crust, enclosed in plastic sheets and folded, are sold as refrigerated dough. They should be allowed to warm to the degree that they are pliable before being unfolded and placed in a pie pan for baking. Pie crust also is marketed as a dry mix that needs only the addition of water to form a dough that can be rolled and placed in pie pans.

OTHER TYPES OF PASTRY AND CRUSTS

Crumb, Cookie, and Sweet Tart Crusts

The bottom crust on pies as well as some other desserts such as cheesecakes may be made from crumbs. Graham cracker crumbs are frequently used; sugar cookies, chocolate sandwich cookies, gingersnaps, and other cookies may be crumbed and used (Figure 19-8). The typical ratio of ingredients in crumb crusts is one part melted butter, two parts sugar, and four parts crumbs [4]. When cookies are used instead of graham cracker crumbs, the amount of sugar may need to be decreased.

The preparation of crumb crusts is generally quick and easy. The crumbs, sugar, and melted butter are

FOCUS ON SCIENCE

How Does the Type of Pie Pan Have an Impact on Color and the Potential Soaking of Crusts?

For well-baked golden bottom crusts, use pans made of heat-resistant glass, dull anodized aluminum enamel, or darkened metal. These types of pie pans absorb heat, thereby ensuring the crusts brown perfectly. Shiny pans reflect heat so bottom crusts are more likely to be soggy. Therefore, the selection of the pan is essential.

FIGURE 19-8 This cream cheese pumpkin dessert has a tasty gingersnap crumb crust. *(Courtesy of McCormick & Company Inc.)*

FIGURE 19-9 This sweet dough tart shell has been filled with a pastry cream and topped with carefully arranged fruit. A fruit glaze will finish this beautiful dessert.

blended. If the mixture is too dry to stick together, additional melted butter may be slowly added until the desired consistency is achieved. Then the crumbs are pressed into the bottom of the pan to a depth between 1/8 and 1/4 inch. This crust may be refrigerated and filled after the butter has firmed, or it can be baked in an oven preheated to 350°F (177°C) for about 10 minutes or until lightly browned and then filled. Baked crusts will be firmer and will provide a stronger crust.

Tart crusts may be made from a sweet dough that usually contains egg yolk [4]. The fat is blended in thoroughly in a mixing procedure similar to making cookies as opposed to the mixing procedure for standard pie pastry. These sweet dough crusts generally are not flaky like other pie crusts, but they have the advantage of being crisp and sturdy. These characteristics are desirable for tarts, which are usually made in a shallow, straight-sided pan (Figure 19-9).

Puff Pastry and Phyllo Dough

Puff pastry is a rich dough that separates into many light, crisp layers when baked. Steam is the leavening agent in this dough, and rolling a sheet of butter into the dough results in the flaky layers that are characteristic of puff

pastry. Making puff pastry from scratch requires care and patience, as the chilled dough must be rolled multiple times to create the layers from the butter that has been folded and rolled into the dough. Alternatively, puff pastry is available frozen for use in creating a number of desserts and other dishes.

Phyllo dough is a paper-thin pastry that is bland in flavor. It is used in Mediterranean, Middle Eastern, and Central Asian dishes [4]. Phyllo dough is generally purchased frozen because of the time and skill required to make this dough. Sheets of phyllo dough may be layered into custard cups, baked, and then filled with a custard or cheese filling and topped with fruit. Phyllo dough is also used for the classic Greek dessert called *baklava*. Frozen phyllo dough should be thawed slowly in the refrigerator because attempts to thaw phyllo dough quickly create difficulties in separating and handling the sheets. While working with phyllo dough, cover it with plastic wrap to prevent it from drying out. Many recipes will call for the dough to be lifted one sheet at a time and placed in the pan and brushed with butter before adding another sheet and repeating the process.

CHAPTER SUMMARY

- Pastries are products made from doughs containing moderate to large amounts of fats and mixed in such a way as to produce flakiness. Pie crust, puff pastry, and phyllo dough are examples.

- Good-quality pastry is tender but does not easily break when served. It is flaky with a blistered surface, slightly crisp, evenly and lightly browned, and pleasantly flavored.

- Factors that affect flakiness are the type and consistency of fat, type of flour, proportion of water, degree of mixing, method of mixing, and number of times the dough is rolled.

- Tenderness is at a maximum when the fat spreads over the flour particles. However, some of the factors that encourage flakiness tend to decrease tenderness.

- Plain pastry contains flour, fat, salt, and water. Plain pastry is leavened primarily by steam produced in a hot oven.

- A standard technique for mixing pie crust includes the following steps: (1) cut fat into the flour until the fat is the size of peas; (2) add water and mix lightly; (3) gather the dough into a ball and refrigerate; (4) roll the dough out on a lightly floured surface; (5) gently fold the pastry, then lift into the pie plate and unfold; and (6) fit the pastry into the pie pan without trapping air or stretching the crust.

- Plain pastry may be baked before filling or after filling, depending on the type of pie being prepared. Methods to prevent the soaking of crusts filled with fruit fillings or custards are suggested.

- Microwave pastry is tender, flaky, and puffy, but does not brown.

- Crumb crusts may be prepared using the following ratio of ingredients: one part butter, two parts sugar, and four parts crumbs. These crusts may be used with or without baking, although a baked crust will generally be firmer.

- Puff pastry is a rich dough that separates into many light, crisp layers when baked. These doughs may be prepared from scratch or purchased frozen and ready to bake. Phyllo dough is typically purchased frozen due to the skill and time required to make this paper-thin dough.

STUDY QUESTIONS

1. Describe desirable characteristics of good-quality pastry.

2. Describe the role of each of the following ingredients in the preparation of good-quality pastry:
   (a) Flour
   (b) Fat
   (c) Water

3. (a) Suggest an appropriate ratio of fat to flour for making pastry.
   (b) Explain how the type of fat and the type of flour used might affect these proportions.

4. (a) Describe several procedures for mixing pastry.
   (b) What techniques of mixing are likely to produce the most flaky pastry? Why?

5. Describe a satisfactory procedure for making pastry with oil. How does this pastry compare with one made using a solid fat?

6. What is the effect of each of the following on tenderness of pastry?
   (a) Type of fat used
   (b) Type of flour used
   (c) Technique of mixing and handling

7. Suggest an appropriate temperature for baking plain pastry. Explain why this temperature may be recommended.

8. What can be done to prevent or minimize the soaking of bottom crusts of custard and fruit pies during baking?

9. What is puff pastry? Phyllo dough?

VEGETABLES AND VEGETABLE PREPARATION 20

What exactly is a vegetable? We can define vegetables broadly as plants or parts of plants that are used as food. However, so broad a definition includes fruits, nuts, and cereals, which, although of vegetable origin, are not commonly classified as vegetables. The term *vegetable* has through usage come to apply in a more narrow sense to those plants or parts of plants that are served either raw or cooked as part of the main course of a meal. Sweet corn and rice are two examples of cereals that, through usage, are sometimes given the place of vegetables on the table.

Regardless of how we define vegetables, we value them for their unique contributions to color, flavor, and texture in our menus. In addition, vegetables are an important part of our daily food intake because of their nutritional merit, particularly in regard to their content of vitamins, minerals, and fiber.

In this chapter, the following topics will be discussed:

- Consumption trends and the nutritional importance of vegetables
- Kinds of vegetables
- Purchasing and storage
- Preparation and quality considerations
- Cooking methods
- Plant proteins and vegetarian diets

CONSUMPTION TRENDS AND NUTRITION

Consumption Trends

Food supply data showed an increase in the availability of vegetables in the United States from 336 pounds per person in 1970 to 415 pounds per person in 2005 [77]. However, consumption is concentrated among a small number of vegetables. The average per capita disappearance data of 2002–2004 show potatoes, tomatoes, sweet corn, and head lettuce as accounting for 61 percent of the total vegetables [36]. Furthermore, the majority of Americans report consuming less than the recommended servings of vegetables [65]. Using the National Health and Nutrition Examination Survey data, researchers reported 40 percent of the individuals in the United States consume five or more servings of fruit and vegetables per day which corresponds to older, lower recommendations [20]. The proportion of older adults who meet the new recommendations given in the *2005 Dietary Guidelines for Americans* ranges from 1 to 17 percent. Americans especially need to increase their consumption of dark green and orange vegetables and legumes since less than one-third of the recommended amounts of these vegetables are being consumed. Americans appear to favor starchy vegetables and are thus eating more than the recommended levels of potatoes and other starchy vegetables.

Households with higher incomes, older members, and these with a college education are more likely to spend more money on vegetables [62]. A greater variety of vegetables is also used in homes where more meals are prepared from scratch. Vegetable preferences vary by age, racial and ethnic differences, region of the United States, and suburban or rural locations. Women over 40 and Asians consume more spinach than other groups. Consumers in the South eat more cabbage, although sauerkraut is more preferred by households in the Midwest and East. Fresh snap beans are consumed at a higher level by consumers in cities compared to those living in suburban or rural areas. Although the consumption of French fries does not vary by income, location does matter. The majority of French fries are consumed away from home, primarily in fast-food establishments [33, 54].

Nutrition

Vegetables offer a number of beneficial qualities to our diets. Vegetables and fruits probably do more than any other group of foods to add appetizing texture, color, and flavor to daily meals. From a health perspective, vegetables have been associated with a reduced risk of certain

TABLE 20-1   Vegetable Subgroups Based on Nutrient Content. Each group should be included several times each week in meals

Vegetable Group	Examples
Dark green	Bok choy, broccoli, collard greens, dark green leafy lettuce, kale, mesclun, mustard greens, romaine lettuce, spinach, turnip greens, watercress
Orange	Acorn squash, butternut squash, carrots, hubbard squash, pumpkin, sweet potatoes
Dry beans and peas *May be purchased dried or canned.*	Black beans, black-eyed peas, garbanzo beans (chickpeas), kidney beans, lentils, lima beans (mature), navy beans, pinto beans, soybeans, split peas
Starchy	Corn, green peas, lima beans (green), potatoes
Other vegetables	Artichokes, asparagus, bean sprouts, beets, Brussels sprouts, cabbage, cauliflower, celery, cucumbers, eggplant, green beans, green or red peppers, iceberg (head) lettuce, mushrooms, okra, onions, parsnips, tomatoes, tomato juice, turnips, wax beans, zucchini

Source: U.S. Department of Agriculture http://www.mypyramid.gov/pyramid/vegetables.html [70]

TABLE 20-2   Excellent and Good Vegetable Sources of Selected Nutrients

Nutrients	Vegetable Sources
Fiber	*Excellent sources:* Navy beans, kidney beans, black beans, pinto beans, lima beans, white beans, soybeans, split peas, chickpeas, black-eyed peas, lentils, artichokes
Folate	*Excellent sources:* Black-eyed peas, cooked spinach, Great Northern beans, asparagus
Potassium	*Good sources:* Sweet potatoes, tomato paste, tomato puree, beet greens, white potatoes, white beans, lima beans, cooked greens, carrot juice
Vitamin A	*Excellent sources:* Sweet potatoes, pumpkin, carrots, spinach, turnip greens, mustard greens, kale, collard greens, winter squash, red peppers, Chinese cabbage
Vitamin C	*Excellent sources:* Red and green peppers, sweet potatoes, kale, broccoli, Brussels spouts, tomato juice, cauliflower

Source: U.S. Centers for Disease Control and Prevention. Reference 67

cancers, type 2 diabetes, stroke, and potentially cardiovascular disease and hypertension [61, 69, 84]. In 2003, FDA issued a dietary guidance statement that may be used in product labels and other print materials. This statement is, "Diets rich in fruits and vegetables may reduce the risk of some types of cancers and other chronic diseases" [78].

The *2005 Dietary Guidelines for Americans* recommend the daily consumption of two and one-half cups of a variety of vegetables for a reference 2,000 calorie intake [68]. More vegetables should be consumed by those with higher caloric needs. Variety in vegetable use may be accomplished by including all five vegetable subgroups in meals or snacks several times each week: dark green, orange, legumes, starchy vegetables, and other vegetables [70]. Examples of vegetables in these five groups are provided in Table 20-1. Individualized food consumption recommendations can be obtained from http://www.mypyramid.gov.

Nutritionally, vegetables are rich in fiber, folate, potassium, vitamin A, vitamin C and other nutrients. The composition and nutritive value of selected vegetables are given in Appendix C. Examples of excellent and good vegetable sources of nutrients are provided in Table 20-2. Many vegetables, as well as fruits, also are rich in

phytochemicals. Phytochemicals such as carotenoids (including lycopene), flavonoids, glucosinolates, phytoestrogens, phenols, sulfides, capsaicin, anthocyanines, tannins, and more have been found to function as antioxidants or anticancer agents [84].

In addition to many vegetables having a high nutrient content, most vegetables are low in calories and thus may be beneficial in maintaining a healthy weight. To promote vegetable consumption among consumers, the 5 A Day program has been updated to the Fruits and Veggies—More Matters™ health initiative launched in March 2007 (Figure 20-1). Along with the *2005 Dietary Guidelines for Americans*, this national initiative by the Produce for Better Health Foundation, the Centers for Disease Control and Prevention (CDC), and other government

FIGURE 20-1 Logo for Fruit and Veggies—More Matters™. *(Courtesy of the Produce for Better Health Foundation)*

and national partners has been designed to help Americans overcome common barriers to eating fruits and vegetables [50].

KINDS OF VEGETABLES

Various parts of plants are used as vegetables. One grouping by plant part is shown in Table 20-3. Technically, some vegetables might be placed under more than one heading.

Leaf Vegetables

Many different types of greens are available for the consumer to purchase or grow in a garden. Although iceberg lettuce is one of the most widely consumed greens, consumers are increasingly choosing romaine, leaf, and other specialty greens such as radicchio, arugula, and red oak. A description of selected leaf vegetables is provided in Table 20-4. Leafy greens are discussed further in Chapter 22.

Leaf vegetables may be generally characterized as being high in water and low in carbohydrate and calories, with only small amounts of protein and little or no fat (Figure 20-2). These vegetables' chief nutritive contribution is providing vitamins and minerals especially iron, vitamin A value, riboflavin, folate, and vitamin C. Leafy greens that are darker green have a higher vitamin A value. Green leaves also contain calcium, but most of the calcium in spinach, chard, and beet greens is combined with oxalic acid in the plant and is not available for absorption from the digestive tract.

To preserve quality, leafy greens should be stored under refrigeration away from ethylene-producing fruits and vegetables such as tomatoes or apples. Ethylene-producing fruits and vegetables will promote premature spoilage. High humidity conditions are preferable to avoid wilting of the lettuce leaves. All leafy lettuce and greens should be washed thoroughly. Submerging the leaves under cool water then lifting out of the water to drain and repeating in fresh water two or three times until thoroughly washed is recommended. A salad spinner is helpful to adequately dry washed lettuce and greens.

Vegetable-Fruits

Tomatoes, cucumbers, peppers, squash, and several other vegetables are classified as vegetable-fruits. Although typically served as vegetables, these vegetable-fruits are botanically classified as fruits because each one develops from a flower. People often do not think of these vegetables as fruits because they do not taste sweet and are generally prepared in combination with other vegetables. Although green and red peppers, string beans, and okra can be classified as vegetable-fruits, they are also seed pods.

Tomatoes may be consumed raw or cooked and are used by food processors for catsup, tomato sauces, and other tomato products. Peppers can be mild or hot and used in many different kinds of foods. See Chapter 8 for a discussion of the types of peppers used for seasoning.

TABLE 20-3 Parts of Plants Commonly Used as Vegetables

Leaves	Seeds	Roots	Tubers	Bulbs	Flowers	Fruits	Stems and Shoots
Beet greens	Beans,	Beet	Ginger root	Chives	Artichoke	Cucumber	Fennel
Bok choy	Dry Corn (a seed	Carrot	Potato (Irish)	Garlic	(French or	Eggplant	Asparagus
(Chinese chard)	of the grass family	Celeriac	Sunchoke	Leek	Globe)	Okra	Celery
Brussels sprouts	frequently served	(Celery root)	(Jerusalem	Onion	Broccoli	Pepper	(a leaf stem)
	as a vegetable)	Jicama	artichoke)	Shallot	Cauliflower	Pumpkin	Kohlrabi
Cabbage	Lentils	Parsnip				Snap beans	
Chard	Peas	Radish				Squash	
Chinese cabbage		Rutabaga				Sweet corn	
		Salsify				(on the cob)	
Collards		Sweet potato				Tomato	
Dandelion greens		Turnip					
Endive							
Escarole							
Kale							
Lettuce							
Mustard greens							
Parsley							
Romaine							
Spinach							
Turnip greens							
Watercress							

TABLE 20-4 Leaf Vegetables

Description

Brussels Sprouts

Very small heads (often one inch across or less). Dark green, compact leaves. Firm texture. Are generally cooked before consumption.

Lettuce

Arugula. Small, flat leaves with long stems and a peppery taste. Often mixed with other salad greens.

Belgian Endive. Elongated head with white compact leaves and creamy yellow tips. Crisp texture, mild and slightly bitter flavor.

Boston and Bibb. Loose heads, buttery texture, and mild flavor.

Chicory or Curly Endive. Narrow leaves with very curly edges. May be dark green on outer leaves to yellow-white in center. Mild to slightly bitter flavor.

Escarole. Loosely bunched, large heads and slightly crumbled green leaves. Milder taste than curly endive.

Frisee. Ivory-yellow, very thin, and ruffled leaves.

Iceberg. Crisp texture and very mild flavor. Pale green leaves on compact head. Least nutritious of the salad greens.

Looseleaf (Oak Leaf, Red Leaf, Green Leaf). Leaves are joined at stem and do not form a head. Oak leaf has a similar shape of the leaves on an oak tree. Red and green leaf lettuce varieties are characterized by color. Texture is crisp but tender.

Radicchio. Maroon-red leaves on a small compact head. Slightly bittersweet distinctive flavor. Tends to be expensive.

Romaine or Cos. Loaf-like, elongated leaves. Dark green. Strong flavor and crispy texture. Often used for Caesar salads.

Cabbage

Green. Light green compact leaves. Round head.

Red. Purple-red leaves. Round, compact head. Sweeter flavor than green cabbage.

Savoy. Pale green color and crinkled leaves. Round to oblong head with loose, compact leaves.

General Tips. Select firm heads, heavy for size. Precut cabbage is best avoided because of reduced vitamin C content. May be eaten raw or cooked.

Chinese Cabbage

Bok Choy. Thick white stalks and large green leaves. Mild flavor and tender-crisp texture. Often stir-fried but may be used raw.

Napa Cabbage or Chinese Cabbage. Tightly packed oblong head. Leaves are pale green and crinkled. Tender crisp with a mild flavor. May be used fresh or cooked.

Cactus Pads or Napales

Broad green pads with tiny thorns. Tender texture. Flavor is a cross between fresh green beans and bell pepper.

General Tips. Dry, limp, or soggy pads should be avoided when purchasing. May develop bronze discoloration if exposed to temperatures that are too cold. Best stored at 41°F (5°C).

Remove thorns or eyes before preparing and rinse under water. May be eaten raw or cooked by lightly steaming or sautéing.

Greens

Beet. Flat, green leaves with thin red stems and red ribs.

Broccoli Raab. Dark green leaves on slender stalks topped with small clusters of tiny buds. Bitter pungent flavor. Used in Italian and Chinese cuisines. Entire plant is consumed. Flavor is best when cooked.

Collard Greens. Loaf-shaped, flat, green leaves

Dandelion. Narrow, dark green, ragged-edged leaves. Thin, white stems. Mild cabbage-like flavor.

Kale. Depending on variety, may have blue-green or yellow-green leaves. Leaves have curly edges and flat centers. Is typically cooked.

Mustard Greens. Large green, curly-edged leaves. Long narrow stems. Have a pungent, peppery flavor.

Swiss Chard. Large dark green leaves with red veins. Thick, white stems. Flavor is mild and sweet with a slight bitterness.

Turnip. Flat, green, slightly fuzzy leaves. Long, narrow green stems.

Spinach

Flat or Smooth Leaf. Dark, green, slightly crinkled leaves.

Savoy. Dark, green, crinkled leaves.

General Tips. Wash thoroughly to remove sand and dirt. Tear off the stems. May be consumed raw or cooked.

Watercress

Dark-green, heart-shaped leaves. Long, thin stalks. Spicy flavor. Soft to slightly crunchy texture.

Source: References 51, 66

Swiss chard

Chinese Cabbage

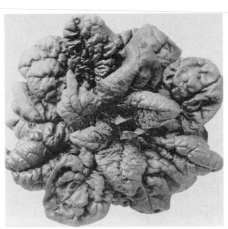

Spinach

Brussels sprouts

Cabbage

FIGURE 20-2 Leaf vegetables. *(Courtesy of W. Atlee Burpee & Co.)*

A description of selected vegetable-fruits is provided in Table 20-5.

Most of the commonly eaten vegetable-fruits (Figure 20-3) are relatively high in water content (92 to 94 percent), with small amounts of carbohydrate. Winter squash is an exception to the usually high water content of this group; it contains only about 85 percent water and 12 percent carbohydrate in the raw state, comparable in carbohydrate content with many of the sweet, fleshy fruits. Cucumbers are particularly low in carbohydrate

TABLE 20-5 Vegetable-Fruits

Name and Description	Selection and Preparation Pointers
Cucumber Dark green skin and firm. Interior is a pale green and moist with seeds running through the center. Often treated with edible wax to reduce moisture loss.	Store under refrigeration in high humidity away from ethylene-producing fruits and vegetables. Wash. Peeling and removal of the seeds is optional depending on preference and recipe. Often consumed raw by simply slicing; may be made into pickles. Cucumber variety is often selected for intended use—fresh or pickled.
Eggplant Usually large (1–5 pounds) with a shiny dark purple skin. Interior is a creamy colored. May be oval or elongated in shape. Excessively large eggplants may be tough and bitter.	Select eggplants with smooth, uniformly colored skin. Store under refrigeration with high humidity away from ethylene-producing fruits and vegetables. Will bruise easily so handle with care. To prepare, wash and slice off ends. To reduce moisture and bitterness, lightly salt sliced eggplant and drain for 30 minutes. May be cooked with or without skin; however, if skin is tough, peeling is preferable. A variety of cooking methods may be used.
Okra An elongated, lantern-shaped vegetable that is 2–7 inches in length. The skin is green and slightly fuzzy. Rows of tiny seeds and a sticky texture are evident when sliced open. Several different varieties are available.	Store under refrigeration with high humidity away from ethylene-producing fruits and vegetables. May be steamed, boiled, pickled, or sautéed. The more it is cut, the stickier it becomes. Is used as a thickener in some recipes due to this quality. Do not cook in iron, copper, or brass pans to avoid darkening of okra.
Pepper Bell peppers may be green, red, or yellow. The red bell peppers are sweeter, milder, and have 11 times more beta carotene than green bell peppers.	Look for firm, fresh-looking, and brightly colored peppers. Shriveled peppers should be avoided. May be consumed raw or cooked in a variety of dishes. To prepare, slice off ends of pepper, remove seed core, and slice off the light colored spins. Cut remaining pepper as desired with knife contact being from the interior of the pepper to the exterior skin. Peppers may be "roasted" by holding over a flame or near a heat element until the skin is blackened. Alternatively, peppers may be roasted under a broiler. Wrap roasted pepper in plastic to "sweat" briefly. Scrape off blackened skin and use pepper as desired.
Pumpkin May range in size from 1–25 pounds. Smaller pumpkins are generally preferred for cooking purposes. Often purchased canned, rather than fresh for use in recipes.	Best stored at 60°–65°F (16°–18°C) with a humidity of 65–70 percent for long-term storage. Higher humidity levels are acceptable for short-term storage. To cook fresh pumpkin, slice in half, remove seeds, pulp, and stringy parts. Cut into smaller segments and peel. Steam or boil until tender and mash or purée in a food processor. The puréed pumpkin then may be used for pies and other recipes. The seeds may be rinsed to remove pulp, then dried with a paper towel. Next toss seeds with seasonings and butter or oil, then roast. The browned and crunchy seeds may be enjoyed as a snack.
Snap or String Beans *Green.* Long straight pods, should snap easily when bent. *Yellow wax.* Long straight pods. Creamy to yellow in color.	Best if stored at 45°–50°F (7°–10°C) in high humidity away from ethylene-producing fruits and vegetables. In home setting, refrigeration will require storage under colder conditions than ideal, thus store for minimum length of time. Cold damaged beans may develop pitting or russeting (browning).
Summer Squash *Pattypan.* Round, squat, small squash with scalloped edges. Yellow or light green color with white flesh. *Yellow crookneck.* Cylindrical shape. Bulb-shaped end. Creamy yellow rind and white flesh. *Zucchini.* Cylindrical, dark green squash with light speckles. Flesh and seeds are white.	Squash should be firm with shiny rinds. Pitting or dull rinds are indications of age and damage. Smaller summer squash are generally higher quality—more tender and better flavor. Ideally should be stored at 45°F (7°C) or warmer. Store away from ethylene-producing fruits and vegetables. May be consumed raw or cooked. The skin, flesh, and seeds may be used.

TABLE 20-5 (Continued)

Winter Squash

Acorn. Acorn shape. Green to yellow-gold hard rind. Flesh is yellow and slightly sweet.	Most winter varieties of winter squash should be stored slightly cooler than room temperature. The rinds should be hard and not tender.
Banana. Large cylindrical-shaped. Creamy yellow, hard rind.	Generally consumed cooked, the rind may be removed before or after cooking. Typically only the flesh of winter squash is used.
Butternut. Dark green hard rind with gray flecks or strips. Slightly sweet, orange flesh.	
Hubbard. Large round squash. Ends taper inward. Rind may be orange, golden, green, or blue-gray.	
Spaghetti. Yellow, semi-hard rind. Large and oblong shape. Yellow flesh separates into spaghetti-like consistency after cooking.	

Tomato

Cherry. Small round tomatoes.	Avoid soft or mushy tomatoes with blemishes.
Grape. Small oblong shape. Concentrated flavor.	Tomatoes should not be refrigerated. Should be stored above 50°F(13°C) to avoid flavor and quality loss. Handle with care to avoid bruising.
Roma. Oblong shape, medium size. Shiny red skin and firm flesh.	May be consumed fresh or cooked. To peel, place cut small "x" at base of tomato and heat in boiling water briefly. Plunge in ice water. The skin will wrinkle and remove very easily.
Round or Globe. Round with shiny red skin and firm flesh. Variety commonly used for slicing.	

Source: References 29, 51, 66

content and high in water content—about 97 percent. Tomatoes and green peppers are vegetable-fruits that are important sources of vitamin C. Pumpkin and yellow squash, tomatoes, and green peppers contain carotenoid pigments, some of which are precursors of vitamin A.

Flowers and Stems

Flowers and stems (Figure 20-4 and Table 20-6) are, in general, high in water and low in carbohydrates. Broccoli has been shown to be a particularly nutritious green vegetable in terms of its vitamin and mineral content and also as a source of phytochemicals. It is one of the richest vegetable sources of vitamin C; even the stems contain this vitamin so, when possible, the stems should be pared and used. Broccoli also provides vitamin A value and contributes some riboflavin, calcium, and iron. Cauliflower and kohlrabi are good sources of vitamin C, and green asparagus has vitamin A value. Figure 20-5 depicts preparation techniques for artichokes.

Roots, Bulbs, and Tubers

Root vegetables include beets, carrots, turnips, rutabagas, and parsnips (Table 20-7). Examples of bulbs, which are enlargements above the roots, are onions, leeks, and shallots (Figure 20-6). The potato is an example of a tuber, which is an enlarged underground stem. Potatoes are consumed by 54 percent of Americans on a daily basis [32]. Over the years, frozen potato usage has increased, and fresh potato usage has declined. About half of the commercial crop of potatoes in the United States is grown in Idaho, Maine, California, and Washington [74].

Bulb, root, and tuber vegetables are generally higher in carbohydrate and lower in water content than leaves,

stems, and flowers. Most of the carbohydrate in potatoes is in the form of starch. Sweet potatoes also contain a fairly large amount of starch but have more sugar than white potatoes. Potatoes (Plate XIV) are significant sources of vitamin C, whereas the yellow carotenoids in sweet potatoes contribute vitamin A value. Selected roots, tubers, and bulbs are described in Tables 20-7 and 20-8.

Characteristics of Potato Varieties. Many different varieties of potatoes are available in the marketplace and most can be classified into five basic types: russet, long white, round red, round white, and yellow flesh. Several varieties of potatoes are pictured in Plate XIV.

Mealiness and waxiness are qualities ascribed to cooked potatoes. A mealy potato separates easily into fluffy particles that feel dry. A type of potato exhibiting this quality to a marked degree is the russet Burbank, which is excellent for baking, mashing, frying, and roasting. On the other hand, a waxy potato is more compact and moist, or almost soggy, and does not separate easily into fluffy particles. Waxy potatoes are therefore not the best choice for mashed or French fried potatoes. The round reds and round whites are generally regarded as waxy potatoes and are especially good for boiling and use in salads or dishes such as scalloped potatoes. The long whites are a good all-purpose potato and function quite well in both boiling and baking.

Potatoes with higher starch content are denser and a higher density potato tends to be mealier. The density of potatoes may be tested by placing a potato in a brine solution of 1 cup salt to 11 cups water. If the potato floats, indicating low solids content, it may be a waxy potato best for boiling; if it sinks, it may be a mealy potato best for

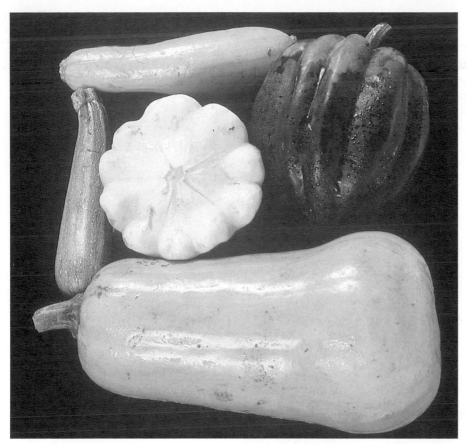

Squash. Clockwise from top: zucchini, yellow, acorn, and spaghetti. Patty pan in center.

Okra

Eggplant

FIGURE 20-3 Vegetable-fruits. *(Squash courtesy of U.S. Department of Agriculture; okra courtesy of W. Atlee Burpee & Co.; and eggplant courtesy of Western Growers Association)*

Kohlrabi

Celery

Cauliflower

Broccoli

FIGURE 20-4 Flowers and stems used as vegetables. *(Courtesy of W. Atlee Burpee & Co.)*

baking. Not all researchers, however, have found a correlation between specific gravity and textural characteristics of potatoes [42].

It has been suggested that the swelling of starch causes the separation of plant cells that occurs in mealy potatoes. The starch granules swell markedly when potatoes are cooked, and water tends to be absorbed when they are boiled. Mealy potatoes that are high in starch content tend to slough off their outer layers when boiled. Storage at temperatures between 50° and 70°F (10° and 21°C) seems to decrease the tendency of the potato to slough during cooking. Also, if the cooking water contains enough calcium salt to maintain or slightly increase the calcium content of the potato, sloughing can be partially controlled.

TABLE 20-6 Flowers, Stems, and Shoots	
Names and Description	**Selection and Preparation Pointers**
FLOWERS	
Artichoke	
Shape and color will vary by variety. Generally green although some may have a tinge of purple. Globe or conical shape with flared petals.	Over-mature artichokes will appear woody.
	Should be stored under refrigeration with high humidity to avoid wilt or mold.
	Wash under running water. Outer, lower petals should be pulled off. Cut stem close to base. Snip off tips of petals if desired. Cook by boiling, steaming, sautéing, or microwaving until a leaf near the center will pull out easily.
	Serve hot or cold. To eat, pull each leaf from the choke. Hold the pointed end and pull the leaf between your teeth to enjoy the edible portion. Discard the leaf. Once all leaves are consumed, scoop out the fuzzy center and discard. The remaining base of the artichoke is edible.
Broccoli	
Compact bud clusters on light green stalks. Bud clusters are a dark green with a purple tinge. Clusters should not be open showing yellow flowers.	Store under refrigeration in high humidity (90–98 percent). Avoid storage with ethylene-producing fruits and vegetables.
	Wash thoroughly. May be consumed raw or cooked. Stems are more tender if peeled.
Cauliflower	
White. Creamy white compact heads with jacket leaves that are bright green and fresh. Heads have appearance of curds.	Gray-brown discoloration or softening suggests potential freeze injury.
	Store under refrigeration in high humidity away from ethylene-producing fruits and vegetables.
Green and Purple. Green is a hybrid of broccoli and cauliflower. Purple is actually a type of broccoli that has an appearance like cauliflower. Purple cauliflower turns green when cooked.	Wash thoroughly. May be consumed raw or cooked.
STEMS AND SHOOTS	
Asparagus	
Green. Spears should be fresh and firm. Tips should be compact and may have a purple tinge.	Select fresh, firm asparagus with compact tips.
White. Spears are thicker and more tender than the green variety. Tips are smooth and rounded.	Store under refrigeration with high humidity. May stand asparagus butt-end down in water. Alternatively, may be stored in a plastic bag for short periods.
	To prepare, wash and snap off ends at the natural breaking point. White asparagus is frequently peeled with a peeler. Green asparagus may be cooked without peeling.
Celery	
Green or pascal is primary variety sold. Light green with long, crisp stalks.	Select celery with compact stalks, firm and crisp ribs, green and not wilted leaves.
	Store under refrigeration with high humidity away from ethylene-producing produce. Store away from onions to avoid odor absorption.
	Wash thoroughly. May be consumed raw or cooked.
Fennel	
Pale green, feathery top. Celerylike stems and bulblike base.	Select fennel with green leaves and firm straight stalks. The bulb should be compact and not spreading. Cut stalks off the bulb and store separately under refrigeration.
	Stalks may be used in soups. Feathery leaves may be used as an herb. The bulb should be washed and trimmed. Bulbs may be used raw, grilled, steamed, or sautéed.
Kohlrabi	
Light green or purple with a globe-shaped root. Leaves and root portion are edible. Bulb flavor is somewhat similar to turnips. Leaves taste like collard greens or kale.	Choose kohlrabi with fresh leaves and smooth bulbs free of cracks. Should be stored under refrigeration in high humidity conditions.
	Leaves are typically cooked. Bulb may used raw or cooked.

Source: References 29, 51, 64, 66

Seeds

Although corn is a cereal product, sweet corn is commonly used as a vegetable in the United States. It is relatively high in carbohydrate, chiefly in the form of starch. Legumes are seeds of the *Leguminosae* family and include many varieties of beans, peas, soybeans, and lentils (Figure 20-7). Legumes will be discussed in more detail later in the chapter. Selected seed vegetables are described in Table 20-9.

FIGURE 20-5 To prepare globe artichokes, (1) cut off the stem about one inch from the base, leaving a stub; (2) cut off about one inch of the top, cutting straight across with a knife; (3) pull off any heavy loose leaves around the bottom; (4) with scissors, clip off the thorny tip of each leaf; (5) drop into boiling, salted water. Season by adding a small clove of garlic, a thick slice of lemon, and one tablespoon of olive or other salad oil for each artichoke. Cover and boil until a leaf can be pulled easily from the stalk or until the stub can be easily pierced with a fork (20 to 45 minutes). Remove carefully from the water. Cut off the stub. *(Courtesy of Western Growers Association)*

Mushrooms

Mushrooms are fungi and not technically vegetables. However, mushrooms are served and used like vegetables and thus will be discussed in this chapter. There is a variety of different kinds of mushrooms, not all of which are edible. Only well-trained experienced individuals should harvest mushrooms from the wild. Poisonous mushrooms growing in the wild can be easily mistaken for edible mushrooms. Selected varieties of edible mushrooms are described in Table 20-10.

Mushrooms that are clean and not soft or show evidence of spoilage should be selected. Store mushrooms in the original container in the refrigerator with high humidity away from foods with strong odors. Mushrooms should be gently cleaned prior to use. Many recommend gently wiping mushrooms with a brush or damp cloth. Others suggest rinsing mushrooms under cool, running water is acceptable. Soaking or submerging in water when cleaning is not recommended. Mushrooms may be served raw or cooked [29, 51, 66].

PURCHASING

Vegetables selected for purchase should be firm, crisp, and bright in color. Size, shape, gloss, color, absence of defects, and freshness are considered. In making selections,

TABLE 20-7 Roots and Tubers	
Name and Description	**Selection and Preparation Pointers**
Beet	
Roots are dark purple-red and round. Tops have green leaves with purple-red stems and veins.	Select smooth, hard, uniformly round beets. Young beets are more tender and may be eaten raw. Medium or large beets are best cooked. Excessively large beets will be undesirably woody.
	Store under refrigeration with high humidity without tops. Store tops separately, then eat as soon as possible.
	Wash and scrub beets before use. Peel after cooking to minimize color loss.
Carrot	
Firm, smooth exterior and crunchy texture. Are orange or orange-red.	Select firm, brightly colored carrots. Avoid soft or wilted roots.
	Bunched carrots are more perishable than topped, thus if purchased with tops, remove before storage. Store under refrigeration with high humidity away from ethylene-producing fruits or vegetables or foods with strong odors.
	May be used raw or cooked. Often peeled but scrubbed peels may be consumed.
Celeriac or Celery Root	
Bulb-shaped, knobby root. Skin is brown and rough. Texture is crisp and flavor is nutty and celerylike.	Select firm, not spongy roots.
May be used cooked or uncooked.	Store under refrigeration with high humidity.
	Scrub, trim top and bottom, quarter, and peel before eating. May be used cooked or uncooked. Overcooked celery root will become mushy.
Ginger Root	
Gnarled light brown rhizome. Rhizomes are underground stems and in the case of ginger are typically referred to as a *root*. Golden to white flesh. Sweet, yet woodsy smell. Sweet, peppery flavor.	Choose roots with fairly smooth light brown skin with minimum knots. Avoid soft or shriveled roots.
	Store at 60°–65°F (16°–18°C) in relatively high humidity. If stored under refrigeration, may soften or shrivel.
	Peel skin from root. May be sliced, grated, or minced. Often used as a flavoring in Asian cuisines.

TABLE 20-7 (Continued)

Name and Description	Selection and Preparation Pointers
Jicama Round, slightly squat shape resembling a turnip. Light brown skin and ivory flesh. Subtle and sweet flavor. Texture is crunchy and juicy.	Select jicama with firm texture and unblemished skin. Store at 60°–65°F (16°–18°C) with moderately high humidity. Typically peeled if consumed raw. May also be cooked.
Parsnip Similar in appearance to a carrot but is creamy beige.	Select medium-sized roots that are fresh and crisp. Store under refrigeration with high humidity away from ethylene-producing produce items. Like carrot, may be peeled or cooked with the skin. May be consumed raw or cooked and may be mashed.
Potato *Russet.* Oblong shape with netted brown skin. White flesh. A mealy, high-starch potato that is good choice for baking, roasting, mashing, and frying. Will be light and fluffy when cooked. Varieties include Burbank, Centennial, Norgold. *Long White.* Oval shape. Thin light tan skin and firm waxy texture. Medium starch good, all-purpose potato. Good choice for boiling, salads, stews, soups, and roasting. Major variety is White Rose. *Round Red.* Rosy red skin. Low in starch and sweet flavor. Often known as "new potatoes." Best for boiling, roasting, or potato salads. Major varieties include La Rouge, Red La Soda, and Red Pontiac. *Round White.* Smooth, light tan skin. Waxy textured, low-starch potato. Good for scalloped potatoes, roasting, and potato salads. Major varieties include Katahdin, Superior, and Chippewa. *Yellow Flesh.* Oval to round shape. Buttery flavor. Dense and creamy texture. Good for baking, mashing, and roasting. Major varieties include Yukon Gold and Yellow Finn. *Purple or Blue.* Deep purple or blue skin and flesh. Have a subtle nutty flavor. Major varieties include Purple Peruvian and All Blue. *Fingerlings.* Heirloom potatoes. Small, oblong potatoes. Firm, flavorful, waxy potatoes.	Select firm and smooth potatoes. Avoid potatoes with excessive soil or with green skins which is evidence of exposure to light. Green areas, if present, must be removed before use. Preferably store at 60°–65°F (16°–18°C) in a dark, well-ventilated area. Refrigerated storage is not recommended because starch in the potato will turn to sugar, affecting flavor and browning when cooked. Sugar will revert to starch when returned to warmer storage. Scrub and cook as desired. May be peeled or consumed with the peel.
Radish *Red Globe.* Red and white radish that is small, round, or oval-shaped. Usually about one inch in diameter. *Black.* Turnip-like size and shape. Often about eight inches in length. Dull black or dark brown skins. Flesh is white and pungent. *Daikons.* Large carrot-shaped radish that is up to 18 inches long. White, juicy flesh is hotter than red globe radishes but milder than black radish.	Select radishes that are hard and solid. Leaves, if attached, should be crisp and green. Radishes with a pithy or spongy texture are old. Store under refrigeration with high humidity. Usually consumed raw but may be cooked for some dishes.
Rutabaga Round with shape like a top. Creamy white to pinkish-red skin with creamy flesh. A cross between a turnip and cabbage.	Select rutabagas that are clean, fairly smooth, without growth cracks or shriveling. Smaller rutabagas are sweeter. Store under refrigeration with high humidity away from ethylene producing produce. Often sold waxed, so wash and peel before cooking. A variety of cooking methods may be used. Overcooking will develop a strong, potentially undesirable flavor
Salsify or Vegetable Oyster *Black.* Sticklike root. Has black skin and cream-colored flesh. *White.* Parsnip-shaped root. Skin has tiny rootlets. Tan skin and off-white flesh	Select firm roots that are not soft or flabby. Store under refrigeration with high humidity. Trim tops and bottoms. Is generally used cooked. Will become mushy if overcooked.

TABLE 20-7 (Continued)

Name and Description	Selection and Preparation Pointers
General information. Both types have a mild oyster flavor with some flavor components similar to artichokes. Texture is crisp like carrots.	
Sweet Potato	
Oblong root vegetable with generally smooth skin. Color may be pale yellow, deep purple, or orange depending on variety. Flesh color will be light yellow, pink, red, or orange.	Select firm, dark orange sweet potatoes without evidence of sprouts, bruises, or decay.
	Store in a cool (60°–65°F/16°–18°C), dry location away from ethylene-producing fruits and vegetables. Do not store in the refrigerator to prevent development of an off-flavor.
Should not be confused with yams which are large starchy roots grown in Africa and Asia.	Wash thoroughly. Cook whole when possible and peel after cooking.
Sunchoke or Jerusalem Artichoke	
Small, knobby tuber. White flesh is nutty, sweet, and crunchy when raw. When baked, similar to potatoes with mild taste of artichokes. Is not a relative to artichokes or from the Middle East, but is a relative of sunflowers and is native to America.	Select firm sunchokes free from mold.
	Store under refrigeration in high humidity. May develop green-tinged skin if exposed to excessive light.
Turnips	
Similar in appearance to a radish but larger. Color is a creamy white to a pinkish-red. Flesh is white.	Select clean, well-shaped turnips without evidence of cracks or shriveling. Smaller turnips are sweeter than large turnips.
	Store under refrigeration with high humidity. Turnip tops should be stored separately from the root.
	May be used cooked or raw.

Source: References 29, 51, 66, 82

Left to right—turnips, beets, rutabaga; parsnips

Left, leeks; right, green onions

FIGURE 20-6 Roots and bulbs used as vegetables. *(Courtesy of United Fresh Fruit and Vegetable Association)*

distinguish between defects that affect appearance only and those that affect edible quality. Vegetables may be highest in quality and lowest in price when locally grown and in season. At the same time, efficient transportation and marketing procedures allow the purchase and enjoyment of a wide variety of good quality vegetables year-round. Quality and prices vary depending on growing conditions, supply, demand, and the distance the produce must be shipped.

Many vegetables are highly perishable and thus are best used when as fresh as possible. Consequently when purchasing, the amount of vegetables that can be stored and used while still at peak quality should be considered. The use of frozen and canned vegetables enables longer storage periods than possible with fresh vegetables. Quality characteristics for specific vegetables may be found in Tables 20-4 through 20-10.

Grades

Fresh, frozen, and canned vegetables and fruits may be graded. Grades specify such characteristics as size, shape, color, texture, general appearance, uniformity, maturity,

TABLE 20-8 Bulbs	
Name and Description	**Selection and Preparation Pointers**
Garlic	
Regular. Firm dry bulbs with cloves covered by a papery skin. May be white or purple. Pungent odor and flavor.	Select firm, plumb bulbs. Avoid shriveled, moldy, soft, or sprouting bulbs. Store in cool, dark location.
Elephant. Larger in size compared to regular garlic.	To prepare, peel papery skin away and remove a clove. Peel off any additional papery layers. Place clove on a cutting board and press with the large flat surface of a chef knife to mash. Slice or mince as desired.
	Alternately may peel away outer papery skin on the garlic bulb. Cut off top of garlic exposing garlic cloves. Lightly oil and roast in oven until soft. Roasted whole garlic may be used as a spread for bread by using a knife to remove garlic from each clove.
Leek	
Long thick white stem and wide green or blue-green tops. Has a mild onionlike flavor. Looks like a giant scallion.	Select leeks with clean, white bottoms and crisp, green, fresh appearing tops.
	Store under refrigeration with high humidity.
	Wash carefully; dirt is likely trapped between overlapping layers of leaves. White bulb and green tops may be used. Often used for seasoning in cooked dishes.
Onion	
Yellow. Full-flavored. Light yellow color.	Select dry onions (red, yellow, or white) that are firm and hard with dry papery skins. Store at 60°–65°F (16°–18°C) with moderate humidity in dark location. After cutting, store in refrigerator.
Red. Purple-red color. Milder in flavor than other kinds.	
White. Full-flavored. White in color.	
Pearl. Small mild-flavored onions. Approximately one-half inch in diameter.	Select scallions with fresh tender green tops and slightly bulb-shaped white ends. Store under refrigeration away from ethylene-producing fruits and vegetables.
Bunch, Green, or Scallions. Small white bulb with bright green, long, slender leaves. Bulb and leaves may be used. Milder flavor than other onions.	Onions may be used raw or in cooked dishes.
Shallot	
Small onion-shaped bulb. Golden brown to reddish-brown papery skin. Bulb consists of cluster of cloves. Flavor is milder and sweeter than other onions.	Select firm shallots that are free of blemishes. Store under refrigeration with high humidity.
	Prepare and use like onions.

Source: References 29, 51, 66

and freedom from defects. A common language is thus provided for wholesale trading and aids in establishing prices based on quality. The U.S. Department of Agriculture (USDA) has established grades for a many food products. Food processors may develop their own grading system, but manufacturers's grades vary between manufacturers and USDA. Thus, when purchasing a "Fancy" or "No. 1" grade, it is important to know if it is a USDA or manufacturer grade designation.

USDA grading is not required by law. USDA grading is voluntary and is provided by request of the food processor or grower. The producer or distributor pays a fee for the USDA grading but can then benefit by the ability to market its product with the USDA grade.

Fresh Vegetable and Fruit Grades. The USDA uniform grade terms for fresh fruits and vegetables are U.S. Fancy, U.S. No. 1, U.S. No. 2, and U.S. No. 3. Only a few vegetables or fruits are packed as the top quality grade U.S. Fancy. The grade most often found is U.S. No. 1. Vegetables with this grade will be tender, fresh-appearing, have

good color, and be relatively free from decay and bruises [73]. The top grade for potatoes is U.S. Extra No. 1, and the second grade is U.S. No. 1. The grade most often found on consumer packages of potatoes is U.S. No. 1 [74].

Generally, potatoes, carrots, and onions are the only fresh vegetables labeled for the consumer with a grade name. Sometimes, consumer fruit packages are marked with a grade, however, this is usually limited to citrus fruits and apples. Because fresh vegetables are perishable, the quality may change between the time of grading and the time of purchase, thereby limiting the usefulness of grades on fresh produce. (See Chapter 4 for a general discussion of grading.)

Canned Vegetable and Fruit Grades. USDA grades of quality have been established for many canned and frozen vegetables and fruits, based on color, uniformity of size, shape, tenderness or degree of ripeness, and freedom from blemishes. The label may designate U.S. Grade A or Fancy, U.S. Grade B or Choice, and U.S. Grade C or Standard [71, 72]. Availability of graded products allows

Sweet corn

Lima beans

Green peas

Pinto beans (far right), soybeans (bottom),
and lentils (left)

FIGURE 20-7 Seed vegetables. *(Courtesy of W. Atlee Burpee & Co.; lima beans, courtesy of the U.S. Department of Agriculture; pintos, soybeans, and lentils, courtesy of Chirs Meister)*

the buyer to select the quality that will be most satisfactory for the intended use. Lower grades of fruits and vegetables are still good and wholesome although they are less perfect than Grade A in color, uniformity, and texture.

When a product has been officially graded under continuous inspection by a USDA inspector, it may carry the official grade name and the statement "Packed under continuous inspection of the U.S. Department of Agriculture" (Figure 20-8). The grade name and the statement may also appear within a shield-shaped outline. Most canned and frozen vegetables and fruits are packed according to grade, whether or not that fact is indicated on the label, and are generally priced according to their quality. Most products marketed are at least Grade B quality, which is quite good. As with fresh produce, the use of the USDA grades is voluntary and is paid for by the packer. The specific brand name of a frozen or canned vegetable or fruit may be an indication of quality, because the packers set their own standards.

Economic Considerations

When purchasing vegetables and fruits, price may be a factor. One argument used by some for the limited consumption of fruits and vegetables is cost. One group of researchers examined the cost of a variety of vegetables and fruits by pound and by serving. Out of the 154 forms of fruits and vegetables priced, more than half cost 25 cents or less per serving [54]. Eight-six percent of the vegetables and 78 percent of the fruits cost less than 50 cents per serving. The decision to purchase frozen,

TABLE 20-9 Seeds

Name and Description	Selection and Preparation Pointers
Corn	
Plump tender yellow, white, or white and yellow kernels. Corn-on-the-cob should have green husks.	Select corn-on-the-cob with fresh, green husks, consistently sized kernels, and silk ends free of decay or worms.
	Store under refrigeration.
Peas	
Snow. Flat green pods with immature peas in interior. Entire pod is edible.	Select green, fresh pods. Green peas should be bulging as evidence of mature peas.
Green. Large, bulging, bright green pods. Mature peas are inside pod. Only the peas are consumed.	Store under refrigeration with high humidity away from ethylene-producing fruits and vegetables.
Snap. Similar in appearance to green peas. Entire pod is edible but should be destringed.	A variety of cooking methods may be used. Snap and snow peas may be consumed raw or cooked. Green peas are typically cooked.

Source: References 51, 66

canned, or fresh is another factor influencing prices. Sixty-three percent of the fruits and 57 percent of the vegetables were least expensive in the fresh form when waste and serving size were taken into consideration.

In seeking various combinations of vegetables in relation to price, 1/2 cup each of broccoli, carrots, potatoes, and cabbage was priced at 27 cents. This combination of vegetables provided 100 percent of the Daily Value of vitamins A and C [54]. By adding three servings of fruit for 37 cents, a total cost of 64 cents for seven servings of fruits and vegetables was found, representing only 12 percent of the total average daily per person expenditure for food. Another group of researchers examined the nutrients per unit cost and concluded fruits and vegetable provide more nutrients per cost than many other foods [12].

Organic

National standards for organic foods were set in place by USDA in 2002 to provide consumers the choice of organic foods in the marketplace. Organic foods must be produced without most conventional pesticides, synthetic fertilizers, sewage sludge, bioengineering, or ionizing radiation [75]. For a product to be labeled as organic, the farm is inspected to certify the farmer is following the USDA organic standards. Companies that handle and process organic foods also must be certified. "Natural" and "organic" do not have the same meaning. Only foods with the organic label have been certified as meeting the USDA standards. For more information about USDA organic food labeling, refer to Chapter 4.

No claims are made by the USDA that organically produced food is safer or more nutritious [75]. However, it is clear that there is a consumer demand for such foods, and the USDA certification provides a uniform standard for consumers who prefer organic foods. Consumers may choose organic foods because of environmental concern, perceived nutritional benefits, perceived flavor, or other reasons. In one study, several types of vegetables were grown conventionally and organically and then compared by consumers in a sensory analysis [91]. The consumer

Bean Sprouts

The technique of sprouting soybean and mung bean seeds was developed by the Chinese centuries ago. Sprouts from many different seeds have become popular as vegetables and are particular favorites at fresh salad bars. The sprouts of some seeds provide significant sources of vitamin C, thiamin, riboflavin, and several minerals [17]. However, due to food safety concerns, current recommendations from the Food and Drug Administration (FDA) suggest that raw bean sprouts, including alfalfa sprouts, should be avoided, especially by individuals at high risk for foodborne illness. Scientists have been exploring methods of destroying pathogenic bacteria on seeds without damaging the ability of the seed to sprout. ■

TABLE 20-10 Mushrooms

Description

Agaricus or White or Button

Most common variety. Creamy white to light brown in color and ranging in size from small to jumbo. Mild, woodsy flavor when raw. May be used raw or cooked.

Chanterelle

Trumpet-shaped. Golden to yellow-orange color with rich, meaty, slightly almond flavor. Should be cooked.

Crimini or Italian Brown

Similar in appearance to agaricus mushroom but is a light tan to brown color. Flavor is earthier than agaricus. May be used raw or cooked.

Enoki

Fragile and flowerlike. Grows in clusters with long, slender stems, and tiny, creamy caps. Light fruity taste. Often used raw.

Morel

Spongelike cap with a short, thick stem. Dark brown color and meaty flavor. Use cooked.

Oyster

Large fluted cap that may be brown to gray. Subtle oyster flavor. Are best when cooked but may be used raw.

Porcini

White to red-brown cap. Meaty texture and nutty flavor. Use cooked.

Portabello

A large mushroom that may be three inches or more in diameter. Is similar to the agaricus and crimini with a meaty texture. Often grilled or roasted.

Shiitake

Large, black-brown, umbrella shaped mushrooms. Rich woodsy flavor. Meaty texture when cooked. Usually used cooked.

Woodgear

Brown, with a floppy cap and short stem. Mild, rich flavor. Usually cooked.

Source: References 51, 66

---

sensory assessment of the conventional and organically grown vegetables did not reveal differences in liking or flavor between the vegetables except for tomatoes. The conventional tomatoes were rated more favorably; however, the researchers noted a potential difference in tomato ripeness may have had an impact on the ratings.

Organic foods do appear to be lower in pesticide residues than conventional foods, but the risk posed by consuming conventional foods may be insignificant [89]. Some studies have found higher nutrient levels in organic foods, although other studies report no differences. Thus, additional research is needed to understand this issue. Overall, in the Institute of Food Technologists' Scientific Status Summary, it was stated that to conclude either conventional or organic food systems to be superior was premature [89].

Biotechnology and Vegetable Production

For centuries humans have exploited the genetic diversity of living systems for improvement of the food supply. Traditional biotechnology works with plant and animal breeding for the selection of desired characteristics. A new biotechnology, often called *genetic engineering*, produces genetic modification at the molecular level.

Biotechnology provides a set of tools for improving the variety and efficiency of food production in less time and with more precision and control than with traditional methods [7, 26]. The American Dietetic Association and a number of other professional organizations and regulatory bodies are supportive of biotechnology [1].

How does genetic engineering work for vegetable crops? It allows controlled insertion of one or two genes into a plant without transferring undesirable characteristics as would likely occur in traditional cross-fertilization methods [7]. Through genetic engineering, soybeans, cottonseed, and corn have been made to tolerate herbicides used to kill weeds and to avoid pests, thus reducing the need for pesticides. Squash, potatoes, and papaya resist plant diseases as the result of genetic engineering.

The development, testing, and sale of genetically modified plants are regulated by the USDA, FDA, EPA, and most state governments. The goal of these agencies is to ensure the safety of genetically engineered foods for consumption by people and animals. These foods must also be judged by government regulators as safe to grow in environment [7]. See Chapters 3 and 14 for additional information about biotechnology and food safety.

(a)

(b)

(c)

FIGURE 20-8 Food products displaying the official USDA certified symbols: (a) USDA shield for products packed under continuous inspection; (b) dates; (c) raisins. *(Courtesy of U.S. Department of Agriculture)*

Partially Processed, Value Added, or Fresh Cuts

Convenience is another factor to consider when purchasing produce. Fresh vegetables and fruits can be pre-trimmed, peeled, cut, sliced, and so on for direct use by consumers in the home or restaurants and other foodservice establishments. Prepared salad mix and peeled baby carrots are examples of these partially processed, value added, or fresh-cut foods. Fresh sliced packaged apples,

offered in a number of quick-service restaurants, is another example of these products.

Food manufacturers are using a variety of technologies to produce minimally processed vegetables and fruits [6, 9], including refrigeration, modified-atmosphere packaging in combination with refrigeration, and heat treatment in combination with hermetic packaging and refrigeration. Custom-tailored packaging films can help to slow the natural degradative changes due to cell

What about Pesticides?

Some people have expressed concern about pesticide residues on vegetables and fruits as marketed. Government studies that have monitored actual pesticide residue levels in foods as prepared and consumed have shown no pesticide residues in more than half of the samples tested and levels below the EPA tolerances in more than 99 percent of the samples tested [28]. Passage by Congress of the Food Quality Protection Act of 1996 reformed some of the past legislation regarding pesticide use in the United States and will enable pesticide regulation to keep pace with scientific advancement [44]. A uniform safety standard has been set for raw and processed foods. FDA regularly monitors pesticide residues on foods. Refer to Chapters 3 and 4 for more information about food safety and the regulation of pesticides. ■

respiration by controlling the oxygen, carbon dioxide, and moisture levels inside the package. Some fresh-cut vegetables have a refrigerated shelf life of up to 21 days because of modified-atmosphere technologies [9].

These minimally processed vegetables and fruits are perishable compared to unprocessed foods because the degradative changes related to senescence in the mature product are enhanced by the physical actions of cutting and slicing. Respiration by the cells increases in response to the injuries [87]. Therefore, partially processed fruits and vegetables must be refrigerated and handled in a sanitary manner to ensure microbiological safety.

Methods of reducing spoilage in partially processed produce foods continue to be investigated. Fresh-cut iceberg lettuce treated with hydrogen peroxide and mild heat was found to maintain a higher level of sensory quality over 15 days of storage as compared to the control [43]. In another study, the effect of low-dose irradiation was compared to acidification, blanching, and chlorination as methods of maintaining the quality of diced celery. The irradiated samples were preferred in sensory tests and maintained color, texture, and aroma longer than the conventionally treated diced celery samples [49].

STORAGE

Fresh vegetables and fruits are perishable and have a limited shelf life. The short storage life of many vegetables is due to their rapid respiration or metabolism. Vegetables and fruits are composed of living, respiring tissue that is also senescing and dying [28]. Thus, when storing vegetables, storage conditions, and the length of storage should be considered so foods may be enjoyed and waste avoided. See Tables 20-4 through 20-10 for storage recommendations for various types of vegetables.

General Conditions

Fresh vegetables of high water content, if allowed to stand long after harvesting without low temperature and high humidity controls, wilt and toughen through loss of moisture, or loss of *turgor* [30]. The flavor is also impaired, mainly because of enzyme actions in the tissues. Leafy greens, in particular, benefit by storage in high humidity conditions. However, excessive moisture can promote spoilage. When vegetables are washed before storage, thorough draining is advised.

Where vegetables are stored is also important. Vegetables stored near strongly flavored foods, such as onions, may absorb unintended flavors. A number of vegetables will spoil more rapidly when stored with other vegetables and fruits that produce ethylene gas. Cucumbers, okra, tomatoes, and a wide variety of fruits such as apples, pears, bananas, berries, pineapples, and plums produce ethylene gas. Ethylene gas can work to your advantage when trying to ripen a vegetable or fruit more rapidly. Placing vegetables or fruits in a paper bag will help to concentrate the ethylene gas.

Temperature

The ideal storage temperature varies from vegetable to vegetable. Several kinds of roots, tubers, and winter squash are typically not refrigerated. Potatoes are generally not stored in the refrigerator to avoid an increase in sugar content because of changes in the metabolism of the plant tissue. Holding at room temperature for several days after refrigeration brings down the elevated sugar content. Thus, when storing for longer periods of time, cold storage can delay sprouting and decay, but warmer storage conditions are necessary before use.

Tomatoes are best stored at room temperature prior to being sliced or otherwise prepared. If tomatoes are picked before being fully ripened, the quality and vitamin

FOCUS ON SCIENCE

What Is Meant by Loss of Turgor?

Turgor is pressure that full vacuoles (composed of water and various solutes) exert on cell walls. This results in a rigid, crisp texture. Turgor is controlled by osmosis in living cells.

Osmosis is the flow of water across a membrane into or out of a cell depending on the concentration of solids such as sugar and salts inside of a cell. Solutes are present inside the cell (vacuole); therefore, pure water flows into the cell. In plant cells, water enters the cell until the inside and outside water potential is equal; however, the cell wall prevents the cell from bursting, resulting in pressure on the cell wall from within. The pressure of each cell wall against its neighbor results in stiffness that allows the plant to stand upright. When vegetables become dehydrated and limp, they will crisp if soaked in water or sprayed with water as is done in many grocery stores.

value will be better if the tomatoes are ripened at room temperature or a little below (59° to 75°F/15° to 24°C) and kept in a lighted place unwrapped. Although the refrigeration of ripe tomatoes has been commonly recommended, researchers found that a trained sensory panel rated the flavor and aroma of tomatoes significantly lower when stored under refrigeration for two days [40]. These researchers concluded that the storage of ripe tomatoes under refrigeration could be an important contributing factor to consumer complaints about tomato flavor.

Many vegetables, such as leafy lettuce and greens, cucumbers, asparagus, celery, beets, carrots, peas, broccoli, cauliflower, and more are best stored under refrigeration. It is interesting to note that refrigeration is useful in conserving vitamin content [5]. Vegetables vary, however, in the extent of change in vitamin C content, even when kept under refrigeration. In one study [15], fresh broccoli did not lose vitamin C when stored up to seven days, whereas green beans lost as much as 88 percent when stored for six days at 36°F (2°C) and 95 to 100 percent relative humidity.

Methods to Extend Storage

A thin coating of a vegetable-oil emulsion on snap beans and other fresh vegetables has been found to decrease the respiration process [57]. When stored at 40°F (4°C), the waxed beans were generally in better condition than the unwaxed beans. Using this procedure to extend storage life and maintain product quality is common in the marketing of fresh vegetables, such as cucumbers and many fruits. In practice, the vegetable or fruit is first washed thoroughly and rinsed, which removes the natural protective wax coating along with dust and dirt. A synthetic edible wax is then applied to restore nature's own coating and extend the shelf life of the product.

Lettuce may be stored in a controlled atmosphere to extend its shelf life [56]. In an atmosphere containing 2.5 percent carbon dioxide and 2.5 percent oxygen, lettuce heads can be stored up to 75 days. The controlled atmosphere combined with polyethylene packaging reduces the rate of respiration in the lettuce tissues (see Chapter 21 for a discussion of controlled atmosphere storage of fruits).

PRELIMINARY VEGETABLE PREPARATION

Most vegetables grow near or in the ground. Thorough washing is therefore needed to remove soil and sand. In washing, the vegetables should be lifted out of the wash water so that the heavier particles of dirt remain in the water (Figure 20-9). More than one washing is recommended, especially for those vegetables such as leafy

FIGURE 20-9 By filling a clean sink with cold water and stirring the greens, they can be efficiently washed.

What Is Solanine, and Is It Toxic?

Solanine is an alkaloid substance that is toxic if consumed in relatively high proportions. So how is it formed? During growth or postharvest storage of potatoes, exposure to light may result in the synthesis of both chlorophyll and alkaloids—specifically, solanine. Solanine has toxic effects, and although the chlorophyll is not harmful, its presence indicates that alkaloid synthesis may have occurred. To avoid solanine, the purchase of green potatoes should be avoided, potatoes should be stored in the dark, and if present, the green areas should be peeled away and discarded.

---

greens to be consumed raw. Pods, such as lima bean and pea pods, should be washed well before being shelled. The removal of all spoiled and discolored portions of vegetables is another part of the preliminary preparation. Leafy vegetables should have all undesirable leaves and coarse stems removed. Some vegetables such as carrots and potatoes may be peeled, or alternatively the skins may be thoroughly washed and consumed. Preparation tips for several kinds of vegetables are provided in Tables 20-4 through 20-10.

Food Safety and Preparation

Vegetables may be contaminated by various microorganisms present in the soil, by postharvest handling, or by improper storage. For example, spores of *Clostridium perfringens* or *Clostridium botulinum* may be present in dirt that clings to some vegetables. E. coli 0157:H7 contamination of spinach and other greens has also occurred and resulted in foodborne illness [10, 79]. From the farm to your fork, many have responsibility for the food safety of produce. The FDA has provided recommendations for good agricultural and manufacturing practices to minimize food safety hazards common to growing, harvesting, packing, and transporting raw vegetables and fruits [80].

As a first food safety step, produce with minimal damage or decay should be selected. Fresh-cut vegetables and fruit must be refrigerated or iced before and after purchase. Vegetables should not come in contact with raw meat, cleaning chemicals, or other items during shopping or storage in the refrigerator to prevent contamination with pathogenic organisms or poisonous chemicals. Hands, sinks, counters, cutting boards, and knives must be clean before preparing vegetables [48, 81]. A cutting board previously used for raw meat then used to prepare salad ingredients has caused many foodborne illnesses.

Vegetables and fruits must be carefully and thoroughly washed in water. Even portions of the plant not consumed should be washed to avoid cross-contamination with the portions of the plant to be consumed. A firm brush is helpful for washing of some vegetables. Other vegetables such as celery and leeks need to be cut apart to allow the wash water to contact fully inner surfaces that may be trapping soil. At this time, the FDA is not recommending the use of vegetable washes or other cleaning chemicals. Lastly, once vegetables have been cut or cooked, refrigeration is necessary [48, 81].

Potatoes with green pigmentation must be peeled. Potatoes become green from exposure to sunlight or artificial light. Greening is accompanied by the formation of solanine, a bitter alkaloid substance that is toxic if consumed in relatively large amounts [74]. Food safety was discussed further in Chapter 3.

Edible Portion and Yield

Some fresh vegetables, depending partly on the way they are trimmed for marketing, may have a relatively high percentage of refuse or waste parts that are thrown away. In quantity food preparation, recipes will note if the ingredient weight or measure has been provided for *edible portion* (EP) or *as purchased* (AP). Edible portion is the amount of the product remaining after cleaning, and as purchased is the amount prior to peeling and cleaning. Whether preparing food at home or in a professional kitchen, an understanding of the amount of waste generated when cleaning vegetables is important because it will affect the quantity of food available for consumption after preparation as well as the cost of the food consumed. Table 20-11 shows the percentage of refuse from some vegetables.

PREPARATION AND QUALITY CONSIDERATIONS

Many people decide what to eat with their eyes. Vegetables therefore must be prepared to preserve pleasing colors. Flavor and texture are also important factors that determine whether we will eat and enjoy a particular vegetable. With the emphasis on the important nutritional contributions of vegetables, preparation techniques that preserve the nutrient value should be used. Both raw and cooked vegetables should retain their attractive and appetizing characteristics until they are served.

Why Cook Vegetables?

Many vegetables are improved in palatability and more easily and completely digested when they are cooked. Some valuable vegetables, such as dried legumes, could

TABLE 20-11 Refuse from Vegetables

Vegetable	Source of Refuse	Refuse (%)
Artichokes	Stem and edible parts of flowers	60
Asparagus	Butt ends	47
Beans, snap	Ends, strings, trimmings	12
Beets, without tops	Parings	33
Broccoli	Leaves, tough stalks, trimmings	39
Brussels sprouts	Outer leaves	10
Cabbage	Outer leaves, core	20
Carrots, raw	Crown, tops, scrapings	11
Cauliflower, raw	Leaf stalks, core, and trimmings	61
Celery	Root and trimmings	11
Chard, Swiss, raw	Tough stem ends, damaged leaves	8
Corn, sweet, raw	Husk, silk, trimmings	35
	Cob	29
Cucumber, pared*	Parings, ends	27
Eggplant, raw	Ends, parings, and trimmings	19
Garlic, raw	Knob and skin	13
Ginger root	Scrapings	7
Lettuce, iceberg	Core	5
Lettuce, Romaine	Core	6
Potatoes	Parings, trimmings	19
Boiled, cooked in skin	Skin and eyes	9
Baked, fresh only	Skin and adhering flesh	23
Shallots, raw	Skins	12
Spinach, raw	Leaves, stems, and roots	28
Squash, summer	Ends	5
Squash, winter, all others, raw	Seeds, rind, and stem	29
Sweet potato, raw	Parings and trimmings	28
Turnip greens, raw	Root, crown, tough stems, and discarded leaves	30
Tomato	Core and stem ends	9

*Refuse will be less when the vegetable is not pared or scraped.

Source: Reference 76

not be masticated or digested in the raw state. The flavors of cooked vegetables are different from those of raw vegetables, adding variety to their use.

Heating improves the utilization of protein from dried legumes, and some of the minerals and vitamins, particularly of soybeans, are more available after the beans are heated [31]. Cooking also causes gelatinization of starch and increases its digestibility. Microorganisms are destroyed by the heating process. Moreover, the bulk of leafy vegetables is greatly decreased, as they wilt during cooking.

Plant Pigments

Much of the appeal of vegetables and fruits is due to their bright colors, which result from the presence of various pigments in the plant tissues. Under appropriate temperatures for postharvest storage, green vegetables have been

reported to undergo little change in color over a 12-day period [19]. Other vegetables also retain color well when stored properly. One challenge of cooking vegetables is to retain these bright colors, because heat and the various conditions of preparation may produce pigment changes that make them dull and less attractive.

Vegetable and fruit pigments include the following:

- chlorophyll—green pigments
- carotenoids—yellow and orange (some are pink or red)
- anthocyanins—red, purple, and blue
- betalains—purplish red (some are yellow)
- anthoxanthins—creamy white to colorless

The yellow-orange and red-blue pigments predominate in fruits. Anthocyanins and anthoxanthins have many similarities in chemical structure. They are called flavonoid pigments and are increasingly being recognized as nutritionally valuable.

Chlorophyll. Chlorophyll plays an important role in photosynthesis, in which the plant uses the energy of the sun's rays with gases from the air to synthesize carbohydrates. Chlorophyll is concentrated in the green leaves, where it is present in tiny bodies called *chloroplasts* [24]. It is mostly insoluble in water. Exposure to acids, alkalies, overcooking, or extended hot holding will chemically change chlorophyll (see Table 20-12).

Heat. Initial heating of green vegetables results in an intensified green color. This brightening of the color is explained in part by the removal of air from the tissues when the green vegetable is heated by steam or boiling water. The removal of air permits greater visibility of the underlying chlorophyll. The bright green color of frozen green vegetables is a result of blanching.

Green beans, broccoli, and other green vegetables will become increasingly olive green in color due to the degradation of chlorophyll to *pheophytin* within as little as five minutes of overcooking. Vegetables should therefore be cooked for the minimum amount of time necessary to tenderize. The hot holding time for vegetables should also be minimized because the same undesirable color changes will occur.

Canned vegetables have been subjected to high heat for extended periods to destroy botulism spores and other microorganisms. This extended cooking causes essentially all of the chlorophyll to degrade to an olive green or olive brown color. *Pyropheophytin* is apparently the major degradation product of chlorophyll in canned vegetables [55]. The differences in color can be readily observed by comparing frozen or fresh green beans or peas with canned.

Acid and Alkalies. Acid contact, like extended exposure to heat, will cause green vegetables to become a dull-green color due to *pheophytin*. Green vegetables may come in contact with acids because of the liberation of acids present in vegetables during cooking or because of the use of an acidic vinaigrette. The length of time vegetables are marinated in a vinaigrette therefore should be kept to minimum. To reduce contact with volatile acids during cooking, remove the pan cover during the first few minutes of cooking to allow some volatile acids to escape.

Alkalies, such as baking soda, have the opposite effect on color. A small amount of baking soda added to green vegetables during cooking will change the chlorophyll to a bright green, more water-soluble pigment called *chlorophyllin*. The use of baking soda in cooking vegetables is not recommended, however, because the flavor, texture, and vitamin content of the vegetables can be adversely affected. Thiamin and vitamin C are particularly susceptible to destruction when baking soda is added during cooking. Texture can become undesirably soft because soda has a disintegrating effect on the hemicelluloses. When green vegetables are properly cooked, and not overcooked, the addition of soda serves no purpose.

Carotenoids. Carotenoids, like chlorophyll, are insoluble in water and are present in the chloroplasts of green leaves. In the autumn, when the chlorophyll disappears, the yellow color can usually be seen. Carotenoids constitute a group of similar pigments, some of which are called *carotenes*. Three of the carotene pigments—α, β, and γ carotene—are found in relatively large amounts in carrots. Other carotenoids, which contain some oxygen in addition to carbon and hydrogen, are called *xanthophylls*. Cryptoxanthin is a xanthophyll that is found in many yellow vegetables. The red pigment of tomatoes, named lycopene, is a carotenoid. Lycopene is also found in watermelon and pink grapefruit and is believed to be an antioxidant that when consumed in the diet correlates with a reduced incidence of cancer and possibly heart attacks [4]. Some of the carotenoid pigments—including α, β, and γ carotene and cryptoxanthin—are be changed into vitamin A in the body and, therefore, contribute substantially to the vitamin A value of the diet.

Carotenoid pigments may lose some of their yellow color when exposed to air because they are susceptible to oxidation. This reaction may occur in vegetables such as

TABLE 20-12 Chlorophyll and Related Compounds		
Compound	Color	Factors Promoting Chlorophyll Degradation
Chlorophyll	Green	
Pheophytin	Dull-olive green	Caused by overcooking, extended hot holding, or contact with acids.
Pyropheophytin	Dull-olive green or olive-brown	Along with pheophytin, is common in canned vegetables. Canned vegetables are heated at high temperatures for extending periods during the canning process.
Chlorophyllin	Bright-green	Caused by exposure to an alkaline, such as baking powder. Use of an alkaline to maintain bright color is not recommended to avoid alkaline-induced nutrient losses.

carrots when they are dehydrated. The carotenoid pigments are quite stable during ordinary cooking procedures. The presence of alkali has little effect on the color. With longer heating, especially with overcooking, the pigments may undergo some chemical change by a process called isomerization in the presence of acid, so that the orange color becomes somewhat more yellow.

Anthocyanins.   The flavonoid pigments are water soluble and found in the cell sap. Common vegetables and fruits colored by anthocyanins include red cabbage, radishes, blackberries, and black raspberries [90].

The pigments in the anthocyanin group of flavonoids are usually red in an acid medium and change to blues and purples as the pH becomes more alkaline. Not all plant anthocyanins behave in the same way with changes of acidity and alkalinity, perhaps as the result of the presence of other pigments or of substances that modify the reactions. Red cabbage is easily changed in color, and it is difficult to retain its typical color while cooking it. The German custom of cooking red cabbage with an apple and adding a small amount of vinegar when served aids in retaining the red color.

When cut with a nonstainless steel knife, red cabbage reveals another property of anthocyanins—the ability to combine with metals to form salts of various colors. The use of lacquered tin for canning red fruits and vegetables prevents the bluish red or violet that results from the combination of anthocyanin pigment with tin or iron. The salts of iron combined with anthocyanins are more blue than those formed with tin.

Betalains.   The pigments in the root tissue of red beets are not chemically similar to those of anthocyanins; they contain nitrogen and are called *betalains* [86]. Some of these pigments are purplish red (red beets), whereas others are yellow (yellow cactus pear). Betalains are stable between pH 3 and 7 [21]. Beets lose much pigment and become pale when they are pared and sliced before cooking, because the pigments are very soluble in water and leach from the tissues. If beets are not peeled and one or two inches of the stem are left intact, they may be cooked in boiling water with a minimal loss of pigment. Beets should therefore be peeled after cooking.

Anthoxanthins.   The anthoxanthin pigments change from white or colorless to yellowish as the pH increases from acidic to alkaline ranges. These pigments are widely distributed in plants and often occur with anthocyanins. They may combine with some metals, such as iron, to form a dark complex. Some combinations with aluminum produce a bright yellow. The anthoxanthin pigments are generally quite stable to heating. If the cooking water is alkaline, however, the pigments may appear yellow. If heating is excessive or prolonged, the pigments also darken. Table 20-13 summarizes the effect of various factors on the color of plant pigments.

Enzymatic Oxidative Browning

Some raw fruits, such as bananas, apples, and peaches, and some pared vegetables, including potatoes and sweet potatoes, darken or discolor on exposure to air. The darkening results from the oxidation of phenolic compounds in the fruit when oxygen from the air is available; the reaction is catalyzed by oxidizing enzymes, called oxidases, present in the plant tissue (see Chapter 9 for a discussion of enzymes). Unattractive, brown pigments are the end products of this enzymatic oxidative reaction.

Methods to Control Browning.   It is, of course, desirable to prevent or control enzymatic darkening because it is aesthetically unappealing both in food freshly prepared

TABLE 20-13 Solubility in Water and Effect of Various Factors on the Color of Plant Pigments

(handwritten annotation: Heating intensifies color)

(handwritten annotation: present in chloroplasts)

Name of Pigment	Color	Solubility in Water	Effect of Acid	Effect of Alkali	Effect of Prolonged Heating	Effect of Metal Ions
Chlorophylls	Green	Slightly	Changes to olive green *pheophytin*	Intensifies green *chlorophyllin*	Olive green *pheophytin* and *pyropheophytin*	
Carotenoids	Yellow and orange; some red or pink	Slightly	Less intense color	Little effect	Color may be less intense*	
Anthocyanins	Red, purple, and blue	Very soluble	Red	Purple or blue	Little effect	Violet or blue with tin or iron
Betalains	Purplish red; some yellow	Very soluble	Little effect	Little effect	Pale if pigment bleeds from tissues	
Anthoxanthins	White or colorless	Very soluble	White	Yellow	Darkens if excessive	Dark with iron; bright yellow with aluminum

*Heating *usually* produces little effect.

Chemical Structures of Plant Pigments

Chlorophyll

Chlorophyll consists of four pyrrole groups in a porphyrin ring with a magnesium molecule in the center chelated to the nitrogens of the pyrroles. The green color of chlorophyll is produced through the resonance of electrons along its conjugated double-bond system. The porphyrin ring can have several different side chains, usually including a long phytol chain. There are a a few different forms that occur naturally, but the most widely distributed in terrestrial plants are chlorophyll a (contains methyl groups; bright blue-green color) and chlorophyll b (contains aldehydes; yellow-green color). The ratio of chlorophyll a to chlorophyll b is 2 : 1.

Carotenoids

Carotenoids are defined by their chemical structure. Carotenoids are responsible for many of the red, orange, and yellow hues of plant leaves, fruits, and flowers, as well as the colors of some birds, insects, fish, and crustaceans. Carotenoids are derived from a 40-carbon polyene chain, which could be considered the backbone of the molecule. The chain may be terminated by cyclic end groups (rings) and may be complemented with oxygen-containing functional groups. The hydrocarbon carotenoids are known as carotenes, whereas oxygenated derivatives of these hydrocarbons are known as xanthophylls. Beta-carotene, the principal carotenoid in carrots, is a familiar carotene, and lutein, the major yellow pigment of marigold petals, is a common xanthophyll. A conjugated double-bond system is responsible for the yellow to red color due to the movement of electrons along the unsaturated chain. Intensity of color is affected by the length of the unsaturated chain along with which the electrons can oscillate and by the shape of the chain which is influenced by the cis and trans configuration of the bonds.

Anthocyanin

Anthocyanins are water-soluble glycosides of polyhydroxyl and polymethoxyl derivatives of 2-phenylbenzopyrylium or flavylium salts. Individual anthocyanins differ in the (a) number of hydroxyl groups present in the molecule; (b) degree of methylation of these hydroxyl groups; (c) nature, number, and location of sugars attached to the molecule; and (d) the number and nature of aliphatic or aromatic acids attached to the sugars in the molecule. Cyanidins and their derivatives are the most common anthocyanins present in vegetables, fruits, and flowers. Anthocyanins share a basic carbon skeleton in which hydrogen, hydroxyl, or methoxyl groups can be found in six different positions. In fruits and vegetables, six basic anthocyanin compounds predominate, differing both in the number of hydroxyl groups present on the carbon ring and in the degree of methylation of these hydroxyl groups.

---

for consumption and in susceptible products held prior to freezing, drying, or canning. Lemon juice, which is highly acidic, evidently interferes with enzyme activity and can be used to coat fruit surfaces to reduce discoloration. Pineapple juice accomplishes the same purpose, although it is less acidic than lemon juice. Pineapple juice contains a sulfhydryl compound that seems to act as an antioxidant in retarding browning. Added vitamin C, either alone or as part of several available commercial products, also aids in reducing discoloration because of its ability to act as an antioxidant. Commercially, sulfur dioxide is sometimes used to inhibit enzyme activity before fruits are dehydrated. Some vegetables, such as potatoes, may be submerged in water to prevent browning.

Sulfites. Sulfites are able to control browning on peeled raw potatoes and other fresh fruits and vegetables. They also have been used for other purposes, such as preventing "black spot" on shrimp and lobster and conditioning doughs. However, some people are sulfite sensitive. The FDA estimates that this sensitivity involves one in a hundred persons in the general population and 5 percent of those with asthma. In 1982, in response to numerous consumer reports, the FDA contracted with the Federation of American Societies for Experimental Biology (FASEB) to examine the link between sulfites and reported health problems. The FASEB concluded in 1985 that, although sulfites are safe for most people, they pose a hazard of unpredictable severity to asthmatics and others who are sensitive to them. In 1986, therefore, the FDA prohibited the use of sulfites to maintain color and crispness on vegetables and fruits meant to be eaten raw, such as those served in salad bars. They also required that the presence of sulfites be disclosed on labels of packaged food. The FDA attempted to rule that sulfiting agents not be allowed on fresh, raw potatoes intended to be cooked and served unpackaged and unlabeled to consumers as, for example, French fries. However, this ruling was not upheld in a court battle in which the fresh potato industry prevailed on procedural grounds. Consumers at risk need to read labels and check carefully, especially when eating away from home [47]. Vitamin C derivatives and citric acid can replace sulfites in retarding undesirable enzymatic browning in fresh fruits and vegetables.

Discoloration in Potatoes after Cooking

Some potatoes darken after cooking, the degree varying with the variety, the locality or soil where grown, the season, and differences in chemical composition. Discoloration is usually found at the stem end of the potato and apparently results from the formation of a dark complex of ferric iron and a polyphenol, probably chlorogenic acid. Addition of a small amount of cream of tartar (about one teaspoon per quart of water) to make the cooking environment more acidic appears to retard the development of after-cooking darkening in susceptible varieties.

Flavor

A wide variation occurs in the flavor of vegetables—some are mild and others, such as asparagus and parsnips, have relatively strong, distinctive flavors. The sugar content is high enough to produce a definite sweet taste in carrots and sweet potatoes, whereas the flavor of spinach includes a slightly bitter component. Onions, garlic, broccoli, and cabbage have distinctive aromas. Vegetables of the cabbage and onion families are sometimes described as strong flavored, but not necessarily in the raw state. The natural flavors that make each vegetable distinctive probably result from mixtures of many compounds, most of them present in tiny amounts. These compounds include aldehydes, alcohols, ketones, organic acids, esters, and sulfur-containing compounds.

When preparing vegetables, the impact on flavor needs to be considered. Overcooking changes the flavor of many vegetables. An "overcooked" vegetable flavor is generally undesirable. For example, compare the differences in flavor among canned, frozen, and fresh vegetables. The amount of water used for cooking also has an influence. When cooking in a large amount of water, more flavor substances will be extracted, and thereby lost. Sugars, acids, and some minerals that contribute to flavor are water soluble and easily extracted from the tissues. Although methods of cooking will be discussed later in the chapter, the method of cooking—boiling, steaming, roasting, or stir-frying—will have an influence on the flavor.

Cabbage Flavors. Vegetables of the cabbage or mustard family, called *Cruciferae*, include cabbage, cauliflower, broccoli, Brussels sprouts, kale, kohlrabi, mustard, rutabaga, and turnips. These vegetables are relatively mild when raw but may develop strong flavors or odors when improperly cooked because of extensive decomposition of certain sulfur compounds [37].

Vegetables of the cabbage family have a milder flavor when cooked (a) until just tender to the fork, (b) in open, uncovered pan, and (c) with enough water to almost cover. Hydrogen sulfide and other volatile sulfur compounds may produce a strong, pungent, sulfurous flavor and odor in overcooked cabbage-family vegetables. Vegetable acids also may aid in the decomposition of the sulfur compounds; therefore leaving the lid off for the first part of cooking to allow some volatile acids to escape, may help to control these changes. A large amount of water dilutes the natural flavors of the vegetables, usually to a substantial degree. The desirability of a milder flavor or stronger natural flavor is a matter of personal preference, however, so preparation techniques may be adjusted to accomplish the desired flavor. The absence of many volatile flavor substances from dehydrated cabbage has been reported [38], which may explain why the dehydrated product is a poor substitute for freshly cooked cabbage in terms of eating quality.

Onion Flavors. The onion family includes onions, leeks, garlic, and chives (Plates II and XIV). These vegetables are usually strong flavored in the raw state, but tend to lose some of their strong flavors when cooked in water. Raw vegetables of the onion family contain derivatives of the sulfur-containing amino acid, cysteine. These compounds are acted on by enzymes in the tissues when

UP CLOSE

The Chemistry of Cabbage Flavors

Chemical substances in vegetables of the cabbage family include *thioglucosides*—compounds which contain a sugar molecule with a sulfur-containing portion. *Sinigrin* is the thioglucoside found in cabbage. When cabbage tissues are damaged by cutting or shredding, an enzyme (a thioglucosidase called *myrosinase*) breaks down the sinigrin to produce a mustard oil, chemically called *allyl isothiocyanate*.

This compound gives a sharp, pungent flavor that is typical of shredded raw cabbage. An amino acid, *S*-methyl-L-cysteine sulfoxide, is also present in raw cabbage and several other members of the cabbage family. On cooking, this compound produces dimethyl disulfide, which contributes to the characteristic and desirable flavor of the cooked vegetable, along with a number of other volatile compounds [37]. ■

the vegetables are peeled or cut to produce volatile sulfur compounds that irritate the eyes and cause tearing or produce biting sensations on the tongue.

The sharp flavor of onions as well as garlic is reduced on cooking. The flavor of onions can be mild when cooked in a large amount of water with the lid of the pan loose or off, or the flavor can be sweeter and more concentrated when cooked in a small amount of water with the lid on. Onions generally tend to increase in sweetness on cooking. Personal preference may determine the cooking method.

Texture

Tender-crisp is often recommended as a desirable end-point texture when cooking vegetables. There are exceptions, of course; a baked potato is expected to be cooked until tender. As with color, the extent to which a particular vegetable is enjoyed will be influenced by texture. **Fiber** components in vegetables are an important contributor to the texture of vegetables.

Fiber Components. Cellulose, a long-chain **polymer** of glucose, is the main structural component of plant cell walls. Other structural compounds include *hemicelluloses* and *pectins*. All of these substances are complex carbohydrates called **polysaccharides** and, because they are not broken down or hydrolyzed by enzymes in the human digestive tract, comprise a major part of dietary fiber [27].

Pectins are found not only in the cell walls but also between the cells, where they act as a cementing substance to bind cells together. Pectic substances include *protopectin*, the insoluble "parent" molecule, *pectinic acid* or *pectin*, and *pectic acid*. *Betaglucans*, which also are fiber components, are glucose polymers with linkages somewhat different from cellulose that make them more soluble in water. They appear to increase cholesterol excretion from the bowel, thus aiding in the prevention of heart disease [2]. A complex noncarbohydrate molecule, *lignin*, is present in woody parts of plants. Various *gums* and *mucilages* are also found in plants as fiber components but are nonstructural polysaccharides.

Influence of Cooking. There appears to be no great loss of **fiber** when vegetables are prepared by typical kitchen methods or commercial processing [92]. Cellulose is somewhat softened by cooking but appears to be mostly indigestible for humans. When calculated on a dry-weight basis, cellulose content seems to increase somewhat when vegetables are boiled, which may result from the liberation of cellulose from the cell walls, making it more available for analysis [22, 23, 39].

The pectic substances, which are part of the intercellular cementing material in plant tissues, may be **hydrolyzed** to a certain extent during cooking, resulting in some cell separation; however, the total pectin content appears to be well retained [92]. In the canning of many vegetables, the solubilization and hydrolysis of pectin apparently contribute to excessive softening. During prolonged cooking at approximately neutral pH, **de-esterification** and de-polymerization (hydrolysis) occur [83].

Alkalies, Acids, and Calcium Salts. Sodium bicarbonate (baking soda) added to cooking water tends to cause the hemicelluloses to disintegrate, producing a soft texture in a short cooking period. Acid, on the other hand, prevents softening of vegetables. Neither of these substances should be added during the cooking of vegetables or legumes.

Calcium salts, as calcium chloride, make vegetable tissues firmer, probably by forming insoluble calcium salts with pectic substances in the plant tissue. Commercially, traces of calcium are added during canning to help preserve the shape and firmness of tomatoes. The FDA allows calcium chloride to be added up to 0.07 percent. It can also be used to make melon rinds firm and brittle for pickling.

Prevention of Nutrient Losses

Nutrient loss can occur during storage, preparation, and cooking. Vitamins may be destroyed by oxidation, lost by leaching into cooking water, or adversely affected by heat.

Storage Losses. Vegetables prepared and used as close to the time of harvest as possible will have higher nutrient levels. Vitamin C losses during storage can vary with losses ranging from 15 percent in green peas and 77 percent for green beans stored under refrigeration for seven days [5]. In one study, 18 percent of vitamin C was lost in broccoli stored under refrigeration for seven days [18]. Losses in B vitamins also occur during storage.

How Cooking Losses Occur. Cooking losses can occur (a) through the dissolving action of water or dilute salt solutions; (b) by chemical decomposition, which may be influenced by the alkalinity or acidity of the cooking medium; (c) by oxidation of specific molecules such as vitamins; (d) by the mechanical loss of solids into the cooking water; and (e) by volatilization. Mechanical losses of nutrients in vegetable cookery are the result of paring, rapid boiling (agitation), and overcooking. Loss of starch and other nutrients occurs from cut surfaces. Losses are greater when parings are thick and when overcooking results in marked disintegration. The chief volatile loss is water, although volatilization of other substances may cause loss of flavor.

Cooking Losses—Water-Soluble Nutrients. Vitamin C is easily oxidized and hence tends to be better retained if conditions favoring oxidation can be eliminated. Covering pans during cooking can have a negative effect on the color and flavor of some vegetables; however, a covered pan hastens cooking, reduces air contact, and thus can be beneficial for nutrient retention. Researchers examining vitamin C losses in broccoli found microwave and pressure cooking did not appreciably affect the vitamin C content. Steaming or boiling, however, were associated with 22 percent and 34 percent loss of vitamin C, respectively [18]. The more alkaline the cooking water, the faster the rate of oxidation of several vitamins, particularly thiamin and vitamin C.

Thiamin is more unstable to heat than riboflavin and niacin, and it appears to be less stable when heated in a water medium than when heated in the dry state. The extent of destruction increases with rising temperature. Riboflavin and niacin are stable to heat even at temperatures above 212°F (100°C).

Cooking Losses—Fat-Soluble Nutrients. Vitamins A and E and the carotenoids, including lycopene, are sensitive to heat, light, oxygen, and pH [5]. These fat-soluble nutrients do not leach into the cooking water like the water-soluble nutrients and appear to be well retained during preparation. Research is ongoing, however, and a study of cooking conditions on lycopene levels in tomatoes found losses of 50 percent or more depending on the method and length of cooking [41].

Influence of Food Production Systems. A comparison was made of vitamin C and folate (a B vitamin) retention in a cook/chill system and cook/hot-hold system. Vegetables reheated after one day of chilled storage had greater losses of both vitamins than those held hot at 162°F (72°C) for 30 minutes. However, the cook/chill vegetables had better vitamin retention than those cooked and held hot for two hours [88]. Holding vegetables hot after cooking causes loss of flavor and nutritive value.

Cooking in batches in food service is an important strategy that results in food with higher nutritional value as well as better sensory qualities because the texture and color are less likely to deteriorate when holding is kept to a minimum. For cooking vegetables in a foodservice operation, convection steaming retained vitamin C well with losses of only 6 to 12 percent. However, when broccoli and cauliflower were held an additional 30 minutes at 145°F (63°C) after cooking, the total loss was 36 to 45 percent [11]. Preservice holding of whipped potatoes in a simulated conventional foodservice system resulted in loss of 36.2 percent of the vitamin C present [59].

Other Changes

Other changes that occur during the cooking of vegetables may have an impact on the water content or starch granules. The water content of vegetables is altered during cooking. Water may be absorbed if the vegetable is cooked submerged in water or, to a lesser extent, in steam. Removal of water occurs during baking. The gelatinization of starch, described as the swelling of starch granules in the presence of moisture, occurs during the cooking of vegetables. This gelatinization may be partial or complete.

SPECIFIC METHODS OF COOKING VEGETABLES

Vegetables may be cooked in a variety of ways. As discussed in the preceding pages, color, texture, flavor, and nutrient retention should be considered when preparing vegetables. The desire for variety is a factor that influences the choice of cooking method. Suitability of the method for the type of vegetable being cooked is a consideration.

Some loss of food value occurs in most methods used in vegetable cookery. For this reason, it is important to serve some vegetables in the raw state. Baking, steaming, stir-frying, and cooking in the skins have been called *conservation methods* of cooking vegetables because food value is retained to a greater extent with these methods.

Broiling and Grilling

High heat is used to cook vegetables when broiled or grilled. Both baking or roasting and grilling result in flavorful vegetables in part due to carmelization. Also, flavors are not diluted in a waterless cooking medium.

Vegetables may be grilled over hot charcoal to develop delicious vegetable dishes (Figure 20-10). The vegetables may be cut in pieces large enough not to drop through the grates, or placed on skewers that can be easily turned on the grill. Lightly brushing the vegetable with an oil and then seasoning with an herb before broiling or grilling will contribute delicious flavors.

Roasting and Baking

Baking or roasting vegetables can be accomplished by the direct heat of the oven, or the vegetable can be pared, sliced, or diced and placed in a covered casserole. In the casserole, however, a moist atmosphere surrounds the vegetable as it cooks. All vegetables that contain a high enough water content to prevent drying and that have little surface exposed to the heat lend themselves well to baking. These include potatoes, sweet potatoes, winter squash, and onions. Vegetables are commonly baked in the skin. Corn on the cob may be shucked and wrapped in foil before baking; or the corn may be baked unshucked. In this case, the silk should first be removed and the ear soaked in water so that the shucks will not burn during the baking process.

Moderately hot oven temperatures, which form steam quickly within the vegetable, give better texture to starchy vegetables than is obtainable at low temperatures. Starchy vegetables, such as potatoes, dry out if overbaked or get soggy if the skin of the vegetable is not opened when baking is finished. Prompt serving of baked vegetables as soon as done is recommended to maintain quality and lessen vitamin losses.

(a)

(b)

FIGURE 20-10 (a) Pita bread topped with tomatoes, basil, and cheese can be grilled for a great appetizer. (b) Grilled garden kabobs are a summertime treat that adds excitement to eating your vegetables. *(Courtesy of Land O'Lakes)*

Pan-Frying and Deep-Frying

Pan-frying (cooking to doneness in a small amount of hot fat) and *deep-fat frying* (cooking submerged in hot fat) are both methods of frying. Potatoes, onions, eggplant, and parsnips are probably more commonly cooked by this method than other vegetables; however, many others could be satisfactorily fried.

Onion rings, eggplant, and zucchini are often battered before being fried in deep fat (Figure 20-11). Carrots, green peppers, parsnips, and mushrooms should be parboiled before being covered with batter and fried in deep fat. There appears to be little loss of vitamins and minerals in the frying of vegetables. Table 20-14 gives approximate temperatures and time periods for deep-fat frying some vegetables and vegetable mixtures. Frying was discussed in more detail in Chapter 10.

Sautéing

Vegetables may be sautéed as a preliminary cooking step in a recipe or as the cooking method for a side dish. The light browning of vegetables such as diced onions, carrots, or celery in a small amount of fat, only enough to coat the bottom of the pan, at a moderately high temperature enhances the flavor and appearance of vegetables. Lightly sautéed vegetables are desirable when preparing soups and sauces with vegetable components.

Quick-cooking vegetables may be sautéed from the raw state when prepared for a vegetable side dish. Vegetables such as carrots may be blanched first and then sautéed to finish. When cooking vegetables with differing cooking times together, the vegetables that will take the longest to cook should be started earlier than the quick-cooking vegetables. Sautéed vegetables should be slightly firm or tender-crisp when done. Vegetables may be sautéed and seasoned with a variety of herbs and sauces for a tasty vegetable dish.

Boiling

Vegetables may be boiled either by partially or completely submerging in water. As a result of extensive water contact, soluble constituents are likely to be lost in the cooking water. Soluble substances in vegetables include water-soluble vitamins, relatively soluble mineral salts, organic acids, flavor substances, and sugars. Much less loss of soluble material occurs if vegetables are boiled in their skins. For example, pared potatoes may lose up to nine times as many minerals and up to four times as much total dry matter as potatoes cooked in their skins.

Blanching.   Blanching is the partial cooking of foods in boiling water for a very brief period. Vegetables may be blanched for several different purposes. Blanching can be used to loosen skins on vegetables such as tomatoes or as a method to set color or soften firm vegetables. Vegetables may also be blanched prior to an additional cooking step such as breading and frying. In this case, blanching will partially cook the vegetable so less cooking is needed during frying, allowing the breading to remain a golden brown. Vegetables to be frozen are blanched to inactive enzymes that will result in undesirable changes during frozen storage.

Parboiling.   Parboiling is similar to blanching, except the cooking time is longer. Parboiling often is used to shorten the final cooking step for vegetables such as broccoli, cauliflower, winter squashes, and root vegetables.

Cooking Losses during Boiling.   Losses of water-soluble constituents, including water-soluble vitamins, vary with the time of cooking and the amount of surface exposed to the water. In general, the more surface exposed and the longer the cooking time, the greater the loss. Losses are also influenced by the amount of cooking

(a)

(b)

(c)

FIGURE 20-11 Onion rings may be made from scratch: (a) dredging the onion rings in flour; (b) dipping in batter; (c) frying.

TABLE 20-14 Approximate Temperatures and Times for Frying Vegetables in Deep Fat

Food	Temperature of Fat		Time (min)
	°F	°C	
Croquettes (cooked mixtures)	375–390	190–199	2–5
French-fried onions, potatoes, and cauliflower	385–395	196–202	6–8
Fritters	360–375	182–190	3–5

water, with more losses occurring as the quantity of cooking water increases. If cooking can be done in little or no water, or if the cooking water is evaporated by the time the vegetable is done, little or no loss of soluble material may occur. Also, cooking waters should be utilized for soups, sauces, and gravies to save valuable nutrients that would otherwise be discarded. It is important to avoid overcooking by bringing vegetables to the just tender stage, as tested with a fork.

In general terms, placing vegetables in just enough boiling water to prevent scorching, covering with a tight-fitting lid, and cooking until just tender constitute an appropriate method for boiling most vegetables to retain maximum flavor, sweetness and aromatic characteristics, and nutritive value. A tightly covered lid will promote more rapid and even cooking. However, some vegetables such as the cabbage-flavored vegetables may develop undesirably strong flavors when covered, and chlorophyll-containing vegetables may develop a dull or olive green color when volatile acids are unable to escape from the covered pan. Thus, some vegetables are best prepared uncovered or with a lid that is slightly offset to allow venting.

Steaming

Steaming consists of cooking in steam, with the vegetable suspended over boiling water in a perforated container (Figure 20-12). Although some tender young vegetables may cook quickly in steam, most vegetables cooked in an ordinary steamer take somewhat longer to cook than those that are boiled. The fact that the vegetable is not actually in water favors the retention of water-soluble constituents.

FIGURE 20-12 These broccoli spears are placed in a perforated pan to be steamed in a commercial foodservice steamer. In the home, small perforated liners are used above boiling water in a saucepan.

Pressure Cooking

Cooking in a pressure saucepan involves cooking in steam, but the steam is confined in the tightly closed pan and a high pressure is created. The cooking temperature rises as the steam pressure rises. At 15 pounds of pressure, the temperature is 250°F (121°C). Small, lightweight pressure saucepans can conveniently be used to cook a variety of foods (Figure 20-13), especially roots, tubers, and legumes. With young, tender vegetables such as spinach, the pressure saucepan may easily result in overcooking, with accompanying loss of color and flavor. The fact that acids released from the vegetable are trapped in the pressure saucepan also contributes to a loss of green color.

Many models of pressure saucepans are adjustable for 5, 10, and 15 pounds of pressure. When the cooking period is completed, the temperature may be quickly reduced by placing the pan in cold water. These features aid in desirable results for various types of vegetables. One disadvantage is the difficulty of testing for doneness during the cooking period if various vegetables are being cooked that require a shorter or longer cooking time than the recommended average time.

Microwave Cooking

Generally both fresh and frozen vegetables can be satisfactorily cooked in a microwave oven. Some vegetables have better color and/or flavor when cooked by microwaves, whereas others have higher-quality characteristics when boiled in a saucepan or cooked by other conventional methods [8, 63]. Whole vegetables or pieces should be of uniform size for the microwave oven to allow more even cooking. Large pieces take longer to cook than small pieces, and microwaving time increases with the amount of food being cooked. Vegetables cooked in their skins should be pricked or cut to allow excess steam to escape. Standing time outside the microwave oven should be considered in the cooking of large vegetables. Microwaving is a good method for cooking corn on the cob. Each cob of corn may be wrapped in waxed paper before microwaving. General principles of microwave cookery were discussed in Chapter 7.

FIGURE 20-13 A pressure saucepan may be used to cook a variety of foods. *(Courtesy of National Presto Industries, Inc.)*

FOCUS ON SCIENCE

tender floweret part in the center of the plate, and the stalk should be positioned near the rim or edge of the plate.

Microwave Cooking of Vegetables

Microwave ovens heat unevenly; therefore the placement of the vegetable in the microwave should be considered. Broccoli, for example, should be positioned on the plate with the

---

Cooking Times for Vegetables

Table 20-15 shows the approximate times for cooking vegetables by several methods. It should be emphasized that all timetables used in cookery are approximate and are to be used merely as guides. In using a timetable, it is best to cook for the minimum time suggested and then test for doneness with a fork before continuing to cook. Variations in the maturity of samples of vegetables, the sizes of whole vegetables or cut pieces, the variety, the temperature of the vegetable when placed in the water as well as the temperature of the water itself, and the amount of water are known factors affecting the time required to cook the vegetable until tender. Some varieties cook in half the time required by other varieties of the same vegetable.

Cooking of Frozen Vegetables

Essentially, the cooking of frozen vegetables is no different from the cooking of fresh vegetables. With the exception of frozen green soybeans, which require almost as long to cook as fresh ones, the cooking time of frozen vegetables is about half that required for fresh vegetables because they have been blanched before freezing. Vegetables may be defrosted before cooking, or the frozen vegetable may be placed in boiling water. Many vegetables cook more uniformly and in slightly shorter time when defrosted, at least partially, before being cooked. To avoid nutrient losses and to reduce handling, however, it is generally recommended most vegetables remain frozen until cooking is started.

Corn on the cob and vegetables frozen in a solid block should be defrosted before cooking. The time required for cooking corn on the cob is not sufficient to defrost the cob. In preparation for freezing, corn on the cob requires a longer blanching time to destroy enzymes than cut corn. This longer blanching time cooks the corn more completely; thus, a short heating period is desirable in the final preparation after freezer storage. Spinach and other leafy vegetables frozen in a solid block are better when partially defrosted before cooking to avoid overcooking the outer leaves before the block is defrosted.

Using a fork to separate and redistribute the unthawed portions in the center midway during the cooking period is an aid in shortening cooking time and increasing the uniformity of cooking.

Cooking of Canned Vegetables

Canned vegetables are already overcooked in the processing; hence, a relatively short reheating time is desirable to avoid further softening of the vegetables. A short heating period is safe for commercially canned foods; however, it is recommended that low-acid, home-canned vegetables be boiled for at least 10 minutes before tasting to destroy **botulinum toxin**, if present [25]. Boiling should be extended by one additional minute for each 1,000-foot increase in elevation. Commercially canned vegetables may be easily heated in the microwave oven or by conventional methods.

PLANT PROTEINS AND VEGETARIAN DIETS

According to a poll of approximately 1,000 men and women over 18 years of age, an estimated 2.3 percent of the U.S. population is vegetarian [60]. Adoption of a vegetarian diet may be motivated by a variety of factors including ecological concerns, religious beliefs, economic considerations, and philosophical or ethical values [3]. The following general classifications of vegetarians have been outlined by the Institute of Food Technologists.

Semi-vegetarian: eats dairy products, eggs, chicken, and fish but no other animal flesh

Pesco-vegetarian: eats dairy products, eggs, and fish but no other animal flesh

Lacto-ovo-vegetarian: eats dairy products and eggs but no animal flesh

Lacto-vegetarian: eats dairy products but no animal flesh or eggs

Ovo-vegetarian: eats eggs but no dairy products or animal flesh

Vegan: eats no animal products of any type

TABLE 20-15 Approximate Cooking Time for Vegetables

Vegetable	Approximate Amount for 4 Servings	Preparation for Cooking	Approximate Amount of Water for Boiling	Amount of Water for Pressure Saucepan	Time (min) Boiling	Steaming	Baking	Pressure Saucepan (15 lb of pressure)
Artichokes,								
French	2 lb	Whole	To cover	1 c	25–40			10
Jerusalem	1 lb	Whole, pared	Partially cover	1 c	20–30	35	30–60	15
Asparagus	1 lb	Woody ends broken off, scales removed	To cover butts	1/3 c	Tips, 5–10 Butts, 10–15	10–15 25–30		Tips, 1–1 1/2 Large tips, 2
Beans, young green or wax	3/4 lb	Whole or broken, strings removed	About half the volume of beans	1/3 c	20–25	25–30		1 1/2–3
Beans, fresh lima	2 lb in pod (2 c shelled)	Shelled	About 2 c	1/3 c	25–35	25–40		2–3 (5 lb pressure)
Beets, young	6 medium or 1 1/2 lb	Whole, skin, root, and 2 in. of stem left on	To cover	3/4 c	30–45	60–75		12, small 18, large
Beet greens	1–1 1/2 lb	Whole leaf with tender stem and midrib	Partially cover	1/2 c	5–15			2
Broccoli	1 medium bunch (1 1/2–2 lb)	Woody stems removed, coarse leaves removed, smaller stems pared and split to hasten cooking	To cover stems	1/3 c	Florets, 5–10 Stems, 10–15			1 1/2–2
Brussels sprouts	3/4–1 qt	Whole, outer leaves removed; larger compact heads may be partially split	Partially cover	1/2 c	10–15			1–2
Cabbage, new green	1 lb	Outer leaves and stalk removed; shredded.	Partially cover	1/2 c	6–9	9–10		1–1 1/2
Mature, white	1 lb	Outer leaves and stalk removed; shredded	Partially cover	1/2 c	8–10	10–12		2–3
Red	1 lb	Outer leaves and stalk removed; shredded; cook with tart apple or add 2–3 Tbsp vinegar after cooking	Partially cover	1/2 c	15–20	25–30		3–4
Carrots, young	1 lb	Whole, skins on or scraped	Partially cover	1/3 c	20–25	25–30	35–45	4
		Scraped, cut into halves or quarters lengthwise or diced			10–15			2–3
Cauliflower	1 1/2–2 lb	Outer leaves and stalks removed; separated into flowerets	Partially cover	1/2c	8–10	10–15		1 1/2
		Whole flower	Partially cover	1/2 c	20–25	25–30		3–4

TABLE 20-15 (Continued)

Vegetable	Approximate Amount for 4 Servings	Preparation for Cooking	Approximate Amount of Water for Boiling	Amount of Water for Pressure Saucepan	Time (min)			
					Boiling	*Steaming*	*Baking*	Pressure Saucepan *(15 lb of pressure)*
Celery	1 medium bunch	Cut into 1/2- to 3/4-in. pieces	1/2-in. depth in pan; add water if needed	1/3 c	15–20	25–30		2–3
Corn, young green	4 ears	On cob or cut off	Cover ears; partially cover cut corn	1/2 c on cob	5–10	10–15		1–2
				1/3 c off cob	5			2
Okra	1 lb	Sliced or whole	Partially cover	1/3 c	10–20	20–25		3 (sliced)
Onions	1 lb	Two outer layers removed Whole, cut into halves or quarters or slices	Cover or partially cover	1/2 c	Whole, 25–35 Quarters, 15–20		45–60	6–7 3
Parsnips	1 lb	Scraped or pared; cooked whole or cut in half lengthwise; woody core removed	Partially cover	1/2 c	15–25	30–35		2 (sliced) 7 (whole)
Peas, green	2 lb in pod	Shelled	1/2- to 1-in. depth in pan; added as needed	1/3 c	10–15	15–20		2–2 1/2 (5 lb pressure)
Potatoes, Irish	1–1 1/2 lb	Whole, with or without skins	Barely cover	1 c	30–35	40	40–60	15
		Pared, cut lengthwise into halves or quarters	Partially cover	3/4 c	20–30	30–35		8
Potatoes, sweet	1–1 1/2 lb	Whole, with or without skins	Barely cover	1 c	30–35	35–40	30–50	8–10
		Pared, halved	Partially cover	1/2 c	20–30	30–35		6–8
Rutabaga	1 1/4 lb	Pared and diced	Partially cover	1/2 c	20–30			6
Spinach	1 lb	Coarse stems and roots removed	1 c per lb or more	1/2 c	3–6	5–10		1–1 1/2
		Stems not removed			8–10	6–12		1–1 1/2
Squash								
Hubbard	1 1/2–2 lb	Pared; cut into 2 × 3-in. pieces	1/2- to 1-in. depth in pan	3/4 c	20–25	30–35		6–8
		Cut into one-portion pieces; rind on					45–60	
summer	1 1/2–2 lb	Pared and sliced	1/2- to 1-in. depth in pan	1/3 c	5–15	10–20	15–20	2
Tomatoes	1 lb	Whole	Little or none	1/4 c	5–10	10	20–30 (whole stuffed)	1–2
Turnips	1 lb	Pared, sliced or diced	Partially cover	1/2 c	15–20	20–25		1 1/2–4
Turnip greens	1–1 1/2 lb			1–2 c	15–25			1–1 1/2

It is the position of the American Dietetic Association that appropriately planned vegetarian diets are healthful, are nutritionally adequate, and provide health benefits in the prevention and treatment of certain diseases [3]. The lesser biological value of most plant proteins in comparison with animal products must be considered in choosing plant foods that will complement each other in essential amino acid content. For example, combining cereal grains that are low in the essential amino acid lysine but supply sufficient methionine with legumes that are lacking in methionine but supply adequate amounts of lysine yields a balanced protein. Vegetarian diets are generally high in dietary fiber and complex carbohydrate and low in fat, as recommended in the Dietary Guidelines for Americans, resulting in potential health benefits.

The food industry has responded to the interests of vegetarians in various ways. Meat analogs made from plant proteins are available as canned or frozen entrees; plant protein concentrates are produced from soy, wheat, peanut, glandless cottonseed, and other sources; tofu and wheat gluten are available; and more manufactured foods free of animal fats and milk proteins are being made. Some vegetarian dishes are shown in Plates XVIII and XIX.

Dried Legumes

Legumes have been the heart of many traditional cuisines for thousands of years [45]. Consumption of legumes in the United States has varied over the years. In 1970, the per capita consumption of legumes based on disappearance data was 6.8 pounds, increasing to 7.8 pounds in 1999, then declining to 6.1 pounds in 2005 [77]. Legumes offer healthful benefits when consumed because they are rich in complex carbohydrate, dietary fiber, and protein, and are low in fat. Legumes are relatively inexpensive as meat substitutes. Legumes include dried beans, peas, and lentils in many different varieties, varying in color, shape, and size. Table 20-16 lists some types of legumes. In the northeastern United States, white beans for baking are the most popular. In the West, especially where there are Hispanic populations, pinto beans are preferred [53]. Black-eyed peas, also known as cowpeas, are favored in the South. Black beans have gained in popularity in trendy restaurants.

Preparation of Legumes

Legumes require cooking before eating. When they are cooked, proteins are made more available, starch is at least partially gelatinized [16], flavor is improved, and some potentially toxic substances are destroyed. A special problem in cooking is offered by the dry seeds—water lost in ripening and drying must be replaced by soaking and by heating. Because legumes are hard and the cellulose and other fiber components are well developed, the legumes must be softened during the cooking process. The ease of softening depends somewhat on how readily the legumes absorb water.

Soaking of Beans.   Prior to cooking, dried legumes are soaked in water. Two methods may be used, overnight soaking in cold water or soaking for one hour in water that was brought to a boil briefly. The rate of hydration is faster in hot water than at room temperature or by the method of soaking all night in cold water [13]. Dry beans absorb as much water in 1 hour, when soaking is started

Type	Description and Use
Black beans	Sometimes called *black turtle-soup beans;* used in thick soups and in Oriental and Mediterranean dishes
Black-eyed peas	Also called *black-eyed beans* or *cowpeas;* small, oval-shaped, and creamy white with a black spot on one side; used primarily as a main-dish vegetable
Garbanzo beans	Also known as *chickpeas;* nut flavored and commonly pickled in vinegar and oil for salads; may also be used as a main-dish vegetable
Great Northern beans	Larger than but similar to pea beans; used in soups, salads, casserole dishes, and baked beans
Kidney beans	Large, red, and kidney shaped; popular for chili con carne; used also in salads and many Mexican dishes
Lima beans	Broad, flat, and in different sizes; used as a main-dish vegetable and in casseroles
Navy beans	Broad term that includes Great Northern, pea, flat small white, and small white beans
Pea beans	Small, oval, and white; hold shape even when cooked tender; used in baked beans, soups, and casseroles
Pinto beans	Beige and speckled; of the same species as kidney beans and red beans; used in salads, chili, and many Mexican dishes
Red and pink beans	Pink beans more delicate in flavor than red beans; both used in many Mexican dishes and chili
Dry split peas	Specially grown whole peas from which skin is removed and then pea broken in half; used mainly for split pea soup but combine well with many different foods
Lentils	Disk shaped and about the size of a pea; short cooking time (about 30 minutes); combine well with many different foods

TABLE 20-16 Some Varieties of Legumes

FOCUS ON SCIENCE

More on the Preparation of Legumes
Acidic Ingredients and Softening of Legumes

Ingredients, such as tomatoes, catsup, molasses, and brown sugar, contain organic acids. These ingredients are added to many dishes containing legumes to boost flavor, but at the same time, they have to be added after the legume has softened. This is because of the pectin content of the legume. If the legume has not softened and the acid ingredient is added too soon, the legume will remain hard.

Rancidity and the Influence of Lipoxygenase

Lipoxygenase is an enzyme that is specific to linoleic (18 : 2) and linolenic (18 : 3) fatty acids. The enzyme supplies the oxygen to the fatty acid and causes rancidity which produces off-flavors. This enzyme is particularly found in fresh peas. Thus it is important that fresh peas are blanched immediately—especially, if they are to be frozen—so that lipoxygenase activity is prevented.

---

by boiling the beans for 2 minutes, as when soaked in cold water for 15 hours. If hot soaked, as generally recommended, beans are cooked in the water used for soaking. Additional water is absorbed during the cooking process, making a gain in weight of 150 to 160 percent (about 4 cups of water per cup of dry beans for both soaking and cooking).

Use of Alkali.   Alkali in the form of baking soda has been used to hasten the softening of dried beans during cooking. Alkali increases water absorption, but it is destructive on the thiamin content of legumes. Another point of objection to the use of baking soda has been the possibility that the bean texture will become too soft. The use of baking soda therefore is not necessary or desirable. If it is used, however, the amount of soda needs to be carefully regulated (1/8 teaspoon per pint of water) to prevent deleterious effects insofar as the flavor and appearance of cooked beans are concerned. In these amounts, baking soda can serve as an aid in softening the seed coats if it is necessary to use hard water to cook the beans.

Soft or Hard Water.   Soft water is preferable for both soaking and cooking dry beans, because the calcium and magnesium salts in hard water may form insoluble salts with pectic substances in the cell walls and between cells in the bean tissue and inhibit proper hydration. There is more water absorbed and fewer hard beans remaining at the end of cooking when soft water rather than hard water is used.

Canned Beans.   One constraint limiting the use of dried beans is the length of preparation time required. Canned beans are convenient and save time in preparation; they may be ready to consume in only the time required to heat. Canned beans, however, may be softer than desired and may not be as bright in color as a bean prepared from dried. For example, black beans may be a richer black color when prepared from dried because some of the black color may be lost in the liquid used in the canning process.

Raffinose and Stachyose.   Legumes contain appreciable amounts of the oligosaccharides raffinose and stachyose, which are not digested by enzymes in the intestinal tract. It is assumed that the flatulence resulting from the ingestion of legumes results from the degradation of these carbohydrates by intestinal microorganisms. It has been suggested, as a result of one study on the carbohydrate content of various legumes after soaking and cooking, that the soaking and cooking water be discarded to maximize the removal of these gas-forming carbohydrates [85]. Flavor substances would then also be discarded, however.

Soybeans

Soybeans are a good source of protein of high biological value and have been used for centuries in various forms as a food staple by millions of people in China and Japan. Soybean products can play an important role in vegetarian diets. These beans were first grown in the United States in the 1920s, primarily because of their oil content. They still supply a large share of the vegetable oil used in this country. In the 1950s, processors began making protein products from soy: soy flour, soy protein concentrate, and isolated soy protein. Later, soy fiber was produced. Varied uses are made of these products in food manufacturing [58]; for example, soy lecithin is widely used in emulsifier systems for processed foods.

In past years, some uses of soybeans in the United States have been limited by their objectionable flavor and odor, sometimes characterized as being "painty" or "beany." Much research has gone into the study of this flavor problem, and several processes have been developed to control it. The off-flavor appears to be caused by the enzyme **lipoxygenase**, and it is now possible to inactivate the enzyme before it can catalyze the off-flavor.

Soy Protein Products.   Soy flour may be made from dehulled soybeans that contain the oil normally present in this product (about 18 percent); however, soy flour is more commonly prepared by grinding soy flakes from which soybean oil has been pressed. When soluble carbohydrates are extracted from defatted soy flour, *soy protein*

HOT TOPICS

Dry Beans—Into the Mainstream?

You may ask, "Who eats beans?" A study conducted by the Economic Research Service of the USDA found people in the southern and western states of the country account for 39 and 38 percent, respectively, of all bean consumption. People of Hispanic heritage represent 11 percent of the U.S. population but account for 33 percent of cooked dry bean consumption. California, Texas, and Florida have a high concentration of Hispanic population [35].

The USDA survey tells us men consume more beans than women. As children grow up, they tend to develop a taste for Mexican-style food and therefore consume more beans. As a whole, cooked dry beans are favored by lower income households. Low income homes tend to consume more pinto and lima beans, whereas black and garbanzo beans might be termed the upscale members of the cooked dry bean community.

Soybeans are in a slightly different category of the many dry bean varieties available. Production and use of soybeans as food began in China before the eleventh century B.C. The Chinese and their neighbors consumed soybeans in traditional foods such as tofu, soy sauce, miso, soy sprouts, and green vegetable soybeans. However, this bean was not grown abundantly throughout the world until the twentieth century [34].

Soy protein foods offer good alternatives to meat, poultry, and other animal-based products because soy has a complete protein profile. With greater emphasis on healthy diets, sales of soy products are increasing and soy is becoming "hot" [52]. The FDA has contributed to this trend by approving a health claim that "25 grams of soy protein a day, as part of a diet low in saturated fat and cholesterol, may reduce the risk of heart disease." No sooner had this regulation been issued, however, than questions arose about certain other components in soy products, particularly isoflavones, thus creating controversy.

The problem is that isoflavones, including genistein and daidzein, are phytoestrogens, a weak form of estrogen that could have a druglike effect in the body, particularly in postmenopausal women. Research is far from conclusive but some studies suggest that high isoflavone levels might even increase rather than diminish the risk of breast cancer in some cases. There is still a lot of emerging data that is confusing, and it is not clear exactly how soy acts.

So what should one do? Common sense and moderation are the best guides. Whole soy protein foods have benefits in promoting a healthy heart. Moderate soy consumption may be linked to a reduced risk of several illnesses, although soy by itself is not a magic food. At least for now it is probably best to leave soy supplements—pills and powders containing high amounts of isoflavones—on the shelf. ∎

---

concentrate is produced. It contains 70 percent or more protein. On further removal of nonprotein substances, *isolated soy proteins* remain, containing 90 percent or more protein. These several soy products are used for various purposes in food processing. Soy flour is shown in the large bowl in Figure 20-14.

Texturized Soy Proteins. Texture is given to soy and other high-protein products by special treatments. In one method, the protein isolate is spun into long fibers by a process similar to the spinning of textile fibers. The wet protein mixture is forced through spinnerettes into a coagulating bath. The resulting fibers are gathered into bundles. Spun protein fibrils may be blended with other ingredients, often using egg albumen as a binding agent, and fabricated into many different foods. Some of these products simulate slices of beef or bacon.

Another method for producing texturized vegetable protein involves the process of *extrusion*. In this procedure, soy flour or protein concentrate is blended with water, flavors, colors, and possibly other additives. The mixture is then fed into a cooking extruder that works the material into a dough. As the dough flows within the channels of an extrusion screw and moves through the small openings of a die, the large protein molecules lose their original structure and form layered masses that cross-link with each other. These masses resist disruption on further heating or processing. The release of pressure as the protein mixture is extruded causes expansion, with tiny air pockets being uniformly dispersed throughout the mass. Texturized soy or vegetable protein (Figure 20-15) is available to the consumer and can be combined with other foods, such as ground beef. Extruded soy protein is used by food processors in such products as meat patties,

FIGURE 20-14 A variety of soy ingredients may be used in food preparation and processing. Top left to right, a glass of soy milk, a bowl of soy flour. Middle left to right, baked goods using soy flour; natto (fermented soybean paste). Bottom left to right, soy nuts; tofu. *(Courtesy of United Soybean Board)*

FIGURE 20-15 TVP (texturized vegetable protein) can be processed from soybeans and comes in different colors and textures. *(Courtesy of United Soybean Board)*

tacos, chili, pizza, lasagna, stews, omelets, and stuffed peppers.

Before texturized soy products are combined with other foods, they are generally hydrated. Both seasoned and unseasoned forms are available. The USDA has written specifications for texturized vegetable protein products that permit their use, on a voluntary basis, in school foodservice and other child-feeding programs. The vegetable protein mixtures are blended in specified amounts up to 30 percent with ground or diced meats in various menu items.

Whole Soybeans.   Acceptable products can be prepared from whole soybeans, including canned soybeans with chicken or pork, vegetarian-style soybeans, and soybean soup [46]. Dry, whole soybeans are shown in Figure 20-16.

Soy Milk.   Soy milk is a common substitute for cow's milk in the United States, and its sales have been increasing in recent years. This product is produced by grinding the softened soybeans and extracting the resulting liquid. Most of the bean's protein, oil, and other solids are present in the milk. To make the soymilk equivalent to cow's milk, it must be fortified with calcium. Commercially, the lipoxygenase enzyme is inactivated to avoid off-flavors. Soy milk in a glass is shown in Figures 20-14 and 20-17.

Tofu.   Tofu (Figures 20-14 and 20-18), also known as soy cheese or bean curd, has a 2,000-year-old tradition as the protein staple for millions of people throughout the Orient. Now it is rising in popularity with Americans. Made by coagulating soy milk with a calcium or magnesium salt and then squeezing out the whey from the curd, tofu is a smooth-textured, bland-flavored, high-moisture product. It is available in different consistencies—silken, soft, firm, and extra firm. The soft, creamy textures blend well with other ingredients, whereas the firmer types can be cubed, sliced, deep fried, and baked. Many interesting dishes can be created with tofu (Figure 20-19). It can be marinated in a soy sauce and spice mixture to give it flavor; used to extend fish and chicken dishes; crumbled in salads; or blended with other ingredients in making salad dressing, dips, and puddings. It can also be used to make an attractive cheesecake (Plate XVIII).

FIGURE 20-16 Soybeans in various stages of development: pods, young beans, and mature beans. *(Courtesy of United Soybean Board)*

FIGURE 20-17 Soy milk and cheese are common substitutes. *(Courtesy of United Soybean Board)*

FIGURE 20-18 Tofu. *(Courtesy of United Soybean Board)*

Fermented Soy Products. Several fermented products are made with soybeans, including *soy sauce*, in which a soybean mash is inoculated with a culture of microorganisms and the mixture is fermented in a salt brine. *Tempeh* is an Indonesian food prepared by mold fermentation of cooked soybeans. *Miso* is a fermented soy paste used as a condiment.

Soybeans and Nutrition. Soybeans are a source of *phytoestrogens*, isoflavonoid compounds having weak estrogenic activity in the body. The physiological effects depend on the amount of soy products consumed, the age of the individual, and probably other factors. In October 1999, the FDA authorized a health claim regarding the association between soy protein and the reduced risk of coronary disease to be used in food labeling. To qualify for this health claim, foods must contain at least 6.25 grams of intact soy protein per serving and also meet other criteria, such as being low in fat, cholesterol, and sodium. Tofu has been reported to contain considerably more isoflavones than a soy drink, but the soy-based formulas that were tested were found to be devoid of these compounds [14].

(a)

(b)

(c)

(d)

FIGURE 20-19 Tofu may be used for a variety of tasty dishes: (a) Tofu stir-fry. (b) This soup has a creamy base that uses soy instead of dairy products. (c) This dairy-free pumpkin pie is lowfat as well. (d) This fiesta scramble may look like ordinary eggs, but in reality it is tofu seasoned with a hint of curry. (*Courtesy of Morinaga Nutritional Foods, maker of Mori-Nu Tofu, www.morinu.com*)

CHAPTER SUMMARY

- Vegetables can be defined broadly as plants or parts of plants that are used as foods. In common usage, vegetables are plants or parts of plants that are served raw or cooked as part of the main course of a meal.

- Vegetables provide vitamins, minerals, starch, protein, and fiber, and many are rich in phytochemicals that appear to offer health benefits. Vegetable consumption has been associated with a reduced risk of certain cancers, type 2 diabetes, stroke and potentially cardiovascular disease, and hypertension. Most Americans consume less than the recommended amount of vegetables.

- Various parts of plants are used as vegetables. Vegetables may be leaves, vegetable-fruits, flowers, stems, roots, bulbs, tubers, and seeds. Leaf vegetables include iceberg lettuce, cabbage, and spinach. Vegetable-fruits are botanically classified as fruits. Cucumbers, eggplant, tomato, squash, and peppers are examples of vegetable-fruits. Flower or stem vegetables include artichokes, broccoli, cauliflower, asparagus, and celery. Roots and tubers include beets, carrots, potatoes, radish, and sweet potatoes. Potatoes may be mealy or waxy. Mealy potatoes are best for baking, and waxy potatoes are best for boiling. Garlic, leeks, onions, and shallots are bulbs. Seed vegetables include sweet corn, peas, and legumes.

- Mushrooms are fungi and not technically vegetables but are often served as vegetables. There are many different kinds of mushrooms. Poisonous mushrooms grow in the wild and can be easily mistaken for edible mushrooms.

- Vegetables selected for purchase generally should be firm, crisp, and bright in color. USDA grades may be used to guide purchasing for some canned and fresh vegetables.

- Price, whether organic, produced by biotechnology, or partially processed, may be considered when purchasing vegetables. Many vegetables are most economical to purchase fresh. Vegetables provide more nutrition per cost than many other foods. USDA organic certification provides a consistent standard to guide purchases. Biotechnology is supported by many professional organizations. Through biotechnology, new plant varieties can be developed. Partially processed or valued-added vegetables such as precut, bagged salad mixes offer convenience for consumers.

- Fresh vegetables and fruits are perishable because they are composed of living, respiring tissue. Ideal storage conditions vary with the type of vegetable. Most vegetables are best stored in refrigerated high humidity conditions to avoid wilting or loss of turgor. Some vegetables, such as potatoes and tomatoes, should be stored at room temperature. The sugar content of potatoes increases when refrigerated. Modified atmosphere packaging, controlled atmosphere, and light waxing are ways to extend storage of some vegetables.

- Preliminary vegetable preparation should include thorough washing because most vegetables grow near or in the ground. For food safety, care should be taken to avoid cross-contamination of vegetables with raw meats or cleaning chemicals during shopping or storage. Vegetables may have a relatively high percentage of refuse or waste after trimming or peeling. Quantity recipes will express the amount of a vegetable in a weight or measure either as edible portion or as purchased.

- Vegetables are cooked to improve palatability, allow for easy and more complete digestion, and to destroy microorganisms. Some vegetables, such as dried legumes, would be difficult to consume if not cooked. Cooking also causes gelatinization of starch and increases digestibility.

- Preparation methods for vegetables should promote the retention of nutrients, while maintaining or developing a desirable color, flavor, texture, and general appearance.

- The cholorophyll pigments in vegetables are green and will degrade to a dull olive color when in contact with acids or when overcooked. Baking soda will change chorophyll to a bright green pigment; however, the use of soda is not recommended when cooking because of adverse effects on the flavor, texture, and vitamin content.

- Carotenoids include the pigments *carotene*, found in carrots; *xanthophylls*, found in many yellow vegetables; and *lycopene*, found in tomatoes, pink grapefruit, and watermelon. Many carotenoid pigments are changed to vitamin A in the body. These pigments are quite stable during ordinary cooking procedures.

- The anthocyanin group of flavonoid pigments is usually red in an acid medium and changes to blues and purples as the pH becomes more alkaline. Red cabbage is a vegetable containing anythocyanin pigments.

- Betalains are often a purple-red color and are found in the root tissue of beets. These pigments are very soluble in water, thus peeling beets after cooking will help to retain color.

- Anthoxanthin pigments change from white to colorless to yellowish as the pH increases from acidic to alkaline ranges. Although these pigments are generally stable to heating, excessive or prolonged heating may cause darkening.

- Some pared vegetables, including potatoes, sweet potatoes, and some raw fruits, will darken or discolor on exposure to air as a result of enzymatic oxidative reactions. Acids found in lemon juice, pineapple juice, and vitamin C will prevent browning. Sulfites control browning and may be used in some food processing applications; however, some people are sulfite sensitive.

- The natural flavors that make each vegetable distinctive probably result from a mixture of many compounds including aldehydes, alcohols, ketones, organic acids, esters, and sulfur-containing compounds.

- Vegetables of the cabbage or mustard family are relatively mild when raw but when overcooked may result in strong, pungent, sulfurous flavor and odor. Vegetables of the onion family are usually strong flavored in the raw state but tend to become milder when cooked.

- Tender-crisp is a desirable texture for many cooked vegetables. Cellulose, hemicelluloses, and pectins are structural compounds in vegetables that comprise a major part of dietary fiber. Betaglucans and lignin also are fiber components. Although there is no great loss of fiber during cooking, some fiber components are softened during cooking. Alkalies (baking soda) will cause hemicelluloses to disintegrate resulting in a soft texture. Acid prevents softening of vegetables. Neither acids nor alkalies are recommended when cooking vegetables. Calcium salts, as calcium chloride, make vegetable tissues more firm.

- Nutrient losses can occur during storage, preparation, and cooking. Vegetables consumed as close to harvest as possible will have higher nutrient levels. Vitamins may be lost two ways during cooking. Vitamins may be destroyed by oxidation or, if water soluble, the vitamins may be dissolved in the cooking water. The stability of vitamins varies by vitamin. Extended hot-holding or chilling and reheating of vegetables will result in increased vitamin losses.

- Vegetables may be cooked by broiling, grilling, roasting, baking, pan-frying, deep-frying, sautéing, broiling, steaming, pressure cooking, or microwave cooking. Frozen vegetables generally require less cooking time than fresh vegetables due to blanching prior to freezing. Canned vegetables should be reheated in a short period of time to avoid additional overcooking. Low-acid, home-canned vegetables, however, should be boiled for 10 minutes to destroy botulinum toxin, if present.

- Vegetarians may be classified as semi-vegetarian, pesco-vegetarian, lacto-ovo-vegetarian, lacto-vegetarian, ovo-vegetarian, or vegan. Vegetarian diets are healthful and nutritionally adequate.

- Legumes are seeds and include many varieties of beans, peas, soybeans, and lentils. Legumes are rich in complex carbohydrates, dietary fiber, and protein, and are low in fat. Legumes contain appreciable amounts of the oligosaccharides raffinose and stachyose, which are not digested by enzymes in the intestinal tract.

- Legumes require cooking before eating. Dried beans are rehydrated by soaking in hot water or cold water before cooking. Canned beans may be used to save time in preparation.

- Soybeans are a good source of protein of high biological value and phytoestrogens. Many types of products including soybean oil, soy milk and cheese, tofu, flour, soy lecithin, and texturized soy protein are available. Fermented products made from soy include soy sauce, tempeh, and miso.

STUDY QUESTIONS

1. What are vegetables? Give definitions.

2. List eight classification groups of vegetables based on the parts of the plant that are used as food. Give examples of vegetables in each category.

3. The composition and nutritive value of vegetables differ depending on the part of the plant used. Indicate which types of vegetables are generally

    (a) High in water content

    (b) High in starch

    (c) High in protein

    (d) High in fiber

    (e) Good sources of vitamins A and C

    (f) Low in kilocalories

4. (a) List at least three plant polysaccharides that are components of dietary (indigestible) fiber.

    (b) Name three pectic substances. What roles do these play in plant structure? Which pectic substance is important in making fruit jellies and jams?

5. The color of fruits and vegetables is due to their content of certain pigments.

    (a) List five groups of plant pigments. Describe the color for each group.

    (b) How do the pigments and/or colors change in the presence of acid and alkali and with prolonged heating?

    (c) Explain why it is important to preserve the natural colors of vegetables and fruits during cooking.

6. Flavor varies from one vegetable to another, and many substances contribute to the characteristic flavors.

    (a) List two different families of vegetables that are considered to be strong flavored and indicate what types of compounds are responsible for these flavors.

    (b) Explain how cooking procedures may change these flavors.

7. (a) Describe the usual characteristics of fresh vegetables of good quality.

    (b) Suggest important factors to consider in purchasing fresh vegetables.

8. Both fresh and processed vegetables and fruits may be graded.

    (a) What advantages result from the use of grades on fresh fruits and vegetables?

(b) What factor most limits the use of consumer grades for fresh fruits and vegetables?

(c) List three USDA grades that may be used on canned and frozen vegetables and fruits. Discuss the value to the consumer of grading these products.

9. Suggest appropriate methods for storing various types of fresh vegetables to retain quality.

10. Describe some advances in biotechnology that can be used to improve some characteristics of vegetables and fruits. Give examples.

11. Why is it important to cleanse fresh vegetables thoroughly as a first step in their preparation?

12. Describe several ways in which losses may occur during the cooking of vegetables.

13. In the following list, check the items that describe what may happen when vegetables are cooked. Correct any incorrect statements.

(a) Starch swells and gelatinizes.

(b) Cellulose fibers harden.

(c) Volatile flavors are trapped inside the cells.

(d) Leafy vegetables become limp.

(e) Cellulose fibers soften slightly.

(f) Intercellular cement is hardened.

(g) Vitamins go off in the steam.

(h) Some vitamins and minerals dissolve in the cooking water.

(i) Texture becomes softer.

(j) Some vitamins are lost by oxidation.

(k) Some volatile flavors are lost.

(l) Chlorophyll may be changed to anthocyanins.

(m) Carotenes may become white.

(n) Some volatile acids are released.

(o) Pheophytin, an olive green pigment, may be produced from chlorophyll.

(p) Proteins are coagulated.

(q) Pectic substances are hydrolyzed or broken down.

14. Outline an appropriate procedure for boiling each of the following vegetables. Explain why you would use the procedure in each case.

(a) A green vegetable such as broccoli

(b) Cabbage

(c) Onions

(d) Beets

15. Describe five appropriate methods for cooking vegetables in addition to boiling.

16. Describe an appropriate method for preparing frozen vegetables and canned vegetables.

17. Explain why frozen vegetables require less time for cooking than similar fresh vegetables.

18. **(a)** Describe characteristics of mealy potatoes and waxy potatoes.

(b) For what uses is each type of potato best suited? Why?

19. Explain why the green pigmentation that sometimes develops on potatoes exposed to light should not be eaten.

20. **(a)** Outline a satisfactory method for cooking dried beans and explain why this procedure would be appropriate.

(b) List and describe several different legumes.

21. Describe various types of vegetarian diets.

22. **(a)** What flavor problem has limited the use of soybeans in the United States in past years? How has it been solved?

(b) Describe several soy products that are available for use in manufactured foods.

(c) Describe two methods by which plant proteins may be texturized. Give examples of the use of these products in food processing and preparation.

(d) What is *tofu*? How might it be used in food preparation?

FRUITS AND FRUIT PREPARATION 21

What are fruits? To answer this question, we might begin by saying that all fruits are produced from flowers and are the ripened ovaries and adjacent tissues of plants. In this respect, from a botanical point of view, some foods used as vegetables, nuts, or grains are fruits of the plants from which they were harvested. However, the foods usually designated and used as fruits in food preparation have some common characteristics in addition to the botanical similarity—they are fleshy or pulpy, often juicy, and usually sweet, with fragrant, aromatic flavors.

Thus, the definition of fruits according to botanical characteristics does not always agree with the classification of common usage. Several fleshy botanical fruits, including tomatoes and squash, are not sweet and are used as vegetables. Cereal grains, nuts, and legumes are dry (not fleshy) fruits and have been classified into separate groups for practical use. Rhubarb, which is not a fruit in the botanical sense, is often used as a fruit in meal preparation.

In this chapter, the following topics will be discussed:

- Fruit classifications
- Fruit consumption, composition, and nutritive value
- Color and flavor
- Ripening
- Selection and storage
- Fruit juices
- Dried, canned, and frozen fruits
- Preparation

FRUIT CLASSIFICATIONS

Fleshy fruits may be classified as simple, aggregate, or multiple, depending on the number of ovaries and flowers from which the fruit develops. *Simple fleshy fruits* develop from a single ovary in one flower and include citrus fruits, drupes, and pomes. Oranges, grapefruit, lemons, and limes are examples of citrus fruits (Figure 21-1). Drupes are fruits in which a stone or pit encloses the seed and include apricots, cherries, peaches, and plums (Plates X and XII). Pomes are fruits that have a core. Apples and pears are pomes (Plates X and XI). *Aggregate fruits* develop from several ovaries in one flower and include raspberries, strawberries, and blackberries. Pineapple and figs are examples of a *multiple fruits* that have developed from a cluster of several flowers.

FRUIT CONSUMPTION, COMPOSITION, AND NUTRITIVE VALUE

Consumption

Two cups of fruit each day are recommended for those consuming a reference 2,000 calorie diet in the *2005 Dietary Guidelines for Americans* [36]. In a telephone interview of 305,504 persons over 18 years of age in 2005, only 33 percent reported consuming fruit two or more times per day [35]. According to U.S. food supply data, Americans consume only 1.4 servings (about three-fourths cup) of fruit per day [12]. Although USDA food supply data reveal an increase in fruit availability over the years, fruit consumption is nevertheless below recommendations. In 2005, 273 pounds of fruit were available annually per capita as compared to 242 pounds in 1970. The top five fruits consumed are oranges, apples, grapes (including wine grapes), and bananas. These fruits account for 74 percent of the per capita consumption of fruits in 2002–2004 [18]. In 2004, 46 percent of the total fruit was consumed fresh and 42 percent as juice [39]. Individualized recommendations for fruit and other food intake can be found at http://www.mypyramid.gov. See Chapter 2 for a discussion about food supply data.

Schematic cross-section of an orange

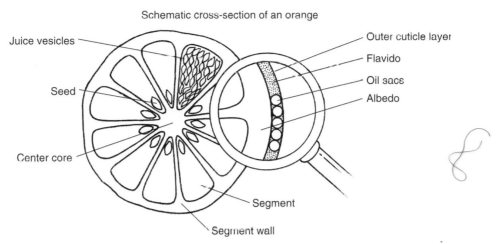

FIGURE 21-1 A cross-section of an orange shows the various parts of the fruit. *(Reprinted from Matthews, R. F., and Braddock, R. J. Recovery and applications of essential oils from oranges.* Food Technology, 41(1), 57. 1987. Copyright © by Institute of Food Technologists)

Composition and Nutritive Value

Most fruits comprise an edible portion combined with some refuse. The refuse or waste may be as high as 33 to 39 percent in certain fruits, such as the banana and pineapple. The chief energy nutrient present is carbohydrate, which occurs mainly as sugars. The caloric value of fruits, as served, is usually higher than that of succulent vegetables because of fruits' higher sugar content. Most fruits have only a trace of fat; two exceptions are coconut (35 percent) and avocado (17 percent). Only a very small amount of protein is found in fruits, and the water content averages about 85 percent. From a nutritional standpoint, fruits are valuable chiefly for vitamin and mineral content, phytochemicals, and indigestible dietary fiber or bulk. Although fruits vary widely in their vitamin content, many fruits are high in vitamin C and vitamin A value, but the B vitamins occur in relatively low concentration. Folic acid is found in oranges.

Variety, growing climate and sunlight, and stage of maturity are significant factors affecting vitamin content in fruits. In addition, handling practices, methods of processing, storage temperatures, and length of storage of fruits may produce a decrease of as much as 50 percent in some vitamin values. The composition and vitamin content of some selected fruits and fruit juices are given in Appendix C.

Vitamin C. Certain fruits are especially valuable sources of vitamin C (Figure 21-2). The most dependable year-round source of vitamin C is probably citrus fruits. Tomatoes, botanically considered fruit, contain only about half as much vitamin C as citrus fruits but are a significant source because of wide use. In season, strawberries and cantaloupe make significant contributions. A generous serving of strawberries may easily provide the recommended daily allowance of vitamin C for an adult. As long as strawberries are not bruised or hulled, they retain vitamin C well. Slicing strawberries rather than crushing them in preparation for certain uses decreases loss of vitamin C.

FOCUS ON SCIENCE

Lowdown on Fruit that Contains Fat

Yes, there are some fruits that contain fat including avocados, coconuts, and olives. Avocados and olives contain a high percent of oleic acid, a monounsaturated fatty acid that is associated with positive nutritive contributions. However, coconut contains a high amount of saturated short-chain fatty acids C-10 (capric acid), C-12 (lauric acid), and C-14 (myristic acid).

(a)

(b)

FIGURE 21-2 Oranges (a) and grapefruit (b) are both rich sources of vitamin C. *(Courtesy of © Sunkist Growers, Inc. All rights reserved.)*

When cantaloupes are at the optimum ripeness for fine flavor, the greatest concentration of vitamin C is highest. The soft center flesh is richer in the vitamin than the harder, firmer flesh near the rind. Honeydew melons rate lower than cantaloupes, and watermelon is a comparatively poor source of vitamin C. The guava is extremely rich in vitamin C, containing an average of 242 milligrams per 100-gram portion of edible fruit. The kiwi is also an excellent source of this vitamin, containing 74.5 mg

of vitamin C per serving, which is nearly equivalent to the amount of vitamin C found in an orange [37].

Vitamin A Value. Yellow fruits contain carotenoid pigments that are precursors of vitamin A. Apricots, cantaloupe, mangoes, and persimmons all contain appreciable amounts of vitamin A value. Nectarines, peaches, star fruit, grapefruit, guavas, mandarin oranges, plantains, plums, and watermelon are examples of other fruits that contain vitamin A value, although to a lesser amount than those previously noted.

Calcium and Iron. Plants tend to concentrate calcium and iron in leaves and phosphorus in seeds. Fruits are therefore not generally considered excellent sources of these minerals. However, blackberries, raspberries, strawberries, dried apricots, prunes, dates, and figs may contribute appreciable amounts of iron to the diet. Of the fruits available year-round, oranges, grapefruit, and figs provide a fair source of calcium.

Fiber. Whole fresh fruits are better sources of fiber than other forms. For example, a whole apple, with peel, has 2 grams of fiber. One-half cup of applesauce provides 0.65 gram of fiber, and 3/4 cup of apple juice supplies only 0.25 gram of fiber [26].

Phytochemicals and Antioxidants. Along with vegetables, fruits appear to provide a protective effect against various types of cancer when consumed in recommended amounts [28, 42]. Phytochemicals, present in many fruits and vegetables, have been identified as being health protective [42]. Watermelon and tomatoes are both rich in lycopene, a phytochemical, that is a red pigment with antioxidant properties [2]. Blueberries are rich in anthocyanins, another natural pigment, that also functions as an antioxidant [20].

COLOR

The pigments that give fruits their characteristic colors are the same as those in vegetables: chlorophyll (green), carotenoids (primarily yellow and orange), anthocyanins

FOCUS ON SCIENCE

What Are Phytochemicals?

Phytochemicals are non-nutritive plant chemicals that have protective or disease-preventative properties. There are more than a thousand known phytochemicals. It is well known

that plants produce these chemicals to protect themselves, but research demonstrates that phytochemicals can protect humans against diseases. Most phytochemicals have antioxidant activity and protect the body's cells against oxidative damage and reduce the risk of developing certain types of cancer. Some of the well-known phytochemicals are lycopene in tomatoes, isoflavones in soy, and flavonoids in fruits. Fruit sources of phytochemicals include blueberries, cranberries, cherries, and apples.

HEALTHY EATING

Fruits—"Feel Good" Foods?

A trend is developing in the fruit field! According to Elizabeth Sloan [27], Americans are in search of a "fruit fix." They hunt for fruit in the bottom of their yogurt and feel *less* guilty when they eat *fruit-covered* cheesecake. Many grocery shoppers say that they are increasing their consumption of fruits and vegetables. We are eating fresh fruits, fruit salads, canned fruits, and frozen fruits and buy more fresh-cut, ready-to-use fruits and vegetables.

Health is one factor that is driving the fruit and vegetable trend. We hear much about reducing fat intake, lowering blood cholesterol, increasing fiber, and losing weight. A number of fruits are promoted for their healthful content of antioxidants—particularly, dried plums, raisins, blueberries, blackberries, raspberries, cherries, and grapes [24].

But there are other factors besides health that are contributing to the trend. American interest in Far Eastern, Caribbean, and Island cuisines has created a requirement for lighter ingredients and sauces and for freshness in foods. Fruits are great tools for chefs in foodservice as they create fruit chutneys, fruit-based salad dressings, and fruit 'n spice sauces. In the future, stir-fries and salads may highlight more fruits; meat and poultry dishes may be smothered in fruit sauces. In addition, there may be more fruit fondues, fruit sorbets, cobblers, and pies made with nontraditional fruit [27].

Indeed, Americans are looking for and finding their "fruit fixes." And food manufacturers have a great incentive to highlight the fruit content of their products as well as to create new and appealing fruit delights. Fruit is truly a potent sign and reminder of healthful, flavorful, and attractive food. ■

FOCUS ON SCIENCE

The Chemistry of Enzymatic Browning

Enzymatic browning takes place when the enzyme polyphenoloxidase (PPO) or other enzymes catalyze the oxidation of phenols in the fruit to form compounds called *quinones*. The quinones can polymerize to form *melanins* which cause the brown pigments.

Chemical Reaction

Phenolic Compound → Diphenol → Quinone → Melanin
(discoloration)

Chlorogenic Acid   PPO; Oxygen; Copper (Cu^{+2}) [co-factor]

Treatments That Will Prevent Enzymatic Browning

- Lemon juice and other acids are used to preserve color in fruit, particularly apples, by lowering the pH and removing the copper site necessary for the enzyme to function.

- Ascorbic acid can inhibit browning by reducing the quinones back to the original phenol compounds.
- Sulfites react with quinines. Therefore, no color pigment is formed.
- Heat will inactivate the enzyme.
- Honey contains short-chain proteins which interact with quinones.

Beneficial and Detrimental Aspects of Enzymatic Browning

Enzymatic browning can be beneficial because of color and flavor development in tea and dried fruits such as figs and raisins. Discoloration in cut fresh fruits and vegetables, as well as seafood such as shrimp, is detrimental.

TABLE 21-1 Methods to Prevent Enzymatic Oxidative Browning	
Method	**Explanation**
Acid pH	Fruit may be dipped in acid solutions composed of ascorbic acid (vitamin C), citric acid, or cream of tartar. Diluted orange, lemon, or pineapple juice may be used for this purpose.
Reduce oxygen contact	Coat or sprinkle fruit with sugar, or submerge in a sugar solution. A salt solution may be used to prevent oxidative browning of potatoes because the salty flavor imparted would be acceptable for potatoes.
Heat (blanching)	Heat will denature the enzymes that cause browning. Thus, fruits or vegetables are often blanched prior to freezing.

(red, purple, and blue), betalains (primarily purple-red), and anthoxanthias (creamy white to colorless). In fruits, the predominant pigments are the yellow-orange carotenoids and the red-blue anthocyanins. Enzymatic oxidative discoloration is also similar for fruits and vegetables. Chapter 20 provided a discussion of these topics, and Table 21-1 offers an overview of methods to prevent oxidative browning.

Mixing various colored fruit juices may sometimes produce surprising, often unattractive results. The tin or iron salts present in canned juices can explain some of the reactions that occur: The metals combine with the anthocyanin pigments to produce violet or blue-green colors. Pineapple juice contains a small amount of iron from the equipment used in its processing and, when added to red or purple fruit juices, changes the color to blue or intensifies the original blue color (Plate XXXII). Usually, acid in the form of lemon juice intensifies the red color of red or blue fruit juice mixtures. Orange juice is best omitted from combinations of red or blue fruit juices because it often produces a brownish color when present in a fairly large quantity. Nevertheless, some very tasty and attractive juice blends, punches, and smoothies can be prepared (Figure 21-3).

The color of canned fruits containing anthocyanin pigments tends to deteriorate on storage whether the container is tin or glass. This deterioration is greater in the presence of light and warm temperatures. Canned or bottled shelf-stable cranberry juice cocktail is an example of a fruit product that will exhibit an unattractive reddish-brown color with extended storage.

FLAVOR

The flavor of fruits, in general, may be described as tart, fragrant, and sweet, these characteristics blending together in a pleasant and refreshing flavor bouquet. The flavor of each fruit is characteristic of that fruit. A ripe banana, for example, is readily identified by its odor and taste, which result from a specific complex combination of flavor components.

Aspartame, a high-intensity sweetener, appears to enhance the fruitiness of natural fruit-flavored systems such as orange and strawberry. The addition of sucrose or table sugar does not produce a similar enhancement of fruit flavor [43].

Aromatic Compounds

Fruits owe their characteristic flavors largely to certain aromatic compounds that are present. Many of these compounds are esters, for example, methyl butyrate that is responsible for the typical odor and flavor of pineapple. Other compounds include aldehydes, such as benzaldehyde derivatives, and various alcohols, which have been

FOCUS ON SCIENCE

Why Do the Blueberries in Muffins Turn Green after Baking?

The next time you make blueberry muffins, read the recipe carefully. If the muffin batter contains buttermilk and baking soda, you may want to reconsider the recipe. Baking soda neutralizes the acid in the buttermilk and makes the pH of the batter alkaline. Therefore, when the blueberries are added to the batter and baked, a green color will develop around the blueberries.

Blueberries contain the anthocyanin pigment. This pigment requires an acidic pH to maintain its blue color. An alkaline pH will turn anthocyanin green. A muffin made with milk and baking powder should give better results.

(a)

(b)

FIGURE 21-3 (a) Raspberry juice, raspberries, bananas, and vanilla yogurt blend to make a beautiful and delicious fruit smoothie. (b) These fruit smoothies, composed of bananas, strawberries, mangoes, and cranberries, also make a wonderful addition to any breakfast. *(Courtesy of Dole Food Company, Inc.)*

found to be responsible for the floral and fruity part of the aroma of apricots [6]. In each fruit, many different compounds contribute to flavor; at least 32 different substances have been identified in the aroma of apricots, for example. In loquat fruit—a tropical or subtropical fruit with a flavor described as being mild, subacid, and applelike—researchers have identified 80 aroma substances. Benzaldehyde was a major aroma compound [11]. Some of the fruit flavor compounds can be synthesized in the laboratory, thus helping to improve the quality of artificial flavorings.

Acids

Also contributing to flavor are organic acids, occurring in fruits in the free form or combined as salts or esters. Malic and citric acids are most commonly present, but tartaric acid is a prominent constituent of grapes. Although mixtures of acids may occur, one component usually predominates in each fruit. Fruits of the plum family and cranberries contain some benzoic acid that cannot be used by the body but is excreted as hippuric acid. Rhubarb contains variable amounts of oxalic acid, depending on the maturity of the plant. Oxalic acid usually combines with calcium in the plant to form insoluble calcium oxalate, which is not absorbed from the digestive tract. Fruits vary in acidity; some of this variation depends on variety and growing conditions. Scores for flavor have been positively correlated with pH in fruits such as peaches and raspberries [29].

Essential Oils

Some fruits, as well as other plants, contain essential oils. Oil of lemon and oil of orange, well-known examples of such oils, occur in the leathery skin of the fruit (see Figure 21-1). They may be expressed and used as flavoring or as the basis of extracts, which are made by combining the oil with alcohol.

Other Components

Sugars, some mineral salts, and a group of phenolic compounds contribute to fruit flavor. Fruits cooked in metal containers may form some acid salts with the metals.

Tin or iron salts in canned fruits may sometimes produce a metallic flavor, but these salts are not harmful. Phenolic compounds impart a bitter taste and produce an astringent or puckery feeling in the mouth. They appear to be present in the largest amount in immature fruits.

CHANGES DURING RIPENING

Fruits are living systems. Respiration occurs in the cells of the fruit as they carry on normal metabolic processes involving growth, maturation, and eventual ripening. Ethylene gas is a ripening hormone produced in small amounts by the cells after the fruit is mature. Without ethylene, the fruit does not ripen. Distinct changes occur in fruits during ripening: (1) a decrease in green color and development of yellow-orange or red-blue colors, (2) a softening of the flesh, (3) the development of characteristic pleasant flavors, and (4) changes in soluble solids such as sugars and organic acids.

Role of Ethylene Gas in Ripening

Ethylene gas, produced naturally by many fruits and vegetables, promotes ripening. Fruits that have been harvested well before ripening has started may be stored in an atmosphere that contains ethylene gas to speed the ripening process. Bananas are generally ripened in this way. This is the same concept that is being applied when fruit is placed in a closed bag to promote ripening. Because apples emit ethylene gas, an apple is sometimes placed in the bag with the fruit to be ripened. Ethylene gas, produced naturally by the fruit, builds up in the closed bag. Alternately, fruit that is fully ripe should not be stored in a closed bag or near apples and other high ethylene-producing fruits and vegetables to reduce ethylene gas exposure. In general, there is no material difference in the gross composition (protein, fat, and carbohydrate) of fruits that ripen naturally and those that ripen by ethylene gas in a controlled atmosphere.

Ethylene production is stimulated when plant tissues are injured. Preparation of fruits and vegetables involves peeling, slicing, and cutting, which injure tissues and

FOCUS ON SCIENCE

Extracting Essential Oils from Lemons and Oranges

A microplane is a good tool to use when grating the rind of an orange or lemon to extract the essential oil contained in the rind. The microplane glides over the surface of the rind to capture the oils. If you go down too far into the pith or white part under the skin, there are bitter compounds (tannins) that will contribute to an off-flavor.

induce ethylene production. When these products are placed in sealed containers, the ethylene accumulates and accelerates undesirable changes in quality such as a decrease in firmness and loss of the pigment chlorophyll. It has been reported that when an absorbent for the ethylene gas (charcoal with palladium chloride) was placed in a small paper packet and enclosed in the package containing the processed fruit, the accumulation of ethylene was deterred, thereby preventing the softening of fruits such as kiwifruits and bananas [1]. Researchers also are exploring the use of an ethylene-inhibiting chemical, 1-methylcyclopropene (MCP), to extend the shelf life of fruits and vegetables [7].

Color

The change in color during ripening is associated with both synthesis of new pigments and breakdown of the green pigment chlorophyll. Chlorophyll may mask yellow carotenoid pigments in the immature fruit. Anthocyanins are probably synthesized as ripening proceeds.

Softening

Involved in the softening of fruits are the pectic substances, the complex insoluble protopectin being degraded to pectin, which is also called *pectinic acid*. Gel-forming properties are characteristic of pectin, making it important in the preparation of jams and jellies. Further softening in ripening fruit produces pectic acid from pectin, with a consequent loss of gelling ability. The breakdown of pectic substances found between plant cells may cause separation of cells as part of the softening process. Many fruits soften faster when the temperature of the surrounding air is increased [4].

Flavor

The development of a characteristic pleasant flavor in ripened fruit involves a decrease in acidity and an increase in sugar, along with the production of a complex mixture of volatile substances and essential oils. Thus, fruit that is not fully ripe may be tart and lack sweetness. In some fruits, such as bananas, the increase in sugar is accompanied by a decrease in starch; however, sugar content increases even in such fruits as peaches, which contain no appreciable amount of starch at any time. Some cell wall polysaccharides may decrease as the sugar content increases. In addition, the phenolic compounds, with their astringent properties, seem to decrease.

Vitamin Content

Ripeness and the method of ripening may influence the vitamin content of fruits. For example, the vitamin C content of bananas is greatest in fully ripe fruits, although the total amount present is relatively small. Vine-ripened tomatoes also have a higher vitamin C value than tomatoes picked green and ripened off the vine.

SELECTION OF FRESH FRUITS

An abundance of fresh fruits is available in U.S. markets year-round. In making selections, the consumer should look for signs of good quality, which are generally evident from the external appearance of the product. These signs include the proper stage of ripeness, good color, freedom from insect damage, and the absence of bruises, skin punctures, and decay. The grading of fruits, which may be useful to the consumer in making selections, was discussed with the grading of vegetables in Chapter 20. Quality may be better and prices lower when fruit is in season in nearby areas. In any case, when the fruit harvest is plentiful, the prices are lowest. Table 21-2 summarizes some points to consider in selecting various fruits.

Apples

Apples are among the most widely used fruits. They rank second in U.S. per capita fruit consumption behind bananas [25]. Apples are found locally in most parts of the United States in many varieties that differ in characteristics and seasonal availability. However, six states—Washington, Michigan, New York, California, Pennsylvania, and Virginia—account for more than 85 percent of the U.S.

FOCUS ON SCIENCE

Pectin Development in Fruit

Protopectin → Pectin (or Pectinic Acid) → Pectic Acid

     Protopectinase   Pectin methyl esterase

During ripening, protopectinase converts protopectin to colloidal pectin (able to gel) or water-soluble pectinic acid. Pectin methyl esterase (pectinase) cleaves the methyl esters from pectin to produce poly D-galacturonic acid or pectic acid, and this substance is partially degraded to monomeric D-galacturonic acid by polygalacturonase. These enzymes act in concert during maturation in determining fruit and vegetable texture. Pectic acid causes a soft, mushy, and mealy texture.

TABLE 21-2 Selection of Fresh Fruits

	Quality Characteristics to Look for during Selection
Fruit	
Apple	Firm, crisp, well colored; mature when picked; varieties vary widely in eating and cooking characteristics (see Table 21-3)
Apricot	Plump, firm, golden yellow; yield to gentle skin pressure when ripe
Avocado	Shape and size vary with variety; may have rough or smooth skin but no dark, sunken spots; yield to gentle skin pressure when ripened and ready for use
Banana	Shipped green and ripened as needed at 60° to 65°F (16° to 18°C); refrigerate only after ripened; firm, yellow, free from bruises
Blueberry	Dark blue, silvery bloom, plump, firm, uniform size. Discard green berries.
Cherry	Very delicate; handle carefully; fresh, firm, juicy, well matured, well colored
Citrus	Firm, well shaped, heavy for size, reasonably smooth-textured skin
Cranberry	Plump, firm, deep red to red-maroon color
Grape	Well colored, plump, firmly attached to stem
Guava	Skin color green to yellow, depending on variety; flesh white to deep pink; round, firm but yielding to slight pressure when ripe
Kiwifruit	Chinese gooseberry renamed kiwifruit; light brown, furry, tender soft skin
Mango	Vary in size and shape; yellowish; firm, smooth skin; ripen at room temperature until yields to slight pressure; soft, aromatic flesh
Nectarine	Plump, rich color, slight softening along "seam," well matured
Papaya	Well shaped; well colored, at least half yellow and not green; smooth, unbruised
Peach	Fairly firm, yellow between red areas, plump, well shaped, "peachy" fragrance
Pear	Firm, well shaped, color appropriate for variety
Pineapple	Well shaped, heavy in relation to size; greenish-brown to golden-brown color, fragrant odor
Plum	Fairly firm to slightly soft; good color for variety; smooth skin
Pomegranates	Unbroken, hard rind covering many seeds; varies in color from yellow to deep red; heavy for size; large sizes juicier; only seeds are edible
Strawberry	Full red color, bright luster, firm flesh, cap stem attached, dry, clean
Variety Fruits	
Atemoya	Small, green, rough skinned; creamy, soft, sweet pulp; large black seeds
Breadfruit	Oval or round, 2–15 pounds; yellowish-green rind with rough surface; white to yellow fibrous pulp; important food in South Sea Islands
Carambola (star fruit)	Waxy, yellow; five fluted sides; tart, sweet-sour flavor
Cherimoya (custard apple)	Almost heart shaped; uniform green when ripe; no mold or cracks at stem end; fresh pineapple-strawberry-banana flavor
Passion fruit (granadilla)	Size and shape of an egg; tough, purple skin; yellowish meat with many black seeds
Kumquat	Small, football shaped, yellow, firm; sweet skin and tart flesh
Loquat	Small, round or oval; pale yellow or orange; somewhat downy surface; thin skin; firm, mealy flesh
Persimmon	Bright orange; Hachiya variety slightly pointed and soft when ripe; Fuyu variety more firm when eaten (like an apple); smooth, rich taste
Plantain	Greenish looking bananas with rough skins and blemishes; frequently used as a vegetable; never eaten raw
Ugli fruit	About the size of a grapefruit; spherical; extremely rough peel, badly disfigured, with light green blemishes that turn orange when fruit is mature; very juicy with orangelike flavor

Source: References 23, 38

apple crop. Washington State is the leading producer of apples (Figure 21-4). Controlled atmosphere storage (discussed later in this chapter) has lengthened their seasons of availability. Of the more than 100 varieties of apples grown in the United States, only about a dozen are commonly marketed [22].

Apples have many culinary uses. They may be served fresh in salads (Figure 21-5) or as desserts and cooked in sauces, pies, and cobblers. Varieties differ in their suitability for being cooked or eaten fresh. Table 21-3 gives some suggestions for use, and Plate X shows several different varieties of apples.

FIGURE 21-4 Apples are picked by hand when ripe.   *(Courtesy of the Washington Apple Commission)*

FIGURE 21-5 This wilted lettuce and apple salad is an attractive and delicious way to serve apples.   *(Courtesy of the Washington Apple Commission)*

Avocados

The bland flavor and smooth texture of avocados blend well with many food combinations. Avocados are unique fruits in that they contain about 17 percent fat. Avocados are available all year, grown in California, Florida, and other countries such as Mexico and Chile [23, 38]. They may be purchased slightly underripe and ripened at room temperature, preferably in a dark place. When ready for use, they should yield to gentle pressure on the skin. Avocados should be refrigerated only after ripening. Figure 21-6 provides suggestions for avocado preparation.

Bananas

Banana plants grow in tropical areas, and bananas of many different varieties are produced. As the plant blooms, a cluster of tiny blossoms emerges, each blossom producing one banana. The fruits grow together on a stem of about 300 bananas. After harvest, the stem is divided into hands, each of which contains 10 to 12 individual bananas. Bananas are picked green and ripen best after harvesting. As they ripen, the skin gradually turns yellow.

Bananas rank second in world fruit production but are first in fruit sales in the United States. They are generally

TABLE 21-3 Desirability of Apple Varieties for Different Uses

Variety	Flavor and Texture	Fresh and in Salads	Pies	Sauces	Baking	Freezing (Slices)	Main Season
Cortland	Mild, tender	Excellent	Excellent	Very good	Good	Very good	Oct. to Jan.
Red Delicious	Sweet, mellow	Excellent	Poor	Fair	Poor	Fair	Sept. to May
Golden Delicious	Sweet, semifirm	Excellent	Very good	Good	Very good	Very good	Sept. to Apr.
Gravenstein	Tart, crisp	Good	Good	Good	Good	Good	July to Sept.
R. I. Greening	Slightly tart, firm	Poor	Excellent	Excellent	Very good	Excellent	Oct. to Mar.
Jonathan	Tart, tender	Very good	Very good	Very good	Poor	Very good	Sept. to Jan.
McIntosh	Slightly tart, tender	Excellent	Excellent	Good	Fair	Good	Sept. to Apr.
Rome Beauty	Slightly tart, firm	Good	Very good	Very good	Excellent	Very good	Oct. to Apr.
Stayman	Tart, semifirm	Excellent	Good	Good	Good	Good	Oct. to Mar.
Winesap	Slightly tart, firm	Excellent	Good	Good	Good	Very good	Oct. to June
Yellow Transparent	Tart, soft	Poor	Excellent	Good	Poor	Poor	July to Aug.
York Imperial	Tart, firm	Fair	Good	Very good	Good	Good	Oct. to May

Source: Reference 31

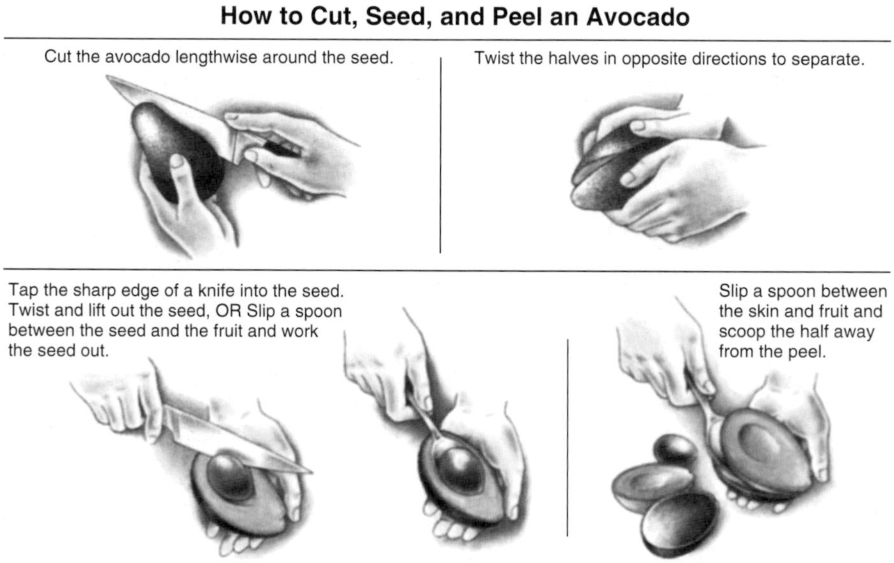

How to Cut, Seed, and Peel an Avocado

Cut the avocado lengthwise around the seed.

Twist the halves in opposite directions to separate.

Tap the sharp edge of a knife into the seed. Twist and lift out the seed, OR Slip a spoon between the seed and the fruit and work the seed out.

Slip a spoon between the skin and fruit and scoop the half away from the peel.

FIGURE 21-6 Preparation of avocado. *(Courtesy of California Avocado Commission)*

available year-round. The United States imports bananas primarily from Costa Rica, Guatemala, Ecuador, Colombia, and Honduras [25]. Until they are fully ripe, they should be kept at room temperature; they do not ripen normally if chilled. When the skin is green tipped, bananas are best for cooking—baking or broiling. Fully yellow bananas are good for eating or using in salads and desserts. Brown-speckled skins indicate very ripe fruit that is excellent for mashing and use in baked products. Skins with a gray appearance have been cold damaged and may not ripen properly.

Bananas have been used to reduce fat in baked products. A fat replacement system composed of banana flakes, cellulose gel, and cellulose gum is being developed. It can replace up to 100 percent of the fat in a baked product

and up to 50 percent of the sugar. No banana flavor is perceptible [32].

Berries

Blueberries, strawberries (Plate XII), cranberries, raspberries, and blackberries are some of the varieties of berries available in the marketplace. Blueberries are available from May through September. Large blueberries are cultivated varieties, and the small berries are wild. High quality blueberries should be a dark blue color with a silvery bloom, which is a natural protective coating [38]. Blueberries should be washed immediately before use, not before storage. Cranberries are marketed primarily from September through January and are a seasonal favorite in many homes over the fall and winter holidays.

Strawberries should have a full red color, firm flesh, and the cap stem attached [38]. Like other berries, strawberries should be washed just before use. Washed berries will mold rapidly during storage. Strawberries are most readily available in May and June, although with transportation from warmer U.S. climates and imports, strawberries can be purchased nearly throughout the year. Blackberries, raspberries, dewberries, and loganberries are similar to each other in structure. These berries should be plump and tender, but not mushy, when purchased.

Cherries

Cherries may be sweet or tart. Tart cherries are generally used for cooking and baking. Sweet cherries include the dark red Bing and Lambert varieties and the yellowish Royal Anne (Plate X). Cherries do not ripen off the trees and decay rapidly. The marketing season, depending on the variety, is from May to August for domestic cherries.

Citrus Fruits

Oranges, lemons, grapefruit, limes, tangerines, kumquats, and tangelos (which are a cross between a tangerine and a grapefruit) are included in the citrus fruit classification. The chief producing areas of these fruits in the United States are Florida, California, Texas, and Arizona. Citrus fruits are a valuable and reliable source of vitamin C in the diet and are also noted for the tart and appetizing flavor they contribute to fruit desserts and salads (Figure 21-7).

In addition to being graded, citrus fruits can be classified on the basis of size, depending on the quantity of fruit required to fill certain standard-size containers. Cartons holding 40 pounds are often used. Large oranges may be 56 count (56 oranges per carton); medium oranges may be 88 count; and small oranges may be 113 or even 138 count. Large oranges are usually about 4 3/8

FIGURE 21-7 Caramelized orange and grapefruit segments with raspberry sorbet make a tasty, light dessert. *(Courtesy of © Sunkist Growers, Inc. All rights reserved.)*

inches in diameter, medium ones about 3 1/2 inches, and small ones about 2 1/2 inches.

Except for making juice, large oranges are generally preferred by consumers over small ones. The most common criticisms of large oranges are excessive waste from thick skins and excessive expense. Large fruit is often classed as fancy fruit, and its price may increase at a faster rate than the edible portion. For juice extraction, small sizes or ungraded stock may be most economical. Generally the juice from small oranges is higher in total solids, acid, and vitamin C than that of medium-size fruit and higher still than that of large fruit. In the purchase of citrus fruits, it should be noted that fruits that are relatively thin skinned, firm, and heavy in relation to size usually contain more juice than thicker-skinned and lighter-weight products. Russeting, which is a tan, brown, or blackish mottling or speckling on the skin of some Florida and Texas oranges and grapefruit, has no effect on eating quality.

Two principal market varieties of oranges are the Valencia and the navel. For juice extraction, the Valencia orange is often preferable; whereas for slicing or sectioning, the navel orange may be more satisfactory. The navel orange is distinguished by the formation of a navel at the apex or blossom end of the fruit. This formation appears to be a tiny orange within a larger one. The navel orange is available from California and Arizona from November until early May and has no seeds, less juice, and a thicker, somewhat more pebbled skin than the Valencia—a skin that is easily removed by hand, and segments that separate easily. Florida and Texas oranges are marketed from early October until late June and include several varieties including Valencias in the spring. Most of the Florida Valencias have yellow skins, much juice, and light-colored juice and pulp. All Valencias have seeds, but the California Valencia has only a few. Valencia oranges have a tendency late in the season to turn from a bright orange to a greenish tinge, particularly around the stem end. This change in color affects only the outer skin and is not an indication of maturity.

Some varieties of grapefruit are classed as seedless, although they often contain a few seeds, and some are seeded. Some grapefruit varieties have white flesh, whereas others have pink or red flesh. Although Florida is the main producer of grapefruit, it is also supplied by Texas, California, and Arizona. Grapefruit is available all year but is most abundant from January through May.

Grapes

Grapes are the leading fruit crop in the world and the second in the United States. California produces 97 percent of the table grapes in the United States. Grapes are also grown in Arizona. Over half of all the grapes grown in the United States are used to make wine [26]. European types of grapes, which are firm fleshed and very sweet, include the Thompson seedless (an early green grape), the Tokay and Cardinal (early, bright red grapes), and the Emperor (late, deep red grape). American types of grapes have softer flesh and are very juicy. The blue-black Concord variety is commonly marketed and is unexcelled for juice and jelly making.

Grapes are picked ripe and thus do not ripen in storage. Like many other fresh fruits, grapes should not be washed until ready to use [23]. When selecting, look for grapes that are well colored, plump, and firmly attached to the stem. Stems should be green and pliable [23].

Melons

Melons (Figure 21-8) are among the most difficult of fruits to select. No absolute guide for selection is available, but desirability is indicated by such qualities as ripeness, heaviness in relation to size, usually a characteristic aroma, characteristic color, and freedom from abnormal shape, decay, and disease. The ripeness of some melons, such as honeydew, crenshaw, casaba, and cantaloupe, is indicated by color and a slight yielding to thumb pressure on the bud end or on the surface. If the melon was mature when picked, it usually shows a round dent where the stem broke away from the melon.

Most cantaloupes are firm and not completely ripe when first displayed in markets. Holding them a few days at room temperature allows the completion of ripening. The color of uncut watermelons is probably the best key to ripeness. A yellowish underside, regardless of the green color of the rest of the melon, is a good sign. Other guides in selection might be a relatively smooth surface, a slight dullness to the rind, and ends of the melon that are filled out and rounded. In cut watermelons, desirable characteristics include firm, juicy flesh with a good red color, dark brown or black seeds, and no white streaks.

Foodborne outbreaks of salmonellosis have been traced to melons, the organisms probably having been introduced from the unwashed rind into the fruit during the cutting of the melons. The microbes will multiply on cut melon if temperatures are suitable for growth [33]. Outbreaks of E. coli 0157:H7 have been associated with cantaloupe from salad bars. The melon may have been inoculated with E. coli by cross-contamination from another product, such as beef, during kitchen preparation. Thus, measures to prevent or reduce the risk of foodborne illness include thorough washing of the melon before cutting, use of good personal hygiene and kitchen sanitation practices, and refrigeration of prepared melons. Food safety was discussed in Chapter 3.

Peaches and Nectarines

Both nectarines and peaches originated in Asia thousands of years ago. Although peaches and nectarines are similar, they each are distinct fruits (Plate X). Nectarines do not have the fuzzy coat of peaches but will have a strong "peachy" fragrance even when only partially ripe. Nectarines and peaches may be freestone or clingstone. The flesh of freestone varieties will separate readily from the flesh and are used most commonly for eating fresh or freezing. The flesh clings to the pit of clingstone varieties. Clingstones are used primarily for canning [38].

An important factor in peach quality is the stage of maturity at harvest. Peaches will ripen off the tree. Once

FIGURE 21-8 A variety of melons include the cantaloupe (front and center); the casaba on the left; a cut honeydew behind the casaba; a cut crenshaw in the rear center; and a Santa Claus or Christmas melon in the upper right. (*Courtesy of the United Fresh Fruit and Vegetable Association*)

(a)

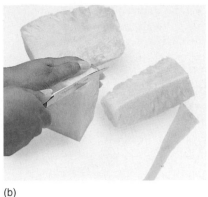
(b)

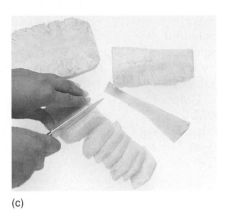
(c)

FIGURE 21-9 Fresh pineapple may be quickly prepared. (a) Slice off leaves and stem end, then stand fruit upright, and cut the peel off in vertical strips. (b) Cut the fruit in quarters, then remove the woody core as shown. (c) Cut the flesh into wedges or chunks as desired. *(Source: Reference 15)*

picked, they are immediately dipped in ice water to remove the field heat and stop the ripening process. Then they are stored at 34° to 40°F (1° to 5°C) to keep ripening at a minimum and retard decay. If peaches are picked too soon, they will never ripen after cold storage, and they will lack flavor [21].

The best quality peaches have a good yellow undercover and yield slightly to finger pressure. The appearance of a peach does not always indicate the flavor, however. Peaches should be eaten at optimum ripeness. To avoid chill injury (brown flesh, lack of juice, and poor flavor), a peach that is not fully ripened should not be refrigerated until after it has been held at room temperature and ripened [23].

Plums

Many varieties of plums are available (Plate X). The peak season for domestic plums is June through September [23]. Plums from Chile are available during the winter months. Plums are highly perishable, thus must be purchased and used at peak quality or spoilage will occur. Plums should range from firm to slightly soft when purchased. Plums that are not fully ripened should not be refrigerated but instead held at 55° to 70°F (13° to 21°C) [23]. Once ripened, the plums may be refrigerated but should be used within a few days.

Pears

The most popular type of pear is the Bartlett. Other varieties of pears, grown primarily in Washington, Oregon, and California, are Anjou, Bosc, Winter Nellis, and Comice (Plate XI) [38]. Pears are generally firm when purchased but will soften at room temperature. Fully ripe pears will be sweet and juicy.

Pineapple

The pineapple plant bears its first fruit 18 to 22 months after planting. Each plant produces a single 4- to 5-pound fruit. The fruit is harvested when the appropriate stage of

sweetness is reached. The optimum flavor is a balance between sweet and tart. The sweetest flavor and brightest yellow color are found at the base of the pineapple fruit.

A ripe pineapple has a rich fragrance. It springs back slightly when touched. Color may vary from green through brown to gold and is not an indication of ripeness [23]. A hard pineapple should be kept at room temperature until it becomes fragrant and springy. Once ripe, it can be refrigerated.

Pineapple is a popular canned fruit. It may be processed as chunks, cubes, slices, or crushed. The preparation of pineapple is shown in Figure 21-9.

Variety Fruits

Many uncommon fruits have appeared on the market throughout the United States in recent years. As consumers become more familiar with these fruits and learn to use them, their market share increases. *Kiwifruit* or Chinese gooseberries, grown in New Zealand and California, have become a widely accepted fruit in a relatively short time. Californian kiwifruit are marketed from October through May. Although the furry skin is edible, most prefer to peel the skin to reveal the bright green flesh (Figure 21-10). Ripe kiwifruit should yield slightly to the touch.

FIGURE 21-10 Kiwifruit has a brown, fuzzy skin on the exterior and bright green flesh and small black seeds on the interior. *(Source: Reference 15)*

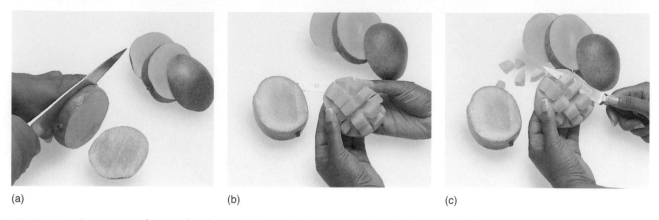

(a) (b) (c)

FIGURE 21-11 A mango can be pitted and cut as follows: (a) Cut along each side of the pit. (b) Cube each section by making crosswise cuts through the flesh, just to the skin. Press up on the skin side to expose the cubes. (c) Cut the cubes off for use in salads and other dishes. *(Source: Reference 15)*

Coconuts are familiar to American consumers as packaged flaked coconut. However, fresh coconuts may be preferred in some recipes due to their flavor. Fresh coconuts are prepared by puncturing the shell through one of the eyes with a ice pick or knife, then draining out the coconut milk. Next the shell is baked in a 350°F (177°C) oven for approximately 15 minutes and placed in the freezer until cool, but not frozen. This heating and cooling process will allow the flesh to separate easily from the shell. Any brown skin remaining on the coconut may be pared or peeled off. The coconut milk and the shredded coconut may be used in many dishes.

Mangoes have become popular with the interest in Caribbean and Mexican cuisines. Mangoes have a spicy, sweet flavor with an acidic note. These fruits are grown primarily in Florida, Mexico, Haiti, and Puerto Rico [22]. Ripe mangoes should have yellow, orange, or red skins and should yield to gentle pressure [23]. The preparation of mangoes is shown in Figure 21-11 [15].

Papayas are available year-round, with supplies peaking in May through September (Plate XIII). A ripe papaya should yield to gentle pressure [23]. Papayas may be eaten raw or used for sauces, sorbets, pickles, or chutneys [15]. The seeds are edible, providing a peppery flavor with a crunch (Figure 21-12). Other exotic fruits

include *passion fruit*, a small egg-shaped fruit with an intense and tart flavor that goes well in fruit punches and juices. The pulp can be used in desserts such as sherbets, ice creams, and parfaits. The *prickly pear* can be chilled, the spines and peel cut away, sliced, and served raw. The *cherimoya* can be chilled, cut in half, and eaten with a spoon. The *carambola*, or star fruit, is recognized by the star shape of a slice. It is very tart, with a sweet-sour flavor, and is often cooked. Only the sweet, juicy seeds of *pomegranates* are consumed. To prepare, bend back the rind and pull out the seeds from the surrounding white membrane [23]. Other variety fruits are listed in Table 21-2 and pictured in Plate XIII.

STORAGE OF FRESH FRUITS

Temperature and Storage Conditions

Fresh fruits are perishable and most require refrigeration. Soft fruits such as berries keep better when spread out on a flat surface. Citrus fruits, except lemons which keep best at a temperature of 55° to 58°F (13° to 15°C), should be refrigerated and covered to avoid drying out. Avocados and bananas are so injured by chilling that they discolor and lose the power of ripening even if they are later held at warmer temperatures. In fact, bananas are injured when held at temperatures lower than 55°F (13°C) *before* ripening. If these and other tropical fruits must be held for any time, they should be ripened before being stored at colder temperatures. After ripening, avocados hold best at about 40°F (4°C). Similarly, peaches, nectarines, and plums should not be refrigerated until after fully ripened, because these fruits can also be cold damaged and fail to ripen properly.

Several fruits, such as grapes and berries, should not be washed until just before use. Grapes and blueberries have a natural protective bloom which should not be washed off prior to storage. Berries, in general, tend to

FIGURE 21-12 Papaya has golden to reddish-pink flesh with dark silver black seeds. *(Source: Reference 15)*

Fruit and Vegetable Imports and Country of Origin Labeling

The variety of fresh fruit in the food supply is supported by the growth of imports. Imported fresh fruit permits Americans to enjoy tropical fruits and fresh fruits that are out of season domestically. In 2005, Mexico, Canada, Chile, China, and Costa Rica were the leading sources of fruit and vegetable imports into the United States [18]. Bananas and table grapes are the top fruit imports.

At this time, some fruits are labeled with the country of origin. In 2008, mandatory country of origin labeling for fruits and vegetables is expected [14]. Labeling was scheduled to take effect originally in 2004, but it was delayed in light of controversy about the cost and the value consumers would place on such labeling. ■

---

mold more rapidly if washed too far ahead of consumption. Apples are not necessarily damaged by advanced washing; however, many apples are marketed with a light coat of wax that will become hazy in appearance if the apples are washed then stored [23].

Methods to Extend Storage

Controlled Atmosphere. Fruits are actively metabolizing tissues and, even after harvesting, continue to respire—to take in oxygen and give off carbon dioxide. Cold temperatures reduce the rate of metabolism and retard ripening but do not completely stop these processes. An additional aid in controlling metabolic changes and thus lengthening the possible storage period, or extending the shelf life, for certain fruits is *controlled atmosphere (CA) storage* [17].

In controlled atmosphere storage, the oxygen in the atmosphere is reduced below the usual 21 percent level to as low as 2 to 3 percent. This markedly lowers the rate of cell metabolism and aging in the fruit, delaying the changes that would normally occur and prolonging the storage life. For example, changes in pigments, decrease

in acid, loss of sugars, and breakdown of pectic substances are retarded in apples stored at 38°F (4°C) in an atmosphere containing 5 percent carbon dioxide and 3 percent oxygen [13].

Each stored fruit has a critical oxygen level, below which injury to the tissues occurs. Relatively high carbon dioxide levels are sometimes used with the low oxygen atmosphere. However, the atmosphere is carefully monitored, and excess carbon dioxide, produced by the fruit during respiration, is removed so that a desirable level of carbon dioxide is constantly maintained. Temperature and humidity are also carefully controlled. Apples that have been stored in a controlled atmosphere are commonly marketed as CA apples. CA apples offer a level of freshness and quality not otherwise available in the spring and summer months.

Modified Atmosphere Packaging. Another preservative technique closely related to controlled atmosphere storage is *modified atmosphere packaging*. This technique involves a modification of the oxygen, carbon dioxide, and water vapor levels in the air surrounding a product

FOCUS ON SCIENCE

Coatings on Fruit to Preserve Quality

Different materials have been used and researched to preserve quality of fruit and vegetables. Wax, parafilm, hydrocolloids, lipids, and protein materials have been explored and

researched for use on fruits and vegetables to extend shelf life. A thin coating of the aforementioned materials is applied on the fruit's surface to decrease the respiration rate (senescence), thereby delaying the ripening process and at the same time maintaining quality, freshness, and extending shelf life.

in a package. A semipermeable film used for packaging allows the natural process of respiration by the fresh or minimally processed fruit to reduce the oxygen and increase the carbon dioxide content of the atmosphere around the fruit. As modified atmosphere packaging systems have become more sophisticated, the package can allow oxygen in while allowing the escape of excess carbon dioxide, water, heat, or ethylene gas [5]. A low storage temperature must still be maintained, because changes in temperature may affect the gas concentrations in the package [30]. The initial microbial load on the fruit or vegetable should be as low as possible, because the modified atmosphere does not stop the growth of microorganisms [16].

Irradiation. Irradiation of fresh fruits, at controlled dosages, can delay senescence, reduce mold growth, and extend shelf life. It may be used in combination with modified atmosphere treatment. Irradiation was discussed further in Chapter 3.

FRUIT JUICES

Fruit juices are an important means of utilizing fresh fruits. The commercial fruit juice industry in the United States has had a spectacular rise since 1925, with fruit juice consumption in this country surpassing that of fruit processed in all other forms. Much of the increase in fruit juice production has been with citrus fruits. After the commercial introduction of frozen orange concentrate in 1945 and 1946, this product became the leader among processed fruits in terms of fresh-weight-equivalent consumed. A large share of the Florida orange crop is used to produce juice. Although frozen concentrated orange juice continues to be produced, single-strength, not-from-concentrate is the most popular for consumer use [8].

Sources of Vitamin C

Some edible material is lost when juices are extracted and the juice is strained, resulting in the total nutritive value of the whole fruit being somewhat higher than the juice coming from it. Regardless, little loss of vitamin C occurs during preparation and processing of citrus juices. The freezing and subsequent storage of orange juice at $0°F$ ($-18°C$) or below does not cause a significant loss of vitamin C, especially if aeration before freezing is avoided. Possibly because of their high acidity, citrus juices tend to retain vitamin C well.

Apple, cranberry, grape, pineapple, and prune juices and apricot nectar contain little vitamin C unless they are fortified with the added vitamin. Vitamin C is added to some juices, partly to increase the nutritive value and partly to improve their appearance, flavor, and stability during storage. The added vitamin C in noncitrus juices may be less stable than the vitamin naturally present in citrus juices. In opened containers stored in a refrigerator, the vitamin C in canned orange juice was found to be more stable, up to 16 days, than that in vitamin C–fortified

HEALTHY EATING

Fruit Juice or Fruit Drink—What Is the Difference?

To be labeled "fruit juice," the product must contain 100 percent juice. When a beverage contains less than 100 percent juice, the name of the product must include the term "drink," "beverage," or "cocktail." Furthermore, any product with a name, label, or flavoring that suggests the product is made with fruits or vegetables must provide a statement of the total percent of juice. Therefore, a product that appears to contain juice, but does not, must indicate "contains no juice."

A product labeled orange juice is a "juice," and a statement indicating 100 percent juice will be found on the label. In contrast, a grape juice drink or cranberry juice cocktail uses the term "drink" or "cocktail"; these products will be less than 100 percent juice. Some of these drinks, beverages,

and cocktails may contain only 20 or 10 percent juice. Although fruit drinks, beverages, and cocktails may contain 100 percent of the daily value of vitamin C because of fortification, consider the other nutrients contained in a juice that will be absent from a drink. Read the ingredient labels, which often show that water and added sugar are key ingredients. It should be noted that cranberry juice cocktail is often sold as a cocktail or blend because of the very tart nature of cranberries.

So what's the difference between a juice and a drink? It is all in the percentage of actual juice! ■

Source: References 40, 41

canned apple juice [19]. Additional vitamin C, calcium, and other nutrients are added to some orange juices.

Juice Processing

Orange Juice. In preparing orange juice concentrate, the fruit is graded, washed, and sanitized before it enters the juice extractors. Juice may be extracted using a machine similar to a kitchen juicer that cuts the fruit in half, then presses the half against a rotating burr. In another commonly used method of extraction, the fruit is penetrated by a porous tube and then crushed. Next the juice is processed to remove the seeds and membranes. During this step, the amount of pulp can be controlled to produce high- or low-pulp juice [8].

Single-strength, not-from-concentrate juice is pasteurized to reduce pathogenic or spoilage organisms and eliminate enzymes that can promote the separation of the pulp [8]. It is then rapidly chilled at about 35°F (1.7°C) before packaging. The package may be lined with a special material that prevents loss of volatile flavor substances in the packaging [9]. Some processors may use aseptic bulk storage in the marketing of chilled, pasteurized, single-strength orange and grapefruit juices.

Frozen, concentrated orange juice is heated to a greater extent than single-strength pasteurized juice. Thermally accelerated short-time evaporators are commonly used to concentrate orange juice. With this process, water is removed until the soluble solids are about 65 percent [8]. To produce the standard three-parts-water-to-one-part juice sold in the marketplace, the juice may be diluted to 42 percent. Frozen concentrated juices should be kept at 0°F (−18°C) or below, both in market channels and in the kitchen, to retard losses of nutritive value, flavor, and other quality characteristics.

Noncitrus Juice. Noncitrus juices may be sold as concentrates. One major advantage of fruit juice concentrates is that the volume is greatly reduced and shipping and handling costs are less. Concentrated juices and fruit purées may be dehydrated by roller or drum drying, spray drying, or foam mat drying. Although some flavor loss occurs in drying, the final product is acceptable.

Cloud or Haze. Cloud or haze, which is a desirable characteristic of citrus juices, is a complex mixture of cellular organelles, color bodies, oil droplets, flavonoids, and cell wall fragments which include pectic substances, cellulose, and hemicelluloses. Pectic substances play an important role in stabilizing the cloudy appearance and also contribute a characteristic body or consistency. Present in cell walls and between cells, pectic substances are released into the juice when extracted. In citrus juices, this cloud may be stabilized by flash-heating to a temperature higher than usual pasteurization temperatures to destroy pectin esterase enzymes that destabilize the cloud by allowing calcium ions to link de-esterified pectin molecules into aggregates which settle out.

Apple and grape juices, however, are preferred as clear. Pectin-degrading enzymes (pectinases) may be added to these juices to aid in the processing. The treated juice is less viscous and can be easily filtered. This process is called *clarification*. The color and flavor of the clarified juices are also stabilized. To increase yield, while still maintaining or improving the quality and stability of the final juice product, enzyme preparations that contain cellulase and hemicellulase activity, as well as pectinase, may be used. These additional enzymes act on the fruit tissue to macerate and further liquefy in order to extract more soluble solids [10]. Additionally, haze formation in apple juice may commonly be the result of a protein–tannin haze [3].

Pasteurized or Treated Juice. Pasteurization is a short, high-heat treatment used to kill potential pathogens in fruit juice. About 98 percent of the juice sold in the United States is pasteurized. Juices also may be treated with ozone, high pressure, or other methods to reduce pathogens. The treatment of juice to kill pathogenic pathogens is important for safety as illustrated by the outbreak of E. coli 0157:H7 illness in 1996 that was linked to the consumption of unpasteurized apple juice. Additional foodborne outbreaks have occurred since 1996 [34].

Juice that has not been pasteurized or otherwise treated to reduce potential pathogens may be sold but must have a label warning the public it has not been pasteurized and may contain harmful bacteria. Juices treated with ozone, UV irradiation, surface treatment of the fruit, or high pressure treatment may be marketed as fresh squeezed. These juices will not be labeled as pasteurized, but unlike unpasteurized and untreated juices, these treated juices are not required to use the warning label [34]. See Chapter 3 for more information on food safety.

DRIED FRUITS

When fruits are preserved by drying, the water content is reduced to less than 30 percent. In some fruits, such as dates, figs, raisins, pears, and peaches, the water content may be only 15 to 18 percent when fruits come from the drying yards and dehydrators. As marketed, these fruits usually contain 28 percent or more moisture; therefore, they may be partially rehydrated before being packaged for the consumer. Dried fruits with 28 to 30 percent water are examples of intermediate-moisture foods that are plastic, easily chewed, and do not produce a sensation of dryness in the mouth, but are microbiologically stable. In vacuum-drying, the water content is reduced to very low levels, about 2.5 to 5 percent. Fruits dried by this method are usually stored in sealed containers to retain the low moisture levels.

Carbohydrate, caloric, and mineral values of dried fruits are higher by weight than those of the corresponding fresh fruits because of the removal of water. Also, the flavor is more concentrated than that of fresh fruit. The vitamin content of fruits is changed in drying depending on the methods of drying and sulfuring. Some fruits, such as apricots and peaches, are subjected to the fumes of sulfur dioxide gas or are dipped in a sulfite solution to prevent darkening of color and to kill insects. Sulfuring aids in the preservation of vitamins A and C, but adversely affects thiamin.

Methods and Storage

The term *dried* is commonly applied to all fruits in which the water content has been reduced to a low level. Sun-drying methods use the sun as a source of heat. Dehydration can also be accomplished by artificial heat under well-controlled conditions of humidity, temperature, and circulation of air. The sanitary practices involved in dehydration with artificial heat and the preservation of such physical properties as color, texture, and flavor in cooked dehydrated fruits may represent possible advantages for this method compared with cooked sun-dried fruits.

Vacuum-drying results in fruit with very low moisture levels, although relatively low temperatures are used in the process. Under vacuum, water evaporates at a lower temperature. These fruits usually have excellent eating quality, and they rehydrate quickly and easily. Fruits may also be freeze-dried.

Because dried fruits are greatly reduced in water content and consequently have increased sugar content, they are resistant to microbial spoilage. Light-colored fruits that have been exposed to sulfur dioxide to prevent darkening also become more insect resistant as a result of the sulfur treatment. Dried fruits should be stored in tightly closed plastic, glass, or metal containers to protect against insect infestation.

Prunes

Prunes are varieties of plums that can be dried without fermenting while still containing the pits. Two main varieties are the French plum, grown chiefly in California and France, and the Italian plum, grown chiefly in Oregon. These fruits are blue or purple on the outside, with greenish yellow to amber flesh. They have a high sugar content, so they produce a sweet-flavored prune when dried.

Before drying, plums are dipped in lye to puncture the skin and make it thinner, thus permitting rapid drying and improving the texture of the skin. Careful washing removes the lye before further processing. Some packaged prunes have been sterilized and packed hot in a package lined with aluminum foil. The residual heat in the pits seems to be sufficient to sterilize the package and also to tenderize the prune fiber to some extent, thus giving the prune its quick-cooking quality.

Prunes are classified according to size, that is, the approximate number to the pound. It is generally conceded that large prunes of the same variety and quality as small prunes have no better flavor than the small fruit.

Large fruit may be preferred for dessert purposes, but it must be remembered that price usually increases with size at a faster rate than the amount of the edible portion. For the making of pulp, small and medium sizes are more economical.

The laxative value of prunes is the result of their fiber content and of a water-soluble extractive, *diphenylisatin*, that stimulates intestinal activity. Prune juice also contains the active laxative agent.

CANNED FRUITS

Canned fruit is essentially cooked fruit that has been sealed and processed for keeping and, as such, represents a widely used convenience food. Flavors and textures are somewhat altered by cooking or canning, and vitamin values may be slightly reduced. The vitamins and minerals that go into solution are conserved because juices are usually eaten with the fruit.

Canned fruits lose nutrients and flavor less readily when stored at relatively low temperatures. If stored for prolonged periods above 72°F (22°C), they deteriorate in quality at a relatively rapid rate.

More "light" canned fruit products are being marketed in response to increasing concerns about health and nutrition. These fruits contain less sugar than the traditional canned products, often because they are packed in their juice with no sugar added. The grading of commercially canned fruits was discussed in Chapter 20, and home canning is explained in Chapter 30.

FROZEN FRUITS

The fruits that are most commonly frozen are cherries (both sour and sweet), strawberries (both sliced in sugar and whole), boysenberries, loganberries, red and black raspberries, blueberries, and sliced peaches. Frozen mixed fruits, rhubarb, plums, black mission figs, cranberries, pineapple, apple slices, and some varieties of melon are also available in some markets. Most frozen fruits are not heated during processing but are often frozen in a sugar syrup. Commercially, small whole fruits may be frozen quickly in liquid nitrogen. No sugar or syrup need be added in this process.

Frozen apples, cherries, and some other fruits used for pies should be partially defrosted to facilitate their use and to drain some of the juice. Otherwise, they are used in the same manner as fresh fruit. If the fruit has been frozen with some sugar or syrup, allowance must be made in adding sugar to prepared products. Rhubarb should be cooked without defrosting. Blueberries and other fruits frozen dry can be used either frozen or thawed in cooked dishes.

Frozen fruits should be moved quickly in market channels with proper precautions for maintaining cold temperatures. They should also be moved quickly from the market to the kitchen freezer to avoid partial thawing and consequent loss of quality on refreezing. For best quality retention, frozen fruits need to be stored at a temperature of 0°F (−18°C) or lower.

All frozen fruits to be used raw should be barely defrosted. If all the crystals have thawed, the fruit tends to become flabby, particularly when using berries or peaches in shortcake, which is often warm when served. The warm shortcake may complete the defrosting. Some frozen fruits, such as peaches and apples, tend to turn brown during frozen storage and after thawing. Use of vitamin C in the syrup aids in the retention of natural color by preventing oxidation.

PREPARATION

Most fresh fruits are generally considered to be at their best in the raw, ripened state and are thus served without cooking when possible. Fresh fruits should always be washed to remove dust, soil, some spray residues, and some microorganisms. See Chapters 3 and 4 for more information on food safety and food regulation. If fruits that brown easily, such as bananas and apples, are to be peeled and cut, they should be dipped in or covered with lemon juice, pineapple juice, or solutions of vitamin C mixtures so that discoloration does not readily occur. The acids and/or antioxidants in these solutions retard the enzyme activity and/or tie up oxygen to prevent brown compounds from forming. Placing the fruit in a sugar syrup or even immersing it in water retards browning to some degree by excluding air. Enzymatic oxidative browning was discussed in Chapter 20.

Citrus fruits are generally peeled, sectioned, sliced, or wedged. When peeling oranges, it is desirable to remove as much of the white membrane between the peel and the fruit as possible because this membrane is bitter and may be tough. The peel may be removed with a knife (Figure 21-13), or oranges may be placed in boiling water briefly and then peeled by hand. This method is best if several oranges are to be peeled because the oranges will peel more easily and quickly when heated.

Some recipes call for orange or lemon zest. Zest is the colored portion of the rind, excluding the white part of the rind. Zest may be prepared using a tool that cuts thin strips of the rind or by using a fine grater.

For some fruits, including green apples and rhubarb, cooking is sometimes desirable or necessary because they are more palatable and digestible when cooked. Cooking is also one way to add variety as fruits are included in daily menus. Overripe fruits may be further preserved by cooking.

Effect of Cooking Medium

The softening and breakage of pieces of fruit or vegetable during cooking is influenced by the cooking medium. If it is desirable to have fruits retain their shape, they may be cooked in a sugar syrup. If sauce is the expected end product, cooking in water hastens disintegration of the tissues.

The reason for these differences lies with the imbalance between sugar concentrations inside the fruit and in the cooking liquid. In uncooked fruit tissue, the cell walls act as *semipermeable membranes*, allowing passage only of water. If there is a difference in sugar concentration within and outside the cells, such as when sugar is sprinkled on fresh strawberries, water exits the cells in an attempt to dilute the concentrated sugar solution that has formed on the surface of the fruit: thus, juice forms when strawberries are left to stand with sugar. The reverse occurs, that is, water enters fruit cells, when fruit is placed in plain water, because the concentration of sugar within the cells is greater than in the water outside the fruit. This movement of water through a semipermeable membrane is *osmosis*.

As fruit is heated, however, the permeability of the cell walls changes to allow not only the passage of water but also the movement of sugar and other small molecules. Simple diffusion then occurs as sugar and water move into or out of tissues. Therefore, in fruit slices cooked in a sugar syrup more concentrated than the 12 to 15 percent sugar solution found naturally in most fruits, sugar moves into the cells, and water moves out into the cooking liquid in an attempt to equalize the sugar concentration throughout (Figure 21-14). Because fruits shrink slightly, they appear shiny and translucent, and the tissue is firm. A desirable proportion of water to sugar for most fruits is about two to one by measure. When the shape of the fruit pieces is to be retained, the fruit should not be stirred during cooking.

Conversely, when fruit is cooked in water alone, sugar moves from the more concentrated solution within the cells to the plain surrounding water, and some water moves back into the tissues (Figure 21-14). Fruits that are to be cooked to a smooth pulp are stewed in water until they attain the desired softness, after which sugar is added. These fruits may be stirred during cooking. The same principles described earlier apply to vegetables cooked in water containing sugar versus plain water. The sugar content of most vegetables, however, is low, and they are usually enjoyed without sweetening.

Contrary to these general principles, some varieties of fruits do not cook to a smooth pulp in any circumstance, and not every variety holds its shape well when cooked in syrup. The final product obtained is therefore partly a matter of choice of variety.

General Cooking Recommendations for Fruits

Cooking of fruits will proceed most evenly when the pan is covered during cooking. The heat source should be regulated so that the liquid in the pan simmers or boils slowly.

Rhubarb is easily overcooked. Using a small amount of water and careful, slow cooking, only until the pieces are tender and partially broken, produces a desirable sauce

To section citrus fruits, pare deeply enough to remove the membrane that covers the pulp.

Cut toward the center along the membrane and remove the section.

For a basketball method of peeling, first slice off the stem end of the orange. Without cutting into the meat, score the peel with a knife. Pull the peel away with the fingers, leaving the white inner skin that clings to the fruit.

FIGURE 21-13 Methods of preparing citrus fruit for serving. *(Courtesy of © Sunkist Growers, Inc. All rights reserved.)*

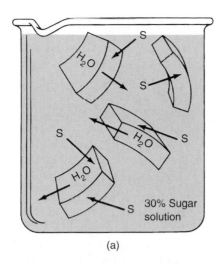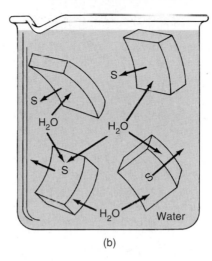

FIGURE 21-14 Cooking of fruit. (a) Apple slices cooked in a sugar solution will retain their shape. Sugar (S) moves into the fruit cells, and some water (H_2O) comes out into the surrounding sugar solution in an attempt to dilute it. (b) Apple slices cooked in plain water tend to break up more as water moves into the cells, expanding them.

from rhubarb. Apples sliced for cooking may sometimes include the skin, for added color, flavor, and nutritive value. After cooking, the fruit may be run quickly through a strainer or food mill to increase the smoothness of the pulp if applesauce is being prepared.

Excess sugar in fruit sauces mars the delicate flavor of many fruits. The desirable amount is often difficult to determine, especially when fruits are made into pies and other products, in which the amount of sugar may not be added gradually until the desired amount is determined. The same variety of apple or other fruits varies in acidity from season to season and at different times during the storage period.

Cooking Dried Fruits

Some of the water that has been removed from fruit in the drying process is returned by soaking. Cooking after soaking softens the tissues. Soaking in hot water for a short time results in good water absorption. The dried fruit, covered with water, may be brought to a boil, immediately covered and removed from the heat source, and then left to stand for 20 to 30 minutes (no longer than one hour). After soaking, the fruit is simmered until the desired degree of softness is achieved. Some commercially available dried fruits are tenderized and have a higher moisture content. They require little or no soaking and a short cooking period.

The higher sugar content of dried fruits reduces the need for additional sweetening. The small amount of sugar that is sometimes used is added at the end of the cooking period. The degree of acidity of the fruit determines the amount of sugar to be used. For example, dried apricots, being much more tart, require more sugar than prunes.

Baking

Some fruits lend themselves well to baking. The aim is to have the fruit hold its form but be cooked until tender throughout. Apples and pears are often baked in their skins (cores removed) to hold in the steam that forms within the fruit and cooks the interior. Pared slices or sections may be baked in a covered casserole (350° to 400°F/ 177° to 204°C oven temperature). Bananas are sometimes baked, although in general they are preferred raw. Rhubarb can also be baked and will keep its shape.

Glazing

A rangetop method known as *glazing* can be satisfactorily used to cook apples. The apples are cored as for baking, and a slit is cut in the skin all around the apple at right angles, or parallel, to the core. The apples are then placed in a saucepan with 1/4 cup of water and 1/8 cup of sugar for each apple in the pan. They are covered and cooked over low heat. The apples are turned once while cooking and are cooked until tender. The cover is removed for the last minute before the apples are done.

Broiling

Bananas, grapefruit halves, and pineapple slices are some of the fruits that can be satisfactorily broiled. To modify the bland flavor of cooked bananas, lemon juice or broiled bacon may be added.

Sautéing

Apples, bananas, and pineapple slices may be prepared by sautéing, or cooking quickly in a small amount of fat. A flavorful fat such as butter is preferred.

CHAPTER SUMMARY

- Using a botanical definition, fruits are produced from flowers and are the ripened ovaries and adjacent tissue of plants. In common usage, fruits are fleshy or pulpy, often juicy, usually sweet, with fragrant, aromatic flavors.

- Fleshy fruits may be classified as simple, aggregate, or multiple. Simple fruits include citrus fruits, drupes, and pomes. Drupes are fruits in which a stone or pit encloses the seed. Pomes have a core.

- Americans consume less fruit than the two cups daily recommended by the *2005 Dietary Guidelines for Americans*. Oranges, apples, wine grapes, bananas, and table grapes are the top five fruits consumed.

- Fruits comprise an edible portion combined with some refuse. The chief energy nutrient is carbohydrate, which occurs primarily as sugars. Fruits are valuable in the diet due to their vitamin, mineral, phytochemicals, and fiber content. Vitamins C and A are prevalent in many fruits.

- The pigments that give fruits their characteristic color are the same as those in vegetables. The yellow-orange carotenoids and the red-blue anthocyanins predominate. The interaction of pigments should be considered when mixing fruit juices. Anthocyanin pigments tend to deteriorate on storage. Methods to prevent enzymatic oxidative browning must be used with some cut fruits.

- The flavor of fruits may be described as tart, fragrant, and sweet. Fruits owe their characteristic flavors largely to aromatic compounds. Other components contributing to fruit flavor include aldehydes, various alcohols, organic acids, essential oils, sugars, mineral salts, and phenolic compounds. Malic, citric, and tartaric acids are common. Oxalic acid is found in rhubarb.

- Fruits are living systems. Respiration occurs in the cells of the fruit as they carry on normal metabolic processes. Distinct changes occur in fruits during ripening: (1) a decrease in green color and development of yellow-orange or red-blue colors, (2) a softening of the flesh, (3) the development of characteristic pleasant flavors, and (4) changes in soluble solids such as sugars and organic acids.

- Ethylene gas is a ripening hormone produced by the cells after the fruit is mature. Bananas are harvested before ripening and are exposed to ethylene gas to speed ripening. Some fruits, such as apples, emit ethylene gas and thus will promote ripening of other fruits stored nearby.

- A wide variety of fruits are available. Some varieties of apples are best for eating out of hand and others for baking. Avocados, bananas, peaches, nectarines are some fruits that should be refrigerated only after ripening. Berries should be washed just before use to avoid premature spoilage. Cherries may be sweet or tart. Tart cherries are generally used for baking. Citrus fruits are high in vitamin C and include oranges, lemons, grapefruit, limes, tangerines, kumquats, and tangelos. Grapes may be consumed as table grapes or made into wine or jellies.

- Many kinds of melons are available, including honeydew, crenshaw, casaba, cantaloupe, and watermelon. The peak season for domestic plums is June through September. Plums should be slightly soft when ripe. A popular type of pear is the Bartlett. Pears will soften at room temperature after purchase. A ripe pineapple has a rich fragrance and springs back slightly when touched. Kiwifruit, fresh coconut, mangoes, papayas, passion fruit, prickly pear, cherimoya, and carambola are fruits that some consumers may consider to be exotic.

- Cold temperatures are desirable for many fruits to slow the rate of metabolism and extend shelf life. Additional methods to extend storage included controlled atmosphere storage, modified atmosphere packaging, and irradiation.

- Fruit juices may be processed as a frozen fruit juice concentrate or a single-strength juice. Cloud or haze is an undesirable characteristic in some juices such as apple juice. Pasteurization or other methods of treatment are important for microbiological safety.

- When fruits are preserved by drying, the water content is reduced to less than 30 percent. Vacuum-dried fruits may have a water content of 2.5 to 5 percent. Fruits may be dried by sun-drying or by artificial heat in controlled conditions of humidity, temperature, and circulation of air.

- Canned fruit is cooked fruit that has been sealed and processed for keeping. Some fruits such as cherries and berries are commonly frozen. Frozen fruits to be used raw should be barely defrosted when served so the fruit will not become excessively soft prior to use.

- When preparing fruits, fresh fruits should be thoroughly washed and peeled, sliced, or trimmed as needed. Some fruits such as apples and bananas will brown readily and should be treated to prevent enzymatic oxidative browning.

- Some fruit may be cooked. To maintain the shape of a fruit, cook in a sugar syrup. If a sauce is the desired product, then cook the fruit in water to hasten the disintegration of the tissues. These different effects are the result of the imbalance between the sugar concentration inside the fruit and in the cooking medium.

- Dried fruits may be soaked in water to rehydrate prior to cooking. The higher sugar content of dried fruits makes the use of additional sweetening unnecessary.

- Other methods of cooking fruits include baking, glazing, broiling, and sautéing.

STUDY QUESTIONS

1. What is a *fruit?* Define a *pome* and a *drupe.* Give examples of each.

2. (a) What is the usual percentage of water found in fruits? What is the usual percentage of carbohydrate? What type of carbohydrate usually predominates in ripe fruits?

   (b) List and be able to recognize fruits that are good sources of vitamin C.

3. Describe common characteristics of fruit flavor. List four types of chemical substances that contribute to the flavor of fruits.

4. (a) What pigments are often present in fruits?

   (b) Explain why pigment content should be considered when mixing various fruit juices to make a fruit drink.

5. Describe the major changes that occur during the ripening of fruit.

6. (a) Describe the usual characteristics of fruits of good quality and suggest appropriate storage conditions to maintain quality.

   (b) What factors are generally monitored during controlled atmosphere storage of fruits and vegetables? Why is this type of storage effective for some fruits?

   (c) Explain what is involved in modified atmosphere packaging.

7. (a) Describe the major steps in the production of orange juice concentrate.

   (b) What contributes to the stability of the hazy cloud characteristic of orange juice? To what treatment may the juice be subjected during processing to maintain cloud formation? Explain why this treatment is effective.

   (c) What special processing that involves enzyme action may be used to produce a sparkling clear fruit juice? Describe and explain.

8. Why are some fruits treated with sulfur before drying? Describe some effects of this process on nutritive value.

9. (a) Compare the general effects of cooking fruits in water and in sugar syrups. Explain what is happening in each case.

   (b) Suggest an appropriate procedure for cooking dried fruits. Explain why you would recommend this procedure.

   (c) Describe several additional methods for cooking fruits.

SALADS AND GELATIN SALADS 22

At one time the term *salad* may have applied only to green leaves or to stalks that were eaten raw (Figure 22-1). Although today we often refer to green leafy vegetables, such as lettuce, endive, and romaine, as *salad greens*, the term *salad* has a much broader meaning. It includes mixtures of meat, fish, poultry, cheese, nuts, seeds, and eggs, as well as all kinds of vegetables and fruits. Often, salads are made with raw or uncooked foods, but they are certainly not limited to these items. A salad may be composed entirely of cooked or canned products, or mixtures of raw and cooked items may be used. A dressing is usually served either mixed with or accompanying the salad. The dressing may be rich and elaborate, or it may be as simple as lemon juice. Congealed salads, prepared with gelatin, that contain a variety of ingredients are yet another type. Gelatin is also used in other recipes including desserts.

The salad is an appealing form in which to use fresh fruits and vegetables. The element of crispness, which most salads introduce, provides an opportunity for greater variation in texture for many menus. Tartness and

appetizing, fresh flavors are easily added to the meal in the form of salads.

In this chapter, the following topics will be discussed:

- Salad use in meals
- Nutritional contribution of salads
- Salad ingredients and preparation
- Gelatin structure, characteristics, and manufacture
- Effect of temperature, concentration, and other factors on gelation
- Gelatin salads and desserts

SALAD USE IN MEALS

The salad may be served at numerous points in a meal. It often accompanies the main course, but is sometimes served as a separate course, either between the main course and the dessert or before the main course. Some salads, especially those with fruit and nuts that are dressed with a rich or somewhat sweet dressing, are appropriately served for dessert. For luncheon or supper, the salad may be the main course, with the remainder of the menu being built around it (Figure 22-2).

The type of salad served depends on its use or position in the meal. The dinner salad is usually a light, crisp, tart accompaniment to the meat or other entree. Heavier, high-calorie salads, such as macaroni and tuna fish or meat and potato, are not appropriately included in a meal already composed of filling, high-protein foods. Instead, meat, poultry, fish, egg, cheese, and potato salads that are combined with some crisp vegetables and relishes are suitable for use as a main course. Some small fish salads of high flavor, such as crab, shrimp, lobster, and anchovy, may serve as an appetizer, similar to cocktails and canapés made with these fish. Usually the amount of fish used is not large, and it is combined with crisp, flavorful foods.

Potato salad may be an accompaniment to cold meats on a supper platter. Used in this way, the starchy potato

FIGURE 22-1 This salad of sweet and bitter greens with balsamic mustard vinaigrette is simple yet flavorful. The greens in this salad include watercress, romaine, and Bibb lettuce.

FIGURE 22-2 A pasta, black bean, and chicken salad with cheese cubes, summer squash, and green peppers is a delicious summer entrée. *(Courtesy of Land O'Lakes)*

functions as it does in the dinner menu. Potato salad is sometimes served hot, as was the original German potato salad.

The fruit salad is particularly suitable as an appetizer or dessert. If kept tart and not too large, it may also be appropriately used as an accompaniment in the dinner menu. A fruit salad can be a popular choice for refreshments at an afternoon or evening party. When a fruit salad is used as dessert, it may be served with a cheese plate and crisp crackers or a sweet creamy yogurt dressing.

NUTRITION

With the emphasis on increasing our consumption of fruits and vegetables as recommended by the *2005 Dietary Guidelines for Americans,* salads can make an impressive contribution to accomplishing this goal. Usually there is a wide variety of produce from which to choose. The majority of salads prepared from fresh fruits and vegetables are comparatively low in kilocalories (not including the dressing, of course) but are important sources of minerals, vitamins, and fiber. Fruit and vegetable salads may also be an excellent source of so-called phytochemicals or "neutraceuticals," which are thought to contribute to a decrease in degenerative diseases such as heart disease and cancer [12]. The green leafy vegetable salads are especially valuable for iron, vitamin A, vitamin C, and beta-carotene.

Starchy salads, such as potato, are higher in kilocalories than salads made with fruits and succulent vegetables. Meat, fish, egg, and cheese salads furnish chiefly protein, although some crisp vegetables often form a part of such mixtures.

The final caloric value of salads, as consumed, is greatly influenced by the type and quantity of dressing used. The amount of fat, usually contained in the salad oil or cream, is the major factor influencing the caloric content of dressings. Cooked dressings, particularly those made with water or milk, have a lower caloric value than mayonnaise and French dressings. French and a variety of commercial salad dressings average 60 to 80 kilocalories per tablespoon. Mayonnaise contains about 100 kilocalories per tablespoon. There are, however, many reduced-fat dressings on the market. Special fat-free dressings may

Salads—Served through the Ages

The salad is not a modern preparation. Green leaves were used by the ancient Romans. Other nationalities from the fifteenth century onward favored the use of flavorful herbs and raw vegetables. The introduction of salads into England was apparently made by Catherine of Aragon, one of the wives of Henry VIII and a daughter of Ferdinand and Isabella of Spain. The origin of present-day meat and fish salads was probably the salmagundi of England, used for many years as a supper dish. This meat dish made use of numerous gar-nishes that are used today, such as hard-cooked eggs, pickles, beets, and anchovies.

The influence of southern France is apparent in the use of French dressing for salads. The original dressing was made of olive oil and was seasoned to perfection. Spain has made the pepper a popular salad vegetable, and the Mediterranean countries introduced garlic flavor. The original German potato salad has many variations today. ■

furnish as little as 6 kilocalories per tablespoon. See Chapter 10 for more information about salad dressings.

SALAD INGREDIENTS

Salad Plants

The best-known salad plant is lettuce, of which there are several types. Iceberg lettuce is a crisphead type and is the most popular of the salad greens. Butterhead types, including Bibb and Boston, have soft, pliable leaves and a delicate, buttery flavor. Another type of lettuce, romaine, or Cos, is characterized by leaves that appear coarse yet are actually tender, sweet, and more flavorful than iceberg lettuce. Leaf lettuce, including both green and red varieties, is a still different type, with leaves loosely branching from the stalk. Endive or chicory, escarole, spinach, sorrel, mustard, and dandelion may be used as salad greens offering yet another dimension to the flavor, taste, and appearance of a salad. Watercress and Chinese cabbage or

HEALTHY EATING

Add a Salad and Reap Nutritional Benefits

Salads can help us to consume more fruits and vegetables and gain the benefit of more vitamins, fiber, and phytochemicals in our diet. Others suggest that consuming a high-volume but low-calorie salad such as green salad with a low-calorie dressing can help to decrease calorie intake. But does it really work?

A group of researchers, using the Third National Health and Nutrition Examination Survey that included 9,406 women and 8,282 men, found the consumption of salads and raw vegetables was positively associated with higher serum levels of folic acid, vitamins C and E, lycopene, and α- and β-carotene [7].

Another group of researchers examined the influence of salad consumption on satiety and how the consumption of a salad as a first course affected food consumption during the remaining meal. Forty-two women participated in this study. These researchers found that consuming a low-energy dense salad as a first course reduced intake during the entire meal [6]. Choose the first course wisely, however; a high-calorie but small salad may result in an overall increase in calories at the meal. ■

FIGURE 22-3 Many different kinds of greens are available: (a) Boston, (b) iceberg, (c) leaf, (d) red oak leaf, (e) romaine, (f) radicchio, (g) dandelion, and (h) spinach.

celery cabbage are also highly acceptable as salad plants. Shredded cabbage may make up the entire salad, as in cole slaw; it may serve as a foundation or bed for other salad ingredients; or it may be part of a vegetable salad mixture. Figure 22-3 shows some of the common salad greens and a more detailed description of several of these was provided in Chapter 20.

Other, very flavorful ingredients include tomatoes, cucumbers, radishes, red and green peppers, green onions, and celery. Many of these vegetables are particularly valuable for their crisp textures. Raw turnip is another interesting ingredient for salads. It can be used in thin slices (often allowed to curl in cold water), sticks, or fine shreds. Raw carrots can be used similarly. Small pieces of raw cauliflower and broccoli florets are also desirable salad components. Foods with very pronounced flavor, such as pineapple, should be used sparingly in mixtures to avoid masking more delicate flavors.

Cooked beets have a desirable texture and flavor for some types of salads; however, because of the soluble red pigment present, they may mar the color of other salad ingredients. If used carefully and kept separate from other ingredients, beets are valuable additions.

Edible flowers may be used as salad ingredients or as garnishes. For example, nasturtium blossoms can be filled with a seafood stuffing and served on a bed of dark green leaves. See Chapter 8 for more information about edible flowers as well as fresh herbs that may be used as salad ingredients.

SALAD PREPARATION

Preparation

Prechilling all salad ingredients, including dressings, canned items such as canned tuna or olives, and vegetable ingredients is a beneficial preparation step. If salad materials are kept ready in the refrigerator, salad preparation becomes a simple, easy procedure. Furthermore, as a food-safety practice, salads will chill more rapidly after preparation if ingredients have been prechilled.

Cleanliness of hands and work areas are of prime importance when preparing salads, especially because many salads are consumed raw and cooking will not destroy pathogenic organisms introduced through poor sanitation. Once the preparation area is sanitary and clean, ingredients should be carefully and thoroughly washed. When washing greens, submersing in cool water then lifting the greens out of the water away from the soil is recommended. Greens should be washed more than once, with extra care given to those greens such as endive and savoy spinach that may easily trap dirt. A salad spinner is helpful in removing excess moisture. Other kinds of vegetables should be carefully cleaned with a small brush and water to remove soil.

For maximum retention of freshness and nutritive value, many salad ingredients should be prepared shortly before the salad is to be made and served. Some vegetables such as green leaves and celery, however, will be crisp and fresh if they are washed, closely wrapped, and chilled in the refrigerator for several hours. The water that clings to leaves and stems after washing helps to develop crispness if enough time is allowed for chilling in the refrigerator. All excess water, however, should be removed from the vegetables before storage to decrease the likelihood of spoilage.

Preparation of Salad Ingredients

Fruit Preparation.   Sections of citrus fruits can be prepared well in advance without significant quality loss. Citrus fruit sections used in salads are usually left whole, but many fruits are cut into bite-sized pieces (Figure 22-4). Canned pineapple, peach, and pear can be cut easily with a fork and may be left whole. Fresh fruits such as apples, bananas, pears, peaches, and nectarines will need to be dipped in an acidic fruit juice, such as diluted orange juice, or lightly sugared to prevent enzymatic oxidative browning unless cut immediately prior to consumption. More information was provided about enzymatic oxidative browning in Chapters 20 and 21.

Vegetable Preparation.   When preparing salad plants, all inedible portions should be removed. Cutting out the core or stem from a head of iceberg lettuce speeds the absorption of water and simplifies separation of the leaves from the head. Firmly striking the core of a head of lettuce on a hard surface loosens the core for easy removal.

Vegetables are left whole or are diced, shredded, sliced, or sectioned, depending on the type of vegetable (Figure 22-5). When vegetables are used in relish or crudité trays, some vegetables such as fresh green beans should be lightly blanched, then chilled. Other vegetables such as carrots are served raw in sticks or sliced thinly and placed in ice water to curl. Because carrots are very firm, they are best used as tiny sticks, thin slices, or shredded, depending on the type of salad. Tiny beets can be left whole; cauliflower and broccoli can be used in separate florets. Tomatoes are often peeled and left whole or cut into wedges or slices. Cucumbers are sliced or diced depending on the type of salad. Celery is usually diced but may be cut into sections that are prepared to form celery curls or cut into shreds. Although green beans in a combination salad are usually cut into short lengths, they may be left whole. Asparagus tips can also be used.

FIGURE 22-4 This salad is composed of sectioned Minneola tangelos, baby field greens, toasted walnuts, crumbled blue cheese, and a grilled chicken breast. *(Courtesy of © Sunkist Growers, Inc. All rights reserved.)*

(a)

(b)

FIGURE 22-5 Fresh vegetables, sometimes called crudités, can be beautifully displayed as a salad or as an accompaniment for a salad. (a) Radish roses, green peppers, celery curls, carrot curls, cauliflower, and carrot sticks. *(Courtesy of Western Growers Association)* (b) Carrots, broccoli, sugar snap peas, cucumbers, zucchini, mushrooms, and cherry tomatoes are artfully arranged with a dip. *(Courtesy of the American Egg Board)*

Peppers are often cut into rings but may be coarsely chopped or slivered for some purposes.

Potatoes used for salad should be of a variety that holds its form when diced. Mealy potatoes tend to form a starchy mass when made into salad; therefore, waxy potatoes are a better choice. Potatoes may be diced before or after cooking; however, dicing before boiling will reduce the amount of handling that is needed after the potatoes are cooked.

In general, vegetables in most mixed salads should be cut into bite-sized pieces so that the use of a knife is not needed when eating the salad. The preferred size of vegetables will vary, however, depending on preferences and the recipe. In most cases, salad ingredients should not be finely minced, because soft foods that are too finely cut tend to form a paste when mixed with salad dressings. Vegetables are often cut finer for molded gelatin salads than for other salads. Cabbage, regardless of how it is used, is more attractive and becomes better seasoned if it is finely shredded. Coarse shreds of cabbage are difficult to chew, particularly if it is a variety that does not become crisp easily.

Meat, Poultry, and Fish Salad Preparation. Meats and chicken used in salads are usually diced, but fish is most often coarsely flaked with a fork. Small shellfish, such as shrimp, may be left whole or diced. Canned salmon and tuna fish are difficult to prepare in a way that retains the form of pieces, although tuna is more firm than salmon. Fish canned with a considerable amount of oil can be washed off with hot water before being chilled. Thus, water-packed fish is preferable, or alternately, the oil may become part of the dressing.

Marinated Salads

Meat, fish, starchy vegetables, and whole firm pieces of more succulent vegetables may be improved by *marinating*, which is the process of coating foods lightly with a dressing or oil (a *marinade*) and letting the mixture stand in the refrigerator for an hour or more before being made into a salad. The major purpose of marinating most salads is to improve the flavor. Many flavorful marinades can be prepared using specialty oils, vinegars, wines, fruit juices, herbs, and spices.

Some pasta salads are marinated overnight in the refrigerator. Due to the absorption of marinade, it is important to cook the pasta only until "tender to the bite," or the pasta will be too soft. Leafy vegetables generally cannot be marinated because they wilt. Also, the color of the vegetables in the salad should be considered. For example, a fresh green bean or broccoli salad will not maintain a bright green color if marinated in an acidic

marinade for more than a few hours (see Chapter 20). Excess marinade is drained off when the salad is prepared.

Arrangement

Whether elaborate or simple, salads should be attractively arranged (Figures 22-4 and 22-6). Whole stuffed tomatoes, halves of peaches or pears, slices of pineapple, and gelatin molds necessarily take on a more fixed appearance than combination salads made from cut pieces. Color can be added by mixing a colorful ingredient in the main body of the salad or by adding a bed of greens and a garnish. The use of contrasting colors and shapes is especially effective. However, some colors may not combine attractively—for example, the clear red lycopene pigment of tomato and the purplish red pigment of beets.

Garnishes

Garnishes are not used solely as decorations but are also edible constituents that form part of the salad. Ripe or stuffed green olives, radishes, and small cheese-stuffed celery stalks often have the effect of garnishes when placed on lettuce beside the salad proper. Sprigs of watercress or parsley, which introduce a darker green color and an interesting leaf design, add appeal to many vegetable salads. Strips of pimiento or a bit of paprika add a touch of color, but too much paprika may be unattractive. Overgarnishing should be avoided. Plates XII and XV illustrate several different types of salads and their arrangements.

Dressing the Salad

A wide variety of salad dressings is available. Most salad dressings are examples of emulsions, either temporary or permanent, and were discussed in Chapter 10.

Certain types of salad, including potato, macaroni, meat, chicken, and fish, and some fruit salads, are improved by being left to stand in the refrigerator for a time with the dressing. These salads are often mixed with the dressing and chilled for several hours before serving. Shredded cabbage may be improved by brief contact with the dressing. For most other leafy salads, however, the texture, appearance, and flavor are better if the dressing is added when the salad is served. The dressing may coat all of the salad ingredients, as when the dressing is applied to

FOCUS ON SCIENCE

Acidic Marinades and Chlorophyll

The addition of an acid to a marinated salad containing a green (chlorophyll) vegetable will turn the chlorophyll to an olive green color (pheophytin). A portion of the chlorophyll

compound undergoes a chemical change because of the amount and contact time with the acidic ingredient.

(a)   (b)

FIGURE 22-6 (a) This Salade Niçoise was prepared by carefully arranging tomato wedges, sliced cucumbers, green beans, wedged hard-cooked eggs, quartered new potatoes, blanched green peppers, artichoke hearts, and fresh grilled tuna over a colorful bed of greens. (b) An attractively arranged mix of baby greens and tomatoes creates a light and juicy summer salad.

a large amount of salad in a bowl either at the table or immediately before serving. The ingredients are tossed with a serving spoon and fork until they are well coated with dressing. Light mixing is necessary to retain the characteristic form of each of the salad plants in the mixture. Alternatively, a small amount of dressing may be applied to individual servings before the salad is placed on the table, or the dressing may be passed for individuals to serve themselves.

Salads and Food Safety

Sanitary food-handling practices and good temperature control are important when preparing and serving salads. The cutting, dicing, and arranging of salads must be done in a way to minimize cross-contamination from hands, cutting boards, kitchen sinks, or other sources. All fruits and vegetables, including melons, need to be stored at or below 41°F (4°C) once peeled, sliced, or otherwise broken apart.

The hot summer months and the popularity of picnics combine to encourage the holding of meat and starchy salads with mayonnaise or creamy salad dressings for extended periods without chilling. Any salad composed of high-protein, neutral pH, and high-moisture foods will spoil readily if temperature abused. Thus, salads have caused outbreaks of food poisoning when held too long without adequate refrigeration. This is why it is particularly important that salads be refrigerated or iced in a cooler, if taken to a picnic, to prevent the growth of any undesirable microorganisms (see Chapter 3). Although mayonnaise has historically been implicated in the outbreak of foodborne illness in some salads, commercial mayonnaise, which is acidic, is not the culprit—rather it is the lack of cleanliness during preparation and temperature control that are to blame.

GELATIN AND GELS

A gel is a special kind of structure that might be described as something between a solid and a liquid. Gels occur in a variety of food products, including most starch-thickened puddings and pie fillings, egg custards, fruit jellies, and gelatin molds used either as salads or as desserts. Starch-thickened mixtures and egg custards are treated in other chapters; gelatin is discussed in this chapter. First, however, let us discuss certain characteristics common to all gels.

Gel Structure and Characteristics

Gels are composed mainly of fluid, but they behave much like rigid solids. These interesting characteristics appear to be the result of their special type of structure. Gels contain long, thin chainlike molecules, called polymers, that are joined or cross-linked at random spots to produce a three-dimensional structure something like a pile of dry brush (Figure 22-7).

Examples of polymers that form gels are (1) the linear protein molecules of gelatin; (2) the amylose fraction of starch with its long chain of glucose molecules linked together; (3) the large protein molecules of egg, which are composed of long chains of amino acids; and (4) the pectin molecules, which are long chains of galacturonic acid and its methyl esters. Pectin is responsible for the setting of fruit jellies and jams.

The polymer network that is responsible for gel formation is immersed in a liquid medium to which it is attracted. In a sense, it traps the liquid in its chainlike network. The liquid and the polymer network then work together—the liquid keeps the polymer network from collapsing into a compact mass, and the network keeps the liquid from flowing away.

HOT TOPICS

Food Safety and Fresh Fruits and Vegetables

Eating fruits and vegetables is associated with a healthy lifestyle. So, what hazards could possibly be connected to these favored foods? Actually, there are several points in the production of fruits and vegetables at which contamination could occur. Potential concerns can include contamination with pathogens directly from improperly treated manure fertilizer or irrigation water that is microbiologically unsafe. In addition, postharvest operations, such as packing, can present potential contamination [5].

In 2006, a foodborne illness outbreak involving fresh spinach occurred. Although in this outbreak no specific error could be identified, it was evident the field had become cross-contaminated with a cattle operation in the local area. A need to examine and further improve agricultural practices to minimize the risk of E. coli 0157:H7 outbreaks has been identified by the FDA [9].

Fresh-cut produce, which has become very popular in the marketplace, can present special food-safety considerations. The process of cutting up fruits and vegetables removes the protective skin and increases the surface area available for contamination. Also, the living tissues begin to respire more rapidly when cut, decreasing the period of peak quality. Modified atmosphere packaging (MAP) helps to control these changes if done properly, and these foods must be kept under refrigeration.

Various washing and sanitizing processes are used in the packing of fresh vegetables and fruits, and newer technologies are being studied. Methods to remove pathogens include physical removal, chlorine dioxide, acidified sodium chlorite, acidic compounds, and ozone. Use of irradiation is another possibility [1], and good manufacturing practices (GMPs) and Hazard Analysis and Critical Control Points (HACCP) programs continue to be the primary pathogen control strategy [5].

Not to be overlooked is your role in the safety of produce. A number of consumers report not washing produce before use, rarely washing melons before preparation, and storing their produce below raw meats in the refrigerator [4]. All of these are hazardous practices that have resulted in foodborne illness. So do your part and follow good food-safety practices when preparing your fresh fruits and vegetables. ■

Gels are sometimes described as mixtures that hold the shape of the container after they are removed from it; however, gels vary from being soft to fairly rigid [8]. Most food gels are relatively soft but are resilient or elastic.

Environmental conditions affect the characteristics of many gels. Some gels shrink or swell with changes in temperature. Many food gels liquefy or melt over a relatively narrow temperature range. The melting and solidifying constitute a reversible process in such gels as gelatin mixtures. Gels may also be affected by pH, becoming softer with greater acidity. Some gels exhibit syneresis. This may occur in overcooked egg mixtures and in some starch and gelatin gels stored in the refrigerator for a few days.

Manufacture of Gelatin

Gelatin is obtained by the hydrolysis of collagen, which is found in the connective tissues of animals. The chief sources of commercial gelatin are animal hides, skins, and bones. The most significant raw material source for edible gelatin in North America is porkskin [2]. The conversion of collagen to gelatin is, in fact, a fundamental part of the cookery of less tender cuts of meat. As cooked meat cools, the formation of a gel from the gelatin produced in the meat juices is often visible.

The industrial manufacture of gelatin comprises three basic stages: (1) the raw material is treated to separate the collagen from the other components present; (2) the purified collagen is converted into gelatin; and (3) the gelatin is purified, refined, and recovered in dry form [13]. The conditions for manufacturing edible gelatin include an acid and a lime treatment, followed by washing and sterilization, to ensure a product of high sanitary quality (Figure 22-8) [2]. The dry form in which gelatin is marketed also favors a low bacterial count. When gelatin is hydrated, however, and used to make a gel, the moist product is a favorable medium for bacterial growth and should be refrigerated as are other perishable foods.

Some concern has been expressed about the safety of gelatin as a result of bovine spongiform encephalopathy (BSE), which is sometimes called "mad cow disease." BSE is a progressive neurological disorder of cattle that was first found in Great Britain in the late 1980s. Epidemiological and laboratory evidence have suggested a causal

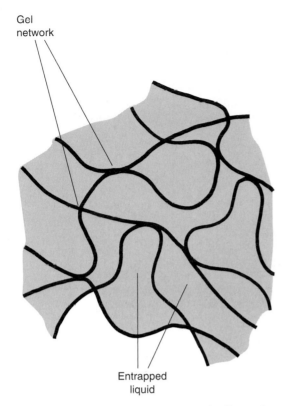

Gel network

Entrapped liquid

FIGURE 22-7 When a gel is formed, a network of long, thin molecules traps liquid in its meshes.

relationship between a variant form of Creutzfeldt-Jacob disease (CJD) in Great Britain and BSE [10]. Guidance has been provided to the industry regarding the sourcing and processing of gelatin to reduce potential risks of BSE [11].

Gelatin is marketed in both granular and pulverized forms. Fine division of the gelatin allows it to be dispersed more easily in hot water. Gelatin mixes, which include sugar, acid, coloring, and flavoring substances, usually contain pulverized gelatin. A good quality of plain gelatin should be as nearly flavorless and odorless as possible.

Uses

Edible gelatin, which has met specified standards of quality, is used to form a basic gel structure. This structure may carry fruits, vegetables, cheese, meats, whipped cream, nuts, and other appropriate foods as various salads and desserts are prepared (Figure 22-9). It may also act as a foam stabilizer in whipped products and as a thickener in some puddings and pies. It is used in the making of certain candies, such as marshmallows, and in some frozen desserts in which it acts to control crystal size.

Gelatin is a highly efficient gelling agent. As little as 1 to 3 parts of gelatin in 97 to 99 parts of water produces a moldable gel.

Nutritive Value

Gelatin is a protein food derived from animal sources, yet it is a protein of low biologic value. It lacks several essential amino acids, particularly tryptophan. Regardless of the quality of protein, the amount of gelatin required to form a gel is so small (one tablespoon per pint of liquid) that its nutritive contribution is insignificant. One tablespoon of granulated gelatin furnishes about 30 kilocalories and 9 grams of protein.

Some gelatin desserts and salads may provide the means by which significant amounts of fresh fruits and vegetables are incorporated into the diet, but it is the added foods rather than the gelatin that are nutritionally valuable.

GELATIN HYDRATION, SWELLING, AND DISPERSION

Dry gelatin hydrates and swells when soaked in cold water. The water molecules are attracted to the gelatin molecules and form a water shell around them. This aids in later dispersion of the gelatin in hot water.

The ease, rapidity, and extent of swelling depend on several factors. If the gelatin is finely granulated or

FOCUS ON SCIENCE

What Is the Difference between Gel Formation Caused by Eggs and That Caused by Pectin?

Eggs

Eggs form a gel based on the sequence of amino acids that are present on the protein chain. Heat allows the chain to denature (unravel), and liquid is trapped. Calcium enhances the mechanism to occur, as observed in baked custard.

Pectin

Pectin, because of its chemical make up, requires both a particular amount of sugar (at least 55 percent) and an acidic pH (3.0 to 3.2) for the chain mechanism to occur to trap liquid and form a gel.

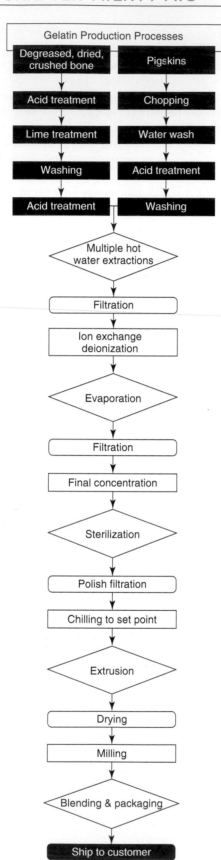

FIGURE 22-8 Gelatin production process. *(Adapted from Gelatin Manufacturers Institute of America, Reference 2)*

pulverized, more surface is exposed to the water. Consequently, the rate of swelling is increased. Directions on packages of most gelatin mixes suggest omitting soaking the mix in cold water and adding boiling water directly to the pulverized gelatin, which has previously been mixed with sugar or nonnutritive sweeteners and flavorings.

The degree of acidity or alkalinity, the kinds of salts present, and the presence of sugar all influence the swelling of gelatin. Sugar and certain salts inhibit swelling, whereas other salts accelerate it. Because the fruit acids and sugar used for flavor are usually not added until the unflavored gelatin has swelled and been dispersed, they do not affect these processes.

When the temperature of soaked gelatin is elevated to 95°F (35°C) or higher, the gelatin molecules separate or disperse. Some hot liquid can be added to the hydrated gelatin to disperse it, after which the remaining liquid can be added cold; or the hydrated gelatin can be suspended over hot water until dispersion takes place, after which all remaining liquid can be added cold. Boiling all of the remaining liquid before adding it is unnecessary and undesirable for two reasons: More time is required to cool the mixture, and some volatile flavor substances are lost with high temperatures.

GELATION

Gelation means gel formation or the stiffening of a gelatin dispersion. Gelation does not occur at a fixed or clearly defined point, but rather is a gradual process. It evidently involves the joining or linking of gelatin molecules in various places to form the three-dimensional "brush-heap" structure that is typical of gels (see Figure 22-7).

Effect of Temperature

Different samples of gelatin set at different temperatures, but all require cooling below the temperature of dispersion, which is 95°F (35°C). Gelatins that require a low temperature to solidify tend to liquefy readily when brought back to room temperature. Gelatin dispersions that have set quickly because they were subjected immediately to very low temperatures also melt more readily at room temperature than similar gelatin mixtures that set at somewhat higher temperatures.

A gelatin dispersion may remain liquid at temperatures that would ordinarily be low enough for gelation if rapidly cooled. Adding ice cubes to the cold water to speed the setting process and then refrigerating is an example of rapid cooling that is sometimes used to set gelatin quickly. If more time is allowed, however, and ice is not used, gelation occurs at a higher (warmer) temperature.

Gelation also occurs more quickly at a cold temperature if the gelatin dispersion stands at room temperature for a time before being chilled. Temperatures required for the solidification of a gelatin dispersion vary from less

Fish Gelatin and Plant-Based Gelatin Substitutes

Some individuals may prefer to use gelatin derived from sources other than pork or beef. Those who follow a vegetarian diet or who avoid pork or beef for religious reasons avoid foods prepared with gelatin or seek other options. Gelatin may be made from fish. Gelatin derived from fish usually has lower melting and gelling temperatures compared to conventional gelatins [3]. These differences are more pronounced when the type of fish used is a cold-water fish as opposed to a warm-water fish. In general, fish gelatins can be more similar to gelatins made with pork skin if the concentration of fish gelatin is increased [14].

Agar and carrageenan are additional options for those who prefer to avoid gelatin made from meat as well as fish. Agar and carrageenan are derived from seaweed and thus are plant based. Compared to other gelatins that melt at temperatures below body temperature, agar and carrageenan gels melt at temperatures higher than body temperature [14]. ■

FIGURE 22-9 Gelatin may be served plain, with fruit, or with vegetable ingredients as is shown in this shimmering gelatin mold. *(Courtesy of United Fresh Fruit and Vegetable Association and Western Growers Association)*

than 50°F (10°C) to approximately 58° to 60°F (14° to 16°C).

Concentration

The concentration of gelatin affects not only the firmness of the gel but also the rate of setting. The higher the concentration, the firmer the gel and the faster the rate of setting.

The usual percentage of gelatin in a gelatin mold of good texture is about 1.5 or 2 percent, depending on the ingredients used in the mixture. One tablespoon (7 grams) of unflavored gelatin per two cups of liquid gives a gelatin concentration of about 1.5 percent. Beating the gelatin dispersion to a foam or sponge increases the volume sufficiently to decrease the firmness of the gel. A higher concentration of gelatin is thus required to produce a firm texture in whipped products. Very weak dispersions of gelatin, such as those used in ice creams, eventually set if given a long time and a low temperature. If excess gelatin is used in ice cream, gumminess increases with longer storage.

FOCUS ON SCIENCE

known as a *sol* (solid in a liquid). Hot liquid is then added to dissolve and disperse the gelatin. As the liquid cools, the gelatin chains come together to form a *gel* (liquid trapped in a solid).

Gelatin: A Sol and a Gel

Gelatin contains amino acids joined in a sequence to form a polypeptide chain called a *primary structure*. When coarse dry gelatin hydrates and swells when soaked in cold water it is

Gels become stiffer with longer standing. Unless a relatively high concentration of gelatin is used, it is usually desirable to allow gelatin mixtures to stand several hours or overnight at a low temperature to develop optimum stiffness.

Degree of Acidity

The fruit juices and vinegar that are frequently added to the gelatin mixtures used for desserts and salads increase the acidity of the dispersions. Too high a concentration of acid can prevent gelation or cause the formation of a soft gel, even when a fairly high concentration of gelatin is present.

Lemon juice and vinegar have a more pronounced effect on gelation than tomato juice and some other fruit juices of lower acidity. Two tablespoons of lemon juice as part of one cup of liquid is usually enough for good flavor unless the dispersion is to be beaten to a foam. In this case, the flavor is diluted. This dispersion forms a more tender gel than one made without acid and yet is usually satisfactorily stiff even when no extra gelatin is added.

Chopped vegetables or diced fruits added to a gelatin mixture mechanically break up the gel and may prevent its setting into a sufficiently firm mass. If, in addition, enough acid is added to give good flavor, the resulting gel may be too weak to be molded. Use of a somewhat higher concentration of gelatin may be necessary in such circumstances. The time required for acid gelatin dispersions to set is greater than that required for neutral ones.

Effect of Salts, Sugar, and Enzymes

Salts. Gel strength is increased when milk is used as a liquid in gelatin mixtures, probably as a result of the salts present in milk. Even hard water that contains minerals produces a firmer gel than distilled water.

Addition of Sugar. Sugar weakens a gelatin gel and retards the rate of setting. Usual recipes for gelatin mixtures have been adjusted so that the weakening effect of sugar is counterbalanced by the firming effect of increased gelatin concentration.

Effect of Enzymes. The bromelain enzyme in fresh pineapple is a proteinase that hydrolyzes protein. Some other tropical fruits, including kiwifruit and papaya, also contain proteinases. If these enzymes are not destroyed by heat before the fruit is added to a gelatin dispersion, they will break down gelatin molecules so that they cannot form a gel. Because the heat of processing has destroyed the enzyme in canned pineapple pieces or juice, these products can be satisfactorily used in gelatin mixtures. Freezing does not affect the activity of the enzyme, however, and thus frozen pineapple cannot be used in a gelatin gel.

GELATIN SALADS AND DESSERTS

Fruit, Vegetable, Meat, and Fish Jellies

Before fruits, vegetables, or other solid food materials are added to a gelatin mixture, they should be thoroughly drained of juices. The juices of fruits and some vegetables may be added as part of the liquid required to disperse the gelatin. Gelatin mixtures should stand until they are thickened and just ready to form a gel before solid food materials are added to them. If the gelatin mixture is too liquid, the added pieces will float. Waiting until the mixture is thickened allows the added materials to be dispersed more evenly throughout the mixture.

Aspics

Aspic is usually a beef-flavored gelatin mixture, although fish and poultry flavors may also be used. Tomato aspic salad is made with unflavored gelatin and seasoned tomato juice. Chopped celery may be added to a tomato aspic salad. As a variation of this salad, avocado slices can be placed in the salad mold before the tomato aspic mixture is poured over them, or the aspic can be layered with a cottage cheese and sour cream mixture to which unflavored gelatin has been added. Aspic is often used to make fancy canapés that may be part of buffet platters (Figure 22-10).

FOCUS ON SCIENCE

gelatin strands which is why resetting a gelatin with acidic ingredients may be less successful. The ability for the gelling mechanism of gelatin to be reversible is very unique to gelatin; it cannot be done to starch or pectin.

My Gelatin Is Set. How Can I Add the Other Food Ingredients?

As long as no excessive acidic ingredients were added to the gelatin mixture, gelatin can be melted by setting it over boiling water, then chilled to reset. Recall that acid weakens the

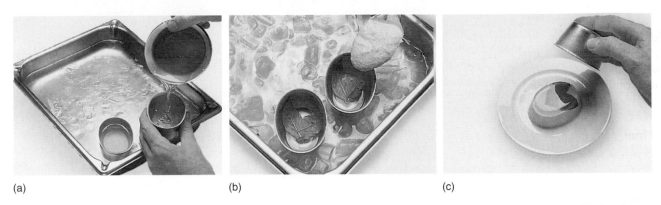

(a)   (b)   (c)

FIGURE 22-10 (a) Cool liquid aspic jelly is poured into the mold. (b) Mold is garnished with vegetable leaves, then filled with a cold mousse. (c) After refrigeration, the mold is dipped in warm water, then inverted onto a plate.

Foams and Sponges

A gelatin dispersion can be beaten to form a foam. It increases two or three times its original volume, depending largely on the stage at which the dispersion is beaten. If beating is not started until the gelatin begins to set, the volume obtained is small, and finely broken bits of solidified gelatin are evident throughout the mass. The best stage for beating is when the dispersion is about the consistency of whipping cream or thin egg whites. The gelatin mixture is elastic and stretches to surround the air bubbles. Beating is continued until the mass is very stiff, to avoid the formation of a clear layer in the bottom of the mold. However, it may be necessary to stop and chill the beaten mixture again in the middle of beating. Just the friction of continued beating can warm the mixture enough to thin it. On standing, the gelatin sets and stabilizes the foam. An increase in gelatin, sugar, and flavoring is required if the gelatin dispersion is to be beaten to a foam because the increased volume of a foam dilutes these ingredients.

To form a sponge, whipped egg white is beaten into the mixture after the syrupy gelatin mixture is beaten until it is thick and foamy. The sponge can be poured into molds and should be refrigerated until it solidifies. There is a danger of salmonella organisms being present in raw egg white. For safety, the egg whites should be pasteurized. Frozen or refrigerated pasteurized eggs may be purchased. As another option, pasteurized egg-white powder can be purchased. This ingredient is used in boxed angel food cake mixes. The dried pasteurized egg white may be more readily available at the retail level, although both dried and frozen or refrigerated pasteurized egg products are available in the commercial environment.

Bavarian and Spanish Creams

Gelatin mixtures that have stood long enough to be thickened and syrupy may have fruit pulp added and whipped cream folded into them to make Bavarian creams. Charlottes are similar to Bavarian creams but may contain a large proportion of whipped cream and are usually molded with lady fingers. Whipped evaporated or dried milk is sometimes substituted for whipped cream in gelatin desserts.

Fillings for chiffon pies have gelatin as a basic foam stabilizer. In the preparation of most chiffon fillings, a cooked custard mixture containing egg yolk and sugar is thickened with gelatin. Whipped egg whites (pasteurized) and possibly whipped cream are folded into the mixture. The gelatin sets and stabilizes the egg and/or cream foam.

Spanish cream is a soft custard made with egg yolks that is set with gelatin. The egg whites are beaten to a stiff foam and folded into the mixture after it is partially set. A danger of salmonella organisms is also present in the making of chiffon pie and Spanish cream if raw egg white, rather than pasteurized egg white, is used. These products should not be made unless pasteurized egg whites are available.

Unmolding the Gel

To unmold a gelatin gel, the mold containing the gel should be dipped for a few moments in lukewarm (not hot) water. One side of the gel should then be carefully loosened with a knife to allow air to come between the gel and the mold. The gel should slide easily from the mold. The mold can be very lightly oiled before the gelatin mixture is placed in it to facilitate removal of the gel.

CHAPTER SUMMARY

- Salads include a wide array of dishes, including mixtures of meat, fish, poultry, cheese, nuts, seeds, and eggs, as well as all kinds of vegetables and fruits. Salads may be served before the main course, as the main course, or as a dessert.

- Salads can contribute to the goal of consuming more fruits and vegetables.

- Many kinds of greens can be used in salads. Vegetables, fruits, and edible flowers provide interesting flavors, colors, and textures in salads.

- Sanitary food-handling practices are important in salad preparation to reduce the risk of foodborne illness. Most salads should be prepared shortly before the salad is to be served. When preparing salad plants, wash thoroughly and remove inedible portions. Storage of the vegetables in the refrigerator after washing will provide an opportunity for the vegetables to crisp.

- Salad ingredients may be marinated to improve flavor. The length of time salad ingredients are marinated varies with the type of ingredient. Excess marinade is drained off during final preparation of the salad.

- Salads should be attractively arranged with a consideration for color and shape. Garnishes provide decoration but are also edible constituents that form part of the salad.

- Many types of salad dressings are available. Dressing may be placed on some salads in advance, and others are added just before service or are provided on the table for individuals to serve themselves.

- Salads should be properly refrigerated and maintained cold to prevent foodborne illness. Special attention is needed to control the temperature of salads at summer picnics. Any salad composed of high-protein, neutral pH, and high-moisture foods will spoil readily if temperature abused.

- A gel is a special kind of structure that might be described as something between a solid and a liquid. Gels occur in a variety of food products, including most starch-thickened puddings and pie fillings, eggs custards, fruit jellies, and gelatin molds.

- Gels are composed of mainly fluid, but they behave much like rigid solids. Gels contain long, thin chain-like molecules, called *polymers*, that are joined or cross-linked at random spots to produce a three-dimensional structure something like a pile of dry brush. Gels may vary from being soft to fairly rigid.

- Gelatin is obtained by the hydrolysis of collagen. The chief sources of commercial gelatin are animal hides, skins, and bones. Gelatin is a protein food derived from animal sources, yet it is a protein of low biological value.

- Gelatin is a highly efficient gelling agent. It may be used in various salads and desserts, as a foam stabilizer, thickener, or to control crystal size in some candies.

- Temperature, concentration, degree of acidity, and presence of salts, sugar, and enzymes influence the strength of the gelatin gel.

- When preparing gelatins with canned fruits, the juice should be drained and then used as part of the measured liquid. Generally, solid ingredients should be added to a gelatin mixture after the gelatin has partially set, or the ingredients will float rather than being evenly dispersed.

- Aspics are usually a beef-flavored gelatin mixture, although fish, poultry, and tomato aspics may also be prepared.

- A gelatin dispersion can be beaten to form a foam. It will increase two to three times its original volume. Bavarian creams include fruit pulp and whipped cream. Spanish creams are prepared with a soft egg custard, whipped egg whites, and gelatin.

STUDY QUESTIONS

1. **(a)** Describe four or five ways in which salads may be used in a meal.

   (b) Describe 10 or 12 different salads. Suggest appropriate uses for them in a menu.

2. **(a)** Describe and be able to identify several leafy plants that can be appropriately used as salad greens.

   (b) Suggest a satisfactory way to prepare these greens for use in salads. Explain why this procedure is effective.

3. Identify and explain several food-safety practices to be observed when preparing and serving salads.

4. Marinating may be appropriate for what types of salads? Explain why.

5. Give several appropriate suggestions for arranging salads as they are served.

6. Gels of various types have common characteristics.

   (a) Give several examples of food products that are gels.

   (b) Describe the theoretical structure of a gel.

   (c) What is *syneresis?*

7. What is *gelatin?* What is its source commercially?

8. In what forms is gelatin usually sold on the market?

9. How should unflavored gelatin be treated—and why—as it is used in the preparation of gelatin gels?

10. Describe what happens as gelatin forms a gel.

11. What is the effect of each of the following on the gelation of gelatin gels?

    (a) Temperature

    (b) Concentration of gelatin

    (c) Addition of acid

    (d) Addition of sugar

    (e) Addition of raw pineapple

12. Describe major characteristics of each of the following gelatin mixtures:

    (a) Aspics

    (b) Foams

    (c) Sponges

    (d) Bavarian creams

    (e) Spanish creams

MILK AND MILK PRODUCTS* 23

Since animals were domesticated centuries ago, the milk from various species such as cow, buffalo, goat, and camel has been used in the diets of people throughout the world. Only cow's milk is of commercial importance in the United States, although small amounts of goat's milk are sold.

The dairy industry has traditionally operated under a philosophy of minimal modification of milk as it is preserved and handled in market channels. Relatively simple processes and physical separations have been used in the manufacture of various dairy products, preserving their natural properties to a large extent. These dairy products are used in our diets as beverages and ingredients in a wide array of dishes. Although butter and ice cream are dairy products, these dairy products were discussed in Chapters 10 and 12.

In this chapter, the following topics will be discussed:

- Consumption trends, nutrition, and composition
- Sanitation, grades, and processing

- Types of milk and cream products
- Food preparation with milk and cream
- Cheese manufacturing and cheese types
- Food preparation with cheese

CONSUMPTION TRENDS AND NUTRITION

Consumption Trends

According to the U.S. Department of Agriculture (USDA) food disappearance data, the annual consumption of milk, including whole, 2 percent, 1 percent, nonfat milk, and buttermilk, has decreased from 269 pounds (34 gallons) per person in 1970 to 181 pounds (23 gallons) per person in 2005 [50]. The kind of milk consumed has changed considerably over the years. Whole milk consumption has decreased while the use of fat-reduced milk has increased (Figure 23-1).

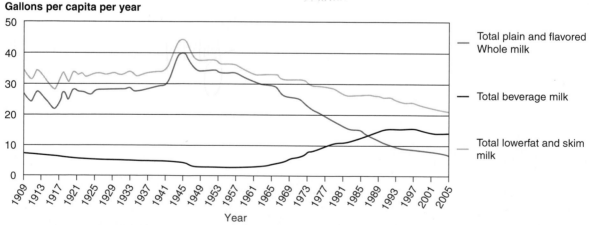

Gallons per capita per year

Low fat and fat free milk include 2% reduced fat milk, low fat milk (1%, 0.5%, and buttermilk), and skim milk (fat-free). Calculated from unrounded data.

FIGURE 23-1 U.S. per capita food availability of milk. *(Courtesy of U.S. Department of Agriculture, Economic Research Service)*

*"Milk products" in the title of this chapter refers to those other than butter and ice cream.

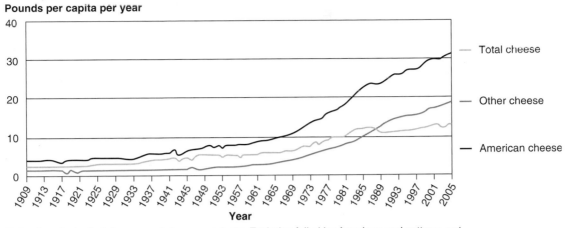

Natural equivalent of cheese and cheese products. Excludes full-skim American and cottage, pot, and baker's cheese. American cheese includes Cheddar, Colby, washed curd, stirred curd, and Monterey jack. Other cheese includes Romano, Parmesan, mozzarella, Ricotta, other Italian cheeses, Swiss, brick, Muenster, cream and Neufchatel, blue, gorgonzola, Edam, Gouda, imports of Gruyere and Emmenthaler, and other miscellaneous cheeses. Swiss cheese includes imports of gruyere and emmenthaler. Calculated from unrounded data.

FIGURE 23-2 U.S. per capita food availability of cheese. *(Courtesy of U.S. Department of Agriculture, Economic Research Service)*

TABLE 23-1 Yogurt, Sour Cream, and Cream Consumption in 1970 and 2005 in Pounds per Capita per Year

Year	Yogurt (excluding frozen)	Cream Cheese	Sour Cream
2005	8.6	8.1	4.4
1970	0.83	4.0	1.1

Source: U.S. Department of Agriculture Food Disappearance Data, Reference 50

In contrast to the downward trend in milk consumption, Americans are consuming record-high levels of cheese. According to the USDA food disappearance data, 17 pounds of cheese were available per capita in 1970 compared to 53 pounds in 2005 [50] (Figure 23-2). Americans simply seem to enjoy the taste of cheese and are increasingly choosing foods such as cheeseburgers, nachos, and an array of Mexican and Italian foods that feature cheese [43]. Pizza sales, ethnic foods, and new manufactured foods, such as frozen products and boxed dry mixes, have contributed to this increase in cheese consumption [7]. Yogurt, sour cream, and cream cheese consumption also have increased since 1970 (Table 23-1).

Nutritive Value

Three cups of milk per day are recommended in the 2005 *Dietary Guidelines for Americans* for most age groups [49]. Milk products are the major source of calcium in the diets of most Americans. The intake of calcium is associated with higher bone density, which is desirable for healthy bones. The Surgeon General of the United States reported an estimated 1.5 million Americans suffer an osteoporosis-related fracture annually, and these numbers are anticipated to double or triple by the year 2020 without positive changes in food consumption and other health habits [51].

Milk provides many nutrients in addition to calcium. The protein in milk is a complete protein, providing all of the essential amino acids. Milk is a good source of the amino acid tryptophan, which is a precursor or provitamin for niacin, so milk is a good source of niacin as well. Milk also provides significant levels of riboflavin, vitamin D (when fortified), vitamin A, phosphorus, and potassium and other nutrients. The Daily Values for a reference 2,000 calorie diet for several nutrients found in milk are presented in Table 23-2.

TABLE 23-2 Daily Values for Nutrients Found in 8 Ounces of Milk Based on a Referent 2,000-Calorie Diet

Nutrient	Daily Value (percent)
Calcium	30
Vitamin D (fortified)	25
Riboflavin	24
Phosphorus	20
Protein	16
Vitamin B$_{12}$	13
Potassium	11
Vitamin A	10
Niacin Equivalent	10

Source: National Dairy Council, Reference 32

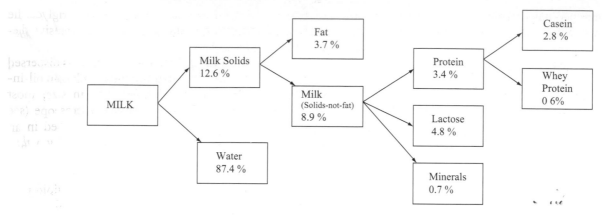

FIGURE 23-3 Composition of milk. *(Source: Adapted from Reference 4)*

The intake of dairy foods is associated with statistically significant increases in the intake of calcium, magnesium, potassium, zinc, iron, vitamin A, riboflavin, and folate [57]. Although milk is not particularly high in iron and folate, those who consume more dairy foods apparently consume higher levels of other high-nutrient foods. Individuals who consume limited a amount of dairy foods do not appear to compensate with other calcium-rich foods and thus have a low calcium intake. The consumption of dairy foods was not found to be associated with higher fat and cholesterol intakes [57].

COMPOSITION AND PROPERTIES OF MILK

An average composition of whole cow's milk is 88 percent water, 3.4 percent protein, 3.7 percent fat, 4.7 percent carbohydrate, and 0.7 percent ash (Figure 23-3). The quantitative composition of milk varies somewhat in response to several physiological and environmental factors. The breed of the cow, the time of milking, the feed consumed, the environmental temperature, the season,

FIGURE 23-4 A Holstein dairy cow poses for a photograph.
(Courtesy of U.S. National Resources Conservation Service; photo by Bob Nichols)

and the age and health of the cow are all factors that can affect the composition of milk [25] (Figure 23-4).

The most variable component of milk is the fat, followed by protein. Carbohydrate and ash or mineral content vary only slightly. Different breeds of cattle may produce milk that varies from 3.5 to 5.0 percent fat. The fat content of pooled market milk is adjusted to a desired level by the dairy processor. Standards for minimum fat content differ somewhat in various states. The composition of some common milk products is given in Appendix C.

Protein

Casein and whey are the two primary types of protein found in milk. Casein and whey are not single proteins, but rather complexes of many closely related protein molecules (Table 23-3). Very small amounts of other proteins are also present in milk. Casein and whey function differently in food preparation and cheese making as will be explained later in the chapter. See Chapter 9 for a more in-depth discussion of proteins.

Casein. About 80 percent of the protein in milk is *casein*. Casein is classified as a phosphoprotein because of the phosphoric acid that is contained in its molecular structure. At the normal acidity of fresh milk (about pH 6.6), casein is largely combined through the phosphoric acid part of its structure with calcium, as calcium caseinate. It is dispersed in the watery portion of milk,

TABLE 23-3 Casein and Whey Proteins in Milk

Casein	Whey
α_{s1}-Casein	β-Lactoglobulin
α_{s2}-Casein	α-Lactalbumin
β-Casein	Serum Albumin
κ-Casein	
γ-Casein	

Source: Reference 18

called *milk serum*. With the addition of sufficient acid to lower the pH to about 4.6 or the addition of an enzyme substance called rennet, casein precipitates as a curd. Rennet is used in cheese making and will be discussed later in the chapter.

Kappa-casein (Table 23-3) plays an important role in stabilizing the tiny casein particles or micelles in a colloidal dispersion. The casein molecules are linked into tiny micelles with the help of colloidal calcium phosphate. These micelles are apparently responsible for the whiteness of milk.

Whey. Whey protein is made up principally of *lactalbumin* and *lactoglobulin* (Table 23-3). Whey proteins are not precipitated by acid or rennet but can be coagulated by heat. These proteins seem to be chiefly responsible for the precipitate that usually forms on the bottom and sides of a container in which milk is heated. Whey proteins are a byproduct of cheese making and are used in a variety of food products.

Fat

The fat in milk (milkfat, butterfat, or cream) is a complex lipid. Milkfat as a whole is composed primarily of triglycerides. In addition to the small amount of phospholipids present, milkfat also contains some sterols—chiefly, cholesterol. The triglycerides are characterized by the presence of many short-chain, saturated fatty acids, such as butyric and caproic acids. These are partly responsible for the relatively low melting point and, therefore, the soft–solid consistency of butter. When butter spoils as a result of hydrolysis of triglyceride molecules, the disagreeable odor and flavor are due primarily to the release of free butyric and caproic acids from the triglyceride molecules. Refer to Chapter 9 for a more extensive discussion on lipids in foods.

Milkfat exists in whole milk as tiny droplets dispersed in the milk serum (watery portion); thus, milk is an oil-in-water emulsion. The fat globules vary in size; most are minute yet easily visible under the microscope (see Figure 23-5). The fat globules remain dispersed in an emulsified form because they are surrounded by a thin film or membrane called the *milkfat globule membrane*. This membrane is composed of a lipid-protein complex and a small amount of carbohydrate [19]. The lipid portion includes phospholipids, triglycerides, and sterols.

Some fat globules in fresh, unprocessed milk are loosely grouped in small clusters. Then, as nonhomogenized milk stands, the fat globules tend to form larger and larger clusters. Because fat is less dense than the watery portion of milk, the fat clusters rise to the surface as cream. The size of the dispersed fat globules in milk is decreased by the process of homogenization. The dispersion is therefore more stable, and the cream no longer rises to the surface on standing. Homogenization is discussed later in the chapter.

Carbohydrate

The chief carbohydrate of milk, lactose or milk sugar, is a disaccharide. On hydrolysis, it yields the monosaccharides glucose and galactose (see Chapter 9 for the chemical structures of disaccharides and monosaccharides). Lactose is the least sweet and also the least soluble of the common sugars. Because of its low solubility, it may crystallize and give some food products a sandy texture when present in too large an amount. For example, when too

UP CLOSE

Casein and Whey in Food Products

Both casein and whey may be isolated and then used in a variety of food products. Isolated casein and caseinate products may be found in such products as imitation cheese, coffee whiteners, dessert toppings, and bakery items.

Whey is a byproduct of cheese making and may be further processed by a procedure involving ultrafiltration to produce whey-protein concentrate (WPC). WPC may be made to contain about 35, 50, or 80 percent protein. Further processing may produce whey protein isolate (WPI), which contains greater than 90 percent protein. These whey products, in dried form, may be used in a wide range of food applications, including the formulation of high-protein beverages that are popular with athletes, and used in bakery products, prepared mixes, soups, confectionery, and margarines [11, 16]. On heating, dispersions of WPC can act as gelling agents. Beta-lactoglobulin accounts for about 50 percent of total whey proteins and is apparently the principal gelling protein in whey [27, 30]. ∎

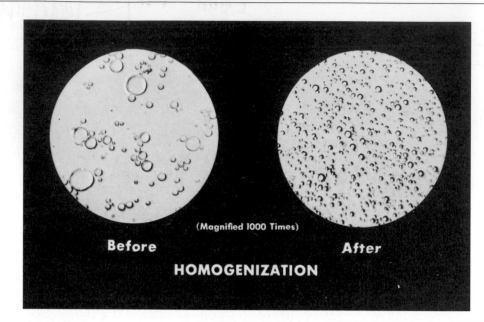

FIGURE 23-5 Homogenization of milk decreases the size of the dispersed fat particles, as shown in this photomicrograph of evaporated milk. *(Courtesy of the Evaporated Milk Association)*

much nonfat dry milk, which is high in lactose, is added to ice cream, the less soluble sugar may produce sandiness at the low temperature required for freezing. Lactose separated from milk finds many uses in the food industry. It may be an ingredient in such products as cooked sausages and hams, confections, and infant formulas.

Lactose Intolerance. The enzyme *lactase*, normally produced in the small intestine, breaks down lactose into its two component simple sugars. In some people, however, this enzyme is present in insufficient quantity for them to handle more than a very small amount of milk sugar without discomfort. Because lactose is poorly digested in people who have an enzyme deficiency, it remains in the intestine and is broken down by microorganisms, producing gas, cramping, and diarrhea. A deficiency of lactase, producing a lactose intolerance, seems to develop quite frequently, even in early childhood, among certain populations, particularly non-Caucasian peoples. People with lactose intolerance may be able to tolerate small amounts of some fermented milk products, such as yogurt and buttermilk, if much of the lactose in these products has been broken down to glucose and galactose. Aged cheese may also be tolerated.

The lactase enzyme has become available commercially, and the dairy industry has produced fluid milks, both whole and reduced-fat, treated with this enzyme so that the lactose content of the milks is reduced, typically by 70 percent [13]. These milks are sweeter tasting because the lactose has been broken down to the sweeter sugars—glucose and galactose. Lactase is also available for home use in liquid and tablet or capsule form. The lactase can be consumed directly or added to regular milk.

Minerals and Vitamins

Calcium, phosphorus, magnesium, and sodium are some of the minerals found in milk. Milk, in particular, is valued for its calcium content. One eight-ounce glass of milk provides approximately 300 milligrams of calcium. Three cups of milk also contains about 95 percent of the phosphorus recommended daily for adults 19 years and older [29].

Water- and fat-soluble vitamins are found in milk. The fat-soluble vitamins A, D, E, and K are carried in the fat globules. Vitamin A, a fat-soluble vitamin, is removed with the cream when reduced-fat milk products are produced. Thus, reduced-fat milk is fortified to replace this vitamin. Vitamins D, E, and K are found in low levels in milk. Milk is commonly fortified with Vitamin D to provide 25 percent of the daily recommendation for this nutrient in an eight-ounce serving [29].

Color

The white appearance of milk is due to the reflection of light by the colloidally dispersed casein micelles and by the calcium phosphate salts. Two yellowish pigments also contribute to the color of milk—carotenes and riboflavin. The fat-soluble carotenes are found in the milkfat and contribute to a yellow, creamy color. Depending on the concentration of carotenes, the intensity of color in milk varies. The concentration of carotenes, in turn, depends on the amount of pigment in the feed of the cow and on its ability to change it to the colorless vitamin A molecule. A greenish-yellow fluorescent color, particularly noticeable in liquid whey, is due to the presence of the water-soluble vitamin, riboflavin.

Flavor

The flavor of milk is bland and slightly sweet because of its lactose content. A major flavor sensation of milk is thought to be its particular mouthfeel, which results from the emulsion of milkfat, as well as from the colloidal structure of the proteins and some of the calcium phosphate. The slight aroma of fresh milk is produced by several low-molecular-weight compounds, such as acetone, acetaldehyde, dimethyl sulfide, methyl ketones, short-chain fatty acids, and lactones. Some of the volatile compounds contributing to the flavor of milk are unique to the fatty portion of milk.

Heat Processing. Heat processing may affect the flavor of milk, the change in flavor being dependent on the time and temperature of heating. The effect on flavor of heating to pasteurize milk, including the use of ultrahigh temperatures for very short periods, is minimal and tends to disappear during storage. Milk sterilized at ultrahigh temperatures tastes very much like conventionally pasteurized milk, although some people may notice a slightly cooked flavor [37].

Other Factors Influencing Flavor. The off-flavors that sometimes occur in milk may result from the feed consumed by the cow, the action of bacteria, chemical changes in the milk, or the absorption of foreign flavors after the milk is drawn. One chemical off-flavor is called *oxidized* flavor [42]. This flavor can result from the oxidation of phospholipids in the milk. Because traces of copper accelerate the development of oxidized flavor, copper-containing equipment is not used in dairies.

An off-flavor may also be produced when milk is exposed to light. This off-flavor, which develops rapidly, involves both milk protein and riboflavin. The amount of riboflavin in milk decreases as the off-flavor develops. Waxed cartons and opaque plastic containers help to protect milk from light, thus reducing riboflavin loss and the development of off-flavors.

pH

Fresh milk has a pH of about 6.6, which is close to the neutral pH of 7. As milk stands exposed to air, its acidity decreases slightly because of the loss of carbon dioxide. Raw milk ordinarily contains bacteria that ferment lactose and produce lactic acid, thus gradually increasing acidity. The "souring" of the milk and a curd is produced by this process. A clean, acidic taste is characteristic. Pasteurized milk does not sour in this way. The heat of pasteurization destroys most of the lactic acid bacteria responsible for the souring process. Instead, pasteurized milk spoils by the action of putrefactive bacteria, which break down the proteins in milk and results in a bitter, unpleasant flavor.

SANITATION, GRADING, AND PROCESSING

Milk is among the most perishable of all foods because it is an excellent medium for the growth of bacteria. Some of these bacteria are harmless, but some may be pathogenic to humans. Quality milk has been produced, processed, and distributed under rigid sanitary conditions so that it has a relatively low bacterial count, is free from disease-producing organisms, has good flavor and appearance, and is of high nutritive value and satisfactory keeping quality. Various controls and treatments for milk have been instituted to ensure quality in this product.

Grade A Pasteurized Milk Ordinance

The Grade A Pasteurized Milk Ordinance is a set of recommendations made by the U.S. Public Health Service—Food and Drug Administration (FDA). This ordinance describes the steps necessary to protect the milk supply. It outlines sanitary practices, which include the following:

Inspection and sanitary control of farms and milk plants

Examination and testing of herds

FOCUS ON SCIENCE

Causes of Off-Flavors in Milk
Action of Copper in Milk

Copper is a metal that will cause a "clipping" action on the triglyceride producing free fatty acids in the milk. Once there are free fatty acids, especially if the fatty acids are unsaturated, they will undergo oxidative rancidity—a procedure that will cause off-flavor and aroma in the milk.

Since riboflavin is a vitamin, how can it produce an off-flavor in the milk?

Riboflavin when exposed to light decomposes to *lumiflavin*. Lumiflavin is a stronger oxidizing agent than riboflavin and can catalyze destruction of a number of vitamins, particularly ascorbic acid. When milk was sold in bottles, this reaction sequence caused a significant problem with loss of nutrients and the development of undesirable flavor known as "sunlight" off-flavor. Opaque milk containers prevent this problem by reducing the light exposure.

Employee instruction on good manufacturing practices

Proper pasteurization and processing

Laboratory examination of milk

Monitoring for chemical, physical, and microbial adulterants

Formulated as a guide to states and other jurisdictions responsible for milk quality, this ordinance has been voluntarily adopted by many state and local governments, and is revised periodically [53]. The majority of people in the United States live in areas where the guidelines of this ordinance are in effect.

Grading

Sanitary codes generally determine the grading of milk. Grades and their meanings may vary according to local regulations unless the pasteurized milk ordinance has

been adopted; in which case, standards are uniform. The most rigid control is placed on the production and processing of Grade A market milk, which is the grade most sold to consumers. The Grade A Pasteurized Milk Ordinance recommends that state health or agriculture departments have programs to monitor regularly the milk supply for the presence of unintentional microconstituents, which include pesticide residues, antibiotics, and radioactivity. In addition, the FDA regularly conducts surveys and other monitoring activities.

The USDA has set quality grade standards for nonfat dry milk and also for butter and some cheeses. In addition, a Quality Approved rating is available for certain products (Figure 23-6). If a manufacturer uses the USDA grade or Quality Approved shield on product labels, the plant must operate under the continuous inspection of USDA agents. The grades for regular nonfat dry milk are U.S. Extra and U.S. Standard. For the instantized

HOT TOPICS

Why Are Some Dairy Products Labeled "from Cows Not Treated with rbST" and What Is rbST?

Dairy processors feel there is a consumer demand for dairy foods produced from cows not treated with rbST and so these products are marketed. Whether or not milk produced without the use of rbST is different is another issue, because the label also reads, "No significant difference has been shown between milk derived from rbST-treated cows and non-rbST-treated cows."

Bovine somatotropin (bST) is a naturally occurring protein hormone in cattle that influences milk production. This hormone can be artificially synthesized (rbST) with biotechnology, and when given to cows, it increases milk production by about 10 percent. Following the evaluation of research on rbST, the FDA found milk and meat from treated animals to be safe for human consumption; therefore in 1993, the FDA approved the use of rbST [2]. A second review of rbST in 1998 affirmed the safety of this protein hormone [56].

Safety questions about rbST linger, however, in part due to information posted on the Internet. The FDA based its assessment on the scientific literature. Scientific journals are *refereed*, which means that a scientific research study, published in a refereed journal, has undergone a *blind* review by other scientists. A research paper based on inadequate research methodology or inappropriate statistical analysis will be rejected for publication. In contrast, anything can be posted on the Internet.

What does this have to do with rbST? The reason product labels must state there is no difference between cows treated with rbST and those not treated is because the findings reported in refereed scientific journals do not reveal differences. Some points to consider:

- The National Institute of Health, World Health Organization, and *Journal of the American Medical Association* are among those in the scientific community who have reviewed the rbST data and concluded milk and meat from rbST cows are safe.

- bST and rbST are protein hormones; thus like insulin, which is a protein hormone, bST and rBST have no activity when taken by mouth.

- bST appears to be species specific and was shown not to influence growth, even when injected into humans.

- bST is a normal hormone for cows which naturally fluctuates in levels over the period of lactation. The milk produced from an rbST-treated cow contains no higher hormone levels than nontreated cows.

- A variety of factors influences the incidence of mastitis in cows, and rbST can be one factor. However, milk from both rbST-treated and -nontreated cows is tested for antibiotic residues. If found, the milk is discarded [1]. ■

FIGURE 23-6 USDA shields indicate quality in dairy products. *(Courtesy of the U.S. Department of Agriculture)*

product, the grade is U.S. Extra. Grading is a voluntary, fee-for-service program.

Pasteurization

Low bacterial count and high standards of production do not always ensure a milk supply that is free from pathogenic organisms. Even under the best sanitary practices, disease-producing organisms may contaminate raw milk [29]. Therefore, milk is pasteurized as a safeguard for consumers. Pasteurization is required by law for all Grade A fluid milk and milk products that enter interstate commerce for retail sale [3].

The pasteurization process involves heating raw milk in properly approved and operated equipment at a sufficiently high temperature for a specified length of time to destroy pathogenic bacteria. It generally destroys 95 to 99 percent of nonpathogenic bacteria as well. Although milk is not completely sterilized by pasteurization, its keeping quality is greatly increased over that of raw milk. Various time and temperature relationships that can be used in pasteurization are provided in Table 23-4.

Various tests can be applied to ascertain the thoroughness of milk pasteurization. For example, measurements can be made of any activity of the enzyme alkaline phosphatase, which is naturally present in milk. If this enzyme is completely inactivated, the milk has been heated sufficiently to destroy any pathogenic microorganisms that might be present.

The temperatures and times for pasteurization do not significantly alter the milk constituents or properties. Whey proteins are denatured only slightly, and minerals are not appreciably precipitated. Vitamin losses range from 0 to 10 percent [3]. Changes in curd characteristics that occur as a result of pasteurization tend toward the production of a finer curd when milk is digested.

Homogenization

If milk was not homogenized, the cream would rise. If you tried to drink a *homogenous* beverage, you would first need to shake your milk, like some salad dressings must be shaken before use. This tendency of the fat globules in whole fluid milk to rise and form a cream line is changed

TABLE 23-4 Times and Temperatures That May Be Used for the Pasteurization of Milk		
Name of Process	**Time and Temperature**	**Comments**
Pasteurization	145°F (63°C) for 30 minutes	These time and temperature combinations are identified in the Grade "A" Pasteurized Milk Ordinance.
	161°F (72°C) for 15 seconds	
	191°F (89°C) for 1.0 seconds	145°F (63°C) for 30 minutes is often called low-temperature, long-time (LTLT) pasteurization.
	194°F (90°C) for 0.5 second	
	201°F (94°C) for 0.1 second	161°F (72°C) for 15 seconds is a high-temperature, short-time (HTST) pasteurization process.
	204°F (96°C) for 0.05 second	
	212°F (100°C) for 0.01 second	
Ultrapasteurization	280°F (138°C) for 2 or more seconds	Product may be stored under refrigeration for an extended period (14 to 28 days).
Ultrahigh-temperature	280° to 302°F (138° to 150°C) for 1 to 2 seconds	Sterilizes the milk. When in aseptic packaging in presterilized containers, this milk may be kept on the shelf without refrigeration for at least three months. After it is opened, however, it must be refrigerated.

Source: References 29, 31, 53

FOCUS ON SCIENCE

More about Pasteurization

Bacteria Found in Milk

Pasteurization is important to destroy pathogenic bacteria that are inherent to milk. *Salmonella dublin*, *Listeria monocytogenes*, *E. coli*, and *Campylobacter jejuni* are bacteria that can pose a problem and are under constant surveillance.

Why is alkaline phosphatase pinpointed when evaluating the effectiveness of milk pasteurization?

Alkaline phosphatase is an enzyme that may not be irreversibly destroyed but only reversibly inactivated by high-temperature, short-time (HTST) pasteurization. This creates a dilemma for the processor when, for example, milk properly pasteurized by an HTST method exhibits a positive phosphatase test (indicative of improper pasteurization) only because of regeneration of this enzyme.

HEALTHY EATING

Raw Milk—What Are the Risks?

The consumption of raw milk or cheese produced from unpasteurized (raw) milk caused 1,007 illnesses, 104 hospitalizations, and two deaths from 1998 to May 2005 [52]. These illnesses and deaths were the result of 45 foodborne illness outbreaks identified by the Centers for Disease Control and Prevention in which raw milk was implicated. Not all foodborne illnesses are reported, and thus the actual numbers of consumers who became ill as the result of consuming raw milk during this time period is likely much higher.

Claims on the Internet about the safety and superior quality of raw milk are not supported by science [3, 52, 54]. One such claim is that pasteurized milk must be fortified by vitamin D because of pasteurization. However, milk, whether raw or pasteurized, is not high in vitamin D. Milk is a logical choice for vitamin D fortification because this vitamin works with calcium to promote healthy bones. See also Chapter 3 for more about food safety. ∎

by homogenization. In this process, fat globules are divided into such small particles that they are dispersed permanently in a very fine emulsion throughout the milk serum (Figure 23-5). Most of the milk marketed in the United States is homogenized.

Homogenization consists of pumping milk or cream under pressures of 2,000 to 2,500 pounds per square inch through tiny openings in a machine called a *homogenizer*. A film of adsorbed protein or lipoprotein immediately surrounds each of the new globules, acting as an **emulsifier**, and prevents them from reuniting. It is estimated that about one-fourth of the protein of milk is adsorbed on the finely dispersed fat particles of homogenized milk.

The increased dispersion of fat imparts richer flavor and increased viscosity to the milk. Because light is scattered more effectively by the greater number of fat globules, homogenized milk is whiter [29]. Homogenized milk is also less likely to develop an oxidized flavor and produces a softer curd in the stomach, thereby aiding digestion.

Fortification

Fortification is the addition of certain nutrients to milk as a means of improving the nutritional value. The principal form of fortification is the addition of about 400 international units (IUs) of vitamin D per quart. In view of the relationship between vitamin D and absorption and utilization of calcium and phosphorus in the body, and because milk is an outstanding source of these minerals, milk is generally regarded as a logical food to fortify with vitamin D. Although the addition of vitamin D is very common, according to the standards of identity for milk vitamin D fortification is optional. Some milk products also may be fortified with nonfat dried milk solids which will increase the protein and calcium content of the milk.

Fat-reduced milk, such as 2 percent milk or nonfat milk, must be fortified with vitamin A. Vitamin A fortification of reduced-fat milk is mandatory because vitamin A, a fat-soluble vitamin, is present only in the fatty portion of milk. Thus, removal of the cream results in the loss of the vitamin A. It is particularly important that nonfat dry milk sent to other countries be fortified with vitamin A because vitamin A deficiencies are common in some developing countries.

TYPES OF MILK PRODUCTS

Milk is marketed in several different forms to appeal to the varied tastes and desires of the consuming public. Packaging of milk in individual milk "chugs" has promoted milk as a grab-and-go beverage (Figure 23-7). Development of new milk products has been motivated by the desire to improve keeping quality, to facilitate distribution and storage, to make maximum use of byproducts, and to utilize surpluses [37]. Cost variations among different forms of milk depend on such factors as supply and demand, production and processing costs, and governmental policies.

Federal standards of identity have been set for a number of milk products that enter interstate commerce. These standards define the composition, the kind and quantity of optional ingredients permitted, and the labeling requirements. The 1990 Federal Nutrition Labeling and Education Act requires that virtually all packaged foods bear nutrition labeling (refer to Chapter 4 for more information about food labeling). State and local agencies are encouraged to adopt the federal standards to enhance uniformity.

Fluid Milk

Fresh fluid milk is commonly labeled according to its content of milkfat. Beginning January 1, 1998, the labeling of fat-reduced milk followed the same requirements that the FDA established several years ago for the labeling of most other foods that are reduced in fat. Therefore, skim milk may be labeled "skim," "fat-free," "zero-fat," or "no-fat" milk. The regulations were also changed to give dairy processors more freedom to devise new formulations, for example, "light" milk with at least 50 percent less fat than

FIGURE 23-7 Milk "chugs" create a convenient way to have milk on the go. A fat-free milk chug is shown here. *(Courtesy of Reiter Dairy)*

whole milk and reformulated milks with reduced-fat content but increased creaminess [22, 35]. The names for milk and fat content are summarized in Table 23-5.

Whole Milk. The term *milk* usually refers to whole milk. According to federal standards, whole milk packaged for beverage use must contain not less than 3.25 percent milkfat and not less than 8.25 percent milk-solids-not-fat, which are mostly protein and lactose [47]. At milk-processing plants, the milk from different suppliers is standardized to one fat level by removing or adding milkfat as necessary.

Fat-Reduced Milks. Milks may be modified in fat content as listed in Table 23-5. The nutrients that lower-fat milk products provide, other than fat, must be at least equal to full-fat milk before vitamins A and D are added. The word *skim* is allowed in the labeling of no-fat milk because consumers realize that skim milk means no fat. *Skim* or *nonfat milk* is milk from which as much fat has been removed as is technologically possible. The fat content is less than 0.5 percent. All of these milks contain at least 8.25 percent milk-solids-not-fat. Addition of

TABLE 23-5 Names for Milk			
Old Name	**New Name**	**Total Fat per 240 mL or 1 Cup**	**Kilocalories per 240 mL or 1 cup**
Milk	Milk	8.0 grams	150
Lowfat 2 percent milk	Reduced-fat or less-fat milk	4.7 grams	122
Lowfat 1 percent milk	Lowfat milk	2.6 grams	102
Skim milk	Fat-free, skim, zero-fat, no-fat, or nonfat milk	less than 0.5 gram	80

Source: Reference 22

vitamin A to low-fat and skim milk is required for milk shipped in interstate commerce.

Flavored Milk and Eggnog. Milk flavored with chocolate, strawberry, or other flavors is available. These dairy products have the same nutritional value as unflavored milk but may have a moderately or significantly higher caloric content due to the added ingredients. Eggnog includes milk, egg yolk, sweeteners, and flavors such as nutmeg and vanilla. It is most often sold during the Thanksgiving and Christmas holiday seasons.

Concentrated Fluid Milk

Evaporated Milk. In the production of evaporated milk, about 60 percent of the water is removed in a vacuum pan at 122° to 131°F (50° to 55°C). A prewarming period of 10 to 20 minutes at 203°F (95°C) is usually effective in preventing coagulation of the protein casein during sterilization. The heat sterilization process occurs after the product is homogenized and canned. In another process, the concentrated milk may be heated in a continuous system at ultrahigh temperatures and then canned aseptically. This product is less viscous, whiter, and tastes more like pasteurized milk than evaporated milk processed by the traditional method. Evaporated milk is fortified with 400 IUs of vitamin D per quart.

Federal standards require that evaporated milk contain not less than 6.5 percent milkfat and not less than 23 percent total milk solids. Evaporated skim milk must contain not less than 20 percent milk solids. In this case, both vitamins A and D must be added [55].

Sweetened Condensed Milk. To prepare sweetened condensed milk, about 15 percent sugar is added to whole or skim milk, which is then concentrated to about one-third of its former volume. Because the 42 percent sugar content of the finished product acts as a preservative, the milk is not sterilized after canning. Federal standards require 28 percent total milk solids. Whole sweetened condensed milk must contain 8 percent milkfat, whereas the skim milk product must have not more than 0.5 percent fat.

Storage and Quality. Sterilized, canned evaporated or condensed milk should keep indefinitely without microbiologic spoilage; however, other changes affect its quality, thus storage beyond one year is not recommended. If allowed to stand for a long time, the homogenized fat particles tend to coalesce, thus breaking the emulsion. The solids begin to settle, and the product may thicken and form clots. To retard these changes, stored cans of evaporated and condensed milk should be turned every few weeks. The vegetable gum carrageenan is often added to evaporated milk as a stabilizer.

Browning of condensed milk and evaporated milk is probably due to the Maillard reaction and occurs during both sterilization and storage. The rate of browning is greater at room temperature and with longer storage time.

Dry Milk

Dairy products may be dried to allow extended storage without the need for refrigeration. Nonfat dried milk is commonly available, but other dried milk products are also available. Whole or lowfat milk, when dried, has a shorter shelf life than nonfat dried milk because the fat is subject to oxidation. Dried buttermilk is available through retail and food distribution channels. It is widely used in commercial flour mixtures. Dried churned buttermilk is an excellent ingredient for use in baked products because it contains phospholipids that function as emulsifiers.

Nonfat dry milk powder is usually made from fresh pasteurized skim milk by removing about two-thirds of the water under vacuum and then spraying this concentrated milk into a chamber of hot filtered air. This process produces a fine powder of very low moisture content, about 3 percent. Nonfat dry milk may also be produced by spraying a jet of hot air into concentrated skim milk (foam spray-drying).

The method of processing has an impact on how easily a dried milk product will reconstitute. Instant nonfat dry milk disperses readily in cold water. To make the instant product, regular nonfat dry milk is remoistened with steam to induce agglomeration of small particles into larger, porous particles that are creamy white and

FOCUS ON SCIENCE

Sweetened Condensed Milk and Lime Juice— Why Does It Thicken?

I was watching a cooking show on television, and Key Lime Pie was being made. The host of the show put lime juice and sweetened condensed milk together and said the two ingredients together will thicken. Why will it thicken?

When the protein casein is concentrated in a product such as sweetened condensed milk, the proteins show a high water-holding capacity by thickening and forming a gel when (a) heated or (b) in contact with an acid. In traditional Key Lime Pie recipes, sweetened condensed milk and lime juice are mixed together, and a gel is formed because of the acid contact when it is allowed to chill.

Temperature Abuse of Milk and Spoilage

Why does milk spoil if I pour any milk that was held at room temperature back into its original carton?

After pasteurization, very little bacteria is left in the milk. Any bacteria that may be introduced may thrive and proliferate if held at room temperature for any length of time because there are few "competitors" in the milk. Additionally, because milk is a source of proteins and nutrients such as minerals and vitamins, it provides a good environment for bacterial growth. Buttermilk and sour cream have a longer shelf life because their pH (acidic) is low enough to prevent microbes from thriving.

Thus, when milk is temperature abused by being left at room temperature, any bacteria present or incidentally added to the milk will grow rapidly. Adding this contaminated milk into the original carton will essentially inoculate the entire carton with bacteria that are likely to cause spoilage.

---

free flowing. The lactose may be in a more soluble form, particularly on the outside of the particles.

To reconstitute instant dried milk, add the powder to water and then shake or stir. For use in flour mixtures and some other products, the dry milk can be mixed with dry ingredients and the water added later. Warm water and agitation are helpful when reconstituting dried milk that is not instant because it will not dissolve as readily as instant dried milk. The quantity of instant milk powder needed to make one quart of fluid milk is usually 1 1/3 cups.

Cultured Milk Products

Cultured or fermented milks are one of the oldest preserved foods, having been used for centuries. Several hundred different cultured milk products are consumed worldwide [21]. Yogurt, buttermilk, and sour cream are among some of the available cultured dairy products. Sour cream will be discussed with other types of creams.

Cultured milk products are prepared by the addition of appropriate bacterial cultures to the fluid milk. The bacteria ferment lactose to produce lactic acid. Lactic acid production lowers the pH of the product to between 4.1 and 4.9 and thus discourages the growth of undesirable microorganisms. Acids, such as lactic and citric, may also be added directly to milk, either with or without the addition of microbial cultures. The development of acidity is responsible for several physical and chemical properties that make the fermented products unique. Each bacterial culture produces its own characteristic flavor components. Some protein hydrolysis occurs, apparently contributing to a softer, more easily digested curd.

Yogurt. Yogurt is a cultured milk product made from whole, lowfat, and skim milk. Even cream can be used to make yogurt. In the production of yogurt, a mixed culture of *Lactobacillus bulgaricus* and *Streptococcus thermophilus* is usually added to the pasteurized milk premix. *Lactobacillus acidophilus* or other strains may be added to the culture, which is then incubated at 108° to 115°F (42° to 46°C) until the desired flavor, acidity, and consistency are attained. After yogurt has reached the desired flavor and consistency, further bacterial activity is retarded by chilling.

A sharp, tangy flavor is characteristic of yogurt. Two general types of yogurt are manufactured: the set style has a firm gel; stirred yogurt has a semiliquid consistency. Yogurt is often marketed with sweetened fruit added

Dry Milk and Shelf Life

Whole dried milk can become rancid and, like nonfat dried milk, can turn a tan or brown color with extended storage. Why does this occur?

Rancidity

Water activity will have an effect on rancidity in dried whole milk. In dried foods with very low moisture content, oxidation proceeds very rapidly. Thus, nonfat dried milk is preferred because there is no fat in the product to become rancid.

Browning

Dried milk, however, will undergo browning due to a Maillard reaction. Maillard browning requires protein (amino acid) and carbohydrate (sugar). In dried milk, the presence of lactose and amino acid (lysine) will cause Maillard browning. Additionally, the nutrient content is compromised because lysine, an essential amino acid, may be lost in the browning reaction.

which may be placed on the bottom of the container or blended throughout. Some yogurt products are labeled to inform the consumer that a significant level of live, active cultures is present. Other yogurts may be heat-treated after fermentation to extend shelf life, but live organisms are then not present in the product as consumed.

The nutrient composition of yogurt reflects the nutrient composition of the milk used in its production; however, a considerable increase in folic acid concentration appears to occur during the fermentation process. Additional calcium is also found in yogurt when milk solids are added [41]. The lactose content of yogurt is reduced during fermentation, because some lactose is hydrolyzed to the monosaccharides glucose and galactose. When the yogurt premix is enriched with nonfat milk solids, however, the initial level of lactose is actually higher than that of ordinary milk: 6 to 8 percent compared to 5 percent in milk. During fermentation, the lactose level of yogurt typically falls to about 4 percent [41]. When microorganisms are still alive and contain the enzyme *lactase*, lactose digestion appears to be enhanced for those who are lactose intolerant.

Buttermilk. The term *buttermilk* was originally used to describe the liquid remaining after cream is churned to produce butter. This liquid is still used for the production of dried buttermilk, a baking ingredient. Today, however, fluid buttermilk is a cultured milk. Cultured buttermilk is usually made from pasteurized lowfat or skim milk, with nonfat dry milk solids added. It can also be made from fluid whole milk or reconstituted nonfat dry milk. If it is made from lowfat or whole milk, it really should be called cultured milk or cultured lowfat milk rather than buttermilk. In the process of manufacturing, a culture of *Streptococcus lactis* is added to the milk to produce the acid and flavor components. The product is incubated at 68° to 70°F (20° to 22°C) until the acidity is 0.8 to 0.9 percent (pH 4.6), expressed as lactic acid [37]. Butter granules or flakes, salt, and a small amount of citric acid may be added to enhance the flavor.

Acidophilus Milks. Lowfat or skim milk may be cultured with *Lactobacillus acidophilus* and incubated at 100°F (38°C) until a soft curd forms. This formulation is then called *acidophilus-cultured milk*. It has an acidic flavor. In another process, a concentrated culture of *L. acidophilus* is grown and then added to pasteurized milk to produce *sweet acidophilus milk*. This product is not acidic in taste, and its consistency is similar to that of fluid milk. Acidophilus milk introduces acidophilus bacteria into the intestine, where it may help to maintain a proper balance of microorganisms.

Kefir. Kefir is a fermented milk beverage that may be made with the milk of cows, sheep, or goats. Soymilk kefir has also been produced [26]. Kefir grains are used to

HEALTHY EATING

Yogurt and Probiotics

Natural yogurt is one of the world's first health foods. It was appreciated in Europe and Asia long before it was introduced into the American market in the 1940s. Since then, however, many changes have been brought about in that first full-fat, simply fermented, unflavored yogurt—lowfat, milder fermentations, heavily flavored with fruit or caramel, sweetened, gelled, spoonable, liquefied, drinkable, and so on. Now the "big" thing is—probiotics! [12].

Probiotics are live microbial food ingredients that have a beneficial effect on the gastrointestinal tract. Evidence suggesting the positive health benefits of probiotics in the diet and the market for cultured dairy foods is growing [12, 20, 38]. *Lactobacillus acidophilus, Lactobacillus reuteri,* and bifidobacteria are normal inhabitants of the intestinal tract, contributing to increased acidity and deterrence of undesirable microbial growth. The addition of safe and suitable microbial organisms to milk products is allowed by the Pasteurized Milk Ordinance. Additional research is necessary to provide sufficient proof for the FDA to approve label claims for nutritional benefits of fermented milk products [14, 17, 44]. At this time, however, evidence is strong for the ability of two **probiotics**, *Streptococcus thermophilus* and *Lactobacillus bulgaricus,* that are used in making yogurt, to digest lactose in the intestinal lumen. Thus, this may be the health claim that may be accepted by regulatory agencies [5]. ■

inoculate the milk with a wider number of cultures than typically found in yogurt. Kefir is tart, slightly carbonated, and mildly alcoholic due to the fermentation process. Like yogurt, kefir has been found to improve lactose digestion in adults who are lactose intolerant [10].

Filled and Imitation Milks

Filled and imitation milks are substitute products. Both are subject to variable state regulations but are not governed by the same rigid sanitation and composition requirements as pasteurized Grade A milk and milk products. Filled and imitation milks are subject to the 1990 Federal Nutrition Labeling and Education Act, under which a substitute food must be nutritionally equivalent to its standardized counterpart except that calories and/or fat may be reduced. Some dairy processors use a special seal on their products to emphasize that their dairy products are real, not imitation. Figure 23-8 shows this seal, which consists of the word _Real_ enclosed in a symbolic drop of milk.

Filled Milk. Filled milk is a substitute that can be made by combining a fat other than milkfat with water, nonfat milk solids, an emulsifier, color, and flavoring. The mixture is heated, under agitation, and then homogenized. The resulting product appears to be very much like milk [6]. Cheese and cultured milk products may be produced from filled milk. This process creates dairylike products that do not contain butterfat or cholesterol. In the past, coconut oil has been the main source of fat in filled milk because of its desirable flavor, even though it is a highly saturated fat. Other sources of fat for filled milk are partially hydrogenated soybean, corn, and cottonseed oils containing approximately 30 percent linoleic acid.

Imitation Milk. Imitation milk resembles milk but usually contains no milk products per se. Such ingredients as water, corn syrup solids, sugar, vegetable fats, and a source of protein are most often used in imitation milk. Derivatives of milk, such as casein, casein salts, and other milk proteins, may be used as the protein source; soy proteins may also be used. Some imitation milk contains whey products. The vegetable fat is often coconut oil.

Types of Cream Products

Cream is the high-fat, liquid product that is separated from whole milk. Cream adds richness and body to foods that are prepared with it and, when whipped, provides a creamy, yet airy delicacy. According to federal standards of identity, cream must contain not less than 18 percent milkfat.

Fluid Cream. Several liquid cream products are marketed, including light or coffee cream containing 18 to 30 percent milkfat, light whipping cream with 30 to 36 percent milkfat, and heavy cream or heavy whipping cream

FIGURE 23-8 Sometimes dairy processors put on their packaged products a special symbol containing the word _Real_. This emphasizes that these products are not imitation.

with not less than 36 percent milkfat [37]. If cream is to be whipped, a minimum of 30 percent milkfat is necessary. Half-and-half is a mixture of milk and cream containing not less than 10.5 percent milkfat but less than 18 percent. This product is commonly used in place of light cream or coffee cream.

The thickness of cream is related to its fat content; it is generally thicker at higher fat levels. Other factors also affect thickness. Cream at room temperature is thinner than cream at refrigerator temperature because chilling makes the fat globules firmer, thereby increasing the **viscosity** of the cream. When chilled to a temperature of 41°F (5°C) and held at that temperature for 24 to 48 hours, cream gradually increases in thickness.

Sour Cream. Commercial sour cream is a cultured or an acidified light cream. A culture of _Streptococcus lactis_ organisms is added to cream, and the product is held at 72°F (22°C) until the acidity, calculated as lactic acid, is at least 0.5 percent [37]. Nonfat milk solids and stabilizing vegetable gums such as carrageenan may be added to sour cream, which can also be produced from half-and-half. If manufacturers use food-grade acid instead of bacteria to make sour cream, the product must be labeled as "acidified sour cream" [47]. _below 36% fat_

Dried Cream. Dried cream is available that may be used reconstituted to liquid form. An instant dry creamed milk made from modified skim milk (calcium reduced), light cream, and lactose has also been manufactured. When it is sprinkled on the surface of a beverage, it disperses quickly.

Nondairy Products. Many nondairy products for whipped toppings, coffee whiteners, sour cream–type mixtures, and snack dip bases have been developed and marketed. Initially, these were promoted as low-cost substitutes for the more expensive natural dairy products. Many of them, particularly whipped toppings and coffee whiteners, have been accepted on their own merits rather

sugar hydrogenated oil

than as substitutes and have taken over much of the market. One advantage of whipped toppings is their stability. Whipped toppings will tolerate overmixing to a greater degree than real whipped cream and will maintain quality during storage for a longer period of time.

Nondairy whipped toppings often contain sugar, hydrogenated vegetable oil, sodium caseinate, and emulsifiers. Whipped toppings are available in a dry form, which is added to cold milk before whipping, and also in a frozen, whipped form. The foam is stable and requires only defrosting before use. Nondairy products resembling whipped cream that contain water, vegetable fat, sugar, sodium caseinate, emulsifiers, and vegetable gums are also available in pressurized cans. These products must be refrigerated. Nondairy coffee whiteners are widely used in hot beverages. They usually contain corn syrup solids, vegetable fat, a source of protein such as sodium caseinate or soy protein, emulsifiers, and salts.

Although nondairy whipped toppings, coffee whiteners, and other products are termed "nondairy," these products often contain casein or whey. Thus, those who are allergic to dairy products often must avoid these nondairy foods as well.

FOOD PREPARATION WITH MILK AND CREAM

Milk and milk products are used to make a wide variety of dishes including salads, soups, entrees, side dishes, desserts, and beverages. When used in cooking, the prevention of curdling is desired. High temperatures, extended hot holding or cooking, and acidic or salty ingredients can all contribute to curdling. The tendency for milk to curdle is diminished by the use of low or moderate temperatures. You may already have observed less curdling of the milk on scalloped potatoes cooked in a low or moderate oven than when a higher temperature is used. In addition, higher fat milk products, such as cream or whole milk, are more stable than lowfat or nonfat milk and thus are less likely to separate.

In the following section, the general effect of heat, acid, enzymes, phenolic compounds, salt, freezing, and whipping on milk during usual food preparation practices is considered. Preparation of white sauces and cream soups, using heated milk, was discussed in Chapter 13, and preparation of hot chocolate containing milk is covered in Chapter 28.

Heat

Heating milk during cooking results in several changes. Proteins coagulate, calcium is less dispersed, fat globules coalesce, surface films may form, and the sugars and protein may brown due to the application of heat.

Protein Coagulation. On heating, the whey proteins lactalbumin and lactoglobulin become insoluble or precipitate. Lactalbumin begins to coagulate at a temperature of 150°F (66°C). The amount of coagulum increases with rising temperature and time of heating. The coagulum that forms appears as small particles rather than a firm mass and collects on the bottom of the pan in which the milk is heated. This collection of particles, of course, contributes to the characteristic scorching of heated milk. You can stir the milk while it heats to lessen the amount of precipitate on the bottom, but some scorching may still occur, particularly if a large quantity of milk is heated at one time. One way to prevent scorching is to heat milk over hot water in a double boiler rather than with direct heat.

Casein, the protein found in the largest amount in milk, does not coagulate at the usual temperatures and times used in food preparation. Although some of its properties may change slightly, it coagulates only when heated to very high temperatures or for a long period at the boiling point. In fact, as long as 12 hours may be required for casein to coagulate when heated at a temperature of 212°F (100°C).

Heating periods that produce casein coagulation are shorter when the concentration of casein is increased above that in regular fluid milk. For example, in the sterilization of canned evaporated milk, it is necessary to take certain measures to prevent coagulation of the casein. One such measure is to prewarm the milk prior to its sterilization.

The coagulation of milk proteins by heat is accelerated by an increase in acidity. This can be observed when preparing cream of tomato soup which curdles easily when heated. Milk protein coagulation is also influenced by the kinds and concentrations of salts present. The salts in such foods as ham hocks and vegetables are partly responsible for coagulation of casein when these products are cooked in milk.

Mineral Changes. The dispersion of calcium phosphate in milk is decreased by heating, and a small part of it is precipitated. Some of the calcium phosphate collects on the bottom of the pan with coagulated whey proteins, and some is probably entangled in the scum on the top surface of the milk.

Coalescence of Fat Globules. The layer of fat that may form on milk that has been boiled results from the breaking of the films of protein that surround the fat globules in the unheated milk. The breaking of films of emulsifying agents permits the coalescence of fat globules.

Surface Film Formation. The composition of the film on heated milk is variable. It may contain coagulated protein, with some precipitated salts and fat globules entangled in the mesh of coagulated matter.

The formation of a film or scum on the surface of heated milk is often troublesome, and it is responsible when milk boils over the sides of the pan. A certain amount of pressure develops under the film, which forces the film upward, and the milk flows over the sides of the pan. A slight film may form at relatively low temperatures, but this may be prevented by a cover on the pan, by dilution of the milk, or by the presence of fat floating on the surface. As the temperature is increased, a tough scum forms that is insoluble and can be removed from the surface. As soon as it is removed, however, another film forms.

Sometimes, to break up the film, the heated milk is beaten with a rotary-type egg beater. This procedure has limited usefulness because of the continuous formation of fresh film; however, foam formation at the surface appears to aid in preventing a really tenacious scum from forming. Whipped cream placed on the surface of hot chocolate is one example of another method used to discourage surface film formation.

Browning. When certain sugars and proteins are heated together, browning occurs. This particular nonenzymatic browning is of the Maillard type. Concentrated milk products such as evaporated milk contain substantial amounts of both protein and the sugar lactose and develop some brown color on heating. This reaction may also occur in dried milk stored for long periods. Heating sweetened condensed milk in a can which has been placed in a pan of water for several hours results in a brown-colored product of thickened consistency and sweet caramel flavor. This "pudding" is sometimes used as a dessert.

Acid Coagulation

Although the protein casein is hardly susceptible to coagulation by heating, it is highly sensitive to precipitation on the addition of acid. The acid may be added as such, or it may be produced by bacteria as they ferment milk sugar. Recall that in cultured milk products, lactic acid is produced, making the product more acidic. The acid curdling of milk is a desirable reaction in making such products as cultured buttermilk, yogurt, sour cream, and some cheeses. Prevention of casein coagulation or curdling, however, is fundamental to the success of such products as cream of tomato soup. Fruit–milk mixtures may also curdle, as you may have noticed when putting cream on fresh fruits or making fruit–milk beverages or sherbets (Figure 23-9).

What Happens When Acid Is Added to Milk? Observe the impact of acid by adding vinegar or lemon juice to milk. Curdling quickly becomes evident. The curdling of milk can be explained scientifically. The pH of milk is normally about 6.6. When the pH reaches about 4.6, the colloidally dispersed casein particles become unstable. These casein proteins adhere and form a coagulum or curd. This probably occurs because the usual negative charge on the casein particles, which causes them to repel each other and remain apart, is neutralized by the acidic hydrogen ion (H^+).

FIGURE 23-9 Dairy products such as frozen yogurt may be blended with fruits to make delicious smoothies. *(Courtesy of Dole Food Company, Inc.)*

A considerable amount of calcium is also released from the casein molecules to the liquid whey. The calcium was bonded through the phosphoric acid groups of casein. The curd then traps the whey in its meshes. The whey, which contains the whey proteins, most of the lactose, and many minerals, is released when the curd is cut or stirred and heated. These processes occur in the manufacture of cheese.

Enzyme Coagulation

A number of enzymes from plant, animal, and microbial sources are capable of clotting milk or producing a curd. A **protease** called *chymosin* is often used in cheese making. It is found in the stomachs of young animals, and its function is to clot milk prior to the action of other protein-digesting enzymes. The name *chymosin* is derived from the Greek word *chyme*, meaning "gastric liquid," and is used in the recommended international enzyme nomenclature [45]. The crude chymosin enzyme is called *rennet*. Rennet has been used for many years in the preparation of most varieties of cheeses. When the sources of rennet became limited, several other nonrennin milk-clotting enzymes were used as rennet substitutes [8]. The FDA has affirmed that use of the chymosin preparation derived by fermentation from the genetically modified *Aspergillus* mold is GRAS (generally regarded as safe). This was one of the first genetically engineered food products to be approved.

Because rennet is an enzyme preparation, it requires specific conditions of temperature and acidity for its action. The optimum temperature is 104° to 108°F (40° to 42°C). Refrigerator temperatures retard its action. No action occurs below 50°F (10°C) or above 149°F (65°C). Rennet acts best in a faintly acid medium, and action does not occur in an alkaline environment.

When casein is precipitated by the action of rennet, the calcium is not released to the whey but remains attached to the casein. Therefore, cheese made with rennet is a much better source of calcium than cheese made by acid precipitation alone. Cottage cheese is often made by acid precipitation. Table C-4 in Appendix C shows that cottage cheese is considerably lower in calcium than Cheddar cheese.

The action of the enzyme bromelin from raw or frozen pineapple in preventing the gelation of gelatin is well known. The enzyme digests proteins and hence changes the gelatin to smaller compounds that do not form a gel. The enzyme bromelin also clots milk but later digests the clot. Other enzymes in fruits are probably responsible for some of the curdling action that occurs when milk or cream and certain fruits are combined. All fruits contain some organic acids, but not always in sufficient concentration to cause the curdling of milk. Destroying the enzymes before combining fruit with milk will, of course, prevent curdling caused by enzyme action.

Coagulation by Phenolic Compounds

Some phenolic-type compounds are present in fruits and vegetables. In fruits, these compounds are found chiefly in the green stages and are present in a greater amount in some varieties than in others. Seeds and stems may contain significant amounts of phenolic substances. Among vegetables, the roots, pods, some seeds, and woody stems are likely to contain more phenolic compounds than other parts of the plant, although distribution is general throughout the plant. Curdling of milk may occur if phenolic-containing foods, such as potatoes, are cooked in the milk; however, the time and temperature of heating also influence curdling. In addition, the low levels of organic acids present in potatoes contribute to curdling.

Coagulation by Salts

The cause of curdling in foods cooked in milk is likely to be a combination of factors. The salts present in the milk, in the food combined with the milk, or added sodium chloride may influence coagulation of the casein. Of the meats commonly cooked in milk, ham usually causes more coagulation than chicken, veal, or pork, although these may vary in their effect. The high sodium chloride content of ham may be responsible for the excessive curdling that occurs when ham is cooked in milk. Processed shrimp can also contain sodium levels that may cause curdling in a milk-based dish.

Freezing

When milk or cream is frozen at a relatively slow rate, the film of protein that acts as an emulsifying agent around the fat globules is weakened or ruptured. As a result, the fat globules tend to coalesce. The oily masses that float on top of hot coffee when previously frozen cream is added demonstrate the cohesion of fat particles that results from freezing. The dispersion of protein and calcium phosphate is also disturbed by freezing. Both constituents tend to settle out on thawing and standing, thus reducing the whiteness of milk. The effects of freezing are not harmful and do not affect food value.

Whipping of Cream

A foam is a dispersion of a gas in a liquid. If the foam is stable, a stabilizing agent is needed to keep the gas dispersed. Certain conditions are necessary for the foam to form in the first place. A foaming agent must be dispersed in the liquid to lower the surface tension of the liquid, and thus allow the liquid to surround the gas bubbles. The stabilizing agent can then act to keep the gas bubbles separated.

When cream is whipped, a foam is formed. The liquid is the water in the cream, the gas is air that is beaten in, and the foaming agent that lowers the surface tension of the water is protein that is dispersed in the cream. During whipping, air bubbles are incorporated and surrounded by a thin liquid film that contains protein. The foam cells are stabilized by coalesced fat globules. The fat globules apparently coalesce because much of the milk fat globule membrane surrounding them and keeping them separated has been removed in the whipping process [24]. At the cold temperature of the whipping cream, the fat globules are solid. Whipping is the first stage of churning cream. If whipping is continued too long, the emulsion breaks, and butter is formed.

Air bubbles in whipped cream must be surrounded by protein films. Because so much of the protein of homogenized cream is used to surround the increased number of fat globules, little protein remains to surround the air bubbles formed in whipping. Therefore, whipping cream is usually not homogenized. Several factors, including temperature, affect the whipping properties of cream.

Temperature and Viscosity. Cream held at a cold temperature (45°F/7°C or below) whips better than cream held at warmer temperatures. Above 50°F (10°C), agitation of cream increases the dispersion of the fat instead of decreasing it. The beater and bowl that are used, as well as the cream, should be chilled. In whipping cream, the aim is to increase clumping of fat particles; at low temperatures, agitation results in clumping. Lower temperatures increase viscosity, which increases the whipping properties of cream. Higher fat content also increases viscosity and furnishes more fat globules for clumping. Because viscosity increases with aging, the whipping property improves with the aging of cream.

Fat Content. A fat content of 30 percent is about the minimum for cream that will whip with ease and produce a stiff product. Increasing the fat up to 40 percent improves the whipping quality of cream, because more solid fat particles are thus available to stabilize the foam.

Amount of Cream Whipped. In whipping large amounts of cream, it is better to do successive whippings of amounts tailored to the size of the whipper used, rather than to whip a large amount at one time. If a very small amount of cream is to be whipped, a small deep bowl should be used so that the beaters can adequately agitate the cream.

Effect of Other Substances. Increased acidity up to the concentration required to produce a sour taste (0.3 percent) has no effect on whipping quality. The addition of sugar decreases both volume and stiffness and increases the time required to whip cream if it is added before whipping. If sugar is to be added, it is best added after the cream is stiff or just prior to serving. If sugar is added just before serving, powdered sugar should be used, because granulated sugar needs more time to dissolve (Figure 23-10).

Whipping of Other Milk Products

Evaporated Milk. When evaporated milk is chilled to the ice crystal stage, it will whip to about three times its original volume. This ability to whip is evidently the result of the higher concentration of milk solids in evaporated milk than in fresh whole milk. The protein in the milk acts as a foaming agent and also aids in stabilizing. This foam, however, is not stable on standing. The addition of acid, such as a small amount of lemon juice (about one tablespoon per cup of undiluted milk), helps to stabilize the protein and makes a more lasting foam.

FIGURE 23-10 This crème Chantilly was made by first whipping heavy chilled cream until thickened. Powdered sugar and vanilla were added, and the mixture was whipped until the consistency shown here. *(Source: Reference 23)*

Nonfat Dry Milk. A light and airy whipped product may be produced by whipping nonfat dry milk. Equal measures of dry milk and very cold water are normally used, with the dry milk being sprinkled over the surface of the water before whipping. This foam is highly unstable, but its stability may be increased somewhat by adding small amounts of an acid substance such as lemon juice before whipping.

Care of Milk

Fundamentals in the care of fluid milk, whether by producer or consumer, are cleanliness, cold temperature, and the prevention of contamination by keeping the milk covered. Milk, being very perishable, should be stored at 41°F (5°C) or below immediately after purchase [34]. It should be returned to the refrigerator immediately after use to prevent warming, which encourages bacterial growth. Milk that has been poured but not used should never be returned to the original container, because it may contaminate the rest of the milk. Milk that has been properly refrigerated should remain fresh for approximately five days [47]. The absorption of other food odors should be avoided by keeping the milk container closed during storage.

Containers or storage conditions that protect milk from exposure to light should be used. Light exposure produces an oxidized off-flavor and reduces riboflavin and vitamin A content. Riboflavin is very unstable to ultraviolet light, which means that milk exposed to light may lose large amounts of this vitamin. Because approximately 38 percent of the riboflavin in the American diet comes from milk and dairy products, it is important to protect the riboflavin in milk. The retention of riboflavin in skim milk placed in blow-molded polyethylene containers and held in a lighted chamber for 5 days has been reported to average 58 percent at the top of the containers compared with 92 percent at the bottom of the containers [39].

Nonfat dry milk should be stored in moisture-proof packages at a temperature no higher than ordinary room temperature. Dry milk takes up moisture and becomes lumpy and stale when exposed to air during storage. Because of the fat content, whole dry milk is not as stable to storage as the nonfat product. Unopened cans of evaporated milk can be stored at room temperature. Once the can is opened, however, it must be treated as fluid milk and refrigerated. When cans of evaporated milk are stored for several months, they should be turned over periodically to retard the settling out of milk solids.

CHEESE

Cheese is a concentrated dairy food defined as the fresh or matured product obtained by draining the whey (the moisture or serum of the original milk) after coagulation of casein, the major milk protein. Many different kinds of cheese may be produced with soft or firm textures, milk, pungent, or sharp flavors. Cheese may be enjoyed as part of a cheese, fruit, and cracker board or as a component of a recipe (Figure 23-11 and Plates XII and XVI). Although in the United States, much of the cheese produced is made from cow's milk, the milk from other animals such as goats is also used.

Composition and Nutritive Value

Cheese is a highly concentrated food; one pound of cheese may contain the protein and fat of one gallon of milk. The protein is of high biologic value, and the fat is largely saturated. Vitamin A is carried in the fat. The addition of salt for flavor, as well as the concentration of the milk that naturally contains sodium, makes cheese a high-sodium food.

The composition of cheese varies widely with the fraction of milk used and the amount of moisture retained. When cheese is made from whole milk, the fat remains with the curd when the whey is drained off. Much of the milk sugar, the soluble salts, and the water-soluble vitamins are drained off in the whey, although even in hard cheeses the whey is never entirely removed. Whey cheeses and concentrated whey added to cheese spreads or cheese foods save some of these valuable nutrients.

Cheese made by rennet coagulation is an excellent source of calcium and phosphorus; however, cheese coagulated by acid alone contains less calcium. The reason for this difference in calcium content is that the lower pH or greater acidity produced by adding acid causes the release of more calcium ions (Ca^{2+}) from the phosphate groups that are part of the casein molecule. Much of this released calcium goes into the whey and is not retained in the curd. Cheddar-type cheese, made chiefly by rennet coagulation of the milk, may retain up to 80 percent of the original milk calcium. Soft cheeses made by acid precipitation, such as cottage cheese, may retain not more than one-fourth to one-half of the milk calcium.

American Cheddar cheese averages, roughly, one-third water, one-third fat, and one-fourth protein. It also contains about 4 percent ash and less than 1 percent carbohydrate, including lactic acid. Cheese made from low-fat or skim milk is lower in fat content than cheese made from whole milk. Cheese containing vegetable oil instead of milkfat is available for those who want to decrease their intake of animal fat.

The moisture content of soft cheese varies from 40 to 75 percent, whereas hard cheeses tend to contain a more nearly uniform amount of water—from 30 to 40 percent. High moisture content is a factor in the perishability of cheese, those with a large amount of moisture being more perishable.

Cheese Manufacture

The manufacture of most types of cheese begins with pasteurized milk and follows steps that include (1) promoting curd formation with acid produced by lactic acid–producing bacteria (a starter culture) and/or a coagulating enzyme; (2) cutting the curd into small pieces to allow the whey to escape; (3) heating the curd to contract the curd particles and hasten the expulsion of whey; (4) draining, knitting or stretching, salting, and pressing the curd; and (5) curing or ripening [36]. Some cheeses, including cottage cheese, cream cheese, and mozzarella, are not ripened. Some kinds of cheese are colored with carotene to give a yellow color.

Curd Formation. The casein forms a curd by acid coagulation or coagulating enzymes. The curds are primarily coagulated casein, with entrapped fat globules if whole milk is used. When coagulated by acid, lactic acid–producing bacteria, also called a *starter culture*, are added to warm milk. Acid-coagulated cheese is usually not ripened. Rennet, obtained from the stomach of calves, is the enzyme used to form a curd in cheese making. The purified enzyme from rennet, chymosin, may also be produced by genetic engineering.

Cutting and Heating Curd. Cutting the curd helps to release the whey from the casein [33]. The curd is cut with knives or wires. Cooking the curd further helps to facilitate curd removal by contracting the curd particles. The curd texture and moisture level are also affected by cooking.

FIGURE 23-11 Cheddar cheese in the pastry and the apple filling of these cheddar apple tarts with apricot-mint glaze creates a warm snack or dessert. *(Courtesy of the American Dairy Association)*

PLATE XVII

Egg dishes.

Frittatas are open faced omelets with hearty fillings cooked into the egg mixture. This frittata is filled with O'Brien potatoes and cheese. (Courtesy of the American Egg Board)

Eggs baked in a rice nest and topped with cheese is an interesting way to serve eggs at dinner. (Courtesy of the American Egg Board)

A potluck classic—Deviled Eggs. (Courtesy of the American Egg Board)

This vegetable scramble pocket is composed of eggs scrambled with carrots, onions, and red and green sweet peppers. The eggs are spooned into a pita pocket and dressed with honey mustard to finish this dish. (Courtesy of the American Egg Board.)

PLATE XVIII

Vegetarian dishes may be very creative and tasty.

Lemon tofu cheesecake combines silken tofu with some low-fat cream cheese. (Courtesy of the United Soybean Board)

Corn-olive cakes are cooked on a lightly oiled griddle and served with salsa. (Courtesy of the California Olive Industry)

Colorful spinach and red bell pepper contrast with dark ripe olives and Jack cheese in rolled flour tortillas spread with reduced-fat cream cheese, making rolled sandwiches. (Courtesy of the California Olive Industry)

Greek-style pizza may be prepared using foccacia bread topped with sour cream, tomatoes, fresh spinach, artichoke hearts, pepperoncini peppers, Greek kalamata olives, and feta cheese. (Courtesy of Land O'Lakes.)

PLATE XIX

Vegetarian dishes.

Meatless vegetarian burgers include fresh mushrooms, olives, onions, and Mozzarella cheese combined with rolled oats and brown rice, bound together with egg whites. (Courtesy of the California Olive Industry)

Jeweled cheese burritos include pinto beans, shredded carrots, red bell peppers, ripe olives, chilies, and Jack cheese in a flour tortilla wrap. (Courtesy of the California Olive Industry)

Tortillas make a delicious covering for these veggie wraps that include bean sprouts, shredded cabbage, and a seasoned rice, textured vegetable protein, and diced firm tofu mixture with hoisin sauce. (Courtesy of the United Soybean Board)

An egg-less salad sandwich is made using tofu. Fooled you didn't it! (Courtesy of Morinaga Nutritional Foods, maker of Mori-Nu Tofu, www.morinu.com)

PLATE XX

Cuts of beef. (Courtesy of the National Live Stock and Meat Board)

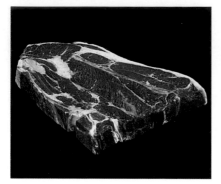

Beef chuck, seven-bone steak

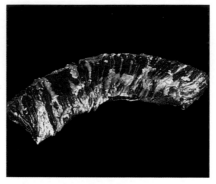

Beef plate, skirt steak boneless (inner diaphragm muscle)

Beef flank steak

Beef loin, tenderloin steak

Beef loin, top sirloin steak boneless

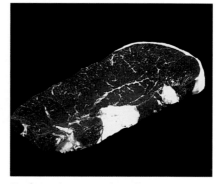

Beef round, top round steak

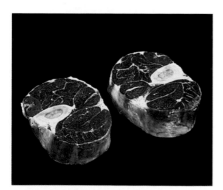

Beef shank, cross cuts

Beef round, eye round roast

Swiss steak piperade uses beef round steak with tomatoes, bell peppers, and seasonings and is served on a bed of cooked farfalle (bowtie) pasta.

PLATE XXI

Cuts of beefsteak. (Courtesy of the National Live Stock and Meat Board)

Beef rib steak

Beef loin, top loin steak

Beef loin, T-bone steak

Beef loin, porterhouse steak

Beef loin, flat-bone sirloin steak

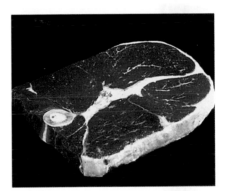

Beef round steak

Beef chuck, arm steak

Beef chuck, blade steak

T-bone steaks, flavored with a pesto composed of parsley, garlic, and olive oil, are grilled with red and green peppers. (Courtesy of Cattlemen's Beef Board through the National Cattlemen's Beef Association.)

PLATE XXII

Cuts of beef. (Courtesy of the National Live Stock and Meat Board)

Beef chuck, top blade pot roast

Beef chuck, shoulder pot roast boneless

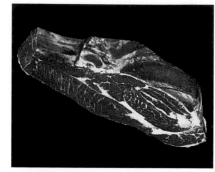

Beef chuck, under-blade pot roast (bottom portion of blade)

Beef chuck, short ribs

Beef brisket boneless

Beef for stew

Beef rib roast, small end

Beef rib eye roast

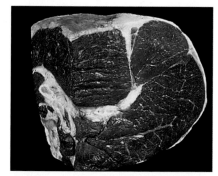

Beef round, rump roast

Beef, round, rump roast boneless

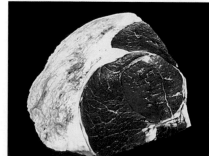

Beef round, tip roast

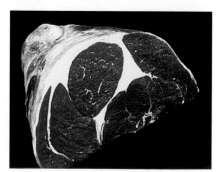

Beef round, heel of round

PLATE XXIII

Cooked beef.

Tropical grilled flank steak is served with fresh fruit salsa, which contains green apple, mango, papaya, pineapple, green and red bell peppers, and cilantro. (Courtesy of National Live Stock and Meat Board.)

Beef, pepper, and mushroom kabobs use beef top sirloin steak. A mixture of oil, lemon juice, mustard, honey, oregano, and pepper coats each kabob before broiling. (Courtesy of National Live Stock and Meat Board.)

Spicy grilled short ribs are marinated in barbecue sauce, lemon juice, minced jalapeno peppers, and green onion for several hours before cooking. (Courtesy of National Live Stock and Meat Board.)

Stir-fried beef gyros in pita pockets are prepared with seasoned beef round tip steaks, pita bread, tomatoes, and cucumber ranch dressing. (Courtesy of Cattlemen's Beef Board through the National Cattlemen's Beef Association.)

PLATE XXIV

Veal.

Veal loin chops

Veal cutlets (thin, boneless leg slices)

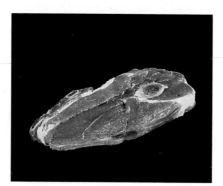

Veal shoulder, arm steak

Veal leg, round steak

Veal Breast with olive-mushroom filling is prepared by spreading the filling over the veal breast then rolling, tying, and cooking in a Marsala wine sauce. (Courtesy of Cattlemen's Beef Board through the National Cattlemen's Beef Association.)

Fruit 'n pecan stuffed veal crown roast is an eye-catching entree. The ribs are stuffed with dried apricots and prunes, celery, onion, toasted pecans, and cooked brown rice. (Courtesy of the National Live Stock and Meat Board.)

PLATE XXV

Cuts of lamb. (Courtesy of the National Live Stock and Meat Board)

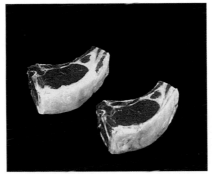

Lamb rib chops

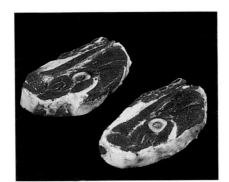

Lamb shoulder, arm chops

Lamb loin chops

Lamb leg, French-style roast

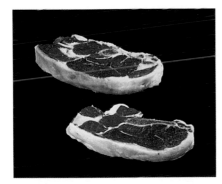

Lamb leg, sirloin chops

Lamb leg, American-style roast

*This sautéed lamb loin with stuffed rösti
potatoes, cherry confit, and fresh asparagus, has been beautifully presented.*

PLATE XXVI

Cuts of pork. (Courtesy of the National Live Stock and Meat Board)

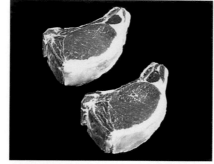

Pork loin, rib chops

Pork loin chops

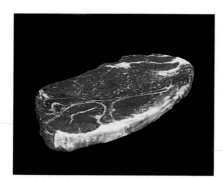

Pork shoulder, blade steak

Pork spare ribs

Pork loin, tenderloin whole

Pork loin, sirloin roast

Smoked ham, shank portion

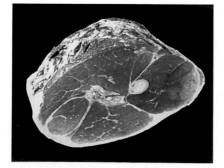

Smoked ham, rump portion

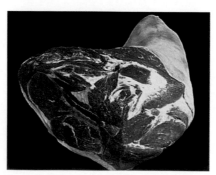

Pork shoulder, arm picnic

Pork shoulder, arm roast

PLATE XXVII

Pork. (Courtesy of The National Pork Board)

A spiral cut ham seasoned with a hot pepper jelly can be prepared quickly.

Boneless pork chops prepared with red and yellow peppers is a tender and tasty dish.

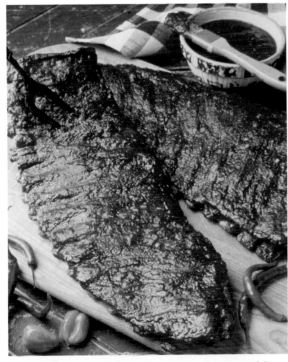

Many different kinds of sauces may be used to create delicious spareribs.

This pork loin roast was prepared with an Italian dressing mix, cumin, and oregano. Fall vegetables are served on the side.

PLATE XXVIII

Poultry.

Turkey sausage vegetable kabobs and plum barbeque chicken can be served for a tasty summer time meal. (Courtesy of Land O'Lakes.)

Chicken breasts may be crusted with herbs for a unique flavor. (Courtesy of the National Chicken Council and U.S. Poultry and Egg Association.)

Roast chicken with fall vegetables. (Courtesy of the National Chicken Council and U.S. Poultry and Egg Association.)

Breaded and baked chicken served with corn on the cob. (Courtesy of the National Chicken Council and U.S. Poultry and Egg Association.)

PLATE XXIX

Poultry.

Bone-in chicken breast glazed and served with fresh fruit. (Courtesy of Dole Food Company, Inc.)

Chicken tenders seasoned with cilantro and served with red beans and rice. (Courtesy of Land O' Lakes.)

Thinly sliced chicken breast or chicken tenders may be used in the preparation of Hunan chicken. (Courtesy of the National Chicken Council and U.S. Poultry and Egg Association.)

Skinless chicken thighs marinated and grilled are served with green beans and walnuts. (Courtesy of the National Chicken Council and U.S. Poultry and Egg Association.)

PLATE XXX

Seafood. (Courtesy of the Florida Department of Agriculture and Consumer Services, Bureau of Seafood and Aquaculture)

Clams

Oysters

Spiny lobster

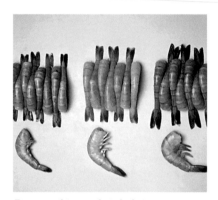

Brown, white, and pink shrimp

Fresh fish—bright scales and firm to the touch

This dish called shrimp tortilla towers is an unique way to present shrimp.

PLATE XXXI

Seafood.

Smoked Spanish mackerel. (Courtesy of the Florida Department of Agriculture and Consumer Services Bureau of Seafood and Aquaculture.)

Stuffed pompano fillets. (Courtesy of the Florida Department of Agriculture and Consumer Services Bureau of Seafood and Aquaculture.)

Sweet 'n sour shrimp. (Courtesy of the Florida Department of Agriculture and Consumer Services Bureau of Seafood and Aquaculture.)

A cobb salad prepared with surimi, hard-boiled eggs, bleu cheese, red peppers, avocado, bacon, and a bed of greens. (Courtesy of Alaska Seafood Marketing Institute.)

Basil broiled fish served with roasted vegetables. (Courtesy of Florida Department of Agriculture and Consumer Services, Bureau of Seafood and Aquaculture.)

PLATE XXXII

Beverages. (Courtesy of Dole Food Company, Inc.)

Blueberries, pineapple, bananas, and milk are blended to create this tropical blueberry smoothie.

A refreshing fruit bowl summer punch is prepared with bananas, frozen yogurt, raspberries, and lemon-lime soda.

A distinctly fall beverage is created with pineapple juice, cinnamon, figs, prunes, raisins, and vanilla extract.

Draining, Knitting, Salting, and Pressing Curd. The curds are drained with a metal strainer or may be dipped out of the vat and placed in perforated molds that will allow further draining of the whey [33]. Knitting occurs when the cheese is packed or, in the case of some types of cheese, is pulled or kneaded. This stage improves texture, permits further lactic acid development, and regulates moisture levels. Salting the curds further draws the whey out of the curds and thus reduces moisture content of the cheese. Salt also adds flavor and suppresses undesirable microorganisms. Pressing the curd into a cloth or a mold, often with external weights, removes additional whey and produces the characteristic shape of the cheese.

Ripening. Ripening refers to the changes in physical and chemical properties, such as aroma, flavor, texture, and composition, that take place between the time of precipitation of the curd and the time when the cheese develops the desired characteristics for its type. Some changes that occur are the (1) formation by bacteria of lactic acid from the lactose; (2) digestion of the protein by enzymes into end products, including peptides and amino acids; (3) development and penetration of molds in mold-ripened cheese; (4) gas formation by certain types of microorganisms used; and (5) development of characteristic flavor and aroma substances, including those developed from the decomposition of fat by lipase enzymes.

Flavor. The flavor of ripened cheese results from a blending of the decomposition and hydrolysis products formed from the milk components. The hydrolysis of protein results in free water-soluble amino acids that give the cheese a softer, more pliable texture, as well as improved flavor. The fat of some cheese is hydrolyzed by enzymes, liberating fatty acids. Most of the small amount of lactose that is present in cheese is converted to other compounds. Lactic acid is formed. A characteristic flavor is developed in each particular type of cheese.

Cooking Quality. The changes that occur in cheese during ripening not only affect flavor and texture but also improve the cooking quality. The increased dispersibility of the protein of ripened cheese contributes to the ease of blending cheese with other food ingredients, particularly for such products as cheese sauce.

Effect of Molds and Other Organisms during Ripening. Various types of organisms produce distinctive flavors, aromas, and textures in cheeses. The *Penicillium roqueforti* or *Penicillium glaucum* types of molds are responsible for the mottled blue-green appearance of blue, Roquefort, Gorgonzola, and Stilton cheeses. The curd is inoculated with pure cultures of the mold, which penetrate during the curing process.

Camembert cheese is inoculated with two molds: *Oidium lactis*, which covers the cheese in the first stages of ripening, and *Penicillium camemberti*, which grows later.

The enzymes produced by the molds penetrate and soften the cheese. Organic acids used as food by the molds gradually disappear, providing a more favorable medium for putrefactive bacteria. The cheese is usually placed in small molds, with the curing agents on the outside surface. They gradually penetrate throughout the cheese during the holding period. Damp caves are used to ripen some types of cheese that depend on mold action for the development of flavor.

Swiss cheese owes its large holes to special gas-forming organisms. These organisms grow and produce carbon dioxide gas during the early stage of ripening, while the cheese is soft and elastic. Limburger cheese owes its characteristic odor to the development of putrefactive bacteria, which are allowed to act over a considerable period. Ordinary Cheddar cheese varies widely in flavor and texture, depending on the organisms that predominate and the length of time of ripening. *Lactobacilli* and *Streptococcus lactis* organisms play major roles in the ripening of good Cheddar cheese. The presence of salt delays bacterial growth and therefore alters the rate of ripening.

Length of Ripening. Mild cheeses, such as brick and Monterey jack, are allowed to ripen for a shorter period than strong cheeses, such as Parmesan. Blue cheese is usually aged three to four months but may be aged up to nine months for more pronounced flavor. Mild Cheddar is ripened for a shorter length of time than sharp Cheddar.

Grades

USDA grade standards U.S. Grade AA and U.S. Grade A have been developed for Swiss, Cheddar, Colby, and Monterey cheese. Cheese bearing these grades must be produced in a USDA-inspected and -approved plant under sanitary conditions. Graders evaluate the flavor and texture of the cheese. Some cheese and cheese products not covered by a U.S. grade standard may be inspected and bear a USDA Quality Approved inspection shield on the label. This shield indicates that the cheese has been manufactured in a plant meeting USDA sanitary specifications and is a cheese of good quality [46].

Types of Cheese Products

The groupings of cheeses may be determined by two factors: the amount of moisture in the finished cheese and the kind and extent of ripening. Based on moisture content, cheese may be classified as soft, semihard, or hard. Based on the kind and extent of ripening, cheese may be classified as unripened, mold ripened, or bacteria ripened. Ripened cheese may be strong and sharp or mild.

More than 2,000 names have been given to cheeses with somewhat different characteristics, but there are only about 10 distinct types of natural cheese. Table 23-6 describes the characteristics of some popular varieties of natural cheeses; some of these are shown in Figure 23-12 and Plate XVI.

TABLE 23-6 Characteristics of Some Popular Varieties of Natural Cheeses

Kind or Name (place of origin)	Kind of Milk Used in Manufacture	Ripening or Curing Time	Flavor	Body and Texture	Color	Retail Packaging	Use
Soft, Unripened Varieties							
Cottage, plain or creamed (unknown)	Cow's milk skimmed; plain curd, or plain curd with cream added	Unripened	Mild, acid	Soft, curd particles of varying size	White to creamy white	Cup-shaped containers, tumblers, dishes	Salads, with fruits, vegetables, sandwiches, dips, cheese cake
Cream, plain (United States)	Cream from cow's milk	Unripened	Mild, acid	Soft and smooth	White	3- to 8-oz. packages	Salads, dips, sandwiches, snacks, cheese cake, desserts
Neufchatel (Nü-shä-tĕl´) (France)	Cow's milk	Unripened	Mild, acid	Soft, smooth, similar to cream cheese but lower in milkfat	White	4- to 8-oz. packages	Salads, dips, sandwiches, snacks, cheese cake, desserts
Ricotta (rĭc ō´-ta) (Italy)	Cow's milk, whole or partly skimmed, or whey from cow's milk with whole or skim milk added; in Italy, whey from sheep's milk	Unripened	Sweet, nutlike	Soft, moist or dry	White	Pint and quart paper and plastic containers, 3-lb metal cans	Appetizers, salads, snacks, lasagna, ravioli, noodles and other cooked dishes, grating, desserts
Firm, Unripened Varieties							
Gjetost* (Yĕt´ŏst) (Norway)	Whey from goat's milk or a mixture of whey from goat's and cow's milk	Unripened	Sweetish, caramel	Firm, buttery consistency	Golden brown	Cubical and rectangular	Snacks, desserts, served with dark breads, crackers, biscuits, or muffins
Mysost (mü sŏst) also called Primost (prē´m-ôst) (Norway)	Whey from cow's milk	Unripened	Sweetish, caramel	Firm, buttery consistency	Light brown	Cubical, cylindrical, pie-shaped wedges	Snacks, desserts, served with dark breads
Mozzarella (mō̆-tsa-rel´la) (Italy)	Whole or partly skimmed cow's milk; in Italy, originally made from buffalo's milk	Unripened	Delicate, mild	Slightly firm, plastic	Creamy white	Small round or braided form, shredded, sliced	Snacks; toasted sandwiches; cheeseburgers; cooking, as in meat loaf; or topping for lasagna, pizza, and casseroles
Soft, Ripened Varieties							
Brie (brē) (France)	Cow's milk	4–8 weeks	Mild to pungent	Soft, smooth when ripened	Creamy yellow interior; edible thin brown and white crust	Circular, pie-shaped wedges	Appetizers, sandwiches, snacks, good with crackers and fruit, dessert
Camembert (kăm´ĕm-bâr) (France)	Cow's milk	4–8 weeks	Mild to pungent	Soft, smooth, very soft when fully ripened	Creamy yellow interior; edible thin white or gray-white crust	Small circular cakes and pie-shaped portions	Appetizers, sandwiches, snacks, good with crackers and fruit such as pears and apples, dessert

Name	Kind of Milk	Ripening Time	Flavor	Body and Texture	Color	Shape and Style	Uses
Limburger (Belgium)	Cow's milk	4–8 weeks	Highly pungent, very strong	Soft, smooth when ripened; usually contains small irregular openings	Creamy white interior; reddish-yellow surface	Cubical, rectangular	Appetizers, snacks, good with crackers, rye, or other dark breads, dessert
Bel Paese† (bĕl pä-ä´-ze) (Italy)	Cow's milk	6–8 weeks	Mild to moderately robust	Soft to medium firm, creamy	Creamy yellow interior; slightly gray or brownish surface sometimes covered with yellow wax coating	Small wheels, wedges, segments	Appetizers, good with crackers, snacks sandwiches, dessert
Brick (United States)	Cow's milk	2–4 months	Mild to moderately sharp	Semisoft to medium firm; elastic, numerous small mechanical openings	Creamy yellow	Loaf, brick, slices, cut portions	Appetizers, sandwiches, snacks, dessert
Muenster (mŭn´stēr) (Germany)	Cow's milk	1–8 weeks	Mild to mellow	Semisoft; numerous small mechanical openings; contains more moisture than brick	Creamy white interior; yellow-tan surface	Circular cake, blocks, wedges, segments, slices	Appetizers, snacks, served with raw fruit, dessert
Port du Salut (por cū sä´t´) (France)	Cow's milk	6–8 weeks	Mellow to robust	Semisoft, smooth, buttery; small openings	Creamy yellow	Wheels and wedges	Appetizers, snacks, served with raw fruit, dessert
Firm, Ripened Varieties							
Cheddar (England)	Cow's milk	1–12 months or longer	Mild to very sharp	Firm, smooth; some mechanical openings	White to medium-yellow-orange	Circular, cylindrical loaf, pie-shaped wedges, oblongs, slices, cubes, shredded, grated	Appetizers, sandwiches, sauces, on vegetables, in hot dishes, toasted sandwiches, grating, cheeseburgers, dessert
Colby (United States)	Cow's milk	1–3 months	Mild to mellow	Softer and more open than Cheddar	White to medium-yellow-orange	Cylindrical, pie-shaped wedges	Sandwiches, snacks, cheeseburgers
Caciocavallo (kä´chō´-kä-al´lō) (Italy)	Cow's milk; in Italy, cow's milk or mixtures of sheep's, goat's, and cow's milk	3–12 months	Piquant, similar to Provolone but not smoked	Firm, lower in milkfat and moisture than Provolone	Light or white interior; clay or tan surface	Spindle- or ten-pin-shaped, bound with cord, cut pieces	Snacks, sandwiches, cooking, dessert; suitable for grating after prolonged curing

TABLE 23-6 (Continued)

Kind or Name (place of origin)	Kind of Milk Used in Manufacture	Ripening or Curing Time	Flavor	Body and Texture	Color	Retail Packaging	Use
Edam (ē´ dăm) (Netherlands)	Cow's milk, partly skimmed	2–3 months	Mellow, nutlike	Semisoft to firm, smooth; small irregularly shaped or round holes; lower milkfat than Gouda	Creamy yellow or medium yellow-orange interior; surface coated with red wax	Cannon ball-shaped loaf, cut pieces, oblongs	Appetizers, snacks, salads, sandwiches, seafood sauces, dessert
Gouda (gou´ -dá) (Netherlands)	Cow's milk, whole or partly skimmed	2–6 months	Mellow, nutlike	Semisoft to firm, smooth; small irregularly shaped or round holes; higher milkfat than Edam	Creamy yellow or medium yellow-orange interior; may or may not have red wax coating	Ball shaped with flattened top and bottom	Appetizers, snacks, salads, sandwiches, seafood sauces, dessert
Provolone (prō-vō-lō-nĕ), also smaller sizes and shapes called Provolette and Provoloncini (Italy)	Cow's milk	2–12 months	Mellow to sharp, smoky, salty	Firm, smooth	Light creamy interior; light brown or golden yellow surface	Pear shaped, sausage and salami shaped, wedges, slices	Appetizers, sandwiches, snacks, soufflé, macaroni and spaghetti dishes, pizza, suitable for grating when fully cured and dried
Swiss, also called Emmentaler (Switzerland)	Cow's milk	3–9 months	Sweet, nutlike	Firm, smooth, with large round eyes	Light yellow	Segments, pieces, slices	Sandwiches, snacks, sauces, fondue, cheeseburgers
Parmesan (pär´-mĕ-zän´) also called Reggiano (Italy)	Partly skimmed cow's milk	14 months to 2 years	Sharp, piquant	Very hard, granular; lower moisture and milkfat than Romano	Creamy white	Cylindrical, wedges, shredded, grated	Grated for seasoning in soups, vegetables, spaghetti, ravioli, breads, popcorn, used extensively in pizza and lasagna
Romano (rō-mä´-nō), also called Sardo Romano and Pecorino Romano (Italy)	Cow's milk; in Italy, sheep's milk (Italian law)	5–12 months	Sharp, piquant	Very hard granular	Yellowish-white interior, greenish-black surface	Round with flat ends, wedges, shredded, grated	Seasoning in soups, casserole dishes, ravioli, sauces, breads, suitable for grating when cured for about 1 year
Sap Sago* (săp´-sä-gō) (Switzerland)	Skimmed cow's milk	5 months or longer	Sharp, pungent, cloverlike	Very hard	Light green by addition of dried, powdered clover leaves	Conical, shakers	Grated to flavor soups, meats, macaroni, spaghetti, hot vegetables; mixed with butter, makes a good spread on crackers or bread

Blue-vein Mold Ripened Varieties

Variety	Kind of milk	Ripening time	Flavor	Body and texture	Color	Shapes	Uses
Blue, spelled Bleu on imported cheese (France)*	Cow's milk	2–6 months	Tangy, peppery	Semisoft, pasty, sometimes crumbly	White interior, marbled or streaked with blue veins of mold	Cylindrical, wedges, oblongs, squares, cut portions	Appetizers, salads, dips, salad dressing, sandwich spreads, good with crackers, dessert
Gorgonzola (gôr-gön-zō'-lä) (Italy)	Cow's milk; in Italy, cow's milk or goat's milk or mixtures of these	3–12 months	Tangy, peppery	Semisoft, pasty, sometimes crumbly, lower moisture than Blue	Creamy white interior, mottled or streaked with blue-green veins of mold; clay-colored surface	Cylindrical, wedges, oblongs	Appetizers, snacks, salads, dips, sandwich spreads, good with crackers, dessert
Roquefort* (rōk'-fẽrt) or (rôk-fôr') (France)	Sheep's milk	2–5 months or longer	Sharp, slightly peppery	Semisoft, pasty, sometimes crumbly	White or creamy white interior, marbled or streaked with blue veins of mold	Cylindrical wedges	Appetizers, snacks, salads, dips, sandwich spreads, good with crackers, dessert
Stilton* (England)	Cow's milk	2–6 months	Piquant, milder than Gorgonzola or Roquefort	Semisoft, flaky; slightly more crumbly than Blue	Creamy white interior; marbled or streaked with blue-green veins of mold	Circular, wedges, oblongs	Appetizers, snacks, salads, dessert

*Imported only.

†Italian trademark—licensed for manufacture in United States; also imported.

Source: Reference 15

FOCUS ON SCIENCE

More about Rennet

Where does rennin (rennet) come from?

Until 1990, rennet was produced the old-fashioned way from abomascums (the last of the four chambers of the stomach of a ruminant animal) and from various "vegetable" rennets (some of which, called *microbial coagulant*, are made from the microorganism *Mucor miehei*). Today, at a cost of one-tenth of that before 1990, chymosin (or rennet) is produced by genetically engineering bacteria into which the gene for this enzyme has been inserted. When the bacteria are grown in large vats, they secrete rennin, which is then purified for cheese making. Rennin is available commercially in tablet or in liquid form.

How does rennet work?

Rennet is an enzyme; therefore, there are specific requirements for its activity—temperature, pH, substrate, and amount. Rennet is specific for its operation in milk to convert it to a gel. Before the addition of rennet, the temperature of the milk should be 104° to 108°F (40°C to 42°C). Because rennet needs a substrate which is calcium and because some calcium may be lost from the solution during pasteurization, a small amount of calcium chloride is added. The calcium chloride aids coagulation and ensures a firm curd that does not fall apart when cut. Lactic acid bacteria also may be added to acidify the milk. One rennet tablet will set five gallons of milk.

Source: Fankhauser, D. B. (2007). *Rennet for Cheese Making*. University of Cincinnati Clermont College. Retrieved April 23, 2008, from http://biology.clc.uc.edu/fankhauser/Cheese/Rennet/Rennet/html

---

Cold-Pack Cheese.   Cold-pack or club cheese is made by grinding and mixing together one or more varieties of cheese without the aid of heat. Acid, water, salt, coloring, and spices may be added, but the final moisture content must not exceed that permitted for the variety of natural cheese from which it was prepared. The cheese is packaged in jars or in moisture-proof packages in retail-size units. Cold-pack cheese food is prepared in the same manner as cold-pack cheese, but it may contain other ingredients such as cream, milk, skim milk, nonfat dry milk, or whey. It may also contain pimientos, fruits, vegetables, or meats, and sweetening agents such as sugar and corn syrup.

Process Cheese.   A significant part of the cheese produced in the United States today is made into pasteurized process cheese and related products. Process cheese is made by grinding and mixing together different samples of natural cheese with the aid of heat and an emulsifying agent, such as sodium salts of phosphoric acid. A selected blend of cheese or portions of the same variety selected at different stages of ripeness are used, and the product is pasteurized before packaging.

After the cheese is melted, it is run into molds that may be jars, glasses, or metal-foil-lined cardboard boxes. As the cheese hardens, it clings closely to the jar or foil, thus preventing molds from attacking the surface. Pasteurization of the cheese destroys bacteria and enzymes, thus stopping all ripening. Process cheese is also sold in individual slices and can be purchased with individual slices separately wrapped. Lowfat (about 8 percent) pasteurized process cheese products in individual slices are available on the market. These products contain skim milk cheese, water, emulsifier salts, flavorings, and a preservative (sorbic acid).

The quality and flavor of process cheese depend on the quality and flavor of the cheese used to make it. Several varieties of cheese are made into pasteurized process cheeses, including Cheddar, Swiss, and brick cheese. Convenience, ease of blending in cooked dishes, and the protection offered by the package against spoilage are factors influencing the consumer's choice to use process cheese. The blend of cheeses is chosen to retain as far as possible the characteristic flavor of the type of cheese used; however, the flavor of the process cheese is seldom, if ever, equal to that of the original product. The characteristic differences in texture of the original cheeses tend to be lost, as the texture of process cheese is more or less uniform and soft. The moisture content of process cheese may not exceed 40 percent.

Process Cheese Foods and Spreads.   Pasteurized process cheese food is produced in a manner similar to process cheese except that it contains less cheese. Cream, milk, skim milk, nonfat milk solids or whey, and sometimes other foods, such as pimientos, may be added to it resulting in a product that is higher in moisture than process cheese. Cheese food is more mild in flavor, melts more quickly, and has a softer texture than process cheese because of its higher moisture content.

Pasteurized process cheese spread generally has a higher moisture and lower milkfat content than process cheese food. A stabilizer is added to prevent separation of ingredients. It is generally more spreadable than process cheese food.

Lowfat Cheese.   Fat-free, "part skim," and lowfat cheeses are available. Lowfat milk is used to make many lowfat cheeses. Reduced-fat cheeses are generally perceived to be less desirable than full-fat cheeses from a

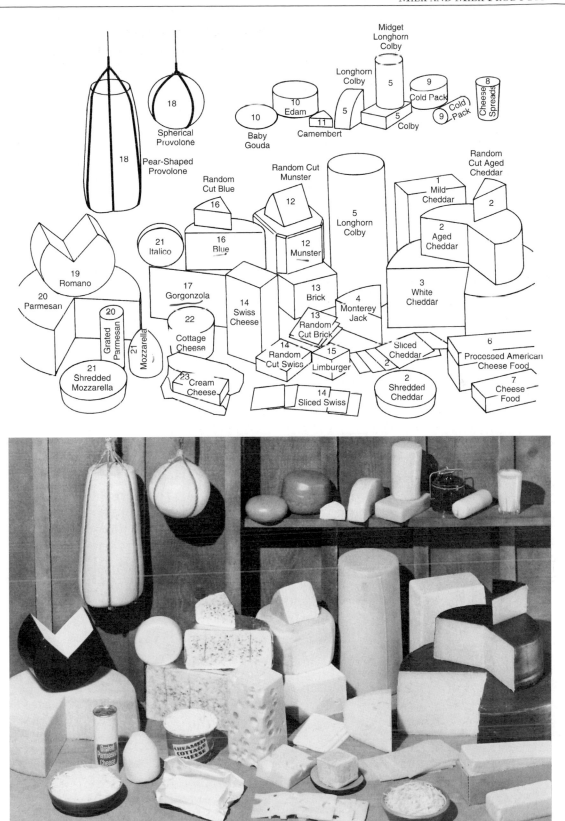

FIGURE 23-12 Many kinds of cheese are available. To identify the cheeses shown here, see the accompanying labeled drawing. *(Courtesy of the American Dairy Association)*

sensory perspective. Researchers have found that reduced-fat cheeses have a texture that was more hard, waxy, chewy, and springy than full-fat cheeses [9]. In addition, reduced-fat cheeses may be less sticky, cohesive, meltable, and smooth.

Researchers are exploring methods of producing higher quality lowfat cheeses. One process involves the removal of fat from a full-fat Cheddar cheese through centrifugation. A high-quality Cheddar cheese with about 16 percent fat, compared to 34 percent fat in full-fat cheese, can be produced using this method [40]. The choice of culture also appears to be important in the production of a flavorful and functional lowfat cheese.

Cheese Storage

Soft and unripened cheeses have limited keeping quality and require refrigeration. The shelf life of cottage cheese may be extended two or three times the usual period by adding carbon dioxide gas and packaging the product in high-barrier material [28]. All cheese is best kept cold. To prevent the surfaces from drying out, the cheese should be well wrapped in plastic wrap or metal foil or kept in the original container if it is one that protects the cheese. In the refrigerator, strong cheeses that are not tightly wrapped may contaminate other foods that readily absorb odors.

Molds are used to make some kinds of cheeses and thus will be found on the exterior or interior of Roquefort, blue, Gorgonzola, Stilton, Brie, and Camembert. Molds used to produce cheese are safe to eat. Wild molds, that are not part of the manufacturing process, are undesirable when growing on the surface of cheeses. Wild molds may be safely cut off of hard cheeses such as Cheddar [48]. However, if soft or shredded cheeses mold, the cheese will need to be discarded because the mold cannot be completely removed.

Freezing is not recommended for most cheeses because, on thawing, they tend to be mealy and crumbly; however, some varieties of cheese can be frozen satisfactorily in small pieces (one pound or less, not more than one inch thick). These varieties include brick, Cheddar, Edam, Gouda, Muenster, Port du Salut, Swiss, provolone, mozzarella, and Camembert. When frozen cheese is to be thawed, it may be taken from the freezer and placed in the refrigerator for several days before using it. This so-called *slow thawing* helps to avoid the detrimental effects of freezing and aids in preserving the original flavor, body, and texture.

Cheese usually exhibits its most distinctive flavor when served at room temperature. The amount of cheese to be used should be removed from the refrigerator about 30 minutes prior to serving [36]. An exception is cottage cheese, which should be served cold.

Cheese in Cooked Foods

Cheese adds flavor, color, and texture to a variety of cooked foods. Many casserole mixtures use cheese, either as a basic component or as a topping. And what would pizza be without cheese? In addition, a cheese tray combined with fresh fruits and/or vegetable relishes makes an easy snack or a colorful dessert (see Figure 23-13).

A hard cheese, such as Cheddar, softens and then melts when it is heated at low to moderate temperatures.

FIGURE 23-13 Cheese and fruit can be served as either a snack or a dessert. These natural cheeses make a wonderful selection when mixed with grapes, pears, apples, or guava. *(Source: Reference 23)*

Further heating results in the separation of fat and the development of a tough, rubbery curd, which will form long strings when manipulated with a spoon. If the cheese has been heated to the latter stage, it will tend to harden on cooling. Finely dividing the cheese by grating or grinding before combining it with other ingredients facilitates melting without overheating. Cheese sauces should be cooked in a double boiler or over low heat with continuous stirring. Well-ripened cheese and process cheese blend better in heated mixtures than mild (less aged) natural cheese and are less likely to produce stringiness.

Welsh rabbit is a thickened cheese sauce with seasonings. It may also contain egg and is usually served over toast. Cheese soufflé is a combination of white sauce and eggs, with grated cheese to give it flavor (Figure 23-14). The white sauce used as a basis may vary in consistency or in amount, but soufflés made with a thick sauce base are usually easier for the inexperienced person to make and tend to shrink less after baking. The baking dish containing the soufflé should be placed in a pan of water during baking to avoid overcooking. Several examples of the use of cheese in cooked foods are illustrated in Figure 23-14.

(a)

(b)

(c)

FIGURE 23-14 (a) These bagels are topped with spinach, Swiss, and provolone cheese. *(Courtesy of the American Dairy Association)*
(b) Cheese soufflé is an egg dish prepared with whipped egg whites, a white sauce, and cheese. *(Courtesy of Kraft Foods)*
(c) Apples and pears are topped with Monterey Jack and cheddar cheeses, then baked with a sugared crumb mixture to create a pleasing dish served with cinnamon-sugared flour tortillas. *(Courtesy of the American Dairy Association)*

CHAPTER SUMMARY

- The annual per capita consumption of milk has decreased. Yogurt and cheese consumption has increased considerably. Milk is rich in calcium and provides a dependable source of ribloflavin, vitamin A, vitamin D (when fortified), and protein.

- Milk is composed of water, carbohydrate, protein, fat, and ash. Casein and whey are the two primary types of protein in milk. Whey protein is a byproduct of cheese making. The milkfat is composed of primarily triglycerides characterized by short-chain saturated fatty acids. The fat in milk is dispersed in milk serum; thus, milk is an emulsion.

- The chief carbohydrate is lactose. Some individuals may be lactose intolerant and may find dairy products such as yogurt, aged cheeses, or lactose-reduced milks to be better tolerated.

- The white appearance of milk is due to the reflection of light by colloidally dispersed casein micelles and calcium phosphate salts. Carotenes and riboflavin are two yellowish pigments that also contribute color to milk.

- The flavor of milk is bland and slightly sweet with a mild aroma. Off-flavors may be produced when milk is exposed to light.

- Fresh milk has a nearly neutral pH. Raw milk gradually increases in acidity on storage because of lactic acid–producing bacteria.

- The Grade A Pasteurized Milk Ordinance provides regulations to protect the milk supply. Sanitary codes generally determine the grading of milk. If a manufacturer of dairy products uses the USDA grade or Quality Approved shield on product labels, the plant must operate under continuous inspection of USDA agents.

- Pasteurization is required by law for all Grade A fluid milk and milk products that enter interstate commerce for retail sale. The pasteurization process involves heating raw milk to a sufficiently high temperature for a specified length of time to destroy pathogenic bacteria.

- Homogenization consists of pumping milk or cream under pressure through tiny openings to increase the dispersion of fat and prevent the cream from separating upon standing.

- Milk is commonly fortified with vitamins A and D. The fortification with vitamin D is optional, but vitamin A fortification is required in lowfat and nonfat milks.

- Milk is marketed as fluid milk, reduced-fat fluid milk, concentrated fluid milk, dry milk, cultured milk products, filled or imitation milks, and cream. Each of these products has specific characteristics.

- Heat, acid, enzymes, phenolic compounds, salt, and freezing have an effect on milk and milk products.

- Several changes may occur when heating milk. Whey proteins coagulate, calcium is less dispersed and may precipitate, fat globules coalesce, surface films may form, and the sugars and proteins may brown.

- Casein is highly sensitive to precipitation on the addition of acid. This acid curdling is desirable when making products such as buttermilk, yogurt, sour cream, and some cheeses.

- A number of enzymes from plant, animal, and microbial sources are capable of clotting or curdling milk. Chymosin or rennin is such an enzyme. The enzyme bromelin, found in fresh pineapple, also clots milk but later digests the clot.

- Phenolic compounds, found in plants, may cause curdling of milk when cooked. Sodium chloride also promotes the coagulation of casein.

- Fat globules tend to coalesce when milk or cream has been frozen. The dispersion of protein and calcium phosphate is also disturbed by freezing.

- Milk products such as cream, evaporated milk, and nonfat dry milk may be whipped to create a foam. Cream that is cold and higher in fat (30 percent or higher) will whip most successfully. Sugar should be added after the cream is stiff.

- Fluid milk should be stored at 41°F (5°C) or below immediately after purchase. The milk container should be closed to prevent absorption of other food odors. Milk should be protected from light to retain the riboflavin. Nonfat dry milk should be stored in moisture-proof packages at room temperature or cooler. Evaporated milk should be turned periodically to retard the settling of milk solids.

- Cheese is a concentrated dairy food defined as the fresh or matured product obtained by draining the whey after coagulation of casein. Cheese manufacture usually involves (1) curd formation with a starter culture and/or a coagulating enzyme; (2) curd cutting to drain the whey; (3) curd heating; (4) draining, knitting or stretching, salting, and pressing; and (5) curing or ripening. The changes in cheese during ripening affect flavor, texture, and improve cooking quality.

- Various types of organisms produce distinctive flavors, aromas, and textures in cheeses. The mottled-green appearance of some cheeses is due to the type of mold used. Swiss cheese owes its large holes to special gas-forming organisms.

- Cheese may be classified by the amount of moisture (soft, semihard, or hard) and the kind and extent of ripening (unripened, mold ripened, or bacteria ripened). USDA grade standards have been developed for some varieties of cheese.

- Cold-pack or club cheese, process cheese, and process cheese foods are made by grinding and mixing together different samples of natural cheese. Additional ingredients and processes are allowed depending on the type of process cheese.

- All cheese should be stored cold although the flavor of many types of cheese is best when served at room temperature. Freezing is generally not recommended; however, some cheeses may be satisfactorily frozen.

- When cooking with cheese, finely dividing the cheese by grating will facilitate melting without overheating. Overheating results in the separation of the fat and the development of a tough, rubbery curd.

STUDY QUESTIONS

1. Describe present trends in the consumption of dairy products in the United States.

2. What is the average percentage composition of whole cow's milk?

3. Name the following items:
   (a) Protein found in milk in largest amount
   (b) Two major whey proteins
   (c) Major carbohydrate of milk
   (d) Two minerals for which milk is considered to be a particularly good source
   (e) Vitamin for which milk is a good source that is easily destroyed when milk is exposed to sunlight

4. Explain why milk is classified as an emulsion. Describe how the fat in milk is dispersed.

5. How do opaque containers help to protect milk against the development of off-flavor? Explain.

6. Describe the purpose, process, and resulting product when milk is
   (a) Pasteurized
   (b) Homogenized
   (c) Fortified

7. Briefly describe the major characteristics of each of the following processed milk products:
   (a) Whole fluid milk
   (b) Skim milk
   (c) Reduced-fat milk
   (d) Lowfat milk
   (e) Ultrahigh-temperature processed milk
   (f) Evaporated milk
   (g) Sweetened condensed milk
   (h) Nonfat dry milk, regular, and instant
   (i) Dried buttermilk (churned)

   (j) Buttermilk (cultured)
   (k) Filled milk
   (l) Yogurt

8. (a) Explain why it is so important that milk be handled properly, both in processing and in the kitchen.
   (b) What does the USDA Quality Approved shield mean when it is placed on certain dairy products?
   (c) What is the Grade A Pasteurized Milk Ordinance?

9. (a) What causes milk to scorch when it is heated over direct heat?
   (b) Which milk proteins coagulate quite easily with heating? Which do not?

10. Suggest ways to prevent or control the formation of a film or scum on the surface of heated milk.

11. (a) Which milk protein coagulates easily with the addition of acid?
    (b) Give examples illustrating when the acid coagulation of milk is desirable and when it is undesirable.

12. (a) What is *rennet?* What does it do to milk?
    (b) What role does rennet play in cheesemaking?
    (c) What is *chymosin?* List two sources.

13. (a) Describe what happens when cream is whipped.
    (b) What conditions should be controlled, and why, if cream is to whip properly?
    (c) Suggest effective procedures for whipping evaporated milk and nonfat dry milk.

14. Describe the general steps usually followed in the manufacture of cheese.

15. (a) What is meant by *ripening* cheese?
    (b) Describe general changes that may occur during the ripening process.

16. Give examples of each of the following types of cheese:
    (a) Soft, unripened
    (b) Firm, unripened
    (c) Soft, ripened
    (d) Semisoft, ripened
    (e) Firm, ripened
    (f) Very hard, ripened
    (g) Blue-vein mold-ripened

17. Describe the major characteristics of the following:
    (a) Cold-pack cheese
    (b) Process cheese

(c) Process cheese food
(d) Process cheese spread

18. (a) Describe what happens when cheese is heated too long or at too high of a temperature.
    (b) Suggest an appropriate way for preparing a cheese sauce. Explain why this method should be effective.

EGGS AND EGG COOKERY 24

Few ingredients in food preparation are as useful in so many different ways as eggs. Used alone or in combination with other foods, eggs may become the major protein dish for a meal. The color, viscosity, emulsifying ability, and coagulability, as well as flavor of eggs, make it possible for eggs to play a variety of roles in cookery processes.

The presence in the yolk of lipoproteins makes the egg yolk especially valuable in the formation of emulsions. (Eggs as emulsifiers were discussed in Chapter 10.) The surface activity of the proteins of egg white, in particular, also makes the egg useful in the production of films that hold air and thus create a foam, such as found in meringues and angel food cake. The leavening of a variety of food mixtures results from this characteristic. An egg white foam used in certain candies also improves the texture by controlling crystallization of sugar.

The ability of egg proteins to coagulate when heated, resulting in thickening or gel formation, contributes much to the characteristic properties of such dishes as custards, puddings, and various sauces. Coagulation of egg protein, along with the viscosity of the uncooked egg, is the basis for the use of egg as a binding agent and as a coating to hold crumbs together for crust formation on breaded foods. Rigidity of cell walls and of crusts in numerous doughs and batters is increased by coagulation of egg.

Use of the egg as a clarifying agent also depends on the coagulation of egg proteins. Broths and coffee may be clarified with eggs. Adding eggs improves the color and flavor of most dishes. Plain eggs—cooked in the shell, scrambled, and fried—also provide eating enjoyment. The egg gives all this to food preparation besides providing a package of essential nutrients that enrich the diet.

Although the eggs of all birds may be eaten, the egg of the chicken is used most often so the focus in this chapter will be on chicken eggs unless otherwise specified. In this chapter, the following topics will be discussed:

- Composition and nutritive value
- Structure
- Quality and sizing
- Food safety of eggs
- Preservation and processing
- Coagulation of eggs in food preparation
- Preparation methods for eggs

COMPOSITION AND NUTRITIVE VALUE

Whole egg contains about 75 percent water, 12 percent protein, 10 percent fat, 1 percent carbohydrate, and 1 percent minerals. The white and the yolk are very different from each other in composition, however, as shown in Table 24-1. Essentially all the fat of the egg is found in the yolk; the white contains a larger percentage of water. The shell makes up about 11 percent of the total weight of the egg and is composed of approximately 95 percent calcium carbonate in crystal form [28].

Although the ratio of white to yolk varies in individual eggs, the white is usually about two-thirds by weight of the total edible portion, and the yolk is approximately one-third. In general, the yolk has higher nutrient density than the white, containing more minerals and vitamins relative to its weight.

In 1967, Americans were eating about 320 eggs per person per year. As concerns about fat and cholesterol in the diet increased, however, the high cholesterol content of egg yolk made it a target. Egg consumption fell to 237 per person in 1996 [27]. More recent research indicates

TABLE 24-1 Chemical Composition of Egg without Shell									
	Amount	Weight (g)	Water (%)	Energy (kcal)	Protein (g)	Fat (g)	Iron (mg)	Vitamin A (retinal equivalent, RE)	Thiamin (mg)	Riboflavin (mg)
Whole egg, large	1	50	75	72	6	5	0.7	95	0.03	0.25
Egg white	1	33	88	15	4	0	trace	0	trace	0.15
Egg yolk	1	17	49	60	3	5	0.6	97	0.03	0.11

Source: *Nutritive Value of Foods*. Home and Garden Bulletin No. 72. Washington, DC: U.S. Department of Agriculture, 1991.

that dietary cholesterol has less effect on serum cholesterol than previously thought, and eggs are getting better press. Eggs have several nutritional and economic advantages, including being a significant source of several vitamins. In 2005, 254 eggs were available in the food supply per person [33].

Proteins

Egg proteins are of excellent nutritional quality, having the highest protein efficiency ratio (PER) of any of the common foods. The major protein in egg white is *ovalbumin*, a protein that is easily denatured by heat. Other egg white proteins are *ovotransferrin, ovomucoid, ovomucin,* and *lysozyme*. Ovomucin, although present in a comparatively small amount, has a large effect on the consistency of thick egg white. It is a very large molecule with a filamentous or fiberlike nature.

The major proteins in egg yolk are lipoproteins, which include *lipovitellin* and *lipovitellinin*. The lipoproteins are responsible for the excellent emulsifying properties of egg yolk when used in such products as mayonnaise. The preparation of mayonnaise was discussed in Chapter 10.

Lipids

The fatty materials in egg yolk, making up about one-third of the weight of fresh yolk, include triglycerides, phospholipids, and cholesterol. One large egg yolk contains about 215 milligrams of cholesterol; the egg white has no cholesterol. Because of the high level of cholesterol in the yolk, the egg has been considered to be an atherogenic food. That concept is now changing. The fatty acid composition of egg yolk may be altered by changing the hen's diet. For example, an increased level of omega-3 fatty acids has been reported to result from the addition of small amounts of menhaden fish oil or special mixtures to the laying hen's diet [37]. Eggs have been introduced into consumer markets that have 195 milligrams of cholesterol per egg, 25 percent less saturated fat, and three times the amount of omega-3 fatty acids as a result of a patented feed program (Figure 24-1) [29].

Pigments

Because certain yellow carotenoid pigments can be converted into vitamin A in the body, the question has been raised of whether more highly colored egg yolks are a better source of vitamin A than pale yolks. The predominant yellow pigment of egg yolk is a *xanthophyll*, which is not changed to vitamin A in the body. Deep-colored yolks, however, are high in vitamin A content because the same rations that produce color in the yolks also contain more provitamin A, which the hen is able to convert into vitamin A and deposit in the yolk. Hens that do not have access to green or yellow feed and that produce pale yolks may be given vitamin A–supplemented rations. The pale yolks are then high in vitamin A. The vitamin A content of egg yolk, therefore, cannot be predicted solely on the basis of the

FOCUS ON SCIENCE

More about Lipoproteins in Eggs

Lipovitellin is a lipoprotein found in egg yolks. It is separated into α- and β-lipovitellins. The lipids in α- and β-lipoproteins include 40 percent neutral proteins and 60 percent phospholipids (emulsifiers). The phospholipid fraction of each protein contains 75 percent phosphatidylcholine, 18 percent phosphatidylethanolamine, and 7 percent sphingomyelin and lysophospholipids.

Source: Pawne, W. D. and Nahai, S. (1985). Chapter 14: Characteristics of edible fluids of animal origins: Eggs. In *Food Chemistry*, edited by O. Fennema, p. 842. New York: Marcel Dekker, Inc.

FOCUS ON SCIENCE

docosahexaenoic (22:6 n-3) acids. These fatty acids are omega-3 fatty acids which are highly unsaturated and associated with health benefits.

What Lipids Are Found in Menhaden Fish Oil?

Menhanden fish oil may be added to the laying hens' diets to promote increased omega-3 fatty acids in the eggs. The lipids found in this fish oil are *eicosapentaenoic* (20:5 n-3) and

[handwritten: 1 egg = 215 mg/cholesterol DV = 300 mg/day]

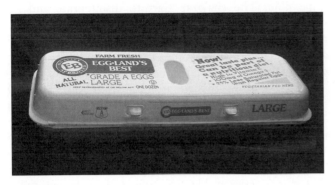

FIGURE 24-1 These grade A large eggs marketed by Eggland are high in vitamin E and omega-3 fatty acids and have 25 percent less saturated fat than regular eggs. *(Courtesy of U.S. Department of Agriculture)*

depth of the yellow color. In practice, egg producers usually feed chickens either sufficient green vegetation or xanthophyll pigments to yield a yolk of medium color intensity.

STRUCTURE

Egg Shell

The egg shell is porous and allows exchange of gases and loss of moisture from the egg. It is brown or white, depending on the breed of the hen. The color of the shell

[handwritten: —can absorb flavor + odors]

has no effect on the flavor, quality, or nutritive value of the contents. An air cell formed at the large end of the egg is produced on cooling by the separation of two thin, fibrous protein membranes that are present between the shell and the egg white (Figure 24-2).

In the past, it has been suggested that the protective dull waxy coat on the outside of the egg, referred to as the *cuticle* or the *bloom*, should not be washed off. When it is washed, the porous shell may then more easily permit bacteria, molds, and undesirable flavors or odors to enter the egg. There also may be a greater evaporation of moisture unless preventative measures are taken. However, dirt or soil on shells is probably the most prominent cause of the bacterial invasion of eggs. In commercial practice, therefore, dirty eggs are washed. The eggs are usually washed in automatic washers using alkaline cleaning compounds. After washing, the eggs may be rinsed with a sanitizing agent. If eggs are washed properly, the undesirable effects of washing are kept at a minimum [16]. To replace the natural bloom, the eggs are lightly oiled before packaging [2].

Albumen, Chalazae, and Membranes

The albumen, usually called the *egg white*, consists of thin and thick portions. The proportions of thin and thick white vary widely in different eggs and change during storage under varying conditions. It has been estimated

THE PARTS OF AN EGG

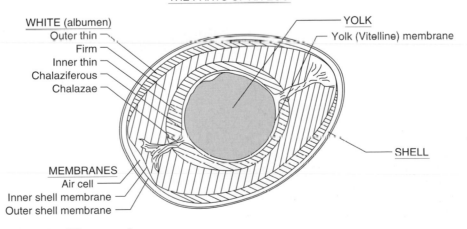

FIGURE 24-2 The parts of an egg.

that about 20 to 25 percent of the total white of fresh eggs (one to five days old) is thin white. Thick white is characterized by a higher content of the protein ovomucin than is found in thin white.

Immediately adjacent to the *vitelline membrane*—the thin membrane that surrounds the egg yolk—is a *chalaziferous* or inner layer of firm white. This chalaziferous layer gives strength to the vitelline membrane and extends into the *chalazae*. The chalazae appear as two small bits of thickened white, one on each end of the yolk, and anchor the yolk in the center of the egg. Chalazae appear to have almost the same molecular structure as ovomucin [15]. Two more membranes are found in eggs. These membranes are called shell membranes and are found adjacent to the shell.

Yolk

The yolk is composed of tiny spheres of various sizes and shapes, closely packed in the vitelline membrane. Protein granules and oil droplets exist within the spheres [26]. Marketed eggs are usually infertile, and the germinal disc on the surface of the yolk does not develop. No difference in nutritive value is noted between infertile and fertilized eggs, but fertile eggs may tend to deteriorate more rapidly. Occasionally a blood spot may be found on a yolk. It is not because the egg has been fertilized but instead is the result of the blood vessel rupture on the surface of the yolk [3]. Blood spots are primarily a cosmetic defect and thus are safe to eat.

EGG QUALITY AND SIZING

Physical Characteristics of Fresh and Deteriorated Eggs

Most eggs reach the stores only a few days after being laid and thus exhibit the characteristics of fresh eggs. A very fresh egg, when broken onto a flat plate, stands up in rounded form due, to a considerable extent, to the viscosity of the thick portion of the egg white. As eggs age, qual-ity deterioration is observable. The proportion of thin white increases, whereas that of thick white decreases in older eggs. This thinning of the thick white appears to involve some changes in the filamentous protein ovomucin. Lysozyme also may be involved.

With aging, the yolk takes up water from the white, and the yolk membrane stretches. When broken out, the deteriorated egg flattens and tends to spread over a level surface. If stretched excessively by movement of water into the yolk, the yolk membrane is weakened and may break when the egg is removed from the shell. Separation of the yolk from the white is thus rendered difficult or impossible. The chalazae start to disintegrate and no longer hold the yolk in the center of the egg, and the yolk moves freely. As an egg ages, especially in a warm, dry atmosphere, moisture escapes through the shell. The air cell, which is very small in a fresh egg, increases in size.

The yolks of fresh eggs are slightly acid (usual pH 6.0 to 6.2), whereas the whites are alkaline (usual pH 7.6 to 7.9). A loss of carbon dioxide from the egg in storage results in increased alkalinity of both white and yolk. The white may eventually reach a pH of 9.0 to 9.7. This increase in pH or alkalinity of eggs during storage may be slowed to an appreciable degree by coating the egg shells with a thin layer of oil on the day the eggs are laid. It has been suggested that damage to some egg white proteins by a very alkaline pH results in angel food cakes of decreased volume [23]. These changes in eggs because of age are summarized in Table 24-2.

Flavor and Odor Deterioration

The flavor and odor of fresh eggs are affected by the feed, the individuality of the hen, and storage conditions. During storage, off-flavors may be produced in eggs by contamination with microorganisms or by the absorption of flavors from the environment. One study of the headspace over scrambled eggs reported the presence of 38 volatile substances, including alcohols, aldehydes, ketones, esters, benzene derivatives, and sulfur-containing compounds [22]. A comparison with the volatile compounds of

---

TABLE 24-2 Physical Changes in Eggs because of Increasing Age

Component	High Quality Fresh Eggs	Poor Quality Older Eggs
Air Cell	Small	Larger
Albumin (Egg Whites)	Egg whites adjacent to the yolk are noticeably thick. Whites of very fresh eggs may appear cloudy.	Egg white is thin and runny.
Yolk	Yolk stands high and round when broken out onto a plate.	Membrane around yolk weakens. Yolk appears more flattened when broken onto a plate.
Chalazae	Chalazae are strong and hold yolk in center of whites within the shell.	Chalazae weaken, and yolk is no longer "centered" in the shell.
pH	Slightly acidic yolks (pH 6.0 to 6.2) Alkaline egg whites (pH 7.6 to 7.9)	Increased alkalinity of whites and yolks (pH of 9.0 to 9.7)

polystyrene packaging materials, commonly used in egg cartons, suggested that some migration of volatile compounds from the packaging into the eggs may have occurred during storage. Further studies of cooked egg flavors will be interesting and useful.

Purchasing Fresh Eggs

Consumers can gauge the freshness of eggs by the pack or expiration date on the egg carton. The "pack date" must be displayed on eggs cartons using the USDA grade shield [34]. The pack date is generally provided using the *Julian date*, which is a three-digit code representing the day of the year; thus, January 1 is 001 and December 31 is 365. Eggs also generally have a "sell-by" or "exp" (expiration date) on the carton. Properly refrigerated eggs should maintain good quality for three to five weeks after purchase [34] or four to five weeks after the Julian date [2]. USDA grades are discussed later in the chapter.

Measuring Quality

Candling is the method used to determine the interior quality of eggs that go into trade channels. Hand candling, shown in Figure 24-3, is rarely used in present commercial grading operations, having been replaced by automated equipment and mass-scanning devices. Candling may still be used for spot checking, however, and is useful for teaching and demonstrating quality determination. When candling by hand, the egg is held to an opening, behind which is a source of strong light. As the light passes through the egg, it shows the quality of the shell, the size of the air cell, the position and mobility of the yolk, blood spots, molds, and a developing embryo, if one is present. As eggs deteriorate and the chalazae weaken, the yolk tends to settle toward the shell rather than remain suspended in the firm white. In such circumstances, the yolk is more fully visible when the egg is candled, in part because the yolk is no longer centered. Dark yolks also cast a more distinct shadow than light

yolks. USDA grades for eggs are based on their candled appearance. In Grade AA eggs, the air cell is about 1/8 inch in depth and the diameter of a dime [2].

Although candling is the best method available for rating unbroken eggs, it may not always be reliable in indicating the quality of the egg when it is opened. Some tests done on the broken-out egg include measurement of the height of the thick white in relation to the weight of the egg (Haugh unit), and measurement of the height of the yolk in relation to the width of the yolk (yolk index). Figure 24-4 shows the operation of an instrument for measuring Haugh units in a broken-out egg.

Grading

The classification of individual eggs according to established standards constitutes grading for quality. The egg grade standards widely used throughout the United States have been formulated by the U.S. Department of Agriculture; these are summarized in Table 24-3.

In grading, the candled appearance of the egg shell, air cell, white, and yolk are considered. According to the results of the candling inspection, the eggs are assigned one of three consumer grades: U.S. Grade AA, U.S. Grade A, or U.S. Grade B. These grades are illustrated by photographs of broken-out eggs in Figure 24-5, and the grade marks are shown in Figure 24-6.

Grades AA and A have a large proportion of thick white that stands up around a firm, high yolk. These eggs are especially good for frying and poaching, when appearance is important. Grade B eggs, which have thinner whites and spread out more, are good for general baking and cooking. Grade B eggs are generally not found in retail stores. The nutritional value for all grades is similar.

Eggs must be held under refrigeration, preferably in a closed carton, to maintain quality. Eggs deteriorate from the time laid until consumed. Figure 24-7 indicates how egg quality decreases with the time of holding. With proper care, however, this decline in quality can be minimized.

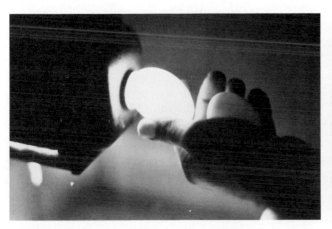

Eggs are held to a bright light during hand candling

Mass scanning devices speed the candling process

FIGURE 24-3 Candling is used to determine the interior quality of eggs. *(Courtesy of the U.S. Department of Agriculture)*

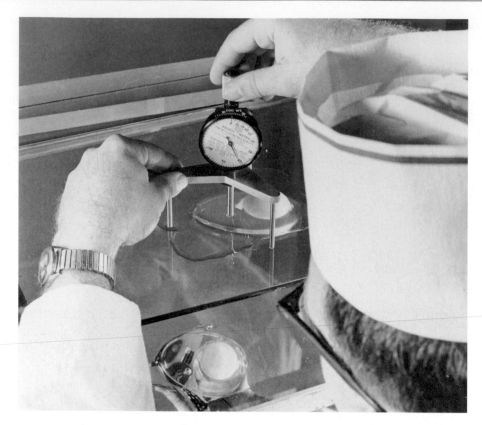

FIGURE 24-4 A micrometer is used to evaluate the quality of an egg that has been removed from the shell. This is done by measuring the height of the thick white. This instrument gives a direct reading in Haugh units. *(Courtesy of the U.S. Department of Agriculture)*

TABLE 24-3 **Summary of U.S. Standards for Quality of Individual Shell Eggs**

| Quality Factor | Specifications for Each Quality Factor | | |
	AA Quality	A Quality	B Quality
Shell	Clean	Clean	Clean to slightly stained
	Unbroken	Unbroken	Unbroken
	Practically normal	Practically normal	Somewhat abnormal
Air Cell	1/8 in. or less in depth	3/16 in. or less in depth	Over 3/16 in. in depth
	Unlimited movement and free or bubbly	Unlimited movement and free or bubbly	Unlimited movement and free or bubbly
White	Thick	Clear	Clear
	Firm	Reasonably firm	Somewhat watery
			Small blood and meat spots may be present
Yolk	Outline slightly defined	Outline fairly well defined	Outline plainly visible
	Practically free from defects	Practically free from defects	Enlarged and flattened
			Clearly visible germ development but no blood

Source: References 8, 32

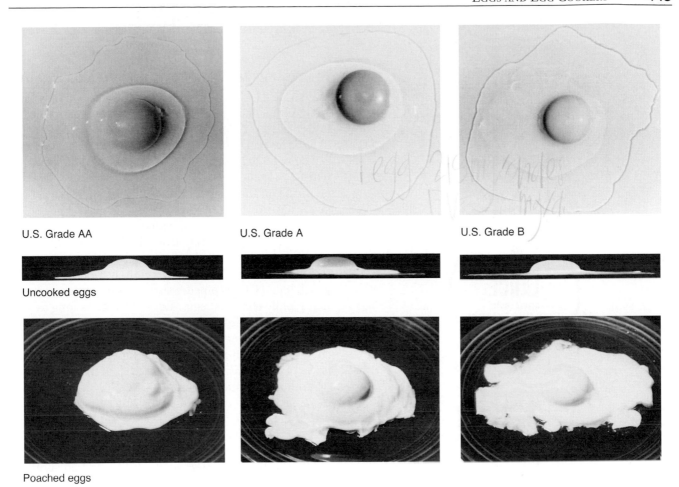

U.S. Grade AA   U.S. Grade A   U.S. Grade B

Uncooked eggs

Poached eggs

FIGURE 24-5 Characteristics of egg quality, with the yolk standing highest on the thick white of the U.S. Grade AA eggs, are evident in broken-out eggs and in poached eggs. *(Courtesy of the U.S. Department of Agriculture)*

Sizing

Separate from the process of grading, eggs are sorted for size into six weight classes, as shown in Figure 24-8. This separation is on the basis of weighing individual eggs. The commercial weighing and packaging of eggs may be automated, as illustrated in Figure 24-9. Within each grade are several sizes usually available on supermarket shelves.

Size relative to cost per dozen is an important factor to consider when buying eggs. Most eggs are marketed in cartons, on which the minimum weight per dozen, in ounces, is usually listed. This weight can be divided into the price per dozen to determine the cost per ounce of egg. The cost per ounce of each of the sizes of eggs can then be compared to determine which is the best buy.

Another point to consider in buying eggs is the use for which they are purchased. There is no one best size to buy. Large eggs may be preferred for table use, but for cooking purposes price in relation to size may be a more important consideration. Recipes calling for a specific number of eggs are usually formulated on the basis of the large size. Actually, measuring or weighing eggs in recipes gives much more uniform results. If jumbo and extra large or small and peewee-size eggs are used in a recipe, some adjustment should be made, reducing or increasing the number of eggs by one-fourth to one-third for the jumbo and extra large or for the small and peewee sizes, respectively. If several eggs are used in a recipe, the potential for error increases.

FOOD SAFETY OF EGGS

About one out of 20,000 eggs produced is contaminated with *Salmonella enteritidis*. With 47 billion shell eggs consumed annually, this translates into about 2.3 million eggs that are positive for *Salmonella enteritidis* [24]. Eggs were estimated to be the cause of 182,000 cases of foodborne illness in 2000 [30].

Unbroken shell eggs may contain salmonella bacteria because *Salmonella enteritidis* may infect the reproductive system of laying hens, which then results in the contamination of the egg in advance of shell formation. These eggs are laid already contaminated with the organism inside the intact shell. Eggs also may become infected from pathogens carried in fecal and dirt contamination on the shell exterior and then move through the shell pores to the inner parts of the eggs [34]. Washing of eggs during processing and a light oil coating to seal the shell reduce this risk. Raw or undercooked eggs and foods

FIGURE 24-6 Three grade marks for eggs graded under federal and state supervision. The marks show both grade and size. *(Courtesy of the U.S. Department of Agriculture)*

containing them have been implicated in about 80 percent of those *S. enteritidis* outbreaks in which a food source was identified [20].

Government Regulation

The U.S. Food and Drug Administration (FDA) and the U.S. Department of Agriculture Food Safety and Inspection Service (FSIS) share federal responsibility for egg safety [5]. A 1999 Egg Safety Action Plan developed by the FDA and FSIS seeks to reduce and eventually eliminate eggs as a source of *Salmonella enteritidis*.

In 2000, the FDA finalized regulations to require safe food-handling instructions on cartons and new refrigeration requirements [36]. Shell eggs are required to have the following statement: "Safe Handling Instructions: To prevent illness from bacteria: keep eggs refrigerated, cook eggs until yolks are firm, and cook foods containing eggs thoroughly." The refrigeration requirements, effective in 2001, specify that untreated shell eggs sold at stores,

roadside stands, and so forth must be held and displayed at or below 45°F (7°C) [35].

Processing and Storage Considerations

If salmonella are present in an egg, the numbers would likely be small at the time of laying and would probably not create a problem if the product were eaten immediately. The real problems occur with the mishandling of the egg at any place along the production line from the hen to the consumer. At warm temperatures, microorganisms can increase rapidly, which is why eggs should always be properly refrigerated.

A cryogenic system of cooling eggs has been developed to cool eggs quickly from the "just-laid" temperature of 110°F (43°C) down to 45°F (7°C) in 80 to 90 seconds [24]. Eggs are conveyed into a cooling tunnel in which liquid CO_2 is piped, creating a vapor/snow mixture that rapidly chills the eggs. Eggs can take as long as 7 to 14 days to cool from 110°F (43°C) to 45°F (7°C) under normal processing and packaging conditions. Quickly cooled eggs are fresher, and microbial testing has shown lower levels of *Salmonella enteritidis*.

Additional methods of processing shell eggs to increase food safety have been developed. Shell eggs may be pasteurized by using a hot-water immersion process that controls time and temperature to result in a 5-log reduction in salmonella [25]. A high-moisture, hot-air method of pasteurization is also being studied. Both of these methods maintain the desirable characteristics of shell eggs, including the whippability of the white. In 2000, the FDA approved use of ionizing radiation on eggs in the shell to reduce *salmonella*. Although irradiation is effective, the white may become slightly opaque and lose some of the whipping ability [25].

Purchasing and Storage Recommendations

Buy eggs at retail from refrigerated cases only; for foodservice, use only eggs delivered under refrigeration [34, 35]. Buy clean eggs with uncracked shells. Refrigerate eggs immediately, in cartons or cases, at 45°F (7°C) or slightly below. Do not wash eggs unless they are to be used immediately. Use shell eggs within three to five weeks. Leftover egg dishes should be stored in small enough containers so cooling down to 41°F (4°C) is rapid.

Handling and Preparation Recommendations

Wash hands, utensils, equipment, and work surfaces before or after contact with eggs [34, 35]. Do not keep eggs out of the refrigerator for more than two hours. Cooked eggs for a picnic should be packed in a cooler with enough ice to keep cool.

Do not eat raw eggs, including foods such as milkshakes, Caesar salad, ice cream, or eggnog made from recipes in which the raw egg ingredients are not cooked. Foods such as ice cream and eggnog should be prepared from a cooked base heated to 160°F (71°C). Prepare

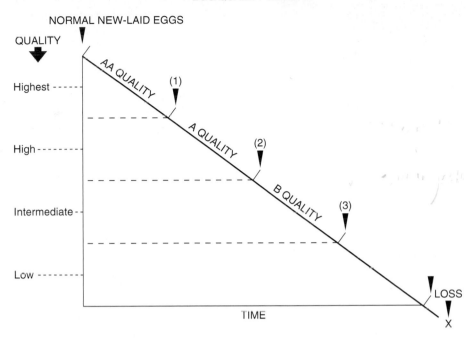

FIGURE 24-7 The graded quality of eggs declines with the time of holding. *(Courtesy of the U.S. Department of Agriculture)*

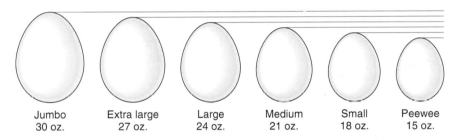

FIGURE 24-8 When purchasing eggs, you should be aware of both size (an indication of quantity) and grade (an indication of quality). There are six sizes shown. The weights shown in the illustrations represent ounces per dozen eggs. *Source: Reference 19*

other foods such as Caesar salad with pasteurized or irradiated eggs.

Cook eggs slowly over moderate heat. An endpoint cooking temperature of 145°F (57°C) is acceptable for eggs that will be immediately consumed. In general, cook at least until the whites are completely coagulated and the yolks are firm. Scrambled eggs should not be runny. Those especially at risk, such as infants, pregnant women, the elderly, or the ill, should avoid eating soft-cooked or runny eggs. However, pasteurized shell eggs or egg products are safe for these individuals. In foodservice, only pasteurized eggs must be used in dishes such as scrambled eggs if a large number of eggs will be pooled. When serving high-risk populations, the use of only pasteurized egg products is recommended.

Casseroles and other dishes containing eggs should be cooked to 160°F (71°C) and checked by thermometer.

Divinity candy and seven-minute frosting are safe when prepared by combining hot sugar syrup with the beaten egg whites. Meringue-topped pies are safe when meringue is placed on a hot filling and baked at 350°F (177°C) for 15 minutes. Cooked eggs and egg-rich foods, such as custards, puddings, and pumpkin pie, should be served immediately after cooking or refrigerated at once for use within three to four days.

PRESERVATION AND PROCESSING

Processed Egg Products

Egg breaking, separation, and pasteurization in preparation for freezing or drying are usually done by egg-processing plants. After washing and candling, the eggs go

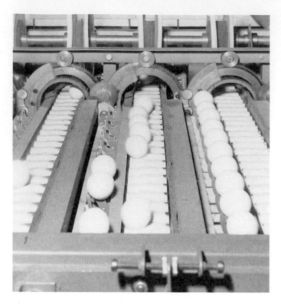

FIGURE 24-9 Eggs are handled and weighed by automatic in-line scales. Eggs of different sizes are weighed and ejected from the line at different points. *(Courtesy of the U.S. Department of Agriculture)*

to egg-breaking machines. Completely automated equipment processes the eggs, removing them from filler flats, washing and sanitizing the outside shells, and breaking and separating the eggs into white, yolks, and mixture of white and yolk. The liquid egg product is then filtered and chilled before further processing. Scrupulous cleanliness must be maintained throughout the process, and contamination from the introduction of unwholesome eggs into the whole egg mass must be avoided. All egg products are monitored for pathogenic organisms, and tests for salmonella are made regularly by the egg products industry and the USDA. Only products negative for salmonella organisms can be sold.

Pasteurized.   Pasteurization is required by the federal government for all processed eggs whether frozen, dried, or liquid to ensure freedom from pathogenic microorganisms. However, eggs must be pasteurized in such a way that, while bacteria are destroyed, the functional properties (whipping and baking performances) are not damaged [17]. The USDA regulates the minimum temperature and holding time for the pasteurization of egg

HOT TOPICS

Focusing on Eggs!

Federal and state governments, the scientific community, and the egg industry are all focusing on eggs—and egg products. Why? Because they want to protect the health of the American people. Eggs—even unbroken, fresh, clean shell eggs—may contain *Salmonella enteritidis* bacteria that can cause foodborne illness. No matter how hard we try to control these tiny organisms, salmonella and other pathogens keep causing major outbreaks. For example, in May 2001 an outbreak occurred in Minneapolis involving raw eggs used in the preparation of Hollandaise sauce for eggs Benedict served at a buffet in a major hotel. At least 46 of those attending the buffet were ill, along with a chef, 8 hotel engineers, and at least 2 waiters [41].

Many government agencies are involved in the regulation—surveillance, inspection, investigation, and enforcement—of our food supply, from farm to table. At the federal level, the Animal and Plant Health Inspection Service (APHIS) monitors the incidence of *Salmonella enteritidis* in flocks of laying hens. The Agricultural Research Service (ARS) conducts research to study the habits of salmonella,

while the National Agricultural Statistics Service (NASS) analyzes the economic impact on the egg-producing industry. The Food Safety and Inspection Service (FSIS) works together with the Food and Drug Administration (FDA) to strengthen regulations with the goal of finally solving the problem of *Salmonella enteritidis* in eggs. The FSIS is also responsible for educating the consumer about the safe handling of eggs. And we should not forget the Agricultural Marketing Service (AMS) that administers the egg-quality grading program. In addition, state agriculture departments and state and local health departments monitor compliance with U.S. standards as eggs are packed, transported, and sold in retail markets.

Even with all of this vigilant surveillance, however, you must focus on safe egg handling and cooking methods. Follow the safe handling instructions now required on all raw, unpasteurized shell eggs sold in retail markets: "To prevent illness from bacteria: Keeps eggs refrigerated, cook eggs until yolks are firm, and cook foods containing eggs thoroughly." Then enjoy your favorite egg recipes. ■

FOCUS ON SCIENCE

What Is a 5-Log Reduction?

At present, FDA regulations cover the pasteurization of eggs, milk, juice, and seafood. In all cases, FDA talks of achieving zero pathogen levels through pasteurization. In practice, what is meant by "zero pathogen level" or "destruction or elimination" of a "[heat resistant] microorganism" is reducing the offending pathogenic microorganism by at least five orders of magnitude, for example, a 100,000-fold reduction, also known as 5-log reduction.

Source: Hansen, M. (2007). Comments of Consumers Union on the Food and Drug Administration's (FDA's) Docket No. 2005N-0272, "Irradiation in the Production, Processing and Handling of Food."

---

products. A summary of pasteurization temperatures is provided in Table 24-4.

Frozen. The functional properties of raw egg whites are not altered by freezing and thawing. However, frozen egg yolks become viscous and gummy on thawing unless they are mixed with sugar, salt, or syrup before freezing (see Chapter 30 for directions on freezing eggs at home). It has been suggested that the freezing process destabilizes the surface of the tiny lipid-protein particles (lipoproteins) in egg yolk. The fragments that are liberated then aggregate on thawing to form a mesh-type structure or gel [18]. Whole mixed eggs are often frozen without added salt or sugar; however, because of the presence of the yolk, they probably retain their culinary qualities better when a stabilizer is added. Cooked egg white is not stable to freezing and thawing. The gel structure of the coagulated protein is damaged by ice crystal formation. Syneresis occurs on thawing.

Egg-processing firms design and produce several specialty egg products, many of which are frozen. Hard-cooked, chopped, and peeled eggs are used for salad bars. Frozen or refrigerated hard-cooked egg rolls or *long eggs* offer the advantage of providing consistently sized sliced eggs for salad garnishes. To make these long eggs, albumen is cooked around a center core of egg yolk that may be approximately 10 inches in length, thus the name. Frozen, precooked products such as egg patties, fried eggs, crêpes, omelets, French toast, quiche, and egg breakfast sandwiches are also available in grocery stores and for foodservice use.

Dried. Drying is a satisfactory method for preserving eggs, either whole or as separated yolks or whites. Spray-dried egg whites and egg yolks have long shelf lives, and are used in many food product formulations. To retain their functional properties, good color, and flavor, and to help control the Maillard reaction during storage, dried whites require treatment to remove the last traces of glucose. Dried eggs keep best if the initial moisture content is low and if they are kept in a tightly sealed container. Low storage temperatures are also important in maintaining the quality of the dried products.

Dried eggs can be reconstituted before use, or they can be sifted with dry ingredients and extra liquid added later to the recipe. General directions for use are to sift prior to

TABLE 24-4 Pasteurization Temperatures for Egg Whites, Yolks, and Whole Eggs	
Type of Egg Product	**Pasteurization Temperatures and Conditions**
Liquid whole egg	140°F (60°C) for not less than 3 1/2 minutes
	Note: Whole egg blends must be heated to a higher temperature.
Egg whites	134°F (57°C) for 3.5 minutes or 132°F for 6.2 minutes (without addition of acid)
	Note: Egg whites become denatured with a loss of foaming ability when pasteurized at temperatures used for whole eggs. Increasing acidity of the whites before pasteurization reduces denaturation.
Egg yolks	140°F (60°C) for 6.2 minutes or 142°F for 3.5 minutes
	Note: The pasteurization temperatures for egg yolks with sugar or with salt added are slightly different.

Source: Reference 6

measuring and to place lightly in a measuring cup or spoon before leveling off the top with a spatula or straight edge. For reconstitution, dried egg should be sprinkled over the surface of lukewarm water, stirred to moisten, and then beaten until smooth. Reconstituted dried whites are beaten very stiff for most, if not all, uses. Dried egg whites are commonly found in angel food cake mixes.

Liquid.   Liquid eggs, broken out of the shell, are available to foodservice operators and food processors, as whole eggs, egg whites, egg yolks, or blended egg products such as scrambled egg mix. When these eggs are pasteurized, any salmonella or other pathogenic organisms that may be present are destroyed, but the product is not sterile. Some microorganisms capable of causing postpasteurization spoilage are still present. Consequently, the shelf life of pasteurized, refrigerated liquid eggs is limited. Shelf lives of 12 days at 36°F (2°C) and 5 days at 48°F (9°C) have been reported. An ultrapasteurization process, with heating at temperatures up to 154°F (68°C) and subsequent aseptic packaging, has been developed for homogenized liquid whole eggs [10]. These products must be refrigerated but have an extended shelf life of six to seven weeks.

Liquid refrigerated egg products offer advantages for use in foodservice operations and food-processing facilities. They may be easily poured, the need for thawing is eliminated, functional properties and quality are maintained, there is no need to dispose of egg shells, and they are pasteurized. Furthermore, quantity foodservice operations would not be able to serve menu items such as scrambled eggs without the use of pasteurized egg products because food-safety regulations prohibit the pooling of shell eggs in quantity.

Egg Substitutes

The food industry has responded to the desire of some consumers to have a low-cholesterol egg product by marketing egg substitutes in both liquid and dry forms. Most of the available egg substitute products contain no egg yolk but have a high concentration of egg white (over 80 percent). To provide yolklike properties to the egg white mixture, various ingredients are used. These include, in different products, corn oil and nonfat dry milk; soy protein isolate, soybean oil, and egg white solids; and calcium caseinate, nonfat dry milk, and corn oil. A few products on the market contain small amounts of egg yolk. Most of the egg substitutes are free, or almost free, of cholesterol and contain considerably less fat, and the fat is more unsaturated than in whole eggs.

When compared with fresh whole eggs, egg substitutes may have somewhat less desirable flavor, aroma, and overall acceptability [9]. Custards made from egg substitute products, however, have been reported to have less sag and spread than those made with whole eggs. One study found in custards prepared with nonfat, 70 percent lactose-reduced milk, that egg substitutes produced less desirable custards than those made with whole eggs [40]. Yellow cakes prepared with egg substitutes were higher in volume than those made with whole eggs, but were less desirable in flavor and overall acceptability.

Commercial Cold Storage

In the past, some eggs produced in the United States were placed in commercial cold storage during periods of higher production. Eggs were stored at 29° to 32°F (–1.5° to 0°C), which is just above their freezing point. Only eggs of original high quality were stored. These eggs remained in desirable condition when the storage room was well controlled for humidity (85 to 90 percent), circulation of air, and freedom from objectionable odors. A controlled atmosphere of carbon dioxide or ozone was advantageous in maintaining quality. Eggs stored under these conditions could be maintained at Grade A quality for as long as six months. However, extended commercial cold storage is rarely used today because modern breeding and flock management have virtually eliminated seasonal differences in production [1].

FOCUS ON SCIENCE

What Are Some of the Ingredients in Egg Substitutes?

Egg substitutes contain modified food starch, xanthan, and guar gum. These hydrocolloids contribute the viscosity to the egg substitute that would otherwise be produced by the yolk, if present. Egg substitutes also contain minerals and vitamins: vitamins A, B_1, B_6, B_{12}; folic acid; and the minerals calcium, iron, and zinc. These nutrients are contained in the yolk, but because it is absent, these are supplemented in the product. These ingredients may be responsible for the off-flavors detected in the egg substitute.

COAGULATION OF EGGS AND EGG FOAMS IN FOOD PREPARATION

Heat Coagulation of Egg Proteins

Both egg white and yolk proteins coagulate when heated and can therefore be used for thickening or gel formation. Upon heating, the egg proteins are denatured and then gradually aggregate to form a three-dimensional gel network. The network is stabilized by cross-bonds that include disulfide linkages and hydrogen bonding [21].

Egg functions best as a thickener when it is beaten only enough to blend the egg mass smoothly. If too much air is incorporated during beating, the egg foam may float on the surface of the mixture to be thickened. The following factors affect the heat coagulation of egg proteins.

Concentration and Part of Egg Used. The temperature at which egg proteins coagulate and the time required for coagulation depend in part on the proportion of egg in any mixture (Table 24-5). Coagulation does not occur instantaneously, but rather proceeds gradually. Egg yolk proteins require a slightly higher temperature for coagulation than those of egg white. Egg white loses its transparency and becomes opaque white on coagulation. Because little color change occurs in egg yolk at the beginning of coagulation, the exact temperature at which thickening starts is more difficult to judge than is the case with egg white. Dilution of egg with an ingredient such as milk increases the temperature at which coagulation occurs.

The texture of coagulated egg yolk, when cooked intact, is crumbly and mealy but solid. When the yolk membrane is ruptured and the stirred yolk is heated, however, the texture of the resulting gel is firm and rubbery. This difference in texture of intact and stirred egg yolk may result from changes that occur in the intricate microstructure of egg yolk with stirring. The tiny discrete granules of the intact yolk may form a highly cross-linked protein network when disrupted [39]. To achieve complete coagulation, a whole egg must be heated to the temperature required for yolk protein coagulation, because whole egg includes the yolk.

Time and Temperature. The rate and amount of coagulation within a given time period will increase with increasing temperature. The character of the coagulum formed when egg white is heated at high temperatures is firm, even tough, compared with the soft, tender, more evenly coagulated product obtained when coagulation takes place at lower temperatures.

The toughness and greater shrinkage of the protein coagulated at a high temperature are the basis for the recommended use of low or moderate temperatures for egg cookery. The temperatures used need not be as low as 158°F (70°C), although that temperature, maintained for a sufficient length of time, eventually brings about complete coagulation of egg proteins. If eggs are cooked in water, the water should not boil. Water at a temperature of about 185°F (85°C) will produce a texture that is tender, yet firm. Coagulation at this temperature takes place in a noticeably shorter time than is required at 158°F (70°C).

For an omelet cooked in a skillet over direct heat, the heat should be kept low so that the mass cooks slowly and can be heated uniformly throughout without toughening the bottom layers. The coagulation of a puffy omelet may be finished in a moderate oven. Oven temperatures from 300° to 350°F (149° to 177°C) have been found to be satisfactory for cooking eggs and egg dishes, although there are indications that somewhat higher temperatures also are satisfactory if time is carefully controlled. Placing egg dishes in a pan of water when baking in an oven will help to protect the egg product from becoming overcooked.

Effect of Rate of Heating. Rapidly heated egg mixtures such as custards coagulate at a higher temperature than similar mixtures that are slowly heated. The fact that the coagulation temperature with rapid heating is very close to the curdling temperature means that a rapidly cooked custard is more likely to curdle than one that is slowly heated. A slowly heated custard can, nevertheless, curdle if it is heated to a temperature that is too high.

Effect of Added Substances. Egg mixtures containing sugar coagulate at a higher temperature. In contrast, slightly acidic egg mixtures coagulate at a lower temperature.

TABLE 24-5 Coagulation Temperature of Egg Proteins in Egg Whites, Yolk, Whole Eggs, and Egg Mixtures	
Portion of the Egg	**Temperature Range for Coagulation**
Egg white, undiluted	140°F (60°C)—Coagulation begins and whites begin to become opaque
	158°F (70°C)—Whites are coagulated and fairly firm
Egg yolk, undiluted	149°F (65°C)—Beginning of coagulation
	158°F (70°C)—Yolk loses its fluidity
One whole egg, diluted with one cup of milk	176°F (80°C)—Approximate temperature of coagulation
	Temperature for coagulation of diluted eggs will vary with the amount of dilution and whether other ingredients are included.

FOCUS ON SCIENCE

Why Do Eggs Become Tough and Rubbery when Overcooked or Cooked at Too High of a Temperature?

The main protein in the egg white is albumin, which is a simple protein. This protein is linear in structure and is easily denatured by heat. When cooking an egg, this protein is the first that undergoes a change; in the presence of extreme heat over a long period, it will produce a tough and rubbery product.

Salts, such as chlorides, phosphates, sulfates, and lactates, aid in gel formation in cooked egg mixtures.

Sugar affects the temperature of coagulation by increasing the heat stability of the proteins. Custards are a typical egg dish that is sweetened. Slightly acidic egg mixtures coagulate more rapidly, at a somewhat lower temperature. Examples of acidic egg mixtures include those with added dates or raisins, omelets made with tomato or orange juice, and Hollandaise sauce containing lemon juice. The coagulum formed in an acidic egg mixture is also more firm than that of less acidic mixtures. The hardness and cohesiveness of egg white gels have been reported to be minimal at pH 6 and increased as the pH was either decreased to 5 or increased to 9 [38]. Too much acid in egg mixtures may cause curdling.

Coagulation by Mechanical Beating and Egg Foams

As egg whites are beaten, they first become foamy and then form soft moist peaks. With additional beating, the peaks become stiffer. Eventually, with overbeating, the foam becomes dry and may appear to be flocculated (Figure 24-10). Part of the protein in the thin films surrounding each of the air bubbles or cells that comprise the structure of a beaten egg white foam is coagulated in the beating process. This provides some rigidity and stabilizes the foam. If the protein becomes overcoagulated, however, the foam takes on a dry, lumpy appearance because of loss of flexibility in the films and the breaking of many air cells. Undesirable effects on both foam volume and stability can be expected when whites are overbeaten. Overbeaten egg whites are brittle, inelastic, and will not blend well with other ingredients. On standing, liquid will separate from the foam.

Egg White Foams. Egg whites, beaten to form moderately stiff peaks, are used in a number of dishes such as soufflés, soft meringues, puffy omelets, and angel food cakes. When a beater is withdrawn from the beaten whites and the tips fall over, the egg whites are described as moderately stiff. The foam should retain a shiny, smooth surface, and the mass should flow very slowly if the bowl is

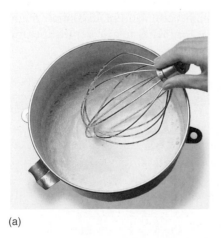

(a)

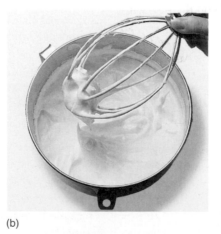

(b)

(c)

FIGURE 24-10 (a) Eggs properly whipped to soft peaks; (b) eggs properly whipped to stiff peaks; (c) spongy, overwhipped eggs. *Source: Reference 19*

partially inverted. Air cells should be quite fine and of even size. Reconstituted dried egg whites, such as those in angel food cake mixes using a two-stage mixing method, are beaten to a very stiff stage, as indicated in the package directions. Stiff peaks will remain standing tall when the beater is removed from the beaten whites.

Beaten Whole Eggs. Whole eggs can be beaten much stiffer than might be expected if beating is continued for a long enough time. As a result of the presence of the fat from the yolk, which retards foam formation, there is little danger of overbeating the whole egg.

Beaten Egg Yolks. Egg yolks increase slightly in volume when beaten. Yolks change to a pale lemon color as air is incorporated, and the mass may become thick and full of fine cells. It is difficult, if not impossible, to beat a small quantity of egg yolk thoroughly unless a small dish of narrow diameter and a small egg beater are used.

Factors Affecting Egg Foams. The freshness of eggs and temperature, as well as the type of beater and bowl, will affect the whipping quality of eggs.

Thin and Thick Whites. The foam produced from the beating of thin whites is more fluffy and has less body than the foam created from thick, viscous whites. Thick whites seem to produce a more stable foam even though thin whites may initially beat to a larger volume. The volume of cooked products, such as angel food cake and meringues, is greater when thick whites are used rather than thin whites.

Temperature. Eggs at room temperature whip more easily, quickly, and to a larger volume than eggs at refrigerator temperature. This may be due to the lower surface tension of the eggs at room temperature.

Type of Beater Used. The type of beater used and the fineness of the wires or blades of the beater can affect the size of the air cells that are obtained and the ease with which the eggs are beaten. Thick blades or wires do not divide egg whites as easily as fine wires, and the resulting air cells are therefore larger. All cells become smaller with longer beating regardless of the type of beater used.

Type of Container in which Eggs Are Beaten. Bowls with small rounded bottoms and sloping sides are preferable to bowls with large flat bottoms because, in the former, the beater can more easily pick up the egg mass. The size of the bowl must obviously be adapted to the amount of egg to be beaten. If whisks are used for beating egg whites, a large platter is preferable to a bowl for holding the whites because of the over-and-over strokes that are used.

Effect of Added Substances. Fat, salt, acid, and sugar will affect egg foams by interfering with whipping, decreasing volume, increasing stability, or increasing the whipping time.

Fat. Fat, in the form of refined cottonseed oil, has been shown to interfere with whipping when present to the extent of 0.5 percent or more. The presence of small amounts of yolk in egg white greatly retards foam formation. This effect is thought to be the result of the fat, probably the lipoproteins, in the egg yolk, which may form a complex with proteins in the white. The directions on packages of angel food cake mix indicate that plastic bowls should not be used for mixing because of the difficulty in removing all fat from the surface of the plastic.

Salt. The addition of a small amount of salt to egg whites (1 gram salt to 40 grams egg white) has been reported to decrease the volume and stability of the foam and to increase the whipping time [12]. Egg white foams are less elastic when they are beaten with salt than when no salt is added.

Acid. The addition of acid or acid salts to egg white decreases the alkalinity of the white and increases the stability of the egg white foam. The whipping time is increased. A stiff and large volume foam results from addition of acid before or shortly after foaming has started. Cream of tartar, which is acidic, is frequently added to egg whites before beating.

Sugar. Sugar retards the denaturation and coagulation of egg proteins and increases the beating time required to attain maximum volume. It is therefore important not to add sugar to egg whites before beating is started, but rather very gradually, possibly one to two tablespoons at a time, after foaming first occurs. In fact, it is probably best, in the preparation of any sugar-containing egg white foam, to beat the whites to soft peaks before adding sugar, with intermittent beating between the additions of sugar. Otherwise, the beating time is considerably prolonged. The presence of sugar in an egg white foam stabilizes the foam as it forms, greatly decreasing the possibility of overbeating. The texture of the foam is also very fine, with many small air cells, and the surface has a shiny, satiny appearance.

SPECIFIC METHODS OF EGG PREPARATION

Poached Eggs

Poaching consists of cooking the edible portion of an egg in hot water, milk, cream, or other liquids. The use of a double boiler will guard against scorching when eggs are poached in milk or cream. A simmering liquid, a temperature of about 185°F (85°C), is recommended when poaching eggs. Higher water temperatures will promote toughening of the proteins and lower temperatures will take more time. Eggs poached in 185°F (85°C) liquids will cook in about five to eight minutes. Because the addition of cold eggs to hot liquid immediately lowers the temperature of the liquid, it is possible to have the temperature of the liquid at the boiling point when the eggs are added. The heat can then be regulated to keep the liquid simmering. If the water is not hot enough when the egg is added, the egg white will spread throughout the liquid in filmy and fragmented layers rather than set quickly and hold its original shape.

The liquid in the pan used for poaching should be deep enough to cover the eggs so that a film of coagulated white may form over the yolk. Salt and acid added to the cooking water are both aids in coagulation but are not necessary. Two teaspoons of vinegar and 1/2 to 1 teaspoon of salt per pint of water can be effective. Eggs poached in salted water are more opaque white and less shiny than eggs poached in unsalted water. The eggs may appear puckered or ruffled as also occurs when poached in boiling water.

There is a wide range of individual preference regarding the desirable characteristics of poached eggs. Many people enjoy a poached egg that is rounded, with a film of coagulated white covering the yolk. The white is completely coagulated but jellylike and tender (Figure 24-5), and the yolk is thick enough to resist flowing. For safety, as discussed earlier in the chapter, the yolk should be thickened and not runny.

The freshness of eggs and thickness of whites have considerable influence on the poached product. For example, eggs with thin whites tend to spread out in thin layers and may fragment into pieces when placed in the hot liquid. The technique of adding the egg to the water also is important to the quality of the cooked egg. It is usually desirable to remove the egg from the shell and place it in a small flat dish from which it can be slipped easily and quickly into the poaching water.

Cooked in the Shell

Eggs may be cooked in the shell to varying degrees of firmness. Eggs prepared for those who are pregnant, elderly, very young, or ill however, should be thoroughly cooked. The usual objective, in any case, is to produce a tender coagulated white and a yolk that is thickened and not runny. Hard-cooked eggs should have a dry, mealy yolk. If the surface of the yolk is green, it is most likely overcooked. Water maintained at a boiling temperature for the entire cooking period has a definite toughening effect on the white. Cooling hard-cooked eggs in cold water immediately after cooking facilitates the removal of the shell. Even so, very fresh eggs (less than 48 hours old) are difficult to peel without considerable white adhering to the shell. Either of the following two methods can be used to ensure satisfactory tenderness of eggs cooked in the shell.

Method I. Place eggs in a single layer in a saucepan and add water until the eggs are covered. Cover and bring just to boiling, then turn off heat. For hard-cooked eggs, allow the eggs to remain in the water for 15 minutes for large eggs. For soft-cooked eggs, let stand in hot water for 4 to 5 minutes. At the end of the designated time for either hard- or soft-cooked eggs, place the eggs in ice water until cool enough to handle [2].

Method II. Add eggs to water at a simmering but not boiling temperature of about 185°F (85°C). Maintain this temperature for at least 7 minutes for hard-cooked eggs.

One group of researchers [14] compared hard-cooked eggs prepared by two different methods.

Method A. Place the eggs in cold water in a covered pan, bring the water to boiling, remove the pan from the heat, and hold for 25 minutes.

Method B. Carefully place the eggs in boiling water, reduce the heat, and simmer (at 185°F or 85°C) eggs for 18 minutes.

In both methods, the eggs were submerged in cold running water for 5 minutes at the end of the cooking period. The researchers reported that Method B produced eggs that were easier to peel and rated higher in all criteria than those prepared by starting with cold water. In another study, boiling for 20 minutes produced hard-cooked eggs that were firmer and exhibited stronger egg odor and more off-flavors than simmering or steaming methods of cooking [31].

In summary, fresh eggs of high quality should be selected for the preparation of hard-cooked eggs. The temperature of the water in which the eggs are cooked should be maintained below the boiling point, and the time of cooking should be no longer than is required to coagulate both the white and the yolk. The eggs should be cooled as quickly as possible after cooking.

Fried Eggs

Fried eggs may be *sunny* side up (not flipped), *over easy* (flipped with a runny yolk but firm white) or *over hard* (flipped with a hard yolk and white). Basted eggs are another variation of fried eggs. Basted eggs are not flipped. The top surface of basted eggs is cooked by either basted fat spooned over the eggs or water added to a pan that is then covered with a lid to create steam. The preparation of over easy eggs is shown in Figure 24-11.

Eggs are fried by heating a small amount of clarified butter or oil in a sauté pan. Only the amount of fat needed to prevent sticking of the eggs is recommended. The pan and fat should be hot enough that the egg begins to fry when added to the pan but not so hot that the fat begins to smoke or brown. Temperatures that are too high will toughen the egg. If the underside of a fried egg is brown and the edges crisp and frilled, the pan and fat were probably too hot, unless, as is true for some people, crispness in a fried egg is preferred.

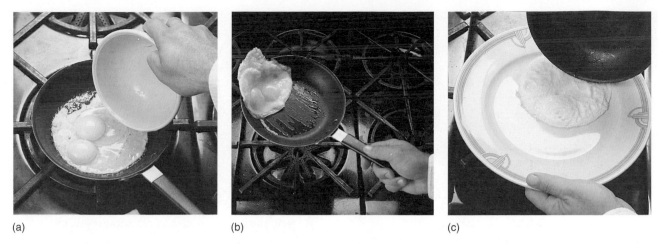

(a)   (b)   (c)

FIGURE 24-11 (a) Pouring eggs into a nonstick sauté pan; (b) eggs are flipped with a quick movement of the wrist; (c) eggs are slid onto a plate. *Source: Reference 19*

Scrambled Eggs

The whites and yolks are mixed together in the preparation of scrambled eggs. If they are thoroughly mixed, the product has a uniform yellow color. Some people like the marbled effect that is produced by mixing yolks and whites only slightly. About one tablespoon of milk is added per egg, with salt and pepper. The mixture is then poured into a warm skillet containing a small amount of melted butter or margarine. As the mixture begins to set under moderate heat, a heat-resistant spatula or an inverted pancake turner may be gently drawn across the bottom, forming large soft curds.

To reduce the risk of foodborne illness, large numbers of broken-out eggs should not be pooled. Thus in the foodservice setting, frozen or refrigerated pasteurized scrambled egg mixes are used. Scrambled eggs can be dressed up for lunch or supper by adding other ingredients (Figure 24-12).

Shirred Eggs

Shirred eggs are cooked and served in the same dish. The dish is coated with butter or margarine, the eggs are broken into it, and the dish is placed in a 325°F (160°C) oven to bake. Additional ingredients such as ham or cheese can be baked with the eggs. Care must be taken not to overcook and thus toughen shirred eggs.

Omelets

The two basic types of omelets are plain or French, and foamy or puffy. The puffy omelet has a more spongy texture than the French omelet because of the greater incorporation of air. Small amounts of liquid may be added to the French omelet. The liquid used in omelets can be water, milk, cream, or acid juices such as tomato and orange. Omelets can be filled with cheese, a mixture of vegetables, or fruits (Figure 24-13).

Proportions for a French Omelet	
4 eggs	1/2 tsp (3 g) salt
4 Tbsp (59 mL) liquid	few grains pepper

Whole eggs are beaten enough to blend white and yolk, then diluted slightly with liquid and seasoned. The mixture is cooked in a lightly greased pan until it is coagulated, after which the omelet is folded (Figure 24-14).

FOCUS ON SCIENCE

What Is Clarified Butter?

Clarified butter also is known as *drawn butter*. The butter has been slowly melted, thereby evaporating most of the water and separating the milk solids from the golden liquid on the surface. The milk solids sink to the bottom of the pan. After any foam is skimmed off the top, the clear (clarified) butter is poured or skimmed off the milky residue and used in cooking. Milk solids burn easily when heated. Therefore, clarified butter has a higher smoke point than regular butter because the milk solids have been removed.

FIGURE 24-12 This egg dish combines scrambled eggs with green and red peppers to create a tasty breakfast dish. *(Courtesy of the American Egg Board)*

FIGURE 24-13 A variety of fillings can be used in a plain omelet. *(Courtesy of the American Egg Board)*

(a)

(b)

(c)

(d)

FIGURE 24-14 The preparation of a folded omelet is shown here. It is similar to a French omelet, except the fillings are added before the omelet is folded.
(a) Lifting the egg from the pan's edges to allow raw egg under the cooked eggs; (b) adding filling; (c) folding the omelet; (d) Placing omelet onto a plate. *Source: Reference 19*

To produce more rapid coagulation, a spatula can be used to carefully lift the edges of the egg mass as it coagulates, thus allowing the liquid portion on top to flow underneath, where it can come in contact with the pan. Another aid is to cover the pan to furnish steam to cook the top surface of the omelet. The omelet should be cooked slowly, keeping the heat low to avoid toughening of the coagulated eggs. The omelet should be cooked uniformly throughout.

Proportions for a Puffy Omelet	
4 eggs	1/2 tsp (3 g) salt
2 to 4 Tbsp (30 to 59 mL) liquid	few grains pepper
1/8 tsp cream of tartar	

The cream of tartar is added to the egg whites, which are beaten until moderately stiff. The liquid, salt, and pepper are added to the egg yolks, and the mixture is beaten until it is lemon colored and so thick that it piles. The beaten yolk mixture is folded into the beaten whites carefully to blend the mass evenly and yet avoid too much loss of air.

The lightly greased pan in which the omelet is cooked should be hot enough to start coagulation, but not hot enough to toughen the coagulated layer in contact with the pan or to brown it excessively. The omelet is cooked slowly until it is light brown underneath.

Several methods can be used to coagulate the top of the foamy omelet.

Method I. Placing a cover on the pan during part of the cooking period forms steam, which cooks the top layer of egg. The cover must not stick to the omelet, as the omelet is likely to collapse when the cover is removed. This method involves some risk, as a covered pan is hotter than an open pan, and overheating may cause the omelet to collapse. If the cover is lifted occasionally and the omelet is cooked successfully by this method, the omelet is usually quite tender and moist, partly because it cooks in less time and partly because less evaporation occurs.

Method II. When the mass is coagulated to within 1/4 to 1/3 inch of the top, the omelet pan can be placed in a moderate oven to dry the top (Figure 24-15).

Method III. Following method I, the pan can be held in a broiler to dry the top. This method must be used with caution, as a broiler flame can easily overheat the mass and cause it to collapse.

Method IV. The omelet can be cooked in an oven at 300° to 350°F (149° to 177°C) for the entire time.

Crêpes

Crêpes are thin, tender pancakes containing a relatively high proportion of egg. They can be filled with a variety of items, including fish, meats, poultry, eggs, cheese, vegetables, and fruits (Figure 24-16). Crêpes can also be served with sweet, dessert-type fillings.

The thin crêpe batter is cooked on medium heat in a seasoned slope-sided omelet or crêpe pan. Enough batter is poured in to cover the bottom of the pan; then the pan is tipped or tilted to allow the batter to move quickly over the bottom. Any excess batter is poured off. The crêpe is cooked until it is lightly browned on the bottom and dry on the top.

Soufflés

The word *soufflé* is French for *puff*. A soufflé is thus a dish that puffs up spectacularly in the oven. Soufflés are similar to foamy omelets, except that they have a thick, white sauce base and contain additional ingredients such as grated cheese, vegetable pulp, or ground meats. Dessert soufflés are sweet and may contain lemon, strawberry, and chocolate.

In the preparation of a soufflé, beaten egg yolks are added to the thick white sauce base. Cheese or other ingredients are then added. A stiffly beaten egg white foam is folded into the white sauce base. The high proportion of egg in the soufflé provides structure as the egg proteins coagulate, and basic principles of egg cookery require moderate cooking temperatures. Soufflés are usually baked, although they can be steamed. When they are baked, the dish containing the soufflé mixture should be placed in a pan of hot water to protect against excessive heating. Soufflés will shrink after removal from the oven and should be served immediately.

Custards

A true custard consists only of eggs, milk, sugar, and flavoring. No starchy agent is added. Custards are of two types: the stirred or soft custard, which is given a creamy consistency by being stirred while it is cooking; and the baked custard, which is allowed to coagulate without stirring, thereby producing a gel. There must be enough egg in the baked custard to produce a firm mass when cooked, particularly if the custard is to be unmolded when served. The proportion of egg to milk is often the same for baked and stirred custards; however, less egg is used in stirred custard when a thin consistency is desired.

Custard dishes can be served as simple egg desserts or can be elegant dishes. Flan, popular in Mexican cuisine, is similar to baked custard. It is a custard baked over a layer of caramelized sugar. Flans are generally unmolded, and the caramelized sugar flows over the top for a delicious and beautiful dessert. Crème brûlée is another type of custard that can be prepared either as a baked or a stirred custard. Crème brûlée is a very rich custard generally

Cook the omelet slowly until it is lightly browned on the bottom.

After drying the top of the omelet in a moderate oven, test it for doneness by inserting a spatula in the center. The spatula should come out clean.

Make a shallow crease across the middle of the omelet.

Fold the omelet over and carefully transfer it to a serving platter.

FIGURE 24-15 Preparation of a puffy omelet. *(Courtesy of the U.S. Poultry and Egg Association)*

composed of egg yolks and heavy cream rather than whole eggs and milk, as in other baked custards. This custard is generally topped with brown or white sugar that is either caramelized under a broiler or with a torch. A description of basic baked and stirred custards follows.

Proportions for Custards	
1 c (237 mL) milk	2 Tbsp (25 g) sugar
1 to 1 1/2 eggs or 2 to 3 yolks	1/4 tsp vanilla or 1/16 tsp nutmeg

(To measure 1/2 egg, mix together white and yolk of whole egg; then divide into two equal portions by measuring 1 Tbsp at a time.)

Baked Custard.   Because the egg is used for thickening, it is beaten only enough to blend the white and yolk well. Sugar can be added to the egg or dissolved in the milk. Milk is usually scalded before being added to the egg mixture. Scalding hastens the cooking and helps retain a mild, sweet flavor, but it does not produce a smoother custard. Flavoring must be added when the mixture is prepared for cooking.

The custard cups should be placed in a pan of hot water as a protection against overheating, even though a moderate oven temperature may be used (about 350°F or 177°C). Custards placed in a pan of very hot water can be baked in a 400°F (204°C) oven for a much shorter time than in a 350°F oven. However, care must be exercised to remove the custard from the oven as soon as it is coagulated to avoid undesirable overcooking.

Why Do Eggs Turn Green?

Usually eggs turn green because of overcooking. Eggs held hot for too long will also turn green. Therefore, hard-cooked eggs should be cooled quickly in cold water to prevent continued cooking. Scrambled eggs held hot in an oven or warmer may also start to develop an olive green shade. Although safe to eat, green eggs are typically considered unattractive. Refrigerated, pasteurized egg products often contain citric acid. Citric acid will make the eggs resistant to turning green even if overcooked.

The science behind green eggs is as follows. Reaction of iron in the yolk with hydrogen sulfide from the white produces the greenish ferrous sulfide (FeS) deposit. Most of the iron in an egg is present in the yolk. Sulfur occurs in about equal amounts in yolk and white, but the sulfur compounds in the white are more labile to heat than those in the yolk.

Hydrogen sulfide (H_2S) is therefore easily formed from the sulfur compounds in the white during prolonged heating and forms even more readily when the pH of the egg is markedly alkaline, as in an older egg.

Ferrous sulfide forms very slowly until the yolk reaches about 158°F (70°C) and seldom occurs in fresh eggs cooked 30 minutes at 185°F (85°C). The green color is less likely to form in rapidly cooked eggs, because the hydrogen sulfide gas is drawn to the lowered pressure at the surface of the cooling egg and thus combines less readily with iron at the surface of the yolk. However, if an egg is cooked 30 minutes in boiling water, the ferrous sulfide will probably form regardless of cooling. Also, in older eggs that are very alkaline, the green color may be produced despite the precautions taken during cooking [4]. ■

The baked custard is done when the tip of a knife inserted halfway between the center and outside comes out clean (Figure 24-17). When custard is overcooked, some clear liquid separates from the gel structure, that is, syneresis occurs. In addition, the custard may appear porous and contain holes, especially on the outer surfaces, when it is unmolded. The top surface may be concave and browned. In an overcooked custard, the egg proteins that form the meshlike gel structure apparently shrink and squeeze out some of the liquid that was held in the mesh.

Soft or Stirred Custard. The mixture of egg, milk, and sugar is prepared in the same manner as for baked custard. The vanilla, because of its volatility, is added after the other ingredients are cooked. Custards that are cooked more slowly coagulate more completely at a lower temperature than custards that are cooked rapidly. There is less danger of curdling, and both consistency and flavor are better in stirred custards cooked relatively slowly. The total cooking time, in a double boiler, should be 12 to 15 minutes, heating more rapidly at first and then more slowly near the end of the cooking period.

Constant stirring is necessary to prevent lumping. Stirring separates the coagulated particles, resulting in a creamy consistency regardless of the amount of egg used. The tendency is to cook a soft custard until it appears as thick as is desired, but caution should be exercised. The custard will be thicker when it is cold. When the custard coats the spoon well, it should be removed from the heat and cooled immediately by either pouring it into a cold dish or suspending it, in the pan used for cooking, in cold water.

Overheating a stirred custard results in curdling. A very slightly curdled custard may be improved if it is

FIGURE 24-16 Chopped hard-cooked eggs and asparagus spears provide the filling for these delicious crêpes, which are topped with a cheese sauce. *(Courtesy of the American Egg Board)*

(a)

(b)

(c)

FIGURE 24-17 (a) A baked custard is done when the tip of the knife, inserted into the custard about halfway between the center and the outside, comes out clean. *(Courtesy of Chris Meister)*
(b) Unmolded baked custards may be served with a fruit sauce. *(Courtesy of the U.S. Poultry and Egg Association)*
(c) This chocolate sponge custard topped with whipped cream and chocolate curls is not only delicious, but pleasing to the eyes as well. *(Courtesy of the American Egg Board)*

beaten with a rotary beater, but this treatment is of no value for excessively curdled custards. In an overcooked custard, the coagulated proteins shrink and separate out from the more liquid portion of the mixture, giving the appearance of curds. Also, the flavor of an overcooked custard tends to be strong and sulfury.

A stirred custard can be used to create some interesting and delicious desserts. For example, hard meringue shells can be filled with crushed or whole sweetened strawberries or other fruit and the custard poured over the fruit. This can then be crowned with a bit of whipped topping. Or, the custard can be flavored with caramelized sugar and poured into individual serving dishes. Small soft meringues that have been previously baked can be placed on top of the custard.

Meringues

Meringues are of two types: the soft meringue used for pies and puddings, and the hard meringue generally used as a crisp dessert base or as a cookie.

Proportions for Soft Meringues	
1 egg white	1/16 tsp cream of tartar (optional)
2 Tbsp (25 g) sugar	1/8 tsp flavoring (if desired)

To produce a soft meringue that is fine textured, tender, cuts easily without tearing, and shows neither syneresis nor **beading** on top of the baked meringue, each of the following items should be considered carefully:

1. When the egg whites are partially beaten (possibly to a soft foam), sugar is gradually added, 1/2 to 1 tablespoon at a time, and the beating is continued until the mixture is stiff but with soft peaks that still tip over.
2. The meringue should be placed on a *hot* filling.
3. The meringue should be baked at 350°F (177°C) for 12 to 15 minutes, depending on the depth of the meringue.

Heating must be sufficient throughout the soft meringue to destroy any salmonella organisms that may be present in the eggs. Meringues baked at moderate oven temperatures may be slightly sticky, compared to those baked at high oven temperatures, but the moderate temperature produces an attractive, evenly browned product that is safe to eat. Two particular problems that may be encountered in making soft meringues are weeping, or leaking of liquid from the bottom of the meringue, and beading [11, 13]. Weeping or syneresis apparently results from undercooking the meringue. It can also occur as a result of underbeating the egg whites. Placing the meringue on a hot filling helps to achieve complete coagulation of the egg proteins. Beading is usually attributed to overcooking or overcoagulation of the egg white

proteins. It can also result from a failure to dissolve the sugar sufficiently when it is beaten into the meringue.

Proportions for Hard Meringues	
1 egg white	1/16 tsp cream of tartar
1/4 c (50 g) sugar	few grains salt
1/8 tsp vanilla	

In the preparation of hard meringues, cream of tartar is added to the egg white, which is beaten until a soft foam begins to form. Flavoring may be added at this point. Sugar is added gradually and beating continued until the mass is very stiff. Portions of the meringue are dropped onto a baking sheet, which may be covered with parchment paper, and shaped into small shells. Meringues are baked at a low oven temperature (about 250°F or 121°C) for 50 to 60 minutes, depending on the size of the meringues, and then left in the oven with the heat turned off for another hour.

If a temperature lower than 250°F (121°C) can be maintained for a longer time, the effect is one of drying instead of baking the meringue and produces even better results. Well-insulated ovens that hold the heat for several hours can be preheated and then turned off entirely.

Desirable hard meringues are crisp, tender, and white in appearance. It is important that they do not show gumminess or stickiness, which results from underbaking. This may occur either from an oven temperature that is too high or a baking time that is too short. When the baking temperature is too high, the meringues are browned on the outside before the interior is dry enough, and the residual moisture produces stickiness.

Microwave Cooking

One thing that the microwave oven does not do successfully is cook an egg in its shell. Steam builds up inside the egg, and it bursts. However, eggs can be satisfactorily cooked in several other ways by microwaves. They can be poached in liquid. The liquid is first brought to a boil in a custard cup. Then the broken-out egg is added and cooked for a short time on medium power. The egg should be cooked until the white is opaque but not set. During a standing period of 2 to 3 minutes, the cooking is completed. Broken-out eggs can also be cooked in individual custard cups without liquid, as shirred eggs are cooked. The yolk membrane should be first pierced with a toothpick to help prevent bursting from steam pent up during cooking.

Because the egg yolk contains more fat than the egg white, it attracts more energy and cooks faster. If an egg is microwaved until the white is completely coagulated, the yolk may toughen.

Scrambled eggs are prepared for the microwave by mixing melted butter, eggs, and milk and cooking on high power for about half the cooking time before breaking up the set parts and pushing them to the center of the dish.

The eggs are stirred once or twice more while the cooking is completed. Again, standing time after cooking is important to finish the cooking without toughening the eggs. Scrambled eggs prepared by microwaves are fluffier and have more volume than conventionally scrambled eggs. Omelets, including fluffy omelets, can also be prepared in the microwave oven.

For fried eggs, a browning dish is necessary. The browning dish is preheated on high, and then the eggs are added. The browning dish absorbs enough energy and produces a hot enough surface to brown the eggs lightly. Egg dishes such as quiche can also be prepared using microwaves.

In hospital foodservice, microwaves are often used to reheat food at the point of serving; however, some questions have been raised concerning the lack of uniformity in heating, which results in lack of confidence in the ability of this heating process to destroy microorganisms sufficiently. It has been found, when reheating scrambled eggs in a microwave oven under actual foodservice operating conditions, that temperature variability in the eggs could be controlled within 9°F (5°C) if voltage to the oven and temperature of the food before heating were rigidly controlled [7]. Careful attention to these factors that affect heating is necessary to ensure safety of the food for service to clients.

CHAPTER SUMMARY

- Eggs function in several roles in food preparation because of the ability to emulsify, foam, form gels, coagulate, and clarify liquids.

- Essentially all of the fat and cholesterol is found in the yolk; the white is higher in water. In general, the yolk has a higher nutrient density than the white. The major protein in the egg white is ovalbumin. Lipoproteins are the major proteins in the yolk. The lipoproteins are responsible for the emulsifying properties of egg yolks. The fatty materials in egg yolk include triglycerides, phospholipids, and cholesterol. The predominant yellow pigment of the egg yolk is xanthophyll. Yellow carotenoid pigments in the yolk may be converted into vitamin A in the body. No difference in nutritive value is noted between infertile and fertilized eggs.

- The egg shell is porous and allows exchange of gases and loss of moisture from the egg. Egg shells may be brown or white, depending on the breed of the chicken. The natural bloom on shells is replaced with a light oil coat after washing to reduce loss of moisture.

- The egg white consists of thin and thick portions. Chalazae are two strands of thickened white that anchor the yolk in the center of the egg. As eggs age, the proportion of thin white increases, the chalazae disintegrate, the yolk absorbs water from the white, the air cell increases in size, and alkalinity increases.

- USDA grades for eggs are based on their candled appearance. Grade AA and A eggs have a large proportion of thick white that stands up around a firm high yolk. USDA grading services are available on a fee-for-service basis.

- Eggs are sorted into six weight classes. Recipes are generally formulated on the basis of the large size. Adjustments in recipes can be made for different sizes of eggs.

- The FDA and FSIS share federal responsibility for egg safety. Since the mid 1980s, *Salmonella enteritidis* has been frequently implicated in foodborne illness. Unbroken shell eggs may contain this bacterium, or the eggs may become infected as contamination on the shell exterior moves through the shell pores into the interior.

- In 2000, the FDA finalized regulations to require safe food-handling instructions on cartons and to specify refrigeration temperature during storage and sale.

- Raw eggs should not be consumed. Pasteurized eggs should be used in recipes such as Caesar dressing. Casseroles and other dishes containing eggs should be cooked to 160°F (71°C). When serving high-risk populations, the use of pasteurized egg products is recommended.

- Egg-processing plants usually do egg breaking, separation, and pasteurization in preparation for liquid refrigerated products (whole eggs, egg whites, egg yolks, or blended products), frozen eggs, or dried eggs. Pasteurization is required by the federal government for all processed eggs.

- The functional properties of raw egg whites are not altered by freezing and thawing. However, frozen egg yolks become viscous and gummy on thawing unless they are mixed with sugar, salt, or syrup before freezing. Drying is a satisfactory method for the preservation of eggs. A variety of egg substitutes are available in the marketplace to offer a low-cholesterol egg substitute.

- Coagulation occurs not instantly, but gradually. Egg yolk protein requires a slightly higher temperature for coagulation compared to egg whites. Diluted egg mixtures require a higher temperature for coagulation. The use of low or moderate temperatures for egg cookery is recommended to avoid toughness and greater shrinkage of egg proteins. Overcooked yolks may develop a green color.

- Factors influencing the coagulation of egg proteins include (a) rate of heating, (b) sugar in the mixture, or (c) acid in the mixture.

- Egg whites coagulate with mechanical beating. First egg whites become foamy, then soft moist peaks form. Stiff peaks form with continued beating, but overbeating will result in a dry, lumpy foam.

- The foam produced from thin whites is more fluffy and has less body than one created from thick, viscous whites. Thick whites produce a more stable foam. Eggs whip more easily and quickly at room temperature. Both whole eggs and egg yolks may be beaten, but with different results than observed with egg whites. Additional factors influencing egg white foams include (a) type of beater used, (b) type of bowl used, or (c) added substances such as fat, salt, acid, and sugar. Cream of tartar and sugar stabilizes egg white foams, but sugar should not be added until later in the whipping process.

- Poached, hard-cooked or soft-cooked in the shell, fried, scrambled, shirred, omelets, crêpes, custards, meringues, as well as many other egg dishes may be prepared.

- Microwave ovens may be used to prepare scrambled, fried, poached, and other egg dishes. However, microwave ovens are not recommended for hard- or soft-cooked eggs in the shell because the shell can burst.

STUDY QUESTIONS

1. (a) Compare the chemical composition of whole egg, egg white, and egg yolk, indicating major differences.

   (b) What major protein is found in egg white?

   (c) What types of proteins predominate in egg yolk?

2. Describe the following parts of an egg and indicate the location for each.

   (a) Cuticle or bloom

   (b) Shell

   (c) Outer membrane

   (d) Inner membrane

   (e) Air cell

   (f) Thin white

   (g) Thick white

   (h) Chalazae

   (i) Vitelline membrane

   (j) Yolk

3. (a) Compare the major characteristics of fresh and deteriorated eggs.

   (b) How can freshness best be maintained in eggs during storage?

4. (a) List the USDA consumer grades for eggs and describe the major characteristics of each grade.

   (b) Describe the process by which eggs are graded.

5. (a) Explain why the FDA has designated shell eggs as a potentially hazardous food.

   (b) Give several suggestions for the safe handling and preparation of shell eggs.

6. (a) Explain why eggs are usually pasteurized before freezing or drying.

   (b) What special problem is usually encountered in the freezing of egg yolks? How can this problem be solved?

7. List several different uses for eggs in food preparation.

8. Egg proteins coagulate on heating and can therefore be used for thickening purposes in cooking. Describe the effect of each of the following factors on the temperature of coagulation:

   (a) Source of egg protein (white or yolk)

   (b) Rate of heating

   (c) Dilution

   (d) Addition of sugar

   (e) Addition of acid

9. Describe the various changes or stages that occur as egg white is mechanically beaten to a very stiff, dry foam.

10. Describe the effect of each of the following on the volume and/or stability of egg white foam:

    (a) Thickness of the white

    (b) Temperature of the white

    (c) Type of beater used

(d) Type of container used

(e) Addition of salt

(f) Addition of acid

(g) Addition of sugar

11. Describe and explain an appropriate procedure for preparing each of the following food items:

(a) Poached eggs

(b) Eggs cooked in the shell

(c) Fried eggs

(d) Scrambled eggs

(e) Omelets, plain or French and foamy or puffy

(f) Shirred and poached eggs cooked by microwaves

12. **(a)** Describe appropriate procedures for preparing stirred custard and baked custard. Explain why each step in the procedures is important.

(b) Why should precautions be taken to avoid overheating custards during preparation? Explain.

13. Describe major differences in preparation and use of soft and hard meringues.

MEAT AND MEAT COOKERY 25

Meat is defined as the flesh of animals used for food. Cattle, swine, and sheep are the chief meat animals in the United States. Small amounts of rabbit and venison are also consumed in the United States; in other parts of the world, horse, dog, llama, and camel are used as meat.

This chapter will focus on meat from cattle, swine, and sheep. In this chapter, the following topics will be discussed:

- Consumption trends and nutrition
- Meat composition and structure
- Meat classifications
- Meat production and marketing
- Purchasing considerations
- Factors affecting tenderness and flavor

- Cured meats
- Storage, safe handling, and preparation of meats
- Soup stock and gravies

CONSUMPTION TRENDS AND NUTRITION

Consumption Trends

For many, meat, poultry, and fish play an important role in meal planning. Changes have occurred, however, over the past two decades in the amounts of these protein-rich foods consumed by Americans. The current trend is toward the consumption of less red meat and more poultry (Figure 25-1) [91]. According to U.S. Department of

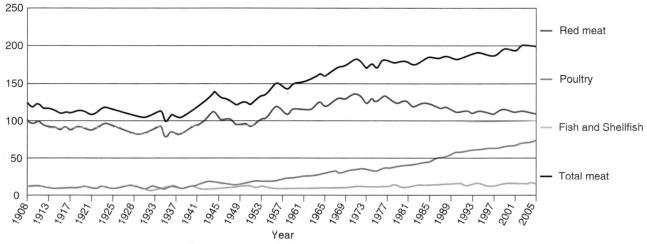

Boneless, trimmed (edible) weight, pounds per capita per year

Red meat commodities include beef, veal, port, lamb, and mutton. Poultry commodities include turkey and chicken. Fish and shellfish include fresh and frozen, canned, and cured products. Figures are calculated on the basis of raw and edible meat. Excludes edible offals, bones, and viscera for red meat and fishery products. Includes skin, neck, and giblets for poultry (chicken and turkey). Excludes game consumption for red meat and fishery products. Excludes use of chicken for commercially-prepared pet food. Calculated from unrounded data.

FIGURE 25-1 U.S. per capita availability of meat. *(Courtesy of U.S. Department of Agriculture, Economic Research Service.)*

What Does It Mean If the Label States "Lean"?

Nutrition claims are regulated by the government. Therefore, terms such as *lean* and *extra lean* have standardized definitions. If you see these terms on a package of beef, here is what they mean.

Lean—100 grams (3.5 ounces) of beef with
- less than 10 grams of fat
- 4.5 grams or less of saturated fat
- less than 95 milligrams of cholesterol

Extra Lean—100 grams (3.5 ounces) of beef with
- less than 5 grams of fat
- less than 2 grams of saturated fat
- less than 95 milligrams of cholesterol ■

Source: Reference 101

Agriculture (USDA) food disappearance data, Americans ate, on an annual per capita basis, 132 pounds of red meat (beef, veal, pork, lamb, and mutton) in 1970 but only 110 pounds in 2005. At the same time, the consumption of poultry increased from 34 pounds per person in 1970 to 74 pounds in 2005. Nevertheless, the total consumption of meat, poultry, and fish increased from 177 pounds per person per year in 1970 to 200 pounds in 2005.

Nutritive Value

Meat is composed of approximately 75 percent water, 20 percent protein, and 5 percent representing fat, carbohydrate, and minerals [105]. The percentage of these components varies depending on the kind of meat and the cut. The protein in meat is of high biological value, including all of the essential amino acids.

Lean meats are a good source of thiamin, riboflavin, and niacin, as well as other members of the B complex. Lean pork is particularly rich in thiamin. Liver and kidney are good dietary sources of riboflavin and are richer in niacin than most other tissues. All meats furnish tryptophan, the amino acid that serves as a precursor of niacin for the body. Liver is a variable but excellent source of vitamin A. Meat is an excellent or good source of iron, zinc, selenium, and phosphorus. Twenty-three percent of the iron in the U.S. food supply is supplied by meat, poultry, fish, and meat alternatives [32]. Some copper and other trace minerals are also supplied by meat.

The monounsaturated, saturated, and polyunsaturated fats are found in meats. Meat also contains cholesterol. The amount of fat in meat can vary significantly by the cut, amount of fat trim, and preparation method. For example, a three-ounce serving of eye round beef roast contains 1.4 grams of saturated fat and 4.0 grams of total fat. This cut of beef is therefore considered lean.

Ground beef is sold with fat content ranging from 70 to 95 percent lean. A three-ounce serving of 95 percent lean ground beef that has been pan-broiled will contain 8 percent of the daily value of total fat based on a 2,000 calorie intake. In contrast, 75 percent lean ground beef will have 21 percent of the daily value of total fat intake [90]. See Appendix C for the nutritive value of selected meats.

COMPOSITION AND STRUCTURE

As purchased, meat is composed of muscle, connective tissue, and fatty or adipose tissue. Muscle is composed of as much as 75 percent water which is held by the proteins in a gel-type structure. The connective tissue is distributed throughout muscle, binding cells and bundles of cells together. It is also present in tendons and ligaments.

Some cuts of meat include bone, and although it is not eaten, it is an important aid in identifying various cuts of meat. Pigments in meat influence our perceptions of quality as well as the type of meat. Beef, pork, and lamb, while all considered red meats, vary in color.

Muscle

Muscle has a complex structure that is important to its function in the living animal, where it performs work by contracting and relaxing. Muscle fibers are the basic structural units of muscle. It is important to pay attention to the how muscles are put together because it affects the quality and cooking characteristics of meat.

The muscle fiber is a long threadlike cell that tapers slightly at both ends (Figure 25-2). It is tiny, averaging about 1/500th inch in diameter and 1 to 2 inches in length. Inside the fiber or cell is an intricate structure.

FOCUS ON SCIENCE

Moist or Dry Heat Cooking Method? Look at the Bones

The bones in a cut of meat can provide a good indicator whether to use moist or dry heat preparation methods. By knowing the location of the retail cut, this will take away the guesswork at the store and being unsure of "How should I prepare this cut of meat?"

Dry heat

- T-bone (short loin)
- Rib bone (rib section)
- Pin, flat, and wedge bones (sirloin)

Moist heat

- Round bone (round)
- Blade bone (chuck)

It includes contractile material called *myofibrils*, surrounded by the **cytoplasmic** substance called *sarcoplasm* (Figure 25-3). There is also a system of tubules and **reticulum** around each myofibril that plays a key role in initiating muscle contraction. In addition, many **mitochondria** act as powerhouses to provide energy for the cell in the form of the high-energy compound adenosine triphosphate **(ATP)**.

If you could look further into the structure of the tiny myofibrils, about 2,000 of which are present in each muscle cell, you would see special proteins. These proteins form thick filaments and thin filaments that are set in an orderly array (Figure 25-4). If you visualize a transverse section cut through the center of a myofibril, it would be similar to that shown in Figure 25-5. The thick filaments are composed primarily of the protein *myosin*, whereas the thin filaments are made up of another protein, *actin* [29].

It is thought that when a muscle contracts, the thick and thin filaments slide together, something like a telescope, thus shortening the length of the muscle. As the thick and thin filaments slide together, they apparently form cross-bridges with each other, thus making a new protein in the shortened myofibril called *actomyosin*. Energy for this process is provided from chemical changes in ATP.

The parallel alignment of the thick and thin filaments in all the myofibrils of a cell produces a pattern of

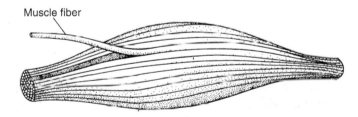

Muscle fiber

FIGURE 25-2 Tiny muscle fibers or cells are combined to form small bundles.

FIGURE 25-3 The muscle fiber or cell consists of many tiny myofibrils held together by the cell membrane. Each myofibril is made up of contractile proteins in a special ordered array, as shown in Figure 25-4.

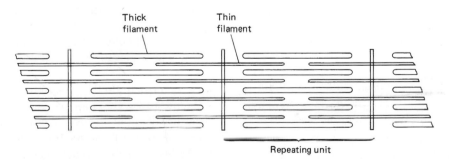

Thick filament   Thin filament

Repeating unit

FIGURE 25-4 Thick and thin, rodlike components or filaments inside the myofibril are composed of protein molecules. Myosin is the protein found in the thick filaments; actin makes up the thin filaments. They are systematically arranged in a cylindrical shape. When muscle contracts, the thin filaments in each repeating unit push together, thus shortening the length of the muscle.

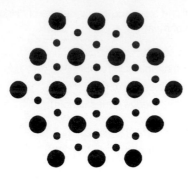

FIGURE 25-5 Transverse section through a cylindrical myofibril. The large dots represent the thick filaments composed of myosin molecules. The smaller dots represent the thin filaments composed of actin.

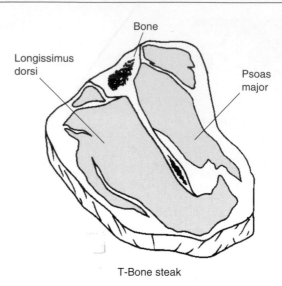

FIGURE 25-7 The major muscles in a T-bone steak.

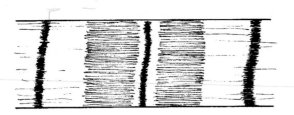

FIGURE 25-6 Representation of a striated muscle showing light and dark bands on the myofibrils (enlarged about 20,000 diameters).

dark and light lines and spaces when viewed under a microscope (see Figure 25-6). The thick filaments are present in the dark bands, and the thin filaments extend into the light bands. The striated pattern continues to repeat itself along the length of the myofibril.

Let us now return to the basic unit—the muscle fiber or cell—and see how these units are built into larger bundles and muscles. Each cell or fiber is surrounded by a fine membrane called the *sarcolemma*. Small bundles of the fibers, surrounded by thin sheaths of connective tissue to hold them together, form primary bundles (each containing 20 to 40 fibers). The primary bundles are then bound together with sheets of connective tissue to form secondary bundles. Secondary bundles bound together by connective tissue form major muscles. The primary bundles comprise the grain of the meat, which may appear to be fine or coarse.

Each major muscle in the animal body has been named. Figure 25-7 shows two of the major muscles in a T-bone steak—the *longissimus dorsi*, which runs along the back of the animal, and the *psoas major* or *tenderloin* muscle, which is particularly valued for its tenderness.

Connective Tissue

As indicated, muscle tissue does not occur without connective tissue, which binds the muscle cells together in various-size bundles. It also makes up the tendons and ligaments of an animal body. Generally, connective tissue has few cells but a considerable amount of extracellular

background material called *ground substance*. Running through and embedded in this matrix of ground substance are long, strong fibrils or fibers. Many of these fibrils contain the protein *collagen*.

Collagen, elastin, and reticulin are three kinds of connective tissue found in meat. Collagen-containing connective tissue is white. Connective tissue that contains another protein, called *elastin*, is yellow. Although collagen fibers are flexible, they do not stretch as much and are not as elastic as elastin fibers. Very little elastin seems to be present in most muscles, particularly those of the loin and round regions, but a considerable amount of elastin may be present in the connective tissue of a few muscles, including some in the shoulder area. A third type of connective tissue fibril, *reticulin*, consists of very small fibers. This type of connective tissue forms a delicate network around the muscle cells.

When connective tissue is heated with moisture, some collagen is hydrolyzed to produce the smaller gelatin molecule. This change accounts for much of the increase in tenderness that occurs in less tender cuts of meat cooked by moist heat. Heating causes only slight softening of elastin, however. If elastin is present in relatively large amounts, it should be trimmed out or tenderized by cutting or cubing (as in the preparation of minute steaks).

In muscles that are used by an animal for locomotion, such as those in the legs, chest, and neck, connective tissue tends to develop more extensively. Less tender cuts of meat usually contain more connective tissue than tender cuts, although this is not the only factor affecting meat tenderness.

Fatty Tissue

Special cells contain large amounts of fat for storage in the body. These cells are embedded in a network of connective tissue to form adipose or fatty tissue. Some hard fats, such as beef suet, have visible sheets of connective tissue separating layers or masses of fat cells. Fat is generally colorless, but in older animals, it becomes yellowish instead of white as **carotenoid pigments** accumulate. The type of cattle feed may also affect the color of the fat.

Fats from different species and from different parts of the same animal differ to some extent in composition. The more brittle, hard fats of beef and mutton contain higher percentages of **saturated fatty acids.** Softer fats contain more **unsaturated fatty acids.** The high melting point of lamb fat causes it to congeal when served unless the meat is very hot. Lard extracted from the fatty tissue around the glandular organs has a somewhat higher melting point than that produced from back fat.

There are three major kinds of fat in meat: *intra*muscular, *inter*muscular, and subcutaneous. Intramuscular fat also is called **marbling.** It is observed as very small streaks of fat between muscle fibers and bundles (Figure 25-8). Marbling is associated with juiciness, flavor, and tenderness [29]. Intermuscular fat is found between individual muscles and may be either a small or relatively large seam of fat. Subcutaneous fat is the fat found under the skin and, if excessive, may be trimmed from the exterior of the muscle before sale to the consumer.

Bone

Long shafts of bone consist chiefly of compact bony tissue. A center canal is filled with yellow marrow. Other bones may be spongy in character and may contain red marrow, which has many blood vessels. Bones or pieces of bone that appear in retail cuts of meat aid in the identification of the cut, giving clues to its location on the carcass. The condition of the backbone or *chine* bone also provides an indication about the age of the animal. Relatively young animals will have backbones that are redder and less hard than backbones from mature animals.

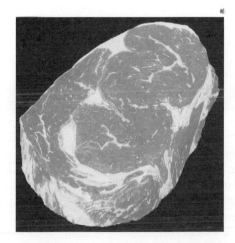

FIGURE 25-8 This steak is well marbled. Fat is distributed throughout the muscle of this beef ribeye steak. *(Courtesy of the National Cattlemen's Beef Association)*

Pigments

The color of meat comes chiefly from the pigment *myoglobin.* Although *hemoglobin* is a red pigment in the blood, it contributes little to the color of meat because much of the blood is drained from the carcass. Myoglobin and hemoglobin are similar in chemical structure. Both contain the protein globin and the iron-containing pigment heme, but myoglobin is smaller. Hemoglobin carries oxygen in the bloodstream, whereas myoglobin holds it in the muscle cells.

The quantity of myoglobin in muscle increases with age; thus, beef has a darker color than veal. The color of meat also varies with the species of animal from which it is obtained. Pork muscle generally contains less myoglobin than beef muscle and appears lighter in color. Different muscles of the same animal may also differ in color.

Myoglobin exists in three primary forms: *oxymyoglobin, deoxymyoglobin,* and *metmyoglobin.* Each of these forms is responsible for a different color, thus meat may appear cherry red, purple-red, or brown. These forms of myoglobin are affected by the presence of oxygen and exposure to light. The form of myoglobin also has an impact on the final appearance of cooked meat. Thus, temperature, not color, is the best indicator of doneness of meats. Table 25-1 provides an overview of each of these forms of myoglobin, and Figure 25-9 depicts the chemical changes associated with the each pigment.

Other factors that influence myoglobin are pH, meat source, packaging, freezing, fat content, and added ingredients [46]. The appearance of the meat when raw as well as when cooked can be influenced by these additional factors (Table 25-2). Thus although color is often used as an indication of quality or cooking doneness, it is not reliable. A thermometer is the only safe and reliable way to assess doneness especially when preparing meats such as ground beef which may result in a foodborne illness if undercooked.

CLASSIFICATION

Beef

Beef is the meat from full-grown cattle. Beef carcasses are classified on the basis of age and sex. A *steer* is a male castrated when young; a *heifer* is a young female that has not yet borne a calf; a *cow* is a female that has borne a calf; a *stag* is a male castrated after maturity; and a *bull* is a mature male that has not been castrated.

Steer carcasses are generally preferred by meat handlers because of their heavier weight and the higher proportion of meat to bone, but steer and heifer carcasses of the same grade are of equal quality. A steer weighs about 1,000 pounds at two years and yields about 450 pounds of meat [101]. The quality of meat from cows is variable, depending on maturity, but is usually inferior to both steer and heifer meat. Stag meat is not normally marketed in the United States, and bull carcasses generally are used in processed meats.

TABLE 25-1 Forms of Myoglobin and Description of Characteristics

Forms	Color	Description of Characteristics
Oxymyoglobin	Bright cherry red	Easily formed in presence of oxygen. The plastic overwrap, often used for retail meat packing, allows oxygen to permeate the wrap, thereby resulting in bright red meat.
		Easily denatured when cooked and may denature to a brown color prematurely before the meat is a safe temperature for consumption.
Deoxymyoglobin	Purple-red	Chemically reduced form. Often observed when packaged in *cryovac,* which is a vacuum-sealed, airtight, plastic package. Exposure to oxygen upon opening of the package will cause the color to "bloom" to a bright red (oxymyoglobin). Also may be observed in an oxygen-permeable package where the exterior of the meat is bright red but the low oxygen interior of the meat is still purple-red.
		This form is least sensitive to heat denaturation, thus meats cooked when purple-red may still appear reddish-pink when at a safe temperature for consumption.
Metmyoglobin	Brown	Formed after a period of storage with exposure to oxygen. Reducing substances are no longer produced in the tissues over time and this oxidized form of myoglobin is produced, resulting in a brown color. Fluorescent light accelerates the formation of metmyoglobin.
		Is not necessarily an indication of spoilage.
		Denatures rapidly when cooked and is likely to appear brown when undercooked.

Source: References 46, 107

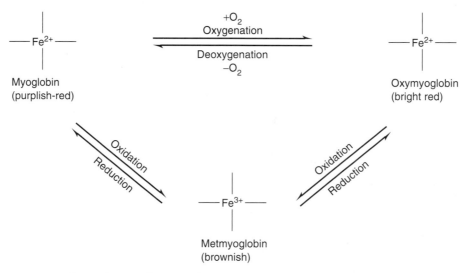

FIGURE 25-9 Some changes that occur in meat pigments.

Veal

Veal is meat from immature bovines. In the wholesale market, veal carcasses are usually from animals of either sex that are at least 3 weeks but generally less than 20 weeks of age [68]. They are fed largely on milk or milk products. The term *calf* or baby beef is applied to animals slaughtered between 5 months and about 10 months of age. The older animals have passed the good veal stage but do not yet possess the properties of good beef.

Lamb and Mutton

Sheep carcasses are classified as lamb, yearling mutton, and mutton according to the age of the animal. Lamb is obtained from young animals of either sex that are less than 12 months of age, although the exact age at which lamb changes to mutton is somewhat indefinite. Mutton carcasses are those that have passed the lamb stage. The usual test for a lamb carcass is the break joint. The feet of a lamb, when broken off sharply, separate from the leg

TABLE 25-2 Additional Factors that Influence Myoglobin in Meats

Factors	Description
pH	Normal muscle pH is around 7, whereas fresh meat pH is 5.4 to 5.6. The pH drops after slaughter due to the breakdown of glycogen to lactic acid. Animals that are active or stressed shortly before slaughter will use glycogen; as a result, the meat will have a higher pH (6.2 or higher). High pH meat will be darker in color and is commonly called dark, dry, firm meat.
	Although the effect is variable, high pH meat tends to brown prematurely when cooked.
Meat source	Higher myoglobin concentrations are found in male animals, extensively used muscles in either sex, and more mature animals.
Modified atmosphere packaging	80 percent oxygen and 20 percent carbon dioxide modified atmosphere packaging promotes *oxymyoglobin* and will stabilize the red color.
	0.4 percent carbon monoxide and 30 percent carbon dioxide with the balance as nitrogen forms *carboxymyoglobin*. This pigment is a stable cherry red color.
	Meat packaged in a modified atmosphere may brown prematurely when cooked.
Freezing	Color may fade or darken with frozen storage. Color changes of meat cooked from frozen or previously frozen meats is variable, but premature browning is common.
Fat content	Lean ground meats tend to appear redder in the raw state due to less "white" fat mixed into the meat. The influence of fat content on browning is apparently limited.
Added ingredients	Salt will cause faster browning of meat.
	Nitrate, used in cured meats, will result in a heat-stable pink color as is commonly observed in ham or smoked turkey.

Source: References 46, 107

Iridescent Colors and Meat

The surface of meat may have shiny, rainbowlike colors. This physical phenomenon is called *iridescence*. It also may be observed in the rainbow of colors in soap bubbles and fish scales. Consumers may conclude meat with green, red, orange, and yellow iridescence is spoiled; however, iridescence is not caused by spoilage or chemical additives.

So what do we know about iridescent colors and meat? Iridescence is primarily associated with light diffraction and the surface microstructure. Meat may be more likely to be iridescent when the meat

- Is from the *semitendinosus* muscle found in the round
- Fibers are more perpendicular to slicing surface
- Is hydrated and has a moist surface
- Is sliced with a very sharp blade such as a very sharp meat slicer ■

Source: Reference 56

above the regular joint. The break shows four distinct ridges that appear smooth, moist, and red with blood. In mutton, the break comes in the true joint, which is below the break joint.

Most of the meat from sheep is marketed as lamb. Relatively little older mutton is sold. The flesh of all carcasses in the mutton class is darker in color than lamb. It is also less tender and has a stronger flavor when it is from animals beyond two years of age.

Pork

Pork is the meat of swine. Good-quality pork is obtained from young animals usually 7 to 12 months of age. In young animals, there is no distinction in quality or grade

MULTICULTURAL CUISINE

Bison

Huge shaggy animals once roamed the land from Canada to Mexico, grazing the great plains and mountain areas. These animals—the scientific species *Bison*—were the center of life for many Native Americans, who used them for food, shelter, and clothing. Buffalo are of the bovine family, as are domestic cattle. Wild West stories relate the thrill of buffalo hunts and the terror when the herds stampeded. From an estimated 60 million animals in earlier times, by 1893 there were only slightly more than 300 bison left in the United States.

Today, however, the bison are coming back, with an estimated 350,000 head in North America [93]. In addition to bison found in public park lands, many are privately owned, raised on the open range, and grain-fed 90 to 120 days before they are slaughtered for food. Some 20,000 are slaughtered each year in the United States, compared to approximately 125,000 cattle per day. Nevertheless, Americans consume approximately one million pounds of bison each month.

As meat, is bison different from beef? Bison is considerably lower in fat, when comparing lean cuts. A 3-ounce portion of roast bison contains about 22 grams protein, 2 grams fat, 66 mg cholesterol, and 145 calories. It is an excellent source of iron and B vitamins, as well as good-quality protein. Some say that bison has a sweeter, richer flavor than beef.

What do you do with bison, once you have made the decision to try it? Well, you should handle bison meat as you would any other type of meat—always following safe food-handling practices. Refrigerate it, properly packaged to prevent any leakage onto other foods, and use within three to five days or freeze it. USDA inspection of bison is voluntary.

Because bison is very lean and lacks marbled fat, it should generally be cooked using low heat and long cooking times. Braising or other moist cooking methods are recommended for roasts and steaks, although broiling or pan-frying may be used on thin-sliced bison. Ground bison should always be cooked to 160°F for safety reasons [93].

As you continue your experiences with new foods, you might like to try "beefalo," a cross between bison and domestic cattle. It has taken years of research to develop this breed, because the natural result of bison–domestic bovine crossbreeding is sterile offspring. Beefalo is also an excellent high-quality protein source with relatively low fat content. Enjoy your journey as you explore more red meat varieties. ∎

---

because of sex, whereas sex differences in older animals are pronounced. Most of the pork marketed in the United States comes from young animals.

MEAT PRODUCTION AND MARKETING

Livestock is raised on farms across America as well as throughout the world. Cattle are grass-fed when young and then may be grown to maturity (often called finished) in feedlots on feed consisting of corn and other grains to promote growth. About three-fourths of the cattle are "finished" in feedlots [101]. Lamb is often finished in feedlots as well. [106].

Antibiotics and Hormones

Antibiotics may be used to treat illnesses in livestock. Antibiotic residues, however, may not be present in the meat when sold. Therefore, the USDA's Food Safety and Inspection Service (FSIS) randomly samples animals at slaughter and also tests for residues [101]. An animal that has been given antibiotics must be off the antibiotics for a specified period of time before it is legal to slaughter the animal.

Hormones may be used in cattle and lambs to promote growth [101, 106]. Three natural hormones and two synthetic hormones have been approved for use in cattle. One hormone has been approved for use in lamb. These hormones are used as an implant in the animal's ear and must be used in accordance with regulations. Hormones are not permitted for use in veal or pork [99, 100].

Animal Welfare and Slaughter

Animals must be handled and slaughtered in accordance with the Humane Methods of Slaughter Act of 1978 [92, 96, 102]. Livestock must be treated humanely. For example, animals must have access to water, access to feed if held for more than 24 hours, and enough space to lie down. Appropriate methods of moving animals and the construction of the pens are given within the regulations. All livestock must be insensible to pain by stunning before being shackled, hoisted, or cut. Shortly after stunning, when the animal is unconscious, a sharp instrument is used to cut the carotid arteries and jugular veins or the blood vessels closer to the heart to bleed the animal [112]. Approximately 50 percent of the blood is drained from the animal. The only exception to the stunning requirement is ritual slaughter in accordance with the Jewish (Kosher slaughter) or Islamic (Halal slaughter) religious faiths [102].

Postmortem Changes

The muscles are soft and pliable before an animal is slaughtered. The metabolism in the cells is interrupted upon death, beginning processes that lead to a stiffening of the carcass known as *rigor mortis*. Postmortem metabolic changes include the (a) accumulation of lactic acid in the muscles resulting in a decrease in pH and (b) disappearance of ATP which is the high-energy compound produced in metabolism in the living animal. The muscle becomes contracted as a result of these changes. The muscle proteins (actin and myosin), which form the thin and thick filaments of the myofibrils in the muscle cell, slide or telescope on each other and bond together, forming actomyosin. Thus, the muscle is no longer extensible.

The time required after the death of the animal for occurrence of the stiffening process is affected by various factors. Both colder and warmer temperatures speed the development of rigor [37, 113]. The species of animal, its age, and its activity just before slaughter also affect the time of onset of rigor. In large animals, such as cattle, rigor begins more slowly and lasts longer than in smaller animals. In beef, the softening of the muscles, signaling the resolution of rigor mortis, occurs within 24 to 48 hours. If meat is separated from the carcass immediately after slaughter and cooked rapidly before rigor has a chance to develop, it will be tender. If the cooking is slow, however, rigor may develop during heating and increase toughness in the cooked meat [37, 42].

If the supply of glycogen in the muscle is low at the time of death, as is the case when much activity occurs just before slaughter, less lactic acid is produced from glycogen. As discussed in Table 25-2, when the pH of the muscle remains high, the meat is an undesirable dark color [46]. The muscle tissue has an increased water-binding capacity resulting in firm meat with a dry, sticky texture because the water is so tightly bound in the muscle [26, 46].

Aging

If meat is allowed to hang under refrigeration for one or two days after slaughter, it will gradually begin to soften as rigor mortis passes. If it is held still longer, a process of ripening or aging occurs. Aging results in an increase in tenderness, improvement of flavor and juiciness, better browning in cooking of both lean and fat, and a loss of red interior color at a lower cooking temperature [43]. Aging too long may result in a strong flavor or development of an off-flavor and off-odor. A major reason for the increase in tenderness during aging appears to be a breakdown of proteins in the myofibrils by enzymes [47]. Aging of beef may also produce some change in **mucoprotein**, which is a component of connective tissue [61].

Meat is commonly aged at approximately 36°F (2°C). However, aging sides of beef at 60°F (16°C) produces changes in tenderness more rapidly than aging at the lower temperature. At the higher temperature, some means of retarding microbial growth is necessary. Aging of meat is a commercial process not accomplished in home kitchens.

Two different methods—dry aging and wet aging—can be used for the postmortem aging of meat. Dry aging is aging meat "as is" under refrigeration, whereas wet aging involves packaging the meat in a vacuum bag and holding it under refrigeration. When these two methods of aging were compared for short-cut strip loins and ribs of beef, it was found that differences in palatability attributes of cooked steaks and roasts were slight [74]. There was, however, one major difference between the two methods: a greater shrink and trim loss was associated with dry aging, making this process more costly and time consuming.

Beef is the only type of meat that is commonly aged, although some consumers also prefer lamb when it is aged. Many cuts of beef are tender after 11 to 14 days of aging; however, other cuts benefit by a longer aging period [18]. Veal is not improved by aging, and the lack of fat on the carcass results in excessive surface drying. Pork is usually obtained from a young, tender animal; thus, toughness is not generally a problem. Aging of pork for more than three or four days may be complicated by the tendency for relatively rapid development of rancidity in the fat during holding.

Packaging

Many supermarkets as well as foodservice operations receive much of their fresh meat in reduced-oxygen barrier bags (*cryovac* packaging). Beef packaged in vacuum barrier bags will be a purplish-red and will not "bloom" to a bright cherry red color until the package is opened. It is this same packaging that is used when beef is wet aged. Most beef sold in supermarkets is a bright red because the oxygen barrier bags have been opened and the meat is portioned and repackaged on a Styrofoam tray with an oxygen-permeable plastic wrap.

Case-ready meat has been proposed for the retail market. Case-ready meat is packaged centrally and then delivered to the retail market ready for the display case. Centralized packaging would move the cutting and packaging steps from the supermarket meat departments into centralized operations. Costs can be reduced, shelf-life extended, and microbiological quality improved [11, 12, 13]. Wal-Mart is reported as using exclusively case-ready meat. Some of the case-ready meat packaging systems are described in Table 25-3.

TABLE 25-3   Types of Case-Ready Meat Packaging Systems

Type of Packaging	Description	Meat Color
Vacuum packaged, reduced oxygen	Heavy plastic bag (*cryovac*) with reduced oxygen levels. Will maintain a relatively long shelf life.	Purplish-red color until the package is opened.
High oxygen modified atmosphere	Oxygen and carbon dioxide are added to the package atmosphere. The package often is a solid plastic tray covered with a barrier clear film. The package volume is approximately double that of the meat to allow adequate head space for the modified atmosphere. The high oxygen levels promote oxidation and thus antioxidants may be used. Wal-Mart uses this packaging method.	Bright red. High oxygen level converts the pigment to brown metmyoglobin over time.
Carbon monoxide, low oxygen modified atmosphere	Up to 0.4 percent of carbon monoxide is added to the package atmosphere. Carbon dioxide levels are also elevated. The package volume is approximately double that of the meat. Shelf life for meat packaged in this way is typically longer than for other methods. The modified atmosphere in this package retards oxidation and the growth of spoilage organism.	A stable red color is produced by the low level of carbon monoxide. Use by dates and other spoilage indicators must be used to assess this product which will retain a bright red color for extended periods.

Source: References 12, 13, 82

Labeling

The FSIS approves labels for meat and poultry products. Each meat or poultry label must contain the following information: (a) product name, (b) producer or distributor name and address, (c) inspection mark (round stamp), (d) ingredient list in order from highest to lowest amounts, (e) net weight, (f) establishment number indicating the plant where the product was processed, and (g) handling instructions for products that require special handling to remain safe. Refer to Chapter 4 for more about government regulation and labeling requirements.

In 1994, the USDA mandated a safe handling label for raw or partially cooked meat and poultry products that are packaged in USDA- or state-inspected processing plants and retail stores (Figure 25-10). These instructions are designed to decrease the risk of foodborne illness attributable to unsafe handling, preparation, and storage

SAFE HANDLING INSTRUCTIONS

This product was prepared from inspected and passed meat and/or poultry. Some food products may contain bacteria that could cause illness if the product is mishandled or cooked improperly. For your protection, follow these safe handling instructions.

- Keep refrigerated or frozen. Thaw in refrigerator or microwave.
- Keep raw meat and poultry separate from other foods. Wash working surfaces (including cutting boards), utensils, and hands after touching raw meat or poultry.
- Cook thoroughly.
- Keep hot foods hot. Refrigerate leftovers immediately or discard.

FIGURE 25-10 The USDA requires safe handling instructions on packages of all raw or partially cooked meat and poultry products. *(Courtesy of the American Meat Institute and the U.S. Department of Agriculture)*

of meat and poultry products, both at foodservice facilities and in private kitchens by educating the consumer. The language and format for the label is specified [53].

Some meat is labeled as "natural." Products labeled natural may not contain artificial color or flavor, preservatives, or other artificial ingredients [101]. Additionally a statement on the package should explain to the consumer what is meant by the term *natural*. Some companies identify their meat as natural to indicate no hormones or antibiotics were used or that the animals were raised in grass and not finished in a feedlot. The terms *natural* and *organic* should not be used interchangeably because specific governmental guidelines have been established for the use of the term *organic*. See Chapter 4 for information about organic food regulations.

Government Regulation, Inspection, and Grading

Regulation.   Several laws have been passed and regulations published, at both the national and local levels, to protect and inform the consumer on the purchasing of meat and poultry products. The aim of these regulations is to protect the public, not only from obvious abnormalities and animal disease, but also from the hazards of pathogenic microorganisms that may be present on carcasses or in processing plants. The USDA has responsibility at the federal level for the inspection, grading, setting of standards, and labeling of all meat and poultry products. The Wholesome Meat Act of 1967 requires that state governments have local programs of meat inspection equal to those of the federal government for meat that is sold within state boundaries. Otherwise, the federal government will assume the responsibility for inspection. State programs are periodically reviewed to see that satisfactory standards are maintained. The Federal Meat Inspection

Act also requires that all meat imported into the United States must comply with the same standards of inspection applied to meat produced in the United States.

Much of the slaughtered meat and poultry goes into processed items, including sausages, ham, pizza, frozen dinners, and soups. The federal inspection program is also responsible for the safety of these products. An in-plant inspector monitors the processing operations (Figure 25-11).

Inspection. The inspection for the wholesomeness of all meats entering interstate commerce by qualified agents of the USDA Food Safety and Inspection Service is required. If meat carcasses pass the inspection process, the inspector's stamp (Figure 25-12) is placed on each wholesale cut of the carcass. This stamp carries numbers to indicate the packer and identify the carcass. If the meat is unsound, it is not permitted to enter retail trade. Consumers should, however, always use safe food-handling practices to protect against foodborne illness (see Chapter 3).

Traditionally, the inspection system relied largely on sight, touch, and smell, which was appropriate in an era when the goal was to protect the public against obvious abnormalities and animal disease. Animals are inspected alive and at various stages of the slaughtering process. The cleanliness and operating procedures of meatpacking plants are also supervised. However, certain hazards cannot easily be observed, particularly contamination of the

Inspection stamp used on meat carcasses.

Seal used on prepared meat products.

FIGURE 25-12 Federal meat inspection stamps. *(Courtesy of the U.S. Department of Agriculture)*

FIGURE 25-11 A USDA inspector is checking pork carcasses. *(Courtesy of U.S. Department of Agriculture)*

animals or processing plants with pathogenic microorganisms—bacteria, parasites, fungi, and viruses—that can cause human illness. Because of the danger of illness for the meat-consuming public, the USDA revised many aspects of the inspection system to detect and reduce the microbial hazards while providing greater assurance that meat and meat products are safe for human consumption. Four essential elements comprise the modernized inspection process [15].

1. All state and federally inspected meat and poultry slaughter and processing plants must have a Hazard Analysis and Critical Control Points (HACCP) plan (see Chapter 3).
2. Each of these meat and poultry plants must develop written sanitation standard operating procedures (SOPs) to show how they will meet daily sanitation requirements.
3. The federal agency tests for salmonella on raw meat and poultry products to verify that pathogen reduction standards for salmonella are being met.
4. Slaughter plants test for generic E. coli on carcasses to verify the process is under control with respect to preventing and removing fecal contamination.

E. coli. In 2002, the regulations designed to reduce the incidence of E. coli 0157:H7 were strengthened [35, 89]. Additional measures continue to be implemented to reduce the incidence of meat contaminated with E. coli 0157:H7. The incident rate was 0.9 illness per 100,000 people in 2005, which is down from 2.1 cases per 100,000 in 1997. The number of recalls of meat following positive test results for E. coli contamination likewise has dropped over the years [103]. Nevertheless, all those who handle raw meat must use safe food-handling and cooking practices to further protect against a potential foodborne illness. See Chapter 3 for a discussion about foodborne illness.

Bovine Spongiform Encephalopathy. Federal agencies including the USDA and the U.S. Department of Health and Human Services (HHS) have worked to prevent bovine spongiform encephalopathy (BSE) from entering the United States. BSE, also sometimes called *mad cow disease*, was found in two U.S. animals, one in 2003 and another in 2005 [40]. Meat from these animals did not enter the food supply.

BSE was first reported in the United Kingdom in 1986 and since that time has been identified in several additional European countries [108, 109]. Since 1989, the United States prohibited the importation of cattle and edible animal products from countries with cases of BSE [71]. The importation of live ruminants and most ruminant products from all of Europe was banned starting in 1997 [108]. Additional preventative measures have included (a) regulations prohibiting the use of most mammalian protein in feeds manufactured for ruminants, (b) FDA inspection of feed mills and rendering facilities, (c) USDA examination of all cattle before approval for food and prohibition of the use of all cattle with neurological diseases, and (d) USDA examination of cattle brains for the presence of BSE [34, 71, 108, 109].

Following the identification of two U.S. cattle that tested positive for BSE, more protective regulations were added. These include the banning of the following from the human food supply: (a) nonambulatory or downer cattle; (b) specific risk materials such as brain, spinal cord, nerves attached to spinal cord, and so forth; and (c) beef processed with mechanical separation [40].

Trichinella spiralis. There is no practical means of inspecting for the presence of the small parasite *Trichinella spiralis*, which may be found in the muscle of pork carcasses. When consumed, this organism causes trichinosis. Regulations for the inspection of meat products containing pork that are usually eaten without cooking require treatment of such products in a way that destroys any live trichinae that may be in the pork muscle tissue. This process can be accomplished in one of three ways: (a) heating uniformly to a temperature of 137°F (59°C), (b) freezing for not less than 20 days at a maximum temperature of 5°F (−15°C), or (c) curing under special methods prescribed by the USDA. Products such as dried and summer sausage, bologna, frankfurter-style sausage, cooked hams, and cooked pork in casings are among those requiring this treatment.

Grades and Grading. A program separate from the inspection service is the USDA system of grading meat. Whereas inspection of meat for wholesomeness is mandatory for all meat as it is slaughtered, grading is voluntary. Although it is not required that meat be graded to be marketed, grading provides a national uniform language for use in the buying and selling of meat. Grades are also useful to the consumer in knowing what quality to expect from purchased meats. The grading program is administered by the USDA, but the cost of the service is borne by those meatpackers who use it. Two types of grading are done: One for yield and the one for quality.

Yield Grades. For beef and lamb, yield grades (Figure 25-13) have been established for use with quality grades. Yield grades are based on cutability, which indicates the proportionate amount of salable retail cuts that can be obtained from a carcass. Yield Grade 1 is for the highest yield; Yield Grade 5, the lowest. A large proportion of edible meat is indicated by a relatively large ribeye area, a thin layer of external fat, and a small amount of fat around the internal organs. The dual system of grading, for both quality and yield, attempts to offer the consumer high-quality meat without excess fat. Both quality and yield grades must be used when beef and lamb are federally graded. Conformation, or shape and build of the animal, is reflected to some degree in the yield grade. A stocky, muscular build usually represents a relatively high proportion of salable meat and receives a high yield grade.

Quality Grades. Quality grades have been established for beef, veal, lamb, and mutton (Figure 25-14). In pork, the grade is determined by class (barrow, gilt, sow, stag, or boar) and consideration of quality and yield [68]. Factors considered in determining the quality grades are associated with palatability or eating quality [88].

Marbling and maturity are the two major considerations in evaluating the quality of beef. Marbling refers to the flecks of fat within the lean muscle. An optimum thickness of surface fat layer also appears to contribute to palatability [23, 85]. The maturity of an animal affects the lean meat texture—the grain generally becoming more coarse with increasing maturity. Fine-textured lean is usually slightly more tender than lean with a very coarse texture. A mature animal develops changes in connective tissue that contribute to decreased tenderness. Characteristics of quality for different kinds of meat are given in Table 25-4.

Table 25-5 shows USDA quality grades for beef, veal, lamb, mutton, and pork. Utility and lower grades of meat are rarely, if ever, sold as cuts in retail stores but instead are used in processed meat products. The appropriate

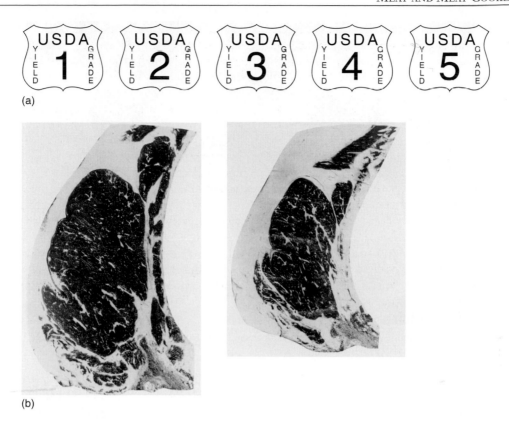

FIGURE 25-13 (a) U.S. yield grades identify carcass differences in cutability: the percentage yields of boneless, closely trimmed retail cuts from the high-value parts of the carcass. (b) Beef rib from Yield Grade 2 (left). Beef rib from Yield Grade 4 (right). *(Courtesy of the U.S. Department of Agriculture)*

USDA quality grade mark is applied to meat with a roller stamp that leaves its mark the full length of the carcass.

Because beef can vary so much in quality, it has eight designated grades, with USDA Prime beef being the highest quality. Only about 7 percent of marketed beef is likely to be graded Prime, and most of this beef is purchased for use in commercial foodservice. USDA Choice grade beef has slightly less marbling than Prime, but is still of very high quality. USDA Select and Standard grades lack the juiciness and quality of the higher grades, but because meat from these grades comes from animals younger than 30 to 42 months, it may be fairly tender. USDA Commercial, Utility, and Cutter grade beef comes from mature animals that are older than 42 months. Thus, slow cooking with moist heat is needed to tenderize these lower grades.

PURCHASING MEAT

Meat Identification

An understanding of meat cuts and relative quality is useful when purchasing meat. Price, tenderness, and recommended preparation methods vary considerably among various cuts. Meat carcasses are first divided into relatively large primal or wholesale cuts, such as the square-cut chuck section of beef. Primal cuts are then further divided into smaller retail cuts. Primal or wholesale and retail cuts of beef, pork, veal, and lamb are shown in Figures 25-15, 25-16, 25-17, and 25-18, respectively.

Division into cuts is made in relation to bone and muscle structure. Muscles found together in any one retail cut generally have similar characteristics of tenderness and texture. The shapes and sizes of bones and muscles in retail cuts act as guides to identification. Figures 25-19 and 25-20 show basic retail meat cuts that can be identified by their characteristic bone shapes. Because the skeletal structure is similar for all meat animals, the basic cuts are similar for beef, pork, veal, and lamb; however, each type of meat carcass is divided in a somewhat different manner.

Some meat cuts are known by different names in various parts of the country. For example, boneless beef top loin steaks are commonly called Delmonico, Kansas City, New York, or strip steaks; flank steak may be called London broil or minute steak. An industrywide Cooperative Meat Identification Standards Committee, organized by the meat industry, has developed standards for the retail meat trade and provided a master list of recommended names for retail cuts of beef, pork, veal, and

Federal inspectors/graders confer in a meat packing plant. Beef carcasses are hanging in the background.

U.S. federal meat quality grade stamps are placed within a shield.

FIGURE 25-14 The meat grading program is administered by the U.S. Department of Agriculture, but the cost of the service is borne by the meatpackers. *(Courtesy of the U.S. Department of Agriculture)*

lamb. The recommended retail package label information includes the species or kind of meat, the primal cut name, and the specific retail name from the master list. A typical label reads "Beef Chuck—Blade Roast." When purchasing meat for foodservice, Institutional Meat Purchase Specifications (IMPS) provide standardized meat cuts by number. Photographs and written descriptions of the IMPS items are provided in the North America Meat Processors Association's *Meat Buyer's Guide* [68]. Photographs of selected beef and pork retail cuts are shown in Plates XX, XXI, XXII, XXIII, XXIV, XXVI, and XXVII.

Beef. Cuts of beef are sometimes classified by most tender, medium tender, and least tender cuts. In general, those muscles that are little used are the most tender. Thus, meat from the rib, short loin, and sirloin are the most tender and also typically cost more per pound than other cuts. Table 25-6 lists the primal cuts by tenderness. There are some exceptions to these general rules. The

top five muscles, in order of tenderness, are given in Table 25-7 and include two individual muscles from the chuck primal. Although the chuck primal in general is not considered to be tender, these two individual muscles are exceptions.

Several popular steaks are cut from the short loin and the sirloin. The short loin and sirloin are cut into steaks as follows: top loin, nearest the rib, then T-bone, porterhouse, and sirloin. The tenderloin muscle, which lies on the underside of the backbone (between the backbone and kidney fat), forms one eye of meat in the loin steaks. It is very small or even nonexistent in the top loin steak area, but increases in size further back, having maximum size in the porterhouse steaks. The tenderloin may be bought as a boneless cut suitable for roasting or cutting into steaks. Because of its tenderness, tenderloin commands a high price.

Veal, Lamb, and Pork. Veal, lamb, and pork carcasses, being smaller than those of beef, are divided into fewer

TABLE 25-4 Indicators of Quality in Beef, Veal, Lamb, and Pork

Meat Classification	Indicators of Good Quality	Indicators of Poor Quality
Beef	Bright red color of lean muscle after the cut surface is exposed to air for a few minutes (meat will be a purplish-red color before exposure to air). Fine-grained and smooth to the touch. Firm fat. Chine or backbone is soft, red, and spongy and shows considerable cartilage.	Darker red color and coarse grain. Lacks smooth, satiny surfaces when cut. Fat is oily or soft in texture. Bones are white, hard, brittle, and show little or no cartilage.
Veal	Grayish-pink flesh and a texture that is fine-grained and smooth to the touch. Interior fat is firm and brittle. Bones are red, spongy, and soft and have an abundance of cartilage.	Either a very pale or a dark color of the lean. Little or no fat distributed throughout the carcass.
Lamb	Pinkish-red color, fine-grained, and smooth-cut surfaces of the flesh. Firm, flaky, and brittle fat. Bones are soft, red, and spongy and show cartilage.	Darker color of the lean, heavier fat layers, and a stronger flavor.
Pork	Grayish-pink color. Fine-grained. Very firm fat, but not brittle as in other types of meats. Soft, red, and spongy bones.	Excess fat distributed in the lean tissues and on the exterior. Color of the lean is darker, the grain is coarser, and the bones may appear less red and spongy. This is particularly true if the meat is from an animal beyond the optimal age limit.

Source: References 51, 68, 88

TABLE 25-5 USDA Quality Grades for Meat

Beef	Veal	Lamb	Mutton	Pork (excludes stag and boar classes)
Prime	Prime	Prime	Choice	U.S. No. 1
Choice	Choice	Choice	Good	U.S. No. 2
Select	Good	Good	Utility	U.S. No. 3
Standard	Standard	Utility	Cull	U.S. No. 4
Commercial	Utility			U.S. Utility
Utility				
Cutter				
Canner				

Source: Reference 68

primal and retail cuts. The loin of pork is a long cut including both the rib and loin sections. The rib and loin sections of veal, lamb, and pork are cut into chops or roasts. The hind legs are also tender enough for roasts. The individual cuts are identical in general shape and characteristics to similar cuts from beef, but less variation exists in the tenderness of cuts from different sections of the animal. All cuts of young pork of good quality, both fresh and cured, are tender. However, like beef, the cuts from the loin primal such as pork chops and pork tenderloin are often preferred.

Lamb and veal are similar to beef in that neck, shoulder or chuck, breast, and shanks may require some moist heat in cooking for tenderness. Some cuts of veal and lamb are shown in Plates XXIV and XXV. Even the most tender cuts of veal may be improved by some application of moist heat to hydrolyze the collagen in connective tissue. The lack of fat marbling in veal may also affect its tenderness. Larding, which involves inserting strips of fat into lean meat, supplies fat and enhances the flavor. The leg, loin, and rib sections of good-quality veal may be satisfactorily roasted.

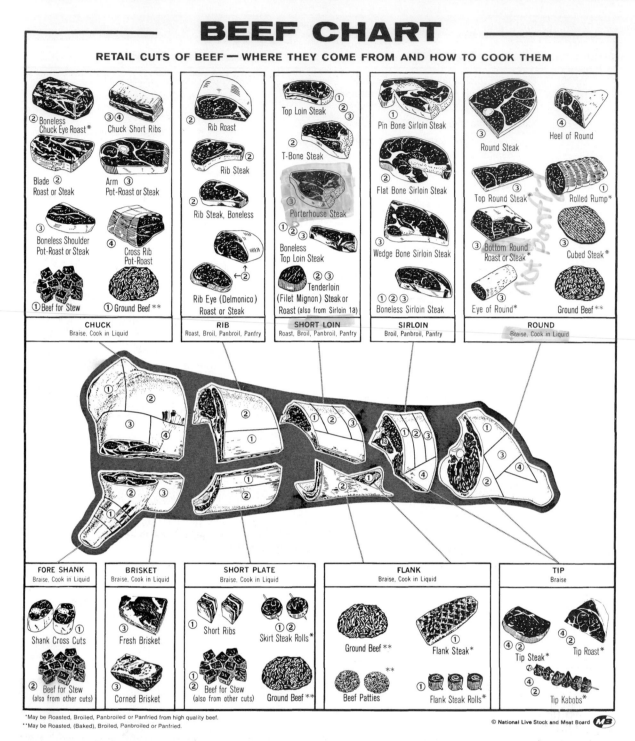

FIGURE 25-15 Primal and retail cuts of beef. *(Courtesy of the National Live Stock and Meat Board)*

Restructured Meat

The market demand for boneless steak meat that can be prepared rapidly cannot always be met with existing high-quality meat supplies at prices that are seen as reasonable by consumers. One way to help supply this potential market is with the production of restructured meats. *Restructuring* is changing the form of soft tissues, including lean, fat, and connective tissue [57]. The process generally begins with flaking, coarse grinding, dicing, or chopping the meat to reduce the particle size. Following this reduction process, it is mixed with small amounts of such substances as salt and phosphates to solubilize muscle proteins on the surface of the meat pieces and to aid in binding the particles together. The meat mass is then formed into the desired shape and size. Through restructuring, less valuable pieces of meat,

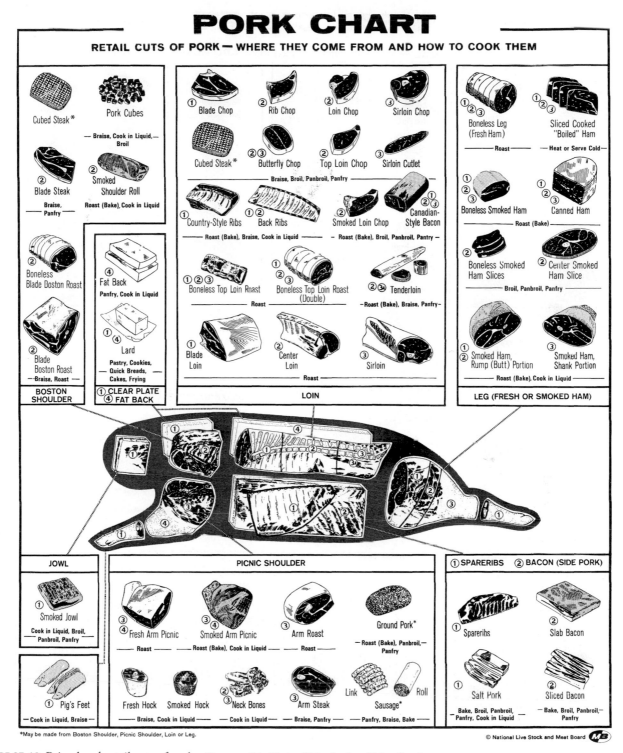

FIGURE 25-16 Primal and retail cuts of pork. *(Courtesy of the National Live Stock and Meat Board)*

including lean trimmings, are upgraded. They are used to produce boneless, uniformly sized steak or roast products that resemble fresh intact muscle in flavor, color, and texture [19]. For example, Canadian-style bacon is a restructured product, whereas Canadian bacon is a smoked and cured whole-muscle pork loin. Canadian bacon is more expensive, but if the intended use is for a sandwich, then Canadian-style bacon may be perfectly acceptable.

The composition of restructured meats can be formulated to meet consumer demands, including lowfat items. The meat pieces used may be trimmed of connective tissue to varying degrees [78], and lean meat from grass-fed animals may be used [77].

VEAL CHART

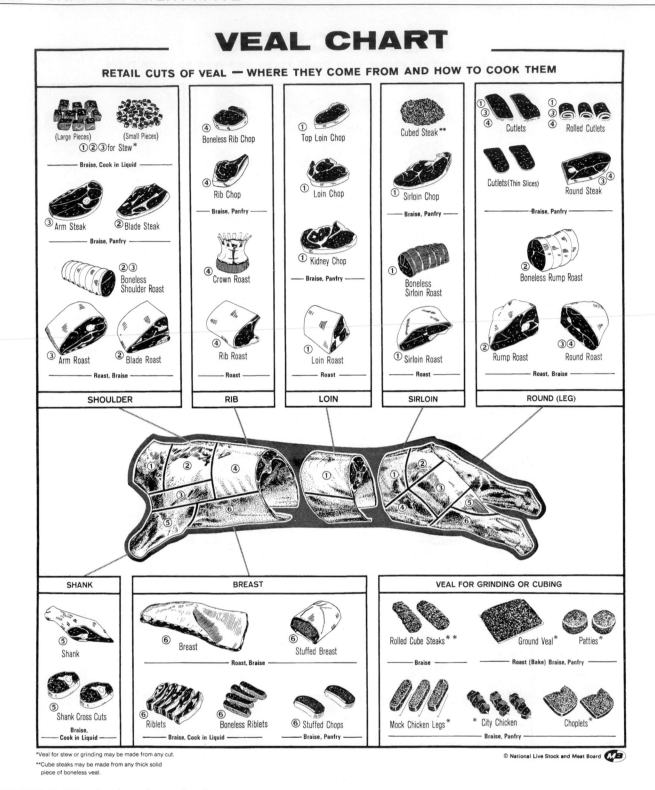

FIGURE 25-17 Primal and retail cuts of veal. *(Courtesy of the National Live Stock and Meat Board)*

Variety Meats

Included in the category of variety meats are sweetbreads, heart, tongue, tripe, liver, kidney, and oxtail (Figure 25-21). Sweetbreads are the thymus gland of the calf or young beef. This gland disappears as the animal matures. The thymus

gland of lamb is sometimes used for sweetbreads but is too small to be of practical value.

The thymus gland has two parts—the heart sweetbread and the throat, or neck, sweetbread. It is white and soft. Tripe is the smooth lining from the first beef

LAMB CHART

RETAIL CUTS OF LAMB — WHERE THEY COME FROM AND HOW TO COOK THEM

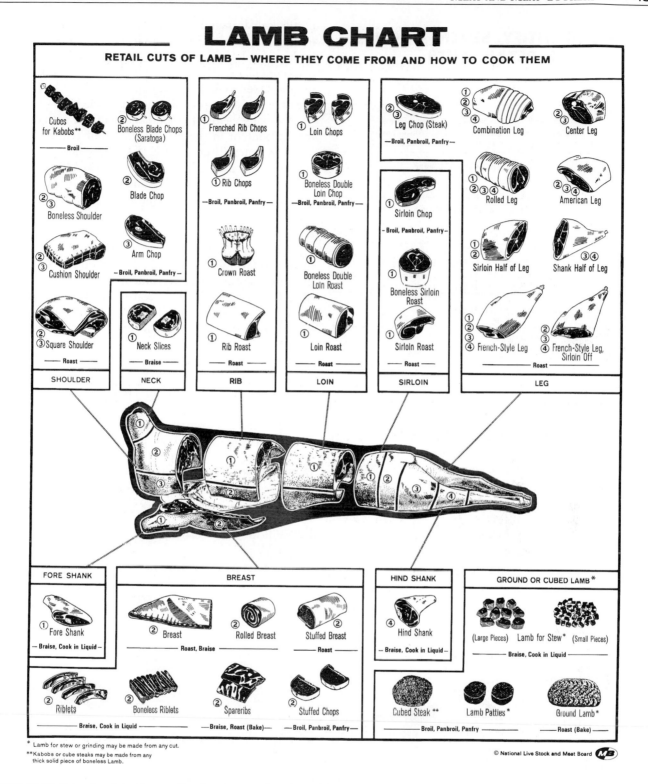

FIGURE 25-18 Primal and retail cuts of lamb. *(Courtesy of the National Live Stock and Meat Board)*

stomach, the honeycombed lining from the second stomach, and the pocket-shaped section from the end of the second stomach. The heart and tongue are much-exercised muscles and therefore are not tender. They, as well as tripe, require relatively long, slow cooking for tenderization. Liver is a fine-textured variety meat. Veal or calf liver, because of its tenderness and mild flavor, is usually preferred to other kinds of liver and for that reason is more expensive. Livers from all meat animals are high in nutritive value. Kidneys from beef and veal consist of irregular lobes and deep clefts. Kidneys from veal are more tender and delicate in flavor than those from beef.

BONES IDENTIFY SEVEN GROUPS OF RETAIL CUTS

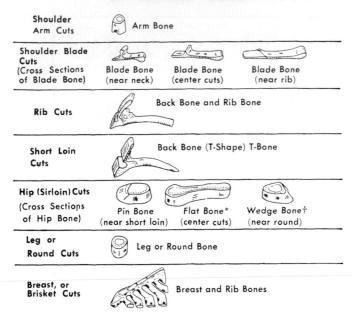

Shoulder Arm Cuts	Arm Bone		
Shoulder Blade Cuts (Cross Sections of Blade Bone)	Blade Bone (near neck)	Blade Bone (center cuts)	Blade Bone (near rib)
Rib Cuts	Back Bone and Rib Bone		
Short Loin Cuts	Back Bone (T-Shape) T-Bone		
Hip (Sirloin) Cuts (Cross Sections of Hip Bone)	Pin Bone (near short loin)	Flat Bone* (center cuts)	Wedge Bone† (near round)
Leg or Round Cuts	Leg or Round Bone		
Breast, or Brisket Cuts	Breast and Rib Bones		

*Formerly part of "double bone" but today the back bone is usually removed leaving only the "flat bone" (sometimes called "pin bone") in the sirloin steak.

†On one side of sirloin steak, this bone may be wedge shaped while on the other side the same bone may be round.

FIGURE 25-19 Basic bone shapes aid in meat cut identification. *(National Live Stock and Meat Board)*

Ground Beef and Hamburger

Ground beef and hamburger are both made from beef that has been ground. Beef fat may be added to "hamburger," but it may not be added to "ground beef" [98]. A processor may add fat if the meat being ground is particularly lean and a higher fat level is desired. A maximum fat content of 30 percent by weight has been set for both ground beef and hamburger ground in federally inspected plants. Most ground beef, however, is prepared in local supermarkets to maintain freshness. The percentage of lean is often provided on the label.

Cooking yields of ground beef increase with decreasing fat content in the raw product, but tenderness and juiciness generally decrease [21]. Ground beef is the most commonly consumed form of red meat in the United States, accounting for approximately 42 percent of total beef consumption [22]. Ground chuck must come specifically from the chuck area of the carcass, and ground round must come only from the round.

Irradiated ground beef may be purchased as one method of avoiding E. coli 0157:H7 (Figure 25-22). The meat industry and the government are pursuing methods of reducing the risk of E. coli 0157:H7–contaminated meat reaching the marketplace. Microbiological product testing has resulted in meat recalls. However, because a small number of organisms can cause disease, irradiation can provide a high level of safety [6, 72]. This extra level of protection may be especially important when serving populations at a high risk for foodborne illness such as children or when preparing ground beef in situations where careful and consistent temperature control may be difficult. In one study, consumers rated irradiated and control ground beef patties equally for overall liking, toughness, flavor, and texture. The irradiated beef patties were rated as juicier than the nonirradiated [110]. See Chapter 3 for a more extensive discussion on food safety.

Economic Considerations

American families tend to spend a substantial percentage of their food money on meats. If this amounts to as much as 38 to 40 percent of the food budget, it is quite possible

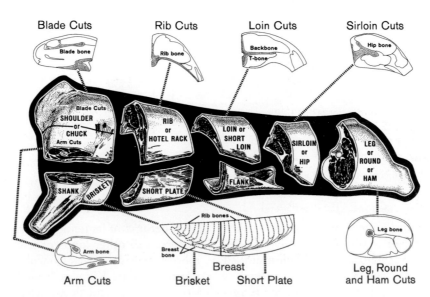

FIGURE 25-20 Seven basic retail cuts of meat. *(National Live Stock and Meat Board)*

TABLE 25-6	Level of Tenderness Associated with Beef Cuts	
Most Tender Cuts	**Medium Tender Cuts**	**Least Tender Cuts**
Rib	Chuck	Flank
Short loin	Rump	Plate
Sirloin	Round	Brisket
		Neck
		Shanks

TABLE 25-7	The Top Five Beef Muscles in Order of Tenderness	
Name of Muscle	**Location of Muscle**	**Retail Name**
Psoas Major	Beef loin, tenderloin	Tenderloin or filet mignon
Infraspinatus	Chuck, beef shoulder, top blade	Flat iron steak
Gluteus Medius	Top sirloin center-cut	
Longissimus Dorsi	Beef rib, ribeye and beef loin strip steak, center-cut	Ribeye steak or strip steak
Triceps Brachii	Chuck, beef shoulder, arm	Ranch steak

Source: Reference 68

that other important food items, such as milk, fruits, and vegetables, are being neglected. Meats are among the most expensive items of the diet. They are well liked, and many families place undue emphasis on the need for meat in every meal.

Considerable variation exists in the percentage of bone, muscle meat, and visible fat among retail cuts. Table 25-8 provides some information about the yield of boneless cooked meat from various cuts. Ground beef yields the largest number of three-ounce servings per pound of beef; short ribs, bone-in, yield the smallest number of servings. In general, the cost per pound of an edible portion is greatest in those cuts that command the

How to Buy a Ham

The first step in purchasing a ham is to understand the terminology. *Fresh ham* refers to the meat from the pork primal called "ham" that has not been cured. The ham primal is the rear leg of the pork. USDA defines a *cured ham* as meat from the ham pork primal.

In common usage, a variety of pork cuts may be cured and called "ham." Curing may be dry or wet. Ingredients used in curing include salt, sodium or potassium nitrate, and other seasonings. Not all hams are fully cooked; therefore, the label must be checked for the statement "cook before eating" to know if the ham needs further cooking or may be consumed as purchased.

There are a variety of hams available in the marketplace. Those hams produced from primal cuts other than the ham primal do not meet USDA definition for ham and usually have a qualifying term such as "cottage." Some of the terminology used for hams includes:

- Capacolla ham—Usually made from the pork shoulder butts. Should always be labeled with "cooked" in product name.
- Cottage ham—Usually not cooked. Is cured pork from the shoulder butt primal and thus does not meet USDA definition for ham.

- Country ham—Uncooked, cured, dried pork from the ham primal or the pork shoulder. Prepared by a dry application of salt or salt and other curing ingredients.
- Ham—Cured leg of pork.
- Ham shank end—From the lower, slightly pointed part of the leg.
- Ham, Smithfield—Aged, dry-cured ham made exclusively in Smithfield, VA.
- Ham, water added—At least 17 percent protein with 10 percent added solution.
- Ham, with natural juices—At least 18.5 percent protein.
- Hickory-smoked ham—Cured ham smoked over burning hickory wood chips in a smokehouse.
- Prosciutto—Italian-style dry-cured ham that is raw. Because of the dry-curing process, it may be consumed without cooking unless otherwise labeled. Prosciutto, Cooked refers to a dry-cured ham that is cooked. ■

Source: Reference 104

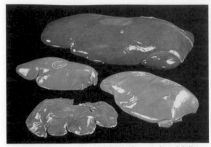

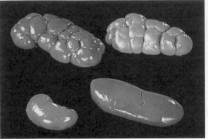

Livers (top, beef, middle left, veal; middle right, lamb; bottom, pork)

Kidneys(top left, beef; top right, veal; lower left, lamb; lower right, pork)

Hearts (in order of size: beef, veal, pork, and lamb)

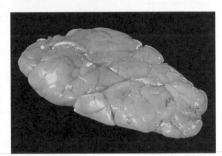

Tongues (in order of size: beef, veal, pork, and lamb)

Sweetbreads

FIGURE 25-21 Variety meats. *(Courtesy of the National Live Stock and Meat Board)*

FIGURE 25-22 Irradiated ground beef can take the worry out of grilling hamburgers by significantly reducing the risk of E. coli 0157:H7. *(Courtesy of Agricultural Research Service, U.S. Department of Agriculture; photo by Stephen Ausmus)*

Ground Beef: Juicy and Lowfat

Researchers continue to explore ways to produce a palatable product with low fat content [33]. Isolated soy protein has been added to lean ground beef, but it has had little or no success in increasing juiciness [54]. The addition of water, up to 10 percent, with or without added phosphate, has been reported to increase juiciness, tenderness, and overall palatability scores in lowfat ground beef patties (10 percent fat). The lowfat patties with added water scored equal in texture and flavor to those containing 22 percent fat [63]. Combinations of unhydrated dietary fiber (from sugarbeets,

oats, or peas), potato starch, and **polydextrose** added to ground beef with 5 to 10 percent fat content produced cooked patties that were similar in texture to control patties containing 20 percent fat. However, the experimental patties were less juicy than the higher-fat product [86]. If the price differential between extra lean and regular ground beef is relatively great, regular ground beef may be purchased, cooked, drained of extra fat, and possibly also rinsed with hot water to substantially reduce its fat content [79]. However, if rinsed, the ground beef should be reheated up to 160°F (71°C). ■

TABLE 25-8 Yield of Boneless Cooked Meat from 1-Pound Retail Cuts of Beef and Veal*

Kind and Cut of Meat	Number of 3 oz Servings	Volume, Chopped or Diced (cups)
Beef		
Brisket		
Bone-in	2	1–1 1/2
Boneless, fresh or corned	3	1 1/2–2
Chuck roast		
Arm		
Bone-in	2 1/2–3	1 1/2–2
Boneless	3 1/2	2
Blade		
Bone-in	2 1/2	1 1/2
Boneless	3–3 1/2	2
Club or T-bone steak, bone-in	2	—
Flank steak, boneless	3 1/2	—
Ground beef	4	—
Porterhouse steak, bone-in	2–2 1/2	—
Rib roast		
Bone-in	2 1/2	1 1/2
Boneless	3	1 1/2–2
Round steak		
Bone-in	3–3 1/2	—
Boneless	3 1/2–4	—
Rump roast		
Bone-in	2 1/2	1 1/2
Boneless	3 1/2	2
Short ribs, bone-in	1 1/2	1
Sirloin steak		
Bone-in	2–2 1/2	—
Boneless	2 1/2–3	—

TABLE 25-8 (Continued)

Kind and Cut of Meat	Number of 3 oz Servings	Volume, Chopped or Diced (cups)
Veal		
Breast		
Bone-in	2	1–1 1/2
Boneless	3	1 1/2–2
Cutlet		
Bone-in	3 1/2	—
Boneless	4	—
Leg roast		
Bone-in	2 1/2	1 1/2
Boneless	3 1/2	2
Loin chops, bone-in	2 1/2–3	—
Loin roast		
Bone-in	2 1/2	1 1/2
Boneless	3 1/2	2
Rib chops, bone-in	2 1/2	—
Rib roast		
Bone-in	2–2 1/2	1–1 1/2
Boneless	3 1/2	2
Shoulder roast		
Bone-in	2 1/2	1 1/2
Boneless	3 1/2	2

*These figures allow no more than 10 percent fat on a cooked bone-in cut and no more than 15 percent fat on a cooked boneless cut.

Source: Used by permission the U.S. Department of Agriculture.

highest prices, and vice versa, but several exceptions occur because of differences in the percentage of bone and fat in the cuts. For example, at the same price per pound, the rump (bone-in) may cost almost double the price of round per pound of edible portions because only about 43 percent of the rump is edible compared with about 76 percent of round. Also, the price per pound of short ribs would need to be quite low for this cut to be a very economical buy in terms of cooked lean meat yield. Therefore, it is important to recognize that cost per pound of meat as purchased is not the sole consideration. The edible yield of the meat must be considered.

The usual amount to buy per serving is 4 ounces of meat with little or no bone, and 3/4 to 1 pound of meat with a high refuse content. One average pork chop is a serving, as is one to two lamb chops, depending on the size and thickness of the chops. In recent years however, portion sizes have increased and have resulted in higher meal costs while not necessarily improving dietary quality. The USDA Food Guide Pyramid (http://www.mypyramid.gov) provides individualized recommendations for serving sizes.

Most of the less expensive cuts of meat are a more economical source of lean than expensive cuts. Retail prices are determined largely by such factors as tenderness, general appearance, and ease or convenience in cooking. The consumer tends to buy on the basis of these qualities to so great an extent that the loins and ribs, which constitute about one-fourth of the beef carcass, represent about one-half of the retail cost. Neither palatability nor food value corresponds directly to market price. Many of the less expensive, less tender cuts of meat have more flavor than tender cuts and, if properly cooked, are delicious. The food value is similar in both tender and less tender lean meat cuts. Thus, consumers have many opportunities to save money when selecting meat cuts.

TENDERNESS AND FLAVOR

Tenderness

One of the most valued attributes of meat is tenderness. The grading of meat by USDA standards does not directly measure this characteristic, although the probability that a beef carcass will be tender is greater in a higher grade than in a lower grade. Pork and lamb, because they are marketed young, are usually tender.

Much more variation exists in beef, and much of the research on tenderness has been concerned with beef cuts. A system of sampling, cooking, and testing beef was developed in the U.S. Meat Animal Research Center in Nebraska that identifies beef carcasses with rib and loin cuts of above-average tenderness [38]. Under this system, a rib steak from a chilled carcass is cooked, then measured for tenderness with an electronic testing machine that provides computer data (Figure 25-23). Research at the Meat Animal Research Center has shown that marbling accounts for only 10 percent of the variation in beef rib-eye tenderness [38]. Thus, a system for more accurately predicting tenderness will be of value.

Taste panels, in studying the tenderness of meat, have described several components of tenderness that are apparent during the biting and chewing of meat. These include the ease with which teeth sink into the meat, or softness, the crumbliness of the muscle fibers, and the amount of connective tissue or the amount of residue remaining after the meat is chewed for a specified time. Each of these components of tenderness may be influenced by various factors operating in the production and preparation of beef and other meats, including, as we have discussed, aging of beef and changes in the muscle proteins producing actomyosin.

Connective Tissue. It is generally agreed that larger amounts of connective tissue in a cut of meat cause decreased tenderness. The least-used muscles of an animal, particularly those in the rib and loin sections, contain less connective tissue than muscles that are used for locomotion (Figure 25-24). The muscles of the rib and

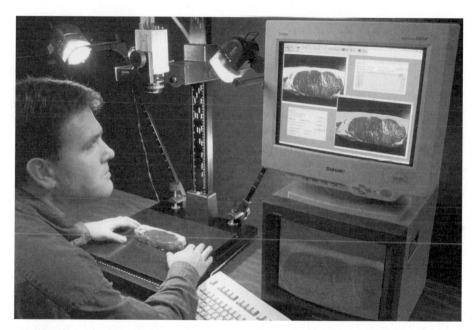

FIGURE 25-23 A food technologist uses a computer program to predict tenderness and beef carcass composition based on test results. *(Courtesy of Agriculture Research Service, U.S. Department of Agriculture; photo by Keith Weller)*

FOCUS ON SCIENCE

How Does the Warner-Bratzler Shear Measure the Tenderness of Meat?

The Warner-Bratzler Shear test has been used to determine the tenderness of meat. Sensory scores have been found to correlate with shear readings. This agreement in tenderness scoring may be because the dull edge which is used to shear the meat simulates the grinding surfaces of the teeth which also are dull.

The following procedure is used:

- A core piece of meat (0.5 to 1 inch in diameter) is placed on the triangular opening of the guillotine fixture.
- An initial rise in the measurement chart is due to the compression of the sample by the blade prior to shearing.
- The tenderness is measured by the final reading as the meat is cut.

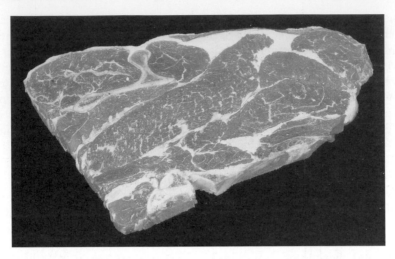

FIGURE 25-24 This beef chuck 7-bone steak has more connective tissue than cuts from the rib and loin. *(Courtesy of the National Cattlemen's Beef Association)*

loin, for example, are more tender than the muscles of the legs and shoulders.

As animals mature and become older, more and stronger connective tissue usually forms in muscle tissues. The cross-links between collagen monomers that comprise the fibrils in connective tissue appear to become less soluble and more resistant to heat as an animal ages. This factor is important in explaining the difference in tenderness between younger and older animals.

The tenderloin muscle, which is not used in locomotion and has little connective tissue, remains tender in animals up to 48 months of age, whereas other muscles with strong connective tissue triple in toughness [83]. The case of veal is different, however. Although it is a very young animal, there is still a relatively high percentage of connective tissue in the muscles because of the lack of time for development of the muscle itself.

Fat and Marbling. The fattening of animals has long been thought to improve the tenderness of meat. It has been suggested that a layer of subcutaneous fat on a carcass delays chilling of the meat, thereby allowing postmortem metabolic changes that result in greater tenderness [23]. The USDA quality grade standards for beef include an estimation of the amount of marbling (the distribution of fat throughout the muscle). Small but statistically significant decreases in tenderness have been found in beef by expert judging panels as marbling decreased from moderately abundant to practically devoid [84]. Juiciness and flavor also decreased. Untrained consumers in San Francisco and Kansas City gave slightly lower scores for overall desirability of top loin beef steaks as the marbling level decreased. In the same study, consumers in Philadelphia rated the steaks with lesser marbling considerably lower than those well marbled, indicating regional differences [81]. Marbling would appear to have an impact on the eating quality of beef steaks, including tenderness, but sometimes this effect on tenderness may be small.

Ground beef is a popular meat product in the United States. When cooked ground beef patties made from raw meat containing 5, 10, 15, 20, 25, and 30 percent fat were compared, it was noted that the lowfat patties (5 and 10 percent) were firmer in texture, less juicy, and less flavorful than the patties with 20 to 30 percent fat [87]. Objective measurements with the Warner-Bratzler and Lee-Kramer shear instruments also showed decreasing tenderness with decreasing fat content.

Other Factors. Carcasses of beef are sometimes subjected to low-voltage electrical stimulation immediately after slaughter to increase tenderness. The beneficial effects may result from an increase in the rate of postmortem metabolism and a disruption of the myofibrils with accelerated enzymatic breakdown of the muscle proteins [27]. Electrical stimulation and 48 hours of aging were reported to have the same tenderizing effect on both steer and bull carcasses as a six-day aging period [31].

The hereditary background of the animal, the management of its feeding, and the size of muscle fibers are other factors that affect meat tenderness. Many of these factors are undoubtedly interrelated, and more research is needed to clarify the whole picture of tenderness in meat. For example, pronounced differences in tenderness are apparent among various muscles of the beef carcass. The tenderloin, or psoas major, and the longissimus dorsi muscles in the rib and loin sections are the most tender; muscles of the round and chuck sections are less tender. These differences in tenderness cannot be completely explained by differences in connective tissue, fat content, or state of muscle contraction [62].

Tenderizing. Because of the lower cost of certain less tender cuts of meat in comparison with more tender pieces, attempts have been made to tenderize the less tender cuts. Grinding and cubing break up the connective tissue and make meat more tender.

Tenderizing compounds containing various enzymes, usually **proteinases**, may be used to hydrolyze some of the proteins in meat. The enzymes include papain and chymopapain from the green papaya fruit, bromelin from pineapple, ficin from figs, and actinidin from kiwifruit. The compounds are applied to the surface of meats prior to cooking. A fork can be used to pierce the meat and allow the material to penetrate a little further. Most of these enzymes act primarily on the muscle cell proteins; bromelin is more active on the collagen of connective tissue. Care must be taken to control excessive action on the meat fibers and prevent the development of a mealy or mushy texture. Little enzymatic action occurs at room temperature, the optimal temperature for papaya enzyme activity being 140° to 160°F (60° to 70°C). This temperature is reached during cooking.

An enzyme mixture may be injected into the bloodstream of the animal just before slaughter. Theoretically, the enzyme is carried to all parts of the body and is evenly distributed throughout the various retail cuts. The enzyme remains inactive until the meat is heated in cooking. Cuts of meat that are usually classified as less tender can be cooked as tender cuts if the beef animals have received enzyme injections. If the enzyme has not been destroyed in cooking, continued tenderization should occur during standing time after cooking.

Flavor

The flavor of meat involves responses from taste and smell and also sensations from pressure-sensitive and heat-sensitive areas of the mouth. Flavor of meat is developed primarily by cooking; raw meat has little aroma and only a bloodlike taste. The flavor of boiled meats differs from that of roasted meats.

The chemistry of meat flavor is highly complex, as many compounds contribute to the characteristic flavor of the cooked product. Some of these flavor compounds are volatile and give rise to odor. One study of the volatile flavor components of fresh beef stew identified 132 different compounds [75].

Although volatile components are possibly the most important part of meat flavor, nonvolatile compounds stimulate taste buds and contribute to the overall flavor complex. The most important taste compounds are inorganic salts, producing a salty taste; sugars, producing a sweet taste; hypoxanthine, contributing some bitterness; organic acids, producing a sour taste; and some nitrogen containing compounds including nucleotides, amino acids, and peptides. In addition to volatile and nonvolatile components of meat flavor, other substances called *flavor potentiators* and *synergists* contribute to taste. Although these substances have no distinctive flavor of their own, they enhance the flavor of other compounds. Flavor potentiators in meat include some amino acids, such as glutamic acid, and certain 5′-nucleotides such as inosinic acid [65].

The feeding management of beef cattle affects the flavor of the meat, particularly the flavor of the fatty portions. Grass- or forage-fed steers have less desirable flavor, characterized as grassy, gamey, and milky-oily, than those animals finished on grain [59, 64]. Serving temperature also affects perceived meat flavor. Beef steaks tasted at 122°F (50°C) are more flavorful and juicy than similar samples tasted at 72°F (22°C) [70]. Not only the temperature, but also the time a meat product is held before serving, can affect flavor. Freshly cooked meat sauce with spaghetti was found to be more flavorful and generally more acceptable to a taste panel than a similar product held hot on a cafeteria counter for 90 minutes [2]. Irradiation of ground beef to reduce foodborne pathogens does not affect the aroma, taste, aftertaste, or texture of ground beef either immediately after irradiation or after frozen storage [28].

Warmed-over flavor is an off-flavor of meats commonly present when meats have been cooked, held under refrigerated or frozen storage, and then reheated. Warmed-over flavor is characterized as "cardboardlike," "painty," or "rancid." These flavors are the result of oxidation. Polyunsaturated fatty acids oxidize more readily than saturated fats, thus those meats with higher levels of polyunsaturated fatty acids are more likely to develop warmed-over flavors. Most prevalent meats with warmed-over flavors are fish, poultry, pork, beef, and lamb in descending order. Oxidation can be reduced by vacuum packaging or covering with a sauce to reduce oxygen exposure. Light exclusion and ingredients such as vitamin E, butylated hydroxyanisol (BHA), citric acid, ascorbic acid, nitrites, and certain spices can also be useful [10]. Oxidation reactions were discussed further in Chapter 10.

FOCUS ON SCIENCE

More about the Causes of Warmed-Over Flavor

Warmed-over flavor (WOF) is caused by unsaturated fatty acids that are found in meat, such as beef, lamb, pork, poultry, and fish. The more unsaturated the fatty acid, the more susceptible it is to degradation during cooking to smaller compounds (aldehydes and ketones). Initially, no flavor changes are evident, but when the food is reheated, the compounds that were formed "volatize" and produce off-flavors in the food. Research has shown that certain spices, such as rosemary, sage, and thyme, contain certain antioxidants that prevent WOF. Covering the food with gravy also acts as a "blanket" to prevent oxidation.

FOCUS ON SCIENCE

What Causes the Red Color in Cured Meat, such as Corned Beef or Bacon?

Nitrite and nitrate are used in the curing process. The following reaction occurs:

$$Mb \rightarrow MetMb^+ \rightarrow NOMetMb^+ \rightarrow NOMb \rightarrow Nitrosylhemochrome$$
$$+NO_2^- \quad +NO \quad reduction \quad heat$$

1. Nitrite (NO_2^-) is an oxidizing agent and rapidly converts myoglobin (Mb) to metmyoglobin ($MetMb^+$).
2. Nitric oxide (NO) then combines with $MetMb^+$ to form nitrosylmetmyoglobin ($NOMetMb^+$).
3. The nitrosylmetmyoglobin ($NOMetMb^+$) is reduced by various reducing agents, such as ascorbate to nitrosylmyoglobin (NOMb).
4. The attractive red color of cured meats before cooking is essentially that of nitrosylmyoglobin (NOMb). It has the red color characteristic of fresh meat oxymyoglobin.
5. Heating converts nitrosylmyoglobin to denatured nitrosylhemochrome which is unstable and characteristically red-pink in cooked cured meats.

CURED MEATS

For centuries, curing has been an important method for preserving meat. At one time, salt (sodium chloride) in comparatively large amounts was the substance used in curing. Today, curing ingredients include sodium nitrite, sugar, and seasonings, in addition to salt. Nitrite reacts with myoglobin, the red pigment of meat, producing nitrosylmyoglobin, which later changes to the characteristic pink color of cured meats during the heating portion of the curing process. The heated pink pigment is nitric oxide hemochrome.

Nitrite

Nitrite is toxic when consumed in excessive amounts. In addition, it has been shown that certain cancer-producing substances, called *nitrosamines,* can be formed in food products or in the acid environment of the stomach by reactions between nitrite and secondary amines. The FDA has therefore limited the amount of nitrite that can be present in a finished cured product. However, in addition to fixing color in cured meats, nitrite contributes to the development of characteristic flavor and inhibits the growth of the bacterium *Clostridium botulinum.* This organism has the ability, under suitable conditions, to produce a deadly toxin. Other ingredients, such as vitamins C and E, are now used with the lesser amounts of nitrite [16]. A 1997 report of analysis for nitrite in cured meats obtained from the marketplace indicated that the current residual nitrite level is approximately one-fifth the level of 25 years ago [17]. The risks from nitrites are considered to be very low at this time. In 2000, a review of data from a long-term rodent study concluded there was no evidence that nitrite is a carcinogen in male and female rats and male mice. The evidence for female mice was insufficient [5]. Research on this subject will no doubt continue.

Salt

Salt in the curing mixture inhibits the growth of undesirable microorganisms during curing and adds flavor. Salt, in sufficient quantities with or without other curing agents, also causes the development of a heated pink pigment. This change in color can occur accidentally and undesirably in products such as meatloaf if the salt content is high enough and the product is not cooked shortly after mixing. Raw, processed turkey breasts may also show this color defect if the amount of salt used in processing was too high. Both of these products will remain pink even if thoroughly cooked. In processed meats, such as ham or smoked turkey, this pink color is expected.

Some processed meats are being produced with lower salt content because of the interest in decreasing the sodium levels in the American diet. Phosphates may also be used in curing solutions to decrease shrinkage in meat by retaining moisture.

Cured Products

Ham, bacon, smoked pork-shoulder picnic, and Canadian bacon are commonly cured pork cuts. Corned beef is the cured brisket of beef. Frankfurters and a variety of sausages are also cured products. The desire to reduce the amount of fat in meats has extended to the cured meat-processing industry. Comminuted emulsion-type products such as wieners, sausages, and bologna can be produced with reduced-fat levels. An increased level of water, with binders such as starch, cereal, soy flour, soy protein concentrate, and nonfat dry milk, can be used to produce texture and sensory properties similar to those of the higher-fat products [36].

During the curing process, the curing mixture may be rubbed dry on the outside of a cut of meat, or the meat may be submerged in a solution of the curing ingredients. The rate of diffusion of the ingredients into the meat is, however, slow. The curing ingredients are much more rapidly and uniformly distributed throughout the meat when they are injected internally. In meat cuts in which the vascular system is still intact, as in hams, briskets, and tongues, the curing solution may be pumped into the arteries. Brine may be injected with needles into other cuts such as bacon. Pumping the curing solution into meat increases the weight of the meat. Federal regulations require that a ham must be "shrunk" back to at least

FOCUS ON SCIENCE

How Do Phosphates Work in Cured Meats?

The addition of appropriate phosphates increases the water-holding capacity of raw and cooked meats. Therefore, phosphates are used in the production of sausages, in the curing of ham, and in poultry and seafoods to decrease drip losses. Sodium tripolyphosphate ($Na_5P_3P_{10}$) is the phosphate most commonly added to processed meat, poultry, and seafood. It often is used in blends with sodium hexametaphosphate [$(NaPO_3)_n$, $n=10$-15] to increase tolerance to calcium ions that exist in brines used in meat curing.

Uncertain of the mechanism, researchers believe that phosphate anions interact with divalent cations and myofibrillar proteins. Binding of polyphosphate anions to proteins and simultaneous cleavage of cross-linkages between actin and myosin result in increased electrostatic repulsion between peptide chains and a swelling of the muscle system. If exterior water is available, it can be taken up in an immobilized state within the loosened protein network.

---

its original fresh weight by the time heating and/or smoking is completed. If not, the ham must be labeled "ham, water added" if it contains up to 10 percent added moisture. Hams labeled "country-style" are processed by using a dry cure, slow smoking, and long drying process. They are firm textured, relatively low in moisture (about 85 percent of the original weight), and always require cooking before eating.

It is no longer necessary to cure ham primarily for preservation purposes, because refrigeration is readily available; thus, ham is cured with more interest in flavor and color. After the injection of curing solution, hams are heated or smoked. During this process, they are heated to an internal temperature of 140°F (60°C), but they need additional cooking before serving. Hams labeled "fully cooked" are heated to an internal temperature of about 150°F (66°C). No additional cooking is required, but they may be cooked further if desired. Canned hams that have been processed at sterilizing temperatures are also available. All processed products containing pork must be treated so that any trichinae present are destroyed, because this organism causes trichinosis in humans.

Sausages and Luncheon Meats

More than 200 varieties of sausages and luncheon meats are marketed in the United States (Figure 25-25). These are made from chopped or ground meat with various seasonings and often contain curing ingredients. Sausages are usually molded in casings, either natural or manufactured, or in metal molds. Many casings are edible, but some, such as the casings used for summer sausage, are not edible and should be removed prior to use.

Amendments to the standards of identity for frankfurters and other similar cooked sausages allow lowfat processed meat products to be included. A maximum combination of 40 percent fat and added water is allowed,

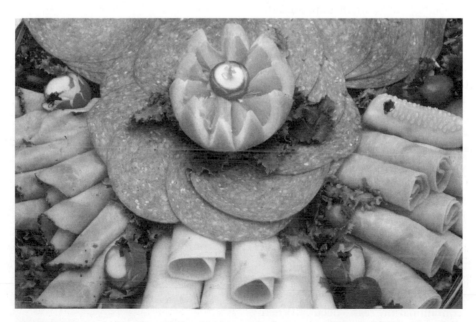

FIGURE 25-25 Agricultural research scientists study the source of flavor differences in deli meats, bologna, and sausages. Consumers have a wide variety of meats from which to choose. *(Courtesy of the Agricultural Research Service, U.S. Department of Agriculture; photo by Scott Bauer)*

with the maximum fat content no more than 30 percent. The maximum allowable level of binders, individually or collectively, is 3.5 percent. Sausages containing more than 3.5 percent of the various binders or more than 2 percent of isolated soy protein or caseinate must be labeled "imitation" [33]. Frankfurters may contain up to 15 percent poultry without special labeling. Turkey is used in the production of a variety of sausages, frankfurters, and luncheon meats, including bologna. Sausages can be classified as follows:

1. Uncooked
   a. Fresh pork sausage in bulk or encased as links
   b. Fresh bratwurst
   c. Bockwurst
2. Cooked
   a. Bologna (small, medium, and large)
   b. Frankfurters (wieners)
   c. Knockwurst
   d. Liver sausage or Braunschweiger
   e. Miscellaneous loaves
3. Semidry or dry
   a. Salami
   b. Cervelat
   c. Pepperoni

Cured Meat Pigments

Cured meat pigments tend to be oxidized and to discolor when exposed to the lighting of display cases in supermarkets. Vacuum packaging in oxygen-impermeable material prevents oxygen from coming in contact with the meat. Such packaging increases the shelf life of processed products such as bacon and luncheon meats by controlling the oxidation of pigments and the development of oxidized off-flavors.

SAFE STORAGE AND PREPARATION OF MEATS

Safe Storage and Handling

Fresh meats are highly perishable. A cold storage temperature that is at or below 40°F (4.5°C) is required. Coolers for meat in foodservice operations should be set at 36°F (2°C) or colder. Meats should not be placed above other foods in the refrigerator, particularly vegetables, unless they are held in a leak-proof container. If bacteria are present on meat and its drippings come in contact with other foods, cross-contamination can occur. When handling meat, everything should be kept clean—hands, utensils, counters, cutting boards, and sinks. In particular, wash, rinse, and sanitize utensils that have touched raw meat before using for cooked meats. Refer to Chapter 3 for more about recommended food safety practices.

Ground meats and variety meats are particularly perishable and should be cooked within one to two days after purchase if they are not frozen. Suggested storage times for some meats are given in Table 25-9. For freezing, meat hould be wrapped tightly in moisture-/vapor-proof material (Figure 25-26). The meat may be divided into serving-size portions before freezing. It should be kept frozen at 0°F (–18°C) until used. Frozen ground meat should be defrosted (a) in the refrigerator, (b) in the microwave and cooked immediately after thawing, or (c) in cold, running water—never at room temperature. Thawing meats at room temperature provides an opportunity for the growth of pathogenic bacteria and thus should not be done.

Preparation and Food Safety

Knowledge of, and adherence to, the recommended endpoint cooking temperatures of meat is necessary to prevent foodborne illness. All raw meats are more or less contaminated with a variety of bacteria, some of which may constitute hazards, particularly if the food is mishandled or undercooked. In addition, flesh foods may contain parasites or the larvae of tapeworms when raw.

Ground Beef. E. coli 0157:H7 caused concern after several outbreaks of hemorrhagic colitis resulting in some deaths were traced to ground beef patties in the early 1990s. Ground beef must be cooked to at least 155°F (68°C) for 15 seconds in foodservice operations and 160°F (70°C) in home kitchens to destroy any E. coli 0157:H7 that may be present (Figure 25-27). The ground

TABLE 25-9 Suggested Storage Periods to Maintain High Quality in Beef and Veal		
	Storage Period	
Product	**Refrigerator** [35° to 40°F (2° to 4°C)]	**Freezer** [0°F (–18°C)]
Fresh meat		
Chops and cutlets	3–5 days	3–4 months
Ground beef or veal	1–2 days	2–3 months
Roasts		
Beef	3–5 days	8–12 months
Veal	3–5 days	4–8 months
Steaks	3–5 days	8–12 months
Stew meat	1–2 days	2–3 months
Variety meats	1–2 days	3–4 months
Cooked meat and meat dishes	1–2 days	2–3 months

Source: Used by permission of the U.S. Department of Agriculture.

Wrapping Instructions

Choose a moisture/vapor-proof freezer wrap to seal out air and lock in moisture. Heavy duty, pliable wraps such as aluminum foil, freezer paper and plastic wrap are good choices for bulky, irregular-shaped beef cuts since they can be molded to the shape of the cut.

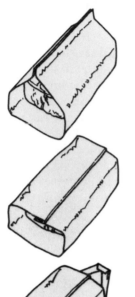

1. Place beef cut in center of wrapping material. When several cuts are packaged together, place a double thickness of freezer wrap between them for easier separation.

2. Bring edges of wrap together over beef. Fold over at least twice, pressing wrap closely to beef to force out air.

3. Smooth ends of wrap, creasing edges to form triangles. Double-fold ends toward package to seal out air.

4. Fold ends under package as shown and seal with continuous strip of freezer tape. Label tape with name of cut, number of servings and date of freezing.

FIGURE 25-26 Wrapping instructions for meat that is to be frozen. *(Courtesy of National Cattlemen's Beef Association)*

beef temperature guidelines should also be applied to beef products that have been punctured, such as blade-tenderized or minute steaks.

One important contributing factor in E. coli 0157:H7 outbreaks associated with ground beef has been undercooking [14]. For safety, ground meat should always be cooked to the recommended internal temperature and checked with a properly calibrated thermometer. In the early 1990s, consumers were told to cook their ground beef until the juices ran clear; however, starting in 1997 the Food Safety and Inspection Service (FSIS) began recommending the use of a food thermometer [76]. This change was made because research conducted at Kansas State University and later confirmed by the

USDA's Agricultural Research Service found that some meat appears to be brown before reaching a safe endpoint temperature. One group of researchers found that nearly 50 percent of the patties tested showed premature browning [45]. This study supported other research [41] that found patties were more likely to brown before reaching a safe internal temperature if the ground beef contains predominately oxymyoglobin (cherry-red) or metmyoglobin (brown) pigments. Alternatively, some lean ground beef or ground beef that contains spices and spice extractives may remain pink at temperatures well above 160°F (70°C). Thus, color is not a reliable indicator of doneness.

Beef Steaks, Pork, and Lamb.   Beef steaks and roasts may be cooked to lower temperatures (145°F or 63°C), because these solid muscle meats will be heated to high enough temperatures to kill bacteria that could be present on the surface. Pork steaks and roasts must be cooked to 145°F (63°C) to destroy *Trichinella spiralis*. Ground pork, like ground beef, must be cooked to 155°F (68°C). Although the infection rate of pork with *Trichinella spiralis* has declined considerably over the years, cooking to recommended temperatures is still advisable. Lamb should be cooked to an endpoint temperature of 145°F (63°C). When cooking any meat in a microwave oven, an endpoint temperature of 165°F (74°C) is recommended [67]. All previously cooked products should be reheated to 165°F (74°C) [67]. Table 25-10 summarizes recommended endpoint cooking temperatures for meats. See Chapter 3 for additional guidance on safe cooking temperatures.

METHODS OF PREPARING AND COOKING MEAT

Meat may be prepared in a variety of ways for consumption. The cut of meat, food preferences, and cuisine will influence the method of cooking. As an initial preparation step, fat and connective tissue may be trimmed from the cut. Safe vegetable dyes are used for the government inspection and grade stamps. Thus, unless preferred, these stamps do not need to be trimmed off. Occasionally, bone splinters may be present and should be removed.

Dry, Moist, and Combination Cooking Methods

Conventional cooking of meat is divided into dry-heat and moist-heat methods. Dry-heat cookery traditionally includes roasting or baking, broiling, and pan-broiling. Frying can also be included in this classification because fat, not moisture, comes in contact with the surface of the meat during cooking. These procedures are discussed in

FIGURE 25-27 USDA reminds consumers through the "Is it done yet" campaign that a thermometer should be used to test doneness of foods. *(Courtesy U.S. Department of Agriculture, Food Safety and Inspection Service.)*

TABLE 25-10	FDA Food Code Minimum Internal Endpoint Cooking Temperatures for Meat
Product	**Minimum Internal Cooking Temperature**
Ground meat (Ground beef, pork, and other meat)	155°F (68°C) for 15 seconds
Pork, beef, veal, lamb	Steaks/chops
	145°F (63°C) for 15 seconds
	Roasts
	145°F (63°C) for 4 seconds
Injected meats (Brined ham or flavor-injected roasts)	155°F (68°C) for 15 seconds
Meat cooked in microwave	165°F (74°C)

Source: Reference 67

more detail later in this chapter under "Specific Cooking Methods."

Moist-heat methods are stewing or cooking in water and pressure cooking (Figure 25-28). Simmering temperatures for stewing are sometimes specified on the assumption that the boiling temperature toughens meat; however, there is apparently little difference in the final tenderness of meats cooked in water at simmering or boiling temperatures.

Braising is often called a combination method of cooking because both dry- and moist-heat methods are used. The braising of large pieces of meat is sometimes called *pot-roasting*. When meats are braised, the surfaces may first be browned using dry heat by pan-broiling or frying before finishing the cooking process with a moist method involving potentially a sauce or steam heat. The term *fricassee* may be applied to braised meats cut into small pieces before cooking.

For many years, dry-heat methods of cooking were generally applied only to tender cuts of meat, whereas moist-heat methods were thought to be necessary to tenderize all less tender pieces. However, roasting less tender cuts with dry heat can be satisfactorily accomplished using very low oven temperatures and long periods of time [50]. The flavors developed in beef during roasting and broiling seem to be favored by most people over those developed in braising or pot-roasting.

FIGURE 25-28 This savory beef stew with roasted vegetables is prepared by lightly browning the beef in oil then simmering until tender. *(Courtesy of the National Cattlemen's Beef Association)*

Not all cuts of meat respond similarly to various cooking methods. Beef loin, a tender cut of meat usually cooked with dry heat, becomes tougher if cooked thoroughly with moist heat [20]. In contrast, bottom round steaks, a less tender cut of meat, become more tender when braised well-done. Thus, moist-heat cooking methods may be unsuitable for some tender cuts. Dry heat can be appropriate for tender and less tender cuts, providing the temperature is reduced and the length of cooking is extended for the less tender cuts. Apparently there is enough water in the meat itself to provide for the hydrolysis of connective tissue during slow cooking of less tender cuts.

Effect of Heat on Meat

Heat produces many changes in meat. Fat melts, myoglobin is denatured, and tenderness changes. Fat melts when meat is heated, and the capacity of the muscle proteins to hold water is lessened, thus causing reduced juiciness and tenderness and increased weight loss. The volume of the meat decreases on cooking. Redness decreases as internal temperature increases. The meat pigment myoglobin appears to be denatured around 140°F (60°C), and denaturation of other proteins seems to be complete by 176°F (80°C) [9]. However, as previously discussed, a brown color is not a reliable indicator of the doneness of ground beef.

Heating causes a decrease in tenderness when the meat reaches from 104° to 140°F (40° to 60°C). This is followed by a gradual increase in tenderness above 140°F (60°C) or even above 122°F (50°C) in young animals. The original toughening appears to be the result of a shortening of the fibers accompanied by hardening as the proteins denature and coagulate. The later tenderizing evidently results from the softening of connective tissue and the hydrolysis to gelatin of some collagen in this tissue [8, 52, 60].

The response of an individual muscle to heating is influenced by the amount of connective tissue; however, the muscle fibers from different muscles may also react differently toward heat. In one study, researchers heated a tender muscle (longissimus dorsi) and less tender muscles (semitendinosus and semimembranosus) of beef to three different internal temperatures. They found that the tender muscle did not change in tenderness with increasing degrees of doneness, but the two less tender muscles increased in tenderness with higher internal temperatures [80]. The less tender muscles contained more connective tissue, which was evidently softened with increased temperatures. A different balance between the hardening of muscle fibers and the softening of connective tissue was achieved in the less tender muscles than in the tender muscle.

Cooking Losses

Cooking losses, including loss of weight and loss of nutrients, increase gradually with increasing internal temperatures [9]. Weight loss results from the formation of drippings, evaporation of water, and evaporation of other volatile substances. When meat is roasted in an open pan, considerable evaporation of water from the meat surface occurs, but nutrients and flavor substances are better retained in the meat than when the meat is cooked in water or steam. As water evaporates, minerals and extractives are deposited on the surface of the meat, which may account in part for the pronounced flavor of the outer brown layer of roasted meat.

Fat losses are less consistent than those of other constituents, probably because of the unequal distribution of fat throughout most pieces of meat. Fat on or near the surface is lost to a greater extent than fat in the interior because of the slowness of heat penetration. Not all fat that liquefies is lost, because some of it can, and does, penetrate to the interior. The fat layer on the outside of meat aids in decreasing water loss by preventing evaporation. Researchers have found that the degree of fat trim on raw beef loin steaks did not significantly affect the sensory characteristics of the cooked meat; however, the fat content of the cooked steak with the fat totally trimmed off was significantly less than the fat content of the steak with regular trim [1]. In cooking ground beef, either as patties or as crumbles, fat losses are greater when the fat content of the raw meat is higher [55].

The final internal temperature to which meat is cooked influences total weight losses. Weight loss increases with increasing internal temperature. Total weight loss is usually greater in moist-heat than in dry-heat methods of cooking meat. Top round steaks showed total cooking losses of 27.5 percent when they were cooked by moist heat compared with 20.6 percent when they were cooked by dry heat [66].

Although some losses of B vitamins, including thiamin, riboflavin, and niacin, occur during cooking, cooked meats are still good sources of these vitamins. Greater vitamin losses occur during braising and stewing than during roasting and broiling, but many are retained in the cooking liquid. Vitamin retention in meats during cooking in water depends on the cooking time, with greater losses occurring as cooking continues. Riboflavin and niacin are more resistant to destruction by heat than thiamin.

Shrinkage

Shrinkage in cooked meats begins at 122° to 140°F (50° to 60°C) because of the shortening of muscle fibers and coagulation of proteins. There is loss of water and melting of fat. The higher the interior temperature of the meat, the greater the shrinkage. Less shrinkage usually occurs in meats roasted at 300° to 350°F (149° to 177°C) than in meats roasted at higher oven temperatures. Meats roasted for the whole cooking time at a high oven temperature may shrink as much as 40 to 60 percent compared with 15 or 20 percent at low temperatures. It is wise to consider excess shrinkage in economic terms, as fewer servings can be obtained from meats that have been allowed to shrink excessively during cooking. Particularly in quantity cookery, the yield of the meat can have a very noticeable impact on the number of servings available after cooking.

Basting

Pouring or spooning liquids such as meat drippings or a marinade over the surface of meat while it is roasting is called *basting*. The major purpose of basting is to keep the surface moist, but the use of a savory liquid also enhances the flavor of the cooked meat. If meats are placed in the roasting pan with the fat layer on top, the melted fat flows over the surface of the roast as it cooks, and self-basting occurs.

Salting

When should meat be salted? There is debate about the answer to this question. Rubs have become popular in the preparation of many meat dishes. Rubs are a mixture of spices and herbs that may be used dry or wet to season meat [51]. Many of the rubs do include salt, and these rubs add a unique flavor to the dish even if it is a large roast that was seasoned with the rub before cooking (Figure 25-29).

Others prefer not to salt their meat before cooking. If the piece of meat is large, the salt will not penetrate a roast to a depth greater than 1/2 inch. Putting a lot of salt on the outer surface may result in an outer layer that is too salty or salty drippings. The outer layer then also becomes crusty. Salt retards the browning of meat, and for that reason, salt may be applied to steaks and chops after they are cooked.

Meatloaves cannot be well seasoned unless salt is mixed with the meat before the loaf is shaped. To season small pieces of meat, as in stew, salt may be added to the cooking water. Total losses from the meat seem to be no greater in salted than in unsalted stews.

Although salting a raw or slightly cooked surface of meat draws juice to the surface, it has not been proven that salting meats before or during cooking results in any greater total losses from the meat than would occur if meats were not salted.

(a)

(b)

FIGURE 25-29 (a) This Italian beef roast was rubbed with a mixture of basil, oregano, salt and pepper prior to roasting. *(Courtesy of the National Cattlemen's Beef Association)*
(b) A purchased Italian seasoning blend was rubbed on this pork loin roast before roasting. *(Courtesy of National Pork Board)*

Juiciness

Juiciness is a highly desirable characteristic in cooked meats. Depending on such factors as the quality of the meat, the amount of marbling, and aging, meats differ in their juiciness. Aged meats are usually the juiciest of meats. The meat from younger animals is often more juicy than that from older animals. The amount of fat in a piece of meat, particularly fat marbled throughout the muscle, may increase the apparent juiciness of meat as it is eaten. In comparing the sensory properties of ground beef patties with three different levels of fat, it was reported that juiciness, as well as tenderness, was associated with the higher amounts of fat [7].

The interior temperature to which meats are cooked affects juiciness, with meats cooked to the rare and medium-done stages being more juicy than well-done meats. In fact, it is difficult to cook meats to a brown interior color without a substantial loss of juiciness.

Meats that are cooked for a long time in moist heat to develop tenderness reach an interior temperature so high that they cannot fail to be dry. If meats are cooked in moisture and are served in the cooking liquid, as Swiss steak is, they may appear to be moist, but that moistness is not juiciness within the meat itself.

Tenderization

Proper cooking contributes to the development of the desirable trait of tenderness in less tender meat and to its preservation in already tender cuts. The tender cuts do not contain large amounts of connective tissue, which may need to be softened by long cooking. Therefore, overcooking of these cuts should be avoided.

Adequate tenderization of connective tissue generally occurs with either the application of moist heat or the use of dry heat for long cooking periods at low temperatures. In either case, tenderization results from hydrolysis of the collagen in connective tissue to produce gelatin. A firming effect that may take place in muscle fibers subjected to long cooking is more than counterbalanced by the softening of connective tissue. However, if the meat is not carved across the grain, producing short muscle fiber segments, the long intact muscle fibers that are separated because of connective tissue disintegration may contribute to apparent toughness as the meat is eaten. Proper carving of meat thus contributes to tenderness as the meat is served.

Less tender cuts of beef can be tenderized to some extent by soaking the meat in an acid-containing marinade for 24 to 48 hours before cooking [39, 73]. The tenderizing effect depends on the concentration of acid present. Marinated beef muscles with a pH of 3.25 have been found to be significantly more tender than those with a pH of 4.25 [73]. At the lower pH, the water-binding capacity of the muscle is increased, the total collagen content is reduced, and cooking losses are decreased. Meats should always be marinated in the refrigerator, not on the counter. Marinade used on raw meat or poultry should not be reused unless it is boiled first to destroy any bacteria.

Meat tenderizers increase the tenderness of meat through enzymatic hydrolysis of proteins in the tissue as the meat is heated [30]. (See "Tenderness and Flavor" earlier in this chapter.)

Specific Cooking Methods

Roasting or Baking. Historically, the term *roasting* was applied to the cooking of large cuts of meat before an open fire. Today the terms *roasting* and *baking* are often used synonymously and apply to the method of placing meat on a rack in an open pan and cooking by the dry heat of an oven. Baking is actually more commonly used with portion cuts and roasting with large pieces of meat (Figures 25-30 and 25-31).

The oven temperature generally recommended for roasting tender cuts of meat is 325°F (177°C). As the oven temperature is increased from 300° to 450°F (149° to 232°C), the cooking time for meats cooked to the same internal temperature is decreased, total cooking losses are increased, and the uniformity of doneness throughout the meat is decreased. Adequate browning for good flavor and attractive appearance occurs at low constant oven temperatures, particularly if temperatures of 325° and 350°F (163° and 177°C) are used. A high temperature at the beginning does not seal in juices.

Meat can also be roasted in a convection oven in which the heated air is constantly recirculated by means of a fan. The cooking process is speeded up in convection ovens, and the roasting time is therefore somewhat less than with a conventional oven.

Cuts of Meat for Roasting. Tender and less tender cuts of meat may be roasted. Less tender cuts of beef are tender and acceptable when roasted at low oven temperatures of

FIGURE 25-30 This roast is being checked for doneness with an instant read thermometer. Notice the temperature is taken in the center of the roast. *Source: Reference 51.*

FIGURE 25-31 This veal roast with apricot thyme chutney is moist and flavorful. *(Courtesy of the National Cattlemen's Beef Association)*

225° to 250°F (107° to 121°C) [69]. The less tender cuts have been found to be more moist and juicy than similar cuts that are braised. The cooking time at the low temperature is considerably extended.

Length of Cooking Time. The length of cooking time may be estimated by minutes per pound guides (Table 25-11). Assessment of doneness is best done by a thermometer near the end of the estimated cooking time because the actual time needed can vary by the (a) shape, thickness, and the proportion of meat to bone and (b) oven load. A standing rib roast cooks in less time than a rolled rib roast because the latter is made more compact by boning and rolling. Large roasts of the same general shape as small roasts require fewer minutes per pound. Additionally, if an oven is heavily loaded or frequently opened, the temperature of the oven may drop and result in a longer cooking time.

Carry-Over Cooking. After a relatively large roast is removed from the oven, it continues to cook as heat continues to penetrate to the center. This effect may be referred to as *carry-over* cooking. The rise in temperature may continue for 15 to 45 minutes or longer and may be from 5° to 10°F (3° to 6°C), depending on the oven temperature at which the meat is roasted, the internal temperature at which the roast is removed from the oven, the size of the roast, and the composition of the meat. Thus, to avoid overcooking, a roast should be removed from the oven at a lower temperature than the desired endpoint to allow for the rise in temperature.

The higher the oven temperature at which the roast is cooked, the greater the increase in internal temperature of the roast after removal from the oven. The lower the internal temperature of the roast when it is removed from the oven, the greater the rise in temperature after removal from the oven. Small, thin roasts may show little or no rise in temperature because of the rapid cooling from the surface.

Thermometer Use. To accurately measure the doneness of meat, a meat thermometer or an instant read

TABLE 25-11 Approximate Roasting Time and Interior Temperature for Some Typical Meat Cuts*

Cut	Weight (lb)	Oven Temperature	Interior Endpoint Cooking Temperature of Meat	Approximate Time per Pound (minutes)
Beef				
Rib roast, bone in	5–6	325°F (163°C)	145°F (63°C) medium rare	23–25
			160°F (71°C) medium	27–30
			170°F (77°C) well done	32–34 (If boneless, add 5–8 minutes per pound)
Round or rump roast	2 1/2–4	325°F (163°C)	145°F (63°C) medium rare	30–35
			160°F (71°C) medium	35–40
Tenderloin, whole	4–6	425°F (218°C)	145°F (63°C) medium rare	45–60 minutes total
Half			160°F (71°C) medium	35–45 minutes total
Veal				
Rib roast	4–5	325°F (163°C)	160°F (71°C) medium	25–27
			170°F (77°C) well done	29–31
Loin	3–4	325°F (163°C)	160°F (71°C) medium	34–36
			170°F (77°C) well done	38–40
Pork, Fresh				
Loin roast, bone-in or boneless	2–5	350°F (176°C)	160°F (71°C) medium	20–30
Boston butt	3–6	350°F (176°C)	160°F (71°C) medium	45
Tenderloin	1/2 to 1 1/2	425°F (218°C)	160°F (71°C) medium	20–30 minutes total
Leg (fresh ham), Whole, bone-in	12–16	350°F (176°C)	160°F (71°C) medium	22–26
Pork, Cured and Fully Cooked				
Whole, bone in	10–14	325°F (163°C)	140°F (60°C)	15–18
Spiral cut, whole or half	7–9	325°F (163°C)	140°F (60°C)	14–18
Arm picnic shoulder, boneless	5–8	325°F (163°C)	140°F (60°C)	25–30
Lamb				
Lamb leg, bone in	5–7	325°F (163°C)	145°F (63°C) medium rare	20–25
			160°F (71°C) medium	25–30
			170°F (77°C) well done	30–35
Lamb leg, boneless rolled	4–7	325°F (163°C)	145°F (63°C) medium rare	25–30
			160°F (71°C) medium	30–35
			170°F (77°C) well done	35–40
Shoulder roast or Shank leg half	3–4	325°F (163°C)	145°F (63°C) medium rare	30–35
			160°F (71°C) medium	40–45
			170°F (77°C) well done	45–50

*If higher or lower temperatures are used for roasting, the times will obviously be somewhat shorter or longer, respectively.
Source: U.S. Department of Agriculture, Food Safety and Inspection Service.

thermometer should be used. The thermometer is inserted in the thickest portion of the meat (Figure 25-30). Meat thermometers may remain in the roast while it is cooking. Instant read thermometers may be used to check the internal temperature at the end of the cooking period but may not be left in the oven. The recommended internal temperatures for fresh beef or lamb cooked to various stages of doneness are as follows [94, 97]:

Medium rare	145°F (63°C)
Medium	160°F (71°C)
Well done	170°F (77°C)

Broiling. In broiling, meats are cooked with a direct heat source, such as a gas flame, live coals, or an electric element, that emits radiant energy (Figure 25-32). Broiling is used for relatively thin cuts of meat such as steaks and chops. It is usually done using the broil setting on a range, with the door closed for a gas range and open for an electric range. Steam may accumulate in an electric oven with the door closed, and steam retards browning. A rack for holding the meat out of the drippings is essential, both to keep the meat from stewing in its juices and to prevent burning of the fat.

The source of heat used for broiling is usually constant, with variation in temperature achieved through regulating the distance of the surface of the meat from the source of radiant heat. The relatively high temperatures normally used in broiling do not seem to toughen the meat, possibly because cooking times are relatively short or because tender cuts of meat are used. Broiling may be used for relatively thin, less tender cuts of meat if they have been treated with meat tenderizers.

The doneness of steaks can be tested in various ways. To avoid cutting the steak or otherwise damaging the appearance, test doneness by using the firmness of the meat as a guide. Rare meat will be soft, but well-done meat will be firm when pressed with a utensil. With experience, the firmness of meat can become a good indication of doneness for steaks. Unlike ground beef that must be tested with a thermometer for doneness, steaks that may be contaminated with E. coli 0157:H7 will have contamination only on the surface, thus an internal temperature lower than 155°F (68°C) is acceptable because the external temperature will exceed that necessarily to destroy E. coli.

Steaks may also be checked for doneness by use of a thermometer, although adequate contact of the thermometer with the interior of the steak will be necessary (see Chapter 3 for descriptions of thermometers). Pulling apart the fibers in the thickest portion to see the color of the juice is yet another option. A cut is sometimes made next to the bone to determine interior color.

Table 25-12 gives the approximate broiling time for some typical cuts. Like the timetable for roasting, it is strictly a guide, not a precise statement of time. The distance of the meat surface from the broiling unit is usually two to five inches. Thicker cuts are placed farther from the heat source than thin cuts to allow more uniform cooking.

Pan Broiling. A variation of broiling is pan-broiling. In this case, heat is applied by means of direct contact with a hot surface such as a heavy pan or a grill. The surface of the pan is lightly oiled to prevent the muscle tissue from sticking. As fat accumulates in the pan during cooking, it should be poured off to avoid frying the meat in its own fat.

Tender beef steaks, lamb chops, and ground beef patties are satisfactorily pan-broiled. Veal, because of its lack of fat, may be somewhat dry when broiled or pan-broiled. Pork chops are tender enough for dry-heat methods of cooking but should be cooked to an internal temperature of 145°F (63°C).

FIGURE 25-32 Grilling is a great choice for these pineapple and soy glazed ribeye steaks. *(Courtesy of the National Cattlemen's Beef Association)*

TABLE 25-12 Approximate Broiling Times for Some Typical Meat Cuts

Cut	Average Weight (lb)	Time (min)		
		Rare	Medium	Well Done
Beef				
Club steak (top loin)				
1 in.	1	14–17	18–20	22–25
1 1/2 in.	1 1/4	25–27	30–35	35–40
Porterhouse				
1 in.	2	19–21	22–25	26–30
1 1/2 in.	2 1/2	30–32	35–38	40–45
Sirloin				
1 in.	3	20–22	23–25	26–30
1 1/2 in.	4 1/2	30–32	33–35	36–40
Ground beef patty, 1 in. thick by 3 1/2 in. diameter	1/4		18–22	24–28
Lamb				
Loin chops				
1 in.	3/16		10–15	16–18
1 1/2 in.	5/16		16–18	19–22
Rib chops				
1 in.	1/8		10–15	16–18
1 1/2 in.	1/4		16–18	19–22
Ground lamb patty				
1 in. thick by 3 1/2 in. diameter	1/4		18–20	22–24

Sautéing and Frying. Sautéing and frying are additional methods that may be used for cooking tender cuts of meat (Figure 25-33). Sautéing and frying are similar, but sautéing uses less fat and a higher temperature compared to frying. Also, pan-fried foods are often lightly dredged in flour or crumbs. In pan-frying, only a small amount of fat (enough to form a layer of melted fat 1/4 to 1/2 inch deep) is used.

Foods may also be deep-fat fried. In deep-fat frying, the melted fat is deep enough to cover the food. Fried food requires draining on absorbent paper to remove excess fat. Meats may be dipped in flour or in egg and crumbs before frying to produce a brown crust on the meat. Frying can also be used to brown meats that are to be braised.

Microwave Cooking. An important advantage of the microwave oven for cooking meat is that it uses substantially less energy for the same degree of doneness than conventional methods, cooking in one-third to one-half the time [49]. Convection ovens also conserve energy because lower cooking temperatures and shorter cooking and preheating times are used.

Some early studies involving comparisons of meat cookery using microwave and conventional ovens often found greater cooking losses and somewhat less palatable products with microwave cooking, particularly when less tender cuts of meat were prepared [48, 58]. Today, microwave ovens with variable power settings allow cooking at different energy levels. Cooking top round roasts of beef, particularly from the frozen state, at simmer power levels produces more palatable products than cooking similar roasts at high power levels. Roasts cooked at the lower power level are often similar in palatability to roasts cooked in conventional ovens [25, 111].

Microwaves do not heat uniformly. Holding roasts for about 30 minutes will allow the heat to distribute throughout the meat. A higher endpoint cooking temperature is recommended for meats cooked by microwave for food-safety reasons. Cooking all meats to a minimum of 165°F (74°C) is recommended [67].

The flavor of microwaved meats may be somewhat different from that of meat cooked by conventional methods. Frequent turning and basting with a sauce ensure full flavor and color development of the surface. Small pieces of meat, particularly, do not brown when cooked in a microwave oven. Various browning elements and special browning grills have been developed by the manufacturers of microwave equipment to solve this problem. The use of browning devices increases fuel consumption by 50 percent

FIGURE 25-33 This Asian beef and broccoli with noodles dish may be stir-fried and ready to eat in about 30 minutes. *(Courtesy of the National Cattlemen's Beef Association)*

or more over cooking by microwaves alone. Total cooking time is also increased [24].

Main dishes containing meat often microwave well; they are prepared rapidly and generally result in a flavorful mixture. Microwaving is also particularly useful for reheating cooked meat and meat dishes, not only because it is rapid but also because it results in minimal **warmed-over flavor** and aroma [44]. Still another convenient use of the microwave oven is for the rapid thawing of frozen meats.

Braising. A combination method of cooking, braising is usually applied to less tender cuts of meat, but may be used for a variety of meats (Figure 25-34). Browning of the meat surface can be accomplished by first frying, pan-broiling, or broiling. The pan or kettle is closely covered, and cooking is continued, with the liquid simmering or slowly boiling until the meat becomes tender. Cuts from the chuck and round of beef are commonly braised. Braising is recommended for veal and pork chops,

although pork chops are also effectively cooked by roasting or baking.

Braising can be done either on the top of the range or in the oven. The cooking time is longer in the oven, using more energy. Because the pan is tightly covered, the meat is cooked in a moist atmosphere even though it is cooked in the oven. The time of cooking depends on the character of the meat and the size of the cut, but braised meat is always cooked well done. The term *pot-roasting* is often used to refer to the braising of large cuts of meat such as beef chuck roasts. Swiss steaks are braised beef steaks.

Meats can be braised with or without added water. When braised without added water, steam from the water in the meat itself can provide the moisture needed to hydrolyze the collagen in connective tissue. Adding small quantities of water frequently rather than a large amount at one time is preferable to retain the brown surface of prebrowned meat.

Stewing. The method of cooking meats in liquid at simmering or slow boiling temperatures is stewing (Figure 25-35). For brown stew, part or all of the meat may be browned before stewing to help develop flavor and color in the stew. If vegetables are used, they should be added just long enough before the stew is to be served so that they are not overcooked.

Pressure Cooking. Cooking meat in a pressure saucepan is a moist-heat method generally used for less tender cuts. Only a relatively short cooking time is necessary because heating produces a temperature higher than that of the usual boiling point of water, which is the temperature used for braising and stewing. The retention of steam within the cooking vessel, which increases the vapor pressure of the water, is responsible for the high temperature. Meats prepared in a pressure saucepan are commonly cooked to a well-done stage. A distinctive steamed flavor can usually be recognized.

Crockery Slow Cooking. Various types of crockery slow-cooking pots are available and are often used for meat cookery. These electric appliances have a low-temperature setting that allows meat and other foods to be cooked for long periods without constant watching. For example, a beef roast can be placed in the cooker with no added liquid, covered, and cooked on the lowest setting for 10 to 12 hours. Meat dishes with added liquid, such as beef stew or Swiss steak, are also satisfactorily cooked in crockery slow cookers. The low setting usually represents a temperature of about 200°F (93°C). The direct heat from the pot, lengthy cooking, and steam created within the tightly covered container combine to destroy bacteria and make this method of cooking meat safe [95].

Grilled Meats and Your Health

Heterocyclic amines (HCAs) and polycyclic aromatic hydrocarbons (PAHs) may be produced when meats are grilled. Both of these chemicals have been associated with a higher potential risk of cancer. HCAs are produced on meats when cooked at high temperatures when grilled, broiled, or fried. PAHs are usually formed when fat drips onto coals or hot stones, producing smoke or flare-ups.

Meat cooked well done, burnt, or charred appears to be the most problematic. Consequently, here are some ways to reduce exposure to heterocyclic amines:

- Grill fruits or vegetables because these foods do not produce HCAs or PAHs.

- Marinate meats because these appear to produce lower levels of these chemicals when grilled.

- Trim the fat from meats and remove the skin from chicken to reduce the amount of fat dripping onto the coals.

- Precook meats in the oven or microwave, then finish on the grill.

- Flip frequently to cook evenly and reduce formation of HCAs

- Do not consume burnt or blackened parts of the meat.

- Do not allow flames from the grill near the meat. ■

Source: References 3, 4

FIGURE 25-34 These pork chops are browned lightly in oil then simmered in salsa to create this easy and tasty dish. *(Courtesy of National Pork Board)*

Cooking in these covered pots is achieved by moist heat. The long cooking period allows the breakdown of the connective tissue to gelatin in less tender meats, thus increasing tenderness.

Cooking Variety Meats

The choice of a cooking method for variety meats is influenced by the tenderness of the various parts. Heart, kidney, tongue, and tripe require cooking for tenderness and are braised or simmered. Older beef liver may also require tenderizing by braising. Sweetbreads and veal or calf liver are tender and may be cooked by dry-heat methods such as broiling or frying. These variety meats may also be cooked by moist-heat methods. Sweetbreads are delicate tissues that are made more firm and white when they are precooked for about 20 minutes at a simmering temperature in salted, acidulated water. After this preliminary treatment, they can be prepared in various ways. Table 25-13 provides suggestions pertinent to the preparation of variety meats.

Cooking Frozen Meats

Frozen meats can be either thawed and cooked or cooked without thawing first. The cooking temperature must be lower, and the time of cooking increased if the meat is frozen when cooking begins. If pieces of frozen meat are large, the cooking time may be considerably longer than for similar thawed or fresh cuts. Frozen roasts require up to 1.5 times as long to cook as unfrozen roasts of the same

STEP 1. Coat beef with seasoned flour, if desired. Brown on all sides in small amount of oil, if desired.

STEP 3. Cover with liquid. Season with additional herbs, if desired.

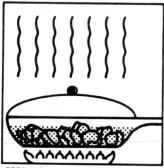

STEP 2. Pour off excess drippings.

STEP 4. Cover utensil and simmer on top of range or in oven until tender. Add vegetables to meat and liquid just long enough before serving to cook through, or until tender.

FIGURE 25-35 Less tender meat may be tenderized by cooking in liquid. *(Courtesy of the National Cattlemen's Beef Association)*

size. If frozen meats are braised, they may be browned at the end of the braising period rather than at the beginning.

There are no appreciable differences in palatability or nutritive value in meats cooked from the thawed or frozen state. Thawed meats are cooked in the same way as fresh meats. Thawing of frozen meat, particularly large pieces of meat, should be done in the refrigerator for microbiological safety. Meats may also be thawed under cold running water or in the microwave if cooked immediately after thawing.

SOUP STOCK AND GRAVY

Soup Stock

A stock is a flavored liquid used chiefly in the making of soups. Beef is the most commonly used meat for stock. Veal produces a very mild stock that may be desirable in some dishes. Lamb and mutton produce excellent broth, but they should be used only when lamb or mutton flavor is desired. The bones and meat

TABLE 25-13 **Variety Meats**		
Name	**Preliminary Preparation**	**Cooking Methods**
Liver	Liver from young animals should be sliced 1/2 in. thick for best results in retaining juiciness. Remove outside membrane, blood vessels, and excess connective tissue. Wash large pieces before removing membrane.	Broil or pan-broil young liver. Fry or bread young liver. Braise whole piece of older beef liver. Grind and make into liver loaf. (Liver is easier to grind if first coagulated in hot water.)
Kidney	Wash kidneys and remove outer membrane. Lamb kidneys may be split in half, and veal kidneys cut into slices. Cook beef kidneys in water for tenderness, changing the water several times.	Young kidneys may be broiled, pan-broiled, made into stew or kidney pie, or ground and made into loaf. Beef kidneys, after being cooked for tenderness, may be cooked in the same way, except that they should not be broiled or pan-broiled.
Sweetbreads	Soak in cold water to remove blood. Remove blood vessels and excess connective tissue. Parboil in salted, acidulated water to make firm and white using 1 tsp salt and 1 Tbsp vinegar per quart of water.	Sweetbreads may be creamed, dipped in egg and crumbs and fried in fat, combined with cooked chicken and creamed or scalloped, or dipped in melted fat and broiled.
Heart	Heart is a muscular organ that is usually cooked by moist-heat methods for tenderness. Wash in warm water and remove large blood vessels.	Stuff with bread dressing and braise until tender. May be cooked in water seasoned with salt, onion, bay leaf, celery, and tomato and served hot or cold.
Tongue	Tongue is a muscular tissue that requires precooking in water for tenderness. After cooking, remove the skin and cut out the roots. Smoked or pickled tongue is usually soaked for several hours before cooking.	May be cooked in water, seasoned with salt, onion, bay leaf, and celery. If it is to be served cold, it is more moist when allowed to cool in the water. After it is cooked in water, the tongue may be covered with brown or tomato sauce and braised in the oven. The cooked tongue may be reheated in a sweet pickling solution. For this method, the tongue is best precooked in plain salted water.
Tripe	Fresh tripe is cooked before selling but requires further cooking in water until tender (1 or more hours).	Serve precooked tripe with well-seasoned tomato sauce. Dip in batter and fry in deep fat. Brush with flavorful fat and broil.

from poultry make desirable broth. Stock may also be made from fish.

Seven principles should be followed to produce high quality stocks: (1) start with cold water, (2) simmer gently, (3) skim frequently, (4) strain carefully, (5) cool quickly, (6) store properly, and (7) degrease [51]. The more surface of the meat that is exposed to the water, the more flavor that is extracted when making stock. For the best stock, then, this means cutting the meat into small cubes or grinding it through a coarse grinder rather than cooking it in one piece. The meat may be soaked for one-half to one hour in cold water; then cooking is started and the water is allowed to simmer three to four hours. Cooking some bone and some fat with the lean meat is thought to improve the flavor.

Vegetables and seasonings should be added during the last hour of cooking to avoid the development of undesirable flavors resulting from the overcooking of some vegetables. When cooking is finished, the stock is poured through a colander to remove the meat, bone, and seasonings. When the stock is cool, the hard fat layer may be removed from the top.

The major difference between brown and white soup stock is that, in the making of brown stock, about one-third of the meat cubes are first browned in a skillet. The vegetables also may be caramelized in the oven or on top of the range for additional flavor and color. The pan is deglazed by adding water to dissolve the brown matter from the pan. The browned meat and water are then added to the soup kettle in which the remaining cubes have been placed in cold water.

The meat left from making soup stock retains many of its nutrients. The flavor is lacking, but other flavors from vegetables and condiments may be added so that the meat can be utilized. For example, it can be cut into small pieces and served in the soup.

Bouillon is prepared by seasoning a soup stock. *Consommé* is an enriched or double-strength bouillon that has been clarified so that it is crystal clear. It can be made from any kind of stock, although beef is most commonly used. One egg white and one crushed shell per quart of broth accomplish clarification. The broth is heated to the boiling point and boiled for a few minutes, after which it is poured through several thicknesses of cheesecloth to strain out the coagulated egg with its adhering particles. The material that is removed from the soup stock by clarifying is chiefly coagulated protein.

Gravy

Gravies or sauces are commonly used as accompaniments to enhance the flavor of meat. The drippings from fried, pan-broiled, or roasted meat and the cooking liquid from stewed or braised meats or poultry can be used to make gravy. Low temperatures for meat cookery usually produce a minimum of brown material. Particularly for the making of gravy, there should be no burned drippings. Gravies and some sauces may be served either thickened or unthickened. *Au jus* gravy goes naturally with roast beef and is unthickened. To thicken gravy, flour or another starch thickener can be added (1 1/2 to 2 tablespoons per cup of liquid) in one of two ways: as a smooth flour and water paste (slurry), or as dry flour stirred into the fat (roux). The latter method is usually preferable when the drippings contain little or no water. Excess fat in the pan should be removed before the flour is added. Once the approximate quantity of gravy desired is determined, two tablespoons of fat should be retained for each cup of gravy. When dry flour and fat in the drippings are blended together and cooked for a few minutes, they form a *roux*. Cold liquid can then be mixed gradually with the hot roux until a smooth gravy is formed. Heating is continued, with stirring, until the **starch gelatinizes** and the mixture thickens. Seasonings may then be added.

In the alternate method of making gravy, a cold slurry of liquid and a thickener, such as flour, are mixed with hot liquid that has been added to the drippings, with constant stirring until the gravy thickens. The liquid used in gravies is usually water, but milk, meat stock, tomato juice, wine, vegetable juice, or other liquids may be used. The gravy will be best if the drippings are rich and flavorful. Gravies should be tasted before serving to make certain that the proper blending of flavors has been achieved.

A great variety of sauces can be served with meats. Sauces may be made from drippings but are often made without any meat components. White sauce (discussed in Chapter 13) may be the basis for some sauces served with meats. Tomato sauces go with meatballs and spaghetti, and mushroom sauce is often served with Swiss steak. Brushing broiled lamb chops with melted butter containing parsley, lemon juice, and white pepper produces a sauce called *maître d'hôtel butter.*

CARVING MEAT

Successful carving of meat partly depends on some knowledge of the anatomy of the cut to be carved. It is important to know something of the location of the joints and the direction in which the muscle fibers run. Insofar as possible, meats should be carved across the grain. Knives for carving should be well sharpened and of good-quality steel that will hold an edge well.

Carving should be done rapidly so that the meat stays warm. Neatness and economy of cutting are also important. If some parts of the meat are better than others, such parts should be divided among those at the table rather than given to the first ones served. Enough meat to serve all at the table should be carved before the host starts to serve the plates. The slices are arranged neatly on the platter. Before inviting guests to be served a second time, the host should be sure that some meat is carved and ready.

Diagrams showing the techniques for carving certain cuts of meat are shown in Figure 25-36.

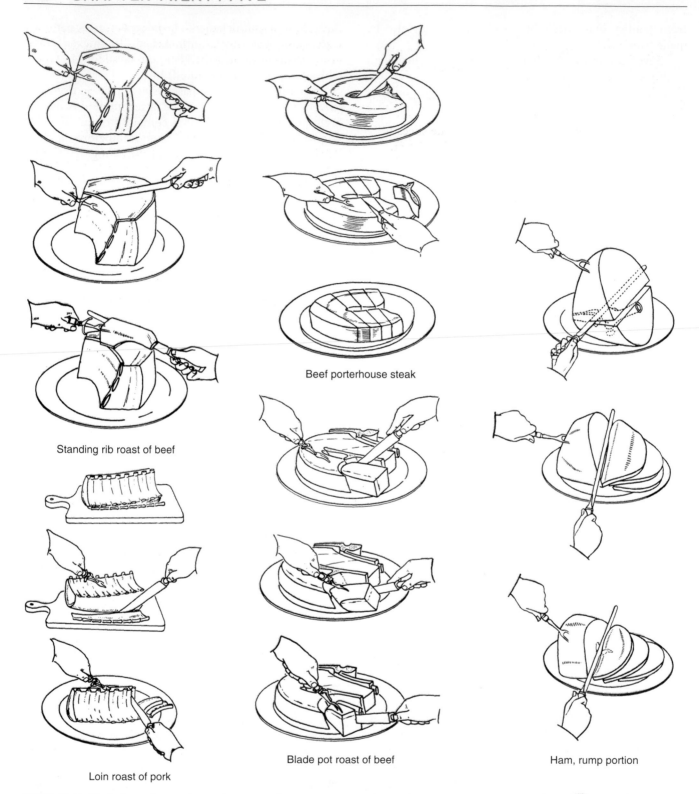

Standing rib roast of beef

Beef porterhouse steak

Loin roast of pork

Blade pot roast of beef

Ham, rump portion

FIGURE 25-36 Techniques for carving various cuts of meat. *(Courtesy of the National Live Stock and Meat Board)*

Beef Steak

Steak is one of the easiest meats to carve. With the steak lying flat on the platter, the fork is inserted in a suitable position for holding the steak firmly. Steaks from the loin (top loin, T-bone, porterhouse, and sirloin) have the bone separated from the meat before the meat is carved. The knife is allowed to follow the bone closely until the meat is completely separated. The meat is then cut into pieces of a suitable size for serving. Porterhouse and T-bone steaks are usually carved so that each person receives some tenderloin and some outer muscle. In this case, steaks are cut with, rather than across, the fiber.

Standing Rib Roast

A standing rib roast is placed before the carver with the rib side to the left. The carver inserts a fork between two ribs. The knife passes from the outer edge toward the ribs in removing a slice of meat. Slices may vary in thickness, but 1/4 to 3/8 inch is desirable. After several slices have been carved, the knife is used to separate the slices from the bone. Each slice is then transferred to the platter.

Rolled Rib Roast

Horizontal slices are cut from the top of a rolled rib roast.

Pot Roasts

Insofar as possible, slices of pot roasts should be cut across the grain. Some cuts used for pot roasts may have fibers running in several directions, in which case it is difficult to carve across the fibers. If the muscles are separated first, cutting across the grain is easier.

Ham

The shank bone of the ham is placed toward the carver's right. The larger muscles of the ham are sliced by cutting straight down from the outer edge to the leg bone. After several slices have been carved, the knife is inserted in the last opening and is allowed to follow the bone, thus separating slices from the bone. Slices can then be lifted out.

Loin Roasts

A loin roast of pork is carved by cutting slices from the end of the roast. The roast is prepared at the market to make carving easy. The rib section has the backbone sawed loose from the ribs. The backbone is removed in the kitchen before the roast is placed on the platter. Cutting is done close along each side of the rib bone. One slice contains the rib, the next is boneless, and so on.

Leg of Lamb

The cushion of a leg of lamb, which is the most meaty portion, lies below the tail. The carver inserts a fork to bring the cushion into an upright position. Slices are then carved as from ham.

CHAPTER SUMMARY

- Meat is the flesh of animals used for food. Meat is composed chiefly of water, protein, fat, and minerals. Lean meats are a good source of thiamin, riboflavin, niacin, iron, zinc, and phosphorus as well as other vitamins and minerals. The percentage of fat in meats varies widely, depending on the cut, amount of trim, and preparation method.

- Structurally, meat is composed of muscle, connective tissue, fatty tissue, and bone. The muscle fiber is a long threadlike cell that tapers slightly at both ends. Inside this cell or fiber is an intricate structure including myofibrils and sarcoplasm. Inside the myofibrils are thick filaments composed of myosin and thin filaments made up of the protein actin. Connective tissue binds the muscle cells together in various-size bundles. Collagen, elastin, and reticulin are three kinds of connective tissue found in meat. Fat is deposited between muscles (marbling), under the skin, and around glandular organs. More brittle fats contain higher percentages of saturated fatty acids.

- The color of meat comes primarily from the pigment myoglobin. Myoglobin exists in three primary forms: oxymyoglobin, deoxymyoglobin, and metmyoglobin.

- Beef carcasses are classified on the basis of age and sex. Veal is the meat from immature bovines that are at least 3 weeks but generally less than 20 weeks of age. Sheep carcasses are classified as lamb, yearling mutton, and mutton according to the age of the animal. Pork is the meat of swine.

- Cattle are grass-fed when young and are often raised to maturity in feedlots on grain-based feed. Antibiotics may be used to treat illnesses, but antibiotic residuals may not be present in the meat when sold. Hormones may be used in cattle and lambs, as regulated by USDA, but not in veal or pork.

- Before an animal is slaughtered, the muscles are soft and pliable. The stiffening of the carcass after death is known as *rigor mortis*. Meat is generally allowed to hang under refrigeration for one or two days after slaughter until the rigor mortis passes. If it is held longer, the process of ripening or aging occurs. Beef is the only type of meat that is commonly aged. Aging of meat can be accomplished by dry aging or wet aging.

- Meat may be sold in various types of packages. Oxygen content within the packaging and whether the atmosphere within the package has been modified will have an impact on color and perishability of the meat.

- The USDA has responsibility at the federal level for the inspection, grading, setting of standards, and labeling of all meat and poultry products. All meats entering interstate commerce must be inspected by the USDA Food Safety and Inspection Service. An inspector's stamp is placed on each wholesale cut of the carcass that passes inspection. A safe-handling label is mandated on meat and poultry products. "Natural" and "organic" may be found on packages, but these terms are not interchangeable.

- Separate from the inspection service is the USDA program for the voluntary system of grading meat. Quality grades have been established, and the appropriate USDA grade mark is applied to the meat carcass. Yield grades are based on cutability, which indicates the proportionate amount of salable retail cuts that can be obtained from a carcass.

- An understanding of the division of the carcass into retail cuts is helpful in understanding the relative quality characteristics and the associated prices. The parts of the body that are affected little by the exercise of the animal will yield the most tender, as well as most expensive, cuts of meat.

- Restructured meat products may be made by flaking, coarse grinding, dicing, or chopping the meat, then binding the particles together into the desired shape and size.

- Variety meats include sweetbreads, heart, tongue, tripe, liver, kidney, and oxtail.

- Ground beef and hamburger are both made from beef, but only hamburger may have beef fat added to the grind. A maximum fat content of 30 percent by weight has been established for ground beef and hamburger. Irradiated ground beef may be purchased to reduce the risk of E. coli.

- When purchasing meat, the yield and cost of the lean portion should be considered.

- Tenderness in meat is influenced by the age of the animal, amount of connective tissue in the cut of meat, and amount of marbling. The hereditary background of the animal, the management of its feeding, and the size of the muscle fibers are additional factors affecting tenderness.

- The flavor of meat is developed primarily by cooking. The feeding management of beef cattle also affects the flavor of the meat.

- Many kinds of cured meats are available in the marketplace. Curing ingredients include sodium nitrite, salt, sugar, and seasonings. Nitrite and salt will react with myoglobin to produce the characteristic pink color of cooked cured meats.

- Fresh meats must be stored at or below 40°F (4.5°C). Meats should not be placed above other foods in the refrigerator to prevent cross-contamination with other foods. Frozen meat should be defrosted in the refrigerator, in the microwave and cooked immediately, or under cold running water.

- Knowledge of and adherence to the recommended endpoint cooking temperatures of meat are necessary to prevent foodborne illness. For food-safety purposes, cook ground beef to 155° to 160°F (68 to 70°C) and beef, pork, or lamb steaks and roasts to 145°F (63°C). Thermometers should be used to test the internal temperature of meats to assess doneness. As high as 50 percent of ground beef has been shown to be brown in color before the meat has reached a safe temperature.

- Meats generally are more appealing and palatable to people when cooked. Conventional cooking is divided into dry-heat and moist-heat methods. Heat causes proteins to denature and coagulate, fats to melt, and color changes to occur. Cooking losses, including loss of weight and nutrients, increase gradually with increasing internal temperatures.

- In preparation of meats, tenderization may be achieved by the use of moist cooking methods if the cut of meat has significant amounts of collagen connective tissue, carving across the grain, or marinating in a mixture that contains acid.

- Commonly used cooking methods for meats include roasting, baking, broiling, pan-broiling, sautéing, frying, microwave cooking, braising, and crockery slow cooking. Cooking charts are available to provide guidance in the amount of time necessary to roast, bake, or grill meat. Thermometers should be used to determine if the desired or safe endpoint cooking temperature has been reached. Roasted meats will continue to rise in temperature after removal from the oven.

- Frozen meats can be either thawed and cooked or cooked without thawing first. The cooking temperature must be lower and the time of cooking increased by as much as 1.5 times if the meat was frozen when cooking started.

- A stock is a flavored liquid used in the making of soups, sauces, and gravies. Beef is the meat commonly used for stock. Bouillon and consommé are made from stocks. Gravies may be made by thickening drippings with a slurry or with a roux, then adding liquid and cooking until the starch is gelatinized.

- Successful carving of meat depends on some knowledge of the anatomy of the cut to be carved. Neatness, economy of cutting, and consideration of the guests to be served are additional important components of carving.

STUDY QUESTIONS

1. **(a)** List the major and minor components of meat.

   (b) The protein content of meat varies with the amount of fat. How much protein is usually present in lean muscle?

   (c) What vitamins and minerals does meat provide in significant amounts?

2. Explain why the color of meat may change from a purplish-red to a bright red when exposed to air. Explain why meat may turn a brownish color when held too long. What is responsible for the typical cured meat color?

3. Meat is basically muscle tissue containing some fat and bone. Briefly describe what meat is like in structure, including each of the following components in your explanation:

   (a) Muscle proteins—myosin and actin

   (b) Myofibrils

   (c) Muscle fibers

   (d) Bundles of muscle fibers (making the grain of the meat)

   (e) Muscles (such as tenderloin and ribeye)

   (f) Connective tissue

   (g) Connective tissue proteins–collagen and elastin

   (h) Fat cells, fatty tissues, and marbling

   (i) Bone

4. **(a)** What is *rigor mortis*? Why is it important in a study of meat?

   (b) Why is beef aged? What changes occur during aging or ripening of meat?

5. List several factors that may affect tenderness of meat. Discuss what effect each factor has on tenderness.

6. Meat and poultry labeling is the responsibility of the USDA.

   (a) What must be included on a meat or poultry label?

   (b) What nutrient content claims can be made?

7. Explain what the round inspection stamp on meat carcasses implies.

8. **(a)** Why are meats graded and by whom are they graded? Is this a mandatory or voluntary program?

   (b) Explain the difference between quality grades and yield grades for meat. What factors are considered in each?

   (c) From the following list of quality grade names, indicate which apply to beef, which to veal, and which to lamb.

(1)	Prime	(6)	Choice
(2)	Select	(7)	Cutter
(3)	Standard	(8)	Canner
(4)	Commercial	(9)	Cull
(5)	Utility	(10)	Good

9. **(a)** Name the primal or wholesale cuts of beef and pork.

   (b) Name several retail cuts that come from each primal cut listed in Question 9a.

   (c) Which primal cuts of beef are usually tender? Which are less tender?

   (d) Be able to identify pictures of each of the following retail cuts of meat:

Beef	Pork
Rib steak and roast	Rib chops
Top loin steak	Loin chops
T-bone steak	Blade steak
Porterhouse steak	Ham
Sirloin steak	
Round steak or roast	
Blade steak or roast	
Arm steak or roast	
Flank steak	
Brisket	
Short ribs	

10. What are *restructured meats?* What advantages do they offer?

11. Name several variety meats. Discuss possible advantages for their use in meal planning.

12. **(a)** Name several cuts of meat that are commonly cured.

    (b) What ingredients are usually used in the curing process? Discuss advantages and disadvantages of the use of nitrite as a curing ingredient.

13. Describe appropriate storage conditions for meat in the kitchen.

14. How does heat generally affect muscle fibers? Connective tissue? Explain why this information is important in deciding how to cook tender and less tender cuts of meat.

15. When meat is cooked by any method, it usually loses weight. Account for this weight or cooking loss.

16. Describe the usual procedures used in cooking meat by each of the following methods. Indicate whether each is a dry-heat or a moist-heat method. Also suggest several cuts of meat that may appropriately be cooked by each of the methods listed.

    (a) Roasting

    (b) Broiling

    (c) Pan-broiling

    (d) Frying

    (e) Microwave cooking

    (f) Braising

    (g) Stewing

    (h) Pressure cooking

17. In roasting, broiling, and pan-broiling, when should meats be salted? why?

18. Describe how frozen meats may be appropriately handled in preparation for cooking.

19. (a) What oven temperatures are most satisfactory when roasting tender cuts of beef? Less tender cuts? Explain why these temperatures are appropriate.

    (b) Why should a meat thermometer be used when roasting meat?

    (c) Explain why ground beef should always be checked with a thermometer to assess when it is safely cooked.

20. What types of compounds appear to be important components of meat flavor?

21. Describe appropriate procedures for the preparation of the following:

    (a) Soup stock

    (b) Gravy

The term *poultry* is used to describe all domesticated birds that are intended for human consumption, including chickens, turkeys, ducks, geese, guinea fowl, squab (young pigeons), and pigeons. Chickens and turkeys are by far the most commonly consumed poultry items in the United States. Poultry is marketed throughout the year in a wide variety of forms, many of which are convenience foods. In this chapter, the following topics will be discussed:

- Consumption, composition, and nutritional value
- Classification and market forms
- Poultry production and marketing
- Government inspection, grading, and oversight of labeling
- Buying of poultry
- Safe storage, handling, and preparation
- Cooking methods

CONSUMPTION

As measured by food supply data, red meat (beef, veal, pork, lamb, and mutton) remains the most commonly consumed meat in the United States at 110 pounds per person in 2005 [24]; however, poultry consumption has increased considerably over the years. Between 1970 and 2005, annual per capita poultry consumption more than doubled; 74 pounds of poultry were available in the food supply in 2005 compared to 34 pounds in 1970. According to 2005 USDA food supply data, chicken accounted for 60 pounds per capita compared to 13 pounds of turkey per capita (Figure 26-1). Like chicken, turkey consumption has doubled since 1970. The popularity of poultry has been influenced by the consumer's perception that it is lowfat, inexpensive, and convenient to prepare compared to other meat [21].

Boneless, trimmed (edible) weight, pounds per capita per year

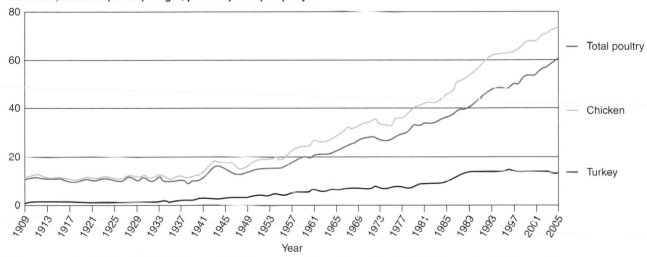

Figures are calculated on the basis of raw and edible meat. Includes skin, neck, and giblets for poultry (chicken and turkey). Excludes use of chicken for commercially-prepared pet food. Calculated from unrounded data.

FIGURE 26-1 U.S. per capita availability of poultry. *(Courtesy of U.S. Department of Agriculture, Economic Research Service)*

COMPOSITION AND NUTRITIVE VALUE

Chicken and turkey meat provides high-quality protein to the diet. When consumed without the skin and prepared with little or no added fat, a 3 1/2 ounce serving of chicken or turkey breast meat will have less than two grams of fat per serving. The cholesterol content of poultry is similar to that found in red meats. Like other meats, poultry provides B vitamins and iron. The iron content of poultry white meat is lower than that in the dark meat such as legs or thighs.

The light meat of poultry, particularly the breast, has shorter, tenderer fibers that are less firmly bound together with connective tissue than those of dark meat. As in mammals, the amount of connective tissue in poultry varies with age; it is more abundant in old birds, especially males.

The fat of poultry is deposited in layers under the skin, in the abdominal cavity, and to a lesser degree in the muscle tissue. Because fat is deposited under the skin, consuming poultry without the skin will lower the fat content considerably. The fat content of the meat is similar if the skin is removed before or after cooking as long as the skin is not consumed [16]. The fat of all types of poultry has a softer consistency and lower melting point than the fat of other meats. Capons have more fat and a more uniform distribution of fat in the flesh than other chickens. Goose and duck are higher in fat than chicken or turkey. Geese, particularly, have a distinctive flavor, which may be objectionable in older birds. The composition of chicken and turkey is given in Appendix C.

Like other meats, myoglobin is responsible for the color of the meat in poultry. Muscles that are used to a greater extent, such as the legs and thighs, have a higher level of myoglobin and will therefore be dark. Birds that fly, such as duck, have only dark meat. The skin of chicken can range in color from a creamy white to yellow. This color difference is due to the feed provided to the bird and is not an indication of differences in nutritional value or flavor [30]. Refer to Chapter 25 for a more in-depth discussion of myoglobin in meat.

CLASSIFICATION AND MARKET FORMS

The market forms of poultry have changed over the years, from the early 1960s when whole dressed chicken accounted for over 80 percent of chicken sales to the present day when the largest share of chicken is marketed as cut-up parts, some of them boneless and skinless. No longer just for holidays, turkey has become popular year-round with about 70 percent of turkey consumption at times other than holidays [17]. The proliferation of quick-service restaurants that sell chicken fillet sandwiches, chicken nuggets, and turkey deli sandwiches along with a wide variety of frozen and fresh convenience foods such as turkey pot pies, chicken enchiladas, and chicken fettuccini have contributed to these changing market trends.

Although chicken and turkey are the most commonly consumed types of poultry, duck, goose, and game birds may also be prepared. Poultry is classified on the basis of age and weight. Younger birds are tenderer than mature birds. Various types and classifications of poultry are provided in Table 26-1.

POULTRY PRODUCTION AND PROCESSING

Production

Georgia, Arkansas, Alabama, North Carolina, and Mississippi are the top five broiler-producing states in the United States [15]. Chickens are raised by farmers under contract with integrated poultry companies. Chickens are housed in *growout houses* where they are free to roam about the house with access to feed and water. Guidelines are in place for the square footage necessary per chicken in the house. If poultry is labeled as *free-range*, access to a yard outside the house is provided [2]. Turkey is raised in similar conditions.

Poultry feed generally consists of corn and soybean meal with added vitamins and minerals. Antibiotics may be used to treat illness or to increase the efficiency of the feed; however, a withdrawal period is required so the birds are free from antibiotic residuals prior to slaughter [28, 30]. Hormones are not permitted for use in poultry.

Processing

Birds are slaughtered after first being anesthetized with an electric current. Many of the processes in poultry plants are automated. Processing equipment includes a picking machine with rotating drums and rubber fingers that remove feathers from the slaughtered and scalded birds, a carousel eviscerator that slides metal spoons into the birds and pulls out the viscera, and a carousel fat remover that removes abdominal fat [5].

Slaughtered, eviscerated poultry are washed with chlorinated water and chilled immediately, usually by immersion of the carcasses in chilled water at less than 36°F (2°C) to control the growth of microorganisms. The U.S. Department of Agriculture (USDA) inspectors monitor the processes and test for salmonella organisms as a measure of the plant's effectiveness in controlling contamination.

A certain number of chickens will leave processing plants with some detectable *Salmonella* bacteria. Some of these bacteria may be firmly attached to or entrapped in poultry skin when they first arrive at the processing plant. The USDA's Food Safety and Inspection Service has approved the use of trisodium phosphate (TSP) to reduce microorganisms [30]. TSP can reduce to less than 5 percent the number of birds containing *Salmonella* without affecting flavor, texture, or appearance.

TABLE 26-1 Poultry Classification

Type	Description	Age	Weight
Young chicken	*White and dark meat. Is lowfat without skin. Cook with a variety of methods.*		
Broiler-fryer	Either sex; tender	9–12 weeks	2 1/2–4 1/2 pounds
Roaster	Either sex; tender	3–5 months	5–8 pounds
Capon	Castrated male; very meaty and tender	16 weeks–8 months	4–10 pounds
Poussin	Small immature birds	<24 days	<1 pound
Rock Cornish game hen	Cross of Cornish chicken with another breed. Either sex; immature; tender	4–7 weeks	<2 pounds
Older chicken	*Flavorful but less tender. Prepare with moist heat.*		
Baking or stewing hen	Mature laying hen; less tender	>10 months	5–6 pounds
Young turkey	*White and dark meat. Lowfat without skin.*		
Fryer-roaster	Either sex, tender	10–12 weeks	4–8 pounds
Young hen	Female; tender	5–7 months	8–16 pounds
Young tom	Male; tender	5–7 months	>16 pounds
Duck	*A dark meat bird. Pekin duck is the most common variety. High percent of bone and fat to meat.*		
Duckling	Either sex; tender	6–8 weeks	3–6 pounds
Roaster duckling	Either sex; younger than mature duck	<16 weeks	4–7 pounds
Goose	*A very fatty dark meat bird. Usually roasted.*		
Young	Either sex; tender	10–16 weeks	10–16 pounds
Mature		>25 weeks	
Domestic game birds			
Guinea fowl or guinea hen	Tender light and dark meat with little fat	11 weeks	2–3 pounds
Pigeon	Squab the most common form; dark, tender meat with little fat	28–30 days	12–16 ounces
Partridge	Usually coarse textured meat; best cooked with moist heat	<1 year	
Pheasant	Mild flavored meat; hen is tenderer than the cock		1.75–4 pounds
Quail	A small lean bird; related to the pheasant		3–7 ounces

Source: References 2, 16, 19, 29, 30

Raw poultry and poultry products may be treated with ionizing radiation to control and reduce the population of pathogens such as *Salmonella*, *Campylobacter*, and *Listeria monocytogenes*. Irradiation of poultry has been approved by the USDA and by the Food and Drug Administration (FDA). Packages must bear an irradiation logo and the statement, "Treated with radiation" or "Treated by irradiation." The shelf life of irradiated chicken has been reported to be as long as 15 days compared with about 6 days for unirradiated carcasses, as evidenced by the bacterial counts [12].

GOVERNMENT REGULATIONS

Inspection

The Wholesome Poultry Products Act, similar to the Wholesome Meat Inspection Act, was enacted in 1968. It requires that all poultry marketed in the United States be inspected for sanitary processing and freedom from disease. This inspection is performed either by agents of the federal government or by adequate state systems. The inspection process in a poultry-production plant is illustrated in Figure 26-2. The handling of both poultry and meat inspection at the federal level is the responsibility of the Food Safety and Inspection Service of the USDA.

All poultry-processing plants must operate under a Hazard Analysis and Critical Control Points (HACCP) plan. The processor must also have written sanitation standard operating procedures (SOPs) for daily operation and must test for certain microorganisms. Pathogen reduction is a major goal of the program.

Figure 26-3 shows the USDA inspection mark. Poultry bearing the official mark, sometimes printed on a tag attached to the wing (Figure 26-4), must come from a healthy flock, be processed under specified sanitary conditions, and be properly packaged and labeled. Only prepared poultry products, not fresh poultry, may contain additives such as a basting solution, salt, or other

FOCUS ON SCIENCE

More about Trisodium Phosphate (TSP)

At present, the mechanism of TSP is not well understood. However, at the cell membrane level, TSP helps to remove fat films and exerts surfactant and detergent effects when at a high pH level (pH = 12). Research also has indicated loss of cell viability and membrane integrity and disruption of cytoplasmic and outer membranes of *Salmonella enteriditis* strains treated with concentrations of TSP at pH 10–11.

Source: Sallam, K. I., and Samejima, K. (2004). Effects of trisodium phosphate and sodium chloride dipping on the microbial quality and shelf life of refrigerated tray-packaged chicken breasts. *Food Science Biotechnology, 13*(4), 425–429.

FIGURE 26-2 (a) A federal inspector examines the poultry in the production room. *(Courtesy of the U.S. Department of Agriculture)*

(b) An Agricultural Research Service engineer is developing a computer-directed scanning system to speed the inspection of the nearly 8 billion chickens processed annually through federally inspected plants in the United States. *(Courtesy of the U.S. Department of Agriculture, U.S. Agriculture Research Service, photo by Keith Weller)*

FIGURE 26-3 U.S. Department of Agriculture inspection mark for poultry. *(Courtesy of the U.S. Department of Agriculture)*

FIGURE 26-4 The wing tag may include the class name—in this case, Frying Chicken—in addition to the inspection mark and the grade mark. *(Courtesy of the U.S. Department of Agriculture)*

approved ingredients [31]. Prepared poultry products, such as canned, boned poultry, frozen dinners and pies, and specialty items, must also be produced with USDA inspection.

Grading

In addition to inspecting for wholesomeness, the USDA has developed voluntary standards for quality grades. These grades—A, B, and C—are placed on the label in a shield-shaped mark (see Figures 26-4 and 26-5). Many states participate in a grading program, and in such states the official stamp reads, "Federal–State Graded." Signs of quality that are evaluated in grading include conformation or shape of the bird, fleshing, distribution and amount of fat, and freedom from pinfeathers, skin and flesh blemishes, cuts, and bruises. Grade A birds will be virtually free from defects [30, 31]. Differences between Grades A and B are shown in Figure 26-6.

Labeling

Fresh and Frozen. The terms *fresh* and *frozen*, as applied to poultry products, were defined in 1997. Fresh poultry must have never been below 26°F (–3°C). Raw poultry held at 0°F (–18°C) or below must be labeled as

FIGURE 26-5 The U.S. Department of Agriculture grade shield denotes that poultry has been graded for quality. Poultry must first be inspected for wholesomeness, however. *(Courtesy of the U.S. Department of Agriculture)*

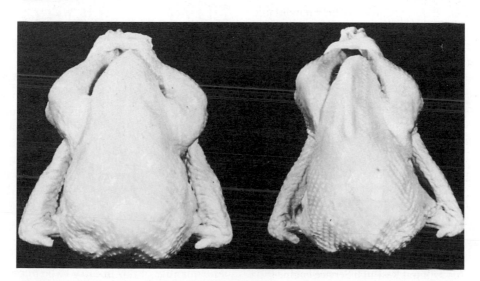

FIGURE 26-6 Grading for quality is not required by law, but many firms choose to have their poultry graded. U.S. Grade A (left) and U.S. Grade B (right) young turkeys are shown. *(Courtesy of the U.S. Department of Agriculture)*

TABLE 26-2 Poultry Labeling Terms	
Basted or self-basted	Products injected or marinated with a solution containing butter or other edible fat, stock or water plus spices, flavor enhancers, and other approved substances. A maximum added weight of 3 percent for bone-in poultry and an added weight of 8 percent for boneless poultry.
Chemical free	This term is not allowed on labels.
Free-range or free-roaming	Poultry has been allowed access to outside.
Halal or Zabiah Halal	Prepared in federally inspected plants and handled according to Islamic rule under Islamic authority.
Kosher	Prepared in federally inspected plants and handled under rabbinical supervision.
Mechanically separated poultry	Effective 1996, poultry product that has been separated from the bone through a sieve or similar device under pressure must be labeled as *mechanically separated chicken or turkey*.
No hormones	Hormones are not allowed in the raising of poultry; therefore if this statement is used on a label it must be followed by the statement, "Federal regulations prohibit the use of hormones."
No antibiotics	May be used if poultry was raised without antibiotics.
Oven prepared	Fully cooked and ready to eat.
Oven ready	Product is ready to cook.
Organic	Specific guidelines under USDA's National Organic Program must be followed in the production and processing of the product. Feed used for the birds must also be organic.
Natural	Contains no artificial flavors, coloring, chemical preservatives, or other artificial or synthetic ingredients. The term *natural* must be explained on the label.

Source: Food Safety and Inspection Service, U.S. Department of Agriculture, References 26, 28

frozen or previously frozen. A third category of poultry is referred to as *hard-chilled* or *previously hard-chilled*. Hard-chilled poultry has been held below 26°F (–3°C) but above 0°F (–18°C). Poultry that has been hard-chilled is not required to have any descriptive label on the product, but it should not be labeled as fresh or frozen, because neither of these categories applies [25, 26].

Absorbed and Retained Water. Under new regulations effective in 2002, poultry products must label the percentage of absorbed or retained water in any raw poultry product as a result of carcass washing, chilling, or other postslaughter processing unless the amount of water retained can be demonstrated to be unavoidable due to meeting food-safety requirements [27]. Poultry has been traditionally chilled using water immersion, which may result in water retention. This new regulation came into effect because of a suit brought by poultry consumers and red meat producers alleging that poultry products containing absorbed water were adulterated (in an economic sense) and misbranded under the 1957 Poultry Products Inspection Act.

Nutrition Labeling. The 1990 Nutrition Labeling and Education Act mandates nutrition labels on processed poultry products. As with meat, merchandisers can choose to provide nutrition information on raw, single-ingredient poultry products such as raw chicken legs. This information may appear on labels, posters, pamphlets, or videos in the store. The nutrient content claims that are allowed for poultry are the same as for meat (see discussion in Chapter 2).

Other Labeling Requirements. As with meat, raw or partially cooked poultry must carry a safe-handling label. The other requirements for a poultry label include the product name, name and address of the producer or distributor, inspection mark, ingredients and net weight, establishment number identifying the plant where the product was processed, and handling instructions. After the product leaves the processing plant, it comes under the jurisdiction of the FDA, which is responsible for preventing the sale of adulterated food, including poultry. Additional information and terms that may appear on a poultry label are provided in Table 26-2.

BUYING POULTRY

Quality and Characteristics of Age

Most poultry sold in retail markets are young, tender birds. In a young bird, the end of the breastbone is pliable, and the wing offers little resistance when bent into an upright position. The skin of a young bird is pliable, soft, and tears easily. An older bird has a hard, calcified breastbone and may show an abundance of long hairs. The skin of older birds is tougher, and the flesh is less tender. Weight varies by breed and is not necessarily an indication of age. In young birds, sex differences are not significant; however, with increase in age, male birds are inferior in flavor to female birds.

Amount to Buy and Economic Considerations

The quantity of raw poultry to be purchased per person is greater than other types of meat because poultry has a relatively high proportion of waste from the raw carcass to the cooked bird. Skin, fat, and bone accounted for about 50 percent of the weight of the cooked chicken. Cooking of poultry, as well as other meats, results in lost moisture and fat which will affect the cooked yield of the meat. The yield of cooked weight for young chickens has been reported to be 65 percent of the raw weight for those that were baked and 73 percent for those that were simmered [14]. Thus, the yield of cooked edible meat from the raw chicken carcass was about 35 percent. Cooking losses vary with the temperature and method of cooking and with the percentage of fat. The high fat content of ducks and geese results in particularly high cooking losses.

General guidelines for the amount of poultry to purchase have been developed [16, 29, 33].

- Fresh or frozen whole turkey—1 pound per person
- Fresh or frozen whole chicken—1/2 pound per person
- Duck or Goose—1 to 1 1/2 pounds per person

Table 26-3 gives the estimated number of servings from a pound of ready-to-cook poultry for additional types of poultry products. To satisfy individual preferences for various poultry parts, pieces of all one kind, such as chicken breasts or drumsticks, are often packaged together and marketed. As Table 26-3 indicates, more poultry is needed per serving when such pieces as wings or thighs are purchased than when breasts, which contain less bone, are bought.

When considering what form of poultry offers the best value, the price per serving rather than the price per pound should be considered. Bone-in chicken will generally cost less than a boneless chicken breast, but the boneless chicken breast will yield more meat per pound. If purchasing a whole chicken versus a whole cut-up chicken, the additional cost per pound for the cut-up chicken reflects convenience. With practice, cutting up a bird can be done easily and will save money. Figure 26-7 shows procedures to follow in cutting up chickens.

TABLE 26-3 Number of Servings from a Pound of Ready-to-Cook (RTC) Poultry

| | **Approximate Servings of Cooked Meat** | | |
Kind and Class	Size of Serving	Number of Servings Per Pound RTC	Approximate Yield of Cooked, Diced Meat (cups)
Chicken			
Whole			
Broiler-fryer	3 oz without bone	2	1 1/4
Roaster	3 oz without bone	2 1/4	1 1/2
Stewing hen	3 oz without bone	2	1 1/4
Pieces			
Breast halves (about 5 3/4 oz each)	1, about 2 3/4 oz without bone	2 3/4	
Drumsticks (about 3 oz each)	2, about 2 1/2 oz without bone	2 1/2	
Thighs (about 3 3/4 oz each)	2, about 3 oz without bone	2 1/4	
Wings (about 2 3/4 oz each)	4, about 2 3/4 oz without bone	1 1/2	
Breast quarter (about 11 oz each)	1, about 4 1/2 oz without bone	1 1/2	
Leg quarter (about 10 3/4 oz each)	1, about 4 1/4 oz without bone	1 1/2	
Turkey			
Whole	3 oz without bone	2 1/4	1 1/4
Pieces			
Breast	3 oz without bone	2 3/4	1 3/4
Thigh	3 oz without bone	2 3/4	
Drumstick	3 oz without bone	2 1/2	
Wing	3 oz without bone	1 3/4	
Ground	3 oz	3 3/4	
Boneless turkey roast	3 oz	3 1/4	
Duckling	3 oz without bone	1	
Goose	3 oz without bone	1 3/4	

(Courtesy of the U.S. Department of Agriculture)

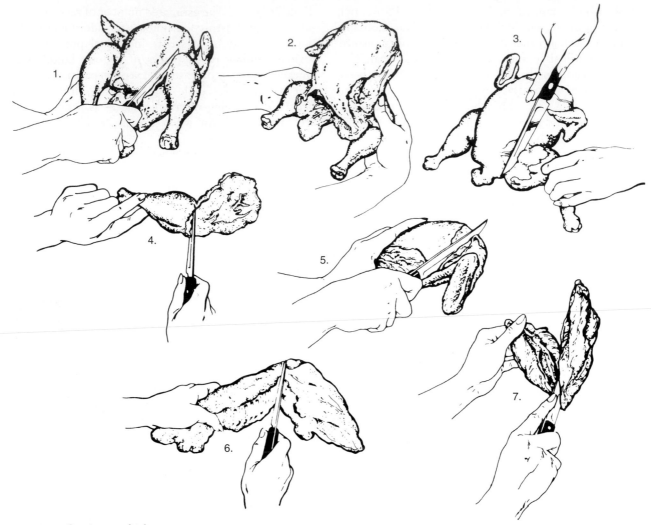

FIGURE 26-7A Cutting up chicken. *(Courtesy of the National Broiler Council)*
1. Place chicken, breast-side up, on cutting board. Cut skin between thighs and body.
2. Grasping one leg in each hand, lift chicken, and bend legs until bones break at hip joints.
3. Remove leg-thigh from body by cutting (from tail toward shoulder) between the joints, close to bones in back of bird. Repeat other side.
4. To separate thighs and drumsticks, locate knee joint by bending thigh and leg together. With skin-side down, cut through joints of each leg.
5. With chicken on back, remove wings by cutting inside of wing just over joint. Pull wing from body and cut from top down, through joint.
6. Separate breast and back by placing chicken on neck-end or back and cutting (toward board) through joints along each side of rib cage.
7. Breast may be left whole or, to cut into halves, place skin-side down on board and cut wishbone in two at V of bone.

SAFE STORAGE AND PREPARATION

Safe Storage and Handling

Chilled, raw poultry is a highly perishable product and should be stored at a refrigerator temperature of 40°F (4°C) or below. Even at refrigerator temperatures, storage time is usually limited to a few days. If poultry must be stored longer than a few days, wrap it in moisture-proof packing to help prevent freezer burn and freeze. Frozen storage should be at or below 0°F (−18°C).

All surfaces, such as countertops and cutting boards, that come into contact with raw poultry during its preparation should be thoroughly cleaned and sanitized before other foods are placed on them. One tablespoon of household bleach in one quart of water may be used to sanitize cutting boards and other work surfaces. Cutting boards made of wood, which may be difficult to sanitize adequately, should not be used for cutting up raw poultry. These precautions are necessary to avoid cross-contamination of cooked poultry and other foods prepared on the same surfaces because raw poultry may be

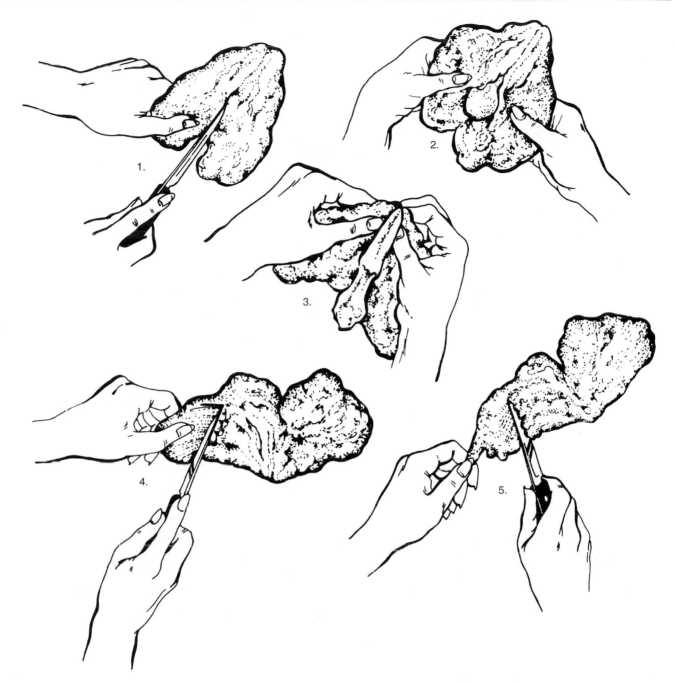

FIGURE 26-7B Boning a whole chicken breast. *(Courtesy of the National Broiler Council)*
1. Place skin-side down on cutting board with widest part nearest you. With point of knife, cut through white cartilage at neck-end of keel bone.
2. Pick up breast and bend back, exposing keel bone.
3. Loosen meat from bone by running thumbs around both sides; pull out bone and cartilage.
4. Working with one side of breast, insert tip of knife under long rib bone inside thin membrane and cut or pull meat from rib cage. Turn breast and repeat on other side.
5. Working from ends of wishbone, scrape all flesh away, and cut bone from meat. (If white tendons remain on either side of breast, loosen with knife and pull out.)

contaminated with *Salmonella* or *Campylobacter* bacteria when brought into the kitchen. A retail study conducted in Minnesota found that 88 percent of the poultry sampled from local supermarkets tested positive for

Campylobacter [8]. *Salmonella* and *Campylobacter* food-borne illness were discussed in Chapter 3.

Washing or rinsing of poultry before cooking is not recommended [30]. Any bacteria that may be present on

HOT TOPICS

Scientists and Chickens—Partners?

It takes a tough scientist to make a tender (and juicy) chicken! Thus says the Agricultural Research Service of the USDA [6]. Brenda Lyon is a food scientist at its research center in Athens, Georgia, where she focuses on the relationships between sensory attributes (eating quality) of poultry meat and production practices (growing and processing the birds).

For over 20 years, Lyon has studied the characteristics of poultry meat. We like our chicken to be tender and moist, but there are many components that affect these characteristics. The amount of force it takes to cut through a piece of poultry—called *shear value*—can be easily measured with a machine. But human subjects, with their senses of smell, taste, touch, and sight, are essential in evaluating aroma, appearance, juiciness, texture, and so on. And it doesn't stop there. For example, characteristics such as mouthfeel, springiness, chewiness, compaction of the meat after chewing, and ease of swallowing all play a part in creating a sensory texture profile.

Now, to be a sensory evaluator in these research projects requires intensive training in order to identify the various characteristics of poultry meat and assign intensity values to them. In Lyon's laboratory, she is a tough trainer. Just how tender is tender; how juicy is juicy—on a scale monitored by a computer?

What is the ultimate goal of this food technology research? It is to assist the poultry producers in bringing to the marketplace a product that consumers will buy, will be nourished by, and will enjoy. Processes developed to handle poultry must ultimately pass the sensory panel test for eating quality.

As an example, it has been found that the amount of time the breast muscles remain on the bone after processing affects the texture and tenderness of the boned meat. It seems the best timing for acceptable tenderness is four to six hours postmortem. Rigor mortis occurs and is dissipated by this time period. Sensory panels found that meat left on the bone for less than four hours was tougher than meat left on the bone longer. This four to six hour period must be integrated into the inspection, chilling, and cutting processes in a poultry plant. Reducing the chilling time to accommodate the deboning process interfered with rigor mortis and made the cooked breast meat tough. The sensory panels were key in determining the real effects of the production processes.

Thus the food scientist and the poultry processor need to work together as partners in order to produce the kind of chicken we all enjoy. Eating quality is the ultimate deciding factor in whether a process is successful. ■

Food technologists discuss the fiber orientation of a Chicken bread sample. *(Courtesy of the U.S. Department of Agriculture, Agricultural Research Service, photo by Peggy Greb)*

the bird will be destroyed by proper cooking. Washing of poultry, prior to preparation, therefore does not affect the safety of the bird after cooking but may result in contamination of other areas in the kitchen which can pose a safety risk [35].

Thawing of Frozen Poultry

Poultry products, like other highly perishable foods, should be thawed one of three ways: (1) under refrigeration, (2) in clean, cold water that is changed every 30 minutes, (3) or in the microwave [28]. Birds thawed under cold water or in the microwave should be cooked immediately after thawing. Birds thawed under refrigeration may be stored in the refrigerator for one to two days prior to cooking. Thawing on the kitchen counter or in warm water are unsafe practices.

When thawing under refrigeration, allow a minimum of 24 hours per 4 to 5 pounds. The bird should be placed at the bottom of the refrigerator in a leakproof container so raw juices from the thawing bird do not contaminate other foods. Birds thawed in water should be in a leakproof package and submerged in cold tap water that is changed every 30 minutes so the water remains clean and cold. Warm water should not be used to thaw a bird because the outer areas of the bird will be exposed to temperatures favorable for rapid bacterial growth. When thawing under cold water, approximately 30 minutes per pound should be adequate.

Safe Endpoint Cooking Temperatures

Poultry should always be cooked to a minimum 165°F (74°C) to destroy any pathogenic organisms that may be present [32]. The temperature of whole birds should be checked in the (a) innermost part of the thigh and wing, and (b) thickest part of the breast. Higher temperatures of 170° to 180°F (77° to 82°C) may be recommended by some sources to ensure an acceptable temperature has been reached throughout the bird or because of personal preferences for a more well-done bird. Color of the meat and juices and looseness of the joints when wiggled are suggestive of doneness, but are not reliable indicators from a food-safety perspective.

Whole turkeys and some roasting chickens may have "pop-up" temperature indicators. These temperature indicators are usually set for a temperature of 185°F (85°C). However, because these indicators are only in one location of the bird, it is still recommended that a thermometer be used to check other areas of the bird to assess doneness [33].

To Stuff or Not to Stuff

Stuffing a bird before roasting is not generally recommended. Bacteria can survive in stuffing that has not reached the safe temperature of 165°F (74°C), potentially resulting in foodborne illness. If a bird is stuffed, the following precautions should be taken. First, stuff the bird loosely immediately before placing in the oven. Do not stuff the bird the night or even hours ahead. Second,

check the temperature of the dressing and see that it is at 165°F (74°C) or higher throughout before removing from the oven to serve. The bird is likely to be well above 165°F (74°C) when the dressing is adequately cooked but should be checked in several locations to be certain.

Although prestuffed fresh birds may be purchased in the marketplace, these are not recommended by the USDA [33]. Frozen, prestuffed birds may also be purchased and are considered safe when cooked from the frozen state. Manufacturer's directions should be followed. The temperature in the center of the stuffing, as measured with a thermometer, should reach 165°F (74°C).

Handling Leftovers

Cooked poultry products are ideal for the growth and/or toxin production of any microorganisms with which they may have been contaminated during handling and serving; therefore, maintaining proper temperature control is essential. Poultry products should always be refrigerated promptly and used within a few days. When a large bird has been prepared, the meat should be removed from the bone, cut into smaller pieces, and refrigerated so the meat cools rapidly.

If cooked poultry will be kept longer than a few days, it should be placed in a moisture-/vapor-proof wrapping or container and frozen. Longer storage periods are possible when raw or cooked poultry is frozen. Better flavor and texture are maintained in the uncooked than in the cooked frozen product when they are to be stored for a few months.

COOKING POULTRY

The fundamental principles of cooking poultry do not differ from those for other meats. Dry-heat methods (broiling, frying, baking, and roasting) are applicable to

Handling Precooked Poultry Products Safely

Processed poultry products are popular for use in the foodservice industry because they are uniform in weight, shape, yield, composition, and cooking requirements. Some of these are distributed in a precooked form that requires only refrigeration rather than freezing. The raw poultry product may be vacuum packaged in a multilaminate film, cooked, and then marketed in the same package. When vacuum packaged, uncured precooked turkey breast rolls were evaluated for microbiologic stability past 30 days of storage at 40°F (4°C), no colonies of **psychrotrophic** aerobic **bacteria** were detected; however, some **mesophilic** anaerobic **bacteria** were present. These findings indicate that precautions should be taken when serving these precooked poultry products to ensure that they are not temperature abused. Thus, they should not be held at higher than refrigerator temperatures for any period that would allow bacteria to multiply, and they must always be refrigerated [22]. ∎

young, tender birds. Moist-heat methods should be applied to older, less tender birds to make them tender and palatable. Most of the poultry sold on the market today is young and tender and can be cooked by dry-heat methods. As with meat, poultry should not be washed in water before cooking.

Roasting

All kinds of young, tender poultry can be roasted or baked (Figure 26-8 and Plates XXVIII and XXIX). Poultry may be roasted in an oven or in an electric roaster. Before roasting, birds may be **trussed** by tying the legs together as well as the wings with thread or butcher's twine to create a more compact shape if desired. Poultry may be roasted with little prepreparation or after brining. Although not ideal, turkey and chicken may be roasted from the frozen state; however, the time required for cooking will be 50 percent more. Lastly, duck and goose are roasted with consideration of their high fat content.

Traditional Roasting. To roast a whole chicken or turkey, the bird should be placed in a relatively shallow roasting pan to allow contact of the hot oven air with the bird. Many sources recommend that 1/2 cup of water be added to the bottom of the pan. The oven temperature for roasting poultry should be no lower than 325°F (163°C) [31]. An aluminum foil tent is sometimes used to cover the breast of turkeys either at the beginning or the end of roasting to prevent overbrowning. Alternatively, the whole bird can be wrapped in foil, although lower palatability for foil-wrapped turkeys versus open pan–roasted

birds has been reported [4]. Palatability is probably similar for birds roasted with the breast either up or down in the roasting rack. Birds may be **basted** during cooking using juices from the roaster pan.

When a minimum endpoint temperature of 165°F (74°C) has been reached, the bird should be removed from the oven and allowed to stand for approximately 20 minutes before carving. This resting period will allow the juices to more readily remain in the meat when sliced. Table 26-4 gives approximate cooking times for unstuffed turkeys. The internal temperature of turkey meat, both whole birds and light or dark meat roasts, appears to be a good guide in cooking. The yield and juiciness of cooked meat decrease as the internal temperature increases from 104° to 194°F (40° to 90°C). At the same time, the scores for odor, flavor, and mealiness increase with increasing temperature [9].

Electric Roaster Ovens. Poultry may be roasted in a large electric roaster. The roaster should be preheated to 325°F (163°C). The lid should remain on throughout cooking to maintain adequate temperature levels.

Brining before Roasting. Poultry can be soaked in a mixture of salt and water, called *brine*. Two cups of salt for two gallons of water is suggested [18]. Other seasonings such as bay leaves, garlic, and peppercorns may be added for additional flavor. To brine a bird, submerge it in the salt-and-water mixture in a large container for 6 to 8 hours while keeping it at or below 40°F (4°C). After brining, remove the bird from the liquid and roast. The bird may cook more rapidly when brined so temperatures should be monitored to avoid overcooking.

Roasting of Duck and Goose. Duck and goose contain a relatively high level of fat under the skin. Therefore, when these birds are roasted, it is recommended that the skin be scored in a crisscross pattern with a knife so the fat can drain off during roasting. Higher oven

FIGURE 26-8 A roasted chicken can be presented on a platter before carving for the diners. *(Courtesy of the National Chicken Council and U.S. Poultry and Egg Association)*

TABLE 26-4 Timetable for Roasting Fresh or Thawed Turkey	
Purchased Weight (lb)	Approximate Roasting Time @ 325°F (Hours)*
8 to 12	2 3/4 to 3
12 to 14	3 to 3 3/4
14 to 18	3 3/4 to 4 1/4
18 to 20	4 1/4 to 4 1/2
20 to 24	4 1/2 to 5

*These times are approximate and should always be used in conjunction with a properly placed thermometer.

(Courtesy of the U.S. Department of Agriculture)

How Does Brining Work?

Starting at the molecular level, poultry and other meats are made up of cells. Within these cells are membranes that allow for the movement of substances in and out. Water is the only substance able to move freely in and out across these borders. Additionally, inside these cells are dissolved solutes (solids) such as salts, potassium, and calcium. If there is only water outside, the balance of solids will be off; some water will go in, and salt will come out.

When the raw poultry is submerged in the brine solution, some of the water will be drawn out of the meat, thereby diluting the brine solution which then results in the brine solution entering into the meat. The salt in the brine solution, once absorbed into the meat, will cause the proteins to unravel or denature into loose coils. During cooking, these proteins will trap water almost like a gel. Therefore, a moist finished product will be the result.

---

temperatures are often used to encourage the rendering of the fat from the bird.

Broiling and Grilling

For broiling or grilling, young tender birds are cut into halves, quarters, or smaller pieces. Small young chickens and small fryer-roaster turkey pieces all may be appropriately broiled or grilled. The pieces are placed on a slotted grid or rack on the broiler pan or on grates over hot coals. Joints may be snapped so that pieces lie flat. With the broiler rack placed five to six inches from the flame or heating element, chicken pieces broiled for 20 to 25 minutes on each side should be cooked well done. Turkey pieces require 30 to 35 minutes on each side. Tongs should be used to turn the poultry pieces during broiling.

Poultry to be broiled or grilled may be marinated. Poultry picks up the flavors of a marinade fairly rapidly, generally in two hours. Extended contact with acid in the marinade may cause the texture of the meat to soften excessively and thus should be avoided [11]. For food safety, leftover marinade should be discarded. The flavor and color of broiled and grilled poultry may also be enhanced by basting during broiling or by applying a coating or breading mixture before cooking. Coating greatly reduces cooking losses not only with broiling but also with other cooking methods [20].

Grilling and Smoking of Whole Turkeys or Chickens

Whole birds may be grilled on a covered gas or charcoal grill. Smaller turkeys, less than 16 pounds, are recommended because a larger bird may take too long to cook and food safety could be compromised [34]. A grill or appliance thermometer should be used to monitor the temperature inside the grill. A temperature of around 300°F (149°C) is desirable.

The bird is cooked by indirect heat inside the grill. With charcoal, the hot coals should be pushed evenly around the edge, and a drip pan with water should be placed in the center. The bird is then placed on the grates above the drip pan, and the lid is placed on the grill. New briquettes must be added every hour to maintain temperature.

For a gas grill with more than one burner, place the turkey to the side away from burners which are turned on. If the grill has only one burner, place a pan of water under the grate to create indirect heat and place the bird on top of the grate in a roasting pan. Likewise, the lid of the grill should be closed to raise the heat within the grill.

Pan-Frying

Pieces of young chickens are frequently fried. The pieces are first coated by being rolled in seasoned flour mixtures, batters, or egg and crumbs [3, 23]. Slow, careful cooking is necessary when pan-frying to prevent overbrowning before the birds are done. Usually, 40 to 60 minutes is required to cook the flesh thoroughly, part of this time with the frying pan covered.

Young chickens may be oven fried at about 400°F (204°C). The pieces are first coated and then placed in a baking pan containing a small amount of oil. The chicken is turned midway through the baking process.

Deep-Fat Frying

To deep-fat fry, the food is submerged in hot oil. Pieces of chicken to be deep-fat fried may be steamed almost done before being dipped in flour, batter, or egg and crumbs and then browned in the heated fat. Deep-fat fried chicken may also be coated and fried from the raw state. It is cooked at 325° to 350°F (165° to 175°C) for 20 to 30 minutes, depending on the size of the chicken piece. Pressure deep-fat fryers have been developed especially for the frying of poultry in the food-processing and food-service industries.

Deep-fat frying of whole turkeys has gained in popularity. Safety should be of prime importance when deep-fat frying a large bird because hot oil can cause severe burns and can catch fire if overheated. Deep-fat frying of turkey in the home setting should be done outdoors. Storage and subsequent disposal of oil must also be considered.

To deep-fat fry a turkey, select a bird that is 12 pounds or less [34]. The cooking oil should be maintained at a temperature of 350°F (175°C) by monitoring with a thermometer designed for deep fat. The length of

FOCUS ON SCIENCE

More on the Deep-Fat Frying of Whole Turkeys

The first step in deep-fat frying a turkey is to determine the correct amount of oil to be used in the fryer. Place the turkey into the pot that will be used for frying and add water just until it barely covers the top of the turkey. The water level should be at least four to five inches below the top of the pot. Remove the turkey from the pot and mark where the water line is. This will be the amount of oil to be used for frying. This precaution will prevent the overflow of the hot oil when the turkey is placed in the fryer, which could lead to fire and severe burning. If the pot is too small to allow a four- to five-inch head space, use a larger pot and measure using the same procedure.

Select a fat with a high smoke point. Peanut oil is usually suggested because it contains a fatty acid of 22 carbons and a high smoke point, which makes it a good choice for frying. Heat the fat to the desired temperature, approximately 350°F (177°C), using a thermometer made for deep-fat frying. The temperature of the oil will drop when the turkey is added, so start timing when the temperature again reaches 350°F (177°C). The cooking time can be estimated by calculating of cook time of three minutes per pound and then adding another five minutes to the total. Therefore, for a 12-pound turkey, the cooking time is calculated as 12 x 3 = 36 + 5 = 41 minutes. Check doneness with a thermometer.

---

cooking time is approximately three to five minutes per pound. The turkey is done when the internal temperature of the bird is at a minimum of 165°F (74°C) as measured with a thermometer.

Braising

The method of braising involves cooking poultry in steam in a covered container. The term *fricassee* is often applied to cut pieces of chicken that are braised. Usually, the pieces are browned by first frying in a small amount of fat. Then, moisture is added, and the poultry is simmered in a covered skillet until tender and well done. Alternatively, the poultry can be cooked until tender and then fried until brown. A sauce or gravy made from the pan liquor is often served over the poultry pieces. Braising tenderizes older, less tender poultry but also is an appropriate method for cooking young birds.

Stewing

For stewing, birds are usually cut into pieces, although whole birds may be cooked in water seasoned with spices and herbs and vegetables. The poultry should be simmered in a relatively large amount of water until tender.

Microwave Cooking

Microwave cooking of poultry is not recommended. Microwave energy is not as effective as conventional cooking for destruction of microorganisms in whole turkeys, in chicken halves, and probably in pieces. In one study, turkeys that had been inoculated with food-poisoning bacteria before cooking were baked in the microwave oven. Roasting to an internal breast temperature of 170°F (77°C) did not completely eliminate the microorganisms [1]. Although the turkeys in this study contained abnormally high numbers of bacteria, it is possible that pathogenic microorganisms present in more usual numbers will survive. In another study, cooking chicken halves in the microwave oven to an internal temperature of 185°F (85°C) was not sufficient to destroy, in more than 50 percent of the chickens, all *Salmonella* organisms with which the birds had been inoculated [13].

Cooking and Color Changes

Discoloration of Poultry Bones.   The bones of frozen young birds are often very dark in color after the birds are cooked. Freezing and thawing break down the blood cells of bone marrow and cause a deep red color to appear [7, 30]. During cooking, the red color changes to brown, although this color change does not affect flavor. Cooking directly from the frozen state has been shown to result in less darkening than rapid or slow thawing [7].

Pink Flesh.   At times the meat of poultry can be a pink color even though it is fully cooked. Reasons for this "pinking" vary. Cured poultry such as smoked turkey is expected to be pink. Some of the reasons why uncured poultry can be pink include (a) genetics, feed, and preslaughter handling; (b) incidental nitrite or nitrate exposure through feed or the environment; (c) carbon monoxide exposure in gas ovens; and (d) smoke exposure during grilling [10]. Pink poultry is safe to eat, providing it has been cooked to a minimum of 165°F (74°C).

CHAPTER SUMMARY

- The term *poultry* is used to describe all domesticated birds that are intended for human consumption, including chickens, turkeys, ducks, geese, guinea fowl, squab (young pigeons), and pigeons. Poultry consumption has increased considerably over the years. Chicken and turkey provide high-quality protein and are lowfat.

- Antibiotics may be used in the raising of poultry, but residuals must not be present in meat. Hormones may not be used. Irradiation has been approved by the USDA and FDA to reduce pathogens such as *Salmonella, Campylobacter,* and *Listeria monocytogenes.*

- The Wholesome Poultry Products Act, passed in 1968, requires that all poultry marketed in the United States be inspected for sanitary processing and freedom from disease. All poultry-processing plants are required to operate under an HACCP plan. Wholesome birds are identified with the USDA inspection mark. USDA has developed voluntary standards for quality grades. These grades—A, B, and C—are placed on the label in a shield-shaped mark.

- *Fresh* and *frozen* are defined for poultry products. Labels on raw poultry products must provide the percentage of absorbed or retained water in the product unless unavoidable due to meeting food-safety requirements. Nutrition labels are mandated on processed poultry products. Other requirements for a poultry label include the product name, name and address of the producer or distributor, inspection mark, ingredients and net weight, establishment number identifying the plant where the product was processed, and handling instructions.

- Most poultry sold in retail markets are young tender birds. In a young bird, the end of the breastbone is pliable, and the wing offers little resistance when bent into an upright position. The skin of a young bird is pliable, soft, and tears easily.

- Poultry has a relatively high proportion of waste from the raw carcass to the cooked bird. Skin, fat, and bone account for about 50 percent of the weight of cooked chicken. Cooking losses vary with the cooking temperature and method and with the percentage of fat in the bird.

- Chilled, raw poultry is highly perishable and may be contaminated with microorganisms. Thus, poultry should be stored under refrigeration and not allowed to drip into other food products to avoid cross-contamination. Cutting boards and other work surfaces should be cleaned and sanitized after contact with raw poultry.

- Cooked or fresh poultry products should be used within a few days or frozen. Only safe methods for thawing frozen poultry should be used.

- Poultry should be cooked to a minimum endpoint temperature of 165°F (74°C) to destroy foodborne pathogens. Stuffing a bird before roasting is generally not recommended. However, if a bird is stuffed, the center of the stuffing must reach a minimum of 165°F (74°C).

- Dry-heat methods are appropriate for young, tender birds. Moist-heat methods should be applied to older, less tender birds. Broiling, frying, braising, and stewing are additional ways in which poultry may be cooked.

- Poultry bones may be discolored and dark when very young birds have been frozen. This color does not affect flavor. Cooking directly from the frozen state may result in less darkening of the bones. Cooked poultry meat may still be slightly pink for a variety of reasons, but it is safe to eat if cooked to the recommended temperature.

STUDY QUESTIONS

1. Poultry may be divided into several groups with respect to type, age, and sex.

   (a) Describe each of the following classes of chickens and turkeys.

Chickens	Turkeys
Broiler-fryer	Fryer-roaster
Roaster	Young hen
Capon	Young tom
Rock Cornish hen	
Baking hen	
Stewing hen or fowl	

   (b) Suggest satisfactory methods of cooking each type of poultry listed in Question 1a. Why is each method appropriate?

2. **(a)** What does the round USDA inspection mark mean when placed on poultry?

   (b) List the USDA grades that may be used on poultry and describe the qualities that are considered in grading.

3. Explain why it is so important to handle poultry properly, both in the raw and in the cooked state.

4. Describe an appropriate method for roasting turkeys. Explain why you would suggest this procedure.

5. Describe general procedures for broiling, frying, braising, and stewing poultry. Why is the microwave cooking of poultry not recommended?

6. Discuss the information and the terminology that is found on the labels of poultry products.

There are thousands of different species of fish worldwide, about 300 of these being within the United States or in the coastal waters surrounding it. Fish live in fresh water or in the seas and oceans. Seafood come to the United States from all over the world, sometimes traveling long distances before being processed, sold, or eaten [10]. About two-thirds of the seafood in the United States is imported [5]. Nevertheless, the U.S. fishing fleet is the fourth largest in the world and represents about 23,000 large vessels and more than 100,000 smaller craft [19].

In 2006, the most popular fish in the United States was shrimp at 4.4 pounds consumed per capita (Figure 27-1).

Tuna was the second most popular fish, after having previously held the number one spot in 2000. The remaining top ten species consumed in the United States in descending order are salmon, pollock, tilapia, catfish, crab, cod, clams, and scallops [20].

In this chapter, the following topics will be discussed:

- Consumption, composition, and nutritive value
- Classifications and market forms
- Harvest and aquaculture
- Government regulations and grading
- Buying of fish and shellfish
- Safe storage, handling, and preparation

FIGURE 27-1 Shrimp can be prepared many ways. In this dish, it is sautéed and served with lemon and orange sections over angel hair pasta. *(Courtesy of © Sunkist Growers, Inc., All rights reserved)*

CONSUMPTION

Compared to the annual per capita consumption of red meats and poultry in the United States, the consumption of fish and shellfish is modest but is increasing. According to U.S. Department of Agriculture (USDA) food disappearance data, 16 pounds of fish and shellfish, fresh, canned, and frozen were available per capita in 2005 compared to 12 pounds in 1970. In contrast, USDA data reveal much higher quantities of other meats per capita. In 2005, 62 pounds of beef, 60 pounds of chicken, and 47 pounds of pork were available per capita in the United States [27].

COMPOSITION AND NUTRITIVE VALUE

The gross composition of seafood is similar to that of lean meat (see Appendix C). Seafood, like red meat and poultry, is a valuable source of good-quality protein. Fish average 18 to 20 percent protein.

Many varieties of fish are lower in fat and cholesterol compared to other meats. Additionally, the small amount of fat present in most kinds of fish is highly unsaturated. Included among the unsaturated fats in fish oil are the omega-3 polyunsaturated fatty acids (PUFA), *eicosapentaenoic acid* (EPA), and *docosahexaenoic acid* (DHA) (see Chapter 9). Seafood is the predominate source of omega-3 fatty acids in the American diet [8].

The consumption of one to two servings of fish per week with reasonably high levels of EPA and DHA has been associated with a reduction in coronary death [17, 18]. DHA also appears to be beneficial for early neurodevelopment. The fat in many common fish contains 8 to 12 percent EPA and 30 to 45 percent total omega-3 PUFA [7], which makes fish an important source of these nutrients. The grams of omega-3 fatty acids found in a three-ounce serving of some commonly consumed kinds of fish are provided in Table 27-1.

All shellfish have some carbohydrate in the form of glycogen. Lobster have less than 1 percent, but abalone, clams, mussels, oysters, and scallops have from 3 to 5 percent. The sweet taste of various shellfish is due to the glucose formed by enzyme action from the glycogen. Shrimp are high in cholesterol compared to beef, chicken, and other seafood products. However, shrimp are very lowfat.

Seafood is an important source of minerals, with oysters being particularly rich in zinc, iron, and copper. Oysters, clams, and shrimp also contain a somewhat higher percentage of calcium than other fish and meats, which are notably low in calcium. Canned fish, such as sardines that are consumed with the bones, are a good source of calcium. Marine fish are a dependable source of iodine. Oysters, clams, and lobsters are the highest in iodine of all seafood. Shrimp ranks next, with crab and other ocean fish last in order.

Fat fish contain more vitamin A than lean varieties. Canned salmon is a fair source of vitamin A and a good source of riboflavin and niacin. The presence in raw fish of the enzyme *thiaminase*, which destroys thiamin, may make the vitamin unavailable if fish is held in the raw state.

TABLE 27-1 Grams of Omega-3 Fatty Acids in Selected Kinds of Seafood	
Seafood Name	**Grams of Omega-3 Fatty Acids per Three-Ounce Serving**
Herring	1.71–1.81
Salmon	0.68–1.83
Oysters	0.37–1.17
Halibut	0.40–1.00
Tuna, canned light	0.26–0.73
Pollock	0.46
Flounder or sole	0.43
Crabs	0.34–0.40
Lobster	0.07–0.41
Shrimp	0.27
Clams	0.24
Cod	0.13–0.24
Grouper	0.21
Catfish	0.15–0.20
Scallops	0.17
Mahi mahi	0.12

Source: Reference 1

FOCUS ON SCIENCE

However, because they are highly unsaturated, they are susceptible to rancidity which will lead to off-aromas and -flavors if the fish is not handled properly. Fish should be chilled immediately when brought home by keeping it on ice in the refrigerator before cooking.

Eicosapentaenoic Acid (EPA) and Docosahexaenoic Acid (DHA)

Eicosapentaenoic acid (EPA) and docosahexaenoic acid (DHA) are both highly unsaturated fatty acids with five and six double bonds, respectively. They also are classified as omega-3 fatty acids which contribute health benefits to the diet.

CLASSIFICATION AND MARKET FORMS

Two major categories for the classification of fish are vertebrate fish with fins and shellfish or invertebrates. The Food and Drug Administration (FDA) provides two useful online resources, the *Seafood List* and the *Regulatory Fish Encyclopedia*, available at http://www.fda.gov [31, 32]. Information about many different kinds of fish as well as acceptable market names is provided. The *Seafood Handbook* is another excellent resource which is especially useful for those who purchase seafood in foodservice organizations [26].

Fin Fish

Fin fish are usually covered with scales and may be further divided into two types: flat and round fish. Round fish swim vertically, whereas flat fish swim in a horizontal position. Some examples of round fish include bass, catfish, cod, haddock, pollock, grouper, mahi-mahi, orange roughy, red snapper, salmon, shark, swordfish, tilapia, trout, tuna, and whitefish. Fish classified as flatfish include flounder, sole, and halibut [11]. Some of the most commonly consumed fin fish are described in Table 27-2.

TABLE 27-2 Description of Selected Popular Fin Fish in the United States

Name of Fish	Description
Tuna	Albacore, bluefin, yellowfin, and skipjack are all varieties of tuna. Tuna may be purchased fresh, frozen, or canned. Bluefin and yellowfin is used in the raw market as sashimi and sushi. "Canned" tuna may be sold in cans or pouches with a water or oil pack. Albacore is known as "white meat tuna." Most of the light meat canned tuna is skipjack, although some may be yellowfin. Light meat tuna is low in mercury compared to albacore.
Salmon	Atlantic, Chinook, chum, coho, pink, and sockeye are all kinds of salmon. Salmon may be purchased fresh, frozen, smoked, or canned. Atlantic salmon is successfully "farmed" in floating net-pens in open bays. Chinook salmon are found in the Pacific Ocean and are known for a buttery, rich taste and red flesh. Chum salmon are also found in the Pacific Ocean and have a lower oil content than other varieties with orange, pink, or red flesh. Coho has a relatively high fat content and a mild flavor. Pink salmon is generally lean and mild flavored. It is often canned.
Pollock	Alaskan pollock is in the cod family. It is a mild, delicate fish that produces a white flesh when cooked. Pollock fillets may be prepared by baking or grilling. It is often used to produce surimi or breaded and battered fish.
Tilapia	Tilapia is commonly farm raised. It is lean, mild, and sweet tasting. After cooking, the flesh is white with tender flakes. It may be purchased fresh, frozen, or as breaded fillets. Poor-quality tilapia may have an off-flavor.
Catfish	Catfish is farmed raised with much of the U.S. catfish produced in the Mississippi Delta. The meat is moist and dense. The cooked meat is white and opaque.
Cod	Cod may be harvested from the Pacific and Atlantic Oceans. Atlantic and Pacific cod are used interchangeably, although there are subtle differences between them. Cod is lean and cooks quickly. The flavor is neutral. The cooked flesh is white.

Source: Reference 26

TABLE 27-3 Some Species of Fish

Species	Weight Range (lb)	Usual Market Form	Suggested Preparation Method
Lean saltwater fish			
Bluefish	1–7	Whole and drawn	Broil, bake, fry
Cod	3–20	Steaks and fillets	Broil, bake, fry, steam
Flounder	1/4–5	Whole, dressed, and fillets	Broil, bake, fry
Haddock	1 1/2–7	Drawn and fillets	Broil, bake, steam
Hake	2–5	Whole, dressed, and fillets	Broil, bake, fry
Halibut	8–75	Steaks	Broil, bake, steam
Rosefish	1/2–1 1/4	Fillets	Bake
Snapper, red	2–15	Drawn, steaks, and fillets	Bake, steam
Whiting	1/2–1 1/2	Whole, dressed, and fillets	Bake, fry
Fat saltwater fish			
Butterfish	1/4–1	Whole and dressed	Broil, bake, fry
Herring	3/4–1	Whole	Bake, fry
Mackerel	3/4–3	Whole, drawn, and fillets	Broil, bake
Salmon	3–30	Drawn, dressed, steaks, and fillets	Broil, bake, steam
Shad	1 1/2–7	Whole and fillets	Bake
Lean freshwater fish			
Brook trout	3/4–8	Whole	Broil, bake, fry
Yellow pike	1 1/2–10	Whole, dressed, and fillets	Broil, bake, fry
Fat freshwater fish			
Catfish	1–10	Whole, dressed, and skinned	Bake, fry
Lake trout	1 1/2–10	Drawn, dressed, and fillets	Bake, fry
Whitefish	2–6	Whole, dressed, and fillets	Broil, bake

Fish are also categorized according to whether they live in *fresh* or *salt* waters. Freshwater fish come from lakes and rivers instead of the oceans. Saltwater fish usually have more distinctive flavor than freshwater fish. Fish with vertebrae are further classified on the basis of their fat content as *lean* or *fat*, lean fish having less than 5 percent fat in their edible flesh. Oily fish, such as salmon, usually have more flavor than lean fish. Examples of lean and fat fish are found in Table 27-3.

What Is Fish Roe?

Roe is the mass of eggs from finfish and consists of sacs of connective tissue enclosing thousands of small eggs. It is important that the sacs remain intact, because the eggs cannot otherwise be held together. Although roe is of minor importance in the marketing of fish, available only during spawning season and very perishable, fresh fish roe is well liked by some people. The most highly prized for flavor is shad roe, although in the Great Lakes area, whitefish roe is also popular. Roe from most fish that are commonly consumed can be eaten. Caviar is sturgeon roe preserved in brine. It is expensive and is used mainly for making appetizers.

A method of cooking that intensifies flavor is preferable for fish roe. It is usually parboiled for two to five minutes, after which it is dipped in cornmeal or in egg and crumbs and fried. Parboiling aids in thorough cooking of the roe without its hardening by being fried too long. ■

Shellfish

Shellfish are of two types: mollusks and crustaceans. The shellfish most commonly marketed in the United States are clams, crab, lobster, oysters, scallops, and shrimp. Clams, oysters, shrimp, and spiny lobster are shown in Plate XXX.

Mollusks. Mollusks have a soft structure and are either partially or wholly enclosed in a hard shell that is largely of mineral composition. Mollusks may be further subdivided into univalves (abalone), bivalves (clams, oysters, and mussels), and cephalopods (squid and octopus).

Univalves. As the name suggests, univalves have a single shell. Abalone are harvested in California and are characterized by a flavor somewhat like lobster [26]. Overcooked abalone will become very tough. Conch provide a firm, lean meat similar in flavor to abalone or clam. They are found in the Caribbean and off the Florida Keys. In the United States, commercial harvesting is banned because conch are endangered in domestic waters [26].

Bivalves. Oysters, clams, mussels, and scallops are all examples of bivalves. Bivalves have two shells connected by a hinge. Oysters can be purchased live in the shell, fresh or frozen shucked (removed from the shell), or canned. Live oysters have a tightly closed shell. Gaping shells indicate that they are dead and therefore no longer usable. Shucked oysters should be plump and have a natural creamy color, with clear liquor.

Several species of clams are used for food. They are marketed live in the shell, fresh or frozen shucked, or canned. Shucked clams should be plump, with clear liquor, and free from shell particles (see Plate XXX). Mussels have a distinctive taste that is a blend of clams and oysters. Mussels have "beards" or byssus threads that should be removed just before cooking [26]. Tightly closed shells of clams and mussels indicate that they are alive and therefore usable.

Scallops are mollusks similar to oysters and clams except that they swim freely through the water by snapping their shells together. The oversize adductor muscle that closes the shell is the only part of the scallop eaten by Americans. Both bay and sea scallops may be found in the marketplace, although only the bay scallop may be found whole and live [26]. Usually both kinds of scallops are sold shucked and cleaned.

Cephalopods. Octopus and squid are cephalopods. Both are characterized by a head with a number of arms attached near the head. Neither has an external shell but instead both have an internal shell called a cuttlebone [11]. Squid often is called *calamari* on menus. To tenderize, octopus must be cooked by simmering or another slow-cooking method. In contrast, squid should be cooked quickly because overcooking will make it tough [26].

Crustaceans. Crustaceans are covered with a crustlike shell and have segmented bodies. Common examples are lobster, crab, shrimp, and crayfish.

Shrimp. Shrimp include the common or white shrimp, which is greenish gray when caught; the brown or Brazilian shrimp, which is brownish red when raw; the pink or coral shrimp; and the Alaska and California varieties, which vary in color and are relatively small. Despite the differences in color in the raw state, cooked shrimp differ little in appearance and flavor. Raw shrimp in the shell are often called *green shrimp*. Shrimp are usually sold with the head and thorax removed. The sand vein should be removed in larger shrimp.

Shrimp are designated by the count per pound as Jumbo, Large, Large Medium, Medium, and Small. The largest size has 15 or fewer shrimp to the pound; the smallest size has 60 or more to the pound. Breaded shrimp, which have been peeled, cleaned, and breaded for frying, are available (Figure 27-2). Prawn are shrimplike crustaceans that are usually relatively large in size.

Lobster. The true lobster, or Northern lobster, is found near the shores of Europe and North America in the cold waters of the North Atlantic Ocean. The spiny or rock lobster is nearly worldwide in its distribution. The spiny lobster may be distinguished by the absence of large, heavy claws and the presence of many prominent spines on its body and legs. Figure 27-3 shows both of these lobsters.

Lobsters are a dark bluish-green when taken from the water but change to a "lobster red" during cooking. Lobsters and crabs must be alive at the time of cooking to ensure freshness. The tail should curl under the body when the live lobster is picked up. Lobsters cooked in the shell are available. They should be bright red in color and have a fresh odor. Frozen lobster tails can be purchased in some markets. The cooked meat, picked from the shells of lobsters and crabs, is marketed fresh, frozen, and canned.

Crab. Blue crabs, constituting about three-fourths of all crab marketed in the United States, come from the Atlantic and Gulf coasts. Blue crabs, if harvested right after molting, are called "soft shell" crabs. Because the shell is so tender, the shell and meat of soft shell crabs are consumed. Fresh-cooked meat from blue crabs may be packed in several grades: lump meat, or solid lumps of white meat from the body of the crab; flake meat, or small pieces of white meat from the rest of the body; lump and flake meat combined; and claw meat, which has a brownish tinge.

Dungeness crabs are found on the Pacific Coast from Alaska to Mexico. Fresh-cooked meat from both the body and claws of Dungeness crabs has a pinkish tinge and is packed as one grade. Jonah crabs are found off New England in the United States and are a less expensive crab

FIGURE 27-2 Breaded shrimp ready for frying. *(Courtesy of the Florida Department of Agriculture and Consumer Services, Bureau of Seafood and Aquaculture)*

Northern lobster.

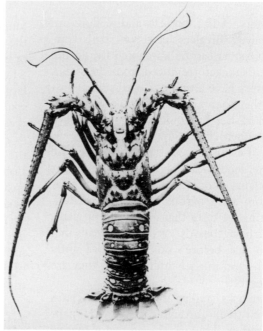

Spiny or rock lobster.

FIGURE 27-3 Two types of lobster. *(Courtesy of the Bureau of Commercial Fisheries, U.S. Department of the Interior)*

meat compared to blue and Dungeness crabs [26]. Dungeness and blue crabs are shown in Figure 27-4.

Market Forms

Several varieties of fin fish, fresh or frozen, are marketed in various forms. Figures 27-5 and 27-6 show some of these. Whole or round fish are marketed just as they come from the water. Drawn fish have had only the entrails removed; dressed fish are scaled and eviscerated and usually have the head, tail, and fins removed. Steaks are cross-cut sections of the larger sizes of dressed fish. Fillets are sides of the fish cut lengthwise away from the backbone. A butterfly fillet is the two sides of a fillet. Sticks are uniform pieces of fish cut lengthwise or crosswise from fillets or steaks; however, some breaded, frozen fish sticks may be made from minced fish. Figure 27-6 shows several forms of fish.

Shellfish are marketed in the shell, shucked (removed from the shell), headless (shrimp and some lobster), or already cooked. When purchased fresh, clams, oysters,

Blue crab.

Dungeness crab.

FIGURE 27-4 The two most common types of crabs available in the United States. *(Courtesy of the Bureau of Commercial Fisheries, U.S. Department of the Interior)*

Whole or round fish.

Drawn fish.

Dressed or pan-dressed fish.

Steaks.

Single fillet.

Sticks.

Butterfly fillet.

FIGURE 27-5 Market forms of fish *(Courtesy of the Bureau of Commercial Fisheries, U.S. Department of the Interior)*

and mussels, should always be alive. Shells should be closed or snap closed when touched. Likewise, fresh lobster should be alive. These kinds of shellfish may also be marketed cooked or frozen.

Many convenience items containing fish are available. Fish may be battered or breaded. The amount of breading should be considered in relation to the fish when comparing prices. Breaded seafood that contains

A drawn fish, with entrails removed.

Filleting a fish.

A whole Red Grouper and fillets.

Steaks cut from tuna loin.

Catfish with fillet, steak, and sticks.

Broiled Florida fish fillets accompanied by fresh seasoned vegetables.

FIGURE 27-6 Fish may be prepared in various forms. *(Courtesy of Florida Department of Agriculture and Consumer Services, Bureau of Seafood and Aquaculture)*

less than 50 percent by weight of seafood must be labeled imitation [26]. Another consideration is whether a breaded seafood item is composed of pieces of fish cut from fillets or if the fish has been flaked and reformed. Breaded flaked fish products should be less expensive than those made from fillets. Smoked seafood may also be purchased.

SEAFOOD HARVEST AND AQUACULTURE

Wild Caught

Seafood are harvested from oceans, rivers, and lakes by commercial fishing operations for sale to the public or by those who fish for sport and personal enjoyment. Commercially, fish may be harvested by trawling, trolling, purse seining, gillnetting, longlining, pot fishing, or dredging [26]. Trawling is accomplished by dragging a large cone-shaped net through the water. When baits or lures are dragged behind the fishing vessel, it is called *trolling*. Salmon may be caught in using this method. Purse seining is used for schools of fish that are encircled with a net, then "pursed" at the bottom. Gillnets catch fish by trapping the fish in the net sized to catch certain varieties and sizes of fish. A long line with baited hooks placed either near the surface or near the bottom, depending on species, is called *longlining*. Crabs and lobsters are harvested by trapping them in a pot or trap placed on the bottom of the ocean. Clams, oysters, mussels, and scallops are caught by dredging a metal rake along the ocean bottom.

Aquaculture

Aquaculture, or fish farming, is not new. It was apparently practiced in China as early as 2000 B.C. Extremely rapid growth has occurred in this industry since the mid-1980s [5]. China, India, Vietnam, Thailand, Indonesia, Bangladesh, Japan, Chile, and Norway lead the world in aquaculture production. The United States is ranked 10th in total aquaculture production [34]. Much of the seafood consumed by Americans is imported. Of this imported seafood, nearly half of it is farmed [33].

Sustainability

The farming and harvesting of seafood with consideration for the long-term health of the ecosystem promote the sustainability of our seafood supplies. Darden Restaurants, operators of Red Lobster restaurants, is an example of one company that has been including sustainability into its purchasing decision-making process [26]. Within the U.S. government under the National Oceanic and Atmospheric Administration (NOAA), *FishWatch* provides information about various seafood species to help consumers make informed decisions about what species may be at risk because of overfishing [35].

GOVERNMENT REGULATION

Inspection and Regulatory Oversight

The FDA maintains an Office of Seafood as part of its regulatory responsibilities. Since December 1997, seafood processors, packers, and warehouses—both domestic and foreign exporters to this country—have been required to follow a Hazard Analysis and Critical Control Points (HACCP) system (see Chapter 3). The HACCP system focuses on identifying and preventing hazards that could cause foodborne illness rather than relying on random sampling of finished seafood products and occasional plant inspections. In 2001, the FDA announced noncompliant firms will be inspected more frequently and laboratory testing will be more extensive with enforcement action when necessary [29].

The FDA also sets standards for seafood contaminants such as pesticide residues and mercury; administers the National Shellfish Sanitation Program with shellfish-producing states and other countries; and analyzes fish and fishery products for toxins, chemicals, and other hazards in agency laboratories [10].

FOCUS ON SCIENCE

Fatty Acids in Farm-Raised Fish

Aqua farms can be based on land or in the ocean. Land-based farms raise thousands of fish in ponds, pools, or concrete tanks. Ocean-based aqua farms are situated close to shorelines. Fish grown in ocean-based farms are grown in net or mesh cages.

Freshwater fish are an enormous part of the world aquaculture production. Their fatty acid contents are in some cases similar to those of marine fish with eicosapentaenoic (20;5n-3) and docosahexaenoic (22;6n-3) acids as reasonably important lipid components. The U.S. channel catfish account for 45 percent of all U.S. aquaculture production.

Source: Ackman, R. G. (1992). *Fatty Acids in Fish and Shellfish*, edited by C. K. Chow, p. 169. New York: Marcel Dekker.

Grading

The NOAA in the U.S. Department of Commerce operates a voluntary seafood inspection and grading program. A fee for the voluntary service is paid by the processor. Fish products meeting the official standards may carry U.S. inspection and grade labels.

Quality grades are determined largely on the basis of appearance, uniformity, absence of defects, character (mainly texture), and flavor and odor of the product. Grades for breaded items also consider the amount of edible fish as compared with the amount of breading and the presence of bone in fish sticks. For most items, specific grades are U.S. Grade A, U.S. Grade B, and Substandard.

BUYING FISH AND SHELLFISH

The first step in purchasing seafood is to assess your retailer. The fresh seafood counter should be clean and without a strong "fishy" odor. Fresh fish does not smell, and thus a strong odor is suggestive of old fish or poorly cleaned display cases. Fresh fish should be in a refrigerated case, often displayed on ice to maintain a temperature just above freezing. Shellfish should have tags that identify the certification number of the processor and the location of harvest. This information should be printed on the label as well.

Freshness

Fresh finfish have firm flesh, a stiff body, and tight scales. The gills are red, and the eyes are bright and unsunken. Pressure on the body does not leave an indentation in the flesh (see Plate XXX) except in the case of fish that has been frozen and thawed. The exterior of fresh fish has little or no slime. Fresh seafood should not smell "fishy," but rather like a "fresh ocean breeze." Stale fish, on the other hand, are flabby, and the eyes are dull and sunken. The scales are easily brushed off, the gills are no longer bright red, and the odor is stale or sour.

Frozen fish should be solidly frozen when purchased, with no discoloration or brownish tinge in the flesh. It should have little or no odor and should be wrapped in a moisture-/vapor-proof material. Frozen fish with frost, ice, or large amounts of ice crystals may have been thawed and refrozen and should not be purchased.

Mollusks in the shell should always be alive when they are purchased. The shells of live mollusks will be tightly closed or will close when tapped lightly or iced. Any mollusks that do not close tightly should be thrown away. Seafood should be bought only from reputable dealers.

HOT TOPICS

Future Fish—Are They Here Now?

From bacteria to plants and, now, to animals—scientists have been moving the technology of genetic modification. Fish make attractive candidates for genetic engineering research. First, they produce eggs in large quantities, and these eggs are released and develop outside the body, where scientists can easily work with them. In the near future, will you be buying genetically modified salmon or trout for your Saturday night dinner? It is not clear just when or if this will happen. AquaBounty Farms of Waltham, Massachusetts, has already developed a salmon that is modified to grow twice as fast as its wild counterpart. AquaBounty Farms has already submitted a premarket application to the FDA, the agency responsible for regulating genetically modified fish [22].

This brings us to the subject of regulation—of genetically modified food products, that is. There are many pros and cons in this area. Some of these have been presented for discussion and debate by the Pew Initiative on Food and Biotechnology, a group funded by the Pew Charitable Trust that attempts to be an independent and objective source of credible information on agricultural biotechnology for both the public and the policymakers.

This group suggests that the application of genetic engineering to animals—including fish—could provide numerous benefits to humankind. But, they say, it is unclear whether regulators presently have the tools they need to evaluate these new products adequately. A new and clearly articulated roadmap may be needed to assess the risk and benefits adequately [23]. What will the future bring? Stay tuned! ■

The area of harvest for shellfish is an important factor influencing the safety of the shellfish, and reputable dealers will provide product from approved sources. When selecting fresh lobster, only lobsters that move when handled and thus are alive should be purchased.

Fish Products

Many value-added fish products are available from which consumers and foodservice establishments can choose.

Minced Fish Products. Included in the technological advances made in the U.S. seafood industry is the production of deboned, minced raw fish from lesser-known species and fillet trimmings. Minced fish has given rise to new families of food products. For example, frozen minced fish blocks are cut into fish sticks and portions. These products can be found on the market in a variety of forms, including crunchy breaded pieces, seafood nuggets, and fish loaf with creamy sauce [15, 24].

A raw material called *surimi* (from the Japanese) offers opportunities for the production of several food items. To prepare surimi, minced fish is first washed to remove fat, blood, pigments, and other undesirable substances, leaving only the myofibrillar proteins of the fish flesh. This material is then frozen with the addition of **cryoprotectants**, such as sucrose and sorbitol or possibly maltodextrins and polydextrose, because the myofibrillar proteins of fish are labile to denaturation on freezing [14].

Further processing and fiberizing produce an elastic and chewy texture in the product that can be made to resemble that of shellfish [12]. Surimi-based fiberized simulated crab legs are shown in Figure 27-7. Japanese techniques in the production of surimi have been Americanized, and several plants are producing surimi and similar products in the United States. Novel snack foods are also produced from surimi [9].

Cured Fish. Although fish may be cured for preservation purposes, the cure often imparts a distinctive flavor of its own that is appreciated for variety. Some hardening and toughening of the outer surface occur when fish is salted, dried, or smoked. Common examples of cured fish are salt cod, mackerel (see Plate XXXI), finnan haddie, and kippered herring. Finnan haddie is haddock that has been cured in brine to which carotene pigment has been added and later smoked. It is preferred lightly cured but does not keep long with a light cure. If finnan haddie is to be kept for some time or shipped long distances, the cure must be stronger. Kippered herring is also lightly brined and smoked. It is often canned to preserve its typical flavor rather than being cured in a heavier brine.

Canned Fish. The principal kinds of canned fish are salmon, tuna, sardines, shrimp, crab, lobster, and clams.

Salmon packing is one of the big industries of the Pacific Northwest. Five principal varieties of salmon are packed, depending on the locality. The five varieties in order of consumer preference are red salmon or sockeye; chinook; coho, medium red or silverside; pink; and chum. The fish with red flesh and high oil content are preferred by consumers, although they are the most expensive.

In the United States, only six species of tuna may be labeled "tuna" when canned: yellowfin, skipjack, albacore, bluefin, Oriental tuna, and little tuna. The related species of bonito and Pacific yellowtail cannot legally be marketed as tuna. Albacore may be labeled "white meat"; the other species are labeled "light meat" tuna. Three different styles of packing for canned tuna are fancy or solid pack, chunk style, and flake or grated style. Each style can be packed in either oil or water. The normal color of precooked or canned tuna is pinkish. Some fish do not develop the pink color, but take on a tan or tannish-green color and then are rejected. These fish are referred to in the industry as *green* tuna.

Tuna is now being sold in flexible retort packaging as an alternative method of providing the consumer with "canned" tuna. The flexible pouches are not packed in oil or water and thus the product is ready to use without draining (see Chapter 2 and Figure 2-9a).

Breaded or Battered Fish Products. A variety of seafood products ranging from shrimp, fillets, fish sticks and more are available that have been breaded or battered. Breaded and battered products should be evenly covered and should separate from other portions easily. If products appear to be frozen together or exhibit excessive amounts of frost, poor temperature control is the likely cause, and the product should be avoided. Breaded and battered fish should remain frozen until cooked [26]. In

FIGURE 27-7 Surimi is made by a special process from mechanically deboned fish flesh. It is used for a variety of fabricated seafood products and can be a tasty addition to an entrée salad. *(Courtesy of Florida Department of Agriculture and Consumer Services, Bureau of Seafood and Aquaculture)*

general, the amount of fish in relation to the amount of breading or batter should be assessed in relation to price.

SAFE STORAGE AND HANDLING

Seafood Safety

When properly handled and thoroughly cooked, fish is safe to eat. Seafood, however, is the most perishable of flesh foods and does present potential hazards if not produced and handled properly. The primary causes of food-borne illness associated with seafood include (a) bacteria or viral contamination, (b) parasites, and (c) shellfish or finfish toxins. These food safety issues are summarized in Table 27-4 and were also discussed in Chapter 3.

Chemicals such as mercury may also be present in some fish in hazardous amounts [6]. The FDA released a consumer advisory for pregnant women in 2001 and again in 2004 about the risks of mercury in fish [28, 30]. In this advisory, the avoidance of shark, swordfish, king mackerel, and tilefish by pregnant women is suggested to reduce mercury exposure. A general recommendation of eating only an average of 12 ounces of fish per week is provided. Local fish advisories should also be checked to assess the risk of mercury contamination from recreationally caught fish. This information may be obtained from the Environmental Protection Agency (EPA) (http://www.epa.gov) or state and local health departments.

These recommendations should be interpreted with a realization most Americans consume far less than 12 ounces of fish per week. Furthermore, the consumption of long-chain omega-3 fatty acids has been associated with health benefits including improved cognitive function in infants [3, 16]. Research into mercury contamination of fish, the potential protective role of selenium, and environmental cleanup is needed [21].

Spoilage of Fish and Storage Recommendations

Fresh fish are extremely perishable and spoil rapidly. In addition to the delicate structure of fish, which makes bacterial invasion easy, it has been shown that rapid spoilage is partly the result of the high degree of activity of the enzymes present in fish. The low temperatures of the natural environment of some fish may account for the unusual activity of the body enzymes. Thus, to maintain quality, fish are stored in flaked ice (cubed ice may bruise the fish) or in a frozen salt solution to achieve a somewhat lower temperature until the fish are ready for sale [13].

When fish spoils, bacteria decompose fish tissue, and a volatile substance called *trimethylamine* is released. Measurement of trimethylamine levels gives an indication of the microbiologic quality of fish [36]. Researchers are developing methods of packaging fish for sale in supermarkets to enhance safety and shelf life. Packaging structures may incorporate antimicrobial compounds or package surfaces that provide spoilage indicators by measuring ammonia, trimethylamine, and dimethylamine [2]. Labels that change colors when a product has been subjected to time and temperature abuse are being tested [2]. Storage recommendations for seafood are provided in Table 27-5.

PREPARATION

Cooking Finfish

Frozen seafood should be thawed in the refrigerator in its own container. Allow about a day for defrosting. Individual steaks or fillets may be cooked either thawed or frozen. If they have been thawed, they may be cooked as fresh fish.

To lend variety to menus, fish may be cooked by either dry- or moist-heat methods. Fish have very little connective tissue, and it is of a kind that is easily hydrolyzed. The structure of fish is delicate and tender, even in the raw state; therefore, the use of moist heat for tenderization purposes is not necessary. In fact, a big problem in fish cookery is retention of the form of the fish, which is done by careful handling. If fish is cooked in water, it is usually necessary to tie the piece of fish in cheesecloth or wrap it in parchment paper to prevent it from falling apart during cooking. Because extractives are low in fish, a method that develops flavor, such as frying, broiling, and baking, is often preferred.

Although overcooking is to be avoided, for optimum food safety, fish must be cooked to a minimum safe temperature of 145°F (63°C). A visual indication of doneness is evident when the flakes separate easily. It should be tested with a fork in a thick portion, as the outer, thin edges cook more readily than the thicker muscles. About 10 minutes of cooking time per one inch of thickness is generally suggested for fish fillets.

If two or more fish fillets have been frozen in a package, it is necessary to partially defrost them to separate them for cooking. For partially or wholly frozen fish, the cooking temperature must be lower and the time of cooking longer than for defrosted fish to permit thawing as the fish cooks. Otherwise, ice may remain in the center of the cut even when the outside is thoroughly cooked.

Broiling

Fish to be broiled may be in the form of fillets, steaks, or boned or unboned whole fish (head removed). Unboned whole fish is cut through the ribs along the backbone, allowing it to lie flat. If the skin has been left intact, the fish is placed skin-side down on the broiler rack. It may later be turned, but turning large pieces of fish is difficult and tends to break the fish apart. Using a relatively low broiling temperature to prevent overbrowning and basting the top surface with fat to keep it moist usually make it possible for fish to be broiled until done without turning (Figure 27-8).

TABLE 27-4 Seafood Food Safety Hazards

Hazard	Type of Seafood Affected	Description	Safeguards
Bacteria			
Vibrio vulnificus and Vibrio parahaemolyticus	Raw or improperly cooked oysters	Naturally found in warm coastal waters. Most prevalent during months of April to October.	Individuals with liver disease, diabetes, suppressed immune system, or other significant health concerns are at highest risk for serious illness and potentially death as the result of Vibrio vulnificus. Anyone in a high-risk group should not eat raw oysters. Cook oysters before consumption. Purchase from approved, reputable suppliers.
Virus			
Hepatitis A and Norovirus	Shellfish contaminated by sewage or by food handler	Primarily found in feces of people infected with these viruses. Thus, sewage contaminated waters or food handlers are usual cause.	Cook shellfish. Purchase from approved reputable suppliers. Use good personal hygiene when handling food and, if ill, do not prepare food for others.
Parasites			
Anisakiasis	Raw and undercooked: herring, cod, halibut, mackerel, and Pacific salmon	Worm-parasite that is found in the environment of certain fish.	Cook fish to 145°F (63°C). If serving undercooked, purchase sushi-grade fish that has been frozen for the approved time and temperature required to destroy this parasite. Purchase from approved suppliers.
Fish Toxins			
Scrombroid or Histamine poisoning	Most commonly found in tuna, bonito, mackerel, and mahi mahi	Found on certain fish when the fish has been temperature-abused.	Not destroyed by cooking, freezing, curing, or smoking. Avoid temperature abuse. Purchase from approved, reputable suppliers.
Ciguatera fish poisoning	Most commonly found in predatory reef fish, including barracuda, grouper, jacks, and snapper	Found on predatory reef fish that have eaten smaller fish who have consumed toxic algae. The algae are naturally found in the environment.	May not be smelled or tasted. Not destroyed by cooking or freezing. Purchase from reputable suppliers who sell fish from safe waters.
Shellfish Toxins			
Paralytic shellfish poisoning	Shellfish found in colder waters, including clams, mussels, oysters, and scallops	This toxin, *saxitoxin,* is found on certain toxic algae found in cold waters.	None of the shellfish toxins may be smelled or tasted and are not destroyed by cooking or freezing.
Neurotoxic shellfish poisoning	Shellfish found in warmer waters, including mussels, clams, and oysters	This toxin, *brevetoxin,* is found on certain toxic algae found in warm waters.	Harvesting of shellfish is closed in areas with toxic algae blooms. Some, although not all, algae blooms may be called "red tide."
Amnesic shellfish poisoning	Shellfish found in coastal waters of the east coast of Canada and Pacific Northwest	This toxin, *domoic acid,* is found in certain toxic algae in cooler coastal waters.	Purchase shellfish from approved, reputable suppliers.

Source: Reference 4

FOCUS ON SCIENCE

Spoilage Indicators for Fish

Some of the visual indicators of fish spoilage can vary with the kind of fish. For example, depending on the species of the fish, the eyes of fresh may be dark. The aroma of the fish, however, is a strong indicator of freshness.

Most marine fish contain a substance called trimethylamine oxide (TMAO). Certain bacteria that occur naturally on the skin and in the gut of fish and in seawater can break down TMAO to trimethylamine (TMA). The amount of TMA produced is a measure of activity of spoilage bacteria in the flesh and therefore an indicator of degree of spoilage.

Bacteria can also generate small amounts of ammonia in spoiling fish, mainly from free amino acids. The amount of ammonia can give an indication to the extent of spoilage. Shellfish may develop more ammonia than most marine fish and at an earlier stage.

TABLE 27-5 Storage Recommendations for Seafood	
Kind of Seafood	**Storage Recommendations**
Fresh Finfish	
Whole, fresh caught	Store at 32°F (0°C). Ice with shaved ice to maintain cold temperatures. Should not sit in water as a result of the melting ice. Alternatively, may be wrapped in moisture-proof packaging and refrigerated. Should be used or frozen within two days. Rapid freezing is desirable to prevent large ice crystals that will contribute to drip loss when thawed.
Fillets and steaks	Store at 32°F (0°C). Wrap in moisture-proof packaging and use within two days or freeze (0°F/−18°C) in vapor-barrier freezer packaging for longer storage. Icing is not recommended unless in moisture-proof packaging because fillets will easily absorb melted water.
Shellfish	
Live clams, oysters, mollusks, lobsters, and crabs	Store at 41°F (5°C) in high humidity. May store with seaweed or damp paper. Do not put in fresh water because these saltwater shellfish will perish. Storage in plastic bags and icing is not recommended. Under good conditions, shellfish may be kept alive for several days. Dead shellfish will need to be discarded.
Shucked oysters, clams, and scallops	Maintain cold temperatures. Set in container on ice to lower temperature. Do not allow direct contact with ice because melting water will be absorbed.

Source: Reference 11

Fish, Shellfish, and Waste

The refuse of fish is rather high, commonly around 50 percent or more by weight. In general, the smaller the fish, the higher the percentage of refuse. The waste is composed chiefly of scales, head, bones, and, in some cases, the skin. In shellfish, the shell constitutes the chief waste; running as high as 60 to 80 percent of the total weight. For example, a lobster weighing 1 1/4 pounds will yield only about 1/4 pound of edible flesh. The only part of the scallop eaten in the United States is the muscle that operates the opening and closing of the shell, with the rest being waste.

Ways to use more of the fish and thereby reduce waste are being explored. Fish byproducts are used to produce gelatin, minced fish, and nutraceuticals such as condroitin sulfate. Fish oil, fishmeal, and fish protein concentrate also provide an opportunity to use more of the fish [25]. Ultimately, will we be able to utilize the entire fish? ■

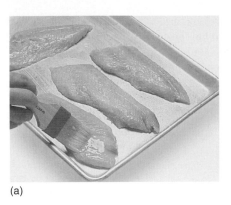
(a)

(b)

(c)

FIGURE 27-8 (a) Brushing the fillets with butter; (b) topping snapper with the tomato concassée; (c) the fish after baking.

Baking

Fish fillets may be used for baking, but often whole fish that have been stuffed and sewed or skewered to prevent loss of stuffing are baked. The fish are usually placed in a shallow, open pan and basted to keep the skin from becoming hard and dry. A moderately heated oven produces the most satisfactory results, especially if the fish are stuffed. Stuffed pompano fillets are shown in Plate XXXI.

Frying

Small whole fish, fillets, or steaks may be fried (Figure 27-9). Pieces of a suitable size for serving are usually dipped in water, milk, or egg mixed with milk, then in a dry ingredient, such as cornmeal, flour, or fine crumbs. If the fish is to be deep-fat fried, the temperature of the fat should not exceed 385° to 395°F (196° to 202°C) so that the fish will be fully cooked by the time it is browned.

FIGURE 27-9 These Florida mullet fillets were breaded in cornmeal and fried in oil until golden brown. Mashed potatoes, fresh sliced tomatoes, and okra are tasty accompaniments.
(*Courtesy of Florida Department of Agriculture and Consumer Services, Bureau of Seafood and Aquaculture*)

Steaming and Simmering

Fish may be cooked by steaming or simmering. These are closely related methods of cookery, varying in the amount of the cooking liquid used. Fish to be steamed may be placed on a rack over a boiling liquid with a tight cover on the pan, and cooked until done. Steaming may also be done in the oven in a covered pan, or the fish may be wrapped tightly in aluminum foil. The foil retains moisture, and the fish cooks in an atmosphere of steam. Finnan haddie, which is a cured fish, retains its characteristic flavor particularly well when it is steamed and served with melted butter.

Fish that are simmered are covered with a liquid and cooked just below the boiling point. The fish hold their form better if tied in cheesecloth, wrapped in parchment paper, or placed in a wire basket in the water. Large, firm-fleshed fish are better cooked by this method, because the flesh does not fall apart as readily as less firm or fatty fish. Adding 3 tablespoons of vinegar, lemon juice, or white wine and 1 1/2 tablespoons of salt per quart of water seasons fish well. Fish cooked in moist heat are usually served with a sauce.

Microwave Cooking

Fish can be prepared in a variety of ways using the microwave oven, including soups and chowders, appetizers, and main dishes. Generally, fillets or steaks are arranged in a baking dish, with the thickest portions toward the outside of the dish. They may be brushed with melted butter or lemon juice, covered with waxed paper, and microwaved on medium-high or high. The dish should be rotated halfway during the cooking period unless a turntable is available.

Cooking Shellfish

Shellfish, the flesh of which appears to differ in structure from that of finfish, are much firmer and are easily toughened by high temperatures. Whether the differences are due to the amount and kind of connective tissue is not certain. Nevertheless, in cooking most shellfish, high

FOCUS ON SCIENCE

Why Do Crustaceans (Shrimp, Lobster, and Crab) Turn Pink when Cooked?

Lobster, shrimp, and crab shell have two colors: blackish and orange-pink (similar to the ones in carrots). Crustaceans look blackish while alive because the orange-pink color exists but is hidden. The blackish color is due to protein chains. These protein chains hide the orange-pink molecules by wrapping around and containing them. When heat is applied, the protein chains uncoil (denature) and release the orange-pink molecules. The orange color is no longer hidden, and the shell turns orange-pink.

---

temperatures and long cooking should be avoided. Moist-heat methods are generally satisfactory, but if the shellfish are cooked in a liquid medium, as in the making of oyster stew, a simmering temperature of 181° to 185°F (82° to 85°C) should be used.

Live lobsters are parboiled in salted water (two teaspoons of salt per quart of water). The water should be boiling when the lobster is added but kept at a simmering temperature once it has been added. Simmering for about 12 minutes is recommended, depending on the size of the lobster. Overcooking toughens the flesh. After parboiling, the flesh is removed from the shell and prepared in any desired manner. The pink coral on the outside adds attractiveness to the lobster meat and should not be discarded. The edible meat is in the claws, which must be cracked to remove the meat, and in the tail. The whole tail may be separated from the body and the segmented shell removed.

Simmering is the basic method of cooking raw shrimp. Depending on the size, the time of cooking is three to five minutes or until the shrimp begin to curl and turn pink. Shrimp can be simmered, the shell removed, and then the sand vein along the back taken out. The sand vein is the intestinal tract located just under the outer curved surface. Alternatively, the shrimp can first be peeled and then simmered. Either way, 1 1/2 pounds of raw shrimp yield about 3/4 pound of cooked ready-to-eat shrimp. The sand vein often remains in canned shrimp and must be removed before this product is used. Large shrimp are often deep-fat fried. Plate XXXI shows sweet-and-sour shrimp served over rice.

CHAPTER SUMMARY

- There are thousands of different species of fish worldwide. Shrimp, tuna, and salmon are among the most popular fish in the United States.

- Many fish are lower in fat and cholesterol compared to other meats. The fat in fish is highly unsaturated. Omega-3 polyunsaturated fatty acids, found in many varieties of fish, have been associated with health benefits.

- Two major categories of fish are vertebrate fish with fins and shellfish. Finfish may be further classified as flat or round fish, lean or fat, and fresh or salt water. Shellfish are subdivided into mollusks and crustaceans. Mollusks may be univalves, bivalves, or cephalopods. The shells of live oysters, clams, and mussels must be closed or snap shut if alive to be suitable for use.

- Fish may be marketed as whole fish, drawn, dressed, steaks, or fillets. Fish may be fresh or frozen. Shellfish are generally marketed in the shell, shucked, headless, or precooked. Roe is the mass of eggs from finfish and consists of sacs of connective tissue enclosing thousands of eggs.

- Seafood are harvested from oceans, rivers, and lakes. Aquaculture or fish farming is increasingly providing the fish for our tables. The consideration of the long-term health of the ecosystem promotes sustainability of our seafood supplies.

- The FDA maintains an Office of Seafood as part of its regulatory responsibility. Seafood processors, packers, and warehouses are required to follow an HACCP system and are inspected by the FDA. The FDA also sets standards for seafood contaminates, administers the National Shellfish Sanitation Program, and analyzes fish and fishery products for hazards.

- The National Oceanic Atmospheric Administration in the U.S. Department of Commerce operates a voluntary system of seafood inspection and grading that is paid for by the processor. Quality grades are determined largely on the basis of appearance, uniformity, absence of defects, character, flavor, and odor of the product.

- The first step in purchasing seafood is to assess the retailer. Fresh finfish have firm flesh, a stiff body, and tight scales. The gills are red, and the eyes are bright and unsunken. Fresh seafood do not smell fishy. Frozen fish should be solidly frozen, with no discoloration or brownish tinge in the flesh. Mollusks in the shell should always be alive when purchased.

- Value-added fish products are available. Minced fish products are used in the production of fish sticks and portions. Surimi is a minced fish product that is processed to produce simulated crab legs. Cured, canned, and breaded fish are additional kinds of fish products.

- Seafood are the most perishable of flesh foods. Bacteria, viruses, natural toxins, and chemical toxins can result in foodborne illnesses associated with the consumption of seafood. The FDA has released a consumer advisory about the risks of mercury in fish.

- Fresh fish should be held at 32°F (0°C). Live shellfish should be stored in a moist environment at 41°F (5°C). If fish are not to be used within two days of purchase, they should be frozen. Rapid freezing is desirable to prevent the formation of large ice crystals.

- Fish may be cooked by dry- or moist-heat methods because it has very little connective tissue. Overcooking should be avoided. Fish is fully cooked when the flakes separate easily. A minimum safe temperature of 145°F (63°C) is recommended.

- Fish may be broiled, baked, fried, steamed, simmered, poached, or cooked in the microwave. Sauces or flavored liquids used during cooking can enhance the flavor.

- Shellfish are much firmer and are easily toughened by high temperatures, thus shrimp, lobster, and clams are often simmered. The water should be boiling when a lobster is added.

STUDY QUESTIONS

1. How do fish and shellfish differ? Suggest subclassifications for both fish and shellfish and give several examples from each group.

2. (a) Describe five market forms in which fish may be sold.

   (b) In what forms may minced fish appear on the retail market?

   (c) What is *surimi*? How is it used in the seafood industry?

3. Why has there been an emphasis in recent years on increasing the consumption of fish in the American diet?

4. (a) Describe characteristics of fresh fish.

   (b) Suggest appropriate procedures for handling and storing fish. Explain why these procedures are necessary.

   (c) Explain why shellfish should never be eaten raw.

   (d) What are some possible causes of illness when seafood are not properly handled or prepared?

5. Describe or identify the following:

   (a) Green shrimp

   (b) Northern lobster

   (c) Spiny or rock lobster

   (d) Scallops

   (e) Fish roe

   (f) Finnan haddie

   (g) Tuna

6. List five principal varieties of salmon.

7. Explain why it is appropriate to cook fish with either dry- or moist-heat methods.

8. Describe satisfactory procedures for cooking fish by each of the following methods:

   (a) Broiling

   (b) Baking

   (c) Frying

   (d) Steaming

   (e) Microwaves

9. What chief precaution should be taken when cooking shellfish? Why?

BEVERAGES 28

A wide variety of commercially produced beverages is on the market. This market continues to diversify, with beverage production increasingly being targeted to specific market segments. This trend toward diversification can be observed even with a basic beverage such as coffee. No longer do we simply ask, "Coffee—black or with cream?" Today, there are flavored coffees, espresso, and more. Unique beverages are available to satisfy and interest consumers with varied preferences and needs. Beverages have been formulated for such groups as children, older people, physically active individuals, and persons with special dietary needs.

In this chapter, the following topics will be discussed:

- Consumption trends of beverages
- Water
- Carbonated beverages
- Functional beverages
- Noncarbonated fruit beverages
- Alcoholic beverages
- Coffee
- Tea
- Cocoa and chocolate

CONSUMPTION TRENDS OF BEVERAGES

Over the years, the beverages we choose have changed. The U.S. Department of Agriculture (USDA) food disappearance data for several beverages are provided in Table 28-1. In the 1940s, 45 gallons of milk were available in the food supply per person compared to only 21 gallons per person in 2005 [44]. In contrast, bottled water consumption has grown dramatically to 25 gallons per capita in 2005 from only 1.6 gallons per capita in 1976. Bottled water represents a $5.2 billion market that is growing nearly 30 percent per year [22].

Carbonated soft drinks are still the most widely consumed beverage in the United States. Although our consumption of coffee has been relatively stable in the last 20 years, our current level of consumption is down from the 1940s when 40 to 45 gallons were reported per capita.

WATER

Only one percent of the water on the earth is available for drinking and other uses [42]. Our water comes from surface water (lakes and rivers) or ground water (wells). Surface water supplies 74 percent of the water used in the United States. The Environmental Protection Agency (EPA) regulates public water systems under the Safe Water Drinking Act. Water quality is also regulated by the Clean Water Act. This federal law governs the control of water pollution.

Bottled water has become the second largest commercial beverage, only surpassed by soft drinks in per capita consumption annually [44]. Bottled water is convenient to carry and may be perceived by some consumers as "better than" tap water. Compared to other beverage choices, water is calorie free, yet thirst quenching. *Enhanced waters*, containing functional ingredients such as vitamins, calcium, or super oxygenation, may become the next big trend in bottled waters [22].

Around 75 percent of the water bottlers use ground water, although the municipal water system is the source of water for other companies [42]. Generally the water is further filtered and treated to offer the quality desired by consumers. Filtering and water treatment methods include distillation, reverse osmosis, absolute 1 micron filtration, and ozonation (Table 28-2). Like other foods, the FDA regulates bottled water. The FDA definitions for types of bottled water are provided in Table 28-3. Seltzer, soda, tonic, and some sparkling waters are considered to be soft drinks and thus will be discussed later in the chapter.

TABLE 28-1 U.S. Per Capita Food Availability of Beverages in Gallons per Year

	2005	1995	1985
Total beverage milk	21.0	23.9	26.7
Tea	7.9	7.9	7.1
Coffee	18.5	15.3	19.3
Bottled water	25.4	11.6	5.1
Diet soft drink	16.0	13.8	10.4
Regular soft drink	35.5	36.8	30.8
Fruit juices	8.2	8.1	7.7
Fruit drinks, cocktails, and ades	13.9	15.0	10.2
Canned or bottled iced tea	0.47	NA	NA
Vegetable juices	21.3	21.8	23.8
Beer	21.3	21.8	23.8
Wine	2.4	1.7	2.4
Distilled spirits	1.4	1.2	1.8

Source: Reference 44

TABLE 28-2 Water Treatment Methods

Water Treatment Methods	Description
Distillation	Water is turned into the vapor and then condensed into water again. Minerals are too heavy to vaporize and thus are left behind.
Reverse osmosis	Water is forced through membranes to remove minerals and other substances.
Absolute 1 micron filtration	Filters are used to remove particles larger than 1 micron.
Ozonation	Ozone gas (O_3) is used as an antimicrobial agent for disinfection purposes. Bottlers often use this method instead of chlorine that may leave a chlorine taste and odor. Ozone may be produced with action of electricity on oxygen.

Source: References 1, 5

TABLE 28-3 FDA Standard Definitions for Types of Bottled Water

Types of Bottled Water	Definitions
Artesian	Water from a well that taps a confined aquifer. When tapped, pressure in the aquifer often pushes the water to the surface. Artesian well water may be more pure; however, there is no guarantee artesian waters are cleaner than water from an unconfined aquifer.
Mineral	Water from an underground source with at least 250 parts per million of total dissolved solids. Minerals and trace elements must be present in the water and not added later.
Purified	Water treated to meet the U.S. Pharmacopeia definition of pure water.
Spring	Water from an underground formation that flows naturally to the earth's surface. May be collected through a borehole if the water obtained is the same as that feeding the spring. Must be collected in the spring.
Well	Water from a hole bored or drilled into an aquifer.
Sparkling	Water that contains the same amount of carbon dioxide as present when it emerged from source. Carbon dioxide may be replaced to obtain the original carbon dioxide levels.

Source: References 1, 15, 42

CARBONATED BEVERAGES

Carbonation is the process of saturating the beverage with carbon dioxide, giving unique zest to the drink. The carbonation also provides protection against bacterial spoilage during storage [17].

The first step in the production of carbonated soft drinks is the preparation of a syrup for sweetening. To this are added flavoring, coloring, acid, and a preservative, with continuous mixing and blending. Finally, the syrup is diluted to the finished beverage level, which is carbonated in a pressurized carbon dioxide vessel, or carbo-cooler. The carbonated beverage is then pumped to the filler, which meters the liquid into a sterile container that is sealed [17]. Many carbonated drinks are made without sugar, using alternative sweeteners such as aspartame. Refer to Chapter 11 for more information about high-intensity, alternative sweeteners.

Sparkling water beverages contain carbon dioxide, a low level of sweetener, which is often fructose, and flavoring. Enticing names such as *summer strawberry*, *wild mountain berry*, *Mexican lime*, *fiesta orange*, and *orchard peach* are often attached to these flavored waters. Club soda is carbonated water with sodium bicarbonate and potassium carbonate added. The original seltzer is simply carbonated water, but seltzers are also sold with sweetener and flavor ingredients added. Tonic water is a carbonated water flavored with quinine.

Many carbonated beverages contain caffeine, including cola drinks, pepper products, and many citrus products. The labeling of caffeine content of beverages is not mandated at this time but has been recommended. The caffeine content of 56 national-brand and 75 private-label, store-brand carbonated beverages was analyzed in a recent study. These researchers found the caffeine content of beverages varied widely, from 4.9 to 74 milligrams of caffeine per 12 ounces of beverage [4]. The caffeine level for the national-brand beverages was found to be more consistent compared to the store brands which could vary by production lot. In another study, carbonated fountain beverages from restaurants were found to contain higher caffeine levels than their canned counterparts, although the fountain items showed more variability [18]. Caffeine content of some carbonated drinks is shown in Table 28-4.

TABLE 28-4 Caffeine Content of Selected Foods and Beverages

	Caffeine (mg)
Coffee (5 oz cup)	
Drip method	110–150
Percolated	64–124
Instant	40–108
Decaffeinated	2–5
Instant decaffeinated	2
Tea (5 oz cup)	
1-minute brew (black)	21–33
3-minute brew (black)	35–46
5-minute brew (black)	39–50
Instant	12–28
Iced tea (12 oz can)	22–36
Chocolate products	
Hot cocoa (6 oz cup)	2–8
Milk chocolate (1 oz)	1–15
Soft drinks (12 oz can)	
Pepsi One	57.1 ± 3.3
Mountain Dew	54.8 ± 2.5
Tab	48.1 ± 1.9
Diet Coke	46.3 ± 1.7
RC Cola	45.2 ± 4.1
Dr. Pepper	42.6 ± 2.0
Sunkist Orange	40.6 ± 0.2
Pepsi	38.9 ± 1.0
Coca-Cola	34.4 ± 1.5
Barq's Root Beer	22.4 ± 1.4

Source: References 2, 4, 18, 41

FUNCTIONAL BEVERAGES

Some beverages that do not fit traditional definitions have been grouped as New Age or functional beverages and are moving into the mainstream. Energy drinks, some isotonic (sport) beverages, herbal and green teas, fortified waters, and some caffeinated drinks are part of this group. The functional beverage market grew 14 percent from 2002 to 2007 [30]. Consumers are interested in functional beverages for a variety of reasons, including the desire to make up for unhealthy eating, supplement healthy habits, avoid empty calories, or to address a specific health issue [30].

Now on the market are bottled waters with added calcium or vitamins and other beverages with antioxidants, fiber, or omega-3 fatty acids [30]. Smart drinks contain substances such as herbal extracts (ginseng, ginkgo leaf, and ma huang), guarana, amino acids, vitamins, minerals, and other ingredients that allegedly stimulate energy and alertness. Some of these ingredients are untested and their short- and long-term effects are controversial. The FDA has relaxed its oversight in this area since passage in 1994 of the Dietary Supplement Health and Education Act [19, 20].

Food processors are faced with some challenges in the formulation of functional beverages. Calcium can result in a chalky mouthfeel, iron and potassium may leave a metallic aftertaste, and other nutrients likewise can cause undesirable flavors [14]. Successful functional beverages will overcome objectionable sensory attributes to result in a pleasing, as well as healthful, beverage.

Sports or Isotonic Beverages

Sports beverages are designed to prevent dehydration during vigorous exercise and to give a quick energy burst. They should have the same osmotic pressure as human blood to allow for rapid absorption. Typically sports beverages have a low level of carbonation and a carbohydrate content of 6 to 8 percent (compared with soft drinks, which have 10 to 12 percent). The sweeteners added to sports drinks are usually glucose, maltodextrins, and sucrose. For electrolyte replacement, sports drinks contain ingredients such as monopotassium phosphate, sodium chloride, sodium citrate, and potassium chloride [17]. The ideal beverage for fluid replacement in athletes during training and competition appears to be one that tastes good, does not cause gastrointestinal discomfort when consumed in large volumes, promotes rapid fluid absorption and maintenance of extracellular fluid volume, and provides energy to working muscles [10].

Energy Drinks

Like other kinds of functional beverages, the popularity of energy drinks has grown considerably. Some of these energy drinks report increased energy and endurance in their advertisements. Ingredients may include B vitamins, botanicals such as ginseng and guarana, D-ribose, L-carnitine, taurine, and peptides [32]. Peer-reviewed research is needed on these and other ingredients found in energy drinks [25].

The term *energy drinks* has also been used to describe beverages with high levels of caffeine and sugar. Some of these beverages have been banned or restricted in European countries. The high levels of caffeine in these beverages can cause a rapid heart rate, hypertension, tremors, or increase the risk of dehydration during exercise [25].

NONCARBONATED FRUIT BEVERAGES

Fruit beverages contain fruit or juice (1.5 to 70 percent) and water, as well as sweeteners, flavoring, coloring, and preservatives. These are not fruit juices, although fruit may be a predominant ingredient. They can be either low calorie or high calorie. Acidulants are normally added. Acidulants contribute to flavor and may act as preservatives to restrict microbial growth by lowering the pH. The addition of flavoring substances strengthens and deepens the flavor of the fruit juice in the drink. The trend in recent years has been toward an increased demand for flavors obtained from natural sources. New Age juice drinks often feature combinations of exotic fruit flavors, such as mango/passion fruit, kiwi/strawberry, and pear/clove [16, 17]. Juice drinks may also contain various vegetable gums, cellulose derivatives, and starch in small amounts to add body and affect the mouthfeel of the beverage [35].

Fruit beverages are susceptible to microbial spoilage and fermentation. Therefore protection by pasteurization or added preservatives is required. Pasteurization is accomplished by heat or microfiltration, with the product often being heated in-line and then placed in aseptic packaging. The approval of hydrogen peroxide as a packaging sterilant in 1984 made possible the packaging of many beverages in laminated boxes, which are available in various sizes. Alternatively, the beverage may be pasteurized by filling the package, closing, and then heating it. A hot-filling method, involving filling the package with the hot product and turning the package so that all sides contact the product, may also be used [17].

Fruit smoothies have become a popular beverage that may be prepared in the home or purchased when eating out. Smoothies are a frozen blended beverage composed of fruit, fruit juices, yogurt, or other dairy ingredients. In the commerial market, a variety of healthy or functional ingredients may be added to create a unique beverage [34]. Fruit smoothies are shown in Figure 28-1.

ALCOHOLIC BEVERAGES

Three general classifications of alcoholic beverages exist: wines, beers, and spirits. Alcoholic beverages are consumed as a drink but may also be used as a flavoring in cooking. Depending on the recipe and method of cooking, residual alcohol may be present in the prepared dish. A brief overview of alcoholic beverages follows.

(a)   (b)

FIGURE 28-1 (a) Bananas, orange juice, strawberries, sherbet, and a lemon-lime carbonated beverage are blended for this smoothie. (b) The fruit garnish may be as tasty as the fruit beverage. *(Courtesy of Dole Food Company, Inc.)*

Wine

Wine is usually made from the juice of grapes. Other fruits such as pears, apples, or cherries may also be used to make wine, however. The process of making wine involves the chemistry of fermentation, as does the making of all alcoholic beverages. The process of fermentation is simple in that yeast acts on sugar, converting it into alcohol and carbon dioxide gas [26]. Finished wines usually contain 10 to 14 percent alcohol.

In wine production, the grapes are crushed to release the juice. If making white wine, the juice is separated from the skins. Next, the wine is fermented in tanks either through the action of natural yeast found on the grape skins or added yeast. During fermentation, other microorganisms may grow and either positively or negatively affect the characteristics of the wine. Once fermentation is complete, red wines are separated from the grape skins. Whether making white or red wines, the yeast and other solids are allowed to settle. These solids are called the *lees* [26]. Additional impurities may be removed from the wine before it is bottled by a process called *fining*. Some wines may undergo a second fermentation to produce desired characteristics. After fermentation, wines are aged to develop the flavor and aroma. Red wines are usually aged longer than white wines. Some wines are aged in oak to add an oaky flavor [29].

Beer

Beer is made from water, hops, and malted barley [29]. Like wine, beer is fermented by yeast to produce an alcohol content of 2 to 6 percent. A vine, called *Humulus lupulus*, produces the small flowers which are the hops used in beer [29].

The first step in brewing beer is to malt the barley by steeping it in water until it begins to germinate. Next, the malt is heated and dried in a process called *kilning*. The dried malt is then cracked in a mill, and hot water is added. The steeping of the malt in the hot water is called *mashing*. During this step, a sweet liquid called *wort* is produced. Brewing is the boiling of the wort, to which the hops have been added. Following brewing, the wort is cooled and strained. Yeast is added to the wort to begin fermentation and produce the beer. The beer is conditioned during storage to develop flavor and filtered to remove particles causing cloudiness. Unlike wine, beers are not aged but instead should be consumed as soon as possible after production. The type of beer, ales or lagers, as well as the unique qualities of an individual beer is affected by variations to the basic brewing process described.

Spirits

Spirits or liquors are alcoholic beverages such as gin, rum, tequila, vodka, whisky, and brandy that have a high alcohol content. These beverages are made by distilling the liquid from grains, vegetables, or other ingredients such as molasses that has been first fermented. Distillation concentrates the alcohol. In the United States, spirits are classified by proof. A spirit that contains 40 percent alcohol by volume would be labeled 80 proof.

COFFEE

The coffee plant is apparently native to Ethiopia and other parts of tropical Africa. It was introduced into the Middle Eastern countries in the fifteenth century, and, later, both the growing of the plant and the custom of coffee drinking spread throughout the eastern hemisphere. Coffee was introduced into Java by the Dutch in the seventeenth century and later into South America. Since that time, Brazil has become the largest coffee-producing country in the world. Central America, Colombia, Hawaii, Africa, and Puerto Rico also have climatic conditions favorable to the growth of a fine grade of mild coffee.

The Coffee Plant

The coffee plant grows 6 to 20 feet high, depending on the species, the country in which it is grown, and the local custom of pruning. There are many varieties of coffee, but only a few are grown for commercial use. The original species native to Ethiopia and the one most commonly grown is *Coffea arabica*, but when grown in different soils, altitudes, and climates, this species takes on different characteristics. Arabica, which is now grown chiefly in Central and South America, has a fine full flavor and aroma. A second hardy variety commonly grown in Africa is *Coffea robusta*. Robusta coffee shrubs are best suited to low elevations (about 1,000 feet), and the beans are not as flavorful or as acid tasting as those from arabica coffee plants.

flavor [41]. Coffee acidity is apparently affected by many factors, including variety, altitude at which the plant is grown, processing of the fruit, age of the beans, and the degree of roasting of the beans.

Volatile Substances. Almost 700 volatile compounds have been identified as contributing to the aroma of coffee [37]. The most desirable aroma comes from a delicate balance in composition of volatiles. Sulfur compounds and phenolic compounds are among the main contributors to the characteristic aroma. Many of the flavor substances in a coffee beverage are lost or changed by heat. Therefore, an extended heating period at a high temperature can remove or destroy the desirable aroma and flavor. Long heating even at a low temperature may have the same effect. Reheating a coffee beverage has been shown to decrease organoleptic acceptance by a judging panel at the same time that a loss of volatile substances was shown by gas chromatographic techniques [40].

Bitter Substances. Bitterness in coffee becomes more pronounced as the polyphenol content increases. Polyphenol solubility apparently increases with temperature, and a boiling temperature releases polyphenols readily from the coffee bean. Caffeine contributes to bitterness. Coffee also contains other substances that produce distinctly bitter tastes.

Caffeine. Pharmacologists classify caffeine as a mild stimulant of the central nervous system and consider it one of the world's most widely used drugs [24]. Caffeine is one of a group of chemical compounds called *methylxanthines*, which occur naturally in the parts of many species of plants, including coffee beans, tea leaves, cocoa beans, and cola nuts. Theobromine, a somewhat milder stimulant than caffeine, is also a methylxanthine and is found in chocolate and cocoa. Table 28-4 gives the caffeine content of some common foods and beverages.

Kinds of Coffee Beverages

Decaffeinated Coffee. Some people want the flavor of the coffee beverage without caffeine. Most of the caffeine can be removed from the green coffee beans to yield decaffeinated coffee. Although decaffeinated coffee generally has good flavor, there is a slight loss of the usual coffee flavor during processing.

Several processes are available for use in accomplishing decaffeination. These extraction processes primarily employ (1) water, (2) steam, (3) carbon dioxide, (4) ethyl acetate, (5) methylene chloride, or (6) coffee oils. The FDA regulates the level of solvent residue that may remain in the decaffeinated bean. Much of the decaffeination of coffee beans is presently being done in Europe.

Instant Coffee Products. Instant or soluble coffee is convenient. It is composed of dry, powdered, water-soluble solids produced by dehydrating very strong, brewed coffee, which is often percolated under vacuum to minimize the loss of flavor substances. Some carbohydrate may be added. The flavor of instant coffee is similar to that of freshly brewed coffee, but the aroma is usually somewhat lacking in comparison with the fresh-brewed beverage. The quality of soluble coffee flavor can be improved by capturing desirable aroma compounds in coffee oil and adding them back to the coffee powder [19].

Some soluble coffees are freeze-dried. In this process, the strong, brewed coffee is first frozen and then dried by vaporization in a vacuum. Like instant coffees produced by other methods, the freeze-dried products are reconstituted by adding boiling water according to directions on the package. Soluble coffees should be kept packaged in water- and airtight containers because they are hygroscopic.

Specialty Coffee Beverages. How Americans drink coffee has changed over the years. The growth of premium, upscale coffee shops such as Starbucks has resulted in the popularity of a wide variety of coffee beverages, many of which are based on espresso [21]. *Espresso* coffee is prepared from a French roast coffee and heated by steam. Expresso is a strongly flavored, rich beverage prepared with special equipment (Figure 28-3). *Espresso machiatto* is espresso with a small amount of steamed milk. *Cappuccino* is prepared with one-third espresso, one-third steamed milk, and one-third foamed milk (Figure 28-4). *Caffè latte* is composed of one-third espresso and two-thirds steamed milk without the foam. A strong coffee with steamed milk is called *café au lait* [28]. Additionally, a variety of flavored coffees such as hazelnut and French vanilla

FIGURE 28-3 An espresso coffee machine *(Courtesy of KRUPS North America)*

Cappuccino.

Caffé latte.

FIGURE 28-4 Cappuccino and caffè latte have become popular coffee beverages. *(Source: Reference 28)*

may be purchased, or coffee beverages may be prepared from sweet, icy, blended coffees.

Iced Coffee. An iced beverage that possesses the maximum flavor is made by pouring a freshly made, strong coffee infusion over crushed ice in a glass. Strong infusions, whether combined hot or cold with ice, are made with a larger-than-usual amount of coffee per cup of water rather than by longer-than-usual infusion periods. Long infusion periods decrease flavor and aroma and increase bitterness. Iced coffee is also available in bottles to be refrigerated and served cold.

Coffee Substitutes. Parched ground cereals and/or roots are used as coffee substitutes. Their flavor is due largely to various products formed during the heating process. **Chicory** is sometimes added to coffee substitutes for a somewhat bitter taste. Chicory can also be blended with coffee. This mixture is preferred over coffee alone by some people. A darker color results from the addition of chicory, but the characteristic coffee flavor and aroma are decreased. The coffee substitutes do not generally produce a stimulating effect as does the caffeine in coffee.

Purchasing and Storage of Coffee

Purchasing. Coffee may be purchased ground or as whole beans. The kind of bean and roast should be considered in relation to your coffee preferences. Whole beans provide an level of freshness difficult to obtain when purchasing a ground coffee. If ground, coffee should be vacuum sealed to reduce exposure to oxygen. Once opened, however, the coffee will begin to lose flavor and quality.

Good grades of coffee are characterized by a sharp, more desirable flavor compared with the flat, neutral flavor of poor grades. A middle grade of coffee, purchased and used fresh, yields a better beverage than a high grade that is stale. Poor grade coffee, although less expensive, may not result in the anticipated cost savings because a larger amount of coffee may be required for an acceptable flavor compared to a high quality coffee.

Storage. The freshness of coffee is an important factor affecting the quality of the coffee beverage. Coffee is best when it is freshly roasted. It deteriorates on standing. Thus for best flavor, whole-bean coffee should be stored

FOCUS ON SCIENCE

How Are Coffees Flavored?

Hazelnut, Irish cream, French vanilla, and other flavors of coffee are available. Flavors may be added to whole or ground coffee. The coffee chosen for flavoring should be a low-acid, full-flavored bean that is a light or medium roast. Espresso, a dark roast, is also sometimes flavored. The amount of flavor added to the beans or ground coffee is usually 2 to 3 percent by weight. So how it is added?

Whole Bean Coffee

- The flavors are suspended in a liquid system composed of propylene glycol or vegetable oil.
- The flavors are atomized—sprayed on or applied in a rotating mixer.

- The beans are likely to have a glossy sheen from the addition of the flavor.

Ground Coffee

- The beans may be flavored before grinding, but the flavor tends to stick to the grinders. Later batches of beans may be contaminated with unintended flavors.
- The addition of dried flavors to ground coffee appears to be a preferable flavoring method to avoid cross-contamination.

Source: Kuntz, L. A. (1996, July). Coffee and tea beverages. *Food Product Design.* Retrieved August 17, 2008, from http://www.foodproductdesign.com/articles/465/465_0796DE.html

for about a week or less in an airtight container [9]. Although coffee beans can be used for several weeks after purchase, the flavor will be less desirable. If a longer storage time is needed, freezer storage is preferable to refrigerated storage because the moisture and odors present in refrigerators will promote quality deterioration.

Ground coffee becomes flat or stale more rapidly than coffee in the bean. The chief cause of staleness has been assumed to be the oxidation of certain coffee constituents. Because ground coffee has a high level of oxygen exposure, it is not surpring that it would deteriorate in quality quickly as compared to whole beans. The oxidation theory seems to be inadequate, however, in explaining all the changes brought about in stale coffee. The fat of coffee apparently does not become rancid in the short time required for coffee to become stale. The effect of oxygen on roasted coffee is rapid during the first three weeks and is thought to affect mainly the flavor constituents. After three weeks, the oxygen probably combines with the oils of the coffee, which results in the development of true rancidity several months later.

Moisture has a pronounced effect in decreasing the storage life of coffee. Tests on volatile substances extracted from coffee show that if the substances are sealed in a vacuum tube, changes are retarded; if the substances are exposed to air, changes occur rapidly; and if the substances are exposed to moisture, the changes are still more pronounced.

Proper sealing of roasted—especially ground—coffee is fundamental. The vacuum type of package from which air is removed before sealing affords more protection than other types of packages. Flavor deterioration in vacuum-packed coffee depends on the extent to which air is removed from the container. Another development involves the use of carbon dioxide gas under pressure in cans after the air is removed.

Grind and Quality

For the best coffee flavor, whole beans should be ground immediately prior to brewing. Coffee grinders are available for home or foodservice use. Coffee may be ground to differing degrees of fineness. Any grind, however, contains particles of many sizes.

Alternately, ground coffee may be purchased. Ground coffees differ basically in the proportion of each size of particles. A *regular grind* contains a higher proportion of coarse particles than a *drip* or *medium grind;* a *fine grind* contains no coarse particles. It is also possible to pulverize coffee, but neither institutional nor home-type brewing equipment is designed for pulverized coffee. Its use in such equipment would result in a bitter-tasting beverage.

Consistency in the grind is important in maintaining consistent quality. As the percentage of large particles in the coffee grind is increased, the brewed beverage is weaker. A foodservice manager should know if the supplier measures and controls consistency of the grind.

Methods of Making Coffee

Good coffee may be brewed by several methods (Figure 28-5). In each method, important factors include control of the water temperature and the time that the coffee is in contact with the water. The temperature of the water should be at least 185°F (85°C) to extract a desirable amount of soluble solids; however, it should not be hotter than 203°F (95°C) to avoid extraction of excessive amounts of bitter substances and loss of many volatile flavor substances.

The amount of coffee used in relation to the water determines the initial strength of the brew. Measures of 1 to 3 tablespoons of coffee per cup (8 ounces) of water yields brews ranging from weak to very strong. Use of 1 1/3 to 1 1/2 tablespoons of coffee per cup of water gives a medium-strength brew. Because coffee "cups" included with many dish or china services are actually only 5-6 ounces, many coffee makers are gauged for this size of "cup." One tablespoon per 6 ounce "cup" of coffee is often recommended but should be adjusted depending on desired strength.

Drip or Filtration. In the drip or filtration method, the water filters through the coffee into the lower compartment of the coffeemaker. In foodservice, an urn is used to make drip or filtered coffee. The upper part of a drip coffeemaker is perforated and holds the coffee grounds, and the lower compartment receives the filtered beverage. The perforations of the upper compartment are covered with thin filter paper or cheesecloth to prevent the passage of coffee grounds into the beverage. If the perforations are too small, the rate of filtration is too slow to yield a desirable beverage.

The drip method probably extracts less of the bitter substances than other methods. If it is not allowed to boil and is not kept hot too long, coffee made by the drip method retains more of the flavor constituents than coffee made by other methods.

Vacuum Filtration. Another type of pot for the filtration method is the vacuum coffeemaker. The upper compartment, which holds the coffee, has an open tube that extends almost to the bottom of the lower compartment. Coffee is usually prevented from passing into the lower compartment by a cloth-covered disk, which is held in place over the tube opening. In some models, a glass rod that fits the tube opening is used instead of the disk. Water is placed in the lower compartment, and the pot is heated until most of the water rises into the upper compartment. The pot is then removed from the source of heat until the water filters through the coffee and passes back into the lower compartment. The upper compartment is removed, and the beverage is carefully reheated to a desirable temperature for serving. The chief difficulties in the use of this method are that the coffee may not be hot when served, or if kept hot, it may boil and lose much of the flavor and aroma.

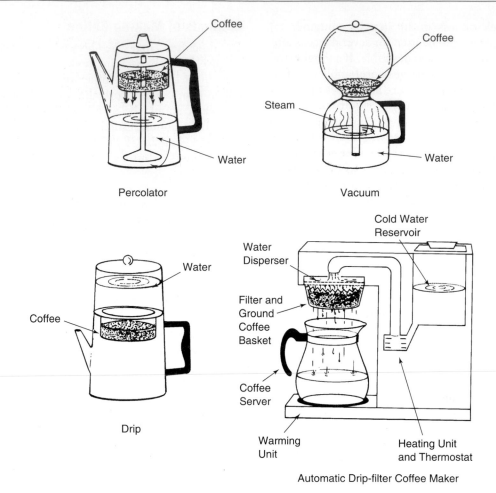

FIGURE 28-5 Types of coffeemakers.

French Press. To make coffee in a French press, a coarse grind is best. Water is brought to a boil, then poured over the coffee grounds in the vessel. After about four minutes, the coffee grounds are "pressed" to the bottom, and the coffee may be served. Some describe the flavor of coffee prepared with a French press as more flavorful; others comment that the coffee can have less clarity. One drawback to this method is that many French press coffeemakers do not have a heat source, and thus the coffee must be served immediately as it will become cold.

Percolation. When coffee is percolated, heated water is forced upward through a tube into the coffee compartment. The water filters through the coffee several times before the beverage is of desirable strength. The water is probably not at the boiling point when it is in contact with the coffee, but the beverage is close to the boiling point when it is ready to be served. Unless the construction of the pot is good and the time of percolating is carefully controlled, much of the flavor and aroma may be lost by this method. The time required varies with the speed of percolation and with the quantity of coffee made. Usually

six to eight minutes is adequate to make four to six cups of coffee.

Steeping. Although steeped coffee is sometimes described as *boiled*, the beverage made by heating the coffee and water together is more desirable in flavor if it is not allowed to boil. Steeping (extracting flavor below the boiling point) extracts much less of the bitter substances from coffee than boiling. Coffee boiled for one minute is distinctly more bitter than coffee heated from 185° to 203°F (85° to 95°C). This method may be convenient for use on picnics and camping excursions. If egg white is mixed with the coffee before the water is added, the temperature must rise high enough to coagulate the dilute solution of egg to clarify the beverage. Boiled coffee made with egg is more bland than that made without egg because of the combination of egg albumin with the polyphenol compounds. The length of steeping varies with the temperature of the water that is mixed with the coffee and with the fineness of the coffee grind. Hot water is preferable because less time is required to make the beverage than when cold water is used. Short infusion periods usually yield better-flavored coffee than longer periods.

Other Factors Affecting Coffee Quality

The Coffee Pot. Pots made of glass, earthenware, or enamelware are good choices for coffeemaking. Some metals form compounds with caffeine and probably with other constituents of coffee and thus are best avoided. Metallic pots impart a metallic flavor to coffee. Stainless steel is resistant to attack and, therefore, its effect on the flavor of coffee is negligible. Chrome and nickel plating show no staining or corrosion when used in a coffee pot.

A clean coffee pot is essential to making a good coffee beverage. The pot should be washed with hot soapy water or scoured as necessary to remove the oily film that collects on the inside. Thorough rinsing is essential. A pot that retains a stale coffee odor is not a clean pot and will mar the flavor of the best-made coffee. Regular cleaning schedules should be employed for coffee-making equipment used in foodservice establishments.

Water. The water used to brew coffee should be free of any undesirable elements picked up in pipelines, boilers, or water tanks. You should never brew coffee with water you would not drink. Soft water or water of low hardness gives coffee a more desirable flavor than very hard or alkaline water. Water having a high carbonate or bicarbonate content and water that has passed through an ion-exchange softening system (and thus is high in sodium ions) will not filter through coffee in a drip or vacuum pot as rapidly as naturally soft water. This means an increase in both the time of contact with the coffee and the amount of material extracted, which can be objectionable.

Temperature. The optimum temperature for brewing a good coffee beverage is probably 185° to 203°F (85° to 95°C). Boiling produces a distinctly bitter beverage. Polyphenol substances are more soluble at boiling than at 203°F (95°C). The longer the heating period, even at lower temperatures, the higher the percentage of bitter substances dissolved and the greater the loss of flavor substances. Nearly all the caffeine is dissolved at 185° to 203°F (85° to 95°C), and not as many flavor substances are lost than as at higher temperatures. Boiling water may be used to start the preparation of coffee, because the temperature drops once the water comes in contact with the coffee and the pot.

TEA

A legend tells us that one day in 2737 B.C. the Chinese emperor Shen Nung was boiling drinking water over an open fire. He believed that drinking boiled water was a healthy practice. Some leaves from a nearby *Camellia sinensis* plant floated into the pot. The emperor drank the mixture and declared that it gave him vigor of body, contentment of mind, and determination of purpose. Today that potion—tea beverage—is widely consumed throughout the world.

Countries that produce the largest volumes of tea are India and China. Other regions of production include Kenya, Sri Lanka, Turkey, Indonesia, Japan, South America, and Bangladesh. Teas vary according to the age of the leaf, the season of plucking, the soil, and climatic conditions, as well as the method of processing.

The Tea Plant

Tea comes from the leaves of *Camellia sinensis*, a white-flowered evergreen (Figure 28-6). The plant is pruned and cultivated to produce many young shoots. Pluckings may extend over a period of several months (Figure 28-7).

After processing, tea leaves are sorted into sizes by a screening procedure. Grades refer to the leaf size and have nothing to do with the quality or flavor of tea. The largest leaves are orange pekoe, pekoe, and pekoe souchong. The smaller or broken leaves are classified as broken orange pekoe, broken pekoe souchong, broken orange pekoe fannings, and fines (also called "dust")[39].

Processing

Three principal types of tea, differentiated by the method of leaf processing, are black, green, and oolong.

Black Tea. About 82 percent of the tea consumed in the United States is black tea [43]. In the traditional method of its manufacture, the leaves are first withered, a process in which excess moisture is removed. The leaves are then rolled in special machines that release enzymes and juices from the leaves. Next, the leaves ferment in a room with controlled temperature and humidity. Finally, they are dried in ovens. A nontraditional method may be used by some processors to speed production by using machines that finely chop the leaves, thereby shortening the time for withering and fermenting [39].

Green Tea. Only about 17 percent of the tea consumed in the United States is green tea [43]. Green tea is produced by first steaming the leaves to inactivate the enzymes and then rolling and drying. The leaf retains much of its original green color, especially the finer leaves. Older leaves often are a blackish-gray color. The beverage made from green tea is greenish-yellow and is distinctly bitter and astringent. It has little aroma and flavor as compared with black tea because the preliminary steaming destroys the enzymes that produce flavor substances during the fermentation of black tea.

Oolong Tea. Oolong tea is a partially fermented tea. The fermentation period is too short to change the color of the leaf completely; it is only partially blackened. The flavor and aroma of this beverage are intermediate between those produced from green and black teas.

FIGURE 28-6 Tea shoots, showing buds and leaves. *(Copyright © Tea and Coffee Trade Journal)*

FIGURE 28-7 Picking tea leaves, two leaves and a bud at a time. The work is done chiefly by women who carry light bamboo baskets strapped to their backs. *(Courtesy of the U.S. Food and Drug Administration. From FDA Consumer, 30:23[2], 1996)*

Composition

The stimulating characteristic of tea comes from its caffeine content. The tea beverage contains less than half as much caffeine as coffee (see Table 28-4). The actual content of caffeine depends on the method of brewing. Longer brewing results in higher caffeine content.

Tea has been reported to contain a significant amount of folacin [3]. A person could obtain up to 25 percent of the Recommended Dietary Allowance (RDA) for folacin by drinking 5 cups of tea per day. Tea appears to have a negative effect on iron absorption when consumed with a meal [12].

FOCUS ON SCIENCE

What Is White Tea?

First it was green tea, and now it is white tea that is gaining consumer interest. So what is white tea? First, it is produced from the leaves of *Camellia sinensis* plant just like black, oolong, and green tea. Like green tea, it is not fermented. The leaves are allowed to dry in the sun. White tea leaves are specifically picked to be those leaves that are young and still covered with a "down," or short, white hairs. The leaves look white because the down gives a silvery or white appearance. The flavor of white teas is described as light and sweet.

Source: Berry, D. (2008, March). Iced tea gets hotter. *Food Product Design.* Retrieved August 17, 2008, from http://www.foodproductdesign.com/articles/beverage/iced-tea-gets-hotter.html

---

The flavor of tea is influenced by the presence of considerable quantities of polyphenolic substances, which are particularly responsible for astringency. Some of the polyphenols are changed in the oxidation process that takes place when black tea is fermented. They contribute to the characteristic aroma and flavor of this tea. Degradation of other substances, including linolenic acid, amino acids, and carotenes, during the manufacture of black tea may also contribute to flavor and aroma.

Market Forms

A wide variety of teas are available on the market. According to the Tea Association of the U.S.A., approximately 65 percent of the tea brewed in the United States is made with the use of tea bags [43]. Loose tea is gaining in popularity, however, while the use of instant tea mix is declining.

Many scented and flavored teas are marketed. These teas contain such flavorings as oils of peppermint, strawberry, orange, or lemon; spices such as cinnamon or cloves; blackberry leaves; almond; and licorice root. As with coffee, decaffeinated tea is also available and may be flavored.

Instant Teas.   Instant teas are dried products prepared from brewed teas. These teas are particularly useful for preparing iced tea. To serve, simply disperse the tea in cold water and add ice. Instant tea mixes may contain sugar, citric acid, maltodextrins, and flavoring such as lemon. Low-calorie tea products sweetened with aspartame or saccharin are also available.

Herbal Teas.   A variety of herbal teas are on the market. These "teas" contain dried leaves of various plants other than tea. Often they are a mixture of several dried plant materials such as strawberry leaves, apples, hibiscus flowers, rose hips, peppermint, ginger, nutmeg, cinnamon, chamomile, and alfalfa. Herbal teas contain no caffeine but often contain substances that have soothing, stimulating, or euphoric effects. Some potential health hazards are associated with their misuse. For example, long-term use of ginseng may produce hypertension, nervousness, sleeplessness, and edema. So-called dieter's teas may contain senna, aloe, buckthorn, and other plant-derived laxatives that, when consumed in excessive amounts, can cause diarrhea, vomiting, nausea, stomach cramps, chronic constipation, fainting, and perhaps death [27].

Considerations for Tea Making

High-quality teas are brewed under similar conditions as those best for the brewing of coffee. Water is preferably soft and just under boiling temperature. Glass, earthenware, enamelware, or other vitrified ware is recommended because metallic pots impart a metallic taste.

Water Quality and Temperature.   Soft water is preferable to hard alkaline water for making tea because the polyphenol substances in tea may interact with certain salts in hard water to produce an undesirable precipitate.

Water just under boiling temperature is best for brewing tea. Boiling water may volatilize flavor and aroma substances. Water should be freshly boiled with enough oxygen still in it to prevent the flat taste that results from the loss of dissolved gases by boiling.

Quantity of Tea and Length of Infusion.   The aim in making tea is to extract the maximum flavor with a minimum of polyphenol compounds, which are bitter. Flavor substances and caffeine are readily extracted by short infusion periods. Strong beverages of good flavor require more of the beverage-making constituents instead of a longer infusion period. The usual proportion of tea per cup of water is about one teaspoon.

Effect of Lemon Juice.   Tea is lightened by the addition of lemon because the oxidized polyphenolic compounds change color in an acid medium. These substances tend to be dark in an alkaline medium.

Tea-Making Methods

Tea may be made with the use of a tea bag or loose tea. This beverage then may be consumed hot or can be iced to make iced tea.

Tea Bags. The tea bag is placed in water just under boiling and remains in contact with the water until the desired strength is achieved. Many foodservice establishments serve those who order tea with a pot of hot water and the tea bags on the side.

Steeping of Loose Tea. To steep tea, the measured tea is placed in a preheated pot, and boiling water is poured into the pot. The pot is then covered and allowed to stand in a warm place until the desired strength is obtained. Steeping periods usually range from two to four minutes, depending on the temperature and the strength desired. If the maximum quantity of tea is used, four minutes may produce a somewhat bitter beverage. The leaves are strained out of the beverage.

Iced Tea. Iced tea, a favorite drink in the United States, is best made from a larger proportion of tea to water than is normally used for hot tea, because melting ice dilutes the beverage. Lengthy steeping to brew a beverage strong enough to stand dilution extracts too many polyphenol substances. It is believed that a cloudy beverage may result from a complex formed between caffeine and some of the polyphenol substances. This complex may form more readily in iced tea than in hot tea. Its formation is encouraged when larger amounts of polyphenol substances are present. Diluting strong infusions while hot helps to prevent cloudiness.

For sweetening iced tea with sugar, an extrafine granulation that is quickly soluble is desirable. If mint flavor is desired in iced tea, the mint leaves can be crushed and added to the tea leaves before the boiling water is added, or a sprig of mint can be served in the glass of iced tea.

Iced tea dispensers may be used in foodservice establishments. Care should be taken to dismantle, clean, and sanitize these dispensers at least once a day, as is recommended by the FDA, to avoid microbial buildup in the tubing connections.

COCOA AND CHOCOLATE

The cacao tree (*Theobroma cacao*) requires very exacting growing conditions and is cultivated only in an area within 20 degrees of the equator. Much of the world cacao crop now comes from West Africa; however, cocoa originated in Latin America, where Brazil and Ecuador are still large producers.

The cultivated cacao tree is deliberately kept pruned to a height of about 19 feet (6 meters) so that the fruits can be harvested with a long stick. The fruits grow directly on the stem or thick branches of the tree. Full-grown fruits are about 8 inches (20 centimeters) long and 4 inches (10 centimeters) across in an oblong shape. Botanically, the leathery fruits are giant berries. Each berry, or pod, contains 30 to 40 seeds or beans occurring in rows and embedded in a white or pinkish pulp (Figure 28-8).

Processing

Cocoa and chocolate are made by grinding the seeds of the cacao tree. To decrease the bitter taste, the seeds are first fermented. The ripe pods are cut from the tree and chopped open. The seeds, surrounded by the gelatinous pulp, are piled into large heaps or put into special boxes and covered with a layer of leaves. Fermentation then begins; the fruit pulp is digested as the temperature rises. This process is completed within five to seven days; the cocoa flavor has begun to develop. The bean has become

(a)

(b)

FIGURE 28-8 (a) Cocoa pods have a hard semiwoody shell. One pod carries anywhere from 20 to 50 beans. (b) Cocoa beans ready for export. (*Courtesy of Chocolate Manufacturers Association*)

dark brown and its shell thinner. Now the beans can be dried easily, preferably outdoors in the sun. After they are dried, the beans are bagged and shipped to the cocoa processor.

There are many varieties of cacao beans, and the great variation in flavor, color, and other characteristics that exists in cocoa and chocolate products is explained, to a large extent, by the characteristics of the various seeds used to make these products. Usually, there is some blending of the beans of different varieties.

The processor cleans the beans and removes impurities and irregularities; then the beans are roasted to further develop flavor characteristics. The beans next go to a winnowing machine, which cracks them and separates the shell from the bean. The cracked kernels are called *nibs*. The nibs go to grinders and various mills that reduce the particle sizes so that they cannot be detected on the tongue. Heat from this process melts the fat, converting the nibs into a suspension of cocoa solids in cocoa butter called *chocolate liquor* [13]. Chocolate liquor can be (1) solidified without the addition of sugar to form unsweetened chocolate, (2) mixed with sugar and fat to produce sweet chocolate, or (3) processed with sugar and milk to produce milk chocolate.

Chocolate. If chocolate is to be produced from the roasted nibs, the ground liquid mass is refined to a smooth, velvety texture and then subjected to a process called *conching*. This process involves heating the liquid chocolate at a carefully controlled temperature while constantly stirring. The mixture is aerated, some volatile acids and moisture are driven off, and flavor is developed [6]. Additional cocoa butter, emulsifiers, sugar, milk solids, and flavorings may be added at this stage before the liquid mass is molded. Chocolate must be carefully tempered at a controlled temperature while it cools to

ensure that a desirable texture results from the proper type of crystallization of the fat in the finished product.

Cocoa. For the making of cocoa, the liquid mass is pumped into presses from which much of the cocoa butter is squeezed out under high pressure. The remaining solids are formed into a cocoa cake, which is further processed. Eventually it is broken up to form a powder.

Natural- and Dutch-Processed Cocoa. Cocoas may be divided into two main classes: natural processed and Dutch processed. Some chocolate is also Dutch processed.

Dutch processing consists of treating the nibs with alkali, the object being to increase the reddish color and the solubility. The latter effect is accomplished only to a slight degree. Dutch-processed cocoa is distinctly darker than natural-processed cocoa. It also has a reddish tinge. The characteristic chocolate flavor is changed by the alkali treatment. The pH of Dutch-processed cocoa is 6.0 to 8.8, and that of natural-processed cocoa is usually 5.2 to 6.0. The color of such products as chocolate cake may range from cinnamon brown to deep mahogany red as the pH changes from acid to alkaline (see Chapter 18).

Composition

Fat. According to the FDA standard of identity, bitter chocolate contains not less than 50 percent and not more than 58 percent by weight of cocoa fat or cocoa butter. The high-fat content of chocolate produces a beverage richer than that made from cocoa. Cocoas vary in fat content. Breakfast cocoa is a relatively high-fat cocoa and must contain at least 22 percent cocoa fat.

When cocoa is substituted for chocolate, particularly in baked products, approximately three tablespoons of cocoa plus one tablespoon of fat are considered to be equivalent to one ounce of chocolate.

FOCUS ON SCIENCE

Putting the Shine on Solid Chocolate

Cocoa butter has a characteristic melting behavior that gives it properties that are significant in chocolate. At ambient temperatures, it is hard and brittle, giving chocolate its characteristic snap, but it also has a steep melting curve that allows for a complete melting at mouth temperature. The melting behavior is related to the chemical composition of cocoa butter: rich in palmitic (24 to 30%), stearic (30 to 36%), and oleic (32 to 39%) acids. The palmitic and stearic acids are found on the 1 and 3

positions on the triacyglycerol. These positions and the amount of fatty acids make it predictable and account for its sharp melting point. When the chocolate melts and solidifies, because of its fatty acid makeup, it can form crystals in many different forms or positions (I through VI). Form V is required for the characteristic chocolate shine that is achieved through a series of cooling and heating processes that have been found to optimize the production. When the fatty acids change position or into another form (VI), white crystals of fat (bloom) appear on the surface of the chocolate. This is because of the fluctuation of temperature during storage or migration of liquid oils from nut centers.

Source: Gunstone, F. D. (2002). Chapter 24. Food applications of lipids. In *Food Lipids*, edited by C. A. Akoh and D. B. Min, p. 742. New York: Marcel Dekker, Inc.

The fat of chocolate contributes much to its eating quality because it has a sharp melting point that is close to body temperature. This results in rapid melting of the chocolate in the mouth with a smooth, velvety feel and the release of flavor substances.

Starch. Cocoa contains about 11 percent starch and chocolate about 8 percent starch. In preparing a beverage from cocoa and chocolate, a method that cooks the starch results in a more homogeneous beverage in which there is less tendency for the cocoa or chocolate to settle out than a method in which no heat is applied.

The thickening effect of starch must be taken into account when cocoa and chocolate are used in flour mixtures, and the amount of flour must be adjusted accordingly. If cocoa is substituted for chocolate directly, on the basis of weight, it thickens more than chocolate.

Flavor and Color. Chocolate, like many foods, contains a large number of flavor molecules; many have not been chemically identified. Volatile compounds make up a large part of the flavor bouquet. Marked changes in the flavor of chocolate and cocoa occur when these products are heated to high temperatures, especially in the absence of water. Bitter, disagreeable flavors develop, and scorching occurs easily.

Both flavor and color are affected by the phenolic compounds present in the cocoa bean. These substances undergo oxidation to form various reddish-brown compounds that are insoluble in water. Some of the astringent phenolic compounds in the fresh unfermented bean have an extremely bitter taste. These undergo a change during fermentation but are present to a small extent in the fermented bean.

Theobromine and Caffeine. Considerably more theobromine than caffeine is found in cocoa and chocolate. Both substances are methylxanthines, but theobromine is a milder stimulant than caffeine. The theobromine and caffeine contents of various foods containing cocoa or chocolate are listed in Table 28-5.

TABLE 28-5 Theobromine and Caffeine Content of Cocoa Products

	Theobromine (mg/serving)	Caffeine (mg/serving)
Dark sweet chocolate, 1 oz	123.5	15.1
Milk chocolate, 1 oz	38.1	5.4
Chocolate fudge topping, 2 Tbsp	62.7	3.5
Brownies, 1 oz	29.4	2.8
Chocolate chip cookies, one serving	17.6	2.1
Chocolate cake with chocolate frosting, 1/12 cake	161.2	15.8
Chocolate pudding, 1/2 cup	87.5	7.0

Source: Reference 11

Chocolate and Tea: Good for Your Health?

Chocolate contains dietary flavonols (epicatechin and catechin) which may be good for your heart [7]. The flavonol content of chocolates is variable, however. The antioxidants appear to be highest in cocoa powder, followed by unsweetened baking chocolate and dark chocolate [36]. Processors are responding to the potential health benefits of chocolate by developing new foods and products with chocolate. As you enjoy that chocolate treat, do keep in mind that, depending on the type of chocolate and the recipe in which the chocolate is found, you are likely to be consuming a high level of fat and calories.

Tea, if unsweetened, does not add calories, yet has polyphenols (epigallocatechin gallate and theaflavin) which are believed to be healthy. Like chocolate, tea has been associated with promoting heart health. In addition, the polyphenols in tea may have a role in the prevention of cancer [31].

As research continues, the role of chocolate and tea in health will be better understood. ∎

Bloom and Storage Recommendations

Bloom. A grayish-white haze, called *bloom*, may sometimes develop on the surface of chocolate. In addition to the appearance defect, the mouthfeel of solid sweetened chocolate may be granular when bloom develops. Because bloom is a quality defect, preventing bloom is an important consideration for both manufacturers and retailers of chocolate. There are two types of bloom. One type arises from changes in the fat crystals with an accumulation of large fat crystals or agglomerates of fat crystals on the surface of the chocolate. These reflect light, creating the appearance that is called *bloom*. Another type of bloom results from the action of moisture on the sugar ingredients in the chocolate [33].

Bloom may occur for a variety of reasons, including incorrect cooling methods, warm or fluctuating storage temperatures, the addition of fats that are incompatible with cocoa butter, and abrasion or finger marking, particularly under warm conditions. The use of proper tempering temperatures and time periods during the manufacturing process and the use of emulsifiers and modifiers retard bloom formation.

Storage. The avoidance of high storage temperatures is essential in maintaining the quality of chocolate and avoiding the development of bloom. Moisture is also detrimental and encourages lumping in cocoas. Both chocolate and cocoa are best stored at a temperature no higher than 65° to 70°F (18° to 21°C) and 50 to 65 percent relative humidity. Milk chocolate absorbs flavors and odors and should be stored where this cannot occur.

Cooking with Chocolate

Chocolate Melting. When chocolate is melted, care must be used to avoid overheating, which may produce a firm, lumpy mass that does not blend with other ingredients. A low to moderate temperature should be applied to chocolate that has been shaved or chopped into pieces. Heating the chocolate over hot water lessens the danger of overheating. However, care should be taken to avoid getting water into the melting chocolate because the chocolate can seize (suddenly harden), thereby becoming stiff rather than smooth throughout. Chocolate can also be easily melted in the microwave oven. The use of chocolate in coating confections was discussed in Chapter 11.

Methods for Making Cocoa Beverage. Cocoa or hot chocolate can be made by a quick method or a syrup method. In the quick method, the hot milk is poured over a cocoa-sugar mixture in the cup. A disadvantage of the quick method is that the starch is not cooked sufficiently to prevent the cocoa from settling out.

In contrast, preparation of the beverage by either a syrup or a paste method produces more desirable body and flavor than usually results from the quick method. In both the syrup and paste methods, a portion of the chocolate is cooked with water and sugar to form a syrup or a paste. The cooking of the mixture cooks the starch found in the cocoa, or in the case of the paste method, cooks the starch in the cocoa and the added starch. The purpose of the cornstarch is to produce a beverage with more body and to prevent most satisfactorily any tendency of the cocoa to settle. With instant cocoa mixes, the addition of a stabilizer or emulsifier may help to keep the particles dispersed. Proportions and instructions for the syrup and paste methods are provided in Table 28-6.

Because milk is a prominent constituent of cocoa or chocolate beverages, scum formation may occur. It can be retarded by covering the pan or by beating the mixture to produce a light foam. Alternatively, the surface of the cocoa can be covered with whipped topping or marshmallows to prevent scum formation. High temperatures, which may scorch both milk and chocolate, should be avoided (see Chapter 23).

TABLE 28-6 Syrup and Paste Methods for the Preparation of Hot Cocoa and Hot Chocolate

Syrup Method for Hot Cocoa or Hot Chocolate

Make a syrup by boiling the ingredients in either of the cocoa or chocolate ingredient lists for one minute. Evaporation will reduce the volume. Add 3/4 cup of hot milk. The syrup can be made in quantity and stored in the refrigerator, then mixed with hot milk when desired.

Cocoa Recipe	Chocolate Recipe
2 tsp to 1 Tbsp cocoa	1/3 oz chocolate, shaved fine
2 tsp to 1 Tbsp sugar	1 to 1 1/2 Tbsp sugar
1/4 cup water	1/3 cup water

Paste Method for Hot Cocoa or Hot Chocolate

Boil all of the ingredients below for 1 to 2 minutes. Combine with 2 cups of hot milk.

1/2 Tbsp corn starch	1 oz chocolate (or 3 Tbsp cocoa)
1/3 cup water	2 Tbsp sugar

CHAPTER SUMMARY

- Most water bottlers use ground water, but some use purified municipal water. The FDA regulates bottled water and defines the terms such as *artesian*, *spring water*, and others.

- Soft drinks have been "carbonated" with carbon dioxide. Sparkling waters such as club soda, seltzer, and tonic water are included in this category of beverages. Many carbonated beverages, including colas and pepper drinks, contain caffeine. Caffeine levels vary by type of beverage, brand, and potentially within a brand.

- Functional beverages include ingredients such as added calcium, vitamins, or herbs. Sports drinks are designed to prevent dehydration during vigorous exercise and to give a quick energy burst. Energy drinks usually contain high levels of caffeine, sugar, and botanicals. Adverse health effects have resulted in the ban of some energy drinks in Europe.

- Fruit beverages contain fruit or juice (1.5 to 70 percent) and water, as well as sweeteners, flavoring, coloring, and preservatives. These are not fruit juices, although fruit may be a predominant ingredient.

- Wines, beers, and spirits are the three general classifications of alcoholic beverages. The process of making alcoholic beverages involves fermentation. In fermentation, yeast acts on sugar, converting it into alcohol and carbon dioxide gas.

- *Coffea arabica* and *Coffea robusta* are two comon coffee plants. Coffee plants produce cherries which must be dry-, wet-, or semidry-processed to remove the fruit, skin, and pulp surrounding the coffee bean. Beans are roasted to develop flavor and aroma. Coffee roasts are classified by the color of the roasted bean.

- Some of the constituents of coffee include acids, volatile substances, bitter substances, and caffeine. Coffee may be decaffeinated.

- Coffee beans should be ground immediately before brewing for optimum quality. Ground coffee becomes flat more rapidly than whole coffee beans. Vacuum packaging helps to protect freshness.

- Coffee may be brewed using drip filtration, vacuum filtration, French press, percolation, or steeping methods. The temperature of the water should be at least 185°F (85°C). Boiling produces a bitter beverage. The use of 1 1/3 to 1/2 tablespoons of coffee per 8-ounce cup of water gives a medium-strength brew.

- Tea comes from the plant *Camellia sinensis*. Three types of tea are black, green, and oolong.

- Soft water is preferable to hard alkaline water for making tea. Water should be freshly boiled. Glass, earthenware, enamelware, or other vitrified ware is recommended. The usual proportion of tea per cup of water is about one teaspoon. The infusion period should be relatively brief for best flavor.

- Iced tea is best made from a larger proportion of tea to water than is used for hot tea to allow for dilution from ice. Diluting strong infusions while hot helps to prevent cloudiness.

- The cacao tree (*Theobroma cacao*) produces the seeds that are processed into chocolate and cocoa through a series of steps. The cracked bean kernels are called *nibs*. The nibs are ground to produce a suspension of cocoa solids in cocoa butter called *chocolate liquor*. Cocoa may be natural processed or Dutch processed.

- If chocolate is produced from the nibs, the ground liquid mass is refined into a smooth, velvety texture through the conching process. Additional cocoa butter, emulsifiers, sugar, milk solids, and flavoring may be added during conching.

- Cocoa contains about 11 percent starch and chocolate about 8 percent starch. The fat level varies with the type of chocolate. FDA standards of identity define the names that may be used for certain chocolate and cocoa products. A number of flavor molecules are found in chocolate. Heating to high temperatures, especially in the absence of water, will result in bitter, disagreeable flavors. Chocolate also contains the stimulants theobromine and caffeine.

- Bloom is a quality defect exhibiting a grayish-white haze and a granular mouthfeel. It may develop as a result of incorrect cooling temperatures, warm or fluctuating cooling temperatures, the addition of incompatible fats, and abrasion or finger marking. Proper storage conditions are needed to maintain chocolate and cocoa quality.

- When cooking with chocolate, overheating should be avoided to prevent the development of a firm, lumpy mass. To make hot chocolate or cocoa beverages, the use of the syrup or paste method is recommended.

STUDY QUESTIONS

1. **(a)** Describe trends in beverage consumption in the United States.

   (b) How are carbonated soft drinks usually processed?

   (c) What roles do sports drinks play in the beverage market?

   (d) How do fruit drinks differ from fruit juices?

   (e) How is wine produced?

2. From what is coffee made? How is it processed to make it ready for use in preparing a beverage?

3. List the constituents of coffee that contribute to its quality as a beverage. Describe the contributions that each constituent makes.

4. Describe conditions that will aid in preserving freshness in coffee, both in the bean and in the ground.

5. **(a)** Describe three methods for preparing coffee.

   (b) What types of material are preferable for coffee pots?

   (c) How does the type of water used affect coffee quality?

   (d) Why should coffee not be boiled? Explain.

   (e) How is instant coffee produced?

6. Describe differences in processing and characteristics of black, green, and oolong teas.

7. **(a)** Describe two appropriate procedures for the preparation of tea.

   (b) Discuss several factors that are important in the preparation of good quality tea and iced tea.

   (c) What cautions should be kept in mind when using various herbal teas?

8. What is the source of chocolate and cocoa? How are they processed?

9. **(a)** How do natural-processed and Dutch-processed cocoa differ?

   (b) How do chocolate and breakfast cocoa differ in fat and in starch content?

   (c) How might cocoa be appropriately substituted for chocolate in a recipe?

10. Describe *bloom* on chocolate and give possible explanations for its development.

11. How should chocolate and cocoa be stored? Why?

12. Suggest a satisfactory method for preparing cocoa beverage. Explain why this is a good method.

FOOD PRESERVATION AND PACKAGING 29

Food preservation has been practiced for thousands of years, but marked changes have occurred as civilization has developed and technology increased. In early historic times, people learned to dry their supplies of fresh meat and fish in the sun and to store food for the cold winter months. Later they discovered how to smoke and salt these products to extend the time that the foods remained edible.

In the early years of American history, particularly on the frontiers, a precise schedule of work was necessary to harvest crops of fruits, vegetables, and grains at just the right time. Much labor was expended in preserving excesses of these crops, often in root cellars and granaries, for later use when nothing could be grown. Animals were slaughtered and processed quickly, usually in cool weather, to decrease spoilage. Canning had not yet been discovered in the very early days of America—that came later, beginning in France about 1810. During early history, much time was required by members of a household, particularly the housewife, for preparing and preserving food.

Today is very different from the early days in America. The basic food preservation methods used in previous years are still utilized. Added, however, is a whole arsenal of technology for ensuring the availability of a large variety of high-quality foods throughout the year. The future is likely to bring the continued development of new nonthermal preservation methods that use such technologies as pulsed electric field and ultrahigh-pressure processing and sterilization [27, 28, 30, 31, 38].

Much of the processing and initial treatment for the preservation of foods in Western countries is done by the food industry. Consumers, as well as foodservice managers, are accustomed to purchasing canned, frozen, fermented, dried, portioned, and packaged foods. The freezer and the microwave oven form a duo that is widely used for the final storage and then rapid heating of the processed and preserved foods that are purchased.

Despite these trends in commercial preservation and packaging of foods, there are still many places in America, particularly in rural areas and smaller towns, where home gardens are popular and the excess produce is canned, frozen, or dried for future use. Thus, a brief discussion of home-canning and -freezing techniques is provided in Chapter 30.

In this chapter, the following topics will be discussed:

- Causes of food spoilage
- Temperature control for preservation
- Moisture control for preservation
- Preservatives
- Irradiation
- Functions of food packaging
- Regulatory requirements for packaging
- Packaging materials and methods of packaging
- Waste management

CAUSES OF FOOD SPOILAGE

When foods spoil, they become inedible or hazardous to eat because of chemical and physical changes that occur within the food. The two major causes of food spoilage are the growth of microorganisms, including bacteria, yeasts, and molds, and the action of enzymes that occur naturally in the food. Additional causes of food spoilage are nonenzymatic reactions such as oxidation and desiccation, mechanical damage such as bruising, and damage from insects and rodents.

Microorganisms

Although microorganisms can cause food spoilage, they also have important advantageous roles in food preservation and processing. For example, certain cheeses, such as Roquefort and Camembert, are ripened by molds; other cheeses are ripened by bacteria. Production of some Oriental foods, including soy sauce, requires fermentation by molds. Yeast is an essential ingredient in bread and is needed by the brewing industry. Buttermilk, yogurt, sauerkraut, and fermented pickles owe their special desirable flavors to bacterial action. (Some basic characteristics of molds, yeasts, and bacteria were described in Chapter 3.)

Enzymes

Enzymes are present in any food that has been living tissue, such as meat, fish, fruits, vegetables, milk, and eggs. Unless undesirable enzyme action is controlled or the enzymes are destroyed (often by heating), they may be responsible for unwanted chemical changes in preserved foods. (General characteristics of enzymes were discussed in Chapter 9.)

Desiccation, Bruising, and Oxidation

Proper packaging of food plays an important role in controlling food spoilage resulting from desiccation, bruising, and damage by insects and rodents. Oxidation of fats may also be retarded to some degree by appropriate packaging, as well as by the control of environmental conditions and the addition of antioxidants. Biodegradable polymer films offer alternative packaging without the environmental problems produced by plastic packaging [22].

Edible films or coatings composed of lipids, resins, polysaccharides, proteins, or combinations of these substances are used on a variety of food products. On fresh fruits and vegetables, for example, films and coatings are (a) moisture barriers and (b) oxygen and carbon dioxide barriers to control respiration in the tissues and reduce postharvest decay [2, 22].

GENERAL METHODS OF FOOD PRESERVATION

All methods used for preserving foods are based on the general principle of preventing or retarding the causes of spoilage—microbial decomposition, enzymatic and nonenzymatic chemical reactions, and damage from mechanical causes, insects, and rodents. When the growth of microorganisms is only retarded or inhibited, preservation is temporary. When spoilage organisms are completely destroyed and the food is protected so that no other microorganisms are permitted to reinfect it, more permanent preservation is achieved.

No method of food preservation improves the original quality of a food product. If a preserved food is to be of satisfactory quality, then the starting material must be fresh, flavorful produce at an optimal stage of ripeness or maturity.

Preservation by Temperature Control

Either cold or hot temperatures can be used to preserve foods. Cold temperatures produce an environment unfavorable to microbial growth, whereas sufficiently high temperatures destroy spoilage agents.

Cold Temperatures. Cold temperatures mainly inhibit the growth of microorganisms, although some destruction of microbial cells occurs at very low temperatures. With chilling, the length of time that the food remains wholesome varies with the temperature employed and with the type of food being chilled. It also depends on the type of packaging, including modified atmosphere packaging and vacuum cooking–packaging, which extend the effective period of refrigerated storage for food. Refrigerated foods with extended shelf life have generally received precooking or minimal processing and include such items as meat, seafood, egg, and vegetable salads; fresh pasta and pasta sauces; soups; and entrees, as well as precut fruits and vegetables. The chief microbiological concern for these products is the growth of psychrotropic and mesophilic pathogens that might occur during extended refrigerated storage or temperature abuse [26].

Refrigeration and Controlled Atmosphere Storage. In most refrigerators, maintenance of a temperature of 41° (5°C), or slightly lower, preserves many foods for only a few days. In cold-storage warehouses, the time is increased. Here the temperature is lower, and the humidity is controlled, both conditions favoring preservation. Control and monitoring of gases in the atmosphere of the cold-storage facility (controlled atmosphere storage) are also used in some cases to retard ripening or maturation changes that decrease the storage life of fresh produce. Apples are often stored in controlled atmosphere storage to maintain quality for extended periods after harvest.

Freezing. Freezing can preserve foods for long, but not indefinite, periods of time provided that the quality of the food is initially good and the temperature of storage is well below the actual freezing temperature of the food. For the highest retention of both flavor and nutritive value in frozen foods, the freezer should be maintained at no higher than 0°F (–18°C) [18]. Care must be exercised in the marketing of frozen foods to ensure that they are held at freezing temperatures at all times as they move through the various market channels to the consumer.

The action of enzymes already present in the tissues is retarded at freezing temperatures. In certain products such as vegetables, however, enzyme action may still produce undesirable effects on flavor and texture during freezer storage. The enzymes, therefore, must be destroyed by heating the vegetables in hot water or steam, a process called *blanching*, before they are frozen.

Thermal Processing. Hot temperatures preserve by destroying both microorganisms and enzymes. Yeasts, molds, and enzymes are readily destroyed at the boiling temperature of water. The heating must be maintained long enough to permit all parts of the food to reach the necessary temperature, however. Heat penetration is sometimes slow in such foods as partially ripe pears or peaches. Bacteria are less readily destroyed than yeasts, molds, and enzymes, the vegetative or active cells being more readily destroyed than spore forms. Many bacterial spores, including spores of *Clostridium botulinum*, are highly resistant to heat, especially in a low-acid environment. Care must be exercised in the heat processing of canned food to ensure destruction of bacterial spores. The leading cause of botulism in the United States is the consumption of inadequately processed home-canned foods, usually low-acid vegetables or meats. *Clostridium botulinum* may also be found in home-prepared garlic-seasoned oils that have been improperly handled.

Canning. Canning as a method of food preservation involves essentially the complete destruction of microorganisms and their spores, as well as enzymes, by the use of high temperatures, followed by sealing of the container to prevent recontamination of the food (Figure 29-1). The food in this case is essentially sterilized.

Retort pouches or packages have been developed as flexible packaging for thermoprocessed foods. Lightweight pouches with a relatively thin cross-section of a food improve the quality of sterilized packaged food because less time is required for complete heat penetration. Energy savings also result. Because the weight of the packages is much less than that of metal cans and lids, the ease of transporting is increased, and the expense is decreased [44]. Tuna in retort packaging made its debut in 2000 [9]. Chapter 2 discussed the use of retort packaged foods in military rations.

Pasteurization. Pasteurization of food products involves the use of temperatures lower than required for sterilization. Foods that are often pasteurized include milk, fruit juices, and eggs that are to be frozen or dried. All pathogenic microorganisms, but not all other microorganisms present, are destroyed by pasteurization. Thus, pasteurization results in a more limited or temporary preservation period than sterilization and canning.

Preservation by Moisture Control

Drying. One of the oldest methods of preserving foods involves the removal of moisture until the product is dry. As practically applied, the food is dried in the sun or by air currents and artificial heat until the moisture content of the food is reduced to a level that inhibits the growth of microorganisms. The actual percentage of moisture varies but is usually under 30 percent. Some dehydrated foods such as dried potato slices contain only 2 to 3 percent moisture. Many commercially dried fruits, with intermediate moisture content of about 15 to 35 or 40 percent, have water activity low enough for preservation yet are pleasant to eat directly without rehydration [14]. Osmotic drying is used in some commercial products such as *craisins*. In osmotic drying, a strong syrup is used to draw water from the food and then the food is finish-dried with air [11].

Some foods can be easily dried at home, including most garden vegetables, fruits, and garden herbs such as parsley and oregano. Drying can be done in driers especially designed for this purpose, in the oven, or, in sunny climates, in trays placed in the sun. Vegetables, with few exceptions, should be blanched before drying to stop the action of enzymes that produce undesirable changes in texture and flavor during storage. Dried vegetables that have been blanched also dry more easily and retain more vitamins. Light-colored fruits, such as apples, apricots, and peaches, are of better quality when they are sulfured

FIGURE 29-1 Bottled green beans are sealed so that recontamination by microorganisms cannot occur. *(Courtesy of the Ball Brothers Company)*

before drying to prevent darkening as a result of the action of oxidizing enzymes. This process involves exposing the fruit to the fumes of burning sulfur or, alternatively, dipping in a weak bisulfite solution.

Freeze-Drying. In the process of freeze-drying, the food product is first frozen, and then placed in a vacuum chamber to which a small amount of heat is applied. Under the reduced pressure of the vacuum, the ice in the frozen food changes directly to water vapor (sublimes) and is carried away by the circulating heated air. The moisture content of the food is thus reduced to 1 to 8 percent. The food remains frozen through most of the drying period; it does not get warm as does food that is subjected to ordinary drying processes. Fresh flavors and textures are therefore better preserved by freeze-drying than by sun-drying or other procedures of artificial drying without vacuum. Commercially, microwaves rather than a conventional heat source may be used in the freeze-drying process [42]. A number of freeze-dried foods for individual use are sold in sporting goods outlets and are used by campers and hikers.

Oxidation during freeze-drying is curbed by the low oxygen tension maintained and sometimes by the breaking of the vacuum with an inert gas rather than air. Freeze-dried meats are similar to fresh meats in flavor and color but may be somewhat tougher and drier. Tenderness is improved if the meat is hydrated in 2 percent brine or if proteolytic enzymes are added to the hydrating liquid. Fruits are another food that is successfully freeze-dried. The browning of freeze-dried fruits can be prevented by treatment with sulfur dioxide.

Freeze-dried foods do not require refrigeration and offer the advantage of being light when transported. Sir Edmund Hillary took 300 pounds of freeze-dried items on his Himalayan mountain-climbing expedition. The products reconstituted to 1,200 pounds and included ham, chicken, chops, steaks, fruits, and vegetables. Although refrigeration is not required, freeze-dried products do tend to deteriorate with long storage unless they are properly packaged.

Use of Preservatives

Adding chemical preservatives to a food product is another method of inhibiting the growth of undesirable microorganisms. Common preservatives, sometimes called *household preservatives*, include acids, salt, sugar, spices, and smoke. It is the phenols in wood smoke that seem to exert the major preservative action.

Acids and Sugar. Vinegar contains acetic acid and is commonly used, along with salt, to pickle vegetables (Figure 29-2). In pickle and sauerkraut fermentations, lactic and other organic acids are produced over time by friendly bacteria present on the vegetables. Not only does the acid prevent unwanted microbial growth, but

FIGURE 29-2 A mixture of salt, vinegar, and water is poured over cucumbers and dill in the preparation of dill pickles. *(Courtesy of the U.S. Department of Agriculture)*

FIGURE 29-3 A good-quality jelly is stiff enough to hold its shape yet is delicate and tender. The jelly is preserved by its content of approximately 65 percent sugar.

additional flavor substances are produced by the desirable bacteria. Sugar in large amounts is used in the production of jellies, jams, and preserves (Figure 29-3). It acts as a preservative by binding the moisture necessary for microbial growth and activity.

Spices. Spices inhibit bacterial growth to some degree but vary in their effectiveness. Ground cinnamon and cloves are more valuable than nutmeg and allspice in quantities that can be used without marring flavor. However, spices themselves are often responsible for introducing bacteria into foods. Oils of spice are sterile and have a more inhibitory effect on microbial growth than ground spices.

Other Preservatives. Numerous preservatives are used as food additives and must be approved for use by the U.S. Food and Drug Administration (FDA). Thorough testing for safety is required before approval is given. (Food additives were discussed in Chapter 8.) Sodium benzoate, used in very small amounts in some margarines, and sodium propionate, used to retard molding in bread, are examples of preservatives that may be added to foods. An antioxidant is a special type of preservative that inhibits the spoilage of fats that may occur from a nonenzymatic oxidative process. The FDA has approved nisin, or *bacteriocin*, a polypeptide antibacterial substance, for use in some pasteurized cheese spreads. It is active only against gram-positive bacteria and is approved for use to inhibit the growth of *Clostridium botulinum* spores. The bacterium *Streptococcus lactis* produces this antibiotic [13, 15].

Preservation by Irradiation

Food is exposed to ionizing radiation to (a) reduce microbial levels, (b) destroy pathogens, (c) extend shelf life, and (d) remove insect infestation [41]. Irradiation has been found to be safe through more than 50 years of research. It has been approved for use in several foods by the FDA and USDA (Table 29-1). The World Health Organiza-

tion (WHO), UN Food and Agricultural Organization (FAO), and International Atomic Energy Agency (IAEA) have concluded irradiated food is safe. Additionally, it has been endorsed by the American Dietetic Association [1] and the American Medical Association [45]. Irradiation of half of all ground beef, poultry, pork, and processed meat has been estimated by the Centers for Disease Control and Prevention (CDC) experts to reduce foodborne illnesses by one million cases [43]. More than 40 food products are irradiated in over 37 countries [45].

Irradiation has been called "cold" pasteurization by some because it destroys microorganisms without heating the food. Sources of radiation energy allowed for food processing include **gamma rays** (produced from cobalt-60 and cesium-137), beta rays generated by electron beams, and x-rays [41]. Electron beams are produced with electricity. Ionizing radiation, produced by one of these methods, has energy high enough to change atoms in the irradiated food by removing an electron to form an **ion**. These freed electrons break chemical bonds in the microbial DNA, thereby killing the microbe. Ionizing radiation does not have enough energy to split atoms in the food and cause it to become **radioactive**. Thus, irradiated foods are not radioactive.

TABLE 29-1 Food Irradiation in the United States

Product	Purpose of Irradiation	Dose Permitted (kGy)**	Date
Wheat and wheat powder	Insect disinfestations, mold control	0.2–0.5	1963
Pork carcasses or fresh noncut processed cuts	Control of *Trichinella spiralis*	0.3–1.0 max.	1985
White potatoes	Sprout inhibition, extend shelf life	0.05–0.15	1964
Herbs, spices, and dry vegetable seasoning	Microbial control, decontamination or disinfestation of insects	30.0 max.	1986
Dry or dehydrated enzyme preparations	Control of insects and microorganisms	10.0 max.	1986
Fruits and vegetables, fresh	Disinfection, delay maturation	1.0 max.	1986
Poultry, fresh or frozen	Control of illness-causing microorganisms such as *Salmonella*	3.0 max	1990
Poultry, fresh or frozen (USDA)	Microbial control	1.5–4.5	1992
Meat, frozen, packaged*	Sterilization	44.0 min.	1995
Animal feed and pet food	*Salmonella* control	2.0–25.0	1995
Meat, uncooked, chilled	Microbial control	4.5 max.	1997
Meat, uncooked, frozen	Microbial control	7.0 max.	1997
Meat, uncooked, chilled (USDA)	Microbial control	4.5 max.	2000
Meat, uncooked, frozen (USDA)	Microbial control	7.0 max.	2000
Shell eggs, fresh	*Salmonella* control	3.0 max	2000
Seeds for sprouting	Microbial control	8.0 max	2000
Molluscan shellfish, fresh or frozen	*Vibrio, Salmonella, Listeria* Control	0.5–7.5	Pending
Ready-to-eat, unrefrigerated meat and poultry products	Microbial control	4.5 max	Pending

*For meats used solely in the National Aeronautics and Space Administration (NASA) space flight programs.

**The amount of radiation energy absorbed is measured in units of grays (or kilograys, meaning 1,000 grays, kGy). One gray equals 1 joule of absorbed energy per kilogram.

Source: References 3, 32, 41

FIGURE 29-4 An irradiated food on the retail market should bear the international symbol along with either of the statements "treated with radiation" or "treated by irradiation."

Irradiated foods marketed for consumers must be labeled with an official logo (Figure 29-4) and the statement "treated with radiation" or "treated by irradiation." Consumer acceptance is important for commercial application of food irradiation. A few stores across the United States have successfully marketed irradiated foods [36]. Early studies of consumer acceptance have indicated that an education program is effective in increasing both consumers' knowledge and their positive attitude toward food irradiation [34, 37]. It is important for consumers to know that irradiation of food can effectively reduce or eliminate pathogens and spoilage microorganisms while maintaining wholesomeness, sensory quality, and nutrient content [16, 24, 32, 41].

PACKAGING OF FOOD

Major changes have occurred in food packaging over the past 20 or 30 years. Some trends in this area include packages that adapt to preserve desirable environments around fresh, chilled, or prepared foods in the supermarket; increased aseptic packaging; a wider variety of packaging materials from which to choose; and the movement for environmentally friendly packaging [25, 35]. Innovations in food packaging, along with new food-processing technologies, have resulted in greater convenience for the consumer, less flavor loss during processing, and savings on materials and energy costs.

Functions of Food Packaging

The main functions of food packaging are to protect the food from contamination, contain the food, and provide information [25]. Additionally, packaging provides convenience by enabling consumers to heat or cook the food in the package. Packages that can be opened and then reclosed or are shatter proof are likewise appreciated by consumers.

Protection. Food packaging provides protection from chemical, biological, and physical influences that may cause deterioration of the product. Tamper-resistant packaging has been developed to protect consumers from willful tampering and adulteration of foods and other products [25].

A variety of chemical changes in food can be controlled or prevented by the type of packaging. Appropriate packaging minimizes reactions that affect the stability or the shelf life of the food products. Water vapor and oxygen are always present in the environment around foods and can affect the stability of packaged food products. The package may provide a barrier to these gases. It acts in some cases to keep moisture in the food and thus prevent desiccation or drying. In other cases, it prevents moisture from entering the package and being absorbed by the food. Certain packages control migration of atmospheric oxygen. The permeability of the package to light may also affect the stability of the food.

Proper packaging keeps biological contaminates at a minimum by providing a barrier to microbes, insects, rodents, or other animals [25]. Packaging can also provide an environment not conducive to the growth of microorganisms and thus reduces microbial decomposition of foods. Both temperature and moisture content can affect the microbes' potential for growth and activity.

Physical protection of the foods helps to prevent breakage, crushing, and other forms of damage that would cause the food to be undesirable or unusable [25]. For example, fresh eggs are protected by cardboard or Styrofoam egg cartoons.

Containment. Food containers hold and separate foods into units of a particular size and weight. Containers provide ease in handling and convenience. From a packaging-waste perspective, large containers result in less environmental waste. Individual or small containers may result in less food waste, however, if the larger container of food cannot be used before quality has deteriorated.

Marketing and Information. The package provides information about the product for the consumer. The food facts nutrition label, package contents, product use, and even recipes may be provided on the label. Innovative packaging can boost sales [25]. Unique codes on package labels enable traceability of the product throughout the distribution process. If a food recall occurs, the products affected by the recall can be identified. See Chapter 4 for information about the regulation of food labels.

Regulatory Requirements

The FDA considers the compatibility of food and its packaging to be a safety issue. The package is a potential source of chemical substances for the food product. Migration of substances from packaging materials does occur and cannot be completely eliminated; thus, the packaging materials are legally considered to be food additives and require premarket safety evaluation and approval by the FDA [19].

FOCUS ON SCIENCE

Food Preservation and Packaging in Space

A unique way to illustrate the main points in this chapter is to identify the particular food preservation and packaging techniques utilized in NASA's astronaut program. In space, food is individually packaged and stowed for easy handling in a zero-gravity environment space. An oven is provided in the space shuttle and the space station to heat foods to their proper temperature. Depending on the mission, there may be no refrigerators in space, so food must be stored and prepared properly to avoid spoilage, especially on longer missions.

Food Packages

On earth, the disposal of food packages is often done without a thought. In space, astronauts throw their food packages away in a trash compactor or inside the space shuttle when they are done eating. Some packaging actually prevents the food from flying away. The food packaging is designed to be flexible, easy to use, as well as maximize space when stowing or disposing food containers.

Rehydratable Food

A variety of foods and beverages may be rehydrated in space travel. Some of these foods include soups, macaroni and cheese, chicken and rice, shrimp cocktail, scrambled eggs, and cereals. Breakfast cereals are prepared by packaging in rehydratable package with nonfat dry milk and sugar, if needed. Water is added to the package just before eating.

Thermostabilized Food

Food is heat processed to destroy undesirable microorganisms and enzymes. Individual servings of thermostabilized foods are available in aluminum or bimetallic cans, plastic cups, or in flexible retort pouches. Cans are easy-open with full panel, pull-out lids. Most of the entrees are packaged in flexible retort pouches that may be heated, cut open with scissors, and eaten directly.

Intermediate Moisture (IM) Food

Intermediate moisture foods are preserved by restricting the amount of water available for microbial growth. Water is removed or restricted with water-binding substances such as sugar or salt. The moisture level of IM foods ranges from 15 to 30 percent.

Natural Form Foods

A variety of natural form, ready-to-eat foods such as nuts, granola bars, and cookies are available. These foods are packaged in flexible pouches and require no further processing.

Irradiated Meat

Beef steaks are cooked, packaged in flexible foil-laminated pouches, and sterilized by exposure to ionizing radiation. These steaks are stable at ambient temperature.

Condiments

Several condiments are provided and include commercially packaged individual packets of catsup, mustard, mayonnaise, taco sauce, and hot pepper sauce. Pepper is dissolved in oil, and the salt is dissolved in water, then packaged in polyethylene dropper bottles. The salt and pepper, as sold on earth, would float around at zero gravity.

Shelf-Stable Tortilla

Tortillas are served instead of bread because the crumbs would float around and go into the equipment. However, tortillas became moldy on long flights. Shelf-stable tortillas were developed that are stabilized by a combination of modified atmosphere packaging, pH (acidic), and water activity. Mold growth is prevented by removing oxygen from the package. This is accomplished by packaging in a high-barrier container in a nitrogen atmosphere with an oxygen scavenger. Water activity is reduced to less than 0.9 in the final product by dough formulation. Reduced water and lower pH inhibit growth of pathogenic clostridia which could be a potential hazard in the anaerobic atmosphere created by modified atmosphere.

Source: NASA. *Food for space flight.* Retrieved April 19, 2008, from http://www.spaceflight.nasa.gov/shuttle/reference/factsheets/food.html

Packaging Materials

Packaging materials should be carefully chosen. Food quality, food processing methods, consumer wants, packaging costs, and environmental impact are all issues to be considered. Food flavors can be adversely affected by the type of packaging. Direct contact of food with packaging materials may result in migration of volatile compounds from the package into the packaged food. The loss of desirable content constituents in the plastic packaging is referred to as *scalping* [8]. Plastic materials such as polyethylene and polypropylene in particular have been implicated in flavor absorption into the plastic [8].

Glass offers the advantage of being chemically inert and thus does not affect flavor. However, glass is heavy and costly to transport. Additionally, it is breakable, which is a significant disadvantage for some packaging needs. Particular types of packaging materials are needed for **aseptic-packaged**, hot-filled, dry-filled–no process, frozen, and retorted foods [10]. Stand-up flexible pouches have gained in popularity as one way to reduce the amount of packaging materials [5].

Paper and Paperboard. A variety of paper and paperboard packages are used. Corrugated boxes, milk cartons, folding cartons, bags, sacks, and wrapping paper are examples of paper and paperboard packages. Paper and paperboard are produced from cellulose fibers derived from wood [25]. Any additives used in the processing of paper intended for food use are regulated by the FDA. Because paper has poor barrier properties, it is treated, coated, laminated, or otherwise processed [25].

Paper and paperboard packages are used for several different types of food products. Paperboard trays, developed for microwave use, may also withstand up to 400°F (204°C) in conventional ovens. A heat-resistant plastic resin is applied to solid, bleached sulfate board, which is formed into trays of various shapes and sizes. These containers can be used for shelf-stable foods, refrigerated foods, and frozen foods [12]. Orange juice and milk cartons of paperboard may have resealable caps for easier opening and pouring.

Rectangular paperboard cartons, laminated with aluminum and/or polyethylene, can be used for the aseptic packaging of products such as fruit juices and drinks [23]. These containers are made in various sizes. An assortment of products, including dry cereals, cake mixes, rice mixes, macaroni and cheese, and so on, are packed in

paperboard cartons. In some cases, inner linings hold the product.

Plastics. Plastics are organic polymers with variable chemical compositions and physical properties. Many different fabrication processes are used to produce the many types and shapes of both rigid and flexible packages used by the packaging industry. Several different kinds of plastics are described in Table 29-2.

Metals. Metals used for packaging include aluminum, aluminum foil, tinplate, and tin-free steel [25]. Aluminum is lightweight, resistant to corrosion, and easily recycled. However, because it cannot be welded, it is used only for seamless containers. Tinplate is produced by coating thin sheets of steel in molten tin. These containers may be heat treated and sealed and thus are useful for sterilized products. Tinplate can be recycled and is less expensive than aluminum. Tin-free steel must be coated with an

---

TABLE 29-2 Kinds of Plastics Commonly Used for Food Packaging

Name	Characteristics	Examples
Polyolefin 　Polyethylene 　Polypropylene	Most widely used food packaging plastics. Flexible, light, strong, stable, resistant to moisture and chemicals. May be recycled or reused.	Milk, juice, and water bottles. Cereal box liners. Margarine tubs and yogurt containers. Trash and grocery bags.
Polyesters 　Polyethylene terephthalate (PETE) 　Polycarbonate 　Polyethylene naphthalate (PEN)	PETE is the most widely used food packaging polyester. Provides good barrier to gases and moisture. Does not have good resistance to bases. Polycarbonate is clear, heat resistant, and durable. Harsh chemicals may release a potentially hazardous chemical, and additional risk assessment has been suggested. PEN performs well at high temperatures but is more expensive than PETE.	PETE is used for plastic carbonated beverage containers, food trays, and thin-oriented films such as used for snack food wrappers. Polycarbonate is often used for returnable or refillable water bottles and sterilizable baby bottles. PEN is well suited for beer and other beverage containers.
Polyvinyl chloride (PVC)	Heavy, stiff, with excellence resistance to chemicals. Is difficult to recycle and should not be incinerated because of chlorine content.	Bottles and packaging films.
Polyvinylidene chloride (PVdC)	Heat sealable and excellent barrier to many substances. Should not be incinerated because of high chlorine content.	Packaging of poultry, cheese, snack foods, tea, coffee, and confections.
Polystyrene	Clear, hard, and brittle. Has a low melting point. May be recycled or incinerated.	Egg cartons, disposable plastic silverware, cups, plates, bottles, and food trays.
Polyamide (nylon)	Good chemical resistance, toughness, and gas permeability.	Boil-in-the-bag packaging.
Ethylene vinyl alcohol (EVOH)	Excellent barrier to oil, fat, and oxygen. Is moisture sensitive.	Multilayered films where not in direct contact with foods.
Laminates and co-extrusions	Lamination is the process of bonding two or more plastics together or bonding a plastic to another material such as paper or aluminum. Co-extrusion is the combination of two or more layers of molten plastics during film manufacturer. Because laminates and co-extrusions include multiple materials, recycling is difficult.	

Source: Reference 25

organic material for corrosion resistance. It cannot be welded. Tin-free steel is used for food cans, trays, and bottle caps.

Metal cans may be flat rectangles, tall and thin, squat, pot-bellied, and many other configurations. The bodies may be three- or two-piece and fabricated from steel or aluminum [9]. Likewise, many different styles of closure may be used. The traditional metal can is made of steel with a thin coating of tin. It generally is cylindrical and is made of three pieces. The two ends are attached to the cylinder, which has a soldered seam. Two-piece cans, with the base and cylinder in one piece, are manufactured; these cans have fewer seams, are more durable, lighter in weight, stack better on shelves, and can be produced more inexpensively than the traditional three-piece cans. The two-piece can may also be shaped as a tray to allow more rapid heat penetration during processing and thus reduce heating time [12].

Combinations of Materials. A combination of two or more materials can provide improved functional properties for food packages. Several films can be laminated together, each layer contributing specific characteristics. For example, containers for aseptic packaging may be fabricated with aluminum foil as a barrier material and polypropylene or polyethylene as heat-sealing and food-contact surfaces. Because foil must be protected from mechanical damage, paperboard is often utilized as the outer layer of this laminate. These packages act as barriers to moisture, oxygen, light, and microorganisms, and have the necessary strength and heat sealability [39]. Individually portioned fruit drinks are often marketed in such packages.

The flexible retort pouch is another example of a package using a combination of materials. It typically consists of three laminated materials held together by adhesives. The outer layer is polyester, which provides strength; the middle layer is aluminum foil, which provides a barrier to moisture, gas, and light; and the inner layer is polyolefin (polyethylene or polypropylene), which provides a good heat seal.

The retort pouch is thin and permits sterilizing temperatures to be reached more quickly throughout the contents than the traditional can. Thus, the processed product is fresher and firmer. The sealed pouch, which can be stored on the shelf, may be heated in boiling water in preparation for serving. The pouch is easily opened by cutting with scissors or tearing across the top [12]. Tuna was introduced in retort packaging in 2000 and is now widely available [9].

Edible Films and Coatings. An edible film is defined as a thin layer of edible material formed on a food as a coating or placed (preformed) on or between food components [22]. Edible coatings and films are not meant to replace nonedible, synthetic packaging materials for prolonged storage of foods. They can, however, act as adjuncts for improving overall food quality and extending shelf life. They may inhibit migration of moisture, oxygen, carbon dioxide, aromas, lipids, and so on; carry food ingredients such as antioxidants, antimicrobials, or flavor; and/or improve mechanical integrity or handling characteristics of the food.

The desired characteristics of the edible film depend on the food product and its primary type of deterioration. For example, if the food is a manufactured product high in polyunsaturated fat, a film extremely resistant to the entrance of oxygen would be desirable to avoid the early development of rancidity. If the product is a fresh fruit or vegetable, however, the film would need to retard moisture loss but allow some permeability of oxygen and carbon dioxide gases as the plant cells continue to respire [21].

Potential edible films include polysaccharides such as starch, high amylose starch, methyl cellulose, alginate, carrageenan, and low-methoxyl pectin; proteins such as collagen, gelatin, wheat gluten, zein from corn, soy protein isolate, whey proteins, and casein; edible waxes; and combinations of these substances [22].

Methods of Packaging

Aseptic Packaging. Aseptic processing involves sterilization of the food product, sterilization of the package or container in which the food will be placed, filling the sterilized container with the sterilized food in an environment in which sterility is maintained, and sealing the container to prevent subsequent contamination [7]. Aseptic processing was developed in the 1940s. Since 1981, when the use of hydrogen peroxide for the sterilization of packaging materials was approved by the FDA, this process has rapidly gained popularity in the United States. In 1995, about 10 billion retail and institutional aseptic packages entered U.S. distribution channels [4]. Superheated steam or dry hot air may be used to sterilize aseptic packages, as well as hydrogen peroxide in combination with heat or ultraviolet light [20]. Hydrogen peroxide together with heat or ultraviolet radiation treatment is commonly used for the sterilization of paper-based packaging. Magnetic resonance imaging (MRI) inspection of aseptically packaged foods has been developed as a technique for the 100 percent inspection of products, at production line speeds, to assure product quality and safety [29].

Food products to be aseptically packaged are pumped through heat exchangers of various types, then into a holding tube, and finally into a cooling section before being packaged. Aseptic packaging of low-acid foods containing particulates requires demonstration of sterility at the center of the food particles, based on a defined microbiological procedure and a mathematical model. Destruction of any *Clostridium botulinum* spores present must be ensured. An aseptic filling process for a low-acid particulate product, specifically potato soup, was accepted by the FDA in 1997 [33]. These types of products have been sold in other countries for several years.

Aseptic sterilization and packaging has several advantages over in-container sterilization, the process used in conventional canning. Processing conditions are independent of container size and, therefore, very large containers can be used. The process is highly automated, resulting in higher productivity. It is also more energy efficient and less expensive. Packaging costs are lower for many container types. Aseptic processing yields higher-quality foods than traditional procedures requiring longer heating. Transport and storage costs are also less than those for frozen foods, as refrigeration is unnecessary [39].

Modified Atmosphere Packaging. Modified atmosphere packaging (MAP) may be defined as the enclosure of food products in gas-barrier materials, in which the gaseous environment has been changed or modified (Figure 29-5). The modification may slow respiration rates of fresh produce, reduce microbial spoilage, and retard deterioration due to enzymatic reactions with the end result of extending the shelf life of the food [17, 40]. The gaseous atmosphere within the package usually contains a reduced amount of oxygen and increased amounts of carbon dioxide and nitrogen. MAP is most commonly applied to fresh-cut produce, which in 1995 approached 10 percent of retail produce sales [4]; however, sandwiches, pastas and sauces, prepared poultry, and lunch

FIGURE 29-5 Precut lettuce is often sold in modified atmosphere packaging. (*Courtesy of the U.S. Department of Agriculture, photograph by Ken Hammond*)

kits also use MAP. MAP may be of two types: high gas permeable or low gas permeable. Respiring products such as fresh produce are packaged in high gas permeable MAP; pasta and other prepared dishes are placed in low gas permeable MAP [6].

Modification of the gas mixture may be accomplished by two different methods: vacuum packaging and gas packaging. Vacuum packaging involves packaging the product in a film with low oxygen permeability, removing air from the package, and sealing it hermetically. Oxygen in the headspace is reduced to less than 1 percent. Carbon dioxide, if it is produced from tissue and microbial respiration, eventually increases to 10 to 20 percent within the headspace. Low oxygen and elevated carbon dioxide extend the shelf life of fresh meat by inhibiting the growth of aerobic microorganisms. The meat must be kept refrigerated. Although this works well for fresh and processed meat products, it cannot be used for crushable items such as pizza, pasta, and baked products [40].

The technique in gas packaging involves removing air from the package and replacing it with a mixture of nitrogen, oxygen, and carbon dioxide. The pressure of gas inside the package is maintained approximately equal to the external pressure. Nitrogen is an inert gas that does not affect the food and has no antimicrobial properties. It is used chiefly as a filler to prevent package collapse in products that can absorb carbon dioxide. Oxygen is generally avoided except for products that continue to respire after packaging, such as fruits and vegetables. It is also used with fresh meat to maintain the red color associated with good-quality meat. Carbon dioxide is bacteriostatic and fungistatic. Its effect depends on several factors, including the microbial load, gas concentration, temperature, and packaging film permeability. Table 29-3 gives some examples of gas mixtures for selected foods [40].

Sous vide. *Sous vide* is a French term meaning "under vacuum." Sous vide processing technology involves the slow, controlled cooking of foods in sealed, evacuated, heat-stable pouches or trays so that the natural flavors are retained, followed by quick chilling, and cold storage at

TABLE 29-3 Gas Mixtures for Selected Food Products

| Product | Temperature (°C) | Gas Concentration (%) | | |
		Oxygen	Carbon Dioxide	Nitrogen
Fresh meat	0–2	70	20	10
Cured meat	1–3	0	50	50
Cheese	1–3	0	60	40
Apples	4–6	2	1	97
Tomatoes	5–10	4	4	92
Baked products	Room temperature	0	60	40
Pizza	Room temperature	0	60	40

Source: Reference 40

TABLE 29-4 Packaging Waste Management Strategies	
Strategy	
Pay-as-you-throw programs	Waste reductions of 14 to 27 percent in communities where consumers pay for trash removal based on amount of trash.
Source reduction	Manufacturers are "lightweighting" packages by making more lightweight containers.
	Glass containers decreased 50 percent in weight (1992–2002).
	Aluminum decreased 26 percent in weight (1975–2005).
	Steel cans decreased 40 percent in weight since 1970.
	One-gallon milk jugs decreased 30 percent in last 20 years.
Reuse	Refillable containers are being produced.
Recycle	30 million tons of containers and packaging recycled in 2005 which represents 40 percent of the packaging generated.
Combustion	Controlled burning of waste in designated facility. Heat can be recovered from combustion to produce energy. Air emissions must be controlled.
Landfills	New landfill technologies are being developed to improve the degradation of waste. Air emissions and potential ground water contamination must be controlled.

Source: Reference 25

32° to 37°F (0° to 3°C). These refrigerated products with extended shelf life can be reheated in a boiling water bath or in a microwave oven. The major microbiological hazard associated with this processing technology is the potential growth and toxin production of *Clostridium botulinum*. Other organisms of public health concern include pathogenic strains of *E. coli*, *Salmonella*, *Staphylococcus*, *Listeria*, and *Yersinia* species. These organisms should all be destroyed during the heating process; however, a Hazard Analysis and Critical Control Points (HACCP) approach at all stages of sous vide processing and handling is essential to promote a reasonable degree of confidence in product safety [40]. The risks involved in temperature abuse continue into the kitchen. Refrigerator temperatures should always be 40°F (4°C) or lower.

Packaging Waste Management

As we evolve into a "throw-away" society, we are producing waste from packaging, as well as from other sources, at a faster rate than we are finding solutions to deal with it. Landfills are quickly being filled up. Industries and legislatures alike are facing the challenge of handling solid waste in an economical and environmentally attractive manner. In 2005, 35 percent of the municipal solid waste was from packaging-related materials including glass, metal, plastic, paper, and paperboard [25]. Of this, food packaging represents about two-thirds of the total volume of package waste [25].

Some strategies include source reduction or eliminating unnecessary packaging and using lighter-weight materials; reusable plastic containers and pallets; recycling, which provides another source of raw materials and decreases the waste going to landfills; incineration, burning waste properly without causing air pollution; and landfilling—the least desirable method but the most commonly used. Table 29-4 provides data about some of these strategies. The success of these strategies will depend on communication between industry and government, the creation of markets for recycled goods, the development of effective disposal systems, and public support of recycling programs.

CHAPTER SUMMARY

- Food preservation has been practiced for thousands of years. Technological advances have permitted the preservation of a wide variety of foods in convenient packaging for use year-round.

- The major causes of food spoilage are growth of microorganisms, enzyme action, oxidation, desiccation, mechanical damage, and infestation by insects or rodents. Some microorganisms have advantageous roles in food preservation and processing.

- Food preservation may be accomplished by temperature control (refrigeration and freezing), thermal processing (canning and pasteurization), drying and freeze-drying, use of preservatives (acids, sugars, spices, or additives), or irradiation.

- Cold temperatures inhibit the growth of microorganisms. Refrigerated foods should be at a temperature at or below 41°F (5°C). Frozen foods should be maintained at or below 0°F (–18°C). Vegetables are generally blanched before they are frozen to destroy enzymes naturally present.

- Hot temperatures preserve by destroying both microorganisms and enzymes. Many bacterial spores are highly resistant to heat; thus, care must be taken in the heat processing of canned foods. Pasteurization of food products involves the use of temperatures lower than those required for sterilization.

- One of the oldest methods of preserving foods involves the removal of moisture until the product is dry. The percentage of moisture in dried foods is usually under 30 percent. Vegetables may be blanched and fruits may be sulfured before drying.

- In the process of freeze-drying, the food product is first frozen, then placed in a vacuum chamber to which a small amount of heat is applied. Fresh flavors and textures are better preserved by freeze-drying than by sun-drying or other drying procedures.

- Acids, salt, sugar, spices, and smoke are common food preservatives. Numerous other preservatives may be used as food additives. The FDA approves these preservatives. Sodium benzoate and sodium propionate are examples of preservatives that may be added to food.

- Irradiation has been found to be safe through more than 50 years of research. Food is irradiated to reduce microbial levels, destroy pathogens, extend shelf life, and remove insect infestation. The FDA approves products that may be irradiated. The sources of radiation allowed for food processing include gamma rays, accelerated electrons, and machine-generated x-rays. Irradiated foods are not radioactive.

- Major changes have occurred in food packaging over the past 20 to 30 years. The main functions of food packaging are to protect from contamination, contain the food, and provide information.

- A variety of packaging materials are available for food products. Paper, plastics, metals, and edible films are all examples of possible packaging materials.

- Aseptic packaging involves the sterilization of the food product, sterilization of the package or container, filling the sterilized container with the sterilized food in an environment in which sterility is maintained, and sealing the container to present subsequent contamination. Aseptic processing yields higher-quality foods than traditional procedures requiring longer heating.

- Modified atmosphere packaging (MAP) may be defined as the enclosure of food products in gas barrier materials, in which the gaseous environment has been changed or modified. Fresh-cut produce, pasta, and other prepared dishes may be packaged using MAP.

- Sous vide is a French term meaning "under vacuum." Sous vide technology involves the slow, controlled heating of foods in sealed, evacuated, heat-stable pouches or trays, followed by quick chilling and cold storage.

- The management of packaging waste may include source reduction, reusable containers, and recycling.

STUDY QUESTIONS

1. Describe several basic causes of food spoilage.

2. Why are enzymes of some concern in preserving foods? Explain.

3. For each of the following general principles of food preservation, describe a specific method of preserving food:

   (a) Use of low temperatures

   (b) Use of high temperatures

   (c) Reduction of moisture

   (d) Addition or development of acid

   (e) Addition of large amounts of sugar

4. (a) What is meant by *ionizing radiation?*

   (b) Describe several uses of low-dose ionizing radiation in the preservation of foods, both short and long term.

   (c) Why might some members of the public be concerned about the safety of irradiated foods? How can these concerns be addressed?

5. (a) Describe several functions of food packages.

   (b) Why does the FDA consider food-packaging materials to be food additives?

   (c) Briefly describe and give examples of how each of the following materials can be used in packaging:

   Paper
   Plastics
   Metals
   Combinations of materials
   Edible films and coatings

6. What is *aseptic packaging?* What advantages does it have for food products?

7. (a) Describe what is meant by *modified atmosphere packaging*.

  (b) What types of foods may benefit from a modified atmosphere and why? Explain.

  (c) What two methods may be employed for the modification of the gaseous atmosphere in a package? Describe them.

  (d) Describe the sous vide processing of food. What precautions must be exercised in its processing and handling?

8. Describe several ways to reduce and manage packaging waste.

FOOD PRESERVATION BY FREEZING AND CANNING 30

Foods may be preserved for extended periods of time by either freezing or canning. In this chapter, the following topics pertaining to the freezing and canning of foods will be discussed:

- History of freezing
- Freezing process
- Changes during freezing, storage, and thawing
- Selection of foods for freezing
- Freezing and storage techniques
- History of canning
- Methods for home canning including boiling water bath and pressure canning
- Containers for canning
- Achieving heat penetration and an effective seal
- Handling after processing of canned foods

FREEZING

Clarence Birdseye, a food technology pioneer, began development of the frozen food industry in the 1920s with the production of frozen fish. He applied his engineering skills to develop plate freezers and blast freezers not unlike those used today. Although interrupted by World War II, the infant frozen food industry grew rapidly during the late 1940s and 1950s [4]. Equipment for rapid freezing and widespread availability of freezers in both home and institutional kitchens contributed importantly to this growth. Since the early days, there have been many improvements in freezing technology. Researchers have studied the freezing process itself in an attempt to understand and minimize the effects on food quality at each stage in the production of frozen foods [19]. A large assortment of frozen foods is marketed. The sweeping success of the microwave oven for reheating frozen foods has also contributed to growth in the frozen food industry.

The frozen food industry continues to work at improving the quality of frozen foods. For example, research concerning the properties and possible applications of "antifreeze" proteins as agents to prevent the growth of large ice crystals during frozen storage may in the future be applied to certain frozen foods. Antifreeze proteins are **glycoproteins** found in fish from southern polar oceans. These proteins now can be synthesized chemically or by genetic engineering [10].

Other areas of research include air-impingement, pressure shift, and extrusion freezing methods [16]. Air-impingement freezing uses thin, high-velocity jets of air directed at the food to accomplish fast cooling rates, resulting in reduced moisture loss and formation of small ice crystals [6, 16]. Pressure-shift freezing uses an increase of pressure to depress the freezing point of water, thereby allowing the product to be cooled to –4°F (–20°C) without the water freezing. When the pressure is released, the water freezes rapidly, and small, uniform ice crystals are formed. Extrusion freezing is being studied as a way to freeze ice cream to –4°F (–20°C) directly from the freezer. Traditionally, ice cream is frozen to 19°F (–7°C), then placed in a hardening room to complete the freezing process. Extrusion freezing has been shown to produce a more uniform crystal size [16].

Producers of frozen foods are concerned with maintaining quality as the food moves through the transport and distribution systems, where it must always be held at low temperatures [3]. Various devices called *time–temperature indicators* (TTIs) have been developed as means of monitoring and controlling critical temperatures during the storage, handling, and distribution of frozen and refrigerated foods [4, 22].

The extent to which home freezing is practiced depends on individual circumstances and objectives. Produce, for example, must be available at advantageous prices in the market or from home gardens to make freezing an economical practice. In any case, however, the freezer contributes to efficient management in meal planning and preparation, and it has the advantage of allowing quantity buying with less frequent purchasing. It also provides convenience in the temporary storage of prepared foods made in larger quantities than are to be consumed immediately.

The Freezing Process

Freezing is the change in physical state from liquid to solid that occurs when heat is removed from a substance. When foods are frozen, they undergo a phase change of liquid water into solid ice. The water molecules reduce their motion and form an organized pattern of crystals. The three stages in the freezing process are as follows:

1. The temperature of the food is lowered to freezing.
2. Ice crystals begin to form as the liquid reaches the freezing point; the temperature required varies with the product to be frozen. For water, the freezing temperature is 32°F (0°C). As ice crystals form from water, the remaining water becomes more concentrated with solute, lowering the freezing point still further. This process is continuous, but the zone of maximum crystal formation in frozen foods is 25° to 31°F (–4° to –0.5°C). See Figure 30-1.
3. After ice formation ceases, the temperature of the frozen product is gradually lowered to the necessary storage temperature.

In a frozen food product, the activity of microorganisms is negligible. Enzymatic processes may continue, although at a reduced rate. Fast freezing and low storage temperatures are favorable for holding enzyme action at a minimum and for the best retention of nutrients. Most vegetables are blanched before freezing to destroy enzymes so that enzymatic action does not produce off-flavors and undesirable texture changes during frozen storage. When the secondary changes in flavor and texture resulting from blanching are unacceptable, such as in freezing strawberries or other fresh fruits, chemicals such as vitamin C (ascorbic acid) may be added to control some of the enzymatic reactions [19]. After thawing, the growth of microorganisms may occur at a rapid rate.

The first commercial method of freezing foods was the slow freezing process sometimes called *sharp freezing*. In this method, foods are placed in refrigerated rooms ranging from 25° to –20°F (–4° to –29°C), but large pieces of food or large containers of food require many hours or days to freeze. Quick-freezing methods use lower temperatures, –25° to –40°F (–32° to –40°C), so the time of freezing is greatly reduced over that required in sharp freezing. Other factors that aid in hastening the freezing process are small masses of foods, contact with freezing coils or metal plates, and rapidly moving currents of frigid air. Figure 30-1 shows the relative differences in time of freezing by quick- and slow-freezing methods. The freezing of food in most home freezers is a relatively slow process.

The process of freezing rapidly at very low temperatures (–76°F/–60°C or lower) is called *cryogenic freezing*. In cryogenic freezers, which use liquid nitrogen or carbon dioxide, the food is cooled so quickly that many tiny ice crystals form simultaneously, producing a much smaller number of large crystals. Tiny ice crystals have a less damaging effect on plant and animal cells than large crystals.

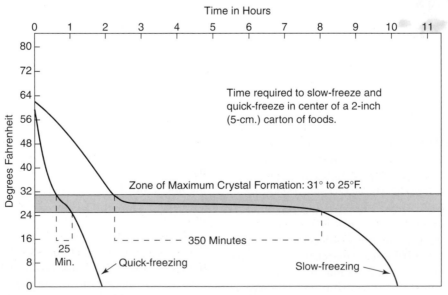

FIGURE 30-1 Diagram showing some differences between quick and slow freezing. *(Courtesy of Frosted Foods Sales Corporation)*

Changes During Freezing, Storage, and Thawing

Changes may occur in many foods that are to be frozen as they are held before freezing. Careful handling, transportation, and storage procedures must be used before and during preparation for freezing if quality loss is to be minimized [19]. Crops should be harvested at the optimal stage of maturity and the produce frozen before the sugar content is reduced or undesirable enzyme activity develops. Such care greatly increases the chances that high-quality frozen produce will result. Many changes still occur in the freezing of food, holding it in frozen storage, and thawing it.

Formation of Ice Crystals. Ice crystal formation, changes in ice crystals during frozen storage, and later thawing all affect the texture of many frozen foods. The effects of freezing depend partly on the nature and state of the material that is frozen. Vegetable and fruit tissues, in particular, decrease in firmness with freezing and thawing. Whether plant tissues are blanched may affect how ice crystals form in the tissues. For example, in unblanched tissue, the cell walls are intact, and the exchange of water through osmosis is possible. If the freezing rate is slow, significant amounts of water may translocate from within cells into the extracellular medium. The formation of ice crystals in extracellular spaces causes injury to the cells. On thawing, not all of the moisture is reabsorbed by the cells.

With rapid freezing, more and smaller ice crystals are formed within cells. These also cause damage to cell structures, although the damage is less when the crystals are small. The loss of water held in the cells (turgor) as the cells are ruptured during freezing is probably responsible for much of the loss of firmness in frozen and thawed plant tissues.

As the temperature is reduced during freezing and more ice crystals form, the concentration of dissolved substances in the unfrozen medium increases, and the viscosity of this unfrozen portion increases. At some temperature, depending on the composition of the system, the viscosity of the unfrozen matrix becomes so high that molecular motion is greatly inhibited. Unfrozen water molecules can then no longer migrate to join ice crystals. Other reaction rates become slowed. The temperature at which this transformation takes place is called the *glass transition temperature* (T_g). The transition state can be detected by observing changes in various dielectric, mechanical, and thermodynamic properties [21]. Frozen storage stability is greatest at or below T_g temperature. This information can be valuable in optimizing storage conditions for particular frozen products as researchers develop methods of modifying T_g [19].

Enzyme Action. Enzymes are present in all living tissue. Respiration, catalyzed by many enzymes, continues in fruits and vegetables after they are severed from the growing plant. These metabolic reactions reduce sugar content, which accounts for the loss of sweetness in such vegetables as peas and corn. Other enzymatic changes also occur. Unless the enzymes responsible for undesirable chemical changes are destroyed before foods are frozen, the foods may show various undesirable color, flavor, and texture changes during freezing, storage, and thawing. Freezing inhibits enzyme action somewhat, but it does not destroy the enzymes.

Vegetables are blanched before freezing to inactivate enzymes that may cause browning, destruction of chlorophyll and carotenoid pigments, or development of unpleasant flavors during storage [2, 18]. In addition, blanching shrinks the vegetable tissues so that they pack more easily, expels air so that the potential for oxidation is lessened, and decreases the microbial load. From the standpoint of both overcooking and loss of soluble nutrients, however, the blanching operation should be as short as possible.

Light-colored fruits, such as peaches and apples, are particularly susceptible to enzymatic oxidative browning in both the fresh and frozen states. The addition of sugar or syrup to the fruit before freezing aids in the retention of color, although darkening may occur if the fruits are held too long. Sugar also aids in preventing marked flavor changes and loss of the natural aroma. The addition of vitamin C to the syrup is effective in preventing browning; it acts as an antioxidant. Citric and other organic acids may also be effective for some fruits by lowering the pH enough to interfere with the activity of the browning enzymes.

Nonenzymatic Oxidation. The process of nonenzymatic oxidation of fatty materials in frozen foods, may occur. Residual oxygen is usually present in frozen foods, and the fat of pork is particularly susceptible to oxidation and the development of rancidity. Bacon does not keep well in frozen storage. Antioxidants may be added to some products commercially to control unwanted oxidation.

Desiccation. If food products to be frozen are not properly packaged with moisture/vapor-proof material, they tend to lose moisture by sublimation. Some of the ice changes directly to water vapor without going through the liquid state, and the water vapor collects to form frost inside the package and/or inside the freezing compartment. Desiccation or dehydration thus occurs.

The term *freezer burn* as applied to frozen foods refers to dehydration resulting in discoloration, change in texture, and off-flavors. This condition is often observed in frozen poultry and other flesh foods as white or brownish dehydrated areas. It also may occur in other foods. Proper packaging is important in the control of freezer burn.

Activity of Microorganisms. Usually present in frozen foods, microorganisms' activity is negligible as

FOCUS ON SCIENCE

Why Are Vegetables, but Not Fruit, Blanched before Freezing?

Vegetables have different characteristics compared to fruits and therefore can be blanched before freezing. Fruits will turn mushy after defrosting if blanched. This change in texture is not a problem for fruits that are going to be cooked after defrosting. However, if frozen fruits are to be used without cooking, they should be treated with some type of antioxidant to prevent discoloration so that a better texture can be maintained after thawing.

---

long as the storage temperature remains below 16° to 10°F (–9° to –12°C). The microorganisms become active at warmer temperatures. They may begin to multiply rapidly as soon as defrosting occurs. It is important that frozen foods be held at optimal, nonfluctuating storage temperatures and be used as soon as they are defrosted.

Selection of Foods for Freezing

Success in freezing depends to a considerable degree on the kinds and varieties of foods selected for freezing. Local agricultural experiment stations are usually able to furnish advice concerning the kinds and varieties of locally grown fruits and vegetables that are best adapted to freezing preservation. The fruits that are least changed in freezing preservation include red tart cherries, cranberries, currants, gooseberries, blueberries, and raspberries. Strawberries and peaches yield frozen products superior to those preserved by other methods. Loganberries, boysenberries, blackberries, dewberries, pineapples, melons, apples, and plums also yield good frozen products.

Although citrus fruits do not freeze well, their juices freeze quite satisfactorily, as do apple cider and other fruit juices. Some fruit juices are concentrated by partial freezing, the ice crystals being removed by straining. Some vegetables do not freeze satisfactorily, including green onions, lettuce and other salad greens, radishes, and raw tomatoes.

Fruits and vegetables should be frozen at the proper stage of maturity. Vegetables should be harvested while they are young and tender, and fruits should be at their optimal stage of ripeness for best flavor, color, and texture. Meats and poultry to be frozen should be of high quality. Fish deteriorates so rapidly that it is best frozen as soon as possible after it is caught.

Techniques for Freezing

Fruits.   Detailed instructions for the freezing of fruits and vegetables are provided in the Cooperative Extension Service, University of Georgia/Athens, Bulletin 989 [1] and the *Ball Blue Book* [12].

Mixing juicy fruits with dry sugar draws out the juices to form a syrup. Alternatively, the fruit can be covered with a sugar syrup. Most fruits require sugar or syrup treatment to protect against enzymatic changes during freezing and storage. Blanching changes the fresh flavor and texture characteristics of fruits and is thus not commonly used. Blueberries and cranberries yield satisfactory products when frozen without sugar or syrup or scalding. Strawberries can be frozen whole, but they retain their best color and flavor in sliced form in sugar or syrup packs.

When syrups are used, they are prepared and chilled prior to packing. Vitamin C may be added to the syrup to control browning of the fruit—approximately 1/2 teaspoon of crystalline vitamin C per quart of syrup. Commercial products containing vitamin C are also available for use in retarding the browning of frozen fruit. Syrup concentrations usually vary from about 30 to 70 percent sugar, although lower concentrations may be preferred from both a flavor and nutritive standpoint.

Vegetables.   Most vegetables yield products of the best quality and flavor when frozen on the day they are harvested. If immediate freezing is impossible, adequate refrigeration is necessary for the interim. The speed at which the vegetables go from garden to freezer is one of the most important factors affecting quality in frozen products. The stage of maturity is also important. For those vegetables that change rapidly in maturity, such as peas, corn, snap beans, lima beans, soybeans, and asparagus, one or two days may mean the difference between a young tender vegetable and one that is tough and of poor quality.

Washing, draining, and sorting of the vegetables usually precede trimming and cutting. To avoid undesirable enzymatic changes, which adversely affect color, flavor, and texture during freezing and frozen storage, most vegetables require blanching to inactivate enzymes. Blanching can be done in boiling water, in steam, or by the application of microwaves. Water-soluble constituents are better retained in steam blanching, but efficient steaming equipment is sometimes difficult to obtain for home use. A tightly closed container is needed that holds enough rapidly boiling water to form steam and a rack to hold the vegetables above the water level. If boiling water is used, enough water should be used so that the boiling does not stop when the vegetables are placed in the water. Wire racks are ideal containers to hold the vegetables. At least one gallon of water per pound of vegetables is needed, and more might be desirable.

Important as the blanching process is, it should not be overdone. The shortest possible time needed to inactivate enzymes should be used to avoid both actual cooking and the loss of water-soluble nutrients. Small quantities of a vegetable are blanched at one time so that all pieces will be quickly, thoroughly, and uniformly heated. After blanching, the vegetables must be cooled quickly in cold running water or ice water to about 50°F (10°C). Chilling is necessary to avoid overheating and to maintain quality. Required times are equal for chilling and blanching.

Prompt freezing is very important in the freezing preservation of foods, particularly vegetables. The sooner vegetables are frozen after blanching, the better the product is likely to be.

Meat, Fish, and Poultry. Meats to be frozen are usually cut into pieces of a suitable size for cooking. The pieces may be steaks, chops, roasts, ground meat, cubes for stews, or other forms. Removal of the bone conserves freezer space. Fish can be boned and packed as fillets or steaks. Poultry can be dressed and left whole for roasting or cut into pieces. Giblets are usually wrapped in parchment and placed inside of whole roasters and broilers. Only high-quality fresh meat products should be frozen.

Careful wrapping or packaging with recommended packaging materials is essential in protecting the products from oxidation and desiccation. More information on the freezing of meat, fish, and poultry is found in the *Ball Blue Book* [12] and in bulletins obtained from county agricultural extension agents [1].

Eggs. Frozen egg whites seem to lose none of the quality needed for culinary uses; however, yolks become gummy and gelled on thawing because of an irreversible change involving the lipoproteins. To be usable, a stabilizer such as sugar, syrup, or salt must be added to yolks. Mixed whole eggs usually have a small amount of stabilizer added because they contain the yolk, but they have been successfully frozen without a stabilizer.

When freezing eggs at home, about 1 tablespoon of sugar or corn syrup or 1/2 teaspoon of salt can be blended with 1 cup of egg yolk before freezing. The use of a small container that makes possible the thawing of only the amount of egg needed is recommended. Defrosted eggs usually have a relatively high bacterial count and deteriorate rapidly after defrosting.

Prepared Foods. On the market are many different frozen prepared foods and meals that require only reheating. Packaging technologies that allow direct heating in the microwave oven or boiling in the bag in which the product was frozen contribute to the wide variety of available choices. Prepared foods that require only thawing, including a variety of baked products, are usually brought into the kitchen for short-term storage only.

Many prepared foods can also be frozen in the kitchen for convenience and efficiency. Various casseroles, main dish items, and plated meals can be prepared in quantity and frozen for future use.

Programs to provide meals for homebound elderly people often involve the preparation and delivery of single meals one to five days a week. Some programs, however, have elected to offer supplementary meals. Plated meals prepared on-site, but not served immediately, may be frozen, decreasing cost and waste in preparation. Freezing practices in such programs have been investigated in a study of time–temperature relationships during the freezing of packaged meals. Similar meals were frozen in a refrigerator-freezer unit, an upright freezer, and a walk-in freezer [23]. Meals packaged in individually divided foil

FOCUS ON SCIENCE

A New Alternative to Blanching: Infrared (IR) Heating

Blanching and dehydration are two essential processes with high energy consumption for fruits and vegetables. Blanching is normally achieved using hot water and steam that can cause loss of nutrients. Because fruit cannot be blanched prior to freezing, infrared (IR) heating is being considered. Intermittent IR heating is an intermittent heat treatment that is able to dry, blanch, and dehydrate fruits and vegetables simultaneously. Studies have shown that IR satisfactorily inactivates enzymes in apples and removes a desirable amount of moisture while preserving surface color in the fruit.

Source: Pan, Z., Olson, D. A., Ameratanga, K., Olsen, C. W., Zhu, Y., and McHugh, T. H. (2005), *Feasibility of using infrared heating and dehydration of fruits and vegetables* (Meeting Paper ASAF No: 056086), 1–13. St. Joseph, MI: American Society of Agricultural Engineers.

containers were positioned either individually or stacked three deep on the freezer shelf. The temperature during the freezing process was recorded in the center meal.

These investigators reported that the temperature in the refrigerator-freezer was 12°F (–11°C), in the upright freezer it was –15°F (–26°C), and in the walk-in freezer it was –9°F (–23°C). The time that the meals spent in the danger zone, 45° to 140°F (7° to 60°C), after placement in the freezer, was longer in the refrigerator-freezer than in the other freezing units and was much longer in all the freezers for the stacked meals than for the single layer. The time in the danger zone was about half as long for pot roast as for oven-baked chicken. It was concluded that freezers that maintain temperatures above 0°F (–18°C) may have difficulty freezing meals within a two-hour period. It was also concluded that stacked meals take considerably longer to exit the danger zone than those that are placed in a single layer. Employees who work in feeding programs for the elderly may need to be trained in the proper handling of food to be frozen [23].

Baked products can be frozen either before or after baking. The storage life of unbaked batters and doughs is usually less than that of the baked products. If frosted or iced cakes are to be frozen, they might be frozen first without wrapping to prevent the wrapping material from sticking to the frosting, and then wrapped and returned to the freezer.

Frozen bread doughs can be made from the usual formulations, provided that the level of yeast is increased to 4 or 5 percent. A short fermentation period is desirable before freezing. If a satisfactory product is to result, sufficient yeast viability must be maintained during freezing and freezer storage to produce adequate amounts of carbon dioxide gas.

Certain foods do not freeze well at home, although commercial processes and materials may produce satisfactory results [15]. For example, cooked egg whites toughen and become rubbery, mayonnaise tends to separate as the emulsion breaks, starch-thickened sauces tend to weep as starch retrogradation occurs, and fried foods often change in flavor when reheated.

Containers

Containers for freezing foods can be made of glass, metal, plastic materials, paper or fiber board, and certain moisture/vapor-proof transparent materials and should have tight-fitting lids or closures. A container that is ideal for freezer use has been described as one that is both airtight to prevent oxidation and moisture/vapor-proof to prevent dehydration. Of course, liquid tightness is necessary for use with liquid foods, such as sugar and syrup packs for fruits.

Freezer space is usually such that cube-shaped containers permit the most efficient use of storage space. It is obvious that rigidity in a container prevents crushing of the products. If containers are made of a material that can be thoroughly cleaned, they may be reused. Moisture/vapor-proof bags are satisfactory if little handling is required.

TABLE 30-1	Size of Container in Relation to Number of Servings
Servings	**Size of Container**
1 or 2	1/2 pt
4	1 pt
8	1 qt

Pliable moisture/vapor-proof bags should have as much air as possible removed from them and should be twisted and tightly closed. Immersing the lower part of the bag and its contents in water while packaging such irregularly shaped items as whole poultry may aid in removing air by the pressure of the water on the bag. Boil-in-the-bag containers are available for home use in freezing prepared foods. These bags may be heat-sealed before freezing.

The size of the container used is important because many frozen foods should not be held after defrosting (see Table 30-1). Containers larger than 1/2 gallon or 5 pounds are not recommended because of the slow rate of freezing.

For dry packs, the cartons can be almost completely filled before freezing. Syrup packs, or juicy products such as sliced strawberries mixed with sugar, should have about 10 percent headspace to allow for expansion of the contents during freezing.

Use and Management of the Home Freezer

A freezer can be a convenience in many ways, but careful planning should go into its selection and use. The needs in each situation differ, and freezer use should be adapted to individual conditions and preferences. A freezer is a considerable investment and should be kept full or nearly full at all times to minimize the cost per unit of food stored. For example, as the stock of frozen garden vegetables and fruits diminishes, it may be possible to buy larger quantities of commercially frozen products at a savings; however, the quality of frozen foods is not maintained indefinitely—it decreases with time. Suggested maximum storage periods for maintaining good quality in commercially frozen foods that are stored in kitchen freezers are provided in Table 30-2.

Time can be saved by doubling or tripling recipes when they are being prepared if they are suitable for freezing. The frozen products can be conveniently served on busy days. Advance planning in meal preparation and entertaining may be simplified with the use of a freezer. An accurate inventory of frozen foods should be kept.

All foods should be stored no higher than 0°F (–18°C) to maintain palatability and nutritive value. Accurate and effective temperature control is therefore important. If a freezer stops running and remains off for an extended period, several alternatives are possible to

TABLE 3C-2 Suggested Maximum Home-Storage Periods to Maintain Good Quality in Commercially Frozen Foods

Food	Approximate Holding Period at 0°F (−13°C) (months)	Food	Approximate Holding Period at 0°F (−18°C) (months)	Food	Approximate Holding Period at 0°F (−18°C) (months)
Fruits and vegetables		Pies (unbaked)		Cooked chicken and turkey	
Fruits		Apple	8	Chicken or turkey dinners (sliced meat and gravy)	6
Cherries	12	Boysenberry	8		
Peaches	12	Cherry	8	Chicken or turkey pies	12
Raspberries	12	Peach	8	Fried chicken	4
Strawberries	12			Fried chicken dinners	4
Fruit juice concentrates		*Meat*			
Apple	12	Beef		*Fish*	
Grape	12	Hamburger or chopped (thin) steaks	3	Fillets	
Orange	12	Roasts	12	Cod, flounder, haddock, halibut, pollock	6
Vegetables		Steaks	12		
Asparagus	8	Lamb		Mullet, ocean perch, sea trout, striped bass	3
Beans	8	Patties (ground meat)	3		
Cauliflower	8	Roasts	12	Pacific Ocean perch	2
Corn	8	Pork, cured	2	Salmon steaks	2
Peas	8	Pork, fresh		Sea trout, dressed	3
Spinach	8	Chops	4		
Frozen desserts					
Ice cream	1				

TABLE 30-2 Continued

Food	Approximate Holding Period at 0°F (−18°C) (months)	Food	Approximate Holding Period at 0°F (−18°C) (months)	Food	Approximate Holding Period at 0°F (−18°C) (months)
Sherbet	1	Roasts	8	Striped bass, dressed	3
		Sausage	2	Whiting, drawn	4
Baked goods		*Veal*			
Bread and yeast rolls		Cutlets, chops	4	*Shellfish*	
White bread	3	Roasts	8	Clams, shucked	3
Cinnamon rolls	2	Cooked meat		Crabmeat	
Plain rolls	3	Meat dinners	3	Dungeness	3
Cakes		Meat pie	3	King	10
Angel	2	Swiss steak	3	Oysters, shucked	4
Chiffon	2			Shrimp	12
Chocolate layer	4	*Poultry*			
Fruit	12	Chicken		*Cooked fish and shellfish*	
Pound	6	Cut up	9	Fish with cheese sauce	3
Yellow	6	Livers	3	Fish with lemon butter sauce	3
Danish pastry	3	Whole	12		
Doughnuts		Duck, whole	6	Fried fish dinner	3
Cake type	3	Goose, whole	6	Fried fish sticks, scallops, or shrimp	3
Yeast raised	3	Turkey			
		Cut up	6	Shrimp creole	3
		Whole	12	Tuna pie	3

Source: Courtesy of the U.S. Department of Agriculture

keep the food from spoiling. If it is available, enough dry ice may be added to the freezer to maintain below freezing temperatures for a few days. Or, the food may be put into insulated boxes or wrapped in newspapers and blankets and rushed to a freezer-locker plant. If the freezer will be off only a few hours, it should simply be kept tightly closed.

Sometimes frozen foods are partially or completely thawed before it is discovered that the freezer is not operating. Although partial thawing and refreezing reduce the quality of most foods, partially thawed foods that still contain ice crystals or foods that are still cold (about 40°F or 4°C) can usually be safely refrozen. Ground meats, poultry, and seafood should not be refrozen if they have thawed completely, because bacteria multiply rapidly in these foods. Each package of meat, vegetable, or cooked food should be carefully examined. If the food is thawed or the color or odor is questionable, the food should be discarded because it may be dangerous.

CANNING

Canning involves two processes: (1) the application to foods of temperatures high enough to destroy essentially all microorganisms present, both vegetative cells and spores, and (2) the sealing of the heated product in sterilized airtight containers to prevent recontamination. The degree of heat and the length of heating vary with the type of food and the kinds of microorganisms likely to occur. Fruits and tomatoes that are sufficiently acid are successfully canned at the temperature of boiling water. The time of boiling depends on the degree of acidity, the consistency of the product, the method of preparation, and other factors. Vegetables, including some low-acid tomatoes, and meats, which are relatively low in acid, must be heated to temperatures higher than that of boiling water at atmospheric pressure. This method involves the use of a pressure canner. Because bacterial spores that may be present are more resistant to heat under conditions of low acidity, the time of heating necessary to destroy them at the temperature of boiling water would likely be several hours. The food would be rather unpalatable after such a prolonged cooking period. Moist heat evidently destroys microorganisms by coagulating proteins and destroys enzymes in a similar manner.

Historical Highlights

The history of canning began about 1795, when the French government offered a prize for the development of a new method of preserving food from one harvest to the next. Nicolas Appert, a Parisian confectioner, worked many years on such a process and finally, in 1809, he successfully preserved some foods by sealing them with corks in glass bottles and heating them for various lengths of time [7]. Appert received financial support from the French government, including an initial cash award (12,000 francs) for his accomplishment.

With contributions from many workers along the way, the canning industry gradually developed until today cans of food are being filled, sealed, and processed by the millions. The tin canister was first developed in England about 1810. Peter Durand, a broker, was granted a patent in London, possibly as an agent or middleman for a French inventor, Phillipe de Girard [8, 9]. Canned foods were produced in England for the British navy in the early 1800s. The retort for pressure canning was developed in Philadelphia around 1874 [11]. Pasteur's work with microorganisms about 1860 began a study of the true causes of food spoilage, and the process of canning was approached on a scientific basis at the turn of the twentieth century.

Various types of batch and continuous **retorts** are used in commercial canning [13]. Some retorts agitate or rotate the cans during processing to increase the rate of heat penetration and to aid in heat distribution. Commercial canning also includes methods that employ higher temperatures and shorter time periods than are used in traditional commercial canning. **Aseptic canning** (discussed in Chapter 29) is also practiced, preserving a fresher flavor for many food products. The variety of equipment available for commercial canning provides the industry with the flexibility it needs to develop and produce unique food products and to select various packaging options. Semirigid and flexible packages, such as the **retort pouch**, can be readily handled to produce shelf-stable foods. In all cases of commercial canning, careful written documentation of temperature distribution during processing must be maintained [17].

Although much of our canned food is now produced commercially, some people still can or bottle foods at home for various reasons, including palatability, economy, and the satisfaction derived from do-it-yourself projects. For those who must restrict their intake of salt and sugar, products may be canned without the addition of these substances. Canning tomatoes from backyard gardens appears to be one of the more popular home food preservation activities.

Methods for Home Canning

High-quality products should always be selected for canning and recommended procedures followed to ensure safe products that do not spoil on storage. Detailed steps to be followed in home canning are given in the Cooperative Extension Service, University of Georgia/Athens, Bulletin 989 [1], the *Ball Blue Book* [12], and the *USDA Complete Guide to Home Canning* [24].

Packing. Only glass jars are generally available for home canning. Foods can be packed into the jars either raw or hot in preparation for the canning processing step (Figure 30-2).

In the raw-pack method of canning, the uncooked food is packed into the container, and the container is filled with boiling liquid. Some headspace should be left

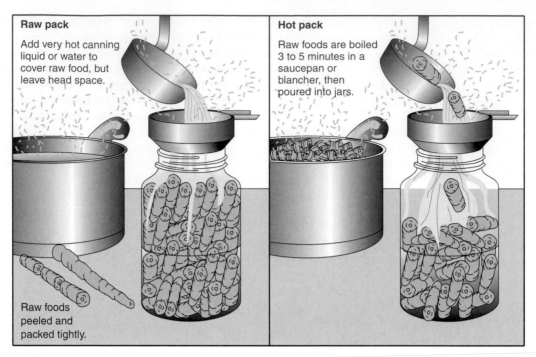

Raw pack

Add very hot canning liquid or water to cover raw food, but leave head space.

Raw foods peeled and packed tightly.

Hot pack

Raw foods are boiled 3 to 5 minutes in a saucepan or blancher, then poured into jars.

FIGURE 30-2 Bottles can be filled by either the raw-pack or the hot-pack method, as illustrated. *(Courtesy of the U.S. Department of Agriculture)*

in the top of the container before sealing; usually 1/2 to 1 inch is suggested. This space allows for the expansion of the jar contents during heating. Glass jars are only partially sealed before processing at the necessary temperature for the recommended time.

In the hot-pack method of canning, the food is heated in syrup, water, steam, or extracted juice before being packed into containers. With this method, the temperature of the food should be at least 170°F (77°C) when packed in the container.

The raw-pack method may have an advantage over the hot-pack method in that large pieces of fruit, such as peach halves, or fragile berries can be placed in jars so that they present an attractive appearance and are closely packed. The hot-pack method may be advantageously used for some foods because it helps to drive out air, wilts or shrinks plant tissues, allows closer packing, and slightly shortens the processing time. The initial temperature of the food is relatively high, and heat penetration is more rapid when the food is packed hot. Pears, apples, and pineapples have a more attractive translucent appearance when prepared by the hot-pack rather than by the raw-pack method. Also, more fruit can be fit into the container.

Processing. The processing of canned fruits, vegetables, and meats is done after these foods have been packed into containers by either the hot- or raw-pack method as described previously. The processing may be accomplished in a boiling water bath for acid fruits and acid tomatoes. For vegetables, meat, fish, and poultry, which

are low in acid, the use of a pressure canner is essential. A higher temperature is required with these products for the complete destruction of bacterial spores. Of particular concern is the destruction of the spores of *Clostridium botulinum*. These spores can vegetate and, under the anaerobic conditions that are found in the sealed cans, may produce a deadly toxin that causes botulism when consumed, even in tiny amounts. In low-acid foods such as vegetables and meats, the temperature of boiling water is not sufficient to ensure spore destruction. A pressure canner, in which higher temperatures can be attained, must be used in the canning of these products.

Boiling Water Bath. High pH or acidic foods may be processed by a boiling water bath. Processing by means of a boiling water bath requires a large boiling water canner (Figure 30-3). The canner must be deep enough so that at least one inch of briskly boiling water will be above the tops of the jars during processing. A fitted lid covers the canner. A rack keeps jars one inch or less above the bottom, thus avoiding breakage and allowing even circulation of heat underneath the jars. Unless the bath has a removable holder for jars, a lifter of some kind is necessary for placing jars into, and removing them from, the boiling water.

The canner should be filled halfway with water. For raw-packed foods, preheat the water to 140°F (60°C); for hot-packed foods, 180°F (82°C). Load the filled jars, fitted with lids, into the canner rack and use the handles to lower the rack into the water, or fill the canner one jar at a time. Add more boiling water so that the water level is at

FIGURE 30-3 The boiling water should extend two inches above the jars in a boiling water canner. A rack in the canner promotes proper water circulation around the jars and allows for easy removal of the jars. *(Courtesy of Alltrista Consumer Products Company, Marketers of Ball brand and Kerr brand home canning products)*

least one inch above the jar tops. Heat on high until the water boils vigorously. Cover the canner and lower the heat to maintain a gentle boil (212°F, 100°C) throughout the processing period [12, 24].

Some varieties of tomatoes now being grown in the United States, including Garden State, Ace, 55VF, and Cal Ace, are lower in acid content than those commonly produced in previous years. These tomatoes are likely to have pH values above 4.6 and are considered to be low-acid foods. If they are to be canned as acid foods in a boiling water canner, they must be acidified with lemon juice or citric acid to a pH of less than 4.6. Two tablespoons of bottled lemon juice or 1/2 teaspoon citric acid per quart of tomatoes will ensure a safe level of acidity [12, 24]. Properly acidified tomatoes can be processed in a boiling water canner. Alternatively, low-acid tomatoes, not treated with lemon juice or citric acid, must be processed in a pressure canner, as are other vegetables and meat products.

Pressure Canning. Low-acid foods, with a pH of higher than 4.6, must be canned with a pressure canner to achieve temperatures higher than 212°F (100°C) [12]. The boiling point of a liquid such as water varies with the atmospheric pressure over its surface. As the atmospheric pressure is decreased with higher altitudes, the boiling point of the liquid is decreased. In a pressure canner, the water vapor or steam that is produced when the water is heated to its normal boiling point is captured inside the canner with its tightly sealed cover, thus increasing the pressure over the surface of the water in the pressure canner. This raises the boiling point of the water, and temperatures higher than the usual boiling point of water can thus be achieved.

Pressure canners in the past were constructed of heavy metal with clamp-on or turn-on lids. They had a dial gauge to indicate pressure. Most pressure canners of today are lightweight, thin-walled kettles with turn-on

lids (Figure 30-4). Their essential features are a *rack* to hold jars off the bottom, a *vent port* (steam vent or petcock) that is left open for a few minutes to drive out air and fill the compartment with steam and then closed with a *counterweight* or *weighted gauge*, and a *safety fuse* or *valve* through which steam may escape if too high a pressure develops within the canner (Figure 30-5). The pressure canner is used primarily to provide a high temperature for the destruction of heat resistant microorganisms and their spores in a shorter time than is possible at the boiling temperature of water.

To operate the pressure canner, put two to three inches of water in the canner and then place filled jars on the rack, using a jar lifter. Space the jars to permit circulation of steam. Fasten the canner lid securely, making sure that the gasket is clean and in place. Leave the petcock open or the weight off the vent port and heat on high until steam flows from the port or petcock. Allow a steady stream of steam to exit from the canner for 10 minutes before closing the petcock or placing the weight on the vent port. The steam drives air out of the canner as completely as possible, or *exhausts* the canner. If the air is not removed, the air in the canner contributes a partial pressure along with the steam, and the temperature inside the canner will not be as high as when all the pressure comes from steam. The food may therefore be underprocessed. Canners are not equipped with thermometers that show the exact interior temperature, so it is important that the canner be properly exhausted. Table 30-3 shows temperatures that are obtainable in a pressure canner at different pressures, provided that no air remains in the canner.

Pressure will build up during the first three to five minutes after closing the vent port. Start the timing process when the pressure gauge shows the desired pressure or when the weighted gauge begins to wiggle or rock. Regulate the source of heat to maintain a steady pressure on the gauge. Rapid and large fluctuations in pressure during processing will cause liquid to be lost from the jars. Weighted gauges should jiggle periodically or rock slowly throughout the process. They allow the release of tiny amounts of steam each time they move and thus control the pressure precisely. Constant watching is not required.

When the processing time is completed, turn off the heat and remove the canner from the heat source, if possible. Let the canner depressurize. *Do not force the cooling process.* Cooling the canner with cold water or opening the vent port or petcock before the canner is depressurized will cause loss of liquid from the jars and the seals may fail. After the canner is depressurized, remove the weight from the vent port or open the petcock, unfasten the lid, and open the canner carefully.

Immediately after processing in either the boiling water canner or the pressure canner, jars that were not tightly closed before processing, as is proper when using self-sealing lids, should now be tightly closed. Sealing occurs automatically with cooling. A vacuum is gradually produced as the jars cool.

(a)

(b)

FIGURE 30-4 A pressure canner is necessary to obtain temperatures higher than 212°F (100°C).
(a) This pressure canner is shown with jars of canned food. *(Courtesy of National Presto Industries)*
(b) Pressure canners are heated on top of the range to achieve the necessary pressure for the canning of low-acid foods such as green beans. *(Courtesy of Alltrista Consumer Products Company, Makers of Ball brand and Kerr brand home canning products)*

The temperature most commonly used for home canning of low-acid foods is 240°F (116°C), corresponding to a pressure of 10 pounds per square inch. However, it has been reported that a higher pressure (15 pounds) and thus a shorter processing time also gives satisfactory results in terms of texture, color, and flavor of vegetables. Asparagus, peas, and strained squash were the vegetables tested [14].

Internal canner temperatures are lower at higher altitudes. Adjustments must therefore be made to compensate.

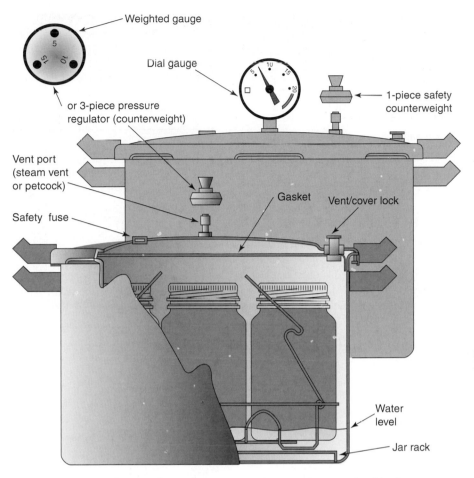

FIGURE 30-5 Essential parts of a pressure canner. Also note the water level in the canner. *(Courtesy of the U.S. Department of Agriculture)*

TABLE 30-3	Temperatures Obtainable at Different Pressures in a Pressure Cooker	
	Temperature	
Pressure (lb)	**°F**	**°C**
5	228	109
10	240	116
15	250	121
20	259	126
25	267	131

If the pressure canner has a pressure gauge, the canner should be checked for accuracy at the beginning of each season. Checking is often done locally through the county cooperative extension service or the home service department of a utility company. The amount and direction of error in the pressure gauge should be noted on a tag tied to the canner. An adjustment should then be made when the canner is used. Weighted-gauge canners cannot be adjusted for altitude. Therefore, at altitudes above 1,000 feet, they must be operated at canner pressures of 10 instead of 5 pounds per square inch or 15 instead of 10 pounds, as indicated in the *Ball Blue Book* [12] and USDA Home Canning Guide [24].

Containers for Canning

Commercial Canning. Containers for commercially canned foods are usually made of tin-plated steel (tin cans), aluminum, or glass. Tin-free steel cans have also been produced. Tin cans are of two types: plain and lacquered. The latter may be coated with the bright, or R, lacquer suitable for all red-colored foods containing anthocyanin pigment and for pumpkin and squash. If anthocyanins are canned in plain tin, they fade and become bluish. Pumpkin and squash tend to corrode plain tin. The dull, or C, lacquer should not be used with acid foods or with meats that contain much fat, as both acid and fat may cause the lacquer to peel. This makes the food unsightly, although it is harmless. The dull, or C, lacquer is used for corn, succotash, and other sulfur-containing foods to prevent dark deposits of tin or iron sulfide on the food and on the can. Tin sulfide, which is brown, and iron sulfide, which is black, are not harmful but detract from the appearance of the food.

FOCUS ON SCIENCE

Canning at High Altitudes

When canning at high altitudes using the boiling water bath or a pressure canner, modifications must be made to the processing times and pressure levels for the food to be safe. Some of the basic differences for high altitude canning are noted below.

Boiling Water Bath—High-Acid Foods

The boiling point of water is lower at high altitudes (at high altitudes, water boils below 212°F/100°C). Therefore the processing time must be increased by 1 minute for each 1,000 feet above sea level if the time is 20 minutes or less. If the processing time is more than 20 minutes, increase time by 2 minutes per 1,000 feet.

Pressure Canner—Required for Low-Acid Foods

All low acid foods must be heated at 240°F (115°C) for the appropriate time in order to destroy heat-resistant bacteria and the spores formed by bacteria. To achieve these temperatures, a steam pressure canner must be used. At sea level, 10 pounds of

steam pressure will produce 240°F (115°C), but at altitudes of 2,000 feet and above, the number of pounds of steam pressure must be increased to reach this temperature. For safe canning at high altitudes, the pressure must be increased by 1/2 pound per 1,000 feet above sea level, as illustrated in the following:

Altitude	Pressure Required
Sea level	10.0 lbs.
2,000 feet	11.0 lbs.
3,000 feet	11.5 lbs.
4,000 feet	12.0 lbs.
5,000 feet	12.5 lbs.
7,000 feet	13.5 lbs.
10,000 feet	15.0 lbs.

Source: Colorado State University Cooperative Extension Resource Center. Prepared by Pat Kendall, Professor of Food Science and Human Nutrition. Colorado State University Cooperative Extension. Retrieved February 27, 2008, from http://cerc.colostate.edu/titles/p41.html

---

Commercial canning in metal has several advantages over glass: Breakage is eliminated, cans are always sealed before processing, heat penetration is more rapid than with glass, the cans may be rapidly cooled after processing by being plunged into cold water, and the cans are generally less expensive. Special flexible packages, such as retort pouches, may also be used for commercial canning to produce shelf-stable foods not requiring refrigeration. These packages are less expensive to process and ship, after the initial expense by the food processor for the necessary processing equipment or modification of conventional equipment [20, 25].

Home Canning. The jars generally available in the United States for home canning are heat-resistant glass jars with self-sealing lids (Figure 30-6). The self-sealing closure for a canning jar has a composition ring in the lid that becomes soft when heated and then hardens, forming a seal on the edge of the jar top when it becomes cold. New lids are required for self-sealing jars each time the jars are used, but the screw bands may be reused over a long period. The lids are placed in simmering, but not boiling water, for at least 10 minutes prior to use according to the manufacturer's directions [12].

For low-acid vegetables and for meats, jars no larger than quart size are recommended because of the danger of poor heat penetration in larger jars. The pint size is

FIGURE 30-6 The most commonly used closure for canning jars is the metal screw band and metal self-sealing lid. Sealing occurs on the top edge of the jar. *(Courtesy of the U.S. Department of Agriculture)*

usually advised for corn, shell beans, and lima beans, in which heat penetration is slow.

Heat Penetration

Heat penetration during canning is affected by such factors as the size of the container, the material from which the container is made, the initial temperature of the food when the processing is started, the temperature used for processing, the fullness of the pack, and the character of the food. Heat penetration is more rapid in smaller containers and in tin than in glass. Starchy vegetables and closely packed leafy vegetables transmit heat poorly. Colloidal starch solutions retard heat penetration more than concentrated sugar solutions.

Heat penetration is more rapid if the food is hot when the processing is started and if a higher temperature is used for processing. In general, the higher the processing temperature, the shorter the required heating time.

Obtaining a Partial Vacuum

A partial vacuum in the sealed jar is important in the canning of food because it helps to maintain an effective seal and it inhibits oxidative changes. A partial vacuum is created when the air within the jar exerts less pressure outward than the atmosphere exerts on the outside of the jar. This vacuum is produced as a result of several events that occur during the canning process. First, food is heated. The application of heat causes internal gases to expand. When the food is heated in a glass canning jar, the gases escape through the partially sealed lid. Formation of an effective vacuum depends largely on this process of *venting*.

After processing is completed and the jar is removed from the canner, sealing occurs. With self-sealing devices, the complete sealing takes place automatically as the softened sealing compound hardens on cooling. During cooling, the contents of the jar contract, leaving a space in the top that is less dense than the atmosphere pressing down on the outside of the lid. Thus, a partial vacuum is formed to aid in keeping the seal tight.

Obtaining an Effective Seal

A good seal is essential in canned foods. All jars should be examined for nicks or rough places on the sealing surfaces that might interfere with a good seal. Lids must fit well. Care should be taken to remove small bits of food from the top of the jar before closing the container, because they interfere with the formation of a complete seal.

After the jars have cooled for 12 to 24 hours, the screw bands may be removed and the jars tested for a complete seal. If the center of the lid is either flat or bulging, it is probably not sealed. It should be concave, that is, pulled down slightly in the center. Try to gently lift the lid off with your fingertips. If the lid does not flex up and down and the lid is tightly attached, then the lid has a good seal [12].

Handling after Processing

Proper handling and storage of canned food are important in maintaining its quality. When glass jars with self-sealing lids are thoroughly cool and have sealed, the screw bands should be removed and rinsed clean so that they can be used again. If they are left on the jars they may stick or rust, making removal difficult. The outside of the jars should be wiped clean of any residual syrup or other material. Containers should be labeled to show the contents and date of processing.

Canned foods should be stored in a cool, dry, dark place. At cool storage temperatures, the eating quality and nutritive value are better maintained. Glass jars, particularly, should be stored in a dark place because light causes fading and discoloration of plant pigments. Properly canned foods may be safely stored for several years, but the quality of the food gradually decreases, especially if storage temperatures are relatively high. Therefore, use of canned foods within a year is generally recommended.

If low-acid vegetables, including low-acid tomatoes, have not been canned according to the recommendations of the USDA, they should be boiled for 10 minutes after opening the can and before tasting any of the food contained in it. For altitudes at and above 1,000 feet, one additional minute should be added per 1,000 feet. This recommendation is for safety in case *Clostridium botulinum* organisms have survived and produced toxin in the sealed jar [12]. Botulism has occurred most commonly from the use of home-canned products.

All canned products should be inspected before use to ensure the vacuum seal is present. Check for signs of mold, gassiness, cloudiness, spurting liquid when the jar is opened, seepage, yeast growth, fermentation, sliminess, and disagreeable odors [12]. All of these are indications of spoilage, and the food should not be used.

CHAPTER SUMMARY

- Freezing is the change in physical state from liquid to solid that occurs when heat is removed from a substance. Most vegetables are blanched before freezing to destroy enzymes that can produce undesirable changes. In fruits, vitamin C may be added to control the enzymatic reactions. The addition of sugar or syrup to fruit before freezing aids in the retention of color and the maintenance of natural flavors and aromas.

- Cryogenic freezing is the process of freezing rapidly at very low temperatures. When food is frozen quickly, tiny ice crystals, less damaging to the food cells, are formed.

- The loss of water held in cells as the cells are ruptured during freezing is probably responsible for much of the loss of firmness in frozen and thawed plant tissues.

- If foods to be frozen are not properly packaged, moisture will be lost by sublimation. Desiccation or dehydration thus occurs. Freezer burn, as applied to frozen foods, refers to dehydration resulting in discoloration, change in texture, and off-flavors.

- The activity of microorganisms is negligible as long as the storage temperature remains below 16° to 10°F (–9° to –12°C). The microorganisms, however, become active at warmer temperatures and begin to multiply rapidly as soon as defrosting occurs.

- Specific techniques for the freezing of fruits, vegetables, meat, fish, poultry, eggs, and prepared foods are recommended for optimum quality. Containers for the freezing of foods should be airtight and moisture/vapor-proof.

- If a freezer stops running and remains off for an extended period, dry ice may be added to maintain freezing temperatures, or the food may be packaged and transported to a freezer-locker plant. Freezers that are off for only a few hours should remain tightly closed.

- Although partial thawing and then refreezing of foods reduces quality, foods that still contain ice crystals may be refrozen. Meats, poultry, and seafood should not be refrozen if complete thawing has occurred. Any questionable food product should be discarded.

- Canning involves two processes: (1) the application to foods of temperatures high enough to destroy essentially all microorganisms present, and (2) the sealing of the heated product in sterilized, airtight containers. The degree of heat and length of heating vary with the type of food and kinds of microorganisms likely to occur.

- Only glass jars manufactured for home canning should be used. Food may be packed into the jars using the raw-pack or hot-pack methods.

- Following packing, foods are processed using a boiling water bath or pressure canning. The boiling water bath requires the use of a large boiling water canner. Only high-acid foods may be processed using the boiling water bath.

- Pressure canning is required for all low-acid foods because these foods must be heated to 240°F (116°C), which may only be achieved in a pressure canner. Some varieties of tomatoes may be low-acid, and therefore it is recommended that all tomatoes be properly acidified with the addition of lemon juice or citric acid if processed using a boiling water canner or are processed using a pressure canner.

- The time of processing varies by altitude. Therefore, when canning, the altitude in your area should be checked and the proper time and pressure guidelines followed.

- Upon the completion of the processing in a pressure canner, the heat should be turned off, and the canner should be allowed to depressurize without using cold water or opening the vent port or petcock to speed the cooling process.

- Immediately after processing in either the boiling water canner or the pressure canner, all jars should be tightly closed. Sealing of the jars occurs automatically with cooling. In home-canned foods, the jars should be tested for a complete seal after the jars have cooled for 12 to 24 hours. The lid should be concave, and it should not lift off with your fingertips.

- Canned foods should be stored in a dry, dark place, at cool storage temperatures to maintain optimum quality. Although properly canned foods may be safely stored for years, the quality declines over time. Thus, use of canned foods within a year is recommended.

- All canned products should be inspected before use to ensure the vacuum seal is still present and to check for signs of spoilage. Low-acid foods, for which the canning process may not have been done according to guidelines, should be boiled for 10 minutes after opening the can and before tasting any of the food. At altitudes above 1,000 feet, additional boiling time is necessary.

STUDY QUESTIONS

1. Discuss differences in methods used, rate and time of freezing, and size of resulting ice crystals between slow freezing and quick freezing.

2. Describe several undesirable changes that may occur during freezing, frozen storage, or thawing of frozen foods.

3. (a) Explain why vegetables should be blanched before freezing.

   (b) Give several suggestions for carrying out the blanching process to ensure that it will accomplish its purpose satisfactorily.

4. What is *freezer burn?* How can it be prevented in frozen foods?

5. How does freezing control the causes of food spoilage and thus preserve foods?

6. Discuss several points that should be considered in selecting foods for freezing.

7. What are two important roles, in addition to sweetening, that are played by sugar or syrup packs in freezing fruits?

8. What general procedures should be followed in the freezing of meat, fish, and poultry?

9. What differences exist between the procedures for freezing egg whites and egg yolks? Why are these different procedures necessary?

10. (a) Why should containers and wrappers used on frozen foods be moisture/vapor-proof?

    (b) Why should headspace be left in containers when freezing foods?

11. List several things that should be considered to make the most effective use of a freezer.

12. Describe some pertinent events in the history of canning that are associated with each of the following names and dates.

    (a) Appert, 1809

    (b) 1810

    (c) 1874

    (d) Pasteur, 1860s

13. Distinguish between the raw-pack and the hot-pack methods of packing canned foods. Discuss advantages of each.

14. Explain why fruits and high-acid tomatoes can be safely canned in a boiling water bath, but vegetables and meat products must be canned in a pressure canner. What might botulism have to do with your explanation?

15. (a) Describe the essential parts of a pressure canner and explain their functions.

    (b) Why is it important to completely exhaust a pressure canner before closing the petcock and building pressure?

    (c) Suggest a possible explanation for the loss of liquid from jars processed in a pressure canner.

16. (a) Of what materials are "tin" cans usually made? Why are their inside surfaces sometimes lacquered with R or C enamel?

    (b) Describe self-sealing lids commonly used on bottled produce. Explain how they work.

    (c) What steps should be taken to ensure that an effective seal is formed in bottled produce?

17. List several factors that may affect the rate of heat penetration as canned foods are processed.

18. Explain how a partial vacuum is formed in canned foods. Why is it important that this occurs?

WEIGHTS AND MEASURES

SYMBOLS FOR MEASUREMENTS

tsp	= teaspoon	cc	= cubic centimeter
Tbsp	= tablespoon	mL	= milliliter
fg	= few grains	L	= liter
fl oz	= fluid ounce	oz	= ounce
c	= cup	lb	= pound
pt	= pint	μg	= microgram
qt	= quart	mg	= milligram
gal	= gallon	g	= gram
		kg	= kilogram
		mm	= millimeter
		cm	= centimeter
		m	= meter

EQUIVALENTS

		Common Use
1 gram	= 0.035 ounce	
1 ounce	= 28.35 grams	30 grams
4 ounces	= 113.40 grams	125 grams
8 ounces	= 226.80 grams	250 grams
1 kilogram	= 2.2 pounds	
1 kilogram	= 1,000 grams	
1 pound	= 0.454 kilogram	
1 pound	= 453.59 grams	450 grams
1 liter	= 1.06 quarts	
1 liter	= 1,000 milliliters	
1 quart	= 0.946 liter	0.95 liter
1 quart	= 946.4 milliliters	950 milliliters
1 cup	= 236.6 milliliters	240 milliliters
1/2 cup	= 118 milliliters	120 milliliters
1 fluid oz	= 29.57 milliliters	30 milliliters
1 tablespoon	= 14.8 milliliters	15 milliliters
1 teaspoon	= 4.9 milliliters	5 milliliters
1 inch	= 2.54 centimeters	2.5 centimeters
1 centimeter	— 0.4 inch	
1 yard	= 0.914 meter	

SOME INGREDIENT SUBSTITUTIONS

For:	Substitute:
1 tablespoon flour (thickener)	1/2 tablespoon cornstarch, potato starch, or arrowroot starch, or 1 tablespoon quick-cooking tapioca
1 cup sifted all-purpose flour	1 cup unsifted all-purpose flour minus 2 tablespoons
1 cup sifted cake flour	7/8 cup or 1 cup minus 2 tablespoons sifted all-purpose flour
1 cup sifted self-rising flour	1 cup sifted all-purpose flour plus 1 1/2 teaspoons baking powder and 1/2 teaspoon salt
1 cup honey	1 1/4 cups sugar plus 1/4 cup liquid
1 cup corn syrup	1 cup sugar plus 1/4 cup liquid
1 cup butter	1 cup margarine or 7/8 cup hydrogenated shortening or 7/8 cup lard
1 ounce baking chocolate	3 tablespoons cocoa plus 1 tablespoon fat
1 ounce semisweet chocolate	1/2 ounce baking chocolate plus 1 tablespoon sugar
1 cup buttermilk	1 cup plain yogurt
1 teaspoon baking powder	1/4 teaspoon baking soda plus 5/8 teaspoon cream of tartar or 1/4 teaspoon baking soda plus 1/2 tablespoon vinegar or lemon juice

STANDARD CAN SIZES

Can Size	Contents (c)	Average Net Weight
8 oz	1	8 oz
Picnic	1 1/4	11 oz
No. 300	1 3/4	15 oz
No. 303	2	16 oz
No. 2	2 1/2	1 lb 4 oz
No. 2 1/2	3 1/2	1 lb 13 oz
No. 3 cylinder	5 1/2	46 fl oz
No. 10	13	6 lb 10 oz

Source: American Home Economics Association. (1993). *Handbook of Food Preparation* (9th ed.). Washington, D.C.: American Home Economics Association.

METRIC CONVERSIONS

		Multiply by
Length	inches to centimeters	2.5
	feet to centimeters	30
	yards to meters	0.9
Volume or Capacity	teaspoons to milliliters	5
	tablespoons to milliliters	15
	fluid ounces to milliliters	30
	cups to liters	0.24
	cups to milliliters	237
	quarts to liters	0.95
	gallons to liters	3.8
Mass or Weight	ounces to grams	28
	pounds to grams	454
	pounds to kilograms	0.45

COMMON MEASUREMENTS
USED IN FOOD PREPARATION

3 tsp	= 1 Tbsp	10 2/3 Tbsp	= 2/3 c
16 Tbsp	= 1 c	2 c	= 1 pt
4 Tbsp	= 1/4 c	4 c	= 1 qt
8 Tbsp	= 1/2 c	4 qt	= 1 gal
12 Tbsp	= 3/4 c	2 Tbsp	= 1 fl oz or 1/8 c
5 1/3 Tbsp	= 1/3 c	8 fl oz	= 1 c or 1/2 pt

APPROXIMATE NUMBER OF CUPS IN
A POUND OF SOME COMMON FOODS

2 1/4 c granulated sugar   2 c butter or margarine
4 c all-purpose flour   4 c grated cheese

WEIGHTS AND MEASURES FOR
SOME FOOD INGREDIENTS

All-purpose flour, sifted	1 lb = 4 c	115 g per c
Whole wheat flour, stirred	1 lb = 3 1/3 c	132 g per c
SAS-phosphate baking powder	14 oz = 2 1/2 c	3.2 g per tsp
Baking soda	1 lb = 2 1/3 c	4 g per tsp
Granulated sugar	1 lb = 2 1/4 c	200 g per c
Brown sugar, packed	1 lb = 2 1/4 c	200 g per c
Salt	1 lb = 1 1/2 c	288 g per c
Margarine	1 lb = 2 c	224 g per c
Hydrogenated fat	1 lb = 2 1/3 c	188 g per c
Oil	1 lb = 2 1/6 c	210 g per c
Eggs, fresh whole	1 lb = 1 3/4 c	248 g per c

TEMPERATURE CONTROL

OVEN TEMPERATURES

Temperatures for cooking can be most accurately controlled when a thermostat or a thermometer is used. Ovens generally have thermostat-controlled heat. They may be checked occasionally with a portable oven thermometer if there is some question about the accuracy of the thermostatic control.

Temperature Range for Ovens

Very low	250–275°F	121–135°C
Low	300–325°F	149–163°C
Moderate	350–375°F	177–191°C
Hot	400–425°F	204–218°C
Very hot	450–500°F	232–260°C

THERMOMETERS FOR OTHER USES

Thermometers are available for reading the temperature of deep fats, sugar syrups, and meats. In taking the temperature of hot fats or of boiling sugar syrups, the bulb of the thermometer should be fully submerged but should not touch the bottom of the utensil. In reading the scale, the eye should be level with the top of the mercury column.

Meat thermometers have a short scale, up to about 212° F (100° C). The bulb is small, and the thermometer is inserted so that the bulb rests in the center of the roast or the muscle being roasted.

CONVERTING FAHRENHEIT AND CELSIUS TEMPERATURES

Formulas

$$1.8 \times °C = °F - 32$$
$$\text{or}$$
$$°C = (°F - 32) \times 5/9$$
$$°F = (°C \times 9/5) + 32$$

The first formula given for temperature conversion can be used for changing either Celsius to Fahrenheit or Fahrenheit to Celsius simply by inserting the known temperature in the appropriate place in the formula and then solving the equation for the unknown.

Conversion Table

°F	°C	°F	°C
50	10.0	200	93.3
60	15.6	210	98.9
70	21.1	212	100.0
80	26.7	215	101.7
90	32.2	220	104.4
100	37.8	230	110.0
110	43.3	235	112.8
120	48.9	240	115.6
130	54.4	245	118.3
140	60.0	248	120.0
150	65.6	250	121.1
160	71.1	252	122.2
170	76.7	255	123.9
180	82.2	260	126.7
190	87.8	270	132.2

NUTRITIVE VALUE OF SELECTED FOODS

TABLE C-1 Vegetables

Vegetable	Approximate Measure	Food Weight (g)	Energy (kcal)	Water (%)	Protein (g)	Carbohydrate (g)	Calcium (mg)	Iron (mg)	Vitamin A Value (IU)	Vitamin A Value (RE)	Thiamin (mg)	Riboflavin (mg)	Ascorbic acid (mg)
Leaves													
Cabbage, raw, finely shredded	1 c	70	15	93	1	4	33	0.4	90	9	0.04	0.02	33
Lettuce, raw, crisphead	1/2 head	135	20	96	1	3	26	0.7	450	45	0.06	0.04	5
Spinach, frozen cooked	1 c	190	55	90	6	10	277	2.9	14,790	1,479	0.11	0.32	23
Vegetable-fruits													
Peppers, green, sweet, raw	1 pod	74	20	93	1	3	3	0.6	390	39	0.06	0.04	95
Squash, winter, baked, cubes	1 c	205	80	89	2	18	29	0.7	7,290	729	0.17	0.05	20
Tomatoes, raw	1	123	25	94	1	5	9	0.6	1,390	139	0.07	0.06	22
Flowers and stems													
Asparagus, cooked from raw, cut	1 c	180	45	92	5	8	43	1.2	1,490	149	0.18	0.22	49
Broccoli, cooked from raw, cut	1 c	155	45	90	5	9	71	1.8	2,180	218	0.13	0.32	97
Cauliflower, cooked from raw	1 c	125	30	93	2	6	34	0.5	20	2	0.08	0.07	69
Celery, raw, outer stalk	1 stalk	40	5	95	Trace	1	14	0.2	50	5	0.01	0.01	3
Bulbs, roots, tubers													
Beets, cooked, diced	1 c	170	55	91	2	11	19	1.1	20	2	0.05	0.02	9
Carrots, cooked from raw, sliced	1 c	156	70	87	2	16	48	1.0	38,300	3,830	0.05	0.09	4
Potatoes, peeled after boiling	1	135	115	77	2	27	11	0.4	0	0	0.14	0.03	18

TABLE C-1 (Continued)

Vegetable	Approximate Measure	Food Weight (g)	Energy (kcal)	Water (%)	Protein (g)	Carbohydrate (g)	Calcium (mg)	Iron (mg)	Vitamin A Value (IU)	Vitamin A Value (RE)	Thiamin (mg)	Riboflavin (mg)	Ascorbic acid (mg)
Sweet potatoes, boiled, peeled	1	151	160	73	2	37	32	0.8	25,750	2,575	0.08	0.21	26
Seeds and pods													
Snap beans, cooked from frozen	1 c	135	35	92	2	8	61	1.1	710	71	0.06	0.10	11
Corn, sweet, cooked from raw	1 ear	77	85	70	3	19	2	0.5	170	17	0.17	0.06	5
Peas, green, cooked from frozen	1 c	160	125	80	8	23	38	2.5	1,070	107	0.45	0.16	16
Peas, split, dry, cooked	1 c	200	230	70	16	42	22	3.4	80	8	0.30	0.18	0
Beans, dry, cooked Pinto	1 c	180	265	65	15	49	86	5.4	Trace	Trace	0.33	0.16	0

Source: Nutritive Value of Foods, Home and Garden Bulletin No. 72. Washington, DC: U.S. Department of Agriculture, 1991.

TABLE C-2   Fruits and Fruit Juices

Fruit	Approximate Measure	Food Weight (g)	Energy (kcal)	Water (%)	Protein (g)	Carbohydrate (g)	Vitamin A Value (IU)	(RE)	Ascorbic Acid (mg)
Apples, raw, unpeeled	1 medium	138	80	84	Trace	21	70	/	8
Apricots, raw	3 apricots	106	50	86	1	12	2,770	277	11
Avocados, raw, California	1 avocado	173	305	73	4	12	1,060	106	14
Bananas, raw, without peel	1 banana	114	105	74	1	27	90	9	10
Blueberries, raw	1 c	145	80	85	1	20	150	15	19
Cantaloupe, raw	1/2 medium	267	95	90	2	22	8,610	861	113
Grapefruit, medium									
White	1/2	120	40	91	1	10	10	1	41
Pink or red	1/2	120	40	91	1	10	310	31	41
Grapefruit juice, frozen concentrate diluted with 3 parts water	1 c	247	100	89	1	24	20	2	83
Grapes, raw, Thompson	10 grapes	50	35	81	Trace	9	40	4	5
Oranges, raw	1 orange	131	60	87	1	15	270	27	70
Orange juice, fresh	1 c	248	110	88	2	26	500	50	124
canned, unsweetened	1 c	249	105	89	1	25	440	44	85
frozen concentrate, diluted with 3 parts water	1 c	249	110	88	2	27	190	19	97
Peaches, raw	1 medium	87	35	88	1	10	470	47	6
Pears, raw	1 pear	166	100	84	1	25	30	3	7
Pineapple, raw, diced	1 c	155	75	87	1	19	40	4	24
Raspberries, red, raw	1 c	123	60	87	1	14	160	16	31
Strawberries, raw, capped	1 c	149	45	92	1	10	40	4	84
Tangerines, raw	1 medium	84	35	88	1	9	770	77	26
Watermelon, raw, wedge, with rind and seeds	4 × 8 in.	482	155	92	3	35	1,760	176	46

Source: Nutritive Value of Foods, Home and Garden Bulletin No. 72. Washington, DC: U.S. Department of Agriculture, 1991.

TABLE C-3 Meat, Fish, and Poultry

Meat	Approximate Measure (oz)	Weight (g)	Food Energy (kcal)	Water (%)	Protein (g)	Fat (g)	Iron (mg)	Thiamin (mg)
Beef, cooked								
Cuts braised, simmered, or pot roasted								
Lean and fat	3	85	325	43	22	26	2.5	0.06
Lean only	2.2	62	170	53	19	9	2.3	0.05
Ground beef, broiled								
Lean	3	85	230	56	21	16	1.8	0.04
Regular	3	85	245	54	20	18	2.1	0.03
Roast, oven-cooked								
Relatively fat, such as rib								
Lean and fat	3	85	315	46	19	26	2.0	0.06
Lean only	2.2	61	150	57	17	9	1.7	0.05
Relatively lean, such as eye of round								
Lean and fat	3	85	205	57	23	12	1.6	0.07
Lean only	2.6	75	135	63	22	5	1.5	0.07
Lamb, cooked								
Leg, roasted								
Lean and fat	3	85	205	59	22	13	1.7	0.09
Lean only	1.6	73	140	64	20	6	1.5	0.08
Liver, beef, fried	3	85	185	56	23	7	5.3	0.18
Pork, fresh, cooked								
Chop, loin, broiled								
Lean and fat	3.1	87	275	50	24	19	0.7	0.87
Roast, rib								
Lean and fat	3	85	270	51	21	20	0.8	0.50
Lean only	2.5	71	175	57	20	10	0.7	0.45
Veal, cooked, bone removed								
Roast, rib, medium fat	3	85	230	55	23	14	0.7	0.11
Poultry								
Chicken, breast, fried, batter-dipped Flesh with skin	4.9	140	365	52	35	18	1.8	0.16
Chicken, drumstick, fried, batter-dipped Flesh with skin	2.5	72	195	53	16	11	1.0	0.08
Chicken, canned, boneless	5	142	235	69	31	11	2.2	0.02
Turkey, roasted, flesh only								
Dark meat	3	85	160	63	24	6	2.0	0.05
Light meat	3	85	135	66	25	3	1.1	0.05
Fish								
Haddock, breaded, fried	3	85	175	61	17	9	1.0	0.06
Tuna, canned in oil								
Drained solids	3	85	165	61	24	7	1.6	0.04
Tuna, canned in water								
Solids and liquid	3	85	135	63	30	1	0.6	0.03
Flounder, baked	3	85	80	78	17	1	0.3	0.05
Salmon, baked	3	85	140	67	21	5	0.5	0.18

Source: Nutritive Value of Foods, Home and Garden Bulletin No. 72. Washington, DC: U.S. Department of Agriculture, 1991.

TABLE C-4 Dairy Products

Product	Approximate Measure	Food Weight (g)	Energy (kcal)	Water (%)	Protein (g)	Fat (g)	Carbohydrate (g)	Calcium (mg)	Vitamin A (IU)	(RE)
Fluid milk										
Whole, 3.3% fat	1 c	244	150	88	8	8	11	291	310	76
Nonfat (skim)	1 c	245	85	91	8	Trace	12	302	500	149
Reduced fat, 2% fat, nonfat milk solids added, less than 10 g of protein per cup	1 c	245	125	89	9	5	12	313	500	140
Buttermilk	1 c	245	100	90	8	2	12	285	80	20
Canned										
Evaporated, unsweetened whole	1 c	252	340	74	17	19	25	657	610	136
Condensed, sweetened	1 c	306	980	27	24	27	166	868	1,000	248
Dry, nonfat, instant	1 c	68	245	4	24	Trace	35	837	1,610 (added)	483
Yogurt, plain (from partially skimmed milk with added milk solids)	1 c	227	145	85	12	4	16	415	150	36
Cream										
Half-and-half	1 c	242	315	81	7	28	10	254	1,050	259
Light, coffee or table	1 c	240	470	74	6	46	9	231	1,730	437
Heavy whipping	1 c	238	820	58	5	88	7	154	3,500	1,002
Cheese										
Cheddar	1 oz	28	115	37	7	9	Trace	204	300	86
Creamed cottage, 4% fat (curd not pressed down), large curd	1 c	225	235	79	28	10	6	135	370	108

Source: Nutritive Value of Foods, Home and Garden Bulletin No. 72, Washington, DC: U.S. Department of Agriculture, 1991.

TABLE C-5 Cereal Products

Product	Approximate Measure	Weight (g)	Food Energy (kcal)	Water (%)	Protein (g)	Carbohydrate (g)	Iron (mg)	Thiamin (mg)	Riboflavin (mg)	Niacin (mg)
Wheat										
Bread, whole wheat	1 slice	25	70	29	3	13	1.0	0.08	0.06	1.1
Bread, white, enriched	1 slice	25	65	37	2	12	0.7	0.12	0.08	0.9
Bulgur, uncooked	1 c	170	600	10	19	129	9.5	0.48	0.24	7.7
Cream of Wheat, quick, enriched, cooked	1 c	244	140	86	4	29	10.9	0.24	0.07	1.5
Flour, whole wheat	1 c	120	400	12	16	85	5.2	0.66	0.14	5.2
Flour, all-purpose, enriched	1 c	125	455	12	13	95	5.5	0.80	0.50	6.6
Flour, cake or pastry, enriched	1 c	96	350	12	7	76	4.2	0.58	0.38	5.1
Raisin Bran	1 oz	28	90	8	3	21	3.5	0.28	0.34	3.9
Shredded Wheat	1 oz	28	100	5	3	23	1.2	0.07	0.08	1.5
Wheaties	1 oz	28	100	5	3	23	4.5	0.37	0.43	5.0
Macaroni, cooked enriched	1 c	130	190	64	7	39	2.1	0.23	0.13	1.8
Noodles (egg), enriched, cooked	1 c	160	200	70	7	37	2.6	0.22	0.13	1.9
Corn										
Cornmeal, whole-ground, dry	1 c	122	435	12	11	90	2.2	0.46	0.13	2.4
Cornmeal, degermed, enriched, cooked	1 c	240	120	88	3	26	1.4	0.14	0.10	1.2
Corn										
tortillas	1	30	65	45	2	13	0.6	0.05	0.03	0.4
Cornflakes										
plain	1 oz	28	110	3	2	24	1.8	0.37	0.43	5.0
sugar covered	1 oz	28	110	3	1	25	1.8	0.37	0.43	5.0
Oats										
Oatmeal or rolled oats, cooked	1 c	234	145	85	6	25	1.6	0.26	0.05	0.3
Rice										
white, enriched, cooked regular	1 c	205	225	73	4	50	1.8	0.23	0.02	2.1
instant	1 c	165	180	73	4	40	1.3	0.21	0.02	1.7
brown	1 c	195	230	70	5	50	1.0	0.18	0.04	2.7

Source: Nutritive Value of Foods, Home and Garden Bulletin No. 72, Washington, DC: U.S. Department of Agriculture, 1991.

REFERENCES

Chapter 1

1. American Dietetic Association. (1999). Position of the American Dietetic Association: Dietary guidance for healthy children aged 2–11 years. *Journal of the American Dietetic Association, 99,* 93–101.

2. Beale, C. L. (2000). A century of population growth and change. *Food Review, 23*(1), 16–22.

3. Blackburn, G. L. (2001). Feeding 9 billion people—A job for food technologists. *Food Technology, 55*(6), 106.

4. Blisard, N. (2000). Food spending by U.S. households grew steadily in the 1990's. *Food Review, 23*(3), 18.

5. Bosley, G. C., and Hardinge, M. G. (1992). Seventh-Day Adventists: Dietary standards and concerns. *Food Technology, 46*(10), 112.

6. Bowers, D. E. (2000). Cooking trends echo changing roles of women. *Food Review, 23*(1), 23–29.

7. Brownell, K. D., and Ludwig, D. S. (2002, June 9). Fighting obesity and the food lobby. *Washington Post.* Retrieved June 16, 2002, from http://www.washingtonpost.com/wp-dyn/articles/A15232-2002jun7.html

8. Chaudry, M. M. (1992). Islamic food laws: Philosophical basis and practical implications. *Food Technology, 46*(10), 92.

9. Clausen, A. (2000). Spotlight on national food spending. *Food Review, 23*(3), 15–17.

10. Costacou, T., Levin, S., and Mayer-Davis, E. J. (2000). Dietary patterns among members of the Catawba Indian nation. *Journal of the American Dietetic Association, 100,* 833–835.

11. Crutchfield, S. R., and Weimer, J. (2000). Nutrition policy in the 1990's. *Food Review, 23*(3), 38–43.

12. DeRovira, D. (1996). The dynamic flavor profile method. *Food Technology, 50*(2), 55.

13. Escobar, A. (1999). Factors influencing children's dietary practices: A review. *Family Economics and Nutrition Review, 12*(3–4), 45–55.

14. Falciglia, G. A., and Norton, P. A. (1994). Evidence for a genetic influence on preference for some foods. *Journal of the American Dietetic Association, 94,* 154.

15. Farah, H., and Buzby, J. (2005). U.S. Food consumption up 16 percent since 1970. *Amber Waves, 3*(6), 5.

16. Gable, S., and Lutz, S. (2001). Nutrition socialization experiences of children in the Head Start program. *Journal of the American Dietetic Association, 101,* 572–577.

17. Gerrior, S., and Bente, L. (2001). Food supply nutrient and diet guidance, 1970–1999. *Food Review, 24*(3), 39–46.

18. Giese, J. (1995). Measuring physical properties of foods. *Food Technology, 49*(2), 54.

19. Guthrie, J. F., Lin, B. H, Reed, J., and Stewart, H. (2005). Understanding economic and behavioral influences on fruit and vegetable choices. *Amber Waves, 3*(2), 36–41.

20. Hampl, J. S., and Sass, S. (2001). Focus groups indicate that vegetable and fruit consumption by food stamp–eligible Hispanics is affected by children and unfamiliarity with non-traditional foods. *Journal of the American Dietetic Association, 101,* 685–687.

21. Harlander, S. K. (1991). Biotechnology: A means for improving our food supply. *Food Technology, 45*(4), 84.

22. Hoch, G. J. (1997). Flavor technology report: Reaction flavors. *Food Processing, 58*(4), 57.

23. Hollingsworth, P. (2001). Supermarket trends. *Food Technology, 55*(3), 20.

24. Hollingsworth, P. (2001). Veggie burgers swerve into the mainstream. *Food Technology, 56*(1), 18.

25. Hollingsworth, P. (2002). One-handed cuisine and other business trends to watch. *Food Technology, 56*(4), 18.

26. Huang, Y., and Ang, C. Y. W. (1992). Vegetarian foods for Chinese Buddhists. *Food Technology, 46*(10), 105.

27. Institute of Food Technologists' Expert Report on Biotechnology and Foods. (2000). Benefits and concerns associated with recombinant DNA biotechnology-derived foods. *Food Technology, 54*(10), 61–80.

28. Institute of Food Technologists' Expert Panel on Food Safety & Nutrition. (1989). Food flavors. *Food Technology, 43*(12), 99.

29. Jackson, M. A. (2000). Getting religion: For your products, that is. *Food Technology, 54*(7), 60–66.

30. Katz, F. (1997). Technology trends. *Food Technology, 51*(6), 46.

31. Kenney, B. F. (1990). Applications of high-performance liquid chromatography for the flavor research and quality control laboratories in the 1990s. *Food Technology, 44*(9), 76.

32. Kittler, P. G., and Sucher, K. P. (2001). *Food and Culture,* 3rd ed. Belmont, CA: Wadsworth.

33. Langen, S. (2002). Consumers want easy meals. *Food Technology, 56*(1), 10.

34. Leland, J. V. (1997). Flavor interactions: The greater whole. *Food Technology, 51*(1), 75.

35. Lin, B. H., Guthrie, J., and Frazao, E. (1999). Nutrient composition of food away from home. In *America's Eating Habits: Changes and Consequences,* edited by E. Frazao. Washington, DC: USDA, ERS, AIB-750.

36. Lin, B. H., Guthrie, J., and Frazao, E. (2001). American children's diets not making the grade. *Food Review, 24*(2), 8–17.

37. Madsen, M. G., and Grypa, R. D. (2000). Spices, flavor systems, and the electronic nose. *Food Technology, 54*(3), 44–46.

38. National Center for Health Statistics. (2005). *Health, United States, 2005: With Chartbook on Trends in the Health of Americans.* Washington DC: Government Printing Office.

39. Nord, M. (2006). More households had difficulty meeting their food needs. *Amber Waves, 4*(1), 5.

40. Pszczola, D. E. (1997). Lookin' good: Improving the appearance of food products. *Food Technology, 51*(11), 39.

41. Popper, R., and Kroll, B. J. (2003). Food preference and consumption among the elderly. *Food Technology, 57*(7), 32–38.

42. Putnam, J., and Allshouse, J. (2001). Imports' share of U.S. diet rises in late 1990's. *Food Review, 24*(3), 15–22.

43. Putnam, J., Kantor, L. S., and Allshouse, J. (2000). Per capita food supply trends: Progress toward dietary guidelines. *Food Review, 23*(3), 2–14.

44. Regenstein, J. M., and Regenstein, C. E. (1979). An introduction to the kosher dietary laws for food scientists and food processors. *Food Technology, 33*(1), 89.

45. Rogers, C. C. (2001). A look at America's children and their families. *Food Review, 24*(2), 2–7.

46. Sloan, A. E. (1999). Bite-size goes big time. *Food Technology, 53*(7), 30.

47. Sloan, A. E. (2000). La cucina latina. *Food Technology, 54*(9), 24–25.

48. Sloan, A. E. (2001). Ethnic foods in the decade ahead. *Food Technology, 55*(10), 18.

49. Sloan, A. E. (2001). More on ethnic foods: Move over, BBQ, Cajun, and Caesar. *Food Technology, 55*(11), 18.

50. Sloan, A. E. (2006). What, when, and where America eats. *Food Technology, 60*(1), 18–27.

51. Story, M., Neumark-Sztainer, D., and French, S. (2002). Individual and environmental influences on adolescent eating behaviors. *Supplement to the Journal of the American Dietetic Association, 102*(3), S40–S51.

52. Szczesniak, A. S. (1963). Classification of textural characteristics. *Journal of Food Science, 28,* 385.

53. Szczesniak, A. S. (1990). Texture: Is it still an overlooked food attribute? *Food Technology, 44*(9), 86.

54. Tegene, A., Wallace, H., Rousu, M., and Shogren, J. (2003). Information sways consumer attitudes toward biotech foods. *Amber Waves, 1*(3), 6.

55. Terry, R. D. (1994). Needed: A new appreciation of culture and food behavior. *Journal of the American Dietetic Association, 94,* 501.

56. Tsung, T., Schmitt, V., and Isz, S. (2001). Electronic tongue: A new dimension in sensory analysis. *Food Technology, 55*(10), 44–50.

57. Uhl, S. (1996). Ingredients: The building blocks for developing "new" ethnic foods. *Food Technology, 50*(7), 79.

58. U.S. Centers for Disease Control. (2006). "Overweight and Obesity: Obesity Trends: U.S. Obesity Trends 1985–2004." Retrieved May 23, 2006, from http://www.cdc.gov/nccdphp/dnpa/obesity/trend/maps/index.htm

59. U.S. Department of Agriculture. (1992, August). *The food guide pyramid.* Home and Garden Bulletin No. 252.

60. U.S. Department of Agriculture. (2004). Official USDA food plans: Cost of food at home at four levels, U.S. average, December 2004. *Family Economics and Nutrition Review, 16*(1), 84.

61. U.S. Department of Agriculture, Economic Research Service. (2007). "Briefing Rooms: Food, CPI, Prices, and Expenditures." Retrieved January 8, 2008, from http:// ers.usda.gov/Briefing/CPIFoodAndExpenditures/

62. U.S. Department of Health and Human Services. (2000). 19—Nutrition and overweight. *Healthy People 2010.* Retrieved May 17, 2002, from http://www.health.gov./healthypeople/document/tableofcontents.htm

63. U.S. Department of Health and Human Services and U.S. Department of Agriculture. "Dietary Guidelines for Americans 2005." Retrieved May 5, 2006, from http://www.healthierus.gov/dietaryguidelines/

64. U.S. Department of Health and Human Services and U.S. Department of Agriculture. "Dietary Guidelines for Americans 2005: Chapter 1—Background and Purpose of the Dietary Guidelines for Americans." Retrieved May 20, 2006, from http://health.gov/dietaryguidelines/dga2005/document/html/chapter1.htm

65. U.S. Department of Health and Human Services and U.S. Department of Agriculture. "Dietary Guidelines for Americans 2005: Executive Summary." Retrieved May 20, 2006, from http://www.health.gov/dietaryguidelines/dga2005/document/html/executivesummary.htm

66. U.S. Department of Health and Human Services and U.S. Department of Agriculture. "Finding Your Way to a Healthier You: Based on the Dietary Guidelines." Retrieved May 5, 2006, from http://www.healthierus.gov/dietaryguidelines

67. van Buren, S. (1992). Analyzing time–intensity responses in sensory evaluation. *Food Technology, 46*(2), 101.

68. Weicha, J. M., Fink, A. K., Wicha, J., and Herbert, J. (2001). Differences in dietary patterns of Vietnamese, White, African-American, and Hispanic adolescents in Worchester, Mass. *Journal of the American Dietetic Association, 101,* 248–251.

69. Yi-Ling, P., Dixon, Z., Himburg, S., and Huffman, F. (1999). Asian students change their eating patterns after living in the United States. *Journal of the American Dietetic Association, 99,* 54–57.

Chapter 2

1. American Dietetic Association. (2001). Position of the American Dietetic Association: Dietetic professionals can implement practices to conserve natural resources and protect the environment. *Journal of the American Dietetic Association, 101,* 1221–1227.

2. American Frozen Food Institute. (n.d.). "History of Frozen Food." Retrieved June 20, 2002, from www.affi.com/factstat-history.asp

3. Bergman, E. A., Buergel, N. S., Englund, T. F., and Femrite, A. (2004, Fall). The relationship between the length of lunch period and nutrient consumption in the elementary school setting. *The Journal of Child Nutrition & Management,* Issue 2. Retrieved June 15, 2006, from http://docs.schoolnutrition.org/newsroom/jcnm/04fall/bergman/bergman2.asp

4. Bergman, E. A., Buergel, N. S., Englund, T. F., and Femrite, A. (2004, Fall). The relationship of meal and recess schedules to plate waste in elementary schools. *The Journal of Child Nutrition & Management*, Issue 2. Retrieved June 15, 2006, from http://docs.schoolnutrition.org/newsroom/jcnm/o4fall/bergman/bergman1.asp

5. Blisard, N. (2000). Food spending by U.S. households grew steadily in the 1990's. *Food Review, 23*(3), 18–22.

6. Bourland, C. T., Fohey, M. F., Rapp, R. M., and Sauer, R. L. (1982). Space shuttle food package development. *Food Technology, 36*(9), 38.

7. Brody, A. L. (2002). Food canning in the 21st century. *Food Technology, 56*(3), 75–78.

8. Brody, A. L. (2004). An astronautical food odyssey. *Food Technology, 58*(3), 64–66.

9. Carlson, A., Kinsey, J., and Nadav, C. (2002). *Family Economics and Nutrition Review, 14*(2), 11–19.

10. Chapman, N. (2005). Securing the future for monitoring the health, nutrition, and physical activity of Americans. *Journal of the American Dietetic Association, 105,* 1196–1200.

11. Davis, D. E., and Stewart, H. (2002). Changing consumer demands create opportunities for U.S. food system. *Food Review, 25*(1), 19–23.

12. Dinkins, J. M. (1997). Food preparers: Their food budgeting, cost-cutting, and meal planning practices. *Family Economics and Nutrition Review, 10*(2), 34.

13. Dyson, L. K. (2000). American cuisine in the 20th century. *Food Review, 23*(1), 2–7.

14. Elitzak, H. (2004). Behind the data: Calculating the food marketing bill. *Amber Waves, 2*(1), 43.

15. Fu, B., and Nelson, P. E. (1994). Conditions and constraints of food processing in space. *Food Technology, 48*(9), 113.

16. Garrett, E. S. (2002). The "shrouded threat" of foodborne parasites. *Food Technology, 56*(4), 20.

17. Hackes, B. L., Shanklin, C. W., Kim, T., and Su, A. Y. (1997). Tray service generates more food waste in dining areas of a continuing-care retirement community. *Journal of the American Dietetic Association, 97,* 879.

18. Harris, J. M. (2002). Food product introductions continue to decline in 2000. *Food Review, 25*(1), 24–27.

19. Hollingsworth, P. (2001). Convenience is key to adding value. *Food Technology, 55*(5), 20.

20. Hollingsworth, P. (2001). Supermarket trends. *Food Technology, 55*(3), 20.

21. Hollingsworth, P. (2002). Surveying the crowded (nutrition) bar scene. *Food Technology, 56*(6), 20.

22. Kantor, L. S., Lipton, K., Manchester, A., and Oliveira, V. (1997). Estimating and addressing America's food losses. *Food Review, 20*(1), 2.

23. Lachance, P. A. (2002). Nutraceuticals, for real. *Food Technology, 56*(1), 20.

24. Liebtag, E. S. (2005). Where you shop matters: Store formats drive variation in retail food prices. *Amber Waves, 3*(5), 13–18.

25. Lin, B. H., Guthrie, J., and Frazao, E. (1999). Nutrient composition of food away from home. In *America's Eating Habits: Changes and Consequences,* edited by E. Frazao. Washington, DC: USDA, ERS, AIB-750.

26. Mermelstein, N. H. (2001). Military and humanitarian rations. *Food Technology, 55*(11), 73–75.

27. Moshfegh, A., Goldman, J., and Cleveland, L. (2005). *What We Eat in America,* NHANES 2001–2002: Usual nutrient intakes from food compared to dietary reference intakes. U.S. Department of Agriculture, Agricultural Research Service.

28. National Aeronautics and Space Administration. (2005). "Station Crew 'Kicks It Up a Notch' with Chef Emeril Lagasse." Retrieved October 8, 2006, from http://www.nasa.gov/mission_pages/station/behindscenes/emeril_ISS_food.html

29. National Aeronautics and Space Administration. (2005). "NASA Facts: Cosmic Cuisine." Retrieved October 8, 2006, from http://www.nasa.gov/pdf/137398main_FS-2005-10-055%20Cuisine_1.pdf

30. National Aeronautics and Space Administration. (2002). "NASA Facts: Space Food." Retrieved October 8, 2006, from http://spaceflight.nasa.gov/spacenews/factsheets/pdfs/food.pdf

31. National Aeronautics and Space Administration. (n.d.). "NASA Facts: Food for Space Flight." Retrieved June 12, 2002, from http://www.jsc.nasa.gov/pao/factsheets/nasapubs/food.html

32. Neff, J. (1996). Will home meal replacement replace packaged foods? *Food Processing, 57*(11), 35.

33. Norton, V. P., and Martin, C. (1991). Plate waste of selected food items in a university dining hall. *School Food Service Research Review, 15*(1), 37.

34. Putnam, J. J. (2000). Major trends in U.S. food supply, 1909–99. *Food Review, 23*(1), 8–14.

35. Putnam, J. J., and Allshouse, J. E. (1999, April). *Food consumption, prices, and expenditures, 1970–97.* Food and Rural Economics Division, Economic Research Service, U.S. Department of Agriculture. Statistical Bulletin No. 965.

36. Pszczola, D. E. (2001). Convenience foods: They've come a long, long way. *Food Technology, 55*(9), 85–94.

37. Regmi, A., and Gehlhar, M. (2001). Consumer preferences and concerns shape global food trade. *Food Review, 24*(3), 2–8.

38. Regmi, A., and Pompelli, G. (2002). U.S. food sector linked to global consumers. *Food Review, 25*(1), 39–44.

39. Sloan, A. E. (1997). What's cooking? *Food Technology, 51*(9), 32.

40. Sloan, A. E. (2000). The top ten functional food trends. *Food Technology, 54*(4), 33.

41. Staff. (2006). Indicators: Food and fiber sector indicators. *Amber Waves, 4*(2), 38.

42. Staff. (2006). Indicators: Food and fiber sector indicators. *Amber Waves, 4*(1), 38.

43. Unnevehr, L., Deaton, L., and Kramer, C. (1994). International trade agreement provides new framework for food-safety regulation. *Food Review, 17*(3), 2.

44. U.S. Department of Agriculture, Agricultural Research Service. (2005). "What We Eat in America, NHANES

2001-2002." Retrieved June 10, 2006, from http://www.ars.usda.gov/services/docs.htm?docid=7674&pf=1&cg_id=0

45. U.S. Department of Agriculture, Agricultural Research Service. (2004). "News and Events: Researchers Develop Improved Food Consumption Method." Retrieved June 1, 2006, from http://www.ars.usda.gov/is/pr/2004/040614.htm

46. U.S. Department of Agriculture, Economic Research Service. (2006). "Food Availability: Documentation." Retrieved June 1, 2006, from http://www.ers.usda.gov/data/foodconsumption/foodavaildoc.htm

47. U.S. Department of Labor, Bureau of Labor Statistics. "Consumer Expenditure Survey." Retrieved June 19, 2006, from http://www.bls.gov/data/home.htm

48. U.S. Department of Labor, Bureau of Labor Statistics. Data. Retrieved April 12, 2008, from http://www.bls.gov/data/home.htm

49. U.S. per capita food consumption. (1997). *Family Economics and Nutrition Review, 10*(1), 38.

Chapter 3

1. Altrekruse, S. F., Yang, S., Timbo, B. B., and Angulo, F. J. (1999). A multistate survey of consumer food-handling and food-consumption practices. *American Journal of Preventative Medicine, 16*(3), 216–221.

2. American Dietetic Association. (2003). Position of the American Dietetic Association on food and water safety. *Journal of the American Dietetic Association, 103,* 1203–1218.

3. American Dietetic Association. (1997). Position of the American Dietetic Association on management of health care food and nutrition services. *Journal of the American Dietetic Association, 97,* 1427–1430.

4. American Dietetic Association. (2000). Position of the American Dietetic Association: Food irradiation. *Journal of the American Dietetic Association, 100,* 246–253.

5. American Dietetic Association. (2006). Position of the American Dietetic Association: Agricultural and food biotechnology. *Journal of the American Dietetic Association,* 106, 285–293.

6. American Society for Microbiology. (2005). "Women Better At Hand Hygiene Habits, Hands Down." Retrieved July 4, 2006, from http://www.asm.org/media/index/asp?bid=38075

7. Anderson, J. B., Shuster, T. A., Hansen, K. E., Levy, A. S., and Volk, A. (2004). A camera's view of consumer food-handling behaviors. *Journal of the American Dietetic Association, 104,* 186–191.

8. Anderson, J. B., Shuster, T. A., Gee, E., Hansen, K., and Mendenhall, V. T. (2000). *A camera's view of consumer food handling and preparation practices.* Final report prepared for the U.S. Food and Drug Administration. North Logan, UT: Spectrum Consulting.

9. Association of Women's Health, Obstetric, and Neonatal Nurses, International Food Information Council, U.S. Department of Agriculture, and U.S. Department of Health and Human Services. (2001, September). *Listeriosis and pregnancy: What is your risk?* Brochure retrieved May 22, 2002, from www.fsis.usda.gov/OA/pubs/lm_tearsheet.htm

10. Auld, G. W., Kendall, P. A., and Chipman, H. (1994). Consumer and producer perceptions and concerns regarding pesticide use. *Food Technology, 48*(3), 100.

11. *Ball Blue Book of Preserving.* (2005). Muncie, IN: Jarden Home Brands.

12. Bennett, G. A., and Richard, J. L. (1996). Influence of processing on *Fusarium* mycotoxins in contaminated grains. *Food Technology, 50*(5), 235.

13. Blackburn, G. L. (2001). Feeding 9 billion people—A job for food technologists. *Food Technology, 55*(6), 106.

14. Bren, L. (2004). Got milk? Make sure it's pasteurized. *FDA Consumer Magazine. 38*(5).

15. Bruhn, C., and Mason, A. (2002). Community leader response to educational information about biotechnology. *Journal of Food Science, 67,* 399–403.

16. Centers for Disease Control and Prevention, Division of Bacterial and Mycotic Diseases. (2006). "Disease Information." Retrieved June 30, 2006, from http://www.cdc.gov/ncidod/dbmd/diseaseinfo/

17. Centers for Disease Control and Prevention, Division of Bacteria and Mycotic Diseases. (2005). "Disease Information: Marine Toxins." Retrieved June 21, 2006, from http://www.cdc.gov/ncidod/dbmd/diseaseinfo/marinetoxins_g.htm

18. Centers for Disease Control and Prevention, Division of Parasitic Diseases. (1999). "Fact Sheet: Trichinosis." Retrieved June 26, 2002, from http://www.cdc.gov/ncidod/dpd/parasites/trichinosis/factsht_trichinosis.htm

19. Centers for Disease Control and Prevention, Division of Parasitic Diseases. (2004). "Fact Sheet: Toxoplasma Infection." Retrieved June 25, 2006, from http://www.cdc.gov/ncidod/dpd/parasites/toxoplasmosis/factsht_toxoplasmosis.htm

20. Chlorine Chemistry Council. (n.d.). "Good Food Starts with a Clean Kitchen." Retrieved July 3, 2006, from http://www.c3.org/chlorine_knowledge_center/poster.html

21. Clark, J. P. (2005). Allergen-safe processing. *Food Technology, 59*(2), 63–64.

22. Clemens, R. A. (2001). Friendly bacteria—a functional food? *Food Technology, 55*(1), 27.

23. Crocco, S. (1981). Potato sprouts and greening potatoes: Potential toxic reaction. *Journal of the American Medical Association, 245,* 625.

24. Cross, H. R. (1996). HACCP: Pivotal change for the meat industry. *Food Technology, 50*(8), 236.

25. Crutchfield, S. R., and Roberts, T. (2000). Food safety efforts accelerate in the 1990's. *Food Review, 23*(3), 44–49.

26. Duxbury, D. (2004). Keeping tabs on *Listeria. Food Technology, 58*(7), 74–76, 80.

27. Educational Foundation of the National Restaurant Association. (2006). *ServSafe Coursebook,* 4th ed. Chicago, IL: National Restaurant Association.

28. Food and Drug Administration. (2005, December). "FDA Warns Consumers to Avoid Drinking Raw Milk." Retrieved July 5, 2006, from http://www.fda.gov/bbs/topics/NEWS/2005/NEW01278.html

29. Food and Drug Administration. (2005, March). "FDA Issues Health Advisory about Certain Soft Cheese Made

from Raw Milk." Retrieved July 5, 2006 from http://www.fda.gov/bbs/topics/news/2005/NEW01165.html

30. Food and Drug Administration, Center for Food Safety and Applied Nutrition. (2004). "Bad Bug Book: Prions and Transmissible Spongiform Encephalopathies." Retrieved June 21, 2006, from http://www.cfsan.fda.gov/~mow/prion.html

31. Food and Drug Administration, Center for Food Safety and Applied Nutrition. (2004, August). "Food Allergen Labeling and Consumer Protection Act of 2004 (Title II of Public Law 108-282)." Retrieved June 12, 2006, from http://www.cfsan.fda.gov/~dms/alrgact.html

32. Food and Drug Administration, Center for Food Safety and Applied Nutrition. (2005). "Commonly Asked Questions about BSE in Products Regulated by FDA's Center For Food Safety and Applied Nutrition (CFSAN)." Retrieved June 21, 2006, from http://www.cfsan.fda.gov/~comm/bsefaq.html

33. Food and Drug Administration, Center for Food Safety and Applied Nutrition. (2005, June). "FDA Pesticide Program Residue Monitoring, 1993–2003." Retrieved July 3, 2006, from http://www.cfsan.fda.gov/~dms/pesrpts.html

34. Food and Drug Administration, Center for Food Safety and Applied Nutrition. (n.d.). "Bad Bug Book." Retrieved June 20, 2006, from http://www.cfsan.fda.gov/~mow/intro.html

35. Food and Drug Administration, Food Safety and Inspection Service, Centers for Disease Control and Prevention. (2004, May 11). "Healthy People 2010 Focus Area Data Progress Review: Focus Area 10: Food Safety." Retrieved June 21, 2006, from http://www.foodsafety.gov/~dms/hp2010.html

36. Food and Drug Administration, U.S. Department of Agriculture, U.S. Environmental Protection Agency, and Centers for Disease Control and Prevention. (1997). "Food Safety from Farm to Table: A National Food Safety Initiative, Report to the President." Retrieved June 24, 2002, from http://vm.cfsan.fda.gov/~dms/fsreport.html

37. Food and Drug Administration, U.S. Department of Agriculture, and Centers for Disease Control and Prevention. (1998). "Guidance for Industry: Guide to Minimize Microbial Food Safety Hazards for Fresh Fruits and Vegetables." Retrieved June 24, 2002, from http://www.cfsan.fda.gov/~dms/prodguid.html

38. Formanek, R. (2001). Food allergies: When food becomes the enemy. *FDA Consumer, 35*(4).

39. Formanek, R. (2001). Highlights of FDA food safety efforts: Fruit juice, mercury in fish. *FDA Consumer, 3*(2).

40. Formanek, R. (2001). Proposed rules issued for bioengineered foods. *FDA Consumer, 35*(2).

41. Fox, J. A. (2002). Influence on the purchase of irradiated foods. *Food Technology, 56*(11), 34–37.

42. Giese, J. (2000). Pesticide analysis. *Food Technology, 54*(12), 64–65.

43. Greger, J. L. (2000). Biotechnology: Mobilizing dietitians to be a resource. *Journal of the American Dietetic Association, 100*, 1306–1308.

44. Greger, J. L., and Baier, M. (1981). Tin and iron content of canned and bottled foods. *Journal of Food Science, 46*, 1751.

45. Hingley, A. (1999). *Campylobacter:* Low-profile bug is food poisoning leader. *FDA Consumer, 33*(5).

46. Institute of Food Technologists' Expert Report on Biotechnology and Foods. (2000). Human food safety evaluation of rDNA biotechnology-derived foods. *Food Technology, 54*(9), 53–61.

47. Institute of Food Technologists' Expert Panel on Food Safety and Nutrition. (1997). Virus transmission via food. *Food Technology, 51*(4), 71.

48. Jackson, G. J. (1997). *Cyclospora*—Still another new foodborne pathogen. *Food Technology, 51*(1), 120.

49. Killinger, K. M., Hunt, M. C., Campbell, R. E., and Kropf, D. H. (2000). Factors affecting premature browning during cooking of store-purchased ground beef. *Journal of Food Science, 65*, 585–587.

50. Lusk, J. L., Fox, J. A., and McIlvain, C. L. (1999). Consumer acceptance of irradiated meat. *Food Technology, 53*(3), 56–59.

51. Mead, P. S., Slutsker, L., Dietz, V., McCaig, L. F., Bressee, J. S., Shapiro, C., Griffen, P. M., and Tauxe, R.V. (1999). Food-related illness and death in the United States. *Emerging Infectious Diseases, 5*, 607–625.

52. Meadows, M. (2004). The FDA and the fight against terrorism. *FDA Consumer Magazine, 38*(11).

53. Meer, R. R., and Misner, S. L. (2000). Food safety knowledge and behavior of expanded food and nutrition education program participants in Arizona. *Journal of Food Protection, 63*, 1725–1731.

54. Mermelstein, N. H. (1993). Controlling *E. coli* 0157:H7 in meat. *Food Technology, 47*(4), 90.

55. Mermelstein, N. H. (2000). E-beam irradiated beef reaches the market, papaya and gamma-irradiated beef to follow. *Food Technology, 54*(7), 88–92.

56. Mermelstein, N. H. (2001). Sanitizing meat. *Food Technology, 55*(3), 64–68.

57. Murphy, P. A., Hendrich, S., Landgren, C., and Bryant, C. M. (2006). Food mycotoxins: An update. *Journal of Food Science, 71*, R51–R65.

58. National Restaurant Association. (2006). "2006 Restaurant Industry Fact Sheet." Retrieved July 3, 2006, from http://www.restaurant.org/research/ind_glance.cfm

59. Nayga, R. M. Jr., Poghosyan, A., and Nichols, J. (2004). Will consumers accept irradiated food products? *International Journal of Consumer Studies, 28*(2), 178–185.

60. Newsome, R. (2006). Understanding mycotoxins. *Food Technology, 60*(6), 51–58.

61. Olsen, S. J., MacKinon, L. C., Goulding, J. S., Bean, N. H., and Slutsker, L. (2000). Surveillance for foodborne disease outbreaks—United States 1993–1997. *Morbidity and Mortality Weekly Report, 49*(SS01): 1–51.

62. Orlandi, P. A., Chu, D. M. Y., Bier, J. W., and Jackson, G. J. (2001). Scientific status summary: Parasites and the food supply. *Food Technology, 56*(4), 72–81.

63. Park, J., and Brittin, H. C. (1997). Increased iron content of food due to stainless steel cookware. *Journal of the American Dietetic Association, 97*, 659.

64. Public Law 107-188. "Public Health Security and Bioterrorism and Response Act of 2002." Retrieved July 5, 2006, from http://www.fda.gov/oc/bioterrorism/PL107-188.html

65. Ralston, K., Starke, Y., Brent, P., and Riggins, T. (2000). Awareness of risks changing how hamburgers are cooked. *Food Review, 23*(2), 44–50.

66. Resurreccion, A. V. A., and Galvez, F. C. F. (1999). Will consumers buy irradiated beef? *Food Technology, 53*(3), 52–55.

67. Shah, N. P. (2001). Functional foods from probiotics and prebiotics. *Food Technology, 55*(11), 46.

68. Shiferaw, B., Yang, S., Cieslak, P., Vugia, D., Marcus, R., Koehler, J., Deneen, V., and Angulo, F. (2000). Prevalence of high-risk food consumption and food handling practices among adults: A multistate survey, 1996–1997. *Journal of Food Protection, 63*, 1538–1543.

69. Siuta-Cruce, P., and Goulet, J. (2001). Improving probiotic survival rates. *Food Technology, 55*(10), 36.

70. Smith, J. S., and Pillai, S. (2004). Irradiation and food safety. *Food Technology, 58*(11), 48–55.

71. Taylor, S. L., and Hefle, S. L. (2001). Food allergies and other sensitivities. *Food Technology, 55*(9), 68–83.

72. Taylor, S. L., and Hefle, S. L. (2005). Allergen control. *Food Technology, 59*(2), 40–43, 75.

73. Teixeira, A., Almonacid, S., and Simpson, R. (2006). Keeping botulism out of canned foods. *Food Technology, 60*(2), 84.

74. Trautman, T. (2005). Labeling food allergens. *Food Technology, 59*(2), 92.

75. U.S. Centers for Disease Control and Prevention. (2006). "BSE (Bovine Spongiform Encephalopathy, or Mad Cow Disease)." Retrieved July 3, 2006, from http://www.cdc.gov/ncidod/dvrd/bse

76. U.S. Centers for Disease Control and Prevention. (2006). Preliminary FoodNet data on the incidence of infection with pathogens transmitted commonly through food—10 states, United States, 2005. *Morbidity and Mortality Weekly Reports, 55*(14), 392–395. Retrieved May 20, 2006, from http://www.cdc.gov/mmwr/preview/mmwrhtml/mm5514a2.htm

77. U.S. Department of Agriculture. (1994). *Complete guide to home canning*. Agriculture Information Bulletin No. 539. Washington, DC: U.S. Government Printing Office.

78. U.S. Department of Agriculture, Food Safety and Inspection Service. (2005). "Fact Sheets: Molds on Foods—Are They Dangerous?" Retrieved July 5, 2006, from http://www.fsis.usda.gov/Fact_Sheets/Molds_on_Food/index.asp

79. U.S. Department of Agriculture, Food Safety and Inspection Service. (2006). "Food Safety Education: Is It Done Yet?" Retrieved July 3, 2006, from http://www.fsis.usda.gov/is_it_done_yet/

80. U.S. Department of Health and Human Services, Food and Drug Administration. (2001). "FDA Publishes Final Rule to Increase Safety of Fruit and Vegetable Juices." Retrieved June 24, 2002, from http://www.cfsan.fda.gov/~lrd/hhsjuic4.html

81. U.S. Department of Health and Human Services and U.S. Environmental Protection Agency. (2004). "What You Need to Know about Mercury in Fish and Shellfish." Retrieved July 3, 2006, from http://www.cfsan.fda.gov/~dms/admehg3.html

82. U.S. Environmental Protection Agency. (2001, June). *Fact sheet: Mercury update: Impact on fish advisories*. EPA 823-F-01-011.

83. Young, A., Taylor, J., and Fix, J. L. (1999, August). A killer in our food. *Detroit Free Press*. Retrieved May 22, 2002, from http://www.freepress.com/outbreak/

Chapter 4

1. Barrows, J. N., Lipman, A. L., and Bailey, C. J. (2003). "Color Additives: FDA's Regulatory Process and Historical Perspectives." (Reprint from *Food Safety Magazine*, October/November 2003 issue). Retrieved July 11, 2006, from http://www.cfsan.fda.gov/~dms/col-regu.html

2. Brecher, S. J., Bender, M. M., Wilkening, V. L., McCabe, N. M., and Anderson, E. M. (2000). Status of nutrition labeling, health claims, and nutrient content claims for processed foods: 1997 food label and package survey. *Journal of the American Dietetic Association, 100*, 1056.

3. Buzby, J. C., and Crutchfield, S. R. (1997). USDA modernizes meat and poultry inspection. *Food Review, 20*(1), 14.

4. Formanek, R. (2001). Proposed rules issued for bioengineered foods. *FDA Consumer, 35*(2).

5. Giese, J. (2000). Pesticide analysis. *Food Technology, 54*(12), 64–65.

6. Griffiths, J. C. (2005). Coloring foods and beverages. *Food Technology, 59*(5) 38–44.

7. Henkel, J. (1996). How to comment on proposals and submit petitions. *FDA Consumer, 30*(3), 6.

8. Hilts, P. J. (2006). The FDA at work: Cutting-edge science promoting public health. *FDA Consumer, 40*(1), 29–35, 39–41.

9. Institute of Food Technologists' Expert Report on Biotechnology and Foods. (2000). Labeling of rDNA biotechnology-derived foods. *Food Technology, 54*(9), 62–74.

10. International Food Information Council and U.S. Food and Drug Administration. (2004). *Food ingredients and colors*. Retrieved July 10, 2006, from http://www.cfsan.fda.gov/~dms/foodic.html

11. Kessler, D. A. (1992). Reinvigorating the Food and Drug Administration. *Food Technology, 46*(8), 20.

12. Looney, J. W., Crandall, P. G., and Poole, A. K. (2001). The matrix of food safety regulations. *Food Technology, 55*(4), 60–76.

13. Meadows, M. (2006). A century of ensuring safe foods and cosmetics. *Food Technology, 40*(1), 7–13.

14. Mermelstein, N. H. (1993). A new era in food labeling. *Food Technology, 47*(2), 81.

15. Mermelstein, N. H. (1993). Nutrition labeling in foodservice. *Food Technology, 47*(4), 65.

16. Mermelstein, N. H. (2001). Terrorism spurs renewed call for single food safety agency. *Food Technology, 55*(11), 32.

17. Montecalvo, J. (2001). The national organic program: An opportunity for industry. *Food Technology, 55*(6), 26.

18. Newberne, P., Smith, R. L., Doull, J., Feron, V. J., Goodman, J. I., Munro, I. C., Portoghese, P. S., Waddell, W. J., Wagner, B. M., Weil, C. S., Adams, T. B., and

Hallagan, J. B. (2000). GRAS flavoring substances, 19. *Food Technology, 54*(6), 66–84.

19. Ohr, L. M. (2004). Nutrition in a nutshell. *Food Technology, 58*(1), 55–59.

20. Newsome, R. (1997). Codex, international trade, and science. *Food Technology, 51*(9), 28.

21. Regenstein, J. (2002). A single food safety agency is not the answer. *Food Technology, 56*(3), 104.

22. Segal, M. (1993, May). Ingredient labeling: What's in a food? *FDA Consumer, Special Edition.* Retrieved July 2, 2002, from http://www.fda.gov/fdac/special/foodlabel/ingred.html

23. Smith, R. L., Cohen, S. M., Doull, J., Feron, V. J., Marnett, L. J., Portoghese, P. S., Waddell, W. J., Wagner, B. M., and Adams, T. B. (2005). GRAS flavoring substances 22. *Food Technology, 59*(8), 24–62.

24. Staff. (2006). FDA milestones. *FDA Consumer, 40*(1), 36–38.

25. Stehlin, D. (1993). A little "lite" reading. *FDA Consumer—Special edition.* Retrieved July 3, 2002, from http://fda.gov/fdac/special/foodlabel/lite.html

26. Swann, J. P. (2001). "History of the FDA." Retrieved June 23, 2002, from http://www.fda.gov/oc/history/history-offda/default/htm

27. The American Dietetic Association. (2000). Position of the American Dietetic Association: Food irradiation. *Journal of the American Dietetic Association, 100*, 246–253.

28. Turner, R. E. (2002). Organic standards. *Food Technology, 56*(6), 24.

29. U.S. Centers for Disease Control and Prevention, Division of Bacterial and Mycotic Disease. (2005). "Food Irradiation." Retrieved June 21, 2006, from http://www.cdc.gov/ncidod/dbmd/diseaseinfo/foodirradiation.htm

30. U.S. Department of Agriculture. (2002). "Organic Food Standards and Labels: The Facts." Retrieved July 11, 2006, from http://www.ams.usda.gov/nop/consumerbrochure.htm

31. U.S. Department of Agriculture. (2005). "Fact Sheets: Irradiation and Food Safety." Retrieved July 10, 2006, from http://www.fsis.usda.gov/Fact_Sheets/Irradiation_and_food_Safety/index.asp

32. U.S. Department of Agriculture. (2005). "Food Irradiation: A Focus on Food Irradiation." Retrieved July 10, 2006, from http://fsrio.nal.usda.gov/document_fsheet.php?product_id=154

33. U.S. Department of Agriculture, Agricultural Marketing Service. (2002). "The National Organic Program: Background Information." Retrieved July 11, 2006, from http://www.ams.usda.gov/nop/FactSheets/Backgrounder.html

34. U.S. Department of Agriculture, Food Safety Inspection Service. (2006). "About FSIS: Celebrating 100 years of FMIA." Retrieved July 7, 2006, from http://www.fsis.usda.gov/About_FSIS/100_Years_FMIA/index.asp

35. U.S. Department of Health and Human Services, Food and Drug Administration. (1996, March). Food standards: Amendment of standards of identify for enriched grain products to require addition of folic acid. *Federal Register, 61*(44), 8781–8797. Retrieved July 2, 2002, from http://www.cfsan.fda.gov/~lrd/fr96305b.html

36. U.S. Department of Health and Human Services, Food and Drug Administration. (2005, April). "Docket No. 2004N-0456: Proposed Rule: Food Labeling." Retrieved July 10, 2006, from http://www.fda.gov/ohrms/dockets/98fr/05-6644.htm

37. U.S. Food and Drug Administration. (1999, May). The food label. *FDA Backgrounder.* Retrieved July 2, 2002, from http://www.cfsan.fda.gov/~dms/fdnewlab.html

38. U.S. Food and Drug Administration. (2005, May). News release: "USDA and HHS Propose to Modernize Principles for Food Standards of Identity." Retrieved July 8, 2006, from http://www.fda.gov/bbs/topics/news/2005/usda_hhs051705.html

39. U.S. Food and Drug Administration. (n.d.) "Laws Enforced by the FDA and Related Statutes." Retrieved July 7, 2006, from http://www.fda.gov/opacom/laws/

40. U.S. Food and Drug Administration, Center for Food Safety and Applied Nutrition. (1995). Office of Seafood Handout: "The Food and Drug Administration's Seafood Regulatory Program." Retrieved July 7, 2006, from http://www.cfsan.fda.gov/~lrd/sea-ovr.html

41. U.S. Food and Drug Administration, Center for Food Safety and Applied Nutrition. (2003). "Claims That Can Be Made for Conventional Foods and Dietary Supplements." Retrieved May 20, 2006, from http://www.cfsan.fda.gov/~dms/hclaims.html

42. U.S. Food and Drug Administration, Center for Food Safety and Applied Nutrition. (2003). "Color Additives: FDA's Regulatory Process and Historical Perspectives." Retrieved July 11, 2006, from http://www.cfsan.fda.gov/~dms/col-regu.html

43. U.S. Food and Drug Administration, Center for Food Safety and Applied Nutrition. (2004, August). "Food Allergen Labeling and Consumer Protection Act of 2004" (Title II of Public Law 108-282). Retrieved June 12, 2006, from http://www.cfsan.fda.gov/~dms/alrgact.html

44. U.S. Food and Drug Administration, Center for Food Safety and Applied Nutrition. (2005). "The 2005 FDA Food Code: Questions and Answers." Retrieved June 21, 2006, from http://www.cfsan.fda.gov/~dms?fc05-qa.html

45. U.S. Food and Drug Administration, Center for Food Safety and Applied Nutrition. (2006). "FDA News: FDA Finalizes Health Claim Associating Consumption of Barley Products with Reduction of Risk of Coronary Heart Disease." Retrieved May 20, 2006, from http://www.fda.gov/bbs/topics/NEWS/2006/New01375.html

46. U.S. Food and Drug Administration, Center for Food Safety and Applied Nutrition. (2006). "Label Claims: Health Claims That Meet Significant Scientific Agreement (SSA)." Retrieved May 20, 2006, from http://www.cfsan.fda.gov/~dms/lab-ssa.html

47. U.S Food and Drug Administration, Center for Food Safety and Applied Nutrition. (2006). "*Trans* Fat Now Listed with Saturated Fat and Cholesterol on the Nutrition Facts Label." Retrieved May 20, 2006, from http://www.cfsan.fda.gov/~dms/transfat.html

48. U.S. Food and Drug Administration, Center for Food Safety and Applied Nutrition. (2006). "100 Years: Working to Keep Food and Cosmetics Safe and Promote Good Nutrition." Retrieved July 5, 2006, from http://www.cfsan.fda/acrobat/100years.pdf

49. U.S. Food Safety Inspection Service. (1999). "Backgrounder: *Codex alimentarius.*" Retrieved July 6, 2002, from http://www.fsis.usda.gov/OA/backgrounder/codex.htm

50. Winter, C. K. (1993). Pesticide residues and the Delaney clause. *Food Technology, 47*(7), 81.

51. Winter, C. K. (1997). Assessing, managing, and communicating chemical food risks. *Food Technology, 51*(5), 85.

52. Wodicka, V. O. (1996). Regulation of food: Where have we been? *Food Technology, 50*(3), 106.

Chapter 5

1. American Association of Family and Consumer Sciences. (2001). *Food: A Handbook of Terminology, Purchasing, and Preparation,* 10th ed. Alexandria, VA: American Association of Family and Consumer Sciences.

2. American Standards Association. (1963). *American Standard Dimensions, Tolerances, and Terminology for Home Cooking and Baking Utensils.* New York: American Standards Association, Inc.

3. Arlin, M. L., Nielsen, M. M., and Hall, F. T. (1964). The effect of different methods of flour measurement on the quality of plain two-egg cakes. *Journal of Home Economics, 56,* 399.

4. Labensky, S. R., and Hause, A. M. (2007). *On Cooking: A Textbook of Culinary Fundamentals,* 4th ed. Upper Saddle River, NJ: Pearson Prentice Hall.

5. Lawless, S. T., Gregoire, M. B., Canter, D. D., and Setser, C. S. (1991). Comparison of cakes produced from computer-generated recipes. *School Food Service Research Review, 15*(1), 23–27.

6. Matthews, R. H., and Batcher, O. M. (1963). Sifted versus unsifted flour. *Journal of Home Economics, 55,* 123.

7. Molt, M. (2006). *Food for Fifty,* 12th ed. Upper Saddle River, NJ: Pearson Prentice Hall.

8. Randal, J. (1994). Going metric: American foods and drugs measure up. *FDA Consumer, 28: 23*(7).

Chapter 6

1. American Association of Family and Consumer Sciences. (2001). *Food: A Handbook of Terminology, Purchasing, and Preparation,* 10th ed. Alexandria, VA: American Association of Family and Consumer Sciences.

2. Labensky, S. R., and Hause, A. M. (2007). *On Cooking: A Textbook of Culinary Fundamentals,* 4th ed. Upper Saddle River, NJ: Pearson Prentice Hall.

3. Molt, M. (2006). *Food for Fifty,* 12th ed. Upper Saddle River, NJ: Pearson Prentice Hall.

Chapter 7

1. American Association of Family and Consumer Sciences. (2001). *Food: A Handbook of Terminology, Purchasing, and Preparation,* 10th ed. Alexandria, VA: American Association of Family and Consumer Sciences.

2. Bowers, D. E. (2000). Cooking trends echo changing roles of women. *Food Review, 23*(1), 23–29.

3. Brody, A. L. (2001). The return of microwavable foods. *Food Technology, 55*(3), 69–70.

4. Carroll, L. E. (1989). Hydrocolloid functions to improve stability of microwavable foods. *Food Technology, 43*(6), 96.

5. Cipra, J. S., and Bowers, J. A. (1971). Flavor of microwave- and conventionally-reheated turkey. *Poultry Science, 50,* 703.

6. Dahl, C. A., and Matthews, M. E. (1980). Effect of microwave heating in cook/chill foodservice systems. *Journal of the American Dietetic Association, 77,* 289.

7. Decareau, R. V. (1992). *Microwave Foods: New Product Development.* Trumbull, CT: Food & Nutrition Press, Inc.

8. Giese, J. H. (1992). Advances in microwave food processing. *Food Technology, 46*(9), 118.

9. Institute of Food Technologists' Expert Panel on Food Safety and Nutrition. (1989). Microwave food processing. *Food Technology, 43*(1), 117.

10. Katz, F. (1999). Microwave packaging addresses speed, clarity, and ease of use. *Food Technology, 53*(7), 106–107.

11. Lindsay, R. E., Krissinger, W. A., and Fields, B. F. (1986). Microwave vs. conventional oven cooking of chicken: Relationship of internal temperature to surface contamination by *Salmonella typhimurium. Journal of the American Dietetic Association, 86,* 373.

12. Mandigo, R. W., and Janssen, T. J. (1982). Energy-efficient cooking systems for muscle foods. *Food Technology, 36*(4), 128.

13. Mermelstein, N. H. (1999). Microwave processing of food. *Food Technology, 53*(7), 114–116.

14. Miller, R. A., and Hoseney, R. C. (1997). Method to measure microwave-induced toughness of bread. *Journal of Food Science, 62,* 1202.

15. National Restaurant Association Educational Foundation. (2006). *ServSafe Coursebook,* 4th ed. Chicago, IL: National Restaurant Association.

16. Pszczola, D. E. (2001). Convenience foods: They've come a long, long way. *Food Technology, 55*(9), 85–94.

17. Ramesh, M. N., Tevini, D., and Wolf, W. (2002). Microwave blanching of vegetables. *Journal of Food Science, 67*(1), 390–398.

18. Ryynanen, S., and Ohlsson, T. (1996). Microwave heating uniformity of ready meals as affected by placement, composition, and geometry. *Journal of Food Science, 61,* 620.

19. Spears, M., and Gregoire, M. (2007). *Foodservice Organizations: A Managerial and Systems Approach,* 6th ed. Upper Saddle River, NJ: Pearson Prentice Hall.

20. Toops, D. (1998). Microwave science's Bob Thompson. New technology zaps microwave inconsistencies. *Food Processing, 59*(1), 45.

21. USDA Food Safety and Inspection Service. (2006, April). "Fact Sheets: Appliance and Thermometers–Cooking Safely in the Microwave Oven." Retrieved July 20, 2006, from http://www.fsis.usda.gov/Fact_Sheets/Cooking_Safelyin_the_Microwave/index.asp

22. USDA Food Safety and Inspection Service, FDA Center for Food Safety and Applied Nutrition. (2000, November). "Food Safety Facts: Cooking Safely in the Microwave." Retrieved July 19, 2006, from http://www.foodsafety.gov/~fsg/fs-mwave.html

23. U.S. Food and Drug Administration, Center for Devices and Radiological Health. (2006, July). "Microwave Oven Radiation." Retrieved July 19, 2006, from http://www.fda.gov/cdrh/consumer/microwave.html

Chapter 8

1. ACH Food Companies, Inc. (2006). "Usage Tips: How to Test for Freshness." Retrieved July 22, 2006, from http://www.spiceadvice.com/usage/index.html

2. American Spice Trade Association. (n.d.). "ASTA Frequently Asked Questions." Retrieved August 17, 2002, from http://astaspice.org/main_faqs.htm

3. American Spice Trade Association. (n.d.) "Spice Definitions and Glossary." Retrieved July 28, 2006, from http://www.astaspice.org/spice/spice_07.htm

4. Augustin, J., Augustin, E., Cutrufelli, R. L., Hagen, S. R., and Teitzel, C. (1992). Alcohol retention in food preparation. *Journal of the American Dietetic Association, 92,* 486.

5. Bosland, P. W. (1996). Capsicums: Innovative uses of an ancient crop. In *Progress in New Crops*, edited by J. Janick, pp. 479–487. Arlington, VA: ASHS Press.

6. Dziezak, J. D. (1989). Spices. *Food Technology, 43*(1), 102.

7. *Fat Replacers*. (1992). Calorie Control Council, Suite 500-G, 5775 Peachtree-Dunwoody Road, Atlanta, GA 30342.

8. Furth, P., and Cox, D. (2004). The spice market expands. *Food Technology, 58*(8), 30–34.

9. Geha, R. S., Beiser, A., Clement, R., Patterson, R., Greenberger, P. A., Grammer, L. C., Ditto, A. M., Harris, K. E., Shaughnessy, M. A., Yarnold, P. R., Corren, J., and Saxon, A. (2000). Supplement–Review of alleged reaction to monosodium glutamate and outcome of a multicenter double-blind placebo-controlled study. *Journal of Nutrition, 130,* 1058S–1062S.

10. Gillette, M. (1985). Flavor effects of sodium chloride. *Food Technology, 39*(6), 47.

11. Institute of Food Technologists' Expert Panel on Food Safety and Nutrition. (1987). Monosodium glutamate (MSG). *Food Technology, 41*(5), 143.

12. International Food Information Council and U.S. Food and Drug Administration. (2004). "Food Ingredients and Colors." Retrieved July 10, 2006, from http://www.cfsan.fda.gov/~dms/foodic.html

13. Labensky, S. R., and Hause, A. M. (2007). *On Cooking: A Textbook of Culinary Fundamentals*, 4th ed. Upper Saddle River, NJ: Pearson Prentice Hall.

14. Loria, C. M., Obarzanek, E., and Ernst, N. D. (2001). Supplement—Choose and prepare foods with less salt: Dietary advice for all Americans. *Journal of Nutrition, 131,* 536S–551S.

15. Marcus, J. B. (2005). Culinary applications of umami. *Food Technology, 59*(5), 24–30.

16. McCormick. (2006). "The Enspicelopedia." Retrieved July 22, 2006, from http://mccormick.com/content.cfm?ID=8291

17. McCormick. (2006). "Toss Old Spices Seasonally." Retrieved July 22, 2006, from http://mccormick.com/content.cfm?ID=11985

18. McCormick. (n.d.). "Hot, Hot, Hot, Stuff!" Retrieved August 2, 2002, from http://www.mccormick.com/content.cfm?ID=9079

19. Meadows, M. (2003). MSG: A common flavor enhancer. *FDA Consumer Magazine, 31*(1).

20. Ortiz, E. L. (1992). *The Encyclopedia of Herbs, Spices, and Flavorings: A Cook's Compendium*. New York: DK Publishing, Inc.

21. Porzio, M. (2004). Flavor encapsulation: A convergence of science and art. *Food Technology, 58*(7), 40–47.

22. Pszczola, D. E. (1997). Salty developments in food. *Food Technology, 51*(10), 79.

23. Pszczola, D. E. (2001). 2001: A spice odyssey. *Food Technology, 55*(1), 36–44.

24. Pszczola, D. E. (2001). Suppliers' night 2000 proves to be a spicy affair. *Food Technology, 55*(1), 68–73.

25. Raghavan, S. (2004). Developing ethnic foods and ethnic flair with spices. *Food Technology, 58*(8), 35–42.

26. Riley, K. A., and Kleyn, D. H. (1989). Fundamental principles of vanilla/vanilla extract processing and methods of detecting adulteration in vanilla extracts. *Food Technology, 43*(10), 64.

27. Rosengarten, F., Jr. (1969). *The Book of Spices*. Wynnewood, PA: Livingston Publishing Company.

28. Sloan, A. E. (2001). Eastern influence. *Food Technology, 55*(3), 18.

29. Sloan, A. E. (2001). Ethnic foods in the decade ahead. *Food Technology, 55*(10), 18.

30. Sloan, A. E. (2001). More on ethnic foods: Move over BBQ, Cajun, and Caesar. *Food Technology, 55*(11), 18.

31. U.S. Food and Drug Administration. (2003, August). "FDA Changes Labeling Requirement for Olestra." Retrieved July 29, 2006, from http://www.fda.gov/bbs/topics/ANSWERS/2003/ANS01245.html

32. U.S. Food and Drug Administration, Center for Food Safety and Applied Nutrition. (n.d.). "EAFUS: A Food Additive Database." Retrieved July 29, 2006, from http://www.cfsan.fda.gov/~dms/eafus.html

33. U.S. Department of Health and Human Services and U.S. Department of Agriculture. "Finding Your Way to a Healthier You: Based on the Dietary Guidelines." Retrieved May 5, 2006, from http://www.health.gov/dietaryguidelines/dga2005/document/html/brochure.htm

Chapter 9

1. American Association of Cereal Chemists. (2001). The definition of dietary fiber. *Cereal Foods World, 46*(3), 112–126.

2. American Association of Family and Consumer Sciences. (2001). *Food: A Handbook of Terminology, Purchasing, and Preparation*, 10th ed. Alexandria, VA: Author.

3. American Dietetic Association. (2002). Position of the American Dietetic Association: Health implications of dietary fiber. *Journal of the American Dietetic Association, 102,* 993–1000.

4. Buswell, A. M., and Rodebush, W. H. (1956). Water. *Scientific American, 194*(4), 2.

5. Carr, J. M. (1993). Hydrocolloids and stabilizers. *Food Technology, 47*(10), 100.

6. Dziezak, J. D. (1991). A focus on gums. *Food Technology, 45*(3), 116.

7. Gordon, D. T. (2002). Intestinal health through dietary fiber, prebiotics, and probiotics. *Food Technology, 56*(4), 23.

8. Hicks, K. B., and Moreau, R. A. (2001). Phytosterols and phytostanols: Functional food cholesterol busters. *Food Technology, 55*(1), 63–67.

9. Hollingsworth, P. (2001). Margarine: The over-the-top functional food. *Food Technology, 55*(1), 59–62.

10. Katz, E. E., and Labuza, T. P. (1981). Effect of water activity on the sensory crispness and mechanical deformation of snack food products. *Journal of Food Science, 46,* 403.

11. U.S. Department of Agriculture. *Nutritive value of foods.* (1991). Home and Garden Bulletin No. 72. Washington, DC: Author.

12. Ohr, L. M. (2002). Circulating heart smart news. *Food Technology, 56*(6), 109–115.

13. Papazian, R. (1998, September). Bulking up fiber's healthful reputation. *FDA Consumer.* Retrieved August 27, 2002, from http://www.cfsan.fda.gov/~dms/fdafiber.html

14. Pszczola, D. E. (1999). Starches and gums move beyond fat replacement. *Food Technology, 53*(8), 74–80.

15. Sanderson, G. R. (1996). Gums and their use in food systems. *Food Technology, 50:* 81(3).

16. Shah, N. P. (2001). Functional foods from probiotics and prebiotics. *Food Technology, 55*(11), 46.

17. U.S. Department of Agriculture, Agricultural Research Service. (2008). "USDA Nutrient Database for Standard Reference," Release 20. Retrieved April 11, 2008, from http://www.ars.usda.gov/Services/docs.htm?docid=8964

Chapter 10

1. Agriculture Marketing Service, U.S. Department of Agriculture. (1995, February). How to buy dairy products. *Home and Garden Bulletin 201.*

2. Akoh, C. C. (1998). Fat replacers. *Food Technology, 52*(3), 47.

3. Allman-Farinelli, M. A., Gomes, K., Favaloro, E. J., and Petocz, P. (2005). A diet rich in high-oleic-acid sunflower oil favorably alters low-density lipoprotein cholesterol, triglycerides, and factor VII coagulant activity. *Journal of the American Dietetic Association, 105,*1071–1079.

4. American Dietetic Association. (2005). Position of the American Dietetic Association: Fat replacers. *Journal of the American Dietetic Association, 105,* 266–275.

5. American Palm Oil Council. (n.d.). "Frequently Asked Questions." Retrieved August 12, 2006, from http://www.americanpalmoil.com/faq.html

6. Berger, K. (1986). Palm oil products. *Food Technology, 40*(9), 72.

7. Bertolli USA. (n.d.). "Olive Oil Varieties." Retrieved August 12, 2006, from http://www.bertolli.us/oliveoil.aspx

8. Binkoski, A. E., Kris-Etherton, P. M., Wilson, T. A., Mountain, M. L., and Nicolosi, R. J. (2005). Balance of unsaturated fatty acids is important to a cholesterol-lowering diet: Comparison of mid-oleic sunflower oil and olive oil on cardiovascular disease risk factors. *Journal of the American Dietetic Association, 105,* 1080–1086.

9. Blumenthal, M. M. (1991). A new look at the chemistry and physics of deep-fat frying. *Food Technology, 45*(2), 68.

10. Caponio, F., and Gomes, T. (2004). Examination of lipid fraction quality of margarine. *Journal of Food Science, 69,* 63–66.

11. Chanmugam, P., Guthrie, J. F., Cecilio, S., Morton, J. F., Basiotis, P. P., and Anand, R. (2003). Did fat intake in the United States really decline between 1989–1991 and 1994–1996? *Journal of the American Dietetic Association, 103,* 867–872.

12. Clark, J. P. (2005). Fats and oil processors adapt to changing needs. *Food Technology, 59*(5), 74–76.

13. Crutchfield, S. R., and Weimer, J. (2000). Nutrition policy in the 1990's. *Food Review, 23*(3), 38–43.

14. Dorko, C. (1994). Antioxidants used in foods. *Food Technology, 48*(4), 33.

15. Drewnowski, A. (1997). Why do we like fat? *Journal of the American Dietetic Association, 97,* S58.

16. Dunford, N. T. (2001). Health benefits and processing of lipid-based nutritionals. *Food Technology, 55*(1), 38–44.

17. Duxbury, D. (2005). Omega-3s offer solutions to *trans* fat substitution problem. *Food Technology, 59*(4), 34–39.

18. Dziezak, J. D. (1986). Preservatives: Antioxidants. *Food Technology, 40*(9), 94.

19. Dziezak, J. D. (1989). Fats, oils, and fat substitutes. *Food Technology, 43*(7), 66.

20. Erickson, M. D., and Frey, N. (1994). Property-enhanced oils in food applications. *Food Technology, 48*(11), 63.

21. Farah, H., and Buzby, J. (2005). U.S. food consumption up 16 percent since 1970. *Amber Waves, 3*(5), 5.

22. Fitzpatrick, M. P., Chapman, G. E., and Barr, S. J. (1997). Lower-fat menu items in restaurants satisfy customers. *Journal of the American Dietetic Association, 97,* 510.

23. Food and Nutrition Board, Institute of Medicine. (2002). "Letter Report on Dietary Reference Intakes for *trans* Fatty Acids." Retrieved August 30, 2002, from http://www.iom.edu/CMS/5410.aspx

24. Fulton, L., and Hogbin, M. (1993). Eating quality of muffins, cakes, and cookies prepared with reduced fat and sugar. *Journal of the American Dietetic Association, 93,* 1313.

25. Giese, J. H. (1993). Alternative sweeteners and bulking agents. *Food Technology, 47*(1), 114.

26. Giese, J. (1996). Fats, oils, and fat replacers. *Food Technology, 50*(4), 78.

27. Hearn, T. L., Sgoutas, S. A., Hearn, J. A., and Sgoutas, D. S. (1987). Polyunsaturated fatty acids and fat in fish flesh for selecting species for health benefits. *Journal of Food Science, 52:* 1209.

28. Hicks, K. B., and Moreau, R. A. (2001). Phytosterols and phytostanols: Functional food cholesterol busters. *Food Technology, 55*(1), 63–67.

29. Hollingsworth, P. (2001). Margarine: The over-the-top functional food. *Food Technology, 55*(1), 59–62.

30. Institute of Food Science and Technology. (1999, June). "Position Statement: *Trans* Fatty Acids (TFA)." Retrieved September 7, 2002, from http://www.ifst.org/hottop9.htm

31. Katz, F. (1997). The move towards genetically improved oils. *Food Technology, 51*(11), 66.

32. Kostas, G. (1997). Low-fat and delicious: Can we break the taste barrier? *Journal of the American Dietetic Association, 97,* S88.

33. Labensky, S. R., and Hause, A. M. (2007). *On Cooking: A Textbook of Culinary Fundamentals,* 4th ed. Upper Saddle River, NJ: Pearson Prentice Hall.

34. Lawson, H. W. (1985). *Standards for Fats and Oils.* Westport, CT: Avi Publishing.

35. Lee, S., and Inglett, G. E. (2006). Functional characterization of steam jet-cooked β-glucan-rich barley flour as an oil barrier in frying batters. *Journal of Food Science, 71(6),* E308–E313.

36. List, G. R. (2004). Decreasing *trans* and saturated fatty acid content in food oils. *Food Technology, 58(1),* 23–31.

37. McComber, D., and Miller, E. M. (1976). Differences in total lipid and fatty acid composition of doughnuts as influenced by lecithin, leavening agent, and use of frying fat. *Cereal Chemistry, 53,* 101.

38. National Sunflower Association. (n.d.). "Sunflower Oil: Your Healthy Choice." Retrieved August 12, 2006, from http://www.sunflowernsa.com/oil/

39. Nettleton, J. (2005). Omega-3 fatty acids in foods and health. *Food Technology, 59(9),* 120.

40. Neuhouser, M. L., Kristal, A. R., and Patterson, R. E. (1999). Use of food nutrient labels is associated with lower fat intake. *Journal of the American Dietetic Association, 99,* 45–50.

41. Ohr, L. M. (2004). Controlling cholesterol. *Food Technology, 58(11),* 73–76.

42. Pszczola, D. E. (2001). Antioxidants: From preserving food quality to quality of life. *Food Technology, 55(6),* 51–59.

43. Pszczola, D. E. (2001). Salad days? Not for these dressings. *Food Technology, 55(4),* 78–86.

44. Pszczola, D. E. (2004). Fats: In *trans*-ition. *Food Technology, 58(4),* 52–63.

45. Pszczola, D. E. (2006). Future strategies for fat replacement. *Food Technology, 60(6),* 61–84.

46. Smouse, T. H. (1979). Review of soybean oil reversion flavor. *Journal of the American Oil Chemists' Society, 56,* 747A.

47. Staff report. (2001). Combining nutrients for health benefits. *Food Technology, 55(2),* 42–47.

48. Szafranski, M., Whittington, J. A., and Bessinger, C. (2005). Pureed cannelloni beans can be substituted for shortening in brownies. *Journal of the American Dietetic Association, 105,* 1295–1298.

49. Szczesniak, A. S. (1990). Texture: Is it still an overlooked food attribute? *Food Technology, 44(9),* 86.

50. Tarrago-Trani, M. T., Phillips, K. M., Lemar, L. E., and Holden, J. M. (2006). New and existing oils and fats used in products with reduced *trans*-fatty acid content. *Journal of the American Dietetic Association, 106,* 867–880.

51. U.S. Department of Agriculture. (2005). "Dietary Guidelines for Americans 2005: Chapter 6, Fats." Retrieved August 19, 2006, from http://health.gov/DIETARY-GUIDELINES/dga2005/document/html/chapter6.htm

52. U.S. Department of Agriculture, Economic Research Service. "Data Sets. Food Availability: Custom Queries." Retrieved August 8, 2006, from http://www.ers.usda.gov/Data/Foodconsumption/FoodAvailQueriable.aspx

53. U.S. Food and Drug Administration, Center for Food Safety and Applied Nutrition. (2006). "Questions and Answers about *Trans* Fat Nutrition Labeling." Retrieved August 1, 2006, from http://www.cfsan.fda.gov/~dms/qatrans2.html

54. Wardlaw, G. M., and Kessel, M. W. (2002). *Perspectives in Nutrition,* 5th ed. New York: McGraw-Hill.

55. Wisconsin Dairy Association. (n.d.). "Key Steps in Butter Production." Retrieved August 12, 2006, from http://www.wisdairy.com/otherdairyproductinfo/butter/butter-basics/KeySteps.aspx

Chapter 11

1. American Dietetic Association. (2004). Position of the American Dietetic Association: Use of nutritive and non-nutritive sweeteners. *Journal of the American Dietetic Association, 104,* 255–275.

2. Awad, A., and Chen, A. C. (1993). A new generation of sucrose products made by cocrystallization. *Food Technology, 47(1),* 146.

3. Bartoshuk, L. M. (1991). Sweetness: History, preference, and genetic variability. *Food Technology, 45(11),* 108.

4. Bell, J. (1993). High intensity sweeteners—A regulatory update. *Food Technology, 47(11),* 136.

5. Blankers, I. (1995). Properties and applications of lactitol. *Food Technology, 49(1),* 66.

6. Carr, J. M., Sufferling, K., and Poppe, J. (1995). Hydrocolloids and their use in the confectionery industry. *Food Technology, 49(7),* 41.

7. Cohen, S. M. (1986). Saccharin: Past, present, and future. *Journal of the American Dietetic Association, 86,* 929.

8. Coulston, A. M., and Johnson, R. K. (2002). Sugar and sugars: Myths and realities. *Journal of the American Dietetic Association, 102,* 351–353.

9. Dziezak, J. D. (1986). Sweeteners and product development. *Food Technology, 40(1),* 112.

10. Dziezak, J. D. (1989). Ingredients for sweet success. *Food Technology, 43(10),* 94.

11. Hardy, S. L., Brennand, C. P., and Wyse, B. W. (1979). Fructose: Comparison with sucrose as sweetener in four products. *Journal of the American Dietetic Association, 74,* 41.

12. Hess, D. A., and Setser, C. S. (1986). Comparison of aspartame- and fructose-sweetened layer cakes: Importance of panels of users for evaluation of alternative sweeteners. *Journal of the American Dietetic Association, 86,* 919.

13. Hoch, G. J. (1997). Sweet anticipation. *Food Processing, 58(12),* 45.

14. Hollingsworth, P. (2002). Artificial sweeteners face sweet 'n sour consumer market. *Food Technology, 56(7),* 24–27.

15. Hollingsworth, P. (2002). Developing and marketing foods for diabetics. *Food Technology, 56(10),* 38.

16. Koivistoinen, P., and Hyvönen, L. (1980). *Carbohydrate sweeteners in foods and nutrition.* New York: Academic Press.

17. Kroger, M., Meister, K., and Kava, R. (2006, April). Low-calorie sweeteners and other sugar substitutes: A review of the safety issues. *Comprehensive Reviews in Food Science and Food Safety, 5,* 35–47.

18. McNutt, K. (2000). What clients need to know about sugar replacers. *Journal of the American Dietetic Association, 100,* 466–469.

19. Mermelstein, N. H. (2002). Formulating foods for diabetics. *Food Technology, 56*(10), 42.

20. Nabors, L. O. (2002). Sweet choices: Sugar replacements for food and beverages. *Food Technology, 56*(7), 28–34, 45.

21. Prakash, I., Corliss, G., Ponakala, R., and Ishikawa, G. (2002). Neotame: The next-generation sweetener. *Food Technology, 56*(7), 36–40, 45.

22. Pszczola, D. E. (1987). American fructose unveils new technologies in HFCS plant. *Food Technology, 41*(10), 50.

23. Pszczola, D. E. (1997). Ingredient developments for confections. *Food Technology, 51*(9), 70.

24. Pszczola, D. E. (1999). Sweet beginnings to a new year. *Food Technology, 53*(1), 70.

25. Pszczola, D. E. (2003). Sweetener + sweetener enhances the equation. *Food Technology, 57*(11), 48–61.

26. Pszczola, D. E. (2006). Synergizing sweetness. *Food Technology, 60*(3), 69–79.

27. Rapaille, A., Gonze, M., and Van der Schueren, F. (1995). Formulating sugar-free chocolate products with maltitol. *Food Technology, 49*(7), 51.

28. Staff. (1987). Crystalline fructose: A breakthrough in corn sweetener process technology. *Food Technology, 41*(1), 66.

29. Staff. (1996). Thaumatin—The sweetest substance known to man has a wide range of food applications. *Food Technology, 50*(1), 74.

30. Staff. (2006). Artificial sweeteners: No calories–sweet! *FDA Consumer, 40*(4), 27–28.

31. Sugar Association. "What Are the Types of Sugar?" Retrieved August 19, 2006, from http://www.sugar.org/consumers/sweet_by_nature.asp?id=275

32. U.S. Department of Agriculture, Economic Research Service. "Data Sets. Food Availability: Custom Queries." Retrieved August 19, 2006, from http://www.ers.usda.gov/Data/FoodConsumption/FoodAvailQueriable.aspx

33. Woodruff, S., and Van Gilder, H. (1931). Photomicrographic studies of sucrose crystals. *Journal of Physical Chemistry, 35,* 1355.

Chapter 12

1. Buck, J. S., Walker, C. E., and Pierce, M. M. (1986). Evaluation of sucrose esters in ice cream. *Journal of Food Science, 51,* 489.

2. Byer, J. (2002). Effect of a starch-lipid fat replacer on the rheology of soft-serve ice cream. *Journal of Food Science, 67,* 2177–2182.

3. Code of Federal Regulations. *Definitions and Standards under the Federal Food, Drug, and Cosmetic Act: Frozen Desserts. Title 21, Part 20.*

4. Goff, D. (n.d.) "Dairy Science and Technology: Ice Cream Defects." Retrieved October 1, 2006, from http://www.foodsci.uoguelph.ca/dairyedu/icdefects

5. Goff, D. (n.d.) University of Guelph (Ontario, Canada). "Dairy Science and Technology: Ice Cream Manufacturer." Retrieved October 1, 2006, from http://www.foodsci.uoguelph.ca/dairyedu/icmanu.html

6. Halford, B. (2004). Ice cream: The finer points of chemistry and flavor release make this favorite treat so sweet. *Chemical and Engineering News, 82*(45), 51–53.

7. Hatchwell, L. C. (1994). Overcoming flavor challenges in low-fat frozen desserts. *Food Technology, 48*(2), 98.

8. International Dairy Foods Association. (2004). "Ice Cream and Frozen Dessert Sales and Consumption." Retrieved October 1, 2006, from http://www.idfa.org/facts/icecream/ic_consumption_2004.pdf

9. International Dairy Foods Association. (n.d.). "Keep It Cool! Tips on Storing and Handling Ice Cream." Retrieved October 1, 2006, from http://idfa.org/facts/icmonth/page9.cfm

10. International Dairy Foods Association. (n.d.) "The History of Ice Cream." Retrieved October 1, 2006, from http://www.idfa.org/facts/icmonth/page7.cfm

11. Keller, S. E., Fellows, J. W., Nash, T. C., and Shazer, W. H. (1991). Application of bulk-free process in aspartame-sweetened frozen dessert. *Food Technology, 45*(6), 100.

12. Keller, S. E., Fellows, J. W., Nash, T. C., and Shazer, W. H. (1991). Formulation of aspartame-sweetened frozen dairy dessert without bulking agents. *Food Technology, 45*(2), 102.

13. Kurtzweil, P. (1998). Skimming the milk label: Fat-reduced milk products join the food labeling fold. *FDA Consumer, 32*(1).

14. Marshall, R. T., Goff, H. D., and Hartel, R. W. (2003). *Ice Cream,* 6th ed. New York: Kluwer Academic/Plenum Publishers.

15. Tharp, B. W., and Gottemoller, T. V. (1990). Light frozen dairy desserts: Effect of compositional changes on processing and sensory characteristics. *Food Technology, 44*(10), 86.

16. Thomas, E. L. (1981). Structure and properties of ice cream emulsions. *Food Technology, 35*(1), 41.

17. U.S. Department of Agriculture, Economic Research Service. (2006). "Data Sets: Food Availability: Custom Queries." Retrieved September 26, 2006, from http://www.ers.usda.gov/Data/FoodConsumption/FoodAvailQueriable.aspx

18. U.S. Food and Drug Administration. (2002, April 1). *Code of Federal Regulations, Title 21, Part 135.3—Frozen Desserts.* Washington, DC: U.S. Government Printing Office, 358–366.

19. Wittinger, S. A., and Smith, D. E. (1986). Effect of sweeteners and stabilizers on selected sensory attributes and shelf life of ice cream. *Journal of Food Science, 51,* 1463.

Chapter 13

1. Alden, L. (2005). Starch thickeners. *The Cook's Thesaurus.* Retrieved October 26, 2006, from http://foodsubs.com/ThickenStarch.html

2. Atwell, W. A., Hood, L. F., Lineback, D. R., Varriano-Marston, E., and Zobel, H. F. (1988). The terminology and methodology associated with basic starch phenomena. *Cereal Foods World, 33,* 306.

3. Banasiak, K. (2005). News: New waxy starch tested. *Food Technology*, *59*(7), 12–14.

4. Bean, M. M., and Yamazaki, W. T. (1978). Wheat starch gelatinization in sugar solutions. I. Sucrose: Microscopy and viscosity effects. *Cereal Chemistry*, *55*, 936.

5. Corn Refiners Association. (2002). "Frequently Asked Questions." Retrieved October 26, 2006, from http://www.corn.org/web/faq.htm

6. Corn Refiners Association. (2002). "The Corn Refining Process." Retrieved October 26, 2006, from http://corn.org/web/process.htm

7. Hansuld, M. K., and Briant, A. M. (1954). The effect of citric acid on selected edible starches and flours. *Food Research*, *19*, 581.

8. Hegenbart, S. (1996, January). Understanding starch functionality. *Food Product Design*. Retrieved October 26, 2006, from http://www.foodproductdesign.com/articles/462/462_0196CS.html

9. Hoch, G. J. (1997). The starch search. *Food Processing*, *58*(5), 60.

10. Holmes, Z. A., and Soeldner, A. (1981). Effect of heating rate and freezing and reheating of corn and wheat starch–water dispersions. *Journal of the American Dietetic Association*, *78*, 352.

11. Holmes, Z. A., and Soeldner, A. (1981). Macrostructure of selected raw starches and selected heated starch dispersions. *Journal of the American Dietetic Association*, *78*, 153.

12. Homesey, C. (2000, September). Starch: Stabilizer solutions. *Food Product Design*. Retrieved October 26, 2006, from http://www.foodproductdesign.com/articles/463/463_0900cs.html

13. International Starch Institute. (1999). "Starch Containing Plants." Retrieved November 4, 2006, from http://www.starch.dk/isi/starch/botany.htm

14. Kuntz, L. A. (2005, September). "Ingredient Insight: A Starch That's Hard to Resist." Retrieved October 26, 2006, from http://www.foodproductdesign.com/articles/0905INI.html

15. Labensky, S. R., and Hause, A. M. (2007). *On Cooking: A Textbook of Culinary Fundamentals*, 4th ed. Upper Saddle River, NJ: Pearson Prentice Hall.

16. Luallen, T. E. (1994). The use of starches in frozen food formulation. *Food Technology*, *48*(5), 39.

17. Messenger, B. (1997). Going native. *Food Processing*, *58*(1), 48.

18. Pszczola, D. E. (1996). Native starches offer functionality comparable to modified starches. *Food Technology*, *50*(12), 75.

19. Pszczola, D. E. (1999). Starches and gums move beyond fat replacement. *Food Technology*, *53*(8), 74–80.

20. Pszczola, D. E. (2000). Less traditional soups and sauces would meet Warhol's approval. *Food Technology*, *54*(3), 74–90.

21. Spies, R. D., and Hoseney, R. C. (1982). Effect of sugars on starch gelatinization. *Cereal Chemistry*, *59*, 128.

22. Waniska, R. D., and Gomez, M. H. (1992). Dispersion behavior of starch. *Food Technology*, *46*(6), 110.

23. Wiesenborn, D. P., Orr, P. H., Casper, H. H., and Tacke, B. K. (1994). Potato starch paste behavior as related to some physical/chemical properties. *Journal of Food Science*, *59*, 644.

24. Yackel, W. C., and Cox, C. (1992). Application of starch-based fat replacers. *Food Technology*, *46*(6), 146.

Chapter 14

1. Al-Babili S., and Beyer, P. (2005). Golden rice—five years on the road—five years to go? *Trends in Plant Science*, *10*(12), 565–573.

2. American Association of Family and Consumer Sciences. (2001). *Food: A Handbook of Terminology, Purchasing, and Preparation*, 10th ed. Alexandria, VA: American Association of Family and Consumer Sciences.

3. American Dietetic Association. (2002). Position of the American Dietetic Association: Health implications of dietary fiber. *Journal of the American Dietetic Association*, *102*, 993–1000.

4. Behall, K. M., Scholfield, D. J., and Hallfrisch, J. (2006). Whole-grain diets reduce blood pressure in mildly hypercholesterolemic men and women. *Journal of the American Dietetic Association*, *106*, 1445–1449.

5. Buzby, J., Farah, H., and Vocke, G. (2005). Will 2005 be the year of the whole grain? *Amber Waves*, *3*(3), 13–17.

6. Carlson, A., Mancino, L., and Lino, M. (2005, August). "Grain Consumption by Americans." USDA Center for Nutrition Policy and Promotion: Nutrition Insight 32. Retrieved November 14, 2006.

7. Carroll, L. E. (1990). Functional properties and applications of stabilized rice bran in bakery products. *Food Technology*, *44*(4), 74.

8. Chinnaswamy, R., and Hanna, M. A. (1987). Nozzle dimension effects on the expansion of extrusion cooked corn starch. *Journal of Food Science*, *52*, 1746.

9. Cleveland, L. E., Moshfegh, A. J., Albertson, A. M., and Goldman, J. D. (2000). Dietary intake of whole grains. *Journal of the American College of Nutrition*, *19*(3), 331S–338S.

10. Comis, D. (2002). Let them eat cake. *Agricultural Research Magazine*, *50*(3).

11. Core, J. (2002). New rice could benefit malnourished populations. *Agricultural Research Magazine*, *50*(9).

12. Dziezak, J. D. (1991). Romancing the kernel: A salute to rice varieties. *Food Technology*, *45*(6), 74.

13. Giese, J. H. (1992). Pasta: New twists on an old product. *Food Technology*, *46*(2), 118.

14. Kahn, C. B., and Penfield, M. P. (1983). Snack crackers containing whole-grain triticale flour: Crispness, taste, and acceptability. *Journal of Food Science*, *48*, 266.

15. Khan, M. N., Des Rosiers, M. C., Rooney, L. W., Morgan, R. G., and Sweat, V. E. (1982). Corn tortillas: Evaluation of corn cooking procedures. *Cereal Chemistry*, *59*, 279.

16. Kurtzweil, P. (1996). How folate can help prevent birth defects. *FDA Consumer*, *30*(7), 7.

17. Marquart, L. and Cohen, E. A. (2005). Increasing whole grain consumption. *Food Technology*, *59*(12), 24–32.

18. Mermelstein, N. H. (2001). Processing pasta for ingredient use. *Food Technology*, *55*(7), 72–75.

19. National Pasta Association. (2002). "Industry Statistics." Retrieved October 7, 2002, from http://www.ilovepasta.org

20. National Pasta Association. (2004). "The Inside Story: How Pasta Is Made." Retrieved November 14, 2006, from http://www.ilovepasta.org/theinsidestory.html

21. Nicklas, T. A., Myers, L., and Berenson, G. S. (1994). Impact of ready-to-eat cereal consumption on total dietary intake of children: The Bogalusa Heart Study. *Journal of the American Dietetic Association*, *94*, 316.

22. North American Millers' Association. (2006). "Corn Milling Process." Retrieved October 26, 2006, from http://www.namamillers.org/ci_products_corn_mill.html

23. Parlin, S. (1997). Rice flour makes its mark. *Food Processing*, *58*(10), 60.

24. Pszczola, D. E. (1998). What's beyond the horizon? *Food Technology*, *52*(9), 94.

25. Pszczola, D. E. (2000). A pasta for all paisans. *Food Technology*, *54*(4), 84–92.

26. Pszczola, D. E. (2001). Rice: Not just for throwing. *Food Technology*, *55*(2), 53–59.

27. Pszczola, D. E. (2005). Ingredients for bread meet changing needs. *Food Technology*, *59*(1), 55–63.

28. Pszczola, D. E. (2005). Never say never: Emerging technologies solve familiar problems. *Food Technology*, *59*(2), 53–67.

29. Raloff, J. (1991). Beyond oat bran. *Food Technology*, *45*(8), 62.

30. Rao, D. R., Patel, G., and Nishimuta, J. F. (1980). Comparison of protein quality of corn, triticale, and wheat. *Nutrition Reports International*, *21*, 923.

31. Riceland Foods, Inc. (2006). "All about Rice: U.S. Production." Retrieved November 24, 2006, from http://www.riceland.com/consumers/all_about/

32. Shoemaker, R., Johnson, D. D., and Golan, E. (2003). Consumers and the future of biotech foods in the United States. *Amber Waves*, *1*(5), 30–36.

33. Slavin, J. (2004). Whole grains and human health. *Nutrition Research Reviews*, *17*, 1–12.

34. Slavin, J., and Kritchevsky, D. (2002). Pass the whole-grain snack food, please. *Food Technology*, *56*(5), 216.

35. Smith Edge, M., Miller Jones, J., and Marquart, L. (2005). A new life for whole grains. *Journal of the American Dietetic Association*, *105*, 1856–1860.

36. Solganik, H. (1997). A toast to tortillas. *Food Processing*, *58*(11), 64.

37. Suszkiw, J. (2002). Rice, Oh so nice. *Agricultural Research Magazine*, *50*(5).

38. Teutonico, R. A., and Knorr, D. (1985). Amaranth: Composition, properties, and applications of a rediscovered food crop. *Food Technology*, *39*(4), 49.

39. U.S. Department of Agriculture. (2005). "Dietary Guidelines for Americans 2005: Chapter 5 Food Groups to Encourage." Retrieved November 24, 2006, from http:// www.health.gov/dietaryguidelines/dga2005/docu ment/html/chapter5.htm

40. U.S. Department of Agriculture. (2006, August). "Genetically Engineered Rice." Fact Sheet Release No. 0306.06.

Retrieved November 24, 2006, from http://www.usda.gov/wps/portal/!ut/p/_s.7_0_A/7_0_1OB/.cmd/ad/.ar/sa.retrievecontent/.c/6_2_1UH/.ce/7_2_5JM/.p/5_2_4TQ/.d/1/_th/J_2_9D/_s.7_0_A/7_0_1OB?PC_7_2_5JM_contentid=2006%2F08%2F0306.xml&PC_7_2_5JM_parentnav=LATEST_RELEASES&PC_7_2_5JM_navid=NEWS_RELEASE

41. U.S. Department of Agriculture, Animal and Plant Health Inspection Service. (2006, August). "BRS Qs & As: Biotechnology Regulatory Services." Retrieved November 24. 2006, from http://www.aphis.usda.gov/publications/biotechnology/content/printable_version/BRS_QA_biotechandusda.pdf

42. U.S. Department of Agriculture, Animal and Plant Health Inspection Service. (2006, April). "Biotechnology Regulatory Services: Coordinated Framework for the Regulation of Biotechnology." Program Aid No. 1862. Retrieved November 24, 2006, from http://www.aphis.usda.gov/publications/biotechnology/content/printable_version/BRS_CoordFrame Bro.pdf

43. U.S. Department of Agriculture, Economic Research Service. "Data Sets. Food Availability: Custom Queries." Retrieved November 14, 2006, from http://www.ers.usda.gov/data/FoodConsumption/FoodAvailQueriable.aspx

44. U.S. Food and Drug Administration. (2006, February 16). "FDA News: FDA Provides Guidance on 'Whole Grain' for Manufacturers." Retrieved November 14, 2006, from http:// www.fda.gov/bbs/topics/news/2006/NEW01317.html

45. U.S. Grains Council. (2006). "Corn: World Corn Production and Trade." Retrieved November 24, 2006, from http://www.grains.org/page.ww?section=Barley%2C+Corn+%26+Sorghum&name=Corn

46. Zhao, Y. H., Manthey, F. A., Chang, S. K. C., Hou, H. J., and Yuan, S. H. (2005). Quality characteristics of spaghetti as affected by green and yellow pea, lentil, and chickpea flours. *Journal of Food Science*, *70*(6), S371–S376.

Chapter 15

1. American Dietetic Association. (2005). Position of the American Dietetic Association: Fat replacers. *Journal of the American Dietetic Association*, *105*, 266–275.

2. Butaki, R. C., and Dronzek, B. (1979). Comparison of gluten properties of four wheat varieties. *Cereal Chemistry*, *56*, 159.

3. Fermin, B. C., Hahm, T. S., Radinsky, J. A., Kratochvil, R. J., Hall, R. E., and Lo, M. Y. (2005). Effect of praline and glutamine on the functional properties of wheat dough in winter wheat varieties. *Journal of Food Science*, *70*(4), E273–E278.

4. Figoni, P. (2004). *How Baking Works: Exploring the Fundamentals of Baking Science*. Hoboken, NJ: John Wiley & Sons, Inc.

5. Gordon, D.T. (1999). What is dietary fiber? *Food Technology*, *53*(6), 242.

6. Hansen, L., and Rose, M. S. (1996). Sensory acceptability is inversely related to development of fat rancidity in bread made from stored flour. *Journal of the American Dietetic Association*, *96*, 792.

7. Hoseney, R. C. (1994). *Principles of Cereal Science and Technology*, 2nd ed. St. Paul, MN: American Association of Cereal Chemists, Inc.

8. Il, B., Daun, H., and Gilbert, S. G. (1991). Water sorption of gliadin. *Journal of Food Science, 56*, 510.

9. Kendall, P. (2003). *High Altitude Baking*. Denver: 3D Press, Inc., Colorado State University Cooperative Extension.

10. Lorenz, K. (1972). Food uses of triticale. *Food Technology, 26*(11), 66.

11. Ma, C., Oomah, B. D., and Holme, J. (1986). Effect of deamidation and succinylation on some physicochemical and baking properties of gluten. *Journal of Food Science, 51*, 99.

12. Mani, K., Tragardh, C., Eliasson, A. C., and Lindahl, L. (1992). Water content, water soluble fraction, and mixing affect fundamental rheological properties of wheat flour doughs. *Journal of Food Science, 57*, 1198.

13. Myhre, D. V. (1970). The function of carbohydrates in baking. *Baker's Digest, 44*(3), 32.

14. Ngo, W., Hoseney, R. C., and Moore, W. R. (1985). Dynamic rheological properties of cake batters made from chlorine-treated and untreated flours. *Journal of Food Science, 50*, 1338.

15. Pomeranz, Y., and MacMasters, M. M. (1968). Structure and composition of the wheat kernel. *Baker's Digest, 42*(4), 24.

16. Psczcola, D. E. (2002). Adding to the family of rice bran extracts. *Food Technology, 56*(1), 66.

17. Psczcola, D. E. (2005). Ingredients for bread meet changing "Kneads." *Food Technology, 59*(1), 55–63.

18. Sanchez-Marroquin, A., Domingo, M. V., Maya, S., and Saldana, C. (1985). Amaranth flour blends and fractions for baking applications. *Journal of Food Science, 50*, 789.

19. Sloan, A. E. (2001). Dietary fiber moves back into the mainstream. *Food Technology, 55*(7), 18.

20. Staff. (1994). Blends reduce fat in bakery products. *Food Technology, 48*(6), 168.

21. Watson, C. A., Shuey, W. C., Crawford, R. D., and Gumbmann, M. R. (1977). Physical dough, baking, and nutritional qualities of straight-grade and extended-extraction flours. *Cereal Chemistry, 54*, 657.

22. Wheat Foods Council. (2005). "Grains of Truth about Wheat Flour." Retrieved November 25, 2006, from http://www.wheatfoods.org/_filelibrary/product/43/wheat_flour.pdf

Chapter 16

1. Figoni, P. (2004). *How Baking Works: Exploring the Fundamentals of Baking Science*. Hoboken, NJ: John Wiley & Sons, Inc.

2. Fulton, L., and Hogbin, M. (1993). Eating quality of muffins, cake, and cookies prepared with reduced fat and sugar. *Journal of the American Dietetic Association, 93*, 1313.

3. Hippleheuser, A. L., Landberg, L. A., and Turnak, F. L. (1995). A system approach to formulating a low-fat muffin. *Food Technology, 49*: 92(3).

4. Holt, S. D., McWatters, K. H., and Resurreccion, A. V. A. (1992). Validation of predicted baking performance of muffins containing mixtures of wheat, cowpea, peanut, sorghum, and cassava flours. *Journal of Food Science, 57*, 470.

5. Labensky, S. R., and Hause, A. M. (2007). *On Cooking: A Textbook of Culinary Fundamentals*, 4th ed. Upper Saddle River, NJ: Pearson Prentice Hall.

6. Matthews, R. H., Kirkpatrick, M. E., and Dawson, E. H. (1965). Performance of fats in muffins. *Journal of the American Dietetic Association, 47*, 201.

7. Polizzotto, L. M., Tinsley, A. M., Weber, C. W., and Berry, J. W. (1983). Dietary fibers in muffins. *Journal of Food Science, 48*, 111.

Chapter 17

1. American Institute of Baking. (n.d.). "Bagels: Frequently Asked Questions." Retrieved November 5, 2002, from http://techserv.aibonline.org

2. Avital, Y., Mannheim, C. H., and Miltz, J. (1990). Effect of carbon dioxide atmosphere on staling and water relations in bread. *Journal of Food Science, 55*, 413.

3. Baguena, R., Soriano, M. D., Martinez-Anaya, M. A., and Benedito de Barber, C. (1991). Viability and performance of pure yeast strains in frozen wheat dough. *Journal of Food Science, 56*, 1690.

4. Cleveland, L. E., Moshfegh, A. J., Albertson, A. M., and Goldman, J. D. (2000). Dietary intake of whole grains. *Journal of the American College of Nutrition, 19*(3), 331S–338S.

5. Collar, C., Mascaros, A. F., and Benedito de Barber, C. (1992). Amino acid metabolism by yeasts and lactic acid bacteria during bread dough fermentation. *Journal of Food Science, 57*, 1423.

6. Dziezak, J. D. (Ed.). (1987). Yeasts and yeast derivatives: Definitions, characteristics, and processing. *Food Technology, 41*(2), 104.

7. Dziezak, J. D. (1991). Enzymes: Catalysts for food processes. *Food Technology, 45*(1), 78.

8. Figoni, P. (2004). *How Baking Works: Exploring the Fundamentals of Baking Science*. Hoboken, NJ: John Wiley & Sons, Inc.

9. Fleischmann's Yeast. (2006). "Yeast: Another Name for Fleischmann's®." Retrieved December 29, 2006, from http://www.breadworld.com/sciencehistory/yeast.asp

10. Gray, J. A., and BeMiller, J. N. (2003). Bread staling: Molecular basis and control. *Comprehensive Reviews in Food Science and Food Safety, 2*, 1–21.

11. Hallberg, L. M., and Chinachoti, P. (2002). A fresh perspective on staling: The significance of starch recrystallization on the firming of bread. *Journal of Food Science, 67*, 1092–1096.

12. Hartnett, D. I., and Thalheimer, W. G. (1979). Use of oil in baked products—Part I: Background and bread. *Journal of the American Oil Chemists' Society, 56*, 944.

13. Hoseney, R. C. (1994). *Principles of Cereal Science and Technology*, 2nd. ed. St. Paul, MN: American Association of Cereal Chemists, Inc.

14. Hoseney, R. C., Lineback, D. R., and Seib, P. A. (1978). Role of starch in baked foods. *Baker's Digest, 52*(4), 11.

15. Labensky, S. R., and Hause, A. M. (2007). *On Cooking: A Textbook of Culinary Fundamentals*, 4th ed. Upper Saddle River, NJ: Pearson Prentice Hall.

16. Marston, P. E., and Wannan, T. L. (1976). Bread baking. *Baker's Digest, 50*(4), 24.

17. Martin, M. L., Zeleznak, K. J., and Hoseney, R. C. (1991). A mechanism of bread firming. I. Role of starch swelling. *Cereal Chemistry, 68*, 498.

18. Miller, R. A., Hoseney, R. C., Graf, E., and Soper, J. (1997). Garlic effects on dough properties. *Journal of Food Science, 62*, 1198–1201.

19. Molt, M. (2006). *Food for Fifty*, 12th ed. Upper Saddle River, NJ: Pearson Prentice Hall.

20. Patrow, C. J., and Marlett, J. A. (1986). Variability in the dietary fiber content of wheat and mixed-grain commercial breads. *Journal of the American Dietetic Association, 86*, 794.

21. Payton, S. B., Baldwin, R. E., and Krause, G. F. (1988). Bread formulation designed for the elderly using response surface methodology. *Journal of Food Science, 53*, 302.

22. Pomeranz, Y. (1980). Molecular approach to breadmaking— An update and new perspectives. *Baker's Digest, 54*(1), 26.

23. Pomeranz, Y., and Finney, K. F. (1975). Sugars in breadmaking. *Baker's Digest, 49*(1), 20.

24. Powers, E. M., and Berkowitz, D. (1990). Efficacy of an oxygen scavenger to modify the atmosphere and prevent mold growth on meal, ready-to-eat pouched bread. *Journal of Food Protection, 53*, 767.

25. Pszczola, D. E. (2002). Bakery ingredients: Past, present, and future directions. *Food Technology, 56*(1), 56–72.

26. Ranhotra, G., Gelroth, J., Novak, F., and Matthews, R. (1985). B vitamins in selected variety breads commercially produced in major U.S. cities. *Journal of Food Science, 50*, 1174.

27. Ranhotra, G., Gelroth, J., Novak, F., and Matthews, R. (1985). Minerals in selected variety breads commercially produced in four major U.S. cities. *Journal of Food Science, 50*, 365.

28. Red Star. (n.d.) "Products." Retrieved December 29, 2006, from http://www.redstaryeast.com/products.html

29. Shogren, M. D., Pomeranz, Y., and Finney, K. F. (1981). Counteracting the deleterious effects of fiber in bread making. *Cereal Chemistry, 58*, 142.

30. Sloan, A. E. (1999). The upper crust. *Food Technology, 53*(10), 26.

31. Sloan, A. E. (2001). Dietary fiber moves back into the mainstream. *Food Technology, 55*(7), 18.

32. Sluimer, P. (2005). *Principles of Breadmaking: Functionality of Raw Materials and Process Steps*. St. Paul, MN: American Association of Cereal Chemists, Inc.

33. Tieckelmann, R. E., and Steele, R. E. (1991). Higher-assay grade of calcium peroxide improves properties of dough. *Food Technology, 45*(1), 106.

34. Trivedi, N. B., Cooper, E. J., and Bruinsma, B. L. (1984). Development and applications of quick-rising yeast. *Food Technology, 38*(6), 51.

35. Unrein, J. (2002). U.S. customers get serious about artisan bread. *Milling and Baking News, 81*(10), 28–91.

36. U.S. Department of Agriculture, Center for Nutrition Policy and Promotion. (2005, August). "Grain Consumption by Americans: Nutrition Insight 32." Retrieved December 15, 2006, from http://www.cnpp.usda.gov/Publications/NutritionInsights/Insight32.pdf

37. U.S. Department of Health and Human Services and U.S. Department of Agriculture (2005, January 12). "Dietary Guidelines for Americans 2005." Retrieved May 5, 2006, from http://www.healthierus.gov/dietary guidelines/

38. Wheat Foods Council. (n.d.). "Commercial Breads." Retrieved November 5, 2002, from http://www.wheatfoods.org/grain_combread.html

39. Wheat Foods Council. (n.d.). "Sourdough." Retrieved November 5, 2002, from http://www.wheatfoods.org/grain_info/sour/html

40. Wu, J. Y., Maningat, J. I., Ponte, J. G., Jr., and Hoseney, R. C. (1988). Short-time breadmaking systems. Effect of formulation, additives, temperature, and flour quality. *Journal of Food Science, 53*, 535.

41. Wyatt, C. J. (1983). Acceptability of reduced sodium in breads, cottage cheese, and pickles. *Journal of Food Science, 48*, 1300.

Chapter 18

1. American Association of Family and Consumer Science. (2001). *Food: A Handbook of Terminology, Purchasing, and Preparation*, 10th ed. Alexandria, VA: American Association of Family and Consumer Sciences.

2. Barmore, M. A. (1936). "The influence of various factors including altitude in the production of angel food cake." Colorado State University Experiment Station Technical Bulletin No. 15.

3. Bean, M. M., Yamazaki, W. T., and Donelson, D. H. (1978). Wheat starch gelatinization in sugar solutions. II. Fructose, glucose, and sucrose: Cake performance. *Cereal Chemistry, 55*, 945.

4. Berglund, P. T., and Hertsgaard, D. M. (1986). Use of vegetable oils at reduced levels in cake, pie crust, cookies, and muffins. *Journal of Food Science, 51*, 640.

5. Briant, A. M., and Willman, A. R. (1956). Whole-egg sponge cakes. *Journal of Home Economics, 48*, 420.

6. Campbell, L. A., Ketelsen, S. M., and Antenucci, R. N. (1994). Formulating oatmeal cookies with calorie-sparing ingredients. *Food Technology, 48*(5), 98.

7. Coleman, P. E., and Harbers, C. A. Z. (1983). High fructose corn syrup: Replacement for sucrose in angel cake. *Journal of Food Science, 48*, 452.

8. Donelson, J. R., Gaines, C. S., and Finney, P. L. (2000). Baking formula innovation to eliminate chlorine treatment of cake flour. *Cereal Chemistry, 77*(1), 53–57.

9. Ebeler, S. E., Breyer, L. M., and Walker, C. E. (1986). White layer cake batter emulsion characteristics: Effects of sucrose ester emulsifiers. *Journal of Food Science, 51*, 1276.

10. Elgidaily, D. A., Funk, K., and Zabik, M. E. (1969). Baking temperature and quality of angel cakes. *Journal of the American Dietetic Association, 54*, 401.

11. Franks, O. J., Zabik, M. E., and Funk, K. (1969). Angel cakes using frozen, foam-spray-dried, freeze-dried, and spray-dried albumen. *Cereal Chemistry, 46*, 349.

12. Fulton, L., and Hogbin, M. (1993). Eating quality of muffins, cake, and cookies prepared with reduced fat and sugar. *Journal of the American Dietetic Association, 93,* 1313.

13. Gaines, C. S., and Donelson, J. R. (1982). Contribution of chlorinated flour fractions to cake crumb stickiness. *Cereal Chemistry, 59,* 378.

14. Gonzales-Galan, A., Wang, S. H., Sgarbieri, V. C., and Moraes, M. A. C. (1991). Sensory and nutritional properties of cookies based on wheat-rice-soybean flours baked in a microwave oven. *Journal of Food Science, 56,* 1699.

15. Hoseney, R. C. (1994). *Principles of Cereal Science and Technology,* 2nd. ed. St. Paul, MN: American Association of Cereal Chemists, Inc.

16. Kim, C. S., and Walker, C. E. (1992). Changes in starch pasting properties due to sugars and emulsifiers as determined by viscosity measurement. *Journal of Food Science, 57,* 1009.

17. Lawless, S. T., Gregoire, M. B., Canter, D. D., and Setser, C. S. (1991). Comparison of cakes produced from computer-generated recipes. *School Food Service Research Review, 15*(1), 23.

18. Marx, J. T., Marx, B. D., and Johnson, J. M. (1990). High-fructose corn syrup cakes made with all-purpose flour or cake flour. *Cereal Chemistry, 67,* 502–504.

19. Matthews, R. H., and Dawson, E. H. (1966). Performance of fats in white cake. *Cereal Chemistry, 43,* 538.

20. McCullough, M. A. P., Johnson, J. M., and Phillips, J. A. (1986). High fructose corn syrup replacement for sucrose in shortened cakes. *Journal of Food Science, 51,* 536.

21. Molt, M. (2006). *Food for Fifty,* 12th ed. Upper Saddle River, NJ: Pearson Prentice Hall.

22. Ngo, W., Hoseney, R. C., and Moore, W. R. (1985). Dynamic rheological properties of cake batters made from chlorine-treated and untreated flours. *Journal of Food Science, 50,* 1338.

23. Nishibori, S., and Kawakishi, S. (1990). Effects of dough materials on flavor formation in baked cookies. *Journal of Food Science, 55,* 409.

24. Paton, D., Larocque, G. M., and Holme, J. (1981). Development of cake structure: Influence of ingredients on the measurement of cohesive force during baking. *Cereal Chemistry, 58,* 527.

25. Prost, C., Lee, C. Y., Giampaoli, P., and Richard, H. (1993). Extraction of cookie aroma compounds from aqueous and dough model system. *Journal of Food Science, 58,* 586.

26. Rankin, L. L., and Bingham, M. (2000). Acceptability of oatmeal chocolate chip cookies prepared using puréed white beans as a fat ingredient substitute. *Journal of American Dietetic Association, 100,* 831–833.

27. Splenda. (n.d.). "Cooking and Baking Tips." Retrieved December 2, 2002, from http://www.splenda.com

28. Swanson, R. B., and Musayac, L. J. (1999). Acceptability of fruit purées in peanut butter, oatmeal, and chocolate-chip reduced-fat cookies. *Journal of the American Dietetic Association, 99,* 343–345.

29. Thomasson, C. A., Miller, R. A., and Hoseney, R. C. (1995). Replacement of chlorine treatment for cake flour. *Cereal Chemistry, 72*(6), 616–620.

Chapter 19

1. Berglund, P. T., and Hertsgaard, D. M. (1986). Use of vegetable oils at reduced levels in cake, pie crust, cookies, and muffins. *Journal of Food Science, 51,* 640.

2. Briant, A. M., and Snow, P. R. (1957). Freezer storage of pie shells. *Journal of the American Dietetic Association, 33,* 796.

3. Hirahara, S., and Simpson, J. I. (1961). Microscopic appearance of gluten in pastry dough and its relation to the tenderness of baked pastry. *Journal of Home Economics, 53,* 681.

4. Labensky, S. R., and Hause, A. M. (2007). *On Cooking: A Textbook of Culinary Fundamentals,* 4th ed. Upper Saddle River, NJ: Pearson Prentice Hall.

5. Matthews, R. H., and Dawson, E. H. (1963). Performance of fats and oils in pastry and biscuits. *Cereal Chemistry, 40,* 291.

6. Miller, B. S., and Trimbo, H. B. (1970). Factors affecting the quality of pie dough and pie crust. *Baker's Digest, 14*(1), 46.

Chapter 20

1. American Dietetic Association. (2006). Position of the American Dietetic Association: Agriculture and food biotechnology. *Journal of the American Dietetic Association, 106,* 285–293.

2. American Dietetic Association. (2002). Position of the American Dietetic Association: Health implications of dietary fiber. *Journal of the American Dietetic Association, 102,* 993–1000.

3. American Dietetic Association. (2003). Position of the American Dietetic Association and Dietitians of Canada: Vegetarian diets. *Journal of the American Dietetic Association, 103,* 748–765.

4. Arnold, J. (2002). Watermelon packs a powerful lycopene punch. *Agricultural Research Magazine, 50*(6).

5. Barrett, D. M. (2007). Maximizing the nutritional value of fruits and vegetables. *Food Technology, 61*(4), 40–44.

6. Bliss, R. M. (2006). Fresh-cuts are popular, any way you slice them. *Agricultural Research Magazine, 54*(7). Retrieved November, 14, 2006, from http://www.ars.usda.gov/is/AR/archive/jul06/produce0706.htm

7. Bren, L. (2003). Genetic engineering: The future of foods? *FDA Consumer Magazine, 37*(6). Retrieved June 3, 2007, from http://www.fda.gov/fdac/features/2003/603_food.html

8. Bowman, F., Page, E., Remmenga, E. E., and Trump, D. (1971). Microwave vs. conventional cooking of vegetables at high altitude. *Journal of the American Dietetic Association, 58,* 427.

9. Brody, A. L. (2005). What's fresh about fresh-cut? *Food Technology, 59*(11), 74–77.

10. Calvin, L., Avendaño, B., and Schwentesius, R. (2007). Outbreak linked to spinach forces reassessment of food safety practices. *Amber Waves, 5*(3), 24–31. Retrieved June 7, 2007, from http://www.ers.usda.gov/AmberWaves/Scripts/print.asp?page=/June07/Features/Spinach.htm

11. Carlson, B. L., and Tabacchi, M. H. (1988). Loss of vitamin C in vegetables during the foodservice cycle. *Journal of the American Dietetic Association, 88,* 65.

12. Darmon, N., Darmon, M., Maillot, M., and Drewnowski, A. (2005). A nutrient density standard for vegetables and fruits: Nutrients per calorie and nutrients per unit cost. *Journal of the American Dietetic Association, 105,* 1881–1887.

13. Dawson, E. H., Lamb, J. C., Toepfer, E. W., and Warren, H. W. (1952). *Development of rapid methods of soaking and cooking dry beans.* Technical Bulletin No. 1051. Washington, DC: U.S. Department of Agriculture.

14. Dwyer, J. T., Goldin, B. R., Saul, N., Gualtieri, L., Barakat, S., and Adlercreutz, H. (1994). Tofu and soy drinks contain phytoestrogens. *Journal of the American Dietetic Association, 94,* 739.

15. Eheart, M. S., and Odland, D. (1972). Storage of fresh broccoli and green beans. *Journal of the American Dietetic Association, 60,* 402.

16. Elbert, E. M., and Witt, R. L. (1968). Gelatinization of starch in the common dry bean, *Phaseolus vulgaris. Journal of Home Economics, 60,* 186.

17. Fordham, J. R., Wells, C. E., and Chen, L. H. (1975). Sprouting of seeds and nutrient composition of seeds and sprouts. *Journal of Food Science, 40,* 552.

18. Galgano, F., Favati, F., Caruso, M., Pietrafesa, A., and Natella, S. (2007). The influence of processing and preserving on the retention of health-promoting compounds in broccoli. *Journal of Food Science, 72*(2), S130–S135.

19. Gnanasekharan, V., Shewfelt, R. L., and Chinnan, M. S. (1992). Detection of color changes in green vegetables. *Journal of Food Science, 57,* 149.

20. Guenther, P. M., Dodd, K. W., Reedy, J., and Krebs-Smith, S. M. (2006). Most Americans eat much less than the recommended amounts of fruits and vegetables. *Journal of the American Dietetic Association, 106,* 1371–1379.

21. Herbach, K. M., Stintzing, F. C., and Carle, R. (2006). Betalain stability and degradation—Structural and chromatic aspects. *Journal of Food Science, 71*(4), R41–R50.

22. Herranz, J., Vidal-Valverde, C., and Rojas-Hidalgo, E. (1981). Cellulose, hemicellulose and lignin content of raw and cooked Spanish vegetables. *Journal of Food Science, 46,* 1927.

23. Herranz, J., Vidal-Valverde, C., and Rojas-Hidalgo, E. (1983). Cellulose, hemicellulose and lignin content of raw and cooked processed vegetables. *Journal of Food Science, 48,* 274.

24. Humphrey, A. M. (2004). Chlorophyll as a color and functional ingredient. *Journal of Food Science, 69*(5), C422–C425.

25. Jarden Corporation. (2005). *Ball Blue Book of Preserving.* Muncie, IN: Jarden Corporation.

26. Institute of Food Technologists' Expert Report on Biotechnology and Foods. (2000). Human food safety evaluation of rDNA biotechnology-derived foods. *Food Technology, 54*(9), 53–61.

27. Institute of Food Technologists' Expert Panel on Food Safety and Nutrition. (1989). Dietary fiber. *Food Technology, 43*(10), 133.

28. Institute of Food Technologists' Expert Panel on Food Safety and Nutrition. (1990). Quality of fruits and vegetables. *Food Technology, 44*(6), 99.

29. Labensky, S. R., and Hause, A. M. (2007). *On Cooking: A Textbook of Culinary Fundamentals,* 4th ed. Upper Saddle River, NJ: Pearson Prentice Hall.

30. Lazan, H., Ali, Z. M., Mohd, A., and Nahar, F. (1987). Water stress and quality during storage of tropical leafy vegetables. *Journal of Food Science, 52,* 1286.

31. Liener, I. (1979). Significance for humans of biologically active factors in soybeans and other food legumes. *Journal of the American Oil Chemists' Society, 56,* 121.

32. Lin, B. H., Lucier, G., Allshouse, J., and Kantor, L. S. (2001). Fast food growth boosts frozen potato consumption. *Food Review, 24*(1), 38–46.

33. Lin, B. H., Reed, J., and Lucier, G. (2004, October). *U.S. fruit and vegetable consumption: Who, what, where, and how much.* Agriculture Information Bulletin Number 792-2. Retrieved May 28, 2007, from http://www.ers.usda.gov/publications/aib792/aib792-2/aib792-2.pdf

34. Liu, K. (2000). Expanding soybean food utilization. *Food Technology, 54*(7), 46.

35. Lucier, G., Lin, B., Allshouse, J., and Kantor, L. S. (2000). *Factors affecting dry bean consumption in the United States.* Vegetable and Specialties Situation and Outlook Report/VGS-280. Retrieved November 25, 2002, from http://ers.usda.gov/briefing/drybeans/

36. Lucier, G., Pollack, S., Ali, M., and Perez, A. (2006, April). *Fruit and vegetable backgrounder/VGS-313-01.* Retrieved May 25, 2007, from http://www.ers.usda.gov/Publications/VGS/Apr06/VGS31301/

37. MacLeod, A. J., and MacLeod, G. (1970). Effects of variations in cooking methods on the flavor volatiles of cabbage. *Journal of Food Science, 35,* 744.

38. MacLeod, A. J., and MacLeod, G. (1970). The flavor volatiles of dehydrated cabbage. *Journal of Food Science, 35,* 739.

39. Matthee, V., and Appledorf, H. (1978). Effect of cooking on vegetable fiber. *Journal of Food Science, 43,* 1344.

40. Maul, F., Sargent, S. A., Sims, C. A., Baldwin, E. A., Balaban, M. O., and Huber, D. J. (2000). Tomato flavor and aroma quality as affected by storage temperature. *Journal of Food Science, 65,* 1228–1237.

41. Mayeaux, M., Xu, Z., King, J. M., Prinyawiwatkul, W. (2006). Effects of cooking conditions on lycopene content in tomatoes. *Journal of Food Science, 71*(8), C461–C464.

42. McComber, D. R., Osman, E. M., and Lohnes, R. A. (1988). Factors related to potato mealiness. *Journal of Food Science, 53,* 1423.

43. McWatters, K. H., Chinnan, M. S., Walker, S. L., Doyle, M. P., and Lin, C. M. (2002). Consumer acceptance of fresh-cut iceberg lettuce treated with 2 percent hydrogen peroxide and mild heat. *Journal of Food Protection, 65,* 1221–1226.

44. Mintzer, E. S., and Osteen, C. (1997). New uniform standards for pesticide residues in food. *Food Review, 20*(1), 18.

45. Morrow, B. (1991). The rebirth of legumes. *Food Technology, 45*(9), 96.

46. Nelson, A. I., Wei, L. S., and Steinberg, M. P. (1971, January). Food products from whole soybeans. *Soybean Digest.*

47. Papazian, R. (1996). Sulfites. *FDA Consumer, 30*(10), 10.

48. Partnership for Food Safety Education. (2004). "Safe Handling of Fresh Produce." Retrieved March 8, 2007, from http://www.fightbac.org/content/view/203

49. Prakash, A., Inthajak, P., Huibregtse, H., Caporaso, F., and Foley, D. M. (2000). Effects of low-dose irradiation and conventional treatments on shelf life and quality characteristics of diced celery. *Journal of Food Science, 65*, 1070–1075.

50. Produce for Better Health Foundation. (2007). "Fruit and Veggies—More Matters™ Background." Retrieved May 25, 2007, from http://www.fruitandveggiesmorematters.org/wp-content/uploads/userfiles/file/pdf/press/fruitsveggies-moremattersbackground.doc

51. Produce Marketing Association. (2002). *The PMA fresh produce manual.* Newark, DE: Author.

52. Pszczola, D. E. (2000). Soy: Why it's moving into the mainstream. *Food Technology, 54*(9), 76.

53. Putnam, J., Kantor, L. S., and Allshouse, J. (2000). Per capita food supply trends: Progress toward dietary guideline. *Food Review, 23*(3), 2–14.

54. Reed, J., Frazao, E., and Itskowitz, R. (2004, July). *How much do Americans pay for fruits and vegetables?* Agricultural Information Bulletin No (AIB790). Retrieved March 31, 2007, from http://www.ers.usda.gov/publications/aib790/

55. Schwartz, S. J., and Von Elbe, J. H. (1983). Kinetics of chlorophyll degradation to pyropheophytin in vegetables. *Journal of Food Science, 48*, 1303.

56. Singh, B., Yang, C. C., Salunkhe, D. K., and Rahman, A. R. (1972). Controlled atmosphere storage of lettuce. 1. Effects on quality and the respiration rate of lettuce heads. *Journal of Food Science, 37*, 48.

57. Singh, R. P., Buelow, R. H., and Lund, D. B. (1973). Storage behavior of artificially waxed green snap beans. *Journal of Food Science, 38*, 542.

58. Slavin, J. (1991). Nutritional benefits of soy protein and soy fiber. *Journal of the American Dietetic Association, 91*, 816.

59. Snyder, P. O., and Matthews, M. E. (1983). Percent retention of vitamin C in whipped potatoes after pre-service holding. *Journal of the American Dietetic Association, 83*, 454.

60. Stahler, C. (2006). How many adults are vegetarian? *The Vegetararian Resource Group Vegetarian Journal* [Online]. Retrieved June 19, 2007, from http://vrg.org/journal/vj2006issue4/vj2006issue4poll.htm

61. Steinmetz, K. A., and Potter, J. D. (1996). Vegetables, fruit, and cancer prevention: A review. *Journal of the American Dietetic Association, 96*, 1027.

62. Stewart, H., Harris, J. M., and Guthrie, J. (2004, October). *What determines the variety of a household's vegetable purchases?* Agriculture Information Bulletin Number 792-3. Retrieved May 28, 2007, from http://www.ers.usda.gov/publications/aib792/aib792-3/aib792-3.pdf

63. Stone, M. B., and Young, C. M. (1985). Effects of cultivars, blanching techniques, and cooking methods on quality of frozen green beans as measured by physical and sensory attributes. *Journal of Food Quality, 7*, 255.

64. The California Artichoke Advisory Board. (n.d.) "Basic Preparation." Retrieved June 1, 2007, from http://www.artichokes.org/basic_prep.html

65. U.S. Centers for Disease Control and Prevention. (2006, November). "5 A Day: Data and Statistics Compared." Retrieved March 31, 2007, from http://apps.nccd.cdc.gov/5ADaySurveillance/

66. U.S. Centers for Disease Control and Prevention. (n.d.) "Fruit and Vegetable of the Month." Retrieved May 30, 2007, from http://www.fruitsandveggiesmatter.gov/month/index.html

67. U.S. Centers for Disease Control and Prevention. (n.d.). "How Many Fruits and Vegetables Do You Need?" Retrieved May 25, 2007, from http://www.fruitsandveggiesmatter.gov/downloads/General_Audience_Brochure.pdf

68. U.S. Department of Agriculture. (2005). "Dietary Guidelines for Americans 2005: Key Recommendations for the General Population." Retrieved May 25, 2007, from http://www.health.gov/dietaryguidelines/dga2005/recommendations.htm

69. U.S. Department of Agriculture. (2005). "Nutrition and Your Health: Dietary Guidelines for Americans: Part D: Science Base. Retrieved May 25, 2007, from http://www.health.gov/dietaryguidelines/dga2005/report/HTML/D6_SelectedFood.htm

70. U.S. Department of Agriculture. (n.d.). Inside the Pyramid: What Foods Are in the Vegetable Group? Retrieved May 25, 2007, from http://www.mypyramid.gov/pyramid/vegetables.html

71. U.S. Department of Agriculture, Agricultural Marketing Service. (1994). *How to buy canned and frozen fruits.* Home and Garden Bulletin No. 261.

72. U.S. Department of Agriculture, Agricultural Marketing Service. (1994). *How to buy canned and frozen vegetables.* Home and Garden Bulletin No. 259.

73. U.S. Department of Agriculture, Agricultural Marketing Service. (1994). *How to buy fresh vegetables.* Home and Garden Bulletin No. 258.

74. U.S. Department of Agriculture, Agricultural Marketing Service. (1994). *How to buy potatoes.* Home and Garden Bulletin No. 262.

75. U.S. Department of Agriculture, Agricultural Marketing Service. (2002, April). "The National Organic Program: Organic Food Standards and Labels: The Facts." Retrieved July 11, 2006, from http://ams.usda.gov/nop/Consumers/brochure.html

76. U.S. Department of Agriculture, Agricultural Research Service. (2002). "USDA National Nutrient Database for Standard Reference, Release 15." Retrieved December 7, 2002, from the Nutrient Data Laboratory website, http://www.nal.usda.gov/fnic/foodcomp

77. U.S. Department of Agriculture, Economic Research Service. (2007). "Data Sets: Food Availability." Retrieved May 25, 2007, from http://www.ers.usda.gov/Data/FoodConsumption/FoodAvailIndex.htm

78. U.S. Food and Drug Administration. (2003). "Dietary Guidance Message about Fruits and Vegetables." Retrieved May 28, 2007, from http://www.cfsan.fda.gov/~dms/lab-dg.html

79. U.S Food and Drug Administration. (2007, March). "FDA Finalizes Report on 2006 Spinach Outbreak." Retrieved June 6, 2007, from http://www.fda.gov/bbs/topics/NEWS/2007/NEW01593.html

80. U.S. Food and Drug Administration and Center for Food Safety and Applied Nutrition. (1998). "Guidance for Industry: Guide to Minimize Microbial Food Safety Hazards for Fresh Fruit and Vegetables." Retrieved November 30, 2002, from http://www.foodsafety.gov/~dms/prodguid.html

81. U.S. Food and Drug Administration, Center for Food Safety and Applied Nutrition. (2005, November). "Safe Handling of Raw Produce and Fresh-Squeezed Fruit and Vegetable Juices." Retrieved March 8, 2007, from http://www.cfsan.fda.gov/~dms/prodsafe.html

82. U.S. Potato Board. (n.d.). "Food Service: Potato Varieties: A Variety for Every Need." Retrieved October 26, 2006, from http://www.healthypotato.com/foodservice/varieties.asp

83. Van Buren, J. P., and Pitifer, L. A. (1992). Retarding vegetable softening by cold alkaline pectin deesterification before cooking. *Journal of Food Science*, 57, 1022.

84. Van Duyn, M. A. S., and Pivonka, E. (2000). Overview of the health benefits of fruit and vegetable consumption for the dietetics professional: Selected literature. *Journal of the American Dietetic Association*, 100, 1511–1521.

85. Vidal-Valverde, C., Frias, J., and Valverde, S. (1993). Changes in the carbohydrate composition of legumes after soaking and cooking. *Journal of the American Dietetic Association*, 93, 547.

86. Von Elbe, J. H., Maing, I., and Amundson, C. H. (1974). Color stability of betanin. *Journal of Food Science*, 39, 334.

87. Watada, A. E., Abe, K., and Yamuchi, N. (1990). Physiological activities of partially processed fruits and vegetables. *Food Technology*, 44(5), 116.

88. Williams, P. G., Ross, H., and Miller, J. C. B. (1995). Ascorbic acid and 5-methyltetrahydrofolate losses in vegetables with cook/chill or cook/hot-hold foodservice systems. *Journal of Food Science*, 60, 541.

89. Winters, C. K., and Davis, S. F. (2006). IFT: Scientific status summary: Organic foods. *Journal of Food Science*, 71(9), R117–R124.

90. Wrolstad, R. E. (2004). Anthocyanin pigments—Bioactivity and coloring properties. *Journal of Food Science*, 71(5), C419–C421.

91. Zhao, X., Chambers, E. IV, Matta, Z., Loughin, T. M., and Carey, E. E. (2007). Consumer sensory analysis of organically and conventionally grown vegetables. *Journal of Food Science*, 72(2), S87–S91.

92. Zyren, J., Elkins, E. R., Dudek, J. A., and Hagen, R. E. (1983). Fiber contents of selected raw and processed vegetables, fruits and fruit juices as served. *Journal of Food Science*, 48, 600.

Chapter 21

1. Abe, K., and Watada, A. E. (1991). Ethylene absorbent to maintain quality of lightly processed fruits and vegetables. *Journal of Food Science*, 56, 1589.

2. Arnold, J. (2002). Watermelon packs a powerful lycopene punch. *Agricultural Research Magazine*, 50(6).

3. Beveridge, T. (1999). Electron microscopic characterization of haze in apple juice. *Food Technology*, 53(1), 44–48.

4. Bourne, M. C. (1982). Effect of temperature on firmness of raw fruits and vegetables. *Journal of Food Science*, 47, 440.

5. Brody, A. L. (2005). What's fresh about fresh-cut. *Food Technology*, 59(11), 74–77.

6. Chairote, G., Rodriguez, F., and Crouzet, J. (1981). Characterization of additional volatile flavor components of apricot. *Journal of Food Science*, 46, 1898.

7. Clark, J. P. (2002). Extending the shelf life of fruits and vegetables. *Food Technology*, 56(4), 98–100, 105.

8. Clark, J. P. (2003). Orange juice processing. *Food Technology*, 57(12), 50–51.

9. Demetrakakes, P. (1996). Unconcentrated effort. *Food Processing*, 57(11), 77.

10. Faigh, J. G. (1995). Enzyme formulations for optimizing juice yields. *Food Technology*, 49(9), 79.

11. Frohlich, O., and Schreier, P. (1990). Volatile constituents of loquat (*Eriobotrya japonica* Lindl.) fruit. *Journal of Food Science*, 55, 176.

12. Guthrie, J. F., Lin, B. H., Reed, J., and Stewart, H. (2005). Understanding economic and behavioral influences on fruit and vegetable choices. *Amber Waves*, 3(2), 36–41.

13. Knee, M. (1971). Ripening of apples during storage. III. Changes in chemical composition of Golden Delicious apples during the climacteric and under conditions simulating commercial storage practice. *Journal of the Science of Food and Agriculture*, 22, 371.

14. Krissoff, B., and Kuchler, F. (2007, May). Mandatory country-of-origin labeling: Will it benefit consumers? *Amber Waves*, 5 (Special Issue), 38–39.

15. Labensky, S. R., and Hause, A. M. (2007). *On Cooking: A Textbook of Culinary Fundamentals*, 4th ed. Upper Saddle River, NJ: Pearson Prentice Hall.

16. Labuza, T. P. (1996). An introduction to active packaging for foods. *Food Technology*, 50(4), 68.

17. Lidster, P. D., Lightfoot, H. J., and McRae, K. B. (1983). Production and regeneration of principal volatiles in apples stored in modified atmospheres and air. *Journal of Food Science*, 48, 400.

18. Lucier, G., Pollack, S., Ali, M., and Perez, A. (2006, April). Fruit and Vegetable Backgrounder/VGS-313-01. Retrieved May 25, 2007, from http://www.ers.usda.gov/Publications/VGS/Apr06/VGS31301/

19. Noel, G. L., and Robberstad, M. T. (1963). Stability of vitamin C in canned apple juice and orange juice under refrigerated conditions. *Food Technology*, 17, 947.

20. Ohr, L. M. (2005). Brain foods. *Food Technology*, 59(7), 69–73.

21. Pratt, S. (1992). The "peachfuzz" plot. *Food Technology*, 46(8), 46.

22. Produce Marketing Association. (1995). *The Foodservice Guide to Fresh Produce*. Newark, DE: Author.

23. Produce Marketing Association. (2002). *The PMA Fresh Produce Manual*. Newark, DE: Author.

24. Pszczola, D. E. (2001). Antioxidants: From preserving food quality to quality of life. *Food Technology*, 55(6), 51.

25. Putnam, J. J., and Allshouse, J. (2001). Imports' share of U.S. diet rises in late 1990's. *Food Review*, 24(3), 15–22.

26. Segal, M. (1988). *Fruit*. U.S. Department of Health and Human Services Publication No. (FDA) 88–2226.

Rockville, MD: U.S. Department of Health and Human Services.

27. Sloan, A. E. (2001). Fruit frenzy. *Food Technology, 55*(12), 14.

28. Steinmetz, K. A., and Potter, J. D. (1996). Vegetables, fruit, and cancer prevention: A review. *Journal of the American Dietetic Association, 96,* 1027.

29. Sweeney, J. P., Chapman, V. J., and Hepner, P. A. (1970). Sugar, acid, and flavor in fresh fruits. *Journal of the American Dietetic Association, 57,* 432.

30. Talasila, P. C., Chau, K. V., and Brecht, J. K. (1995). Design of rigid modified atmosphere packages for fresh fruits and vegetables. *Journal of Food Science, 60,* 758.

31. *The Buying Guide for Fresh Fruits, Vegetables, Herbs, and Nuts,* 8th ed. (1986). Shepherdstown, WV: Blue Goose Growers, Inc.

32. Toops, D. (1997). Going bananas. *Food Processing, 58*(8), 51.

33. U.S. Centers for Disease Control and Prevention. (2002, November 22). Multistate outbreaks of *Salmonella* serotype Poona infections associated with eating cantaloupe from Mexico—United States and Canada, 2000–2002. *MMWR Weekly, 51*(46), 1044–1047. Retrieved June 28, 2007, from http://www.cdc.gov/mmwr/preview/mmwrhtml/mm5146a2.htm

34. U.S. Centers For Disease Control and Prevention. (2005, December). "Preventing Health Risks Associated with Drinking Unpasteurized or Untreated Juice." Retrieved June 28, 2007, from http://www.cdc.gov/foodborne/juice_spotlight.htm

35. U.S. Centers for Disease Control and Prevention. (2007, March 16). Fruit and vegetable consumption among adults – United States, 2005. *MMWR Weekly, 56*(10), 213–217. Retrieved June 28, 2007, from http://www.cdc.gov/mmwr/preview/mmwrhtml/mm5610a2.htm

36. U.S. Department of Agriculture. (2005). "Dietary Guidelines for Americans 2005: Key Recommendations for the General Population." Retrieved May 25, 2007, from http://www.health.gov/dietaryguidelines/dga2005/recommendations.htm

37. U.S. Department of Agriculture, Agricultural Research Service. (2002). "USDA National Nutrient Database for Standard Reference," Release 15. Retrieved December 7, 2002, from the Nutrient Data Laboratory website, http://www.nal.usda.gov/fnic/foodcomp

38. U.S. Department of Agriculture, Agricultural Marketing Service. (1994). *How to buy fresh fruits.* Home and Garden Bulletin No. 260.

39. U.S. Department of Agriculture, Economic Research Service. (2006). "Table 39—Per Capita Consumption of Major Food Commodities." Retrieved May 27, 2007, from http://ers.usda.gov/publications/agoutlook/aotables/2006/05May/aotab39.xls

40. U.S. Food and Drug Administration, Center for Food Safety and Applied Nutrition. (1999, June). "A Food Labeling Guide. Chapter II—Name of Food." Retrieved June 29, 2007, from http://www.cfsan.fda.gov/~dms/flg-2.html

41. U.S. Government Printing Office. (2001, April 1). "Code of Federal Regulations: 21CFR102.33—Beverages That Contain Fruit or Vegetable Juice." Retrieved June 27, 2007, from http://ecfr.gpoaccess.gov/cgi/t/text/text-idx?c=ecfr&sid=8c5344f04a8ae103e5b0ff5a17c7fa97&rgn=div8&view=text&node=21:2.0.1.1.3.2.1.5&idno=21

42. Van Duyn, M. A. S., and Pivonka, E. (2000). Overview of the health benefits of fruit and vegetable consumption for the dietetics professional: Selected literature. *Journal of the American Dietetic Association, 100,* 1511–1521.

43. Wiseman, J. J., and McDaniel, M. R. (1991). Modification of fruit flavors by aspartame and sucrose. *Journal of Food Science, 56,* 1668.

Chapter 22

1. Clark, J. P. (2002). Extending the shelf life of fruits and vegetables. *Food Technology, 56*(4), 98.

2. Gelatin Manufacturers Institute of America. (2001). "How We Make Gelatin." Retrieved December 21, 2002, from http://www.gelatin-gmia.com/html/rawmaterials.html

3. Gudmundsson, M. (2002). Rheological properties of fish gelatins. *Journal of Food Science, 67*(6), 2172–2176.

4. Li-Cohen, A. E., and Bruhn, C. M. (2002). Safety of consumer handling of fresh produce from the time of purchase to the plate: A comprehensive consumer survey. *Journal of Food Protection, 65*(8), 1287–1296.

5. Oria, M. (2001). Report addresses safety of fruit and vegetables. *Food Technology, 55*(11), 22.

6. Rolls, B. J., Roe, L. S., and Meengs, J. S. (2004). Salad and satiety: Energy density and portion size of a first-course salad affect energy intake at lunch. *Journal of the American Dietetic Association, 104,* 1570–1576.

7. Su, L. J., and Arab, L. (2006). Salad and raw vegetable consumption and nutritional status in the adult U.S. population: Results from the Third National Health and Nutrition Examination Study. *Journal of the American Dietetic Association, 106,* 1394–1404.

8. Tanaka, T. (1981). Gels. *Scientific American, 244*(1), 124.

9. The FDA: Fresh leafy greens grown in the United States are safe. (2006) *FDA Consumer, 40*(6), 11.

10. U.S. Centers for Disease Control. (2001). "Questions and Answers Regarding Bovine Spongiform Encephalopathy (BSE) and Creutzfeldt-Jacob Disease (CJD)." Retrieved December 20, 2002, from http://www.cdc.gov/ncidod/diseases/cjd/bse_cjd_qu.htm

11. U.S. Food And Drug Administration. (1997, December). "Guidance for Industry: The Sourcing and Processing of Gelatin to Reduce the Potential Risk Posed by Bovine Spongiform Encephalopathy (BSE) in FDA-Regulated Products for Human Use." Retrieved December 20, 2002, from http://www.fda.gov/opacom/morechoices/industry/guidance/gelguide.htm

12. Van Duyn, M. A. S., and Pivonka, E. (2000). Overview of the health benefits of fruit and vegetable consumption for the dietetics professional: Selected literature. *Journal of the American Dietetic Association, 100,* 1511–1521.

13. Ward, A. G., and Courts, A. (Eds.). (1977). *The Science and Technology of Gelatin.* New York: Academic Press.

14. Zhou, P., and Regenstein, J. M. (2007). Comparison of water gel desserts from fish skin and pork gelatins using instrumental measurements. *Journal of Food Science, 72*(4), C196–C201.

Chapter 23

1. Barbano, D. (1995). "Cornell University: bST Fact Sheet." Retrieved July 14, 2007, from http://www.cfsan.fda.gov/~ear/CORBST.html

2. Blayney, D. P. (1994). Milk and biotechnology: Maintaining safe, adequate milk supplies. *Food Review,* 17(2), 27.

3. Bren, L. (2004). Got milk? Make sure it's pasteurized. *FDA Consumer Magazine,* 38(5).

4. Chandan, R. (1997). *Dairy-based ingredients.* St. Paul, MN: Eagan Press.

5. Clemens, R. A. (2001). Friendly bacteria: A functional food? *Food Technology,* 55(1), 27.

6. Council on Foods and Nutrition. (1969). Substitutes for whole milk. *Journal of the American Medical Association,* 208, 58.

7. Enns, C. W., Goldman, J. D., and Cook, A. (1997). Trends in food and nutrient intakes by adults: NFCS 1977–78, CSFII 1989–91, and CSFII 1994–95. *Family Economics and Nutrition Review,* 10(4), 2.

8. Gupta, C. B., and Eskin, N. A. M. (1977). Potential use of vegetable rennet in the production of cheese. *Food Technology,* 31(5), 62.

9. Gwartney, E. A., Foegeding, E. A., and Larick, D. K. (2002). The texture of commercial full-fat and reduced-fat cheese. *Journal of Food Science,* 67, 812–816.

10. Hertzler, S. R., and Clancy, S. M. (2003). Kefir improves lactose digestion and tolerance for adults with lactose maldigestion. *Journal of the American Dietetic Association,* 103, 582–587.

11. Hoch, G. J. (1997). Whey to go. *Food Processing,* 58(3), 51.

12. Hollingsworth, P. (2001). Culture wars. *Food Technology,* 55(3), 43–46.

13. Holsinger, V. H., and Kligerman, A. E. (1991). Applications of lactase in dairy foods and other foods containing lactose. *Food Technology,* 45(1), 92.

14. Hoover, D. G. (1993). Bifidobacteria: Activity and potential benefits. *Food Technology,* 47(6), 120.

15. *How to buy cheese.* (1974). Home and Garden Bulletin No. 193. Washington, DC: U.S. Department of Agriculture.

16. Huffman, L. M. (1996). Processing whey protein for use as a food ingredient. *Food Technology,* 50(2), 49.

17. Hughes, D. B., and Hoover, D. G. (1991). Bifidobacteria: Their potential for use in American dairy products. *Food Technology,* 45(4), 74.

18. Jensen, R. G. (Ed.). (1995). *Handbook of Milk Composition.* New York: Academic Press.

19. Kanno, C., Shimomura, Y., and Takano, E. (1991). Physicochemical properties of milkfat emulsions stabilized with bovine milkfat globule membrane. *Journal of Food Science,* 56, 1219.

20. Katz, F. (2001). Active cultures add function to yogurt and other foods. *Food Technology,* 55(3), 46–49.

21. Kroger, M., Kurmann, J. A., and Rasic, J. L. (1989). Fermented milks—Past, present, and future. *Food Technology,* 43(1), 92.

22. Kurtzweil, P. (1998). Skimming the milk label. *FDA Consumer,* 32(1), 22.

23. Labensky, S. R., and Hause, A. M. (2007). *On Cooking: A Textbook of Culinary Fundamentals,* 4th ed. Upper Saddle River, NJ: Pearson Prentice Hall.

24. Lee, S. Y., and Morr, C. V. (1993). Fixation staining methods for examining microstructure in whipped cream by electron microscopy. *Journal of Food Science,* 58, 124.

25. Light, A., Heymann, H., and Holt, D. L. (1992). Hedonic responses to dairy products: Effects of fat levels, label information, and risk perception. *Food Technology,* 46(7), 54.

26. Liu, J. R., and Lin, C. W. (2000). Production of kefir from soymilk with or without added glucose, lactose, or sucrose. *Journal of Food Science,* 65(4), 716–719.

27. Mangino, M. E. (1992). Gelation of whey protein concentrates. *Food Technology,* 46(1), 114.

28. Mermelstein, N. H. (1997). Extending dairy product shelf life with carbon dioxide. *Food Technology,* 51(12), 72.

29. Miller, G. D., Jarvis, J. K., and McBean, L. D. (2007). *Handbook of Dairy Foods and Nutrition,* 3rd ed. Boca Raton, FL: CRC Press Taylor and Frances Group.

30. Mulvihill, D. M., and Kinsella, J. E. (1987). Gelation characteristics of whey proteins and beta-lactoglobulin. *Food Technology,* 41(9), 102.

31. National Dairy Council. (2000). "Newer Knowledge of Dairy Foods / Milk: V. Protecting the Quality of Milk and Other Dairy Foods." Retrieved July 5, 2007, from http://www.nationaldairycouncil.org/NationalDairyCouncil/Nutrition/Products/knowledge.htm

32. National Dairy Council. (2004). "Nutrition and Product Information: Milk's Unique Nutrient Package." Retrieved July 6, 2007, from http://www.nationaldairy council.org/NationalDairyCouncil/Nutrition/Products/Milks-Nutrient-Package.htm

33. National Dairy Council. (2007). "Newer Knowledge of Dairy Foods / Cheese. Retrieved July 5, 2007, from http:// nationaldairycouncil.org/NationalDairyCouncil/Nutrition/Products/cheesePage1.htm

34. National Restaurant Association Educational Foundation. (2006). *ServSafe Coursebook,* 4th ed. Chicago, IL: National Restaurant Association Educational Foundation.

35. Neff, J. (1997). Fattening up a new dairy niche. *Food Processing,* 58(1), 45.

36. National Dairy Council. (1992). *Newer Knowledge of Cheese.* Rosemont, IL: Author.

37. National Dairy Council. (1993). *Newer Knowledge of Milk.* Rosemont, IL: Author.

38. Ohr, L. M. (2002). Improving the gut feeling. *Food Technology,* 56(10), 67–70.

39. Palanuk, S. L., Warthesen, J. J., and Smith, D. E. (1988). Effect of agitation, sampling location, and protective films on light-induced riboflavin loss in skim milk. *Journal of Food Science,* 53, 436.

40. Pszczola, D. E. (2001). Say cheese with new ingredient developments. *Food Technology,* 55(12), 56–66.

41. Savaiano, D. A., and Levitt, M. D. (1984). Nutritional and therapeutic aspects of fermented dairy products. *Contemporary Nutrition* (General Mills Nutrition Department), 9(6).

42. Shipe, W. F., Bassette, R., Deane, D. D., Dunkley, W. L., Hammond, E. G., Harper, W. J., Kleyn, D. H., Morgan,

M. E., Nelson, J. H., and Scanlan, R. A. (1978). Off-flavors of milk: Nomenclature, standards, and bibliography. *Journal of Dairy Science, 61*, 855.

43. Sloan, E. A. (2000). Say cheese! *Food Technology, 54*(6), 18–19.

44. Speck, M. L., Dobrogosz, W. J., and Casas, I. A. (1993). *Lactobacillus reuteri* in food supplementation. *Food Technology, 47*(7), 90.

45. Staff. (1989). Rennet containing 100% chymosin increases cheese quality and yield. *Food Technology, 43*(6), 84.

46. U.S. Department of Agriculture. (1995). *How to buy cheeses.* Home and Garden Bulletin No. 193.

47. U.S. Department of Agriculture. (1995). *How to buy dairy products.* Home and Garden Bulletin No. 255.

48. U.S. Department of Agriculture. (2002, April). "Molds on Food: Are They Dangerous?" Retrieved August 20, 2002, from http://www.fsis.usda.gov/OA/pubs/molds.htm

49. U.S. Department of Agriculture. (2005). "Nutrition and Your Health: Dietary Guidelines for Americans: Part D. Science Base." Retrieved April 6, 2008, from http://www.health.gov/dietaryguidelines/dga2005/report/HTML/D6_SelectedFood.htm

50. U.S. Department of Agriculture, Economic Research Service. (2007). "Data Sets. Food Availability: Custom Queries." Retrieved July 6, 2007, from http://www.ers.usda.gov/Data/FoodConsumption/FoodAvailQueriable.aspx

51. U.S. Department of Health and Human Services. (2004). *Bone Health and Osteoporosis: A Report of the Surgeon General.* Rockville, MD: U.S. Department of Health and Human Services, Office of the Surgeon General.

52. U.S. Food and Drug Administration. (2007, March). "FDA News: FDA and CDC Remind Consumers of the Dangers of Raw Milk." Retrieved June 28, 2007, from http://www.fda.gov/bbs/topics/NEWS/2007/NEW01576.html

53. U.S. Food and Drug Administration, Center for Food Safety and Applied Nutrition. (2004, March). "Grade 'A' Pasteurized Milk Ordinance" (2003 revision). Retrieved July 8, 2007, from http://www.cfsan.fda.gov/~ear/pmo03.html

54. U.S. Food and Drug Administration, Center for Food Safety and Applied Nutrition. (2006, October). "Food Facts: The Dangers Of Raw Milk: Unpasteurized Milk Can Pose a Serious Health Risk." Retrieved July 4, 2007, from http://www.cfsan.fda.gov/~dms/rawmilk.html

55. U.S Food and Drug Administration, Center for Food Safety and Applied Nutrition. (2006, April). "Title 21—Food and Drugs, Subchapter B—Food for Human Consumption, Part 131—Milk and Cream." Retrieved July 12, 2007, from http://www.accessdata.fda.gov/scripts/cdrh/cfdocs/cfcfr/CFRSearch.cfm?fr=131.130

56. U.S. Food and Drug Administration, Center for Veterinary Medicine. (1999, February). "Report on the Food and Drug Administration's Review of the Safety of Recombinant Bovine Somatotropin." Retrieved July 14, 2007, from http://www.fda.gov/cvm/RBRPTFNL.htm

57. Weinberg, L. G., Berner, L. A., and Groves, J. E. (2004). Nutrient contributions of dairy foods in the United States, Continuing Survey of Food Intakes by Individuals, 1994–1996, 1998. *Journal of the American Dietetic Association, 104*, 895–902.

Chapter 24

1. American Egg Board. (2002, September). "Egg Industry Fact Sheet." Retrieved from http://www.aeb.org/eii/facts/industry-facts-06-2002.htm

2. American Egg Board. (1994, April). *Eggcyclopedia*, 3rd ed. Chicago, IL: American Egg Board.

3. American Egg Board. (n.d.) "Basic Egg Facts." Retrieved from http://www.aeb.org/LearnMore/EggFacts.htm

4. Baker, R. C., Darfler, J., and Lifshitz, A. (1967). Factors affecting the discoloration of hard-cooked egg yolks. *Poultry Science, 46*, 664.

5. Bufano, N. S. (2000). Keeping eggs safe from farm to table. *Food Technology, 54*(8), 192.

6. Code of Federal Regulations. (1997, January 7). *Inspection of eggs and egg products: Pasteurization of eggs.* 7CFR59.570.

7. Cremer, M. L. (1981). Microwave heating of scrambled eggs in a hospital foodservice system. *Journal of Food Science, 46*, 1573.

8. U.S. Department of Agriculture. (1990). *Egg grading manual.* Agriculture Handbook No. 75. Washington, DC: Author.

9. Gardner, F. A., Beck, M. L., and Denton, J. H. (1982). Functional quality comparison of whole egg and selected egg substitute products. *Poultry Science, 61*, 75.

10. Giese, J. (1994). Ultrapasteurized liquid whole eggs earn 1994 IFT Food Technology Industrial Achievement Award. *Food Technology, 48*(9), 94.

11. Gillis, J. N., and Fitch, N. K. (1956). Leakage of baked soft meringue topping. *Journal of Home Economics, 48*, 703.

12. Hanning, F. (1945). Effect of sugar or salt upon denaturation produced by beating and upon the ease of formation and the stability of egg white foams. *Iowa State College Journal of Science, 20*, 10.

13. Hester, E. E., and Personius, C. J. (1949). Factors affecting the beading and leaking of soft meringues. *Food Technology, 3*, 236.

14. Irmiter, T. F., Dawson, L. E., and Reagan, J. G. (1970). Methods of preparing hard cooked eggs. *Poultry Science, 49*, 1232.

15. Itoh, T., Miyazaki, J., Sugawara, H., and Adachi, S. (1987). Studies on the characterization of ovomucin and chalaza of the hen's egg. *Journal of Food Science, 52*, 1518.

16. Kinner, J. A., and Moats, W. A. (1981). Effect of temperature, pH, and detergent on survival of bacteria associated with shell eggs. *Poultry Science, 60*, 761.

17. Kline, L., and Sugihara, T. F. (1966, August). Effects of pasteurization on egg products. *Baker's Digest, 40*, 40.

18. Kurisaki, J., Kaminogawa, S., and Yamauchi, K. (1980). Studies on freeze-thaw gelation of very low density lipoprotein from hen's yolk. *Journal of Food Science, 45*, 463.

19. Labensky, S. R., and Hause, A. M. (2007). *On Cooking: A Textbook of Culinary Fundamentals*, 4th ed. Upper Saddle River, NJ: Pearson Prentice Hall.

20. Lin, C. T. J., Morales, R. A., and Ralston, K. (1997). Raw and undercooked eggs: A danger of salmonellosis. *Food Review, 20*(1), 27.

21. Margoshes, B. A. (1990). Correlation of protein sulfhydryls with the strength of heat-formed egg white gels. *Journal of Food Science, 55*, 1753.

22. Matiella, J. E., and Hsieh, T. C. Y. (1991). Volatile compounds in scrambled eggs. *Journal of Food Science, 56,* 387.

23. Meehan, J. J., Sugihara, T. F., and Kline, L. (1962). Relationships between shell egg handling factors and egg product properties. *Poultry Science, 41,* 892.

24. Mermelstein, N. H. (2000). Cryogenic system rapidly cools eggs. *Food Technology, 54*(6), 100–103.

25. Mermelstein, N. H. (2001). Pasteurization of shell eggs. *Food Technology, 55*(12), 72–73, 79.

26. Mineki, M., and Kobayashi, M. (1997). Microstructure of yolk from fresh eggs by improved method. *Journal of Food Science, 62,* 757.

27. Neff, J. (1998). The great egg breakthrough. *Food Processing, 59*(1), 25.

28. Parsons, A. H. (1982). Structure of the eggshell. *Poultry Science, 61,* 2013.

29. Pszczola, D. E. (1999). Waking up breakfast foods. *Food Technology, 53*(3), 60–67.

30. Schroeder, C. M., Naugle, A. L., Schlosser, W. D., Hogue, A. T., Angulo, F. J., Rose, J. S., Ebel, E. D., Disney, W. T., Holt, K. G., and Goldman, D. P. (2005). Estimate of illnesses from *Salmonella Enteritidis* in eggs, United States, 2000. *Emerging Infectious Diseases* [on-line], *11*(1). Retrieved February 9, 2008, from http://www.cdc.gov/ncidod/eid/vol11no01/04-0401.htm

31. Sheldon, B. W., and Kimsey, H. R., Jr. (1985). The effects of cooking methods on the chemical, physical, and sensory properties of hard-cooked eggs. *Poultry Science, 64,* 84.

32. U.S. Department of Agriculture. (1995). *How to buy eggs.* Home and Garden Bulletin No. 264.

33. U.S. Department of Agriculture, Economic Research Service. (2007). "Food Availability (Per Capita) Data System." Retrieved February 14, 2008, from http://ers.usda.gov/data/FoodConsumption/

34. U.S. Department of Agriculture, Food Safety Inspection Service. (2002, October). "Focus on Shell Eggs." Retrieved December 30, 2002, from http://fsis.usda.gov/OA/pubs/shelleggs.htm

35. U.S. Food and Drug Administration, Center for Food Safety and Applied Nutrition. (2007, March). "Food Safety Facts for Consumers: Playing It Safe with Eggs." Retrieved April 6, 2008, from http://www.cfsan.fda.gov/~dms/fs-eggs.html

36. U.S. Health and Human Services. (2000, November). "FDA Finalizes Safe Handling Labels and Refrigeration Requirements for Marketing Shell Eggs." Retrieved December 29, 2002, from http://www.cfsan.fda.gov/~lrd/hhseggs2.html

37. Van Elswyk, M. E., Sams, A. R., and Hargis, P. S. (1992). Composition, functionality, and sensory evaluation of eggs from hens fed dietary menhaden oil. *Journal of Food Science, 57,* 342.

38. Woodward, S. A., and Cotterill, O. J. (1986). Texture and microstructure of heat-formed egg white gels. *Journal of Food Science, 51,* 333.

39. Woodward, S. A., and Cotterill, O. J. (1987). Texture and microstructure of cooked whole egg yolks and heat-formed gels of stirred egg yolk. *Journal of Food Science, 52,* 63.

40. Wu, V. T., Brochetti, D., and Duncan, S. E. (1998). Sensory characteristics and acceptability of lactose-reduced baked custards made with an egg substitute. *Journal of the American Dietetic Association, 98,* 1467–1469.

41. Zottola, E. A. (2001). Reflections on *Salmonella* and other "wee beasties" in foods. *Food Technology, 55*(9), 60.

Chapter 25

1. Akinwunmi, I., Thompson, L. D., and Ramsey, C. B. (1993). Marbling, fat trim, and doneness effects on sensory attributes, cooking loss, and composition of cooked beef steaks. *Journal of Food Science, 58,* 242.

2. Al-Obaidy, H. M., Khan, M. A., and Klein, B. P. (1984). Comparison between sensory quality of freshly prepared spaghetti with meat sauce before and after hot holding on a cafeteria counter. *Journal of Food Science, 49,* 1475.

3. American Cancer Society. (2005). "Harmful Chemicals in Grilled Meats." Retrieved September 12, 2007, from http://www.cancer.org/docroot/PED/content/PED_11_1_Harmful_Chemicals_in_Grilled_Meats.asp

4. American Institute for Cancer Research. (2001). "The Facts about Grilling." Retrieved September 12, 2007, from http://www.aicr.org/site/DocServer/FactsAboutGrilling.pdf?docID=1081

5. Archer, D. L. (2001). Nitrite and the impact of advisory groups. *Food Technology, 55*(3), 26.

6. Archer, D. L. (2000). *E. coli* 0157:H7—Searching for solutions. *Food Technology, 54*(10), 142.

7. Berry, B. W., and Leddy, K. F. (1984). Effects of fat level and cooking method on sensory and textural properties of ground beef patties. *Journal of Food Science, 48,* 1715.

8. Bouton, P. E., Harris, P. V., and Ratcliff, D. (1981). Effect of cooking temperature and time on the shear properties of meat. *Journal of Food Science, 46,* 1082.

9. Bowers, J. A., Craig, J. A., Kropf, D. H., and Tucker, T. J. (1987). Flavor, color, and other characteristics of beef longissimus muscle heated to seven internal temperatures between 55° and 85°C. *Journal of Food Science, 52,* 533.

10. Brewer, M. S., and Decker, E. (1998). "Facts: What Is 'Warmed-Over Flavor'?" Retrieved October 10, 2007, from http://www.meatscience.org/Pubs/factsheets/q-warmover.pdf

11. Brody, A. L. (2002). The case for—or against—case-ready fresh red meat in the United States. *Food Technology, 54*(8), 153–156.

12. Brody, A. L. (2004). The case for case-ready meat. *Food Technology, 58*(8), 84–86.

13. Brody, A. L. (2007). Case-ready packaging for red meat. *Food Technology, 61*(3), 70–72.

14. Buchanan, R. L., and Doyle, M. P. (1997). Foodborne disease significance of *Escherichia coli* 0157:H7 and other enterohemorrhagic *E. coli*. *Food Technology, 51*(10), 69.

15. Buzby, J. C., and Crutchfield, S. R. (1997). USDA modernizes meat and poultry inspection. *Food Review, 20*(1), 14.

16. Cassens, R. G. (1995). Use of sodium nitrite in cured meats today. *Food Technology, 49*(7), 72.

17. Cassens, R. G. (1997). Residual nitrite in cured meat. *Food Technology, 51*(2), 53.

18. Cattlemen's Beef Board. (n.d.) "Industry Guide for Beef Aging." Retrieved August 10, 2007, from http://www.beefresearch.org/CMDocs/BeefResearch/Industry%20-Guide%20for%20Beef%20Aging.pdf

19. Costello, C. A., Penfield, M. P., and Riemann, M. J. (1985). Quality of restructured steaks: Effects of days on feed, fat level, and cooking method. *Journal of Food Science, 50,* 685.

20. Cover, S., and Hostetler, R. L. (1960). *Beef tenderness.* Texas Agricultural Experiment Station Bulletin No. 947. College Station, TX: Texas Agricultural Experiment Station.

21. Cross, H. R., Berry, B. W., and Wells, L. H. (1980). Effects of fat level and source on the chemical, sensory, and cooking properties of ground beef patties. *Journal of Food Science, 45,* 791.

22. Davis, C. G., and Lin, B. H. (2005). "Factors Affecting U.S. Beef Consumption." U.S. Department of Agriculture, LPD-M-135-02. Retrieved September 23, 2007, from http://www.ers.usda.gov/publications/ldp/Oct05/ldpm13502/ldpm13502.pdf

23. Dolezal, H. G., Smith, G. C., Savell, J. W., and Carpenter, Z. L. (1982). Comparison of subcutaneous fat thickness, marbling and quality grade for predicting palatability of beef. *Journal of Food Science, 47,* 397.

24. Drew, F., and Rhee, K. S. (1979). Microwave cookery of beef patties: Browning methods. *Journal of the American Dietetic Association, 74,* 652.

25. Drew, F., Rhee, K. S., and Carpenter, Z. L. (1980). Cooking at variable microwave power levels. *Journal of the American Dietetic Association, 77,* 455.

26. Egbert, W. R., and Cornforth, D. P. (1986). Factors influencing color of dark cutting beef muscle. *Journal of Food Science, 51,* 57.

27. Fabiansson, S., and Libelius, R. (1985). Structural changes in beef longissimus dorsi induced by postmortem low voltage electrical stimulation. *Journal of Food Science, 50,* 39.

28. Fan, X., Niemira, B. A., Rajkowski, K. T., Phillips, J., and Sommers, C. H. (2004). Sensory evaluation of irradiated ground beef patties for the National School Lunch Program. *Journal of Food Science, 69*(9), S384–S387.

29. Feiner, G. (2006). *Meat Products Handbook: Practical Science and Technology.* Boca Raton, FL: CRC Press.

30. Fogle, D. R., Plimpton, R. F., Ockerman, H. W., Jarenback, L., and Persson, T. (1982). Tenderization of beef: Effect of enzyme, enzyme level, and cooking method. *Journal of Food Science, 47,* 1113.

31. Gariepy, C., Amiot, J., Pommier, S. A., Flipot, P. M., and Girard, V. (1992). Electrical stimulation and 48 hours aging of bull and steer carcasses. *Journal of Food Science, 57,* 541.

32. Gerrier, S., and Bente, L. (2001). Food supply nutrients and dietary guidance, 1970–1999. *Food Review, 24*(3), 39–46.

33. Giese, J. H. (1992). Developing low-fat meat products. *Food Technology, 46*(4), 100.

34. Giese, J. H. (2001). It's a mad, mad, mad, mad cow test. *Food Technology, 55*(6), 60–62.

35. Giese, J. H. (2002). Washington news. *Food Technology, 56*(10), 22.

36. Gravely, M. H. (1993). Understanding the new meat and poultry labels. *Food News for Consumers, 10*(1–2), 8.

37. Hamm, R. (1982). Postmortem changes in muscle with regard to processing of hot-boned beef. *Food Technology, 36*(11), 105.

38. Hardin, B. (1999). Predicting tenderness in beefsteaks. *Agricultural Research Magazine, 47*(11).

39. Howat, P. M., Sievert, L. M., Myers, P. J., Koonce, K. L., and Bidner, T. D. (1983). Effect of marination upon mineral content and tenderness of beef. *Journal of Food Science, 48,* 662.

40. Hueston, W., and Byrant, C. M. (2005). Transmissible spongiform encephalopathies. *Journal of Food Science, 70*(5), R77–R87.

41. Hunt, M. C., Sorheim, O., and Slinde, E. (1999). Color and heat denaturation of myoglobin forms. *Journal of Food Science, 60,* 1175–1196.

42. Jacobs, D. K., and Sebranek, J. G. (1980). Use of prerigor beef for frozen ground beef patties. *Journal of Food Science, 45,* 648.

43. Jennings, T. G., Berry, B. W., and Joseph, A. L. (1978). Influence of fat thickness, marbling, and length of aging on beef palatability and shelf-life characteristics. *Journal of Animal Science, 46,* 658.

44. Johnston, M. B., and Baldwin, R. E. (1980). Influence of microwave reheating on selected quality factors of roast beef. *Journal of Food Science, 45,* 1460.

45. Killinger, K. M., Hunt, M. C., Campbell, R. E., and Kropf, D. H. (2000). Factors affecting premature browning during cooking of store-purchased ground beef. *Journal of Food Science, 65,* 585–587.

46. King, N. J., and White, R. (2006). Does it looked cooked? A review of factors that influence cooked meat color. *Journal of Food Science, 71*(4), R31–R40.

47. Koohmaraie, M., Seideman, S. C., Schollmeyer, J. E., Dutson, T. R., and Babiker, A. S. (1988). Factors associated with the tenderness of three bovine muscles. *Journal of Food Science, 53,* 407.

48. Korschgen, B. M., Baldwin, R. E., and Snider, S. (1976). Quality factors in beef, pork, and lamb cooked by microwaves. *Journal of the American Dietetic Association, 69,* 635.

49. Korschgen, B. M., Berneking, J. M., and Baldwin, R. E. (1980). Energy requirements for cooking beef rib roasts. *Journal of Food Science, 45,* 1054.

50. Laakkonen, E., Wellington, G. H., and Sherbon, J. W. (1970). Low-temperature, long-time heating of bovine muscle. 1. Changes in tenderness, water-binding capacity, pH and amount of water-soluble components. *Journal of Food Science, 35,* 175.

51. Labensky, S. R., and Hause, A. M. (2007). *On Cooking: A Textbook of Culinary Fundamentals,* 4th ed. Upper Saddle River, NJ: Pearson Prentice Hall.

52. Leander, R. C., Hedrick, H. B., Brown, M. F., and White, J. A. (1980). Comparison of structural changes in bovine longissimus and semitendinosus muscles during cooking. *Journal of Food Science, 45,* 1.

53. Lin, J. C., and Kaufman, P. (1995). Food companies offer views of safe handling label for meat and poultry. *Food Review, 18*(3), 23.

54. Liu, M. N., Huffman, D. L., Egbert, W. R., McCaskey, T. A., and Liu, C. W. (1991). Soy protein and oil effects on

chemical, physical and microbial stability of lean ground beef patties. *Journal of Food Science, 56,* 906.

55. Love, J. A., and Prusa, K. J. (1992). Nutrient composition and sensory attributes of cooked ground beef: Effects of fat content, cooking method, and water rinsing. *Journal of the American Dietetic Association, 92,* 1367.

56. Mancini, R. (2007). "Iridescence: A Rainbow of Colors, Causes, and Concerns." National Cattlemen's Beef Association. Retrieved October 14, 2007, from http://www.beefresearch.org/CMDocs/BeefResearch/Beef%20Iridescence.pdf

57. Mandigo, R. W. (1986). Restructuring of muscle foods. *Food Technology, 40*(3), 85.

58. Marshall, N. (1960). Electronic cookery of top round of beef. *Journal of Home Economics, 52,* 31.

59. Maruri, J. L., and Larick, D. K., (1992). Volatile concentration and flavor of beef as influenced by diet. *Journal of Food Science, 57,* 1275.

60. McDowell, M. D., Harrison, D. L., Pacey, C., and Stone, M. B. (1982). Differences between conventionally cooked top round roasts and semimembranous muscle strips cooked in a model system. *Journal of Food Science, 47,* 1603.

61. McIntosh, E. N. (1967). Effect of postmortem aging and enzyme tenderizers on mucoprotein of bovine skeletal muscle. *Journal of Food Science, 32,* 210.

62. McKeith, F. K., de Vol, D. L., Miles, R. S., Bechtel, P. J., and Carr, T. R. (1985). Chemical and sensory properties of thirteen major beef muscles. *Journal of Food Science, 50,* 869.

63. Miller, M. F., Andersen, M. K., Ramsey, C. B., and Reagan, J. O. (1993). Physical and sensory characteristics of low-fat ground beef patties. *Journal of Food Science, 58,* 461.

64. Mitchell, G. E., Reed, A. W., and Rogers, S. A. (1991). Influence of feeding regimen on the sensory qualities and fatty acid contents of beef steaks. *Journal of Food Science, 56,* 1102.

65. Moody, W. G. (1983). Beef flavor: A review. *Food Technology, 37*(5), 227.

66. Moore, L. J., Harrison, D. L., and Dayton, A. D. (1980). Differences among top round steaks cooked by dry or moist heat in a conventional or a microwave oven. *Journal of Food Science, 45,* 777.

67. National Restaurant Association Educational Foundation. (2006). *ServSafe Coursebook,* 4th ed. Chicago, IL: National Restaurant Association Education Foundation.

68. North American Meat Processors Association (NAMP). (2007). *The Meat Buyers Guide.* Hoboken, NJ: John Wiley & Sons, Inc.

69. Nielsen, M. M., and Hall, F. T. (1965). Dry-roasting of less tender beef cuts. *Journal of Home Economics, 57,* 353.

70. Olson, D. G., Caporaso, F., and Mandigo, R. W. (1980). Effects of serving temperature on sensory evaluation of beef steaks from different muscles and carcass maturities. *Journal of Food Science, 45,* 627.

71. Omaye, S. T. (2001). Preventing BSE in the U.S. *Food Technology, 55*(4), 26.

72. Omaye, S. T. (2001). Shiga-toxin–producing *Escherichia coli:* Another concern. *Food Technology, 55*(5), 26.

73. Oreskovich, D. C., Bechtel, P. J., McKeith, F. K., Novakofski, J., and Basgall, E. J. (1992). Marinade pH affects textural properties of beef. *Journal of Food Science, 57,* 305.

74. Parrish, F. C., Jr., Boles, J. A., Rust, R. E., and Olson, D. G. (1991). Dry and wet aging effects on palatability attributes of beef loin and rib steaks from three quality grades. *Journal of Food Science, 56,* 601.

75. Peterson, R. J., and Chang, S. S. (1982). Identification of volatile flavor compounds of fresh, frozen beef stew and a comparison of these with those of canned beef stew. *Journal of Food Science, 47,* 1444.

76. Ralston, K., Starke, Y., Brent, P., and Riggins, T. (2000). Awareness of risks changing how hamburgers are cooked. *Food Review, 23*(2), 44–50.

77. Rathje, W. L., and Ho, E. E. (1987). Meat fat madness: Conflicting patterns of meat fat consumption and their public health implications. *Journal of the American Dietetic Association, 87,* 1357.

78. Recio, H. A., Savell, J. W., Branson, R. E., Cross, H. R., and Smith, G. C. (1987). Consumer ratings of restructured beef steaks manufactured to contain different residual contents of connective tissue. *Journal of Food Science, 52,* 1461.

79. Rhee, K. S. (1994). Reducing fat in ground meat cookery. *Food and Nutrition News, 66*(5), 37.

80. Sanderson, M., and Vail, G. E. (1963). Fluid content and tenderness of three muscles of beef cooked to three internal temperatures. *Journal of Food Science, 28,* 590.

81. Savell, J. W., Branson, R. E., Cross, H. R., Stiffler, D. M., Wise, J. W., Griffin, D. B., and Smith, G. C. (1987). National consumer retail beef study: Palatability evaluations of beef loin steaks that differed in marbling. *Journal of Food Science, 52,* 517.

82. Sebranek, J. G., Hunt, M. C., Cornforth, D. P., and Brewer, M. S. (2006). Carbon monoxide packaging of fresh meat. *Food Technology, 60*(5), 184.

83. Shorthose, W. R., and Harris, P. V. (1990). Effect of animal age on the tenderness of selected beef muscles. *Journal of Food Science, 55,* 1.

84. Smith, G. C., Carpenter, Z. L., Cross, H. R., Murphey, C. E., Abraham, H. C., Savell, J. W., Davis, G. W., Berry, B. W., and Parrish, F. C., Jr. (1984). Relationship of USDA marbling groups to palatability of cooked beef. *Journal of Food Quality, 7,* 289.

85. Tatum, J. D., Smith, G. C., and Carpenter, Z. L. (1982). Interrelationships between marbling, subcutaneous fat thickness and cooked beef palatability. *Journal of Animal Science, 54,* 777.

86. Troutt, E. S., Hunt, M. C., Johnson, D. E., Claus, J. R., Kastner, C. L., and Kropf, D. H. (1992). Characteristics of low-fat ground beef containing texture-modifying ingredients. *Journal of Food Science, 52,* 19.

87. Troutt, E. S., Hunt, M. C., Johnson, D. E., Claus, J. R., Kastner, C. L., Kropf, D. H., and Stroda, S. (1992). Chemical, physical, and sensory characterization of ground beef containing 5 to 30 percent fat. *Journal of Food Science, 57,* 25.

88. U.S. Department of Agriculture. (1995, July). *How to buy meat.* Home and Garden Bulletin Number 265.

89. U.S. Department of Agriculture. (2002, September). "News Release: USDA Strengthens Food Safety Policies."

Release No. 0405.02. Retrieved September 26, 2002, from http://www.usda.gov/news/releases/2002/09/0405.htm

90. U.S. Department of Agriculture, Agricultural Research Service. (2006). "USDA National Nutrient Database for Standard Reference," Release 19. Retrieved August 14, 2007, from http://www.ars.usda.gov/main/site_main.htm?modecode=12354500

91. U.S. Department of Agriculture, Economic Research Service. (2007). "Data Sets. Food Availability: Custom Queries." Retrieved August 3, 2007, from http://www.ers.usda.gov/data/foodconsumption/FoodAvailQueriable.aspx

92. U.S. Department of Agriculture, Food Safety Inspection Service. (1998, March). "Special Survey on Humane Slaughter and Ante-Mortem Inspection." Retrieved September 3, 2007, from http://www.fsis.usda.gov/oa/pubs/antemort.pdf

93. U.S. Department of Agriculture, Food Safety and Inspection Service. (2000, May). "Focus on: Bison." Retrieved January 9, 2003, from http://www.fsis.usda.gov/OA/pubs/focusbison.htm

94. U.S. Department of Agriculture, Food Safety and Inspection Service. (2000, May). "Focus on: Lamb . . . From Farm to Table." Retrieved January 9, 2003, from http://www.fsis.usda.gov/OA/pubs/focuslamb.htm

95. U.S. Department of Agriculture, Food Safety and Inspection Service. (2000, July). "Focus on: Slow Cooker Safety." Retrieved January 9, 2003, from http://www.fsis.usda.gov/OA/pubs/slocookr.htm

96. U.S. Department of Agriculture, Food Safety and Inspection Service. (2001, June). "Fact Sheets: Key Facts: Humane Slaughter." Retrieved September 3, 2007, from http://www.fsis.usda.gov/Fact_Sheets/Key_Facts_Humane_Slaughter/index.asp

97. U.S. Department of Agriculture, Food Safety and Inspection Service. (2003, February). "Focus on Beef . . . From Farm to Table." Retrieved March 18, 2008, from http://www.fsis.usda.gov/Fact_Sheets/Beef_from_Farm_to_Table/index.asp

98. U.S. Department of Agriculture, Food Safety and Inspection Service. (2002, July). "Focus on Ground Beef." Retrieved August 10, 2007, from http://www.fsis.usda.gov/Fact_Sheets/Ground_Beef_and_Food_Safety/index.asp

99. U.S. Department of Agriculture, Food Safety and Inspection Service. (2006, October). "Meat Preparation: Veal from Farm to Table." Retrieved September 3, 2007, from http://www.fsis.usda.gov/Fact_Sheets/Veal_from_Farm_to_Table/index.asp

100. U.S. Department of Agriculture, Food Safety and Inspection Service. (2003, February). "Safety of Fresh Pork . . . From Farm to Table." Retrieved September 3, 2007, from http://www.fsis.usda.gov/Fact_Sheets/Pork_from_Farm_to_Table/index.asp

101. U.S. Department of Agriculture, Food Safety and Inspection Service. (2003, February). "Fact Sheets: Beef . . . From Farm to Table." Retrieved August 10, 2007, from http://www.fsis.usda.gov/Fact_Sheets/Beef_from_Farm_to_Table/index.asp

102. U.S. Department of Agriculture, Food Safety and Inspection Service. (2005, January). "Livestock Inspector Training." Retrieved September 3, 2007, from http://www.fsis.usda.gov/PDF/LSIT_HumaneHandling.pdf

103. U.S. Department of Agriculture, Food Safety and Inspection Service. (2007, February). "Timeline of events related to *E. coli* 0157:H7." Retrieved March 18, 2008, from http://www.fsis.usda.gov/Science/Ecoli_0157_Timeline/index.asp

104. US. Department of Agriculture, Food Safety Inspection Service. (2007, April). "Fact Sheets: Ham and Food Safety." Retrieved September 29, 2007, from http://www.fsis.usda.gov/Fact_Sheets/Ham/index.asp

105. U.S. Department of Agriculture, Food Safety and Inspection Service. (2007, April). "Fact Sheets: Water in Meat and Poultry." Retrieved August 10, 2007, from http://www.fsis.usda.gov/Fact_Sheets/Water_in_Meats/index.asp

106. U.S. Department of Agriculture, Food Safety and Inspection Service. (2007, May). "Meat Preparation: Lamb from Farm to Fork." Retrieved September 3, 2007, from http://www.fsis.usda.gov/Fact_Sheets/Lamb_from_Farm_to_Table/index.asp

107. U.S. Department of Agriculture, Food Safety and Inspection Service. (2008, January). "Fact Sheets: The Color of Meat and Poultry." Retrieved March 18, 2008, from http://www.fsis.usda.gov/Fact_Sheets/Color_of_Meat_&_Poultry/index.asp

108. U.S. Department of Health and Human Services. (2001, August). "Federal Agencies Take Special Precautions to Keep "Mad Cow Disease" Out of the United States." Retrieved June 23, 2002, from http://www.hhs.gov/news/press/2001pres/01fsbse.html

109. U.S. Food and Drug Administration. (2002, February). "Keeping the U.S. Free of "Mad Cow Disease—FDA's Actions to Keep Out Disease That's Stalked Europe." Retrieved November 15, 2002, from http://www.fda.gov/opacom/factsheets/justthefacts/8BSE.html

110. Vickers, Z. M., and Wang, J. (2002). Liking of ground beef patties is not affected by irradiation. *Journal of Food Science*, *67*, 380–383.

111. Voris, H. H., and van Duyne, F. O. (1979). Low wattage microwave cooking of top round roasts: Energy consumption, thiamin content and palatability. *Journal of Food Science*, *44*, 1447.

112. Warriss, P. D. (2000). *Meat Science: An Introductory Text*. New York: CABI Publishing.

113. Yu, L. P., and Lee, Y. B. (1986). Effects of postmortem pH and temperature on bovine muscle structure and meat tenderness. *Journal of Food Science*, *51*, 774.

Chapter 26

1. Aleixo, J. A. G., Swaminathan, B., Jamesen, K. S., and Pratt, D. E. (1985). Destruction of pathogenic bacteria in turkeys roasted in microwave ovens. *Journal of Food Science*, *50*, 873.

2. Brewer, V. "An Introduction to Chicken Production: A Brief Insight into the Modern Chicken and Egg Industries." Retrieved December 29, 2007, from http://www.nationalchickencouncil.com/consumerinfo/docs/Introductionto ChickenProduction.pdf

3. Cunningham, F. E., and Tiede, L. M. (1981). Influence of batter viscosity on breading of chicken drumsticks. *Journal of Food Science*, *46*, 1950.

4. Deethardt, D., Burrill, L. M., Schneider, K., and Carlson, C. W. (1971). Foil-covered versus open-pan procedure for roasting turkey. *Journal of Food Science*, *36*, 624.

5. Demetrakakes, P. (1997). Speeding pullets. *Food Processing, 58*(9), 67.

6. Durham, S. (2002). It takes a tough scientist to make a tender (and juicy) chicken. *Agricultural Research Magazine, 50*(2).

7. Hatch, V., and Stadelman, W. J. (1972). Bone darkening in frozen chicken broilers and ducklings. *Journal of Food Science, 37*, 850.

8. Hingley, A. (1999). *Campylobacter*: Low-profile bug is food poisoning leader. *FDA Consumer, 33*(5).

9. Hoke, I. M., McGeary, B. K., and Kleve, M. K. (1967). Effect of internal and oven temperatures on eating quality of light and dark meat turkey roasts. *Food Technology, 21*, 773.

10. Holownia, K., Chinnan, M. S., and Reynolds, A. E. (2003). Pink color defect in poultry white meat as affected by endogenous conditions. *Journal of Food Science, 68*(3), 742–747.

11. Labensky, S. R., and Hause, A. M. (2007). *On Cooking: A Textbook of Culinary Fundamentals*, 4th ed. Upper Saddle River, NJ: Pearson Prentice Hall.

12. Lamuka, P. O., Sunki, G. R., Chawan, C. B., Rao, D. R., and Shackelford, L. A. (1992). Bacteriological quality of freshly processed broiler chickens as affected by carcass pretreatment and gamma irradiation. *Journal of Food Science, 57*, 330.

13. Lindsay, R. E., Krissinger, W. A., and Fields, B. F. (1986). Microwave vs. conventional oven cooking of chicken: Relationship of internal temperature to surface contamination by *Salmonella*. *Journal of the American Dietetic Association, 86*, 373.

14. Meiners, C., Crews, M. G., and Ritchey, S. J. (1982). Yield of chicken parts: Proximate composition and mineral content. *Journal of the American Dietetic Association, 81*, 435.

15. National Chicken Council. (2007). "Top 25 Broiler Producing States." Retrieved December 28, 2007, from http://www.nationalchickencouncil.com/statistics/stat_detail.cfm?id=9

16. National Chicken Council. (n.d.). *Chicken: Consumer's Guide to Buying, Preparing, Storing, Serving, Enjoying.* Washington, DC: Author.

17. National Turkey Federation. (2002). "Consumer Statistics." Retrieved January 17, 2003, from http://www.eatturkey.com/consumer/stats/stats.html

18. National Turkey Federation. (2004). "Brine Roasted Turkey." Retrieved December 28, 2007, from http://www.eatturkey.com/consumer/cookinfo/brine.html

19. North American Meat Processors Association (NAMP). (2007). *The Meat Buyer's Guide.* Hoboken, NJ: John Wiley & Sons, Inc.

20. Proctor, V. A., and Cunningham, F. E. (1983). Composition of broiler meat as influenced by cooking methods and coating. *Journal of Food Science, 48*, 1696.

21. Putnam, J. J., and Allshouse, J. E. (1999). *Food consumption, prices, and expenditures, 1970–1997.* Food and Rural Economics Division, Economic Research Service, U.S. Department of Agriculture. Statistical Bulletin No. 965.

22. Smith, D. M., and Alvarez, V. B. (1988). Stability of vacuum cook-in-bag turkey breast rolls during refrigerated storage. *Journal of Food Science, 53*, 46.

23. Suderman, D. R., and Cunningham, F. E. (1980). Factors affecting adhesion of coating to poultry skin, effect of age, method of chilling, and scald temperature on poultry skin ultrastructure. *Journal of Food Science, 45*, 444.

24. U.S. Department of Agriculture, Economic Research Service. (2006). "Data Sets. Food Availability: Custom Queries." Retrieved December 30, 2007, from http://www.ers.usda.gov/Data/foodconsumption/FoodAvailQueriable.aspx

25. U.S. Department of Agriculture, Food Safety and Inspection Service. (1999, October). "The Poultry Label Says 'Fresh.'" Retrieved January 14, 2003, from http://fsis.usda.gov/OA/pubs/freshlabel.htm

26. U.S. Department of Agriculture, Food Safety and Inspection Service. (2001, January). "Meat and Poultry Labeling Terms." Retrieved January 14, 2003, from http://fsis.usda.gov/OA/pubs/lablterm.htm

27. U.S. Department of Agriculture, Food Safety and Inspection Service. (2001, April). "USDA Rule on Retained Water in Meat and Poultry." Retrieved January 14, 2003, from http://fsis.usda.gov/oa/background/waterretention.html

28. U.S. Department of Agriculture, Food Safety and Inspection Service. (2001, October). "Turkey . . . From Farm to Freezer." Retrieved December 28, 2007 from http://www.fsis.usda.gov/Fact_Sheets/Turkey_from_Farm_to_Freezer/index.asp

29. U.S. Department of Agriculture, Food Safety and Inspection Service. (2006, April). "Duck and Goose from Farm to Table." Retrieved December 28, 2007, from http://www.fsis.usda.gov/Fact_Sheets/Duck_&_Goose_from_Farm_to_Table/index.asp

30. U.S. Department of Agriculture, Food Safety and Inspection Service. (2006, April). "Focus on: Chicken." Retrieved December 30, 2007, from www.fsis.usda.gov/Fact_Sheets/Chicken_Food_Safety_Focus/index.asp

31. U.S. Department of Agriculture, Food Safety and Inspection Service. (2006, April). "Food Safety of Turkey . . . From Farm to Table." Retrieved December 28, 2007, from http://www.fsis.usda.gov/Fact_Sheets/Turkey_from_Farm_to_Table/index.asp

32. U.S. Department of Agriculture, Food Safety and Inspection Service. (2006, April). "Single Minimum Internal Temperature Established for Cooked Poultry." Retrieved May 20, 2006, from http://www.fsis.usda.gov/News_&_Events/NR_040506_01/index.asp

33. U.S. Department of Agriculture, Food Safety and Inspection Service. (2006, July). "Let's Talk Turkey—A Consumer Guide to Safely Roasting a Turkey." Retrieved December 28, 2007, from http://www.fsis.usda.gov/Fact_Sheets/Lets_Talk_Turkey/index.asp

34. U.S. Department of Agriculture, Food Safety and Inspection Service. (2006, October). "Turkey: Alternate Routes to the Table." Retrieved December 28, 2007, from http://www.fsis.usda.gov/Fact_Sheets/Turkey_Alt_Routes/index.asp

35. Woodburn, M. (1989). Myth: Wash poultry before cooking. *Diary, Food, and Environmental Sanitation, 9*, 65–67.

Chapter 27

1. American Heart Association. (2007). "Fish, Levels of Mercury and Omega-3 Fatty Acids." Retrieved January 21, 2008,

from http://www.americanheart.org/print_presenter.jhtml?identifier=3013797

2. Brody, A. L. (2001). Is something fishy about packaging? *Food Technology, 55*(4), 97–98.

3. Crawford, L. M. (2004, March). "Fish Is an Important Part of a Balanced Diet." Retrieved January 5, 2008, from http://www.fda.gov/oc/opacom/hottopics/mercury/mercuryop-ed.html

4. Educational Foundation of the National Restaurant Association. (2006). *ServSafe Coursebook*, 4th ed. Chicago, IL: National Restaurant Association.

5. Flick, G. J. (2002). U.S. aquaculture is fighting an upstream battle. *Food Technology, 56*(9), 124.

6. Foulke, J. (1994). Mercury in fish. *FDA Consumer, 28*(7), 5.

7. Hearn, T. L., Sgoutas, S. A., Hearn, J. A., and Sgoutas, D. S. (1987). Polyunsaturated fatty acids and fat in fish flesh for selecting species for health benefits. *Journal of Food Science, 52*, 1209.

8. Institute of Medicine. (2006, October). "Seafood Choices: Balancing Benefits and Risks." Retrieved January 18, 2008, from http://www.nmfs.noaa.gov/fishwatch/docs/seafood_choices.pdf

9. Karmas, E., and Lauber, E. (1987). Novel products from underutilized fish using combined processing technology. *Journal of Food Science, 52*, 7.

10. Kurtzweil, P. (1997). Critical steps toward safer seafood. *FDA Consumer, 31*(7), 10.

11. Labensky, S. R., and Hause, A. M. (2007). *On Cooking: A Textbook of Culinary Fundamentals*, 4th ed. Upper Saddle River, NJ: Pearson Prentice Hall.

12. Lee, C. M. (1984). Surimi process technology. *Food Technology, 38*(11), 69.

13. Lee, C. M., and Toledo, R. T. (1984). Comparison of shelf life and quality of mullet stored at zero and subzero temperature. *Journal of Food Science, 49*, 317.

14. MacDonald, G. A., and Lanier, T. (1991). Carbohydrates as cryoprotectants for meats and surimi. *Food Technology, 45*(3), 150.

15. Martin, R. E. (1988). Seafood products, technology, and research in the U.S. *Food Technology, 42*(3), 58.

16. Morissey, M. T. (2006). Mercury in seafood: Facts and discrepancies. *Food Technology, 6*(8), 132.

17. Mozaffarian, D., Bryson, C. L., Lemaitre, R. N., Burke, G. L., and Siscovick, D. S. (2005). Fish intake and risk of incident heart failure. *Journal of the American College of Cardiology, 45*(12), 2015–2121.

18. Mozaffarian, D., and Rimm, E. B. (2006). Fish intake, contaminants, and human health: Evaluating the risks and benefits. *The Journal of the American Medical Association, 296*, 1885–1899.

19. National Fisheries Institute, Inc. (2003). "About Our Industry: Harvesting." Retrieved January 20, 2003, from http://www.nfi.org/?a=about&b=Harvesting

20. National Fisheries Institute, Inc. (2007). "Top 10 U.S. Consumption by Species Chart." Retrieved January 4, 2008, from http://www.aboutseafood.com/media/top_10.cfm

21. Omaye, S. T. (2001). Shark-fin soup and methylmercury: To eat or not to eat. *Food Technology, 55*(10), 26.

22. Pew Initiative on Food and Biotechnology. (2003). "Biotech and the Deep Blue Sea." Retrieved February 1, 2003, from http://pewagbiotech.org/buzz/display/php3?storyID=47

23. Pew Initiative on Food and Biotechnology. (2003). "Future Fish: Issues in Science and Regulation of Transgenic Fish." Retrieved February 1, 2003, from http://pewagbiotech.org/research/fish

24. Regenstein, J. M. (1986). The potential for minced fish. *Food Technology, 40*(3), 101.

25. Regenstein, J. M. (2004). Total utilization of fish. *Food Technology, 58*(3), 28–30.

26. Seafood Business. (2005). *Seafood Handbook*. Portland, ME: Diversified Business Communications.

27. U.S. Department of Agriculture, Economic Research Service. "Data Sets. Food Availability: Custom Queries." Retrieved January 15, 2007, from http://www.ers.usda.gov/Data/foodconsumption/FoodAvailQueriable.aspx

28. U.S. Department of Health and Human Services and U.S. Environmental Protection Agency. (2004, March). "What You Need to Know about Mercury in Fish and Shellfish." Retrieved January 4, 2008, from http://www.cfsan.fda.gov/~dms/admehg3.html

29. U.S. Food and Drug Administration. (2001, February). "FDA's Seafood HACCP Program: Mid-Course Correction." Retrieved June 23, 2002, from http://www.cfsan.fda.gov/~comm/shaccp1.html

30. U.S. Food and Drug Administration. (2001, March). "An Important Message for Pregnant Women and Women of Childbearing Age Who May Become Pregnant about the Risks of Mercury in Fish." Retrieved January 21, 2003, from http://cfsan.fda.gov/~dms/admehg.html

31. U.S. Food and Drug Administration, Center for Food Safety and Applied Nutrition. (2005, October). "Search the Seafood List." Retrieved January 5, 2008, from http://www.cfsan.fda.gov/~frf/seaintro.html

32. U.S. Food and Drug Administration, Center for Food Safety and Applied Nutrition. (n.d.). Regulatory fish encyclopedia (RFE) browse page. Retrieved January 5, 2008, from http://www.cfsan.fda.gov/~frf/rfe0.html

33. U.S. National Oceanic and Atmospheric Administration. (2007). "U.S. Aquaculture." Retrieved January 31, 2008, from http://aquaculture2007.noaa.gov/pdf/bkgdAQsuccess607.pdf

34. U.S. National Oceanic and Atmospheric Administration. (2007, October). "Aquaculture in the United States." Retrieved January 31, 2008, from http://aquaculture.noaa.gov/us/welcome.html

35. U.S. National Oceanic and Atmospheric Administration, National Marine Fisheries Service. (n.d.) "FishWatch: U.S. Seafood Facts." Retrieved January 19, 2008, from http://www.nmfs.noaa.gov/fishwatch/about_us.htm

36. Wong, K., and Gill, T. A. (1987). Enzymatic determination of trimethylamine and its relationship to fish quality. *Journal of Food Science, 52*, 1.

Chapter 28

1. Bullers, A. C. (2002). Bottled water: Better than tap? *FDA Consumer Magazine, 36*(4).

2. Bunker, M. L., and McWilliams, M. (1979). Caffeine content of common beverages. *Journal of the American Dietetic Association, 74,* 28.

3. Chen, T., Lui, C. K. F., and Smith, C. H. (1983). Folacin content of tea. *Journal of the American Dietetic Association, 82,* 627.

4. Chou, K. H., and Bell, L. N. (2007). Caffeine content of prepackaged national-brand and private-label carbonated beverages. *Journal of Food Science, 72*(6), C337–C342.

5. Clark, J. P. (2004). Ozone—Cure for some sanitation problems. *Food Technology, 58*(4), 75–76.

6. Clark, J. P. (2007). Lessons from chocolate processing. *Food Technology, 61*(12), 89–91.

7. Clemons, R., and Pressman, P. (2005). Chocolate and affairs of the heart. *Food Technology, 59*(9), 21.

8. Coffee Review. (2008). "Processing: Fruit Removal and Drying." Retrieved March 19, 2008, from http://www.coffeereview.com/reference.cfm?ID=134

9. Coffee Review. (2008). "Buying and Storing: Keeping It Fresh." Retrieved March 19, 2008, from http://www.coffeereview.com/reference.cfm?ID=157

10. Coleman, E. (1991). Sports drink research. *Food Technology, 45*(3), 104.

11. Craig, W. J., and Nguyen, T. T. (1984). Caffeine and theobromine levels in cocoa and carob products. *Journal of Food Science, 49,* 302.

12. Disler, P. B., Lynch, S. R., Charlton, R. W., Torrance, J. D., and Bothwell, T. H. (1975). The effect of tea on iron absorption. *Gut, 16,* 193.

13. Dziezak, J. S. (1989). Ingredients for sweet success. *Food Technology, 43*(10), 94.

14. Eckert, M. and Riker, P. (2007). Overcoming challenges in functional beverages. *Food Technology, 61*(3), 20–26.

15. Electronic Code of Federal Regulations. (1995, November). "Title 21: Food and Drugs, Part 165. Beverages." Retrieved March 19, 2008, from http://ecfr.gpoaccess.gov/cgi/t/text/text-idx?c=ecfr&sid=3a07994396118e00ba4cae642612b1d9&rgn=div5&view=text&node=21:2.0.1.1.37&idno=21

16. Giese, J. (1995). Developments in beverage additives. *Food Technology, 49*(9), 64.

17. Giese, J. H. (1992). Hitting the spot: Beverages and beverage technology. *Food Technology, 46*(7), 70.

18. Grand, A. N., and Bell, L. N. (1997). Caffeine content of fountain and private-label store brand carbonated beverages. *Journal of the American Dietetic Association, 97,* 179.

19. Hollingsworth, P. (1997). Beverages: Redefining New Age. *Food Technology, 51*(8), 44.

20. Hollingsworth, P. (2000). Functional beverage juggernaut faces tighter regulations. *Food Technology, 54*(11), 50–54.

21. Hollingsworth, P. (2002). Burgers or biscotti? The fast-food market is changing. *Food Technology, 56*(9), 20.

22. Hollingsworth, P. (2002). Profits pouring from bottled water. *Food Technology, 56*(5), 18.

23. Hughes, W. J., and Thorpe, T. M. (1987). Determination of organic acids and sucrose in roasted coffee by capillary gas chromatography. *Journal of Food Science, 52,* 1078.

24. Institute of Food Technologists' Expert Panel on Food Safety and Nutrition. (1987). Evaluation of caffeine safety. *Food Technology, 41*(6), 105.

25. Kanter, M. A. (2005). Energy drinks: A lot of "bull." *Food Technology, 59*(12), 104.

26. Kolpan, S., Smith, B. H., and Weiss, M. A. (2002). *Exploring Wine: The Culinary Institute of America's Complete Guide to the Wines of the World,* 2nd ed. New York: John Wiley & Sons, Inc.

27. Kurtzweil, P. (1997). Dieter's brews make tea time a dangerous affair. *FDA Consumer, 31*(5), 6.

28. Labensky, S. R., and Hause, A. M. (2003). *On Cooking: A Textbook of Culinary Fundamentals,* 3rd ed. Upper Saddle River, NJ: Pearson Prentice Hall.

29. Labensky, S. R., and Hause, A. M. (2007). *On Cooking: A Textbook of Culinary Fundamentals,* 4th ed. Upper Saddle River, NJ: Pearson Prentice Hall.

30. Lal, G. G. (2007). Getting specific with functional. *Food Technology, 61*(12), 24–31.

31. Ohr, L. M. (2004). All tea'd up. *Food Technology, 58*(7), 71–72.

32. Ohr, L. M. (2007). Energy boosters. *Food Technology, 61*(4), 69–73

33. Pszczola, D. E. (1997). The bloom is off the chocolate. *Food Technology, 51*(3), 28.

34. Pszczola, D. E. (1999). Sipping into the mainstream. *Food Technology, 53*(11), 78–92.

35. Pszczola, D. E. (2001). How ingredients help solve beverage problems. *Food Technology, 55*(10), 61–74.

36. Pszczola, D. E. (2006). Thinking outside the box (of chocolates). *Food Technology, 60*(9), 50–61.

37. Sakano, T., Yamamura, K., Tamon, H., Miyahara, M., and Okazaki, M. (1996). Improvement of coffee aroma by removal of pungent volatiles using A-type zeolite. *Journal of Food Science, 61,* 473.

38. Schenker, S., Heinemann, C., Huber, M., Pompizzi, R., Perren, R., and Escher, F. (2002). Impact of roasting conditions on the formation of aroma compounds in coffee beans. *Journal of Food Science, 67,* 60–66.

39. Segal, M. (1996). Tea, a story of serendipity. *FDA Consumer, 30*(2), 22.

40. Segall, S., Silver, C., and Bacino, S. (1970). The effect of reheating upon the organoleptic and analytical properties of beverage coffee. *Food Technology, 24*(11), 54.

41. Sivetz, M. (1972). How acidity affects coffee flavor. *Food Technology, 26*(5), 70.

42. Tarver, T. (2007). Scientific status summary. "Just add water": Regulating and protecting the most common ingredient. *Journal of Food Science, 73*(1), R1–R13.

43. Tea Association of the U.S.A. Inc. (2007). "Tea Fact Sheet." Retrieved March 19, 2008, from http://www.teausa.com/general/501g.cfm

44. U.S. Department of Agriculture, Economic Research Service. (2007). "Food Availability (Per Capita) Data System." Retrieved March 15, 2008, from http://ers.usda.gov/data/FoodConsumption/

Chapter 29

1. American Dietetic Association. (2003). Position of the American Dietetic Association: Food irradiation. *Journal of the American Dietetic Association. 100,* 246–253.

2. Baldwin, E. A., Nisperos, M. O., Hagenmaier, R. D., and Baker, R. A. (1997). Use of lipids in coatings for food products. *Food Technology, 51*(6), 56.

3. Blumenthal, D. (1990). *Food irradiation*. Department of Health and Human Services Publication No. (FDA) 91–2241.

4. Brody, A. L. (1996). Integrating aseptic and modified atmosphere packaging to fulfill a vision of tomorrow. *Food Technology, 50*(4), 56.

5. Brody, A. L. (2000). Has the stand-up flexible pouch come of age? *Food Technology, 54*(7), 94–95.

6. Brody, A. L. (2000). Smart packaging becomes Intelli-pac™. *Food Technology, 54*(6), 104–107.

7. Brody, A. L. (2000). The when and why of aseptic packaging. *Food Technology, 54*(9), 101–102.

8. Brody, A. L. (2002). Flavor scalping: Quality loss due to packaging. *Food Technology, 56*(6), 124–125.

9. Brody, A. L. (2002). Food canning in the 21st century. *Food Technology, 56*(3), 75–78.

10. Cabes, L. J., Jr. (1985). Plastic packaging used in retort processing: Control of key parameters. *Food Technology, 39*(12), 57.

11. Clark, J. P. (2002). Drying still being actively researched. *Food Technology, 56*(9), 97–101.

12. Clausen, S., Barclay, M. J. A., and Wolf-Novak, L. C. (1986). Food packaging: A consideration for procurement. *Journal of the American Dietetic Association, 86*, 362.

13. Delves-Broughton, J. (1990). Nisin and its uses as a food preservative. *Food Technology, 44*(11), 100.

14. Gee, M., Farkas, D., and Rahman, A. R. (1977). Some concepts for the development of intermediate moisture foods. *Food Technology, 31*(4), 58.

15. Giese, J. (1994). Antimicrobials: Assuring food safety. *Food Technology, 48*(6), 102.

16. Henkel, J. (1998). Irradiation: A safe measure for safer food. *FDA Consumer, 32*(3), 12.

17. Hintlian, C. B., and Hotchkiss, J. H. (1986). The safety of modified atmosphere packaging: A review. *Food Technology, 40*(12), 70.

18. Institute of Food Technologists' Expert Panel on Food Safety and Nutrition. (1986). Effects of food processing on nutritive values. *Food Technology, 40*(12), 109.

19. Institute of Food Technologists' Expert Panel on Food Safety and Nutrition. (1988). Migration of toxicants, flavors, and odor-active substances from flexible packaging materials to food. *Food Technology, 42*(7), 95.

20. Ito, K. A., and Stevenson, K. E. (1984). Sterilization of packaging materials using aseptic systems. *Food Technology, 38*(3), 60.

21. Kester, J. J., and Fennema, O. R. (1986). Edible films and coatings: A review. *Food Technology, 40*(12), 47.

22. Krochta, J. M., and De Mulder-Johnston, C. (1997). Edible and biodegradable polymer films: Challenges and opportunities. *Food Technology, 51*(2), 61.

23. Lisiecki, R., Spisak, A., Pawloski, C., and Stefanovic, S. (1990). Aseptic package addresses a variety of needs. *Food Technology, 44*(6), 126.

24. Lusk, J. L., Fox, J. A., and McIlvain, C. L. (1999). Consumer acceptance of irradiated meat. *Food Technology, 53*(3), 56–59.

25. Marsh, K., and Bugusu, B. (2007). Food packaging—Roles, materials, and environmental issues. *Journal of Food Science, 72*(3), R39–R55.

26. Marth, E. H. (1998). Extended shelf life refrigerated foods: Microbiological quality and safety. *Food Technology, 52*(2), 57.

27. Mermelstein, N. H. (1997). High-pressure processing reaches the U.S. market. *Food Technology, 51*(6), 95.

28. Mermelstein, N. H. (1998). Interest in pulsed electric field processing increases. *Food Technology, 52*(1), 81.

29. Mermelstein, N. H. (1999). Magnetic resonance imaging provides 100 percent inspection. *Food Technology, 53*(11), 94–97.

30. Mertens, B., and Knorr, D. (1992). Developments of non-thermal processes for food preservation. *Food Technology, 46*(5), 124.

31. Meyer, R. S., Cooper, K. L., Knorr, D., and Lelieveld, H. L. M. (2000). High pressure sterilization of foods. *Food Technology, 54*(11), 67–72.

32. Olson, D. G. (1998). Irradiation of food. *Food Technology, 52*(1), 56.

33. Palaniappan, S., and Sizer, C. E. (1997). Aseptic process validated for foods containing particulates. *Food Technology, 51*(8), 60.

34. Pohlman, A. J., Wood, O. B., and Mason, A. C. (1994). Influence of audiovisuals and food samples on consumer acceptance of food irradiation. *Food Technology, 48*(12), 46.

35. Pszczola, D. E. (1995). Packaging takes an active approach. *Food Technology, 49*(8), 104.

36. Pszczola, D. E. (1997). 20 ways to market the concept of food irradiation. *Food Technology, 51*(2), 46.

37. Resurreccion, A. V. A., and Galvez, F. C. F. (1999). Will consumers buy irradiated beef? *Food Technology, 53*(3), 52–55.

38. Sizer, C. E., Balasubramaniam, V. M., and Ting, E. (2002). Validating high pressure processes for low-acid foods. *Food Technology, 56*(2), 36–42.

39. Smith, J. P., Ramaswamy, H. S., and Simpson, B. K. (1990). Developments in food packaging technology. Part 1: Processing/cooking considerations. *Trends in Food Science and Technology, 1*(5), 107.

40. Smith, J. P., Ramaswamy, H. S., and Simpson, B. K. (1990). Developments in food packaging technology. Part 2: Storage aspects. *Trends in Food Science and Technology, 1*(5), 111.

41. Smith, J. S., and Pillai, S. (2004). Scientific status summary: Irradiation and food safety. *Food Technology, 58*(11), 48–55.

42. Sunderland, J. E. (1982). An economic study of microwave freeze-drying. *Food Technology, 36*(2), 50.

43. Tauxe, R. V. (2001). Food safety and irradiation: Protecting the public from foodborne infections. *Emerging Infectious Diseases, 7*(3), 516–521. Retrieved April 5, 2008, from http://www.cdc.gov/ncidod/eid/vol7no3_supp/tauxe.htm

44. Tuomy, J. M., and Young, R. (1982). Retort-pouch packaging of muscle foods for the Armed Forces. *Food Technology, 36*(2), 68.

45. U.S. Department of Agriculture. (2005). "Fact Sheets: Irradiation and Food Safety." Retrieved April 5, 2008, from http://www.fsis.usda.gov/Fact_Sheets/Irradiation_and_Food_Safety/index.asp

Chapter 30

1. Andress, E. L., and Harrison, J. A. (1999). *So easy to preserve*, Bulletin 989, 4th ed. Athens, GA: Cooperative Extension Service, The University of Georgia/Athens.

2. Barrett, D. M., and Theerakulkait, C. (1995). Quality indicators in blanched, frozen, stored vegetables. *Food Technology, 49*(1) 62.

3. Bramsnaes, F. (1981). Maintaining the quality of frozen foods during distribution. *Food Technology, 35*(4), 38.

4. Brody, A. L. (1996). Chills: A chronology of IFT's refrigerated and frozen foods division. *Food Technology, 48*(12), 50.

5. Brody, A. L. (2001). What's active about intelligent packaging. *Food Technology, 55*(6), 75–78.

6. Clark, J. P. (2002). Developments in food freezing. *Food Technology, 56*(10), 76–77.

7. Corcos, A. (1975). A note on the early life of Nicolas Appert. *Food Technology, 29*(5), 114.

8. Cowell, N. D. (1995). Who introduced the tin can?—A new candidate. *Food Technology, 49*(12), 61.

9. Cowell, N. D. (2007). More light on the dawn of canning. *Food Technology, 61*(5), 40–45.

10. Feeney, R. E., and Yeh, Y. (1993). Antifreeze proteins: Properties, mechanism of action, and possible applications. *Food Technology, 47*(1), 82.

11. Goldblith, S. A. (1972). Controversy over the autoclave. *Food Technology, 26*(12), 62.

12. Jarden Home Brands. (2005). *Ball Blue Book of Preserving.* Muncie, IN: Author.

13. Kimball, R. N., and Heyliger, T. L. (1990). Verifying the operation of steam retorts. *Food Technology, 44*(12), 100.

14. Lazaridis, H. N., and Sander, E. H. (1988). Home-canning of food: Effect of a higher process temperature (121° C) on the quality of low-acid foods. *Journal of Food Science, 53*, 985.

15. Luallen, T. E. (1994). The use of starches in frozen food formulation. *Food Technology, 48*(5), 39.

16. Mermelstein, N. H. (2001). What's happening in freezing research. *Food Technology, 55*(10), 81–83.

17. Park, D. J., Cabes, L. J., Jr., and Collins, K. M. (1990). Determining temperature distribution in rotary, full-immersion, hot-water sterilizers. *Food Technology, 44*(12), 113.

18. Poulsen, K. P. (1986). Optimization of vegetable blanching. *Food Technology, 40*(6), 122.

19. Reid, D. S. (1990). Optimizing the quality of frozen foods. *Food Technology, 44*(7), 78.

20. Roop, R. A., and Nelson, P. E. (1982). Processing retort pouches in conventional sterilizers. *Journal of Food Science, 47*, 303.

21. Roos, Y. H., Karel, M., and Kokini, J. L. (1996). Glass transitions in low moisture and frozen foods: Effects on shelf life and quality. *Food Technology, 50*(11), 95.

22. Taoukis, P. S., Fu, B., and Labuza, T. P. (1991). Time-temperature indicators. *Food Technology, 45*(10), 70.

23. Thole, C., and Gregoire, M. B. (1992). Time-temperature relationships during freezing of packaged meals in feeding programs for the elderly. *Journal of the American Dietetic Association, 92*, 350.

24. U.S. Department of Agriculture. (1994, September). *Complete guide to home canning.* Agriculture Information Bulletin No. 539.

25. Williams, J. R., Steffe, J. F., and Black, J. R. (1981). Economic comparison of canning and retort pouch systems. *Journal of Food Science, 47*, 284.

WEB RESOURCES

Chapter 1

U.S. government individual dietary recommendations.

http://www.mypyramid.gov

U.S. government information about the *2005 Dietary Guidelines*.

http://www.healthierus.gov/dietaryguidelines

Healthy People 2010.

http://www.health.gov

Institute of Food Technologists.

http://www.ift.org

The American Dietetic Association.

http://www.eatright.org

National Restaurant Association information about meals consumed in restaurants and other data about Americans' eating habits.

http://www.restaurant.org

Chapter 2

U.S. Department of Agriculture. Has a variety of food-related topics including "food consumption" for food disappearance data. Also data and articles in the publication *Amber Waves* are available on this website.

http://www.usda.gov

The Economic Research Service, under the U.S. Department of Agriculture, provides on-line access to the "food disappearance" or "food supply" data.

http://www.ers.usda.gov/Data/FoodConsumption/FoodAvailIndex.htm

USDA Food Surveys Research Group. Links for the "What We Eat in America" surveys, nutrient content of foods, and more.

http://www.ars.usda.gov/main/site_main.htm?modecode=12355000

National Aeronautics and Space Administration. Information about the space program and food in space.

http://www.nasa.gov

Chapter 3

U.S. Department of Agriculture. Topics related to food safety and food regulation.

http://www.usda.gov

Food and Drug Administration.

http://www.fda.gov

Food and Drug Administration, Center for Food Safety and Applied Nutrition. Information about a wide variety of topics pertaining to food safety and nutrition.

http://www.cfsan.fda.gov

Centers for Disease Control and Prevention. Foodborne illness outbreaks and information about microorganisms.

http://www.cdc.gov

Partnership for Food Safety Education. Information for consumers and educators about food safety.

http://www.fightbac.org

A gateway to U.S. government food-safety information.

http://www.foodsafety.gov

National Center for Home Food Preservation. Source for information about home canning and food preservation and includes links to government, university, and industry food preservation websites.

http://www.homecanning.com

Food Safety Network. Information for students, researchers, and consumers. Includes news releases on outbreaks, research, government oversight of food safety, and more.

http://www.foodsafetynetwork.ca/en/

Chapter 4

U.S. Food and Drug Administration and the FDA Center for Food Safety and Nutrition.

http://www.fda.gov and http://www.cfsan.fda.gov

U.S. Department of Agriculture. Addresses for the USDA Food Safety and Inspection Service and Agricultural Marketing Service (AMS). More information about the National Organic Program found on the AMS website.

http://www.usda.gov, http://www.fsis.usda.gov, and http://www.ams.usda.gov

Environmental Protection Agency.

http://www.epa.gov

Centers for Disease Control and Prevention.

http://www.cdc.gov

Chapter 5

American Association of Family and Consumer Sciences. Includes resources for home food preparation.

http://www.aafcs.org/

American National Standards Institute (ANSI). This private, nonprofit organization administers the U.S. voluntary standardization and conformity assessment system.

http://www.ansi.org/

National Institute of Standards and Technology, an agency of the Commerce Department's Technology Administration. Many links with metric conversions, educational resources, and other information about the use of metric (including food preparation applications).

http://ts.nist.gov/WeightsAndMeasures/Metric/mpo_home. cfm

U.S. Metric Association. A nonprofit organization that promotes the use of metric in the United States. Educational materials and links to other metric resources.

http://lamar.colostate.edu/~hillger/

Science Made Simple. Includes easy-to-use weight and measurement conversion calculator.

http://www.sciencemadesimple.com/conversions.html

Lists of sites providing recipes that may be of interest. In general, companies, associations, and sites affiliated with well-known magazines generally offer well-tested recipes.

http://www.cooksillustrated.com/Default.asp, http://www. epicurious.com, http://www.bettycrocker.com/, http:// www.bhg.com/, http://www.landolakes.com/, http:// www.mccormick.com/

Chapter 6

Cook's Illustrated. Has tests of cooking and food preparation equipment and the results.

http://www.cooksillustrated.com/testinghome.asp

Chapter 7

U.S. Food and Drug Administration, Center for Devices and Radiological Health. Information about FDA oversight of microwaves ovens.

http://www.fda.gov/cdrh/consumer/microwave.html

USDA Food Safety and Inspection Service. Information about cooking safely in microwave ovens.

http://www.fsis.usda.gov/Fact_Sheets/
Cooking_Safely_in_the_Microwave/index.asp

USDA Food Safety and Inspection Service and FDA Center for Food Safety and Applied Nutrition. Food safety information for cooking with a microwave oven.

http://www.foodsafety.gov/~fsg/fs-mwave.html

Chapter 8

American Spice Trade Association. A spice library, history, equivalency chart and other information about spices and spice trade.

http://astaspice.org

McCormick & Co., Inc. Featured is a spice encyclopedia, recipes, cooking tips, and other suggestions.

http://www.mccormick.com

ACH Food Companies, Inc. Information about spices and herbs.

http://www.spiceadvice.com

FDA's *"Everything" Added to Food in the United States* (EAFUS) Food Additive Database.

http://www.cfsan.fda.gov/~dms/eafus.html

Chapter 9

Nutrient Data Laboratory, U.S. Department of Agriculture, Agriculture Research Service. *USDA National Nutrient Database for Standard Reference, Release 20* may be searched online or software may be downloaded to search the database on your own computer.

http://www.ars.usda.gov/nutrientdata

Chapter 10

Food and Drug Administration, Center for Food Safety and Applied Nutrition. Information about trans fatty acids and labeling.

http://www.cfsan.fda.gov

American Heart Association.

http://www.americanheart.org

National Heart, Lung, and Blood Institute, National Institutes of Health. The National Cholesterol Education Program.

http://www.nhlbi.nih.gov/chd/

Fats of Life Newsletter. Information provided for consumers about dietary fats.

http://www.fatsoflife.com

Chapter 11

The Sugar Association. Information about processing, types of sugar, and cooking with sugar (including candy making).

http://www.sugar.org

American Sugar Alliance. Information about the U.S. sweetener industry.

http://www.sugaralliance.org

National Confectioners Association and Chocolate Manufacturers Association. FAQs about chocolate and candy.

http://www.candyusa.org/

Chapter 12

International Dairy Foods Association. Information about ice cream.

http://www.idfa.org

Dairy Science and Technology Department at the University of Guelph. Extensive information about ice cream preparation, manufacturer, ingredients, and quality.

http://www.foodsci.uoguelph.ca/dairyedu

National Dairy Council.

http://nationaldairycouncil.org

Chapter 13

National Starch and Chemical Company.

http://www.foodstarch.com/

A food starch dictionary.

http://www.foodinnovation.com/dictionary/a.asp

Corn Refiners Association. Information about corn wet milling and aspects of the corn refining industry.

http://www.corn.org

Chapter 14

Wheat Foods Council. Contains information about a variety of wheat foods including health information.

http://www.wheatfoods.org

Popcorn Board. Information about popcorn including recipes.

http://www.popcorn.org

National Pasta Association. Cooking tips, history, and recipes.

http://www.llovepasta.org

USA Rice Federation and Riceland Foods. Information about U.S. rice production, types of rice, and preparation of rice.

http://www.usarice.com and http://www.riceland.com

North American Millers' Association. Information about the milling of several different grains.

http://www.namamillers.org

Chapter 15

North American Millers' Association. Information about the milling of grains.

http://www.namamillers.org

Colorado State University Cooperative Extension Resource Center. High-altitude food preparation guidelines.

http://www.cerc.colostate.edu/titles/P41.html

Home Baking Association. Baking tips and resources for educators. Helpful materials for those teaching children how to bake.

http://homebaking.org

Chapter 16

Home Baking Association. Recipes, educator resources, and links to industry partners.

http://www.homebaking.org

American Institute of Baking (AIB) provides training, education, and conducts research for the baking industry.

http://www.aibonline.org/

Nestle USA. Features baking tips and recipes.

http://www.verybestbaking.com/

Land O'Lakes, Inc. A wide variety of recipes and food preparation information.

http://www.landolakes.com

Clabber Girl. Recipes and baking tips.

http://www.clabbergirl.com/

Chapter 17

Kansas Wheat Commission. Information about kinds of wheat and baking, along with bread recipes.

http://www.kswheat.com

Fleischmann's Yeast Company. Information, tips, and recipes (including bread machine recipes) for the beginning and experienced baker.

http://www.breadworld.com/

Red Star Yeast page. Recipes, the science of yeast, and baking tips.

http://www.redstaryeast.com

Home Baking Association. Recipes, educator resources, and links to industry partners.

http://www.homebaking.org

American Institute of Baking (AIB). AIB provides training, education, and conducts research for the baking industry.

http://www.aibonline.org/

Chapter 18

Colorado State University Cooperative Extension Resource Center. High altitude food preparation guide.

http://cerc.colostate.edu/titles/P41.html

Home Baking Association. Recipes, educator resources, and links to industry partners.

http://www.homebaking.org

Nestlé USA. Features baking tips and recipes.

http://www.verybestbaking.com/

Land O' Lakes, Inc. A wide variety of recipes and food preparation information.

www.landolakes.com

Betty Crocker, General Mills, Inc. Many home-sized recipes.

www.bettycrocker.com

Epicurious. A wide variety of recipes.

http://eat.epicurious.com

Splenda® brand no-calorie sweetener. Product information and recipes.

www.splenda.com

Chapter 20

The Produce for Better Health Foundation. Educational information promoting fruit and vegetable consumption.

http://www.fruitsandveggiesmorematters.org

Fruits and vegetable information developed in cooperation with several agencies and organizations. Features a fruit and a vegetable of the month and tips to promote fruit and vegetable consumption.

http://www.fruitsandveggiesmatter.gov/

U.S. Department of Agriculture. Individualized guidance on foods to consume based on the *2005 Dietary Guidelines for Americans*.

http://www.mypyramid.gov

Frieda's Specialty Produce Company. Credited with popularizing the kiwi fruit in the United States. Information about exotic fruits and vegetables, recipes, industry links, and products for purchase.

http://www.friedas.com/

California Artichoke Association. Recipes and preparation tips.

http://www.artichokes.org

Mushroom Council. Information about varieties of mushrooms and preparation.

http://www.mushroomcouncil.com

U.S. Potato Board. Recipes and information about potatoes.

http://www.uspotatoes.com

Idaho Potato Commission. Tips and recipes.

http://www.idahopotato.com/

United Soybean Board. A wide variety of information, including recipes that use soybeans.

http://www.soybean.org/ and http://www.unitedsoybean.org

Mori-Nu Company. Information about soy and tofu, including many recipes featuring tofu.

http://www.morinu.com/

U.S.A. Dry Pea and Lentil Council. Recipes, cooking tips, and information about varieties of dry peas and lentils.

http://www.pea-lentil.com/

Additional councils, commissions, and associations with information about other vegetables can be found by searching on the Internet.

Chapter 21

The Produce for Better Health Foundation. Educational information for promoting fruit and vegetable consumption.

http://www.fruitsandveggiesmorematters.org

Fruits and Veggies Matter. Developed in cooperation with several agencies and organizations. Features a fruit and a vegetable of the month and tips to promote fruit and vegetable consumption.

http://www.fruitsandveggiesmatter.gov/

U.S. Department of Agriculture. Provides individualized guidance on foods to consume based on the *2005 Dietary Guidelines for Americans*.

http://www.mypyramid.gov

Frieda's Specialty Product Company. Credited with popularizing the kiwi fruit in the United States. Information about exotic fruits and vegetables, recipes, industry links, and products for purchase.

http://www.friedas.com/

Dole Food Company, Inc. Many recipes, a kid's page, and produce information.

http://www.dole.com/

Washington Apple Commission. Features recipes, description of apple varieties, and crop statistics.

http://www.bestapples.com

Pear Bureau Northwest. Provides recipes and information about pears.

http://www.usapear.com/

Northwest Cherry Growers. Information about varieties of cherries.

http://www.nwcherries.com/

Sunkist Growers, Inc. Citrus fruit information and recipes.

http://www.sunkist.com/

California Strawberry Commission. Facts about strawberries and recipes.

http://www.calstrawberry.com/

California Cling Peach Board. Information for consumers, students, and industry as well as several recipes.

http://www.calclingpeach.com/

Florida Citrus. Recipes and citrus FAQ.

http://www.floridajuice.com/

Texas Produce Association. Information about several kinds of fruits as well as vegetables grown in Texas.

http://www.texasproduceassociation.com/

Chapter 22

Dole Food Company, Inc. Features salad recipes and other information.

http://www.dolesalads.com/

Gelatin Manufacturers Institute of America. Information and pictures about gelatin manufacture.

http://www.gelatin-gmia.com

Chapter 23

National Dairy Council.

http://www.nationaldairycouncil.org

American Dairy Association. Descriptions of types of cheese and recipes.

http://www.ilovecheese.com

Wisconsin Milk Marketing Board. Recipes, a cheese encyclopedia, and information about cheese making.

http://www.wisdairy.com

Chapter 24

American Egg Board. Recipes, food safety, nutrition, egg facts, and more.

http://www.aeb.org/

Chapter 25

U.S. Department of Agriculture. Information about the inspection and grading of meat.

http://www.usda.gov

U.S. Department of Agriculture. Meat preparation fact sheet with information about game such as venison, pheasant, wild boar, and other game animals.

http://www.fsis.usda.gov/Fact_Sheets/Farm_Raised_Game/index.asp

Food Safety Inspection Service, U.S. Department of Agriculture. Information about the inspection of meat.

http://www.fsis.usda.gov

Agricultural Marketing Service, U.S. Department of Agriculture. Information about the grading and marketing of meat.

http://www.ams.usda.gov

National Cattlemen's Beef Association. Recipes, nutrition, purchasing, storage, food safety and additional topics about beef and veal.

http://www.beef.org

National Pork Producers Council. Pork facts, figures, and recipes.

http://www.nppc.org/

National Pork Board. Features many recipes and other consumer tips about using pork.

http://www.otherwhitemeat.com

American Lamb Board. Recipes and information about lamb.

http://www.americanlambboard.org/

American Lamb Council. Many recipes using lamb.

http://www.lambinfo.com

National Hot Dog and Sausage Council. Many fun facts and trivia about hot dogs and sausages along with recipes.

http://www.hot-dog.org/

North American Meat Processors Association. This nonprofit industry organization publishes the NAMP *Meat Buyers Guide*.

http://www.meatami.com/

American Meat Institute. Meat and poultry association. Industry-related information.

http://www.namp.com/

Chapter 26

The National Chicken Council and the U.S. Poultry and Egg Association. Cooking tips, poultry statistics, nutrition information, and recipes.

http://www.eatchicken.com/

National Turkey Federation. Recipes, chef demonstrations, and other helpful information.

http://www.eatturkey.com/

Chapter 27

Center for Food Safety and Applied Nutrition, U.S. Food and Drug Administration. Links to many government documents relating to the regulation and food safety of seafood.

http://vm.cfsan.fda.gov/seafood1.html

Seafood Products Research Center, Center for Food Safety and Applied Nutrition. *Regulatory Fish Encyclopedia.* Photographs of many kinds of fish including the common and scientific names.

http://vm.cfsan.fda.gov/~frf/rfe0.html

National Oceanic and Atmospheric Administration (NOAA) Seafood Inspection Program. Through the 1946 Agricultural Marketing Act, NOAA provides a voluntary inspection service to the industry. Grading and certification services also are provided. Information about the seafood program and consumer tips for purchasing and storage of seafood.

http://www.noaa.gov/ and http://seafood.nmfs.noaa.gov/

Environmental Protection Agency. Information about water quality and fish advisories.

http://www.epa.gov

http://www.epa.gov/mercury/advisories.htm

http://www.epa.gov/waterscience/fish/advisories/2006/index.html

Alaska Seafood Marketing Institute. Recipes, nutrition information, industry statistics, and educator resources.

http://www.alaskaseafood.org/

Division of Florida Aquaculture and Florida Department of Agriculture and Consumer Services. Information about shellfish and other Florida aquaculture.

http://www.floridaaquaculture.com/ and http://www.fl-seafood.com/

National Fisheries Institute. Trade association. Industry information and statistics.

http://aboutseafood.com

Chapter 28

Tea Association, Tea Council, and Special Tea Institute. Information about tea.

http://www.teausa.com

National Coffee Association of USA, Inc. Information about the purchase, storage, and preparation of coffee as well as coffee drinking trends.

http://www.ncausa.org

Specialty Coffee Association.

http://www.scaa.org

Coffee Review. Information about coffee and coffee buying.

http://www.coffeereview.com/index.cfm

The World Cocoa Foundation. Background about the manufacture of cocoa including several pictures of cocoa processing.

http://www.chocolateandcocoa.org/

National Confectioner's Association and Chocolate Manufacturer's Association. FAQs about chocolate and candy.

http://www.candyusa.org/

Chapter 30

National Center for Home Food Preservation. This center was established through the Cooperative State Research, Education and Extension Service, U.S. Department of Agriculture (CSREES-USDA).

http://www.uga.edu/nchfp/

U.S. Department of Agriculture, National Agriculture Library. Web page entitled "Consumer Corner: Food Storage and Preservation" includes links to a number of food preservation resources.

http://fnic.nal.usda.gov/nal_display/index.php?info_center=4&tax_level=3&tax_subject=358&topic_id=1610&level3_id=5942&level4_id=0&level5_id=0&placement_default=0

Home Food Preservation. The USDA Complete Guide to Home Canning.

http://foodsafety.cas.psu.edu/canningguide.html

Jarden Home Brands. This company produces Ball® and Kerr® products.

http://www.freshpreserving.com/

β-amylase   an enzyme that hydrolyzes starch by breaking off two glucose units at a time, thus producing maltose

5′-ribonucleotides   compounds similar to the RNA found in all body cells; certain ones have been shown to act as flavor enhancers

5-log reduction   represents a reduction in organisms by a factor of 100,000-fold. This reduction represents a risk of less than one in 100,000. This reduction is accepted as making a product safe to eat when the pathogenic organism is one, such as salmonella, that requires a large number of microorganisms to cause illness.

acculturation   the adaptation of a cultural group that has moved into a new area or country to the practices common in the new location

adsorption   the collection of a substance on the surface of a particle or globule without being taken in and incorporated into the globule

aftertaste   a taste that remains in the mouth after a food has been swallowed

agglomerate   to gather into a cluster, mass, or ball

agglutination   the sticking together, as with glue

albumins   simple proteins that are soluble in water

alcohols   chemical compounds characterized by an –OH group

aldehydes   chemical compounds characterized by a $\overset{O}{\underset{}{\|}}$ group (–C–H)

alginate and carrageenan   vegetable gums produced from seaweed

amino acids   small organic molecules, containing both an amino group ($-NH_2$) and an organic acid group (–COOH), that constitute the basic building blocks of proteins

amino group   a chemical group ($-NH_2$) characteristic of all amino acids

amphiphilic   liking or being attracted to both water and fat

amylase   an enzyme that breaks down or hydrolyzes starch to produce dextrins, maltose, and glucose

amylopectin   a fraction of starch with a highly branched and bushy type of molecular structure

amylose   the long-chain or linear fraction of starch

anaphylactic shock   a multiple system reaction including the gastrointestinal tract, the skin, the respiratory tract, and the cardiovascular system that may be the result of a severe allergic reaction; severe hypotension and cardiovascular or respiratory collapse can occur within minutes, resulting in death

anaphylactoid reactions   generally involve several systems, including the gastrointestinal tract, the skin, the respiratory tract, and the cardiovascular system; death can occur within minutes of consuming an offending food

antioxidant   a substance that can stop the uptake of oxygen. For example, high-fat products develop off-flavors and off-odors due to the uptake of oxygen in a process called an oxidation reaction

antioxidants   a substance that retards or stops the development of oxidative rancidity; added to fatty foods in very small amounts

appetite   a desire or craving either for food in general or for some specific food

aromatic   having an aroma or fragrance; an ingredient added to enhance the natural aromas of food. Most herbs and spices, along with some vegetables, are aromatic.

aromatic compounds   compounds that have an aroma or odor

aseptic   free from disease-producing microorganisms; filling a container that has been previously sterilized without recontaminating either product or container is an aseptic process

aseptic canning   a process in which the food material and the container are sterilized separately, and the container is filled without recontamination

aseptic packaging   a process that involves sterilizing the product and the package separately, filling the package without recontaminating the product, and sealing

aspartame   a high-intensity sweetener with the trade name Nutrasweet™

astringency   the puckering, drawing, or shrinking sensation produced by certain compounds in food

atherogenic   capable of contributing to the development of atherosclerosis (fatty deposits in the walls of the arteries)

atmospheric pressure   downward pressure from the weight of the atmosphere (gas surrounding the earth); this pressure decreases at higher elevations

ATP   adenosine triphosphate, a compound containing high-energy phosphate bonds in which the body cell traps energy from the metabolism of carbohydrate, fat, or protein; the energy in ATP is then used to do mechanical or chemical work in the body

basted   food moistened with pan drippings, melted fats, or other liquids during the cooking process

beading   the appearance of tiny droplets of syrup on the surface of a baked meringue as it stands

biotechnology   the use of biological systems and organisms to produce goods and services; may include biology, genetics, and biochemistry processes

birefringence   the ability of a substance to refract light in two directions; this produces a dark cross on each starch granule when viewed with a polarizing microscope

blanch to heat for a few minutes by immersing in boiling water, surrounding with steam, or applying microwaves

botulinum toxin a very potent toxin produced by *Clostridium botulinum* bacteria; in a low-acid environment, the high temperatures achieved in a pressure canner are required for complete destruction of the spores of this microbe

botulism a serious illness resulting from consumption of a deadly toxin produced by the anaerobic bacterium *Clostridium botulinum*

bound water water that is held so tightly by another molecule (usually a large molecule such as a protein) that it no longer has the properties of free water

braise to cook meat or poultry slowly in a small amount of liquid or in steam in a covered utensil after first browning

brown roux equal parts, by weight, of flour and fat that are cooked together until a dark color and nutty aroma develop. A brown roux enhances the color and flavor of sauces and gravies.

buffer a substance that resists changes in pH

bulking agent a substance used in relatively small amounts to affect the texture and body of some manufactured foods made without sugar or with reduced amounts; it compensates to some degree for the nonsweetening effects of sugar in a food product

butyric acid a saturated fatty acid with four carbon atoms that is found in relatively large amounts in butter

calorie a unit of heat measurement; in this chapter, we are referring to the small calorie used in chemistry; the kilocalorie (1 kilocalorie is equal to 1000 small calories) is used in nutrition

capon a male bird castrated when young

caproic acid a saturated fatty acid with six carbon atoms; as a free fatty acid, it has an unpleasant odor

caramelization the development of brown color and caramel flavor as dry sugar is heated to a high temperature; chemical decomposition occurs in the sugar

carbonyl group a ketone ($C=O$) or an aldehyde ($HC=O$) group

carcinogen a cancer-causing substance

carotenes yellow-orange, fat-soluble pigments

carotenoid pigments fat-soluble, yellow-orange pigments that are produced by plants; may be stored in the fatty tissues of animals

carotenoids yellow-orange-red, fat-soluble pigments found in some plant materials such as fruits and vegetables; for example beta-carotene

casein a major protein found in milk

catalyst a substance that changes the rate of a chemical reaction without being used up in the reaction; enzymes are catalysts

catalyze to make a reaction occur at a more rapid rate by the addition of a substance, called a catalyst, which itself undergoes no permanent chemical change

cellulase and hemicellulase enzymes that hydrolyze cellulose and hemicellulose, respectively

certified colors synthetic colors tested on a batch-by-batch basis and certified by the FDA as having met set standards

chelate to attach or bind a substance and hold it tightly so it does not react as usual; for example, to bind iron and copper atoms and hold them so they cannot act as pro-oxidants

chicory a plant whose root is roasted and ground for use as a coffee substitute

chlorogenic acid polyphenolic organic acid

clarify to make clear a cloudy liquid such as heated soup stock by adding raw egg white and/or egg shell; as the proteins coagulate, they trap tiny particles from the liquid that can then be strained out

Clostridium botulinum a spore-forming, anaerobic bacterium that can produce a very potent toxin that causes botulism

coagulate to produce a semi-solid, firm mass or gel by denaturation of protein molecules followed by formation of new cross-links

coagulation usually a change in proteins after denaturation, with new bonds being formed between protein chains, resulting in precipitation or gel formation; often accomplished by heating

collagen a fibrous type of protein molecule found in the connective tissue of animals; produces gelatin when it is partially hydrolyzed

colloidal usually refers to the state of subdivision of dispersed particles; intermediate between very small particles in true solution and large particles in suspension

colloidal structure characterized by dispersed particles which are immediate in size between very small particles in true solution and large particles in suspension. The particle size is generally 1 millimicron to 0.1 micron.

comminute to reduce to small, fine particles

complex carbohydrates carbohydrates made up of many small sugar units joined together, for example, starch and cellulose

controlled atmosphere storage the monitoring and control of content of gases in the storage warehouse atmosphere; a low oxygen content slows down plant respiration and delays senescence (aging)

convenience foods foods that are partially or completely prepared by the food processor, with little or no additional food preparation required of the consumer

covalent bond a strong chemical bond that joins two atoms together

cream of tartar potassium acid tartrate, the partial salt of tartaric acid, an organic acid

critical control point any point in the process where loss of control may result in a health risk

critical temperature the temperature above which a gas can exist only as a gas, regardless of the pressure, because the motion of the molecules is so violent

cross-contamination contamination of one substance by another; for example, cooked chicken is contaminated with *Salmonella* organisms when it is cut on the same board used for cutting raw chicken

cryoprotectants substances that offer protection to such sensitive molecules as proteins during freezing and frozen storage

crystalline the aggregation of molecules of a substance in a set, ordered pattern, forming individual crystals

crystallization the formation of crystals from the solidification of dispersed elements in a precise, orderly structure

crystallize to form crystals, each of which consists of an orderly array of molecules in a pattern characteristic of that particular substance

cuisine a style of cooking or manner of preparing food

culture a way of life in which there are common customs for behavior and in which there is a common understanding among members of the group

cytoplasm pertaining to the protoplasm of a cell, exclusive of the nucleus

daily values nutrient standards used for labeling purposes; they include Daily Reference Values (DRVs) and Reference Daily Intakes (RDIs)

de-esterification the removal of the methyl ester groups from the galacturonic acid building blocks of the pectin molecule

dehydrogenase an enzyme that catalyzes a chemical reaction in which hydrogen is removed, similar to an oxidation reaction

demographic the statistical study of populations

denaturation a change in a protein molecule, usually by unfolding of the amino acid chains, with a decrease in solubility

density mass or weight per unit of volume

desiccation the process of drying as moisture is lost

dextrinization the process in which starch molecules are broken down into dextrins. Dextrins are polysaccharides composed of many glucose units, but are smaller than starch molecules.

dextrins polysaccharides, somewhat smaller in size than starch, resulting from the partial hydrolysis of starch; produced by dry roasting alone or with trace amounts of an acid catalyst

diffusion the movement of a substance from an area of higher concentration to an area of lower concentration

diglyceride glycerol combined with two fatty acids; usually present with monoglycerides in an emulsifier mixture

disaccharide a sugar composed of two simple sugars or monosaccharides

disappearance data data about food that "disappears" into the nation's food distribution system; quantities calculated from beginning inventories, annual production, imports, and exports

disodium 5'-inosinate and disodium 5'-guanylate two of the 5'-ribonucleotides that appear to have the greatest strength as flavor enhancers

disulfide linkages bonding through two sulfur atoms (–S–S–)

emulsifier a substance that is active at the interface between two immiscible liquids, being attracted somewhat to each liquid; it acts as a bridge between them, allowing an emulsion to form

emulsifying agent a substance that allows an emulsion to form because it has some characteristics of each of the two immiscible liquids and forms a bridge between them

emulsion the dispersion of one substance within another with which it ordinarily does not mix (is immiscible). For example, oil and water or vinegar generally do not mix; however, in a product such as mayonnaise (containing oil and vinegar), an emulsion is formed.

encapsulate to enclose in a capsule; flavoring materials may be combined with substances such as gum acacia or modified starch to provide an encapsulation matrix and then spray-dried

enriched enriched foods have had nutrients added so that the food meets the specified legal minimum or maximum levels of nutrients normally found in the food before processing. For example, flour and grain products are enriched to replace the nutrients lost when the bran and germ were removed to produce white flour.

enteropathogenic causing illness in the intestinal tract

enzymatic oxidative browning the browning of cut surfaces of certain fruits and vegetables catalyzed by enzymes in the presence of oxygen. For example, sliced apples will brown even after a relatively brief period of air contact.

enzymatic reactions those that are *catalyzed* by enzymes, which are special proteins produced by living cells; a catalyst changes the rate of a reaction without itself undergoing permanent change

enzymes protein molecules produced by living cells that act as organic catalysts and change the rate of a reaction without being used up in the process

epidemiology the study of causes and control of diseases prevalent in human population groups

espagnole sauce pronounced ess-span-yol, this is a classic brown sauce composed of brown stock, brown roux, mirepoix (diced onions, carrots, celery), and tomato purée.

essential oils concentrated flavoring oils extracted from food substances, such as oil of orange or oil of peppermint

ester a type of chemical compound that results from combination of an organic acid (–COOH) with an alcohol (–OH)

ethnic pertains to basic divisions of humankind into groups that are distinguished by customs, characteristics, language, and so on

ethylene a small gaseous molecule (C_2H_4) produced by fruits and vegetables as an initiator of the ripening process

farm-value share the proportion of the retail price of food that is received by the farmer

fatty acid a chemical molecule consisting of carbon and hydrogen atoms bonded in a chainlike structure; combined through its acid group (–COOH) with the alcohol glycerol to form triglycerides

Federal Register provides citizens with official text of federal laws, presidential documents, and administrative regulations and notices. Also included are descriptions of federal organizations, programs, and activities. The *Federal Register* may be accessed on the Internet.

fermentation the transformation of organic molecules into smaller ones by the action of microorganisms; for example, yeast ferments glucose to carbon dioxide and alcohol

ferric iron iron with a valence of 3^+ (Fe^{3+})

ferrous containing iron

fiber Dietary fiber is nondigestible carbohydrates (including cellulose, hemicelluloses, and pectin) and lignin (a noncarbohydrate material found particularly in woody parts of plants) that are intrinsic and intact in plants; functional fiber consists of isolated nondigestible carbohydrates that have beneficial physiological effects in humans; and total fiber is the sum of dietary fiber and functional fiber.

flavonoid pigments a group of plant pigments with similar chemical structures; they include both anthoxanthins, which are white, and anthocyanins, which are red-blue

flavor profile an outline of the major flavor components and their intensities that are blended to form the overall flavor sensation created by a food

flocculated separated into small woolly or fluffy masses

foam the dispersion of a gas in a liquid, such as a beaten egg-white mixture

food additive a substance, other than usual ingredients, that is added to a food product for a specific purpose, such as flavoring, preserving, stabilizing, thickening

food allergy an abnormal immune response to components in food (usually proteins); symptoms can include gastrointestinal, cutaneous, and respiratory responses or other symptoms such as laryngeal edema, anaphylatic shock, or hypotension

food infection illness produced by the presence and growth of pathogenic microorganisms in the gastrointestinal tract; they are often, but not necessarily, present in large numbers

food intolerances abnormal responses to food that do not involve the immune system

food intoxication illness produced by microbial toxin production in a food product that is consumed; the toxin produces the illness

food safety a judgment of the acceptability of the risk involved in eating a food; if risk is relatively low, a food substance may be considered safe

food security access to enough nourishment, at all times, for an active healthy life

FoodNet the Foodborne Disease Active Surveillance Network, a project with the FDA, USDA, Centers for Disease Control and Prevention (CDC), and 10 states. Foodborne illness outbreaks are documented and tracked.

FORC-G Foodborne Outbreak Response Coordinating Group, a project with the USDA, FDA, and EPA

fortified fortified foods have had ingredients, not normally found in the food, added to improve nutritional content. For example, orange juice is fortified with calcium because calcium is a nutrient not significantly found in oranges.

freeze-drying a drying process that involves first freezing the product and then placing it in a vacuum chamber; the ice sublimes (goes from solid to vapor phase without going through the liquid phase); the dried food is more flavorful and fresher in appearance because it does not become hot in the drying process

freezer burn characterized by grayish-brown or white leathery surfaces of meat that has been frozen and allowed air

contact with the meat. Prevent by freezing in airtight packaging.

freezing mixtures mixtures of crushed ice and salt that become very cold, below the freezing point of plain water, because of the rapid melting of the ice by the salt and the attempt of the system to reach equilibrium; freezing mixtures are used to freeze ice creams in ice cream freezers

functional foods any food that has a positive impact on an individual's health, physical performance, or state of mind in addition to its normal nutritive value; sometimes called *nutraceuticals*

galacturonic acid a chemical molecule very similar to the sugar galactose and containing an organic acid (carboxyl) group in its chemical structure

gamma rays one of three kinds of rays emitted by radioactive substances

gastroenteritis inflammation of the gastrointestinal tract

gel a colloidal dispersion that shows some rigidity and will, when unmolded, keep the shape of the container in which it had been placed

gelatinization the sum of changes that occur in the first stages of heating starch granules in a moist environment; includes swelling of granules as water is absorbed and disruption of the organized granule structure

gelatinization of starch the swelling of starch granules when heated in the presence of water

generic a class of packaged food products that do not carry a specific brand name

genetic engineering the use of recombinant DNA or rDNA technology to modify plants and microorganisms genetically. Genetic engineering or modification allows for the efficient transfer of genetic material compared to traditional cross-breeding, which may require multiple generations

germination the sprouting of a seed

globulins simple proteins that are soluble in dilute salt solutions

glucoamylase an enzyme that hydrolyzes starch by breaking off one glucose unit at a time, thus producing glucose immediately

glucose a monosaccharide or simple sugar that is the basic building unit for starch

glucose isomerase an enzyme that changes glucose to fructose

gluten a protein found in wheat that gives structure to baked products

glycemic response the rise in blood glucose after consumption of a food. The consumption of some foods (such as sugar or high sugar containing foods) results in a greater rise in blood glucose compared to other foods.

glycogen a complex carbohydrate—a polysaccharide—used for carbohydrate storage in the liver and muscles of the body; sometimes called *animal starch*

glycoproteins proteins composed of amino acid chains with a carbohydrate moiety, such as a galactose derivative, attached at certain points

goitrogen a substance that is capable of causing enlargement (goiter) of the thyroid gland in the neck area

good manufacturing practices recommended rules for maintaining sanitation, safety, and quality assurance to be followed in a food-processing plant

grade a symbol, such as Grade A or No. 1, that indicates that the food product carrying this label has met specified predetermined standards of quality

grading the examining of food products and classifying them according to quality, such as Grade A, B, or C, based on defined standards

GRAS the list of food additives that are "generally recognized as safe" by a panel of experts; this list is maintained and periodically reevaluated by the FDA

guarana a South American berry with alleged aphrodisiac qualities; the seeds of the berry contain caffeine

hazard a source of danger, long- or short-term, such as microbial food poisoning, cancer, birth defects, and so on

headspace the volume above a liquid or solid in a container

hedonic having to do with pleasure; a hedonic scale indicates how much a person likes or dislikes a food

hedonic scale a rating scale indicating the degree of liking, usually involving a range from 1 for "dislike extremely" to 7 for "like extremely"

hemorrhagic colitis bleeding and inflammation of the colon or large intestine

hepatitis inflammation of the liver

hermetic completely sealed so as to keep air or gas from getting in or out

hermetic packaging packaging that is airtight

hexose a simple sugar or monosaccharide with six carbon atoms

high risk or potentially hazardous foods these foods support the rapid growth of microorganisms. Potentially hazardous foods are generally moist, high in protein, and have a neutral or slightly acidic pH. Examples include milk and milk products, sliced melons, garlic and oil mixtures, poultry, meat, seafood, sprouts and raw seeds, baked or boiled potatoes, shell eggs, tofu, soy-protein foods, cooked rice, beans, or other heat-treated plant foods

home meal replacement prepared foods purchased to be consumed at home that have similar characteristics to food that may be prepared in the home. Roasted chickens purchased in a foodservice establishment or a grocery store are an example of a home meal replacement food.

homogenization a process used to subdivide particles, usually fat globules, into very small, uniform-sized pieces. Milk is homogenized to prevent the separation of the cream from nonfat milk.

homogenization of whole milk a process in which whole milk is forced, under pressure, through very small openings, dividing the fat globules into very tiny particles

"hot" peppers peppers that contain a substance known as capsaicin, which gives them the highly pungent characteristic called "hot." This substance also stimulates the flow of saliva. "Hotter" peppers contain more capsaicin, concentrated mainly in the thin tissues or veins where the seeds are attached to the spongy central portion.

humectant a substance that can absorb moisture readily

hydration capacity the ability of a substance, such as flour, to absorb water

hydrocolloids large molecules, such as those that make up vegetable gums, that form colloidal dispersions, hold water, and often serve as thickeners and stabilizers in processed foods

hydrogen bond the relatively weak chemical bond that forms between a hydrogen atom and another atom with a slight negative charge, such as an oxygen or a nitrogen atom; each atom in this case is already covalently bonded to other atoms in the molecule of which it is part

hydrolysis the breaking of a chemical linkage between basic units of a more complex molecule to yield smaller molecules; water participates in the reaction and becomes part of the end products

hygroscopic tending to attract or absorb moisture from the atmosphere

idiosyncratic illnesses illnesses attributed to food although the mechanism for the illness is unknown; sulfite-induced asthma is a documented idiosyncratic illness

immiscible describing substances that cannot be mixed or blended

induction coil a coiled apparatus made up of two coupled circuits; interruptions in the direct current in one circuit produce an alternating current of high electrical potential in the other

inspection the examining of food products or processes carefully and critically in order to assure proper sanitary practices, labeling, and/or safety for the consumer

interesterification the hydrolysis of the ester bond between glycerol and the fatty acid. The ester bond is reformed among the mixed free fatty acids and glycerol.

inulin a complex carbohydrate (a polysaccharide) found in the roots of some plants that yields fructose when broken down or hydrolyzed

invert sugar composed of glucose and fructose; formed from sucrose heated in water, water and an acid, or with an enzyme called invertase (sucrase); desirable in food products because it resists crystallization and retains moisture

invisible fat fat that occurs naturally in food products such as meats, dairy products, nuts, and seeds

iodized salt table salt to which small amounts of a stabilized iodide compound have been added to increase dietary iodine and prevent goiter (enlargement of the thyroid gland); its use is encouraged particularly in areas where the soil is deficient in iodine

ion an electrically charged atom or group of atoms; the electrical charge results when a neutral atom or group of atoms loses or gains one or more electrons; loss of electrons results in a positively charged ion

irradiation the treatment of food by electron beams, gamma rays, or x-rays to reduce significantly bacteria, virus, or fungus contamination

isomer a molecule that is chemically identical to another with a different structure and thus different properties

isomerization a molecular change resulting in a molecule containing the same elements in the same proportions but having a slightly different structure and, hence, different properties; in carotenoids, heat causes a change in the position of the double bonds between carbon atoms

jaundice a condition in which the skin and eyeballs become abnormally yellow due to the presence of bile pigments in the blood

ketones chemical compounds characterized by a $(-\overset{\overset{\textstyle O}{\|}}{C}-)$ group

kilocalorie one kilocalorie is equal to 1000 small calories; the small calorie is used in chemistry, whereas the kilocalorie is used in nutrition

kinetic motion the very rapid vibration and movement of tiny molecules or ions dispersed in true solution

labile unstable

lacquered tin an enamel coating on the inside of tin cans

lacquered tin-coated cans an inner lacquer or enamel coating; the coating is of variable composition and overlies the basic tin-coated steel, protecting certain canned foods from discoloration

lacto-ovo vegetarians those who consume milk, eggs, and products derived from them as well as vegetable foods

latent heat the heat or energy required to change the state of a substance, that is, from liquid to gas, without changing the temperature of the substance

LDL cholesterol cholesterol that is combined with low-density lipoproteins in the blood; sometimes called the "bad cholesterol," in contrast to the "good cholesterol" combined with blood high-density lipoproteins

legume any of a large family of plants characterized by true pods enclosing seeds; dried beans and peas

lignin a woody, fibrous, noncarbohydrate material produced in mature plants; component of the fiber complex

linoleic acid a polyunsaturated fatty acid with 18 carbon atoms and two double bonds

linolenic acid a polyunsaturated fatty acid with 18 carbon atoms and 3 double bonds between carbon atoms; omega-3 fatty acid

lipase an enzyme that catalyzes the hydrolysis of triglycerides to yield glycerol and fatty acids

lipids a broad group of fatlike substances with similar properties

lipoprotein a lipid or fatty substance combined with a protein; egg yolk contains lipoproteins that combine phospholipids with protein

lipoxygenase an enzyme that catalyzes the oxidation of unsaturated fatty acids

lycopene a reddish, fat-soluble pigment of the carotenoid type

Maillard reaction the carbonyl group of a sugar combines with the amino group of a protein, initiating a series of chemical reactions which result in a brown color and change in flavor; it may occur in relatively dry foods in long storage as well as in foods heated to high temperatures

maltase an enzyme that hydrolyzes maltose to glucose

maltodextrins a mixture of small molecules resulting from starch hydrolysis, having a dextrose equivalent (DE) of less than 20

maltose a disaccharide or double sugar composed of two glucose units

marbling the distribution of fat throughout the muscles of meat animals

marinated to soak in a prepared liquid for a time, in this case for seasoning purposes

mass the tendency of an object to remain at rest if it is stationary or to continue in motion if it is already moving; mass can be determined by measuring the force with which an object is attracted to the earth, i.e., by measuring its weight

maturing agent a substance that brings about some oxidative changes in white flour and improves its baking properties

mechanically separated meat may be separated from the bone by forcing the bones with the attached meat through a sieve. Mechanically separated meat will be a paste-like product. Mechanically separated beef is prohibited for human food use. Mechanically separated pork and poultry may be used for human food but must be listed on the label.

melting point the temperature at which a solid fat becomes a liquid oil

meniscus the curved upper surface of a column of liquid

mesophilic bacteria bacteria that grow best at moderate temperatures

mesophilic microorganisms organisms that grow at moderate temperatures

metabolic having to do with any of the chemical changes that occur in living cells

metabolic food disorders the result of inherited defects in the ability to metabolize some components of a food or from a genetically determined enhanced sensitivity due to an altered metabolic pattern; lactose intolerance is an example of a metabolic food disorder

methyl ester the chemical combination of methyl alcohol with an organic acid, such as galacturonic acid

methyl ester of galacturonic acid Ester is the chemical word used to describe the linkage between an organic acid group (–COOH) and an alcohol group (–OH); in this case, the alcohol is methanol (which contains only one carbon atom) and the acid is galacturonic acid.

micelles a colloidal particle

microbiology the branch of biology that deals with microorganisms

microencapsulation A coating is applied to very fine particles of a probiotic culture, which protects them until an appropriate time for their release in the gastrointestinal (GI) tract

middlings the relatively fine wheat endosperm which must be further reduced by rollers to produce flour, also called *midds*.

mirepoix two parts diced onion, one part diced carrots, and one part diced celery. One cup of mirepoix would include

1/2 cup onion, 1/4 cup carrots, 1/4 cup celery. Is used to flavor sauces and soups.

mitochondria sausage-shaped bodies in the cell cytoplasm that contain the enzymes necessary for energy metabolism

modified atmosphere packaging the enclosure of food products in gas-barrier materials in which the gaseous environment has been changed or modified in order to extend shelf life

moisture/vapor-proof materials materials that are relatively impermeable to water vapor and other gases; they are desirable for wrapping frozen foods to minimize the loss of moisture, particularly from sublimation

molecule the smallest particle of a substance that can exist separately and still preserve its characteristic properties. For example, a molecule of water (H_2O) still exhibits the chemical and physical properties of water. Molecules are composed of atoms bonded together. If the atoms are alike (as in oxygen formation, O_2) the resulting molecule is called a compound.

mollusks a type of shellfish characterized by a soft, unsegmented body enclosed in a shell of one or more pieces; examples are oysters and clams

monoglyceride glycerol combined with one fatty acid; used as an emulsifier

monosaccharide a simple sugar unit, such as glucose

monounsaturated a fatty acid with one double bond between carbon atoms; capable of binding more hydrogen

monounsaturated fatty acid a fatty acid with one double bond between carbon atoms

mouth feel how a food feels in the mouth (i.e. gritty, creamy, or lumpy)

mucoprotein a complex or conjugated protein containing a carbohydrate substance combined with a protein

mycotoxins toxins produced by molds

nitrogen base a molecule with a nitrogen-containing chemical group that makes the molecule alkaline

noncariogenic not contributing to the development of caries in teeth

nonenzymatic oxidation an oxidation reaction that occurs spontaneously and is not catalyzed by enzymes, for example, oxidation of fats that results in rancidity

nonvolatile not able to vaporize or form a gas at ordinary temperatures

nutrition labeling a special type of food labeling, in addition to basic requirements concerning net contents and manufacturer, that gives information about the nutrient and caloric content of the food on a per-serving basis

objective evaluation having to do with a known object as distinguished from existing in the mind; in food science, measurement of the characteristics of food with a laboratory instrument such as a pH meter to indicate acidity or a viscometer to measure viscosity or consistency

odor a smell, pleasant or unpleasant, perceived through stimulation of the olfactory center

olfactory having to do with the sense of smell

oligofructose an oligosaccharide; a carbohydrate molecule made up of a small number of fructose molecules linked together

oligosaccharide the general term for sugars composed of a few—often between 3 and 10—simple sugars or monosaccharides

omega-3 fatty acids polyunsaturated fatty acids that have the first double bond on the third carbon atom from the methyl ($-CH_3$) end of the carbon chain

omega-3 PUFA a group of polyunsaturated fatty acids that have the first double bond on the third carbon atom from the end of the carbon chain; also called n-3 fatty acids

omega-6 polyunsaturated fatty acids (PUFA) polyunsaturated fatty acids that have the first double bond on the sixth carbon atom from the methyl ($-CH_3$) end of the carbon chain

organic acid an acid containing carbon atoms, for example, citric acid and acetic acid

organic acids generally weak acids characterized by a carboxyl

$$\overset{\displaystyle O}{\underset{\displaystyle (-C-H)}{\|}} \text{ group}$$

organic polymers large carbon-containing molecules made up of many small molecules linked together

osmosis the movement of water through a semipermeable membrane; as ice crystals form extracellularly, the concentration of solute in this area is increased, and water then moves out of the cell in an attempt to equalize the solute concentration

ovalbumin a major protein found in egg white

ovary part of the seed-bearing organ of a flower; an enlarged hollow part containing ovules that develop into seeds

oven spring the rapid increase in volume in a loaf of bread during the first few minutes of baking

oxalic acid an organic acid that forms an insoluble salt with calcium

oxidase an enzyme that catalyzes an oxidation reaction

oxidation a chemical reaction that involves the addition of oxygen

oxidation reactions chemical reactions in which oxygen is added or hydrogen is removed or electrons are lost

palatable pleasing to the taste

papillae small, nipplelike projections of various shapes on the surface of the tongue

pasteurization a mild heat treatment that destroys microorganisms that may cause disease but does not destroy all microorganisms in the product

pasteurize to treat with mild heat to destroy pathogens—but not all microorganisms—present in a food product

pathogenic microorganisms that cause disease may be called pathogens or pathogenic microorganisms

pathogenic bacteria bacteria that can cause disease

pathogenic microorganisms microbes capable of causing disease

pearled a process that removes the outer hull, leaving a small, round, light "pearl" of grain

pectin a complex carbohydrate (polysaccharide) composed of galacturonic acid subunits, partially esterified with methyl alcohol and capable of forming a gel

pectin esterase　an enzyme that catalyzes the hydrolysis of a methyl ester group from the large pectin molecule, producing pectic acid; pectic acid tends to form insoluble salts with such ions as calcium (Ca^{2+}); these insoluble salts cause the cloud in orange juice to become destabilized and settle

pectinase　an enzyme that hydrolyzes the linkages that hold the small building blocks of galacturonic acid together in the pectic substances, producing smaller molecules

pentosans　complex carbohydrates (polysaccharides) that yield five-carbon sugars (pentoses) when hydrolyzed

pentose　a simple sugar or monosaccharide with five carbon atoms

peptide　a chemical molecule composed of amino acids linked together

peptide linkage　linkage between two amino acids that connects the amino group of one and the acid (carboxyl) group of the other

pH　expression of the degree of acidity on a scale of 1 to 14, 1 being most acid, 7 neutral, and 14 most alkaline

phenolic compound　an organic compound that includes in its chemical structure an unsaturated ring with –OH groups on it; polyphenols have more than one –OH group

phenylketonuria (PKU)　a genetic disease characterized by an inborn error in the body's ability to metabolize the amino acid phenylalanine

phospholipid　a type of lipid characterized chemically by glycerol combined with two fatty acids, phosphoric acid, and a nitrogen-containing base, for example, lecithin

phytochemicals　biochemical substances, other than vitamins, of plant origin that appear to have a positive effect on health; they include phenolic compounds, terpenoids, pigments, and other antioxidants.

phytoestrogens　substances found in plant foods, such as soybeans, that have an estrogenlike effect on the body when consumed in the diet.

plant exudates　materials that ooze out of certain plants; some that ooze from certain tree trunks and branches are gums

plastic　able to be molded into various shapes without shattering as a force is applied; plastic fats can be mixed or creamed

plastic fat　a fat that can be molded or shaped, such as hydrogenated shortening, margarine, or butter

plasticity　the ability to be molded or shaped; in plastic fats, both solid crystals and liquid oil are present

poach　to cook in a hot liquid, carefully handling the food to retain its form

polar　having two opposite natures, such as both positive and negative charges

polar materials　chemical molecules that have electric charges (positive or negative) and tend to be soluble in water

polarized light　light that vibrates in one plane

polydextrose　a bulking agent made from an 89 : 10 : 1 mixture of glucose, sorbitol, and citric acid; in body metabolism, it yields one kilocalorie per gram

polymer　a large molecule formed by linking together many smaller molecules of a similar kind

polymerization　the formation of large molecules by combining smaller chemical units

polymers　molecules of relatively high molecular weight that are composed of many small molecules acting as building blocks

polyol　a sugar alcohol

polyphenol　a phenol compound with more than one –OH group attached to the unsaturated ring of carbon atoms; some produce bitterness in coffee and tea

polysaccharide　a complex carbohydrate made up of many simple sugar (monosaccharide) units linked together; in the case of starch, the simple sugars are all glucose

polyunsaturated fats　fats that contain a relatively high proportion of polyunsaturated fatty acids, which have two or more double bonds between carbon atoms; these fatty acids are shaped differently from saturated fatty acids because of the double bonds

polyunsaturated fatty acids　fatty acids that have two or more double bonds between carbon atoms; they could hold more hydrogen atoms if these bonds were broken

pooled　a term used to describe when several eggs are cracked out into a bowl. Several eggs "pooled" in one bowl increase contamination risk because one contaminated egg will contaminate the entire bowl of eggs.

potassium bromate　an oxidizing substance often added to bread dough to strengthen the gluten of strong or high-protein flour

prebiotics　nondigestible foods that beneficially affect the host by selectively stimulating the growth and/or activity of one or more bacteria in the colon.

precipitate　to become insoluble and separate out of a solution or dispersion

precursor　something that comes before; in flavor study, it is a compound that is nonflavorful but can be changed, usually by heat or enzymes, into a flavorful substance

precursors　a substance that "comes before"; a precursor of vitamin A is a substance out of which the body cells can make vitamin A

probiotic　live microorganism food ingredients that enhance human health by improving intestinal microbial balance

proofing　the last rising of bread dough after it is molded into a loaf and placed in the baking pan

pro-oxidant　a substance that encourages the development of oxidative rancidity

protease　an enzyme that hydrolyzes protein

protein efficiency ratio　a measure of protein quality assessed by determining the extent of weight gain in experimental animals when fed the test item

proteinase　an enzyme that hydrolyzes protein to smaller fragments, eventually producing amino acids

protozoa　one-celled animals

P/S ratio　the ratio of polyunsaturated to saturated fatty acids in a food, also sometimes calculated for a total diet; for example, a diet sometimes prescribed for certain individuals with high blood lipids may have a P/S ratio of 3 : 1 or 3

psychrotrophic bacteria   bacteria that grow best at cold temperatures (cold-loving bacteria)

psychrotropic microorganisms   organisms that can grow at refrigerator temperatures

PulseNet   a national network of public health laboratories to "fingerprint" bacteria that may be foodborne, a project with the FDA, USDA, CDC, and all 50 states. Enables tracking of a foodborne illness outbreak to a single source or indicates more than one outbreak has occurred from multiple sources.

pungency   a sharp, biting quality

putrefactive fermentations   decomposition of organic matter by microorganisms, producing foul-smelling end products

quick service restaurants   foodservices that provide limited, but fast, service. Menu selections are few and include foods that may be prepared and served quickly.

radioactive   giving off radiant energy in the form of particles or rays, such as alpha, beta, and gamma rays, by the disintegration of atomic nuclei (the central part of atoms)

rancidity   the deterioration of fats, usually by an oxidation process, resulting in objectionable flavors and odors

raw starch flavor   an undercooked starch in a sauce, gravy, or soup will reduce the flavor of the other ingredients and will provide a flat flavor. You can learn to identify this flavor by tasting a product shortly after the starch has been added, then by tasting it again as cooking proceeds. A fully cooked product should have no raw starch flavor.

reducing substance   a molecule that has an effect opposite that of an oxidizing agent; hydrogen or electrons are gained in a reaction involving a reducing substance

reducing substances   chemical molecules that can supply hydrogen or electrons to prevent or reverse oxidation; the reduced state of iron is the ferrous form (Fe^{2+})

reducing sugar   a sugar with a free aldehyde or ketone group that has the ability to chemically "reduce" other chemical compounds and thus become oxidized itself; glucose, fructose, maltose, and lactose, but not sucrose, are reducing sugars

reduction reactions   chemical reactions in which there is a gain in hydrogen or in electrons

rehydrate   to add water to replace that lost during drying

respiration   a metabolic process by which cells consume oxygen and give off carbon dioxide; continues after harvest

reticulum   a netlike sheath

retort   pressure canning equipment used in commercial canning operations to process low-acid foods at high temperatures

retort pouch   a flexible, laminated package made of special materials that withstands high-temperature processing in a commercial pressure canner called a retort

retrogradation   the process in which starch molecules, particularly the amylose fraction, reassociate or bond together in an ordered structure after disruption by gelatinization; ultimately, a crystalline order appears

reverse osmosis   a process of "dewatering" whereby ions and small molecules do not pass through a membrane but water does pass through

risk   a measure of the probability and severity of harm to human health

roux   a thickening agent made by heating a blend of fat and flour

ruminant   an animal with four stomachs; for example, cattle, sheep, goats, deer, and elk

ruminant animal   an animal with multiple stomachs, one of which is called a *rumen*, where bacterial action occurs on the food that has been eaten; the animal—for example, a cow—"chews its cud" (material regurgitated and chewed a second time)

salmonella   bacteria, some strains of which can cause illness in humans; because the microorganisms themselves produce the gastrointestinal symptoms, the illness is called a food infection

salmonellosis   illness produced by ingestion of *Salmonella* organisms

salt   a chemical compound derived from an acid by replacement of the hydrogen (H^+), wholly or in part, with a metal or an electrically positive ion, for example, sodium citrate

saturated fatty acid   a fatty acid with no double bonds between carbon atoms; it holds all of the hydrogen that can be attached to the carbon atoms

saturated solution   a solution containing all of the solute that it can dissolve at that temperature

Scoville Heat Units   a measurement of chili pungency that was developed through taste testing of a trained sensory panel. High performance liquid chromatography is now used to measure a chili's "heat."

secondary amines   derivatives of ammonia (NH_3) in which two of the hydrogen atoms are replaced by other carbon-containing chemical groups

senescing   growing old or aging

sensory   having to do with the senses (sight, taste, smell, hearing, touch); connected with receiving and transmitting sense impressions

septicemia   the presence of pathogenic microorganisms in the blood

shear   term used to describe various kinds of agitation or stirring that a starch mixture may be subjected to during cooking and processing. Excessive shear will damage the starch granule causing loss of viscosity.

shelf-stable foods   foods that can be stored at room temperature

shred   the area on the sides of a loaf of bread, just above the pan, where the dough rises in the oven before the crust is formed; a desirable shred is even and unbroken

slurry   a thin mixture of water and a fine insoluble material such as flour

smoke point   the temperature at which smoke comes continuously from the surface of a fat heated under standardized conditions

solute   a dissolved or dispersed substance

solution   a mixture resulting from the dispersion of small molecules or ions (called the *solute*) in a liquid such as water (called the *solvent*)

solvent the liquid in which another substance is dissolved

sorbitol a sugar alcohol similar to glucose in chemical structure but with an alcohol group (–C–OH) replacing the aldehyde group (H–C=O) of glucose

soy milk the liquid produced by cooking, mashing, and straining soybeans

specifications a written description of the food or product that is desired. Generally used in foodservice purchasing. This written description must be thorough so that the desired characteristics, quality, and packaging of the item are clearly understood.

sponge the mixture of liquid, yeast, sugar, and part of the flour to make a thin batter that is held at a lukewarm temperature to allow yeast activity for a period before the remaining ingredients are added to form a dough

spore an encapsulated, resistant form of a microorganism

stabilizer a water-holding substance, such as a vegetable gum, that interferes with ice crystal formation and contributes to a smooth texture in frozen desserts

standard of identity a standard set by the U.S. Food and Drug Administration to specifically describe a food; to be labeled as such, a food must meet these specifications

standard operating procedures written instructions for performing a certain process; they must be followed exactly and a record kept of completion of the task

starch gelatinization the swelling of starch granules when heated with water, often resulting in thickening

starch granule a particle formed in the plant seed or root when starch is stored; composed of millions of starch molecules laid down in a very organized pattern; the shape of the granule is typical for each species

steep to soak

sterilization the complete destruction of microorganisms in a medium

sterilize to destroy essentially all microorganisms

sterol a type of fat or lipid molecule with a complex chemical structure, for example, cholesterol

stew to simmer in a small to moderate quantity of liquid

streams the various product flows in a mill which vary by particle size, ash content, and component of the wheat kernel.

sublimation a solid, such as ice, goes directly to the vapor state (water vapor) without going through the liquid state; in the freezer, sublimed water may collect as frost

succulent having juicy tissues; not dry

sulfhydryl compound a chemical substance that contains an –SH group

surface activity the lowering of the surface tension of a liquid because of agents that tend to concentrate at the surface

surface tension tension created over the surface of a liquid because of the greater attraction of the liquid molecules for each other than for the gaseous molecules in the air above the liquid

syneresis separation or "weeping" of liquid from a gel

synergism an interaction in which the effect of the mixture is greater than the effect of the sum of component parts

synthetic compounds those produced by chemically combining two or more simple compounds or elements in the laboratory

tactile having to do with the sense of touch

tallow is fat extracted from sheep or cattle. Tallow is highly saturated and is desirable for some purposes because of its meaty flavor.

taste sensations perceived through stimulation of taste buds on the tongue; primary tastes are sweet, salty, sour, and bitter

taste bud a group of cells, including taste cells, supporting cells, and nerve fibers

taste pore a tiny opening from the surface of the tongue into the taste bud

taste receptor tiny ends of the taste cells that come in contact with the substance being tasted

temper or tempering gradual warming of beaten eggs before adding to a hot liquid. If a recipe states to temper the eggs, when the mixture (usually milk and starch) is thoroughly hot, pour one-fourth or more of the hot mixture slowly into the beaten eggs while mixing. Complete the process by pouring this hot mixture containing eggs into the pan and finish cooking.

temperature danger zone a range of temperatures which allow rapid growth of bacteria and, in some cases, toxin production

texture arrangement of the parts of a material showing the structure; the texture of baked flour products such as a slice of bread may be fine and even or coarse and open; the texture of a cream sauce may be smooth or lumpy

toxin-mediated infections illness produced when a food containing pathogenic organisms is consumed; these organisms then produce illness-causing toxins in the intestines

translucency partial transparency

triglyceride glycerol combined with three fatty acids; most food fats are triglycerides

trussed poultry tied with thread or butcher's twine into a more compact shape. The legs are tied together, then the string is pulled up across the leg and thigh joints up above the wings. Trussing a bird promotes even cooking and helps to retain moisture.

tuber a short, thickened, fleshy part of an underground stem, such as a potato; new plants develop from the buds or eyes

ultrafiltration filtration through an extremely fine filter

unsaturated fatty acid a general term used to refer to any fatty acid with one or more double bonds between carbon atoms; capable of binding more hydrogen at these points of unsaturation

vacuum-drying drying a product in a vacuum chamber in which water vaporizes at a lower temperature than at atmospheric pressure

value added term used to describe a food to which value has been added, often by processing. Lettuce, for example, can be purchased as a head or chopped, washed, and ready to serve.

vapor pressure   the pressure produced over the surface of a liquid as a result of a change in some of the molecules from a liquid to a vapor or gaseous state

vegans   those who exclude from their diet all products that are not of plant origin

vegetable gums   polysaccharide substances that are derived from plants, including seaweed and various shrubs or trees, have the ability to hold water, and often act as thickeners, stabilizers, or gelling agents in various food products; for example, algin, carrageenan, and gum arabic

vegetable-fruit   botanically, a fruit is the ovary and surrounding tissues, including the seeds, of a plant; a vegetable-fruit is the fruit part of a plant that is not sweet and is usually served with the main course of a meal, for example, squash, cucumbers, and tomatoes

viscoelastic   ability of a material to stretch, hold shape, and partially bounce back to original shape; a substance that is both viscous and elastic

viscosity   resistance to flow; thickness or consistency

visible fat   refined fats and oils used in food preparation, including edible oils, margarine, butter, lard, and shortenings

warmed-over flavor   describes the rapid onset of lipid oxidation that occurs in cooked meats during refrigerated storage; oxidized flavors are detectable after only 48 hours

waxy maize   a waxy variety of corn; the starch of this variety contains only the amylopectin fraction

yeast autolysate   the preparation of yeast in which the cells have been destroyed; contains many flavorful substances

yeast fermentation   a process in which enzymes produced by the yeast break down sugars to carbon dioxide and alcohol, and also produce some flavor substances